THE KLEINMAN EDITION

קיצור

KITZUR
SHULCHAN ARUCH

שלחן ערוך

The ArtScroll® Series

Rabbi Nosson Scherman / Rabbi Meir Zlotowitz
General Editors

A PROJECT OF THE

Mesorah Heritage Foundation

BOARD OF TRUSTEES

RABBI REUVEN FEINSTEIN
Rosh HaYeshivah, Yeshiva of Staten Island

JOEL L. FLEISHMAN Chairman
Director, Sam & Ronnie Heyman Center on Ethics,
Public Policy, and the Professions, Duke University

RABBI NOSSON SCHERMAN
General Editor, ArtScroll Series

HOWARD TZVI FRIEDMAN
Founding Partner, Lanx Management, LLC

JUDAH I. SEPTIMUS ESQ, C.P.A.

JOSEPH C. SHENKER
Senior Chair, Sullivan & Cromwell

JAMES S. TISCH
Chairman and CEO, Loews Corp.

RABBI GEDALIAH ZLOTOWITZ
President

RABBI DAVID FEINSTEIN ל"צז
Rosh HaYeshivah, Mesivtha Tifereth Jerusalem

RABBI MEIR ZLOTOWITZ ל"ז
Founder

AUDIT COMMITTEE

SAMUEL ASTROF
CFO/COO (Ret.) The Jewish
Federations of North America;
Partner (Ret.) Ernst & Young, LLP

JOEL L. FLEISHMAN
Director, Sam & Ronnie Heyman Center on Ethics,
Public Policy, and the Professions, Duke University

JUDAH I. SEPTIMUS ESQ, C.P.A.

JOSEPH C. SHENKER
Senior Chair, Sullivan & Cromwell

JAMES S. TISCH
Chairman and CEO, Loews Corp.

INTERNATIONAL BOARD OF GOVERNORS

JAY SCHOTTENSTEIN *(Columbus, OH)*
Chairman

STEVEN ADELSBERG
SIMCHA APPLEGRAD
MOSHE BEINHORN
RABBI RAPHAEL B. BUTLER
EDWARD MENDEL CZUKER *(Los Angeles)*
REUVEN D. DESSLER *(Cleveland)*
URI DREIFUS
YITZCHOK GANGER
MEIR R.Y. GRAFF *(Los Angeles)*
YITZCHOK MENACHEM HAAS
HASHI HERZKA
JACOB HERZOG *(Toronto)*
AMIR JAFFA *(Cleveland)*
ELAN JAFFA
JACK JAFFA
LLOYD F. KEILSON
MICHAEL KEST *(Los Angeles)*
ELLY KLEINMAN
ROBERT LOWINGER
EZRA MARCOS *(Tel Aviv)*
RABBI MEYER H. MAY *(Los Angeles)*
ASHER D. MILSTEIN

ANDREW J. NEFF
AARON J. ORLOFSKY *(Silver Spring)*
BARRY M. RAY *(Chicago)*
ZVI RYZMAN *(Los Angeles)*
JOSEPH A. SCHOTTENSTEIN
JONATHAN R. SCHOTTENSTEIN
JEFFREY A. SCHOTTENSTEIN
HERBERT E. SEIF *(Englewood, NJ)*
NATHAN B. SILBERMAN
ADAM M. SOKOL
A. JOSEPH STERN
JACQUES STERN *(Sao Paulo)*
ELLIOT TANNENBAUM
THOMAS J. TISCH
GARY TORGOW *(Detroit)*
STANLEY WASSERMAN *(New Rochelle)*
CHAIM WEALCATCH *(Baltimore)*
JOSEPH H. WEISS
MICHAEL WEISZ
STEVEN (CHANOCH) WEISZ
SHLOMO WERDIGER

קיצור שלחן ערוך

SHULCHAN ARUCH

VOLUME 2 כרך ב

SIMANIM 35-71 סימנים לה־עא

The ArtScroll® Series

Published by

Mesorah Publications, ltd

THE KLEINMAN EDITION

KITZUR

THE CODE OF JEWISH LAW

by Rabbi Shlomo Ganzfried

TRANSLATED AND ELUCIDATED,
INCLUDING RULINGS OF
THE MISHNAH BERURAH AND IGROS MOSHE

by a team of Torah Scholars
under the General Editorship of

Rabbi Eliyahu Meir Klugman

Rabbi Yosaif Asher Weiss
Editorial Director

FIRST EDITION
Sixteen Impressions ... August 2009 — December 2022
Seventeenth Impression ... May 2024

Published and Distributed by
MESORAH PUBLICATIONS, Ltd.
313 Regina Avenue / Rahway, New Jersey 07065

Distributed in Europe by
LEHMANNS
Unit E, Viking Business Park
Rolling Mill Road
Jarrow, Tyne & Wear NE32 3DP
England

Distributed in Australia & New Zealand by
GOLDS WORLD OF JUDAICA
3-13 William Street
Balaclava, Melbourne 3183
Victoria Australia

Distributed in Israel by
SIFRIATI / A. GITLER — BOOKS
POB 2351
Bnei Brak 51122

Distributed in South Africa by
KOLLEL BOOKSHOP
Northfield Centre, 17 Northfield Avenue
Norwood 2192, Johannesburg, South Africa

ARTSCROLL® SERIES / THE KLEINMAN EDITION
KITZUR SHULCHAN ARUCH — CODE OF JEWISH LAW
VOL. 2 — SIMANIM 35-71

© *Copyright 2009, by* MESORAH PUBLICATIONS, Ltd.
313 Regina Avenue / Rahway, N.J. 07065 / (718) 921-9000 / FAX (718) 680-1875

ALL RIGHTS RESERVED. *The Hebrew text of the Kitzur Shulchan Aruch has been edited,*
corrected, and newly set; the English translation and commentary —
including introductory material, notes, and insights –
as well as the typographic layout and cover artwork, have been written, designed,
edited and/or revised as to content, form and style.
Additionally, new fonts have been designed for the texts and commentaries.
All of the above are fully protected under this international copyright.

> **No part of this volume may be reproduced**
> **IN ANY FORM, including SCANNING, PHOTOCOPYING, OR FOR USE**
> **WITH DIGITAL RETRIEVAL SYSTEMS, AS AN AUDIO OR VIDEO RECORDING**
> **— EVEN FOR PERSONAL, STUDY GROUP OR CLASSROOM USE —**
> **without WRITTEN permission from the copyright holder,**
> *except by a reviewer who wishes to quote brief passages*
> *in connection with a review written for inclusion in magazines or newspapers.*

NOTICE IS HEREBY GIVEN THAT THE PUBLICATION OF THIS WORK
INVOLVED EXTENSIVE RESEARCH AND COSTS,
AND THE RIGHTS OF THE COPYRIGHT HOLDER WILL BE STRICTLY ENFORCED

ITEM CODE: KSA2
ISBN 10: 1-4226-0858-1
ISBN 13: 978-1-4226-0858-6

Typography by CompuScribe at ArtScroll Studios, Ltd.
313 Regina Avenue / Rahway, N.J. 07065 / (718) 921-9000
Bound by Sefercraft, Quality Bookbinders, Ltd. Rahway, NJ

This edition is dedicated in loving memory of our grandparents,
kedoshim who lived their lives and died al Kiddush Hashem.
We were not privileged to know them,
but their influence and inspiration still shape our lives.

Aleksander and Sima Leah Kleinman (Weiss) ז"ל הי"ד
ר' אלכסנדר ב"ר צבי אריה ז"ל הי"ד
מרת סימא לאה בת ר' אברהם ע"ה הי"ד

He was born in what was then Russian Carpathia. Livelihood was difficult. Six days a week were a struggle, but for this deeply spiritual, quiet chassidisher Yid, Shabbos was a day of bliss, in shul, beis medrash, and at the Shabbos table. The heartfelt zemiros and divrei Torah at the Shabbos tisch made the weekday hardship disappear.

She worked hard to help support the family, but Yiddishkeit was never a burden. It was an honor and a joy. She was wise and talented. Her neighbors in Brod and the surrounding area came to her for practical insight, chizuk, and medical advice.

Theirs was a home where shemiras halashon and dikduk b'mitzvos were paramount, and where there was one priority: that their sons must have the finest possible yeshivah education, and that their daughter be a true bas Yisrael.

Rabbi Elimelech and Yita Brocha Fischman ז"ל הי"ד
הרב אלימלך ב"ר ישראל ז"ל הי"ד
מרת יוטא ברכה בת ר' אברהם ע"ה הי"ד

He was born near Marmarosh-Sighet. A talmid of the Kedushas Yom Tov and the Arugas Habosem, he won early recognition as an exceptional talmid chacham. He was a brave yarei Shamayim who was freed from army service because he refused to cut his beard and payos, despite being threatened with prison — and even a bullet.

She descended from a family of distinguished rabbis, among them Rav Chaim Yoseph Gottlieb, the Stropkover Rav זצ"ל, a descendant of the Sh'lah Hakadosh.

He was a chavrusa and respected colleague of the future Satmar Rav, R' Yoel זצ"ל. Then he became gabbai to the legendary chassidic master, R' Shayaleh Keresztirer זצ"ל and his successors. Our zaide wrote many sefarim, including Lechem Abirim al haTorah. He was a renowned baal tefillah, and composer of soul-stirring niggunim. People traveled from afar to spend Yomim Tovim in Keresztur to hear his davening.

She stood proudly by his side to keep a home known for its vibrant spirit of Yiddishkeit, where they raised a houseful of children who distinguished themselves for their erudition and askanus.

יהי זכרם ברוך

משפחת קליינמאן
The Kleinman Family

מכתב ברכה
Letter of Approbation
HaGaon HaRav David Feinstein שליט״א

מתיבתא תפארת ירושלים
Mesivtha Tifereth Jerusalem of America
145 East Broadway / New York, N.Y. 10002
(212) 964-2830
Fax: (212) 349-5213

Rabbi David Feinstein
Rosh HaYeshiva

בס״ד

הנה ראינו במשך השנים את הסייעתא דשמיא של חברת ארטסקרול-מסורה במה שמוציאים לאור את הש״ס בבלי וירושלמי בתרגום וביאור השוה לכל נפש ועוד ספרים קדושים במטרה לעזור לצמאים לדבר ה׳.

ועל כן אמינא יישר כחם שמוציאים לאור בלשון המדוברת ע״י חבר תלמידי חכמים את הספר ״קיצור שולחן ערוך״ כפי שהוגה על ידי המחבר זצ״ל בחייו. והוסיפו לזה ביאורים נחוצים ופסקי הדינים במקומות שבעל המשנה ברורה זצ״ל חולק עליו, וגם פסקי דינים של אאמו״ר בעל האגרות משה זצ״ל, ועל ידי זה יהי׳ לפני הלומד שלשת הדיעות של בעלי הוראה אלו.

יתן השי״ת שיראו ברכה מרובה בעמלם ויצליחו ללמד דעת את המוני בית ישראל הרוצים ללמוד דבר ה׳ זו הלכה במתכונת של ספר ״קיצור שולחן ערוך״.

וע״ז באעה״ח ביום ד׳ לפ׳ משנה התורה, ג׳ אלול תשס״ח

נאום דוד פיינשטיין

TABLE OF CONTENTS

xix	PREFACE
1	DEFINITION OF TERMS

לה/35 הלכות חלה
THE LAWS OF CHALLAH

5

§1 The Mitzvah / §2 The Amount of Dough / §3 Loaves Become Combined by the Vessel / §4-5 Sourdough / §6 Dough Intended To Be Cooked / §7 Dough Kneaded With Fruit Juice / §8 *Challah*: The Woman's Mitzvah / §9 If One Failed To Set Aside *Challah* Before Shabbos

לו/36 הלכות מליחה
THE LAWS OF SALTING

13

§1-5 Soaking Before Salting / §6 The Vessel Used for Soaking / §7 After Soaking / §8 The Salt / §9-11 The Salting Process / §12 Rinsing After Salting / §13 Removing the Head / §14 Utensil Used for Salting / §15 Salting the Head / §16 The Bones / §17 The Legs / §18 The Heart / §19 The Lungs / §20-22 The Liver / §23 The Spleen / §24 The Rectum and Intestines / §25 Milk in the Calf's Stomach / §26 Eggs Found in Poultry / §27 Meat That Has Sat for Three Days / §28 Singeing Poultry

לז/37 טבילת כלים
THE LAWS OF IMMERSING UTENSILS

25

§1 The Mitzvah / §2 Immersing in Rivers / §3 Wood, Earthenware, and Porcelain Utensils / §4 A Nonkosher Utensil / §5-7 Situations of Halachic Doubt / §8-9 The Utensil's Function / §10-11 The Immersion / §12 A Minor / §13 Immersing on Shabbos and Yom Tov

לח/38 הלכות פת עכו״ם – בישולי עכו״ם וחלב עכו״ם
THE LAWS OF THE BREAD OF AN IDOLATER, FOODS COOKED BY AN IDOLATER, AND THE MILK OF AN IDOLATER

33

§1 Bread of an Idolater / §2 Participation of a Jew / §3-4 Breads Included in the Prohibition / §5 Dough Prepared by a Jew / §6 Food Cooked by an Idolater / §7-8 Food Cooked by a Maidservant / §9 When an Idolater Cooks for One Who Is Ill / §10-11 Foods Included in the Prohibition / §12 Beer and Other Beverages / §13 Milk of an Idolater / §14 Cheese of an Idolater / §15 Butter of an Idolater

לט/39 דין מי שרוצה לאכול או לשתות קודם הסעודה   45

LAWS GOVERNING ONE WHO WISHES TO EAT OR DRINK BEFORE A MEAL

§1 Foods and Drinks Before a Meal / §2 Wine and Liquor / §3 Baked Goods

מ/40 הלכות נטילת ידים לסעודה   52

LAWS OF WASHING THE HANDS FOR A MEAL

§1 Obligation of Washing the Hands / §2-3 Criteria for the Vessel / §4-6 Procedure for Washing the Hands / §7 Immersing the Hands / §8-10 Criteria for the Water / §11-12 Clean Hands / §13 Human Force / §14 When Water Is Not Available / §15 Using the Bathroom Before a Meal / §16 One Who Must Wash His Hands During the Meal / §17 Food Dipped in Liquid / §18-19 Which Liquids Are Included / §20 Foods Commonly Eaten With Cutlery / §21 Salt; Liquor

מא/41 הלכות בציעת הפת וברכת המוציא   69

LAWS OF BREAKING BREAD AND THE HAMOTZI BLESSING

§1 The Blessing /§2 Interruption After *Netilas Yadayim* /§3-4 Cutting the Bread /§5 Reciting the Blessing /§6 Salt /§7 Distributing the Bread / §8-10 Order of Precedence of Breads

מב/42 הלכות סעודה   79

LAWS OF PROPER CONDUCT FOR A MEAL

§1 Feeding Animals First / §2-3 Proper Manners in Eating and Drinking / §4 Severe Attitude / §5 Speaking, Torah, and Prayer During a Meal / §6-7 Two People Eating Together / §8-11 Respect for Food / §12 Modesty in Drinking / §13 Staring at One Who Is Eating / §14 Giving Food to the Server / §15 Giving Food to the Non-Observant / §16 Women Drinking / §17-18 Proper Behavior for a Guest / §19-21 Leaving During a Meal / §22 Interruptions During a Meal / §23 Ending the Meal

מג/43 הלכות ברכות לדברים שאוכלים ושותים בתוך הסעודה   91

THE LAWS OF BLESSINGS FOR FOODS THAT ONE EATS OR DRINKS DURING A MEAL

§1 Food That Is Considered "Part of the Meal" / §2 Beverages; Wine; Liquor / §3-5 Fruits / §6 Baked Goods / §7 Coffee After the Meal

מד/44 דין מים אחרונים וברכת המזון   99

THE LAWS OF MAYIM ACHARONIM AND BIRCAS HAMAZON

§1-2 Procedure for *Mayim Acharonim* / §3 Leaving Bread on the Table / §4 Removing the Knives / §5 Obligation for a *Kezayis* / §6 Position While Reciting *Bircas HaMazon* / §7 Amen After *HaRachaman* / §8-9 Waiting or Leaving Before *Bircas HaMazon* / §10 Laws of

Shabbos and Festival Additions / §11 One Who Is in Doubt / §12-15 Compensatory Blessing / §16 Omitting *Al HaNissim* / §17 A Meal That Lasts Into the Night / §18 When Eating With an Idolater

מה/45 הלכות ברכות הזמון
THE LAWS OF THE ZIMUN BLESSING

114

§1 *Zimun* Upon a Filled Cup / §2-3 Pouring the Cup / §4 The Condition of the Cup; Taking and Holding the Cup / §5 The Leader / §6 The *Zimun* Blessing /§7 Reciting the *Bircas HaMazon* With a *Zimun* / §8-9 Drinking the Cup / §10 Joining a Group at the End of the Meal / §11 Separating a Group of Three or More / §12-13 *Zimun* With Ten / §14 Forming a Group of Ten / §15 How a Group Is Joined / §16 When Some of the Group Recited *Bircas HaMazon* / §17 Reciting *Zimun* During a Meal / §18 Large Feasts / §19 Joining Two Groups Together / §20 *Zimun* Response for One Who Did Not Eat / §21 One Group, Different Foods / §22 Women, Minors / §23 Who May Be Joined to a *Zimun*

מו/46 הלכות מאכלות אסורות
THE LAWS OF FORBIDDEN FOODS

134

§1 Bloodspots in Eggs / §2 The Blood of Fish / §3 Blood Inside the Mouth / §4 Blood in Milk / §5 Meat and Dairy: the Prohibition / §6-7 Keeping Meat and Dairy Apart / §8 Separate Utensils / §9-12 Waiting Between Meat and Dairy / §13 Sharp Foods / §14 Milk Substitutes / §15 Changing the Use of a Utensil / §16-19 Food Left in the Hands of an Idolater / §20 Cooking in the Presence of an Idolater / §21 Eating Food of Non-observant Jews / §22 Leaving Utensils With Idolaters / §23-24 Situations of *Tereifah* / §25-27 Dairy or Meaty Bread / §28 Castrated Chicken / §29 Fattened Geese / §30 Pot-coverings / §31-33 Vermin in Water or Vinegar / §34-36 Fruit Infestation / §37 Wheat and Flour Infestation / §38-39 When Infestation Occurs / §40-41 Infestation in Nuts or Preserved Fruits / §42 Cutting an Infested Food / §43-44 Vermin in Fish or Cheese / §45 The Need for Vigilance / §46 Asking a Rav

מז/47 הלכות סתם יינם והכשר הכלים ממנו
THE LAWS OF WINE OF IDOLATERS, AND RENDERING UTENSILS USED WITH SUCH WINE FIT FOR KOSHER USE

159

§1 The Prohibition Nowadays / §2 Therapeutic Bath / §3 Cooked Wine / §4 Mixed Into a Cooked food / §5 Diluted Wine and Raisin Wine / §6 *Temed* / §7 Vats of Pressed Grapes / §8 Peels and Seeds / §9 If an Idolater Added Water / §10 Wine Vinegar / §11 Whiskey / §12 Tartar / §11 Indirect Contact / §14 Shipping Wine / §15 Producing Kosher Wine / §16 Utensils Used for Short-term / §17 Storage Utensils / §18 Glass Utensils / §19 Residual Moisture / §20 Hot Wine / §21 Winemaking Equipment / §22 After Twelve Months

TABLE OF CONTENTS xiv

מח/48 דיני ברכות על מאכלים מחמשת מיני דגן
168
LAWS OF BERACHOS UPON FOODS MADE OF THE FIVE SPECIES OF GRAINS

§1-4 Laws of *Pas Haba'ah B'kisnin* / §5-6 Cooked or Fried Dough / §7 Cooked or Fried Bread / §8 Proper Blessing on Mixture of Dough Products and Liquid / §9 Food Made From Bread Crumbs / §10 Predominance of Grain Products in Mixtures

מט/49 דין ברכת היין וברכת הטוב והמטיב
183
THE HALACHOS OF THE BLESSING FOR WINE AND THE BLESSING OF HATOV VEHAMEITIV

§1-3 Which Wines Require *Borei Pri HaGafen* / §4-6 Blessing Upon Wine Exempts All Beverages / §7 Reciting the Blessing During a Meal / §8-12 Reciting *HaTov VeHaMeitiv* Upon a Second Wine / §13-14 Drinking With Another / §15 Reciting *HaTov VeHaMeitiv* for Others / §16 The Cup of *Bircas HaMazon*

נ/50 כללים בברכה ראשונה מברכת הנהנין
193
GENERAL RULES OF BLESSINGS BEFORE FOOD, DRINK, AND FRAGRANCES

§1 Obligation To Bless Hashem Before Eating / §2 When in Doubt as to the Proper Blessing / §3 Reciting the Blessing While Holding the Item, or in Its Presence / §4 Dropping the Item After Reciting the Blessing / §5 Pause Between Blessing and Eating / §6 Pouring out Harmful Water / §7 Tasting / §8 Eating for Medicinal Purposes / §9 Eating or Drinking To Dislodge an Item From One's Throat / §10 Reciting the Blessing After Putting the Item in One's Mouth / §11-12 Reciting One Blessing for Two Items / §13-16 Change of Location After Reciting the Blessing

נא/51 כללים בברכה אחרונה
206
GENERAL RULES OF BERACHAH ACHARONAH

§1 *Borei Nefashos* / §2 Minimum Amount for *Berachah Acharonah* / §3 A Complete Item / §4-6 Combinations and Time Frame for the Minimum Amount / §7 Blessing Upon the Seven Species / §8-9 Variations of the *Mei'ein Shalosh* Blessing / §10 Like *Bircas Ha-Mazon* / §11 Version and Explanation of *Borei Nefashos* / §12 *Mei'ein Shalosh* and *Borei Nefashos* / §13 Reciting the Blessing in the Place Where One Ate / §14-15 Reciting the Blessing After Digestion

נב/52 דיני ברכת "בורא פרי העץ" ו"בורא פרי האדמה" ו"שהכל"
217
LAWS OF THE BOREI PRI HA'EITZ, BOREI PRI HA'ADAMAH, AND SHEHAKOL BLESSINGS

§1 Fruits and Vegetables / §2 Non-Plant Foods / §3 Mushrooms and Truffles / §4-6 Commonly Eaten Cooked or Raw / §7 Inferior Fruit / §8 Wild Plants / §9 Ancillary Growths / §10 Seeds / §11 Almonds / §12-14 Unripe Fruit / §15 Sucking Juice From an Inedible Fruit /

XV ✑ TABLE OF CONTENTS

§16 Recognizable Form / §17 Rice, Millet / §18 Sugar, Cinnamon, Licorice

נג/53 דין רוטב ומשקה של פירות וירקות — 230
THE LAW REGARDING BROTH AND JUICE OF FRUITS AND VEGETABLES

§1 Fruit Juice, Wine, Olive Oil / §2-3 Broth / §4 Water Used for Pickling / §5 Other Liquids / §6 Raisin Wine

נד/54 דין עיקר וטפל — 237
THE LAW OF PRIMARY AND SUBORDINATE FOODS

§1-4 One Food Eaten as a Result of Another / §5 Foods Cooked Together / §6 Solid and Liquid / §7 Spices With Sugar / §8 Olive Oil / §9 Preserves

נה/55 דין קדימה בברכות — 245
THE LAW OF PRECEDENCE OF BLESSINGS

§1 Different Types of Fruits / §2-3 The Seven Species / §4 *Ha'eitz*, *Ha'adamah* and *Shehakol* / §5 *Mezonos*, *Hamotzi* and *Hagafen*

נו/56 דיני טעות בברכות — 251
THE LAW REGARDING AN ERROR IN BLESSINGS

§1 *Mezonos* and *Hamotzi*; *Hagafen* on Grapes / §2 *Ha'adamah* and *Ha'eitz* / §3 *Ha'eitz* on Wine / §4 *Shehakol* / §5 Error in Intent / §6 Within the Time of *K'dei Dibbur* / §7 After the Time of *K'dei Dibbur*

נז/57 דין בירך על מאכל או משקה ואחר כך הביאו לו עוד — 257
THE LAW OF ONE WHO RECITED A BLESSING ON FOOD OR DRINK AND WAS SUBSEQUENTLY BROUGHT MORE

§1 Purchasing or Slicing Additional Bread / §2 Specific Intent / §3 No Specific Intent / §4 More Important Fruit / §5 Different Types / §6 A Guest / §7 Multiple Cups of Wine

נח/58 דין ברכת הריח — 263
THE LAWS OF BLESSINGS FOR FRAGRANCES

§1 The Blessing Upon Fragrance / §2 Fragrant Fruit / §3 Fragrant Trees / §4 Fragrant Herbs / §5 Non-plant Fragrances / §6 Balsam Oil / §7 Reciting the Wrong Blessing / §8 Fragrant Water or Oil / §9 Precedence of Blessings / §10 Incense / §11 Intended for Fragrance / §12 Spice Shop / §13 Fragrance Without a Source / §14 Forbidden Sources of Fragrance

נט/59 דין ברכת "שהחיינו" ו"הטוב והמטיב" — 272
THE LAWS OF THE SHEHECHEYANU AND THE HATOV VEHAMEITIV BLESSINGS

§1 Blessings Over Good Tidings / §2 Blessing Over Bad Tidings / §3 Long-term Consequences / §4 Everything for the Good / §5 Upon the Birth of a Son / §6 Upon the Death of a Relative / §7-9 Upon Purchasing an Item / §10 Upon Receiving a Gift / §11 Upon Acquiring Torah Books / §12 Insignificant Acquisitions / §13 "Wear Out and Replace!" / §14-17 Upon Enjoying New Fruits / §18 *Shehecheyanu* on Fragrance / §19 Enjoying God's Bounty / §20-21 Seeing a Friend After an Absence

287　　　　　　　　　　　　　　　　　　דין ברכות הראיה　　**ס/60**

THE LAWS OF BLESSINGS OVER SEEING [VARIOUS PHENOMENA AND EVENTS]

§1 Upon Seeing Fruit Trees Blossoming / §2-3 Upon Witnessing Natural Phenomena / §4 Upon Seeing a Rainbow / §5 Upon Seeing Oceans and Tall Mountains / §6-7 The Blessing of the Sun / §8 At the Location of a Personal Miracle / §9 Upon Seeing Great Scholars / §10 Upon Seeing a King / §11 Upon Seeing Graves / §12 Interval Between Blessings / §13-14 Upon Seeing Unusual Creations / §15 Upon Seeing Beautiful Creations

299　　　　　　　ברכת הגומל ועוד קצת ברכות פרטיות　　**סא/61**

BIRCAS HAGOMEIL AND OTHER BLESSINGS FOR SPECIFIC SITUATIONS

§1 Who Is Obligated To Recite the *HaGomeil* Blessing / §2 When and Where To Recite the Blessing / §3 Proper Procedures for One Who Experienced a Miracle / §4 Prayer Before a Medical Procedure or Taking Medicine / §5 Proper Response When Another Person Sneezes / §6 Futile Prayers / §7 Prayer When Measuring Grain / §8 Bar Mitzvah Blessing and Feast / §9-10 Blessings Upon Rain

308　　　　　　　　　　　　　　　הלכות משא ומתן　　**סב/62**

THE LAWS OF BUSINESS TRANSACTIONS

§1-5 Overcharging and Underpaying / §6 The Permissibility of Sales Promotions / §7-8 Accuracy of Scales / §9-10 Measuring Practices / §11-12 The Prohibition Against Owning Inaccurate Instruments of Measure / §13-14 Interfering With the Transactions of Another Jew / §15 Withdrawing From a Transaction / §16-17 Upholding Commitments Made to Others / §18 The Order of Precedence When Selling to Others

321　　　　　אסור להונות בדברים ולגנוב דעת הבריות　　**סג/63**

THE PROHIBITION OF VERBAL ABUSE AND DECEIVING PEOPLE

§1 The Severity of Hurting Verbally / §2-3 Examples of Hurting Verbally / §4-5 The Prohibition of Deception

325　　　　　　　שלא לעשות סחורה בדבר האסור　　**סד/64**

NOT TO CONDUCT BUSINESS WITH A FORBIDDEN ITEM

§1 Designated as Food / §2 A Forbidden Item Acquired Incidentally / §3 Collecting a Loan / §4 Forbidden by Rabbinic Law

xvii TABLE OF CONTENTS

סה/65 הלכות רבית   328
THE LAWS OF INTEREST (RIBBIS)

§1 The Stringency of the Prohibition of *Ribbis* / §2 One Who Accepted *Ribbis* / §3 Stipulated After the Loan / §4 Borrower Adds on His Own / §5 Gift of *Ribbis* / §6 Advanced and Deferred *Ribbis* / §7 Exchanging Loans / §8 Benefiting the Lender / §9 Words of *Ribbis* / §10 Benefit of Gratitude / §11 A *Se'ah* for a *Se'ah* / §12 Collateral / §13 Known Market Price / §14-15 Selling Promissory Notes / §16-17 Advancing Funds / §18-20 Purchasing Merchandise for Resale in Another Place / §21 Renting Real Estate / §22 Laborer / §23 Dowry / §24-29 Transactions Involving an Idolater / §30 An Apostate

סו/66 הלכות עיסקא   355
THE LAWS OF ISKA

§1 The *Iska* / §2-3 Permissible Stipulations and the *Heter Iska* / §4 Acquiring a Portion of the Profit / §5 After the Due Date / §6 Text of the *Heter Iska* / §7 Oral *Heter Iska* / §8 *Heter Iska* for Advancing Payment for Merchandise / §9 Writing an Ordinary Promissory Note / §10 When There Is No Business Venture / §11 Extending the Due Date / §12 Raising Animals

סז/67 הלכות נדרים ושבועות   367
THE LAWS OF VOWS AND OATHS

§1-2 Avoiding Vows and Oaths / §3 Vows for Charity / §4 Oaths or Vows Relating to Mitzvos / §5 Proper Vows / §6 Expressed Correctly / §7 Behavior That Constitutes a Vow / §8 Annulling a Vow / §9 Minimum Age / §10-11 Revoking Vows

סח/68 דין תפלת הדרך ושאר דברים שצריכין ליזהר בדרך   377
LAWS OF THE WAYFARER'S PRAYER
AND OTHER MATTERS THAT ONE MUST
OBSERVE WHEN TRAVELING

§1-2 When To Recite *Tefillas HaDerech* / §3 Adjacent to Another Blessing / §4 Reciting While Riding / §5 Once a Day / §6 Practices When Embarking on a Journey / §7 Ensuring Proper *Kashrus* / §8 Praying While Traveling / §9-10 Eating and *Bircas HaMazon* / §11 Leaving on Friday / §12 Protecting One's Money on Shabbos

סט/69 דיני תפלת מנחה   388
THE LAWS OF THE MINCHAH PRAYER

§1 Special Diligence With Regard to the *Minchah* Prayer / §2 Time of *Minchah* / §3 Engaging in Other Activities Before *Minchah* / §4 Washing the Hands for *Minchah* / §5 *Ashrei* and *Kaddish* / §6 When the Congregation Begins Late / §7 One Who Arrives Late for *Minchah* / §8 *Tachanun* and *Kaddish* at Night / §9 Reciting *Minchah* After the Congregation Ushered in Shabbos or the Festival

ע/70   דיני תפלת מעריב   398
THE LAWS OF THE MAARIV PRAYER

§1 Proper Time for *Maariv* and *Shema* / §2 Eating Before *Maariv*; Latest Time for *Maariv* / §3 Arriving Late to *Maariv* / §4 *Baruch* HASHEM *Le'Olam* and Announcements Before *Shemoneh Esrei* / §5 Waiting for the Last Person

עא/71   סדר הלילה   404
THE NIGHTTIME ROUTINE

§1 Learning Torah at Night / §2 The Evening Meal / §3 Introspection and Repentance / §4 The Bedtime *Shema* / §5 Proper Sleeping Position

411   APPENDIX A — SHIURIM: HALACHIC MEASUREMENT EQUIVALENTS

413   APPENDIX B — ZEMANIM: DIVISION OF HALACHIC TIMES THROUGHOUT THE DAY

419   APPENDIX OF KITZUR'S EDITORIAL GLOSSES

426   APPENDIX D — *HETER ISKA*

427   INDEX

447   THE TWENTY-FOUR BOOKS OF TANACH

xix  PUBLISHER'S PREFACE

❧ Publisher's Preface

It is with great pleasure that MESORAH HERITAGE FOUNDATION presents the second volume of a major ArtScroll project: the five-volume **KLEINMAN EDITION of the KITZUR SHULCHAN ARUCH — CODE OF JEWISH LAW.**

This classic work of halachah was written by Rabbi Shlomo Ganzfried זצ״ל in 1864. His goal was to provide a concise, clear guide that covers virtually the complete spectrum of Jewish law. This is especially important — even vital — for the typical school, shul, and household. Because the "Kitzur" provides a good, general knowledge of the corpus of Halachah, it has been part of the standard curriculum of yeshivos and day schools for generations. As an important and authoritative reference guide in the home, the Kitzur is especially important when a halachic question arises and people need to know quickly what to do. It can be every family's first reference and, as many leading rabbis have said, it lets people understand when to ask and how to ask if they have to consult a halachic authority and how to formulate the question.

The popularity of the Kitzur in Jewish communities around the world proves that Rabbi Ganzfried's classic work still fills a major need. It was reprinted twenty times in the author's lifetime, and many more times since then. It has been universally embraced by all segments of Ashkenazic Jewry, and it has achieved the unusual distinction of winning the respect of scholar and layman alike. In fact, the greatness of the Kitzur is perhaps appreciated most by halachic experts, because they can best see how the author was able to distill complex subjects into clear and deceptively simple language.

ArtScroll's Kleinman Edition of the Kitzur Shulchan Aruch has been carefully designed to combine the best of the old and the new. For the text, we use the Lemberg edition of 1884 — the last edition of the Kitzur that was annotated and approved by the author himself, and which includes his own corrections to earlier editions. We have been faithful to the text and spelling of the Lemberg edition, with the exception of obvious typographical errors, which have been corrected. We are grateful to the MUNK FAMILY of Bnei Brak for lending us their rare copy of that edition לעילוי נשמת הרב ר׳ אליקים ישראל הכהן מונק זצ״ל.

For ease of reading, we present a fully vowelized text of the Kitzur. Under the Hebrew text this edition provides a phrase-by-phrase translation and elucidation, following the much-admired integrated style that is familiar to anyone who has used a volume of ArtScroll's Schottenstein Edition of the Talmud, or the Rashi or Ramban commentaries on the Torah. Also included are notes that provide necessary explanations. Another very important feature is that topics are introduced with background information, so that the reader can have a clear understanding of the relevant laws.

This edition includes another important new feature, which will make this work much more useful to its readership: it contains relevant rulings from the *Mishnah Berurah*, where his rulings differ from those of the Kitzur. We have also included relevant rulings from the *Igros Moshe* of *Rabbi Moshe Feinstein* זצ״ל, where they differ from the Kitzur.

The volume also contains appendices that provide more detailed explanations of the measurements and *shiurim* used by the Kitzur. Also included are the original editorial glosses written by the author himself, which appeared in his 1884 edition.

THE KLEINMAN EDITION OF KITZUR SHULCHAN ARUCH is dedicated by our dear friends, THE KLEINMAN FAMILY, in memory of their grandparents. The Kleinmans are renowned throughout the Torah world for their warmth, integrity, judgment, and generosity. In America and Israel, their names are synonymous with concern for the health of Torah institutions and projects. ArtScroll / Mesorah readers are grateful to them for their dedication of important and popular projects, including individual Talmud volumes, three series of THE KLEINMAN EDITION OF A DAILY DOSE OF TORAH, the INTERACTIVE MISHKAN DVD and the beautiful, full-color books on THE MISHKAN, in both English and Hebrew editions, and the KLEINMAN EDITION OF THE MIDRASH. To us, it is gratifying that these personal friends have become an integral part of our work.

We hope that this work will be of great value to the Jewish public, and find a place in every Jewish home, school, library, and shul.

ACKNOWLEDGMENTS

We are deeply grateful to those who have been instrumental in creating this second volume of the KLEINMAN EDITION of the KITZUR SHULCHAN ARUCH / CODE OF JEWISH LAW.

HAGAON HARAV DAVID FEINSTEIN שליט״א, a founding trustee of the foundation, the Rosh Yeshivah of Mesivtha Tifereth Jerusalem and one of the world's leading *poskim,* has been a guide and counselor from the inception of Mesorah Publications thirty-two years ago. He recognized the importance of the project and provided invaluable guidance and counsel.

RABBI ELIYAHU MEIR KLUGMAN, an American-born Rosh Yeshivah and *moreh hora'ah* now living in Jerusalem, is the General Editor of this project and reviews the work for halachic accuracy; RABBI YOSAIF ASHER WEISS, Rosh Yeshivas Ohr HaDaas, Staten Island, serves as the Editorial Director, in addition to serving as the General Editor of the Kleinman Edition of the *Daily Dose of Torah — Limud Yomi* series, and as an editor of the Schottenstein Editions of Talmud Bavli and Yerushalmi. RABBI CHAIM MALINOWITZ, one of the primary editors of the Schottenstein Editions of Bavli and Yerushalmi, and a *rav* in Beit Shemesh, reviews and comments upon the entire manuscript. We are proud and fortunate that three scholars of such distinction oversee this project, assuring its halachic, pedagogic, and literary excellence.

We are grateful to the outstanding Torah scholars who contribute their talents to the writing and editing of this project: RABBI ELIEZER HERZKA, RABBI DOVID ARYEH KAUFMAN, RABBI SHMUEL KIRZNER, RABBI ELI LEFKOWITZ, RABBI MORDECHAI

xxi PUBLISHER'S PREFACE

SONNENSCHEIN, and RABBI YEHUDA WISCHNITZER; RABBI NOSSON KLUGMAN, who reviewed the manuscript and prepared the appendices; and RABBI MOSHE YEHUDA GLUCK, who has composed a comprehensive index. RABBI AVROHOM SHERESHEVSKY and RABBI MENACHEM DAVIS reviewed the manuscript and corrected the *nikud.*

MRS. AHUVA WEISS provided skilled literary editing; MRS. CHUMIE LIPSCHITZ paginated with her customary typographic skill; MRS. TZIPORAH FRANKEL and MRS. RACHEL GROSSMAN of Jerusalem provided editorial expertise; SURY REINHOLD and DEVOIRY WEISBLUM typed and corrected the manuscript; MRS. MINDY STERN and MRS. ESTHER FEIERSTEIN proofread and made many important suggestions.

Our dear friend and colleague RABBI SHEAH BRANDER has set the standard for graphics beauty for over thirty years. The clarity of the page design of this work is further testimony to his expertise and vision. ELI KROEN designed the sculpted embossed cover with his customary imagination and good taste.

RABBI GEDALIAH ZLOTOWITZ, a key member of the Artscroll administration, was the first to see the value of this project, and encouraged it from its inception.

The stellar staff members mentioned above, as well as the publishers, are grateful to the people who coordinate the production of, and facilitate the communication between, staff members on two continents. SHMUEL BLITZ, director of our Jerusalem office, is an indispensable colleague who, as per the popular saying, uncomplicates problems; AVROHOM BIDERMAN and MENDY HERZBERG oversee the often complex task of keeping the workflow smooth and efficient.

We are profoundly grateful to all the staff members who enable ArtScroll/Mesorah to carry out its mission of maintaining the highest possible standard of quality in bringing Torah classics to the English-speaking public with clarity and accuracy.

We express our appreciation to the trustees and committee members of the MESORAH HERITAGE FOUNDATION. They are all accomplished, busy men who contribute time and expertise to the cause of Torah literacy.

Finally, אחרון אחרון חביב, we thank Hashem Yisbarach for the indescribable privilege of bringing His Word to His people. May He bless all those who take part in this work with good health and the ability to continue to serve Him.

Rabbi Meir Zlotowitz / Rabbi Nosson Scherman

Elul 5769 / September 2009

THE KLEINMAN EDITION

קיצור

KITZUR
SHULCHAN ARUCH

שלחן ערוך

1 DEFINITION OF TERMS

כְּלָלִים / KELALIM

DEFINITION OF TERMS

[This list of definitions was written by the author of the Kitzur, and he placed it at the beginning of the volume to aid the reader.]

עַל אֵיזֶה דְבָרִים שֶׁיָּבֹאוּ כַּמָּה פְּעָמִים בְּסֵפֶר זֶה שֶׁלֹּא אֶצְטָרֵךְ לְפָרְשָׁם בְּכָל מָקוֹם
Definitions **for some terms used often in this work,** presented here **so that I will not need to explain them at each place** they are used.[1]

אֲגוּדָל / AGUDAL

❑ אֲגוּדָל — The term **agudal**[2] הַיְינוּ שֶׁמּוֹדְדִין בְּאֶצְבַּע אֲגוּדָל — **means, that one measures with the finger called *agudal*** (הוּא הָאֶצְבַּע הָעָב, דוימען פינגער — **this is the thick finger, the thumb),** בִּמְקוֹם הָרָחָב — **at its wide point,** שֶׁהוּא בִמְקוֹם הַקֶּשֶׁר שֶׁבֵּין שְׁנֵי הַפְּרָקִים — **which is at the place of the joint between the two sections** of the finger. (וְעַיֵּין סִימָן ט׳ סְעִיף ג׳ — **See Siman 9, *se'if* 3.**[3] שׁוּב הֶרְאַנִי נֶכְדִּי הַבָּחוּר יְחֶזְקֵאל בנעט נֵרוֹ יָאִיר מַה שֶּׁכָּתַב הַשַּׁ״ךְ סִימָן מ״ו סְעִיף קָטָן י״ג — **My grandson, Master Yechezkel Banet, may his light illuminate, later showed me what the *Shach* wrote in 46:13,** וּמַה שֶּׁכָּתַב הַפְּרִי מְגָדִים שָׁם — **and what the *Pri Megadim* wrote there;** וְאָנוּ הַנִּרְאֶה לְעֵינֵינוּ כָּתַבְנוּ — **we have written though, that which appears to our eyes** to be the law.) וּמוֹדְדִין בְּאֶצְבַּע שֶׁל אָדָם בֵּינוֹנִי — **One measures** the thumb-breadth **with the thumb of an average person,** וְהוּא כְּמוֹ שִׁבְעָה גַּרְעִינֵי שְׂעוֹרָה — **which is similar** in size **to seven kernels of barley** מוּנָּחִים זֶה אֵצֶל זֶה בְּרָחְבָּן — **placed near each other widthwise.** וְכֵן בְּמָקוֹם שֶׁנִּזְכָּר סְתָם אֶצְבַּע — **Similarly, wherever the word 'finger' is mentioned,** as a description for a size, **without specifying** which finger, הַכַּוָּונָה הִיא לְרוֹחַב אֶצְבַּע אֲגוּדָל כָּזֶה — **the intention is** to refer **to the size of this finger, the thumb.**

טֶפַח / TEFACH

❑ טֶפַח הוּא אַרְבָּעָה אֲגוּדָלִין — The *tefach* [pl. *tefachim*] **is** the size of **four thumb-breadths.**

אַמָּה / AMAH

❑ אַמָּה הִיא שִׁשָּׁה טְפָחִים — The **amah is six *tefachim.*** (וְהִיא לְעֵרֶךְ אַמָּה בעמיש — **This is approximately** the size of **a Bohemian cubit,** שֶׁהִיא שְׁלֹשָׁה רֶבַע אַמָּה ווינער הַנְּהוּגָה בִּמְדִינָתֵנוּ — **which is equivalent to three-quarters of the Viennese cubit that is commonly used in our country.**)[4] לִפְעָמִים מְשַׁעֲרִין הָאַמָּה בְּשִׁשָּׁה טְפָחִים דְּחוּקוֹת זוֹ

---

1. It should be noted that many of the terms and measurements mentioned here are discussed at greater length in Appendices A and B of this volume.

2. This term, as well as the *tefach, amah, mil, and parsah* that follow (all based upon the *tefach*), refer to spatial measurements.

3. There, Kitzur cites opinions that one measures the *agudal* at the narrowest point of the thumb. Kitzur rules that it is appropriate to follow this opinion when it leads to stringency.

4. The Viennese cubit to which Kitzur refers is equivalent to 30 2/3 in., or 77.92 cm. Thus, three-quarters of this cubit is approximately 23 in., or 58 cm.

לְזוֹ — Sometimes, the *amah* must be measured with six *tefachim* each pushed closely **to the next; וְנִקְרָאָה אַמָּה עֲצֵבֶת — this is called the "compact"** (literally, sad) ***amah.*** **וְלִפְעָמִים מְשַׁעֲרִין הָאַמָּה בְּשִׁשָּׁה טְפָחִים רְוָוחוֹת — Other times one must measure the *amah* with six *tefachim*** placed near each other **loosely; וְנִקְרָאָה אַמָּה שׂוֹחֶקֶת — this is called a "loose"** (literally, *happy*) ***amah.*** **זֶה וָזֶה לְהַחֲמִיר —** Depending on the case, **each** size of *amah* **is used when** this will result **in a stringency**[5] **(רמב"ם סוֹף פֶּרֶק י"ז מֵהִלְכוֹת שַׁבָּת — *Rambam, Hilchos Shabbos,* end of Chapter 17).**

מִיל / MIL

☐ **מִיל הוּא שְׁנֵי אֲלָפִים אַמָּה —** The ***mil*** **is** the equivalent of **two thousand *amos.*** **(וְהוּא שִׁיעוּר הִילּוּךְ אָדָם בֵּינוֹנִי — It is the amount that an average person walks ח"י מִינוּטִין —** in **eighteen minutes.)**

פַּרְסָה / PARSAH

☐ **פַּרְסָה הִיא אַרְבָּעָה מִיל —** The ***parsah*** **is** the equivalent of **four *mil.*** **(שִׁיעוּר הִילּוּךְ שָׁעָה וְחוֹמֶשׁ —** It is **the amount** that **one can walk in one and one-fifth hours,** i.e., seventy-two minutes.**)**

בֵּין הַשְּׁמָשׁוֹת / BEIN HASHEMASHOS

☐ **בֵּין הַשְּׁמָשׁוֹת — *Bein Hashemashos*[6] הִיא י"ג מִינוּטִין וַחֲצִי — is the thirteen-and-a-half-minute period קוֹדֶם צֵאת הַכּוֹכָבִים — before the stars emerge.**[7]

כְּדֵי דִיבּוּר / K'DEI DIBBUR

☐ **כְּדֵי דִיבּוּר — *K'dei dibbur* הַיְינוּ שִׁיעוּר שֶׁיְּכוֹלִין לוֹמַר שְׁלֹשָׁה תֵיבוֹת אֵלּוּ — is the amount** of time **during which one could say these three words: שָׁלוֹם עָלֶיךָ רַבִּי — *Shalom alecha rebbi*** ("Peace unto you, my master").[8] **וְתוֹךְ כְּדֵי דִיבּוּר פֵּירוּשׁוֹ —** When we say that something should be ***toch k'dei dibbur*** (*within k'dei dibbur*), **this means שֶׁלֹּא יִשְׁהֶה כָּל כָּךְ — that he should not wait as long as this time** of "*k'dei dibbur*."

בֵּיצָה / BEITZAH

☐ **בֵּיצָה הִיא שֶׁל תַּרְנְגוֹלֶת —** The ***beitzah***[9] **is** the egg **of a chicken. עִם קְלִיפָּתָהּ —** It is measured **with its shell,**[10] **לֹא גְדוֹלָה וְלֹא קְטַנָּה אֶלָּא בֵּינוֹנִית —** and refers to **neither a large egg nor to a small egg, but to an average**-sized **egg.**

---

5. Where the *amah* size is a minimum requirement, such as the obligation to distance oneself four *amos* from certain objects when reciting *Shema* (see 5:8), one must assume that the size required is the "loose" *amah,* and move away the distance of four of the larger *amos.* Where the *amah* is used as a maximum size, such as in a *succah,* whose *s'chach* may not be higher than twenty *amos,* one must assume that anything larger than the compact *amah* is too large.

6. This refers to a time period during the evening. There is ambiguity regarding whether it should be considered the end of the day or the beginning of the night; see further, Appendix B.

7. According to this ruling, the day extends until thirteen and one-half minutes before the stars emerge. See *Mishnah Berurah* (233:14 and 261:23), who writes that the day ends at sunset, and *bein hashemashos* begins then; see further, Appendix B.

8. [This refers to an increment of time, and is between one and two seconds.]

9. The *beitzah,* or egg, is the basic unit for measuring volume.

10. See, however, Kitzur 40:1 and note 8 there.

כְּזַיִת / KEZAYIS

☐ **כְּזַיִת הוּא כְּמוֹ חֲצִי בֵיצָה — The *kezayis* is equivalent to one-half of** the volume of **the *beitzah*. (וְעַיֵּין סִימָן קי״ט סְעִיף ז׳ — See,** however, ***Siman* 119 *se'if* 7).**[11]

רְבִיעִית / REVI'IS

☐ **רְבִיעִית הִיא כְּמוֹ בֵּיצָה וּמֶחֱצָה — The** ***revi'is***[12] **is equivalent to a *beitzah* and a half. וְהַמְּדִידָה הִיא כָּךְ — The** process of **measuring is as follows: מְמַלֵּא כְּלִי בְּמַיִם וּמְעָרֶה אֶת הַמַּיִם לִכְלִי אַחֵר — One** completely **fills a vessel with water, and then pours the water into another vessel. וְאַחַר כָּךְ יִתֵּן לְתוֹךְ כְּלִי זֶה שֶׁעֵירָה מִמֶּנּוּ אֶת הַמַּיִם — Thereafter, one places into this vessel from which he poured out the water, שְׁלֹשָׁה בֵיצִים — three eggs. וְאַחַר כָּךְ יַחֲזוֹר לְתוֹכוֹ אֶת הַמַּיִם — One then pours the water back into it** (i.e., into the vessel containing the eggs). **וְהַמַּיִם שֶׁיּוֹתִירוּ הַחֲצִי מֵהֶם הוּא רְבִיעִית — Half of the water that remains,** which will not fit back into its original container due to the eggs that are now in it, **is the volume of a *revi'is*.**[13] **וְכֵן כְּשֶׁיִּתֵּן לְתוֹךְ הַכְּלִי בֵּיצָה אַחַת — Similarly, when he places one egg into the vessel** from which he has poured out the water, **אֲזַי הַמַּיִם שֶׁיּוֹתִירוּ הַחֲצִי מֵהֶם הוּא כְּזַיִת — then half of the water that remains,** displaced by the egg, **is the volume of a *kezayis*. (עַיֵּין טוּר וְשֻׁלְחָן עָרוּךְ אוֹרַח חַיִּים סִימָן תנ״ו** — See *Tur* and *Shulchan Aruch, Orach Chaim, Siman* 456.)[14]

פְּרָס / PERAS

☐ **פְּרָס הוּא אַרְבָּעָה בֵיצִים בֵּינוֹנִים — The *peras* is the** dry **volume of four medium-sized eggs. וְיֵשׁ אוֹמְרִים שְׁלֹשָׁה גְּדוֹלִים קְצָת — And some** authorities **say,** the volume of **three slightly large** eggs.[15]

יֵשׁ אוֹמְרִים — There are those who say כִּי הַבֵּיצִים אֲשֶׁר בִּזְמַנֵּינוּ נִתְקַטְּנוּ הַרְבֵּה מִן הַבֵּיצִים אֲשֶׁר הָיוּ בִּזְמַן הַגְּמָרָא — that the eggs of our day are much smaller than the eggs that were extant **in the time of the Talmud, וְאֵינָהּ רַק כְּמוֹ חֲצִי בֵיצָה שֶׁנִּזְכְּרָה בַּגְּמָרָא וּפוֹסְקִים הָרִאשׁוֹנִים ז״ל — and** that **our egg is equivalent only to half** the volume **of the egg that was mentioned in the Talmud and** by the **early authorities, may their memories be blessed. נִמְצָא לְפִי זֶה — According to this, it would emerge כִּי בְּכָל מָקוֹם שֶׁנִּזְכָּר כְּזַיִת — that whenever *kezayis* is mentioned, הוּא כְּמוֹ בֵּיצָה שְׁלֵמָה — it would be equivalent to a whole egg, וּכְבֵיצָה הוּא כְּמוֹ שְׁנֵי בֵיצִים — *and a kebeitzah* would be equivalent to two** of today's **eggs; וּרְבִיעִית הִיא כְּמוֹ שְׁלֹשָׁה בֵּיצִים — and the *revi'is* would be equivalent to three eggs. וְהַמַּחְמִיר תָּבֹא עָלָיו בְּרָכָה — He who is stringent**

11. There, Kitzur cites opinions that the *kezayis* is slightly less than one third of a *beitzah*. Kitzur rules that if one has difficulty using the larger amount, he may rely on that opinion when the *kezayis* requirement is of rabbinic nature.

12. The *revi'is* is a unit of measurement for liquid volume.

13. Due to the irregular shape of eggs, one cannot accurately determine their volume unless one measures the amount of fluid they would displace. Since the *revi'is* is the volume of one and a half eggs, and since we have no method of determining the volume of half an egg, we must use three eggs and divide the displaced water.

14. There, the *Tur* states that this is the preferred method of determining the volume of the egg.

15. See *Mishnah Berurah* (612:8), who states that where the size given pertains to a Scriptural obligation, one must use the more stringent size; where it pertains to a rabbinic obligation, one may use the more lenient size.

in this matter, **blessings should come upon him** (עַיֵּין צל״ח פְּסָחִים דַּף קט״ז וַחֲתַם סוֹפֵר אוֹרַח חַיִּים סִימָן קכ״ז וְסִימָן קפ״א וְאִמְרֵי אֵשׁ אוֹרַח חַיִּים סִימָן ל״ג ל״ד **— see *Tzlach* to *Pesachim* 116, and *Chasam Sofer, Orach Chaim* §127 and §181; see also *Imrei Eish, Orach Chaim* §33, 34).**

כִּמְלֹא לוּגְמָיו / CHEEKFUL

❑ **כִּמְלֹא לוּגְמָיו — A cheekful**[16] **הוּא מַשְׁקֶה שֶׁנּוֹטֵל בְּפִיו וּמְסַלְּקָהּ לְצַד אֶחָד וְנִרְאֶה מְלֹא לוּגְמָיו — is the fluid that one takes into his mouth and then moves it to one side,** filling it **so that his cheek appears full. וְזֹאת מְשַׁעֲרִין בְּכָל אָדָם לְפִי מַה שֶּׁהוּא — This is measured with each person, according to his own size, הַגָּדוֹל לְפִי גָדְלוֹ וְהַקָּטָן לְפִי קָטְנוֹ — the large person's** cheekful **commensurate with his large size, and the small person's commensurate with his small size. וּבְאָדָם בֵּינוֹנִי הוּא רוֹב רְבִיעִית — The average person's cheekful will contain most of a *revi'is.***

חֲמֵשֶׁת מִינֵי דָגָן / FIVE SPECIES OF GRAIN

❑ **חֲמֵשֶׁת מִינֵי דָגָן הֵן — The five species of grain are: חִטָּה — wheat, וּשְׂעוֹרָה — barley,** (ספעלץ, שְׁקוֹרִין דונקעל) **כּוּסְמִין — spelt,** (האבער) **שִׁבּוֹלֶת שׁוּעָל — oats,** (קארען, ראגען) **וְשִׁיפוֹן — and rye.**

16. Regarding the requirement that one drink the *kiddush* wine, as well as for other laws, it is not considered that one has drunk unless one ingests a cheekful of fluid.

סימן לה

הִלְכוֹת חַלָּה[1]

וּבוֹ ט׳ סְעִיפִים

א. עִיסָּה מֵחֲמֵשֶׁת מִינֵי דָגָן[2] חַיֶּיבֶת בְּחַלָּה[3]. קוֹדֶם שֶׁמַּפְרִישִׁין הַחַלָּה מְבָרְכִין בָּרוּךְ אַתָּה ה׳ אֱלֹהֵינוּ מֶלֶךְ הָעוֹלָם אֲשֶׁר קִדְּשָׁנוּ בְּמִצְוֹתָיו וְצִוָּנוּ לְהַפְרִישׁ חַלָּה[4]. וְנוֹטְלִין

SIMAN 35

THE LAWS OF CHALLAH

CONTAINING 9 *SE'IFIM*

§**1** The Mitzvah / §**2** The Amount of Dough / §**3** Loaves Become Combined by the Vessel / §**4-5** Sourdough / §**6** Dough Intended To Be Cooked / §**7** Dough Kneaded With Fruit Juice / §**8** *Challah*: The Woman's Mitzvah / §**9** If One Failed To Set Aside *Challah* Before Shabbos

The Torah (*Bamidbar* 15:17-21) commands that when kneading dough, one must set aside a portion of the dough to be given to the Kohen. This portion is called *challah.*[1] In order for the *challah* to be eaten by the Kohen, the *challah,* as well as the Kohen, must be *tahor* (in a state of ritual purity). *Challah* that became *tamei* (ritually impure) may not be eaten and must be burned. Since nowadays we are unable to maintain the required level of purity, the *challah* must be burned after it is set aside from the dough. Biblically, the mitzvah of *challah* applies only in Eretz Yisrael and only when all of the Jewish people reside there. Nevertheless, the Sages extended the requirement to separate *challah* to apply in all places and at all times (*Yoreh Deah* 322:2).

§1 עִיסָּה מֵחֲמֵשֶׁת מִינֵי דָגָן — **A dough** that has been kneaded **from** one of **the five types of grain**[2] חַיֶּיבֶת בְּחַלָּה — **is subject to the obligation of** setting aside ***challah.***[3] קוֹדֶם שֶׁמַּפְרִישִׁין הַחַלָּה מְבָרְכִין — **Prior to the separation of *challah,* one recites the blessing:** בָּרוּךְ אַתָּה ה׳ אֱלֹהֵינוּ מֶלֶךְ הָעוֹלָם אֲשֶׁר קִדְּשָׁנוּ בְּמִצְוֹתָיו וְצִוָּנוּ לְהַפְרִישׁ חַלָּה — *Baruch Atah Ado-noy, Elokeinu Melech HaOlam, asher kideshanu bemitzvosav, vetzivanu lehafrish challah,* ***Blessed are You, Hashem, our God, King of the universe, Who has sanctified us with His commandments and has commanded us to separate challah.***[4] וְנוֹטְלִין

---

1. Literally, *challah* means "loaf," a reference to the portion separated and given to the Kohen (see *Rashi* to *Bamidbar* 15:20, s.v. ראשית ערסתכם). [The loaves of bread eaten on Shabbos are also referred to as *challos* based on the literal translation of the term, even though they are obviously not the *challah* discussed in our *siman* (see below, 72:6).]

2. The five grains are wheat, barley, oats, spelt, and rye. Dough made from a combination of these grains is also subject to the *challah* obligation, if together these grains comprise the minimum amount set forth in the *se'if* that follows (*Yoreh Deah* 324:2).

3. See Appendix of Kitzur's editorial glosses regarding a dough supplemented with potatoes.

4. Some add the words מִן הָעִסָּה, *from the dough,* at the end of the blessing. [If one is separating *challah* after the bread has been baked (see below, *se'if* 3) those words should not be added.]

LAWS OF CHALLAH — SIMAN 35:2 6

כְּזַיִת מִן הָעִיסָּה[5] וְשׂוֹרְפִין אוֹתָהּ בָּאֵשׁ. וְהַמִּנְהָג לְשָׂרְפָהּ בַּתַּנּוּר שֶׁיֹּאפוּ שָׁם אֶת הַלֶּחֶם.[6]

ב. כַּמָּה שִׁיעוּר הָעִיסָּה שֶׁיִּתְחַיֵּיב בְּחַלָּה? כֹּל שֶׁנַּעֲשָׂה מֵחֲמֵשֶׁת רְבָעִים קֶמַח, וְהֵם כְּמוֹ מ״ג בֵּיצִים וְחוֹמֶשׁ בֵּיצָה[7] (וְעַיֵּין בִּכְלָלִים אֵיךְ מוֹדְדִין)[8].

כְּזַיִת מִן הָעִיסָּה — One then **takes from the dough** a piece the size of **a *kezayis*,**[5] וְשׂוֹרְפִין אוֹתָהּ בָּאֵשׁ — **and burns it in the fire.** וְהַמִּנְהָג לְשָׂרְפָהּ בַּתַּנּוּר שֶׁיֹּאפוּ שָׁם אֶת הַלֶּחֶם — **The custom is to burn it in the oven where they will bake the bread.**[6]

§2 כַּמָּה שִׁיעוּר הָעִיסָּה — **What is the amount of dough** שֶׁיִּתְחַיֵּיב בְּחַלָּה — **that is subject to the obligation of** setting aside ***challah*?** כֹּל שֶׁנַּעֲשָׂה מֵחֲמֵשֶׁת רְבָעִים קֶמַח — **Any dough that has been made from five *reva'im* of flour.** וְהֵם כְּמוֹ מ״ג בֵּיצִים וְחוֹמֶשׁ בֵּיצָה — **This is equivalent to** the volume of **forty-three and one-fifth eggs.**[7] (וְעַיֵּין בִּכְלָלִים אֵיךְ מוֹדְדִין — See ***Kelalim*, Definition of Terms,** for instructions on **how to measure** egg-volumes.)[8]

---

5. Although nowadays the mitzvah can be fulfilled by separating even the smallest amount, the custom is to separate the volume of at least a *kezayis* (an olive's volume) of dough (see *Rama* 322:5), which is approximately .6 to 1.1 fl. oz. (17.3-33.3 cc); see Appendix A.

After separating challah, it is proper to declare: הֲרֵי זוֹ חַלָּה ["This is *challah*"] (*Shaarei Tzedek [Chochmas Adam]* 14:32; *R' Akiva Eiger* to *Yoreh Deah* 328:1; see also *Mishnah Berurah* 457:14).

6. That is, it is thrown into [the fire in the oven] before the bread is baked in the oven (see *Rama, Yoreh Deah* 322:5). One should bear in mind that since *challah* may not be eaten, it has the status of other prohibited foods, and it must not come into contact with food or utensils in a manner that would cause them to become prohibited. For this reason, before putting *challah* into the oven, it should be completely wrapped in aluminum foil, so that the oven should not absorb the flavor of the *challah,* which could in turn be absorbed by the food later baked in the oven. If one is unable to burn the *challah* properly, some authorities permit wrapping it and burying it (see *Chazon Ish, Demai* 15:1).

7. The Gemara (*Eruvin* 83b) derives this amount from the term עֲרִסֹתֵיכֶם, *your dough,* appearing in the passage that sets forth the *challah* obligation, that was transmitted to the Jewish people in the Wilderness. This amount is calculated based on another verse (*Shemos* 16:36) that describes the size of the daily portion of manna that each person received as a tenth of an *eiphah*, which is equivalent to 43 ⅕ eggs. [One *eiphah* = three *se'ah*; one *se'ah* = six *kavin*; one *kav* = four *lugin*; one *log* = six egg-volumes. Thus one *eiphah* = 3 x 6 x 4 x 6 = 432 egg volumes. One tenth of that is 43.2 egg volumes.] See also *Shabbos* 15a. [The expression "five *reva'im*" means "five quarters" (5/4) and refers to 1¼ *kavin;* however, the *kav* used in that calculation was a larger one, equivalent to 34.56 egg-volumes, so that 1¼ of those *kavin* equals 43.2 egg-volumes.]

8. Since the minimum amount of dough from which *challah* must be taken is a measure of volume (43.2 egg-volumes), and not weight, and the weight of a given volume of flour varies with the species of grain and its quality, therefore, weight is not an accurate means of determining whether a portion of flour is sufficiently large to be subject to *challah* (*Rambam Commentary* to *Eduyos* 1:2; see *Mishnah Berurah* 456:3).

Nevertheless, the Rabbis of each generation may use contemporary weights in presenting the *challah* obligation to the masses, provided they remain vigilant in noting any change in circumstances (see *Chazon Ish, Orach Chaim* 39:8). Therefore, many authorities have provided a minimum amount as a weight measure as well (see, for example, *Rambam,* ibid. and *Hilchos Bikkurim* 6:15).

Furthermore, since some uncertainty exists with regard to the determination of the exact measure, many authorities offer two weights, a lesser amount, at which point one should separate *challah* but not recite the blessing, and a greater amount, at which point one is required to recite the blessing as well.

According to R' Chaim Na'eh, one is required to separate *challah* without a blessing

ג. הַמַּצּוֹת[9] שֶׁאוֹפִין לְפֶסַח, אַף עַל פִּי שֶׁבְּכָל עִיסָּה בִּפְנֵי עַצְמָהּ לֹא הָיָה שִׁיעוּר חַלָּה[10], מִכָּל מָקוֹם כֵּיוָן שֶׁמְּנִיחִין אוֹתָן לְתוֹךְ כְּלִי אֶחָד, הַכְּלִי מְצָרְפָן, וְחַיָּיבִין בְּחַלָּה[11]. וּצְרִיכִין לְהַשְׁגִּיחַ שֶׁיִּהְיוּ כָּל הַמַּצּוֹת מוּנָּחוֹת בְּתוֹךְ הַכְּלִי[12]. וְאַף עַל פִּי שֶׁקְּצָת מִן הַמַּצָּה בְּתוֹךְ הַכְּלִי וּקְצָתָהּ בּוֹלֶטֶת חוּץ לַכְּלִי, גַּם כֵּן מִצְטָרְפוֹת. אֲבָל אִם מַצּוֹת שְׁלֵמוֹת מוּנָּחוֹת רַק לְמַעְלָה, וְלֹא בְּתוֹךְ הַכְּלִי, אֵינָן מִצְטָרְפוֹת. וַאֲפִילוּ כִּיסָּה אוֹתָן בְּמַפָּה, לֹא

---

§3 If two doughs were kneaded separately, each one containing less than the minimum amount for the *challah* requirement, and were subsequently joined together, they are subject to the *challah* requirement.[9] This *se'if* introduces a ramification of this law pertaining to bread that was already baked.

הַמַּצּוֹת שֶׁאוֹפִין לְפֶסַח — The matzah that is baked for Pesach is also subject to the *challah* obligation. **אַף עַל פִּי שֶׁבְּכָל עִיסָּה בִּפְנֵי עַצְמָהּ לֹא הָיָה שִׁיעוּר חַלָּה** — Even though the size of **each dough** kneaded for matzah **on its own contains less than the** minimum **amount** that subjects it **to the *challah*** obligation,[10] **מִכָּל מָקוֹם כֵּיוָן שֶׁמְּנִיחִין אוֹתָן לְתוֹךְ כְּלִי אֶחָד — nevertheless, since** after baking the matzos, **they are placed into one vessel, הַכְּלִי מְצָרְפָן — the vessel combines them** into one unit, **וְחַיָּיבִין בְּחַלָּה — and** thus, **they** all **become subject to the *challah* obligation.**[11] **וּצְרִיכִין לְהַשְׁגִּיחַ שֶׁיִּהְיוּ כָּל הַמַּצּוֹת מוּנָּחוֹת בְּתוֹךְ הַכְּלִי — Care must be taken** to ensure **that all the matzos are placed within the vessel.**[12] **וְאַף עַל פִּי שֶׁקְּצָת מִן הַמַּצָּה בְּתוֹךְ הַכְּלִי וּקְצָתָהּ בּוֹלֶטֶת חוּץ לַכְּלִי — Even if part of the matzah is in the vessel and part protrudes outside of the vessel** (i.e., above the walls of the vessel), **גַּם כֵּן מִצְטָרְפוֹת — they also combine** together. **אֲבָל אִם מַצּוֹת שְׁלֵמוֹת מוּנָּחוֹת רַק לְמַעְלָה, וְלֹא בְּתוֹךְ הַכְּלִי — However, if there are entire matzos situated only above, but not within, the vessel, אֵינָן מִצְטָרְפוֹת — they do not combine** with the others for the minimum amount required to set aside *challah*. **וַאֲפִילוּ כִּיסָּה אוֹתָן בְּמַפָּה, לֹא**

---

from flour that weighs 3 lb. 9 oz. (1.61 kg.) or more. According to Chazon Ish, one who kneads as little as 2 lb. 10.3 oz. (1.2 kg.) of flour should separate *challah* without reciting a blessing. [R' Chaim Na'eh agrees that a scrupulous individual should follow the ruling of Chazon Ish in this.]

In order to recite the blessing, one must knead a dough from flour weighing 3 lb. 10.8 oz. (1.66 kg.), according to R' Chaim Na'eh, and 4 lb. 15.4 oz. (2.25 kg.), according to Chazon Ish.

9. See *Yoreh Deah* 325-326 for the details of this law.

10. Kitzur explains below (110:4) that when kneading dough for the Pesach matzah, the custom is not to knead dough larger than the size that would be obligated in *challah*. Since it is difficult to be certain that one has measured accurately, the dough for matzah is generally made slightly smaller than this size.

11. The *challah* obligation is expressed in the Torah (*Bamidbar* 15:20) as applying to dough. Thus, initially, one should separate *challah* from the dough before it is baked. Nevertheless, where *challah* has not been set aside earlier, it is separated after the baking has been completed (see *Yoreh Deah* 327:5; *Orach Chaim* 457:1 with *Mishnah Berurah* §5). Similarly, when a dough was not subject to the *challah* requirement because it contained less than the minimum amount of dough subject to the requirement of *challah*, it can still become subject to that requirement after baking, if joined in a vessel with similar loaves from which *challah* has not been separated. Therefore, the matzos are subject to the requirement of *challah* if they are placed into one vessel after they are baked.

12. If a few matzos are in a large vessel, one must make sure that the matzos are touching each other in the vessel; see *Mishnah Berurah* 457:7.

מְהַנֵּי[13]. אֲבָל אִם מֵנִיחַ הַמַּצּוֹת בְּסָדִין, וּמְכַסֶּה אוֹתָן גַּם כֵּן עִם הַסָּדִין, נֶחְשָׁב הַסָּדִין כְּמוֹ כְּלִי וּמְצָרְפָן, וְאַף שֶׁבָּאֶמְצַע מְגוּלִּים. רַק יִזָּהֵר שֶׁלֹּא תֵצֵא מַצָּה שְׁלֵמָה חוּץ לַכִּיסּוּי.

ד. שְׂאוֹר שֶׁנּוֹטְלִין מִן הָעִיסָּה כְּדֵי לְחַמֵּץ בּוֹ עִיסָּה אַחֶרֶת, צְרִיכִין לִיקַּח קוֹדֶם שֶׁמַּפְרִישִׁין הַחַלָּה[14]. אֲבָל שְׂאוֹר שֶׁנּוֹטְלִין לְחַמֵּץ בּוֹ מַשְׁקֶה שֶׁקּוֹרִין בארשט, צְרִיכִין לִיקַּח לְאַחַר שֶׁהִפְרִישׁוּ חַלָּה[15].

מְהַנֵּי — **Even if he covered them** all **with a cloth, it is not effective** to combine them.[13] אֲבָל אִם מֵנִיחַ הַמַּצּוֹת בְּסָדִין — **Nevertheless, if he places** all of **the matzos in a sheet,** וּמְכַסֶּה אוֹתָן גַּם כֵּן עִם הַסָּדִין — **and also covers them with the sheet** by folding the sheet over the matzos, נֶחְשָׁב הַסָּדִין כְּמוֹ כְּלִי וּמְצָרְפָן — then **the sheet has the effect of a vessel, and combines them,** וְאַף שֶׁבָּאֶמְצַע מְגוּלִּים — **even if they are uncovered** somewhat on top, **in the center,** where the ends of the sheet do not reach. רַק יִזָּהֵר שֶׁלֹּא תֵצֵא מַצָּה שְׁלֵמָה חוּץ לַכִּיסּוּי — **But he should be careful that an entire matzah not protrude from the covering.**

§4 In Kitzur's time, bakers would leave a portion of dough unbaked, whereupon it would become very sour (fermented). This dough (which is known as sourdough, or starter dough) would be used as a leavening agent for subsequent batches of dough. This *se'if* addresses the proper manner to comply with the *challah* obligation with regard to this dough.

שְׂאוֹר שֶׁנּוֹטְלִין מִן הָעִיסָּה — **Sourdough that is taken from the dough,** כְּדֵי לְחַמֵּץ בּוֹ עִיסָּה אַחֶרֶת — **so as** to be used **to make another dough leaven,** צְרִיכִין לִיקַּח קוֹדֶם שֶׁמַּפְרִישִׁין הַחַלָּה — **must be taken before the *challah*** of the dough it is taken from **is set aside.**[14] אֲבָל שְׂאוֹר שֶׁנּוֹטְלִין לְחַמֵּץ בּוֹ מַשְׁקֶה שֶׁקּוֹרִין בארשט — **However, sourdough that is being taken to be used to ferment the beverage called "borscht"** צְרִיכִין לִיקַּח לְאַחַר שֶׁהִפְרִישׁוּ חַלָּה — **must be removed** from the dough only ***after*** **they have set aside *challah*.**[15]

§5 On Pesach, the Torah prohibits owning all *chametz* (leavened grain products), including sourdough. Therefore, in order to bake bread after Pesach, the baker must acquire sourdough from a non-Jewish source. This affects the procedure

---

13. See *Beur Halachah* (457:1 s.v. שיתן and s.v. והסל מצרפם) for further discussion.

14. Although *challah* may be separated from one dough for another dough, nevertheless, this is effective only if the dough that is being separated as *challah* is itself subject to the *challah* obligation. Thus, in this case, if *challah* had already been set aside from the initial dough before the sourdough was taken from it, the sourdough would no longer be subject to the *challah* requirement. One would then be unable to take *challah* from the second dough, for perhaps the piece of dough that is being designated as *challah* is the sourdough from the first dough, which is no longer subject to the *challah* obligation and cannot be separated as *challah* for the second dough. Therefore, one must set aside the sourdough *before challah* is taken from the original dough. Then, when the sourdough is added to a new dough as a leavening agent, it is subject to the *challah* requirement of the new dough. In this way, the new dough will not contain any portion that is not subject to the *challah* requirement.

15. When using the sourdough to initiate the fermentation process in a beverage, *challah* must be taken *before* separating the sourdough from the original dough, for once the sourdough is mixed into the beverage, *challah* will no longer be taken, as beverages are not subject to the *challah* requirement. Therefore, one cannot set aside a portion of dough to be used in this manner until the *challah* obligation is satisfied.

ה. לְאַחַר פֶּסַח, שֶׁלּוֹקְחִין שְׂאוֹר מֵעַכּוּ״ם לְחַמֵּץ בּוֹ הָעִיסָּה, צְרִיכִין לִיזָּהֵר לְהַפְרִישׁ חַלָּה יוֹתֵר גְּדוֹלָה מִמַּה שֶּׁהָיָה הַשְּׂאוֹר[16].

ו. הָעוֹשֶׂה עִיסָּה כְּדֵי לְבַשְּׁלָהּ אוֹ לְטַגְּנָהּ, מַפְרִישִׁין מִמֶּנּוּ חַלָּה בְּלֹא בְּרָכָה[17]. וְאִם עוֹשִׂין לֶאֱפוֹת קְצָת מִמֶּנָּה, אֲפִילוּ דָּבָר מוּעָט, מַפְרִישִׁין מִמֶּנּוּ חַלָּה בִּבְרָכָה[18].

---

for separating *challah,* as will be explained in this *se'if*:

לְאַחַר פֶּסַח — **After Pesach,** שֶׁלּוֹקְחִין שְׂאוֹר מֵעַכּוּ״ם לְחַמֵּץ בּוֹ הָעִיסָּה — **when we purchase sourdough from an idolater** to use **for leavening the dough,** צְרִיכִין לִיזָּהֵר — **we must be careful** לְהַפְרִישׁ חַלָּה יוֹתֵר גְּדוֹלָה מִמַּה שֶּׁהָיָה הַשְּׂאוֹר — **to set aside** as ***challah*** a portion of dough **larger than the size of the sourdough.**[16]

§6 הָעוֹשֶׂה עִיסָּה — **One who makes dough** כְּדֵי לְבַשְּׁלָהּ אוֹ לְטַגְּנָהּ — **for the purpose of cooking it or frying it** מַפְרִישִׁין מִמֶּנּוּ חַלָּה בְּלֹא בְּרָכָה — separates ***challah*** **from it, without** reciting the **blessing.**[17] וְאִם עוֹשִׂין לֶאֱפוֹת קְצָת מִמֶּנָּה — **If one makes** the dough **intending to bake a portion of it,** אֲפִילוּ דָּבָר מוּעָט — **even** if he intends to bake **only a small portion,** מַפְרִישִׁין מִמֶּנּוּ חַלָּה בִּבְרָכָה — **he must set aside *challah*** **from this** dough **with the blessing.**[18]

---

16. Dough kneaded when in the possession of an idolater is not subject to the *challah* obligation. Thus, when using sourdough purchased from an idolater, we are faced with a problem similar to that addressed in the previous *se'if* (see above, note 14). How can *challah* be taken from dough that has been leavened by sourdough purchased from an idolater? Perhaps the portion designated as *challah* will be the sourdough itself! Since this sourdough is not subject to the *challah* requirement, it cannot be used to satisfy the *challah* obligation for the dough kneaded by a Jew. [Here we cannot resolve the problem as we did earlier, by taking out the sourdough before *challah* is separated from the original dough. Since an idolater kneaded the original dough, it never was, and never will be, subject to the *challah* obligation.] In this case, we are required to separate a portion larger than the sourdough as *challah.* In this way, even if the sourdough itself is the piece being set aside as *challah,* along with it there will also be a portion of dough that has definitely *not* come from the idolater, and is therefore subject to the *challah* obligation. Thus, the *challah* obligation for this dough will be satisfied. (Although, the custom [as cited by Kitzur above, *se'if* 1] is to set aside a full *kezayis* of *challah*, nevertheless, with regard to the concern that we are faced with here, we may rely on its minimum requirement; see above, note 5. See Appendix of Kitzur's editorial glosses to *se'if* 1.)

17. When one mixes flour and water into dough with the intention of baking bread with it, the dough becomes obligated in *challah.* This obligation remains even if he ultimately changed his mind and did not bake it into bread, but cooked or fried the dough instead. However, if at the time of kneading, one planned to prepare the dough by cooking or frying, and did not plan to bake it into bread, there is uncertainty among the authorities regarding its status. Some authorities (*Tosafos* and others, cited by *Beis Yosef, Yoreh Deah* 329:3) maintain that if at the time of kneading, one planned to cook or fry it, and not to bake it into bread, and, he indeed cooked or fried it, it is nevertheless subject to the mitzvah of *challah. Shulchan Aruch* (*Yoreh Deah* 329:3), however, rules that since it was never destined to be baked, it did not become subject to the *challah* obligation. Therefore, although *challah* is set aside from such dough (to comply with the stringent opinion), nevertheless, a blessing is not recited, to avoid the possibility of reciting a blessing in vain (see *Shach* 329:4.)

If one changed his mind, and decided to bake the dough, *challah* must be taken with a blessing, even though he originally intended to cook or fry it (*Yoreh Deah* 329:2).

Note that these laws apply to a mixture that has a dough-like consistency. A cake batter, although also subject to the *challah* requirement, is not subject to this requirement unless it is being baked (*Yoreh Deah* 329:2); *challah* is separated after baking it.

18. Since he will be baking a portion, and it

ז. אִם הָעִיסָּה נִילוֹשׁ בְּבֵיצִים, אוֹ בִּשְׁאָר מֵי פֵירוֹת[19], יֵשׁ בּוֹ כַּמָּה סְפֵקוֹת[20], וְלָכֵן צָרִיךְ לְעָרֵב בָּעִיסָּה בִּשְׁעַת לִישָׁה קְצָת מַיִם, אוֹ חָלָב, אוֹ דְּבַשׁ דְּבוֹרִים, אוֹ יַיִן, אוֹ שֶׁמֶן זַיִת, דְּאָז מַפְרִישִׁין מִמֶּנּוּ חַלָּה בִּבְרָכָה[21].

§7 **אִם הָעִיסָּה נִילוֹשׁ בְּבֵיצִים, אוֹ בִּשְׁאָר מֵי פֵירוֹת — If the dough is kneaded with eggs or other fruit juices,**[19] **יֵשׁ בּוֹ כַּמָּה סְפֵקוֹת — there are a number of uncertainties** regarding its *challah* obligation.[20] **וְלָכֵן צָרִיךְ לְעָרֵב בָּעִיסָּה — Therefore, one must mix into the dough** **בִּשְׁעַת לִישָׁה — at the time that it is kneaded** **קְצָת מַיִם, אוֹ חָלָב, אוֹ דְּבַשׁ דְּבוֹרִים, אוֹ יַיִן, אוֹ שֶׁמֶן זַיִת — a bit of water, milk, bees' honey, wine, or olive oil.** **דְּאָז מַפְרִישִׁין מִמֶּנּוּ חַלָּה בִּבְרָכָה — For then,** if one of these liquids is an ingredient in the dough, **one must** certainly **set aside *challah* from this** dough, and do so **with the blessing.**[21]

§8 Although the mitzvah of *challah* is incumbent upon the owner of the dough, he may appoint another adult Jew to perform the mitzvah on his behalf. One may not, however, perform the mitzvah on behalf of the owner without being specifically appointed. In this *se'if* we will see an exception to this rule.

---

does have the properties of dough, it is certainly subject to the *challah* obligation, even if he intends to cook or fry the greater portion and the portion that is baked contains less than the minimum amount delineated in *se'if* 2 (*Yoreh Deah* 329:4).

19. In this context, any beverage other than those listed further in this *se'if* is referred to as fruit juice. [It should be noted, that with regard to the *challah* obligation, there is no difference whether the blessing recited when eating the final product is *hamotzi* or *mezonos*; see below, *Siman* 48, for the particulars of those blessings.]

20. There is disagreement among the authorities regarding the *challah* obligation of dough kneaded with a liquid other than those five mentioned further in this *se'if.* While some authorities (*Yoreh Deah* 329:9) maintain that this dough is subject to the *challah* requirement, others (*Rosh,* cited by *Shach* ad loc.) maintain that it is not. Moreover, a food does not contract *tumah* (ritual impurity) from coming into contact with something *tamei* unless it has first come into contact with water, grape juice, wine, or other liquids specified further in this *se'if.* Thus, if the dough was kneaded with a liquid other than those liquids, the *challah* that was removed from it is *tahor.* Now *challah* that is *tahor* may not be burned. On the other hand, it may not be eaten by a Kohen, as the Kohen is *tamei* and is forbidden to eat *challah.*

This poses a dilemma with regard to disposing of the *challah.* Kitzur will explain how this may be avoided.

21. By adding even a small amount of any of these liquids, both of the issues raised in the previous note are resolved. For a dough containing even a small amount of these liquids becomes subject to the *challah* obligation. And when any of these liquids are added, the dough can contract *tumah,* and the *challah* taken from it can thus be burned [as it contracts *tumah* when touched] (see *Mishnah Berurah* 462:20 with *Shaar HaTziyun* §27; see *Shulchan Aruch* there §5 for another solution).

In the event that one did knead dough with eggs or other fruit juices without mixing in water or another liquid listed in this *se'if,* he is required to set aside *challah* (*Yoreh Deah* 329:9; *Shaar HaTziyun* 462:27; see *Shach* and other commentaries to *Yoreh Deah* ad loc. with regard to whether a blessing is recited). In such a case, we are lenient with regard to *challah* that is set aside outside of Eretz Yisrael, and it is given to a Kohen who is under nine years old, who does not contract *tumah* that disqualifies one from eating such *challah* (*Rama* 329:10; *Mishnah Berurah* 462:20).

According to some authorities (see *Beis Hillel* to *Yoreh Deah* 329:9), it is preferable not to recite a blessing unless *water* (as opposed to the other four liquids) was mixed into the dough; see *Pri Megadim, Mishbetzos Zahav* 462:2).

ח. מִצְוַת הַפְרָשַׁת חַלָּה שַׁיָּיכָה לְהָאִשָּׁה בַּעֲלַת הַבַּיִת[22]. אַךְ אִם הָאִשָּׁה אֵינָהּ בְּבֵיתָהּ, וְיֵשׁ לָחוּשׁ כִּי בְעוֹד שֶׁתָּבֹא תִּתְקַלְקֵל הָעִיסָה, אָז יְכוֹלָה גַּם הַמְשָׁרֶתֶת, אוֹ אָדָם אַחֵר לְהַפְרִישׁ.

ט. שָׁכַח לְהַפְרִישׁ חַלָּה בְּעֶרֶב שַׁבָּת[23]: בְּחוּצָה לָאָרֶץ אוֹכְלִין בְּשַׁבָּת[24], וּמַנִּיחִין חֲתִיכָה אַחַת, וּמַפְרִישִׁין מִמֶּנָּה חַלָּה בְּמוֹצָאֵי שַׁבָּת[25]. וּצְרִיכָה שֶׁתְּהֵא חֲתִיכָה כְּדֵי לְהַפְרִישׁ מִמֶּנָּה חַלָּה וְיִשָּׁאֵר מִמֶּנָּה עוֹד חוּלִין, דְּבָעִינַן שֶׁיִּהְיוּ שִׁירֶיהָ נִיכָּרִין[26]. וְעֶרֶב פֶּסַח

מִצְוַת הַפְרָשַׁת חַלָּה שַׁיָּיכָה לְהָאִשָּׁה בַּעֲלַת הַבַּיִת — **The mitzvah of setting aside** ***challah*** **belongs to the woman** who is the **lady of the house.**[22] אַךְ אִם הָאִשָּׁה אֵינָהּ בְּבֵיתָהּ — **However, if the woman is not at home,** וְיֵשׁ לָחוּשׁ כִּי בְעוֹד שֶׁתָּבֹא תִּתְקַלְקֵל הָעִיסָה — **and there is** reason for **concern that by the time she comes** home, **the dough will spoil,** אָז יְכוֹלָה גַּם הַמְשָׁרֶתֶת, אוֹ אָדָם אַחֵר לְהַפְרִישׁ — **then the** Jewish **maidservant, or another person may set aside** *challah.*

§9 שָׁכַח לְהַפְרִישׁ חַלָּה בְּעֶרֶב שַׁבָּת — **If one forgot to set aside** ***challah*** **on Erev Shabbos** (i.e., Friday),[23] בְּחוּצָה לָאָרֶץ — then, if the dough was kneaded **outside of Eretz Yisrael,** אוֹכְלִין בְּשַׁבָּת — **one may eat** from it **on Shabbos** even before *challah* is set aside.[24] וּמַנִּיחִין חֲתִיכָה אַחַת — However, **one must leave over one piece,** וּמַפְרִישִׁין מִמֶּנָּה חַלָּה בְּמוֹצָאֵי שַׁבָּת — **and separate** ***challah*** **from it after Shabbos has ended.**[25] וּצְרִיכָה שֶׁתְּהֵא חֲתִיכָה כְּדֵי לְהַפְרִישׁ מִמֶּנָּה חַלָּה וְיִשָּׁאֵר מִמֶּנָּה עוֹד חוּלִין — **The piece** left over **must be** large **enough so that one can set aside** ***challah*** **from it, and some will still remain** that is fit for **non-sacred** use. דְּבָעִינַן — **For we require** שֶׁיִּהְיוּ שִׁירֶיהָ נִיכָּרִין — **that the portion that remains** after *challah* has been set aside **be identifiable.**[26] וְעֶרֶב פֶּסַח

---

22. As explained below, 72:6, women have a unique responsibility with regard to this mitzvah.

23. As stated earlier (*se'if* 3 and note 11), when *challah* was not set aside from dough, the obligation must be fulfilled after baking. However, on Shabbos one may not set aside *challah.* The reason for this is that since one is not permitted to partake of the bread before setting aside *challah,* it appears as though one is "fixing" the bread, and this is [Rabbinically] forbidden on Shabbos (see *Mishnah Berurah* 261:4).

24. As indicated in the introduction to our *Siman,* dough kneaded outside of Eretz Yisrael was never included in the Biblical obligation of *challah,* and the source of the obligation is Rabbinic. Therefore, when necessary (as on Shabbos), one may partake of the bread even before setting aside *challah,* and leave over some of the bread from which to separate *challah* after Shabbos (as will be explained by Kitzur). However, if the dough was kneaded in Eretz Yisrael, where the requirement is based upon a Biblical obligation, *challah* must be set aside before one may partake of it. Since this is prohibited on Shabbos, one may not eat these loaves on Shabbos.

25. With regard to a similar situation on Yom Tov, see below, 98:11.

26. One cannot set aside an entire dough for the *challah* obligation; a portion of dough not designated as *challah* must remain after *challah* has been separated. Even if the bread was originally larger (as in this case, where he is setting aside *challah* after most of the bread has been eaten), something must remain of the bread *after challah* is set aside. Therefore, one should leave over slightly more than the amount that he will be separating as *challah* (*Mishnah Berurah* 506:22). According to the custom cited by Kitzur in *se'if* 1, one should leave over somewhat more than a *kezayis*-sized piece, so that the portion he will set aside as *challah* can be the size of a *kezayis.*

שֶׁחָל לִהְיוֹת בְּשַׁבָּת וְשָׁכְחוּ לְהַפְרִישׁ חַלָּה מִן הַחַלּוֹת שֶׁאָפוּ לִכְבוֹד שַׁבָּת, יֵשׁ בָּזֶה מְבוּכָה גְדוֹלָה[27], עַל כֵּן צָרִיךְ כָּל אִישׁ לְהִזָּהֵר בְּעֶרֶב שַׁבָּת וּלְהַזְכִּיר עַל הַפְרָשַׁת חַלָּה (וְעַיֵּין לְקַמָּן סוֹף סִימָן קט״ו)[28].

שֶׁחָל לִהְיוֹת בְּשַׁבָּת — If, when Erev Pesach falls on Shabbos, **וְשָׁכְחוּ לְהַפְרִישׁ חַלָּה מִן הַחַלּוֹת שֶׁאָפוּ לִכְבוֹד שַׁבָּת** — they forgot to set aside *challah* from the loaves that they baked in honor of Shabbos, **יֵשׁ בָּזֶה מְבוּכָה גְדוֹלָה** — there is a great **dilemma** regarding how to resolve this issue.[27] **עַל כֵּן צָרִיךְ כָּל אִישׁ לְהִזָּהֵר בְּעֶרֶב שַׁבָּת** — Therefore, each person must take care on Erev Shabbos **וּלְהַזְכִּיר עַל הַפְרָשַׁת חַלָּה** — **to remind** his household **about** the requirement of **setting aside** ***challah*** **(וְעַיֵּין לְקַמָּן סוֹף סִימָן קט״ו** — **see further, end of *Siman* 115).**[28]

27. If one baked *chametz* (i.e., leavened) loaves for use on this Shabbos, but did not set aside *challah* from them, he will not be able to set aside *challah* from these loaves after Shabbos. Since Pesach immediately follows this Shabbos, he will no longer be permitted to have any remnant of the loaves in his possession, since all *chametz* must be removed from one's possession before Pesach. Although the authorities offer a number of suggestions that can be followed in this situation, there is no clear solution. See next note.

28. There (115:6), Kitzur cites the position of *Magen Avraham* that if one did forget, there is no recourse other than to give all of the bread to an idolater as a gift before the time that it is forbidden to own *chametz*. See notes there for further discussion.

13 LAWS OF SALTING — SIMAN 36:1

סימן לו

הִלְכוֹת מְלִיחָה

וּבוֹ כ״ח סְעִיפִים

א. קוֹדֶם שֶׁמּוֹלְחִין אֶת הַבָּשָׂר צְרִיכִין לְהָדִיחַ אוֹתוֹ יָפֶה יָפֶה בְּמַיִם[1]. שׁוֹרִין אוֹתוֹ בְּמַיִם לְעֵרֶךְ חֲצִי שָׁעָה, וְצָרִיךְ שֶׁהַמַּיִם יְכַסּוּ כָּל הַבָּשָׂר. בְּמָקוֹם שֶׁיֵּשׁ דָּם בְּעַיִן עַל הַבָּשָׂר,

SIMAN 36

THE LAWS OF SALTING

CONTAINING 28 *SE'IFIM*

§1-5 Soaking Before Salting / **§6** The Vessel Used for Soaking / **§7** After Soaking / **§8** The Salt / **§9-11** The Salting Process / **§12** Rinsing After Salting / **§13** Removing the Head / **§14** Utensil Used for Salting / **§15** Salting the Head / **§16** The Bones / **§17** The Legs / **§18** The Heart / **§19** The Lungs / **§20-22** The Liver / **§23** The Spleen / **§24** The Rectum and Intestines / **§25** Milk in the Calf's Stomach / **§26** Eggs Found in Poultry / **§27** Meat That Has Sat for Three Days / **§28** Singeing Poultry

It is prohibited to consume blood of both animals and poultry. This prohibition applies to any blood that has either emerged from the meat at one point or has pooled in some of the animal's blood vessels, but does not apply to blood that had been absorbed and remained absorbed in its place in the meat of the animal. In the process of cooking, blood emerges from the meat and from the blood vessels. This blood is prohibited, and if reabsorbed into the meat, can cause the meat to become prohibited. In addition, some of the blood may become absorbed into the utensils in which the meat is cooked, and cause those utensils to be prohibited for further use.

To prevent this, before cooking meat, one must extract all the blood that is absorbed within the meat. The Sages determined that proper salting of meat prior to cooking, when accompanied by thorough rinsing, effectively extracts blood. Alternatively, the meat can be roasted over a fire, which also draws out the blood. These procedures, known as *kashering*, and the laws that are relevant to this process, are outlined in this *Siman*.

§1 קוֹדֶם שֶׁמּוֹלְחִין אֶת הַבָּשָׂר — **Before salting meat,** צְרִיכִין לְהָדִיחַ אוֹתוֹ יָפֶה יָפֶה בְּמַיִם — **one must rinse it extremely well in water.**[1] שׁוֹרִין אוֹתוֹ בְּמַיִם לְעֵרֶךְ חֲצִי שָׁעָה — To accomplish this, **one must soak it in water for approximately half an hour,** וְצָרִיךְ שֶׁהַמַּיִם יְכַסּוּ כָּל הַבָּשָׂר — **and it is necessary** for this process **that the water cover the entire** piece of **meat.** בְּמָקוֹם שֶׁיֵּשׁ דָּם בְּעַיִן עַל הַבָּשָׂר — **Where**

1. Meat must be soaked prior to salting for several reasons. The two primary reasons are: (1) Soaking softens the meat and thus enables the salt to draw out the blood. (2) Salt draws out only moist blood. Without soaking, the dried blood on the surface of the meat will remain there and then be absorbed into the meat at the conclusion of the salting process (see *Yoreh Deah* 69:1 with commentaries and *Pri Megadim*, Introduction to Laws of Salting).

צְרִיכִין לְשַׁפְשְׁפוֹ בְּמֵי הַשְׁרִיָּה וְלַהֲסִירוֹ. וְכֵן בְּעוֹפוֹת צְרִיכִין לְשַׁפְשֵׁף הֵיטֵב בִּמְקוֹם הַשְּׁחִיטָה, וְכֵן מִבִּפְנִים בְּמָקוֹם שֶׁיֵּשׁ דָּם בְּעַיִן. וְלִפְעָמִים נִמְצָא בְּבָשָׂר אוֹ בְּעוֹף מָקוֹם שֶׁנִּצְרַר בּוֹ דָּם מֵחֲמַת מַכָּה — צְרִיכִין לַחְתּוֹךְ הַמָּקוֹם הַזֶּה וְלַהֲסִירוֹ קוֹדֶם הַשְׁרִיָּה[2]. כְּשֶׁהַמַּיִם קָרִים מְאוֹד יַנִּיחֵם תְּחִלָּה בְּמָקוֹם חַם קְצָת לְהָפִיג צִינָּתָן קוֹדֶם שֶׁשּׁוֹרִין בָּהֶן אֶת הַבָּשָׂר כִּי מֵחֲמַת הַקְּרִירוּת שֶׁבַּמַּיִם יִתְקַשֶּׁה הַבָּשָׂר וְלֹא יֵצֵא אַחַר כָּךְ הַדָּם בִּמְלִיחָה (בֵּית יוֹסֵף).

ב. אִם שָׁכְחוּ וְנִשְׁרָה הַבָּשָׂר בְּמַיִם מֵעֵת לְעֵת, הַבָּשָׂר וְגַם הַכְּלִי אָסוּר[3]. וְכָבֵד שֶׁנִּשְׁרָה בְּמַיִם מֵעֵת לְעֵת יַעֲשֶׂה שְׁאֵלַת חָכָם[4].

---

there is visible blood on the surface of the **meat,** **צְרִיכִין לְשַׁפְשְׁפוֹ בְּמֵי הַשְׁרִיָּה וְלַהֲסִירוֹ** — **one must rub it with the water** in which it is being **soaked, and remove** the blood. **וְכֵן בְּעוֹפוֹת** — **Similarly,** before salting **poultry,** **צְרִיכִין לְשַׁפְשֵׁף הֵיטֵב בִּמְקוֹם הַשְּׁחִיטָה** — **one must rub the place of the slaughter** (i.e., the cut in the neck) **well** to remove all blood. **וְכֵן מִבִּפְנִים בְּמָקוֹם שֶׁיֵּשׁ דָּם בְּעַיִן** — **Similarly,** one must rub the **internal** meat surfaces **where there is visible blood.** **וְלִפְעָמִים נִמְצָא בְּבָשָׂר אוֹ בְּעוֹף** — **Sometimes there is found, within meat or poultry,** **מָקוֹם שֶׁנִּצְרַר בּוֹ דָּם מֵחֲמַת מַכָּה** — **a spot where blood has coagulated** under the flesh **as a result of a wound.** **צְרִיכִין לַחְתּוֹךְ הַמָּקוֹם הַזֶּה וְלַהֲסִירוֹ קוֹדֶם הַשְׁרִיָּה** — In this case **one must cut** open **this spot, and remove** the gathered blood **before soaking** the meat.[2] **כְּשֶׁהַמַּיִם קָרִים מְאוֹד** — **When the water** to be used for soaking **is very cold,** **יַנִּיחֵם תְּחִלָּה בְּמָקוֹם חַם קְצָת** — **one should first place** the water **in a slightly warm spot,** **לְהָפִיג צִינָּתָן קוֹדֶם שֶׁשּׁוֹרִין בָּהֶן אֶת הַבָּשָׂר** — in order **to lessen the coldness** of the water **before soaking the meat in it.** **כִּי** — **For** if this is not done, **מֵחֲמַת הַקְּרִירוּת שֶׁבַּמַּיִם** — **as a result of the coldness of the water** **יִתְקַשֶּׁה הַבָּשָׂר** — **the meat will harden,** **וְלֹא יֵצֵא אַחַר כָּךְ הַדָּם בִּמְלִיחָה** — **and the blood will not come out afterward when it is salted** (**בֵּית יוֹסֵף** — *Beis Yosef, Yoreh Deah* §69 s.v. כיצד).

§2 **אִם שָׁכְחוּ** — **If they forgot** to remove the meat **וְנִשְׁרָה הַבָּשָׂר בְּמַיִם מֵעֵת לְעֵת** — **and the meat soaked in the water for twenty-four hours,** **הַבָּשָׂר וְגַם הַכְּלִי אָסוּר** — both **the meat and the vessel** in which it soaked **are forbidden.**[3] **וְכָבֵד שֶׁנִּשְׁרָה בְּמַיִם מֵעֵת לְעֵת** — **If liver has soaked in water for twenty-four hours,** **יַעֲשֶׂה שְׁאֵלַת חָכָם** — **one must consult a competent halachic authority.**[4]

---

2. Coagulated blood is not extracted in the salting process. One must therefore remove it before the salting can begin.

Shulchan Aruch (*Yoreh Deah* 67:4) offers another solution: One should make cuts in the meat in the place of the wound before salting the meat. The salt will thus draw out the blood from that area as well. One who purchases salted meat or poultry and finds an area that is discolored due to the coagulation of blood should consult a halachic authority.

3. After soaking for twenty-four hours, the meat and the vessel both absorb the taste of the blood, and become prohibited. The meat may not be eaten, and the vessel may not be used to prepare other foods (see *Yoreh Deah* 105:1).

4. At times, liver may be treated more leniently with regard to this law. For being that it is saturated with blood, it may, in the process of soaking, only expel blood and not reabsorb any of the blood in the water. Since the halachah is dependent on the specific circumstances of each situation, one must consult a competent halachic authority each time that this occurs.

ג. בְּעֶרֶב שַׁבָּת שֶׁאֵין לוֹ פְּנַאי, אוֹ בְּעִנְיָן אַחֵר שֶׁהַשָּׁעָה דְחוּקָה, דַּי לְשַׁפְשֵׁף הֵיטֵב אֶת הַבָּשָׂר בְּמַיִם וְיִשְׁרֶה אַךְ מְעַט בְּמַיִם. וּכְשֶׁאֵין אַדְמוּמִית בְּמַיִם יְכוֹלִין לְמְלוֹחַ אוֹתוֹ.

ד. אִם לְאַחַר הַשְּׁרִיָּה חָתְכוּ חֲתִיכָה אַחַת לִשְׁתַּיִם, צְרִיכִין לְהָדִיחַ הֵיטֵב מְקוֹם הַחֲתָךְ מִפְּנֵי הַדָּם שֶׁיֶּשְׁנוֹ שָׁם[5].

ה. בָּשָׂר שֶׁנִּקְרַשׁ מֵחֲמַת הַקּוֹר — צְרִיכִין לְהַשְׁגִּיחַ שֶׁיִּפָּשֵׁר[6], אֲבָל לֹא יַנִּיחוּהוּ אֵצֶל תַּנּוּר שֶׁהוּסַּק[7]. וּבִשְׁעַת הַדְּחָק יְכוֹלִין לְשָׁרוֹתוֹ בְּמַיִם פּוֹשְׁרִין[8].

ו. הַכְּלִי הַמְיוּחָד לִשְׁרִיַּית בָּשָׂר, אֵין לְהִשְׁתַּמֵּשׁ בּוֹ דָּבָר אַחֵר שֶׁל מַאֲכָל[9].

---

§3 **בְּעֶרֶב שַׁבָּת שֶׁאֵין לוֹ פְּנַאי — When, on Erev Shabbos** (i.e., Friday), **one does not have** enough **time** to soak the meat for a half-hour before salting, due to the impending arrival of Shabbos, **אוֹ בְּעִנְיָן אַחֵר שֶׁהַשָּׁעָה דְחוּקָה — or in another situation when there is time pressure, דַּי לְשַׁפְשֵׁף הֵיטֵב אֶת הַבָּשָׂר בְּמַיִם — it is sufficient to rub the meat thoroughly** while rinsing it **with water, וְיִשְׁרֶה אַךְ מְעַט בְּמַיִם — and** then **soak it in water for only a short time; וּכְשֶׁאֵין אַדְמוּמִית בְּמַיִם — once no redness** remains **in the water** with which one is rinsing the meat, **יְכוֹלִין לְמְלוֹחַ אוֹתוֹ — they may salt the meat.**

§4 **אִם לְאַחַר הַשְּׁרִיָּה חָתְכוּ חֲתִיכָה אַחַת לִשְׁתַּיִם— If, after the soaking, they cut one piece** of meat **into two, צְרִיכִין לְהָדִיחַ הֵיטֵב מְקוֹם הַחֲתָךְ — they must rinse the place of the cut** very **well** before salting, **מִפְּנֵי הַדָּם שֶׁיֶּשְׁנוֹ שָׁם — because of the blood that is present** in that area.[5]

§5 **בָּשָׂר שֶׁנִּקְרַשׁ מֵחֲמַת הַקּוֹר** — Regarding **meat that has become frozen due to the cold, צְרִיכִין לְהַשְׁגִּיחַ שֶׁיִּפָּשֵׁר — care must be taken** to ensure **that it is thawed** before it is salted.[6] **אֲבָל לֹא יַנִּיחוּהוּ אֵצֶל תַּנּוּר שֶׁהוּסַּק — However, one should not place it near a heated oven.**[7] **וּבִשְׁעַת הַדְּחָק יְכוֹלִין לְשָׁרוֹתוֹ בְּמַיִם פּוֹשְׁרִין — In pressing situations, one may soak it in warm water.**[8]

§6 **הַכְּלִי הַמְיוּחָד לִשְׁרִיַּית בָּשָׂר — The vessel that is designated for the soaking of meat אֵין לְהִשְׁתַּמֵּשׁ בּוֹ דָּבָר אַחֵר שֶׁל מַאֲכָל — should not be used for any other food-related purpose.**[9]

---

5. When meat is cut, the blood that had previously been absorbed within the piece is now on the surface of the cut. Having emerged from the meat, the blood becomes prohibited (see introduction to this *Siman*). One must therefore rinse the area of the cut before salting to prevent that blood from becoming reabsorbed into the meat, thus rendering the meat prohibited.

6. When the meat is frozen, the salt cannot penetrate it. One must thaw the meat to a point that it is no longer hard.

7. The heat from the oven can cause the blood to become so deeply absorbed into the meat that even subsequent salting will not be able to draw it out. [See below, *se'if* 28, where this issue arises again.]

8. Warm water is generally to be avoided because one may inadvertently use water that is too hot. Hot water can have the same effect as placing the meat near an oven: the heat will cause the blood to become absorbed to the point that it cannot be drawn out by the subsequent salting process. Thus, one may use warm water only in pressing circumstances.

9. Since the regular use of this vessel is for soaking meat, we are concerned that it may

ז. לְאַחַר שֶׁנִּשְׁרָה הַבָּשָׂר צְרִיכִין לְהַטִּיף מִמֶּנּוּ הַמַּיִם כְּדֵי שֶׁלֹּא יִמַּס הַמֶּלַח מִן הַמַּיִם וְלֹא יוֹצִיא אֶת הַדָּם וּצְרִיכִין לְהַשְׁגִּיחַ שֶׁלֹּא יִתְיַבֵּשׁ הַבָּשָׂר לְגַמְרֵי בִּכְדֵי שֶׁלֹּא יִפּוֹל הַמֶּלַח מֵעָלָיו.

ח. הַמֶּלַח לֹא יְהֵא דַק מְאוֹד כְּקֶמַח, דְּאִם כֵּן נָמֵס מִיָּד עַל הַבָּשָׂר וְאֵינוֹ מוֹצִיא דָם. וְגַם לֹא יְהֵא גַּס מְאוֹד, שֶׁמָּא יִפּוֹל מֵעַל הַבָּשָׂר. אֶלָּא יְהֵא בֵּינוֹנִי, כְּמוֹ הַמֶּלַח שֶׁנַּעֲשָׂה עַל יְדֵי בִּישׁוּל, וִיהֵא יָבֵשׁ שֶׁיִּתְפַּזֵּר הֵיטֵב.

ט. צְרִיכִין לְפַזֵּר הַמֶּלַח עַל הַבָּשָׂר בְּכָל הַצְּדָדִין, שֶׁלֹּא יִשָּׁאֵר שׁוּם מָקוֹם בְּלִי מֶלַח[10]. וְלָכֵן, הָעוֹפוֹת צְרִיכִין לְפַתּוֹחַ אוֹתָן הֵיטֵב, כְּדֵי שֶׁיּוּכַל לְמָלְחָן הֵיטֵב גַּם מִבִּפְנִים[11].

---

§7 **לְאַחַר שֶׁנִּשְׁרָה הַבָּשָׂר צְרִיכִין לְהַטִּיף מִמֶּנּוּ הַמַּיִם — After the meat has soaked, one must** allow **the water to drip off of it** before putting salt on the meat **כְּדֵי שֶׁלֹּא יִמַּס הַמֶּלַח מִן הַמַּיִם — so that the salt should not be dissolved by the** remaining **water.** **וְלֹא יוֹצִיא אֶת הַדָּם** — For if the salt dissolves, **it cannot extract the blood.** **וּצְרִיכִין לְהַשְׁגִּיחַ שֶׁלֹּא יִתְיַבֵּשׁ הַבָּשָׂר לְגַמְרֵי** — However, **care must be taken** to ensure **that the meat does not become fully dry,** **בִּכְדֵי שֶׁלֹּא יִפּוֹל הַמֶּלַח מֵעָלָיו — in order that the salt should not fall off of it.**

§8 **הַמֶּלַח לֹא יְהֵא דַק מְאוֹד כְּקֶמַח — The salt** used **should not be very fine, like flour,** **דְּאִם כֵּן נָמֵס מִיָּד עַל הַבָּשָׂר וְאֵינוֹ מוֹצִיא דָם — for if** it is **so fine, it will immediately dissolve upon the meat, and will not extract any blood.** **וְגַם לֹא יְהֵא גַּס מְאוֹד — It should also not be very coarse,** **שֶׁמָּא יִפּוֹל מֵעַל הַבָּשָׂר** — for if it is too coarse, **it may fall off the meat.** **אֶלָּא יְהֵא בֵּינוֹנִי — Rather, it should be** of **average**-sized crystals, **כְּמוֹ הַמֶּלַח שֶׁנַּעֲשָׂה עַל יְדֵי בִּישׁוּל — similar to the salt formed when** saltwater **is cooked.** **וִיהֵא יָבֵשׁ שֶׁיִּתְפַּזֵּר הֵיטֵב — It should** also **be dry, so that it should spread well.**

§9 **צְרִיכִין לְפַזֵּר הַמֶּלַח עַל הַבָּשָׂר בְּכָל הַצְּדָדִין — One must spread the salt upon the meat on all sides,** **שֶׁלֹּא יִשָּׁאֵר שׁוּם מָקוֹם בְּלִי מֶלַח — so that no spot remains without salt.**[10] **וְלָכֵן, הָעוֹפוֹת צְרִיכִין לְפַתּוֹחַ אוֹתָן הֵיטֵב — Therefore,** when salting **poultry, one must open** the fowl **well,** **כְּדֵי שֶׁיּוּכַל לְמָלְחָן הֵיטֵב גַּם מִבִּפְנִים — in order to be able to salt them properly, even inside.**[11]

---

not be cleaned properly, and food placed into it will become soiled with blood. The custom is not to use the vessel even for cold food, and even if it was washed out well (*Nidchei Yisrael* 31:3). However, in the event that one did use it even for hot food, the food is permitted, provided that the vessel was cleaned well before this use and there was no residue of blood. [The soaking that is done in this vessel generally does not impart a forbidden taste of blood to the vessel since it is soaked in cold water and for only a short time.] (*Shach, Yoreh Deah* 69:7; *Taz* 69:5; see also below, *se'if* 14.) If the vessel was not clean, a halachic authority is to be consulted.

10. As long as the meat is salted on all sides, the blood will be drawn out, even the meat is thick. However, if one of the sides is left unsalted, the salt will not draw out all of the blood, even if it is a thin piece of meat (*Aruch HaShulchan* 69:28). See *Rama, Yoreh Deah* 69:4, regarding what one should do in the event that both sides were not covered with salt.

11. After its innards are removed, a bird is hollow. In order to ensure that all the bird's blood will be extracted, one must salt it both inside and outside.

י. הַבָּשָׂר בְּמִלְחוֹ, צָרִיךְ לְהַנִּיחַ בְּמָקוֹם שֶׁיּוּכַל הַדָּם לָזוּב מִמֶּנּוּ הֵיטֵב[12]. וְלָכֵן, לֹא יַעֲמִיד אֶת הַסַּל עִם הַבָּשָׂר עַל גַּבֵּי קַרְקַע, כִּי לֹא יוּכַל הַדָּם לָזוּב הֵיטֵב. וַאֲפִילוּ לְאַחַר שֶׁכְּבָר שֶׁהָה הַבָּשָׂר בְּמִלְחוֹ שִׁיעוּר מְלִיחָה[13] קוֹדֶם הֲדָחָה, לֹא יִתְּנֵהוּ בְּמָקוֹם שֶׁאֵין הַדָּם יָכוֹל לָזוּב הֵיטֵב[14]. וּכְשֶׁמּוֹלְחִין עַל גַּבֵּי דַף, צְרִיכִין לְהַנִּיחוֹ בְּשִׁיפּוּעַ כְּדֵי שֶׁיָּזוּב הֵיטֵב, וְשֶׁלֹּא יִהְיֶה בּוֹ גּוּמָּא שֶׁיִּתְקַבֵּץ בּוֹ צִיר[15]. וְהַמּוֹלֵחַ עוֹפוֹת, אוֹ דוֹפֶן שְׁלֵמָה שֶׁיֵּשׁ לוֹ תּוֹךְ וּבֵית קִיבּוּל, צָרִיךְ לַהֲפוֹךְ צַד הֶחָלָל לְמַטָּה, כְּדֵי שֶׁיּוּכַל הַדָּם לָזוּב הֵיטֵב[16].

יא. יְהֵא הַבָּשָׂר מוּנָּח בְּמִלְחוֹ שִׁיעוּר שָׁעָה, וּבִשְׁעַת הַדְּחָק דַּי כ״ד מִינוּטִין[17].

יב. לְאַחַר שֶׁהָיָה הַבָּשָׂר מוּנָּח בְּמִלְחוֹ כְּשִׁיעוּרוֹ, יְנַפֵּץ מִמֶּנּוּ הַמֶּלַח הֵיטֵב,

---

§10 **הַבָּשָׂר בְּמִלְחוֹ, צָרִיךְ לְהַנִּיחַ בְּמָקוֹם** — **One must place the salt**-covered **meat** **שֶׁיּוּכַל הַדָּם לָזוּב מִמֶּנּוּ הֵיטֵב** — **in a position where the blood can drain from it well.** **וְלָכֵן** — **Therefore,** when salting meat in a basket, **לֹא יַעֲמִיד אֶת הַסַּל עִם הַבָּשָׂר עַל גַּבֵּי קַרְקַע** — **one should not place the basket containing the meat upon the ground,** **כִּי לֹא יוּכַל הַדָּם לָזוּב הֵיטֵב** — **for the blood will not be able to drain well.**[12] **וַאֲפִילוּ לְאַחַר שֶׁכְּבָר שֶׁהָה הַבָּשָׂר בְּמִלְחוֹ שִׁיעוּר מְלִיחָה** — **Even after** the meat has remained **in its salt for the amount of** time required for proper **salting,**[13] **קוֹדֶם הֲדָחָה** — as long as the salt is still on it, **before it has been rinsed** a second time (see *se'if* 12), **לֹא יִתְּנֵהוּ בְּמָקוֹם שֶׁאֵין הַדָּם יָכוֹל לָזוּב הֵיטֵב** — **one should not put it in a place where the blood cannot drain well.**[14] **וּכְשֶׁמּוֹלְחִין עַל גַּבֵּי דַף** — **When salting upon a board,** **צְרִיכִין לְהַנִּיחוֹ בְּשִׁיפּוּעַ** — **one must place** the board **on an incline** **כְּדֵי שֶׁיָּזוּב הֵיטֵב** — **so that** the blood can **drain well.** **וְשֶׁלֹּא יִהְיֶה בּוֹ גּוּמָּא שֶׁיִּתְקַבֵּץ בּוֹ צִיר** — When using a board one must also ensure **that there is no groove** in the board **into which** the **brine** (i.e., the salt-blood mixture) **can gather.**[15] **וְהַמּוֹלֵחַ עוֹפוֹת, אוֹ דוֹפֶן שְׁלֵמָה** — **One who is salting poultry or an entire side** of an animal **שֶׁיֵּשׁ לוֹ תּוֹךְ וּבֵית קִיבּוּל** — **that has an interior** that can function as **a receptacle,** **צָרִיךְ לַהֲפוֹךְ צַד הֶחָלָל לְמַטָּה** — **must turn the** open **side of the hollow downward,** **כְּדֵי שֶׁיּוּכַל הַדָּם לָזוּב הֵיטֵב** — **in order that the blood** can **drain properly.**[16]

§11 **יְהֵא הַבָּשָׂר מוּנָּח בְּמִלְחוֹ שִׁיעוּר שָׁעָה** — **The meat should remain in the salt for an hour.** **וּבִשְׁעַת הַדְּחָק דַּי כ״ד מִינוּטִין** — However, **in a pressing situation, it is enough** to leave it in the salt for **twenty-four minutes.**[17]

§12 **לְאַחַר שֶׁהָיָה הַבָּשָׂר מוּנָּח בְּמִלְחוֹ כְּשִׁיעוּרוֹ** — **After the meat has remained in salt for the required amount** of time, **יְנַפֵּץ מִמֶּנּוּ הַמֶּלַח הֵיטֵב** — **one should**

---

12. When the basket is placed on the ground, the blood that drains from the meat has nowhere to flow, and remains in the basket, where it can be reabsorbed into the meat.

13. See following *se'if.*

14. Until the blood is rinsed off the meat, one must keep the meat in a position that will prevent it from reabsorbing the blood.

15. Here too, we are concerned that if the meat sits in the brine, it will reabsorb the blood.

16. Before an animal is cut up, it has a curved shape, and, if placed with the cavity facing up, fluid can gather inside it. Therefore, one must place it with the cavity facing downward, to ensure that the brine containing blood does not become absorbed into the meat.

17. See *Mishnah Berurah* 459:15.

וּמְדִיחִין אוֹתוֹ ג׳ פְּעָמִים בְּמַיִם הֵיטֵב הֵיטֵב[18]. וְאִשָּׁה יִרְאַת ה׳ יֵשׁ לָהּ לְהַשְׁגִּיחַ בְּעַצְמָהּ עַל הֲדָחַת הַבָּשָׂר, כִּי לִפְעָמִים הַמְשָׁרֶתֶת אֲשֶׁר בְּכָתֵף תִּשָּׂא אֶת הַמַּיִם תְּצַמְצֵם, וִיכוֹלִין לָבֹא חַס וְשָׁלוֹם לְאִיסּוּר דָּם. וּצְרִיכִין לִיזָּהֵר שֶׁלֹּא לְהָנִיחַ אֶת הַבָּשָׂר בְּתוֹךְ כְּלִי בְּלִי מַיִם קוֹדֶם שֶׁהוּדַח[19].

יג. צְרִיכִין לִיזָּהֵר בְּעוֹפוֹת לְהָסִיר אֶת הָרֹאשׁ קוֹדֶם הַשְּׁרִיָּה[20]. וְאִם נִמְלַח הָעוֹף עִם הָרֹאשׁ, יַעֲשֶׂה שְׁאֵלַת חָכָם. וְכֵן צְרִיכִין לִיזָּהֵר בָּזֶה בִּבְהֵמָה[21].

יד. בָּשָׂר שֶׁלֹּא נִמְלַח עֲדַיִין, לֹא יָנִיחוּ אוֹתוֹ בְּמָקוֹם שֶׁלִּפְעָמִים יֵשׁ שָׁם מֶלַח[22].

---

brush off the salt well, **וּמְדִיחִין אוֹתוֹ ג׳ פְּעָמִים בְּמַיִם הֵיטֵב הֵיטֵב** — **and rinse** the meat **with water three times, extremely well.**[18] **וְאִשָּׁה יִרְאַת ה׳** — **The woman who fears God** **יֵשׁ לָהּ לְהַשְׁגִּיחַ בְּעַצְמָהּ עַל הֲדָחַת הַבָּשָׂר** — **should herself supervise the rinsing of the meat,** **כִּי לִפְעָמִים הַמְשָׁרֶתֶת אֲשֶׁר בְּכָתֵף תִּשָּׂא אֶת הַמַּיִם תְּצַמְצֵם** — **for sometimes, the maidservant, who carries the water on her shoulders, will skimp** and not use the amount of water necessary to properly rinse the meat, **וִיכוֹלִין לָבֹא חַס וְשָׁלוֹם לְאִיסּוּר דָּם** — **and they can** thus **come, God forbid, to violate** the **prohibition** of eating **blood.** **וּצְרִיכִין לִיזָּהֵר** — **One must** also **be careful** **שֶׁלֹּא לְהָנִיחַ אֶת הַבָּשָׂר בְּתוֹךְ כְּלִי בְּלִי מַיִם** — **not to place the meat into a vessel without water** **קוֹדֶם שֶׁהוּדַח** — **before it has been rinsed** from the salt.[19]

§13 **צְרִיכִין לִיזָּהֵר בְּעוֹפוֹת** — **One must take care,** when salting **poultry,** **לְהָסִיר אֶת הָרֹאשׁ קוֹדֶם הַשְּׁרִיָּה** — **to remove the head before the soaking.**[20] **וְאִם נִמְלַח הָעוֹף עִם הָרֹאשׁ** — **If the bird was salted with the head** attached, **יַעֲשֶׂה שְׁאֵלַת חָכָם** — **one must consult a competent halachic authority** how to proceed. **וְכֵן צְרִיכִין לִיזָּהֵר בָּזֶה בִּבְהֵמָה** — **Similarly, one must be careful about this** when salting **an animal.**[21]

§14 **בָּשָׂר שֶׁלֹּא נִמְלַח עֲדַיִין, לֹא יָנִיחוּ אוֹתוֹ** — **One should not place meat that has not yet been salted** **בְּמָקוֹם שֶׁלִּפְעָמִים יֵשׁ שָׁם מֶלַח** — **in a spot that sometimes contains salt.** [22]

---

18. If the blood is not properly rinsed away, it will be reabsorbed into the meat, or absorbed into the pot in which the meat is cooked.

With regard to this rinsing, there is no option of an abbreviated process as described above, *se'if* 3, with regard to the pre-salting rinsing.

19. As Kitzur explained in *se'if* 10, if the meat sits in a vessel before it is rinsed, it might reabsorb some of the blood that emerges from it.

20. There are two large blood vessels in the neck that run alongside the windpipes, through which all the blood of the body courses. When an animal is slaughtered, much of the blood from the body of the animal may become pooled in these blood vessels. In the event that the animal is salted whole, this blood (which is not extracted during the salting process) will remain in the animal unless the blood vessels are first cut open and the blood drained (*Yoreh Deah* 22:2). Therefore, when preparing poultry, which is often cooked whole, the head must be severed before salting. After this is done, the salt can extract any residual blood.

21. Although animals are not subject to the requirement of cutting open its veins since they are usually cut into sections before salting (*Yoreh Deah* 22:2), nevertheless, Kitzur urges that even with animals, the head should be severed, to ascertain that the blood that gathers in the veins of the neck be able to flow out.

22. Some salt may have remained there, and in turn, salt the meat that is placed there. Since it was unknown that there was salt in that spot, the meat will not be rinsed after this "salting," and the meat will reabsorb the blood that this salt extracted.

וְיֵשׁ לְיַיחֵד כְּלִי לְבָשָׂר לְחוּד, שֶׁלֹּא לְהָנִיחַ בִּכְלִי זֶה יְרָקוֹת אוֹ פֵּירוֹת, וְכַיּוֹצֵא בוֹ דְּבָרִים שֶׁדַּרְכָּן לֶאֱכוֹל בְּלֹא הֲדָחָה, כִּי דָם מִן הַבָּשָׂר נִדְבָּק בַּכְּלִי וּמִן הַכְּלִי נִדְבָּק בָּהֶם[23].

טו. הָרֹאשׁ — צְרִיכִין לְחָתְכוֹ קוֹדֶם שְׁרִיָּה, וְלִיקַּח אֶת הַמּוֹחַ וְלִקְרוֹעַ אֶת הַקְּרוּם שֶׁעָלָיו, וְלִשְׁרוֹתוֹ וּלְמָלְחוֹ בִּפְנֵי עַצְמוֹ[24]. וְאֶת הָרֹאשׁ צְרִיכִין לְמָלְחוֹ מִבִּפְנִים וּמִבַּחוּץ[25]. וִיכוֹלִין לְמָלְחוֹ גַּם עַל הַשְּׂעָרוֹת[26].

טז. עֲצָמוֹת שֶׁיֵּשׁ בָּהֶן מוֹחַ — אִם עֲדַיִין הֵן דְּבוּקוֹת בַּבָּשָׂר, מוֹלְחָן עִם הַבָּשָׂר בְּיַחַד כְּמוֹ שֶׁהֵן. אֲבָל אִם נִפְרְדוּ מִן הַבָּשָׂר, יִמְלְחֵם בִּפְנֵי עַצְמָם, וְלֹא יוּנְחוּ בְּמִלְחָן אֵצֶל הַבָּשָׂר[27].

יז. רַגְלֵי בְּהֵמוֹת — צְרִיכִין לַחְתּוֹךְ רָאשֵׁי הַטְּלָפַיִם קוֹדֶם הַשְּׁרִיָּה, לְמַעַן יוּכַל

וְיֵשׁ לְיַיחֵד כְּלִי לְבָשָׂר לְחוּד — **It is proper to designate a vessel specifically** in which to put **meat** before it is salted, **שֶׁלֹּא לְהָנִיחַ בִּכְלִי זֶה יְרָקוֹת אוֹ פֵּירוֹת, וְכַיּוֹצֵא בוֹ** — **and not to place in this vessel any vegetables or fruit or the like, דְּבָרִים שֶׁדַּרְכָּן לֶאֱכוֹל בְּלֹא הֲדָחָה** — i.e., **items that are eaten without** prior **rinsing. כִּי דָם מִן הַבָּשָׂר נִדְבָּק בַּכְּלִי** — **For blood from the meat may adhere to the vessel, וּמִן הַכְּלִי נִדְבָּק בָּהֶם** — **and from the vessel, it may adhere to these** foods.[23]

§15 הָרֹאשׁ — צְרִיכִין לְחָתְכוֹ קוֹדֶם שְׁרִיָּה — **The head must be cut into pieces before it is soaked. וְלִיקַּח אֶת הַמּוֹחַ וְלִקְרוֹעַ אֶת הַקְּרוּם שֶׁעָלָיו** — **And** one is required **to take the brain and tear the membrane that is on it, וְלִשְׁרוֹתוֹ וּלְמָלְחוֹ בִּפְנֵי עַצְמוֹ** — **and to soak it and salt it by itself** (i.e., separately from the head).[24] **וְאֶת הָרֹאשׁ צְרִיכִין לְמָלְחוֹ מִבִּפְנִים וּמִבַּחוּץ** — **And one must salt the head** both **on the inside and on the outside,**[25] **וִיכוֹלִין לְמָלְחוֹ גַּם עַל הַשְּׂעָרוֹת** — **and one can salt it even upon the hairs.**[26]

§16 עֲצָמוֹת שֶׁיֵּשׁ בָּהֶן מוֹחַ — The law with regard to **bones that have marrow within them** is as follows: **אִם עֲדַיִין הֵן דְּבוּקוֹת בַּבָּשָׂר** — **If** the bones **are still attached to the meat, מוֹלְחָן עִם הַבָּשָׂר בְּיַחַד כְּמוֹ שֶׁהֵן** — **one may salt them as is, together with the meat. אֲבָל אִם נִפְרְדוּ מִן הַבָּשָׂר** — **However, if they have become separated from the meat, יִמְלְחֵם בִּפְנֵי עַצְמָם** — **one should salt them separately, וְלֹא יוּנְחוּ בְּמִלְחָן אֵצֶל הַבָּשָׂר** — **and they should not remain alongside the meat while in their salt.**[27]

§17 רַגְלֵי בְּהֵמוֹת — When salting **the legs of animals, צְרִיכִין לַחְתּוֹךְ רָאשֵׁי הַטְּלָפַיִם קוֹדֶם הַשְּׁרִיָּה** — **one must cut off the tips of the hooves before soaking them, לְמַעַן**

23. See *se'if* 6, with note 9.

24. The brain is surrounded by a membrane that contains blood. If the brain is salted as is, the extracted blood would collect in the skull, which, due to its shape, will hold the blood and prevent it from draining away. In order to properly extract the blood from the brain, one must first remove the brain from the skull. One must then tear its membrane, so that the blood that is collected in it will have an opening through which to drain (*Yoreh Deah* 71:3).

25. I.e., after the brain has been removed, the skull itself must be salted on both sides, inside and out (as with all meat; see above, *se'if* 9).

26. The hair on the outside of the head does not prevent the salt from extracting the blood.

27. When the bones are not attached to the meat and they are salted together, there is a possibility that the blood that emerges from the meat will be absorbed by the bones (see *Shach, Yoreh Deah* 71:11; see also *Pri Chadash* 71:10).

הַדָּם לָזוּב מֵהֶם[28]. וּצְרִיכִין לְהַנִּיחַ אוֹתָן בְּאוֹפֶן שֶׁיּוּכַל הַדָּם לָזוּב. וִיכוֹלִין לְמָלְחוֹ גַּם עַל הַשְּׂעָרוֹת.

יח. הַלֵּב – צְרִיכִין לִקְרוֹעַ קוֹדֶם הַשְּׁרִיָּה, שֶׁיֵּצֵא הַדָּם מִמֶּנּוּ[29].

יט. הָרֵיאָה – נוֹהֲגִין גַּם כֵּן לְחָתְכָהּ וְלִפְתּוֹחַ הַקְּנוֹקָנוֹת הַגְּדוֹלוֹת שֶׁבָּהּ קוֹדֶם הַשְּׁרִיָּה[30].

כ. הַכָּבֵד יֵשׁ בּוֹ הַרְבֵּה דָם, לְפִיכָךְ לְכַתְּחִלָּה[31] אֵין לוֹ תַקָּנָה לְבַשְּׁלוֹ עַל יְדֵי מְלִיחָה, אֶלָּא צְרִיכִין לִצְלוֹתָהּ עַל הָאֵשׁ[32]. אֲבָל צְרִיכִין מִקּוֹדֶם לְחָתְכָהּ הֵיטֵב, וּלְהַנִּיחָהּ בְּחִיתּוּכָהּ עַל הָאֵשׁ, לְמַעַן יִשְׁאַב הָאֵשׁ הֵיטֵב כָּל הַדָּם שֶׁבָּהּ. וּמְדִיחִין אוֹתָהּ קוֹדֶם שֶׁמְּנִיחִין אוֹתָהּ

וּצְרִיכִין לְהַנִּיחַ אוֹתָן יוּכַל הַדָּם לָזוּב מֵהֶם — so that the blood can drain from them.[28] **בְּאוֹפֶן שֶׁיּוּכַל הַדָּם לָזוּב** — Furthermore, **one must position them in a manner that will enable the blood to drain.** **וִיכוֹלִין לְמָלְחוֹ גַּם עַל הַשְּׂעָרוֹת** — **One may salt** a leg **even** by placing the salt **upon the hairs** of the leg.

§18 **הַלֵּב – צְרִיכִין לִקְרוֹעַ קוֹדֶם הַשְּׁרִיָּה** — **One must tear** open **the heart before the soaking,** **שֶׁיֵּצֵא הַדָּם מִמֶּנּוּ** — **so that the blood should come out of it.**[29]

§19 **הָרֵיאָה – נוֹהֲגִין גַּם כֵּן לְחָתְכָהּ** — **It is the custom to also cut** open **the lung,** **וְלִפְתּוֹחַ הַקְּנוֹקָנוֹת הַגְּדוֹלוֹת שֶׁבָּהּ** — **and to open its larger tubes** **קוֹדֶם הַשְּׁרִיָּה** — **before soaking** it.[30]

§20 **הַכָּבֵד יֵשׁ בּוֹ הַרְבֵּה דָם** — **There is much blood in the liver.** **לְפִיכָךְ לְכַתְּחִלָּה אֵין לוֹ תַקָּנָה לְבַשְּׁלוֹ עַל יְדֵי מְלִיחָה** — **Therefore, initially,**[31] **it cannot be made fit for cooking by** the **salting** process; **אֶלָּא צְרִיכִין לִצְלוֹתָהּ עַל הָאֵשׁ** — **rather, one must roast it over the fire.**[32] **אֲבָל צְרִיכִין מִקּוֹדֶם לְחָתְכָהּ הֵיטֵב** — **But one must first cut it well,** **וּלְהַנִּיחָהּ בְּחִיתּוּכָהּ עַל הָאֵשׁ** — **and place it with the cut side over the fire,** **לְמַעַן יִשְׁאַב הָאֵשׁ הֵיטֵב כָּל הַדָּם שֶׁבָּהּ** — **so that the fire properly draw out all the blood that is within it.** **וּמְדִיחִין אוֹתָהּ קוֹדֶם שֶׁמְּנִיחִין אוֹתָהּ**

---

28. The hooves are hard and smooth, and nothing can flow through them. Like the skull (see above, *se'if* 15), they can serve as a vessel. Their tips must therefore be cut off before the salting (*Shach, Yoreh Deah* 71:3).

29. When the animal is slaughtered, blood flows toward the heart, and pools there. Since salt is ineffective at extracting pooled blood, one must tear the heart open before salting it to drain the blood that has collected there. One may then proceed to salt it to extract the blood that is absorbed within its meat (*Yoreh Deah* 72:1).

However, in general, one should refrain from eating the heart of an animal or fowl, since it can cause memory loss (see Kitzur above, 32:9).

30. Although the lungs and bronchia are soft, and their blood can be extracted by the salting process, nevertheless, since they can hold blood due to their shape, the custom is to cut them open before salting to facilitate the draining of the blood.

31. Kitzur is citing verbatim the words of *Shulchan Aruch* [who in certain cases permits the liver even if it was not salted; see *Yoreh Deah* 73:1 with *Shach* §6]. *Ashkenazic* custom, however, is to prohibit the liver and any other food cooked with it, as well as the utensils, even after the fact, even if it was cut open and salted for a full hour and washed off properly afterward, as long as it was not roasted properly (*Chochmas Adam* 34:11; see also *Nidchei Yisrael* 32:7). A halachic authority should be consulted (see *Rama* ibid. with commentaries).

32. Roasting draws out the blood from the liver. This method may be used to draw out blood of other meat as well.

עַל הָאֵשׁ[33], וּכְשֶׁמּוּנַּחַת עַל הָאֵשׁ מוֹלְחִין אוֹתָהּ שָׁם קְצָת[34]. וְצוֹלִין אוֹתָהּ עַד שֶׁתְּהֵא רְאוּיָה לַאֲכִילָה[35], וְאַחַר כָּךְ מְדִיחִין אוֹתָהּ יָפֶה מִן הַדָּם שֶׁפָּלְטָה, וְיֵשׁ לִיזָּהֵר לַהֲדִיחָהּ ג׳ פְּעָמִים. וְאַחַר כָּךְ יְכוֹלִין לְבַשְּׁלָהּ.

כא. צְרִיכִין לִיזָּהֵר לִצְלוֹתָהּ דַּוְקָא עַל הָאֵשׁ וְלֹא בְּתַנּוּר גָּרוּף. וְכֵן לֹא יִכְרְכוּ אוֹתָהּ בִּנְיָיר לִצְלוֹתָהּ כָּךְ, וַאֲפִילוּ בִּנְיָיר גָּרוּעַ (פליס פאפיר)[36] (עַיֵּין בְּסֵפֶר פִּתְחֵי תְּשׁוּבָה)[37].

כב. אֲבָל אֵין לִמְלוֹחַ כָּבֵד קוֹדֶם צְלִיָּה, כְּדֶרֶךְ שֶׁמּוֹלְחִין בָּשָׂר[38]. וּמִכָּל שֶׁכֵּן שֶׁאֵין לִמְלוֹחַ כָּבֵד עִם בָּשָׂר בְּיַחַד[39].

וּכְשֶׁמּוּנַּחַת עַל הָאֵשׁ — One is to rinse the liver **before placing it over the fire,**[33] **עַל הָאֵשׁ מוֹלְחִין אוֹתָהּ שָׁם קְצָת — and salt it a bit while it is placed over the fire.**[34] **וְצוֹלִין אוֹתָהּ עַד שֶׁתְּהֵא רְאוּיָה לַאֲכִילָה — One** then **roasts it until it is fit to be eaten.**[35] **וְאַחַר כָּךְ מְדִיחִין אוֹתָהּ יָפֶה מִן הַדָּם שֶׁפָּלְטָה — Afterward, one rinses it well,** to clean it **from the blood that it has discharged. וְיֵשׁ לִיזָּהֵר לַהֲדִיחָהּ ג׳ פְּעָמִים — One should take care to rinse it three times, וְאַחַר כָּךְ יְכוֹלִין לְבַשְּׁלָהּ — after which one may cook it** as he wishes.

§21 צְרִיכִין לִיזָּהֵר לִצְלוֹתָהּ דַּוְקָא עַל הָאֵשׁ — One must be careful to roast the liver **only over the fire, וְלֹא בְּתַנּוּר גָּרוּף — and not in a "shoveled out" oven** (i.e., an oven that has had the coals cleared out from it). **וְכֵן לֹא יִכְרְכוּ אוֹתָהּ בִּנְיָיר לִצְלוֹתָהּ כָּךְ — Similarly, they should not wrap it in paper and roast it like that** (i.e., while it is wrapped), **וַאֲפִילוּ בִּנְיָיר גָּרוּעַ (פליס פאפיר) — even in poor**-quality **paper.**[36] (**עַיֵּין בְּסֵפֶר פִּתְחֵי תְּשׁוּבָה** — See *sefer Pischei Teshuvah* 73:1.)[37]

§22 אֲבָל אֵין לִמְלוֹחַ כָּבֵד קוֹדֶם צְלִיָּה, כְּדֶרֶךְ שֶׁמּוֹלְחִין בָּשָׂר — However, one may not salt the liver before roasting it, **in the manner that one salts meat,**[38] **וּמִכָּל שֶׁכֵּן שֶׁאֵין לִמְלוֹחַ כָּבֵד עִם בָּשָׂר בְּיַחַד — and certainly one should not salt liver together with meat.**[39]

---

33. Although fire draws out any blood absorbed *within* the liver, it causes blood *on its surface* to become absorbed by the liver. One must therefore rinse the liver well to remove the blood on its surface.

34. Some authorities maintain that fire is effective in removing blood from meat only if the meat has been salted. See below, *se'if* 22, that the liver may not be salted before the roasting begins.

35. Most authorities rule that it is sufficient to roast the liver for half of the time that it would take for it to be fully roasted (*Shach* 76:14). *Taz* (69:54) writes that the custom is to roast it until it is dry on the outside, at which point it can be assumed that it is dry throughout.

36. When the liver is wrapped, the emerging blood will pool in the paper.

37. *Pischei Teshuvah* there cites the various views regarding the issues discussed in this *se'if.* One should not place the liver on the floor of the oven, for the blood will not be able to drain properly (see *Pischei Teshuvah* there and *Nidchei Yisrael* 32:7).

38. There are two reasons for this: 1) If one would salt the liver first, he may come to cook it with meat. 2) Salting the liver draws its blood out onto its surface, and the fire can then cause the blood on the surface to become reabsorbed into the liver; see above, note 34 (*Taz* 73:7; *Shach* loc. cit. §16). The liver is therefore salted only slightly, and only while it is roasting, as set out above, *se'if* 20.

39. Because of the abundance of blood that the liver contains, we are concerned that if salted together with meat, the meat will absorb some of the blood that emerges from the liver during the salting process.

כג. הַטְּחוֹל – דִּינוֹ כִּשְׁאָר בָּשָׂר, רַק צְרִיכִין לְהָסִיר מִמֶּנּוּ קוֹדֶם שְׁרִיָּה אֶת הַקְּרוּם שֶׁעָלָיו, שֶׁאָסוּר מִשּׁוּם חֵלֶב[40] (גַּם צְרִיכִין לְנַקְּרָן מִשּׁוּם הַגִּידִין)[41]. נוֹטֵל רֹאשׁ הַגִּיד וּמוֹשֵׁךְ אוֹתוֹ וְנִמְשָׁכִין עִמּוֹ ג׳ חוּטִין שֶׁבְּתוֹכוֹ. וְצָרִיךְ לִיזָּהֵר שֶׁלֹּא יַפְסִיק שׁוּם חוּט, וְאִם נִפְסַק, צָרִיךְ לְשָׁרֵשׁ אַחֲרָיו.

כד. הַחַלְחוֹלֶת וּשְׁאָר מֵעַיִים – מוֹלְחִין בְּצַד הַחִיצוֹן שֶׁהַשּׁוּמָּן דָּבוּק שָׁם[42]. דִּינֵי הַכְּחָל בְּיוֹרֶה דֵעָה סִימָן צ׳[43].

כה. קֵיבָה שֶׁל עֵגֶל שֶׁנִּמְצָא בוֹ חָלָב, שׁוֹפְכִין אֶת הֶחָלָב קוֹדֶם שְׁרִיָּה[44] וַהֲרֵי הוּא כִּשְׁאָר בָּשָׂר.

---

§23 הַטְּחוֹל – דִּינוֹ כִּשְׁאָר בָּשָׂר — The halachah of the spleen is the same as that for **other** cuts of **meat, רַק צְרִיכִין לְהָסִיר מִמֶּנּוּ קוֹדֶם שְׁרִיָּה אֶת הַקְּרוּם שֶׁעָלָיו — except that before soaking it, one must remove the membrane from upon it, שֶׁאָסוּר מִשּׁוּם חֵלֶב — as** the membrane **is prohibited, because of** the prohibition against eating ***cheilev*** (i.e., forbidden fats).[40] **(גַּם צְרִיכִין לְנַקְּרָן מִשּׁוּם הַגִּידִין — One must also purge it of** the membrane's **sinews.)**[41] **נוֹטֵל רֹאשׁ הַגִּיד וּמוֹשֵׁךְ אוֹתוֹ — One takes the top of the sinew and pulls it, וְנִמְשָׁכִין עִמּוֹ ג׳ חוּטִין שֶׁבְּתוֹכוֹ — and the three strands that are within** the spleen **come along with it. וְצָרִיךְ לִיזָּהֵר שֶׁלֹּא יַפְסִיק שׁוּם חוּט — One must be careful that no strand** of the membrane **breaks, וְאִם נִפְסַק, צָרִיךְ לְשָׁרֵשׁ אַחֲרָיו — and if it does break, one must root it out.**

§24 הַחַלְחוֹלֶת וּשְׁאָר מֵעַיִים — When salting **the rectum and the rest of the intestines, מוֹלְחִין בְּצַד הַחִיצוֹן שֶׁהַשּׁוּמָּן דָּבוּק שָׁם — one salts them on the outer side, where the fat adheres** to them.[42]
דִּינֵי הַכְּחָל בְּיוֹרֶה דֵעָה סִימָן צ׳ — The laws of the preparation of the **udder are** found **in *Yoreh Deah, Siman* 90.**[43]

§25 קֵיבָה שֶׁל עֵגֶל שֶׁנִּמְצָא בוֹ חָלָב — Regarding the **stomach of a calf in which milk was found, שׁוֹפְכִין אֶת הֶחָלָב קוֹדֶם שְׁרִיָּה — one must pour out the milk before it is soaked,**[44] **וַהֲרֵי הוּא כִּשְׁאָר בָּשָׂר — and** then **it is** treated **like other meat.**

---

40. See *Vayikra* 3:17. The Torah prohibits eating certain of the animal's fats. Included in this prohibition is part of the membrane that surrounds the spleen. These parts must be removed before the salting process, since the salt draws out some of the essence of the *chailev,* which is then absorbed into the spleen, causing it to become forbidden.

41. These sinews are also classified as *chailev.*

42. These organs have no blood internally, aside from the blood that is contained in the fat that is within them. They must therefore be salted on the outside, where most of the fat lies. Although these organs are hollow, and we have seen earlier (*se'if* 9) that salting must be done on all sides, here salting it on one side is sufficient since even the fat on these organs contains only a small amount of blood (*Yoreh Deah* 75:1, *Shach* §7, *Taz* §3).

43. Although, Biblically, the prohibition of cooking milk with meat and of eating and having benefit from milk cooked with meat (see below, 46:5) applies only to milk that was milked from an animal while it was alive and not to milk in the udder of a slaughtered animal, the Sages nevertheless required that milk be removed from the udder (see *Yoreh Deah* §90).

44. This is to avoid creating a forbidden mixture of milk and meat.

כו. בֵּצִים שֶׁנִּמְצְאוּ בְּתוֹךְ עוֹפוֹת, בֵּין שֶׁהֵם קְטַנִּים מְאוֹד, בֵּין שֶׁנִּגְמְרוּ לְגַמְרֵי עִם קְלִיפָּתָן, צְרִיכִין שְׁרִיָּה וּמְלִיחָה וַהֲדָחָה[45]. אֲבָל לֹא יִמְלְחֵם אֵצֶל הַבָּשָׂר, אֶלָּא יַנִּיחֵם בְּמָקוֹם שֶׁלֹּא יָזוּב עֲלֵיהֶם הַדָּם מִן הַבָּשָׂר[46]. וּבֵצִים אֵלּוּ, אֲפִילוּ נִגְמְרוּ לְגַמְרֵי, אָסוּר לְאָכְלָן בְּחָלָב[47].

כז. בָּשָׂר שֶׁשָּׁהָה ג׳ מֵעֵת לְעֵת[48] אָסוּר לְבִישּׁוּל, אֶלָּא אִם כֵּן נִשְׁרָה בֵּינְתַּיִם[49].

כח. נוֹהֲגִין בְּעוֹפוֹת שֶׁלְּאַחַר שֶׁהֵסִירוּ הַנּוֹצוֹת מְהַבְהֲבִין אוֹתָן בָּאוּר לְהָסִיר

§26 **בֵּצִים שֶׁנִּמְצְאוּ בְּתוֹךְ עוֹפוֹת — Eggs that are found inside birds** after they are slaughtered, **בֵּין שֶׁהֵם קְטַנִּים מְאוֹד, בֵּין שֶׁנִּגְמְרוּ לְגַמְרֵי עִם קְלִיפָּתָן —** regardless of **whether they are very small, or fully developed, including their shell, צְרִיכִין שְׁרִיָּה וּמְלִיחָה וַהֲדָחָה — require soaking, salting, and rinsing.**[45] **אֲבָל לֹא יִמְלְחֵם אֵצֶל הַבָּשָׂר — However, one should not salt them near meat** that is being salted. **אֶלָּא יַנִּיחֵם בְּמָקוֹם שֶׁלֹּא יָזוּב עֲלֵיהֶם הַדָּם מִן הַבָּשָׂר — Rather, he should place them in a spot where the blood** discharged **from the meat** that is being salted **will not flow upon them.**[46] **וּבֵצִים אֵלּוּ, אֲפִילוּ נִגְמְרוּ לְגַמְרֵי, אָסוּר לְאָכְלָן בְּחָלָב — These eggs, even** if **fully developed** when found inside the bird, **may not be eaten with milk.**[47]

§27 **בָּשָׂר שֶׁשָּׁהָה ג׳ מֵעֵת לְעֵת — Meat that has sat for three full days** (i.e., seventy-two hours)[48] without being salted **אָסוּר לְבִישּׁוּל — may not be cooked** even if it was subsequently salted, **אֶלָּא אִם כֵּן נִשְׁרָה בֵּינְתַּיִם — unless it had been soaked in the interim.**[49]

§28 **נוֹהֲגִין בְּעוֹפוֹת — It is the practice** when preparing **fowl, שֶׁלְּאַחַר שֶׁהֵסִירוּ הַנּוֹצוֹת מְהַבְהֲבִין אוֹתָן בָּאוּר — that after the feathers are removed, one singes**

---

45. Eggs that have been laid are not considered to be "meat" and therefore do not require any part of the salting process. However, when eggs are still part of the bird at the time that it is slaughtered, they are considered part of the mother, and are treated as meat. As such, they must be salted in the same manner as all other meat.

46. Since the eggs do not contain any significant amount of blood, we are concerned that they may absorb the blood that emerges from the meat with which it is salted; see *Yoreh Deah* 75:1, *Taz* §5.

47. See below, 46:5, where Kitzur outlines the prohibition against eating meat and milk together. Since these eggs have not been laid, they are to be treated as "meat" and may not be eaten with milk.

48. The 72-hour time period begins immediately after the death of the animal (*Igros Moshe, Yoreh Deah* I, §27).

49. After three days, the blood dries and hardens, and can no longer be extracted by the salting process. If this occurs, the meat may no longer be salted, only roasted in a manner similar to the process used for liver; see above, *se'ifim* 20-22. Here, however, one may not cook it even after roasting it (*Shulchan Aruch* 69:12). If the meat was soaked within the three-day period, the blood does not harden.

The meat must be soaked well, not just washed. There is a dispute among the authorities with regard to how long it must be soaked, with the minimum ranging from one half-hour (*Taz* 69:33), or slightly less (*Shach,* according to *Aruch HaShulchan* 69:76), to an hour or two (*Shach* 69:53, according to *Pri Megadim*). After the soaking, the time period for salting is extended by another period of slightly less than 72 hours (*Shulchan Aruch* 69:13) from the end of the soaking (*Aruch HaShulchan* ibid.). This extension through soaking can be done more than once (*Gilyon Maharsha* loc. cit. s.v. להשהותו). Regarding a situation where the third day was Shabbos, see below, 80:57.

אֶת הַנִּשְׁאָר[50]. וּצְרִיכִין לִיזָּהֵר שֶׁלֹּא לְהַבְהֲבָן כִּי אִם בְּשַׁלְהֶבֶת שֶׁל קַשׁ וְתֶבֶן. וְלֹא יַעֲשׂוּ שַׁלְהֶבֶת גְּדוֹלָה. וְיִזָּהֲרוּ לְהוֹלִיךְ הָעוֹפוֹת אָנֶה וָאָנָה לְבַל יִתְחַמְּמוּ[51].

the birds **with fire,** **לְהָסִיר אֶת הַנִּשְׁאָר** — in order **to remove** the stubble **that remains.**[50] **וּצְרִיכִין לִיזָּהֵר** — However, **one must be careful** **שֶׁלֹּא לְהַבְהֲבָן כִּי אִם בְּשַׁלְהֶבֶת שֶׁל קַשׁ וְתֶבֶן** — **not to singe them** with any flame **besides the flame** of burning **hay or straw,** **וְלֹא יַעֲשׂוּ שַׁלְהֶבֶת גְּדוֹלָה** — **and not to make a large flame.** **וְיִזָּהֲרוּ לְהוֹלִיךְ הָעוֹפוֹת אָנֶה וָאָנָה** — **They should** also **be careful to move the birds back and forth** within the flames, **לְבַל יִתְחַמְּמוּ** — **so they should not become heated.**[51]

50. This is generally done before the salting process.

51. When meat is heated before salting, the blood on the surface of the meat becomes absorbed deeply into the meat and does not emerge in the salting process (see above, note 7). When singeing the feathers, one must therefore use a fuel such as straw (which generates less heat), limit the size of the flame, and constantly move the bird about.

25 LAWS OF IMMERSING UTENSILS — SIMAN 37:1

סימן לז
טְבִילַת כֵּלִים
וּבוֹ י״ג סְעִיפִים

א. הַלּוֹקֵחַ כֵּלִים הַשַּׁיָּיכִים לִסְעוּדָה מֵעַכּוּ״ם[1], אֲפִילוּ הֵם כֵּלִים חֲדָשִׁים, אִם הֵם שֶׁל מִינֵי מַתָּכוֹת אוֹ זְכוּכִית[2], אָסוּר לְהִשְׁתַּמֵּשׁ בָּהֶן שׁוּם תַּשְׁמִישׁ, אֲפִילוּ בְּצוֹנֵן, עַד שֶׁטּוֹבְלִין אוֹתָן בְּמַעְיָן, אוֹ בְּמִקְוֶה בְּמָקוֹם שֶׁכָּשֵׁר לִטְבִילַת אִשָּׁה נִדָּה[3], כְּדֵי שֶׁיֵּצְאוּ מִטּוּמְאָתוֹ שֶׁל עַכּוּ״ם לִקְדוּשָּׁתוֹ שֶׁל יִשְׂרָאֵל. וְקוֹדֶם הַטְּבִילָה מְבָרְכִין עַל כְּלִי אֶחָד ״אֲשֶׁר קִדְּשָׁנוּ בְּמִצְוֹתָיו וְצִוָּנוּ עַל טְבִילַת

SIMAN 37
THE LAWS OF IMMERSING UTENSILS
CONTAINING 13 *SE'IFIM*

§1 The Mitzvah / §2 Immersing in Rivers / §3 Wood, Earthenware, and Porcelain Utensils / §4 A Nonkosher Utensil / §5-7 Situations of Halachic Doubt / §8-9 The Utensil's Function / §10-11 The Immersion / §12 A Minor / §13 Immersing on Shabbos and Yom Tov

§1 **הַלּוֹקֵחַ כֵּלִים הַשַּׁיָּיכִים לִסְעוּדָה מֵעַכּוּ״ם** — When **someone purchases utensils whose function relates to a meal,**[1] **from an idolater,** **אֲפִילוּ הֵם כֵּלִים חֲדָשִׁים** — **even if they are new utensils,** and there is no concern that they were used for nonkosher food, **אִם הֵם שֶׁל מִינֵי מַתָּכוֹת אוֹ זְכוּכִית** — **if they are** made **of any type of metal or glass,**[2] **אָסוּר לְהִשְׁתַּמֵּשׁ בָּהֶן שׁוּם תַּשְׁמִישׁ** — **he is forbidden to use them for any** food **purpose,** **אֲפִילוּ בְּצוֹנֵן** — **even for cold** foods, **עַד שֶׁטּוֹבְלִין אוֹתָן בְּמַעְיָן** — **until he immerses them in a spring,** **אוֹ בְּמִקְוֶה בְּמָקוֹם שֶׁכָּשֵׁר לִטְבִילַת אִשָּׁה נִדָּה** — **or in a** *mikveh* (ritual bath) **that is valid for the immersion of a woman who is a** *niddah*.[3] **כְּדֵי שֶׁיֵּצְאוּ מִטּוּמְאָתוֹ שֶׁל עַכּוּ״ם** — This immersion is required, **so that** the utensils **will emerge** thereby **from the spiritual impurity of** having been owned by **an idolater,** **לִקְדוּשָּׁתוֹ שֶׁל יִשְׂרָאֵל** — and enter **into the holiness of** being owned by **a Jew.**

וְקוֹדֶם הַטְּבִילָה מְבָרְכִין — **Before the immersion, one is to recite a blessing.** **עַל כְּלִי אֶחָד** — **When immersing one utensil,** one recites: **״אֲשֶׁר קִדְּשָׁנוּ בְּמִצְוֹתָיו וְצִוָּנוּ עַל טְבִילַת**

---

1. This will be further explained below, *se'ifim* 8 and 9.

2. Immersion of metal utensils is a Biblical requirement. Glass utensils are not included in the Biblical obligation to immerse utensils, but require immersion by Rabbinic enactment (see *Pri Chadash* 120:3). Rabbi Moshe Feinstein writes (*Igros Moshe, Yoreh Deah* III, §22) that utensils made of aluminum, a metal not mentioned in the Torah, also require immersion by Rabbinic enactment. [See also *Igros Moshe*, ibid. §23 regarding immersing disposable containers.]

3. A *niddah* is a woman who has experienced a menstrual flow. (The laws of *niddah* are discussed below, *Simanim* 153-162.) The immersion of a woman who is a *niddah* is Biblically mandated, and necessary in order for her to terminate her *niddah* status. As such, a *mikveh* used by a *niddah* has more stringent requirements than a *mikveh* used by men, for whom no Biblical obligation applies to their immersion nowadays (see *Yoreh Deah* §201).

LAWS OF IMMERSING UTENSILS — SIMAN 37:2-3 26

כֶּלִי". וְעַל שְׁתַּיִם אוֹ יוֹתֵר, מְבָרְכִין "אֲשֶׁר קִדְּשָׁנוּ בְּמִצְוֹתָיו וְצִוָּנוּ עַל טְבִילַת כֵּלִים"[4].

ב. כֵּיוָן שֶׁהַכֵּלִים צְרִיכִין טְבִילָה דַּוְקָא בְּמָקוֹם שֶׁכָּשֵׁר לִטְבִילַת נָשִׁים, לָכֵן צְרִיכִין לִיזָּהֵר שֶׁלֹּא לְהַטְבִּילָן בִּנְהָרוֹת בְּשָׁעָה שֶׁהֵן גְּדוֹלוֹת מִגְּשָׁמִים וְהַפְשָׁרַת שְׁלָגִים. וְזֶה שְׁכִיחַ מְאוֹד קוֹדֶם פֶּסַח, שֶׁהַנְּהָרוֹת גְּדוֹלוֹת וְטוֹבְלִין שָׁם כֵּלִים, וְאֵינוֹ נָכוֹן. עַיֵּין לְקַמָּן סִימָן קס"ב[5].

ג. כְּלֵי עֵץ אֵינָן צְרִיכִין טְבִילָה. וְאִם יֵשׁ עֲלֵיהֶם חֲשׁוּקֵי בַרְזֶל, צְרִיכִין טְבִילָה בְּלֹא בְּרָכָה. כְּלֵי חֶרֶס גַּם כֵּן אֵינָן צְרִיכִין טְבִילָה. וְאִם מְצוּפִּין מִבִּפְנִים בְּאֵבָר[6]

"כֶּלִי" — *Baruch Atah Ado-noy, Elokeinu Melech HaOlam asher kideshanu bemitzvosav, vetzivanu al tevilas keli, Blessed are You, Hashem, our God, King of the Universe,* ***Who has sanctified us with His commandments and has commanded us regarding the immersion of a utensil.*** וְעַל שְׁתַּיִם אוֹ יוֹתֵר, מְבָרְכִין — **When immersing two or more utensils one recites the** following **blessing:** "אֲשֶׁר קִדְּשָׁנוּ בְּמִצְוֹתָיו וְצִוָּנוּ עַל טְבִילַת כֵּלִים" — *Baruch Atah Ado-noy, Elokeinu Melech HaOlam, asher kideshanu bemitzvosav, vetzivanu al tevilas keilim, Blessed are You, Hashem, our God, King of the Universe,* ***Who has sanctified us with His commandments and has commanded us regarding the immersion of utensils.***[4]

§2 כֵּיוָן שֶׁהַכֵּלִים צְרִיכִין טְבִילָה דַּוְקָא — **Since utensils require immersion specifically** בְּמָקוֹם שֶׁכָּשֵׁר לִטְבִילַת נָשִׁים — **in a place that is valid for the immersion of women,** לָכֵן צְרִיכִין לִיזָּהֵר — **therefore, one must be careful** שֶׁלֹּא לְהַטְבִּילָן בִּנְהָרוֹת — **not to immerse them in rivers** בְּשָׁעָה שֶׁהֵן גְּדוֹלוֹת מִגְּשָׁמִים וְהַפְשָׁרַת שְׁלָגִים — **when they are swollen from rain or melting snow.** וְזֶה שְׁכִיחַ מְאוֹד קוֹדֶם פֶּסַח — **This is a very common** situation **before Pesach,** שֶׁהַנְּהָרוֹת גְּדוֹלוֹת — **when the rivers are swollen,** וְטוֹבְלִין שָׁם כֵּלִים — **and people immerse utensils there;** וְאֵינוֹ נָכוֹן — **however, it is not a proper** practice. עַיֵּין לְקַמָּן סִימָן קס"ב — **See below, 162:12.**[5]

§3 כְּלֵי עֵץ אֵינָן צְרִיכִין טְבִילָה — **Wooden utensils do not require immersion.** וְאִם יֵשׁ עֲלֵיהֶם חֲשׁוּקֵי בַרְזֶל — However, **if they have iron hoops on them** צְרִיכִין טְבִילָה בְּלֹא בְּרָכָה — **they require immersion,** but **without** reciting the **blessing.** כְּלֵי חֶרֶס גַּם כֵּן אֵינָן צְרִיכִין טְבִילָה — **Earthenware utensils, too, do not require immersion.** וְאִם מְצוּפִּין מִבִּפְנִים בְּאֵבָר — However, **if they are coated** only **on the inside**

---

4. Utensils manufactured by idolaters require immersion with a blessing. If the utensils were manufactured by a Jew, they do not require immersion. [This is true even if the manufacturer is non-observant or a Shabbos desecrator, and even if the workers in the factory are idolaters (see *Igros Moshe, Orach Chaim* III, §4).] If one does not know if the manufacturer of a utensil is Jewish, he must still immerse the utensil (even if it is made of a material that requires immersion only by Rabbinic decree; see above, note 2). However, since there is a doubt whether immersion is required, he should not recite the blessing. Nevertheless, utensils manufactured in countries where all or most manufacturers are idolaters require immersion with a blessing.

There is halachic doubt whether utensils that were manufactured by a Jew and sold to an idolater require immersion. Therefore, one who purchases them from an idolatrous merchant should immerse them without reciting a blessing (*Igros Moshe, Yoreh Deah* III, §21).

5. There, Kitzur provides some background for this law, and suggests what one can do if the swollen river is the only place available for a woman to perform her immersion.

שֶׁקּוֹרִין גְלֶעזִירְט, צְרִיכִין טְבִילָה בְּלֹא בְרָכָה[7], וְכֵן כְּלֵי פּוֹרְצֶלַיְין[8].

ד. אִם הוּא כְּלִי יָשָׁן שֶׁנִּשְׁתַּמֵּשׁ בּוֹ הָעַכּוּ״ם בְּאוֹפֶן שֶׁצָּרִיךְ הֶכְשֵׁר[9] בְּהַגְעָלָה[10] אוֹ לִיבּוּן[11], צְרִיכִין לְהַכְשִׁירוֹ מִקּוֹדֶם וְאַחַר כָּךְ לְטָבְלוֹ[12].

ה. אִם שָׁאַל אוֹ שָׂכַר כְּלִי מֵעַכּוּ״ם, אֵינָהּ צְרִיכָה טְבִילָה[13]. וְאִם שׁוֹאֵל אוֹ שׂוֹכֵר כֵּלִים מֵחֶנְוָנִי יִשְׂרָאֵל, צְרִיכִין טְבִילָה בְּלֹא בְרָכָה[14]. וְהַחֶנְוָנִי יוֹדִיעַ זֹאת לְמִי שֶׁיִּקְנֶה

---

with lead,[6] **שֶׁקּוֹרִין גְלֶעזִירְט — which they call "*glazeert,*"** **צְרִיכִין טְבִילָה בְּלֹא בְרָכָה — they require immersion without** reciting the **blessing.**[7] **וְכֵן כְּלֵי פּוֹרְצֶלַיְין — The same** applies to utensils of **porcelain.**[8]

§4 אִם הוּא כְּלִי יָשָׁן — If it is an old (i.e., used) **utensil,** **שֶׁנִּשְׁתַּמֵּשׁ בּוֹ הָעַכּוּ״ם — which the idolater had used** **בְּאוֹפֶן שֶׁצָּרִיךְ הֶכְשֵׁר — in a manner that would require that it be rendered fit for kosher use**[9] **בְּהַגְעָלָה אוֹ לִיבּוּן — by** either ***hagalah*** (purging with hot water)[10] **or *libun*** (fire-purging),[11] **צְרִיכִין לְהַכְשִׁירוֹ מִקּוֹדֶם — one must first render it** fit for **kosher** use, **וְאַחַר כָּךְ לְטָבְלוֹ — and then immerse it.**[12]

§5 אִם שָׁאַל אוֹ שָׂכַר כְּלִי מֵעַכּוּ״ם — If one borrowed or rented a utensil from an idolater, **אֵינָהּ צְרִיכָה טְבִילָה — it does not require immersion.**[13] **וְאִם שׁוֹאֵל אוֹ שׂוֹכֵר כֵּלִים מֵחֶנְוָנִי יִשְׂרָאֵל — However, if one borrows or rents utensils** (made by an idolater) **from a Jewish shopkeeper,** **צְרִיכִין טְבִילָה בְּלֹא בְרָכָה — they require immersion without** reciting a **blessing.**[14] **וְהַחֶנְוָנִי יוֹדִיעַ זֹאת לְמִי שֶׁיִּקְנֶה**

---

6. If they are coated only on the outside, they do not require immersion. If they are coated both on the inside and the outside, they must certainly be immersed and the blessing must be recited. Kitzur here discusses a utensil that is coated only on the inside.

7. [It should be noted that the "coating" of which Kitzur speaks was of a more substantial nature than the glazes found on contemporary china. Perhaps for this reason, the prevalent custom today is not to immerse china.]

8. Porcelain utensils do not require immersion, but, as with earthenware, if the inside was coated with a material that requires immersion, they are to be immersed without a blessing. Here too, if they were coated both on the inside *and* the outside with a substance that would require immersion, a blessing must be recited upon immersing them (see, however, previous note).

9. A utensil must undergo one of the following processes if it was used in a certain manner, e.g., to cook or contain hot food.

10. *Hagalah*, purging with water, is generally accomplished by placing the utensil into a pot of boiling water, which causes the utensil to expel any tastes it has absorbed. (The laws of purging are discussed in detail below, *Siman* 116.)

11. If the nonkosher taste became absorbed in a utensil through a use that did not involve liquid (for example, if nonkosher meat was broiled on a grill), it must be purged with *libun* (heating the utensil intensely directly over the fire).

12. If one immerses the utensils before purging them of the nonkosher flavor, his action appears paradoxical, as he is attempting to purify them (through *tevilah*) while at the same time retaining their nonkosher impurities (*Shach, Yoreh Deah* 121:4; *Taz* 121:1).

13. Since it still belongs to the idolater. [However, if it may have been used for nonkosher food, one must perform *hagalah* or *libun*, as the case requires.]

14. In this case, there is a difference of opinion among the authorities whether such utensils require immersion (see *Yoreh Deah* 120:8). The borrower or renter must therefore immerse them in order to fulfill his possible requirement. Nevertheless, no blessing is recited to avoid the possibility of reciting a blessing in vain.

If one was served kosher food in kosher

אַחַר כָּךְ, שֶׁלֹּא יַטְבִּלֵיהוּ שֵׁנִית בִּבְרָכָה[15] **(ט״ז).**

ו. יִשְׂרָאֵל הַמַּחֲזִיק הוטע שֶׁעוֹשִׂין שָׁם כְּלֵי זְכוּכִית, וְהַפּוֹעֲלִים הֵם אֵינָם יְהוּדִים, הַכֵּלִים שֶׁנַּעֲשִׂים שָׁמָּה צְרִיכִין טְבִילָה בְּלֹא בְרָכָה[16]**.**

ז. יִשְׂרָאֵל שֶׁנָּתַן כֶּסֶף אוֹ שְׁאָר מִינֵי מַתָּכוֹת לְאוּמָּן עַכּוּ״ם שֶׁיַּעֲשֶׂה לוֹ כְלִי, אוֹ שֶׁיְּתַקֵּן לוֹ כְלִי שֶׁהָיָה נָקוּב וְלֹא הָיָה מַחֲזִיק רְבִיעִית[17]**, צָרִיךְ גַּם כֵּן טְבִילָה בְּלֹא בְרָכָה**[18]**.**

אַחַר כָּךְ — And the shopkeeper should inform whoever will later purchase the utensil that it has been immersed previously, **שֶׁלֹּא יַטְבִּלֵיהוּ שֵׁנִית בִּבְרָכָה — in order that** the purchaser **not immerse it a second time with a blessing**[15] **(ט״ז — *Turei Zahav*,** *Yoreh Deah* 120:10).

§6 יִשְׂרָאֵל הַמַּחֲזִיק הוטע שֶׁעוֹשִׂין שָׁם כְּלֵי זְכוּכִית — If a Jew has a factory in which glass utensils are manufactured, וְהַפּוֹעֲלִים הֵם אֵינָם יְהוּדִים — and the workers are not Jews, הַכֵּלִים שֶׁנַּעֲשִׂים שָׁמָּה צְרִיכִין טְבִילָה בְּלֹא בְרָכָה — then **the utensils that are manufactured there require immersion, without** reciting the **blessing.**[16]

§7 יִשְׂרָאֵל שֶׁנָּתַן כֶּסֶף אוֹ שְׁאָר מִינֵי מַתָּכוֹת לְאוּמָּן עַכּוּ״ם — If a Jew gave silver, or other types of metal, to an idolatrous craftsman, שֶׁיַּעֲשֶׂה לוֹ כְלִי — to make a utensil for him אוֹ שֶׁיְּתַקֵּן לוֹ כְלִי שֶׁהָיָה נָקוּב — or to repair for him a utensil that had developed **a hole, וְלֹא הָיָה מַחֲזִיק רְבִיעִית — and** the vessel in its broken state **could not hold a *revi'is*,**[17] **צָרִיךְ גַּם כֵּן טְבִילָה בְּלֹא בְרָכָה —** then, upon completion, this utensil **also requires immersion without** reciting the **blessing.**[18]

---

dishes in a Jewish establishment where the dishes have not been immersed, the halachah is as follows: If the food is liquid, such as soup or a drink, which cannot be served without the bowl or cup, it is forbidden to eat or drink from this utensil if it was not immersed. If the food is a solid, then in cases of pressing need, one may consider the plate upon which it is resting unnecessary to the meal, and eat the food that is on the plates either with his hands, or with cutlery made of a material that does not require immersion (*Igros Moshe, Yoreh Deah* III, §22).

15. The second Jew who purchases the utensil should not recite a blessing when immersing the utensil, for after the borrower or renter immersed it, there may be no need for another immersion. He must therefore be told that it has been immersed, so that he will not recite the blessing upon immersing it himself.

16. Some authorities hold that the worker has acquired a degree of ownership in the utensils due to the improvements that he contributed to them. Accordingly, the utensils require immersion. Others hold that the utensils remain under the complete ownership of the Jewish proprietor of the factory, and therefore do not require immersion. The utensils must therefore be immersed, but a blessing should not be recited.

In modern factories, utensils are usually not made individually by the worker, but by machine. In addition, the workers are not paid for each individual utensil made, but by the day or week. Rabbi Moshe Feinstein therefore holds that in this case, one is not required to immerse the utensils (*Igros Moshe, Orach Chaim* III, §4).

17. Between 2.9 fl. oz. and 5.1 fl. oz. (17.3-33.3 cc.); see Appendix A. A container that is broken to the extent that it can no longer contain an amount as small as a *revi'is* loses its status as a utensil, and, upon being repaired is considered a new utensil; see following note.

18. In both instances, it is unclear whether it is considered a utensil in which the idolater has ownership. If, due to the improvement contributed by the idolater, we consider the craftsman to have acquired a degree of ownership in it (see above, note 16), then it requires immersion. However, if the improvement does not grant him even partial ownership of the utensil, it does not require immersion. Because of this uncertainty, the utensil must be immersed, but a blessing should not be recited (see *Shach, Yoreh Deah* 120:21; *Taz* loc. cit. §12).

ח. אֵין צָרִיךְ טְבִילָה אֶלָּא כְּלִי שֶׁמִּשְׁתַּמְּשִׁים בּוֹ לְמַאֲכָל שֶׁהוּא רָאוּי לְאָכְלוֹ מִיָּד בְּלִי שׁוּם תִּיקּוּן אַחֵר[19]. אֲבָל הַבַּרְזִלִּים שֶׁמְּתַקְּנִים בּוֹ אֶת הַמַּצּוֹת, וְשֶׁחוֹתְכִין בּוֹ אֶת הָעִיסָּה, וְהַמַּחַט שֶׁתּוֹפְרִין בָּהּ מוּלְיָיתָא, וְכַיּוֹצֵא בָּהֶן, אֵינָן צְרִיכִין טְבִילָה[20]. אֲבָל סַכִּין שֶׁל שְׁחִיטָה וְסַכִּין שֶׁמַּפְשִׁיטִין בּוֹ, כֵּיוָן שֶׁאֶפְשָׁר לְהִשְׁתַּמֵּשׁ בְּסַכִּין זֶה לְמַאֲכָל שֶׁנִּגְמַר, וְכֵן טַסִּים (בלעכין) שֶׁמַּנִּיחִים עֲלֵיהֶם מַצּוֹת, צְרִיכִין טְבִילָה בְּלֹא בְּרָכָה[21]. וּדְרייפוס שֶׁמַּעֲמִידִין עָלָיו אֶת הַקְּדֵרָה, כֵּיוָן שֶׁאֵין הַמַּאֲכָל בְּעַצְמוֹ נוֹגֵעַ בּוֹ, אֵין צָרִיךְ טְבִילָה. אֲבָל שַׁפּוּד שֶׁל מַתָּכוֹת שֶׁצּוֹלִין עָלָיו בָּשָׂר צָרִיךְ טְבִילָה בִּבְרָכָה[22]. יֵשׁ אוֹמְרִים דִּכְלֵי זְכוּכִית גְּדוֹלוֹת (פלאשן בוטעלן) שֶׁאֵין שׁוֹתִין מִתּוֹכָן, רַק שֶׁמַּחֲזִיקִין בָּהֶן אֶת הַמַּשְׁקָאוֹת

§8 **אֵין צָרִיךְ טְבִילָה — There is no need to immerse** all utensils that come into contact with any food; **אֶלָּא כְּלִי שֶׁמִּשְׁתַּמְּשִׁים בּוֹ לְמַאֲכָל — rather, only a utensil that is used for food שֶׁהוּא רָאוּי לְאָכְלוֹ מִיָּד — that is ready to be eaten immediately, בְּלִי שׁוּם תִּיקּוּן אַחֵר — without any further preparation,** requires immersion.[19] **אֲבָל הַבַּרְזִלִּים שֶׁמְּתַקְּנִים בּוֹ אֶת הַמַּצּוֹת — However, the iron** utensils **with which the** unbaked **matzos are prepared, וְשֶׁחוֹתְכִין בּוֹ אֶת הָעִיסָּה — and with which the dough is cut, וְהַמַּחַט שֶׁתּוֹפְרִין בָּהּ מוּלְיָיתָא — and the needle with which stuffed** birds **are sewn** before being cooked, **וְכַיּוֹצֵא בָּהֶן — and the like, אֵינָן צְרִיכִין טְבִילָה — do not require immersion.**[20] **אֲבָל סַכִּין שֶׁל שְׁחִיטָה — But a slaughtering knife, וְסַכִּין שֶׁמַּפְשִׁיטִין בּוֹ — or a knife used for skinning** animals, **כֵּיוָן שֶׁאֶפְשָׁר לְהִשְׁתַּמֵּשׁ בְּסַכִּין זֶה לְמַאֲכָל שֶׁנִּגְמַר — since such a knife could be used for prepared food, וְכֵן טַסִּים (בלעכין) שֶׁמַּנִּיחִים עֲלֵיהֶם מַצּוֹת — and similarly the trays upon which** unbaked **matzos are placed** during preparation, **צְרִיכִין טְבִילָה בְּלֹא בְּרָכָה — require immersion without** reciting the **blessing.**[21] **וּדְרייפוס שֶׁמַּעֲמִידִין עָלָיו אֶת הַקְּדֵרָה —** Regarding **a tripod upon which the pot is placed** while cooking, the law is **כֵּיוָן שֶׁאֵין הַמַּאֲכָל בְּעַצְמוֹ נוֹגֵעַ בּוֹ —** that **since the food itself does not come in contact with it, אֵין צָרִיךְ טְבִילָה — it does not require immersion. אֲבָל שַׁפּוּד שֶׁל מַתָּכוֹת שֶׁצּוֹלִין עָלָיו בָּשָׂר — However, an iron spit, upon which meat is roasted, צָרִיךְ טְבִילָה בִּבְרָכָה — requires immersion, with a blessing.**[22] **יֵשׁ אוֹמְרִים דִּכְלֵי זְכוּכִית גְּדוֹלוֹת — Some** authorities **say that large glass utensils (פלאשן בוטעלן — i.e., jugs and bottles) שֶׁאֵין שׁוֹתִין מִתּוֹכָן — from which one does not drink, רַק שֶׁמַּחֲזִיקִין בָּהֶן אֶת הַמַּשְׁקָאוֹת — but** people use to **hold beverages in them,**

19. This includes not only utensils like dishes and cutlery, which are used primarily for fully prepared food, but even utensils such as pots, since the pot is in contact with food that is ready to be eaten when the cooking is completed. Only utensils that are used to process food so that they can *later* be prepared, but never come in contact with prepared foods (such as those Kitzur mentions below), do not require immersion. See further.

20. Since these utensils are used only during the preliminary stages of food preparation; see previous note.

21. Although these utensils are used primarily before the food is ready for eating, since they can also be used with food that is completely prepared, one should immerse them, but not recite the blessing.

22. As with a pot, although the meat is placed upon the spit before it is ready to be eaten, since at the time it is removed from the spit it has become "table ready," the spit requires immersion.

A bread toaster does not require immersion; since its purpose is to dry out bread that is already baked and ready to eat, it is not considered a meal utensil (*Igros Moshe, Yoreh Deah* III, §24).

לְעָרוֹת מֵהֶן לְתוֹךְ הַכּוֹסוֹת, לָא חֲשִׁיבֵי כְּלֵי סְעוּדָה וְאֵין צְרִיכִין טְבִילָה. וְיֵשׁ אוֹמְרִים דִּצְרִיכִין טְבִילָה (עַיֵּין יַד אֶפְרַיִם) וְיֵשׁ לְהַטְבִּילָן בְּלֹא בְּרָכָה[23].

ט. רֵחַיִים שֶׁל פִּלְפְּלִין צָרִיךְ טְבִילָה מִשּׁוּם הַמַּתָּכוֹת[24], אֲבָל הַתַּחְתּוֹן שֶׁמְּקַבֵּל אֶת הַתַּבְלִין, כֵּיוָן שֶׁהוּא שֶׁל עֵץ אֵין צָרִיךְ טְבִילָה. וְרֵחַיִים שֶׁל קַאווע יֵשׁ לִטְבּוֹל בְּלֹא בְּרָכָה[25] (עַיֵּין פִּתְחֵי תְּשׁוּבָה סְעִיף קָטָן ח׳).

י. צְרִיכִין לְהַשְׁגִּיחַ קוֹדֶם הַטְּבִילָה שֶׁיְּהֵא הַכְּלִי נָקִי וְלֹא יְהֵא עָלָיו שׁ[וּ]ם לִכְלוּךְ אוֹ חֲלוּדָה (אַךְ רוֹשֶׁם חֲלוּדָה, אוֹ שַׁחֲרוּרִית בְּעָלְמָא, שֶׁדַּרְכּוֹ בְּכָךְ וְאֵין מַקְפִּידִין עָלָיו אֵינוֹ מַזִּיק)[26]. וּצְרִיכִין לִטְבּוֹל כָּל הַכְּלִי בְּפַעַם אַחַת שֶׁיְּהֵא כּוּלּוֹ בַּמַּיִם. וּכְלִי שֶׁיֵּשׁ לוֹ יָד

לְעָרוֹת מֵהֶן לְתוֹךְ הַכּוֹסוֹת — and to pour from them into cups, לָא חֲשִׁיבֵי כְּלֵי סְעוּדָה וְאֵין צְרִיכִין טְבִילָה — are not considered "utensils that pertain to the meal," and do not require immersion. וְיֵשׁ אוֹמְרִים דִּצְרִיכִין טְבִילָה— Other authorities **say that they do require immersion (עַיֵּין יַד אֶפְרַיִם — see *Yad Efraim*,** *Yoreh Deah* 120:1). **וְיֵשׁ לְהַטְבִּילָן בְּלֹא בְּרָכָה** — Therefore, **one should immerse them without** reciting the **blessing.**[23]

§9 רֵחַיִים שֶׁל פִּלְפְּלִין צָרִיךְ טְבִילָה מִשּׁוּם הַמַּתָּכוֹת — A peppermill requires immersion because of the metal blades.[24] **אֲבָל הַתַּחְתּוֹן שֶׁמְּקַבֵּל אֶת הַתַּבְלִין — However, the lower** section (i.e., the receptacle), **which receives the** ground **spice, כֵּיוָן שֶׁהוּא שֶׁל עֵץ אֵין צָרִיךְ טְבִילָה — since it is** made from **wood, does not require immersion. וְרֵחַיִים שֶׁל קַאווע יֵשׁ לִטְבּוֹל בְּלֹא בְּרָכָה — A coffee-grinder should be immersed, without** reciting the **blessing**[25] **(עַיֵּין פִּתְחֵי תְּשׁוּבָה סְעִיף קָטָן ח׳ — see *Pischei Teshuvah* 120:8** for further discussion).

§10 צְרִיכִין לְהַשְׁגִּיחַ קוֹדֶם הַטְּבִילָה שֶׁיְּהֵא הַכְּלִי נָקִי — One must take care to ensure **that before the immersion the utensil is clean, וְלֹא יְהֵא עָלָיו שׁ[וּ]ם לִכְלוּךְ אוֹ חֲלוּדָה — and that there is no dirt or rust on it. (אַךְ רוֹשֶׁם חֲלוּדָה — However, a mark** left by **rust** that has been removed, **אוֹ שַׁחֲרוּרִית בְּעָלְמָא — or a mere** presence of **blackness, שֶׁדַּרְכּוֹ בְּכָךְ וְאֵין מַקְפִּידִין עָלָיו — which is normal and is not objected to, אֵינוֹ מַזִּיק — does not interfere** with the immersion.)[26] **וּצְרִיכִין לִטְבּוֹל כָּל הַכְּלִי בְּפַעַם אַחַת — One must immerse the entire utensil at once, שֶׁיְּהֵא כּוּלּוֹ בַּמַּיִם — so that all of it is in the water. וּכְלִי שֶׁיֵּשׁ לוֹ יָד — A utensil that**

---

23. Rabbi Moshe Feinstein writes (*Igros Moshe, Yoreh Deah* II, §40) that one who buys whiskey or coffee in glass bottles or other food items in cans from an idolater is not required to immerse those bottles or containers before using them for other food. This is because these bottles and containers have no intrinsic value to the idolatrous seller, and are purely intended for the sake of containing the food or drink inside them. It is only in the hands of the Jewish purchaser and user that they gain the status and importance of utensils in their own right when he decides to use them to hold other foods afterward. They are thus deemed utensils made by a Jew, which do not require immersion.

24. See *Chochmas Adam* (73:10).

25. The coffee-grinder, like the slaughtering knife (see previous *se'if*), is mostly used for unfinished food, as the coffee must be cooked after it is ground. Nevertheless, since the grinder is occasionally used for other foods that can be eaten immediately after grinding, it requires immersion.

26. All sides of the utensil must be submerged in the *mikveh*. If dirt or rust is on the utensil, it is a *chatzitzah*, interposition, between the water and the utensil, which invalidates the immersion. Even if the dirt covers only a small area and would normally be ignored, it should preferably be removed. However, if the immersion was performed without removing it, it is deemed insignificant, and the immersion is valid.

צָרִיךְ לִהְיוֹת עִם הַיָּד בְּפַעַם אַחַת כּוּלּוֹ בַּמַּיִם[27]. וְהָאָדָם הַטּוֹבֵל וְאוֹחֵז הַכְּלִי בְּיָדוֹ צָרִיךְ לִטְבּוֹל מִתְּחִלָּה יָדוֹ בְּמָקוֹם שֶׁהוּא טוֹבֵל, וְלֹא יֶאֱחוֹז אֶת הַכְּלִי בְּכֹחַ, אֶלָּא בְּדִיבּוּק בֵּינוֹנִי[28]. וְאִם טוֹבְלִין עַל יְדֵי מַה שֶּׁקּוֹשְׁרִין אֶת הַכְּלִי בְּחֶבֶל, כְּגוֹן שֶׁטּוֹבְלִין בִּבְאֵר, צְרִיכִין לְהַשְׁגִּיחַ שֶׁיִּהְיֶה הַקֶּשֶׁר רָפוּי, שֶׁיּוּכְלוּ הַמַּיִם לָבֹא בְּכָל מְקוֹם הַכְּלִי[29].

יא. אִם טוֹבֵל כֵּלִים שֶׁפִּיהֶם צַר, צָרִיךְ לְהַשְׁגִּיחַ שֶׁיִּהְיוּ בַּמַּיִם עַד שֶׁיִּתְמַלְאוּ מַיִם, כִּי צְרִיכִין שֶׁיָּבוֹאוּ הַמַּיִם עַל הַכְּלִי מִבִּפְנִים וּמִבַּחוּץ.

יב. קָטָן וּקְטַנָּה (עַיֵּין לְקַמָּן סִימָן ס״ז סְעִיף ט׳)[30] אֵינָן נֶאֱמָנִין עַל טְבִילַת כֵּלִים[31].

---

has a handle צָרִיךְ לִהְיוֹת עִם הַיָּד בְּפַעַם אַחַת כּוּלּוֹ בַּמַּיִם — **must be** submerged **in the water in its entirety at one time, with the handle.**[27] וְהָאָדָם הַטּוֹבֵל וְאוֹחֵז הַכְּלִי בְּיָדוֹ — **The person who is immersing the utensil, and holding it in his hand,** צָרִיךְ לִטְבּוֹל מִתְּחִלָּה יָדוֹ בְּמָקוֹם שֶׁהוּא טוֹבֵל — **must first dip his hand into** the water **where he will immerse** the utensil, וְלֹא יֶאֱחוֹז אֶת הַכְּלִי בְּכֹחַ — **and he should not grasp the utensil with force,** אֶלָּא בְּדִיבּוּק בֵּינוֹנִי — but **rather with an average grip.**[28] וְאִם טוֹבְלִין עַל יְדֵי מַה שֶּׁקּוֹשְׁרִין אֶת הַכְּלִי בְּחֶבֶל — Similarly, **if they are immersing by means of a rope tied to the utensil,** כְּגוֹן שֶׁטּוֹבְלִין בִּבְאֵר — **for example, if they are immersing in a well,** צְרִיכִין לְהַשְׁגִּיחַ שֶׁיִּהְיֶה הַקֶּשֶׁר רָפוּי — **they must see to it that the knot is loose,** שֶׁיּוּכְלוּ הַמַּיִם לָבֹא בְּכָל מְקוֹם הַכְּלִי — **so that the water can come over the entire surface of the utensil.**[29]

§11 אִם טוֹבֵל כֵּלִים שֶׁפִּיהֶם צַר — **If one is immersing utensils with narrow openings,** צָרִיךְ לְהַשְׁגִּיחַ שֶׁיִּהְיוּ בַּמַּיִם עַד שֶׁיִּתְמַלְאוּ מַיִם — **he must take care** to ensure **that they remain in the water until they become filled with water,** כִּי צְרִיכִין שֶׁיָּבוֹאוּ הַמַּיִם עַל הַכְּלִי מִבִּפְנִים וּמִבַּחוּץ — **for it is necessary that the water cover** the entire surface of the utensil, both **inside and outside.**

§12 קָטָן — **A boy** who is less than thirteen years old וּקְטַנָּה — **and a girl** who is less than twelve years old (עַיֵּין לְקַמָּן סִימָן ס״ז סְעִיף ט׳ — **see below, 67:9**)[30] אֵינָן נֶאֱמָנִין עַל טְבִילַת כֵּלִים — **are not trusted regarding the immersion of utensils.**[31]

---

27. Regarding an electric appliance that is used for cooking or baking, the part that comes into contact with the food must be immersed. If the appliance has two connected parts, the food receptacle and the part that houses the electrical components, then if the part with the electrical components does not touch the food, the two parts are considered to be two separate utensils even if they are connected. In such a case, it suffices to completely immerse the part that touches the food (*Igros Moshe, Yoreh Deah* I, §57-58).

28. The hand that holds the utensil can also be considered a *chatzitzah,* interposition, as it prevents the water from reaching the utensil. If the hand that holds the utensil is wet with the water of the *mikveh,* however, it is considered as though the water of the *mikveh* has reached even the part of the utensil that is within the person's grasp. He should therefore dip his hand into the *mikveh* before grasping the utensil. He must hold it loosely, however, so that the water of the *mikveh* should penetrate his grasp (see *Taz, Yoreh Deah* 120:4).

29. Therefore, if, in order to lower a utensil into the *mikveh* for immersion, a rope must be tied to it, one must be certain that the rope is not tied too tightly; if the rope is too tight, it would be a *chatzitzah* between the water and the utensil.

30. There, Kitzur explains that in order to be considered an adult one must be of age and have exhibited halachically recognized signs of maturity.

31. Although a minor is qualified to perform an immersion, he is not believed to testify that it

יג. אָסוּר לְהַטְבִּיל כְּלִי בְּשַׁבָּת וְיוֹם טוֹב[32]. וְאִם שָׁכַח לְהַטְבִּילוֹ מִקּוֹדֶם, יִתְּנֵהוּ לְנָכְרִי בְּמַתָּנָה וְיַחֲזוֹר וְיִשְׁאָלֶנּוּ מִמֶּנּוּ[33] (עַיֵּין טוּרֵי זָהָב סְעִיף קָטָן י״ח)[34]. וְאִם הוּא כְּלִי שֶׁרָאוּי לְהָבִיא בּוֹ מַיִם, בְּמָקוֹם שֶׁמּוּתָּר[35] לְטַלְטֵל יִשְׁאַב בּוֹ מַיִם וְיָבִיא לְבֵיתוֹ, דְּלָא מִחֲזֵי כְּמַטְבִּיל[36]. וְלֹא יְבָרֵךְ עָלָיו[37].

§13 אָסוּר לְהַטְבִּיל כְּלִי בְּשַׁבָּת וְיוֹם טוֹב — **It is prohibited to immerse a utensil on Shabbos or Yom Tov** (festival day).[32] וְאִם שָׁכַח לְהַטְבִּילוֹ מִקּוֹדֶם — Therefore, **if one forgot to immerse** the utensil **before** Shabbos or Yom Tov, יִתְּנֵהוּ לְנָכְרִי בְּמַתָּנָה וְיַחֲזוֹר וְיִשְׁאָלֶנּוּ מִמֶּנּוּ — **he should give it to an idolater as a gift, and then borrow it from him.**[33] (עַיֵּין טוּרֵי זָהָב סְעִיף קָטָן י״ח) — **See** ***Turei Zahav****, Yoreh Deah* 120:**18.**[34]) וְאִם הוּא כְּלִי שֶׁרָאוּי לְהָבִיא בּוֹ מַיִם — **If** the utensil that was not immersed before Shabbos **can be used to bring water,** בְּמָקוֹם שֶׁמּוּתָּר לְטַלְטֵל — then, if it is **in a place that one may carry** on Shabbos,[35] יִשְׁאַב בּוֹ מַיִם וְיָבִיא לְבֵיתוֹ — **he may draw water with it** (immersing it totally in the water), **and bring it home**, thus in effect also immersing the utensil. דְּלָא מִחֲזֵי כְּמַטְבִּיל — This is permitted, **as it does not appear as though he is immersing** the utensil for halachic reasons.[36] וְלֹא יְבָרֵךְ עָלָיו — However, **he should not recite a blessing over the immersion.**[37]

---

was performed. If, however, an adult observes a child immersing a utensil, the immersion is valid (*Rama, Yoreh Deah* 120:14).

32. As one is prohibited from using the utensil until after it is immersed, the immersion appears to be "fixing" the utensil, and is Rabbinically prohibited on Shabbos and Yom Tov (see *Beitzah* 18a).

33. A utensil that belongs to an idolater [in which no nonkosher taste is absorbed] may be used by a Jew even without immersion; see above, *se'if* 5.

This solution can also be used on a weekday as well if one cannot immerse a utensil because there is no suitable place to perform the immersion (*Rama* 120:16).

34. *Taz* (*Turei Zahav*) outlines some limitations regarding this solution. *Mishnah Berurah* (323:35) citing the opinion of this *Taz*, rules that if one follows this solution, then he must immerse the utensils after Shabbos or Yom Tov, but not recite the blessing.

35. See below, *Siman* 82, regarding the laws governing where one may carry items on Shabbos. [On Yom Tov, it is permitted to carry an item that is needed (see below, 98:1).]

36. As explained above, note 32, immersion is prohibited on Shabbos and Yom Tov because one appears to be "fixing" the utensil. In this case, however, since he can immerse it in such a manner that it seems as though he is performing a common task, it is permitted; see *Beur Halachah* (323:7 s.v. מותר להטביל).

37. If one would recite a blessing, it would be obvious that he is immersing the utensil in order to permit its use. See *Mishnah Berurah* (323:36), who rules that since immersing a utensil on Shabbos requires that one refrain from reciting the blessing, one should not avail himself of this solution unless he has no other utensil to use.

33 BREAD, COOKED FOOD, AND MILK OF AN IDOLATER — SIMAN 38:1

סימן לח

הִלְכוֹת פַּת עַכּוּ"ם — בִּשׁוּלֵי עַכּוּ"ם וַחֲלֵב עַכּוּ"ם[1]

וּבוֹ ט"ו סְעִיפִים

SIMAN 38

THE LAWS OF THE BREAD OF AN IDOLATER, FOODS COOKED BY AN IDOLATER, AND THE MILK OF AN IDOLATER

CONTAINING 15 *SE'IFIM*

§1 Bread of an Idolater / **§2** Participation of a Jew / **§3-4** Breads Included in the Prohibition / **§5** Dough Prepared by a Jew / **§6** Food Cooked by an Idolater / **§7-8** Food Cooked by a Maidservant / **§9** When an Idolater Cooks for One Who Is Ill / **§10-11** Foods Included in the Prohibition / **§12** Beer and Other Beverages / **§13** Milk of an Idolater / **§14** Cheese of an Idolater / **§15** Butter of an Idolater

The dietary laws that are included in this *Siman* are not Biblically mandated. Rather, the Sages, recognizing the risks inherent in social interaction with idolaters, sought to erect barriers between Jews and their idolatrous neighbors. Understanding that mealtimes provide unique opportunities for social relationships that might lead to intermarriage, they enacted a series of dietary laws that were designed to prevent Jews from sharing meals with idolaters. These included prohibiting a Jew to eat bread baked by an idolater or food cooked by an idolater, even if it has been ascertained that all of the ingredients were kosher.[1]

Also of concern to the Sages was the milk of idolaters, due to the possibility that it might contain milk of nonkosher animals. The Sages therefore instituted that one may not drink an idolater's milk unless a Jew observed the milking, in which case one can be certain that it is the milk of a kosher animal. Due to a concern with regard to the cheesemaking process, they also prohibited cheese of an idolater.

§1 *Se'ifim* 1-5 outline the laws of bread baked by an idolater. In earlier times, the Rabbinical Court issued a decree prohibiting the consumption of any bread baked by idolaters. At a later point, another Rabbinical Court partially suspended this prohibition.[2] Authorities differ regarding the level of prohibition that remains.

---

1. Throughout this *Siman,* when the term פַּת כָּשֵׁר, "*kosher,*" or *acceptable,* bread, is used by the Kitzur, it refers to bread baked by a Jew. All foods discussed in this *Siman* must of course contain only kosher ingredients, and be prepared with kosher utensils, in order to be permitted. [See below, note 10.]

2. In general, a later court may not abolish a decree enacted by an earlier court. However, in cases where the original decree was not upheld by a majority of the Jewish people even at the time when it was instituted, due to the difficulty involved in compliance, a later court may abolish the decree under certain limited

BREAD, COOKED FOOD, AND MILK OF AN IDOLATER — SIMAN 38:1 34

א. אָסְרוּ[2,3] חֲכָמִים לֶאֱכוֹל פַּת שֶׁל עַכּוּ"ם. וְיֵשׁ מְקוֹמוֹת שֶׁמְּקִילִין וְלוֹקְחִין פַּת מִנַּחְתּוֹם עַכּוּ"ם, בְּמָקוֹם שֶׁאֵין שָׁם נַחְתּוֹם יִשְׂרָאֵל[4], אוֹ אֲפִילוּ יֵשׁ, אֶלָּא שֶׁאֵין הַפַּת יָפָה כְּמוֹ זֶה[5]. אֲבָל בְּפַת שֶׁל בַּעֲלֵי בָתִּים עַכּוּ"ם אֵין מְקִילִין, אַךְ בִּשְׁעַת הַדְּחָק[6]. וּמִי שֶׁהוּא בְדֶרֶךְ, אִם יָכוֹל לְהַשִּׂיג פַּת כָּשֵׁר, צָרִיךְ לְהַמְתִּין עַד פַּרְסָה[7,8]. וְלָא מִיקְרֵי פַּת בַּעַל הַבַּיִת,

As a result, traditions regarding certain aspects of this prohibition vary from place to place.[3]

אָסְרוּ חֲכָמִים לֶאֱכוֹל פַּת שֶׁל עַכּוּ"ם — The Sages prohibited eating the bread of an idolater. **וְיֵשׁ מְקוֹמוֹת שֶׁמְּקִילִין** — However, **there are places where** the custom is to be **lenient** in regard to this prohibition, **וְלוֹקְחִין פַּת מִנַּחְתּוֹם עַכּוּ"ם, בְּמָקוֹם שֶׁאֵין שָׁם נַחְתּוֹם יִשְׂרָאֵל — and they purchase bread from an idolatrous baker**[4] **if there is no Jewish baker,** **אוֹ אֲפִילוּ יֵשׁ** — **or,** they purchase from an idolatrous baker **even if there is a Jewish baker,** **אֶלָּא שֶׁאֵין הַפַּת יָפָה כְּמוֹ זֶה — if the bread** of the Jewish baker **is not as good as this** bread of the idolatrous baker.[5] **אֲבָל בְּפַת שֶׁל בַּעֲלֵי בָתִּים עַכּוּ"ם — However, regarding an idolater's homemade bread** **אֵין מְקִילִין — they are not lenient,** **אַךְ בִּשְׁעַת הַדְּחָק — with the exception of a pressing situation.**[6] **וּמִי שֶׁהוּא בְדֶרֶךְ** — Since one should not be lenient in a non-pressing situation, therefore with regard to **one who is on a journey,** **אִם יָכוֹל לְהַשִּׂיג פַּת כָּשֵׁר — if,** by proceeding further along his journey **he will be able to acquire acceptable** (i.e., Jewish-baked) **bread,** **צָרִיךְ לְהַמְתִּין עַד פַּרְסָה— he must delay** his meal and travel **up to a *parsah***[7] to purchase bread that was baked by a Jew, rather than eat bread that was baked by an idolater.[8]

וְלָא מִיקְרֵי פַּת בַּעַל הַבַּיִת — Even bread baked at home **is not considered "homemade**

circumstances (see *Avodah Zarah* 36a). The blanket prohibition against all bread baked by an idolater was such a decree; bread is a basic staple of life, and when a Jewish baker was not available, it was found to be too difficult for most people to comply with this prohibition.

3. See *Beur HaGra, Yoreh Deah* 112:5.

4. I.e., one who baked the bread to sell, in contrast with home-baked bread. Kitzur defines this term further in this *se'if.*

5. The social contact that this law was designed to prevent (see introduction to this *Siman*) is a matter of greater concern if it involves interaction during mealtime, as interaction over meals can lead to socializing, and ultimately to intermarriage. Accordingly, some authorities hold that nowadays the prohibition against bread baked by an idolater applies only to home-baked bread, which lends itself to situations of social interaction. Bread baked for commercial purposes poses less of a concern (see *Avodah Zarah* 35b and *Tosafos* s.v. מכלל; *Rosh, Avodah Zarah* 2:27).

See below, 72:6, where Kitzur writes that for the Shabbos meals, it is preferable not to rely on this leniency; rather, one should use only bread baked by a Jew. This is one reason for the custom for housewives to bake loaves of bread (known as *challah*) in honor of Shabbos (see *Magen Avraham* 242:4). See below, 130:2, with regard to a similar custom during the Ten Days of Repentance (from Rosh Hashanah to Yom Kippur).

6. I.e., the prohibition against eating the homemade bread of an idolater was lifted in cases where obtaining Jewish-baked bread would entail great difficulty. [The punctuation of this clause follows the first edition of Kitzur. In a number of other editions (including that of Rabbi D. Feldman), the phrase אַךְ בִּשְׁעַת הַדְּחָק appears at the beginning of the following sentence, thus reading: *However, in a pressing situation, or someone who is on a journey* ...]

7. Between 2.4 and 2.87 miles (3.84-4.6 km.); see Appendix A.

8. However, if it would be necessary to travel farther than this, it is considered a pressing situation, and one is not required to do so. See *Chochmas Adam* 65:4.

35 BREAD, COOKED FOOD, AND MILK OF AN IDOLATER — SIMAN 38:2-3

אֶלָּא אִם עֲשָׂאוֹ בִּשְׁבִיל בְּנֵי בֵיתוֹ. אֲבָל אִם עֲשָׂאוֹ לִמְכּוֹר, מִיקְרֵי נַחְתּוֹם, אַף עַל פִּי שֶׁאֵין דַּרְכּוֹ בְּכָךְ. וְכֵן נַחְתּוֹם שֶׁעֲשָׂאוֹ לִבְנֵי בֵיתוֹ מִיקְרֵי בַּעַל הַבַּיִת[9]. יֵשׁ מִי שֶׁאוֹמֵר דִּבְמָקוֹם שֶׁאֵין נַחְתּוֹם מָצוּי מוּתָּר, אֲפִילוּ בְּפַת שֶׁל בַּעַל הַבַּיִת, וְאֵינוֹ צָרִיךְ לְהַמְתִּין עַל פַּת כָּשֵׁר, וְכֵן נוֹהֲגִין.

ב. אִם יִשְׂרָאֵל הִשְׁלִיךְ אֲפִילוּ רַק עֵץ אֶחָד לְתוֹךְ הַתַּנּוּר בְּהֶיסֵּקוֹ, מוּתָּר הַפַּת, וְלֹא הָוֵי פַּת עכו״ם[10].

ג. לֹא אָסְרוּ פַּת שֶׁל עכו״ם אֶלָּא שֶׁל חֲמֵשֶׁת מִינֵי דָגָן, אֲבָל פַּת קִטְנִיּוֹת (טענגרא קיקריץ מעלייא)[11] אֵינוֹ בִּכְלַל פַּת, וְגַם אֵינוֹ אָסוּר מִשּׁוּם בִּישּׁוּלֵי עכו״ם,

---

bread" for the purposes of this halachah, אֶלָּא אִם עֲשָׂאוֹ בִּשְׁבִיל בְּנֵי בֵיתוֹ — **unless he made it for the members of his household.** אֲבָל אִם עֲשָׂאוֹ לִמְכּוֹר, מִיקְרֵי נַחְתּוֹם — **However, if he made it** with intention **to sell** it, **he is considered a "baker,"** אַף עַל פִּי שֶׁאֵין דַּרְכּוֹ בְּכָךְ — **even though** baking **is not his regular vocation.** וְכֵן נַחְתּוֹם שֶׁעֲשָׂאוֹ לִבְנֵי בֵיתוֹ — **Similarly, if a baker made** the bread **for the members of his household,** מִיקְרֵי בַּעַל הַבַּיִת — **he is considered a homemaker** with respect to that bread.[9] יֵשׁ מִי שֶׁאוֹמֵר — **There are those who say** דִּבְמָקוֹם שֶׁאֵין נַחְתּוֹם מָצוּי — **that in a place where there is no baker to be found,** מוּתָּר אֲפִילוּ בְּפַת שֶׁל בַּעַל הַבַּיִת — **even "homemade bread" is permitted,** וְאֵינוֹ צָרִיךְ לְהַמְתִּין עַל פַּת כָּשֵׁר — **and one is not required to wait for acceptable bread** to be brought from elsewhere; וְכֵן נוֹהֲגִין — **and this is the accepted practice.**

§2 אִם יִשְׂרָאֵל הִשְׁלִיךְ אֲפִילוּ רַק עֵץ אֶחָד — **If a Jew threw even just one** piece of **wood** לְתוֹךְ הַתַּנּוּר בְּהֶיסֵּקוֹ — **into the oven while it was** being **heated,** מוּתָּר הַפַּת — **the bread baked** from that fire **is permitted** וְלֹא הָוֵי פַּת עכו״ם — **and is not** considered **bread of an idolater.**[10]

§3 לֹא אָסְרוּ פַּת שֶׁל עכו״ם — The Sages **did not prohibit** all **bread baked by an idolater,** אֶלָּא שֶׁל חֲמֵשֶׁת מִינֵי דָגָן — rather, **only that which was made from the "five species of grain"** (wheat, barley, oats, spelt, and rye) אֲבָל פַּת קִטְנִיּוֹת — **However, bread made from legumes** (טענגרא קיקריץ מעלייא — such as corn[11]) אֵינוֹ בִּכְלַל פַּת — **is not** considered **bread.** וְגַם אֵינוֹ אָסוּר מִשּׁוּם בִּישּׁוּלֵי עכו״ם — **This bread is also not prohibited under** the prohibition against eating **food cooked by an**

---

9. As explained in note 5, there is greater concern regarding social interaction with idolaters when the interaction includes partaking of their household meals. Therefore, when bread was baked with the intention that it would be sold, even if a private person baked it, it is considered "baker's bread," since bread that was intended for sale will not lead to socializing. For the same reason, bread baked by a baker for his household's needs is not viewed as "baker's bread" but as "homemaker's bread" (see *Shach, Yoreh Deah* 112:11 and *Gra* ibid. §9).

10. By throwing a piece of wood onto the fire, or by participating in some other part of the baking process (i.e., stoking the fire, placing the bread inside the oven), the Jew demonstrates his awareness that the bread of an idolater is forbidden. This recognition itself accomplishes the goal of having the Jew see himself as apart from the idolaters and from their food (*Yoreh Deah* 112:9; *Levush* ad loc.). See note 27. [Note that bread baked by an idolater is forbidden even if it was baked under supervision of a Jew.]

11. See below, *Siman* 52, note 49.

BREAD, COOKED FOOD, AND MILK OF AN IDOLATER — SIMAN 38:4-5 36

דְהָא אֵינוֹ עוֹלֶה עַל שֻׁלְחַן מְלָכִים[12].

ד. פַּת שֶׁפָּנָיו טוּחִים בְּבֵיצִים אָסוּר[13] מִשּׁוּם הַבֵּיצִים שֶׁעָלָיו דְּהָוֵי לֵיהּ בִּישׁוּלֵי עַכּוּ״ם[14]. וְאוֹתָן רְקִיקִים שֶׁנֶּאֱפִים עַל בַּרְזֶל וְיֵשׁ לָחוּשׁ שֶׁנִּמְשַׁח הַבַּרְזֶל בְּאֵיזֶה שֻׁמָּן אֲסוּרִים בְּכָל עִנְיָן, מִשּׁוּם בְּלִיעַת אִיסוּר[15].

ה. פַּת יִשְׂרָאֵל שֶׁאֲפָאוֹ עַכּוּ״ם גָּרַע מִפַּת עַכּוּ״ם, וְאָסוּר מִשּׁוּם בִּישׁוּלֵי עַכּוּ״ם, אִם לֹא הִכְשִׁיר אֶת הַתַּנּוּר בְּהַשְׁלָכַת עֵץ[16]. וּצְרִיכִין לִיזָּהֵר בָּזֶה כְּשֶׁשּׁוֹלְחִין לֶאֱפוֹת

---

idolater (see below, *se'if* 6), דְהָא אֵינוֹ עוֹלֶה עַל שֻׁלְחַן מְלָכִים — **for it is not brought upon the table of royalty.**[12]

§4 פַּת שֶׁפָּנָיו טוּחִים בְּבֵיצִים אָסוּר — **Bread whose surface is coated with eggs is prohibited** under all circumstances,[13] מִשּׁוּם הַבֵּיצִים שֶׁעָלָיו — **because of the eggs that are on top of it.** דְּהָוֵי לֵיהּ בִּישׁוּלֵי עַכּוּ״ם — **For** the **eggs are "food cooked by an idolater."**[14] וְאוֹתָן רְקִיקִים שֶׁנֶּאֱפִים עַל בַּרְזֶל — **Those wafers** (or pancakes) **that are baked on iron** griddles, וְיֵשׁ לָחוּשׁ שֶׁנִּמְשַׁח הַבַּרְזֶל בְּאֵיזֶה שֻׁמָּן — in a situation **where one must be concerned that** perhaps **the iron was smeared with** nonkosher **fat,** אֲסוּרִים בְּכָל עִנְיָן — **are** also **prohibited under all circumstances,** מִשּׁוּם בְּלִיעַת אִיסוּר — **for** concern that **they absorbed forbidden** food.[15]

§5 פַּת יִשְׂרָאֵל שֶׁאֲפָאוֹ עַכּוּ״ם — **Bread of a Jew that was baked by an idolater** (i.e., the idolater baked a Jew's dough) גָּרַע מִפַּת עַכּוּ״ם — **is dealt with more severely than the bread of an idolater,** וְאָסוּר מִשּׁוּם בִּישׁוּלֵי עַכּוּ״ם — **and is prohibited under the injunction** against **"food cooked by an idolater,"** אִם לֹא הִכְשִׁיר אֶת הַתַּנּוּר בְּהַשְׁלָכַת עֵץ — **unless** the Jew **had made the oven suitable** for baking permitted bread **by throwing** in **a** piece of **wood.**[16] וּצְרִיכִין לִיזָּהֵר בָּזֶה כְּשֶׁשּׁוֹלְחִין לֶאֱפוֹת

---

12. "Bread" made of legumes is not forbidden under the category of "bread of an idolater" because it is not classified as a bread. Here, Kitzur explains that it is also not forbidden under the category of "foods cooked by an idolater" because it does not fit the criteria of that prohibition either. As Kitzur writes below, *se'if* 6, in order to be prohibited as food cooked by an idolater, the food must be sufficiently significant that it would be "brought upon a royal table," a quality that bread made of legumes does not possess.

13. Whether baked for use at home or to be sold, and even in pressing circumstances.

14. The distinction between whether an item was homemade or baked by a baker does not apply to the prohibition against food that an idolater cooked. The reason that certain leniencies developed with regard to the bread of an idolater is based upon the fact that bread is a necessary staple (see above, note 2). However, in regard to the prohibition against food cooked by an idolater there was no such difficulty, as only bread is considered critical to survival. Therefore, food that was cooked by an idolater, even for commercial purposes, is prohibited. In our case, even if the bread was baked for commercial purposes, and would not be prohibited as the bread of an idolater, the egg that is placed upon it is governed by the law of "food cooked by an idolater," which prohibits even food that is commercially prepared (*Rama* 112:6 and *Shach* ibid. §17).

Bagels, although they are cooked before being baked, are nevertheless governed by the laws of "*bread* of an idolater," and are not prohibited as "*food* cooked by an idolater" (*Igros Moshe, Yoreh Deah* II, §33 and IV, §4).

15. Even if these wafers or pancakes would not be included in the prohibition against idolatrous bread, they are prohibited in any event, because they absorbed the nonkosher fat that was smeared onto the griddles. [This concern does not exist in regard to bread, as it is generally not baked upon a fat-coated surface.]

16. As was explained above (note 2), the leniency that developed with regard to "baker's

37 BREAD, COOKED FOOD, AND MILK OF AN IDOLATER — SIMAN 38:6

אוֹ לִצְלוֹת אֵצֶל נַחְתּוֹם עַכּוּ״ם שֶׁהַיִּשְׂרָאֵל יַשְׁלִיךְ עֵץ לְתוֹךְ הַתַּנּוּר, אוֹ שֶׁיָּנִיחַ הַיִּשְׂרָאֵל אֶת הַפַּת אוֹ אֶת הַמַּחֲבַת לְתוֹךְ הַתַּנּוּר[17].

ו. דָּבָר שֶׁאֵינוֹ נֶאֱכָל כְּמוֹ שֶׁהוּא חַי, וְגַם עוֹלֶה עַל שֻׁלְחַן מְלָכִים[18] לְלַפֵּת בּוֹ אֶת הַפַּת, אוֹ לְפַרְפֶּרֶת, שֶׁבִּישְּׁלוֹ אוֹ צְלָאוֹ עַכּוּ״ם[19], אֲפִילוּ בִּכְלֵי יִשְׂרָאֵל וּבְבֵית יִשְׂרָאֵל[20], אָסוּר מִשּׁוּם בִּישּׁוּלֵי עַכּוּ״ם. אֲבָל דָּבָר שֶׁהוּא נֶאֱכָל כְּמוֹ שֶׁהוּא חַי[21], אוֹ

אוֹ לִצְלוֹת אֵצֶל נַחְתּוֹם עַכּוּ״ם — And one must be careful about this when sending food **to be baked or roasted by a baker who is an idolater, שֶׁהַיִּשְׂרָאֵל יַשְׁלִיךְ עֵץ לְתוֹךְ הַתַּנּוּר** — to ensure **that a Jew throws a** piece of **wood into the oven, אוֹ שֶׁיָּנִיחַ הַיִּשְׂרָאֵל אֶת הַפַּת אוֹ אֶת הַמַּחֲבַת לְתוֹךְ הַתַּנּוּר — or that the Jew places the bread or the frying pan into the oven.**[17]

§6 The next seven *se'ifim* present the laws of "food cooked by an idolater."

דָּבָר שֶׁאֵינוֹ נֶאֱכָל כְּמוֹ שֶׁהוּא חַי — Any food **item that is not eaten it its raw state, וְגַם עוֹלֶה עַל שֻׁלְחַן מְלָכִים — and also, that would be brought upon the table of royalty**[18] **לְלַפֵּת בּוֹ אֶת הַפַּת, אוֹ לְפַרְפֶּרֶת — as an accompaniment to bread or as an appetizer, שֶׁבִּישְּׁלוֹ אוֹ צְלָאוֹ עַכּוּ״ם — that was cooked or roasted**[19] **by an idolater, אֲפִילוּ בִּכְלֵי יִשְׂרָאֵל וּבְבֵית יִשְׂרָאֵל — even** if it was cooked or roasted **in the utensil of a Jew, and in the house of a Jew,**[20] **אָסוּר מִשּׁוּם בִּישּׁוּלֵי עַכּוּ״ם— is prohibited, due to** the injunction against eating **"food cooked by an idolater." אֲבָל דָּבָר שֶׁהוּא נֶאֱכָל כְּמוֹ שֶׁהוּא חַי — However, something that is eaten** even **in its raw state,**[21] **אוֹ**

---

bread," is due to the great need for bread, and the excessive hardship that would be caused by prohibiting it. In the situation described in this *se'if,* where the Jew already prepared the dough, it would hardly take effort for him to bake it (or at least to throw in a piece of wood). This bread is therefore not governed by the leniencies of "bread of an idolater," but by the more stringent law of "food cooked by an idolater" (*Shach* 112:7). As we have seen in the previous *se'if* (see note 14), food that is cooked by an idolater is prohibited, even if cooked for commercial purposes. [See note 27.]

17. See Appendix of Kitzur's editorial glosses, where he cites a ruling from below, 72:2, that a Jew who desecrates Shabbos publicly is legally equivalent to an idolater, and food items that he bakes or cooks are prohibited. (See, however, *Igros Moshe, Yoreh Deah* I, §45, for a somewhat more lenient position.)

18. Most authorities maintain that these criteria (that the food is not eaten raw and would be brought upon the table of kings), vary according to time and place. Thus, even if a food was once brought upon the table of royalty, if in another day and age it is not served at a royal meal, then at that later time it would not be included in this prohibition and would be permitted if cooked by an idolater. Similarly, if in some countries fish is eaten raw, but in others fish is eaten only when cooked, then, in the former countries fish is not included in the prohibition, but in the latter it would be prohibited (see *Chochmas Adam* 66:4 and *Aruch HaShulchan* 113:12,18).

19. The prohibition includes baked or fried foods as well, but not smoked or pickled food (*Rashi* to *Avodah Zarah* 38a; *Shulchan Aruch* and *Rama, Yoreh Deah* 113:13).

20. As explained in the introduction to this *Siman*, the prohibitions against the bread and cooked food of an idolater were enacted to prevent unwanted relationships with idolaters that could lead to intermarriage. An additional reason cited that pertains more exclusively to the food cooked by an idolater is the concern that the Jew might be served nonkosher food. Although neither of these reasons would apply to food cooked in the house of a Jew, the food is prohibited in any case (see *Tur, Yoreh Deah* §113).

21. If a food is eaten when raw, the cooking is considered insignificant. When prohibiting the food cooked by an idolater, the Sages included only those foods whose cooking is a significant part of their preparation.

Even if its preparation requires that it be

BREAD, COOKED FOOD, AND MILK OF AN IDOLATER — SIMAN 38:7 38

שֶׁהוּא דָבָר שֶׁאֵינוֹ חָשׁוּב וְאֵינוֹ עוֹלֶה עַל שֻׁלְחַן מְלָכִים[22], אֵין בּוֹ מִשּׁוּם בִּישׁוּלֵי עַכּוּ״ם. וְאֵין[23] לָחוּשׁ לְהַכֵּלִים[24], דִּסְתָם כֵּלִים אֵינָן בְּנֵי יוֹמָא[25].

ז. שִׁפְחָה עַכּוּ״ם בְּבֵית יִשְׂרָאֵל הַמְבַשֶּׁלֶת בִּשְׁבִיל הַיִּשְׂרְאֵלִים, נוֹהֲגִין לְהָקֵל[26], מִפְּנֵי שֶׁאִי אֶפְשַׁר שֶׁלֹּא יְחַתֶּה אֶחָד מִבְּנֵי הַבַּיִת בָּאֵשׁ[27].

שֶׁהוּא דָבָר שֶׁאֵינוֹ חָשׁוּב — **or something that is not significant,** **וְאֵינוֹ עוֹלֶה עַל שֻׁלְחַן מְלָכִים** — **which** therefore **would not be brought upon the table of kings,**[22] **אֵין בּוֹ מִשּׁוּם בִּישׁוּלֵי עַכּוּ״ם** — even if it is cooked by an idolater, **is not included in the prohibition against "food cooked by an idolater"** and may be eaten. **וְאֵין לָחוּשׁ לְהַכֵּלִים** — In these cases, one may eat food prepared by an idolater even if prepared with his own utensils,[23] **and there is no** need for **concern because of the utensils** that may have absorbed the taste of nonkosher food and infused that taste into the food,[24] **דִּסְתָם כֵּלִים אֵינָן בְּנֵי יוֹמָא** — **as utensils of unknown status are not** assumed to be **within a day** of the previous time they were used.[25]

§7 **שִׁפְחָה עַכּוּ״ם בְּבֵית יִשְׂרָאֵל** — Regarding **an idolatrous maidservant in the house of a Jew,** **הַמְבַשֶּׁלֶת בִּשְׁבִיל הַיִּשְׂרְאֵלִים** — **who cooks for the Jews** that reside there, **נוֹהֲגִין לְהָקֵל** — **the custom is to be lenient,**[26] **מִפְּנֵי שֶׁאִי אֶפְשַׁר שֶׁלֹּא יְחַתֶּה אֶחָד מִבְּנֵי הַבַּיִת בָּאֵשׁ** — **for it is impossible that not** even a **single** Jewish **household member will stoke the fire** at some point.[27]

---

mixed with other ingredients, if it does not require cooking, it is not included in this prohibition (*Mishnah Berurah* 203:11).

22. Since one generally would not serve such foods to a guest, there is no concern that partaking of such foods cooked by an idolater would lead to unwanted socializing (*Beis Yosef, Yoreh Deah* §113).

23. As long as one is sure that all the ingredients are kosher. However, there are other factors involved that can easily change the ruling in a specific case. It is therefore imperative that one consult a halachic authority *each time* such a question arises.

24. I.e., presumably, these utensils were used for cooking nonkosher food, and absorbed nonkosher taste. The concern would then be that when kosher food is cooked in them, they would impart some of that taste into the food and render it nonkosher.

25. Nonkosher taste that is absorbed within a utensil is considered spoiled after a 24-hour period. If a nonkosher taste that is deemed spoiled enters a kosher food (e.g., by way of cooking with such a utensil), it does not render it forbidden. [Initially, however, it is prohibited for one to use utensils that have absorbed nonkosher food even after 24 hours have passed.] Since, in the absence of definitive knowledge, we may rely on the assumption that the utensil that was used to prepare the food was not used in the previous 24 hours, any food prepared by the idolater with those utensils is permitted. See above, note 23.

26. *Bach* (beginning of *Siman* 113 s.v. שלקות) writes that in this case one must walk in and out of the room, to ensure that the maidservant does not put nonkosher food into the pot.

One may not allow such a housekeeper to be alone in one's home where there is a concern that she may cook in the kitchen and cause the utensils to become forbidden by cooking prohibited foods, or meat and milk together (see *Igros Moshe, Yoreh Deah* I, §61).

27. As we have seen in *se'if* 2, the prohibition against bread baked by an idolater does not apply where a Jew participated in the baking (i.e., such as by adding a piece of wood to the fire). This leniency applies also to the prohibition against food cooked by an idolater. For this reason, one may partake of food cooked by an idolatrous maidservant, since we assume that one of the Jewish residents of the home will have at least stoked the flame.

Note that this leniency applies in those places where the fire in the oven is lit most of the day and is continuously being stoked. Nowadays, however, with gas ranges and

39 BREAD, COOKED FOOD, AND MILK OF AN IDOLATER — SIMAN 38:8-9

ח. אֲבָל אִם הִיא מְבַשֶּׁלֶת בִּשְׁבִיל עַצְמָהּ לְבַדָּהּ, אֵין רְגִילוּת שֶׁיְּחַתֶּה יִשְׂרָאֵל, וְאֶפְשַׁר דְּלָא מְהַנֵּי בָּזֶה חִיתּוּי, דִּגְרַע מֵאִלּוּ מְבַשֶּׁלֶת בִּשְׁבִיל יִשְׂרָאֵל[28]. וְלָכֵן, אִם בִּשְּׁלָה דְּבָרִים שֶׁיֵּשׁ בָּהֶם מִשּׁוּם בִּישׁוּלֵי עכו"ם, לֹא לְבַד הַתַּבְשִׁיל אָסוּר, אֶלָּא גַּם הַקְּדֵירָה נֶאֶסְרָה לְבַשֵּׁל בָּהּ לְכַתְּחִלָּה[29], וּבְדִיעֲבַד יַעֲשֶׂה שְׁאֵלַת חָכָם.

ט. עכו"ם שֶׁבִּישֵּׁל בְּשַׁבָּת בִּשְׁבִיל חוֹלֶה, הַתַּבְשִׁיל אָסוּר בְּמוֹצָאֵי שַׁבָּת, אֲפִילּוּ לְהַחוֹלֶה אִם אֶפְשָׁר בְּתַבְשִׁיל אַחֵר[30] (עַיֵּין פְּרִי חָדָשׁ יוֹרֶה דֵעָה סוֹף

---

§8 אֲבָל אִם הִיא מְבַשֶּׁלֶת בִּשְׁבִיל עַצְמָהּ לְבַדָּהּ — **However, if she** (the idolatrous maidservant) **is cooking for herself alone,** אֵין רְגִילוּת שֶׁיְּחַתֶּה יִשְׂרָאֵל — **it is not common for the Jews to stoke** the fire. וְאֶפְשַׁר דְּלָא מְהַנֵּי בָּזֶה חִיתּוּי — **Moreover, it is possible that stoking will not be effective** to make the food permitted **in this case,** דִּגְרַע מֵאִלּוּ מְבַשֶּׁלֶת בִּשְׁבִיל יִשְׂרָאֵל — **for this situation is worse than when she is cooking for the Jew.**[28] וְלָכֵן, אִם בִּשְּׁלָה דְּבָרִים שֶׁיֵּשׁ בָּהֶם מִשּׁוּם בִּישׁוּלֵי עכו"ם — **Therefore, if she cooked** food **items that are included in the prohibition against food cooked by an idolater** (i.e., they are not eaten raw and would be brought upon the table of royalty), לֹא לְבַד הַתַּבְשִׁיל אָסוּר — **not only will the** food that was **cooked be prohibited,** אֶלָּא גַּם הַקְּדֵירָה נֶאֶסְרָה לְבַשֵּׁל בָּהּ לְכַתְּחִלָּה — **but the pot** that she used **also becomes prohibited to cook in initially.**[29] וּבְדִיעֲבַד — **After the fact** (i.e., if a Jew did cook in the pot after the maid cooked in it for herself), יַעֲשֶׂה שְׁאֵלַת חָכָם — **one should consult a competent halachic authority** about the status of the food cooked in the pot by the Jew.

§9 עכו"ם שֶׁבִּישֵּׁל בְּשַׁבָּת בִּשְׁבִיל חוֹלֶה — If **an idolater cooked on Shabbos for one who is ill,** הַתַּבְשִׁיל אָסוּר בְּמוֹצָאֵי שַׁבָּת — **the cooked** food **is prohibited at the close of Shabbos,** אֲפִילּוּ לְהַחוֹלֶה — **even for the one who is ill,** אִם אֶפְשָׁר בְּתַבְשִׁיל אַחֵר — **if it is possible** to feed him **other cooked** food.[30] (עַיֵּין פְּרִי חָדָשׁ יוֹרֶה דֵעָה סוֹף

---

electronic ignition of the flame, this leniency regarding an idolatrous maidservant in a Jewish home does not apply.

28. Some authorities maintain that even if the Jew stoked the fire, the food is permitted only because the maid was cooking as part of her service to her employer. According to this view, in the situation where she was cooking for herself, the food would not be permitted even if we were certain that a Jew stoked the flame (see *Shach, Yoreh Deah* 113:7,20).

29. Prohibited food that is cooked becomes absorbed in the walls of the pot that was used, and is transmitted into any food that is later cooked in that pot, causing that food to be become prohibited as well. Therefore, the pot must be properly purged of the nonkosher taste that is absorbed in it. [The procedure for purging is described below, *Siman* 116. With regard to a utensil that absorbed the taste of food cooked by an idolater, there are a number of possible leniencies regarding this procedure; see *Mishnah Berurah* 328:63, citing *Yoreh Deah* 113:16 and *Shach* §21.]

30. Generally, even one who has fallen ill (and his life is not in danger) may not eat nonkosher food, even that which is forbidden Rabbinically (see below, 192:5). In contrast, food cooked by an idolater may be eaten by an ill person if he cannot obtain food cooked by a Jew. The reason for this difference is that food cooked by an idolater is not intrinsically nonkosher; it is forbidden only because of the person who prepared it. Thus, on Shabbos, when food cannot be cooked by a Jew, an ill person may eat food cooked by an idolater. However, he may eat that food only as long as other food is not available. After Shabbos, when a Jew can again cook for him, he may no longer eat the food cooked by an idolater. See below, 91:16, and *Mishnah Berurah* 328:63; cf. ibid. 318:14.

BREAD, COOKED FOOD, AND MILK OF AN IDOLATER — SIMAN 38:10-12 40

סִימָן קי״ג), וּבַכֵּלִים יֵשׁ לְהַתִּיר אַחַר מֵעֵת לְעֵת[31].

י. בֵּיצָה, אַף עַל פִּי שֶׁרְאוּיָה לְגָמְעָהּ חַיָּה, מִכָּל מָקוֹם כֵּיוָן דְּזֶה הָוֵי רַק אֲכִילָה עַל יְדֵי הַדְּחָק, אִם בִּשֵּׁל הָעַכּוּ״ם, אֲסוּרָה[32]. וְכֵן כָּל כַּיּוֹצֵא בָּזֶה.

יא. פֵּירוֹת שֶׁלֹּא נִתְבַּשְּׁלוּ בְּאִילָן כָּל צָרְכָּן, וְאֵינָן נֶאֱכָלִין חַיִּין אֶלָּא עַל יְדֵי הַדְּחָק, שֶׁהָאוּמָּנִים מְטַגְּנִים אוֹתָן בְּצוּקֶר, אֲסוּרִין מִשּׁוּם בִּישׁוּלֵי עַכּוּ״ם[33].

יב. שֵׁכָר שֶׁל תְּבוּאָה וְשֶׁל דְּבַשׁ נוֹהֲגִין בּוֹ הֶיתֵּר לִשְׁתּוֹתוֹ, אֲפִילוּ בְּבַיִת שֶׁמּוֹכְרִין אוֹתוֹ הָעַכּוּ״ם[34], וְאֵין בּוֹ מִשּׁוּם בִּישׁוּלֵי עַכּוּ״ם, דְּהַתְּבוּאָה בְּטֵלָה בְּמַיִם[35],

---

סִימָן קי״ג — See *Pri Chadash, Yoreh Deah* 113:26.) וּבַכֵּלִים יֵשׁ לְהַתִּיר אַחַר מֵעֵת לְעֵת — **As for the utensils, they are permitted** for use **after twenty-four hours.**[31]

§10 בֵּיצָה, אַף עַל פִּי שֶׁרְאוּיָה לְגָמְעָהּ חַיָּה — **An egg, although it can be swallowed when raw,** מִכָּל מָקוֹם כֵּיוָן דְּזֶה הָוֵי רַק אֲכִילָה עַל יְדֵי הַדְּחָק — **nevertheless, since it is only eaten** that way **in pressing situations,** אִם בִּשֵּׁל הָעַכּוּ״ם, אֲסוּרָה — **if an idolater cooks it, it is prohibited.**[32] וְכֵן כָּל כַּיּוֹצֵא בָּזֶה — **The same** law **applies to all similar situations.**

§11 פֵּירוֹת שֶׁלֹּא נִתְבַּשְּׁלוּ בְּאִילָן כָּל צָרְכָּן — **Fruits that have not fully ripened** while **on the tree,** וְאֵינָן נֶאֱכָלִין חַיִּין אֶלָּא עַל יְדֵי הַדְּחָק — **and are not eaten raw** in that state **other than in pressing** situations, שֶׁהָאוּמָּנִים מְטַגְּנִים אוֹתָן בְּצוּקֶר— which have been prepared by idolatrous **professional cooks** who **fried them with sugar,** אֲסוּרִין מִשּׁוּם בִּישׁוּלֵי עַכּוּ״ם — **are prohibited, due to** the prohibition against **food cooked by an idolater.**[33]

§12 שֵׁכָר שֶׁל תְּבוּאָה וְשֶׁל דְּבַשׁ נוֹהֲגִין בּוֹ הֶיתֵּר לִשְׁתּוֹתוֹ — **It is the custom to permit** the drinking of **beer** that is made **from grain or honey,** אֲפִילוּ בְּבַיִת שֶׁמּוֹכְרִין אוֹתוֹ הָעַכּוּ״ם — **even in the house where the idolaters sell it,**[34] וְאֵין בּוֹ מִשּׁוּם בִּישׁוּלֵי עַכּוּ״ם — **and there is no prohibition of "food cooked by an idolater,"** דְּהַתְּבוּאָה בְּטֵלָה בְּמַיִם — **for the grain is** considered to be **nullified in the water.**[35]

---

31. In this situation, a number of halachic factors coincide to allow this leniency. [In brief: (1) The food was cooked on Shabbos for an ill person; (2) the issue is only one of absorbed taste; and (3) 24 hours have passed since the taste was absorbed; see *Chochmas Adam* 66:12.]

Some authorities hold, however, that these utensils do need to be purged after the idolater cooked in them. Still others are even more lenient than Kitzur, and hold that one may use these utensils without purging even *within* 24 hours. According to *Mishnah Berurah* (328:63), there is sufficient basis for one who wishes to rely on this opinion to do so.

32. As Kitzur explained in *se'if* 6, when food that does not require cooking is cooked by an idolater, it is not prohibited, because the idolater's cooking was not an act of significance. Where a food is *usually* cooked, even if in a pressing or unusual situation it might be eaten raw, the cooking is significant, and the food becomes forbidden when cooked by an idolater.

33. See previous note.

34. This is a reference to a separate prohibition, in which one may not drink certain beverages in the home or business of an idolater, to prevent the possibility of intermarriage. Kitzur rules like *Rama* (*Yoreh Deah* 114:1), that beer made from grain or honey was not included in this prohibition (see *Avodah Zarah* 31b and *Yoreh Deah* 114:1 with *Rama*; *Aruch HaShulchan* 114:10-11). [See the end of this *se'if* for further parameters of this prohibition.] Above, Kitzur explains why this beverage is not subject to the general prohibition of food cooked by an idolater.

35. There are two components to beer: the

41 BREAD, COOKED FOOD, AND MILK OF AN IDOLATER — SIMAN 38:13

רַק שֶׁצְּרִיכִין לַחְקוֹר אִם אֵין מַעֲמִידִין אוֹתָן בְּשִׁמְרֵי יַיִן[36]. וּבְמָקוֹם שֶׁיִּשְׂרְאֵלִים מְזַלְזְלִין וּמְקִילִין בְּיַיִן שֶׁל עַכּוּ״ם יֵשׁ לְבַעַל נֶפֶשׁ לְהַחְמִיר עַל עַצְמוֹ גַּם בְּשֵׁכָר[37]. וּבְעִנְיַן שְׁתִיַּית קאפע (בְּלֹא חָלָב, דְּעִם חָלָב וַדַּאי אָסוּר[38]) וְכֵן טשאקאלאדע וְטהע אֵצֶל עַכּוּ״ם, שׁוֹמֵר נַפְשׁוֹ יִרְחַק אֶת עַצְמוֹ (פִּתְחֵי תְּשׁוּבָה סִימָן קי״ד בְּשֵׁם פָּנִים מְאִירוֹת). וְיֵשׁ מַתִּירִין לִשְׁתּוֹת דֶּרֶךְ אַרְעַי, אֲבָל דֶּרֶךְ קְבִיעוּת אָסוּר (יַד אֶפְרַיִם בְּשֵׁם מהריעב״ץ)[39].

יג. חָלָב שֶׁחֲלָבָהּ עַכּוּ״ם וְאֵין יִשְׂרָאֵל רוֹאֵהוּ אֲסוּרָה[40], אֲפִילוּ לַעֲשׂוֹת מִמֶּנָּה

רַק שֶׁצְּרִיכִין לַחְקוֹר — **Nevertheless, one must investigate,** and determine אִם אֵין מַעֲמִידִין אוֹתָן בְּשִׁמְרֵי יַיִן — **that they were not fermented with wine sediment.**[36] וּבְמָקוֹם שֶׁיִּשְׂרְאֵלִים מְזַלְזְלִין וּמְקִילִין בְּיַיִן שֶׁל עַכּוּ״ם — However, **in a place where the Jews are lax and lenient regarding** the prohibition against the **wine of idolaters,** יֵשׁ לְבַעַל נֶפֶשׁ לְהַחְמִיר עַל עַצְמוֹ גַּם בְּשֵׁכָר — **then a scrupulous individual should be stringent** and refrain from partaking of their **beer as well.**[37]

וּבְעִנְיַן שְׁתִיַּית קאפע — **Regarding drinking coffee** (בְּלֹא חָלָב — even **without milk,** דְּעִם חָלָב וַדַּאי אָסוּר — as coffee **with milk would certainly be prohibited**[38]), וְכֵן טשאקאלאדע וְטהע— **and similarly** hot **chocolate or tea,** אֵצֶל עַכּוּ״ם — **at** the home or place of **an idolater,** שׁוֹמֵר נַפְשׁוֹ יִרְחַק אֶת עַצְמוֹ — **he who** wishes to **guard his soul will distance himself** from doing so (פִּתְחֵי תְּשׁוּבָה סִימָן קי״ד בְּשֵׁם פָּנִים מְאִירוֹת — *Pischei Teshuvah, Siman* 114:1 citing *Panim Me'iros* 2:62). וְיֵשׁ מַתִּירִין לִשְׁתּוֹת דֶּרֶךְ אַרְעַי — However, **some** authorities **permit drinking** these beverages at the home or place of an idolater, but only **in a casual manner,** informally. אֲבָל דֶּרֶךְ קְבִיעוּת אָסוּר — **But** if done **in a formal** setting, **it is prohibited** (יַד אֶפְרַיִם בְּשֵׁם מהריעב״ץ — *Yad Efraim,* citing R' Yaakov Emden 2:142).[39]

§13 חָלָב שֶׁחֲלָבָהּ עַכּוּ״ם — **Milk that was milked by an idolater,** וְאֵין יִשְׂרָאֵל רוֹאֵהוּ — **without being overseen by a Jew,** אֲסוּרָה, אֲפִילוּ לַעֲשׂוֹת מִמֶּנָּה גְּבִינָה — **is prohibited** for drinking[40] and it is **even** prohibited to **make cheese from**

---

fermented grain and the water in which it is brewed. Since it is consumed as a beverage, the water is considered to be its primary component. Water does not require cooking to be consumed, and its cooking is therefore considered insignificant (as above, *se'if* 6). Beer is therefore not included in the prohibition against food cooked by an idolater (*Tosafos, Avodah Zarah* 31b s.v. ותרוייהו, cited by *Taz* 114:1; see also below, note 39). The same applies to the other beverages that will be mentioned in this *se'if.*

36. It is prohibited to drink the wine of an idolater (see *Siman* 47 for the particulars of this prohibition). If the wine of an idolater is used to ferment the beer, the beer becomes prohibited.

37. In this case, it is prohibited to drink even the beer of these Jews. We are concerned that while drinking their beer, perhaps one would be led into partaking of their wine as well. Since these Jews are not scrupulous about avoiding the wine of idolaters, perhaps the wine they will serve was actually purchased from an idolater, and is prohibited (*Shach, Yoreh Deah* 114:4).

38. If taken with milk, the coffee would certainly be prohibited due to the separate prohibition against drinking the milk of an idolater (see next *se'if*).

39. While these drinks, like beer, are not prohibited under the category of "foods cooked by an idolater," some authorities hold that they are among the beverages that one may not drink at the home or business of an idolater (see above, note 34). However, the prohibition against drinking certain beverages at the home or business of an idolater applies only to drinking in a formal setting (i.e., a sit-down drinking session); see *Yoreh Deah* 114:1.

40. As explained in the introduction to this

BREAD, COOKED FOOD, AND MILK OF AN IDOLATER — SIMAN 38:13 42

גְּבִינָה[41]. וּלְכַתְּחִלָּה צָרִיךְ הַיִּשְׂרָאֵל לִהְיוֹת בִּתְחִלַּת הַחֲלִיבָה וְיִרְאֶה שֶׁהַכְּלִי הוּא נָקִי. וְנָהֲגוּ לְהַחֲמִיר שֶׁלֹּא יַחֲלוֹב לְתוֹךְ הַכְּלִי שֶׁדַּרְכּוֹ שֶׁל הָעַכּוּ״ם לַחֲלוֹב לְתוֹכוֹ[42]. וּשְׁפָחוֹת שֶׁחוֹלְבוֹת הַבְּהֵמוֹת בְּבֵית יִשְׂרָאֵל אוֹ בְּדִיר שֶׁלָּהֶם, כָּל מָקוֹם שֶׁאֵין בֵּית עַכּוּ״ם מַפְסִיק, וְאֵין לָחוּשׁ לִבְהֵמָה טְמֵאָה, מוּתָּר אֲפִילוּ לְכַתְּחִלָּה לְהַנִּיחָן לַחֲלוֹב[43]. אֲבָל אִם בֵּית עַכּוּ״ם מַפְסִיק, צָרִיךְ שֶׁיְּהֵא שָׁם יִשְׂרָאֵל[44], וַאֲפִילוּ קָטָן אוֹ קְטַנָּה בְּנֵי ט׳ שָׁנָה סַגִּי.

---

it.[41] **וּלְכַתְּחִלָּה** — **Ideally,** **צָרִיךְ הַיִּשְׂרָאֵל לִהְיוֹת בִּתְחִלַּת הַחֲלִיבָה** — **the Jew should be present at the beginning of the milking,** **וְיִרְאֶה שֶׁהַכְּלִי הוּא נָקִי** — **to see that the vessel** into which one milks **is clean** from any nonkosher milk. **וְנָהֲגוּ לְהַחֲמִיר** — **It is customary to be stringent** **שֶׁלֹּא יַחֲלוֹב לְתוֹךְ הַכְּלִי שֶׁדַּרְכּוֹ שֶׁל הָעַכּוּ״ם לַחֲלוֹב לְתוֹכוֹ** — and **not milk into the vessel that an idolater usually milks into.**[42] **וּשְׁפָחוֹת שֶׁחוֹלְבוֹת הַבְּהֵמוֹת** — Regarding **maidservants** who are idolaters that **milk the animals** of their Jewish employers **בְּבֵית יִשְׂרָאֵל אוֹ בְּדִיר שֶׁלָּהֶם** — **in the home of Jews or in their corrals,** **כָּל מָקוֹם שֶׁאֵין בֵּית עַכּוּ״ם מַפְסִיק** — the halachah is that **in a place where no home of an idolater is** situated **between** the home of the Jew and the site of the milking, **וְאֵין לָחוּשׁ לִבְהֵמָה טְמֵאָה** — **and there is no concern that** there was **a nonkosher animal** there, **מוּתָּר אֲפִילוּ לְכַתְּחִלָּה לְהַנִּיחָן לַחֲלוֹב** — **it is permitted, even initially, to allow them to milk.**[43] **אֲבָל אִם בֵּית עַכּוּ״ם מַפְסִיק** — **However, if the home of an idolater is** situated **between** the home of the Jew and the site of the milking, **צָרִיךְ שֶׁיְּהֵא שָׁם יִשְׂרָאֵל** — **then it is necessary that a Jew be present** to oversee the milking.[44] **וַאֲפִילוּ קָטָן אוֹ קְטַנָּה בְּנֵי ט׳ שָׁנָה סַגִּי** — For this supervision, **even minors,** including **a boy or girl** who are **nine years** of age, **are sufficient.**

Siman, the Sages were concerned that the idolaters might add the milk of nonkosher animals into the kosher milk that is purchased from them. The Sages therefore prohibited the milk belonging to idolaters, unless the milking was supervised by a Jew.

According to Rabbi Moshe Feinstein, commercial milk produced by reputable companies in the United States is permitted, even without supervision of the milking by a Jew, even if the company is owned by an idolater. This is because the producers would not use the milk of any other animal and sell it as cow's milk, due to the strict government regulations. Just as when a Jew supervises the milking to ensure that no other milk is added, the milk is permitted, so too, a clear knowledge (based on government requirements) that the milk is from kosher animals is tantamount to Jewish supervision. Clearly, this applies only if there are indeed strong government regulations in place ensuring that no milk from nonkosher animals can be used, such that the producers will comply. Rabbi Feinstein writes, however, that although such commercial milk is halachically permissible, it is proper for a scrupulous individual (*baal nefesh*) to act stringently and use only milk that was produced under Jewish supervision (*Igros Moshe, Yoreh Deah* I, §47-49; III, §16, IV, §5).

41. That is, a Jew may not take milk of an idolater and process it into cheese. [In the following *se'if*, Kitzur discusses the cheese that an idolater produces from milk that was milked under the supervision of a Jew.]

42. This is out of concern that the utensil might retain some residue of nonkosher milk (*Rama* 115:1).

43. In such a case, she will refrain from adding any other milk for fear that the Jew may discover her action (*Beur HaGra* 116:7).

44. In this case she is less afraid of being discovered, and we are thus concerned that she might add nonkosher milk (see *Rama, Yoreh Deah* 115:1).

43 BREAD, COOKED FOOD, AND MILK OF AN IDOLATER — SIMAN 38:14-15

יד. גְּבִינוֹת הָעַכּוּ״ם אֲסוּרָה[45]. וְאִם הַיִּשְׂרָאֵל רוֹאֶה הַחֲלִיבָה וַעֲשִׂיַּית הַגְּבִינוֹת, אִם הַגְּבִינוֹת בִּשְׁעַת עֲשִׂיָּיתָן הֵן שֶׁל יִשְׂרָאֵל, מוּתָּרוֹת. אֲבָל אִם הֵן בִּשְׁעַת עֲשִׂיָּיתָן שֶׁל עַכּוּ״ם אֲסוּרוֹת[46].

טו. הַחֶמְאָה תַּלְיָא בְּמִנְהַג הַמְּקוֹמוֹת: יֵשׁ מְקוֹמוֹת שֶׁאֵין אוֹכְלִין חֶמְאָה שֶׁל עַכּוּ״ם[47], וְיֵשׁ מְקוֹמוֹת שֶׁאוֹכְלִין אוֹתָהּ[48]. וּמִי שֶׁהוֹלֵךְ מִמָּקוֹם שֶׁאֵין אוֹכְלִין אוֹתָהּ לְמָקוֹם שֶׁאוֹכְלִין אוֹתָהּ, אַף עַל פִּי שֶׁדַּעְתּוֹ לַחֲזוֹר לִמְקוֹמוֹ, אוֹכֵל שָׁם עִמָּהֶם[49].

§14 **גְּבִינוֹת הָעַכּוּ״ם אֲסוּרָה — Cheeses of an idolater are prohibited.**[45] **וְאִם הַיִּשְׂרָאֵל רוֹאֶה הַחֲלִיבָה וַעֲשִׂיַּית הַגְּבִינוֹת — However, if a Jew supervises the milking,** and also **the making of the cheeses, אִם הַגְּבִינוֹת בִּשְׁעַת עֲשִׂיָּיתָן הֵן שֶׁל יִשְׂרָאֵל, מוּתָּרוֹת —** then, **if the cheeses belonged to a Jew at the time they were made, they are permitted. אֲבָל אִם הֵן בִּשְׁעַת עֲשִׂיָּיתָן שֶׁל עַכּוּ״ם אֲסוּרוֹת — However, if at the time they were made the cheeses belonged to an idolater, they are prohibited.**[46]

§15 **הַחֶמְאָה תַּלְיָא בְּמִנְהַג הַמְּקוֹמוֹת** — The law regarding **butter** of an idolater **depends upon the custom of the** communities in various **places. יֵשׁ מְקוֹמוֹת שֶׁאֵין אוֹכְלִין חֶמְאָה שֶׁל עַכּוּ״ם** — For **there are** some **places** where the custom is **not to eat the butter of idolaters,**[47] **וְיֵשׁ מְקוֹמוֹת שֶׁאוֹכְלִין אוֹתָהּ — and there are** other **places where** they are lenient, and **they eat it.**[48] **וּמִי שֶׁהוֹלֵךְ מִמָּקוֹם שֶׁאֵין אוֹכְלִין אוֹתָהּ — One who goes from a place where** the custom is **not to** eat the butter of an idolater **לְמָקוֹם שֶׁאוֹכְלִין אוֹתָהּ — to a place where** the custom is **to eat it, אַף עַל פִּי שֶׁדַּעְתּוֹ לַחֲזוֹר לִמְקוֹמוֹ — even if he intends to return to his** original **place, אוֹכֵל שָׁם עִמָּהֶם — may eat** the butter **in accordance with the local custom** while he is **there.**[49]

---

45. Cheese is made by introducing an enzyme (known as rennin or chymosin) into milk. This enzyme is found inside the stomach lining of a young animal; it was therefore the practice to put the stomach of a slaughtered animal into milk, causing the milk to coagulate into cheese. [See *Taz* (*Yoreh Deah* 115:9) regarding why this does not also present a problem of a forbidden milk and meat mixture.] If the stomach used came from a prohibited animal, the cheese produced thereby is forbidden. The Sages prohibited all cheese of an idolater, even that which was produced from milk supervised by a Jew (see previous *se'if*), out of concern that the idolater will produce the cheese by placing it in the stomach of a forbidden animal (*Yoreh Deah* 115:2).

46. In the case of cheese that belongs to an idolater and was also produced by idolaters, the Sages prohibited the cheese even if a Jew oversaw the entire process. However, if the cheese, when it was first made, belonged to a Jew, it is not included in this prohibition, and is permitted, provided that there was Jewish supervision of the milking and the production of the cheese. Cf. *Rama, Yoreh Deah* 115:2 and *Igros Moshe, Yoreh Deah* I, §50.

47. According to this tradition, the Sages prohibited the butter of an idolater as well, out of concern that perhaps a small amount of nonkosher milk adhered to it (*Tur, Yoreh Deah* §115).

48. Those who hold this tradition maintain that the Sages did not include butter in their prohibition against the milk of an idolater. The reason for this is that butter does not form when nonkosher milk is used (see *Taz* 115:12 and *Shach* 115:27). Therefore, the person producing butter will be careful to avoid putting in any nonkosher milk (*Pri Chadash* 115:21). [Note that if a Jew acquired [from an idolater] milk that is subject to the prohibition regarding milk of an idolater, it remains forbidden even if the Jew produced butter from it (*Rama* 115:1).]

49. This halachah, whose source is *Rama* (*Yoreh Deah* 115:3), is not referring to the two differing customs mentioned earlier in this *se'if* regarding the prohibition against butter of an idolater. [In that case, as in all cases where one travels temporarily to a place with a more

BREAD, COOKED FOOD, AND MILK OF AN IDOLATER — SIMAN 38:15 44

וְהַהוֹלֵךְ מִמָּקוֹם שֶׁאוֹכְלִין אוֹתָהּ לְמָקוֹם שֶׁאֵין אוֹכְלִין אוֹתָהּ אָסוּר לְאָכְלָהּ שָׁם. כָּעֵת נִשְׁמַע שֶׁמְּזַיְּיפִין אֶת הַחֶמְאָה בְּשׁוּמַּן חֲזִיר, עַל כֵּן שׁוֹמֵר נַפְשׁוֹ יִרְחַק.

וְהַהוֹלֵךְ מִמָּקוֹם שֶׁאוֹכְלִין אוֹתָהּ — One who goes from a place where they eat it לְמָקוֹם שֶׁאֵין אוֹכְלִין אוֹתָהּ — to a place where they do not eat it, אָסוּר לְאָכְלָהּ שָׁם — may not eat it while **there.**

כָּעֵת נִשְׁמַע שֶׁמְּזַיְּיפִין אֶת הַחֶמְאָה בְּשׁוּמַּן חֲזִיר — Of late, it has been heard, that they deceitfully substitute that which they sell as **butter with the fat of swine** (i.e., lard). **עַל כֵּן שׁוֹמֵר נַפְשׁוֹ יִרְחַק — Therefore, one who** wishes to **guard his soul will distance** himself from butter whose ingredients are not known.

---

lenient custom than his own, he must continue to hold his own more stringent custom; see *Orach Chaim* 468:4 and *Mishnah Berurah* ad loc. §19.] Rather, this halachah refers to a place that follows the more *lenient* custom regarding the primary question of butter of an idolater, but where they nevertheless refrain from eating such butter out of concern for a local problem: Where there are not many milk-producing animals, the idolaters place their milk in the same utensils that are used for their other food. Because of this, the Jews of that area do not eat butter made by an idolater. If a Jew from that place goes to another place in which there is no such concern (e.g., there are many milk-producing animals, and they have designated utensils for the butter), he may eat the butter of that place. The specific concern of his hometown does not apply to the new place, and the custom of his hometown is to be lenient regarding the primary question of butter of an idolater (see *Taz* 115:13 and *Gra* ibid. §21).

45 ONE WHO WISHES TO EAT OR DRINK BEFORE A MEAL — SIMAN 39

סִימָן לט

דִּין מִי שֶׁרוֹצֶה לֶאֱכוֹל אוֹ לִשְׁתּוֹת קוֹדֶם הַסְּעוּדָּה[1,2,3,4,5,6]

וּבוֹ ג׳ סְעִיפִים

SIMAN 39

LAWS GOVERNING ONE WHO WISHES TO EAT OR DRINK BEFORE A MEAL

CONTAINING 3 *SE'IFIM*

§1 Foods and Drinks Before a Meal / §2 Wine and Liquor / §3 Baked Goods

After completing four *Simanim* pertaining to food preparation, in this *Siman* and in those that follow, Kitzur discusses halachos that relate to eating a meal.

Before eating or drinking, one must recite the *berachah rishonah* (*first-blessing;* the blessing recited before eating or drinking) appropriate to that particular food or beverage.[1] Similarly, after one has eaten the minimum amount that subjects him to recite a *berachah acharonah* (*final-blessing;* the blessing recited after eating or drinking), he is obligated to recite the *berachah acharonah* that is appropriate for that food.[2] As will be explained in *Siman* 43, foods that are eaten within the context of a meal that one is eating with bread do not generally require their own individual *berachos*: The obligation of *berachah rishonah* at such a meal is fulfilled by the blessing of *hamotzi*[3] recited upon the bread at the beginning of the meal, and the obligation of *berachah acharonah* is fulfilled with the recitation of *Bircas HaMazon* (Grace After Meals) at the conclusion of the meal.[4]

In certain circumstances, even foods eaten *before* a meal can be considered to be "part of the meal" with regard to the obligation of *berachah acharonah,* with the *Bircas HaMazon* recited at the end of the forthcoming meal serving as the *berachah acharonah* for these foods as well.[5] In this *Siman,* Kitzur outlines the various circumstances that affect the requirement of a *berachah acharonah* for food that is eaten before a meal.[6]

---

1. See below, *Siman* 50, for general rules of *berachah rishonah*, and *Simanim* 48-49 and 52-57 for detailed halachos.

2. See below, *Siman* 51, for general halachos of *berachah acharonah.*

3. The blessing upon bread concludes with the words: הַמּוֹצִיא לֶחֶם מִן הָאָרֶץ, *Who brings forth bread from the earth.*

4. *Bircas HaMazon*, Grace After Meals, is the *berachah acharonah* that one must recite upon eating bread. (The halachos of *Bircas HaMazon* are discussed below, in *Siman* 44.) While most foods eaten within the course of a bread meal are covered by the recitation of *Bircas HaMazon*, some foods eaten during the meal require their own *berachah rishonah* but not their own *berachah acharonah*, while others require both; these halachos are the subject of *Siman* 43.

5. A *berachah rishonah*, however, is always required on such food.

6. The halachos pertaining to the blessings on food are highly specific to the exact circumstances in which the halachah is set. A variation in ingredients, custom, method of

ONE WHO WISHES TO EAT OR DRINK BEFORE A MEAL — SIMAN 39:1   **46**

א. הָרוֹצֶה[7] לֶאֱכוֹל קוֹדֶם נְטִילַת יָדַיִם[8] דְּבָרִים שֶׁיֹּאכַל מִמִּינִים אֵלּוּ גַּם בְּתוֹךְ הַסְּעוּדָה[9], בֵּין שֶׁהֵם דְּבָרִים שֶׁצְּרִיכִין לְבָרֵךְ עֲלֵיהֶם תּוֹךְ הַסְּעוּדָה[10], כְּגוֹן פֵּירוֹת, בֵּין שֶׁהֵם דְּבָרִים שֶׁאֵין צְרִיכִין לְבָרֵךְ עֲלֵיהֶם תּוֹךְ הַסְּעוּדָה[11], כְּגוֹן מִינֵי לִפְתָּן וּמִינֵי קִטְנִיּוֹת[12] וְעֶרְדֶעפְּפֶעל, וְכֵן אִם רוֹצֶה לִשְׁתּוֹת אֵיזֶה מַשְׁקֶה

§1 Kitzur begins the *Siman* by addressing the law with regard to *berachah acharonah,* in a case in which, before one's meal, one eats a type of food that will be eaten during the meal as well. According to some authorities, when the type of food that one eats before the meal will be eaten during the meal, the two acts of eating are considered to be one, and the *Bircas HaMazon* recited at the conclusion of the meal exempts even that which was eaten before the meal from its own *berachah acharonah.* Accordingly, one would not have to recite a *berachah acharonah* on whatever food he eats before the meal if he is planning to eat the same type of food during the meal. Other authorities maintain that this factor alone is not sufficient to connect the two acts of eating and a separate *berachah acharonah* is required before he begins his meal.[7] **הָרוֹצֶה לֶאֱכוֹל קוֹדֶם נְטִילַת יָדַיִם** — **One who wishes to eat before washing the hands** for a meal,[8] **דְּבָרִים שֶׁיֹּאכַל מִמִּינִים אֵלּוּ גַּם בְּתוֹךְ הַסְּעוּדָה** — **certain foods, of a type that he will also be eating during the meal** itself;[9] **בֵּין שֶׁהֵם דְּבָרִים שֶׁצְּרִיכִין לְבָרֵךְ עֲלֵיהֶם תּוֹךְ הַסְּעוּדָה** — regardless of **whether they are foods that,** if eaten **during a meal, one would be required to recite a blessing upon them,**[10] **כְּגוֹן פֵּירוֹת** — **such as fruits,** **בֵּין שֶׁהֵם דְּבָרִים** — **or whether they are foods** **שֶׁאֵין צְרִיכִין לְבָרֵךְ עֲלֵיהֶם תּוֹךְ הַסְּעוּדָה** — upon which **one need not recite a blessing** when eaten during a meal,[11] **כְּגוֹן מִינֵי לִפְתָּן** — **such as types of condiments,** **וּמִינֵי קִטְנִיּוֹת וְעֶרְדֶעפְּפֶעל** — **or types of legumes**[12] **and potatoes;** **וְכֵן אִם רוֹצֶה לִשְׁתּוֹת אֵיזֶה מַשְׁקֶה** — **and likewise,** if

---

preparation, intention, etc., from one case to the next, can cause a significant change in the halachah. The halachos set forth here are to be learned with the purpose of acquiring or reviewing the basic guidelines and determinants that govern the many aspects of the halachos pertaining to blessings. The application of any halachah to a specific case, as with all matters of practical halachah, requires that a competent halachic authority be consulted.

7. See *Shaar HaTziyun* 176:8; *Mishnah Berurah* 174:25.

8. *Siman* 40, below, sets out the halachos of *netilas yadayim* (washing the hands) before eating bread.

9. The halachah described in this *se'if* does not include foods that are subject to the *borei minei mezonos* blessing (see below, note 26), which are discussed below, *se'if* 3. With regard to food eaten before the meal as an appetizer, see *se'if* 2.

10. Certain foods require a *berachah rishonah* even when they are eaten during the course of

a meal; see below, 43:3. The reason that this is a factor is explained below, note 13.

11. See below, 43:1.

Mishnah Berurah (176:2 אות ד׳) points out that when the table is set and one is ready to start eating right away, he may not eat other foods, but must begin his meal with bread. This is because one can just as easily wait the short time until starting the meal, in which case that food will not require its own *berachah rishonah.* Eating before the meal under such circumstances causes an unnecessary blessing to be recited, which is forbidden (see above, 6:4). [According to some authorities, this does not apply to foods that one prefers to eat specifically before the meal begins.] The halachos in this *Siman* refer to a case where one would not have been able to immediately begin his meal. [On the other hand, if one will not be starting his meal for some time, the dispute cited here does not apply, and he is required to recite a *berachah acharonah* as well. See end of *se'if* 3.]

12. Such as peas or beans.

47 ONE WHO WISHES TO EAT OR DRINK BEFORE A MEAL — SIMAN 39:1

(חוּץ מִן הַיַּיִן) קוֹדֶם נְטִילַת יָדַיִם וְגַם בְּתוֹךְ הַסְּעוּדָה יִשְׁתֶּה, יֵשׁ בָּזֶה מַחֲלוֹקֶת הַפּוֹסְקִים אִם הַדְּבָרִים שֶׁאָכַל אוֹ שָׁתָה קוֹדֶם נְטִילַת יָדַיִם נִפְטָרִים בְּבִרְכַּת הַמָּזוֹן, כְּמוֹ שֶׁנִּפְטָרִים אֵלּוּ שֶׁאָכַל בְּתוֹךְ הַסְּעוּדָה, אוֹ שֶׁאֵלּוּ שֶׁאֲכָלָן קוֹדֶם נְטִילַת יָדַיִם אֵינָן נִפְטָרִים בְּבִרְכַּת הַמָּזוֹן[13]. וְלָכֵן יֵשׁ לִמְנוֹעַ מִזֶּה, וְלֹא יֹאכַל וְלֹא יִשְׁתֶּה מֵהֶם רַק קוֹדֶם הַסְּעוּדָה, וִיבָרֵךְ בְּרָכָה אַחֲרוֹנָה, וְלֹא יֹאכַל וְלֹא יִשְׁתֶּה מֵהֶם בְּתוֹךְ הַסְּעוּדָה[14]. וְאִם לֹא בֵּירַךְ תְּחִלָּה בְּרָכָה אַחֲרוֹנָה יְבָרֵךְ בְּתוֹךְ הַסְּעוּדָה, אוֹ אֲפִילוּ לְאַחַר בִּרְכַּת הַמָּזוֹן[15].

one wishes to drink any beverage (חוּץ מִן הַיַּיִן — **except for wine,** which will be discussed below, *se'if* 2), **קוֹדֶם נְטִילַת יָדַיִם — before washing** his **hands** for the meal, **וְגַם בְּתוֹךְ הַסְּעוּדָה יִשְׁתֶּה — and he plans to drink during the meal as well, — יֵשׁ בָּזֶה מַחֲלוֹקֶת הַפּוֹסְקִים — there is a dispute among the halachic authorities regarding this** case: **אִם הַדְּבָרִים שֶׁאָכַל אוֹ שָׁתָה קוֹדֶם נְטִילַת יָדַיִם — Are those items that he ate or drank before washing** his **hands נִפְטָרִים בְּבִרְכַּת הַמָּזוֹן — exempted** from the obligation of a *berachah acharonah* **by** his recitation of the ***Bircas HaMazon*** at the conclusion of the upcoming meal, **כְּמוֹ שֶׁנִּפְטָרִים אֵלּוּ שֶׁאָכַל בְּתוֹךְ הַסְּעוּדָה — just as those** foods **that are eaten during the meal are exempted** by *Bircas HaMazon* and do not require their own *berachah acharonah;* **אוֹ — or** do we say **שֶׁאֵלּוּ שֶׁאֲכָלָן קוֹדֶם נְטִילַת יָדַיִם — that those** foods **that he ate before washing** his **hands** for the meal **אֵינָן נִפְטָרִים בְּבִרְכַּת הַמָּזוֹן — are not exempted** from their own *berachah acharonah* **by** his subsequent recitation of ***Bircas HaMazon*?**[13]

וְלָכֵן — Therefore, to avoid a case of halachic doubt, **יֵשׁ לִמְנוֹעַ מִזֶּה — one should refrain from** entering into **this** situation. **וְלֹא יֹאכַל וְלֹא יִשְׁתֶּה מֵהֶם רַק קוֹדֶם הַסְּעוּדָה — He should eat or drink these** foods or beverages **only** ***before*** **the meal, וִיבָרֵךְ בְּרָכָה אַחֲרוֹנָה — and** then **he should recite a** ***berachah acharonah*****, וְלֹא יֹאכַל וְלֹא יִשְׁתֶּה מֵהֶם בְּתוֹךְ הַסְּעוּדָה —** and **he should not eat or drink these** same types of foods or beverages **during the** subsequent **meal.**[14]

וְאִם לֹא בֵּירַךְ תְּחִלָּה בְּרָכָה אַחֲרוֹנָה — If, in this case, **he did not recite the** ***berachah acharonah*** **first,** i.e., before the meal, **יְבָרֵךְ בְּתוֹךְ הַסְּעוּדָה — he should recite it** even **during the meal, אוֹ אֲפִילוּ לְאַחַר בִּרְכַּת הַמָּזוֹן — or,** if he did not recite it until the meal ended, he should recite it **even after** he recites ***Bircas HaMazon.***[15]

---

13. As explained in the introduction to this *se'if*, the question disputed by the authorities is if the two acts of eating can be considered as one, since he is eating the same type of food both before and during the meal.

Kitzur emphasizes that this doubt applies whether the food in question is fruit, condiments, or vegetables, for the following reason: Some authorities rule that even if merely eating the same type of food does not link the eating that took place before the meal with that of the meal itself, nevertheless, in a case where a person is planning on eating foods that require a *berachah rishonah* even when eaten during a meal, such as fruits, and he plans on eating this food both before the meal and during the meal, the *berachah rishonah* that he recites on the fruit before the meal "covers" the fruit that he will eat during the meal as well. In that case, the *berachah* is enough to join the two acts of eating, and the *Bircas HaMazon* that exempts the fruit eaten during the meal exempts the fruit eaten before the meal as well. Kitzur, by stating that he refers even to fruit, indicates that he nevertheless considers all these instances to be cases of halachic doubt. (*Mishnah Berurah* does offer a ruling on this question, as set out below, note 16).

14. Alternatively, he can make sure that before the meal he eats less than the amount that would obligate him to recite a *berachah acharonah*; see 51:2.

15. In this case, the eating done before the meal has no connection at all with the eating

ONE WHO WISHES TO EAT OR DRINK BEFORE A MEAL — SIMAN 39:2 48

וְאִם אָכַל אוֹ שָׁתָה מִמִּינִים אֵלּוּ גַּם בְּתוֹךְ הַסְּעוּדָה יְהַדֵּר אַחַר בִּרְכַּת הַמָּזוֹן לֶאֱכוֹל אוֹ לִשְׁתּוֹת אֵיזֶה דָּבָר וּלְבָרֵךְ בְּרָכָה אַחֲרוֹנָה לִפְטוֹר גַּם מַה שֶּׁאָכַל אוֹ שָׁתָה קוֹדֶם נְטִילַת יָדַיִם[16].

ב. אִם[17] רוֹצֶה לִשְׁתּוֹת יַיִן קוֹדֶם נְטִילַת יָדַיִם, אֲפִילּוּ לֹא יִשְׁתֶּה יַיִן בְּתוֹךְ הַסְּעוּדָה, מִכָּל מָקוֹם יֵשׁ אוֹמְרִים כֵּיוָן דְּהַיַּיִן בָּא לִפְתּוֹחַ הַבְּנֵי מֵעַיִים[18] וּלְהַמְשִׁיךְ תַּאֲוַת הָאֲכִילָה

וְאִם אָכַל אוֹ שָׁתָה מִמִּינִים אֵלּוּ — **If he did** eat or drink before the meal and also **ate or drank those types** of foods **גַּם בְּתוֹךְ הַסְּעוּדָה** — **during the meal as well,** thus placing himself in the case of halachic doubt described above with regard to his obligation to recite a *berachah acharonah* on that which he ate earlier, **יְהַדֵּר אַחַר בִּרְכַּת הַמָּזוֹן** — **he should endeavor, after** reciting ***Bircas HaMazon*** on the meal, **לֶאֱכוֹל אוֹ לִשְׁתּוֹת אֵיזֶה דָּבָר** — **to eat or drink something** that requires the same *berachah acharonah* as that of the foods he ate earlier, **וּלְבָרֵךְ בְּרָכָה אַחֲרוֹנָה** — **and** then **to recite** that ***berachah acharonah*** on the food he eats after the meal. **לִפְטוֹר גַּם מַה שֶּׁאָכַל אוֹ שָׁתָה קוֹדֶם נְטִילַת יָדַיִם** — In that way, **this** *berachah acharonah* **exempts that which he ate or drank before washing** his **hands** for the meal from its possible obligation of a *berachah acharonah.*[16]

§2 Even if, close to one's meal, one eats food that he will *not* eat during the meal, if the purpose of this food is to stimulate the appetite for the meal itself, according to some authorities this eating is considered "part of the meal" and does not require a separate *berachah acharonah.* Other authorities maintain that this factor does not connect the appetizer food to the meal with regard to the obligation to recite a *berachah acharonah.*[17]

The subject of this *se'if* is wine, which can serve to stimulate the appetite, and is therefore included in the above dispute among the authorities.

אִם רוֹצֶה לִשְׁתּוֹת יַיִן קוֹדֶם נְטִילַת יָדַיִם — **If one wishes to drink wine before washing** his **hands** for the meal, **אֲפִילּוּ לֹא יִשְׁתֶּה יַיִן בְּתוֹךְ הַסְּעוּדָה** — **even if he will not drink wine during the** upcoming **meal** as well, **מִכָּל מָקוֹם יֵשׁ אוֹמְרִים** — **nevertheless, some authorities say** **כֵּיוָן דְּהַיַּיִן בָּא לִפְתּוֹחַ הַבְּנֵי מֵעַיִים** — **that since the wine serves to "open" the digestive system**[18] **וּלְהַמְשִׁיךְ תַּאֲוַת הָאֲכִילָה** — **and to stimulate the**

---

of the meal itself, and the recitation of *Bircas HaMazon* cannot apply to it [even after the fact] (see *Mishnah Berurah* 176:2 אות א׳).

16. In summary, Kitzur does not rule on the question of whether one is obligated to recite a *berachah acharonah* when he has eaten the same type of food during the meal as beforehand, whether or not they are foods that would require their own *berachah rishonah* when eaten during a bread meal. One is therefore advised to avoid this situation; if one does find himself in this situation, he is encouraged to bring himself into a situation where a *berachah acharonah* would be required regardless.

Mishnah Berurah, however, does offer a ruling in this situation. The ruling depends on whether the foods that were eaten during the meal require their own *berachah rishonah* even when eaten during a bread meal: When the foods would *not* require their own *berachah rishonah* during a meal, one is required to recite the *berachah acharonah* on the food that he ate earlier (see 176:2 and *Shaar HaTziyun* §8). However, if the foods would require their own *berachah rishonah* even during the meal, and the *berachah* that he recited upon these foods before the meal exempts those foods that he will eat during the meal from their obligation of a *berachah rishonah* (see above, note 13), then the procedure described here is unnecessary. The two acts of eating are considered to be one, and the *Bircas HaMazon* recited at the end of the meal exempts the food he eats before the meal as well (*Mishnah Berurah* 176:2 אות א׳).

17. See *Mishnah Berurah* 176:2 אות ג׳, *Shaar HaTziyun* ibid. §9. See also *Beur Halachah* to 174:6 s.v. ואפילו.

18. Literally, *to open his innards.*

אם כֵּן הֵם בִּכְלַל הַסְּעוּדָה וְנִפְטָרִים בְּבִרְכַּת הַמָּזוֹן, וְיֵשׁ אוֹמְרִים דַּאֲפִילּוּ אִם שׁוֹתֶה יַיִן גַּם בְּתוֹךְ הַסְּעוּדָה מִכָּל מָקוֹם אֵין הַיַּיִן שֶׁלִּפְנֵי הַמָּזוֹן נִפְטָר בְּבִרְכַּת הַמָּזוֹן[19]. וְלָכֵן יֵשׁ לִמְנוֹעַ מִלִּשְׁתּוֹת קוֹדֶם נְטִילַת יָדַיִם, אֶלָּא אִם כֵּן יִשְׁתֶּה כּוֹס יַיִן גַּם לְאַחַר בִּרְכַּת הַמָּזוֹן, שֶׁיְּבָרֵךְ אַחֲרָיו עַל הַגֶּפֶן[20] וְיִפְטוֹר גַּם מַה שֶּׁשָּׁתָה קוֹדֶם נְטִילַת יָדַיִם[21]. וְאִם רוֹצֶה לִשְׁתּוֹת יֵין שָׂרָף קוֹדֶם הַסְּעוּדָה, בֵּין שֶׁיִּשְׁתֶּה גַּם בְּתוֹךְ הַסְּעוּדָה, בֵּין לֹא יִשְׁתֶּה, יִזָּהֵר שֶׁלֹּא לִשְׁתּוֹת קוֹדֶם הַסְּעוּדָה רַק פָּחוֹת מִכְּזַיִת[22], אֲבָל אִם

appetite, אם כֵּן הֵם בִּכְלַל הַסְּעוּדָה — **any** drinking of wine before the meal **is therefore** considered to be **part of the meal,** וְנִפְטָרִים בְּבִרְכַּת הַמָּזוֹן — **and is exempted** from its own obligation of a *berachah acharonah* **by** the recitation of ***Bircas HaMazon*** at the end of the meal. וְיֵשׁ אוֹמְרִים — **However, some** authorities **say** דַּאֲפִילּוּ אִם שׁוֹתֶה יַיִן גַּם בְּתוֹךְ הַסְּעוּדָה — **that even if he *will* drink wine during the meal,** מִכָּל מָקוֹם — **nevertheless,** אֵין הַיַּיִן שֶׁלִּפְנֵי הַמָּזוֹן נִפְטָר בְּבִרְכַּת הַמָּזוֹן — **wine that one drinks before a meal is not exempted** from the obligation of *berachah acharonah* **by** the recitation of ***Bircas HaMazon.***[19]

וְלָכֵן — **Therefore,** to avoid a situation of doubt, יֵשׁ לִמְנוֹעַ מִלִּשְׁתּוֹת קוֹדֶם נְטִילַת יָדַיִם — **one should refrain from drinking** wine **before washing the hands** for the meal, אֶלָּא אִם כֵּן — **unless** יִשְׁתֶּה כּוֹס יַיִן גַּם לְאַחַר בִּרְכַּת הַמָּזוֹן — **he drinks a cup of wine also after** ***Bircas HaMazon,*** שֶׁיְּבָרֵךְ אַחֲרָיו עַל הַגֶּפֶן — **upon which he will** be obligated to **recite** the ***Al HaGefen*** blessing,[20] and thus brings upon himself an independent obligation to recite that *berachah acharonah.* וְיִפְטוֹר גַּם מַה שֶּׁשָּׁתָה קוֹדֶם נְטִילַת יָדַיִם — **This** blessing **will also exempt** the possible obligation to recite a *berachah acharonah* upon **what he drank before washing** the **hands** for the meal.[21]

Like wine, liquor too can serve as an appetizer. Therefore:

וְאִם רוֹצֶה לִשְׁתּוֹת יֵין שָׂרָף קוֹדֶם הַסְּעוּדָה — **If he wishes to drink liquor before the meal,** בֵּין שֶׁיִּשְׁתֶּה גַּם בְּתוֹךְ הַסְּעוּדָה, בֵּין לֹא יִשְׁתֶּה — **whether he will drink** liquor **during the meal or not,** יִזָּהֵר— **he should take care** שֶׁלֹּא לִשְׁתּוֹת קוֹדֶם הַסְּעוּדָה — **not to drink before the meal** an amount upon which he would be obligated to recite a *berachah acharonah,* רַק פָּחוֹת מִכְּזַיִת — but **only** drink **less than a *kezayis.***[22] אֲבָל אִם

19. According to this view, the fact that a food serves as an appetizer does not render it halachically "part of the meal" (see note 16). According to *Mishnah Berurah* (176:2 אות א׳), since wine requires a *berachah rishonah* when one drinks it during a meal (see Kitzur below, 43:2), if one is planning to drink wine during the meal, he need not recite a *berachah acharonah* on the wine that he drank before the meal in any event; see also *Shulchan Aruch* 299:8 and *Mishnah Berurah* ibid. §27.

20. עַל הַגֶּפֶן, *for the vine,* is the *berachah acharonah* that one recites after drinking wine; see below, 51:7.

21. Kitzur advises this course of action with regard to the wine that one drinks for *Kiddush* on Shabbos as well; see below, 77:10. *Beur Halachah* writes (174:6 s.v. וכן) that in a case where one did drink wine before the meal and therefore has a doubtful obligation to recite a *berachah acharonah* on wine (such as when drinking the wine of *Kiddush* on Shabbos), he should specifically have in mind that the *Bircas HaMazon* he recites at the conclusion of his meal apply to the wine that he drank before the meal as well. [In this situation, his recitation of the full *Bircas HaMazon* exempts his obligation to recite *Al HaGefen* as well; see *Shulchan Aruch* 208:17.]

22. A *berachah acharonah* is recited only upon eating or drinking a minimum amount. In general, for foods, this amount is a *kezayis.* See below, 51:2, which states that according to some, the minimum amount with regard to beverages is also a *kezayis.* In order to avoid any question of an obligation to recite a

ONE WHO WISHES TO EAT OR DRINK BEFORE A MEAL — SIMAN 39:3 50

שָׁתָה כְּזַיִת אוֹ יוֹתֵר נָפַל לִידֵי סָפֵק בְּרָכָה אַחֲרוֹנָה[23].

ג. אִם רוֹצֶה לֶאֱכוֹל קוֹדֶם נְטִילַת יָדַיִם מִינֵי מְזוֹנוֹת[24], כְּגוֹן הָאנִיג קִיכְעֶן, אַייעֶר קִיכְעֶן, וְכַדּוֹמֶה, שֶׁבְּרָכָה אַחֲרוֹנָה שֶׁלָּהֶם הִיא "עַל הַמִּחְיָה"[25], בֵּין שֶׁיֹּאכַל מֵהֶם גַּם בְּתוֹךְ הַסְּעוּדָה, בֵּין שֶׁלֹּא יֹאכַל מֵהֶם בְּתוֹךְ הַסְּעוּדָה, מִכָּל מָקוֹם הֵן נִפְטָרִים בְּבִרְכַּת הַמָּזוֹן (כִּי בִרְכַּת הַמָּזוֹן פּוֹטֶרֶת בִּרְכַּת "עַל הַמִּחְיָה")[26]. וּבִלְבַד שֶׁלֹּא יַפְסִיק הַרְבֵּה בֵּין אֲכִילָה זוֹ לִנְטִילַת יָדַיִם, אֲבָל אִם צָרִיךְ לְהַפְסִיק הַרְבֵּה צָרִיךְ לְבָרֵךְ תְּחִלָּה בִּרְכַּת "עַל הַמִּחְיָה" עַל מַה שֶׁאָכַל.

שָׁתָה כְּזַיִת אוֹ יוֹתֵר — However, if he drank a *kezayis* or more, נָפַל לִידֵי סָפֵק בְּרָכָה אַחֲרוֹנָה — he has fallen into a situation of halachic **doubt regarding** his obligation to recite **a *berachah acharonah.***[23]

§3 אִם רוֹצֶה לֶאֱכוֹל קוֹדֶם נְטִילַת יָדַיִם מִינֵי מְזוֹנוֹת — If one wishes to eat before washing the **hands** for the meal, **types of *mezonos*** foods,[24] **כְּגוֹן הָאנִיג קִיכְעֶן — such as honey cake, אַייעֶר קִיכְעֶן — egg-*kichel,* וְכַדּוֹמֶה — and the like, שֶׁבְּרָכָה אַחֲרוֹנָה שֶׁלָּהֶם הִיא "עַל הַמִּחְיָה"** — foods **whose *berachah acharonah* is *Al HaMichyah,***[25] **בֵּין שֶׁיֹּאכַל מֵהֶם גַּם בְּתוֹךְ הַסְּעוּדָה** — then, **whether he will also eat these** foods **during the meal בֵּין שֶׁלֹּא יֹאכַל מֵהֶם בְּתוֹךְ הַסְּעוּדָה — or he will not eat them during the meal, מִכָּל מָקוֹם — in all such cases, הֵן נִפְטָרִים בְּבִרְכַּת הַמָּזוֹן — they are exempted** from their own obligation of a *berachah acharonah* **through** the recitation of the ***Bircas HaMazon*** after the meal. **כִּי בִרְכַּת הַמָּזוֹן פּוֹטֶרֶת בִּרְכַּת "עַל הַמִּחְיָה")** — This is **because** the recitation of ***Bircas HaMazon* can exempt** one from his obligation to recite **an *Al HaMichyah* blessing.)**[26] **וּבִלְבַד** — One can rely on his recitation of *Bircas HaMazon,* **provided שֶׁלֹּא יַפְסִיק הַרְבֵּה בֵּין אֲכִילָה זוֹ לִנְטִילַת יָדַיִם — that he does not make a lengthy interruption between this eating** before the meal **and washing** the **hands** for the meal; **אֲבָל אִם צָרִיךְ לְהַפְסִיק הַרְבֵּה — but if he will make a lengthy interruption צָרִיךְ לְבָרֵךְ תְּחִלָּה בִּרְכַּת "עַל הַמִּחְיָה" עַל מַה שֶּׁאָכַל** — then **he must first recite the *Al HaMichyah***

---

berachah acharonah after drinking the liquor, one should drink less than .6 fl. oz. (17.3 cc.), the amount of a *kezayis* according to some authorities; see Appendix A.

23. In accordance with the rule of סָפֵק בְּרָכוֹת לְהָקֵל, *a doubtful obligation with regard to blessings is decided leniently*, a *berachah acharonah* should not be recited in this case.

24. I.e., baked goods, upon which one recites the *berachah rishonah* that concludes with בּוֹרֵא מִינֵי מְזוֹנוֹת, *Who created species of nourishment*; see below, *Siman* 48.

25. עַל הַמִּחְיָה, *for the nourishment*, is recited after eating baked goods; see below, 51:8.

26. If one mistakenly recited *Bircas HaMazon* after eating *mezonos*, he has fulfilled his *berachah acharonah* obligation and need not recite *Al HaMichyah* (see *Mishnah Berurah* 208:75). In cases where the recitation of *Bircas HaMazon* would be used to exempt a doubtful obligation of *Al HaMichyah*, when reciting the *Bircas HaMazon* one should specifically intend to fulfill his [doubtful] obligation also with regard to the *mezonos* food that he has eaten (see *Mishnah Berurah* 176:2).

According to *Mishnah Berurah*, there are certain cases when one eats *mezonos* before a meal (but does not eat it during the meal), where one should preferably recite *Al HaMichyah* immediately; for details, see *Mishnah Berurah* 176:2 with *Beur Halachah* and *Shaar HaTziyun* ad loc. See also *Igros Moshe, Orach Chaim* III, §33, who writes similarly that in certain cases, one should recite an *Al HaMichyah* on a *mezonos* snack before he begins the meal. See *Igros Moshe* there for an extensive treatment of these halachos.

51 ONE WHO WISHES TO EAT OR DRINK BEFORE A MEAL — SIMAN 39:3

וַאֲפִילוּ יֹאכַל מִמִּינִים אֵלּוּ גַּם בְּתוֹךְ הַסְּעוּדָּה[27].

blessing on that which he ate before the meal, **וַאֲפִילוּ יֹאכַל מִמִּינִים אֵלּוּ גַּם בְּתוֹךְ הַסְּעוּדָּה** — **even if he will also eat these types** of foods **during the meal.**[27]

27. Regarding the obligation of *berachah acharonah* in the common case of eating baked goods before the meal after reciting *Kiddush* on Shabbos day, see below, 77:14, with notes.

LAWS OF WASHING THE HANDS FOR A MEAL — SIMAN 40:1 52

סימן מ

הִלְכוֹת נְטִילַת יָדַיִם לִסְעוּדָה[1,2,3]

וּבוֹ כא סְעִיפִים

א. הָרוֹצֶה לֶאֱכוֹל פַּת שֶׁמְּבָרְכִין עָלָיו הַמּוֹצִיא[4], צָרִיךְ לִיטּוֹל יָדָיו מִקּוֹדֶם.[5]

SIMAN 40

LAWS OF WASHING THE HANDS FOR A MEAL

CONTAINING 21 *SE'IFIM*

§1 Obligation of Washing the Hands / **§2-3** Criteria for the Vessel /**§4-6** Procedure for Washing the Hands / **§7** Immersing the Hands / **§8-10** Criteria for the Water / **§11-12** Clean Hands / **§13** Human Force / **§14** When Water Is Not Available / **§15** Using the Bathroom Before a Meal / **§16** One Who Must Wash His Hands During the Meal / **§17** Food Dipped in Liquid / **§18-19** Which Liquids Are Included / **§20** Foods Commonly Eaten With Cutlery / **§21** Salt; Liquor

The laws of *netilas yadayim* (washing the hands) have their origin in the laws of *tumah* v'*taharah,* "ritual purity and impurity," that were once an integral part of the daily lives of the Jewish people in earlier times, when the Temple stood. To avoid possible pitfalls associated with eating food with impure hands, the Sages instituted the obligation to purify the hands by washing them in the prescribed manner before eating bread (*se'ifim* 1-16), [1] as well as before eating any food that was commonly dipped in liquid (*se'ifim* 17-21).[2] Although most applications of the halachos of *tumah* are no longer applicable today, we are enjoined to adhere to these procedures so that we will be accustomed to these practices when the laws of *tumah* will again become applicable, with the rebuilding of the Temple.

Another reason for the enactment of *netilas yadayim* is to preserve the cleanliness of the food that one eats. Concern for cleanliness and hygiene is not only a physical issue. It is, in fact, of important spiritual value as well, and is associated with purity and holiness.[3]

§1 הָרוֹצֶה לֶאֱכוֹל פַּת — One who wishes to eat bread שֶׁמְּבָרְכִין עָלָיו הַמּוֹצִיא — upon which the appropriate **blessing is *hamotzi*[4] צָרִיךְ לִיטּוֹל יָדָיו מִקּוֹדֶם — must**

---

1. *Terumah,* the portion of the crop given to the Kohen, must be kept *tahor* (in a ritually pure state). In order that Kohanim be accustomed to washing their hands before eating it, the Sages instituted that all people wash their hands before eating bread, which is the primary *terumah* food. Likewise, special care must be taken when eating food dipped in liquid (see below), since while dipping it, one is liable to touch the liquid, and liquid contracts and transmits *tumah,* ritual impurity, more readily than other food or objects (see *Mishnah Berurah* 158:1,11).

2. *Mishnah Berurah* 158:1. See, however, below, *se'if* 17 and note 74 there, which states that according to some opinions it is no longer obligatory to wash before eating foods dipped in liquid.

3. *Mishnah Berurah* 158:1; *Aruch HaShulchan* 158:2.

4. The blessing ending הַמּוֹצִיא לֶחֶם מִן הָאָרֶץ, *Who brings forth bread from the earth,* is recited

53 LAWS OF WASHING THE HANDS FOR A MEAL — SIMAN 40:2

אִם הַפַּת גָּדוֹל כְּבֵיצָה[6] מְבָרֵךְ עַל הַנְּטִילָה[7]. וּבְפָחוּת מִזֶּה אֵין מְבָרְכִין עַל הַנְּטִילָה[8].

ב. נְטִילַת יָדַיִם צָרִיךְ לִהְיוֹת דַּוְקָא מִן הַכְּלִי[9], וְצָרִיךְ שֶׁיִּהְיֶה הַכְּלִי שָׁלֵם בְּלִי שׁוּם נֶקֶב, אוֹ סֶדֶק מְפוּלָּשׁ. וְגַם לְמַעְלָה יִהְיֶה שָׁוֶה בְּלִי שׁוּם חָרִיץ, אוֹ בְּלִיטָה[10].

first wash his hands.[5] **אִם הַפַּת גָּדוֹל כְּבֵיצָה** — **If the bread** that he will be eating **is** at least **as large as the volume of an egg,**[6] **מְבָרֵךְ עַל הַנְּטִילָה** — **he must recite a blessing upon the washing;**[7] **וּבְפָחוּת מִזֶּה** — **if it is smaller than this** size **אֵין מְבָרְכִין עַל הַנְּטִילָה** — he must still wash, but **he does not recite a blessing upon the washing.**[8]

§2 In the following *se'ifim,* Kitzur sets out the *optimal* way of performing *netilas yadayim* with regard to the appropriate vessel, amount of water, and procedure to be followed. Kitzur does not address the many halachos that apply to one who cannot follow these procedures due to lack of water, appropriate vessel, or any other reason. These halachos are addressed at length in *Orach Chaim* §158-§165 and *Mishnah Berurah* there.

נְטִילַת יָדַיִם צָרִיךְ לִהְיוֹת — ***Netilas yadayim* must be** performed **דַּוְקָא מִן הַכְּלִי** — **specifically** by pouring the water **from a vessel.**[9] **וְצָרִיךְ שֶׁיִּהְיֶה הַכְּלִי שָׁלֵם** — **The vessel must be whole** **בְּלִי שׁוּם נֶקֶב, אוֹ סֶדֶק מְפוּלָּשׁ** — **without any hole or crack that** completely **penetrates** the wall of the vessel. **וְגַם לְמַעְלָה יִהְיֶה שָׁוֶה** — **Also, the** surface at the **top** of the vessel **must be even,** **בְּלִי שׁוּם חָרִיץ, אוֹ בְּלִיטָה** — **without any crevice or protrusion.**[10]

---

when eating bread baked from any of five specific types of grain; see 41:1 with notes. See below, 48:1-4, where Kitzur states that certain baked goods, while classified as "bread-type" foods (פַּת), do not have the halachic status of "bread," and one recites *hamotzi* on such baked goods only when they are eaten as a full meal. Here we learn that the obligation of *netilas yadayim* is dependent on the blessing that is recited upon the food being eaten: Whenever one recites *hamotzi* on the food, one must wash his hands prior to eating it.

5. Even one who is planning to use only one hand to eat must wash both of his hands (*Mishnah Berurah* 158:4).

6. See note 8. Even if no single piece of bread is the size of an egg, as long as the amount of bread he is eating totals at least the volume of an egg, he must recite the blessing upon washing (*Mishnah Berurah* 158:10).

7. The blessing of *al netilas yadayim,* regarding washing the hands; see below, *se'if* 5.

8. Food smaller than the size of an egg is not susceptible to *tumah* by Biblical law (*Mishnah Berurah* 158:9); see introduction to this *Siman. Mishnah Berurah* (ibid.) writes that with regard to this halachah the volume of the egg is measured without its shell. According to the measurements of the Chazon Ish, one should not recite a blessing unless one is eating bread in the volume of 90 cc [3 fl. oz.] (see *Shiurin Shel Torah* §26).

According to Rabbi Moshe Feinstein, although it is better to eat a piece of bread the size of an egg in order to avoid halachic doubt as to whether one is required to recite a blessing or not, nevertheless, if one wants to eat only a *kezayis* of bread (according to R' Moshe Feinstein, approximately 1 fl. oz. [29.6 cc]; see Appendix A), he is still required to recite the blessing of *netilas yadayim* (*Igros Moshe, Orach Chaim* II, §53; IV, §41). Initially, one should wash *netilas yadayim* even if he will be eating less than a *kezayis.* In that case, all agree that no blessing is recited (*Mishnah Berurah* 158:10; see also *Igros Moshe* ibid.).

9. One may not wash his hands by taking the water in the palm of one hand and pouring it onto the other (see *Shulchan Aruch* 159:6).

10. Any point of the vessel's height that cannot hold water does not have the halachic status of a vessel, and one may not wash by pouring the water from that point and higher. When a vessel has, on one side, a cutout opening or a protrusion that is lower than the top of the vessel (to aid the pouring),

LAWS OF WASHING THE HANDS FOR A MEAL — SIMAN 40:3-4 54

וְאוֹתָן קַנְקַנִּים שֶׁיֵּשׁ לָהֶם כְּמִין מַרְזֵב בּוֹלֵט בְּגוֹבַהּ לִשְׂפַת הַכְּלִי, שֶׁיּוֹצְקִין מִמֶּנּוּ דֶּרֶךְ שָׁם, אֵין נוֹטְלִין מִמֶּנּוּ לְיָדַיִם דֶּרֶךְ שָׁם, כִּי שָׁם אֵין לוֹ דִּין כְּלִי, כֵּיוָן שֶׁאֵינוֹ מַחֲזִיק שָׁם מַשְׁקִים[11]. אֶלָּא, צְרִיכִין לִיטּוֹל דֶּרֶךְ שְׂפַת הַכְּלִי מָקוֹם שֶׁמַּחֲזִיק מַשְׁקִין[12].

ג. כְּלִי שֶׁאֵינוֹ יָכוֹל לַעֲמוֹד אֶלָּא עַל יְדֵי סְמִיכָה — [13]אִם מִתְּחִילָּתוֹ נַעֲשָׂה כָּךְ לְהִשְׁתַּמֵּשׁ בּוֹ עַל יְדֵי סְמִיכָה, יֵשׁ לוֹ דִּין כְּלִי. אֲבָל אִם לֹא נַעֲשָׂה לְהִשְׁתַּמֵּשׁ בּוֹ כָּךְ, כְּגוֹן, כִּיסּוּי כְּלִי, אֵין נוֹטְלִין מִמֶּנּוּ. וְיֵשׁ בָּזֶה כַּמָּה חִילּוּקֵי דִינִים בְּשׁוּלְחָן עָרוּךְ.

וְאוֹתָן קַנְקַנִּים — Consequently, regarding **those jars** **שֶׁיֵּשׁ לָהֶם כְּמִין מַרְזֵב** — **that have a spout** on one side **בּוֹלֵט בְּגוֹבַהּ לִשְׂפַת הַכְּלִי** — **protruding above the upper lip of the vessel,** **שֶׁיּוֹצְקִין מִמֶּנּוּ דֶּרֶךְ שָׁם** — **through which the water is poured,** **אֵין נוֹטְלִין מִמֶּנּוּ לְיָדַיִם דֶּרֶךְ שָׁם** — **one should not wash his hands using** the spout, **כִּי שָׁם אֵין לוֹ דִּין כְּלִי** — **because there,** at the level of the spout itself, **it does not have the halachic status of a vessel,** **כֵּיוָן שֶׁאֵינוֹ מַחֲזִיק שָׁם מַשְׁקִים** — **since the vessel cannot hold liquids there,** at the level of the spout.[11] **אֶלָּא** — **Rather,** **צְרִיכִין לִיטּוֹל דֶּרֶךְ שְׂפַת הַכְּלִי** — **one must wash by** pouring the water over **the lip of the vessel** on the other, lower, side, **מָקוֹם שֶׁמַּחֲזִיק מַשְׁקִין** — which is **a place** on the vessel **that can hold liquid.**[12]

§3 **כְּלִי שֶׁאֵינוֹ יָכוֹל לַעֲמוֹד** — Regarding **a vessel that cannot stand** upright **אֶלָּא עַל יְדֵי סְמִיכָה** — **unless it is supported,**[13] **אִם מִתְּחִילָּתוֹ נַעֲשָׂה כָּךְ** — the law is that **if it was made this way originally,** **לְהִשְׁתַּמֵּשׁ בּוֹ עַל יְדֵי סְמִיכָה** — **to be used while supported,** **יֵשׁ לוֹ דִּין כְּלִי** — **then it has the halachic status of a vessel.** **אֲבָל אִם לֹא נַעֲשָׂה לְהִשְׁתַּמֵּשׁ בּוֹ כָּךְ** — **However, if it was not made to be used in this way** — **כְּגוֹן, כִּיסּוּי כְּלִי** — **for example, the cover of a vessel** that can hold liquid when held in an inverted position, but was not made for that purpose — **אֵין נוֹטְלִין מִמֶּנּוּ** — **one may not wash from it.**

וְיֵשׁ בָּזֶה כַּמָּה חִילּוּקֵי דִינִים בְּשׁוּלְחָן עָרוּךְ — This law **has many halachic details** that are set out **in *Shulchan Aruch,*** 159:3-5.

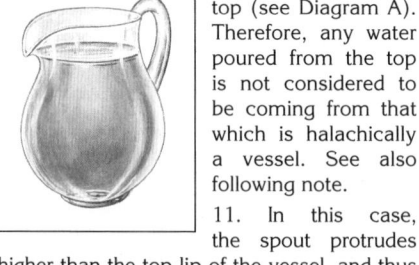

A

the vessel cannot hold water up to the top (see Diagram A). Therefore, any water poured from the top is not considered to be coming from that which is halachically a vessel. See also following note.

11. In this case, the spout protrudes higher than the top lip of the vessel, and thus the vessel cannot hold liquid at that level (see Diagram B). Any water poured from the spout is therefore not considered to be coming from "a vessel."

12. Here Kitzur explains that although the spout that is above the lip of the vessel is not halachically considered a vessel, one may pour from the lower "lip" of the vessel, since at that point the vessel does hold water.

B

13. That is, when the vessel is not supported, any liquid inside it would spill out and the vessel would not contain a *revi'is* [between 2.9 and 5.1 fl. oz. (86.4-150 cc); see Appendix A] (*Shulchan Aruch* 159:3).

ד. שִׁיעוּר הַמַּיִם קָשֶׁה לְשַׁעֵר בְּצִמְצוּם[14]. וּצְרִיכִין לִשְׁפּוֹךְ עַל כָּל יָד מַיִם בְּשֶׁפַע, דְּאָמַר רַב חִסְדָּא: "אֲנָא מְשָׁאִי מְלֹא חָפְנַי מַיָּא וְיָהֲבֵי לִי מְלֹא חָפְנַי טִיבוּתָא"[15]. וְנוֹטְלִין תְּחִלָּה יַד יָמִין, וְאַחַר כָּךְ יַד שְׂמֹאל (כִּדְלְעֵיל סִימָן ב'). וְיָבֹאוּ הַמַּיִם עַל כָּל הַיָּד, דְּהַיְינוּ עַד הַקָּנֶה שֶׁל זְרוֹעַ[16]. לֹא יִשָּׁאֵר מָקוֹם בְּלִי מַיִם, וְעַל כֵּן יַפְרִיד קְצָת הָאֶצְבָּעוֹת וְיַגְבִּיהֵם קְצָת כְּלַפֵּי מַעְלָה, בִּכְדֵי שֶׁיַּגִּיעוּ הַמַּיִם בְּכָל אוֹרֶךְ הָאֶצְבָּעוֹת וּבְרֹאשָׁן וּבְרָחְבָּן סָבִיב. וְיָבֹאוּ הַמַּיִם בִּשְׁפִיכָה אַחַת, וְלָכֵן אֵין לִיטּוֹל יָדָיו מִכְּלִי שֶׁפִּיו צַר וְאֵין הַמַּיִם יוֹרְדִין בְּבַת אַחַת[17]. וְנָכוֹן לִשְׁפּוֹךְ עַל כָּל יָד ב' פְּעָמִים[18].

---

§4 שִׁיעוּר הַמַּיִם — **The amount of water** necessary for *netilas yadayim* קָשֶׁה לְשַׁעֵר בְּצִמְצוּם — **is difficult to figure precisely.**[14] וּצְרִיכִין לִשְׁפּוֹךְ Therefore, **it is necessary to pour** עַל כָּל יָד מַיִם בְּשֶׁפַע — **a generous amount of water upon each hand,** דְּאָמַר רַב חִסְדָּא — **as Rav Chisda said** (*Shabbos* 62b): אֲנָא מְשָׁאִי מְלֹא חָפְנַי מַיָּא — **"I washed** my hands **with full handfuls of water,** וְיָהֲבֵי לִי מְלֹא חָפְנַי טִיבוּתָא — **and they gave me** from Heaven **full handfuls of prosperity."**[15]

וְנוֹטְלִין תְּחִלָּה יַד יָמִין — **One should wash the right hand first** וְאַחַר כָּךְ יַד שְׂמֹאל — **and afterward, the left hand** (כִּדְלְעֵיל סִימָן ב' — **as above, 2:3,** with regard to *netilas yadayim* performed upon arising in the morning). וְיָבֹאוּ הַמַּיִם עַל כָּל הַיָּד — **The water should cover the entire** surface of the **hand,** דְּהַיְינוּ — **that is,** עַד הַקָּנֶה שֶׁל זְרוֹעַ — **until the wrist.**[16]

לֹא יִשָּׁאֵר מָקוֹם בְּלִי מַיִם — **No area** on the hand **should remain without water,** וְעַל כֵּן — **therefore,** in order to accomplish this, יַפְרִיד קְצָת הָאֶצְבָּעוֹת — **one should separate the fingers slightly,** וְיַגְבִּיהֵם קְצָת כְּלַפֵּי מַעְלָה — **and lift them slightly upward** בִּכְדֵי שֶׁיַּגִּיעוּ הַמַּיִם בְּכָל אוֹרֶךְ הָאֶצְבָּעוֹת — **so that the water reaches the entire length of the fingers,** וּבְרֹאשָׁן וּבְרָחְבָּן סָבִיב — **and the top** of the fingers, **and all around their width.**

וְיָבֹאוּ הַמַּיִם בִּשְׁפִיכָה אַחַת — **The water should come** over his hands **in one** unbroken **stream.** וְלָכֵן אֵין לִיטּוֹל יָדָיו — **Therefore, one should not wash his hands** מִכְּלִי שֶׁפִּיו צַר — **from a vessel that has a narrow opening,** וְאֵין הַמַּיִם יוֹרְדִין בְּבַת אַחַת — **from which the water does not come out** all **at once.**[17] וְנָכוֹן — **It is proper** לִשְׁפּוֹךְ עַל כָּל יָד ב' פְּעָמִים — **to pour** from the cup **onto each hand twice.**[18]

---

14. The minimum amount of water required to wash both hands is the total of one *revi'is* [see previous note] (*Shulchan Aruch* 160:13). However, one who uses only this amount of water encounters many complex halachic issues that are avoided by using at least a *revi'is for each hand* (see *Mishnah Berurah* 158:37). In addition, when using only the minimum amount, it is very difficult to completely cover the entire surface of the hand (*Beur Halachah* to 161:4, end of s.v. וראוי לנהוג וכו').

15. Nevertheless, ideally, one should not serve Hashem for the purpose of receiving Heavenly reward, but solely for the sake of the honor of Hashem, and the reward will come on its own.

If one does wash with a generous amount of water, and does not become rich as a result, this is due to his sins that prevent him from attaining his reward in this way (see *Mishnah Berurah* 158:38).

16. For further discussion regarding the area of the hand that the water must reach, see Appendix of Kitzur's editorial glosses.

17. *Mishnah Berurah* (162:30), however, rules that one may wash his hands with two consecutive acts of pouring as well, as long as there was no interruption at all between them. Nevertheless, he discourages the use of various utensils that have narrow openings, since there are those who take a stringent stand on this matter (see *Shaar HaTziyun* there §28-29).

18. If water is not available, one is not required to make an effort to find enough water to pour

LAWS OF WASHING THE HANDS FOR A MEAL — SIMAN 40:5 56

ה. לְאַחַר שֶׁנָּטַל שְׁתֵּי יָדָיו יְשַׁפְשְׁפֵם בְּיַחַד[19] וְיַגְבִּיהֵם נֶגֶד רֹאשׁוֹ, כְּמוֹ שֶׁאָמַר הַכָּתוּב "שְׂאוּ יְדֵכֶם" וְגוֹ'[20], וְקוֹדֶם שֶׁמְּנַגְּבָן יְבָרֵךְ "אֲשֶׁר קִדְּשָׁנוּ בְּמִצְוֹתָיו וְצִוָּנוּ[21] עַל נְטִילַת יָדָיִם". [וְאַף עַל גַּב דְּכָל הַמִּצְוֹת מְבָרֵךְ עֲלֵיהֶם קוֹדֶם עֲשִׂיָּתָן (כִּדְלְעֵיל סִימָן ט' סְעִיף ח'), מִכָּל מָקוֹם בִּנְטִילַת יָדַיִם, כֵּיוָן שֶׁלִּפְעָמִים אֵין יָדָיו נְקִיּוֹת קוֹדֶם נְטִילָה[22], לָכֵן תִּקְּנוּ בְּכָל נְטִילַת יָדַיִם לְבָרֵךְ אַחַר הַנְּטִילָה. וְעוֹד, דְּגַם נִיגּוּב הַיָּדַיִם הוּא מִן הַמִּצְוָה[23].] וּמִי שֶׁנּוֹהֵג לִשְׁפּוֹךְ עַל כָּל יָד ב' פְּעָמִים, יִשְׁפּוֹךְ תְּחִלָּה עַל כָּל יָד פַּעַם אַחַת

---

§5 לְאַחַר שֶׁנָּטַל שְׁתֵּי יָדָיו — **After washing both of his hands,** יְשַׁפְשְׁפֵם בְּיַחַד — **he should rub them together**[19] וְיַגְבִּיהֵם נֶגֶד רֹאשׁוֹ — **and lift them up to the level of his head,** כְּמוֹ שֶׁאָמַר הַכָּתוּב — **as the verse says** (*Tehillim* 134:2): "שְׂאוּ יְדֵכֶם" וְגוֹ' — ***Lift your hands*** **etc.**[20] וְקוֹדֶם שֶׁמְּנַגְּבָן — **And before one dries them,** יְבָרֵךְ — **he should recite the** following **blessing:** "אֲשֶׁר קִדְּשָׁנוּ בְּמִצְוֹתָיו וְצִוָּנוּ עַל נְטִילַת יָדַיִם"— *Baruch Atah Hashem, Elokeinu Melech HaOlam, asher kideshanu bemitzvosav, vetzivanu al netilas yadayim, Blessed are You, Hashem, our God, King of the universe,* ***Who has sanctified us with His commandments and has commanded us***[21] ***regarding washing the hands.***

[וְאַף עַל גַּב דְּכָל הַמִּצְוֹת — **Although** when it comes to the blessings on **all the mitzvos,** מְבָרֵךְ עֲלֵיהֶם קוֹדֶם עֲשִׂיָּתָן — **the blessing is recited upon them preceding their performance** (כִּדְלְעֵיל סִימָן ט' סְעִיף ח') — **as** explained **above,** ***Siman*** **9,** ***se'if*** **8),** מִכָּל מָקוֹם בִּנְטִילַת יָדַיִם — **nevertheless, with regard to** the mitzvah **of** ***netilas yadayim,*** כֵּיוָן שֶׁלִּפְעָמִים — **since at times** אֵין יָדָיו נְקִיּוֹת קוֹדֶם נְטִילָה — **his hands are not clean before he washes** them,[22] לָכֵן תִּקְּנוּ בְּכָל נְטִילַת יָדַיִם — the Sages **therefore instituted** that **for every** ***netilas yadayim*** לְבָרֵךְ אַחַר הַנְּטִילָה — **the blessing should be recited after the washing.** וְעוֹד — **Furthermore,** there is an aspect of "*prior to their performance*" that is fulfilled here as well, דְּגַם נִיגּוּב הַיָּדַיִם הוּא מִן הַמִּצְוָה — **for the drying of the hands,** which one does after reciting the blessing, **is also** a part **of the mitzvah** of *netilas yadayim.*][23]

וּמִי שֶׁנּוֹהֵג — **One who is accustomed** לִשְׁפּוֹךְ עַל כָּל יָד ב' פְּעָמִים — **to pour twice on each hand,** יִשְׁפּוֹךְ תְּחִלָּה עַל כָּל יָד פַּעַם אַחַת — **should first pour one time on**

---

a second time, as long as he pours a *revi'is* of water at once (*Mishnah Berurah* 162:21).

19. To completely remove all dirt from his hands (*Mishnah Berurah* 162:24).

20. The full verse in *Tehillim* reads: שְׂאוּ יְדֵכֶם קֹדֶשׁ וּבָרְכוּ אֶת ה', *Lift your hands in holiness and bless Hashem.* The mitzvah of *netilas yadayim* is alluded to by the verse's use of the word קֹדֶשׁ, *in holiness,* since washing before eating upholds the values of holiness and cleanliness; see introduction to this *Siman.* Thus, we see from the verse that we are to raise our hands at the time of *netilas yadayim,* a mitzvah that promotes holiness.

21. Although the mitzvah of *netilas yadayim* is of Rabbinic origin, we still say that it was Hashem Who "*has commanded us regarding washing the hands,*" for Hashem commanded us to obey the legislation of the Sages (*Devarim* 17:11), who instituted *netilas yadayim* (*Mishnah Berurah* 158:6).

22. E.g., one had used the bathroom, or touched a part of his body that is usually covered (see above, 2:9), in which case he may not recite a blessing until he washes his hands (*Mishnah Berurah* 158:40).

23. Thus, his blessing is still made prior to at least part of the mitzvah. For this reason one must be careful to recite the blessing before drying his hands. Nevertheless, one who did not recite the blessing before drying his hands may still recite the blessing until he has recited the *hamotzi* blessing on the bread (*Mishnah Berurah* 158:44).

57 LAWS OF WASHING THE HANDS FOR A MEAL — SIMAN 40:6-7

וִישַׁפְשְׁפֵם וִיבָרֵךְ, וְאַחַר כָּךְ יִשְׁפּוֹךְ פַּעַם שֵׁנִית עַל כָּל יָד[24] וְיִזָּהֵר לְנַגֵּב יָדָיו יָפֶה[25] וְלֹא יְנַגְּבֵם בַּחֲלוּקוֹ מִשּׁוּם דְּקָשֶׁה לְשִׁכְחָה.

ו. אִם לְאַחַר שֶׁשָּׁפַךְ הַמַּיִם עַל יָדוֹ אַחַת, נָגַע שָׁם בְּיָדוֹ הַשְּׁנִיָּה, אוֹ אָדָם אַחֵר נָגַע שָׁם, אֲזַי נִטְמְאוּ הַמַּיִם שֶׁעַל יָדוֹ[26] וְצָרִיךְ לְנַגְּבָן וְלִיטוֹל פַּעַם שֵׁנִית. אַךְ, אִם אֵירַע לוֹ כֵן לְאַחַר שֶׁכְּבָר בֵּירַךְ, לֹא יְבָרֵךְ שֵׁנִית.

ז. מִי שֶׁאֵין לוֹ כְּלִי יָכוֹל לִטְבּוֹל יָדָיו בְּנָהָר, אוֹ בְּמִקְוֶה הַכְּשֵׁרָה לִטְבִילַת נָשִׁים[27] (וְעַיֵּין לְקַמָּן סִימָן קס״ב דִּין הַנְּהָרוֹת)[28], אוֹ בְּמַעְיָן, אֲפִילּוּ אֵין בּוֹ מ׳

---

each hand, **וִישַׁפְשְׁפֵם — and** then **rub them, וִיבָרֵךְ — and recite the blessing, וְאַחַר כָּךְ יִשְׁפּוֹךְ פַּעַם שֵׁנִית עַל כָּל יָד — and after that** he should **pour the second time on each hand.**[24]

וְיִזָּהֵר — He should take care לְנַגֵּב יָדָיו יָפֶה — to dry his hands well.[25] **וְלֹא יְנַגְּבֵם בַּחֲלוּקוֹ — One should not dry them on his cloak, מִשּׁוּם דְּקָשֶׁה לְשִׁכְחָה — because** doing so **has the negative effect of** causing **forgetfulness.**

§6 אִם לְאַחַר שֶׁשָּׁפַךְ הַמַּיִם עַל יָדוֹ אַחַת — If, after he poured the water on one hand, נָגַע שָׁם בְּיָדוֹ הַשְּׁנִיָּה — he touched the hand that he had already washed **with his other, unwashed hand, אוֹ אָדָם אַחֵר נָגַע שָׁם — or if another person,** who did not wash *netilas yadayim,* **touched** the hand that he had already washed, **אֲזַי נִטְמְאוּ הַמַּיִם שֶׁעַל יָדוֹ — then the water on his hand becomes ritually impure.**[26] **וְצָרִיךְ לְנַגְּבָן — He must** then **dry** the water from his hands **וְלִיטוֹל פַּעַם שֵׁנִית — and wash a second time. אַךְ, אִם אֵירַע לוֹ כֵן — However, if this happened to him לְאַחַר שֶׁכְּבָר בֵּירַךְ — after he had already recited the blessing, לֹא יְבָרֵךְ שֵׁנִית —** he should wash again, but **he should not recite the blessing a second time.**

§7 מִי שֶׁאֵין לוֹ כְּלִי — One who does not have a vessel with which to wash **יָכוֹל לִטְבּוֹל יָדָיו בְּנָהָר — can** fulfill the requirement of *netilas yadayim* by **immersing his hands in a river אוֹ בְּמִקְוֶה הַכְּשֵׁרָה לִטְבִילַת נָשִׁים — or in a *mikveh* that is valid for women's immersion**[27] **(וְעַיֵּין לְקַמָּן סִימָן קס״ב דִּין הַנְּהָרוֹת) — see below, *Siman* 162,** *se'ifim* 12-13, **for the halachah regarding** the suitability of **rivers** for immersion).[28] **אוֹ בְּמַעְיָן — Or,** he may immerse his hands **in a spring, אֲפִילּוּ אֵין בּוֹ מ׳**

---

24. The accepted custom is to pour twice on each hand and then to recite the blessing (*Mishnah Berurah* 158:41). [By washing each hand twice, one avoids the potential halachic issue involved with touching the water on the handle of the washing cup; see ibid. 162:49.]

25. Eating without drying one's hands is considered repulsive behavior (*Mishnah Berurah* 158:46). See *Shulchan Aruch* 158:12 with *Mishnah Berurah,* and *Beur Halachah* ibid. s.v. כאלו, for other reasons to dry one's hands after washing.

26. The unwashed hand is considered to be in an impure state until it is washed. It therefore transmits *tumah* to the water on the washed hand, which in turn transmits *tumah* to the hand that was washed (*Mishnah Berurah* 162:46). Note that an unwashed hand transmits impurity to the water only when one is involved in performing *netilas yadayim;* one who touches water when he is not performing *netilas yadayim* does not transmit impurity to the water and the water is not disqualified; see below, *se'if* 9.

27. I.e., it fulfills all the requirements necessary for it to be used for the ritual immersion required to purify a woman from her *niddah* (menstrual impurity) state; see below, 162:14. See also above, *Siman* 37, note 3.

28. Kitzur specifically addresses the issue that arises when the rivers become swollen due to the rainwater or melting snow (see also above, 37:2).

LAWS OF WASHING THE HANDS FOR A MEAL — SIMAN 40:7 58

סְאָה[29], רַק שֶׁמִּתְכַּסִּים בּוֹ יָדָיו בְּפַעַם אַחַת[30], וּמְבָרֵךְ גַּם כֵּן "עַל נְטִילַת יָדַיִם"[31]. וּבִשְׁעַת הַדְּחָק יָכוֹל לִטְבּוֹל יָדָיו גַּם בְּשֶׁלֶג, אִם יֵשׁ עַל פְּנֵי הָאָרֶץ הַרְבֵּה כְּמוֹ שִׁיעוּר מִקְוֶה[32]. וְאִם[33] צָרִיךְ לִיטּוֹל יָדָיו מִתּוֹךְ פלומפ[34], יָנִיחַ יָדוֹ אַחַת סָמוּךְ לָאָרֶץ וּבְיָדוֹ הַשְּׁנִיָּה יִמְשׁוֹךְ לְהָבִיא עָלָיו אֶת הַמַּיִם, וְאַחַר כָּךְ יַחֲלִיף יָדָיו, אוֹ שֶׁחֲבֵרוֹ יִמְשׁוֹךְ לוֹ. אֲבָל אִם הַיָּדַיִם גְּבוֹהִים מִן הָאָרֶץ, לֹא עָלְתָה לוֹ נְטִילָה

סְאָה — **even if it does not contain forty *se'ah***[29] of water, **רַק שֶׁמִּתְכַּסִּים בּוֹ יָדָיו בְּפַעַם אַחַת** — **as long as his hands can be** completely **covered** by the water in the spring **at one time.**[30] **וּמְבָרֵךְ גַּם כֵּן "עַל נְטִילַת יָדַיִם"** — When washing his hands with these methods, **he should also recite the blessing of *al netilas yadayim.***[31]

וּבִשְׁעַת הַדְּחָק — **In a case of pressing need,** where no water is available, **יָכוֹל לִטְבּוֹל יָדָיו גַּם בְּשֶׁלֶג** — **he may also immerse his hands in snow, אִם יֵשׁ עַל פְּנֵי הָאָרֶץ הַרְבֵּה** — **if there is as much snow upon the ground כְּמוֹ שִׁיעוּר מִקְוֶה** — **as the amount** of water necessary **for a *mikveh*** (forty *se'ah*).[32]

וְאִם צָרִיךְ לִיטּוֹל יָדָיו מִתּוֹךְ פלומפ — **If** he has no other option,[33] and **he must wash his hands from a pump,**[34] **יָנִיחַ יָדוֹ אַחַת סָמוּךְ לָאָרֶץ** — **he should place one hand near the ground, וּבְיָדוֹ הַשְּׁנִיָּה** — **and with his second hand יִמְשׁוֹךְ לְהָבִיא עָלָיו אֶת הַמַּיִם** — **he should draw** the pump **to bring the water upon his** hand, **וְאַחַר כָּךְ יַחֲלִיף יָדָיו** — **and afterward he should switch hands; אוֹ שֶׁחֲבֵרוֹ יִמְשׁוֹךְ לוֹ** — **or,** he should **have his fellow draw** the water **for him,** so he can have both hands close to the ground. **אֲבָל אִם הַיָּדַיִם גְּבוֹהִים מִן הָאָרֶץ** — **However, if his hands were** not positioned near the ground, but **above the ground, לֹא עָלְתָה לוֹ נְטִילָה** — **the**

---

29. Forty *se'ah* is the minimum amount of water required for a *mikveh*. (There is a difference of opinion among contemporary authorities as to the equivalent of forty *se'ah* in modern measurements. According to many opinions it is approximately 200 gallons; however, some views require as much as 255 gallons [approximately 965 liters]; see *Taharas Mayim* 2:5; *Mikveh Mayim*, Vol. 3, Ch. 3.) A spring, however, may be used for an immersion that is valid for *netilas yadayim* even if it contains less than that amount.

30. He need not actually immerse both hands at once; however, there must be enough water that he would be able to do so (*Mishnah Berurah* 159:80).

31. However, when immersing one's hands in water that would be disqualified for washing but qualified for immersing, one should recite the blessing of *al tevilas yadayim*, "regarding immersing the hands" (*Mishnah Berurah* 159:97).

32. It is not necessary that the forty *se'ah* of snow be completely gathered together in one place. One may immerse his hands even in a shallow covering of snow, as long as it is connected to forty *se'ah* of snow. There must, however, be at least enough snow gathered together in that place to cover his hands (*Mishnah Berurah* 160:58).

33. If a vessel is available, one should not wash directly from the pump (*Shaar HaTziyun* 159:45).

34. Kitzur is discussing a mechanism that draws water from an underground spring. In this case, the water that is drawn from the pump is connected via the direct stream of water to the water of the spring. The pump is not considered a "vessel," for it does not actually hold the water. It is therefore not qualified to be used for the *netilas yadayim* that requires a vessel. However, if one's hand is completely covered by the flow from the pump, and the water is directly connected to the water in the spring, he is considered to have *immersed* his hand in the spring, which, as Kitzur has explained in this *se'if,* is a valid method of washing the hands (see *Mishnah Berurah* 159:47).

[Note: Each pump mechanism must be examined separately to ascertain that it is appropriate to be used for *netilas yadayim*, in light of the many halachos that affect the qualification of the water for *netilas yadayim;* see, for example, *Shaar HaTziyun* 159:45.]

(סִידּוּר דֶּרֶךְ הַחַיִּים עַיֵּין שָׁם)[35].

ח. מַיִם שֶׁנִּשְׁתַּנּוּ מַרְאֵיהֶן, בֵּין מֵחֲמַת מְקוֹמָם, בֵּין מֵחֲמַת אֵיזֶה דָּבָר שֶׁנָּפַל לְתוֹכָן[36], פְּסוּלִין לִנְטִילַת יָדַיִם[37], אֲבָל אִם נִשְׁתַּנּוּ מֵחֲמַת עַצְמָן[38] כְּשֵׁרִים[39]. מַיִם שֶׁנַּעֲשָׂה בָּהֶם מְלָאכָה, כְּגוֹן, שֶׁהוּדְחוּ בָּהֶם כֵּלִים[40], אוֹ שֶׁשָּׁרוּ בָּהֶם יְרָקוֹת[41], אוֹ שֶׁנָּתְנוּ בָּהֶם כֵּלִים עִם מַשְׁקִים לְצַנְּנָן[42], אוֹ שֶׁמָּדַד בָּהֶן מִדּוֹת[43], גַּם כֵּן פְּסוּלִין[44].

---

washing is not effective for him and he must wash again (סִידּוּר דֶּרֶךְ הַחַיִּים עַיֵּין שָׁם — *Siddur Derech HaChaim*; **see there,** *Dinei Kli HaRa'ui LeTevilah* §9, for further discussion.)[35]

§8 מַיִם שֶׁנִּשְׁתַּנּוּ מַרְאֵיהֶן — **Water that has become discolored,** בֵּין מֵחֲמַת מְקוֹמָם — **whether as a result of** conditions in **the place** where it was stored, בֵּין מֵחֲמַת אֵיזֶה דָּבָר שֶׁנָּפַל לְתוֹכָן — **or as a result of something that fell into it,**[36] פְּסוּלִין לִנְטִילַת יָדַיִם — **is disqualified for** use for ***netilas yadayim.***[37] אֲבָל אִם נִשְׁתַּנּוּ מֵחֲמַת עַצְמָן — **However, if it became discolored by itself,** without any external cause,[38] כְּשֵׁרִים — **it is** still **fit** for use for *netilas yadayim.*[39]

מַיִם שֶׁנַּעֲשָׂה בָּהֶם מְלָאכָה — **Water that was used to perform a function,** כְּגוֹן, שֶׁהוּדְחוּ בָּהֶם כֵּלִים — **for example,** water **in which vessels were rinsed**[40] אוֹ שֶׁשָּׁרוּ בָּהֶם יְרָקוֹת — **or vegetables were soaked in it,**[41] אוֹ שֶׁנָּתְנוּ בָּהֶם כֵּלִים עִם מַשְׁקִים — **or a container** filled **with** warm **liquid was put in** the water לְצַנְּנָן — for the water **to cool off** the liquid,[42] אוֹ שֶׁמָּדַד בָּהֶן מִדּוֹת — or it was used **to measure** the true capacity of **measures,**[43] גַּם כֵּן פְּסוּלִין — all such water **is also disqualified.**[44]

---

35. Ritual immersion is effective only if it takes place on the ground. Since this *netilas yadayim* is actually an immersion (see previous note), one must position his hands near the ground at the time that they are covered by the water from the spring (*Mishnah Berurah* 159:47).

36. E.g., ink or dye fell into them, or they became darkened due to smoke (*Mishnah Berurah* 160:3).

37. If the water returns to its natural color, it may be used (*Mishnah Berurah* 160:5).

38. Such as standing water in a warm place, that often develops a green coloring (*Mishnah Berurah* 160:2). Water that is discolored from dirt or mud is not disqualified, since water naturally has earth mixed into it (see, however, below, *se'if* 10). Furthermore, such discoloration usually clears up when the water stands for some time (ibid §3).

39. The halachos set out here with regard to discolored water refer only to water being used in a vessel for washing *netilas yadayim;* water that is used for immersion (such as in the previous *se'if*) is subject to different criteria (see *Mishnah Berurah* 160:4).

40. Or to rinse off one's hand; see following *se'if.*

41. To prevent them from wilting. According to some opinions, however, if the vegetables were clean and fresh when they were put in, and the entire purpose of the soaking was only to prevent them from wilting, the water does not become disqualified. *Mishnah Berurah* (160:11) writes that if one already washed his hands with such water, he may eat, but if other water becomes available, he should wash again, but not recite the blessing.

42. E.g., a hot baby bottle was put in a container of water to cool it off.

43. One who wishes to ascertain how much a certain measuring cup contains, can do this by taking a known quantity of water and pouring it into the measuring cup. Water that was used in this way has performed a function and cannot be used for *netilas yadayim* (see *Magen Avraham* 160:5; glosses of *R' Akiva Eiger* ibid. §2; *Tiferes Yisrael* to *Yadayim* Ch. 1, §25).

44. When water is used by a person and performs a function for him, the water is considered from that time onward to be like waste water, and is disqualified for use for *netilas yadayim* (*Mishnah Berurah* 160:6).

LAWS OF WASHING THE HANDS FOR A MEAL — SIMAN 40:9-11 60

וְיֵשׁ פּוֹסְלִין גַּם מַיִם שֶׁנִּמְאֲסוּ, כְּגוֹן, שֶׁשָּׁתָה מֵהֶם כֶּלֶב, אוֹ חֲזִיר וְכַדּוֹמֶה, מִשּׁוּם דְּנַעֲשׂוּ כְּשׁוֹפְכִין. וְיֵשׁ לָחוּשׁ לְדִבְרֵיהֶם[45].

ט. מִי שֶׁלֹּא נָטַל יָדָיו וְנָגַע בְּמַיִם, לֹא נִטְמְאוּ הַמַּיִם[46]. וְלָכֵן הַיּוֹצֵא מִבֵּית הַכִּסֵּא יָכוֹל לִשְׁאוֹב מַיִם בְּחָפְנָיו מִן הֶחָבִית לִרְחוֹץ יָדָיו[47] וְהַנִּשְׁאָרִים כְּשֵׁרִים לִנְטִילַת יָדַיִם. אֲבָל, אִם שִׁכְשֵׁךְ יָדָיו בְּתוֹךְ הֶחָבִית לְנַקּוֹתָן, וַאֲפִילוּ טָבַל בּוֹ רַק אֶצְבָּעוֹ הַקְּטַנָּה לְנַקּוֹתָהּ, נִפְסְלוּ כָּל הַמַּיִם מִפְּנֵי שֶׁנַּעֲשָׂה בָהֶם מְלָאכָה.

י. מַיִם מְלוּחִים, סְרוּחִים, וּמָרִים, אוֹ עֲכוּרִים — אִם אֵין רְאוּיִן לִשְׁתִיַּית כֶּלֶב, פְּסוּלִים לִנְטִילַת יָדַיִם.

יא. קוֹדֶם הַנְּטִילָה צְרִיכִין לְהַשְׁגִּיחַ עַל הַיָּדַיִם שֶׁיִּהְיוּ נְקִיּוֹת בְּלִי שׁוּם חֲצִיצָה[48]. וּמִי

וְיֵשׁ פּוֹסְלִין גַּם מַיִם שֶׁנִּמְאֲסוּ — **Some** authorities **also disqualify water that has become repulsive,** כְּגוֹן, שֶׁשָּׁתָה מֵהֶם כֶּלֶב — **for example,** water **from which a dog drank,** אוֹ חֲזִיר וְכַדּוֹמֶה — **or** from which **a pig** drank, **or the like,** מִשּׁוּם דְּנַעֲשׂוּ כְּשׁוֹפְכִין — **because** when it becomes repulsive **it becomes like waste water.** וְיֵשׁ לָחוּשׁ לְדִבְרֵיהֶם — **It is proper to be concerned for this opinion** and avoid using such water.[45]

§9 מִי שֶׁלֹּא נָטַל יָדָיו — If **one who did not wash his hands** וְנָגַע בְּמַיִם — **touched water,** לֹא נִטְמְאוּ הַמַּיִם — **the water does not** thereby **become ritually impure.**[46] וְלָכֵן — **Therefore,** הַיּוֹצֵא מִבֵּית הַכִּסֵּא — **one who leaves the bathroom** יָכוֹל לִשְׁאוֹב מַיִם בְּחָפְנָיו מִן הֶחָבִית — **may scoop out** (lit., *draw*) **water from a barrel with his hands,** לִרְחוֹץ יָדָיו — and use that water **to wash his hands,**[47] וְהַנִּשְׁאָרִים — **and the remainder** of the water in the barrel כְּשֵׁרִים לִנְטִילַת יָדַיִם — **is** still **qualified** to be used **for** ***netilas yadayim.*** אֲבָל, אִם שִׁכְשֵׁךְ יָדָיו בְּתוֹךְ הֶחָבִית — **However, if he rubbed his hands** in the water **in the barrel** לְנַקּוֹתָן — **to clean them,** וַאֲפִילוּ טָבַל בּוֹ רַק אֶצְבָּעוֹ הַקְּטַנָּה — **even if he only dipped his small finger in** the barrel לְנַקּוֹתָהּ — **for the purpose of cleaning it,** נִפְסְלוּ כָּל הַמַּיִם — **all** of the **water** in the barrel **becomes disqualified** for *netilas yadayim,* מִפְּנֵי שֶׁנַּעֲשָׂה בָהֶם מְלָאכָה — **because the water has been used to perform a function** (see previous *se'if*).

§10 מַיִם מְלוּחִים — With regard to **water that is salty,** סְרוּחִים — **putrid,** וּמָרִים — **bitter,** אוֹ עֲכוּרִים — **or muddied,** אִם אֵין רְאוּיִן לִשְׁתִיַּית כֶּלֶב — **if they** are contaminated to the point that they are **not fit to be drunk by a dog,** פְּסוּלִים לִנְטִילַת יָדַיִם — they **are disqualified** for use **for** ***netilas yadayim.***

§11 קוֹדֶם הַנְּטִילָה — **Before washing** *netilas yadayim* צְרִיכִין לְהַשְׁגִּיחַ עַל הַיָּדַיִם שֶׁיִּהְיוּ נְקִיּוֹת — **one must take care** to ensure **that his hands are clean,** בְּלִי שׁוּם חֲצִיצָה — **and** that they **do not have any** matter stuck to them that would constitute an **interposition** between his hands and the water.[48] וּמִי

45. In a pressing situation, one may rely on the opinion that holds such repulsive waters to be acceptable (*Mishnah Berurah* 160:23).

46. Water is susceptible to *tumah* from unwashed hands only when it is on the hands during *netilas yadayim* (as above, *se'if* 6). Water sitting in a container that is touched by an unwashed hand does not become impure (*Magen Avraham* 160:15).

47. He should ensure that the water with which he washes does not fall back into the barrel (see *Mishnah Berurah* 160:54).

48. See following *se'if,* which states that it is considered an interposition only when he minds having that substance on his hand.

61 LAWS OF WASHING THE HANDS FOR A MEAL — SIMAN 40:12

שֶׁצִּפָּרְנֵי אֶצְבְּעוֹתָיו גְּדוֹלוֹת צָרִיךְ לְדַקְדֵּק לְנַקּוֹת שֶׁלֹּא יְהֵא בְּתַחְתֵּיהֶן טִיט וְצוֹאָה[49], מִשּׁוּם דְּהָוֵי חֲצִיצָה[50]. וְכֵן צָרִיךְ לְהָסִיר הַטַּבָּעוֹת[51] שֶׁלֹּא יִהְיוּ חֲצִיצָה[52].

יב. מִי שֶׁיָּדָיו צְבוּעוֹת, אִם אֵין שָׁם מַמָּשׁוּת הַצֶּבַע כִּי אִם חֲזוּתָא בְּעָלְמָא, לֹא הָוֵי חֲצִיצָה[53]. אֲבָל אִם יֵשׁ עֲלֵיהֶם מַמָּשׁוּת הַצֶּבַע, אֲפִילוּ רַק מְעַט, הָוֵי חֲצִיצָה. אַךְ אִם הוּא אוּמָּן בְּכָךְ, דְּהַיְינוּ, שֶׁהוּא צַבָּע, וְכֵן מִי שֶׁהוּא טַבָּח וְיָדָיו מְלוּכְלָכוֹת מִדָּם, אוֹ שֶׁהוּא סוֹפֵר וְאֶצְבְּעוֹתָיו מְלוּכְלָכוֹת מִדְּיוֹ, וְהוּא רָגִיל בְּכָךְ וְכָל בַּעֲלֵי אוּמָּנוּת זֹאת אֵין מַקְפִּידִין בְּכָךְ, לֹא הָוֵי חֲצִיצָה, אֶלָּא אִם כֵּן הוּא בְּרוֹב הַיָּד[54].

שֶׁצִּפָּרְנֵי אֶצְבְּעוֹתָיו גְּדוֹלוֹת — One who has long fingernails צָרִיךְ לְדַקְדֵּק לְנַקּוֹת — must be careful to clean his nails **שֶׁלֹּא יְהֵא בְּתַחְתֵּיהֶן טִיט וְצוֹאָה — so that there should not be any mud or collected dirt**[49] **underneath them, מִשּׁוּם דְּהָוֵי חֲצִיצָה — for that would constitute an interposition.**[50] **וְכֵן צָרִיךְ לְהָסִיר הַטַּבָּעוֹת — Likewise, one must remove the rings** from one's fingers[51] **שֶׁלֹּא יִהְיוּ חֲצִיצָה — so that they** will **not be an interposition** between the hand and the water.[52]

§12 **מִי שֶׁיָּדָיו צְבוּעוֹת** — The law regarding **one whose hands are colored** depends on the following: **אִם אֵין שָׁם מַמָּשׁוּת הַצֶּבַע — If there is no substance to the coloring כִּי אִם חֲזוּתָא בְּעָלְמָא — but only mere appearance, לֹא הָוֵי חֲצִיצָה** — then this coloring **does not constitute an interposition.**[53] **אֲבָל אִם יֵשׁ עֲלֵיהֶם מַמָּשׁוּת הַצֶּבַע — However, if there is actual substance of the coloring on** his hands, **אֲפִילוּ רַק מְעַט — even if only a little** (i.e., it covers only a minority of his hand), **הָוֵי חֲצִיצָה — it constitutes an interposition. אַךְ — However, אִם הוּא אוּמָּן בְּכָךְ — if his occupation involves** handling **this** type of substance, **דְּהַיְינוּ, שֶׁהוּא צַבָּע — that is,** for example, **he is a dyer, וְכֵן מִי שֶׁהוּא טַבָּח — or similarly, one who is a butcher וְיָדָיו מְלוּכְלָכוֹת מִדָּם — and his hands are soiled with blood, אוֹ שֶׁהוּא סוֹפֵר — or he is a scribe וְאֶצְבְּעוֹתָיו מְלוּכְלָכוֹת מִדְּיוֹ — and his fingers are soiled with ink,** the law is **וְהוּא רָגִיל בְּכָךְ — that if he is used to** having **this** material on his hands, **וְכָל בַּעֲלֵי אוּמָּנוּת זֹאת — and all people of this occupation אֵין מַקְפִּידִין בְּכָךְ — do not mind** if their hands are soiled **in this** way, **לֹא הָוֵי חֲצִיצָה** — then **it does not constitute an interposition אֶלָּא אִם כֵּן הוּא בְּרוֹב הַיָּד — unless** the substance **covers the majority of the hand.**[54]

---

49. *Mishnah Berurah* 161:2.

50. However, one whose fingernails are short need not check and remove any of the dirt that commonly collects under the fingernails, since most people do not mind its presence there (*Rama* 161:1; *Mishnah Berurah* ibid. §9-10).

51. Even if the ring is loose and water can reach the hand, it must be removed, since it is difficult to determine how loose the ring must be to allow the water to reach every part of the finger (*Rama* 161:3; *Mishnah Berurah* ibid. §18).

52. Although, in general, a woman does not mind the presence of a ring on her finger, it is still considered an interposition, since there are times when she does not wish to wear the ring, such as when she kneads dough (*Mishnah Berurah* 161:19; see there regarding the halachah of a man's ring).

53. When one's hands are covered with ink that is still wet, it is not considered an interposition. Even if the ink is dry, it is an interposition only if there is some tangible substance left on his hand (*Igros Moshe, Orach Chaim* II, §110).

54. The rule with regard to interpositions is as follows: If the substance is one that the person minds having on his flesh, *or* if it covers the majority of the hand (even if he does not mind having it), it is considered an interposition, and it must be removed before washing. Thus, if

LAWS OF WASHING THE HANDS FOR A MEAL — SIMAN 40:13 62

וְכֵן, מִי שֶׁיֵּשׁ לוֹ מַכָּה עַל יָדוֹ וְעָלֶיהָ רְטִיָּה שֶׁמִּצְטַעֵר לַהֲסִירָהּ, לֹא הָוֵי חֲצִיצָה[55]. וְעַיֵּין עוֹד בְּסִימָן קס״א דִּינֵי חֲצִיצָה בִּטְבִילַת נָשִׁים וְהוּא הַדִּין לִנְטִילַת יָדַיִם.

יג. הַמַּיִם צְרִיכִין שֶׁיָּבֹאוּ עַל הַיָּדַיִם מִכֹּחַ גַּבְרָא, אֲבָל אִם הַמַּיִם בָּאִים מֵאֲלֵיהֶם לֹא הָוֵי נְטִילָה. וְחָבִית שֶׁיֵּשׁ בּוֹ בַּרְזָא[56] וְהֵסִיר אֶת הַבַּרְזָא, אֲזַי הַמַּיִם הַבָּאִים בְּכֹחַ הָרִאשׁוֹן, דְּהַיְינוּ, קִילּוּחַ הָרִאשׁוֹן לְבַדּוֹ נֶחְשָׁב מִכֹּחַ גַּבְרָא, אֲבָל הַמַּיִם הַבָּאִים אַחַר כָּךְ אֵינָם נֶחְשָׁבִים מִכֹּחַ גַּבְרָא, אֶלָּא כְּאִלּוּ בָּאוּ מֵאֲלֵיהֶם. וְלָכֵן, מִי שֶׁהוּא רוֹצֶה לִיטּוֹל אֶת יָדָיו דֶּרֶךְ הַבַּרְזָא צָרִיךְ לֵידַע שֶׁבְּקִילּוּחַ הָרִאשׁוֹן נִתְכַּסֶּה כָּל הַיָּד[57], וְיִסְתּוֹם אֶת הַבַּרְזָא

וְכֵן — **Similarly,** **מִי שֶׁיֵּשׁ לוֹ מַכָּה עַל יָדוֹ** — **one who has a wound on his hand** **וְעָלֶיהָ רְטִיָּה שֶׁמִּצְטַעֵר לַהֲסִירָהּ** — **and there is a dressing** upon it **that is painful to remove,** **לֹא הָוֵי חֲצִיצָה** — the dressing **does not constitute an interposition.**[55] **וְעַיֵּין עוֹד בְּסִימָן קס״א** — **See further in** ***Siman*** **161** **דִּינֵי חֲצִיצָה בִּטְבִילַת נָשִׁים** — regarding **the laws of interposition with regard to women's immersion,** **וְהוּא הַדִּין לִנְטִילַת יָדַיִם** — **and those same halachos apply to** ***netilas yadayim.***

§13 **הַמַּיִם צְרִיכִין שֶׁיָּבֹאוּ עַל הַיָּדַיִם** — **The water** of *netilas yadayim* **must come onto the hands** **מִכֹּחַ גַּבְרָא** — **as a result of human force;** **אֲבָל אִם הַמַּיִם בָּאִים מֵאֲלֵיהֶם** — **but if the water comes by itself** **לֹא הָוֵי נְטִילָה** — **it is not a valid washing** for *netilas yadayim.* **וְחָבִית שֶׁיֵּשׁ בּוֹ בַּרְזָא** — **A barrel that has a plug,**[56] **וְהֵסִיר אֶת הַבַּרְזָא** — **and one removed the plug,** thus releasing the water in the barrel, **אֲזַי הַמַּיִם הַבָּאִים בְּכֹחַ הָרִאשׁוֹן** — **then the water that comes forth from the first force,** **דְּהַיְינוּ, קִילּוּחַ הָרִאשׁוֹן לְבַדּוֹ** — **that is, the first stream** of water **only,** **נֶחְשָׁב מִכֹּחַ גַּבְרָא** — **is considered** to have come **from a human force.** **אֲבָל הַמַּיִם הַבָּאִים אַחַר כָּךְ** — **But the water that flows out after this** **אֵינָם נֶחְשָׁבִים מִכֹּחַ גַּבְרָא** — **is not considered** to have come **from human force;** **אֶלָּא כְּאִלּוּ בָּאוּ מֵאֲלֵיהֶם** — **rather,** it is considered **as if it came by itself.** **וְלָכֵן** — **Therefore,** **מִי שֶׁהוּא רוֹצֶה לִיטּוֹל אֶת יָדָיו** — **one who wishes to wash his hands** **דֶּרֶךְ הַבַּרְזָא** — **by way of** removing **the plug** from a barrel of water **צָרִיךְ לֵידַע** — **must know** for sure **שֶׁבְּקִילּוּחַ הָרִאשׁוֹן נִתְכַּסֶּה כָּל הַיָּד** — **that with the first stream** of water **the entire hand will be covered.**[57] **וְיִסְתּוֹם אֶת הַבַּרְזָא** — After that first stream, **he should close** the hole with **the plug**

---

a person has dried ink on a small part of his hand, if he is not a scribe (and therefore minds if there is ink there), the ink constitutes an interposition. If he is a scribe, and he does not mind having dried ink on his hands, it is considered an interposition only if the ink covers a majority of his hand (see *Mishnah Berurah* 161:1). For further discussion, see Appendix of Kitzur's editorial glosses.

55. Since he cannot take the bandage off without causing himself pain, there is no concern that he will remove it during the meal and that the food will touch that part of the hand. That part of the hand is therefore not included in the obligation of *netilas yadayim,* and hence the dressing is not considered an interposition. [However, one must take care to pour at least a *revi'is* of water on that hand. It is also proper that the soiled dressing be covered during the meal. If the dressing comes off during the meal, he must wash again.] A dressing that is not painful to remove must be removed prior to washing (see *Mishnah Berurah* 162:68,71; 161:5). A scab that is painful to remove (and one therefore certainly does not mind its continued presence on his hand), is also not considered an interposition (*Rama* 161:2; *Mishnah Berurah* ibid. §16).

56. I.e., a plug or spigot placed in the hole of a barrel.

57. Since the entire hand must be covered by water at one time; see above, *se'if* 4.

63 LAWS OF WASHING THE HANDS FOR A MEAL — SIMAN 40:14

וְיַחֲזוֹר וְיִפְתְּחֵהוּ לִשְׁפִיכָה שְׁנִיָּה[58]. וּמִי שֶׁאֵינוֹ יוֹדֵעַ לְשַׁעֵר, אֵין לוֹ לִיטוֹל יָדָיו בְּדֶרֶךְ זֶה. וּמִכָּל שֶׁכֵּן שֶׁאֵין לִיטוֹל יָדָיו מִן הַכִּיּוֹר שֶׁיֵּשׁ לוֹ בַּרְזָא קָטָן וְהַקִּילוּחַ הוּא דַק[59].

יד. אָסוּר לֶאֱכוֹל בְּלֹא נְטִילָה, אֲפִילּוּ אִם רוֹצֶה לִכְרוֹךְ יָדָיו בְּמַפָּה. וְאִם הוּא בְּדֶרֶךְ וְאֵין לוֹ מַיִם — אִם יוֹדֵעַ כִּי בְּעוֹד דֶּרֶךְ ד׳ מִילִין לְפָנָיו[60], אוֹ מִיל[61] לְאַחֲרָיו[62], יִמְצָא מַיִם, מְחוּיָּב לָלֶכֶת לְפָנָיו ד׳ מִילִין, אוֹ לַחֲזוֹר לְאַחֲרָיו מִיל, לִיטוֹל יָדָיו לַאֲכִילָה[63]. אֲבָל, אִם גַּם שָׁמָּה לֹא יִמְצָא מַיִם, אוֹ שֶׁהוּא עִם חֲבוּרָה וּמִתְיָרֵא לְהִפָּרֵד מֵהֶם, וְכֵן מִי שֶׁיֵּשׁ לוֹ שְׁאָר אוֹנֶס שֶׁאֵינוֹ יָכוֹל לִיטוֹל יָדָיו, יִכְרוֹךְ יָדָיו בְּמַפָּה,

---

וְיַחֲזוֹר וְיִפְתְּחֵהוּ לִשְׁפִיכָה שְׁנִיָּה — **and open it again for a second pouring** on the hand.[58] וּמִי שֶׁאֵינוֹ יוֹדֵעַ לְשַׁעֵר — **One who cannot figure** the amount of water that will flow in this way אֵין לוֹ לִיטוֹל יָדָיו בְּדֶרֶךְ זֶה — **should not wash his hands** for *netilas yadayim* **using this method.** וּמִכָּל שֶׁכֵּן שֶׁאֵין לִיטוֹל יָדָיו מִן הַכִּיּוֹר — **Certainly, one should not wash his hands from a basin** שֶׁיֵּשׁ לוֹ בַּרְזָא קָטָן — **that has a small plug,** וְהַקִּילוּחַ הוּא דַק — **and** when it is removed **the stream** of water **will be narrow,** and unable to cover the hand.[59]

§14 אָסוּר לֶאֱכוֹל בְּלֹא נְטִילָה — **It is forbidden to eat** bread **without washing** *netilas yadayim,* אֲפִילּוּ אִם רוֹצֶה לִכְרוֹךְ יָדָיו בְּמַפָּה — **even if one wishes to wrap his hands in a cloth** so that they do not touch the food. וְאִם הוּא בְּדֶרֶךְ — **If he is traveling** וְאֵין לוֹ מַיִם — **and he has no water,** אִם יוֹדֵעַ — **if he knows** כִּי בְּעוֹד דֶּרֶךְ ד׳ מִילִין לְפָנָיו — **that in another four** ***mil*** or less[60] along the route that lies **ahead of him,** אוֹ מִיל לְאַחֲרָיו — **or** up to **a** ***mil***[61] **behind him,** i.e., out of his way,[62] יִמְצָא מַיִם — **he would find water,** מְחוּיָּב לָלֶכֶת לְפָנָיו ד׳ מִילִין — **then he is obligated to go four** ***mil*** **ahead of him** אוֹ לַחֲזוֹר לְאַחֲרָיו מִיל — **or to turn back** and **go a** ***mil*** **behind him** לִיטוֹל יָדָיו לַאֲכִילָה — in order **to wash his hands for eating.**[63] אֲבָל, אִם גַּם שָׁמָּה לֹא יִמְצָא מַיִם — **However, if he will not find water there either,** אוֹ שֶׁהוּא עִם חֲבוּרָה — **or if he is** traveling **with a group** וּמִתְיָרֵא לְהִפָּרֵד מֵהֶם — **and he is afraid to be separated from them** (e.g., due to the danger involved in traveling alone), וְכֵן מִי שֶׁיֵּשׁ לוֹ שְׁאָר אוֹנֶס — **as well as one who is subject to any other unavoidable circumstance,** שֶׁאֵינוֹ יָכוֹל לִיטוֹל יָדָיו — the result of which is **that he cannot wash his hands,** יִכְרוֹךְ יָדָיו בְּמַפָּה — then **he should wrap his hands in a cloth,**

---

58. This procedure should then be repeated twice more to wash the second hand.

59. *Mishnah Berurah* (159:64; 162:30) writes that if no other vessel is available he may use this one by opening and closing the plug or spigot in quick succession enough times that every part of his hand is covered by water that comes out in the first stream after he opens the plug or spigot.

60. A *mil* is 2000 *amos* (approximately .6 mile-.7 mile [.96 km. — 1.15 km.]). It takes 18 minutes to walk one *mil,* 72 minutes to walk four. According to *Beur Halachah* (163:1 s.v. ברחוק), one who is traveling by train [or, in our times, by car], must travel the time that it takes to walk four *mil.*

61. Or, 18 minutes; see previous note.

62. לְאַחֲרָיו, *behind him,* refers to any direction that is not on his planned trip. Thus, he need travel only up to a *mil* out of his way to obtain water. Similarly, if he is staying in a place that does not have water, he need only travel up to a *mil* (*Mishnah Berurah* 163:3).

63. If he is unsure whether he will find water even after traveling this distance, and he is very hungry, he need not wait (*Mishnah Berurah* 163:3; *Beur Halachah* 163:1 s.v. אם אין מים).

LAWS OF WASHING THE HANDS FOR A MEAL — SIMAN 40:15-16 64

אוֹ יִלְבַּשׁ בָּתֵּי יָדַיִם (האנדשוה) וְיֹאכַל כָּךְ[64].

טו. הָעוֹשֶׂה צְרָכָיו קוֹדֶם אֲכִילָה, שֶׁהוּא צָרִיךְ לִיטוֹל יָדָיו לְבִרְכַּת "אֲשֶׁר יָצַר"[65], וְגַם צָרִיךְ לִיטוֹל יָדָיו לִסְעוּדָה, יֵשׁ בָּזֶה כַּמָּה סְפֵיקוֹת[66]. עַל כֵּן הַנָּכוֹן שֶׁיִּטּוֹל תְּחִלָּה יָדָיו שֶׁלֹּא כְּדִין נְטִילַת יָדַיִם לִסְעוּדָה, דְּהַיְינוּ, שֶׁיִּשְׁפּוֹךְ רַק מְעַט מַיִם לְחָפְנוֹ אַחַת וִישַׁפְשֵׁף שְׁתֵּי יָדָיו בְּמַיִם אֵלּוּ[67] וִינַגְּבֵם הֵיטֵב וִיבָרֵךְ "אֲשֶׁר יָצַר", וְאַחַר כָּךְ יִטּוֹל יָדָיו כְּדִין נְטִילַת יָדַיִם לִסְעוּדָה וִיבָרֵךְ "עַל נְטִילַת יָדָיִם".

טז. מִי שֶׁבְּאֶמְצַע סְעוּדָה[68] נָגַע בְּגוּפוֹ בִּמְקוֹמוֹת הַמְכוּסִּים, אוֹ שֶׁחִיכֵּךְ בְּרֹאשׁוֹ,

---

אוֹ יִלְבַּשׁ בָּתֵּי יָדַיִם (האנדשוה) — or he should wear gloves, וְיֹאכַל כָּךְ — and eat that way without touching the food.[64]

§15 הָעוֹשֶׂה צְרָכָיו קוֹדֶם אֲכִילָה — One who relieves himself before eating, שֶׁהוּא צָרִיךְ לִיטוֹל יָדָיו לְבִרְכַּת "אֲשֶׁר יָצַר" — so that he must now **wash his hands before reciting the** ***Asher Yatzar*** **blessing,**[65] **וְגַם צָרִיךְ לִיטוֹל יָדָיו לִסְעוּדָה — and he must also wash his hands for a meal, יֵשׁ בָּזֶה כַּמָּה סְפֵיקוֹת — there are many halachic doubts regarding** the blessing upon **this** washing were he to wash only once for both obligations.[66] **עַל כֵּן הַנָּכוֹן — Therefore, the appropriate** procedure **is שֶׁיִּטּוֹל תְּחִלָּה יָדָיו שֶׁלֹּא כְּדִין נְטִילַת יָדַיִם לִסְעוּדָה — to wash one's hands first** in a way that is **not in accord with the halachos of** ***netilas yadayim*** **for a meal: דְּהַיְינוּ — That is, שֶׁיִּשְׁפּוֹךְ רַק מְעַט מַיִם לְחָפְנוֹ אַחַת — he should pour only a bit of water onto one of his cupped hands, וִישַׁפְשֵׁף שְׁתֵּי יָדָיו בְּמַיִם אֵלּוּ — and rub his two hands** together **with this water.**[67] **וִינַגְּבֵם הֵיטֵב — He should** then **dry them well, וִיבָרֵךְ "אֲשֶׁר יָצַר" — and recite the** ***Asher Yatzar*** **blessing, וְאַחַר כָּךְ יִטּוֹל יָדָיו — and then wash his hands** again **כְּדִין נְטִילַת יָדַיִם לִסְעוּדָה — in accordance with the halachos of** ***netilas yadayim*** **for a meal, וִיבָרֵךְ "עַל נְטִילַת יָדָיִם" — and then recite the blessing of** ***al netilas yadayim.***

§16 מִי שֶׁבְּאֶמְצַע סְעוּדָה — One who, during a meal, נָגַע בְּגוּפוֹ בִּמְקוֹמוֹת הַמְכוּסִּים — touched his body in a place that is usually covered,[68] **אוֹ שֶׁחִיכֵּךְ בְּרֹאשׁוֹ —**

---

64. *Beur Halachah* (ibid.) cites *Ritva,* who writes that one should not rely on this opinion, even when he will certainly not find water within the above distances, unless it is of great necessity for him to eat (e.g., he is weak from the journey).

65. After relieving oneself, one is obligated to wash his hands and recite the *Asher Yatzar* (*Who fashioned*) blessing; see above, 4:6.

66. The obligation to recite the *Asher Yatzar* blessing begins immediately upon washing after relieving oneself. However, when washing for a meal, one may not interrupt between washing and reciting the blessing of *al netilas yadayim,* nor should one interrupt between washing and eating the bread (see below, 41:2). This would seem to preclude reciting the *Asher Yatzar* blessing until after eating some of the bread. However, it is better not to wait so long from the time he washed his hands to recite *Asher Yatzar.* Therefore, were he to wash his hands only once, he would be placing himself in a halachically untenable position (*Mishnah Berurah* 165:2; see next note).

67. See above, *se'if* 2, which states that this manner of washing is invalid for *netilas yadayim* for a meal. One first washes his hands in this manner, for if he were to wash in a manner that would satisfy the obligation of *netilas yadayim* for a meal, even if his intention when washing the first time was not for *netilas yadayim,* he would not be permitted to recite the blessing of *al netilas yadayim* when washing his hands (that are known to be ritually pure) immediately afterward (see *Mishnah Berurah* 165:2).

68. Certain areas of the body are considered

65 LAWS OF WASHING THE HANDS FOR A MEAL — SIMAN 40:17

אוֹ שֶׁהִשְׁתִּין מַיִם, צָרִיךְ לִיטוֹל יָדָיו פַּעַם שֵׁנִית, אֲבָל לֹא יְבָרֵךְ עֲלֵיהֶם. וְכֵן, אֲפִילוּ אִם עָשָׂה צְרָכָיו וְנוֹטֵל יָדָיו בְּאֶמְצַע הַסְּעוּדָה, אֵינוֹ צָרִיךְ לְבָרֵךְ "עַל נְטִילַת יָדַיִם"[69].

יז. הָאוֹכֵל[70] דָּבָר שֶׁטִּבּוּלוֹ בְּמַשְׁקֶה, אוֹ שֶׁבָּאָה מַשְׁקֶה עַל הַמַּאֲכָל[71] וַעֲדַיִין הוּא לַח מִן הַמַּשְׁקֶה, אַף עַל פִּי שֶׁהוּא אֵינוֹ נוֹגֵעַ בִּמְקוֹם הַמַּשְׁקֶה[72], מִכָּל מָקוֹם צָרִיךְ לִיטוֹל יָדָיו תְּחִלָּה[73], רַק לֹא יְבָרֵךְ "עַל נְטִילַת יָדַיִם". וְהַרְבֵּה מְקִילִין בְּדָבָר זֶה, אֲבָל כָּל יְרֵא שָׁמַיִם יֵשׁ לוֹ לְהַחֲמִיר עַל עַצְמוֹ[74].

---

or scratched his head, **אוֹ שֶׁהִשְׁתִּין מַיִם** — **or urinated, צָרִיךְ לִיטוֹל יָדָיו פַּעַם שֵׁנִית — must wash his hands** for *netilas yadayim* **a second time, אֲבָל לֹא יְבָרֵךְ עֲלֵיהֶם — but he should not recite the blessing upon** this washing. **וְכֵן, אֲפִילוּ אִם עָשָׂה צְרָכָיו — Likewise, even if he relieved himself** (i.e., defecated), **וְנוֹטֵל יָדָיו בְּאֶמְצַע הַסְּעוּדָה** — **and** therefore **washes his hands during the meal, אֵינוֹ צָרִיךְ לְבָרֵךְ "עַל נְטִילַת יָדַיִם" — he should not recite the blessing of *al netilas yadayim*** on this washing.[69]

§17 **הָאוֹכֵל דָּבָר שֶׁטִּבּוּלוֹ בְּמַשְׁקֶה — One who eats** any food[70] **that is** commonly **dipped in liquid, אוֹ שֶׁבָּאָה מַשְׁקֶה עַל הַמַּאֲכָל — or a food upon which liquid was poured,**[71] **וַעֲדַיִין הוּא לַח מִן הַמַּשְׁקֶה — and,** at the time when he is eating the food that was dipped or upon which liquid was poured, **it is still wet from the liquid, אַף עַל פִּי שֶׁהוּא אֵינוֹ נוֹגֵעַ בִּמְקוֹם הַמַּשְׁקֶה — even if he does not touch the place** on the food **that has the liquid** on it (i.e., the part that is wet),[72] **מִכָּל מָקוֹם — nevertheless, צָרִיךְ לִיטוֹל יָדָיו תְּחִלָּה — he must wash his hands before** eating it.[73] **רַק לֹא יְבָרֵךְ "עַל נְטִילַת יָדַיִם" — However, he should not recite the blessing of *al netilas yadayim*. וְהַרְבֵּה מְקִילִין בְּדָבָר זֶה — Many are lenient with regard to this** practice and do not wash before eating such foods; **אֲבָל כָּל יְרֵא שָׁמַיִם יֵשׁ לוֹ לְהַחֲמִיר עַל עַצְמוֹ — however, every God-fearing person should act stringently with himself** and wash.[74]

---

halachically to be "usually covered" regardless of how people of the region dress. Other areas of the body depend on the prevalent custom; see *Orach Chaim* 4:21; *Mishnah Berurah* 4:53-54; *Beur Halachah* to 4:21 s.v. צריך ליזהר.

69. According to *Mishnah Berurah* (164:13), one who defecates or actually soils his hands (in a manner that would require *netilas yadayim;* see *Mishnah Berurah* there and *Beur Halachah* 164:2, s.v. לחזור) during a meal must recite a blessing upon washing *netilas yadayim* a second time. When washing in these circumstances, one needs to wash only once; he first recites *al netilas yadayim,* then *Asher Yatzar* (*Mishnah Berurah* 165:2). See below, 42:22, regarding the obligation of *netilas yadayim* for one who diverted his attention from the meal and then wishes to continue eating.

70. Even fruit, vegetables, or meat (*Mishnah Berurah* 158:11).

71. This also includes fruits or vegetables that were immersed in [or washed with] water to clean them before eating (*Mishnah Berurah* 158:12). The law of our *se'if* applies only in cases where it is customary for the food to be dipped or to have liquid poured on it (*Mishnah Berurah* 158:12).

72. E.g., he eats it with a fork, or he only dips part of it in the liquid (but see below, *se'if* 20, regarding foods that are ordinarily eaten with utensils).

73. See introduction to this *Siman* for the reason for this obligation. All of the halachos of *netilas yadayim* for bread apply to this washing (*Mishnah Berurah* 158:20).

74. According to some authorities, this halachah applied only when people were able to avoid the *tumah* caused by eating impure foods. Since nowadays most people are considered ritually impure, one need not wash before eating such food (see introduction to this *Siman*). In recognition of this opinion,

LAWS OF WASHING THE HANDS FOR A MEAL — SIMAN 40:18-19 66

יח. מַשְׁקִים לְעִנְיָן זֶה הֵמָּה שִׁבְעָה. אֵלּוּ הֵן: יַיִן, וְכֵן חוֹמֶץ מִיַּיִן, דְּבַשׁ דְּבוֹרִים, שֶׁמֶן זַיִת, חָלָב, וּבִכְלָל[75] זֶה גַּם מֵי חָלָב, טַל, דָּם שֶׁל בְּהֵמָה חַיָּה וְעוֹף (וְהַיְינוּ כְּשֶׁאוֹכְלִין לִרְפוּאָה)[76], מַיִם. וְסִימָנָם יָ״ד שַׁחַ״ט דָּ״ם[77]. אֲבָל שְׁאָר מֵי פֵּירוֹת, אֲפִילּוּ בְּמָקוֹם שֶׁרְגִילִין לַעֲשׂוֹת מַשְׁקִים לִשְׁתִיָּה מִסְּחִיטַת אֵיזֶה פֵּירוֹת, אֵין לָהֶם דִּין מַשְׁקֶה לְעִנְיָן זֶה.

יט. פֵּירוֹת שֶׁמְּרוּקָּחִין בְּצוּקֶער אֵין צְרִיכִין נְטִילַת יָדַיִם, כִּי הַצוּקֶער לֹא הָוֵי מַשְׁקֶה. וְגַם הַלַּחְלוּחִית שֶׁיָּצָא מִן הַפֵּירוֹת לֹא הָוֵי מַשְׁקֶה, שֶׁהוּא מֵי פֵּירוֹת. אֲבָל אִם מְרוּקָּחִין בִּדְבַשׁ, אִם נִקְרַשׁ הַדְּבַשׁ הֵיטֵב, אֲזַי יָצָא מִכְּלַל מַשְׁקֶה וְנַעֲשָׂה אוֹכֶל, וְאֵין צָרִיךְ נְטִילַת יָדַיִם. אֲבָל אִם לֹא נִקְרְשׁוּ הֵיטֵב, אֶלָּא נִתְעַבּוּ מְעַט וַעֲדַיִין הֵם

---

§18 מַשְׁקִים לְעִנְיָן זֶה הֵמָּה שִׁבְעָה — **There are seven "liquids"** that qualify **with regard to this** halachah. אֵלּוּ הֵן — **They are:** (1) יַיִן, וְכֵן חוֹמֶץ מִיַּיִן — **wine, and similarly, wine vinegar;** (2) דְּבַשׁ דְּבוֹרִים — **bees' honey;** (3) שֶׁמֶן זַיִת — **olive oil;** (4) חָלָב — **milk,** וּבִכְלָל זֶה גַּם מֵי חָלָב — **and whey**[75] **is also included in this** category; (5) טַל — **dew;** (6) דָּם שֶׁל בְּהֵמָה חַיָּה וְעוֹף — **blood of an animal, beast, or fowl** (וְהַיְינוּ כְּשֶׁאוֹכְלִין לִרְפוּאָה) — **that is, when one eats it for medicinal purposes);**[76] (7) מַיִם — **and water.** וְסִימָנָם — **A mnemonic to** aid in remembering **these** seven **is:** יָ״ד שַׁחַ״ט דָּ״ם — *YaD SHaCHaT DaM.*[77] אֲבָל שְׁאָר מֵי פֵּירוֹת — **However, other fruit juices,** אֲפִילּוּ בְּמָקוֹם שֶׁרְגִילִין לַעֲשׂוֹת מַשְׁקִים לִשְׁתִיָּה — **even where it is common to produce drinks** מִסְּחִיטַת אֵיזֶה פֵּירוֹת — **by squeezing out certain fruits,** אֵין לָהֶם דִּין מַשְׁקֶה לְעִנְיָן זֶה — **do not have the halachic status of a liquid with regard to this** law.

§19 Kitzur discusses the halachic status of preserves with regard to this law.

פֵּירוֹת שֶׁמְּרוּקָּחִין בְּצוּקֶער — **Fruits that are preserved in sugar** ("preserves"), אֵין צְרִיכִין נְטִילַת יָדַיִם — **do not require** *netilas yadayim* כִּי הַצוּקֶער לֹא הָוֵי מַשְׁקֶה — **because the sugar is not a liquid,** וְגַם הַלַּחְלוּחִית שֶׁיָּצָא מִן הַפֵּירוֹת — **and the moisture that exuded from the fruits** לֹא הָוֵי מַשְׁקֶה — **is also not considered a liquid** in regard to this halachah, שֶׁהוּא מֵי פֵּירוֹת — **since it is fruit juice** (see previous *se'if*). אֲבָל אִם מְרוּקָּחִין בִּדְבַשׁ — **However, if they are preserved in honey** then the law is אִם נִקְרַשׁ הַדְּבַשׁ הֵיטֵב — that **if the honey has hardened well,** אֲזַי יָצָא מִכְּלַל מַשְׁקֶה — **then it loses its status as a liquid,** וְנַעֲשָׂה אוֹכֶל — **and attains** the status of **a** solid **food** וְאֵין צָרִיךְ נְטִילַת יָדַיִם — **and** therefore **does not require** *netilas yadayim.* אֲבָל אִם לֹא נִקְרְשׁוּ הֵיטֵב — **However, if** the honey **did not totally harden** אֶלָּא נִתְעַבּוּ מְעַט — **but only thickened somewhat** וַעֲדַיִין הֵם

---

we do not recite the blessing of *al netilas yadayim* when washing for this food. However, since many later authorities hold that this *netilas yadayim* is required nowadays like *netilas yadayim* before eating bread, Kitzur encourages the God-fearing person to adhere to this practice (see also *Mishnah Berurah* 158:20).

75. Whey is the watery part of milk that separates from the curds during cheese-making.

76. Under normal circumstances, it is forbidden to consume blood (see introduction to *Siman* 36). An ill person, however, may consume blood in certain circumstances; see below, 192:5,7.

77. Each of the letters in this mnemonic represents the first letter in the Hebrew word of one of the liquids, in the order listed above.

67 LAWS OF WASHING THE HANDS FOR A MEAL — SIMAN 40:20-21

נִיגָּרִים[78], צְרִיכִין נְטִילַת יָדַיִם. וְכֵן חֶמְאָה, שֶׁהוּא בִּכְלַל הֶחָלָב, אִם הִיא קְרוּשָׁה, אֵינָהּ מַשְׁקֶה רַק אוֹכֶל, אֲבָל אִם הִיא נִימּוֹחָה, הֲרֵי הִיא מַשְׁקֶה[79].

כ. דְּבָרִים שֶׁדַּרְכָּן לְאָכְלָן בְּלֹא כַּף וּמַזְלֵג, אֲפִילוּ הוּא אוֹכֵל עַל יְדֵי כַּף אוֹ מַזְלֵג, צָרִיךְ נְטִילַת יָדַיִם. אֲבָל דָּבָר שֶׁאֵין דַּרְכּוֹ לֶאֱכוֹל רַק עַל יְדֵי כַּף, כְּגוֹן, לְבִיבוֹת וְכַיּוֹצֵא בָּזֶה, וְכֵן פֵּירוֹת מְרוּקָּחִין בִּדְבַשׁ בְּמָקוֹם שֶׁאֵין דַּרְכָּן לְאָכְלָן רַק עַל יְדֵי כַּף אוֹ מַזְלֵג, אֵין צָרִיךְ נְטִילַת יָדַיִם[80].

כא. מֶלַח שֶׁנַּעֲשָׂה מִמַּיִם הָוֵי בִּכְלַל מַיִם (כִּי הַמַּיִם אַף עַל פִּי שֶׁנִּקְרְשׁוּ לֹא יָצְאוּ מִכְּלַל מַשְׁקֶה)[81]. וְלָכֵן, הַטּוֹבֵל צְנוֹן וְכַדּוֹמֶה בְּמֶלַח זֶה צָרִיךְ נְטִילַת יָדַיִם.

נִיגָּרִים — and it is still fluid,[78] **צְרִיכִין נְטִילַת יָדַיִם** — then, in this case, the fruits **do require** *netilas yadayim.* **וְכֵן — Likewise, חֶמְאָה, שֶׁהוּא בִּכְלַל הֶחָלָב — butter, which is included in** the category of **"milk,"** (one of the seven liquids, see above, previous *se'if*), **אִם הִיא קְרוּשָׁה — if it has solidified אֵינָהּ מַשְׁקֶה רַק אוֹכֶל — it is not** considered **a liquid, but** rather **a** solid **food. אֲבָל אִם הִיא נִימּוֹחָה — However, if it is melted, הֲרֵי הִיא מַשְׁקֶה — then it is** considered **a liquid.**[79]

§20 **דְּבָרִים שֶׁדַּרְכָּן לְאָכְלָן** — Regarding those food **items that are commonly eaten** with one's hands, **בְּלֹא כַּף וּמַזְלֵג — without** using **a spoon or a fork,** the halachah if such a food was dipped in liquid is **אֲפִילוּ הוּא אוֹכֵל עַל יְדֵי כַּף אוֹ מַזְלֵג** — that **even if** one **eats** it **with a spoon or fork, צָרִיךְ נְטִילַת יָדַיִם — it requires** *netilas yadayim.* **אֲבָל דָּבָר — However, an item שֶׁאֵין דַּרְכּוֹ לֶאֱכוֹל רַק עַל יְדֵי כַּף — that is commonly eaten only with a spoon, כְּגוֹן, לְבִיבוֹת וְכַיּוֹצֵא בָּזֶה — such as dumplings and the like, וְכֵן פֵּירוֹת מְרוּקָּחִין בִּדְבַשׁ — as well as fruits preserved in honey, בְּמָקוֹם שֶׁאֵין דַּרְכָּן לְאָכְלָן — in a place where it is uncommon to eat them** directly with the hands, **רַק עַל יְדֵי כַּף אוֹ מַזְלֵג —** but **only with a spoon or fork, אֵין צָרִיךְ נְטִילַת יָדַיִם — do not require** *netilas yadayim.*[80]

§21 **מֶלַח שֶׁנַּעֲשָׂה מִמַּיִם — Salt that is produced by** the evaporation of **water הָוֵי בִּכְלַל מַיִם — is included in** the category of the liquid **"water,"** one of the seven liquids enumerated above in *se'if* 18 (**כִּי הַמַּיִם — for water, אַף עַל פִּי שֶׁנִּקְרְשׁוּ — even when frozen, לֹא יָצְאוּ מִכְּלַל מַשְׁקֶה — does not cease to be classified as a liquid).**[81] **וְלָכֵן — Therefore, הַטּוֹבֵל צְנוֹן וְכַדּוֹמֶה בְּמֶלַח זֶה — one who dips a radish, or the like, in this** type of **salt, צָרִיךְ נְטִילַת יָדַיִם — is**

---

78. *Mishnah Berurah* (158:14) writes that it is considered liquid if it is טוֹפֵחַ עַל מְנָת לְהַטְפִּיחַ (i.e., *moist enough* [that an object that touches it will be able] *to moisten* [a third object]).

79. *Mishnah Berurah* (158:16) cites *Chayei Adam* 36:6, who maintains that butter can be considered a liquid only if it was melted in a pan before becoming a part of the food. However, if it was solid and then it was melted directly onto a food, it retains its identity as a solid food, and it does not require *netilas yadayim*. See below, *se'if* 21 and note 81, regarding the halachah of ice.

80. Even if he does happen to touch the food with his hands, while it is on the spoon, in the course of eating it (*Mishnah Berurah* 158:26).

81. Kitzur holds that unlike honey and butter, which when hardened are halachically considered a solid (above, *se'if* 19), water retains the halachic status of a liquid even when it is frozen into ice. Thus, salt that is produced from water has the same halachah as water despite the fact that it is solid in form. According to *Mishnah Berurah,* however, ice is not regarded as water, and is not a liquid with regard to this halachah (see *Shaar HaTziyun* 158:16). Thus, *Mishnah Berurah* rules (158:18) that only wet salt is regarded as a liquid.

LAWS OF WASHING THE HANDS FOR A MEAL — SIMAN 40:21 68

יַיִן שָׂרָף שֶׁנַּעֲשָׂה מִתְּבוּאָה אוֹ מִפֵּירוֹת אֵינוֹ מַשְׁקֶה לְעִנְיָן זֶה, דְּלֹא הָוֵי רַק זֵיעָה מִן הַתְּבוּאָה וּמִן הַפֵּירוֹת, וְאַף עַל פִּי שֶׁיֵּשׁ בּוֹ גַּם מַיִם וּמָזוּג גַּם כֵּן בְּמַיִם, מִכָּל מָקוֹם הֵם הַמִּיעוּט[82]. וְלָכֵן, הַטּוֹבֵל בּוֹ אֵיזֶה דָּבָר וְאוֹכְלוֹ אֵין צָרִיךְ נְטִילַת יָדַיִם. אֲבָל יַיִן שָׂרָף שֶׁנַּעֲשָׂה מִן הַחַרְצַנִּים וְהַזָּגִים אוֹ מִן הַשְּׁמָרִים[83] שֶׁל יַיִן נִרְאֶה דְּהָוֵי מַשְׁקֶה.

---

required to wash *netilas yadayim* before eating it.

יַיִן שָׂרָף שֶׁנַּעֲשָׂה מִתְּבוּאָה אוֹ מִפֵּירוֹת — Liquor that is produced from grain or fruit אֵינוֹ מַשְׁקֶה לְעִנְיָן זֶה — is not classified as **a liquid with regard to this** halachah, **דְּלֹא הָוֵי רַק זֵיעָה מִן הַתְּבוּאָה וּמִן הַפֵּירוֹת — for** the liquor **is** considered to be mere **"sweat"** (i.e., moisture) **of the grain or the fruit. וְאַף עַל פִּי שֶׁיֵּשׁ בּוֹ גַּם מַיִם — Even though there is also water present in** the liquor during the time of production **וּמָזוּג גַּם כֵּן בְּמַיִם — and it is also diluted with water** afterward, **מִכָּל מָקוֹם הֵם הַמִּיעוּט — nevertheless,** it is not considered a liquid, since the water **is a minority** ingredient of the liquor.[82] **וְלָכֵן — Therefore, הַטּוֹבֵל בּוֹ אֵיזֶה דָּבָר — one who dips any** food **item into** liquor **וְאוֹכְלוֹ — and eats it** that way **אֵין צָרִיךְ נְטִילַת יָדַיִם — is not required to wash** ***netilas yadayim.*** **אֲבָל — However, יַיִן שָׂרָף שֶׁנַּעֲשָׂה** — with regard to **liquor that is produced מִן הַחַרְצַנִּים וְהַזָּגִים — from the seeds and skins** of grapes **אוֹ מִן הַשְּׁמָרִים שֶׁל יַיִן — or from the lees**[83] **of wine, נִרְאֶה דְּהָוֵי מַשְׁקֶה — it would seem that it is** to be considered **a liquid** with regard to this halachah.

---

82. Hence, if water constitutes a majority of the liquor, it would be considered a liquid, and one would be required to wash *netilas yadayim* before eating food dipped into it (*Mishnah Berurah* 158:26).

83. Lees are the sediment that result from fermentation of an alcoholic beverage.

69 LAWS OF BREAKING BREAD AND THE HAMOTZI BLESSING — SIMAN 41:1-2

סימן מא

הִלְכוֹת בְּצִיעַת הַפַּת וּבִרְכַּת הַמּוֹצִיא

וּבוֹ י׳ סְעִיפִים

א. עַל לֶחֶם גָּמוּר שֶׁהוּא מֵחֲמֵשֶׁת מִינֵי דָגָן[1] מְבָרְכִין לְפָנָיו הַמּוֹצִיא[2] וּלְאַחֲרָיו בִּרְכַּת הַמָּזוֹן[3] (וְדִין פַּת הַבָּאָה בְכִיסְנִין[4] יְבוֹאָר בְּסִימָן מ״ח).

ב. יֵשׁ לִיזָּהֵר שֶׁלֹּא לְהַפְסִיק בֵּין נְטִילַת יָדַיִם[5] לְהַמּוֹצִיא, אֲבָל מוּתָּר לוֹ לַעֲנוֹת אָמֵן עַל אֵיזֶה בְּרָכָה שֶׁהוּא שׁוֹמֵעַ. וּשְׁהִיָּה[6] כְּדֵי הִילּוּךְ כ״ב אַמָּה[7], אוֹ מִבַּיִת לְבַיִת

SIMAN 41

LAWS OF BREAKING BREAD AND THE HAMOTZI BLESSING

CONTAINING 10 *SE'IFIM*

§1 The Blessing / **§2** Interruption After *Netilas Yadayim* / **§3-4** Cutting the Bread / **§5** Reciting the Blessing / **§6** Salt / **§7** Distributing the Bread / **§8-10** Order of Precedence of Breads

§1 עַל לֶחֶם גָּמוּר — **Upon actual bread** שֶׁהוּא מֵחֲמֵשֶׁת מִינֵי דָגָן — **that is** made from one of **the five species of grain**[1] מְבָרְכִין לְפָנָיו הַמּוֹצִיא — **one recites, before** eating **it,** the ***hamotzi*** blessing,[2] וּלְאַחֲרָיו בִּרְכַּת הַמָּזוֹן — **and after** eating **it,** ***Bircas HaMazon*** (Grace After Meals).[3] (וְדִין פַּת הַבָּאָה בְכִיסְנִין — **The halachah regarding** the blessings to be recited before and after eating ***pas habaah b'kisnin*** ("*kisnin*-bread")[4] יְבוֹאָר בְּסִימָן מ״ח — **will be explained in *Siman* 48,** *se'ifim* 1-4.)

§2 יֵשׁ לִיזָּהֵר — **It is proper to take care** שֶׁלֹּא לְהַפְסִיק בֵּין נְטִילַת יָדַיִם לְהַמּוֹצִיא — **not to make** any **interruption between** washing ***netilas yadayim***[5] **and** reciting the ***hamotzi*** blessing. אֲבָל מוּתָּר לוֹ לַעֲנוֹת אָמֵן — **However, he is permitted to respond** with **"Amen"** עַל אֵיזֶה בְּרָכָה שֶׁהוּא שׁוֹמֵעַ — **on any blessing that he hears** during that time. וּשְׁהִיָּה כְּדֵי הִילּוּךְ כ״ב אַמָּה — **A delay** between drying the hands and reciting the *hamotzi* blessing[6] **of the amount of time** that it takes **to walk twenty-two *amos*,**[7] אוֹ מִבַּיִת לְבַיִת — **or** actually walking **from one house to**

1. The five species of grain are: Wheat, barley, spelt, oats, and rye. Kitzur uses the term לחם גמור, *actual bread*, to exclude grain preparations that are classified as *pas habaah b'kisnin*, as noted at the end of this *se'if*.

2. בָּרוּךְ אַתָּה ה׳ אֱלֹהֵינוּ מֶלֶךְ הָעוֹלָם הַמּוֹצִיא לֶחֶם מִן הָאָרֶץ, *Blessed are You, HASHEM, our God, King of the universe, Who brings forth bread from the earth.*

3. The laws of *Bircas HaMazon* are set out in *Siman* 44.

4. In general terms, this refers to certain types of baked goods that do not usually serve as the main bread of a meal. See 48:2 for the exact definition of *kisnin*-bread and the parameters of its laws.

5. *Washing the hands* [for a meal]. The laws of *netilas yadayim* are explained in the previous *Siman*.

6. *Mishnah Berurah* 166:4.

7. [Approximately 12 seconds. For the length of an *amah*, see Appendix A.] This refers even to one who remains in the same place for this amount of time (*Mishnah Berurah* 166:5).

LAWS OF BREAKING BREAD AND THE HAMOTZI BLESSING — SIMAN 41:3 70

אֲפִילוּ הִילוּךְ מְעַט, וְכֵן אִם דִּיבֵּר[8] מַה שֶּׁאֵינוֹ לְצָרְכֵי הַסְּעוּדָה[9] מִקְּרֵי הֶפְסֵק. וּבְדִיעֲבַד אִם הִפְסִיק לֵית לָן בָּהּ, וּבִלְבַד שֶׁלֹּא עָשָׂה אֵיזֶה מַעֲשֶׂה בֵּינְתַיִם, אוֹ שֶׁהִפְלִיג בִּדְבָרִים, דְּאָז הָוֵי הֶיסֵּחַ הַדַּעַת וְצָרִיךְ נְטִילָה שֵׁנִית (וְעַיֵּין לְקַמָּן סִימָן מ״ב סְעִיף כ״ב)[10].

ג. בּוֹצֵעַ בַּפַּת בְּמָקוֹם הַמּוּבְחָר שֶׁבּוֹ מִפְּנֵי כְּבוֹד הַבְּרָכָה. וְהַמּוּבְחָר הוּא הַמָּקוֹם הַקָּשֶׁה שֶׁשָּׁם נֶאֱפָה הֵיטֵב, וְהוּא הַמָּקוֹם שֶׁכְּנֶגֶד הַמִּתְבַּקֵּעַ, כִּי בְּמָקוֹם שֶׁמַּתְחִיל לֶאֱפוֹת נִדְחָק הָעִיסָּה עַד שֶׁמִּתְבַּקֵּעַ הַצַּד שֶׁכְּנֶגְדּוֹ[11]. אַךְ זָקֵן, שֶׁקָּשֶׁה לוֹ לֶאֱכוֹל פַּת קָשָׁה,

---

another אֲפִילוּ הִילוּךְ מְעַט — **even** if it is only **short walk** (i.e., less than twenty-two *amos*), וְכֵן אִם דִּיבֵּר — also **if one spoke**[8] מַה שֶּׁאֵינוֹ לְצָרְכֵי הַסְּעוּדָה — **about things that were not for the purpose of the meal;**[9] מִקְּרֵי הֶפְסֵק— any of these **are considered an interruption,** and should be avoided between *netilas yadayim* and *hamotzi.* וּבְדִיעֲבַד אִם הִפְסִיק — However, **after the fact, if he did interrupt** during this time לֵית לָן בָּהּ — **we have no** issue **with it,** and he need not wash again, וּבִלְבַד שֶׁלֹּא עָשָׂה אֵיזֶה מַעֲשֶׂה בֵּינְתַיִם — **as long as he did not engage in any activity between** washing his hands and reciting the *hamotzi* blessing, אוֹ שֶׁהִפְלִיג בִּדְבָרִים — **and he did not talk extensively** regarding things unrelated to the meal; דְּאָז הָוֵי הֶיסֵּחַ הַדַּעַת — **for** if he did so, **then it is considered a diversion** of his **attention** from his hands, וְצָרִיךְ נְטִילָה שֵׁנִית — **and he is required to wash a second time** (וְעַיֵּין לְקַמָּן סִימָן מ״ב סְעִיף כ״ב — **see below, 42:22**).[10]

§3 בּוֹצֵעַ בַּפַּת — **One should cut the bread** בְּמָקוֹם הַמּוּבְחָר שֶׁבּוֹ — **at its choicest part** מִפְּנֵי כְּבוֹד הַבְּרָכָה — **because** this is a show of **respect for the blessing.** וְהַמּוּבְחָר הוּא הַמָּקוֹם הַקָּשֶׁה — **The choicest part is the part** of the bread **that is hardest,** שֶׁשָּׁם נֶאֱפָה הֵיטֵב — **since** it is **there** that **it is baked thoroughly.** Kitzur now explains how to identify the part of the bread that is most well done: וְהוּא הַמָּקוֹם — **This is the part** of the bread שֶׁכְּנֶגֶד הַמִּתְבַּקֵּעַ — **that is opposite the** place where its surface is **cracked.** כִּי בְּמָקוֹם שֶׁמַּתְחִיל לֶאֱפוֹת — It can be concluded that this is where the bread began to bake (and hence, the part that is the most well done), **for in the area** of the bread **where it begins to bake,** נִדְחָק הָעִיסָּה — **the dough** expands and **presses** inward, עַד שֶׁמִּתְבַּקֵּעַ הַצַּד שֶׁכְּנֶגְדּוֹ — **until the** surface on the **opposite side** of this area **cracks** from the pressure of the expanding dough.[11] אַךְ זָקֵן — **However, an elderly person,** שֶׁקָּשֶׁה לוֹ לֶאֱכוֹל פַּת קָשָׁה — **for whom it is**

---

8. Even if he spoke only a small amount, and even if he spoke words of Torah (*Mishnah Berurah* 166:2).

Even a prayer on behalf of one's sustenance (which one should recite before one's meal each day; see *Mishnah Berurah* 166:3) should preferably not be said until after reciting the *hamotzi* blessing (in the event that it was not said before *netilas yadayim*); see *Mishnah Berurah* ibid.

Mishnah Berurah (166:5) writes that when there is no reason to wait, it is best to recite *hamotzi* immediately upon drying the hands, without any delay.

9. An interruption for the purpose of the meal, however (for example, if one requests, that salt be brought to the table; see below *se'if* 6), is not considered an interruption; see *Orach Chaim* 167:6.

10. There, Kitzur sets out which cases require one to wash again due to a lack of mindfulness about the state of his hands. See also note 62 there.

11. [It should be noted that our breads are not baked as were the breads that Kitzur is discussing. Our breads are more uniformly baked and thus there is no part of the crust that is more thoroughly baked. See *Mishnah Berurah* 167:3, which states that care must be taken not to cut the bread where it is burned.]

71 LAWS OF BREAKING BREAD AND THE HAMOTZI BLESSING — SIMAN 41:3

יִבְצַע בִּמְקוֹם הָרַךְ. וּמֵהְיוֹת כִּי אֵין לְהַפְסִיק בִּשְׁהִיוֹת הַחִיתּוּךְ בֵּין בִּרְכַּת הַמּוֹצִיא לַהֲאֲכִילָה, עַל כֵּן חוֹתֵךְ מְעַט סָבִיב הַפַּת כְּעֵין טַבַּעַת[12] בְּעִנְיָן שֶׁאִם יֹאחֵז בִּפְרוּסָה יַעֲלֶה כָּל הַכִּכָּר עִמּוֹ, שֶׁאִם לֹא כֵן חָשׁוּב כִּפְרוּסָה[13] וַאֲנַן בָּעֵינַן שֶׁיְּבָרֵךְ בִּרְכַּת הַמּוֹצִיא בְּעוֹד שֶׁהַפַּת שָׁלֵם[14], וְיַנִּיחֶנָּה מְחוּבֶּרֶת לַפַּת, וִיבָרֵךְ בִּרְכַּת הַמּוֹצִיא, וְאַחַר שֶׁסִּיֵּים הַבְּרָכָה יַפְרִידֶנָּה כְּדֵי שֶׁתִּכְלֶה הַבְּרָכָה בְּעוֹד שֶׁהַפַּת שָׁלֵם. וְכֵן כְּשֶׁבּוֹצֵעַ מִכִּכָּר שֶׁאֵינוֹ שָׁלֵם לֹא יַחְתּוֹךְ לְגַמְרֵי קוֹדֶם הַבְּרָכָה, כְּדֵי שֶׁתְּהֵא בִּשְׁעַת הַבְּרָכָה יוֹתֵר גָּדוֹל[15]. וּבְשַׁבָּת[16] לֹא יַחְתּוֹךְ כְּלָל בַּכִּכָּר עַד אַחַר הַבְּרָכָה, כְּדֵי שֶׁיִּהְיוּ הַכִּכָּרוֹת שְׁלֵמוֹת

---

difficult to eat hard bread, יִבְצַע בִּמְקוֹם הָרַךְ — **should** cut and eat **the soft part** of the bread.

וּמֵהְיוֹת כִּי אֵין לְהַפְסִיק — Since one should not interrupt, בִּשְׁהִיוֹת הַחִיתּוּךְ — even **with an** unnecessary **delay** caused **by cutting** the bread, בֵּין בִּרְכַּת הַמּוֹצִיא לַהֲאֲכִילָה — **between the** ***hamotzi*** **blessing and the eating** of the bread, עַל כֵּן — **therefore,** חוֹתֵךְ מְעַט סָבִיב הַפַּת — before reciting the *hamotzi* blessing **one should make a small cut around the bread** כְּעֵין טַבַּעַת — **as in the shape of a ring,** i.e., circling the entire loaf.[12] However, one must take care not to make this cut too deep: בְּעִנְיָן שֶׁאִם יֹאחֵז בִּפְרוּסָה — The cut should be made **so that if he were to hold** the bread by **the piece** to be cut, יַעֲלֶה כָּל הַכִּכָּר עִמּוֹ — it would be connected strongly enough that **the rest of the loaf would come up with it.** שֶׁאִם לֹא כֵן— **for if it would not,** but would rather break off when lifted in this way, חָשׁוּב כִּפְרוּסָה— then **it is considered to be** already **broken** off,[13] וַאֲנַן בָּעֵינַן — **and,** for the honor of the blessing, **we endeavor** whenever possible שֶׁיְּבָרֵךְ בִּרְכַּת הַמּוֹצִיא — **that one should recite the** ***hamotzi*** **blessing** בְּעוֹד שֶׁהַפַּת שָׁלֵם — **while the bread is still whole.**[14]

וְיַנִּיחֶנָּה מְחוּבֶּרֶת לַפַּת — After making this initial cut, **he should leave** the piece **connected to** the main part of **the bread** וִיבָרֵךְ בִּרְכַּת הַמּוֹצִיא — **and recite the** ***hamotzi*** **blessing.** וְאַחַר שֶׁסִּיֵּים הַבְּרָכָה — Only **after he completes** the recitation of **the blessing** יַפְרִידֶנָּה — **should he separate** the piece, כְּדֵי שֶׁתִּכְלֶה הַבְּרָכָה — **so that the blessing is concluded** בְּעוֹד שֶׁהַפַּת שָׁלֵם— **while the bread is still whole.** וְכֵן — **Similarly,** כְּשֶׁבּוֹצֵעַ מִכִּכָּר שֶׁאֵינוֹ שָׁלֵם — **when cutting a loaf that is not whole:** לֹא יַחְתּוֹךְ לְגַמְרֵי קוֹדֶם הַבְּרָכָה — **he should not cut** the piece off **completely before the blessing** is concluded, כְּדֵי שֶׁתְּהֵא בִּשְׁעַת הַבְּרָכָה יוֹתֵר גָּדוֹל — **so that at the time** that **the blessing** is recited, the bread **will be larger.**[15] וּבְשַׁבָּת — When cutting the bread **for the Shabbos** meal,[16] לֹא יַחְתּוֹךְ כְּלָל בַּכִּכָּר — **he should not cut the loaf at all,** i.e., even this initial cut, עַד אַחַר הַבְּרָכָה — **until after** the recitation of **the blessing,** כְּדֵי שֶׁיִּהְיוּ הַכִּכָּרוֹת שְׁלֵמוֹת מַמָּשׁ — **so that the** two **loaves are completely**

---

12. This is a preliminary cut, made to shorten the time it takes to cut the bread when he concludes the blessing. The reason that the bread is not completely cut before the blessing is so that the blessing can be recited upon a whole loaf, as Kitzur proceeds to explain.

13. Even if one were able to lift the bread by the main part and the piece to be cut would not break off, it is still considered to be already broken, if, when lifting it by the smaller piece, the rest of the loaf would fall off (*Mishnah Berurah* 167:6).

14. See below, *se'if* 8.

15. Even though it is not a whole loaf, one should still not cut off a piece before reciting the blessing, since it shows greater respect for the blessing when it is recited on a larger piece of bread (see below, *se'if* 8).

16. Or when cutting for a festival meal (*Mishnah Berurah* 167:10).

LAWS OF BREAKING BREAD AND THE HAMOTZI BLESSING — SIMAN 41:4 72

מַמָּשׁ[17] (עַיֵּין לְקַמָּן סִימָן ע״ז סְעִיף י״ז)[18]. וְגַם בְּחוֹל אִם הוּא עוּגָה דַקָּה יְבָרֵךְ קוֹדֶם הַבְּצִיעָה, כֵּיוָן שֶׁאֵין שְׁהִיָּה בַּשְּׁבִירָה.

ד. לֹא יִבְצַע פְּרוּסָה קְטַנָּה[19], מִפְּנֵי שֶׁנִּרְאֶה כְּצַר עַיִן, וְלֹא פְּרוּסָה יוֹתֵר מִכְּבֵיצָה[20], לְפִי שֶׁנִּרְאֶה כְּרַעַבְתָן[21]. וְדַוְקָא כְּשֶׁאוֹכֵל לְבַדּוֹ, אֲבָל אִם אוֹכֵל עִם הַרְבֵּה בְּנֵי אָדָם וְצָרִיךְ לִיתֵּן מִן הַפְּרוּסָה לְכָל אֶחָד כְּזַיִת[22], מוּתָּר לִבְצוֹעַ כְּפִי מַה שֶּׁצָּרִיךְ לוֹ[23]. וּבְשַׁבָּת, אֲפִילוּ אִם אוֹכֵל לְבַדּוֹ, מוּתָּר לִבְצוֹעַ כְּפִי מַה שֶּׁצָּרִיךְ לְכָל הַסְּעוּדָה, מִפְּנֵי

---

whole[17] (עַיֵּין לְקַמָּן סִימָן ע״ז סְעִיף י״ז — see below, 77:17).[18] וְגַם בְּחוֹל — When eating **during the weekday as well,** אִם הוּא עוּגָה דַקָּה — **if** he is eating **a small roll** יְבָרֵךְ קוֹדֶם הַבְּצִיעָה — **he should recite the blessing before cutting** the bread at all, כֵּיוָן שֶׁאֵין שְׁהִיָּה בַּשְּׁבִירָה — **since there is no** significant **delay** caused **when breaking** off a piece from the small roll.

§4 לֹא יִבְצַע פְּרוּסָה קְטַנָּה — **One should not cut off a small piece**[19] from the loaf, מִפְּנֵי שֶׁנִּרְאֶה כְּצַר עַיִן — **for he would appear miserly;** וְלֹא פְּרוּסָה יוֹתֵר מִכְּבֵיצָה — he should **also not** cut off **a piece larger than** the size of **an egg,**[20] לְפִי שֶׁנִּרְאֶה כְּרַעַבְתָן — **for he would appear gluttonous.**[21] וְדַוְקָא כְּשֶׁאוֹכֵל לְבַדּוֹ — **However,** this applies **only when he is eating alone;** אֲבָל אִם אוֹכֵל עִם הַרְבֵּה בְּנֵי אָדָם — **but if he is eating with many people,** וְצָרִיךְ לִיתֵּן מִן הַפְּרוּסָה — **and he must give from the piece** that he cuts from the loaf לְכָל אֶחָד כְּזַיִת — at least **a** ***kezayis*** **to each person,**[22] מוּתָּר לִבְצוֹעַ כְּפִי מַה שֶּׁצָּרִיךְ לוֹ — **it is permitted for him to cut** a larger piece, **corresponding to the amount that he needs** to distribute to all of those partaking of the meal.[23]

וּבְשַׁבָּת — When cutting bread **for** the **Shabbos** meal, אֲפִילוּ אִם אוֹכֵל לְבַדּוֹ — **even if he is eating alone,** מוּתָּר לִבְצוֹעַ — **it is permitted for him** to initially **cut** a piece כְּפִי מַה שֶּׁצָּרִיךְ לְכָל הַסְּעוּדָה — large **enough for his needs for the entire meal.** מִפְּנֵי

---

17. The Shabbos and festival meals must begin with the recitation of the *hamotzi* blessing upon two whole loaves of bread; see below, 77:17. In this case, the need to have whole loaves outweighs the stringency of shortening the cutting time (see *Mishnah Berurah* 167:10).

18. There, Kitzur writes that although one should not make this initial cut, it is customary to mark the loaf with the knife so that he will not have to spend time looking for the proper place to cut.

19. Smaller than a *kezayis* [the volume of an olive — between .6 and 1.1 fl. oz. (17.3-33.3 cc.); see Appendix A] (*Mishnah Berurah* 167:8).

20. This is equivalent to twice the *kezayis* measurement; see previous note. Kitzur refers here to the piece from which he is planning to eat. However, he may cut a larger piece and then cut smaller pieces from it (*Mishnah Berurah* 167:9).

21. That is, he should not initially cut from the loaf a piece large enough to suffice for the entire meal. Rather, he should cut off a piece smaller than the size of an egg from which to eat right away, and then cut off from the loaf as necessary for the rest of the meal.

22. He should not give less than a *kezayis,* so that he does not appear miserly. Also, ideally one should eat a full *kezayis* right after reciting the *hamotzi* blessing (*Mishnah Berurah* 167:15; see also following *se'if*).

23. When one person recites the *hamotzi* blessing on behalf of many people, he should initially give each of them from the piece that he cuts off after reciting *hamotzi.* Thus, he must cut a piece large enough to enable him to distribute a *kezayis* to each person from it (*Mishnah Berurah* 167:14; see *Kaf HaChaim* 167:19).

73 LAWS OF BREAKING BREAD AND THE HAMOTZI BLESSING — SIMAN 41:5

כְּבוֹד הַשַּׁבָּת לְהַרְאוֹת חֲבִיבַת סְעוּדַּת שַׁבָּת שֶׁחָפֵץ לֶאֱכוֹל בָּהּ הַרְבֵּה. יֵשׁ לֶאֱכוֹל אֶת הַפְּרוּסָה שֶׁבָּצַע עָלֶיהָ קוֹדֶם שֶׁיֹּאכַל פַּת אַחֵר, וְהוּא מִשּׁוּם חִבּוּב מִצְוָה כֵּיוָן שֶׁבֵּירַךְ עָלֶיהָ[24]. וְטוֹב לִיזָּהֵר שֶׁלֹּא יִתֵּן מִמֶּנָּה[25] לְנָכְרִי, אוֹ לִבְהֵמָה וְעוֹף[26].

ה. קוֹדֶם שֶׁיְּבָרֵךְ, יִתֵּן שְׁתֵּי יָדָיו עַל הַפַּת, שֶׁיֵּשׁ בָּהֶן י׳ אֶצְבָּעוֹת כְּנֶגֶד י׳ מִצְוֹת הַתְּלוּיוֹת בְּפַת: "לֹא תַחֲרֹשׁ בְּשׁוֹר וּבַחֲמֹר"[27] (דברים כב, י), כִּלְאַיִם[28], לֶקֶט[29], שִׁכְחָה[30], פֵּאָה[31], "לֹא תַחְסֹם" (שם כה, ד)[32]**, תְּרוּמָה[33], מַעֲשֵׂר רִאשׁוֹן[34], מַעֲשֵׂר שֵׁנִי[35],**

כְּבוֹד הַשַּׁבָּת — This is permitted **because** it is **an honor for the Shabbos** **לְהַרְאוֹת חֲבִיבַת סְעוּדַּת שַׁבָּת** — **to show** his **love for** the mitzvah of eating **the Shabbos meal**, **שֶׁחָפֵץ לֶאֱכוֹל בָּהּ הַרְבֵּה** — **that he wishes to eat a large amount during the meal.** **יֵשׁ לֶאֱכוֹל אֶת הַפְּרוּסָה שֶׁבָּצַע עָלֶיהָ** — Even during the week, **it is proper to eat the piece that he cut off** after reciting the *hamotzi* blessing **קוֹדֶם שֶׁיֹּאכַל פַּת אַחֵר** — **before eating other bread; וְהוּא מִשּׁוּם חִבּוּב מִצְוָה** — **this** is done **as** a show **of love for the mitzvah, כֵּיוָן שֶׁבֵּירַךְ עָלֶיהָ** — **since the blessing was recited upon this** piece.[24] **וְטוֹב לִיזָּהֵר** — **It is proper to take care** **שֶׁלֹּא יִתֵּן מִמֶּנָּה לְנָכְרִי** — **not to give** any of the *hamotzi* piece[25] **to an idolater** **אוֹ לִבְהֵמָה וְעוֹף** — **or to an animal or bird.**[26]

§5 קוֹדֶם שֶׁיְּבָרֵךְ — **Before reciting the blessing** **יִתֵּן שְׁתֵּי יָדָיו עַל הַפַּת** — **he should place both of his hands on the bread, שֶׁיֵּשׁ בָּהֶן י׳ אֶצְבָּעוֹת** — **for** the two hands **have ten fingers** **כְּנֶגֶד י׳ מִצְוֹת הַתְּלוּיוֹת בְּפַת** — **corresponding to the ten mitzvos involved in** the production of **bread:** **"לֹא תַחֲרֹשׁ בְּשׁוֹר וּבַחֲמֹר"** — (1) ***You shall not plow with an ox and a donkey*** *together* (*Devarim* 22:10);[27] **כִּלְאַיִם** — (2) **forbidden mixtures;**[28] **לֶקֶט** — (3) **gleanings;**[29] **שִׁכְחָה** — (4) **forgotten produce;**[30] **פֵּאָה** — (5) **edge;**[31] **לֹא תַחְסֹם** — (6) ***You shall not muzzle*** *an ox in its threshing* (ibid. 25:4);[32] **תְּרוּמָה** — (7) ***terumah;***[33] **מַעֲשֵׂר רִאשׁוֹן** — (8) **the "first" tithe;**[34] **מַעֲשֵׂר שֵׁנִי** — (9) **the "second" tithe;**[35]

---

24. It is an expression of love for the mitzvah of the *hamotzi* blessing to eat the "piece of *hamotzi*" (that is, the piece that he cut after reciting the blessing) with an appetite. He should therefore eat that piece before any other (*Rama* 167:20). *Mishnah Berurah* (167:97) cites *Shelah*, who states that one should also leave over a bit of the *hamotzi* piece to eat after he finishes the rest of his food, so that the taste of the *hamotzi* piece will remain in his mouth.

25. After reciting the blessing, one cuts off a larger piece and then cuts a smaller one from that to eat. This halachah refers to both of those pieces (*Mishnah Berurah* 167:97).

26. To do this would detract from the honor of the mitzvah (*Mishnah Berurah* ibid.).

27. See below, *Siman* 175:2 ff.

28. In Eretz Yisrael, it is forbidden to plant different kinds of crops together; see *Vayikra* 19:19. See below, *Siman* 174:3, for the law outside of Eretz Yisrael.

29. When reaping, one may not gather the ears of grain that fall from the reaper; they must be left for the poor; see *Vayikra* 19:9. [Generally, this law as well as those that follow (with the exception of *challah;* see introduction to *Siman* 35) are in effect only in Eretz Yisrael.]

30. Bundles of harvest that are forgotten in the field must be left for the poor; see *Devarim* 24:19.

31. A portion of the standing crop must be left unharvested and abandoned for the poor; see *Vayikra* 19:9.

32. See below, *Siman* 186, for further discussion of this prohibition.

33. The portion of the crop that is given to the Kohen; see *Bamidbar* 18:12.

34. A tenth of the crop that is given to the Levi; see *Bamidbar* 18:24.

35. An additional tenth of the crop that must be taken to Jerusalem for consumption there.

LAWS OF BREAKING BREAD AND THE HAMOTZI BLESSING — SIMAN 41:5 74

חַלָּה[36]. וְלָכֵן יֵשׁ י׳ תֵּיבוֹת בְּבִרְכַּת הַמּוֹצִיא, וְי׳ תֵּיבוֹת בְּפָסוּק (תהלים קמה, טו) ״עֵינֵי כֹל אֵלֶיךָ יְשַׂבֵּרוּ״[37], וְי׳ תֵּיבוֹת בְּפָסוּק (דברים ח, ח) ״אֶרֶץ חִטָּה וּשְׂעֹרָה״[38], וְי׳ תֵּיבוֹת בְּפָסוּק (בראשית כז, כח) ״וְיִתֶּן לְךָ״[39]. וּכְשֶׁיֹּאמַר אֶת הַשֵּׁם יַגְבִּיהַּ אֶת הַלֶּחֶם. וּבְשַׁבָּת יַגְבִּיהַּ שְׁתֵּיהֶן. וִיבָרֵךְ בְּכַוָּנָה. וִידַקְדֵּק לְהוֹצִיא הֵיטֵב אֶת הַהֵ״א שֶׁל ״הַמּוֹצִיא״[40], וְיִתֵּן רֶיוַח קְצָת בֵּין תֵּיבַת ״לֶחֶם״ לְתֵיבַת ״מִן״, שֶׁלֹּא לְהַבְלִיעַ אֶת הַמֵּ״ם[41]. וּלְאַחַר הַבְּרָכָה, יֹאכַל מִיָּד, כִּי אָסוּר לְהַפְסִיק בֵּין הַבְּרָכָה לִתְחִלַּת הָאֲכִילָה, אֲפִילּוּ לַעֲנִיַּת אָמֵן[42].

יֵשׁ י׳ תֵּיבוֹת בְּבִרְכַּת הַמּוֹצִיא — **חַלָּה** — (10) and *challah.*[36] **וְלָכֵן** — Therefore, **there are ten words in the *hamotzi* blessing,** **וְי׳ תֵּיבוֹת בְּפָסוּק** — **and ten words in the verse** that speaks of Hashem's providing nourishment (*Tehillim* 145:15): **״עֵינֵי כֹל אֵלֶיךָ יְשַׂבֵּרוּ״** — ***The eyes of all look to You with hope*** *and You give them their food in its proper time;*[37] **וְי׳ תֵּיבוֹת בְּפָסוּק** — **and ten words in the verse** describing the produce of the Land of Israel (*Devarim* 8:8): **״אֶרֶץ חִטָּה וּשְׂעֹרָה״** — ***A land of wheat, barley,*** *grape, fig and pomegranate; a land of oil-olives and date-honey;*[38] **וְי׳ תֵּיבוֹת בְּפָסוּק** — **and ten words in the verse** that refers to the blessings of the land (*Bereishis* 27:28): **״וְיִתֶּן לְךָ״** — ***And may*** *God* ***give you*** *of the dew of the heavens and of the fatness of the earth, and abundant grain and wine.*[39]

וּכְשֶׁיֹּאמַר אֶת הַשֵּׁם — **When one recites the Name of Hashem** in the blessing, **יַגְבִּיהַּ אֶת הַלֶּחֶם** — **he should lift the bread;** **וּבְשַׁבָּת יַגְבִּיהַּ שְׁתֵּיהֶן** — **on Shabbos,** when one recites the blessing upon two loaves, **he should lift both** of them.

וִיבָרֵךְ בְּכַוָּנָה — **One should recite the blessing with concentration,** **וִידַקְדֵּק לְהוֹצִיא הֵיטֵב** — **and be meticulous to pronounce well** **אֶת הַהֵ״א שֶׁל ״הַמּוֹצִיא״** — **the** letter *hei* of the word ***hamotzi;***[40] **וְיִתֵּן רֶיוַח קְצָת** — **and he should pause slightly** **בֵּין תֵּיבַת ״לֶחֶם״ לְתֵיבַת ״מִן״** — **between reciting the word *"lechem"* and the word "*min*,"** **שֶׁלֹּא לְהַבְלִיעַ אֶת הַמֵּ״ם** — **so as not to swallow one of the "*mem*"s.**[41]

וּלְאַחַר הַבְּרָכָה, יֹאכַל מִיָּד — **After** reciting **the blessing, he should immediately eat,** **כִּי אָסוּר לְהַפְסִיק** — **for it is forbidden to make an interruption** **בֵּין הַבְּרָכָה לִתְחִלַּת הָאֲכִילָה** — **between** his recitation of **the blessing and his eating** of the bread, **אֲפִילּוּ לַעֲנִיַּת אָמֵן** — **even to respond with "Amen"** to any blessing.[42]

During the third and sixth years of the *shemittah* cycle (the seven-year cycle that ends with the *shemittah* year), *maasar ani* (the pauper's tithe) is substituted for *maaser sheni*. See *Devarim* 14:22-23; 28-29.

36. A portion of dough set aside for the Kohen; see *Siman* 35.

37. The full verse reads: עֵינֵי כֹל אֵלֶיךָ יְשַׂבֵּרוּ וְאַתָּה נוֹתֵן לָהֶם אֶת אָכְלָם בְּעִתּוֹ, *The eyes of all look to You with hope and You give them their food in its proper time.*

38. The full verse reads: אֶרֶץ חִטָּה וּשְׂעֹרָה וְגֶפֶן וּתְאֵנָה וְרִמּוֹן אֶרֶץ זֵית שֶׁמֶן וּדְבָשׁ, *A land of wheat, barley, grape, fig, and pomegranate; a land of oil-olives and date-honey.*

39. The full verse reads: וְיִתֶּן לְךָ הָאֱלֹהִים מִטַּל הַשָּׁמַיִם וּמִשְׁמַנֵּי הָאָרֶץ וְרֹב דָּגָן וְתִירֹשׁ, *And may God give you of the dew of the heavens and of the fatness of the earth, and abundant grain and wine.* For an in-depth explanation of the correlation between the ten fingers and the ten mitzvos of bread, and to the above verses, see *Bach* §167 s.v. ומ״ש ויתן שתי ידיו.

40. This is the first syllable of the word "*hamotzi.*"

41. The last letter of the word לֶחֶם (*bread*) and the first letter of the word מִן (*from*) are both *mem* (pronounced like the English "m"). If one were to recite the words without any pause, one of the *mems* would not be pronounced, and the words would sound like *"lechemin."*

42. I.e., until he chews and swallows at least some of the bread (*Mishnah Berurah* 167:35). Thus, if many people are dining together, and

75 LAWS OF BREAKING BREAD AND THE HAMOTZI BLESSING — SIMAN 41:6-7

וְיֵשׁ לֶאֱכוֹל כְּזַיִת בְּלִי הֶפְסֵק, (וְעַיֵּין לְקַמָּן סִימָן נ׳ סְעִיף ה׳)[43].

ו. מִצְוָה לְהָבִיא עַל הַשֻּׁלְחָן מֶלַח קוֹדֶם שֶׁיִּבְצַע, וְיִטְבּוֹל פְּרוּסַת הַמּוֹצִיא בְּמֶלַח[44], לְפִי שֶׁהַשֻּׁלְחָן דּוֹמֶה לְמִזְבֵּחַ, (וְעַיֵּין לְקַמָּן סִימָן מ״ד)[45], וְהָאֲכִילָה לְקָרְבָּן[46], וְנֶאֱמַר (וַיִּקְרָא ב, יג) ״עַל כָּל קָרְבָּנְךָ תַּקְרִיב מֶלַח״. וּלְפִי שֶׁהַשֻּׁלְחָן דּוֹמֶה לְמִזְבֵּחַ, טוֹב לִיזָּהֵר שֶׁלֹּא לַהֲרוֹג עָלָיו כִּנָּה[47].

ז. אִם מְחַלֵּק פְּרוּסוֹת הַמּוֹצִיא לְהַמְסוּבִּין, לֹא יִזְרְקֵן, דְּאָסוּר לִזְרוֹק אֶת הַפַּת[48].

וְיֵשׁ לֶאֱכוֹל כְּזַיִת — It is proper to eat a *kezayis* of bread **בְּלִי הֶפְסֵק** — without interruption (**וְעַיֵּין לְקַמָּן סִימָן נ׳ סְעִיף ה׳** — see below, 50:5).[13]

§6 מִצְוָה לְהָבִיא עַל הַשֻּׁלְחָן מֶלַח — **One should bring salt to the table** **קוֹדֶם שֶׁיִּבְצַע** — **before breaking bread,** **וְיִטְבּוֹל פְּרוּסַת הַמּוֹצִיא בְּמֶלַח** — **and he should dip the piece upon which the** ***hamotzi*** was recited **into the salt.**[44] **לְפִי שֶׁהַשֻּׁלְחָן דּוֹמֶה לְמִזְבֵּחַ** — This is **because the table is like the Altar** in the *Beis HaMikdash* (**וְעַיֵּין לְקַמָּן סִימָן מ״ד** — **see below, 44:4**),[45] **וְהָאֲכִילָה לְקָרְבָּן** — **and the eating** around the table **is like a sacrifice** offered upon the Altar,[46] **וְנֶאֱמַר** — **and the verse states** (*Vayikra* 2:13): **״עַל כָּל קָרְבָּנְךָ תַּקְרִיב מֶלַח״** — ***On your every offering shall you offer salt.*** **וּלְפִי שֶׁהַשֻּׁלְחָן דּוֹמֶה לְמִזְבֵּחַ** — For this reason **too** — that is, **because the table is like the Altar** — **טוֹב לִיזָּהֵר** — **it is** also **proper to take care** **שֶׁלֹּא לַהֲרוֹג עָלָיו כִּנָּה** — **not to kill a louse upon it.**[47]

§7 אִם מְחַלֵּק פְּרוּסוֹת הַמּוֹצִיא לְהַמְסוּבִּין — **When one distributes the pieces upon which** ***hamotzi*** was recited **to those dining** with him, **לֹא יִזְרְקֵן** — **he should not throw** the pieces to them, **דְּאָסוּר לִזְרוֹק אֶת הַפַּת** — **for it is forbidden to throw bread.**[48]

---

each person recites a *hamotzi* on his own bread, they must take care not to respond with Amen to each other's blessings after reciting their *hamotzi* blessing, before eating some of the bread (*Mishnah Berurah* 167:35). See below, 50:5, which states that ideally, one should not wait (even without talking) longer than *k'dei dibbur* [lit., *the amount (of time) of an utterance*; approximately 1-2 seconds; see *Kelalim*] after reciting *hamotzi,* before partaking of the bread.

43. There, Kitzur sets out the halachos regarding one who did interrupt between his recitation of the blessing of *hamotzi* and his eating.

Rabbi Moshe Feinstein (*Igros Moshe, Orach Chaim* IV, §41) writes that one should take care to eat a *kezayis* of bread within three minutes at one point during the meal. [Generally, any food eaten within the context of a meal that has bread is exempt from a separate obligation to recite upon it a *berachah rishonah* (first-blessing) or *berachah acharonah* (final-blessing); see below, *Siman* 43. However, these foods are exempt only if the bread was eaten during this time span. See also below, *Siman* 43, note 4, for further discussion of this topic.]

44. Based upon Kabbalistic reasons, one should dip the bread into the salt three times (*Mishnah Berurah* 167:33).

45. Kitzur explains there that just as the sacrifices offered on the Altar would atone for the sins of the Jewish people, so too one's table atones for his sins, since it is a place around which he hosts guests. *Mishnah Berurah* (167:30) writes that the table atones for one's sins, as it were, since he gives of his bread to the poor (see *Rashi* and *Tosafos* to *Chagigah* 27a s.v. שלחנו). See also *Shaar HaTziyun* 167:25, which states that the table has the power of atonement when one recites words of Torah around it (see below, 42:5).

46. Since he eats to strengthen himself so that he can be healthy and strong to serve Hashem (*Mishnah Berurah* 167:31; see above, 31:2).

47. Killing a louse on the table does not conform to the proper respect one must show to the table upon which one eats, which is likened to the Altar.

48. See below, 42:9. It is also a lack of respect

וְגַם לֹא יִתְּנֵהוּ לְתוֹךְ יָדוֹ[49], אֶלָּא יַנִּיחֶנָּה לְפָנָיו.

ח. מִצְוָה לִבְצוֹעַ עַל הַפַּת הֶחָשׁוּב יוֹתֵר[50]. וְלָכֵן, אִם יֵשׁ לְפָנָיו חֲתִיכָה פַּת וּפַת שָׁלֵם, וְדַעְתּוֹ לֶאֱכוֹל תּוֹךְ הַסְּעוּדָה מִשְּׁתֵּיהֶן[51], וּשְׁתֵּיהֶן מִמִּין אֶחָד[52], אַף עַל פִּי שֶׁהַפַּת הַשָּׁלֵם הוּא קָטָן יוֹתֵר מִן הַחֲתִיכָה, וְגַם אֵינוֹ נָקִי[53] כְּמוֹ הַחֲתִיכָה, מִכָּל מָקוֹם יִבְצַע עַל הַשָּׁלֵם, דְּהוּא חָשׁוּב יוֹתֵר[54]. אֲבָל אִם אֵינוֹ מִמִּין אֶחָד, אֶלָּא שֶׁהַשָּׁלֵם מִמִּין גָּרוּעַ, כְּגוֹן שֶׁהַשָּׁלֵם הוּא פַּת כּוּסְמִין וְהַחֲתִיכָה הוּא פַּת חִטִּים, אֲפִילוּ הִיא קְטַנָּה, מְבָרֵךְ עַל שֶׁל חִטִּים[55]. וְאִם הַשָּׁלֵם הוּא שֶׁל שְׂעוֹרִים,

---

וְגַם לֹא יִתְּנֵהוּ לְתוֹךְ יָדוֹ — Also, he should not put the piece directly **into the hand** of the recipient;[49] **אֶלָּא יַנִּיחֶנָּה לְפָנָיו — rather, he should place it down before him.**

§8 **מִצְוָה לִבְצוֹעַ — It is a mitzvah to break** the bread, i.e., to recite the blessing, **עַל הַפַּת הֶחָשׁוּב יוֹתֵר — upon the bread that is more significant.**[50] **וְלָכֵן — Therefore, אִם יֵשׁ לְפָנָיו חֲתִיכָה פַּת — if one has before him a cut piece of bread וּפַת שָׁלֵם — and a whole** loaf or roll **of bread, וְדַעְתּוֹ לֶאֱכוֹל תּוֹךְ הַסְּעוּדָה מִשְּׁתֵּיהֶן — and he plans on eating from both during the meal,**[51] **וּשְׁתֵּיהֶן מִמִּין אֶחָד — and they are both** made **of the same type** of grain,[52] **אַף עַל פִּי שֶׁהַפַּת הַשָּׁלֵם** — then the halachah is that **even if the whole bread הוּא קָטָן יוֹתֵר מִן הַחֲתִיכָה — is smaller than the cut piece, וְגַם אֵינוֹ נָקִי כְּמוֹ הַחֲתִיכָה — and also not as fine**[53] **as the cut piece, מִכָּל מָקוֹם — nevertheless, יִבְצַע עַל הַשָּׁלֵם — he should break** the bread, i.e., recite the blessing, **upon the complete one, דְּהוּא חָשׁוּב יוֹתֵר — since it is** considered the **more significant** one.[54]

אֲבָל אִם אֵינוֹ מִמִּין אֶחָד — However, if the two breads before him **were not made of the same type** of grain, **אֶלָּא שֶׁהַשָּׁלֵם מִמִּין גָּרוּעַ** — but **rather, the whole** bread **was** made **of an inferior type — כְּגוֹן — for example, שֶׁהַשָּׁלֵם הוּא פַּת כּוּסְמִין — if the whole one was spelt bread וְהַחֲתִיכָה הוּא פַּת חִטִּים — and the cut piece was wheat bread — אֲפִילוּ הִיא קְטַנָּה** — then, **even if** the cut piece **was smaller מְבָרֵךְ עַל שֶׁל חִטִּים — he should recite the blessing upon** the bread made **of wheat** (although it is not whole and it is smaller).[55] **וְאִם הַשָּׁלֵם הוּא שֶׁל שְׂעוֹרִים — If the whole** bread **was**

---

for the mitzvah to throw the piece upon which *hamotzi* was recited (*Mishnah Berurah* 167:88).

49. It is proper to avoid placing the bread in his hand, since it is the custom to place the bread into the hand of a mourner (see *Mishnah Berurah* 167:90).

50. This *se'if* discusses four qualities of bread that determine its significance: (1) the grain with which the bread is made; (2) whether the loaf of bread or roll is whole or broken; (3) the quality of the flour from which the bread is made; and, (4) the size of the bread. This *se'if* sets out the priorities among these qualities.

51. See below, *seif* 10.

52. Of the five species of grain (listed above, note 1), some are considered more significant, as will be explained later in this *se'if.*

53. Literally, *clean.* Flour from which all the bran was sifted out is considered fine; coarser flour includes some level of bran as well.

54. The quality of "wholeness" takes precedence over the qualities of fineness of the flour and of the size of the pieces. One therefore recites the blessing upon the whole loaf despite it being coarser and smaller than the cut piece.

55. Two species of grain, wheat and barley, are mentioned by name in the verse that enumerates the seven species with which Eretz Yisrael was blessed (*Devarim* 8:8). The other three species of grain are considered inferior to these two. This halachah teaches that the species of a grain is the predominant consideration in the precedence of breads, and outweighs all others. Thus, one who has one bread of any

77 LAWS OF BREAKING BREAD AND THE HAMOTZI BLESSING — SIMAN 41:9

אַף עַל פִּי שֶׁהוּא גָרוּעַ מֵחִטִּין, מִכָּל מָקוֹם כֵּיוָן שֶׁגַּם שְׂעוֹרָה נִזְכָּר בְּפֵירוּשׁ בַּפָּסוּק, וְגַם הוּא שְׁלֵמָה, לָכֵן יְרֵא שָׁמַיִם יֵשׁ לַחֲלוֹק כָּבוֹד גַּם לָזֶה שֶׁל שְׂעוֹרִים וְשָׁלֵם[56]. כֵּיצַד עוֹשֶׂה? מֵנִיחַ אֶת הַחֲתִיכָה תַּחַת הַשְּׁלֵמָה וּבוֹצֵעַ מִשְּׁתֵּיהֶן יַחַד[57]. אִם שְׁתֵּיהֶן שְׁלֵמוֹת, אוֹ שְׁתֵּיהֶן חֲתִיכוֹת, וּשְׁתֵּיהֶן מִמִּין אֶחָד, יְבָרֵךְ עַל הַנָּקִי יוֹתֵר. וְאִם שְׁתֵּיהֶן שָׁווֹת בִּנְקִיּוּת, יְבָרֵךְ עַל הַיּוֹתֵר גָּדוֹל[58].

ט. אִם יֵשׁ לְפָנָיו פַּת יִשְׂרָאֵל וּפַת עַכּוּ״ם, וְאֵינוֹ נִזְהָר מִפַּת עַכּוּ״ם[59], אִם שְׁתֵּיהֶן

---

made **from barley,** **אַף עַל פִּי שֶׁהוּא גָרוּעַ מֵחִטִּין — even though it is inferior to wheat,** **מִכָּל מָקוֹם — nevertheless,** **כֵּיוָן שֶׁגַּם שְׂעוֹרָה נִזְכָּר בְּפֵירוּשׁ בַּפָּסוּק — since barley is also mentioned explicitly in the verse** that enumerates the seven species with which Eretz Yisrael was blessed (*Devarim* 8:8), **וְגַם הוּא שְׁלֵמָה — and it is also whole,** **לָכֵן יְרֵא שָׁמַיִם יֵשׁ לַחֲלוֹק כָּבוֹד — therefore, a God-fearing person should show respect** **גַּם לָזֶה שֶׁל שְׂעוֹרִים וְשָׁלֵם — to the whole** loaf of **barley bread as well.**[56] **כֵּיצַד עוֹשֶׂה — How should he do** this? **מֵנִיחַ אֶת הַחֲתִיכָה תַּחַת הַשְּׁלֵמָה — He should place the cut piece underneath the whole** bread, **וּבוֹצֵעַ מִשְּׁתֵּיהֶן יַחַד — and,** holding both, recite the blessing and **break both of them together.**[57]

אִם שְׁתֵּיהֶן שְׁלֵמוֹת — If both breads before him **are whole,** **אוֹ שְׁתֵּיהֶן חֲתִיכוֹת — or both are cut pieces,** **וּשְׁתֵּיהֶן מִמִּין אֶחָד — and they are both** made **of the same type** of grain, **יְבָרֵךְ עַל הַנָּקִי יוֹתֵר —** then **he should recite the blessing upon** the one made of **the finer** flour. **וְאִם שְׁתֵּיהֶן שָׁווֹת בִּנְקִיּוּת — If they are both equally fine,** **יְבָרֵךְ עַל הַיּוֹתֵר גָּדוֹל — he should recite the blessing upon the one that is larger.**[58]

§9 **אִם יֵשׁ לְפָנָיו — If** a person **has before him** two breads, **פַּת יִשְׂרָאֵל וּפַת עַכּוּ״ם — bread** baked **by a Jew and** kosher **bread** baked **by an idolater,** **וְאֵינוֹ נִזְהָר מִפַּת עַכּוּ״ם — and he does not avoid bread** baked **by an idolater,**[59] then the halachah is as follows: **אִם שְׁתֵּיהֶן שְׁלֵמוֹת — If both** breads **are whole**

---

of the other species (spelt, rye, or oat) and another of wheat or barley, recites the blessing upon the one of wheat or barley, even if the latter is cut, smaller, and coarser (see *Mishnah Berurah* 168:3).

56. In the verse listing the species of the Land of Israel, wheat is mentioned before barley. Therefore, all other things being equal, bread made of wheat takes precedence over one made of barley. In this case, however, the barley bread has the additional quality of being whole, in contrast to the wheat bread that is cut. This, together with the fact that barley is mentioned explicitly in that verse, is a reason that a God-fearing person should also show respect for the barley bread (see *Mishnah Berurah* 168:3). [Note that the rye bread sold commercially today is produced with a majority of wheat flour, and should be treated as wheat bread.]

57. I.e., he takes a piece from each of the breads (see *Beur HaGra* 168:1).

58. To summarize: Above all, one must consider which grain the bread is made of. If it is made of wheat or barley, it takes precedence over a bread of a different species of grain, regardless of other considerations. If the two breads are made of the same type of grain, one should recite the blessing upon the bread that is whole. If they are both whole or both broken, he should recite the blessing upon the one made of the finer flour. If they are both equal in that respect as well, then he should recite the blessing upon the larger one (see *Mishnah Berurah* 168:15).

59. See above, 38:1, where Kitzur sets out the prohibition of bread baked by an idolater, and discusses the custom in certain places to be lenient with regard to such bread.

LAWS OF BREAKING BREAD AND THE HAMOTZI BLESSING — SIMAN 41:10 78

שְׁלֵמוֹת, אוֹ שְׁתֵּיהֶן פְּרוּסוֹת וְגַם שָׁווֹת בִּגְדוֹלוֹת וְהֵן מִמִּין אֶחָד, יְבָרֵךְ עַל פַּת יִשְׂרָאֵל. וְאִם זֶה שֶׁל יִשְׂרָאֵל אֵינוֹ נָקִי כְּמוֹ שֶׁל עַכּוּ״ם, יְבָרֵךְ עַל אֵיזֶה מֵהֶן שֶׁיִּרְצֶה. וְאִם הַבַּעַל הַבַּיִת נִזְהָר מִפַּת עַכּוּ״ם, אֶלָּא שֶׁהוּבָא בִּשְׁבִיל אוֹרֵחַ, יֵשׁ לְסַלְּקוֹ מִן הַשֻּׁלְחָן עַד לְאַחַר בִּרְכַּת הַמּוֹצִיא[60].

י. כָּל דִּין קְדִימַת הֶחָשׁוּב אֵינוֹ אֶלָּא אִם בְּדַעְתּוֹ לֶאֱכוֹל בְּתוֹךְ הַסְּעוּדָה מִשְׁתֵּיהֶן, אֲבָל אִם אֵין דַּעְתּוֹ לֶאֱכוֹל בְּתוֹךְ הַסְּעוּדָה רַק מִפַּת אַחַת, יִבְצַע עַל זֶה שֶׁהוּא רוֹצֶה לֶאֱכוֹל, וְאֵין מַשְׁגִּיחִין בָּזֶה עַל הַחֲשִׁיבוּת[61].

אוֹ שְׁתֵּיהֶן פְּרוּסוֹת — or they are **both cut pieces,** **וְגַם שָׁווֹת בִּגְדוֹלוֹת** — **and they are also the same size** **וְהֵן מִמִּין אֶחָד** — **and of the same type** of grain, **יְבָרֵךְ עַל פַּת יִשְׂרָאֵל** — then **he should recite the blessing upon the bread** baked **by a Jew.** **וְאִם זֶה שֶׁל יִשְׂרָאֵל** — However, **if this** bread baked **by a Jew** **אֵינוֹ נָקִי כְּמוֹ שֶׁל עַכּוּ״ם** — is made from flour that **is not as fine as that of the** bread baked by the **idolater,** **יְבָרֵךְ עַל אֵיזֶה מֵהֶן שֶׁיִּרְצֶה** — **he may recite the blessing upon whichever one he wants.** **וְאִם הַבַּעַל הַבַּיִת נִזְהָר מִפַּת עַכּוּ״ם** — **If the host avoids bread** baked **by an idolater,** **אֶלָּא שֶׁהוּבָא בִּשְׁבִיל אוֹרֵחַ** — and the bread baked by an idolater was **brought** to the table not for the host, **but for the guest** who does eat such bread, **יֵשׁ לְסַלְּקוֹ מִן הַשֻּׁלְחָן** — **it is proper to remove** the bread baked by an idolater **from the table** **עַד לְאַחַר בִּרְכַּת הַמּוֹצִיא** — **until after the** ***hamotzi*** **blessing** is recited.[60]

§10 **כָּל דִּין קְדִימַת הֶחָשׁוּב** — **The entire halachah regarding giving precedence to the** more **significant** bread **אֵינוֹ אֶלָּא אִם בְּדַעְתּוֹ לֶאֱכוֹל בְּתוֹךְ הַסְּעוּדָה מִשְׁתֵּיהֶן** — applies **only if he plans to eat from both of them during the meal.** **אֲבָל אִם אֵין דַּעְתּוֹ לֶאֱכוֹל בְּתוֹךְ הַסְּעוּדָה רַק מִפַּת אַחַת** — **However, if he plans to eat during the meal from only one bread,** **יִבְצַע עַל זֶה שֶׁהוּא רוֹצֶה לֶאֱכוֹל** — **he should** recite the blessing upon, and **break,** the bread **that he wants to eat** **וְאֵין מַשְׁגִּיחִין בָּזֶה עַל הַחֲשִׁיבוּת** — **and we do not take into account the significance** of each bread **in this** case.[61]

---

60. That is, while the host is reciting the blessing on behalf of all of those present, the bread baked by an idolater should be removed from the table (see *Mishnah Beruarah* 168:19 for discussion; cf. *Shulchan Aruch* 168:5). *Mishnah Berurah* (ibid.) writes that where it is customary for each person to recite his own blessing of *hamotzi,* the host should recite the blessing upon the bread baked by the Jew, and the guest should recite the blessing on the bread baked by the idolater.

61. When one wishes to eat one bread and not the other, he may recite the blessing upon the one that he wishes to eat, even if they are both on the table. However, if he has no preference, he should recite the blessing and eat the one that is more significant according to the rules set forth above (*Mishnah Berurah* 168:5).

79 LAWS OF PROPER CONDUCT FOR A MEAL — SIMAN 42:1-2

סימן מב

הִלְכוֹת סְעוּדָה

וּבוֹ כ״ג סְעִיפִים.

א. מִי שֶׁיֵּשׁ לוֹ בְּהֵמוֹת אוֹ עוֹפוֹת שֶׁמְּזוֹנוֹתֵיהֶן עָלָיו, אָסוּר לוֹ לֶאֱכוֹל כְּלוּם עַד שֶׁיִּתֵּן לָהֶם מַאֲכָל[1], דִּכְתִיב (דברים יא, טו) ״וְנָתַתִּי עֵשֶׂב בְּשָׂדְךָ לִבְהֶמְתֶּךָ וְאָכַלְתָּ וְשָׂבָעְתָּ״ — הִקְדִּימָה הַתּוֹרָה מַאֲכַל בְּהֵמָה לְמַאֲכַל הָאָדָם. וְלִשְׁתִיָּה — הָאָדָם קוֹדֵם, דִּכְתִיב (בראשית כד, מו) ״שְׁתֵה וְגַם גְּמַלֶּיךָ אַשְׁקֶה״[2]. וְכֵן כְּתִיב (במדבר כ, ח) ״וְהִשְׁקִיתָ אֶת הָעֵדָה וְאֶת בְּעִירָם״.

ב. לֹא יֹאכַל אָדָם וְלֹא יִשְׁתֶּה דֶּרֶךְ רַעַבְתָנוּת. לֹא יֹאכַל מְעוּמָּד וְלֹא יִשְׁתֶּה מְעוּמָּד.

SIMAN 42

LAWS OF PROPER CONDUCT FOR A MEAL

CONTAINING 23 *SE'IFIM*

§1 Feeding Animals First / **§2-3** Proper Manners in Eating and Drinking / **§4** Severe Attitude / **§5** Speaking, Torah, and Prayer During a Meal / **§6-7** Two People Eating Together / **§8-11** Respect for Food / **§12** Modesty in Drinking / **§13** Staring at One Who Is Eating / **§14** Giving Food to the Server / **§15** Giving Food to the Non-Observant / **§16** Women Drinking / **§17-18** Proper Behavior for a Guest / **§19-21** Leaving During a Meal / **§22** Interruptions During a Meal / **§23** Ending the Meal

§1 **מִי שֶׁיֵּשׁ לוֹ בְּהֵמוֹת אוֹ עוֹפוֹת — One who has animals or fowl שֶׁמְּזוֹנוֹתֵיהֶן עָלָיו — that he is responsible for feeding אָסוּר לוֹ לֶאֱכוֹל כְּלוּם — is forbidden to eat at all עַד שֶׁיִּתֵּן לָהֶם מַאֲכָל — until he gives them food,**[1] **דִּכְתִיב — as it is written** (*Devarim* 11:15): **״וְנָתַתִּי עֵשֶׂב בְּשָׂדְךָ לִבְהֶמְתֶּךָ — *I shall provide grass in your field for your cattle,* וְאָכַלְתָּ וְשָׂבָעְתָּ״ — *and you will eat and you will be satisfied.* הִקְדִּימָה הַתּוֹרָה מַאֲכַל בְּהֵמָה לְמַאֲכַל הָאָדָם** — We see that in this verse, **the Torah precedes** mention of **the animal's food before** mention of **people's food. וְלִשְׁתִיָּה — However, with regard to drinking הָאָדָם קוֹדֵם — the** needs of a **person come first, דִּכְתִיב — as it is written** (*Bereishis* 24:46): **״שְׁתֵה וְגַם גְּמַלֶּיךָ אַשְׁקֶה״ — *Drink, and I will even water your camels.*[2] וְכֵן כְּתִיב** — This can like**wise** be learned from that which **is written** (*Bamidbar* 20:8): **״וְהִשְׁקִיתָ אֶת הָעֵדָה וְאֶת בְּעִירָם״ — *... and you shall give drink to the assembly and to their animals.***

§2 **לֹא יֹאכַל אָדָם וְלֹא יִשְׁתֶּה — A person should not eat or drink דֶּרֶךְ רַעַבְתָנוּת — in a gluttonous manner. לֹא יֹאכַל מְעוּמָּד — He should not eat** while **standing וְלֹא יִשְׁתֶּה מְעוּמָּד — nor should he drink** while **standing. וִיהֵא**

---

1. Children who cannot take food for themselves must be provided for, even before one provides for his animals (*Igros Moshe, Orach Chaim* II, §52).

2. In this verse, Rivkah assures Eliezer that she will draw water for him and for his camels. Here, with regard to drinking, Eliezer's needs are mentioned before that of his animals.

וִיהֵא שֻׁלְחָנוֹ נָקִי וּמְכוּסֶּה יָפֶה, אֲפִילוּ אִם אֵין לוֹ לֶאֱכוֹל רַק דָּבָר שֶׁאֵינוֹ חָשׁוּב. לֹא יֶאֱחוֹז פְּרוּסָה גְדוֹלָה כְּבֵיצָה[3] וְיֹאכַל מִמֶּנָּה. וְלֹא יֶאֱחוֹז הַמַּאֲכָל בְּיָדוֹ אַחַת וְיִתְלוֹשׁ מִמֶּנּוּ בְּיָדוֹ הַשֵּׁנִית[4]. לֹא יִשְׁתֶּה כּוֹס יַיִן בְּפַעַם אַחַת[5], וְאִם שָׁתָה הֲרֵי זֶה גַּרְגְּרָן[6]. בִּשְׁנֵי פְעָמִים — זֶהוּ דֶּרֶךְ אֶרֶץ. וּבִשְׁלֹשָׁה פְּעָמִים — הֲרֵי זֶה מִגַּסֵּי הָרוּחַ, אִם לֹא כְּשֶׁהוּא כּוֹס גָּדוֹל בְּיוֹתֵר, יָכוֹל לִשְׁתּוֹתוֹ אֲפִילוּ בְּכַמָּה פְעָמִים. וְכֵן כּוֹס קָטָן מְאוֹד[7] יָכוֹל לִשְׁתּוֹתוֹ בְּפַעַם אַחַת[8].

ג. לֹא יִשּׁוֹךְ פְּרוּסָה וִינִיחֶנָּה עַל גַּבֵּי הַשֻּׁלְחָן, אוֹ יִתְּנֶנָּה לַחֲבֵרוֹ, אוֹ לְתוֹךְ הַקְּעָרָה, כִּי שֶׁמָּא הוּא מָאוּס לַחֲבֵרוֹ[9]. וְלֹא יִשְׁתֶּה מִכּוֹס וְיִתֵּן לַחֲבֵירוֹ לִשְׁתּוֹת הַמּוֹתָר,

---

שֻׁלְחָנוֹ נָקִי — His table should be clean וּמְכוּסֶּה יָפֶה — and covered nicely, אֲפִילוּ אִם אֵין לוֹ לֶאֱכוֹל — even if he has nothing to eat רַק דָּבָר שֶׁאֵינוֹ חָשׁוּב — except an insignificant item. **לֹא יֶאֱחוֹז פְּרוּסָה גְדוֹלָה כְּבֵיצָה — He should not take hold of a piece of food as large as an egg**[3] **וְיֹאכַל מִמֶּנָּה — and eat** directly **from it** (i.e., bite into it), **וְלֹא יֶאֱחוֹז הַמַּאֲכָל בְּיָדוֹ אַחַת — and he should not** take **hold** of **the food with one hand** **וְיִתְלוֹשׁ מִמֶּנּוּ בְּיָדוֹ הַשֵּׁנִית — and tear from it with his other hand.**[4] **לֹא יִשְׁתֶּה כּוֹס יַיִן בְּפַעַם אַחַת — One should not drink** down **an entire cup of wine at one time;**[5] **וְאִם שָׁתָה — if he did drink** it in this way, **הֲרֵי זֶה גַּרְגְּרָן — he is** considered **a glutton.**[6] **בִּשְׁנֵי פְעָמִים** — Drinking **by** lifting his cup (i.e., bringing it to his mouth) **twice** **זֶהוּ דֶּרֶךְ אֶרֶץ — constitutes proper manners.** **וּבִשְׁלֹשָׁה פְּעָמִים** — One who drinks it **by** lifting his cup **three times**, drinking a small amount each time, **הֲרֵי זֶה מִגַּסֵּי הָרוּחַ — is** considered **from among the haughty.** **אִם לֹא** — These classifications hold true, **unless** **כְּשֶׁהוּא כּוֹס גָּדוֹל בְּיוֹתֵר — it is a very large cup,** **יָכוֹל לִשְׁתּוֹתוֹ אֲפִילוּ בְּכַמָּה פְעָמִים** — in which case **he may even drink it by** lifting his cup **several times;** **וְכֵן כּוֹס קָטָן מְאוֹד — and likewise,** when drinking from **a very small cup**[7] **יָכוֹל לִשְׁתּוֹתוֹ בְּפַעַם אַחַת — he may drink it** down **at one time,** without violating proper manners.[8]

§3 **לֹא יִשּׁוֹךְ פְּרוּסָה — One should not bite** into **a piece** of bread **וִינִיחֶנָּה עַל גַּבֵּי הַשֻּׁלְחָן — and then place it on the table,** **אוֹ יִתְּנֶנָּה לַחֲבֵרוֹ — or give it to his fellow,** **אוֹ לְתוֹךְ הַקְּעָרָה — or** put it **on the** serving **dish,** **כִּי שֶׁמָּא הוּא מָאוּס לַחֲבֵרוֹ — because it may be repulsive to his fellow.**[9] **וְלֹא יִשְׁתֶּה מִכּוֹס — He should not drink from a cup** **וְיִתֵּן לַחֲבֵירוֹ לִשְׁתּוֹת הַמּוֹתָר — and then give the rest to his**

---

3. Between 1.2 and 2.2 fl. oz. (34.6-66.6 cc.). According to *Mishnah Berurah* (*Shaar HaTziyun* 170:19), it is only prohibited when the piece that one is holding is *larger* than the size of an egg.

4. I.e., in the manner of one who uses both of his hands to forcefully tear something apart (*Mishnah Berurah* 170:25).

5. That is, to lift the cup to his mouth and completely drain it.

6. One who drinks most of the cup, but leaves over a bit, is not included in this definition (*Magen Avraham* cited by *Mishnah Berurah* 170:20). [However, he has not exhibited proper manners, as described further in this *se'if*.]

7. A cup that holds less than a *revi'is* [between 2.9-5.1 fl. oz. (86.4-150 cc.); see Appendix A] (*Mishnah Berurah* 170:22).

8. This rule depends on other factors as well, such as the strength of the beverage and the size of the person. A person may drink a weaker wine even with one swallow, while a strong liquor may require a person to stop in the middle of drinking even a very small amount. A larger person may also drink down a regular-size cup of wine at one time; see *Mishnah Berurah* 170:22 and *Shaar HaTziyun* §20.

9. *Mishnah Berurah* (170:36) differentiates between the piece that he bit off and the piece

81 LAWS OF PROPER CONDUCT FOR A MEAL — SIMAN 42:4-5

כִּי יֵשׁ לְכָל אָדָם לִיזָּהֵר שֶׁלֹּא לִשְׁתּוֹת מִשִּׁיּוּרֵי כּוֹס שֶׁשָּׁתָה חֲבֵרוֹ, וְזֶה שֶׁמָּא מֵחֲמַת הַבּוּשָׁה יִשְׁתֶּה בְּעַל כָּרְחוֹ.

ד. לֹא יְהֵא אָדָם קַפְּדָן בִּסְעוּדָתוֹ[10], כִּי הָאוֹרְחִים וּבְנֵי הַבַּיִת מִתְבַּיְּישִׁים אָז לֶאֱכוֹל, כִּי חוֹשְׁבִים פֶּן מִתְרַגֵּז וּמַקְפִּיד עַל אֲכִילָתָן[11].

ה. אֵין מְשִׂיחִין בִּסְעוּדָה, אֲפִילוּ בְּדִבְרֵי תוֹרָה, מִפְּנֵי הַסַּכָּנָה שֶׁמָּא יַקְדִּים קָנֶה לְוֶשֶׁט[12], וַאֲפִילוּ מִי שֶׁנִּתְעַטֵּשׁ, אָסוּר לוֹמַר לוֹ אָסוּתָא. אֲבָל שֶׁלֹּא בִּשְׁעַת אֲכִילָה[13], מִצְוָה לוֹמַר עַל הַשֻּׁלְחָן דִּבְרֵי תוֹרָה[14]. וְיֵשׁ לִיזָּהֵר בָּזֶה מְאוֹד, וּמִנְהָג טוֹב לוֹמַר אַחַר אֲכִילַת פְּרוּסַת הַמּוֹצִיא "מִזְמוֹר לְדָוִד ה׳ רֹעִי לֹא אֶחְסָר" (תהלים כג), שֶׁהוּא תוֹרָה וְגַם תְּפִלָּה

---

fellow to drink, **כִּי יֵשׁ לְכָל אָדָם לִיזָּהֵר — because every person should take care שֶׁלֹּא לִשְׁתּוֹת מִשִּׁיּוּרֵי כּוֹס — not to drink from that which is left in the cup שֶׁשָּׁתָה חֲבֵרוֹ — from which his fellow drank; וְזֶה שֶׁמָּא מֵחֲמַת הַבּוּשָׁה — and this** person to whom he is giving the cup, **may, due to the embarrassment** involved in refusing the cup, **יִשְׁתֶּה בְּעַל כָּרְחוֹ** — feel compelled to **drink it against his will.**

§4 **לֹא יְהֵא אָדָם קַפְּדָן בִּסְעוּדָתוֹ — A person should not have a severe attitude at his meals**[10] **כִּי הָאוֹרְחִים וּבְנֵי הַבַּיִת — because the guests and the members of the household מִתְבַּיְּישִׁים אָז לֶאֱכוֹל — will then be reluctant to eat, כִּי חוֹשְׁבִים פֶּן מִתְרַגֵּז — because they** may **think that** the master of the house **is upset** with them **וּמַקְפִּיד עַל אֲכִילָתָן — or annoyed at their eating.**[11]

§5 **אֵין מְשִׂיחִין בִּסְעוּדָה — One should not converse** while eating **during a meal, אֲפִילוּ בְּדִבְרֵי תוֹרָה — even in words of Torah, מִפְּנֵי הַסַּכָּנָה — because of the danger** involved, **שֶׁמָּא יַקְדִּים קָנֶה לְוֶשֶׁט — lest the food enter the windpipe instead of the esophagus.**[12] **וַאֲפִילוּ מִי שֶׁנִּתְעַטֵּשׁ, — Even when one sneezes, אָסוּר לוֹמַר לוֹ אָסוּתָא — it is forbidden to wish him "good health." אֲבָל שֶׁלֹּא בִּשְׁעַת אֲכִילָה — However,** at points during the meal **when it is not a time of eating,**[13] **מִצְוָה לוֹמַר עַל הַשֻּׁלְחָן דִּבְרֵי תוֹרָה — it is a mitzvah to speak words of Torah at the table,**[14] **וְיֵשׁ לִיזָּהֵר בָּזֶה מְאוֹד — and one should be very careful to do this. וּמִנְהָג טוֹב — It is a proper custom לוֹמַר אַחַר אֲכִילַת פְּרוּסַת הַמּוֹצִיא — to recite, after eating the piece** of bread **upon which the *hamotzi*** blessing was recited, **"מִזְמוֹר לְדָוִד ה׳ רֹעִי לֹא אֶחְסָר"** — the Psalm beginning ***A Psalm by David. HASHEM is my shepherd, I shall not lack*** (*Tehillim* Ch. 23), **שֶׁהוּא תוֹרָה — since** reciting **this** Psalm **constitutes** speaking words of **Torah** **וְגַם תְּפִלָּה**

---

from which he bit. The piece that he bit off may not be placed on the table at all. The larger piece from which he bit off the smaller piece may be placed on the table, but not on the serving plate or before his fellow.

10. I.e., he should not become easily angry or upset (see *Shulchan Aruch* 170:6).

11. Furthermore, if the household members fear the wrath of the master of the house, they will refrain from giving any food of the meal to the poor (*Mishnah Berurah* 170:18).

12. Literally, *lest the windpipe precede the esophagus*, that is, it will precede it in receiving the food. When one talks, the covering of the windpipe (the epiglottis) is opened, allowing food to enter (*Mishnah Berurah* 170:2).

13. For example, between courses (*Mishnah Berurah* 170:1).

14. For example, one can study a Mishnah, halachah, Aggadah (homiletic teaching), or a work of *mussar* (ethical reproach) (*Mishnah Berurah* 170:1).

LAWS OF PROPER CONDUCT FOR A MEAL — SIMAN 42:6-7 82

עַל מְזוֹנוֹתָיו[15]. וּלְאַחַר גְּמַר הַסְּעוּדָה נוֹהֲגִין לוֹמַר בְּחוֹל "עַל נַהֲרוֹת בָּבֶל" וְגוֹ' (שם קלז), וּבְשַׁבָּת וְיוֹם טוֹב, וְכָל הַיָּמִים שֶׁאֵין אוֹמְרִים בָּהֶם תַּחֲנוּן[16], אוֹמְרִים "שִׁיר הַמַּעֲלוֹת בְּשׁוּב ה' " וְגוֹ' (שם קכו)[17]. וּכְשֶׁלּוֹמֵד עַל הַשֻּׁלְחָן מִתּוֹךְ הַסֵּפֶר, צָרִיךְ לְהַשְׁגִּיחַ מְאוֹד כִּי שְׁכִיחַ לִהְיוֹת בִּסְפָרִים תּוֹלָעִים קְטַנִּים וְיוּכַל לָבֹא לִידֵי אִיסּוּר, חַס וְשָׁלוֹם[18].

ו. שְׁנַיִם שֶׁיּוֹשְׁבִין עַל הַשֻּׁלְחָן, אֲפִילּוּ כָּל אֶחָד קְעָרָה שֶׁלּוֹ לְפָנָיו, אוֹ בְּמִינֵי פֵּירוֹת שֶׁיֵּשׁ לְכָל אֶחָד חֶלְקוֹ לְפָנָיו, מִכָּל מָקוֹם הַגָּדוֹל פּוֹשֵׁט יָדוֹ תְּחִלָּה. וְהַשּׁוֹלֵחַ יָדוֹ בִּפְנֵי מִי שֶׁגָּדוֹל מִמֶּנּוּ, הֲרֵי זֶה גַּרְגְּרָן.

ז. שְׁנַיִם שֶׁאוֹכְלִים מִתּוֹךְ קְעָרָה אַחַת וְהִפְסִיק אֶחָד מִלֶּאֱכוֹל כְּדֵי לִשְׁתּוֹת,

---

עַל מְזוֹנוֹתָיו — and it is also a prayer for one's sustenance.[15] **וּלְאַחַר גְּמַר הַסְּעוּדָה — After the conclusion of the meal,** before *Bircas HaMazon* (Grace after Meals), **נוֹהֲגִין לוֹמַר בְּחוֹל — it is customary to recite during the week "עַל נַהֲרוֹת בָּבֶל" וְגוֹ'** — the Psalm, ***By the rivers of Babylon* etc.** (ibid. Ch. 137). **וּבְשַׁבָּת וְיוֹם טוֹב — And on Shabbos and festivals וְכָל הַיָּמִים שֶׁאֵין אוֹמְרִים בָּהֶם תַּחֲנוּן — and all days on which the *Tachanun* prayer is not recited,**[16] **אוֹמְרִים "שִׁיר הַמַּעֲלוֹת בְּשׁוּב ה' " וְגוֹ'** — before *Bircas HaMazon* **we recite** the Psalm, ***A song of ascents. When Hashem will return* etc.** (ibid. Ch. 126).[17] **וּכְשֶׁלּוֹמֵד עַל הַשֻּׁלְחָן מִתּוֹךְ הַסֵּפֶר — When one studies by the table from a book, צָרִיךְ לְהַשְׁגִּיחַ מְאוֹד — he must be very vigilant, כִּי שְׁכִיחַ לִהְיוֹת בִּסְפָרִים תּוֹלָעִים קְטַנִּים — for it is common for there to be small worms in the books, וְיוּכַל לָבֹא לִידֵי אִיסּוּר, חַס וְשָׁלוֹם** — and if they get into his food, **he can come to** violate **a prohibition** by eating the worms, **God forbid.**[18]

§6 **שְׁנַיִם שֶׁיּוֹשְׁבִין עַל הַשֻּׁלְחָן** — When **two people are sitting at a table** for a meal, **אֲפִילּוּ כָּל אֶחָד קְעָרָה שֶׁלּוֹ לְפָנָיו — even if each one has his own dish before him, אוֹ בְּמִינֵי פֵּירוֹת — or** if they were sitting down to eat **fruit שֶׁיֵּשׁ לְכָל אֶחָד חֶלְקוֹ לְפָנָיו — and each one has his own portion before him, מִכָּל מָקוֹם — nevertheless, הַגָּדוֹל פּוֹשֵׁט יָדוֹ תְּחִלָּה — the more prominent** of the two **is to reach** for the food **first. וְהַשּׁוֹלֵחַ יָדוֹ בִּפְנֵי מִי שֶׁגָּדוֹל מִמֶּנּוּ — One who reaches** for the food **before one more prominent than he הֲרֵי זֶה גַּרְגְּרָן — is** considered **a glutton.**

§7 **שְׁנַיִם שֶׁאוֹכְלִים מִתּוֹךְ קְעָרָה אַחַת** — If **two people are eating from one dish, וְהִפְסִיק אֶחָד מִלֶּאֱכוֹל כְּדֵי לִשְׁתּוֹת — and one of them stopped eating** momentarily

---

15. It is a worthy practice to pray for one's sustenance before or during each meal (see *Mishnah Berurah* 166:3).

16. The laws of the *Tachanun* prayer are discussed in *Siman* 22. The specific times that *Tachanun* is not recited are set out in that *Siman, se'if* 8.

17. By reciting these Psalms we remember the destruction of the *Beis HaMikdash* at each meal (see *Mishnah Berurah* 1:11). On Shabbos and Yom Tov, rather than focusing on the bitterness felt by the Jewish people immediately following the Destruction of the *Beis HaMikdash* [which is the theme of *By the rivers of Babylon* etc.], we focus on the rejoicing that will take place at the time of the future Redemption.

18. It is forbidden to ingest any vermin; for more details regarding this prohibition, see below, 46:31-45.

83 LAWS OF PROPER CONDUCT FOR A MEAL — SIMAN 42:8-9

אוֹ לַעֲשׂוֹת אֵיזֶה דָּבָר קָטָן[19], דֶּרֶךְ אֶרֶץ הוּא שֶׁגַּם הַשֵּׁנִי יַמְתִּין עָלָיו. אֲבָל אִם הֵמָּה שְׁלֹשָׁה, אֵין הַשְּׁנַיִם פּוֹסְקִין בִּשְׁבִיל הָאֶחָד.

ח. עוֹשֶׂה[20] אָדָם צְרָכָיו בְּפַת[21], וְהָנֵי מִילֵּי דְּלָא מְמְאִיס בֵּיהּ, אֲבָל מִידֵי דִּמְאִיס בֵּיהּ, לֹא. הִלְכָּךְ, אֵין סוֹמְכִין בּוֹ אֶת הַקְּעָרָה, אִם הִיא מְלֵאָה דָּבָר, שֶׁאִם יִפּוֹל עַל הַפַּת יִמָּאֵס. וּכְשֶׁאוֹכְלִין אֵיזֶה תַּבְשִׁיל עִם חֲתִיכוֹת פַּת וְהַפַּת הוּא לוֹ בִּמְקוֹם כַּף[22], צָרִיךְ לִיזָּהֵר לֶאֱכוֹל בְּכָל פַּעַם קְצָת מִן הַפַּת[23], וְהַנִּשְׁאָר לוֹ מִן הַפַּת גַּם כֵּן יֹאכַל אוֹתוֹ אַחַר כָּךְ[24].

ט. אָסוּר לִזְרוֹק פַּת, אֲפִילוּ בְּמָקוֹם שֶׁאֵינוֹ נִמְאָס[25], כִּי הַזְּרִיקָה הִיא בִּזָּיוֹן[26].

---

to take a drink **אוֹ לַעֲשׂוֹת אֵיזֶה דָּבָר קָטָן — or to perform some small task,**[19] **דֶּרֶךְ אֶרֶץ הוּא — it is proper manners שֶׁגַּם הַשֵּׁנִי יַמְתִּין עָלָיו — for the second person to also** stop eating from the dish and **wait for him. אֲבָל אִם הֵמָּה שְׁלֹשָׁה — However, if there were three** people eating from one dish and one of them paused momentarily, **אֵין הַשְּׁנַיִם פּוֹסְקִין בִּשְׁבִיל הָאֶחָד — the** other **two need not stop** and wait **for the one.**

§8 Not only is destroying food forbidden by the Torah (see *Rambam, Hilchos Melachim* 6:10), it is also forbidden to act in a way that denigrates the gift of food that Hashem has bestowed upon us.[20] The following four *se'ifim* discuss the parameters of these two prohibitions:

עוֹשֶׂה אָדָם צְרָכָיו בְּפַת — A person may use bread for all his needs.[21] **וְהָנֵי מִילֵּי** — However, **this** permit **applies only דְּלָא מְמְאִיס בֵּיהּ** — to such use **that does not render** the bread **repulsive, אֲבָל מִידֵי דִּמְאִיס בֵּיהּ, לֹא — but** a use **that would render** the bread **repulsive is not** permitted. **הִלְכָּךְ — Therefore, אֵין סוֹמְכִין בּוֹ אֶת הַקְּעָרָה — one should not support a dish with** bread **אִם הִיא מְלֵאָה דָּבָר — if** the dish **is filled with an item שֶׁאִם יִפּוֹל עַל הַפַּת יִמָּאֵס — that, if it would fall onto the bread,** the bread **would become repulsive. וּכְשֶׁאוֹכְלִין אֵיזֶה תַּבְשִׁיל עִם חֲתִיכוֹת פַּת — When** one is **eating any cooked food with pieces of bread וְהַפַּת הוּא לוֹ בִּמְקוֹם כַּף — and he is using the bread as his spoon,**[22] **צָרִיךְ לִיזָּהֵר — he must take care לֶאֱכוֹל בְּכָל פַּעַם קְצָת מִן הַפַּת — to eat some of the bread each time** that he brings the food to his mouth,[23] **וְהַנִּשְׁאָר לוֹ מִן הַפַּת — and anything that remains of the bread גַּם כֵּן יֹאכַל אוֹתוֹ אַחַר כָּךְ — should also be eaten after** he is finished eating the dish.[24]

§9 אָסוּר לִזְרוֹק פַּת — It is forbidden to throw bread, אֲפִילוּ בְּמָקוֹם שֶׁאֵינוֹ נִמְאָס — even if it is thrown **in a way that does not render it repulsive,**[25] **כִּי הַזְּרִיקָה הִיא בִּזָּיוֹן — for** the act of **throwing** itself **is a degradation** of the bread.[26]

---

19. But not if he stopped to talk (*Mishnah Berurah* 170:12).

20. See *Rashi* to *Taanis* 20b s.v. אין מאכילין.

21. For example, to cover a utensil (see *Mishnah Berurah* 171:7). Other uses are mentioned later in this *se'if.* The halachos mentioned in this *se'if* apply to all foods, not only to bread (see *Mishnah Berurah* 171:2-3,17).

22. That is, he uses the bread to scoop up the food.

23. Using the bread as a mere implement is degrading for the bread. By eating some of the bread each time, he does not appear to be using the bread, but rather to be using the food as a condiment for the bread (*Mishnah Berurah* 171:17).

24. He must eat it because it has been rendered repulsive and would no longer be eaten by someone else (see *Mishnah Berurah* 171:18).

25. Such as when throwing it onto a clean table.

26. Because of the importance of bread, even

LAWS OF PROPER CONDUCT FOR A MEAL — SIMAN 42:10 84

וּשְׁאָר מִינֵי אוֹכָלִים — אִם נִמְאָסִין עַל יְדֵי הַזְּרִיקָה, אָסוּר לְזָרְקָן. אֲבָל אִם אֵינָן נִמְאָסִין, כְּגוֹן, אֱגוֹזִים וְכַדּוֹמֶה, מוּתָּר[27]. לֹא יֵשֵׁב עַל שַׂק[28] שֶׁיֵּשׁ בּוֹ פֵּירוֹת שֶׁנִּמְאָסִים עַל יְדֵי כָּךְ[29]. אֵין נוֹטְלִין אֶת הַיָּדַיִם בְּיַיִן, אוֹ בִשְׁאָר מַשְׁקֶה, מִשּׁוּם בִּזָּיוֹן[30]. כְּשֶׁרוֹאֶה אֵיזֶה אוֹכֶל מוּנָח עַל הָאָרֶץ, צָרִיךְ לְהַגְבִּיהוֹ. מַאֲכָל שֶׁהוּא רָאוּי לְאָדָם אֵין מַאֲכִילִין אוֹתוֹ לִבְהֵמָה, מִשּׁוּם בִּיזּוּי אוֹכָלִין[31].

י. אִם צָרִיךְ לַעֲשׂוֹת אֵיזֶה רְפוּאָה בְּפַת אוֹ בִשְׁאָר דְּבַר מַאֲכָל, אַף עַל פִּי שֶׁנִּמְאָס בְּכָךְ, מוּתָּר[32].

וּשְׁאָר מִינֵי אוֹכָלִים — Regarding **other kinds of food** the halachah is: **אִם נִמְאָסִין עַל יְדֵי הַזְּרִיקָה** — **If they are rendered repulsive by being thrown** **אָסוּר לְזָרְקָן** — then **it is forbidden to throw them;** **אֲבָל אִם אֵינָן נִמְאָסִין** — **however, if they are not rendered repulsive** thereby, **כְּגוֹן, אֱגוֹזִים וְכַדּוֹמֶה** — **such as** is the case with **nuts and the like,** **מוּתָּר** — then **it is permitted.**[27]

לֹא יֵשֵׁב עַל שַׂק שֶׁיֵּשׁ בּוֹ פֵּירוֹת — **One should not sit on a sack**[28] **that contains fruit,** **שֶׁנִּמְאָסִים עַל יְדֵי כָּךְ** — **since the fruit is rendered repulsive through this.**[29]

אֵין נוֹטְלִין אֶת הַיָּדַיִם בְּיַיִן — **One should not wash his hands with wine** **אוֹ בִשְׁאָר מַשְׁקֶה** — **or other beverages,** **מִשּׁוּם בִּזָּיוֹן** — **because of the degradation** to the beverage.[30] **כְּשֶׁרוֹאֶה אֵיזֶה אוֹכֶל** — **When** a person **sees any food** **מוּנָח עַל הָאָרֶץ** — **lying on the ground,** **צָרִיךְ לְהַגְבִּיהוֹ** — **he must pick it up.**

מַאֲכָל שֶׁהוּא רָאוּי לְאָדָם — **Food that is fit to** be eaten by **people** **אֵין מַאֲכִילִין אוֹתוֹ לִבְהֵמָה** — **should not be fed to animals,** **מִשּׁוּם בִּיזּוּי אוֹכָלִין** — **because** such action is **a denigration of** the **food.**[31]

§10 **אִם צָרִיךְ לַעֲשׂוֹת אֵיזֶה רְפוּאָה בְּפַת** — **If one needs to use bread for medicinal purposes,** **אוֹ בִשְׁאָר דְּבַר מַאֲכָל** — **or to use any other food** for such purposes, **אַף עַל פִּי שֶׁנִּמְאָס בְּכָךְ** — **even if it becomes repulsive through such use,** **מוּתָּר** — **it is permitted.**[32]

---

the act of throwing it is considered to be degrading to it. However, as Kitzur continues, this is not the case with other food (see *Mishnah Berurah* 171:9).

27. *Mishnah Berurah* (171:11, 21) writes that even nuts that are still covered with their shell may be thrown *only* onto a clean surface, since they are liable to be discarded if they become dirty (cf. *Shaar HaTziyun* there §19).

28. Or on any container, if his weight will affect the contents (see *Mishnah Berurah* 171:12).

29. One may sit on a sack of produce that will not be affected by his weight, such as a sack of hard beans (*Shulchan Aruch* 171:2).

30. This is forbidden even if he is doing this simply to clean his hands, and not in order to fulfill the obligation of *netilas yadayim* [i.e., washing one's hands before eating bread; see *Siman* 40] (*Shulchan Aruch* 171:1). [*Netilas yadayim* must be performed with water. See *Mishnah Berurah* 171:8 and *Shulchan Aruch* 160:12 with *Mishnah Berurah* regarding whether washing may be performed with other beverages when no water is available.]

31. *Mishnah Berurah* (171:11; see *Shaar HaTziyun* there §13) cites *Machatzis HaShekel*, which states that (according to one understanding of *Rashi* to *Taanis* 20b s.v. אין מאכילין), when one has only food that is fit for a person, he may feed it to his animals. This would explain the custom of some to feed bread to birds.

32. *Mishnah Berurah* (171:4) adds that it is permitted to use food for any human need as long as it is common to use the food in that way. [For example, if it is common to use oil as a skin softener, it is permitted to use it in that way.]

85 LAWS OF PROPER CONDUCT FOR A MEAL — SIMAN 42:11-14

יא. יִזָּהֵר מְאוֹד בְּפֵירוּרִין שֶׁלֹּא יִזְרְקֵם[33], דְּקָשֶׁה לַעֲנִיּוּת, אֶלָּא יְקַבְּצֵם וְיִתְּנֵם לָעוֹפוֹת.

יב. הַשּׁוֹתֶה מַיִם — לֹא יִשְׁתֶּה בִּפְנֵי רַבִּים[34], אֶלָּא יַהֲפוֹךְ פָּנָיו[35]. וּבִשְׁאָר מַשְׁקִין אֵין צָרִיךְ לַהֲפוֹךְ פָּנָיו.

יג. אֵין מִסְתַּכְּלִין בִּפְנֵי הָאוֹכֵל וְהַשּׁוֹתֶה, וְלֹא בְחֶלְקוֹ שֶׁלְּפָנָיו, כְּדֵי שֶׁלֹּא לְבַיְּישׁוֹ.

יד. כָּל מַאֲכָל וּמַשְׁקֶה שֶׁמְּבִיאִין לִפְנֵי הָאָדָם שֶׁיֵּשׁ לוֹ רֵיחַ[36], וְהָאָדָם תָּאֵב לוֹ, צָרִיךְ לִיתֵּן מִמֶּנּוּ מִיָּד דָּבָר מוּעָט[37] לְהַמְשַׁמֵּשׁ[38], לְפִי שֶׁמַּזִּיק לְאָדָם שֶׁרוֹאֶה לְפָנָיו

---

§11 יִזָּהֵר מְאוֹד בְּפֵירוּרִין — **One should take great care with** bread **crumbs** שֶׁלֹּא יִזְרְקֵם — **not to throw them** to a place where they will be trampled,[33] דְּקָשֶׁה לַעֲנִיּוּת — **since this** action **has the negative effect of** causing **poverty.** אֶלָּא — **Rather,** יְקַבְּצֵם וְיִתְּנֵם לָעוֹפוֹת — **he should gather them and give them to birds.**

§12 הַשּׁוֹתֶה מַיִם — **One who is drinking water** לֹא יִשְׁתֶּה בִּפְנֵי רַבִּים — **should not drink facing the public;**[34] אֶלָּא יַהֲפוֹךְ פָּנָיו — **rather, he should turn his face** to the side before drinking.[35] וּבִשְׁאָר מַשְׁקִין — **With regard to other beverages,** אֵין צָרִיךְ לַהֲפוֹךְ פָּנָיו — **he need not turn his face** to the side.

§13 אֵין מִסְתַּכְּלִין בִּפְנֵי הָאוֹכֵל וְהַשּׁוֹתֶה — **One should not stare into the face of one who is eating or drinking,** וְלֹא בְחֶלְקוֹ שֶׁלְּפָנָיו — **nor at his portion** that is **before him,** כְּדֵי שֶׁלֹּא לְבַיְּישׁוֹ — **so as not to cause him embarrassment.**

§14 כָּל מַאֲכָל וּמַשְׁקֶה שֶׁמְּבִיאִין לִפְנֵי הָאָדָם שֶׁיֵּשׁ לוֹ רֵיחַ — **If any food or drink is served to a person** and it is of a type **that produces a** savory **aroma,**[36] וְהָאָדָם תָּאֵב לוֹ — **such that a person craves it,** צָרִיךְ לִיתֵּן מִמֶּנּוּ מִיָּד דָּבָר מוּעָט — **he must immediately give a bit of that food**[37] לְהַמְשַׁמֵּשׁ — **to the server,**[38] לְפִי שֶׁמַּזִּיק לְאָדָם — **for it is harmful to a person** שֶׁרוֹאֶה לְפָנָיו

---

33. *Mishnah Berurah* 180:10. One may, however, discard such crumbs into water, since they would not be put in a position of being trampled and degraded. Some authorities forbid the discarding of an amount of crumbs that equal a *kezayis* [between .6 and 1.1 fl. oz. (17.3-33.3 cc.); see Appendix A], even when they will not be trampled (ibid.).

34. This practice reflects a modest bearing (see *Rashi* to *Bechoros* 44b s.v. ואין שותין מים). *Mishnah Berurah* (170:13) cites this practice only with regard to Torah scholars.

35. *Mishnah Berurah* (170:13) cites an opinion stating that this does not apply during a meal; cf. Appendix of Kitzur's editorial glosses, where Kitzur does not make this differentiation.

36. Or a pungent taste (*Mishnah Berurah* 169:1).

37. If he is served many foods that have a savory aroma, then he must give a bit of each one to the server (*Beur Halachah* to 169:1 s.v. כל דבר).

38. One must likewise give food to the one who cooks it (*Beur Halachah* to 169:1 s.v. לשמש). *Beur Halachah* writes (ibid.) that the Gemara (*Kesubos* 61a) indicates that one is obligated to give to anyone who may be there at the time and can smell the food, for they too are at risk of the danger described in the halachah above. *Beur Halachah* suggests that the widespread custom that one who enters a person's house during mealtime is invited to partake of the meal, has its roots in this halachah.

LAWS OF PROPER CONDUCT FOR A MEAL — SIMAN 42:15-17 86

מַאֲכָל שֶׁהוּא מִתְאַוֶּה לוֹ וְאֵינוֹ אוֹכֵל מִמֶּנּוּ[39], (עַיֵּין לְעֵיל סִימָן ל״ג סְעִיף ד׳)[40].

טו. לֹא יִתֵּן אָדָם לֶאֱכוֹל אֶלָּא לְמִי שֶׁיּוֹדֵעַ בּוֹ שֶׁיִּטּוֹל יָדָיו וִיבָרֵךְ[41].

טז. אִשָּׁה שֶׁאֵין בַּעְלָהּ עִמָּהּ אֵין לָהּ לִשְׁתּוֹת יַיִן. וְאִם הִיא בְּמָקוֹם אַחֵר שֶׁלֹּא בְּבֵיתָהּ[42], אֲפִילּוּ אִם בַּעְלָהּ עִמָּהּ, אֲסוּרָה לִשְׁתּוֹת. וְהוּא הַדִּין שְׁאָר מַשְׁקִין הַמְשַׁכְּרִין. וְאִם הִיא רְגִילָה לִשְׁתּוֹת יַיִן בִּפְנֵי בַעְלָהּ, מוּתֶּרֶת לִשְׁתּוֹת מְעַט שֶׁלֹּא בִּפְנֵי בַעְלָהּ.

יז. אָסוּר לָאוֹרְחִים לִיטּוֹל כְּלוּם מִמַּה שֶּׁלִּפְנֵיהֶם לִיתֵּן בְּיַד בְּנוֹ, אוֹ בִתּוֹ, שֶׁל בַּעַל

מַאֲכָל שֶׁהוּא מִתְאַוֶּה לוֹ — when he sees in front of him food that he craves וְאֵינוֹ אוֹכֵל מִמֶּנּוּ — and he does not eat from it[39] (עַיֵּין לְעֵיל סִימָן ל״ג סְעִיף ד׳ — see above, 33:4).[40]

§15 לֹא יִתֵּן אָדָם לֶאֱכוֹל — One should not give anyone **to eat אֶלָּא לְמִי שֶׁיּוֹדֵעַ בּוֹ — unless he knows about him שֶׁיִּטּוֹל יָדָיו וִיבָרֵךְ — that he will wash his hands** (if it is bread), **and recite a blessing** upon the food.[41]

§16 אִשָּׁה שֶׁאֵין בַּעְלָהּ עִמָּהּ — A woman whose husband is not with her אֵין לָהּ לִשְׁתּוֹת יַיִן — should not drink wine. וְאִם הִיא בְּמָקוֹם אַחֵר — If she is in another place, שֶׁלֹּא בְּבֵיתָהּ — that is, she is lodging[42] **away from her home, אֲפִילּוּ אִם בַּעְלָהּ עִמָּהּ —** then **even if her husband is with her אֲסוּרָה לִשְׁתּוֹת — she is forbidden to drink** wine; **וְהוּא הַדִּין — the same halachah applies שְׁאָר מַשְׁקִין הַמְשַׁכְּרִין —** to any **other intoxicating beverages. וְאִם הִיא רְגִילָה לִשְׁתּוֹת יַיִן — However, if she is accustomed to drinking wine בִּפְנֵי בַעְלָהּ — in the presence of her husband, מוּתֶּרֶת לִשְׁתּוֹת מְעַט —** then **she is permitted to drink a small amount שֶׁלֹּא בִּפְנֵי בַעְלָהּ — when her husband is not present** as well.

§17 אָסוּר לָאוֹרְחִים — It is forbidden for guests לִיטּוֹל כְּלוּם מִמַּה שֶּׁלִּפְנֵיהֶם — to take any food **that was** put **before them לִיתֵּן בְּיַד בְּנוֹ, אוֹ בִתּוֹ, שֶׁל בַּעַל**

---

39. However, if the server will be sitting down to eat with them afterward, he need not be given to eat first (*Mishnah Berurah* 169:3). Even when the food does not have an aroma, it is the manner of the pious to give some of each type of food to the server right away, since it is painful to see others eating without being able to eat (*Shulchan Aruch* 169:1; *Mishnah Berurah* 169:4). *Beur Halachah* to 169:1 s.v. מיד writes that it seems that this too applies only in cases where the server will not later be given the same foods that he is serving, since this can cause an intense craving for those foods. However, when he usually receives the same food afterward, he need not be given first.

40. There, Kitzur writes how one who smells such an aroma can save himself from danger.

41. See also above, 40:14. One need not have specific knowledge about each particular individual; one may rely on an assumption that the person will keep the halachah (*Beur Halachah* to 169:2 s.v. למי שיודע). However, one may not give to someone about whom there is reason to doubt that he will recite the blessing.

When performing the mitzvah of *tzedakah* (charity) by giving food to a poor person, one need not have definite knowledge of his level of observance before giving to him. Furthermore, if the poor person does not refuse to recite a blessing out of wickedness, but merely cannot recite a blessing, one is still obligated to give him food (*Mishnah Berurah* 169:11).

[R' Moshe Feinstein, in *Igros Moshe*, *Orach Chaim* V, §13 discusses certain circumstances under which one would be allowed to serve food to a non-observant person; see there at length.]

42. See *Mishnah Berurah* 170:13.

87 LAWS OF PROPER CONDUCT FOR A MEAL — SIMAN 42:18-19

הַבַּיִת, כִּי שֶׁמָּא אֵין לְבַעַל הַבַּיִת יוֹתֵר מִמַּה שֶׁהֵבִיא לִפְנֵיהֶם וְיִתְבַּיֵּישׁ שֶׁלֹּא יִהְיֶה לָהֶם דַּי. אֲבָל אִם יֵשׁ עַל הַשֻּׁלְחָן מוּכָן הַרְבֵּה, מוּתָּר.

יח. הַנִּכְנָס לְבַיִת — לֹא יֹאמַר "תְּנוּ לִי לֶאֱכוֹל", עַד שֶׁיֹּאמְרוּ לוֹ הֵם[43]. אָסוּר לֶאֱכוֹל מִסְּעוּדָה שֶׁאֵינָהּ מַסְפֶּקֶת לִבְעָלֶיהָ, שֶׁזֶּהוּ אֲבַק גָּזֵל[44], אַף עַל פִּי שֶׁהַבַּעַל הַבַּיִת מַזְמִינוֹ לֶאֱכוֹל עִמּוֹ. וְהוּא עָוֹן גָּדוֹל, וּמִן הַדְּבָרִים שֶׁקָּשֶׁה לָשׁוּב עֲלֵיהֶם[45].

יט. אָסוּר לָצֵאת מִמְּקוֹמוֹ קוֹדֶם שֶׁיְּבָרֵךְ בִּרְכַּת הַמָּזוֹן, וַאֲפִילוּ לָלֶכֶת בְּאֶמְצַע הַסְּעוּדָה לְחֶדֶר אַחֵר לִגְמוֹר שָׁם סְעוּדָתוֹ, אוֹ שֶׁיַּחֲזוֹר אַחַר כָּךְ לְכָאן לִגְמוֹר סְעוּדָתוֹ[46]. וַאֲפִילוּ לָלֶכֶת רַק חוּץ לְפִתְחוֹ וְלַחֲזוֹר אַחַר כָּךְ לְכָאן לִגְמוֹר סְעוּדָתוֹ

כִּי שֶׁמָּא אֵין לְבַעַל הַבַּיִת — **and give it to the son or daughter of the host,** הַבַּיִת — **because** we are concerned that **the host may not have any more** מִמַּה יוֹתֵר — **than that which he served them,** שֶׁהֵבִיא לִפְנֵיהֶם — וְיִתְבַּיֵּישׁ שֶׁלֹּא יִהְיֶה לָהֶם דַּי — **and he will then be embarrassed when they do not have enough** food. אֲבָל — **However,** אִם יֵשׁ עַל הַשֻּׁלְחָן מוּכָן הַרְבֵּה — **if there is a large amount** of food **prepared on the table,** מוּתָּר — **this is permitted.**

§18 הַנִּכְנָס לְבַיִת — **One who enters the house** of another לֹא יֹאמַר — **should not say,** "תְּנוּ לִי לֶאֱכוֹל" — **"Give me** food **to eat!,"** עַד שֶׁיֹּאמְרוּ לוֹ הֵם — but should wait **until they tell him** that it is time for the meal.[43]

אָסוּר לֶאֱכוֹל — **It is forbidden** for a guest **to eat** מִסְּעוּדָה שֶׁאֵינָהּ מַסְפֶּקֶת לִבְעָלֶיהָ — **from a meal that does not suffice for its owner,** i.e., when the host does not have enough to eat himself, שֶׁזֶּהוּ אֲבַק גָּזֵל — **for such action has a trace of theft,**[44] אַף עַל פִּי שֶׁהַבַּעַל הַבַּיִת מַזְמִינוֹ לֶאֱכוֹל עִמּוֹ — **even if the host invites him to eat with him.** וְהוּא עָוֹן גָּדוֹל — **This is a great sin** וּמִן הַדְּבָרִים שֶׁקָּשֶׁה לָשׁוּב עֲלֵיהֶם — **and is of those sins from which it is difficult to repent.**[45]

§19 אָסוּר לָצֵאת מִמְּקוֹמוֹ — **It is forbidden** for one **to leave his place** during or after a meal קוֹדֶם שֶׁיְּבָרֵךְ בִּרְכַּת הַמָּזוֹן — **before reciting** ***Bircas HaMazon.*** וַאֲפִילוּ לָלֶכֶת בְּאֶמְצַע הַסְּעוּדָה — It is **even** forbidden **to go during a meal** לְחֶדֶר אַחֵר לִגְמוֹר שָׁם סְעוּדָתוֹ — **to another room to finish his meal there,** אוֹ שֶׁיַּחֲזוֹר אַחַר כָּךְ לְכָאן לִגְמוֹר סְעוּדָתוֹ — **or to** go to another room and **afterward return to** his original place **to finish his meal.**[46] וַאֲפִילוּ לָלֶכֶת רַק חוּץ לְפִתְחוֹ — **Even to go just outside his door** וְלַחֲזוֹר אַחַר כָּךְ לְכָאן לִגְמוֹר סְעוּדָתוֹ — **and to return afterward** to his place **to**

---

43. After he is served, he may begin to eat right away, and need not wait to be told to eat (*Mishnah Berurah* 170:30). When one is a paying guest, he may request his food (ibid. §29).

44. Literally, *the dust of theft.*

45. One who does this will often not realize that he has done anything wrong, since he ate only after being invited, and it is therefore not likely that he will repent (see *Rambam, Hilchos Teshuvah* 4:4). [The invitation does not absolve him of wrongdoing, as it was extended out of embarrassment, and was not sincerely meant.]

46. One is required to recite *Bircas HaMazon* in the place where he ate. It is therefore forbidden to leave that place, lest he not return to recite *Bircas HaMazon*, or forget to recite it entirely. Although one may recite *Bircas HaMazon* in the second place if he ate bread there, ideally one should recite it before he leaves the first place of eating (*Mishnah Berurah* 178:33). [See *Rama* 178:2 and *Beur Halachah* ibid. s.v. עוברת regarding leaving the place of a meal to perform a mitzvah. See also below, *se'if* 21, regarding one who had in mind when he began his meal to go to another place before reciting *Bircas HaMazon*.]

LAWS OF PROPER CONDUCT FOR A MEAL — SIMAN 42:19 88

יֵשׁ לִיזָּהֵר מִזֶּה[47]. עָבַר וְיָצָא, בֵּין שֶׁהוּא גוֹמֵר סְעוּדָתוֹ בְּמָקוֹם שֶׁהוּא שָׁם, בֵּין שֶׁהוּא חוֹזֵר לְכָאן לִגְמוֹר סְעוּדָתוֹ, אֵינוֹ צָרִיךְ לַחֲזוֹר וּלְבָרֵךְ הַמּוֹצִיא[48], דְּכֵיוָן שֶׁקָּבַע סְעוּדָתוֹ עַל הַפַּת[49], אַף עַל פִּי שֶׁשִּׁינָּה מְקוֹמוֹ, מִכָּל מָקוֹם נֶחְשָׁב הַכֹּל לִסְעוּדָה אַחַת[50], רַק שֶׁיִּזָּהֵר לֶאֱכוֹל לְכָל הַפָּחוֹת כְּזַיִת[51] פַּת בְּמָקוֹם שֶׁיְּבָרֵךְ בִּרְכַּת הַמָּזוֹן[52]. אֲבָל בִּשְׁאָר

---

finish his meal יֵשׁ לִיזָּהֵר מִזֶּה — is something that **one should take care not to do.**[47] עָבַר וְיָצָא — **If he violated** this halachah **and did leave** his place, בֵּין שֶׁהוּא גוֹמֵר סְעוּדָתוֹ בְּמָקוֹם שֶׁהוּא שָׁם — **whether he finishes his meal in the place where he is** now בֵּין שֶׁהוּא חוֹזֵר לְכָאן לִגְמוֹר סְעוּדָתוֹ — **or whether he returns to** his original place **to finish his meal,** אֵינוֹ צָרִיךְ לַחֲזוֹר וּלְבָרֵךְ הַמּוֹצִיא — **he need not recite the *hamotzi* blessing again** before continuing to eat bread.[48]

Ordinarily, leaving the place in which one recited a blessing upon food is seen as the conclusion of his eating session, and thus the blessing ceases to be effective. If he would like to continue eating elsewhere, or even if he would return to his original place, a new blessing would be required. As we have seen, in the above case the blessing is still effective. Kitzur now explains why:

דְּכֵיוָן שֶׁקָּבַע סְעוּדָתוֹ עַל הַפַּת — **Since he was eating a bread meal,**[49] אַף עַל פִּי שֶׁשִּׁינָּה מְקוֹמוֹ — **even though he changed his** eating **place** during the meal, מִכָּל מָקוֹם נֶחְשָׁב הַכֹּל לִסְעוּדָה אַחַת — **nevertheless, all** that he eats in both places **is considered to be one meal.**[50] רַק שֶׁיִּזָּהֵר — **However, he must take care** לֶאֱכוֹל לְכָל הַפָּחוֹת כְּזַיִת פַּת — **to eat at least a *kezayis***[51] **of bread** בְּמָקוֹם שֶׁיְּבָרֵךְ בִּרְכַּת הַמָּזוֹן — **in the place where he will recite *Bircas HaMazon.***[52] אֲבָל בִּשְׁאָר

---

47. When one leaves the room momentarily there is no concern that he will forget to recite *Bircas HaMazon*. However, there is an opinion that leaving the room even momentarily when eating a bread meal interrupts the effect of his original blessing, and if he wishes to continue eating he must recite another blessing. Ideally, one should not put himself in this situation (even though the halachah does not follow this opinion; see further in this *se'if*). See Appendix of Kitzur's editorial glosses. *Mishnah Berurah* (178:34), however, rules that one may leave the room for a moment.

48. Regarding one who leaves *and* decides to end his meal without eating anything more, see *Rama* 178:2 and *Beur Halachah* ibid. s.v. אם הסיח דעתו.

49. Literally, *he established his meal upon bread.*

50. *Mishnah Berurah* (in his introduction to *Siman* 178) explains that the difference between bread and other foods is that there is an obligation to recite *Bircas HaMazon* in the place where one ate (see below, 44:9). Since even if one leaves the room he must return to recite *Bircas HaMazon,* leaving the room is not considered a termination of his eating session. Even when one eats in the second place, it is considered a continuation of the meal, since he is required to eat some bread in the new place in order to recite *Bircas HaMazon* there (see continuation of this *se'if*). [If one ate less than a *kezayis* of bread, in which case there is no obligation to recite *Bircas HaMazon,* leaving the room does effect an interruption in his eating (*Mishnah Berurah* 178:28).]

51. Between .6 and 1.1 fl. oz. (17.3-33.3 cc.); see Appendix A.

52. In the case discussed in this *se'if,* where the person left during a meal and wishes to continue it elsewhere (as well as in the case of *se'if* 21, below), one must eat at least a *kezayis* of bread in the second place. However, if a person completed his meal and neglected to recite *Bircas HaMazon* before leaving, he may recite *Bircas HaMazon* in the second place even if he ate less than a *kezayis* of bread there; see below, 44:9 and *Mishnah Berurah* 184:9. (For further discusson, see *Pri Megadim, Mishbetzos Zahav* 178:9, and *Derech HaChaim* הלכות נטילת ידים לסעודה, איזה דברים נקראים הפסק בסעודה, דין א'.)

89 LAWS OF PROPER CONDUCT FOR A MEAL — SIMAN 42:20-22

דְּבָרִים אֵינוֹ כֵּן (וְעַיֵּין לְקַמָּן סִימָן נ׳ סְעִיף י״ג)[53].

כ. אִם אוֹכְלִין בַּחֲבוּרָה וְיָצְאוּ קְצָת מֵהֶם עַל דַּעַת שֶׁיַּחְזְרוּ לְכָאן, כֵּיוָן שֶׁנִּשְׁאַר אֲפִילוּ רַק אֶחָד מֵהֶן כָּאן בִּמְקוֹמוֹ, לֹא נִתְבַּטֵּל הַקְּבִיעוּת[54], וּכְשֶׁחוֹזְרִין לִקְבִיעוּתָן חוֹזְרִין וְלֹא הָוֵי הֶפְסֵק.

כא. אִם בִּשְׁעַת בִּרְכַּת הַמּוֹצִיא הָיְתָה דַּעְתּוֹ לָלֶכֶת אַחַר כָּךְ לְבֵית אַחֵר לִגְמוֹר שָׁם סְעוּדָתוֹ[55] וּלְבָרֵךְ שָׁם בִּרְכַּת הַמָּזוֹן, נוֹהֲגִין לְהַתִּיר, וְצָרִיךְ לִיזָּהֵר לֶאֱכוֹל גַּם שָׁם לְכָל הַפָּחוֹת כְּזַיִת פַּת. וְאֵין לַעֲשׂוֹת כֵּן אֶלָּא לְעֵת הַצּוֹרֶךְ, לִסְעוּדַּת מִצְוָה[56].

כב. הַמִּתְפַּלֵּל בְּתוֹךְ הַסְּעוּדָה — כְּשֶׁחוֹזֵר לֶאֱכוֹל, אֵין צָרִיךְ לְבָרֵךְ עוֹד הַמּוֹצִיא.

דְּבָרִים אֵינוֹ כֵּן — However, with regard to foods other than bread, **the halachah is not like this** (וְעַיֵּין לְקַמָּן סִימָן נ׳ סְעִיף י״ג — **see below, 50:13,** for the halachah as it pertains to other foods).[53]

§20 אִם אוֹכְלִין בַּחֲבוּרָה — **If** a few **people are eating** together **as a group,** וְיָצְאוּ קְצָת מֵהֶם — **and some of them left** עַל דַּעַת שֶׁיַּחְזְרוּ לְכָאן — **with the intention to return to** their original place, כֵּיוָן שֶׁנִּשְׁאַר אֲפִילוּ רַק אֶחָד מֵהֶן כָּאן בִּמְקוֹמוֹ — **as long as even only one person remains there in his place,** לֹא נִתְבַּטֵּל הַקְּבִיעוּת — **the meal is not** considered to have **ended**[54] even for those who left; וּכְשֶׁחוֹזְרִין לִקְבִיעוּתָן חוֹזְרִין — thus, **when they return, they are** considered to be **returning to their original meal** וְלֹא הָוֵי הֶפְסֵק — **and** their leaving **does not constitute an interruption** to the meal.

§21 אִם בִּשְׁעַת בִּרְכַּת הַמּוֹצִיא — **If, at the time one** recited **the** ***hamotzi*** **blessing,** הָיְתָה דַּעְתּוֹ לָלֶכֶת אַחַר כָּךְ — **he planned to go after** eating some of the meal לְבֵית אַחֵר לִגְמוֹר שָׁם סְעוּדָתוֹ — **to another house to conclude his meal there**[55] וּלְבָרֵךְ שָׁם בִּרְכַּת הַמָּזוֹן — **and to recite** ***Bircas HaMazon*** **there,** נוֹהֲגִין לְהַתִּיר — **it is customary to permit** him to do this. וְצָרִיךְ לִיזָּהֵר — When one does this, however, **one must take care** לֶאֱכוֹל גַּם שָׁם לְכָל הַפָּחוֹת כְּזַיִת פַּת — **to eat at least a** ***kezayis*** **of bread** in the second place **as well.** וְאֵין לַעֲשׂוֹת כֵּן — However, **one should not do this** אֶלָּא לְעֵת הַצּוֹרֶךְ, לִסְעוּדַּת מִצְוָה — **except when it is necessary for a mitzvah meal.**[56]

§22 הַמִּתְפַּלֵּל בְּתוֹךְ הַסְּעוּדָה — The law regarding **one who recites** one of the daily **prayers during a meal is** כְּשֶׁחוֹזֵר לֶאֱכוֹל — **that when he returns** to the meal **to eat,** אֵין צָרִיךְ לְבָרֵךְ עוֹד הַמּוֹצִיא — **he need not recite the** ***hamotzi*** **blessing again.**

---

53. According to Kitzur, bread is unique among all foods due to its special requirement to recite *Bircas HaMazon* in the place where one ate. However, some authorities hold that since one who eats grain products or fruit of the Seven Species must also recite the *berachah acharonah* (final blessing) in the place where he ate (see below, 51:13), leaving that place before reciting the *berachah acharonah* does not constitute an interruption in his eating session (as explained above, note 50). See further below, *Siman* 50, note 51.

54. Literally, *the [eating] session is not terminated.*

55. See *Mishnah Berurah* 178:33. See also Kitzur below, 135:3, who writes that one should also have this in mind during the washing of *netilas yadayim.*

56. *Mishnah Berurah* makes no such stipulation when discussing this allowance (see 178:33,40).

LAWS OF PROPER CONDUCT FOR A MEAL — SIMAN 42:23 90

וְכֵן אִם יָשַׁן בְּתוֹךְ הַסְּעוּדָה שֵׁינַת אַרְעַי[57], אַף עַל פִּי שֶׁנִּמְשַׁךְ אֵיזֶה זְמַן[58], לֹא מִיקְרֵי הֶפְסֵק. וְכֵן אִם הִפְסִיק בִּשְׁאָר דִּבְרֵי רְשׁוּת[59], כְּגוֹן, שֶׁהוּצְרַךְ לִנְקָבָיו וְכַיּוֹצֵא בָזֶה. וּמִכָּל מָקוֹם בְּכָל אֵלּוּ בָּעֵי נְטִילַת יָדַיִם מֵחָדָשׁ, מִשּׁוּם דַּהֲוֵי הֶיסֵּחַ הַדַּעַת, אֶלָּא אִם כֵּן שָׁמַר יָדָיו[60]. אַךְ לֹא יְבָרֵךְ עַל הַנְּטִילָה[61], כִּי מִשּׁוּם הֶיסֵּחַ הַדַּעַת אֵין מְבָרְכִין עַל הַנְּטִילָה[62].

כג. מִשֶּׁגָּמַר סְעוּדָתוֹ וְנָתַן דַּעְתּוֹ לְבָרֵךְ בִּרְכַּת הַמָּזוֹן, אִם חוֹזֵר וְרוֹצֶה לֶאֱכוֹל, אוֹ לִשְׁתּוֹת, יֵשׁ בָּזֶה הַרְבֵּה חִילּוּקֵי דִינִים לְעִנְיַן הַבְּרָכוֹת[63], עַל כֵּן יֵשׁ לִמְנוֹעַ מִזֶּה. אֶלָּא, מִיָּד כְּשֶׁנָּתַן דַּעְתּוֹ לְבָרֵךְ בִּרְכַּת הַמָּזוֹן, יְבָרֵךְ בִּרְכַּת הַמָּזוֹן.

וְכֵן אִם יָשַׁן בְּתוֹךְ הַסְּעוּדָה שֵׁינַת אַרְעַי — Likewise, if one took a nap during the meal,[57] **אַף עַל פִּי שֶׁנִּמְשַׁךְ אֵיזֶה זְמַן — even if it lasted some time,**[58] **לֹא מִיקְרֵי הֶפְסֵק — it is not considered an interruption** with regard to the *hamotzi* blessing. **וְכֵן — It is likewise** not considered an interruption **אִם הִפְסִיק בִּשְׁאָר דִּבְרֵי רְשׁוּת — if he interrupted** the meal **to attend to any other non-mandatory matter,**[59] **כְּגוֹן, שֶׁהוּצְרַךְ לִנְקָבָיו וְכַיּוֹצֵא בָזֶה — for example, if he attended to his bodily needs, or the like. וּמִכָּל מָקוֹם — Nevertheless, בְּכָל אֵלּוּ בָּעֵי נְטִילַת יָדַיִם מֵחָדָשׁ — in all of these** cases, **a new** ***netilas yadayim*** **is necessary מִשּׁוּם דַּהֲוֵי הֶיסֵּחַ הַדַּעַת — because,** during these activities, **he diverted his attention** from the cleanliness of his hands, **אֶלָּא אִם כֵּן שָׁמַר יָדָיו — unless he** specifically **watched his hands** to make sure that they did not touch anything unclean.[60] **אַךְ לֹא יְבָרֵךְ עַל הַנְּטִילָה — However,** although he must wash, **he does not recite the blessing** (*al netilas yadayim*) **upon this washing,**[61] **כִּי מִשּׁוּם הֶיסֵּחַ הַדַּעַת אֵין מְבָרְכִין עַל הַנְּטִילָה — for we do not recite a blessing upon a washing that is necessitated by his diverting attention** from the cleanliness of his hands.[62]

§23 מִשֶּׁגָּמַר סְעוּדָתוֹ — From the time **when one has concluded his meal וְנָתַן דַּעְתּוֹ לְבָרֵךְ בִּרְכַּת הַמָּזוֹן — and decided to recite *Bircas HaMazon,* אִם חוֹזֵר וְרוֹצֶה לֶאֱכוֹל, אוֹ לִשְׁתּוֹת — if he wishes to eat or drink again, יֵשׁ בָּזֶה הַרְבֵּה חִילּוּקֵי דִינִים לְעִנְיַן הַבְּרָכוֹת — there are many detailed halachos that pertain to this** situation **with regard to the** requirements of reciting **blessings** on that which he will eat or drink.[63] **עַל כֵּן יֵשׁ לִמְנוֹעַ מִזֶּה — One should therefore refrain from** entering into **this** situation. **אֶלָּא — Rather, מִיָּד כְּשֶׁנָּתַן דַּעְתּוֹ לְבָרֵךְ בִּרְכַּת הַמָּזוֹן — as soon as he decides** to recite ***Bircas HaMazon,*** **יְבָרֵךְ בִּרְכַּת הַמָּזוֹן — he should recite *Bircas HaMazon.***

57. I.e., he did not go to bed for a regular sleeping session (שינת קבע); rather, he simply fell asleep at the table (see *Mishnah Berurah* 178:48).

58. Even if he slept in this manner for about an hour (*Mishnah Berurah* 178:48).

59. That is, any interruption that is not set by Rabbinic law to be performed at that time of the meal. Prayer, although required to be done by a certain time, is not a set part of the meal and therefore does not constitute an interruption with regard to the blessing. See *Beur Halachah* to 178:7 s.v. דברי רשות.

60. One who attends to his bodily needs must wash *netilas yadayim* in any case; see above, 40:16. According to *Mishnah Berurah* 178:47, one need not wash his hands again when he stopped the meal only to pray in the place where he was eating. However, when going to the synagogue for prayers during a meal, he must wash his hands again upon his return.

61. See above, 40:16, with note 69.

62. According to *Beur Halachah* (178:1 s.v. המוציא), one who left during the meal for an extended amount of time, and diverted his attention from the cleanliness of his hands, must wash *netilas yadayim* again upon returning to his meal, *and* recite the blessing. See also *Mishnah Berurah* 164:13.

63. See *Shulchan Aruch* 179:1-3. In such a situation, he may also be required to wash *netilas yadayim* again; see *Mishnah Berurah* 179:9.

91 BLESSINGS ON FOODS OR DRINKS DURING A MEAL — SIMAN 43:1

סימן מג

הִלְכוֹת בְּרָכוֹת לִדְבָרִים שֶׁאוֹכְלִים וְשׁוֹתִים בְּתוֹךְ הַסְּעוּדָה

וּבוֹ ז׳ סְעִיפִים.

א. כָּל מַה שֶּׁאוֹכְלִים בְּתוֹךְ הַסְּעוּדָה[1] מִדְּבָרִים שֶׁרְגִילִים לְאָכְלָם בְּתוֹךְ הַסְּעוּדָה לִשְׂבּוֹעַ[2], כְּגוֹן, בָּשָׂר וְדָגִים וּמִינֵי לְפְתָּן דַּיְיסָא מִינֵי לְבִיבוֹת[3], אֲפִילוּ דְבָרִים שֶׁאוֹכְלִים בְּלֹא לֶחֶם, כּוּלָּם אֵינָן צְרִיכִין בְּרָכָה, לֹא לִפְנֵיהֶם, וְלֹא לְאַחֲרֵיהֶם, שֶׁכֵּיוָן שֶׁאוֹכְלִין אוֹתָן לִשְׂבּוֹעַ הֲרֵי הֵן בִּכְלַל הַסְּעוּדָה, וְכָל הַסְּעוּדָה נִגְרֶרֶת אַחַר הַלֶּחֶם שֶׁהוּא עִיקַּר חַיֵּי הָאָדָם[4],

SIMAN 43

THE LAWS OF BLESSINGS FOR FOODS THAT ONE EATS OR DRINKS DURING A MEAL

CONTAINING 7 *SE'IFIM*

§1 Food That Is Considered "Part of the Meal" / §2 Beverages; Wine; Liquor / §3-5 Fruits / §6 Baked Goods / §7 Coffee After the Meal

§1 כָּל מַה שֶּׁאוֹכְלִים בְּתוֹךְ הַסְּעוּדָה — **Any** foods **eaten during a meal,**[1] מִדְּבָרִים שֶׁרְגִילִים לְאָכְלָם בְּתוֹךְ הַסְּעוּדָה לִשְׂבּוֹעַ — if they are **items that are ordinarily eaten during a meal for the purpose of satisfying** one's hunger,[2] כְּגוֹן — **such as** בָּשָׂר וְדָגִים — **meat, fish,** וּמִינֵי לְפְתָּן — **types of condiments,** דַּיְיסָא — **cereal,** מִינֵי לְבִיבוֹת — or different **types of pancakes,**[3] אֲפִילוּ דְבָרִים שֶׁאוֹכְלִים בְּלֹא לֶחֶם — **even** if they are **items that are not** necessarily **eaten** together **with bread,** כּוּלָּם אֵינָן צְרִיכִין בְּרָכָה — **they all do not require** their own **blessing,** לֹא לִפְנֵיהֶם, וְלֹא לְאַחֲרֵיהֶם — **neither prior to** eating **them** (*berachah rishonah — first blessing*) **nor after** eating **them** (*berachah acharonah — final blessing*). שֶׁכֵּיוָן שֶׁאוֹכְלִין אוֹתָן לִשְׂבּוֹעַ — The reason **for this is, since these foods are eaten to satisfy** hunger הֲרֵי הֵן בִּכְלַל הַסְּעוּדָה — **they are considered part of the meal,** וְכָל הַסְּעוּדָה נִגְרֶרֶת אַחַר הַלֶּחֶם — and anything that is considered part of the meal is not viewed independently, **for the entire meal is** considered **subordinate to the bread** with which the meal begins, שֶׁהוּא עִיקַּר חַיֵּי הָאָדָם — **since bread is man's primary source of sustenance.**[4]

1. With regard to these halachos, a "meal" refers to a meal that began with bread; see *Mishnah Berurah* 177:3.

2. For further discussion of this classification, see Appendix of Kitzur's editorial glosses.

3. Other examples include eggs, cooked vegetables, and cheese; see *Shulchan Aruch* 177:1 and *Shaarei Teshuvah* ad loc.

4. This rule applies only if one eats a *kezayis* of bread within the time span of *achilas pras* (literally, *the amount* [of time it takes] *to eat a half-loaf* [of bread]), referring to the standard loaf in the times of the Mishnah. [This time span ranges from 2 to 9 minutes according to the various authorities, and also varies in different situations. According to Rabbi Moshe Feinstein (*Igros Moshe, Orach Chaim* IV, §41), one must eat the *kezayis* within three minutes in order to exempt the requirement to recite a blessing upon other foods of the meal.]

If, during the meal, one does not eat a *kezayis* within that time span, then blessings are required before and after all the other foods consumed during the meal. [This can have practical consequences when one is eating a large meal, but receives only a small portion of bread or *challah*.]

Therefore, one must make up his mind

BLESSINGS ON FOODS OR DRINKS DURING A MEAL — SIMAN 43:2 92

וְלָכֵן כּוּלָּן נִפְטָרִין בְּבִרְכַּת הַמּוֹצִיא[5] וּבְבִרְכַּת הַמָּזוֹן[6]. וַאֲפִילּוּ אִם נִשְׁלְחוּ לוֹ מִבָּתִּים אֲחֵרִים, אֵין צָרִיךְ לְבָרֵךְ עֲלֵיהֶם, דִּסְתָמָא דַּעַת הָאָדָם עַל כָּל מַה שֶּׁיָּבִיאוּ לוֹ[7].

ב. וְכֵן אֵינוֹ צָרִיךְ לְבָרֵךְ עַל כָּל מִינֵי מַשְׁקִין, שֶׁהַמַּשְׁקִין גַּם כֵּן בִּכְלַל הַסְּעוּדָה הֵן, דְּאֵין דֶּרֶךְ אֲכִילָה בְּלֹא שְׁתִיָּה, חוּץ מֵעַל הַיַּיִן, לְפִי שֶׁהַיַּיִן הוּא דָבָר חָשׁוּב (שֶׁבְּכַמָּה מְקוֹמוֹת מְחוּיָּבִין לְבָרֵךְ עָלָיו, אַף עַל פִּי שֶׁאֵינוֹ צָרִיךְ לִשְׁתּוֹת כְּגוֹן קִידּוּשׁ וְהַבְדָּלָה) צְרִיכִין לְבָרֵךְ עָלָיו גַּם בְּתוֹךְ הַסְּעוּדָה[8]. וְאִם בֵּירַךְ עַל הַיַּיִן קוֹדֶם נְטִילַת

וְלָכֵן — **Therefore,** **כּוּלָּן נִפְטָרִין** — **all of these** foods **are exempted** from a *berachah rishonah* **בְּבִרְכַּת הַמּוֹצִיא** — **by the *hamotzi* blessing** that is recited prior to eating the bread,[5] **וּבְבִרְכַּת הַמָּזוֹן** — **and** they are exempted from a *berachah acharonah* **by the *Bircas HaMazon*** (Grace After Meals)[6] recited at the conclusion of the meal.

וַאֲפִילּוּ אִם נִשְׁלְחוּ לוֹ מִבָּתִּים אֲחֵרִים — **Even in the case that** after he began his meal, food **was sent to him from other houses,** **אֵין צָרִיךְ לְבָרֵךְ עֲלֵיהֶם** — **he need not recite a** separate **blessing upon them,** **דִּסְתָמָא דַּעַת הָאָדָם** — **because the unspecified intention of a person** when reciting a blessing at the beginning of a meal **is** **עַל כָּל מַה שֶּׁיָּבִיאוּ לוֹ** — that the blessing is **to** encompass **whatever** foods **they will bring him** in the course of that meal.[7]

§2 **וְכֵן** — **Likewise,** **אֵינוֹ צָרִיךְ לְבָרֵךְ עַל כָּל מִינֵי מַשְׁקִין** — **one need not recite a** separate **blessing for any type of beverage** that he drinks during the meal, **שֶׁהַמַּשְׁקִין גַּם כֵּן בִּכְלַל הַסְּעוּדָה הֵן** — **for the beverages are also** considered **part of the meal,** **דְּאֵין דֶּרֶךְ אֲכִילָה בְּלֹא שְׁתִיָּה** — **as it is uncommon to eat without drinking.** **חוּץ מֵעַל הַיַּיִן** — **The exception** to this rule is **wine,** **לְפִי שֶׁהַיַּיִן הוּא דָבָר חָשׁוּב** — **for wine is** especially **significant** (**שֶׁבְּכַמָּה מְקוֹמוֹת מְחוּיָּבִין לְבָרֵךְ עָלָיו** — as evidenced by the fact that **in many instances one is required to recite the blessing over wine** **אַף עַל פִּי שֶׁאֵינוֹ צָרִיךְ לִשְׁתּוֹת** — **even when he has no need to drink** at the time; **כְּגוֹן קִידּוּשׁ וְהַבְדָּלָה** — **for example,** the obligation to recite ***Kiddush*** on Shabbos **and *Havdalah*** at the conclusion of Shabbos over wine) **צְרִיכִין לְבָרֵךְ עָלָיו גַּם בְּתוֹךְ הַסְּעוּדָה** — Therefore, **one must recite a blessing upon** drinking **wine even during a meal.**[8]

וְאִם בֵּירַךְ עַל הַיַּיִן קוֹדֶם נְטִילַת יָדַיִם — **However, if one recited the blessing for** drinking

---

before the meal that he will eat a *kezayis* of bread, and be sure to do so within the time span of *achilas pras,* in order to exempt all the foods consumed during the meal from their individual blessings (see *Igros Moshe, Orach Chaim* III, §33).

One who eats any amount of bread must wash *netilas yadayim* and recite *hamotzi* on the bread. See above, 40:1 with note 8, with regard to the amount of bread that requires the *netilas yadayim* blessing.

5. See above, 41:1. However, foods that are not usually eaten as part of a meal to satisfy hunger are not subordinate to the bread. The halachos of these foods are set out below, *se'ifim* 3-7.

6. The laws of *Bircas HaMazon* are set out in *Siman* 44.

7. A blessing can only exempt food that a person intended to eat at the time of the blessing (see below, *Siman* 57). Here we learn that since it is not uncommon for one to receive food from a friend or neighbor during his meal, we consider it as if he specifically intended to eat anything that may be brought to him throughout his meal; see *Levush* 177:3.

8. Because of its significance, it is not deemed subordinate to the bread and requires its own blessing.

93 BLESSINGS ON FOODS OR DRINKS DURING A MEAL — SIMAN 43:2

יָדַיִם[9] וְהָיָה דַעְתּוֹ לִשְׁתּוֹת גַּם בְּתוֹךְ הַסְּעוּדָה, אוֹ שֶׁהוּא רָגִיל בְּכָךְ לִשְׁתּוֹת יַיִן בְּתוֹךְ הַסְּעוּדָה, אֵין צָרִיךְ לְבָרֵךְ עָלָיו שֵׁנִית, כִּי נִפְטַר בִּבְרָכָה שֶׁבֵּירַךְ עָלָיו לִפְנֵי הַסְּעוּדָה[10] (וְעַיֵּין לְעֵיל סִימָן ל״ט סְעִיף ב׳)[11]. וְיֵין שָׂרָף בִּמְדִינָתֵינוּ[12], דְּאֵין דֶּרֶךְ לִשְׁתּוֹתוֹ תָּמִיד בְּתוֹךְ הַסְּעוּדָה, הָוֵי סָפֵק אִם הוּא בִּכְלַל הַסְּעוּדָה, אוֹ לֹא[13]. וְלָכֵן, אִם דַּעְתּוֹ לִשְׁתּוֹת יֵין שָׂרָף בְּתוֹךְ הַסְּעוּדָה, יִשְׁתֶּה מְעַט קוֹדֶם נְטִילַת יָדַיִם[14], דְּהַיְינוּ פָּחוֹת מִכְּזַיִת[15] וִיבָרֵךְ עָלָיו וִיכַוֵּין לִפְטוֹר גַּם מַה שֶּׁיִּשְׁתֶּה בְּתוֹךְ הַסְּעוּדָה. וְאִם לֹא עָשָׂה כֵן, יְבָרֵךְ

---

wine before washing his **hands** for a meal.[9] **וְהָיָה דַעְתּוֹ לִשְׁתּוֹת גַּם בְּתוֹךְ הַסְּעוּדָה — and** when he recited the blessing **his intent was to drink** wine **during the meal as well, אוֹ — or,** even if one did not specifically intend to drink wine during the meal, **שֶׁהוּא רָגִיל בְּכָךְ לִשְׁתּוֹת יַיִן בְּתוֹךְ הַסְּעוּדָה — but he is accustomed to drinking wine in the course of his meal, אֵין צָרִיךְ לְבָרֵךְ עָלָיו שֵׁנִית — he need not recite a second blessing** upon wine that he drinks during the meal, **כִּי נִפְטַר — for it is exempted** from a *berachah rishonah* **בִּבְרָכָה שֶׁבֵּירַךְ עָלָיו לִפְנֵי הַסְּעוּדָה — by the blessing recited upon the wine before the meal**[10] **(וְעַיֵּין לְעֵיל סִימָן ל״ט סְעִיף ב׳ — see above, 39:2).**[11] **וְיֵין שָׂרָף בִּמְדִינָתֵינוּ** — Regarding **liquor,** as it is served **in our country,**[12] **דְּאֵין דֶּרֶךְ לִשְׁתּוֹתוֹ תָּמִיד בְּתוֹךְ הַסְּעוּדָה — where it is not the standard practice to always drink it during the meal** (as it is with beverages in general), **הָוֵי סָפֵק אִם הוּא בִּכְלַל הַסְּעוּדָה, אוֹ לֹא — it is a case of** halachic **doubt as to whether it is** considered **a part of the meal or not,** and consequently whether it requires its own *berachah rishonah* when served during a meal.[13] **וְלָכֵן — Therefore,** to avoid this situation, **אִם דַּעְתּוֹ לִשְׁתּוֹת יֵין שָׂרָף בְּתוֹךְ הַסְּעוּדָה — if one is planning to drink liquor during the meal, יִשְׁתֶּה מְעַט קוֹדֶם נְטִילַת יָדַיִם — he should drink a little before** he **washes** his **hands** for the meal;[14] — **דְּהַיְינוּ פָּחוֹת מִכְּזַיִת — that is,** he should drink **less than a *kezayis***[15] **וִיבָרֵךְ עָלָיו — and recite the *berachah*** *rishonah* (i.e., *shehakol*) **upon it** beforehand. **וִיכַוֵּין לִפְטוֹר — And he should have in mind** that this blessing **should exempt גַּם מַה שֶּׁיִּשְׁתֶּה בְּתוֹךְ הַסְּעוּדָה — the** obligation to recite a blessing upon the **liquor that he will drink during the meal as well. וְאִם לֹא עָשָׂה כֵן — If he did not do this,** and he is now in the middle of his meal and wishes to drink liquor, **יְבָרֵךְ**

---

9. That is, in close proximity to the meal (*Beur Halachah* to 174:4 s.v. לפני המזון). This halachah is also applicable when one recites *Kiddush* on wine before the Shabbos or Yom Tov meal; see below, 77:11, and *Mishnah Berurah* 174:8.

10. A blessing exempts that which one plans to eat or drink when he recites the blessing. In this case, if it is his custom to drink wine during the meal, it is considered as if he had planned to drink the wine at the time that he recited the blessing before the meal.

11. Regarding the requirement of a *berachah acharonah* after wine that one drinks before a meal.

12. The Kitzur was written in Hungary.

13. Whereas other beverages, which serve to aid eating or to satisfy thirst brought on by eating, are always considered to be a part of the meal, liquor is not always served for this purpose. It is therefore unclear whether it can be included in the halachah governing other beverages, which, as explained in the beginning of this *se'if,* is based upon the fact that one generally drinks while eating a meal.

14. He should drink it in the place where he will be eating the meal (*Shulchan Aruch* 174:7).

15. As noted by Kitzur above (39:2), in order to avoid any question of an obligation to recite a *berachah acharonah* after drinking the liquor, one should drink less than .6 fl. oz. (17.3 cc.), the amount of a *kezayis* according to some authorities; see Appendix A.

BLESSINGS ON FOODS OR DRINKS DURING A MEAL — SIMAN 43:3 94

מִתְחִלָּה עַל קְצָת צוּקֶר[16] וְיִפְטוֹר אֶת הַיַּיִן שָׂרָף[17]. וְיֵשׁ נוֹהֲגִין לִטְבּוֹל מְעַט פַּת בְּתוֹכוֹ[18]. אֲבָל יֵשׁ מְפַקְפְּקִין עַל זֶה (עַיֵּין מַחֲצִית הַשֶּׁקֶל סִימָן קע״ז סְעִיף קָטָן ג׳)[19].

ג. אִם רוֹצֶה לֶאֱכוֹל בְּתוֹךְ הַסְּעוּדָה פֵּירוֹת[20] בְּלֹא פַּת, כֵּיוָן שֶׁאֵין הַפֵּירוֹת מֵעִיקַּר הַסְּעוּדָה[21], לָכֵן אֲפִילוּ אִם הָיוּ מוּנָּחִין עַל הַשֻּׁלְחָן קוֹדֶם בִּרְכַּת הַמּוֹצִיא, מִכָּל מָקוֹם אֵינָן נִפְטָרִין בְּבִרְכַּת הַמּוֹצִיא, וְצָרִיךְ לְבָרֵךְ עֲלֵיהֶם בְּרָכָה רִאשׁוֹנָה,

---

מִתְחִלָּה עַל קְצָת צוּקֶר — **he should first recite a *berachah* rishonah on some sugar,**[16] וְיִפְטוֹר אֶת הַיַּיִן שָׂרָף — **having in mind** that this blessing **should exempt the liquor as well.**[17] וְיֵשׁ נוֹהֲגִין לִטְבּוֹל מְעַט פַּת בְּתוֹכוֹ — **Some have the practice to dip some bread into the liquor,** so as to avoid the halachic doubt regarding the *berachah rishonah* on the liquor;[18] אֲבָל יֵשׁ מְפַקְפְּקִין עַל זֶה — **however, there are** authorities **who have reservations about** the efficacy of **this** solution (עַיֵּין מַחֲצִית הַשֶּׁקֶל סִימָן קע״ז סְעִיף קָטָן ג׳ — see *Machatzis HaShekel* 177:3).[19]

§3 אִם רוֹצֶה לֶאֱכוֹל בְּתוֹךְ הַסְּעוּדָה — **If a person wishes to eat, during a meal,** פֵּירוֹת בְּלֹא פַּת — **fruits,**[20] eaten **separately from the bread,** the law is as follows: כֵּיוָן שֶׁאֵין הַפֵּירוֹת מֵעִיקַּר הַסְּעוּדָה — **Since the fruits are not a primary** component **of the meal,**[21] לָכֵן — **therefore,** אֲפִילוּ אִם הָיוּ מוּנָּחִין עַל הַשֻּׁלְחָן — **even if they were placed on the table** קוֹדֶם בִּרְכַּת הַמּוֹצִיא — **before the *hamotzi* blessing** was recited, מִכָּל מָקוֹם — **nevertheless,** אֵינָן נִפְטָרִין בְּבִרְכַּת הַמּוֹצִיא — **they are not exempt** from their own *berachah rishonah* **by the *hamotzi* blessing,** וְצָרִיךְ לְבָרֵךְ עֲלֵיהֶם בְּרָכָה רִאשׁוֹנָה — **and one must recite a *berachah rishonah* upon** eating **them.**

---

16. Sweets, which are not eaten to satisfy one's hunger, require a *berachah rishonah* even when eaten during the meal; see *Mishnah Berurah* 177:4.

17. *Mishnah Berurah* (174:39) points out that this case of doubt is usually avoided at the Shabbos meal since the meal is often immediately preceded by *Kiddush*. As set out below, 49:4-5, one who recites a blessing upon wine need not recite a blessing on any other beverages that he consumes afterward (pursuant to the conditions set out there). Thus, if he recited the *Kiddush* upon wine, all beverages that he subsequently drinks, before or during the meal, do not require a separate blessing. If one recited *Kiddush* on beer or the like, upon which the *shehakol* blessing is recited (see below, 52:2), he has certainly exempted the liquor from its own blessing (which is also *shehakol*) during the meal.

18. According to this reasoning, eating the liquor together with the bread makes the liquor subordinate to the bread, and it would therefore be exempt from its own *berachah rishonah* (see below, *Siman* 54, for the halachos of blessings upon "primary" and "subordinate" foods).

19. *Machatzis HaShekel* writes that there are halachic authorities who maintain that when eating something that has no connection to the meal itself, one must recite a *berachah rishonah* even if he eats it with bread; cf. below, *se'if* 3; *Mishnah Berurah* 212:5. [Even according to those who hold that in this case the liquor is indeed considered subordinate, dipping the bread into the liquor would exempt the liquor only if he dips it both at the beginning of his eating and at the end; see below, *se'if* 3, and *Shaar HaTziyun* 174:45.]

Regarding beverages that are served at the end of a meal, see below, *se'if* 7.

20. This includes any food that is eaten as a treat or dessert, and not for the purpose of satisfying hunger (*Mishnah Berurah* 177:4).

21. I.e., they are not items ordinarily eaten during a meal for the purpose of satisfying one's hunger (as described at the beginning of this *Siman*). (Regarding those locales in which fruit is eaten for satiety, and is considered one of the primary courses of the meal, see *Beur Halachah* 177:1 s.v. כגון תאנים; see also following *se'if*.)

95 BLESSINGS ON FOODS OR DRINKS DURING A MEAL — SIMAN 43:3

אֲבָל בְּרָכָה אַחֲרוֹנָה אֵינָן צְרִיכִין, כִּי נִפְטָרִין בְּבִרְכַּת הַמָּזוֹן. וְאִם אֵינוֹ רוֹצֶה לֶאֱכוֹל בְּלֹא פַּת, רַק עִם פַּת, אֵין צָרִיךְ לְבָרֵךְ עֲלֵיהֶם, כִּי הֵם טְפֵלִים לְהַפַּת[22]. וְאִם רוֹצֶה לֶאֱכוֹל קְצָתָן עִם פַּת וּקְצָתָן בְּלֹא פַּת, צָרִיךְ לִיזָּהֵר לֶאֱכוֹל תְּחִלָּה בְּלֹא פַּת וִיבָרֵךְ עֲלֵיהֶם, וְאַחַר כָּךְ יָכוֹל לְאָכְלָן גַּם עִם פַּת. אֲבָל אִם יֹאכַל תְּחִלָּה עִם פַּת, וְאַחַר כָּךְ יֹאכַל בְּלֹא פַּת, אִבָּא סְפֵיקָא בִּבְרָכָה[23]. וְיֵשׁ שֶׁרְגִילִין לֶאֱכוֹל בֵּין מַאֲכָל לְמַאֲכָל אֵיזֶה דָּבָר שֶׁמַּמְשִׁיךְ תַּאֲוַת הָאֲכִילָה, כְּגוֹן, זַיִת מָלוּחַ, לִימוֹנִים מְלוּחִים, צְנוֹן וְכַדּוֹמֶה — זֶהוּ נִקְרָא מֵחֲמַת הַסְּעוּדָה, כֵּיוָן שֶׁעַל יְדֵי כֵן הוּא יֹאכַל יוֹתֵר.

אֲבָל בְּרָכָה אַחֲרוֹנָה אֵינָן צְרִיכִין — However, they do not require a separate ***berachah*** *acharonah,* **כִּי נִפְטָרִין בְּבִרְכַּת הַמָּזוֹן — for they are exempted by** the *Bircas HaMazon* recited at the conclusion of the meal.

וְאִם אֵינוֹ רוֹצֶה לֶאֱכוֹל בְּלֹא פַּת — If one does not want to eat any of the fruit **unaccompanied by bread, רַק עִם פַּת — but** would **rather** eat all of the fruit together **with bread, אֵין צָרִיךְ לְבָרֵךְ עֲלֵיהֶם —** in that case, **he need not recite a *berachah*** *rishonah* **on** the fruits **כִּי הֵם טְפֵלִים לְהַפַּת — since they are** considered **subordinate to the bread** with which he is eating them.[22] **וְאִם רוֹצֶה לֶאֱכוֹל — If he would like to eat קְצָתָן עִם פַּת וּקְצָתָן בְּלֹא פַּת — some** of the fruits **with bread and some of them without bread, צָרִיךְ לִיזָּהֵר — he must take care לֶאֱכוֹל תְּחִלָּה בְּלֹא פַּת — to first eat** some of the fruits **without bread, וִיבָרֵךְ עֲלֵיהֶם — and recite a *berachah*** *rishonah* **upon them, וְאַחַר כָּךְ — and** only **after that יָכוֹל לְאָכְלָן גַּם עִם פַּת — may he eat the fruits with the bread, as well. אֲבָל אִם יֹאכַל תְּחִלָּה עִם פַּת — But if he** does the opposite and **begins to eat** the fruit together **with the bread, וְאַחַר כָּךְ יֹאכַל בְּלֹא פַּת — and afterward eats** them **without the bread, אִבָּא סְפֵיקָא בִּבְרָכָה — there would be a** case of **doubt with regard to the** requirement of reciting a ***berachah*** *rishonah* on the fruits that he eats without the bread.[23]

An exception to the above halachah:

וְיֵשׁ שֶׁרְגִילִין לֶאֱכוֹל — There are those who are accustomed to eating בֵּין מַאֲכָל לְמַאֲכָל — between courses אֵיזֶה דָּבָר שֶׁמַּמְשִׁיךְ תַּאֲוַת הָאֲכִילָה — something to arouse the appetite, כְּגוֹן, זַיִת מָלוּחַ — such as pickled olives, לִימוֹנִים מְלוּחִים — pickled lemons, צְנוֹן — radish, וְכַדּוֹמֶה — or the like. זֶהוּ נִקְרָא מֵחֲמַת הַסְּעוּדָה — Although fruits ordinarily require a *berachah rishonah* even during the meal, **these are considered** to be eaten **as a result of the meal** (i.e., as an integral part of the meal), **כֵּיוָן שֶׁעַל יְדֵי כֵן הוּא יֹאכַל יוֹתֵר — since as a result** of eating any of

---

22. Even if the fruit is not subordinate to the bread with which he began his meal, it is subordinate to the bread that he is actually eating together with the fruit. See below, *Siman* 54.

23. There are differing opinions regarding how much of the fruit must be eaten with the bread in order to consider it subordinate to the bread. According to some, it is sufficient to begin eating the fruit with the bread, while others hold that one must both begin and end the eating of the fruit with bread. Still others hold that even if one begins and ends with the bread, whatever fruit is eaten without the bread in the middle of the meal requires a *berachah rishonah* (see *Mishnah Berurah* 177:10 and *Beur Halachah* to 177:1 s.v. ובסוף). Kitzur does not decide among these opinions, and therefore writes that this situation is one of halachic doubt. *Mishnah Berurah* writes (ibid.) that, when possible, one should recite a *berachah rishonah* on the fruit before eating it with the bread (as the Kitzur writes here). However, if he already began eating the fruit (with bread), he may continue eating without making a blessing [even without bread], but should try at least to also conclude the course of fruit by eating it with bread.

BLESSINGS ON FOODS OR DRINKS DURING A MEAL — SIMAN 43:4-5 96

וְלָכֵן אֵין צָרִיךְ לְבָרֵךְ עָלָיו, שֶׁהַפַּת פּוֹטְרוֹ (עַיֵּין מָגֵן אַבְרָהָם סִימָן קע״ד סְעִיף קָטָן י״א)[24].

ד. אִם קוֹבֵעַ עִיקַר סְעוּדָתוֹ עַל הַפֵּירוֹת שֶׁיֹּאכְלֵם עִם הַפַּת, כֵּיוָן שֶׁהֵם עִיקַר הַסְּעוּדָה, נִפְטָרִים בְּבִרְכַּת הַמּוֹצִיא, אֲפִילוּ לֹא הָיוּ אָז עַל הַשֻּׁלְחָן. רַק צָרִיךְ[25] שֶׁתְּחִלַּת אֲכִילַת הַפֵּירוֹת יִהְיֶה עִם הַפַּת[26] וְאַחַר כָּךְ גַּם מַה שֶּׁיֹּאכַל בְּלֹא פַּת אֵינוֹ צָרִיךְ לְבָרֵךְ עֲלֵיהֶם.

ה. פֵּירוֹת[27] הַמְבוּשָׁלִין לְצָרְכֵי הַסְּעוּדָה[28] כְּמוֹ שֶׁרְגִילִין לְבַשֵּׁל (צו שפייז),

---

these foods, **he will eat more** of the meal. **וְלָכֵן אֵין צָרִיךְ לְבָרֵךְ עָלָיו — Therefore, one need not recite a** ***berachah*** *rishonah* **upon** eating one of these items, **שֶׁהַפַּת פּוֹטְרוֹ — since the** blessing recited upon the **bread exempts it** from its own requirement (**עַיֵּין מָגֵן אַבְרָהָם סִימָן קע״ד סְעִיף קָטָן י״א — see** ***Magen Avraham*** **174:11**).[24]

§4 **אִם קוֹבֵעַ עִיקַר סְעוּדָתוֹ עַל הַפֵּירוֹת — If one designates fruits as the main** course **of the meal,** **שֶׁיֹּאכְלֵם עִם הַפַּת — so that he will be eating the fruits to accompany the bread,** **כֵּיוָן שֶׁהֵם עִיקַר הַסְּעוּדָה** — in this case, **since the fruits are the primary component of the meal,** **נִפְטָרִים בְּבִרְכַּת הַמּוֹצִיא — they are** considered a part of the bread meal, and they are thus **exempted** from the requirement of a separate *berachah rishonah* **by the** ***hamotzi*** **blessing** recited on the bread, **אֲפִילוּ לֹא הָיוּ אָז עַל הַשֻּׁלְחָן — even if the fruits were not present on the table at the time** the *hamotzi* blessing was recited. **רַק צָרִיךְ — However,** in order to exempt the fruits according to all opinions,[25] **it is necessary** **שֶׁתְּחִלַּת אֲכִילַת הַפֵּירוֹת יִהְיֶה עִם הַפַּת — that one begin eating the fruits together with the bread.**[26] **וְאַחַר כָּךְ — After this** has been done, **גַּם מַה שֶּׁיֹּאכַל בְּלֹא פַּת — even that which he eats without bread** **אֵינוֹ צָרִיךְ לְבָרֵךְ עֲלֵיהֶם — he does not need to recite a** separate **blessing upon.**

§5 Although fruit is generally not considered part of the meal, it can be served during the meal in a way that (according to some authorities[27]) its presentation clearly demonstrates that it is one of the regular courses of the meal, and is therefore exempt from the requirement of a *berachah rishonah*:

פֵּירוֹת הַמְבוּשָׁלִין לְצָרְכֵי הַסְּעוּדָה — Regarding **fruits that were cooked for the purpose** of eating during **the meal,** [28] **כְּמוֹ שֶׁרְגִילִין לְבַשֵּׁל (צו שפייז) — such as is customary**

---

24. *Magen Avraham* rules according to the authorities who exempt food that was served to stimulate the appetite, and discusses the application of this halachah to liquor served at different times during the meal.

25. See *Shulchan Aruch* 177:3.

26. In the previous *se'if,* the fruit was not served as a primary accompaniment to the meal, and therefore Kitzur would hold that one should both begin and conclude his course of fruit with bread. In this case, since the fruit is served as a primary component of the meal, Kitzur stipulates only that he begin eating the fruit with bread. However, this condition is not satisfied by taking a small taste of the bread together with the fruit and then eating the fruit by itself for the rest of the meal. Rather, he must eat a significant amount with bread, so that his eating them together will signify that the fruit is the primary accompaniment of the bread; see *Beur Halachah* 177:3 s.v. טוב שיאכל.

27. See *Yad Ketanah,* cited in *Mishnah Berurah* 177:4.

28. This is in contrast to cooked fruit that is sometimes served by itself as a dessert (compote); see *Mishnah Berurah* 177:4 and *Shaar HaTziyun* §7.

97 BLESSINGS ON FOODS OR DRINKS DURING A MEAL — SIMAN 43:6

בֵּין עִם בָּשָׂר, בֵּין בְּלֹא בָשָׂר, יֵשׁ לֶאֱכוֹל מֵהֶם בַּתְּחִלָּה וּבַסּוֹף קְצָת עִם פַּת וּבָאֶמְצַע יָכוֹל לֶאֱכוֹל מֵהֶן גַּם בְּלֹא פַּת, וְאֵינָן צְרִיכִין בְּרָכָה[29].

ו. מַעֲשֵׂה אוֹפֶה, צוקער קיבען[30], טארט[31], מאנדיל קיבען[32] וְכַדּוֹמֶה — אִם אוֹכֵל מֵהֶן מֵחֲמַת רְעָבוֹן כְּדֵי לִשְׂבּוֹעַ מֵהֶן, אֵינוֹ צָרִיךְ לְבָרֵךְ עֲלֵיהֶן, אֲבָל אִם אוֹכֵל מֵהֶן רַק לְתַעֲנוּג יֵשׁ סָפֵק בִּבְרָכָה[33]. וְעַל כֵּן, רָאוּי לְאָדָם לְכַוֵּין בִּשְׁעַת בִּרְכַּת הַמּוֹצִיא לִפְטוֹר כָּל מַה שֶּׁיֹּאכַל מִמִּינִים אֵלּוּ[34].

---

to cook a side dish to be served with the main dish, בֵּין עִם בָּשָׂר, בֵּין בְּלֹא בָשָׂר — **whether** it is cooked **with or without meat,** יֵשׁ לֶאֱכוֹל מֵהֶם בַּתְּחִלָּה וּבַסּוֹף — **one should both begin and conclude his eating** of these fruits קְצָת עִם פַּת — by eating **a bit of them with bread,** וּבָאֶמְצַע — **and** that which he eats **in between** יָכוֹל לֶאֱכוֹל מֵהֶן גַּם בְּלֹא פַּת — **he may eat even without bread;** וְאֵינָן צְרִיכִין בְּרָכָה — **and** eaten in this way, **none of the fruits require a** separate ***berachah*** *rishonah.*[29]

§6 מַעֲשֵׂה אוֹפֶה — **Baked goods,** צוקער קיבען — **such as sugar cake,**[30] טארט — **torte,**[31] מאנדיל קיבען — **almond cake,**[32] וְכַדּוֹמֶה — **and the like,** אִם אוֹכֵל מֵהֶן מֵחֲמַת רְעָבוֹן — **if one eats them** during a meal that begins with bread **because he is hungry,** כְּדֵי לִשְׂבּוֹעַ מֵהֶן — **so that he can satisfy** his hunger **with them,** אֵינוֹ צָרִיךְ לְבָרֵךְ עֲלֵיהֶן — they are considered part of the meal, and **one need not recite a** separate ***berachah*** *rishonah* **upon them.** אֲבָל אִם אוֹכֵל מֵהֶן רַק לְתַעֲנוּג — **However, if one eats them** during the meal **only for pleasure,** יֵשׁ סָפֵק בִּבְרָכָה — **there is a** halachic **doubt regarding the** requirement of a separate ***berachah*** *rishonah.*[33] וְעַל כֵּן — **Therefore,** רָאוּי לְאָדָם לְכַוֵּין בִּשְׁעַת בִּרְכַּת הַמּוֹצִיא — **it is proper for a person to have in mind, when reciting the** ***hamotzi*** **blessing,** לִפְטוֹר כָּל מַה שֶּׁיֹּאכַל מִמִּינִים אֵלּוּ — **to** thereby **exempt anything that he will eat of this type** of food from the requirement of a *berachah rishonah.*[34]

---

29. According to one opinion, fruit served as one of the dishes of the meal is considered part of the meal, and is subordinate to the bread. According to this opinion, one may eat the fruit without bread and not be required to recite a blessing upon it. However, since in order to account for the opinion that disagrees, and holds that in this case a *berachah rishonah* is still required on the fruit, Kitzur writes that the fruit should be eaten in the above manner. Eaten in this way, most authorities hold that any fruit, even when not part of the meal, is exempt from a requirement of a *berachah rishonah* (unless it is clearly a dessert; see above, note 23).

Another way to avoid all doubt would be to first recite a *berachah rishonah* on a raw fruit (that clearly requires a *berachah rishonah* even when eaten during a meal), so that the *berachah* upon the raw fruit exempts the cooked fruit as well (*Mishnah Berurah* 177:4).

30. I.e., yeast cake sprinkled with sugar.

31. I.e., sponge cake (especially jam- or cream-filled).

32. A cake with slivered almond topping.

33. Some authorities hold that when eaten during a meal only for pleasure they are not considered part of the meal. Others hold that even in this case they are considered part of the meal, and one does not recite a separate *berachah rishonah* upon eating these baked goods.

34. See below, 56:1, where Kitzur states that if one recited *hamotzi* upon baked goods whose *berachah* is *mezonos* (*pas habaah bekisnin*), he need not recite another blessing.

See *Beur Halachah* (168:8 s.v. טעונים ברכה לפניהם) for further discussion of the halachah regarding eating baked goods during a meal, as well as certain *mezonos* foods upon which there is no halachic doubt.

BLESSINGS ON FOODS OR DRINKS DURING A MEAL — SIMAN 43:7 98

ז. אִם לְאַחַר גְּמַר הַסְּעוּדָה, קוֹדֶם בִּרְכַּת הַמָּזוֹן, שׁוֹתֶה קאפע כְּדֵי לְעַכֵּל הַמָּזוֹן שֶׁאָכַל[35], צָרִיךְ לְבָרֵךְ עָלָיו בְּרָכָה רִאשׁוֹנָה, כִּי מַה שֶּׁהוּא בָּא לְעַכֵּל אֵינוֹ נֶחְשָׁב מִצָּרְכֵי הַסְּעוּדָה, וּמִכָּל מָקוֹם טוֹב לְבָרֵךְ עַל מְעַט צוקער בִּרְכַּת שֶׁהַכֹּל[36] לִפְטוֹר גַּם אֶת הַקאפע[37].

§7 אִם לְאַחַר גְּמַר הַסְּעוּדָה — **If, after the conclusion of the meal,** קוֹדֶם בִּרְכַּת הַמָּזוֹן — **before** one recites ***Bircas HaMazon*** שׁוֹתֶה קאפע כְּדֵי לְעַכֵּל הַמָּזוֹן שֶׁאָכַל — **he drinks coffee**[35] to help **digest the food that he ate,** צָרִיךְ לְבָרֵךְ עָלָיו בְּרָכָה רִאשׁוֹנָה — **he must recite a *berachah rishonah* upon the coffee.** כִּי מַה שֶּׁהוּא בָּא לְעַכֵּל — This is **because that which serves** only **to aid digestion** אֵינוֹ נֶחְשָׁב מִצָּרְכֵי הַסְּעוּדָה — **is not considered** to be one **of the components of the meal** itself. וּמִכָּל מָקוֹם — **Nevertheless,** טוֹב לְבָרֵךְ עַל מְעַט צוקער בִּרְכַּת שֶׁהַכֹּל — **it is a worthy practice to recite the *shehakol* blessing on a bit of sugar**[36] לִפְטוֹר גַּם אֶת הַקאפע — **and** thereby **exempt the** requirement to recite the *berachah rishonah* upon **the coffee as well.**[37]

35. See *Mishnah Berurah* (174:39), who writes that one who drinks liquor after he finished the meal (before *Bircas HaMazon*) for the purpose of aiding digestion would certainly have to recite a *berachah rishonah* on it.

36. See above, note 16.

37. The proper *berachah rishonah* for both coffee and sugar is *shehakol* (see below, 52:18 and 53:3). [See above, note 17, which states that on Shabbos and Yom Tov, when *Kiddush* is recited before the meal, this is not necessary, because the blessing on the wine exempts other beverages.]

99 LAWS OF MAYIM ACHARONIM AND BIRCAS HAMAZON — SIMAN 44

סימן מד

דִּין מַיִם אַחֲרוֹנִים וּבִרְכַּת הַמָּזוֹן[1,2,3,4]

וּבוֹ יח סְעִיפִים

SIMAN 44

THE LAWS OF MAYIM ACHARONIM AND BIRCAS HAMAZON

CONTAINING 18 *SE'IFIM*

§1-2 Procedure for *Mayim Acharonim* / **§3** Leaving Bread on the Table / **§4** Removing the Knives / **§5** Obligation for a *Kezayis* / **§6** Position While Reciting *Bircas HaMazon* / **§7** Amen After *HaRachaman* / **§8-9** Waiting or Leaving Before *Bircas HaMazon* / **§10** Laws of Shabbos and Festival Additions / **§11** One Who Is in Doubt / **§12-15** Compensatory Blessing / **§16** Omitting *Al HaNissim* / **§17** A Meal That Lasts Into the Night / **§18** When Eating With an Idolater

The basic commandment to recite a blessing to Hashem after a meal[1] is of Biblical origin, as the Torah states (*Devarim* 8:10): וְאָכַלְתָּ וְשָׂבָעְתָּ וּבֵרַכְתָּ אֶת ה' אֱלֹהֶיךָ עַל הָאָרֶץ הַטֹּבָה, *And you shall eat and you shall be satisfied and you shall bless Hashem, your God, for the goodly land that He gave you.* This obligation is fulfilled with the recitation of *Bircas HaMazon*, Grace After Meals. *Bircas HaMazon* consists of four blessings,[2] and is followed by a series of detailed supplications, most of which begin with the word הָרַחֲמָן, *The Compassionate One.*

Before reciting *Bircas HaMazon*, the Sages instituted that one wash his hands. This hand-washing is referred to as *mayim acharonim*, literally, *final waters* [in contrast with the initial hand washing (*netilas yadayim*), required before beginning a meal; see above, *Siman* 40]. Two reasons are given for this obligation: (1) It removes any greasy matter that is present upon one's fingers, in respect for the recitation of *Bircas HaMazon*. (2) The Sages were concerned that some Sodomite salt[3] may have been mixed with the table salt and remained on the fingers. Since this substance can pose a danger to one's eyesight if it comes in contact with the eyes, the Sages instituted that the hands be washed at the end of every meal to remove all traces of this salt.[4]

---

1. For the purposes of this halachah, a "meal" must include a minimum amount of bread (see below, *se'if* 5). In certain circumstances, eating other kinds of baked goods as a meal is also subject to this halachah; see below, 48:1.

2. The first three blessings — the Blessing for the One Who nourishes [בִּרְכַּת הַזָּן], the Blessing for the Land [בִּרְכַּת הָאָרֶץ], and the Blessing for the One Who rebuilds Jerusalem [בּוֹנֵה יְרוּשָׁלָיִם] — are all Biblical in origin. The fourth blessing, the Blessing for the One Who is good and Who confers good [הַטּוֹב וְהַמֵּטִיב], was added by the Sages (see *Berachos* 48b; *Mishnah Berurah* 191:2).

3. *Rashi* to *Menachos* 21a (s.v. שאינה שובתת) states that Sodomite salt came from the shores of "the sea," presumably a reference to the Dead Sea that fills the valley that once contained the city of Sodom.

4. *Chullin* 105a-b.

LAWS OF MAYIM ACHARONIM AND BIRCAS HAMAZON — SIMAN 44:1-2 100

א. בְּדִין מַיִם אַחֲרוֹנִים[5] הַרְבֵּה מְקִילִים, אֲבָל נָכוֹן לְכָל יְרֵא שָׁמַיִם לִיזָּהֵר בָּהֶם[6]. וְאֵין צְרִיכִין לִיטּוֹל אֶלָּא עַד פֶּרֶק ב׳ מִן הָאֶצְבָּעוֹת[7]. וְיַשְׁפִּיל יָדָיו קוֹדֶם שֶׁמְּנַגְּבָן[8]. וְהַמְבָרֵךְ הוּא[9] נוֹטֵל בָּרִאשׁוֹנָה[10].

ב. אֵין נוֹטְלִין עַל גַּבֵּי קַרְקַע בְּמָקוֹם שֶׁבְּנֵי אָדָם הוֹלְכִין, מִפְּנֵי שֶׁרוּחַ רָעָה שׁוֹרָה עַל מַיִם אֵלּוּ[11], אֶלָּא יִטּוֹל לְתוֹךְ כְּלִי[12], אוֹ תַּחַת הַשֻּׁלְחָן[13]. וּמְנַגֵּב יָדָיו, וְאַחַר

This *Siman* details the entire procedure of *mayim acharonim* and *Bircas HaMazon,* with particular focus on the variations of the text of *Bircas HaMazon* on Shabbos and festivals:

§1 בְּדִין מַיִם אַחֲרוֹנִים — **With regard to the law of** washing ***mayim acharonim,*** הַרְבֵּה מְקִילִים — **many** people **are lenient** in fulfilling this requirement.[5] אֲבָל נָכוֹן לְכָל יְרֵא שָׁמַיִם — **However, it is proper for every God-fearing** person לִיזָּהֵר בָּהֶם — **to be scrupulous with regard to** *mayim acharonim.*[6] וְאֵין צְרִיכִין לִיטּוֹל — **One need not wash** the entire hand, אֶלָּא עַד פֶּרֶק ב׳ מִן הָאֶצְבָּעוֹת — but **only until the second** (i.e., middle) **joint of the fingers.**[7] וְיַשְׁפִּיל יָדָיו קוֹדֶם שֶׁמְּנַגְּבָן — **He should lower his hands before he dries them.**[8] וְהַמְבָרֵךְ הוּא נוֹטֵל בָּרִאשׁוֹנָה — **The one who will recite the blessings** of *Bircas HaMazon* (i.e., the leader of the *zimun*)[9] **washes his hands first.**[10]

§2 אֵין נוֹטְלִין עַל גַּבֵּי קַרְקַע — **One should not wash** *mayim acharonim* **on the ground** בְּמָקוֹם שֶׁבְּנֵי אָדָם הוֹלְכִין — **in a place where people walk,** מִפְּנֵי שֶׁרוּחַ רָעָה שׁוֹרָה עַל מַיִם אֵלּוּ — **for a** ***ruach raah*** (spirit of impurity) **rests upon these waters.**[11] אֶלָּא יִטּוֹל לְתוֹךְ כְּלִי — **Rather, he should wash into a vessel,**[12] אוֹ תַּחַת הַשֻּׁלְחָן — **or under the table.**[13] וּמְנַגֵּב יָדָיו — After washing **he should dry his hands** וְאַחַר

---

5. See *Shulchan Aruch* (181:10). *Mishnah Berurah* (181:22) explains that this is because nowadays the reasons for the institution of *mayim acharonim* (cited in the introduction to this *Siman*) do not apply: Sodomite salt is not prevalent, and people are generally not particular about any food residue that remains on their hands after eating.

6. *Mishnah Berurah* (181:22), citing *Magen Avraham* and Vilna Gaon, stresses the importance of adhering to this halachah. Furthermore, *Shulchan Aruch* (181:10) writes that one who has a fastidious nature and is particular about any food residue on his hands is certainly required to wash *mayim acharonim.*

7. [The thumb is washed until the first joint.] This is the area of the hand that generally comes into contact with food. If one was aware that a larger area of his hand touched the food, he should wash that part as well (*Mishnah Berurah* 181:10).

There is no requisite amount of water for this function; whatever amount of water effectively cleans the fingers is sufficient. *Mishnah Berurah* (ibid.), however, bemoans the practice of many individuals who wash *mayim acharonim* with a minimal amount of water that barely covers the fingertips, rendering the washing completely ineffective (ibid. §19).

8. This facilitates the flow of water (and any accompanying dirt or grease) off his fingertips (*Shulchan Aruch* 181:5).

9. *Zimun* is a procedure performed when at least three men ate together. See next *Siman* for the laws and requirements of *zimun.*

10. See *Shulchan Aruch* (181:6) with *Mishnah Berurah* (181:12). For further discussion regarding the order of washing *mayim acharonim*, see Appendix of Kitzur's editorial glosses.

11. [This spirit of impurity may cause harm to one who walks over that spot; see *Magen Avraham* 181:2.]

12. It is preferable not to allow the water to subsequently spill onto the ground [where people walk] (see *Beur Halachah* 181:2 s.v. אלא).

13. Where people do not walk. Even if the

101 LAWS OF MAYIM ACHARONIM AND BIRCAS HAMAZON — SIMAN 44:3

כָּךְ מְבָרֵךְ בִּרְכַּת הַמָּזוֹן. וְלֹא יַפְסִיק[14] בֵּין הַנְּטִילָה לְבִרְכַּת הַמָּזוֹן[15].

ג. אֵין לְהָסִיר הַמַּפָּה וְהַלֶּחֶם עַד לְאַחַר בִּרְכַּת הַמָּזוֹן, שֶׁיְּהֵא פַּת מוּנָּח עַל הַשֻּׁלְחָן בִּשְׁעַת בִּרְכַּת הַמָּזוֹן[16] לְהַרְאוֹת כִּי יֵשׁ שֶׁפַע מֵאֵת ה׳ יִתְבָּרֵךְ שְׁמוֹ לֶאֱכוֹל וּלְהוֹתִיר[17], וּכְמוֹ שֶׁאָמַר אֱלִישָׁע לִמְשָׁרְתוֹ (מלכים־ב ד, מג) **״כִּי כֹה אָמַר ה׳ אָכוֹל וְהוֹתֵר״[18]. וְעוֹד, מִשּׁוּם דְּהַבְּרָכָה אֵינוֹ שׁוֹרָה עַל דָּבָר רֵיק, אֶלָּא כְּשֶׁיֵּשׁ שָׁם אֵי זֶה דָּבָר, כְּמוֹ שֶׁאָמַר אֱלִישָׁע לְאֵשֶׁת עוֹבַדְיָה** (שם פסוק ב) **״מַה יֶּשׁ (ליכי) (לָךְ) בַּבָּיִת״[19].**

כָּךְ מְבָרֵךְ בִּרְכַּת הַמָּזוֹן — **and then recite** ***Bircas HaMazon.*** **וְלֹא יַפְסִיק בֵּין הַנְּטִילָה לְבִרְכַּת הַמָּזוֹן** — **He should not interrupt** unnecessarily[14] **between the washing** of his hands **and** ***Bircas HaMazon.***[15]

§3 **אֵין לְהָסִיר הַמַּפָּה וְהַלֶּחֶם** — **One should not remove the tablecloth and the bread** from the table **עַד לְאַחַר בִּרְכַּת הַמָּזוֹן** — **until after** the completion of ***Bircas HaMazon,*** **שֶׁיְּהֵא פַּת מוּנָּח עַל הַשֻּׁלְחָן** — **so that bread will be on the table** **בִּשְׁעַת בִּרְכַּת הַמָּזוֹן** — **while** ***Bircas HaMazon*** is being recited.[16] **לְהַרְאוֹת כִּי יֵשׁ שֶׁפַע מֵאֵת ה׳ יִתְבָּרֵךְ שְׁמוֹ**— This is in order **to demonstrate that there is** such **an abundance** of food **from Hashem, may His Name be blessed,** **לֶאֱכוֹל וּלְהוֹתִיר** — that one has enough **to eat and to leave over,**[17] **וּכְמוֹ שֶׁאָמַר אֱלִישָׁע לִמְשָׁרְתוֹ** — **as the Prophet Elisha said to his attendant** (*II Melachim* 4:43): **״כִּי כֹה אָמַר ה׳ אָכוֹל וְהוֹתֵר״** — ***for thus said*** *Hashem:* ***Eat and leave over!***[18] **וְעוֹד, מִשּׁוּם דְּהַבְּרָכָה אֵינוֹ שׁוֹרָה עַל דָּבָר רֵיק** — **In addition,** another reason for leaving bread on the table is **because blessing cannot take effect upon something empty;** **אֶלָּא כְּשֶׁיֵּשׁ שָׁם אֵי זֶה דָּבָר** — blessing can take effect **only when there is something** upon which the blessing can take effect, **כְּמוֹ שֶׁאָמַר אֱלִישָׁע לְאֵשֶׁת עוֹבַדְיָה** — **as** the Prophet **Elisha said to the wife of Ovadiah** (ibid. v. 2): **״מַה יֶּשׁ (ליכי) (לָךְ) בַּבָּיִת״**— ***What have you in the house?***[19]

---

table is later moved, presumably the water will have dried by then (*Mishnah Berurah* 181:4).

14. Even to speak words of Torah (*Mishnah Berurah* 181:24).

15. If many people are present, those who wash first experience a delay between their washing and their recitation of *Bircas HaMazon* (while everyone else is washing). *Beur Halachah* (s.v. מן הקטן) therefore suggests that in this case a number of cups of *mayim acharonim* be distributed around the table to expedite the process.

16. If one did remove the bread, he should not bring it back to the table for *Bircas HaMazon,* provided there are some small pieces still left on the table. If, however, the table was completely cleared, he may bring bread to the table for *Bircas HaMazon* (see *Shulchan Aruch* 180:2, *Mishnah Berurah* §4-5).

17. Furthermore, when one leaves the tablecloth and bread on the table during *Bircas HaMazon,* it is clear that he is thanking Hashem for the meal he has just eaten (*Mishnah Berurah* 180:1).

18. The many disciples of Elisha faced a situation where they had an insufficient amount of food for all of them. Elisha declared in the Name of Hashem that not only would the food they had suffice for all the disciples, but they would even have enough to leave over. See *II Melachim* 4:38-44.

19. As detailed in *II Melachim* 4:1-7, Elisha performed a miracle for the impoverished widow of Ovadiah; he caused the one jug of oil that the woman possessed to produce a continuous stream of oil that filled all her containers, providing her with a large amount of oil to sell. Elisha began by asking the woman what she had in the house, since no blessing can take place if there is nothing upon which it can take effect. For this reason, we leave bread on the table so that the blessing can take effect on it.

Additionally, bread must be left on the table so that one should have something available to give should a needy person arrive (*Mishnah Berurah* 180:2).

LAWS OF MAYIM ACHARONIM AND BIRCAS HAMAZON — SIMAN 44:4-5 102

ד. נוֹהֲגִין לְהָסִיר אֶת הַסַּכִּינִים מֵעַל הַשֻּׁלְחָן קוֹדֶם בִּרְכַּת הַמָּזוֹן, אוֹ לְכַסּוֹתָן, כִּי הַשֻּׁלְחָן דּוֹמֶה לְמִזְבֵּחַ וּבַמִּזְבֵּחַ נֶאֱמַר (דברים כז, ה) "לֹא תָנִיף עֲלֵיהֶם בַּרְזֶל", לְפִי שֶׁהַבַּרְזֶל מְקַצֵּר יָמָיו שֶׁל אָדָם, וְהַמִּזְבֵּחַ מַאֲרִיךְ יְמֵי הָאָדָם, וְאֵינוֹ בְּדִין שֶׁיּוּנַף הַמְקַצֵּר עַל הַמַּאֲרִיךְ[20]. וְגַם, הַשֻּׁלְחָן מַאֲרִיךְ יָמָיו שֶׁל אָדָם וּמְכַפֵּר עֲווֹנוֹתָיו[21] בְּהַכְנָסַת אוֹרְחִים, שֶׁגָּדוֹל כֹּחָהּ שֶׁל לְגִימָה שֶׁמַּשְׁרָה שְׁכִינָה[22]. וְנָהֲגוּ בְּהַרְבֵּה מְקוֹמוֹת שֶׁלֹּא לְכַסּוֹתָן בְּשַׁבָּת וְיוֹם טוֹב, כִּי בְּחוֹל מְכַסִּין אוֹתָן מִפְּנֵי שֶׁהֵן כֹּחוֹ שֶׁל עֵשָׂו[23] וּבְשַׁבָּת וְיוֹם טוֹב אֵין שָׂטָן[24] וְאֵין פֶּגַע רַע, וּמִנְהָגָן שֶׁל יִשְׂרָאֵל תּוֹרָה הִיא.

ה. אֲפִילּוּ לֹא אָכַל רַק כְּזַיִת פַּת[25], צָרִיךְ לְבָרֵךְ בִּרְכַּת הַמָּזוֹן[26].

---

§4 נוֹהֲגִין לְהָסִיר אֶת הַסַּכִּינִים מֵעַל הַשֻּׁלְחָן — **It is customary to remove the knives from the table** קוֹדֶם בִּרְכַּת הַמָּזוֹן — **before** ***Bircas HaMazon,*** אוֹ לְכַסּוֹתָן — **or to cover them.** כִּי הַשֻּׁלְחָן דּוֹמֶה לְמִזְבֵּחַ — The reason for this is **because one's table is likened to the Altar** in the Temple, "וּבַמִּזְבֵּחַ נֶאֱמַר "לֹא תָנִיף עֲלֵיהֶם בַּרְזֶל — **and regarding the Altar it is stated** (*Devarim* 27:5): ***You shall not raise iron upon them*** (i.e., to cut the stones from which the Altar is built), לְפִי שֶׁהַבַּרְזֶל מְקַצֵּר יָמָיו שֶׁל אָדָם — **because** the **iron** sword **shortens the life of man,** וְהַמִּזְבֵּחַ מַאֲרִיךְ יְמֵי הָאָדָם — **and the Altar lengthens the life of man,** וְאֵינוֹ בְּדִין — **and it is not proper** שֶׁיּוּנַף הַמְקַצֵּר עַל הַמַּאֲרִיךְ — **for** metal, **which shortens** life, **to be wielded on** the Altar **that lengthens** life.[20] וְגַם, הַשֻּׁלְחָן מַאֲרִיךְ יָמָיו שֶׁל אָדָם — **The table** upon which one eats is **also** included in this, as it **lengthens the life of man** וּמְכַפֵּר עֲווֹנוֹתָיו — **and atones for his sins**[21] בְּהַכְנָסַת אוֹרְחִים — **through** the mitzvah of **inviting guests,** שֶׁגָּדוֹל כֹּחָהּ שֶׁל לְגִימָה — **for great is the power of** providing **food** to travelers and guests, שֶׁמַּשְׁרָה שְׁכִינָה — **for it causes the Divine Presence to reside** in this world.[22] וְנָהֲגוּ בְּהַרְבֵּה מְקוֹמוֹת — **In many places it is customary** שֶׁלֹּא לְכַסּוֹתָן בְּשַׁבָּת וְיוֹם טוֹב — **not to cover** the knives **on Shabbos and festivals,** כִּי בְּחוֹל מְכַסִּין אוֹתָן — **because during the week we cover them** מִפְּנֵי שֶׁהֵן כֹּחוֹ שֶׁל עֵשָׂו — **because they** represent **the power of Eisav,**[23] וּבְשַׁבָּת וְיוֹם טוֹב אֵין שָׂטָן וְאֵין פֶּגַע רַע — **but on Shabbos and festivals there is no** influence of ***Satan,***[24] **or** other **tragic occurrence,** so we do not have to cover the knives. וּמִנְהָגָן שֶׁל יִשְׂרָאֵל תּוֹרָה הִיא — **And the customs of Israel are** to be respected like the laws of the **Torah.**

§5 אֲפִילּוּ לֹא אָכַל רַק כְּזַיִת פַּת — **Even if one ate only a** ***kezayis*** **of bread,**[25] צָרִיךְ לְבָרֵךְ בִּרְכַּת הַמָּזוֹן — **he must recite** ***Bircas HaMazon.***[26]

---

20. Mishnah, *Middos* 3:4.

21. See *Chagigah* 27a with *Rashi* and *Tosafos.*

22. For a full explanation of this idea, see *Sanhedrin* 103b-104a.

23. Yitzchak blessed his son Eisav with the words: וְעַל חַרְבְּךָ תִחְיֶה, *By your sword, you shall live* (*Bereishis* 27:40).

24. *Satan* is the guardian angel of Eisav (see *Bereishis* 32:25, with *Kli Yakar*).

25. Between 1 & 1.1 fl. oz. (29.6-33.3 cc.); see further, *Mishnah Berurah* 486:1. The *kezayis* must be eaten within the time span of *achilas pras* (literally, *the amount* [of time it takes] *to eat a half-loaf* [of bread]), referring to the standard loaf in the times of the Mishnah. According to Rabbi Moshe Feinstein (*Igros Moshe, Orach Chaim* IV, §41), with regard to these halachos, this is calculated as close to three minutes.

26. If one eats to satiety, the obligation to recite *Bircas HaMazon* is of Biblical origin. When one eats, but is not fully sated, if he has eaten a *kezayis* or more, he is required to recite *Bircas HaMazon* by Rabbinic decree (*Mishnah Berurah* 184:22, *Beur Halachah* s.v. בכזית). One who eats less than a *kezayis* recites no blessing afterward.

103 LAWS OF MAYIM ACHARONIM AND BIRCAS HAMAZON — SIMAN 44:6-7

ו. לֹא יְבָרֵךְ מְעוּמָּד, וְלֹא מְהַלֵּךְ, אֶלָּא מְיוּשָּׁב. וַאֲפִילוּ הָיָה הוֹלֵךְ בְּתוֹךְ בֵּיתוֹ כְּשֶׁאָכַל, אוֹ שֶׁהָיָה עוֹמֵד, אוֹ מֵיסֵב, כְּשֶׁצָּרִיךְ לְבָרֵךְ, צָרִיךְ לֵישֵׁב כְּדֵי לְכַוֵּין דַּעְתּוֹ בְּיוֹתֵר[27]. וְגַם לֹא יְהֵא מֵיסֵב, שֶׁהוּא דֶּרֶךְ גַּאֲוָה, אֶלָּא יֵשֵׁב וְיִלְבּוֹשׁ מַלְבּוּשׁ הָעֶלְיוֹן, וְגַם יָנִיחַ הַכּוֹבַע בְּרֹאשׁוֹ, שֶׁיְּהֵא מוֹרָא שָׁמַיִם עָלָיו[28] וִיעוֹרֵר הַכַּוָּנָה. וִיבָרֵךְ בְּאֵימָה וּבְיִרְאָה, וְלֹא יַעֲשֶׂה שׁוּם דָּבָר בְּשָׁעָה שֶׁהוּא מְבָרֵךְ[29].

ז. נוֹהֲגִין שֶׁהַשּׁוֹמְעִים עוֹנִין אָמֵן לְאַחַר הָרַחֲמָן שֶׁבְּבִרְכַּת הַמָּזוֹן[30], מִשּׁוּם דְּאִיתָא בְּמִדְרָשׁ[31] כְּשֶׁשּׁוֹמֵעַ אֶחָד מִתְפַּלֵּל דָּבָר אוֹ מְבָרֵךְ לְיִשְׂרָאֵל, אֲפִילוּ בְּלֹא הַזְכָּרַת הַשֵּׁם, חַיָּיב לַעֲנוֹת אָמֵן.

---

§6 **לֹא יְבָרֵךְ מְעוּמָּד, וְלֹא מְהַלֵּךְ — One should not recite *Bircas HaMazon*** while **standing, nor** while **walking, אֶלָּא מְיוּשָּׁב —** but **rather,** while **sitting. וַאֲפִילוּ הָיָה הוֹלֵךְ בְּתוֹךְ בֵּיתוֹ כְּשֶׁאָכַל — Even if he was walking about his house while he was eating, אוֹ שֶׁהָיָה עוֹמֵד, אוֹ מֵיסֵב — or he was standing or reclining** while eating, **כְּשֶׁצָּרִיךְ לְבָרֵךְ — when** the time comes that **he must recite *Bircas HaMazon*, צָרִיךְ לֵישֵׁב כְּדֵי לְכַוֵּין דַּעְתּוֹ בְּיוֹתֵר — he must sit so that he can concentrate intently** on what he is saying.[27]

וְגַם לֹא יְהֵא מֵיסֵב — Additionally, one should not be in a reclining position while reciting the blessing, **שֶׁהוּא דֶּרֶךְ גַּאֲוָה — for this is arrogant conduct. אֶלָּא יֵשֵׁב — Rather, he should sit** upright, **וְיִלְבּוֹשׁ מַלְבּוּשׁ הָעֶלְיוֹן — and wear an outer garment** (i.e., a jacket); **וְגַם יָנִיחַ הַכּוֹבַע בְּרֹאשׁוֹ — he should also place a hat on his head** for this recitation, **שֶׁיְּהֵא מוֹרָא שָׁמַיִם עָלָיו — so that the fear of Heaven should be upon him.**[28] **וִיעוֹרֵר הַכַּוָּנָה — One should arouse** his **concentration וִיבָרֵךְ בְּאֵימָה וּבְיִרְאָה — and recite *Bircas HaMazon* with awe and reverence, וְלֹא יַעֲשֶׂה שׁוּם דָּבָר — and he should not do anything** else **בְּשָׁעָה שֶׁהוּא מְבָרֵךְ — while he is reciting *Bircas HaMazon*.**[29]

§7 **נוֹהֲגִין שֶׁהַשּׁוֹמְעִים עוֹנִין אָמֵן — It is customary for those listening to respond Amen לְאַחַר הָרַחֲמָן שֶׁבְּבִרְכַּת הַמָּזוֹן —** after each *HaRachaman*, ***The Compassionate One*** supplication **in *Bircas HaMazon*,**[30] **מִשּׁוּם דְּאִיתָא בְּמִדְרָשׁ — because it is stated in the Midrash**[31] **כְּשֶׁשּׁוֹמֵעַ אֶחָד מִתְפַּלֵּל דָּבָר אוֹ מְבָרֵךְ לְיִשְׂרָאֵל — that if one hears another person praying or blessing a Jew, אֲפִילוּ בְּלֹא הַזְכָּרַת הַשֵּׁם— even if** the prayer or blessing **does not mention Hashem's Name, חַיָּיב לַעֲנוֹת אָמֵן — he is obligated to respond Amen.**

He must, however, wash *netilas yadayim* without a blessing (see above, 40:1) and recite the *hamotzi* blessing prior to even such a small snack. See also above, *Siman* 43 note 4.

27. If one was eating while on the road, he may recite *Bircas HaMazon* while walking, for it would be difficult to concentrate while preoccupied with his delay. If, however, he had sat down to eat, he must recite *Bircas HaMazon* while seated (*Shulchan Aruch* 183:11 with *Mishnah Berurah* §36).

28. A head covering is conducive to greater fear of Heaven; see *Shabbos* 156b.

29. See above, 6:1, which states that one may not engage in any action while reciting any blessing.

30. This refers to a series of supplications beginning with the word הָרַחֲמָן, *The Compassionate One*; see introduction to this *Siman*.

31. See *Rus Rabbah*, Introduction §4, and *Sifri* to *Devarim* 32:20.

LAWS OF MAYIM ACHARONIM AND BIRCAS HAMAZON — SIMAN 44:8-9 104

ח. עָבַר וְשָׁהָה מִלְּבָרֵךְ בִּרְכַּת הַמָּזוֹן עַד שִׁיעוּר עִיכּוּל, דְּהַיְינוּ שֶׁמַּתְחִיל לִהְיוֹת רָעֵב, אֵין לוֹ עוֹד תַּקָּנָה לְבָרֵךְ[32]. יֵשׁ אוֹמְרִים דְּשִׁיעוּר עִיכּוּל הוּא שָׁעָה וְחוֹמֶשׁ[33]. וּמִכָּל מָקוֹם בִּסְעוּדוֹת גְּדוֹלוֹת לִפְעָמִים יוֹשְׁבִים בֵּין הָאֲכִילָה לְבִרְכַּת הַמָּזוֹן יוֹתֵר מִזְּמַן זֶה, וְהַיְינוּ, מִפְּנֵי שֶׁגַּם בֵּינְתַיִים עוֹסְקִים בִּשְׁתִיָּה וּבְפַרְפְּרָאוֹת, וּמִכָּל מָקוֹם הַנָּכוֹן שֶׁלֹּא לִשְׁהוֹת הַרְבֵּה.

ט. עָבַר וְיָצָא מִמְּקוֹמוֹ קוֹדֶם שֶׁבֵּירַךְ בִּרְכַּת הַמָּזוֹן — אִם יֵשׁ לוֹ בְּמָקוֹם שֶׁהוּא שָׁם קְצָת פַּת[34], יֹאכַל שָׁם[35] וְאֵין צָרִיךְ לְבָרֵךְ עָלָיו בִּרְכַּת הַמּוֹצִיא

---

§8 **עָבַר וְשָׁהָה מִלְּבָרֵךְ בִּרְכַּת הַמָּזוֹן** — **If, in violation** of the halachah, **one delayed reciting** ***Bircas HaMazon*** **עַד שִׁיעוּר עִיכּוּל** — **until** after **the amount of time** has passed **that** the food **is** already **digested,** **דְּהַיְינוּ שֶׁמַּתְחִיל לִהְיוֹת רָעֵב** — **which is when one begins to feel hungry** again, **אֵין לוֹ עוֹד תַּקָּנָה לְבָרֵךְ** — **there is no longer any way to rectify** this and **to recite** ***Bircas HaMazon.***[32]

יֵשׁ אוֹמְרִים — **Some say** **דְּשִׁיעוּר עִיכּוּל הוּא שָׁעָה וְחוֹמֶשׁ** — **that the amount** of time in which **digestion** occurs **is one and one fifth hours** (72 minutes). **וּמִכָּל מָקוֹם** — **Nevertheless,** **בִּסְעוּדוֹת גְּדוֹלוֹת** — **at lengthy meals** **לִפְעָמִים יוֹשְׁבִים בֵּין הָאֲכִילָה לְבִרְכַּת הַמָּזוֹן** — **people will sometimes sit between eating** the meal **and** ***Bircas HaMazon*** **יוֹתֵר מִזְּמַן זֶה** — **for longer than this time** of 72 minutes. **וְהַיְינוּ, מִפְּנֵי שֶׁגַּם בֵּינְתַיִים עוֹסְקִים בִּשְׁתִיָּה וּבְפַרְפְּרָאוֹת** — **This is** acceptable, **because in the meantime they also engaged in drinking and** eating **appetizers.**[33] **וּמִכָּל מָקוֹם** — **Nevertheless,** **הַנָּכוֹן שֶׁלֹּא לִשְׁהוֹת הַרְבֵּה** — **it is proper not to wait** a **long** time from when the meal has concluded until *Bircas HaMazon* is recited.

§9 It has been taught above, 42:19, that one may not leave the place where he ate before reciting *Bircas HaMazon*. The following *se'if* discusses the law regarding one who left his place.

עָבַר— **If one transgressed** **וְיָצָא מִמְּקוֹמוֹ קוֹדֶם שֶׁבֵּירַךְ בִּרְכַּת הַמָּזוֹן** — **and left his place** of eating **before he recited** ***Bircas HaMazon,*** **אִם יֵשׁ לוֹ בְּמָקוֹם שֶׁהוּא שָׁם קְצָת פַּת** — **if he has a small amount of bread**[34] **in the place where he is** now, **יֹאכַל שָׁם** — **he should eat it there.**[35] **וְאֵין צָרִיךְ לְבָרֵךְ עָלָיו בִּרְכַּת הַמּוֹצִיא** — **He need not**

---

32. *Mishnah Berurah* (ibid. §20) points out that this applies only after one has eaten his fill. In a case where a person did not have enough food when he ate, and therefore began to feel hungry immediately after eating, one cannot take his feeling of hunger as an indication that the food he has eaten is already digested. In this case, many authorities hold that one may recite *Bircas HaMazon* in any case until 72 minutes have passed from his meal (see further in Kitzur). Nevertheless, *Mishnah Berurah* writes that in such a case, where one did not eat his fill and then waited before reciting *Bircas HaMazon*, and is unable to determine whether his food has digested, he should, if possible, eat another *kezayis* of bread upon which he can then certainly recite *Bircas HaMazon*. [He need not recite a new blessing of *hamotzi* before eating that bread, unless he had diverted his attention from eating further.]

33. See *Mishnah Berurah* 184:18.

34. For this purpose, even less than a *kezayis* will suffice, as it is considered an extension of his original meal. However, any food other than bread will not serve this purpose (*Mishnah Berurah* 184:9). See also above, 42:19, 21.

35. Eating bread in one's current location helps only if one is still sated from his original meal. If, however, he is hungry again, he can no longer recite *Bircas HaMazon* for the food that he has eaten earlier (as explained in the previous *se'if*), and if he wishes to eat any bread, he must recite the *hamotzi* blessing again

105 LAWS OF MAYIM ACHARONIM AND BIRCAS HAMAZON — SIMAN 44:10

(כְּמוֹ שֶׁנִּתְבָּאֵר בְּסִימָן מ״ב סְעִיף י״ט), וִיבָרֵךְ אַחַר כָּךְ בִּרְכַּת הַמָּזוֹן שָׁם. וְאִם אֵין לוֹ שָׁם פַּת כְּלָל, צָרִיךְ לַחֲזוֹר לִמְקוֹמוֹ לְבָרֵךְ[36]. וְאִם הוּא רָחוֹק כָּל כָּךְ שֶׁיֵּשׁ לָחוּשׁ שֶׁעַד שֶׁיַּחֲזוֹר לִמְקוֹמוֹ יִשְׁהֶה שִׁיעוּר עִיכּוּל, יְבָרֵךְ בְּמָקוֹם שֶׁהוּא שָׁם[37].

י. בְּשַׁבָּת שֶׁחָל בּוֹ רֹאשׁ חֹדֶשׁ, אוֹ יוֹם טוֹב, אוֹ חוֹל הַמּוֹעֵד[38], אוֹמְרִים תְּחִלָּה ״רְצֵה״, וְאַחַר כָּךְ ״יַעֲלֶה וְיָבֹא״[39], מִפְּנֵי שֶׁהַשַּׁבָּת תָּדִיר וּמְקוּדָּשׁ יוֹתֵר מֵהֶם[40].

---

recite the blessing of *hamotzi* on this bread כְּמוֹ שֶׁנִּתְבָּאֵר בְּסִימָן מ״ב סְעִיף י״ט) — **as was already explained in 42:19),** וִיבָרֵךְ אַחַר כָּךְ בִּרְכַּת הַמָּזוֹן שָׁם — **and after** eating it, **he is to recite *Bircas HaMazon* there.**

וְאִם אֵין לוֹ שָׁם פַּת כְּלָל — **If he has no bread there at all,** צָרִיךְ לַחֲזוֹר לִמְקוֹמוֹ לְבָרֵךְ — **he must return to the place** where he originally ate **in order to recite *Bircas HaMazon.***[36] וְאִם הוּא רָחוֹק כָּל כָּךְ — **If he is so far away** שֶׁיֵּשׁ לָחוּשׁ שֶׁעַד שֶׁיַּחֲזוֹר לִמְקוֹמוֹ — **that there is reason for concern that by the time he returns to his** original **place** יִשְׁהֶה שִׁיעוּר עִיכּוּל — **he will have already waited the amount** of time **for digestion to occur** (i.e., 72 minutes), יְבָרֵךְ בְּמָקוֹם שֶׁהוּא שָׁם — **then he should recite the blessing** of ***Bircas HaMazon*** **where he is** now.[37]

§10 On Shabbos, Rosh Chodesh, and festivals, additional prayers are added to *Bircas HaMazon* before the blessing of *U'venei Yerushalayim (Rebuild Jerusalem).* The prayer of *Retzei* (*May it please You)* is inserted on Shabbos and the prayer of *Yaaleh VeYavo (May there rise and come)* is added on Rosh Chodesh and festivals. Kitzur now discusses these insertions:

בְּשַׁבָּת שֶׁחָל בּוֹ רֹאשׁ חֹדֶשׁ — **On a Shabbos that coincides with Rosh Chodesh** אוֹ יוֹם טוֹב, אוֹ חוֹל הַמּוֹעֵד — or with **Yom Tov or Chol HaMoed,**[38] in which case both the *Retzei* and *Yaaleh VeYavo* prayers must be recited, אוֹמְרִים תְּחִלָּה ״רְצֵה״ — **one should first recite** the prayer of ***Retzei*** וְאַחַר כָּךְ ״יַעֲלֶה וְיָבֹא״— **and after that** the ***Yaaleh VeYavo*** prayer;[39] מִפְּנֵי שֶׁהַשַּׁבָּת תָּדִיר וּמְקוּדָּשׁ יוֹתֵר מֵהֶם — the prayer for Shabbos takes precedence, **for Shabbos is more frequent,**[40] **and has greater holiness than those** other days.

(*Mishnah Berurah* 184:10).

36. In pressing circumstances, however, one may rely on the lenient opinions that permit him to recite *Bircas HaMazon* where he is presently. However, this applies only if he left the place in which he ate without intending to violate the halachah that forbids him to leave before reciting *Bircas HaMazon* (i.e., he did not know the halachah, or forgot). If he willfully violated that halachah, he is obligated to return to recite *Bircas HaMazon* in all circumstances (*Shulchan Aruch* 184:1; *Mishnah Berurah* 184:7).

37. In a case where one is required to return to his original place, if he nevertheless recited *Bircas HaMazon* in the second location, even in intentional violation of the halachah, he has fulfilled the obligation of *Bircas HaMazon*, and he does not have to go back and repeat it in his original place (*Mishnah Berurah* 184:5).

38. The first two and final two days of Pesach and Succos (in Eretz Yisrael, the first day and the last day) are Yom Tov. The intermediate days, known as Chol HaMoed, have a partial status of Yom Tov (see *Siman* 104 for its laws). *Yaaleh VeYavo* is recited throughout the festival.

39. If one switched the order, he need not repeat either one (*Mishnah Berurah* 188:13).

40. In general, that which occurs more frequently takes precedence over that which is less frequent; see, for example, above, 10:2.

41. See above, note 26.

LAWS OF MAYIM ACHARONIM AND BIRCAS HAMAZON — SIMAN 44:11-12 106

יא. מִי שֶׁשָּׁכַח וְנִסְתַּפֵּק לוֹ אִם בֵּירַךְ בִּרְכַּת הַמָּזוֹן אוֹ לֹא — אִם הוּא שָׂבֵעַ (דְּאָז בִּרְכַּת הַמָּזוֹן דְּאוֹרַיְיתָא)[41], צָרִיךְ לְבָרֵךְ פַּעַם שֵׁנִית[42]. וְכֵן אִם נִרְדַּם בְּשֵׁינָה בְּאֶמְצַע בִּרְכַּת הַמָּזוֹן וּכְשֶׁהֵקִיץ אֵינוֹ יוֹדֵעַ הֵיכָן פָּסַק, צָרִיךְ לַחֲזוֹר לְרֹאשׁ בִּרְכַּת הַמָּזוֹן[43]. וְאִשָּׁה שֶׁנִּסְתַּפְּקָה אִם בֵּירְכָה אוֹ לֹא אֵינָהּ צְרִיכָה לְבָרֵךְ פַּעַם שֵׁנִית[44].

יב. טָעָה[45] בְּשַׁבָּת וְלֹא אָמַר "רְצֵה", אוֹ בְּיוֹם טוֹב וְלֹא אָמַר "יַעֲלֶה וְיָבֹא", אִם נִזְכַּר קוֹדֶם שֶׁהִזְכִּיר אֶת הַשֵּׁם מִן הַבְּרָכָה שֶׁל "בָּרוּךְ אַתָּה ה' בּוֹנֵה בְּרַחֲמָיו יְרוּשָׁלָיִם"[46],

---

§11 מִי שֶׁשָּׁכַח **— One who forgot,** וְנִסְתַּפֵּק לוֹ אִם בֵּירַךְ בִּרְכַּת הַמָּזוֹן אוֹ לֹא **— and is in doubt whether he recited *Bircas HaMazon* or not,** אִם הוּא שָׂבֵעַ **— if he is sated** from his meal, (דְּאָז בִּרְכַּת הַמָּזוֹן דְּאוֹרַיְיתָא **— in which case** his obligation to recite ***Bircas HaMazon* is Biblically** mandated),[41] צָרִיךְ לְבָרֵךְ פַּעַם שֵׁנִית **— he must recite *Bircas HaMazon* a second time.**[42]

וְכֵן אִם נִרְדַּם בְּשֵׁינָה **— Likewise, if he dozed off** בְּאֶמְצַע בִּרְכַּת הַמָּזוֹן **— in the middle** of reciting ***Bircas HaMazon,*** וּכְשֶׁהֵקִיץ אֵינוֹ יוֹדֵעַ הֵיכָן פָּסַק **— and when he awakens, he does not know where he left off,** צָרִיךְ לַחֲזוֹר לְרֹאשׁ בִּרְכַּת הַמָּזוֹן **— he must go back to the beginning of *Bircas HaMazon.***[43] וְאִשָּׁה שֶׁנִּסְתַּפְּקָה אִם בֵּירְכָה אוֹ לֹא **— A woman who is unsure if she recited *Bircas HaMazon* or not,** אֵינָהּ צְרִיכָה לְבָרֵךְ פַּעַם שֵׁנִית **— need not recite *Bircas HaMazon* a second time.**[44]

§12 If one omitted *Retzei* or *Yaaleh VeYavo* when reciting *Bircas HaMazon* following the first two meals on Shabbos or Yom Tov, or if he is unsure if he included those passages (see *Mishnah Berurah* 188:16), he must recite the *Bircas HaMazon* again from the beginning.[45] However, in certain circumstances, one can correct the omission by adding a compensatory blessing:

טָעָה בְּשַׁבָּת **— If one erred on Shabbos** when reciting *Bircas HaMazon,* וְלֹא אָמַר "רְצֵה" **— and did not recite** the prayer of ***Retzei,*** אוֹ בְּיוֹם טוֹב **— or,** if he erred **on** Yom Tov, וְלֹא אָמַר "יַעֲלֶה וְיָבֹא" **— and did not recite** the ***Yaaleh VeYavo*** prayer, אִם נִזְכַּר קוֹדֶם שֶׁהִזְכִּיר אֶת הַשֵּׁם **— if he became aware** of his omission **before he mentioned the Name** of Hashem מִן הַבְּרָכָה שֶׁל "בָּרוּךְ אַתָּה ה' בּוֹנֵה בְּרַחֲמָיו יְרוּשָׁלָיִם" **— in the blessing of *Blessed are You, Hashem, Who rebuilds Jerusalem in His mercy,***[46]

---

42. It must be recited in its entirety; see *Mishnah Berurah* 184:13. If he did not eat to satiety, but ate only a *kezayis*, his obligation to recite *Bircas HaMazon* is Rabbinic in origin (see above, note 26). In general, in cases of a doubt as to a Rabbinic obligation, we rule leniently; thus, in this case he would not have to recite *Bircas HaMazon*. However, a God-fearing person in this situation should wash *netilas yadayim,* recite *hamotzi,* eat another *kezayis* of bread, and then recite *Bircas HaMazon*; he thus certainly fulfills his obligation without having recited any unnecessary blessings (ibid. §15).

43. If one is *certain* that he did recite part of *Bircas HaMazon*, he need not repeat that part (*Beur Halachah* 188:6 s.v. לחזור).

44. Although women are certainly obligated to recite *Bircas HaMazon,* it is an unresolved question whether their obligation to recite *Bircas HaMazon* is Biblical in origin (see *Shulchan Aruch* 186:1 with *Mishnah Berurah*). Therefore, if a woman is in doubt whether she recited *Bircas HaMazon,* she is not obligated to recite it again (see above, note 42). See *Mishnah Berurah* (186:3) regarding a woman who wishes to recite it in this situation.

45. If one is unsure if he recited the added passage, it is assumed that he did not (*Mishnah Berurah* 188:16).

46. This blessing is the concluding portion of the third blessing of *Bircas HaMazon; Retzei* and

107 LAWS OF MAYIM ACHARONIM AND BIRCAS HAMAZON — SIMAN 44:12

אוֹמֵר שָׁם "רְצֵה", אוֹ "יַעֲלֶה וְיָבֹא", וְאַחַר כָּךְ "וּבְנֵה" וְכוּ', אֲבָל אִם לֹא נִזְכַּר עַד לְאַחַר שֶׁהִזְכִּיר אֶת הַשֵּׁם, מְסַיֵּים אֶת הַבְּרָכָה "בּוֹנֵה בְרַחֲמָיו יְרוּשָׁלָיִם. אָמֵן"[47]. וְאוֹמֵר שָׁם בְּשַׁבָּת: "בָּרוּךְ אַתָּה ה' אֱלֹהֵינוּ מֶלֶךְ הָעוֹלָם אֲשֶׁר נָתַן שַׁבָּתוֹת לִמְנוּחָה לְעַמּוֹ יִשְׂרָאֵל[48] בְּאַהֲבָה לְאוֹת וְלִבְרִית. בָּרוּךְ אַתָּה ה' מְקַדֵּשׁ הַשַּׁבָּת". וּבְיוֹם טוֹב אוֹמֵר שָׁם: "בָּרוּךְ אַתָּה ה' אֱלֹהֵינוּ מֶלֶךְ הָעוֹלָם אֲשֶׁר נָתַן יָמִים טוֹבִים לְעַמּוֹ יִשְׂרָאֵל לְשָׂשׂוֹן וּלְשִׂמְחָה, אֶת יוֹם חַג (פְּלוֹנִי) הַזֶּה[49]. בָּרוּךְ אַתָּה ה' מְקַדֵּשׁ יִשְׂרָאֵל וְהַזְּמַנִּים". וְאִם חָל יוֹם טוֹב בְּשַׁבָּת וְשָׁכַח "רְצֵה" וְגַם "יַעֲלֶה וְיָבֹא", אוֹמֵר: "בָּרוּךְ אַתָּה ה' אֱלֹהֵינוּ מֶלֶךְ הָעוֹלָם אֲשֶׁר נָתַן שַׁבָּתוֹת לִמְנוּחָה לְעַמּוֹ יִשְׂרָאֵל

אוֹמֵר שָׁם "רְצֵה" — **he should recite *Retzei* there,** i.e., before he continues to recite the blessing, **אוֹ "יַעֲלֶה וְיָבֹא"** — **or** in the event that he forgot ***Yaaleh VeYavo,*** he should recite it there, **וְאַחַר כָּךְ "וּבְנֵה" וְכוּ'** — **and, afterward,** continue with the words *U'venei Yerushalayim,* ***Rebuild*** *Jerusalem* **etc.**

אֲבָל אִם לֹא נִזְכַּר עַד לְאַחַר שֶׁהִזְכִּיר אֶת הַשֵּׁם — **However, if he did not become aware** of his omission **until after he mentioned the Name** of Hashem in the blessing of *Who rebuilds Jerusalem,* **מְסַיֵּים אֶת הַבְּרָכָה "בּוֹנֵה בְרַחֲמָיו יְרוּשָׁלָיִם. אָמֵן"** — **he should** continue and **complete the blessing** of ***Who rebuilds Jerusalem in His mercy, Amen.***[47] **וְאוֹמֵר שָׁם בְּשַׁבָּת** — Then, if **it is Shabbos,** and he didn't recite *Retzei,* **he should recite there** the following compensatory blessing: **"בָּרוּךְ אַתָּה ה' אֱלֹהֵינוּ מֶלֶךְ הָעוֹלָם** — ***Blessed are You, Hashem, our God, King of the Universe,*** **אֲשֶׁר נָתַן שַׁבָּתוֹת לִמְנוּחָה לְעַמּוֹ יִשְׂרָאֵל** — ***Who gave Shabbosos for rest to His people Israel,***[48] **בְּאַהֲבָה לְאוֹת וְלִבְרִית** — ***with love, for a sign and for a covenant.*** **בָּרוּךְ אַתָּה ה' מְקַדֵּשׁ הַשַּׁבָּת"** — ***Blessed are You, Hashem, Who sanctifies the Shabbos.***

וּבְיוֹם טוֹב אוֹמֵר שָׁם — If one omitted *Yaaleh VeYavo* **on Yom Tov, he should recite at that point:** **"בָּרוּךְ אַתָּה ה' אֱלֹהֵינוּ מֶלֶךְ הָעוֹלָם** — ***Blessed are You, Hashem, our God, King of the Universe,*** **אֲשֶׁר נָתַן יָמִים טוֹבִים לְעַמּוֹ יִשְׂרָאֵל** — ***Who gave Yamim Tovim to His people Yisrael,*** **לְשָׂשׂוֹן וּלְשִׂמְחָה** — ***for happiness and gladness,*** **אֶת יוֹם חַג (פְּלוֹנִי) הַזֶּה** — ***this festival day of*** *(such-and-such).*[49] **בָּרוּךְ אַתָּה ה' מְקַדֵּשׁ יִשְׂרָאֵל וְהַזְּמַנִּים"** — ***Blessed are You, Hashem, Who sanctifies Israel and the [festive] seasons.***

וְאִם חָל יוֹם טוֹב בְּשַׁבָּת — **If a Yom Tov coincides with Shabbos,** **וְשָׁכַח "רְצֵה" וְגַם "יַעֲלֶה וְיָבֹא"** — **and he forgot** to recite ***Retzei*** **and also** forgot to recite ***Yaaleh VeYavo,*** **אוֹמֵר: "בָּרוּךְ אַתָּה ה' אֱלֹהֵינוּ מֶלֶךְ הָעוֹלָם** — **he should recite:** ***Blessed are You, Hashem, our God, King of the Universe,*** **אֲשֶׁר נָתַן שַׁבָּתוֹת לִמְנוּחָה לְעַמּוֹ יִשְׂרָאֵל** — ***Who gave***

Yaaleh VeYavo are inserted in the third blessing before the words *U'venei Yerushalayim,* "Rebuild Jerusalem."

47. *Mishnah Berurah* (188:22) rules that if one became aware that he forgot to recite *Retzei* immediately after saying the Name of Hashem (i.e., after saying the words, *Baruch Atah Hashem*) in the blessing of *Bonei Yerushalayim,* he should conclude with the words לַמְּדֵנִי חֻקֶּיךָ, *teach me Your statutes,* and then recite *Retzei* and continue as usual. [The words בָּרוּךְ אַתָּה ה' לַמְּדֵנִי חֻקֶּיךָ, *Blessed are You, Hashem, teach me Your statutes,* is a full verse from *Tehillim* (119:12). In this way he avoids reciting the Name of Hashem in vain; see above, 6:4.]

48. Some texts read "שֶׁנָּתַן" instead of "אֲשֶׁר נָתַן"; see *Shulchan Aruch* 188:6.

49. He should recite here the name of the appropriate festival. With regard to Rosh Hashanah, see below, *se'if* 14.

LAWS OF MAYIM ACHARONIM AND BIRCAS HAMAZON — SIMAN 44:13 108

בְּאַהֲבָה לְאוֹת וְלִבְרִית, וְיָמִים טוֹבִים לְשָׂשׂוֹן וּלְשִׂמְחָה, אֶת יוֹם חַג (פְּלוֹנִי) הַזֶּה. בָּרוּךְ אַתָּה ה׳ מְקַדֵּשׁ הַשַּׁבָּת וְיִשְׂרָאֵל וְהַזְּמַנִּים״. וְאִם אָמַר ״רְצֵה״ וְלֹא אָמַר ״יַעֲלֶה וְיָבֹא״, אוֹמֵר כְּמוֹ בְּיוֹם טוֹב לְבַד. וְאִם אָמַר ״יַעֲלֶה וְיָבֹא״ וְלֹא ״רְצֵה״, אוֹמֵר כְּמוֹ בְּשַׁבָּת בִּלְבַד.

יג. אִם לֹא נִזְכַּר עַד לְאַחַר שֶׁהִתְחִיל הַבְּרָכָה שֶׁלְּאַחֲרֶיהָ, שֶׁהִיא ״בָּרוּךְ אַתָּה ה׳ אֱלֹהֵינוּ מֶלֶךְ הָעוֹלָם, הָאֵל, אָבִינוּ״ וְכוּ׳, אֲפִילוּ לֹא אָמַר רַק (תיבות) [תֵּיבַת] ״בָּרוּךְ״ בִּלְבַד (בְּשֻׁלְחָן עָרוּךְ שֶׁל הַתַּנְיָא), שׁוּב אֵין לוֹ תַּקָּנָה בִּבְרָכוֹת ״אֲשֶׁר נָתַן ...״, וְלָכֵן, אִם הוּא בִּשְׁתֵּי סְעוּדּוֹת הָרִאשׁוֹנוֹת, חוֹזֵר לְרֹאשׁ בִּרְכַּת הַמָּזוֹן. וּכְשֶׁלֹּא אָמַר עֲדַיִין רַק ״בָּרוּךְ אַתָּה ה׳ ״, יְסַיֵּים ״לַמְּדֵנִי חֻקֶּיךָ״[50], כְּדֵי שֶׁלֹּא יְהֵא לְבַטָּלָה, וְאַחַר כָּךְ חוֹזֵר לְרֹאשׁ בִּרְכַּת הַמָּזוֹן. אֲבָל בִּסְעוּדָּה שְׁלִישִׁית, שֶׁאֲפִילוּ בְּשַׁבָּת אֵינוֹ מְחוּיָּב לֶאֱכוֹל פַּת דַּוְקָא[51],

---

Shabbosos for rest to His people Israel, בְּאַהֲבָה לְאוֹת וְלִבְרִית— *with love, for a sign and for a covenant,* וְיָמִים טוֹבִים לְשָׂשׂוֹן וּלְשִׂמְחָה — *and festivals, for happiness and gladness,* אֶת יוֹם חַג (פְּלוֹנִי) הַזֶּה — *this festival day of* (such-and-such). בָּרוּךְ אַתָּה ה׳ — *Blessed are You,* Hashem, מְקַדֵּשׁ הַשַּׁבָּת וְיִשְׂרָאֵל וְהַזְּמַנִּים״ *— Who sanctifies the Shabbos and Israel and the [festive] seasons.*
וְאִם אָמַר ״רְצֵה״— If he recited *Retzei* **וְלֹא אָמַר ״יַעֲלֶה וְיָבֹא״ — but did not recite** *Yaaleh VeYavo,* **אוֹמֵר כְּמוֹ בְּיוֹם טוֹב לְבַד — he should recite** the compensatory blessing **as if it were only a Yom Tov.** **וְאִם אָמַר ״יַעֲלֶה וְיָבֹא״ וְלֹא ״רְצֵה״— If he said** *Yaaleh VeYavo* **and not** *Retzei,* **אוֹמֵר כְּמוֹ בְּשַׁבָּת בִּלְבַד — he should recite the** compensatory blessing **as if it were only Shabbos.**

§13 **אִם לֹא נִזְכַּר — If one did not become aware** of his omission **עַד לְאַחַר שֶׁהִתְחִיל הַבְּרָכָה שֶׁלְּאַחֲרֶיהָ — until after he began the blessing following** *Who rebuilds Jerusalem,* **שֶׁהִיא — that is:** ״בָּרוּךְ אַתָּה ה׳ אֱלֹהֵינוּ מֶלֶךְ הָעוֹלָם, הָאֵל, אָבִינוּ״ וְכוּ׳ — ***Blessed are You,*** **Hashem, *our God, King of the Universe, the Almighty, our Father,* etc.,** **אֲפִילוּ לֹא אָמַר רַק (תיבות) [תֵּיבַת] ״בָּרוּךְ״ בִּלְבַד — even if he said only the word** *Baruch,* ***Blessed,*** **(בְּשֻׁלְחָן עָרוּךְ שֶׁל הַתַּנְיָא** — this point is **from the** ***Shulchan Aruch*** **of** the author of **the** *Tanya,* 188:9), **שׁוּב אֵין לוֹ תַּקָּנָה — at this point, he no longer has a way to rectify** his omission **בִּבְרָכוֹת ״אֲשֶׁר נָתַן ...״ — by** reciting **the** compensatory **blessing of** *Asher nasan,* ***Who gave,*** etc. **וְלָכֵן, אִם הוּא בִּשְׁתֵּי סְעוּדּוֹת הָרִאשׁוֹנוֹת — Therefore, if he was** reciting *Bircas HaMazon* **at** one **of the first two meals** of Shabbos or Yom Tov, **חוֹזֵר לְרֹאשׁ בִּרְכַּת הַמָּזוֹן — he must return to the beginning of** ***Bircas HaMazon.*** **וּכְשֶׁלֹּא אָמַר עֲדַיִין רַק ״בָּרוּךְ אַתָּה ה׳ ״** — In the above case, **if he said only** the words ***Blessed are You,* Hashem,** from the beginning of the blessing, **יְסַיֵּים ״לַמְּדֵנִי חֻקֶּיךָ״ — he should conclude** with the words *Lamdeini Chukecha,* ***teach me Your statutes,***[50] **כְּדֵי שֶׁלֹּא יְהֵא לְבַטָּלָה — so that** Hashem's Name **should not be** recited **in vain,** **וְאַחַר כָּךְ חוֹזֵר לְרֹאשׁ בִּרְכַּת הַמָּזוֹן — and after that, he should return to the beginning of** ***Bircas HaMazon.*** **אֲבָל בִּסְעוּדָּה שְׁלִישִׁית — However,** if this occurs **at the third meal** of Shabbos, **שֶׁאֲפִילוּ בְּשַׁבָּת אֵינוֹ מְחוּיָּב לֶאֱכוֹל פַּת דַּוְקָא — since even on Shabbos, one is not specifically obligated to eat bread**[51]

---

50. See above, note 47. See Appendix of Kitzur's editorial glosses and *Mishnah Berurah* 188:23 with *Beur Halachah* 188:6 s.v. עד שהתחיל, regarding this halachah.

51. I.e., according to some authorities one may fulfill his obligation of a third meal by eating other foods; see below, 77:16.

וּמִכָּל שֶׁכֵּן בְּיוֹם טוֹב[52], וּבִרְכַּת הַמָּזוֹן אֵינוֹ חוֹבַת הַיּוֹם עָלָיו, לָכֵן אֵינוֹ חוֹזֵר לְרֹאשׁ, אֶלָּא גוֹמֵר כָּךְ בִּרְכַּת הַמָּזוֹן. אֲבָל אִם נִזְכַּר בְּמָקוֹם שֶׁיָּכוֹל לְתַקֵּן בְּבִרְכַּת "אֲשֶׁר נָתַן" וְכוּ', מְחוּיָּב לְתַקֵּן[53], אֲפִילוּ בְּכַמָּה סְעוּדוֹת שֶׁאָכַל[54].

יד. טָעָה בְּרֹאשׁ חֹדֶשׁ וְלֹא אָמַר "יַעֲלֶה וְיָבֹא" — אוֹמֵר: "בָּרוּךְ אַתָּה ה' אֱלֹהֵינוּ מֶלֶךְ הָעוֹלָם[55] אֲשֶׁר נָתַן רָאשֵׁי חֳדָשִׁים לְעַמּוֹ יִשְׂרָאֵל לְזִכָּרוֹן", וְאֵינוֹ חוֹתֵם[56] (אֵין חִילּוּק בָּזֶה בֵּין יוֹם בֵּין בְּלַיְלָה)[57]. וּבְחוֹל הַמּוֹעֵד אִם לֹא אָמַר "יַעֲלֶה וְיָבֹא", יֹאמַר: "בָּרוּךְ אַתָּה ה' אֱלֹהֵינוּ מֶלֶךְ הָעוֹלָם אֲשֶׁר נָתַן מוֹעֲדִים לְעַמּוֹ יִשְׂרָאֵל לְשָׂשׂוֹן וּלְשִׂמְחָה,

---

at that meal, **וּמִכָּל שֶׁכֵּן בְּיוֹם טוֹב — and certainly on Yom Tov,** when one need not eat a third meal at all,[52] **וּבִרְכַּת הַמָּזוֹן אֵינוֹ חוֹבַת הַיּוֹם עָלָיו — and *Bircas HaMazon*** is therefore **not a requirement of the day, לָכֵן אֵינוֹ חוֹזֵר לְרֹאשׁ — therefore, he does not return to the beginning** of *Bircas HaMazon* if he forgot to recite *Retzei* or *Yaaleh VeYavo*; **אֶלָּא גוֹמֵר כָּךְ בִּרְכַּת הַמָּזוֹן — rather, he completes *Bircas HaMazon* as is,** without going back. **אֲבָל אִם נִזְכַּר — However, if he becomes aware** of his omission **בְּמָקוֹם שֶׁיָּכוֹל לְתַקֵּן בְּבִרְכַּת "אֲשֶׁר נָתַן" וְכוּ' — at a place where he is able to rectify** his mistake **by** reciting **the** compensatory **blessing of *Who gave*** etc.,[53] **מְחוּיָּב לְתַקֵּן — he must rectify** his omission, **אֲפִילוּ בְּכַמָּה סְעוּדוֹת שֶׁאָכַל — even at any** of the additional **meals he has eaten.**[54]

§14 טָעָה בְּרֹאשׁ חֹדֶשׁ — If one erred on Rosh Chodesh וְלֹא אָמַר "יַעֲלֶה וְיָבֹא" — and he did not recite *Yaaleh VeYavo*, and he realized after he mentioned the Name of Hashem in the blessing of *Who rebuilds Jerusalem in His mercy*, but before beginning the following blessing, **אוֹמֵר** — after completing *Who rebuilds Jerusalem in His mercy, Amen,* **he should recite** the following blessing: **"בָּרוּךְ אַתָּה ה' אֱלֹהֵינוּ מֶלֶךְ הָעוֹלָם — *Blessed are You, Hashem, our God, King of the Universe,*[55] אֲשֶׁר נָתַן רָאשֵׁי חֳדָשִׁים לְעַמּוֹ יִשְׂרָאֵל לְזִכָּרוֹן" — *Who gave Roshei Chodoshim to His people Israel as a remembrance,* וְאֵינוֹ חוֹתֵם — and he does not conclude** with a blessing.[56] **(אֵין חִילּוּק בָּזֶה בֵּין יוֹם בֵּין בְּלַיְלָה — There is no difference whether this occurs during the night or day** of Rosh Chodesh.)[57]

וּבְחוֹל הַמּוֹעֵד אִם לֹא אָמַר "יַעֲלֶה וְיָבֹא" — On Chol HaMoed, if he did not recite *Yaaleh VeYavo*, יֹאמַר: "בָּרוּךְ אַתָּה ה' אֱלֹהֵינוּ מֶלֶךְ הָעוֹלָם — he should recite: *Blessed are You, Hashem, our God, King of the Universe,* אֲשֶׁר נָתַן מוֹעֲדִים לְעַמּוֹ יִשְׂרָאֵל — *Who gave appointed festivals to His people Yisrael,* לְשָׂשׂוֹן וּלְשִׂמְחָה — *for happiness*

---

52. All agree that a third meal on the festivals is not obligatory (*Mishnah Berurah* 188:31).

53. See above, *se'if* 12.

54. Even if they are certainly optional (such as the third meal on Yom Tov, or the fourth meal on Shabbos).

55. See Appendix of Kitzur's editorial glosses.

56. That is, this blessing does not contain the concluding blessing that the earlier blessing did (above, *se'if* 12: בָּרוּךְ אַתָּה ה' מְקַדֵּשׁ..., *Blessed are You, Hashem, Who sanctifies* ...).

57. Although with regard to whether *Shemoneh Esrei* is repeated if one omitted *Yaaleh VeYavo* on Rosh Chodesh, there is a difference between the day *Shemoneh Esrei* and the night *Shemoneh Esrei* (see above, 19:10), that is only with regard to *repeating* a prayer. Here, however, the issue is rectifying his omission by adding a blessing. This may be done at any meal, whether by day or at night (*Beur Halachah* 188:7 s.v. בין בלילה).

LAWS OF MAYIM ACHARONIM AND BIRCAS HAMAZON — SIMAN 44:15 110

אֶת יוֹם חַג (פְּלוֹנִי) הַזֶּה. בָּרוּךְ אַתָּה ה׳ מְקַדֵּשׁ יִשְׂרָאֵל וְהַזְּמַנִּים״[58]. וּבְרֹאשׁ הַשָּׁנָה אוֹמֵר: ״בָּרוּךְ אַתָּה ה׳ אֱלֹהֵינוּ מֶלֶךְ הָעוֹלָם אֲשֶׁר נָתַן יָמִים טוֹבִים לְעַמּוֹ יִשְׂרָאֵל, אֶת יוֹם הַזִּכָּרוֹן הַזֶּה. בָּרוּךְ אַתָּה ה׳ מְקַדֵּשׁ יִשְׂרָאֵל וְיוֹם הַזִּכָּרוֹן״. וְאִם לֹא נִזְכַּר עַד לְאַחַר שֶׁהִתְחִיל הַבְּרָכָה שֶׁלְּאַחֲרֶיהָ, אֵינוֹ חוֹזֵר לְרֹאשׁ[59].

טו. רֹאשׁ חֹדֶשׁ שֶׁחָל בְּשַׁבָּת וְשָׁכַח ״רְצֵה״ וְגַם ״יַעֲלֶה וְיָבֹא״ וְנִזְכַּר וְאוֹמֵר ״בָּרוּךְ אַתָּה ה׳ אֱלֹהֵינוּ מֶלֶךְ הָעוֹלָם אֲשֶׁר נָתַן ...״, כּוֹלֵל גַּם רֹאשׁ חֹדֶשׁ בֵּין בַּפְּתִיחָה בֵּין בַּחֲתִימָה וְאוֹמֵר: ״אֲשֶׁר נָתַן שַׁבָּתוֹת לִמְנוּחָה לְעַמּוֹ יִשְׂרָאֵל בְּאַהֲבָה לְאוֹת וְלִבְרִית, וְרָאשֵׁי חֳדָשִׁים לְזִכָּרוֹן. בָּרוּךְ אַתָּה ה׳ מְקַדֵּשׁ הַשַּׁבָּת וְיִשְׂרָאֵל וְרָאשֵׁי חֳדָשִׁים״. אַף עַל פִּי שֶׁבְּרֹאשׁ חֹדֶשׁ לְבַד אֵינוֹ חוֹתֵם, הָכָא כֵּיוָן שֶׁהוּא חוֹתֵם בִּשְׁבִיל שַׁבָּת,

---

and gladness, אֶת יוֹם חַג (פְּלוֹנִי) הַזֶּה — *this festival day of (such-and-such).* בָּרוּךְ אַתָּה ה׳ — *Blessed are You, Hashem,* מְקַדֵּשׁ יִשְׂרָאֵל וְהַזְּמַנִּים״ — *Who sanctifies Yisrael and the [festive] seasons.*[58] **וּבְרֹאשׁ הַשָּׁנָה אוֹמֵר** — If he omitted *Yaaleh VeYavo* **on Rosh Hashanah, he should recite:** ״בָּרוּךְ אַתָּה ה׳ אֱלֹהֵינוּ מֶלֶךְ הָעוֹלָם — *Blessed are You, Hashem, our God, King of the Universe,* אֲשֶׁר נָתַן יָמִים טוֹבִים לְעַמּוֹ יִשְׂרָאֵל — *Who gave Yamim Tovim to His people Yisrael,* אֶת יוֹם הַזִּכָּרוֹן הַזֶּה — *this Day of Remembrance.* בָּרוּךְ אַתָּה ה׳ — *Blessed are You, Hashem,* מְקַדֵּשׁ יִשְׂרָאֵל וְיוֹם הַזִּכָּרוֹן״ — *Who sanctifies Yisrael and the Day of Remembrance.* **וְאִם לֹא נִזְכַּר — If,** either on Chol HaMoed or Rosh Hashanah, **he did not become aware** of his omission **עַד לְאַחַר שֶׁהִתְחִיל הַבְּרָכָה שֶׁלְּאַחֲרֶיהָ — until after he began the next blessing, אֵינוֹ חוֹזֵר לְרֹאשׁ — he does not return to the beginning** of *Bircas HaMazon.*[59]

§15 רֹאשׁ חֹדֶשׁ שֶׁחָל בְּשַׁבָּת — If Rosh Chodesh coincides with Shabbos, וְשָׁכַח ״רְצֵה״ וְגַם ״יַעֲלֶה וְיָבֹא״ — and one forgot to recite **both** ***Retzei*** **and** ***Yaaleh VeYavo,*** **וְנִזְכַּר וְאוֹמֵר — and he becomes aware** of his omission **and recites:** ״בָּרוּךְ אַתָּה ה׳ אֱלֹהֵינוּ מֶלֶךְ הָעוֹלָם אֲשֶׁר נָתַן ...״ — ***Blessed are You, Hashem, our God, King of the Universe, Who gave*** etc., **כּוֹלֵל גַּם רֹאשׁ חֹדֶשׁ בֵּין בַּפְּתִיחָה בֵּין בַּחֲתִימָה — he should include** the mention of **Rosh Chodesh both in the opening and the closing** of the compensatory blessing. **וְאוֹמֵר: ״אֲשֶׁר נָתַן שַׁבָּתוֹת לִמְנוּחָה לְעַמּוֹ יִשְׂרָאֵל — He should** thus **recite:** ***Who gave Shabbosos for rest to his people Israel,*** בְּאַהֲבָה לְאוֹת וְלִבְרִית — ***with love, for a sign and for a covenant,*** וְרָאשֵׁי חֳדָשִׁים לְזִכָּרוֹן — ***and Roshei Chodoshim for a remembrance.*** בָּרוּךְ אַתָּה ה׳ — ***Blessed are You,*** *Hashem,* מְקַדֵּשׁ הַשַּׁבָּת וְיִשְׂרָאֵל וְרָאשֵׁי חֳדָשִׁים״ — ***Who sanctifies the Shabbos and Israel and Roshei Chodoshim.*** **אַף עַל פִּי שֶׁבְּרֹאשׁ חֹדֶשׁ לְבַד — Although when it is only Rosh Chodesh, אֵינוֹ חוֹתֵם — one does not conclude** with the full text (*Blessed are You, Hashem, Who sanctifies ...*), **הָכָא כֵּיוָן שֶׁהוּא חוֹתֵם בִּשְׁבִיל שַׁבָּת — here, since he**

---

58. *Mishnah Berurah* (188:27) rules that on Chol HaMoed, one should not recite the concluding blessing of בָּרוּךְ אַתָּה ה׳ מְקַדֵּשׁ יִשְׂרָאֵל וְהַזְּמַנִּים, *Blessed are You, Hashem, Who sanctifies Yisrael and the [festive] seasons.*

59. If one was ill and was required to eat on Yom Kippur, he must recite *Bircas HaMazon* with *Yaaleh VeYavo.* However, if one forgot to recite it in its proper place [i.e., he realized after he mentioned the Name of Hashem in the blessing of *Who rebuilds Yerushalayim in His mercy*], he should continue without reciting a compensatory blessing (*Mishnah Berurah* 188:19).

111 LAWS OF MAYIM ACHARONIM AND BIRCAS HAMAZON — SIMAN 44:16

מַזְכִּיר גַּם רֹאשׁ חֹדֶשׁ. אִם אָמַר "רְצֵה" וְלֹא אָמַר "יַעֲלֶה וְיָבֹא" וְלֹא נִזְכַּר עַד לְאַחַר שֶׁהִתְחִיל הַבְּרָכָה שֶׁלְּאַחֲרֶיהָ, אֵינוֹ חוֹזֵר לְרֹאשׁ. (דְּהָא שֶׁל שַׁבָּת אָמַר[60] וּבִשְׁבִיל רֹאשׁ חֹדֶשׁ אֵינוֹ חוֹזֵר וְאִם אָמַר יַעֲלֶה וְיָבֹא וְלֹא אָמַר רְצֵה וְהוּא חוֹזֵר לְרֹאשׁ צָרִיךְ לוֹמַר גַּם יַעֲלֶה וְיָבֹא[61] וְהוּא הַדִּין לְחוֹל־הַמּוֹעֵד וְרֹאשׁ הַשָּׁנָה.)

טז. בַּחֲנוּכָּה וּפוּרִים אִם שָׁכַח לוֹמַר "עַל הַנִּסִּים" וְלֹא נִזְכַּר עַד לְאַחַר שֶׁאָמַר אֶת הַשֵּׁם מֵחֲתִימַת הַבְּרָכָה, שֶׁאָמַר "בָּרוּךְ אַתָּה ה'"[62], אֵינוֹ חוֹזֵר, אַךְ בְּתוֹךְ

---

concludes with the full version of the blessing **on account of Shabbos,** **מַזְכִּיר גַּם רֹאשׁ חֹדֶשׁ** — **he also mentions Rosh Chodesh** in the conclusion.

"אִם אָמַר "רְצֵה" וְלֹא אָמַר "יַעֲלֶה וְיָבֹא — **If,** when Rosh Chodesh coincides with Shabbos, **one recited *Retzei* but not *Yaaleh VeYavo,*** **וְלֹא נִזְכַּר עַד לְאַחַר שֶׁהִתְחִיל הַבְּרָכָה שֶׁלְּאַחֲרֶיהָ** — **and he did not become aware** of his mistake **until he began the next blessing,** **אֵינוֹ חוֹזֵר לְרֹאשׁ** — **he does not return to the beginning** of *Bircas HaMazon.* **(דְּהָא שֶׁל שַׁבָּת אָמַר[60]** — **For he has** fulfilled the obligation to make mention **of Shabbos by reciting** *Retzei,* **וּבִשְׁבִיל רֹאשׁ חֹדֶשׁ אֵינוֹ חוֹזֵר** — **and in order** to make mention **of Rosh Chodesh,** by reciting *Yaaleh VeYavo,* **one does not repeat** the *Bircas HaMazon.* **וְאִם אָמַר יַעֲלֶה וְיָבֹא וְלֹא אָמַר רְצֵה** — **If, however, one recited *Yaaleh VeYavo,* but did not recite *Retzei,*** **וְהוּא חוֹזֵר לְרֹאשׁ** — in which case **he returns to the beginning** of *Bircas HaMazon,* **צָרִיךְ לוֹמַר גַּם יַעֲלֶה וְיָבֹא** — **he must recite *Yaaleh VeYavo* as well.**[61] **וְהוּא הַדִּין לְחוֹל־הַמּוֹעֵד וְרֹאשׁ הַשָּׁנָה** — **The same applies on Chol HaMoed or Rosh Hashanah** that coincides with Shabbos, when one is required to repeat *Bircas HaMazon* if he forgot *Retzei,* but not if he forgot *Yaaleh VeYavo* (see previous *se'if*).)

§16 On Chanukah and Purim, the עַל הַנִּסִּים, *For the Miracles,* prayer is added to *Bircas HaMazon* in the second blessing: נוֹדֶה לְךָ, *We thank You.* This prayer begins with a general statement of thanks for miracles that Hashem has performed for the Jewish people, and is followed by a detailed description of the miracles of the individual festival. On Chanukah, the description begins with the words בִּימֵי מַתִּתְיָהוּ, *In the days of Mattisyahu,* and on Purim, it begins בִּימֵי מָרְדְּכַי, *In the days of Mordechai.* **בַּחֲנוּכָּה וּפוּרִים** — **On Chanukah and Purim,** **"אִם שָׁכַח לוֹמַר "עַל הַנִּסִּים** — **if one forgot to recite** the additional prayer of *Al HaNissim,* ***For the miracles,*** in *Bircas HaMazon,* **וְלֹא נִזְכַּר** — **and he did not become aware** of his omission **עַד לְאַחַר שֶׁאָמַר אֶת הַשֵּׁם מֵחֲתִימַת הַבְּרָכָה** — **until after he said the Name** of Hashem **in the conclusion of the** second **blessing** of *Bircas HaMazon,* **"שֶׁאָמַר "בָּרוּךְ אַתָּה ה'** — i.e., **he said *Blessed are You, Hashem,***[62] **אֵינוֹ חוֹזֵר** — **he does not return** to the beginning of *Bircas HaMazon.* **"אַךְ בְּתוֹךְ "הָרַחֲמָן** — **However, in the** section of the ***HaRachaman***

---

60. Due to an apparent printer's error, the words in brackets were omitted in the Lemberg edition of Kitzur.

61. Although he had already recited *Yaaleh VeYavo* the first time he recited *Bircas HaMazon,* he must repeat it, since the first recitation of *Bircas HaMazon* was completely invalid (*Mishnah Berurah* 188:29).

62. The second blessing of *Bircas HaMazon* concludes with בָּרוּךְ אַתָּה ה' עַל הָאָרֶץ וְעַל הַמָּזוֹן, *Blessed are You, Hashem, for the Land and for the nourishment. Al HaNissim* is recited in the middle of the blessing, immediately prior to the words וְעַל הַכֹּל, *For everything.* One who realizes that he forgot *Al HaNissim* before uttering Hashem's Name, recites *Al HaNissim* at that point. [He then continues וְעַל הַכֹּל, *For everything,* etc.]

״הָרַחֲמָן״[63] יֹאמַר: ״הָרַחֲמָן הוּא יַעֲשֶׂה לָנוּ נִסִּים וְנִפְלָאוֹת כְּמוֹ שֶׁעָשָׂה לַאֲבוֹתֵינוּ בַּיָּמִים הָהֵם בַּזְּמַן הַזֶּה בִּימֵי מַתִּתְיָהוּ״ וְכוּ׳, ״בִּימֵי מָרְדְּכַי״ וְכוּ׳.

יז. הָיָה אוֹכֵל בְּשַׁבָּת וְחָשְׁכָה לוֹ, כֵּיוָן שֶׁעֲדַיִין הוּא לֹא הִתְפַּלֵּל עַרְבִית, אוֹמֵר ״רְצֵה״[64], וְכֵן בְּיוֹם טוֹב, רֹאשׁ חֹדֶשׁ, וַחֲנוּכָּה וּפוּרִים, כֵּיוָן שֶׁהַתְחָלַת הַסְּעוּדָה הָיְתָה בַּיּוֹם, צָרִיךְ לְהַזְכִּיר מֵעִנְיַן הַיּוֹם, אַף עַל פִּי שֶׁמְּבָרֵךְ בַּלַּיְלָה[65]. וְאִם אָכַל בְּעֶרֶב רֹאשׁ חֹדֶשׁ וְנִמְשְׁכָה סְעוּדָתוֹ גַּם תּוֹךְ הַלַּיְלָה וְאָכַל גַּם בַּלַּיְלָה כְּזַיִת פַּת, צָרִיךְ לוֹמַר ״יַעֲלֶה וְיָבֹא״, וְכֵן בַּחֲנוּכָּה וּפוּרִים. וְאִם הִתְחִיל לֶאֱכוֹל בְּשַׁבָּת וְנִמְשְׁכָה

---

supplications[63] יֹאמַר: ״הָרַחֲמָן הוּא יַעֲשֶׂה לָנוּ נִסִּים וְנִפְלָאוֹת — **he should recite:** ***The Compassionate One! May He perform for us miracles and wonders*** כְּמוֹ שֶׁעָשָׂה לַאֲבוֹתֵינוּ בַּיָּמִים הָהֵם בַּזְּמַן הַזֶּה — ***as He performed for our forefathers in those days, at this time.*** בִּימֵי מַתִּתְיָהוּ״ וְכוּ׳ — On Chanukah, he then continues ***In the days of Mattisyahu*** **etc.,** ״בִּימֵי מָרְדְּכַי״ וְכוּ׳ — and on Purim, he continues ***In the days of Mordechai*** **etc.**

§17 הָיָה אוֹכֵל בְּשַׁבָּת — **If one was eating on Shabbos** afternoon, וְחָשְׁכָה לוֹ — **and nightfall** (when Shabbos ends) **arrived,** כֵּיוָן שֶׁעֲדַיִין הוּא לֹא הִתְפַּלֵּל עַרְבִית — **since he did not yet recite** the ***Maariv*** prayer, אוֹמֵר ״רְצֵה״ — **he recites** ***Retzei*** in *Bircas HaMazon.*[64] וְכֵן בְּיוֹם טוֹב — **And likewise,** if this situation occurs **on Yom Tov,** רֹאשׁ חֹדֶשׁ, וַחֲנוּכָּה וּפוּרִים — or **Rosh Chodesh, Chanukah, or Purim,** he should insert the appropriate passages for those occasions even though nightfall has arrived. כֵּיוָן שֶׁהַתְחָלַת הַסְּעוּדָה הָיְתָה בַּיּוֹם — The reason for this is, **since the beginning of the meal took place during the day,** צָרִיךְ לְהַזְכִּיר מֵעִנְיַן הַיּוֹם — **one is required to mention** the passage **that is relevant to that day,** אַף עַל פִּי שֶׁמְּבָרֵךְ בַּלַּיְלָה — **even though one is reciting** ***Bircas HaMazon*** **at night.**[65]

וְאִם אָכַל בְּעֶרֶב רֹאשׁ חֹדֶשׁ — **If one was eating on Erev Rosh Chodesh** (the day before Rosh Chodesh), וְנִמְשְׁכָה סְעוּדָתוֹ גַּם תּוֹךְ הַלַּיְלָה — **and his meal extended into the night,** וְאָכַל גַּם בַּלַּיְלָה כְּזַיִת פַּת — **and during the night he also ate a** ***kezayis*** **of bread,** צָרִיךְ לוֹמַר ״יַעֲלֶה וְיָבֹא״ — **he should recite** ***Yaaleh VeYavo*** in *Bircas HaMazon.* וְכֵן בַּחֲנוּכָּה וּפוּרִים — **Likewise, with regard to** one who is eating on the day before **Chanukah or Purim,** and he eats bread after nightfall, he should include *Al HaNissim* in *Bircas HaMazon.*

וְאִם הִתְחִיל לֶאֱכוֹל בְּשַׁבָּת — **If one began eating on Shabbos** afternoon, וְנִמְשְׁכָה

---

63. He should recite it in the section of those *HaRachaman* supplications that pertain to various holidays and festivals, after the words בְּעֵינֵי אֱלֹהִים וְאָדָם, *in the eyes of God and man,* (see *Mishnah Berurah* 682:5).

64. Since the meal began during the day, he has become obligated to mention the holiness of the day (with *Retzei*); this obligation does not end with nightfall. However, if he were to have prayed *Maariv* [it would be an acknowledgment of the conclusion of Shabbos and] it would appear contradictory to recite *Retzei* afterward (*Mishnah Berurah* 188:32). See also ibid. 424:2.

65. If in this situation one recited *Bircas HaMazon* over a cup of wine (see below, 45:1), he should not include the addition for Shabbos in the *al hagefen* blessing that he recites after drinking the wine (see below, 51:8-9 regarding this blessing and its Shabbos and festival additions). Additionally, if Saturday night is Rosh Chodesh, he *should* include the addition for Rosh Chodesh in the *al hagefen* blessing (see Appendix of Kitzur's editorial glosses).

113 LAWS OF MAYIM ACHARONIM AND BIRCAS HAMAZON — SIMAN 44:18

סְעוּדָתוֹ תּוֹךְ הַלַּיְלָה וְאָכַל גַּם בַּלַּיְלָה כְּזַיִת פַּת וּלְמָחָר הוּא רֹאשׁ חֹדֶשׁ, אוֹמֵר "רְצֵה" וְגַם "יַעֲלֶה וְיָבֹא", וְכֵן בַּחֲנוּכָּה וּפוּרִים. וְיֵשׁ חוֹלְקִין, מִשּׁוּם דְּהָוֵי כְּתַרְתֵּי דְּסָתְרֵי[66], עַל כֵּן יֵשׁ לִמְנוֹעַ שֶׁלֹּא לֶאֱכוֹל אָז בַּלַּיְלָה.

יח. אִם יֵשׁ עוֹבֵד כּוֹכָבִים בַּבַּיִת כְּשֶׁמְּבָרֵךְ בִּרְכַּת הַמָּזוֹן, יֹאמַר "אוֹתָנוּ בְּנֵי בְרִית כּוּלָּנוּ יַחַד"[67].

סְעוּדָתוֹ תּוֹךְ הַלַּיְלָה — **and his meal extended into the night,** **וְאָכַל גַּם בַּלַּיְלָה כְּזַיִת פַּת** — **and during the nighttime he also ate a** ***kezayis*** **of bread,** **וּלְמָחָר הוּא רֹאשׁ חֹדֶשׁ** — **and the next day** (i.e., Saturday night) **is Rosh Chodesh,** **אוֹמֵר "רְצֵה" וְגַם "יַעֲלֶה וְיָבֹא"** — **he should recite both** ***Retzei*** **and** ***Yaaleh VeYavo*** in *Bircas HaMazon.* **וְכֵן בַּחֲנוּכָּה וּפוּרִים** — **Likewise,** if **Chanukah or Purim** begin after Shabbos, he should recite both *Retzei* and *Al HaNissim* in *Bircas HaMazon.* **וְיֵשׁ חוֹלְקִין** — **Some** authorities **disagree** with this ruling, **מִשּׁוּם דְּהָוֵי כְּתַרְתֵּי דְּסָתְרֵי** — **because** reciting **the two** passages **seems contradictory.**[66] **עַל כֵּן יֵשׁ לִמְנוֹעַ שֶׁלֹּא לֶאֱכוֹל אָז** — **Therefore,** to avoid any question, **one should refrain from eating then** (i.e., when one of these days follows Shabbos), **בַּלַּיְלָה** — once **night** has arrived.

§18 **אִם יֵשׁ עוֹבֵד כּוֹכָבִים בַּבַּיִת** — **If there is an idolater in the house,** **כְּשֶׁמְּבָרֵךְ בִּרְכַּת הַמָּזוֹן** — **when one recites** ***Bircas HaMazon*** **יֹאמַר "אוֹתָנוּ בְּנֵי בְרִית כּוּלָּנוּ יַחַד"** — **he should recite:** *The Compassionate One! May He bless ...* ***us members of the covenant, all together ...***[67]

---

66. In the *Retzei* passage, one refers to the day being Shabbos, and in the *Yaaleh VeYavo* passage, one refers to the holiness of Rosh Chodesh, which begins only once Shabbos ends! (see *Mishnah Berurah* 188:33). *Mishnah Berurah* (ibid.) rules in a case when Chanukah or Purim follows Shabbos, since the recitation of *Al HaNissim* is not an absolute obligation (in contrast to that of *Yaaleh VeYavo*), only *Retzei* should be recited.

67. I.e., in the *HaRachaman* section of *Bircas HaMazon*, where our text reads כֵּן יְבָרֵךְ אוֹתָנוּ כֻּלָּנוּ יַחַד, *So may He bless us all together*, one should add the words בְּנֵי בְרִית, *members of the covenant.* For one who practices idolatry and denies the belief in Hashem as the source of all blessings is certainly not deserving of being included in the blessing together with those who place their trust in Him.

LAWS OF THE ZIMUN BLESSING — SIMAN 45:1 114

סימן מה

הִלְכוֹת בִּרְכּוֹת הַזִּימּוּן[1,2]

וּבוֹ כ״ג סְעִיפִים

א. שְׁלֹשָׁה שֶׁאָכְלוּ בְּיַחַד צְרִיכִין לְבָרֵךְ בְּזִימּוּן, וּמִצְוָה[3] שֶׁיְּבָרְכוּ עַל

SIMAN 45

THE LAWS OF THE ZIMUN BLESSING

CONTAINING 23 *SE'IFIM*

§1 *Zimun* Upon a Filled Cup / **§2-3** Pouring the Cup / **§4** The Condition of the Cup; Taking and Holding the Cup / **§5** The Leader / **§6** The *Zimun* Blessing / **§7** Reciting the *Bircas HaMazon* With a *Zimun* / **§8-9** Drinking the Cup / **§10** Joining a Group at the End of the Meal / **§11** Separating a Group of Three or More / **§12-13** *Zimun* With Ten / **§14** Forming a Group of Ten / **§15** How a Group Is Joined / **§16** When Some of the Group Recited *Bircas HaMazon* / **§17** Reciting *Zimun* During a Meal / **§18** Large Feasts / **§19** Joining Two Groups Together / **§20** *Zimun* Response for One Who Did Not Eat / **§21** One Group, Different Foods / **§22** Women, Minors / **§23** Who May Be Joined to a *Zimun*

If three or more men have participated in a meal that requires *Bircas HaMazon*, Grace After Meals, to be recited, a special formula is added at the beginning of *Bircas HaMazon,* in which one of the men formally "invites" the others to join him in the recitation of *Bircas HaMazon.* This formula is referred to as the blessing of *zimun*, literally, *invitation.*

Ideally, when the *zimun* is performed, the leader then recites the entire *Bircas HaMazon* aloud, and all those present listen carefully so they may be exempted by his recitation.[1] Indeed, this is how the *zimun* was practiced in earlier times. However, nowadays, we are concerned that the participants will become distracted and not listen carefully to every word of *Bircas HaMazon*, and thereby not fulfill their basic obligation. Therefore, the accepted custom is to have the leader recite the *zimun,* and then the others recite *Bircas HaMazon* along with him.[2]

Preferably, the *zimun* should be recited over a cup of wine or other qualifying beverage, and Kitzur begins the *Siman* with a full discussion of this topic:

§1 שְׁלֹשָׁה שֶׁאָכְלוּ בְּיַחַד — Three people who have eaten together צְרִיכִין לְבָרֵךְ בְּזִימּוּן — must recite *Bircas HaMazon* with *zimun.* וּמִצְוָה שֶׁיְּבָרְכוּ עַל הַכּוֹס — It is a mitzvah,[3] when there is a *zimun*, **to recite *Bircas HaMazon* over a**

---

1. This follows the rule of שׁוֹמֵעַ כְּעוֹנֶה, *listening is like responding.* In many cases, one can fulfill his obligation to recite a blessing or prayer by listening intently to another's recitation, provided that the one reciting the blessing has intent to exempt the listener, and the listener has the intent to be exempted by the other's recitation.

2. See note 39 below.

3. *Mishnah Berurah* (182:4) writes that the

115 LAWS OF THE ZIMUN BLESSING — SIMAN 45:1

הַכּוֹס[4]. אִם אֶפְשָׁר, צְרִיכִין לְהַדֵּר שֶׁיִּהְיֶה כּוֹס יַיִן, וְאִם אִי אֶפְשָׁר בְּיַיִן, יִהְיֶה שֵׁכָר אוֹ מֶעד אוֹ יַיִן שָׂרָף כְּשֶׁהוּא חֲמַר מְדִינָה, דְּהַיְינוּ שֶׁאֵין יַיִן גָּדֵל שָׁם כְּדֶרֶךְ יוֹם מִן הָעִיר, וְעַל כֵּן הוּא בְּיוֹקֶר וּרְגִילִים לִשְׁתּוֹת מַשְׁקִים אֵלּוּ בִּמְקוֹם יַיִן[5]. וְיֵשׁ אוֹמְרִים דְּבִרְכַּת הַמָּזוֹן אֲפִילּוּ בְּיָחִיד טְעוּנָה כּוֹס[6]. וְנוֹהֲגִין הַמְדַקְדְּקִין כְּשֶׁמְּבָרְכִין בְּיָחִיד שֶׁלֹּא לֶאֱחוֹז הַכּוֹס בַּיָּד רַק מַנִּיחִין אוֹתוֹ עַל הַשֻּׁלְחָן לִפְנֵיהֶם.

---

cup.[4] **אִם אֶפְשָׁר — If possible,** **צְרִיכִין לְהַדֵּר שֶׁיִּהְיֶה כּוֹס יַיִן — one should endeavor that it be a cup of wine.** **וְאִם אִי אֶפְשָׁר בְּיַיִן — If it is impossible to** perform the *zimun* with **wine,** **יִהְיֶה שֵׁכָר אוֹ מֶעד אוֹ יַיִן שָׂרָף — it should be** recited over a cup of **beer, mead, or whiskey,** **כְּשֶׁהוּא חֲמַר מְדִינָה — if it is *chamar medinah,*** "wine" of the province. **דְּהַיְינוּ שֶׁאֵין יַיִן גָּדֵל שָׁם — This means that** the grapes from which the **wine** is produced **do not grow in that area,** **כְּדֶרֶךְ יוֹם מִן הָעִיר — within a day's travel from the city.** **וְעַל כֵּן הוּא בְּיוֹקֶר — Therefore,** wine **is expensive** in this place, **וּרְגִילִים לִשְׁתּוֹת מַשְׁקִים אֵלּוּ — and it is common to drink these beverages** (i.e., beer, mead, or whiskey) **בִּמְקוֹם יַיִן — instead of wine.**[5] **וְיֵשׁ אוֹמְרִים — Some** authorities **say** **דְּבִרְכַּת הַמָּזוֹן אֲפִילּוּ בְּיָחִיד — that even the *Bircas HaMazon*** recited **by an individual** **טְעוּנָה כּוֹס — requires** recitation over **a cup.**[6] **וְנוֹהֲגִין הַמְדַקְדְּקִין — And it is the practice of those who are scrupulous** in their mitzvah observance, **כְּשֶׁמְּבָרְכִין בְּיָחִיד — when reciting *Bircas HaMazon* alone,** **שֶׁלֹּא לֶאֱחוֹז הַכּוֹס בַּיָּד —** to recite it over a cup, but **not to grasp the cup in their hand;** **רַק מַנִּיחִין אוֹתוֹ עַל הַשֻּׁלְחָן לִפְנֵיהֶם — rather, they leave it on the table in front of them.**

---

custom is to be lenient unless wine or *chamar medinah* (see further) is readily available. Rabbi Moshe Feinstein (*Igros Moshe, Yoreh Deah* III, §52:3) asserts that it is not necessary to recite *Bircas HaMazon* over a cup of wine even when ten people are present. Nevertheless, one who wishes to perform the mitzvah in an enhanced manner and recite *Bircas HaMazon* over a cup of wine should stipulate that his actions should not constitute a vow [see below, 67:4] (see *Igros Moshe* ibid. for further discussion).

4. That is, the leader of the *zimun* holds a cup while reciting *Bircas HaMazon.* [Kitzur will immediately discuss what the cup is to contain.]

5. *Mishnah Berurah* (182:7) defines *chamar medinah* as the primary drink of the locale, even if wine is available (but not in abundance). *Rambam* (cited in *Beur Halachah* 272:9 s.v. שמקדשין על שכר) writes that a beverage is considered *chamar medinah* if it is the most popular drink of that region, regardless of the availability of wine. The exception is water, which can never be considered *chamar medinah* (*Shulchan Aruch* 182:2).

Rabbi Moshe Feinstein (*Igros Moshe, Orach Chaim* II, §75) defines *chamar medinah* as a drink that is not served to quench one's thirst, but is served at an occasion such as a meal, or to honor one's guests. Based on this, he concludes that carbonated beverages (e.g., soda) that are drunk primarily to quench one's thirst and for refreshment are classified as water and cannot be considered *chamar medinah.*

If one has two [*chamar medinah*] beverages available, he should use the one that he enjoys drinking more. Certainly, if he drank from one type of beverage during the meal because he is fond of that drink, it should be used for the recitation of *Bircas HaMazon* (see *Mishnah Berurah* 182:9).

6. The general consensus of halachic authorities is that it is unnecessary for an individual to recite *Bircas HaMazon* over a cup (*Mishnah Berurah* 182:4).

ב. מוזגים את הכוס[7] תְּחִלָּה וְאַחַר כָּךְ נוטלין לְיָדַיִם[8].

ג. יַיִן שֶׁשָּׁתוּ מִמֶּנּוּ – כָּל הַנִּשְׁאָר בַּכְּלִי נַעֲשָׂה פָּגוּם[9] וּפָסוּל לְבִרְכַּת הַמָּזוֹן[10] עַד שֶׁיְּתַקְּנוּ[11]. דְּהַיְינוּ, שֶׁנּוֹתֵן לְתוֹכוֹ קְצָת יַיִן, אוֹ קְצָת מַיִם שֶׁאֵינָם פְּגוּמִים[12]. וְכֵיוָן שֶׁצָּרִיךְ לְמַלֹּאות אֶת הַכּוֹס לְשֵׁם בְּרָכָה[13], לָכֵן אִם הַכּוֹס פָּגוּם וְהוּא מְתַקְּנוֹ צָרִיךְ לְשָׁפְכוֹ לְתוֹךְ קַנְקַן וּמִתּוֹךְ הַקַּנְקַן לְתוֹךְ הַכּוֹס לְשֵׁם בְּרָכָה[14].

---

§2 מוזגים את הכוס תְּחִלָּה — The cup of wine **should be poured**[7] **first,** וְאַחַר כָּךְ נוטלין לְיָדַיִם — **and afterward they should wash their hands** in fulfillment of the mitzvah of *mayim acharonim* (*final waters*).[8]

§3 יַיִן שֶׁשָּׁתוּ מִמֶּנּוּ — Regarding **wine from which one drank,** כָּל הַנִּשְׁאָר בַּכְּלִי — **all** the wine **remaining in the vessel** from which he drank נַעֲשָׂה פָּגוּם — **is rendered** *pagum, blemished,*[9] וּפָסוּל לְבִרְכַּת הַמָּזוֹן — **and is disqualified for** the blessing of *Bircas HaMazon*[10] עַד שֶׁיְּתַקְּנוּ — **until its** status **is remedied.**[11] דְּהַיְינוּ, שֶׁנּוֹתֵן לְתוֹכוֹ קְצָת יַיִן — **This is** accomplished **by adding a small amount of wine into** the cup אוֹ קְצָת מַיִם שֶׁאֵינָם פְּגוּמִים — **or a small amount of water that is not *pagum*** itself.[12] וְכֵיוָן שֶׁצָּרִיךְ לְמַלֹּאות אֶת הַכּוֹס — **However, since it is necessary to fill the cup** לְשֵׁם בְּרָכָה — **for the sake of the blessing** of *Bircas HaMazon,*[13] לָכֵן אִם הַכּוֹס פָּגוּם — **therefore, if the cup** of wine **was *pagum*** וְהוּא מְתַקְּנוֹ — **and one is remedying it,** צָרִיךְ לְשָׁפְכוֹ לְתוֹךְ קַנְקַן — **it is necessary to** also **pour** the *pagum* wine **into the bottle,** וּמִתּוֹךְ הַקַּנְקַן לְתוֹךְ הַכּוֹס — **and** then pour wine **from the bottle** back **into the cup,** לְשֵׁם בְּרָכָה — so the cup will have been filled **for the sake of the blessing.**[14]

---

7. Lit., *diluted.* In earlier times, wine was produced in concentrated form and was diluted prior to consumption.

8. There should be no interruption between washing *mayim acharonim* and *Bircas HaMazon* (see *Magen Avraham,* beginning of 181; see above, 44:1-2, for the halachos of *mayim acharonim*).

9. The wine is disqualified if one drank even a small amount directly from the container (*Mishnah Berurah* 182:17). However, if one poured some wine into a cup or into his hand, or even if he dipped his finger in the bottle and tasted it, the remainder is not rendered *pagum (Shulchan Aruch* 182:3 and *Mishnah Berurah* §18).

10. *Rambam* (*Hil. Shabbos* 29:16) writes that the reason for this disqualification is that the remaining wine is viewed as being a mere "leftover" (see also *Maharam Chalavah* to *Pesachim* 105b and *Magen Avraham* 182:10). This wine is disqualified from any mitzvah use, such as *Kiddush* and *Havdalah* (see below, *Siman* 77 and *se'if* 7 there), as well as for *Bircas HaMazon.* However, it is certainly fit for regular consumption, and one recites the *borei pri hagafen* blessing over it (*Shaar HaTziyun* 182:15).

11. According to *Shulchan Aruch* (182:7), if one has no alternative, he may recite *Bircas HaMazon* over a cup of wine that is *pagum. Mishnah Berurah* (182:32) explains that the requirement to use non-*pagum* wine is only in an ideal situation (לְכַתְּחִלָּה); hence, it is better to use *pagum* wine than nothing at all. Furthermore, one can improve the halachic status of the wine slightly by pouring it into a smaller cup that will be completely filled by the wine, as long as the cup contains a *revi'is* (between 2.9 fl. oz. and 5.1 fl. oz. [86.4 – 150 cc.]; see Appendix A).

12. Other [non-*pagum*] beverages may also be used. When using water [or any other beverage] to remedy the *pagum* status of the wine, one must take care that the taste of the wine is not ruined by this addition (*Mishnah Berurah* 182:30).

13. See following *se'if.*

14. He is thus filling the cup entirely for the sake of the blessing. See *Mishnah Berurah* 182:27 with *Shaar HaTziyun* §24 for another reason for doing this; see also *Shulchan Aruch HaRav* 182:5.

ד. הַכּוֹס שֶׁמְּבָרְכִין עָלָיו צָרִיךְ שֶׁיְּהֵא שָׁלֵם. וַאֲפִילוּ נִשְׁבַּר רַק הַבָּסִיס שֶׁל מַטָּה פָּסוּל, וַאֲפִילוּ פְּגִימָה כָּל שֶׁהוּא בִּשְׂפַת הַכְּלִי[15], אוֹ שֶׁנִּסְדַּק, פָּסוּל[16]. וְטָעוּן הֲדָחָה מִבִּפְנִים וּשְׁטִיפָה מִבַּחוּץ, אוֹ מְקַנְּחוֹ יָפֶה שֶׁיְּהֵא נָקִי[17]. וְשׁוֹפֵךְ מִן הַקַּנְקַן לְתוֹכוֹ לְשֵׁם בְּרָכָה[18], וִיהֵא מָלֵא[19] וְהַמְבָרֵךְ מְקַבְּלוֹ בִּשְׁתֵּי יָדָיו (לְהַרְאוֹת חֲבִיבוּת הַכּוֹס שֶׁהוּא חוֹשֵׁק לְקַבְּלוֹ בְּכָל כֹּחוֹ), וּכְדִכְתִיב (תהלים קלד, ב) "שְׂאוּ יְדֵיכֶם קֹדֶשׁ וּבָרְכוּ אֶת ה'"[20], וּמֵסִיר אַחַר כָּךְ יָדוֹ הַשְּׂמָאלִית וְאוֹחֲזוֹ רַק בִּימִינוֹ לְבַדָּהּ בְּלִי סִיּוּעַ הַשְּׂמָאלִית (שֶׁלֹּא יְהֵא נִרְאֶה כְּמַשּׂוֹי עָלָיו). וְנוֹתֵן עֵינָיו בּוֹ, כְּדֵי

---

§4 **הַכּוֹס שֶׁמְּבָרְכִין עָלָיו — The cup over which the blessing is recited צָרִיךְ שֶׁיְּהֵא שָׁלֵם — must be complete. וַאֲפִילוּ נִשְׁבַּר רַק הַבָּסִיס שֶׁל מַטָּה — Even if just the lower base is broken, פָּסוּל** — the cup **is disqualified** and cannot be used for this purpose. **וַאֲפִילוּ פְּגִימָה כָּל שֶׁהוּא בִּשְׂפַת הַכְּלִי — Even** if there is **a minute nick on the rim of the vessel,**[15] **אוֹ שֶׁנִּסְדַּק — or if** the cup **is cracked, פָּסוּל — it is disqualified.**[16] **וְטָעוּן הֲדָחָה מִבִּפְנִים — The inside** of the cup **requires washing וּשְׁטִיפָה מִבַּחוּץ — and the outside, rinsing,** before it is used as the cup of blessing. **אוֹ מְקַנְּחוֹ יָפֶה — Alternatively, he may wipe it thoroughly שֶׁיְּהֵא נָקִי — so that it will be clean.**[17] **וְשׁוֹפֵךְ מִן הַקַּנְקַן לְתוֹכוֹ — One should pour** the wine **from the bottle into** the cup **לְשֵׁם בְּרָכָה — for the purpose of the blessing** of *Bircas HaMazon,*[18] **וִיהֵא מָלֵא — and it should be filled** to the top.[19] **וְהַמְבָרֵךְ — The one leading the** *zimun* blessing **מְקַבְּלוֹ בִּשְׁתֵּי יָדָיו — should take** the cup **in both his hands** (**לְהַרְאוֹת חֲבִיבוּת הַכּוֹס — to demonstrate his love for the** mitzvah of reciting *Bircas HaMazon* over a **cup** of wine, **שֶׁהוּא חוֹשֵׁק לְקַבְּלוֹ בְּכָל כֹּחוֹ** — such **that he desires to receive it with all his strength). וּכְדִכְתִיב** — An allusion to this practice is found in Scripture, **as it is written** (*Tehillim* 134:2): **"שְׂאוּ יְדֵיכֶם קֹדֶשׁ וּבָרְכוּ אֶת ה'"—** ***Raise your hands in holiness, and bless*** ***HASHEM.***[20] **וּמֵסִיר אַחַר כָּךְ יָדוֹ הַשְּׂמָאלִית — After** grasping it **with both hands, he should remove his left hand וְאוֹחֲזוֹ רַק בִּימִינוֹ לְבַדָּהּ — and hold it with the right** hand **only, בְּלִי סִיּוּעַ הַשְּׂמָאלִית — without the assistance of the left** hand (**שֶׁלֹּא יְהֵא נִרְאֶה כְּמַשּׂוֹי עָלָיו — to avoid giving the impression that** holding the cup **is a burden for him). וְנוֹתֵן עֵינָיו בּוֹ — He should look at** the cup **כְּדֵי**

---

15. See *Mishnah Berurah* (183:11). There are those who in fact consider a cup that has even a nick on its rim that would catch a fingernail passing over it as not being whole. However, *Pri Megadim* (*Mishbetzos Zahav* 183:1) cited in *Shaar HaTziyun* (ibid. §9) refers to this opinion as a "stringency."

16. Even if no piece is actually missing from the cup itself and the contents do not leak from the crack it should still not be used initially (*Mishnah Berurah* 183:11, *Shaar HaTziyun* 183:11). *Mishnah Berurah* (ibid. §10) writes that if one has no other cup, he may use a cup with one of the defects mentioned in this *se'if.* However, if there is a hole toward the bottom of the cup so that it cannot retain a *revi'is* (see note 11), it may not be used (*Shaar HaTziyun* ibid. §14).

17. If the cup is completely clean and sparkling, one need not wash it (*Mishnah Berurah* 183:3).

18. I.e., the cup should be filled close to the time of the blessing, and not well in advance (*Mishnah Berurah* 183:8, see *Shaar HaTziyun* 183:7).

19. *Mishnah Berurah* (183:9) comments that although this is ideal, it is not mandatory. If one does not fill the cup all the way to the top in order to avoid spillage, it may still be considered "full" (see also ibid. 182:32).

20. The plural form of the word יְדֵיכֶם, *your hands,* indicates that one should use both his hands when blessing Hashem, i.e., when receiving the cup of wine.

שֶׁלֹּא יַסִּיחַ דַּעְתּוֹ מִמֶּנּוּ[21]. וּמַחֲזִיקוֹ לְמַעְלָה מִן הַשֻּׁלְחָן[23] טֶפַח[22], דִּכְתִיב (שם קטז, יג) "כּוֹס יְשׁוּעוֹת (אקרא) [אֶשָּׂא] וּבְשֵׁם ה' אֶקְרָא". וְאִיטֵּר יָד יֹאחֲזוֹ בְּיָמִין דִּידֵיהּ, שֶׁהוּא שְׂמֹאל שֶׁל כָּל אָדָם[24]. וְיֵשׁ לְהָסִיר מִן הַשֻּׁלְחָן הַכֵּלִים הָרֵיקִים.

ה. אִם בְּנֵי הַמְסִיבָּה שָׁוִים בְּמַעֲלָה וְיֵשׁ בֵּינֵיהֶם כֹּהֵן, מִצְוָה לְכַבְּדוֹ בְּבִרְכַּת הַמָּזוֹן, שֶׁנֶּאֱמַר (ויקרא כא, ח), "וְקִדַּשְׁתּוֹ"[25]. אֲבָל אִם יֵשׁ בֵּינֵיהֶם אָדָם גָּדוֹל וְחָשׁוּב[26], יְבָרֵךְ הוּא[27]. וְנוֹהֲגִין לָתֵת לְאָבֵל[28] לְבָרֵךְ, וְדַוְקָא כְּשֶׁשָּׁוִים

שֶׁלֹּא יַסִּיחַ דַּעְתּוֹ מִמֶּנּוּ — so that he does not become distracted from the blessing that he is reciting.[21] **וּמַחֲזִיקוֹ לְמַעְלָה מִן הַשֻּׁלְחָן טֶפַח — He should hold it one *tefach***[22] **above the table.**[23] **דִּכְתִיב** — An allusion to this practice is found in Scripture, **as it is written** (ibid.116:13): **"כּוֹס יְשׁוּעוֹת (אקרא) [אֶשָּׂא] וּבְשֵׁם ה' אֶקְרָא" — *I will raise the cup of salvations and the Name of Hashem I will invoke.*** **וְאִיטֵּר יָד — A left-handed person** **יֹאחֲזוֹ בְּיָמִין דִּידֵיהּ — should hold** the cup **in *his* "right" hand,** **שֶׁהוּא שְׂמֹאל שֶׁל כָּל אָדָם — which is the left hand of all** other **people.**[24] **וְיֵשׁ לְהָסִיר מִן הַשֻּׁלְחָן** — Before beginning *Bircas HaMazon* **one should remove from the table** **הַכֵּלִים הָרֵיקִים — the empty dishes** that are left over from the meal.

§5 אִם בְּנֵי הַמְסִיבָּה שָׁוִים בְּמַעֲלָה — If all **those participating in the meal are of equal stature** **וְיֵשׁ בֵּינֵיהֶם כֹּהֵן — and there is a Kohen among them,** **מִצְוָה לְכַבְּדוֹ בְּבִרְכַּת הַמָּזוֹן — it is a mitzvah to honor him with** leading the recitation of ***Bircas HaMazon,*** **שֶׁנֶּאֱמַר, "וְקִדַּשְׁתּוֹ" — as it is stated** (*Vayikra* 21:8): ***and you shall sanctify him,*** i.e., the Kohen.[25] **אֲבָל אִם יֵשׁ בֵּינֵיהֶם אָדָם גָּדוֹל וְחָשׁוּב — However, if there is among them a great and prominent person,**[26] **יְבָרֵךְ הוּא — he should be the one to recite *Bircas HaMazon.***[27] **וְנוֹהֲגִין לָתֵת לְאָבֵל לְבָרֵךְ — It is customary to accord a mourner**[28] the opportunity to **recite *Bircas HaMazon,*** **וְדַוְקָא כְּשֶׁשָּׁוִים**

---

21. *Mishnah Berurah* 183:17.

22. Between 3.2 in. and 3.8 in. (8 cm.- 9.6 cm.); see Appendix A.

23. This is done so that those assembled should be able to see it clearly (*Mishnah Berurah* 183:16).

24. An ambidextrous person should hold the cup in his right hand. According to the Vilna Gaon, the entire procedure for receiving and holding the cup is not mandatory; however, it is the preferred way of beautifying this mitzvah (*Mishnah Berurah* 183:20).

Shelah, citing mystical sources, recommends that one hold the cup in the palm of his (right) hand, with his fingers raised around the bottom of the cup. One should not wear gloves while holding the cup (*Mishnah Berurah* ibid. §15).

25. If the Kohen wishes to waive the honor, he may do so (*Magen Avraham* cited in *Mishnah Berurah* 201:13). This is in contrast to the honor accorded to a Kohen at the Reading of the Torah, where the Kohen is not permitted to waive this honor of precedence (see above, 23:9). If there is no Kohen present, it is proper to give this honor to a Levi, if he is of equal stature to the others (*Mishnah Berurah* ibid.). Even if there is a Kohen present, if there is a guest present who has eaten from the food of the host, the host may honor him to lead the *zimun.* This is because a guest has a special opportunity during *Bircas HaMazon* to bless his host for the food he has eaten (see *Shulchan Aruch* 201:1 for the text of this blessing). See *Beur Halachah* 201:1 s.v. בא for further discussion.

26. This refers to one who is great in Torah knowledge (*Mishnah Berurah* 201:1).

27. If there are two Torah scholars present, and the less learned one is a Kohen, it is preferable for the greater scholar to defer the honor to the Kohen, thus fulfilling the mitzvah of honoring a Kohen [who is also a] Torah scholar. As a reward for doing so, he will merit to live long (*Mishnah Berurah* 201:12).

28. I.e., one who is within the twelve-month

בְּמַעֲלָה[29]. וְרָאוּי לְכַבֵּד בְּבִרְכַּת הַמָּזוֹן לְמִי שֶׁהוּא טוֹב עַיִן[30] שׂוֹנֵא בֶּצַע וְגוֹמֵל חֶסֶד בְּמָמוֹנוֹ שֶׁנֶּאֱמַר (משלי כב, ט) "טוֹב עַיִן הוּא יְבֹרָךְ", אַל תִּקְרֵי "יְבֹרָךְ" אֶלָּא "יְבָרֵךְ"[31].

ו. הַמְבָרֵךְ יֹאמַר מִתְּחִלָּה "הַב לָן וּנְבָרֵךְ" כִּי כָל מִילֵּי דִקְדוּשָּׁה בָּעֵי הַזְמָנָה[32], אוֹ יֹאמַר כְּמוֹ שֶׁנּוֹהֲגִין לוֹמַר בִּלְשׁוֹן אַשְׁכְּנַז "רַבּוֹתַי וויר ווילֶען בֶּענְשֶׁען", וְהַמְסוּבִּין[33] עוֹנִין "יְהִי שֵׁם ה' מְבֹרָךְ מֵעַתָּה וְעַד עוֹלָם" (תהלים קיג, ב). וְאַחַר כָּךְ אוֹמֵר הַמְבָרֵךְ "בִּרְשׁוּת וְכוּ' נְבָרֵךְ שֶׁאָכַלְנוּ" וְכוּ'[34]. וְהַמְסוּבִּין אוֹמְרִים

בְּמַעֲלָה — **but only if** those present **are of equal stature.**[29] וְרָאוּי לְכַבֵּד בְּבִרְכַּת הַמָּזוֹן לְמִי **It is proper to honor, with leading** the recitation of ***Bircas HaMazon,* someone** שֶׁהוּא טוֹב עַיִן — **who is generous,**[30] שׂוֹנֵא בֶּצַע — **despises** wrongful **profit,** וְגוֹמֵל חֶסֶד בְּמָמוֹנוֹ — **and practices kindness with his own money,** שֶׁנֶּאֱמַר — **as it is stated** (*Mishlei* 22:9): "טוֹב עַיִן הוּא יְבֹרָךְ" — ***One with a good eye will be blessed*** (*yevorach*); אַל תִּקְרֵי "יְבֹרָךְ" אֶלָּא "יְבָרֵךְ" — **do not read** the word as ***yevorach*,** meaning, "will be blessed," **rather** read it as ***yevareich*,** meaning "shall bless"; i.e., he should be accorded the honor of leading the *Bircas HaMazon* blessing.[31]

§6 The following four *sei'fim* detail the procedure of the *zimun* blessing, from the opening words until the conclusion of *Bircas HaMazon* and the drinking of the wine: הַמְבָרֵךְ יֹאמַר מִתְּחִלָּה — **The one leading the blessing should first say:** "הַב לָן וּנְבָרֵךְ" — *Hav lan u'nevareich,* ***Give us** the cup of wine **and we will recite Bircas HaMazon,*** כִּי כָל מִילֵּי דִקְדוּשָּׁה בָּעֵי הַזְמָנָה — **for all matters of sanctity require** some form of **preparation.**[32] אוֹ יֹאמַר כְּמוֹ שֶׁנּוֹהֲגִין לוֹמַר בִּלְשׁוֹן אַשְׁכְּנַז — **Or he may say, as is customarily said in the German** (Yiddish) **language:** "רַבּוֹתַי וויר ווילֶען בֶּענְשֶׁען" — *Rabbosai, vir (mir) villen bentchen,* ***Gentlemen, we wish to recite the blessing.*** וְהַמְסוּבִּין עוֹנִין — **The diners**[33] **respond:** "יְהִי שֵׁם ה' מְבֹרָךְ מֵעַתָּה וְעַד עוֹלָם" — ***Let the Name of Hashem be blessed from this time until eternity!*** (*Tehillim* 113:2). וְאַחַר כָּךְ אוֹמֵר הַמְבָרֵךְ — **After that, the one leading the blessing says:** "בִּרְשׁוּת וְכוּ' נְבָרֵךְ שֶׁאָכַלְנוּ" וְכוּ' — ***With the permission,* etc., *let us bless [He]** of Whose **we have eaten*** **etc.**[34] וְהַמְסוּבִּין אוֹמְרִים — **The diners**

---

mourning period for a parent (*Mishnah Berurah* 201:1).

29. *Mishnah Berurah* (210:1) writes that the mourner is given precedence only when they have all eaten their own food. However, if there is a guest who has eaten the host's food, the host may accord that person the honor (see above, note 25).

30. Literally, *one who has a good eye.*

31. The word יְבֹרָךְ is written without a *vav,* and can therefore be vowelized as יְבָרֵךְ. Thus, the verse can be understood as saying, *One with a good eye shall* ***bless*** (*Maharsha* to *Sotah* 38b). [The intent of the one invoking a blessing affects its potency. Hence, in order for a blessing to effectively bring forth God's bounty, it must be said by a person who truly desires good for his fellow (*Maharsha* ibid., *Maharal* in *Nesivos Olam, Nesiv Ayin Tov*).]

32. These words serve as an introduction to the actual *zimun* blessing, which begins with the words נְבָרֵךְ שֶׁאָכַלְנוּ מִשֶּׁלּוֹ, *Let us bless [He] of Whose we have eaten. Mishnah Berurah* (192:2) explains that one must prepare himself in order to experience the sanctity of the mitzvah.

33. Literally, *those who are reclining.* [In Talmudic times, people would dine while reclining on couches.]

34. The full phrase is: בִּרְשׁוּת מָרָנָן וְרַבָּנָן וְרַבּוֹתַי, נְבָרֵךְ שֶׁאָכַלְנוּ מִשֶּׁלּוֹ, *With the permission of the distinguished people, rabbis, and gentlemen, let us bless [He] of Whose we have eaten.* See below, *se'if* 12, for the wording of the blessing when there are ten men present.

״בָּרוּךְ שֶׁאָכַלְנוּ״ וְכוּ׳[35]. וְחוֹזֵר הַמְבָרֵךְ וְאוֹמֵר גַּם הוּא ״בָּרוּךְ שֶׁאָכַלְנוּ״ וְכוּ׳. וְנוֹהֲגִין בִּקְצָת מְקוֹמוֹת שֶׁלְּאַחַר שֶׁסִּיֵּם הַמְבָרֵךְ ״וּבְטוּבוֹ חָיִינוּ״ עוֹנִין הַמְסוּבִּין אָמֵן, וּבִקְצָת מְקוֹמוֹת לֹא נָהֲגוּ לוֹמַר אָמֵן[36]. גַּם יֵשׁ מִנְהָגִים שׁוֹנִים בְּעִנְיַן אֲמִירַת ״בָּרוּךְ הוּא וּבָרוּךְ שְׁמוֹ״. יֵשׁ נוֹהֲגִין שֶׁהַמְבָרֵךְ אוֹמְרוֹ, אֲפִילוּ כְּשֶׁמְּזַמְּנִין רַק בִּשְׁלֹשָׁה, וְיֵשׁ אוֹמְרִים שֶׁאֵין לְאָמְרוֹ אֶלָּא כְּשֶׁמְּזַמְּנִין בַּעֲשָׂרָה, שֶׁמַּזְכִּיר אֶת הַשֵּׁם[37], אָז יֹאמְרוֹ. וְכֵן יֵשׁ לִנְהוֹג. וְהַמְסוּבִּין לֹא יֹאמְרוּהוּ[38], וּמִכָּל שֶׁכֵּן מִי שֶׁמְּבָרֵךְ בִּרְכַּת הַמָּזוֹן בְּלֹא זִמּוּן שֶׁלֹּא יֹאמְרוֹ.

ז. הַמְבָרֵךְ יְבָרֵךְ בְּקוֹל וְהַמְסוּבִּין יֹאמְרוּ עִמּוֹ מִלָּה בְּמִלָּה בְּלַחַשׁ, וּבְסוֹף כָּל בְּרָכָה יַקְדִּימוּ לְסַיֵּים קוֹדֶם לְהַמְבָרֵךְ, כְּדֵי שֶׁיַּעֲנוּ אָמֵן עַל בִּרְכָתוֹ[39].

---

respond: ״בָּרוּךְ שֶׁאָכַלְנוּ״ וְכוּ׳ — *Blessed is [He] of Whose we have eaten,* etc.[35] וְחוֹזֵר הַמְבָרֵךְ וְאוֹמֵר גַּם הוּא — **The leader of the blessing then says as well:** ״בָּרוּךְ שֶׁאָכַלְנוּ״ וְכוּ׳ — ***Blessed is [He]***, etc.

וְנוֹהֲגִין בִּקְצָת מְקוֹמוֹת — **It is customary in some places** שֶׁלְּאַחַר שֶׁסִּיֵּם הַמְבָרֵךְ ״וּבְטוּבוֹ חָיִינוּ״ — **that after the leader of the blessing has concluded** the words ***and through His goodness we live,*** עוֹנִין הַמְסוּבִּין אָמֵן — **the diners respond with Amen.** וּבִקְצָת מְקוֹמוֹת — However, **in some places** לֹא נָהֲגוּ לוֹמַר אָמֵן — **they do not follow the custom to respond Amen.**[36] גַּם יֵשׁ מִנְהָגִים שׁוֹנִים — **In addition, there are various customs** בְּעִנְיַן אֲמִירַת ״בָּרוּךְ הוּא וּבָרוּךְ שְׁמוֹ״ — **with regard to saying** *Baruch Hu U'Varuch Shemo*, ***Blessed is He and blessed is His Name,*** following the *zimun* blessing, before beginning *Bircas Hamazon*: יֵשׁ נוֹהֲגִין שֶׁהַמְבָרֵךְ אוֹמְרוֹ — **Some have the custom that the one who leads the *zimun* blessing recites it** אֲפִילוּ כְּשֶׁמְּזַמְּנִין רַק בִּשְׁלֹשָׁה — **even when the *zimun* is being performed with only three** people. וְיֵשׁ אוֹמְרִים שֶׁאֵין לְאָמְרוֹ — **And some say that it should not be said** אֶלָּא כְּשֶׁמְּזַמְּנִין בַּעֲשָׂרָה — **unless the *zimun* is being recited with ten** people; שֶׁמַּזְכִּיר אֶת הַשֵּׁם — **when the Name** of Hashem **is mentioned,**[37] אָז יֹאמְרוֹ — **then** *Baruch Hu U'Varuch Shemo, Blessed is He and Blessed is His Name* **is recited;** וְכֵן יֵשׁ לִנְהוֹג — **and this is how one should conduct** himself. וְהַמְסוּבִּין לֹא יֹאמְרוּהוּ — **However, the diners should not say it,** only the one leading the *zimun*.[38] וּמִכָּל שֶׁכֵּן — **Certainly,** מִי שֶׁמְּבָרֵךְ בִּרְכַּת הַמָּזוֹן בְּלֹא זִמּוּן — **one who is reciting *Bircas HaMazon* without a** *zimun* שֶׁלֹּא יֹאמְרוֹ — **should not recite it.**

§7 הַמְבָרֵךְ יְבָרֵךְ בְּקוֹל — **The one leading the blessing should recite *Bircas HaMazon* aloud,** וְהַמְסוּבִּין יֹאמְרוּ עִמּוֹ מִלָּה בְּמִלָּה בְּלַחַשׁ — **and the diners should recite** the *Bircas HaMazon* **along with him quietly, word by word.** וּבְסוֹף כָּל בְּרָכָה — **At the conclusion of each blessing** יַקְדִּימוּ לְסַיֵּים קוֹדֶם לְהַמְבָרֵךְ — **they should hasten** their pace in order **to conclude before the one reciting the blessing** aloud, כְּדֵי שֶׁיַּעֲנוּ אָמֵן עַל בִּרְכָתוֹ — **so that they may respond with Amen to his blessing.**[39]

---

35. The full phrase is: בָּרוּךְ שֶׁאָכַלְנוּ מִשֶּׁלּוֹ וּבְטוּבוֹ חָיִינוּ, *Blessed is [He], of Whose we have eaten and through His goodness we live.*

36. *Mishnah Berurah* (192:3) writes that this is the prevalent custom.

37. See below, *se'if* 12.

38. *Mishnah Berurah* (192:4) writes that the common custom is that the leader does say *Baruch Hu U'Varuch Shemo* even when there are only three present. See also Appendix of Kitzur's editorial glosses.

39. The practice of many people, to immediately begin reciting *Bircas HaMazon* aloud when the leader finishes the *zimun* blessing, is improper. As a minimum, the one leading the

ח. אַחַר בִּרְכַּת הַמָּזוֹן, מְבָרֵךְ עַל הַכּוֹס שֶׁבֵּירַךְ עָלָיו[40] וְשׁוֹתֶה שִׁיעוּר רְבִיעִית[41], כְּדֵי שֶׁיּוּכַל לְבָרֵךְ בְּרָכָה אַחֲרוֹנָה[42]. אִם כּוֹסוֹת שֶׁל הַמְסוּבִּין הֵן פְּגוּמוֹת[43], צָרִיךְ הַמְבָרֵךְ לִיתֵּן מִכּוֹסוֹ מְעַט לְתוֹךְ כּוֹסוֹת שֶׁלָּהֶם אַחַר שֶׁבֵּירַךְ בּוֹרֵא פְּרִי הַגָּפֶן, קוֹדֶם שֶׁיִּשְׁתֶּה הוּא, כְּדֵי שֶׁיְּבָרְכוּ גַּם הֵם עַל כּוֹסוֹת שֶׁאֵינָן פְּגוּמוֹת. וְכֵן אִם כּוֹסוֹת שֶׁלָּהֶן רֵיקָנוֹת נוֹתֵן לְתוֹכָן מְעַט מִכּוֹס שֶׁל בְּרָכָה. וְלֹא יִטְעֲמוּ עַד שֶׁיִּטְעוֹם הַמְבָרֵךְ. אֲבָל אִם יֵשׁ לָהֶן כּוֹסוֹת בִּפְנֵי עַצְמָן וְאֵינָן פְּגוּמוֹת, אֵין הַמְבָרֵךְ צָרִיךְ לִיתֵּן לָהֶם מִכּוֹס שֶׁלּוֹ, וִיכוֹלִין לִטְעוֹם קוֹדֶם שֶׁיִּטְעוֹם הוּא, וְכֵן נָכוֹן. וְטוֹב, אִם אֶפְשָׁר, שֶׁיִּהְיֶה לְכָל אֶחָד כּוֹס מָלֵא[44].

---

§8 אַחַר בִּרְכַּת הַמָּזוֹן — **After** the conclusion of ***Bircas HaMazon,*** מְבָרֵךְ עַל הַכּוֹס שֶׁבֵּירַךְ עָלָיו — the one who led the *zimun* **recites the** *borei pri hagafen* **blessing over the cup** of wine **on which he recited *Bircas HaMazon,***[40] וְשׁוֹתֶה שִׁיעוּר רְבִיעִית — **and drinks the amount of a *revi'is***[41] כְּדֵי שֶׁיּוּכַל לְבָרֵךְ בְּרָכָה אַחֲרוֹנָה — **so that he will be able to recite a *berachah acharonah*** (final blessing) on the wine.[42] אִם כּוֹסוֹת שֶׁל הַמְסוּבִּין הֵן פְּגוּמוֹת — **If the cups of the diners are** ***pagum,***[43] צָרִיךְ הַמְבָרֵךְ לִיתֵּן מִכּוֹסוֹ מְעַט — **it is necessary for the leader of the blessing to pour a small amount** of wine **from his cup** לְתוֹךְ כּוֹסוֹת שֶׁלָּהֶם — **into their cups** אַחַר שֶׁבֵּירַךְ בּוֹרֵא פְּרִי הַגָּפֶן — **after he has recited the blessing of** ***borei pri hagafen,*** קוֹדֶם שֶׁיִּשְׁתֶּה הוּא — but **before he drinks,** כְּדֵי שֶׁיְּבָרְכוּ גַּם הֵם — **so that they too may recite a blessing** עַל כּוֹסוֹת שֶׁאֵינָן פְּגוּמוֹת — **over cups** of wine **that are not *pagum.*** וְכֵן אִם כּוֹסוֹת שֶׁלָּהֶן רֵיקָנוֹת — **Likewise, if their cups are empty,** נוֹתֵן לְתוֹכָן מְעַט מִכּוֹס שֶׁל בְּרָכָה — **he should pour a small amount** of wine **from the cup** over which **the blessing** was recited **into them.** וְלֹא יִטְעֲמוּ עַד שֶׁיִּטְעוֹם הַמְבָרֵךְ — **They should not drink** from their wine **until** after **the leader has drunk** from his. אֲבָל אִם יֵשׁ לָהֶן כּוֹסוֹת בִּפְנֵי עַצְמָן — **However, if they have their own cups** of wine וְאֵינָן פְּגוּמוֹת — **and the cups are not *pagum,*** אֵין הַמְבָרֵךְ צָרִיךְ לִיתֵּן לָהֶם מִכּוֹס שֶׁלּוֹ — **the one who led the blessing need not give them from** the wine in **his cup,** וִיכוֹלִין לִטְעוֹם קוֹדֶם שֶׁיִּטְעוֹם הוּא — **and they may drink of** their wine **before he drinks.** וְכֵן נָכוֹן — **This is** the **proper** practice; וְטוֹב אִם אֶפְשָׁר — **it is best, if possible,** שֶׁיִּהְיֶה לְכָל אֶחָד כּוֹס מָלֵא — **that each** of those present **should have a full cup** before him.[44]

---

zimun should recite the first blessing of *Bircas HaMazon* aloud, and those present should say it along with him silently, word by word (see below, *se'if* 18). See *Mishnah Berurah* (183:28) for further discussion.

40. Even if he recited a blessing for wine during the meal, a new blessing is now required due to the interruption caused by the recital of *Bircas HaMazon* (*Mishnah Berurah* 190:1). [If the cup contains a beverage other than wine or grape juice, the *shehakol* blessing should be recited.]

41. Between 2.9 fl. oz. and 5.1 fl. oz. (86.4 – 150 cc.); see Appendix A.

42. See below, 51:2. The final blessing for wine is *Al HaGefen* (51:7).

43. See above, *se'if* 3. It was customary in some places to pour a cup for each one of the diners (see *Mishnah Berurah* 182:23); this custom is not prevalent today. See next note.

44. See *Taz* 182:4 and *Pri Megadim* there for the reason.

ט. אִם הַמְבָרֵךְ אֵינוֹ רוֹצֶה לִשְׁתּוֹת, יֵשׁ אוֹמְרִים דְּיָכוֹל לִיתֵּן לְאִישׁ אַחֵר מִן הַמְסוּבִּין שֶׁיְּבָרֵךְ "בּוֹרֵא פְּרִי הַגָּפֶן" וְיִשְׁתֶּה שִׁיעוּר רְבִיעִית וִיבָרֵךְ בְּרָכָה אַחֲרוֹנָה. וְיֵשׁ אוֹמְרִים דְּאֵין לַעֲשׂוֹת כֵּן, אֶלָּא דַּוְקָא הַמְבָרֵךְ בְּזִימּוּן הוּא יְבָרֵךְ עַל הַכּוֹס. וְכֵן נָכוֹן לַעֲשׂוֹת[45].

י. שְׁנַיִם שֶׁאָכְלוּ בְּיַחַד מִצְוָה לָהֶם לְבַקֵּשׁ שְׁלִישִׁי שֶׁיִּצְטָרֵף עִמָּהֶם לְזִימּוּן[46], וַאֲפִילּוּ אִם בָּא הַשְּׁלִישִׁי לְאַחַר שֶׁהַשְּׁנַיִם כְּבָר גָּמְרוּ מִלֶּאֱכוֹל, אֶלָּא שֶׁאִם הָיוּ מְבִיאִין לָהֶם עוֹד אֵיזֶה דָּבָר לְקִינּוּחַ סְעוּדָה הָיוּ אוֹכְלִין[47], מִצְוָה עֲלֵיהֶם לְצָרֵף אֶת זֶה הַשְּׁלִישִׁי לְזִימּוּן, דְּהַיְינוּ שֶׁיִּתְּנוּ לוֹ לֶאֱכוֹל כְּזַיִת[48] שֶׁיִּתְחַיֵּיב בִּבְרָכָה אַחֲרוֹנָה[49]

---

§9 אִם הַמְבָרֵךְ אֵינוֹ רוֹצֶה לִשְׁתּוֹת — **If the leader does not wish to drink** the wine, יֵשׁ אוֹמְרִים — **some** authorities **say** דְּיָכוֹל לִיתֵּן לְאִישׁ אַחֵר מִן הַמְסוּבִּין — **that he may give** it **to another one of the diners,** שֶׁיְּבָרֵךְ "בּוֹרֵא פְּרִי הַגָּפֶן" — for him **to recite the blessing of** *borei pri hagafen* וְיִשְׁתֶּה שִׁיעוּר רְבִיעִית — **and drink the amount of a** *revi'is* of wine, וִיבָרֵךְ בְּרָכָה אַחֲרוֹנָה — **and** then **recite the** *berachah acharonah.* וְיֵשׁ אוֹמְרִים — However, **some** authorities **say** דְּאֵין לַעֲשׂוֹת כֵּן — **that this should not be done;** אֶלָּא דַּוְקָא הַמְבָרֵךְ בְּזִימּוּן — **rather, only the one who recited the** *zimun* **blessing** הוּא יְבָרֵךְ עַל הַכּוֹס — **should himself recite the blessing** of *borei pri hagafen* **over the cup** of wine; וְכֵן נָכוֹן לַעֲשׂוֹת — **and such is the proper practice.**[45]

§10 As mentioned above, the *zimun* blessing is recited only when a minimum of three people have eaten together. In the next several *sei'ifim,* Kitzur explains the importance of forming and retaining this group so that the mitzvah can be performed properly:

שְׁנַיִם שֶׁאָכְלוּ בְּיַחַד — **If two people have eaten together,** מִצְוָה לָהֶם לְבַקֵּשׁ שְׁלִישִׁי — **it is a mitzvah for them to seek a third** person שֶׁיִּצְטָרֵף עִמָּהֶם לְזִימּוּן — **to be joined with them** as one group **so they may** recite **the** *zimun* blessing.[46] וַאֲפִילּוּ אִם בָּא הַשְּׁלִישִׁי — **Even if the third person arrives** לְאַחַר שֶׁהַשְּׁנַיִם כְּבָר גָּמְרוּ מִלֶּאֱכוֹל — **after the** first **two have finished eating,** אֶלָּא שֶׁאִם הָיוּ מְבִיאִין לָהֶם — **but** they are not completely sated, such that **if they would be served** עוֹד אֵיזֶה דָּבָר לְקִינּוּחַ סְעוּדָּה — **something more for dessert** הָיוּ אוֹכְלִין — **they would** be able to **eat it,**[47] then they are not considered to have completed concluded their meal. מִצְוָה עֲלֵיהֶם — Therefore, **it is a mitzvah for them** לְצָרֵף אֶת זֶה הַשְּׁלִישִׁי לְזִימּוּן — **to have the third person join them so** that they may recite **the** *zimun.* דְּהַיְינוּ שֶׁיִּתְּנוּ לוֹ לֶאֱכוֹל כְּזַיִת — This is accomplished **by giving** the third person **a** *kezayis*[48] of food **to eat** שֶׁיִּתְחַיֵּיב בִּבְרָכָה אַחֲרוֹנָה — **so that he will become obligated** to recite a *berachah acharonah,*[49]

---

45. See Appendix of Kitzur's editorial glosses for further discussion.

46. I.e., if there is another person in the house, he should be offered something to eat in order to join them for this purpose, as will be detailed by Kitzur. However, if an individual eats a meal alone, he need not seek two more people in order to recite the *zimun* blessing (*Mishnah Berurah* 193:7-8).

47. That is, if they were brought something that arouses their appetite they would be capable of eating even a small amount of it (see *Shulchan Aruch* 197:1 with *Mishnah Berurah* §2).

48. Between .6 & 1.1 fl. oz. (17.3-33.3 cc.); see Appendix A.

49. I.e., the appropriate *berachah acharonah* for that which he ate, whether bread (*Bircas HaMazon*), or other food, as Kitzur continues. See below, 51:2, which states that the obligation to

123   ⌒⟩   LAWS OF THE ZIMUN BLESSING — SIMAN 45:11

וְיִצְטָרֵף עִמָּהֶם. יֵשׁ אוֹמְרִים דְּבָעִינַן דַּוְוקָא פַּת. וְיֵשׁ אוֹמְרִים דְּסַגִּי גַּם בִּשְׁאָר מִינֵי
דָּגָן. וְיֵשׁ אוֹמְרִים דַּאֲפִילוּ פֵּירוֹת אוֹ יְרָקוֹת סַגִּי. וְיֵשׁ אוֹמְרִים עוֹד דַּאֲפִילוּ אֵינוֹ אוֹכֵל,
רַק שׁוֹתֶה רְבִיעִית⁵⁰ מֵאֵיזֶה מַשְׁקֶה חוּץ מִן הַמַּיִם⁵¹, מִצְטָרֵף. וְכֵן נוֹהֲגִין. וְאַף עַל פִּי
שֶׁלֹּא אָכַל, אֶלָּא שָׁתָה, יָכוֹל לוֹמַר "שֶׁאָכַלְנוּ", כִּי שְׁתִיָּה בִּכְלַל אֲכִילָה⁵². וּלְאַחַר
שֶׁסִּיְּימוּ "הַזָּן אֶת הַכֹּל", אָז יְבָרֵךְ הוּא בְּרָכָה אַחֲרוֹנָה עַל מַה שֶּׁאָכַל אוֹ שָׁתָה. וְאִם
בָּא הַשְּׁלִישִׁי לְאַחַר שֶׁכְּבָר נָטְלוּ יְדֵיהֶם בְּמַיִם אַחֲרוֹנִים, שׁוּב אֵינוֹ מִצְטָרֵף עִמָּהֶם.

יא. שְׁלֹשָׁה שֶׁאָכְלוּ בְּיַחַד, כֵּיוָן שֶׁנִּתְחַיְּיבוּ בְּזִימוּן, אֵינָם רַשָּׁאִים לֵיחָלֵק. וְכֵן אַרְבָּעָה,
אוֹ חֲמִשָּׁה, אֲפִילוּ אֶחָד מֵהֶם אֵינוֹ רַשָּׁאי לְבָרֵךְ בִּפְנֵי עַצְמוֹ, שֶׁכּוּלָּן נִתְחַיְּיבוּ

וְיִצְטָרֵף עִמָּהֶם — and this allows him to combine with them to form a *zimun.* יֵשׁ
אוֹמְרִים — Some authorities say   דְּבָעִינַן דַּוְוקָא פַּת — that the third person must
specifically eat bread in order to join the meal;   וְיֵשׁ אוֹמְרִים — some say   דְּסַגִּי
גַּם בִּשְׁאָר מִינֵי דָּגָן — that it is sufficient even if he eats other grain products;   וְיֵשׁ
אוֹמְרִים — some say   דַּאֲפִילוּ פֵּירוֹת אוֹ יְרָקוֹת סַגִּי — that even if he eats fruits or
vegetables, it is sufficient;   וְיֵשׁ אוֹמְרִים עוֹד — some say yet further,   דַּאֲפִילוּ אֵינוֹ
אוֹכֵל — that even if he does not eat anything,   רַק שׁוֹתֶה רְבִיעִית מֵאֵיזֶה מַשְׁקֶה
but only drinks a *revi'is*[50] of any beverage   חוּץ מִן הַמַּיִם — with the exception of
water,[51]   מִצְטָרֵף — he can be considered joined to the group,   וְכֵן נוֹהֲגִין — and
this last opinion is the accepted custom.   וְאַף עַל פִּי שֶׁלֹּא אָכַל — Even though he
did not eat,   אֶלָּא שָׁתָה — but only drank,   יָכוֹל לוֹמַר "שֶׁאָכַלְנוּ" — he may still
recite the words of the *zimun* blessing that refer to eating, "*Blessed is [He] of Whose we
have eaten,*"   כִּי שְׁתִיָּה בִּכְלַל אֲכִילָה — because drinking is included in the category
of "eating."[52]   וּלְאַחַר שֶׁסִּיְּימוּ "הַזָּן אֶת הַכֹּל" — If he ate something that does not
require *Bircas HaMazon,* after the other two have concluded the first blessing of *Bircas
Hamazon, Hazan es hakol, Who provides sustenance for all,*   אָז יְבָרֵךְ הוּא בְּרָכָה
אַחֲרוֹנָה — the third person should then recite a *berachah acharonah*   עַל מַה שֶּׁאָכַל
אוֹ שָׁתָה — upon that which he ate or drank.   וְאִם בָּא הַשְּׁלִישִׁי — However, if the third person arrives   לְאַחַר שֶׁכְּבָר נָטְלוּ יְדֵיהֶם
בְּמַיִם אַחֲרוֹנִים — after the first two have washed *mayim acharonim,*   שׁוּב אֵינוֹ
מִצְטָרֵף עִמָּהֶם — he can no longer join with them in their meal, and they cannot recite
the *zimun.*

§11 שְׁלֹשָׁה שֶׁאָכְלוּ בְּיַחַד — Three people who have eaten together,   כֵּיוָן שֶׁנִּתְחַיְּיבוּ
בְּזִימוּן — since they are obligated to recite the *zimun* blessing,   אֵינָם רַשָּׁאִים
לֵיחָלֵק — they are not permitted to separate, because if the group is dissolved, the
zimun is no longer possible.   וְכֵן אַרְבָּעָה, אוֹ חֲמִשָּׁה — Likewise, when four or five
people have eaten together,   אֲפִילוּ אֶחָד מֵהֶם אֵינוֹ רַשָּׁאי לְבָרֵךְ בִּפְנֵי עַצְמוֹ — even one
of them is not permitted to recite *Bircas HaMazon* on his own, even though the rest
of them would still be able to perform the *zimun,*   שֶׁכּוּלָּן נִתְחַיְּיבוּ בְּזִימוּן — because
all of them are obligated to recite the *zimun.* Therefore, even though his reciting of

---

recite a *berachah acharonah* begins only after
eating at least a *kezayis* of food.

50. See below, 51:2, which states that one
must recite a *berachah acharonah* on a

beverage only if one drank a *revi'is.*
51. See Appendix of Kitzur's editorial glosses.
52. The word אֲכִילָה, *eating,* can refer to drinking as well; see *Shevuos* 22b.

בְּזִימּוּן. אִם הֵם שִׁשָּׁה, אוֹ יוֹתֵר עַד עֲשָׂרָה, יְכוֹלִין לֵיחָלֵק, שֶׁיִּשָּׁאֵר זִימּוּן לְכָל חֲבוּרָה.

יב. אִם הֵם עֲשָׂרָה נִתְחַיְּיבוּ לְבָרֵךְ בְּשֵׁם, דְּהַיְינוּ שֶׁהַמְבָרֵךְ אוֹמֵר "נְבָרֵךְ אֱלֹהֵינוּ שֶׁאָכַלְנוּ מִשֶּׁלּוֹ"[53] (וכו'). וְלֹא יֹאמַר "נְבָרֵךְ לֵאלֹהֵינוּ". וְהַמְסוּבִּים אוֹמְרִים "בָּרוּךְ אֱלֹהֵינוּ שֶׁאָכַלְנוּ מִשֶּׁלּוֹ" וכו'[54]. וְכֵיוָן שֶׁנִּתְחַיְּיבוּ לְבָרֵךְ בְּשֵׁם, אֲסוּרִין לֵחָלֵק[55], אֶלָּא אִם כֵּן הֵם עֶשְׂרִים, אוֹ יוֹתֵר, אָז מוּתָּרִין לֵיחָלֵק, שֶׁיִּשָּׁאֵר לְכָל חֲבוּרָה זִימּוּן בְּשֵׁם.

יג. אִם טָעָה הַמְזַמֵּן בַּעֲשָׂרָה, וְגַם הָעוֹנִים, וְלֹא הִזְכִּירוּ אֶת הַשֵּׁם בְּבִרְכַּת הַזִּימּוּן, אֵינָם יְכוֹלִים לַחֲזוֹר וּלְזַמֵּן בְּשֵׁם, כֵּיוָן שֶׁכְּבָר יָצְאוּ יְדֵי חוֹבַת זִימּוּן אֶלָּא שֶׁבִּטְּלוּ מִצְוַת הַזְכָּרַת הַשֵּׁם, וּמְעֻוָּת שֶׁלֹּא יוּכַל לִתְקֹן הוּא[56]. אֲבָל אִם הָעוֹנִים

Bircas HaMazon on his own does not cause the others to lose their opportunity for *zimun*, he must remain in order to fulfill his *own* obligation. **אִם הֵם שִׁשָּׁה, אוֹ יוֹתֵר עַד עֲשָׂרָה — But if they are** a group of **six or more up until** a group of **ten, יְכוֹלִין לֵיחָלֵק — they may separate** into two groups of at least three each, **שֶׁיִּשָּׁאֵר זִימּוּן לְכָל חֲבוּרָה —** because enough people **will remain in each group to perform the** ***zimun.***

§12 אִם הֵם עֲשָׂרָה — If they are ten who have eaten together, **נִתְחַיְּיבוּ לְבָרֵךְ בְּשֵׁם — they are obligated to recite the** *zimun* **blessing with** Hashem's **Name. דְּהַיְינוּ שֶׁהַמְבָרֵךְ אוֹמֵר — That is, the leader of the blessing says: "נְבָרֵךְ אֱלֹהֵינוּ שֶׁאָכַלְנוּ מִשֶּׁלּוֹ" (וכו') —** ***Let us bless our God, of Whose we have eaten,***[53] **etc. וְלֹא יֹאמַר "נְבָרֵךְ לֵאלֹהֵינוּ" —** But **he should not say:** ***Let us bless "to" our God.*** **וְהַמְסוּבִּים אוֹמְרִים — The diners reply: "בָּרוּךְ אֱלֹהֵינוּ שֶׁאָכַלְנוּ מִשֶּׁלּוֹ" וכו' —** ***Blessed is our God, of Whose we have eaten*** etc.[54] **וְכֵיוָן שֶׁנִּתְחַיְּיבוּ לְבָרֵךְ בְּשֵׁם — Since they are obligated to recite the** *zimun* **blessing with** Hashem's **Name, אֲסוּרִין לֵחָלֵק — they are forbidden to separate** into more than one group,[55] **אֶלָּא אִם כֵּן הֵם עֶשְׂרִים, אוֹ יוֹתֵר — unless there are twenty or more** people in that group, **אָז מוּתָּרִין לֵיחָלֵק — at which point they may separate** into two groups of ten or more each, **שֶׁיִּשָּׁאֵר לְכָל חֲבוּרָה זִימּוּן בְּשֵׁם —** because enough people **will remain in each group to recite the** ***zimun*** **with** Hashem's **Name.**

§13 אִם טָעָה הַמְזַמֵּן בַּעֲשָׂרָה — If the one leading the ***zimun*** **with ten** people **erred, וְגַם הָעוֹנִים — and those who responded** to his blessing erred **as well, וְלֹא הִזְכִּירוּ אֶת הַשֵּׁם בְּבִרְכַּת הַזִּימּוּן — and they did not mention the Name** of Hashem **in** the *zimun* blessing, **אֵינָם יְכוֹלִים לַחֲזוֹר וּלְזַמֵּן בְּשֵׁם — they may not return** to the beginning **and recite the** ***zimun*** again **with the Name** of Hashem. **כֵּיוָן שֶׁכְּבָר יָצְאוּ יְדֵי חוֹבַת זִימּוּן —** This **is because they have fulfilled their obligation of** ***zimun,*** **אֶלָּא שֶׁבִּטְּלוּ מִצְוַת הַזְכָּרַת הַשֵּׁם — but they have lost the mitzvah of mentioning the Name** of Hashem, **וּמְעֻוָּת שֶׁלֹּא יוּכַל לִתְקֹן הוּא — and it is a** ***twisted thing [that] cannot be made straight.***[56] **אֲבָל אִם הָעוֹנִים — However, if those who** are **to respond**

---

53. [This is the entire declaration; וכו' (*etc.*) was added in error.]

54. This is then repeated by the leader. Each time, the word אֱלֹהֵינוּ, *our God*, is added to the standard blessing.

55. The *zimun* blessing for three people does not contain Hashem's Name, whereas the Name is added for ten or more. Since the blessing is more exalted when ten people eat together, it is prohibited to disband the group if not enough people will remain in order to allow the mention of the Name of Hashem in the blessing. See *Mishnah Berurah* (193:16).

56. The phrase used here is a verse in *Koheles*

125 LAWS OF THE ZIMUN BLESSING — SIMAN 45:14-15

עֲדַיִין לֹא עָנוּ אַחֲרָיו, כֵּיוָן שֶׁעֲדַיִין לֹא נִתְקַיְּימָה מִצְוַת זִימּוּן, יַחֲזוֹר הַמְבָרֵךְ וִיזַמֵּן בְּשֵׁם[57].

יד. אִם שִׁבְעָה אָכְלוּ פַּת וּשְׁלֹשָׁה אָכְלוּ פֵּירוֹת, אוֹ שָׁתוּ מַשְׁקִין, בְּעִנְיָן שֶׁחַיָּיבִין בִּבְרָכָה אַחֲרוֹנָה[58], יְכוֹלִין לְזַמֵּן בְּשֵׁם (בְּכָאן כּוּלֵּי עָלְמָא מוֹדוּ דְּסַגֵּי בְּפֵירוֹת וּבְמַשְׁקֶה)[59]. וּמִצְוָה לְהַדֵּר אַחַר עֲשָׂרָה לְבָרֵךְ בְּשֵׁם. אֲבָל אִם רַק שִׁשָּׁה אָכְלוּ פַּת אֵינָם יְכוֹלִים לְזַמֵּן בְּשֵׁם, דְּרוּבָּא דְּמִינְכַּר בָּעִינַן[60].

טו. כֹּל שֶׁאָכְלוּ בְּיַחַד, אֲפִילוּ לֹא אָכְלוּ כָּל הַסְּעוּדָה בְּיַחַד, אֶלָּא שֶׁיָּשְׁבוּ לֶאֱכוֹל

עֲדַיִין לֹא עָנוּ אַחֲרָיו — **have not yet responded to him,** **כֵּיוָן שֶׁעֲדַיִין לֹא נִתְקַיְּימָה מִצְוַת זִימּוּן** — **since the mitzvah of *zimun* has not yet been fulfilled,** **יַחֲזוֹר הַמְבָרֵךְ וִיזַמֵּן בְּשֵׁם** — **the leader should go back** to the beginning **and** recite the ***zimun*** **with the Name** of Hashem.[57]

§14 **אִם שִׁבְעָה אָכְלוּ פַּת** — **If seven** people **have eaten bread,** **וּשְׁלֹשָׁה אָכְלוּ פֵּירוֹת** — **and three** others **have eaten fruit** **אוֹ שָׁתוּ מַשְׁקִין** — **or have drunk a beverage** **בְּעִנְיָן שֶׁחַיָּיבִין בִּבְרָכָה אַחֲרוֹנָה** — **in a manner that they are obligated** to recite a *berachah acharonah*,[58] **יְכוֹלִין לְזַמֵּן בְּשֵׁם** — **they may** form a group of ten and thus **recite the *zimun* with the Name** of Hashem. (**בְּכָאן כּוּלֵּי עָלְמָא מוֹדוּ** — **In this** situation, **all agree** **דְּסַגֵּי בְּפֵירוֹת וּבְמַשְׁקֶה** — **that** partaking of **fruits or beverages is sufficient** for the three additional members to become joined as a group of ten.)[59] **וּמִצְוָה לְהַדֵּר אַחַר עֲשָׂרָה לְבָרֵךְ בְּשֵׁם** — **It is a mitzvah to seek** people to complete the **ten** necessary **to recite the** *zimun* **blessing with the Name** of Hashem. **אֲבָל אִם רַק שִׁשָּׁה אָכְלוּ פַּת** — **However, if only six** of the ten present **have eaten bread,** **אֵינָם יְכוֹלִים לְזַמֵּן בְּשֵׁם** — **they may not recite the *zimun* with the Name** of Hashem, **דְּרוּבָּא דְּמִינְכַּר בָּעִינַן** — **because** in order to warrant the mention of Hashem's Name **a distinctive majority is necessary.**[60]

§15 As we have seen previously (*se'ifim* 11-12), once a group has eaten together and has become obligated in *zimun,* they may not separate in a manner that will cause the members of the group to lose their opportunity for *zimun*. In this *se'if,* Kitzur defines the criteria that determine whether a group is considered to be joined as one for this purpose.

כֹּל שֶׁאָכְלוּ בְּיַחַד — In **any** situation **where** [a minimum of three] people **have eaten together,** **אֲפִילוּ לֹא אָכְלוּ כָּל הַסְּעוּדָה בְּיַחַד** — **even if they did not eat the entire meal together,** **אֶלָּא שֶׁיָּשְׁבוּ לֶאֱכוֹל** — **but they sat down to eat**

1:15, and refers to (among other things) a lost opportunity to perform a mitzvah that cannot be regained; see *Berachos* 26a and *Chagigah* 9b.

57. If the assembled did respond with Hashem's Name, then when the leader repeats the second sentence of the blessing (see above, *se'if* 6), he should recite Hashem's Name: בָּרוּךְ אֱלֹהֵינוּ שֶׁאָכַלְנוּ מִשֶּׁלּוֹ וּבְטוּבוֹ חָיִינוּ, *Blessed is our God of Whose we have eaten and through His goodness we live* (*Mishnah Berurah* 192:10).

58. I.e., a *kezayis* of fruit or a *revi'is* of drink; see below, 51:2. [See *Beur Halachah* 197:2 s.v. שיש בו רביעית, which indicates that if one had less than a *revi'is* of drink, he may possibly be allowed to join a group of ten; see also *Beur Halachah* 197:2 s.v. כזית ירק.]

59. This is in contrast to above, *se'if* 10, where Kitzur cited a dispute whether eating fruit or drinking a beverage is sufficient to enable a third person to become part of a group of three.

60. I.e., at least seven participants must have eaten bread.

וּבֵרְכוּ בִּרְכַּת הַמּוֹצִיא, אֲפִילּוּ כָּל אֶחָד אוֹכֵל מִכִּכָּר שֶׁלּוֹ, כֵּיוָן שֶׁנִּקְבְּעוּ יַחַד, בֵּין בִּשְׁלֹשָׁה בֵּין בַּעֲשָׂרָה, אֵינָן רַשָּׁאִין לֵיחָלֵק[61]. וַאֲפִילּוּ אֶחָד רוֹצֶה לִגְמוֹר סְעוּדָתוֹ קוֹדֶם שֶׁיִּגְמְרוּ הָאֲחֵרִים, אֵינָן רַשָּׁאִין לֵיחָלֵק[62]. אֲבָל אִם לֹא קָבְעוּ עַצְמָם בִּתְחִלַּת הַסְּעוּדָה, אֶלָּא שֶׁלְּאַחַר שֶׁשְּׁנַיִם כְּבָר אָכְלוּ, אֲפִילּוּ לֹא אָכְלוּ עֲדַיִין רַק כְּזַיִת, וּבָא הַשְּׁלִישִׁי וְקָבַע עִמָּהֶם, אִם גָּמַר סְעוּדָתוֹ עִמָּהֶם, חַיָּיבִים בְּזִימּוּן. אֲבָל אִם רָצָה לִגְמוֹר סְעוּדָתוֹ קוֹדֶם לָהֶן, כֵּיוָן שֶׁלֹּא הִתְחִיל עִמָּהֶם וְגַם לֹא גָּמַר עִמָּהֶם, רַשַּׁאי לֵיחָלֵק וּלְבָרֵךְ בִּפְנֵי עַצְמוֹ[63]. וּמִכָּל מָקוֹם מִצְוָה הִיא לְהַמְתִּין שֶׁיְּבָרְכוּ בְּזִימּוּן. אִם הוּא אוֹנֵס,

וּבֵרְכוּ בִּרְכַּת הַמּוֹצִיא — and recited the blessing of *hamotzi* upon the bread, **אֲפִילּוּ כָּל אֶחָד אוֹכֵל מִכִּכָּר שֶׁלּוֹ — even if each** person **is eating from his own loaf** of bread, **כֵּיוָן שֶׁנִּקְבְּעוּ יַחַד** — the halachah is that **since they have set themselves together** at the onset of the meal, **בֵּין בִּשְׁלֹשָׁה בֵּין בַּעֲשָׂרָה — whether they are** a group of **three or** a group of **ten, אֵינָן רַשָּׁאִין לֵיחָלֵק — they may not separate.**[61] **וַאֲפִילּוּ אֶחָד רוֹצֶה לִגְמוֹר סְעוּדָתוֹ — Even if one of them wishes to conclude his** meal **קוֹדֶם שֶׁיִּגְמְרוּ הָאֲחֵרִים — before the others have concluded** theirs, **אֵינָן רַשָּׁאִין לֵיחָלֵק — they are not permitted to separate.**[62] **אֲבָל אִם לֹא קָבְעוּ עַצְמָם בִּתְחִלַּת הַסְּעוּדָה — However, if they did not set themselves** down together **at the beginning of the meal, אֶלָּא שֶׁלְּאַחַר שֶׁשְּׁנַיִם כְּבָר אָכְלוּ — but rather, after two** people **already** began **to eat, אֲפִילּוּ לֹא אָכְלוּ עֲדַיִין רַק כְּזַיִת — even if they had eaten only a *kezayis*, וּבָא הַשְּׁלִישִׁי וְקָבַע עִמָּהֶם — a third** person **arrived and set** himself down **with them, אִם גָּמַר סְעוּדָתוֹ עִמָּהֶם** — then, **if he completed his meal with them, חַיָּיבִים בְּזִימּוּן — they are obligated to perform the *zimun*** together, **אֲבָל אִם רָצָה לִגְמוֹר סְעוּדָתוֹ קוֹדֶם לָהֶן — but if** the third person **wishes to conclude his meal before them, כֵּיוָן שֶׁלֹּא הִתְחִיל עִמָּהֶם — since he did not begin** eating **with them, וְגַם לֹא גָּמַר עִמָּהֶם — and also did not conclude** his meal **with them, רַשַּׁאי לֵיחָלֵק וּלְבָרֵךְ בִּפְנֵי עַצְמוֹ — he is permitted to separate** from them **and recite *Bircas HaMazon* on his own.**[63] **וּמִכָּל מָקוֹם — Nevertheless, מִצְוָה הִיא לְהַמְתִּין — it is a mitzvah** for the individual **to wait** for the other two to complete their meal **שֶׁיְּבָרְכוּ בְּזִימּוּן — so that they may recite the *zimun*** blessing.

אִם הוּא אוֹנֵס — If one of the diners who ate together **is forced** to leave before the

61. When people set themselves down together to eat a meal at one table, they are considered one group for *zimun* purposes. Members of a household who are eating with the head of the household are considered to be one group even if they are not seated at the same table (*Mishnah Berurah* 193:18). Travelers who eat together in one vehicle may also recite the *zimun* blessing after their meal. However, even if ten are present in such a situation, they should omit mention of Hashem's Name (ibid. §26).

62. One who attends a meal such as a wedding or other event from which he needs to leave early, and cannot wait for the *zimun* at the end of the meal, should stipulate specifically before he sits down to eat, that he does not intend to join together with the others present. In this case, he can recite *Bircas HaMazon* on his own, and is not required to wait for the *zimun* at the end of the meal (*Igros Moshe, Orach Chaim* I, §56).

63. The other two may also conclude their meal without waiting for the third person. However, if they finished eating, but did not recite *Bircas HaMazon* until the third person also completed his meal, and the first two would still have an interest in eating a bit of dessert at that point, if it were served (see above, *se'if* 10), they must now recite the *zimun* together (*Mishnah Berurah* 193:19).

אוֹ מִתְיָירֵא מֵהֶפְסֵד, אֲפִילוּ קָבַע עַצְמוֹ עִמָּהֶם בִּתְחִלָּה, מוּתָּר לִגְמוֹר סְעוּדָתוֹ קוֹדֶם לָהֶם וּלְבָרֵךְ בִּפְנֵי עַצְמוֹ[64]. אֲבָל אִם אֵין הַדָּבָר נָחוּץ, צָרִיךְ לְהַחֲמִיר.

טז. שְׁלֹשָׁה שֶׁאָכְלוּ בְּיַחַד וְשָׁכַח אֶחָד מֵהֶם[65] וּבֵירַךְ בִּרְכַּת הַמָּזוֹן בִּפְנֵי עַצְמוֹ, יְכוֹלִין לְזַמֵּן לְאַחַר שֶׁגָּמַר זֶה בִּרְכַּת הַמָּזוֹן וְיַעֲנֶה גַּם הוּא "בָּרוּךְ שֶׁאָכַלְנוּ" וְכוּ'[66]. אֲבָל אִם זֶה נִצְטָרֵף לְזִימּוּן עִם שְׁנַיִם אֲחֵרִים[67], שׁוּב אֵינוֹ יָכוֹל לְהִצְטָרֵף לְזִימּוּן עִם אֵלוּ. וְאִם שְׁנַיִם בֵּרְכוּ, אֲפִילוּ בִּפְנֵי עַצְמָן, בָּטֵל זִימּוּן.

יז. שְׁלֹשָׁה שֶׁאָכְלוּ וּשְׁנַיִם גָּמְרוּ סְעוּדָתָן וְרוֹצִים לְבָרֵךְ וְאֶחָד עֲדַיִין לֹא גָמַר סְעוּדָתוֹ

---

other two have completed their meal, **אוֹ מִתְיָירֵא מֵהֶפְסֵד** — **or he fears he will suffer a** financial **loss** if he does not leave immediately, **אֲפִילוּ קָבַע עַצְמוֹ עִמָּהֶם בִּתְחִלָּה** — **even if he set himself** down to eat **with them at the beginning** of his meal, **מוּתָּר לִגְמוֹר סְעוּדָתוֹ קוֹדֶם לָהֶם** — **he is permitted to conclude his meal before them** **וּלְבָרֵךְ בִּפְנֵי עַצְמוֹ** — **and recite** ***Bircas HaMazon*** **on his own.**[64] **אֲבָל אִם אֵין הַדָּבָר נָחוּץ** — **However, if the issue is not pressing,** **צָרִיךְ לְהַחֲמִיר** — **one must be stringent** and remain for the *zimun.*

§16 **שְׁלֹשָׁה שֶׁאָכְלוּ בְּיַחַד** — Regarding **three** people **who have eaten together** and are obligated to join in *zimun,* **וְשָׁכַח אֶחָד מֵהֶם** — **and one of them forgot**[65] about this obligation **וּבֵירַךְ בִּרְכַּת הַמָּזוֹן בִּפְנֵי עַצְמוֹ** — **and recited** ***Bircas HaMazon*** **on his own,** **יְכוֹלִין לְזַמֵּן** — the halachah is that **they may** still **perform the** ***zimun*** together, **לְאַחַר שֶׁגָּמַר זֶה בִּרְכַּת הַמָּזוֹן** — **after the one** who forgot to wait **completes** ***Bircas HaMazon.*** **וְיַעֲנֶה גַּם הוּא** — **He also responds** with **"בָּרוּךְ שֶׁאָכַלְנוּ" וְכוּ'** — ***Blessed is*** *He of Whose* ***we have eaten*** etc.[66] **אֲבָל אִם זֶה נִצְטָרֵף לְזִימּוּן עִם שְׁנַיִם אֲחֵרִים** — **However, if he had joined two others to recite the** ***zimun,***[67] **שׁוּב אֵינוֹ יָכוֹל לְהִצְטָרֵף לְזִימּוּן עִם אֵלוּ** — **he can no longer join for the** ***zimun*** **with these** two from the first group. **וְאִם שְׁנַיִם בֵּרְכוּ** — **If two** of the original three **recited** ***Bircas HaMazon,*** **אֲפִילוּ בִּפְנֵי עַצְמָן** — **even if** they did so **on their own,** i.e., they did not join with another person to perform *zimun* as a group of three, **בָּטֵל זִימּוּן** — the opportunity to recite **the** ***zimun*** **is lost.**

§17 **שְׁלֹשָׁה שֶׁאָכְלוּ** — If **three** people **have eaten** together **וּשְׁנַיִם גָּמְרוּ סְעוּדָתָן** **וְרוֹצִים לְבָרֵךְ** — **and two** of them **have completed their meal and wish to recite** ***Bircas HaMazon,*** **וְאֶחָד עֲדַיִין לֹא גָמַר סְעוּדָתוֹ** — **and one has not yet completed his**

---

64. *Mishnah Berurah* (200:5) writes that in this case, it is preferable that the other two interrupt their meal to allow the *zimun* to be recited by the third (although they are not obligated to do so; see following *se'if*).

65. The same law applies to one who intentionally did not wait for the *zimun* (*Beur Halachah* 194:1 s.v. שכח).

66. After the *zimun* blessing, the other two continue with *Bircas HaMazon.* The same halachah applies when the group is larger; for example, if a group of four were eating and two people mistakenly recited *Bircas HaMazon* by themselves (without a *zimun*), they may rejoin the previous group to recite the *zimun* (*Beur Halachah* 194:1 s.v. אחד; see there for further discussion). If three people out of a group of ten recited *Bircas HaMazon,* they may rejoin the group and recite the *zimun* with the Name of Hashem (ibid.).

67. I.e., he joined two others who were eating and recited the *zimun* with them.

וְאֵינוֹ רוֹצֶה לְבָרֵךְ, צָרִיךְ הוּא לְהַפְסִיק מִסְּעוּדָתוֹ כְּדֵי שֶׁיְּבָרְכוּ בְּזִימּוּן[68] וְיַעֲנֶה גַּם הוּא עִמָּהֶם וְיוֹצֵא יְדֵי זִימּוּן, וְיַמְתִּין עַד שֶׁסִּיֵּים הַמְבָרֵךְ "הַזָּן אֶת הַכֹּל", וְאַחַר כָּךְ יָכוֹל לֶאֱכוֹל. וְאֵין צָרִיךְ לְבָרֵךְ בְּרָכָה רִאשׁוֹנָה, כֵּיוָן שֶׁדַּעְתּוֹ הָיָה לֶאֱכוֹל עוֹד[69]. וּכְשֶׁיִּגְמוֹר סְעוּדָתוֹ יְבָרֵךְ בִּרְכַּת הַמָּזוֹן. אֲבָל שְׁנַיִם אֵינָן צְרִיכִין לְהַפְסִיק בִּשְׁבִיל אֶחָד[70], אֶלָּא אִם יִרְצוּ לַעֲשׂוֹת לוֹ לִכְבוֹדוֹ לִפְנִים מִשּׁוּרַת הַדִּין. וַעֲשָׂרָה שֶׁאָכְלוּ בְּיַחַד צְרִיכִין אַרְבָּעָה לְהַפְסִיק בִּשְׁבִיל שִׁשָּׁה, שֶׁהֵם הָרוֹב. וְאֵינָם צְרִיכִין לְהַמְתִּין רַק עַד שֶׁאָמַר "בָּרוּךְ אֱלֹהֵינוּ" וּלְאַחַר שֶׁגָּמְרוּ הֵם סְעוּדָתָן יְזַמְּנוּ לְעַצְמָן בְּלִי הַזְכָּרַת הַשֵּׁם[71].

וְאֵינוֹ רוֹצֶה לְבָרֵךְ — and does not yet **wish to recite *Bircas HaMazon*, צָרִיךְ הוּא לְהַפְסִיק מִסְּעוּדָתוֹ —** the **one** who has not yet completed his meal **must interrupt his meal כְּדֵי שֶׁיְּבָרְכוּ בְּזִימּוּן — so that they may recite *Bircas HaMazon* with a** *zimun*.[68] **וְיַעֲנֶה גַּם הוּא עִמָּהֶם — He should respond** to the *zimun* **with them, וְיוֹצֵא יְדֵי זִימּוּן — thus fulfilling his obligation of *zimun*. וְיַמְתִּין עַד שֶׁסִּיֵּים הַמְבָרֵךְ — He should then wait until the leader has completed "הַזָּן אֶת הַכֹּל"** — the first blessing of *Bircas HaMazon,* with the words ***Hazan es hakol,*** **וְאַחַר כָּךְ יָכוֹל לֶאֱכוֹל — and afterward he may** resume **eating. וְאֵין צָרִיךְ לְבָרֵךְ בְּרָכָה רִאשׁוֹנָה — He need not recite** another ***berachah rishonah*** (first blessing) on the food that he is eating, **כֵּיוָן שֶׁדַּעְתּוֹ הָיָה לֶאֱכוֹל עוֹד — since his intention was to continue eating.**[69] **וּכְשֶׁיִּגְמוֹר סְעוּדָתוֹ יְבָרֵךְ בִּרְכַּת הַמָּזוֹן — When he concludes his meal, he recites *Bircas HaMazon*** himself.

אֲבָל שְׁנַיִם — However, if two people wish to continue eating and one does not, **אֵינָן צְרִיכִין לְהַפְסִיק בִּשְׁבִיל אֶחָד —** the **two are not required to interrupt their meal for the one** person,[70] **אֶלָּא אִם יִרְצוּ לַעֲשׂוֹת לוֹ לִכְבוֹדוֹ — unless they wish to do so to accord him respect לִפְנִים מִשּׁוּרַת הַדִּין —** and go **beyond the boundary of** what is required by **law.**

וַעֲשָׂרָה שֶׁאָכְלוּ בְּיַחַד — If **ten** people **have eaten together** and some wish to recite *Bircas HaMazon,* **צְרִיכִין אַרְבָּעָה לְהַפְסִיק בִּשְׁבִיל שִׁשָּׁה — four** of them **must interrupt** their meal **for the sake of** the other **six, שֶׁהֵם הָרוֹב — because** the six **are the majority. וְאֵינָם צְרִיכִין לְהַמְתִּין רַק עַד שֶׁאָמַר "בָּרוּךְ אֱלֹהֵינוּ" —** Those four **have to wait only until** they have all **said, *Blessed is our God*** etc., and they may then resume eating. **וּלְאַחַר שֶׁגָּמְרוּ הֵם סְעוּדָתָן — After they have completed their meal, יְזַמְּנוּ לְעַצְמָן — they should recite** *Bircas HaMazon* preceded by **the *zimun*** blessing **on their own, בְּלִי הַזְכָּרַת הַשֵּׁם — without mentioning the Name** of Hashem in the *zimun* blessing.[71]

---

68. *Beur Halachah* (200:1 s.v.שאכלו כאחד) is uncertain whether two people who have no urgent reason for departing may compel their colleague to interrupt his meal. However, in any case, since he is the minority, it is proper for him to interrupt his meal in any case.

69. In certain cases, when a person prepares to recite *Bircas HaMazon*, he has thus halachically concluded his meal, and may not continue to eat without reciting the appropriate blessings upon each food (see above, 42:23). Here, Kitzur explains that since he had intended to continue the meal, his response to the *zimun* blessing does not constitute a conclusion to his meal, and he may continue as before, without reciting any blessings on the food that he eats. Nevertheless, *Mishnah Berurah* (200:7) writes that if, when responding to the *zimun*, he did not intend to continue eating, he must wash *netilas yadayim* and recite the blessing of *hamotzi* again before resuming his meal.

70. However, if they have finished eating, they may not wait any longer to delay the third person (*Beur Halachah* 200:1 s.v. עד שיגמרו).

71. See *Mishnah Berurah* 200:9.

יח. בִּסְעוּדוֹת גְּדוֹלוֹת שֶׁהַרְבֵּה מְסוּבִּין שָׁם, יֵשׁ לִבְחוֹר שֶׁיְּבָרֵךְ מִי שֶׁקּוֹלוֹ חָזָק כְּדֵי שֶׁיִּשְׁמְעוּ כָּל הַמְסוּבִּין מִן הַמְבָרֵךְ לְכָל הַפָּחוֹת עַד "הַזָּן אֶת הַכֹּל". וְאִם אִי אֶפְשָׁר בְּכָךְ, יְבָרְכוּ בַּחֲבוּרוֹת שֶׁל עֲשָׂרָה עֲשָׂרָה.

יט. שְׁתֵּי חֲבוּרוֹת שֶׁאוֹכְלִין בְּבַיִת אֶחָד, אוֹ בִּשְׁנֵי בָתִּים, אִם מִקְצָתָן רוֹאִים אֵלּוּ אֶת אֵלּוּ, מִצְטָרְפוֹת לְזִימּוּן[72]. וְאִם לָאו, אֵלּוּ מְזַמְּנִין לְעַצְמָן וְאֵלּוּ מְזַמְּנִין לְעַצְמָן. וְאִם יֵשׁ שַׁמָּשׁ אֶחָד לִשְׁתֵּיהֶן, הוּא מְצָרְפָן[73], וּכְגוֹן שֶׁנִּכְנְסוּ מִתְּחִלָּה עַל דַּעַת לְהִצְטָרֵף יַחַד[74]. וְכָל הֵיכָא שֶׁמִּצְטָרְפוֹת צְרִיכִין שֶׁיִּשְׁמְעוּ כּוּלָּן מִן הַמְבָרֵךְ לְכָל הַפָּחוֹת עַד "הַזָּן אֶת הַכֹּל".

כ. מִי שֶׁהוּא אֵצֶל הַמְבָרְכִים בְּזִימּוּן וְהוּא לֹא אָכַל וְלֹא שָׁתָה עִמָּהֶם[75], כְּשֶׁהוּא שׁוֹמֵעַ

---

§18 בִּסְעוּדוֹת גְּדוֹלוֹת שֶׁהַרְבֵּה מְסוּבִּין שָׁם — **At large feasts at which there are many people dining,** יֵשׁ לִבְחוֹר שֶׁיְּבָרֵךְ מִי שֶׁקּוֹלוֹ חָזָק — **someone with a strong voice should be selected to lead the blessing,** כְּדֵי שֶׁיִּשְׁמְעוּ כָּל הַמְסוּבִּין מִן הַמְבָרֵךְ — **so that all those participating in the meal will hear** the blessing **from the one leading the blessing,** לְכָל הַפָּחוֹת עַד "הַזָּן אֶת הַכֹּל" — **at least until** the completion of the first blessing of *Bircas HaMazon*, ***Hazan es hakol.*** וְאִם אִי אֶפְשָׁר בְּכָךְ — **If this is not possible,** יְבָרְכוּ בַּחֲבוּרוֹת שֶׁל עֲשָׂרָה עֲשָׂרָה — **they should recite the** *zimun* and *Bircas HaMazon* blessings **in groups of ten.**

§19 שְׁתֵּי חֲבוּרוֹת שֶׁאוֹכְלִין בְּבַיִת אֶחָד — If there are **two groups eating in one house,** אוֹ בִּשְׁנֵי בָתִּים — **or in two** separate **houses,** אִם מִקְצָתָן רוֹאִים אֵלּוּ אֶת אֵלּוּ — **if some members** of each group **can see each other,** מִצְטָרְפוֹת לְזִימּוּן — **they may join** as one group in order **to** recite the ***zimun***;[72] וְאִם לָאו — **if they cannot** see each other, אֵלּוּ מְזַמְּנִין לְעַצְמָן — **these should recite the** ***zimun*** **on their own,** וְאֵלּוּ מְזַמְּנִין לְעַצְמָן — **and these should recite the** ***zimun*** **on their own.** וְאִם יֵשׁ שַׁמָּשׁ אֶחָד לִשְׁתֵּיהֶן — **If there is one server for both** groups, הוּא מְצָרְפָן — **his** presence **joins them together** to be considered one group.[73] וּכְגוֹן שֶׁנִּכְנְסוּ מִתְּחִלָּה — However, this is only **in a case where they initially entered** עַל דַּעַת לְהִצְטָרֵף יַחַד — **with the intention of joining together** as one group.[74]

וְכָל הֵיכָא שֶׁמִּצְטָרְפוֹת — **In any situation where** two groups **are joined,** צְרִיכִין שֶׁיִּשְׁמְעוּ כּוּלָּן מִן הַמְבָרֵךְ — **they must all hear from the leader of the** *zimun* **blessing** לְכָל הַפָּחוֹת עַד "הַזָּן אֶת הַכֹּל" — **at least until the** completion of the first blessing of *Bircas HaMazon*, ***Hazan es hakol.***

§20 מִי שֶׁהוּא אֵצֶל הַמְבָרְכִים בְּזִימּוּן — **One who is together with those who are reciting the** ***zimun*** **blessing,** וְהוּא לֹא אָכַל וְלֹא שָׁתָה עִמָּהֶם — **and he did not eat or drink with them,**[75] כְּשֶׁהוּא שׁוֹמֵעַ שֶׁהַמְבָרֵךְ אוֹמֵר — **when he hears the leader**

---

72. See *Beur Halachah* (195:1 s.v. שתי חבורות), who rules that the two groups may be joined by using this method only if each group consists of three or more.

73. Sharing a server connects the two groups even if the server is not eating, and even if the groups are in two rooms and cannot see each other (*Mishnah Berurah* 195:4,5).

74. *Mishnah Berurah* (195:6) cites many authorities who maintain that if the two groups are in one house this condition is unnecessary.

75. See above, *se'if* 10.

שֶׁהַמְבָרֵךְ אוֹמֵר "נְבָרֵךְ שֶׁאָכַלְנוּ מִשֶּׁלּוֹ", עוֹנֶה הוּא "בָּרוּךְ וּמְבוֹרָךְ שְׁמוֹ תָּמִיד לְעוֹלָם וָעֶד"[76]. וְאִם מְזַמְּנִין בַּעֲשָׂרָה וְאוֹמֵר הַמְבָרֵךְ "נְבָרֵךְ אֱלֹהֵינוּ" וְכוּ' עוֹנֶה גַּם הוּא "בָּרוּךְ אֱלֹהֵינוּ וּמְבוֹרָךְ שְׁמוֹ תָּמִיד לְעוֹלָם וָעֶד". וְאִם בָּא לְאַחַר שֶׁכְּבָר אָמַר הַמְבָרֵךְ "נְבָרֵךְ" וְכוּ' וְשׁוֹמֵעַ שֶׁהָעוֹנִים אוֹמְרִים "בָּרוּךְ שֶׁאָכַלְנוּ" וְכוּ', אוֹ "בָּרוּךְ אֱלֹהֵינוּ שֶׁאָכַלְנוּ" וְכוּ', עוֹנֶה אַחֲרֵיהֶם "אָמֵן"[77].

כא. שְׁלֹשָׁה שֶׁאָכְלוּ כָּל אֶחָד מִכִּכָּר שֶׁלּוֹ וְאֶחָד מֵהֶם אָכַל פַּת עַכּוּ"ם וּשְׁנַיִם נִזְהָרִים מִפַּת עַכּוּ"ם[78], מִכָּל מָקוֹם מִצְטָרְפִין לְזִימּוּן, וִיבָרֵךְ זֶה שֶׁאָכַל פַּת עַכּוּ"ם[79], שֶׁהוּא יָכוֹל לֶאֱכוֹל גַּם עִם הָאֲחֵרִים. וְכֵן אִם אֶחָד אוֹכֵל מַאַכְלֵי חָלָב וּשְׁנַיִם

---

say, **"נְבָרֵךְ שֶׁאָכַלְנוּ מִשֶּׁלּוֹ"** — ***Let us bless [He] of Whose we have eaten,*** **עוֹנֶה הוּא** — **he should respond** with: **"בָּרוּךְ וּמְבוֹרָךְ שְׁמוֹ תָּמִיד לְעוֹלָם וָעֶד"** — ***Blessed is [He] and blessed is His Name continuously, for ever and ever.***[76] **וְאִם מְזַמְּנִין בַּעֲשָׂרָה** — **If they were reciting the** ***zimun*** **with ten** people, **וְאוֹמֵר הַמְבָרֵךְ "נְבָרֵךְ אֱלֹהֵינוּ" וְכוּ'** — **and the leader of the blessing** therefore **said,** ***Let us bless our God,*** etc. **עוֹנֶה גַּם הוּא** — **he should also respond** by mentioning the Name of Hashem: **"בָּרוּךְ אֱלֹהֵינוּ וּמְבוֹרָךְ שְׁמוֹ תָּמִיד לְעוֹלָם וָעֶד"** — ***Blessed is our God and blessed is His Name continuously, for ever and ever.*** **וְאִם בָּא לְאַחַר שֶׁכְּבָר אָמַר הַמְבָרֵךְ "נְבָרֵךְ" וְכוּ'** — **If he arrives after the leader has already said** the first phrase of ***Let us bless,*** etc. **וְשׁוֹמֵעַ שֶׁהָעוֹנִים אוֹמְרִים** — **and he hears those who are responding saying, "בָּרוּךְ שֶׁאָכַלְנוּ" וְכוּ'** — ***Blessed is [He]*** *of Whose* ***we have eaten*** **etc., אוֹ "בָּרוּךְ אֱלֹהֵינוּ שֶׁאָכַלְנוּ" וְכוּ'** — **or,** if there are ten, ***Blessed is our God*** *of Whose* ***we have eaten*** etc., **עוֹנֶה אַחֲרֵיהֶם "אָמֵן"** — **he should respond** with **Amen.**[77]

§21 **שְׁלֹשָׁה שֶׁאָכְלוּ כָּל אֶחָד מִכִּכָּר שֶׁלּוֹ** — **Three** people **who have each eaten from** his own loaf of bread, **וְאֶחָד מֵהֶם אָכַל פַּת עַכּוּ"ם** — **and one of them has eaten bread** baked **by an idolater,**[78] **וּשְׁנַיִם נִזְהָרִים מִפַּת עַכּוּ"ם** — **and the** other **two** people **are careful not to eat bread** baked **by an idolater,**[79] **מִכָּל מָקוֹם מִצְטָרְפִין לְזִימּוּן** — **nevertheless, they may join** as a group for the purpose of reciting the ***zimun.*** **וִיבָרֵךְ זֶה שֶׁאָכַל פַּת עַכּוּ"ם** — **The one who has eaten the bread** baked **by an idolater should recite the** *zimun* **blessing, שֶׁהוּא יָכוֹל לֶאֱכוֹל גַּם עִם הָאֲחֵרִים** — **because he is able to eat with the others,** i.e., he is able to eat their bread as well as his own. **וְכֵן אִם אֶחָד אוֹכֵל מַאַכְלֵי חָלָב** — **Likewise, if one is eating dairy foods, וּשְׁנַיִם**

---

76. Even though he did not eat, it is not proper to ignore an invitation to bless Hashem (*Mishnah Berurah* 198:2).

77. Since he did not hear the leader's invitation of *Let us bless,* he cannot respond with *Blessed is* etc. (*Mishnah Berurah* 198:3). However, Amen is always an appropriate response to a blessing (see above, 44:7).

If one hears the leader repeat the last phrase of בָּרוּךְ שֶׁאָכַלְנוּ מִשֶּׁלּוֹ וּבְטוּבוֹ חָיִינוּ, *Blessed is [He] of Whose we have eaten and through His goodness we live*, or even a portion of this phrase, he should respond with Amen again (*Mishnah Berurah* 198:4).

78. Customs vary with regard to eating bread baked by a baker who is an idolater. See above, 38:1-5, for a discussion of the customs and extent of this law.

79. We have seen above (*se'if* 15) that even if each member of the group ate his own food, it is considered a group with regard to the halachos of *zimun*. However, this is true only if there is at least one person in the group who could partake of the food of the others as well. However, if all the members of the group are not able to partake of one another's food, it does not qualify as a group that can recite the *zimun* together (*Mishnah Berurah* 196:8,9).

מַאַכְלֵי בָשָׂר[80], מִצְטָרְפִין, וִיבָרֵךְ זֶה שֶׁאָכַל מַאַכְלֵי חָלָב, שֶׁהוּא יָכוֹל לֶאֱכוֹל גַּם עִם הָאֲחֵרִים[81]. אַךְ אִם זֶה שֶׁאוֹכֵל מַאַכְלֵי חָלָב אֵינוֹ שׁוֹתֶה יַיִן, אוֹ שֶׁאֵין כָּאן אֶלָּא שֵׁכָר שֶׁהוּא חָדָשׁ[82] וְהוּא נִזְהָר מֵחָדָשׁ, מוּטָב שֶׁיְּבָרֵךְ זֶה שֶׁאָכַל בָּשָׂר בְּכוֹס מִלְּבָרֵךְ בְּלֹא כוֹס. וְאִם אֶחָד אָכַל גְּבִינָה קָשָׁה[83] וּשְׁנַיִם בָּשָׂר, יֵשׁ אוֹמְרִים דְּאֵינָן מִצְטָרְפִין, וְיֵשׁ אוֹמְרִים דְּמִכָּל מָקוֹם מִצְטָרְפִין, כֵּיוָן שֶׁיְּכוֹלִין לֶאֱכוֹל מִלֶּחֶם אֶחָד[84]. וְיֵשׁ לְהָקֵל.

כב. נָשִׁים שֶׁאָכְלוּ עִם אֲנָשִׁים שֶׁנִּתְחַיְּבוּ בְּזִימּוּן נִתְחַיְּבוּ גַּם הֵנָּה וּצְרִיכוֹת לִשְׁמוֹעַ בִּרְכַּת הַזִּימּוּן[85]. קָטָן נוֹהֲגִין שֶׁאֵין מִצְטָרְפִין לְזִימּוּן עַד שֶׁהוּא בֶּן י״ג

מַאַכְלֵי בָשָׂר — **and the other two are eating meat foods,**[80] **מִצְטָרְפִין** — **they may join** as one group, **וִיבָרֵךְ זֶה שֶׁאָכַל מַאַכְלֵי חָלָב** — **and the one who has eaten dairy foods should lead the blessing, שֶׁהוּא יָכוֹל לֶאֱכוֹל גַּם עִם הָאֲחֵרִים** — **because he is also able to eat with the others,** i.e., he is able to eat the meat food after he finishes his dairy foods.[81] **אַךְ אִם זֶה שֶׁאוֹכֵל מַאַכְלֵי חָלָב** — **However, if the one who has eaten dairy foods אֵינוֹ שׁוֹתֶה יַיִן** — **does not drink wine, אוֹ שֶׁאֵין כָּאן אֶלָּא שֵׁכָר** — **or if there is** no beverage upon which to recite *Bircas HaMazon* available **here except beer שֶׁהוּא חָדָשׁ** — **that is *chadash*,**[82] **וְהוּא נִזְהָר מֵחָדָשׁ** — **and he is careful not** to eat or drink ***chadash*** products, then he should not be the one to lead the *zimun*. **מוּטָב שֶׁיְּבָרֵךְ זֶה שֶׁאָכַל בָּשָׂר בְּכוֹס** — Rather, **it is better to have the one who has eaten meat recite the blessing over a cup, מִלְּבָרֵךְ בְּלֹא כוֹס** — **than to recite the blessing without a cup. וְאִם אֶחָד אָכַל גְּבִינָה קָשָׁה** — **If one has eaten hard cheese,**[83] **וּשְׁנַיִם בָּשָׂר** — **and two** have eaten **meat, יֵשׁ אוֹמְרִים דְּאֵינָן מִצְטָרְפִין** — **some** authorities **say that they are not** considered **joined together** as a single group for the purpose of *zimun*. **וְיֵשׁ אוֹמְרִים דְּמִכָּל מָקוֹם מִצְטָרְפִין** — However, **some say that nevertheless, they are** considered **joined together** as a single group, **כֵּיוָן שֶׁיְּכוֹלִין לֶאֱכוֹל מִלֶּחֶם אֶחָד** — **since they are able to eat from one bread.**[84] **וְיֵשׁ לְהָקֵל** — **One may be lenient** in this situation, and perform *zimun*.

§22 נָשִׁים שֶׁאָכְלוּ עִם אֲנָשִׁים שֶׁנִּתְחַיְּבוּ בְּזִימּוּן — **Women who have eaten** together **with men who are obligated to perform *zimun*, נִתְחַיְּבוּ גַּם הֵנָּה** — **also become obligated וּצְרִיכוֹת לִשְׁמוֹעַ בִּרְכַּת הַזִּימּוּן** — **and they must listen to the *zimun* blessing.**[85] **קָטָן נוֹהֲגִין שֶׁאֵין מִצְטָרְפִין לְזִימּוּן** — With regard to **a minor, the custom is that he cannot join** a group to allow the ***zimun*** to be recited, **עַד שֶׁהוּא בֶּן י״ג**

---

80. See below, 46:6-7, regarding how two people may eat at the same table when one is eating dairy foods and the other meat.

81. See below, 46:9,11, which states that one who ate meat may not eat dairy foods for another six hours, but one who ate dairy foods need not wait (see there for the necessary procedure).

82. The Torah (*Vayikra* 23:14) prohibits the consumption of the new crop of grain, known as *chadash* ("new"), until the second day of Pesach. In *Siman* 172, Kitzur discusses the prohibition and the reasons why nowadays many are lenient with regard to this prohibition.

83. Although one is generally not required to wait to eat meat after eating dairy, if one eats certain varieties of aged hard cheeses, he must wait six hours (see below, 46:11).

84. The bread must be free of any meat or dairy residue (see below, 46:7). *Mishnah Berurah* (196:9) indicates that one of them must actually have eaten from such bread, and only then can they be considered one group.

85. If three men are not present, a combination of men and women may not form a group for the purpose of *zimun*. However, once there is a requisite number of men, the women who are part of this group are also obligated in

שָׁנָה וְיוֹם אֶחָד[86]. אָז מִצְטָרֵף וְיָכוֹל לְבָרֵךְ גַּם הוּא בְּזִימּוּן, אַף עַל פִּי שֶׁלֹּא נִבְדַּק אִם הֵבִיא שְׂעָרוֹת[87].

כג. מִי שֶׁאֵינוֹ קוֹרֵא קְרִיאַת שְׁמַע שַׁחֲרִית וְעַרְבִית[88], אוֹ שֶׁהוּא עוֹבֵר עֲבֵירוֹת בְּפַרְהֶסְיָא[89], אֵינוֹ מִצְטָרֵף לְזִימּוּן. גֵּר גָּמוּר[90] מִצְטָרֵף לְזִימּוּן וְגַם הוּא יָכוֹל לְבָרֵךְ וְלוֹמַר "עַל שֶׁהִנְחַלְתָּנוּ לַאֲבוֹתֵינוּ"[91], דִּכְתִיב בְּאַבְרָהָם (בראשית יז, ה)

שָׁנָה וְיוֹם אֶחָד — **until he** has reached the age of **thirteen years and one day.**[86] אָז מִצְטָרֵף — **At that point, he may join** a group to allow the *zimun* to be recited, וְיָכוֹל לְבָרֵךְ גַּם הוּא בְּזִימּוּן — **and he also may lead the recitation of the *zimun* blessing,** אַף עַל פִּי שֶׁלֹּא נִבְדַּק — **even though he was not examined** אִם הֵבִיא שְׂעָרוֹת — to determine **if he has exhibited two** pubic **hairs.**[87]

§23 מִי שֶׁאֵינוֹ קוֹרֵא קְרִיאַת שְׁמַע שַׁחֲרִית וְעַרְבִית — **One who does not recite the** *Shema* in the **morning and evening,**[88] אוֹ שֶׁהוּא עוֹבֵר עֲבֵירוֹת בְּפַרְהֶסְיָא — **or he publicly transgresses prohibitions,**[89] אֵינוֹ מִצְטָרֵף לְזִימּוּן — **cannot be counted as part of** a group to allow the ***zimun*** to be recited. גֵּר גָּמוּר — **A convert** who has undergone the **complete**[90] conversion process מִצְטָרֵף לְזִימּוּן — **may join** a group to allow the ***zimun*** to be recited, וְגַם הוּא יָכוֹל לְבָרֵךְ וְלוֹמַר — **and he may also recite *Bircas HaMazon* and say** the phrase, "עַל שֶׁהִנְחַלְתָּנוּ לַאֲבוֹתֵינוּ" — ***because You have given our forefathers as a heritage.***[91] דִּכְתִיב בְּאַבְרָהָם — **For it is written**

---

zimun, and they should respond accordingly (see *Mishnah Berurah* 199:17).

In most places, the family does not generally join together for the meal during the week, and the lady of the house is involved during the meal with preparing and serving the meal. Therefore, she does not intend to join as one of the participants of the meal in a manner that would require her to join in the *zimun*. This is especially true if she has young children who require her attention at that time. However, on Shabbos, or even during the week if she has time to participate in the meal, she is indeed subject to the obligation, and, in such a case, a husband must call his wife to the table to respond to the *zimun* blessing (see *Igros Moshe, Orach Chaim* V, §9.10).

86. It is not necessary for the day to be complete. As soon as he enters his 14th year (i.e., on his 13th birthday) he is considered an adult; see above, 15:2; see also note 9 there. See next note.

87. A boy becomes an adult when he reaches 13 years of age and has grown two pubic hairs (see *Even HaEzer* 155:17-18). For all matters that pertain to Rabbinic laws (such as the recitation of the *zimun* blessing), we assume that when a boy has turned 13, he has already grown these hairs (see *Mishnah Berurah* 199:27 with *Shaar HaTziyun* §19).

88. For the halachos of the recitation of *Shema* in the morning and evening, see above, *Siman* 17, and below, 70:1.

89. This applies even if he has [deliberately] transgressed a well-known prohibition just once. Although this person is still considered a Jew and may be counted for a *minyan* (quorum for prayer) even if he has committed many sins, the Sages did not allow him to join as part of a group for *zimun*. Joining for a *zimun* indicates a level of social connection that one is to avoid with a person who flagrantly sinned in public (*Beur Halachah* 199:3 s.v. ע״ה גמור). [See there regarding whether such a person may serve as the tenth man to allow the *zimun* to be recited with Hashem's Name.]

See *Beur Halachah* 199:3 s.v. מזמנין עליו, who writes that even though we may not count such a person in a *zimun*, he is certainly not exempt from his *own* requirement of *zimun*. Therefore, if there are three people there besides him or if three such people ate together, they are certainly obligated to join in *zimun*.

90. As opposed to one who was circumcised but has not as yet immersed himself in a *mikveh*.

91. This phrase is recited at the beginning of the second blessing, נוֹדֶה לְךָ, *We thank You*,

"כִּי אַב הֲמוֹן גּוֹיִם נְתַתִּיךָ"[92] וְדַרְשִׁינַן (ברכות יג, א): לְשֶׁעָבַר הָיָה אָב לַאֲרָם[93], מִכָּאן וְאֵילָךְ לְכָל הַגּוֹיִם[94].

---

with regard to the patriarch **Avraham** (*Bereishis* 17:5): **"כִּי אַב הֲמוֹן גּוֹיִם נְתַתִּיךָ"** — ***for I have made you the father of a multitude of nations,***[92] **וְדַרְשִׁינַן — and we expound** (*Berachos* 13a) **this** verse to mean: **לְשֶׁעָבַר הָיָה אָב לַאֲרָם — In the past,** Avraham **was a father** only **to** the nation **of Aram,**[93] **מִכָּאן וְאֵילָךְ לְכָל הַגּוֹיִם** — but **from this point onward,** he is a father **to all nations.**[94]

---

and refers to the Land of Israel, which Hashem promised to our forefathers. A convert, who does not descend from our forefathers, may nevertheless recite this phrase, as Kitzur explains.

92. In this verse Hashem changes his name from אַבְרָם, *Avram,* to אַבְרָהָם, *Avraham.* The full verse reads: וְלֹא יִקָּרֵא עוֹד אֶת שִׁמְךָ אַבְרָם וְהָיָה שִׁמְךָ אַבְרָהָם כִּי אַב הֲמוֹן גּוֹיִם נְתַתִּיךָ, *Your name shall no longer be called Avram, but your name shall be Avraham, for I have made you the father of a multitude of nations.*

93. The original name, אַבְרָם, *Avram,* is a contraction of אַב אֲרָם, *father of Aram,* signifying that he was the guiding light of his native country, Aram.

94. The name אַבְרָהָם, *Avraham,* is a contraction of אַב הֲמוֹן, *father of a multitude.* Avraham is referred to as the father of all nations since he taught the world belief in Hashem (see *Rambam, Commentary to Mishnah, Bikkurim* 1:4). Since Avraham is referred to as the father of all nations, a convert descended from any nation may refer to Avraham as his forefather.

LAWS OF FORBIDDEN FOODS — SIMAN 46   **134**

﴾ סימן מו ﴿
הִלְכוֹת מַאֲכָלוֹת אֲסוּרוֹת
וּבוֹ מ"ו סְעִיפִים

﴾ SIMAN 46 ﴿
THE LAWS OF FORBIDDEN FOODS
CONTAINING 46 *SE'IFIM*

§1 Bloodspots in Eggs / §2 The Blood of Fish / §3 Blood Inside the Mouth / §4 Blood in Milk / §5 Meat and Dairy: the Prohibition / §6-7 Keeping Meat and Dairy Apart / §8 Separate Utensils / §9-12 Waiting Between Meat and Dairy / §13 Sharp Foods / §14 Milk Substitutes / §15 Changing the Use of a Utensil / §16-19 Food Left in the Hands of an Idolater / §20 Cooking in the Presence of an Idolater / §21 Eating Food of Non-observant Jews / §22 Leaving Utensils With Idolaters / §23-24 Situations of *Tereifah* / §25-27 Dairy or Meaty Bread / §28 Castrated Chicken / §29 Fattened Geese / §30 Pot-coverings / §31-33 Vermin in Water or Vinegar / §34-36 Fruit Infestation / §37 Wheat and Flour Infestation / §38-39 When Infestation Occurs / §40-41 Infestation in Nuts or Preserved Fruits / §42 Cutting an Infested Food / §43-44 Vermin in Fish or Cheese / §45 The Need for Vigilance / §46 Asking a Rav

In this *Siman*, Kitzur presents some of the laws of various dietary commandments. These include the prohibition against ingesting blood (stated in *Vayikra 7*:26), the prohibitions against mixtures of meat and dairy (found in *Shemos* 23:19), the prohibition against eating the meat of an animal that is *tereifah* [i.e., that had one of numerous specific mortal defects] (found in *Shemos* 22:30), and the prohibitions against eating vermin that infest food (found in *Vayikra* 11:10, 20, 23, 41-44). He then proceeds to discuss the various foods in which such infestation is common.

Kitzur includes in this *Siman* certain Rabbinic laws pertaining to kosher food that has been left in the hands of an idolater or that has been in contact with nonkosher food, and pertaining to the trustworthiness of a non-observant Jew in regard to *kashrus* issues. These laws were instituted to ensure the kosher status of the food eaten by an observant Jew.

In addition to the laws included in this *Siman*, Kitzur presents other aspects of dietary law throughout this *sefer*. In *Siman* 36, Kitzur outlines the required method to ensure that meat does not contain any blood, and discusses aspects of the prohibition against eating *cheilev* (forbidden fats). In *Siman* 38, he presents the laws pertaining to food that is owned or prepared by idolaters; in *Siman* 47, he discusses the laws pertaining to their wine; and in *Simanim* 172-173, Kitzur includes the prohibition against *chadash* ("new" grain) and *orlah* (fruits of the first three years of a tree). [Additionally, there exist prohibitions against eating nonkosher

135 ❧ LAWS OF FORBIDDEN FOODS — SIMAN 46:1

א. דָּם הַנִּמְצָא בְּבֵיצִים אָסוּר, וְלִפְעָמִים כָּל הַבֵּיצָה אֲסוּרָה.[1] וְלָכֵן, כְּשֶׁעוֹשִׂים מַאֲכָל עִם בֵּיצִים, יֵשׁ לִבְדּוֹק אוֹתָן.[2]

animals, birds, and fowl; the prohibition against *eiver min hachai* (a limb from a living creature); and the prohibition against *neveilah*, i.e., the meat of an animal (or bird) that did not undergo proper *shechitah* (ritual slaughter). Kitzur does not address these prohibitions in this work.]

The Talmud (*Yoma* 39a) relates that, in addition to the prohibitions involved in the consumption of nonkosher food, such consumption leads to a "dullness of the heart," i.e., an inability to attain one's spiritual potential. For this reason, *Rama* rules (*Yoreh Deah* 81:7) that even very young children should be stopped from eating nonkosher foods, and an infant should not nurse from a woman who must consume those foods due to illness. This is but one indication of the significance that is attached to these laws.

[It should be noted that the kosher dietary laws are many and varied, and clearly could not all be discussed comprehensively in a work of this nature. The prohibitions that Kitzur chose to discuss reflected the time and place in which the work was authored. In modern times, with the complexity of the production of many processed food items, proper observance of dietary laws requires broad knowledge and Rabbinic guidance. By no means can one consider himself to be "keeping kosher" if he limits his observance to the strictures discussed by Kitzur.]

§1 The Torah (*Vayikra* 7:26) forbids the blood of animals and birds. This prohibition has ramifications in regard to other types of blood as well.

דָּם הַנִּמְצָא בְּבֵיצִים אָסוּר — Blood that is found in eggs is prohibited for consumption, וְלִפְעָמִים כָּל הַבֵּיצָה אֲסוּרָה — and sometimes, when blood is found in it, the entire egg is prohibited.[1] וְלָכֵן, כְּשֶׁעוֹשִׂים מַאֲכָל עִם בֵּיצִים — Therefore, when preparing a food with eggs, יֵשׁ לִבְדּוֹק אוֹתָן — one should examine them to ensure that they are free of blood.[2]

---

1. This is due to the concern that the blood is indicative of a developing embryo. If the blood is in the yolk, the entire egg is prohibited. If the blood is in the white, there are various opinions as to when it suffices to remove the bloody spot and when the entire egg is prohibited (*Yoreh Deah* 66:3). It is therefore customary to refrain from eating any egg in which blood has been found (*Rama* ibid.).

Nowadays, most eggs are unfertilized and cannot produce embryos. Therefore, if one finds blood in such an egg, technically he would be required only to discard the blood, and he would then be permitted to consume the rest. Nevertheless, since an egg is inexpensive, the widespread custom is to act stringently and discard the entire egg. If, however, the egg was mixed with another egg or into a batter, that egg should be removed (to the extent possible) and the remainder of the mixture is permitted (*Igros Moshe, Orach Chaim* III, §61, *Yoreh Deah* I, §36).

2. This remains the custom, even though nowadays the majority of eggs are unfertilized (ibid.). If an egg was mixed into a batter without having been checked, the mixture is permitted, since most eggs do not have blood spots (*Rama, Yoreh Deah* 66:4). This is especially true nowadays, when eggs are generally unfertilized.

ב. דַּם דָּגִים מוּתָּר, אַךְ אִם קִבְּצוֹ בִּכְלִי, אָסוּר, מִפְּנֵי מַרְאִית הָעַיִן[3]. לְפִיכָךְ, אִם נִיכָּר שֶׁהוּא מִדָּגִים, כְּגוֹן שֶׁיֵּשׁ בּוֹ קַשְׂקַשִּׂים, מוּתָּר.

ג. אִם נָשַׁךְ כִּכָּר וְכַדּוֹמֶה וְיָצָא דָּם מִשִּׁינָּיו עַל גַּבֵּי הַכִּכָּר, צָרִיךְ לַחְתּוֹךְ מְקוֹם הַדָּם וּלְזָרְקוֹ[4]. אֲבָל הַדָּם שֶׁבֵּין הַשִּׁינַּיִם מוֹצְצוֹ בְּחוֹל, כֵּיוָן שֶׁלֹּא פֵּירַשׁ[5] (וְלֹא בְּשַׁבָּת כְּמוֹ שֶׁיִּתְבָּאֵר לְקַמָּן בְּסִימָן פ׳ סְעִיף נ״ד)[6].

ד. לִפְעָמִים נִמְצָא דָּם בְּתוֹךְ הֶחָלָב, שֶׁהַדָּם יָצָא עִם הֶחָלָב מִדַּדֵּי הַבְּהֵמָה, וּצְרִיכִין לַעֲשׂוֹת בָּזֶה שְׁאֵלַת חָכָם[7].

ה. בָּשָׂר בְּחָלָב אָסוּר בַּאֲכִילָה וּבְבִישּׁוּל וּבַהֲנָאָה[8,9], וְלָכֵן אִם נֶאֱסַר אֵיזֶה

---

§2 דַּם דָּגִים מוּתָּר — **The blood of fish is permitted.** אַךְ אִם קִבְּצוֹ בִּכְלִי — **However, if one gathered it into a vessel,** אָסוּר, מִפְּנֵי מַרְאִית הָעַיִן — **it is prohibited** for consumption, **due to the appearance** of wrongdoing.[3] לְפִיכָךְ, אִם נִיכָּר שֶׁהוּא מִדָּגִים — **Therefore, if it is apparent that this is** the blood **of fish,** כְּגוֹן שֶׁיֵּשׁ בּוֹ קַשְׂקַשִּׂים — **for example, there are scales in it,** מוּתָּר — then **it is permitted** even though it has been gathered in a vessel.

§3 אִם נָשַׁךְ כִּכָּר וְכַדּוֹמֶה — **If one bit into a loaf** of bread **or the like,** וְיָצָא דָּם מִשִּׁינָּיו עַל גַּבֵּי הַכִּכָּר — **and blood came out of his teeth onto the loaf,** צָרִיךְ לַחְתּוֹךְ מְקוֹם הַדָּם וּלְזָרְקוֹ — **he must cut off the bloody part** of the loaf **and discard it.**[4] אֲבָל הַדָּם שֶׁבֵּין הַשִּׁינַּיִם — **As for blood** emanating from the gums **that is** still **between** one's **teeth,** מוֹצְצוֹ בְּחוֹל, כֵּיוָן שֶׁלֹּא פֵּירַשׁ — **on a weekday, one may suck** and swallow **it, since it has not exited** his body.[5] (וְלֹא בְּשַׁבָּת — **But** one may **not** do so **on Shabbos,** כְּמוֹ שֶׁיִּתְבָּאֵר לְקַמָּן בְּסִימָן פ׳ סְעִיף נ״ד — **as will be explained below, in 80:54).**[6]

§4 לִפְעָמִים נִמְצָא דָּם בְּתוֹךְ הֶחָלָב — **Sometimes, blood is found in milk,** שֶׁהַדָּם יָצָא עִם הֶחָלָב מִדַּדֵּי הַבְּהֵמָה — **because the blood emerged from the animal's udders along with the milk.** וּצְרִיכִין לַעֲשׂוֹת בָּזֶה שְׁאֵלַת חָכָם — **In this** situation, **one must inquire of a halachic authority** regarding the status of the milk.[7]

§5 Another category of prohibited food is that of meat and dairy mixtures: בָּשָׂר בְּחָלָב אָסוּר בַּאֲכִילָה וּבְבִישּׁוּל וּבַהֲנָאָה — With respect to a mixture of **meat and milk, it is prohibited to eat, cook, or derive benefit** from it.[8] However, the prohibition regarding benefit does not apply in all cases.[9] וְלָכֵן — **Therefore,** אִם נֶאֱסַר אֵיזֶה

---

3. Since an observer might think that this is animal blood, its consumption is prohibited. [It should be noted that whenever the Sages imposed a restriction in order to avoid the perception of a violation, the restriction applies even when nobody else is present (*Beitzah* 9a). Thus, consumption of gathered fish blood is prohibited even in absolute privacy. See similarly below, note 32.]

4. For people might think it is animal blood.

5. Since the blood is not visible (i.e., it cannot be seen even when someone else is present), this case does not lend itself to the appearance of wrongdoing [unlike the case in note 3] (*Rashi* to *Kesubos* 60a; see *Gilyon Maharsha* to *Yoreh Deah* 66:10).

6. Sucking blood from a wound on Shabbos is considered חוֹבֵל, *wounding* (see *Magen Avraham* 328:53 and *Mishnah Berurah* 328:147).

7. See Appendix of Kitzur's editorial glosses for further discussion.

8. Each of these acts is prohibited independently (see *Yoreh Deah* 87:1).

9. When a milk-and-meat mixture is prohibited

דָּבָר מִתַּעֲרוֹבֶת בָּשָׂר בְּחָלָב צְרִיכִים לַעֲשׂוֹת שְׁאֵלָה מַה לַעֲשׂוֹת בּוֹ, כִּי לִפְעָמִים נֶאֱסָר גַּם בַּהֲנָאָה, וְלִפְעָמִים אֵינוֹ נֶאֱסָר בַּהֲנָאָה.

ו. שְׁנֵי יִשְׂרְאֵלִים הַמַּכִּירִים זֶה אֶת זֶה, אֲפִילּוּ הֵם מַקְפִּידִים זֶה עַל זֶה, אָסוּר לָהֶם לֶאֱכוֹל בְּשֻׁלְחָן אֶחָד זֶה בָּשָׂר וְזֶה מַאֲכַל חָלָב[10] עַד שֶׁיַּעֲשׂוּ אֵיזֶה הֶיכֵּר, כְּגוֹן שֶׁיֹּאכַל כָּל אֶחָד עַל מַפָּה שֶׁלּוֹ[11], אוֹ שֶׁיַּנִּיחוּ עַל הַשֻּׁלְחָן בֵּין הַמַּאֲכָלִים אֵיזֶה דָּבָר שֶׁאֵין דַּרְכּוֹ לִהְיוֹת שָׁם[12]. וְיִהְיוּ זְהִירִים שֶׁלֹּא לִשְׁתּוֹת מִכְּלִי אֶחָד מִפְּנֵי שֶׁהַמַּאֲכָל נִדְבָּק בַּכְּלִי[13].

דָּבָר מִתַּעֲרוֹבֶת בָּשָׂר בְּחָלָב — if something became prohibited on account of a mixture of meat and milk (e.g., a meat-and-milk mixture fell into another cooked dish, rendering that food prohibited), **צְרִיכִים לַעֲשׂוֹת שְׁאֵלָה מַה לַעֲשׂוֹת בּוֹ — one must inquire** of a halachic authority **what to do with it, כִּי לִפְעָמִים נֶאֱסָר גַּם בַּהֲנָאָה** — for **sometimes it becomes prohibited even for benefit, וְלִפְעָמִים אֵינוֹ נֶאֱסָר בַּהֲנָאָה — and sometimes it does not become prohibited for benefit,** but only for consumption.

§6 The Rabbis instituted certain safeguards to protect against inadvertent mixing of milk and meat:

שְׁנֵי יִשְׂרְאֵלִים הַמַּכִּירִים זֶה אֶת זֶה — Two Jews who are acquainted with each other, אֲפִילּוּ הֵם מַקְפִּידִים זֶה עַל זֶה — even if they act grudgingly toward each other, אָסוּר לָהֶם לֶאֱכוֹל בְּשֻׁלְחָן אֶחָד זֶה בָּשָׂר וְזֶה מַאֲכַל חָלָב — are prohibited from eating together **at one table,** if **this one** is eating **meat and that one** is eating **a dairy food,**[10] **עַד שֶׁיַּעֲשׂוּ אֵיזֶה הֶיכֵּר — unless they make some** distinctive **reminder** that will alert each of them to avoid eating the other's food. **כְּגוֹן — An example** of this reminder would be **שֶׁיֹּאכַל כָּל אֶחָד עַל מַפָּה שֶׁלּוֹ — that each one should eat upon his own tablecloth,**[11] **אוֹ שֶׁיַּנִּיחוּ עַל הַשֻּׁלְחָן בֵּין הַמַּאֲכָלִים — or that they should place upon the table, between the** meat and dairy **foods, אֵיזֶה דָּבָר שֶׁאֵין דַּרְכּוֹ לִהְיוֹת שָׁם — something that would usually not be** found **there,** to serve as a reminder not to eat the other type of food.[12] **וְיִהְיוּ זְהִירִים שֶׁלֹּא לִשְׁתּוֹת מִכְּלִי אֶחָד** — They also **must be careful not to drink from the same vessel, מִפְּנֵי שֶׁהַמַּאֲכָל נִדְבָּק בַּכְּלִי — for the food** that one eats commonly **adheres to the vessel** from which he drinks, and thus they may consume a mixture of meat and milk.[13]

Biblically (viz., when the meat of an animal was cooked with milk or a milk product), then it is prohibited even for benefit. When the prohibition of a mixture is Rabbinic in origin (e.g., when poultry is cooked with milk, or when meat and milk are mixed but not cooked together), then it is prohibited only for consumption but permitted for benefit.

10. When acquaintances eat at the same table, they sometimes share their food. This gives rise to the concern that the one eating meat might mistakenly partake of his fellow's dairy food and vice versa. To preclude this possibility, the Sages forbade two people who are familiar with each other from eating meat and dairy at the same table. This applies even when the acquaintances are begrudging types who would charge each other for any food eaten (as long as they would not prevent each other from taking food in the first place; *Pri Toar* 88:2). Two wayfarers who do not know each other are exempt from this restriction (*Chullin* 107b; *Shach, Yoreh Deah* 88:2).

11. Or each of them uses a different type of placemat.

12. Such as a loaf of bread from which they are not eating, or a candlestick. The article must have some height (*Yoreh Deah* 88:2 with *Taz* §4).

13. Even if they are sitting at separate tables, and even if they are not acquainted with each other, they may not drink from the same vessel (*Shach* 88:8).

ז. וְכָל שֶׁכֵּן שֶׁצְּרִיכִין לִיזָּהֵר שֶׁלֹּא לֶאֱכוֹל מִכִּכָּר אַחַת עִם בָּשָׂר וְעִם חָלָב[14]. וְכֵן נוֹהֲגִין לְיַחֵד כֵּלִים לְמֶלַח אֶחָד לְמַאַכְלֵי בָשָׂר וְאֶחָד לְמַאַכְלֵי חָלָב, כִּי לִפְעָמִים טוֹבְלִים בְּמֶלַח וְנִשְׁאָרִים שִׁיּוּרֵי מַאֲכָל בַּמֶּלַח[15].

ח. נוֹהֲגִין[16] לִרְשׁוֹם אֶת הַסַּכִּין הַמְיוּחָד לְמַאַכְלֵי חָלָב, וְכֵן כָּל כְּלֵי חָלָב, שֶׁלֹּא יָבֹאוּ לִידֵי חִילּוּף[17].

---

§7 וְכָל שֶׁכֵּן שֶׁצְּרִיכִין לִיזָּהֵר — **Certainly, one must** also **be careful** שֶׁלֹּא לֶאֱכוֹל מִכִּכָּר אַחַת עִם בָּשָׂר וְעִם חָלָב — **not to eat from a single** portion-sized **loaf of bread with** both a **meat** meal **and a dairy** meal.[14] וְכֵן נוֹהֲגִין לְיַחֵד כֵּלִים לְמֶלַח — **Similarly, it is customary to designate** separate **salt-receptacles,** אֶחָד לְמַאַכְלֵי בָשָׂר וְאֶחָד לְמַאַכְלֵי חָלָב — **one for** use with **meat foods and one for** use with **dairy foods,** כִּי לִפְעָמִים טוֹבְלִים בְּמֶלַח — **for sometimes one dips** food **into salt** וְנִשְׁאָרִים שִׁיּוּרֵי מַאֲכָל בַּמֶּלַח — **and** some **remnants of the food remain in the salt.** These remnants might then be transferred to the other type of food, when it is dipped into the salt.[15]

§8 נוֹהֲגִין לִרְשׁוֹם אֶת הַסַּכִּין הַמְיוּחָד לְמַאַכְלֵי חָלָב — It is the established custom to have separate sets of knives (and other utensils) for meat and dairy.[16] When these utensils are of similar appearance, **it is customary to mark the knife that is designated for dairy foods,** וְכֵן כָּל כְּלֵי חָלָב — **and similarly,** to mark **all the** other **utensils** designated for **dairy** use, with an identifying feature, שֶׁלֹּא יָבֹאוּ לִידֵי חִילּוּף — **so that they should not become interchanged** with the knives and other utensils designated for meat use.[17]

---

14. The bread used for a meat meal may not be used for a dairy meal (and vice versa), because of the concern that it was touched by a moist piece of meat (or a dairy food) and some residue adhered to it (*Tur, Yoreh Deah* 91:3). This refers only to an individual slice of bread (or a small roll) that one intended to eat with the meat (or dairy) meal, such that he did not guard it from becoming meaty. When partaking of a large loaf of bread intended for use with both meat and dairy meals, one is usually careful not to let meat or dairy come in contact with it. Thus, it may be used for both types of meals. Nevertheless, it is commendable to use different loaves (*Igros Moshe, Yoreh Deah* I, §38). Further details of this law are discussed in *se'if* 12.

15. This refers to salt receptacles into which one dips the food, not to saltshakers. Nevertheless, it is common practice to have separate saltshakers for meat and dairy.

16. See *Rama, Yoreh Deah* 89:4. The reason is that when a utensil is used for a hot or sharp food (see note 30 below), it absorbs some flavor of the food. Should the utensil later be used for hot food of the opposite type, it would impart the flavor it had absorbed into that food and could render it prohibited. Even if used exclusively for cold foods, there is a concern for residue remaining on the utensil, which might be transferred to the other type of food. Further details of this law are discussed in *se'if* 12.

17. The mark need not necessarily indicate that the utensil is designated for dairy use. Since it is universally accepted to mark dairy utensils, any marked utensil is assumed to have been designated for dairy use (see *Rama* ibid.).

If utensils were interchanged (e.g., a meat dish was cooked in a dairy pot or stirred with a dairy spoon), or if a pot became splattered with food of the opposite type, the status of the utensil and the food depends on numerous factors. These include the nature of the utensil (i.e., whether it is a pot, a serving utensil, or a plate), when it was last used for hot food, and the temperature of the food at the time of the mishap, among other factors. Indeed, countless possible mishaps can occur in the kitchen, and each situation is subject to its own law. Therefore, whenever a meat, dairy, or *pareve* utensil comes into contact with food of another type, proper halachic guidance must be sought

ט. אָכַל בָּשָׂר, אוֹ אֲפִילוּ רַק תַּבְשִׁיל שֶׁל בָּשָׂר, לֹא יֹאכַל מַאֲכְלֵי חָלָב עַד שֶׁיִּשְׁהֶה שֵׁשׁ שָׁעוֹת. וְהַלּוֹעֵס לְתִינוֹק צָרִיךְ גַּם כֵּן לְהַמְתִּין[18]. אַף עַל פִּי שֶׁשָּׁהָה כְּשִׁיעוּר, אִם מָצָא בָּשָׂר בֵּין הַשִּׁינַּיִם[19] צָרִיךְ לַהֲסִירוֹ, אֲבָל אֵינוֹ צָרִיךְ לְהַמְתִּין אַחַר כָּךְ, רַק יְקַנֵּחַ אֶת פִּיו וְיִדִיחוֹ. דְּהַיְינוּ, שֶׁיֹּאכַל מְעַט פַּת[20] וִיקַנֵּחַ בּוֹ פִּיו, וְגַם מְדִיחוֹ בְּמַיִם, אוֹ בִּשְׁאָר מַשְׁקֶה.

§9 **אָכַל בָּשָׂר, אוֹ אֲפִילוּ רַק תַּבְשִׁיל שֶׁל בָּשָׂר — If one ate meat, or even only a meaty food dish** (e.g., food cooked with meat gravy), **לֹא יֹאכַל מַאֲכְלֵי חָלָב עַד שֶׁיִּשְׁהֶה שֵׁשׁ שָׁעוֹת — he should not eat** any **dairy foods until he waits six hours. וְהַלּוֹעֵס לְתִינוֹק — Similarly, one who pre-chews** meat **for a baby** but does not swallow it **צָרִיךְ גַּם כֵּן לְהַמְתִּין — must also wait** six hours before partaking of dairy foods.[18] **אַף עַל פִּי שֶׁשָּׁהָה כְּשִׁיעוּר — Now, even if one waited the requisite amount** of time, **אִם מָצָא בָּשָׂר בֵּין הַשִּׁינַּיִם — if he** subsequently **found meat between** his **teeth, צָרִיךְ לַהֲסִירוֹ — he must remove it** before eating dairy.[19] **אֲבָל אֵינוֹ צָרִיךְ לְהַמְתִּין אַחַר כָּךְ — However, one is not required to wait** an additional six hours **afterward** (i.e., after removing the meat from his teeth); **רַק יְקַנֵּחַ אֶת פִּיו וְיִדִיחוֹ** — rather, **he must merely wipe out his mouth and rinse it. דְּהַיְינוּ — That is, שֶׁיֹּאכַל מְעַט פַּת וִיקַנֵּחַ בּוֹ פִּיו — he should eat some bread**[20] **and with it wipe out his mouth, וְגַם מְדִיחוֹ בְּמַיִם, אוֹ בִּשְׁאָר מַשְׁקֶה — and also rinse** the mouth **by** drinking **water or some other beverage.** He is then permitted to eat dairy immediately.

---

regarding the status of both the utensil and the food. [For comprehensive discussion of these laws, the reader is referred to *The Kosher Kitchen* by Rabbi Binyomin Forst, ArtScroll Mesorah Publications, 2009.]

18. There are two reasons given for the required wait. One reason is that meat leaves a fatty residue and a lingering taste in the throat for some time, and to ensure that the residue not mix with the dairy food eaten afterward, one must wait six hours for it to dissolve (*Rashi, Chullin* 105a).

The other reason is that meat particles might remain lodged between one's teeth, and might then mix with the dairy food, but after six hours these particles decay to the point that they are no longer classified as meat (*Rambam, Hil. Maachalos Asuros* 9:28).

According to the first reason, one must wait six hours even if he eats a meaty food dish rather than actual meat (since the food leaves a fatty residue in the throat), but one need not wait six hours if he merely chews meat and does not swallow it. According to the second reason, the opposite is true: One need not wait if he eats a meaty dish (since there is no concern for meat becoming lodged between his teeth), but one must wait if he chews actual meat even though he does not swallow it. The halachah follows both reasons; hence, we abide by the stringencies emerging from both reasons (*Tur, Yoreh Deah* 89:1). Therefore, one must wait six hours even if he ate a meaty dish, and even if he merely chewed meat. [If, however, one merely tasted meat with his tongue and then removed it from his mouth, he need not wait six hours, though he must wipe out and rinse his mouth, as described below (*Pri Chadash* 89:18, *Aruch HaShulchan* 89:14).]

19. This follows the first reason mentioned in the preceding note. According to the second reason, one would not be required to remove the meat particles, for once six hours have passed they are presumed to have decayed to the point that they are no longer considered meat (*Tur* ibid.).

20. Or any other solid food, except flour, dates, and green vegetables (*Shulchan Aruch, Yoreh Deah* 89:2). The food must be swallowed, not merely chewed (*Pri Toar* 89:7).

21. The meat residue that may have remained

י. אִם לֹא הָיָה בַּתַּבְשִׁיל לֹא בָשָׂר וְלֹא שׁוּמָּן שֶׁל בָּשָׂר, אֶלָּא שֶׁנִּתְבַּשֵּׁל בִּקְדֵירָה שֶׁל בָּשָׂר, אֲפִילוּ לֹא הָיְתָה מוּדַחַת יָפֶה, מוּתָּר לֶאֱכוֹל אַחֲרָיו חָלָב[21].

יא. אָכַל גְּבִינָה — מוּתָּר לֶאֱכוֹל אַחֲרָיו בָּשָׂר מִיָּד בִּסְעוּדָה אַחֶרֶת[22], וּבִלְבַד שֶׁיִּבְדּוֹק יָדָיו אִם אֵין שׁוּם דָּבָר מֵהַגְּבִינָה נִדְבָּק בָּהֶם, אוֹ יִרְחָצֵם בְּמַיִם, וְגַם יְנַקֵּר שִׁינָּיו וְיָדִיחַ פִּיו[23]. וְאִם הָיָה הַגְּבִינָה קָשָׁה, דְּהַיְינוּ, שֶׁהוּעַמְדָה בְּקֵיבָה וִישָׁנָה שִׁשָּׁה חֳדָשִׁים[24], אוֹ

---

§10 אִם לֹא הָיָה בַּתַּבְשִׁיל לֹא בָשָׂר וְלֹא שׁוּמָּן שֶׁל בָּשָׂר — **If the food dish** that one ate **did not contain** any actual **meat or meat gravy,** אֶלָּא שֶׁנִּתְבַּשֵּׁל בִּקְדֵירָה שֶׁל בָּשָׂר — **but was** merely **cooked in a pot** that had been used **for meat,** אֲפִילוּ לֹא הָיְתָה מוּדַחַת יָפֶה — then, **even if** the pot **had not been rinsed well,** מוּתָּר לֶאֱכוֹל אַחֲרָיו חָלָב — **it is permitted to eat dairy** immediately **after** eating **that** food.[21]

§11 אָכַל גְּבִינָה — If **one ate** soft **cheese,** מוּתָּר לֶאֱכוֹל אַחֲרָיו בָּשָׂר מִיָּד — **he is permitted to eat meat immediately thereafter,** בִּסְעוּדָה אַחֶרֶת — **at another meal.**[22] וּבִלְבַד שֶׁיִּבְדּוֹק יָדָיו — However, this is **provided that he** first **examines his hands** אִם אֵין שׁוּם דָּבָר מֵהַגְּבִינָה נִדְבָּק בָּהֶם — to ensure **that no residue of cheese remains adhered to them,** אוֹ יִרְחָצֵם בְּמַיִם — **or that he washes them in water.** וְגַם יְנַקֵּר שִׁינָּיו וְיָדִיחַ פִּיו — **Also, he must clean between his teeth and rinse his mouth** before partaking of the meat.[23]

Hard cheese is subject to a more stringent standard:

וְאִם הָיָה הַגְּבִינָה קָשָׁה — **However, if it was hard cheese,** דְּהַיְינוּ, שֶׁהוּעַמְדָה בְּקֵיבָה וִישָׁנָה שִׁשָּׁה חֳדָשִׁים — **that is** to say, **it was set with the stomach** of an animal **and was aged for six months,**[24] אוֹ שֶׁהִיא מְתוּלַּעַת — **or it is**

---

in the pot is not considered sufficiently significant to require a waiting period. The food cooked in the improperly rinsed pot may not, however, be eaten together *with* a dairy food (see *Shach, Yoreh Deah* 89:19).

22. That is, after he recites *Bircas HaMazon,* or a *berachah acharonah,* for the dairy meal [and follows the cleansing procedure that will be described], he is permitted to eat meat. *Mishnah Berurah* (494:16), however, rules that after cleansing the hands and mouth as Kitzur will describe, one may eat meat even during the same meal as soft cheese.

23. A denture wearer who drinks hot milk or eats a hot dairy dish is permitted to eat meat immediately afterward, as long as he cleanses his hands and dentures of any dairy residue [just as one is required to cleanse his own teeth after drinking hot milk or eating a hot dairy dish]. He does not have to be concerned that the dentures absorbed flavor of the hot milk and require *kashering,* because generally speaking, if one can drink the milk, it is not hot enough to impart flavor [i.e., it is not *yad soledes bo*] (*Igros Moshe, Orach Chaim* I, §5).

24. Rennet, an enzyme found in the stomach of some animals, causes milk to curdle; thus, in earlier times, cheese was made by placing the stomach of a slaughtered animal into milk. [See *Taz* (*Yoreh Deah* 115:9) regarding why this does not create a forbidden mixture of milk and meat.] When aged for six months, cheese becomes very strong, and it leaves behind residual fat and flavor that last several hours. Therefore, after eating this type of cheese, one is required to wait six hours before eating meat (see *Taz* 89:4, *Aruch HaShulchan* 89:11). The same rule applies if the cheese was hardened without being set in an animal's stomach, whether with rennet or with artificial enzymes. As long as it is aged six months or more, it is considered "hard cheese" and requires a six-hour wait before meat may be consumed (see *Shach* 89:15; but see *Pri Megadim, Mishbetzos Zahav* 89:4).

Nowadays, many hard cheeses are not aged six months. However, there are some aged cheeses on the market, such as aged cheddar (as opposed to ordinary cheddar), and Swiss cheese produced in Switzerland. ["Swiss cheese" produced in the United States,

שֶׁהִיא מְתוּלַּעַת[25], אִם רוֹצֶה לֶאֱכוֹל אַחַר כָּךְ מַאֲכָלֵי בָשָׂר, צָרִיךְ גַּם כֵּן לְהַמְתִּין שֵׁשׁ שָׁעוֹת.

יב. מִי שֶׁאָכַל גְּבִינָה וְרוֹצֶה לֶאֱכוֹל בָּשָׂר[26], צָרִיךְ לְבַעֵר מֵעַל הַשֻּׁלְחָן שִׁיּוּרֵי פַּת שֶׁאֲכָלוֹ עִם הַגְּבִינָה[27]. וְאָסוּר לֶאֱכוֹל גְּבִינָה עַל מַפָּה שֶׁאָכְלוּ בָשָׂר, וְכֵן לְהִיפּוּךְ. גַּם אָסוּר לַחְתּוֹךְ בְּסַכִּין שֶׁל בָּשָׂר פַּת לְאָכְלוֹ עִם גְּבִינָה, וְכֵן לְהִיפּוּךְ, וַאֲפִילוּ אִם הַסַּכִּין נָקִי[28]. וּבִשְׁעַת הַדְּחָק, כְּגוֹן שֶׁהוּא בְדֶרֶךְ, מוּתָּר לוֹ לַחְתּוֹךְ בְּסַכִּין שֶׁל בָּשָׂר כְּשֶׁהוּא נָקִי וּמְקוּנָּח הֵיטֵב הֵיטֵב לֶאֱכוֹל עִם גְּבִינָה, וְכֵן בְּהִיפּוּךְ[29].

יג. אִם חָתַךְ בְּסַכִּין שֶׁל בָּשָׂר בְּצָלִים, אוֹ שְׁאָר דָּבָר חָרִיף[30], וּנְתָנָם לְמַאֲכַל חָלָב,

---

wormy,[25] אִם רוֹצֶה לֶאֱכוֹל אַחַר כָּךְ מַאֲכָלֵי בָשָׂר — then **if one wishes to eat meaty foods afterward,** צָרִיךְ גַּם כֵּן לְהַמְתִּין שֵׁשׁ שָׁעוֹת — **he must also wait six hours.**

§12 מִי שֶׁאָכַל גְּבִינָה וְרוֹצֶה לֶאֱכוֹל בָּשָׂר — **One who ate cheese and wishes to eat meat** afterward[26] צָרִיךְ לְבַעֵר מֵעַל הַשֻּׁלְחָן שִׁיּוּרֵי פַּת שֶׁאֲכָלוֹ עִם הַגְּבִינָה — **must remove from the table** any **remnants of the bread that he ate with the cheese.**[27] וְאָסוּר לֶאֱכוֹל גְּבִינָה עַל מַפָּה שֶׁאָכְלוּ בָשָׂר — **Additionally, it is prohibited to eat cheese on the tablecloth** upon **which meat was eaten,** וְכֵן לְהִיפּוּךְ — **and likewise, the reverse** (eating meat on a dairy tablecloth) is prohibited. גַּם אָסוּר לַחְתּוֹךְ בְּסַכִּין שֶׁל בָּשָׂר פַּת לְאָכְלוֹ עִם גְּבִינָה — **It is also prohibited to cut with a meat knife the bread** that one intends **to eat with cheese,** וְכֵן לְהִיפּוּךְ — **and likewise, the reverse** is prohibited. וַאֲפִילוּ אִם הַסַּכִּין נָקִי — This is prohibited **even if the knife is clean.**[28] וּבִשְׁעַת הַדְּחָק, כְּגוֹן שֶׁהוּא בְדֶרֶךְ — **However, in a time of pressing need, such as when one is on the road** and has no other knife, מוּתָּר לוֹ לַחְתּוֹךְ בְּסַכִּין שֶׁל בָּשָׂר — **he is permitted to cut** bread **with a meat knife** כְּשֶׁהוּא נָקִי וּמְקוּנָּח הֵיטֵב הֵיטֵב — **that is clean and has been wiped extremely well,** לֶאֱכוֹל עִם גְּבִינָה — even if he wishes **to eat** the bread **with cheese,** וְכֵן בְּהִיפּוּךְ — **and likewise, the reverse** (to cut bread with a clean dairy knife in order to eat the bread with meat) is permitted.[29]

§13 אִם חָתַךְ בְּסַכִּין שֶׁל בָּשָׂר בְּצָלִים, אוֹ שְׁאָר דָּבָר חָרִיף — **If one cut onions or some other sharp** food **item**[30] **with a meat knife,** וּנְתָנָם לְמַאֲכַל חָלָב — **and put the**

---

however, is generally not aged six months (see *The Kosher Kitchen*, by Rabbi Binyomin Forst, ArtScroll Mesorah Publications, 2009, p. 140).]

25. Under certain conditions, it is permitted to eat worms that form in cheese, as elaborated below, *se'if* 44. Eating wormy cheese is akin to eating meat in that it requires a six-hour wait before consumption of the opposite kind (in this case, meat) is permitted (*Mishbetzos Zahav* ibid.).

26. At another meal, as described in the preceding *se'if*.

27. As mentioned in *se'if* 7, bread left over from a dairy meal may not be eaten with a meat meal. These bread remnants must be removed from the table (*Shulchan Aruch, Yoreh Deah* 89:4).

28. It is obviously prohibited to cut the cheese itself with a meat knife, and vice versa (ibid.).

29. Even if the knife is clean and even in a time of pressing need, it is still prohibited to cut cheese itself with a meat knife, or vice versa, (see *Shach* 89:22 with *Pri Megadim*).

30. "Sharp foods" include, but are not limited to, garlic, radish, fresh and pickled olives, lemon, salty herring, and horseradish. [A sharp food has a greater capacity than a bland food to extract flavor from a utensil. Thus, when cut with a meat knife, even one that is not *ben-yomo* (i.e., it was not used in 24 hours), it may have absorbed meat flavor.]

אוֹ בְּהִיפּוּךְ, צָרִיךְ לַעֲשׂוֹת שְׁאֵלַת חָכָם[31].

יד. הָעוֹשֶׂה תַּבְשִׁיל מִבָּשָׂר בַּחֲלֵב שְׁקֵדִים, צָרִיךְ לְהָנִיחַ בְּתוֹכוֹ שְׁקֵדִים, מִפְּנֵי מַרְאִית הָעַיִן[32].

טו. נוֹהֲגִין שֶׁלֹּא לְהַגְעִיל כְּלִי חָלָב לְהִשְׁתַּמֵּשׁ בּוֹ בְּבָשָׂר, אוֹ אִיפְּכָא. (עַיֵּין מָגֵן אַבְרָהָם סִימָן תקי״ט סְעִיף קָטָן י״א וּבְמַחֲצִית הַשֶּׁקֶל)[33].

טז. יַיִן וּבָשָׂר וַחֲתִיכַת דָּג שֶׁאֵין בּוֹ סִימָן שֶׁמַּפְקִידִין אוֹ שׁוֹלְחִין בְּיַד עַכּוּ״ם,

---

onions or other sharp food into a dairy dish, **אוֹ בְּהִיפּוּךְ** — **or** one did **the reverse** (i.e., he cut a sharp food item with a dairy knife and added it to a meat dish), **צָרִיךְ לַעֲשׂוֹת שְׁאֵלַת חָכָם** — **he must inquire of a halachic authority** regarding the status of the food, the pot in which it was cooked, and the utensil with which it was served.[31]

§14 **הָעוֹשֶׂה תַּבְשִׁיל מִבָּשָׂר בַּחֲלֵב שְׁקֵדִים** — **One who makes a meat dish with almond "milk"** **צָרִיךְ לְהָנִיחַ בְּתוֹכוֹ שְׁקֵדִים** — **must place almonds in it,** **מִפְּנֵי מַרְאִית הָעַיִן** — **because** it is necessary to avoid **the appearance** of wrongdoing.[32]

§15 When a dairy utensil is accidentally used for meat, or vice versa, it often becomes unfit for use, since it has absorbed both dairy and meat flavor. One can rectify the utensil by purging its absorbed flavor through the process of *kashering,* which is described in *Siman* 116. Here, Kitzur discusses whether *kashering* may be used to change an ordinary dairy utensil to meat use and vice versa:
נוֹהֲגִין שֶׁלֹּא לְהַגְעִיל כְּלִי חָלָב לְהִשְׁתַּמֵּשׁ בּוֹ בְּבָשָׂר — **The custom is not to purge a dairy utensil** of the dairy taste it has absorbed **so as to use it with meat,** **אוֹ אִיפְּכָא** — **or** to do **the reverse** (i.e., purge a meat utensil for use with dairy). (**עַיֵּין מָגֵן אַבְרָהָם סִימָן תקי״ט סְעִיף קָטָן י״א וּבְמַחֲצִית הַשֶּׁקֶל** — **See** *Magen Avraham* **509:11 and** *Machatzis HaShekel* ad loc.)[33]

§16 Kitzur now turns to the rules of ensuring the kosher status of food entrusted to one who does not observe these laws:
יַיִן וּבָשָׂר וַחֲתִיכַת דָּג שֶׁאֵין בּוֹ סִימָן — **Wine, meat, or a piece of fish that does not have an identifying characteristic,** **שֶׁמַּפְקִידִין אוֹ שׁוֹלְחִין בְּיַד עַכּוּ״ם** — **that one deposits**

---

31. Various factors can influence the law in this situation. Among these is how sharp the food was, when the knife was last used, and whether the knife was clean. Due to the intricacy of the laws involved, one must consult a halachic authority.

32. Almond "milk" is non-dairy, and thus, may be consumed with meat. However, since the observer will not recognize it as almond milk, and may suspect the person of mixing milk with meat, one must place some almonds in the milk to indicate that it is a non-dairy almond product (see *Shach, Yoreh Deah* 87:6). This applies not only when the meat is cooked in almond milk, but also when it is cooked by itself and served with almond milk (see *Aruch HaShulchan* 87:16). The same applies to any other form of non-dairy "milk"; when offered at a meat meal, there must be an indication that it is a non-dairy product. [It should be noted that whenever the Sages imposed a restriction in order to avoid a perception of wrongdoing, that restriction applies even when nobody is present to observe the act (see note 3 above). Thus, the preceding rules apply even to a meal eaten in privacy.]

33. However, if one is *kashering* his utensils so as to use them for Pesach, he may at the same time change their designation from meat to dairy or vice versa (*Mishnah Berurah* 451:19, citing *Teshuvos Chasam Sofer, Yoreh Deah* §110).

וּמִכָּל שֶׁכֵּן בְּיַד יִשְׂרָאֵל חָשׁוּד[34], צָרִיךְ שְׁנֵי חוֹתָמוֹת[35]. אֲבָל יַיִן מְבוּשָּׁל, וְכֵן הַחוֹמֶץ שֶׁל יַיִן, וְחָלָב וּפַת וּגְבִינָה סַגִּי בְּחוֹתָם אֶחָד[36].

יז. אִם שׁוֹלֵחַ אוֹ מַפְקִיד אֵיזֶה דָּבָר בְּשַׂק, צָרִיךְ שֶׁיִּהְיוּ (התפורות) [הַתְּפִירוֹת] מִבִּפְנִים[37] וּלְקָשְׁרוֹ וּלְחָתְמוֹ[38].

יח. אִם אֵירַע שֶׁשָּׁלַח עַל יְדֵי עַכּוּ"ם בְּהֵמָה אוֹ עוֹף שְׁחוּטִים, אוֹ שְׁאָר דָּבָר, בְּלֹא חוֹתָם, יַעֲשֶׂה שְׁאֵלַת חָכָם[39].

---

with **or sends** for delivery **in the hand of an idolater,** **וּמִכָּל שֶׁכֵּן בְּיַד יִשְׂרָאֵל חָשׁוּד** — **and certainly in the hand of a Jew who is suspect** of being lax in his observance of dietary laws,[34] **צָרִיךְ שְׁנֵי חוֹתָמוֹת** — **requires two** identifying **seals** in order to be permitted.[35] **אֲבָל יַיִן מְבוּשָּׁל, וְכֵן הַחוֹמֶץ שֶׁל יַיִן** — **However,** for **cooked wine, and similarly,** for **wine vinegar,** **וְחָלָב וּפַת וּגְבִינָה** — **or** for **milk, bread, or cheese** that are entrusted to an idolater or a suspect Jew, **סַגִּי בְּחוֹתָם אֶחָד** — **a single seal suffices.**[36]

§17 **אִם שׁוֹלֵחַ אוֹ מַפְקִיד אֵיזֶה דָּבָר בְּשַׂק** — **If one sends or deposits** with an idolater or a suspect Jew **something** that is **contained in a sack,** **צָרִיךְ שֶׁיִּהְיוּ (התפורות) [הַתְּפִירוֹת] מִבִּפְנִים** — **it is necessary that the stitches** of the sack **be on the inside,**[37] **וּלְקָשְׁרוֹ וּלְחָתְמוֹ** — **and** it is also necessary **to tie** the opening of the sack **and seal it.**[38]

§18 **אִם אֵירַע** — **If it occurred** **שֶׁשָּׁלַח עַל יְדֵי עַכּוּ"ם** — **that one sent with an idolater** or a suspect Jew **בְּהֵמָה אוֹ עוֹף שְׁחוּטִים, אוֹ שְׁאָר דָּבָר** — **a slaughtered animal or bird, or some other** food **item,** **בְּלֹא חוֹתָם** — **without a seal,** **יַעֲשֶׂה שְׁאֵלַת חָכָם** — then **one must ask a halachic authority** whether it can be used.[39]

---

34. See *Rama, Yoreh Deah* 118:1.

35. The Sages were concerned that the idolater or suspect Jew might desire the food entrusted to him, and he might take it and replace it with a similar nonkosher item. They therefore prohibited consumption of any food left in the care of an idolater or suspect Jew, unless it was enclosed in a sealed wrapping that leaves evidence in case of tampering. This pertains to cases in which the nonkosher replacement item would be forbidden Rabbinically. With respect to foods that are prohibited Biblically, such as meat or fish, the Sages were even more cautious and required that the food be enclosed in a *double*-sealed wrapping (*Rashba, Avodah Zarah* 39a, cited by *Tur* and *Shulchan Aruch, Yoreh Deah* 118:1; for another explanation, see *Rashi, Avodah Zarah* 39b, cited by *Tur* ibid.). [The Sages also required a double-seal for wine, even though the prohibition of the wine would be only Rabbinic (see next *Siman*), because they were especially concerned that an idolater might desire wine to use as an idolatrous libation (*Rashba* ibid. cited by *Beis Yosef* ibid.).]

36. In these cases, the nonkosher replacement food would be prohibited only by Rabbinic law.

37. A seal at the opening of the sack is useless if the sack can be opened from the bottom by undoing its stitches. One must therefore turn the stitches to the inner side of the sack, where they cannot be tampered with.

38. A knot with a seal counts as a single seal. For foods requiring a double seal, one must place an additional sealed wrapping around the food before placing it in the sack (*Aruch HaShulchan* 118:17).

39. Depending on where the idolater carried the food, whether it is recognized to be the food that was sent, and other factors, it may be permitted after the fact. A halachic authority must be consulted.

יט. גְּבִינוֹת וּשְׁאָר דְּבָרִים שֶׁהֵם בִּידֵי עַכּוּ"ם, אַף עַל פִּי שֶׁהֵם בְּחוֹתָם אוֹ בִּדְפוּס שֶׁהֵם כְּשֵׁרִים, כֹּל שֶׁלֹּא יָדַעְנוּ מִי חֲתָמָן, אֲסוּרִין[40].

כ. יֵשׁ לִיזָּהֵר שֶׁלֹּא לְבַשֵּׁל אוֹ לִצְלוֹת יִשְׂרָאֵל וְעַכּוּ"ם שְׁתֵּי קְדֵירוֹת זוֹ אֵצֶל זוֹ, זֶה בְּשַׂר כָּשֵׁר וְזֶה בְּשַׂר טְרֵיפָה, אִם הַקְּדֵרוֹת אוֹ הַמַּחֲבוֹת מְגוּלּוֹת[41]. וְכֵן יֵשׁ לִיזָּהֵר שֶׁלֹּא לְהַנִּיחַ הַקְּדֵרוֹת אֵצֶל הַשְּׁפָחוֹת כְּשֶׁאֵין יִשְׂרָאֵל בַּבַּיִת וְאֵינוֹ יוֹצֵא וְנִכְנָס[42].

כא. מִי שֶׁאֵין מַכִּירִין אוֹתוֹ שֶׁהוּא מוּחְזָק בְּכַשְׁרוּת — אָסוּר לִקְנוֹת מִמֶּנּוּ יַיִן, אוֹ שְׁאָר דְּבָרִים, שֶׁיֵּשׁ לָחוּשׁ בָּהֶם לְאִיסּוּר[43]. מִיהוּ, אִם נִתְאָרַח אֶצְלוֹ, אוֹכֵל עִמּוֹ,

---

§19 **גְּבִינוֹת וּשְׁאָר דְּבָרִים שֶׁהֵם בִּידֵי עַכּוּ"ם** — **Cheeses and other** food **items that are in the hands of an idolater,** **אַף עַל פִּי שֶׁהֵם בְּחוֹתָם** — **even if they are sealed** in the manner in which Jews seal foods, **אוֹ בִּדְפוּס שֶׁהֵם כְּשֵׁרִים** — **or** it is **printed** upon them **that they are kosher,** **כֹּל שֶׁלֹּא יָדַעְנוּ מִי חֲתָמָן, אֲסוּרִין** — **as long as we do not know who sealed them** or printed on them, **they are prohibited.**[40]

§20 Next, Kitzur discusses precautions that were instituted to safeguard against the mingling or interchanging of kosher and nonkosher foods:

יֵשׁ לִיזָּהֵר — **Care should be taken** **שֶׁלֹּא לְבַשֵּׁל אוֹ לִצְלוֹת יִשְׂרָאֵל וְעַכּוּ"ם שְׁתֵּי קְדֵירוֹת זוֹ אֵצֶל זוֹ** — **that a Jew and an idolater not cook or roast two pots next to each other,** **זֶה בְּשַׂר כָּשֵׁר וְזֶה בְּשַׂר טְרֵיפָה** — with **this one** containing **kosher meat and that one** containing **nonkosher meat,** **אִם הַקְּדֵרוֹת אוֹ הַמַּחֲבוֹת מְגוּלּוֹת** — **if the pots or frying pans are uncovered.**[41] **וְכֵן יֵשׁ לִיזָּהֵר** — **Similarly, care should be taken** **שֶׁלֹּא לְהַנִּיחַ הַקְּדֵרוֹת אֵצֶל הַשְּׁפָחוֹת** — **not to leave pots** of food cooking **in the care of** idolatrous **maidservants** **כְּשֶׁאֵין יִשְׂרָאֵל בַּבַּיִת** — **when there is no Jew in the house** **וְאֵינוֹ יוֹצֵא וְנִכְנָס** — **and** a Jew **is not** even **going and coming.**[42]

§21 **מִי שֶׁאֵין מַכִּירִין אוֹתוֹ שֶׁהוּא מוּחְזָק בְּכַשְׁרוּת** — Regarding **one who is not known to be observant** of the laws of *kashrus,* **אָסוּר לִקְנוֹת מִמֶּנּוּ יַיִן** — **it is prohibited to purchase from him wine** **אוֹ שְׁאָר דְּבָרִים, שֶׁיֵּשׁ לָחוּשׁ בָּהֶם לְאִיסּוּר** — **or anything else about which there could be concern that it is prohibited.**[43] **מִיהוּ, אִם נִתְאָרַח אֶצְלוֹ** — **However, if one is his guest,** **אוֹכֵל עִמּוֹ** — **one may eat with him** of

---

40. We must be concerned that perhaps an idolater wrapped and sealed the foods in the manner of Jews, or he obtained a stamp with which he imprinted "Kosher" on the foods (see *Rama, Yoreh Deah* 118:9 and 118:13). [Nowadays, we rely on *kashrus* certification symbols printed on food packages if these are copyrighted and their misuse makes a perpetrator liable to prosecution by the government, so one would be afraid to forge them.]

41. We must be concerned that some of the nonkosher food or liquid will splatter onto the kosher food or pot (*Shach* 118:36; cf. *Beur HaGra* 118:35). After the fact, however, if the pots were cooked alongside each other and no splattering was observed, the kosher food is permitted (*Shulchan Aruch, Yoreh Deah* 118:11).

42. We must be concerned that the maidservant will add something nonkosher to the food when no one is present. When a Jew comes and goes, however, even if he is not constantly present, we assume that she will not tamper with the cooking food, out of fear of his imminent entry (see *Yoreh Deah* 118:12). [Even if there is no food cooking, one may not leave a non-Jewish housekeeper alone in one's home, when there is no Jew coming and going, in a situation where there is concern that she might use a pot to cook something nonkosher, such as meat and dairy together, and this would render the pot forbidden. For discussion, see *Igros Moshe, Yoreh Deah* I, §61. See also *se'if* 22.]

43. This applies even to food that is prohibited by Rabbinic decree (*Shach* 119:3).

כֹּל שֶׁלֹּא נוֹדַע לוֹ שֶׁהוּא חָשׁוּד[44].

כב. יֵשׁ לִיזָּהֵר מִלְּהַנִּיחַ בְּבֵית עַכּוּ"ם כְּלִי שֶׁיֵּשׁ לָחוּשׁ שֶׁמָּא נִשְׁתַּמֵּשׁ בּוֹ, וַאֲפִילוּ נְתָנוֹ לְאוּמָּן לְתַקְּנוֹ, אִם יֵשׁ לָחוּשׁ שֶׁמָּא נִשְׁתַּמֵּשׁ בּוֹ, יַעֲשֶׂה שְׁאֵלַת חָכָם[45].

כג. לִפְעָמִים[46] לוֹקְחִין עוֹף כְּפוּת וּמַשְׁלִיכִין אוֹתוֹ אַרְצָה וְאַחַר כָּךְ שׁוֹחֲטִים אוֹתוֹ, וְהוּא אִיסּוּר גָּמוּר, כִּי בְּהֵמָה אוֹ עוֹף שֶׁנָּפַל אֵין לוֹ הֶיתֵּר עַד שֶׁרוֹאִין אַחַר כָּךְ שֶׁהָלַךְ ד' אַמּוֹת הִילּוּךְ יָפֶה[47]. וְגַם בִּכְבָשִׂים וּבַעֲגָלִים צְרִיכִין לִיזָּהֵר בָּזֶה מְאוֹד.

כד. בִּימֵי הַקַּיִץ שָׁכִיחַ מְאוֹד בְּבַר־אַוְזוֹת שֶׁנִּמְצָאוּ בּוּעוֹת קְטַנּוֹת כְּמִין יַבֶּלֶת

---

his food, כֹּל שֶׁלֹּא נוֹדַע לוֹ שֶׁהוּא חָשׁוּד — **as long as he is not known to be suspect** of violating the *kashrus* laws.[44]

§22 יֵשׁ לִיזָּהֵר — **Care should be taken** מִלְּהַנִּיחַ בְּבֵית עַכּוּ"ם — **to avoid leaving in an idolater's house** כְּלִי שֶׁיֵּשׁ לָחוּשׁ שֶׁמָּא נִשְׁתַּמֵּשׁ בּוֹ — **a** food **utensil** about which **there is** room for **concern that it might have been used** for nonkosher food. וַאֲפִילוּ נְתָנוֹ לְאוּמָּן לְתַקְּנוֹ — **And even if one gave it to a craftsman to fix,** אִם יֵשׁ לָחוּשׁ שֶׁמָּא נִשְׁתַּמֵּשׁ בּוֹ — **if,** when one retrieves it, **there is** room for the **concern that perhaps it was used,** יַעֲשֶׂה שְׁאֵלַת חָכָם — **one must inquire of a halachic authority** as to the permissibility of the utensil.[45]

§23 We now turn to the laws of *tereifah*:[46]

לִפְעָמִים — **Sometimes** לוֹקְחִין עוֹף כְּפוּת וּמַשְׁלִיכִין אוֹתוֹ אַרְצָה — **people take a bound fowl and throw it to the ground** to stun it, וְאַחַר כָּךְ שׁוֹחֲטִים אוֹתוֹ — **and then they slaughter it.** וְהוּא אִיסּוּר גָּמוּר — **But this is absolutely forbidden,** כִּי בְּהֵמָה אוֹ עוֹף שֶׁנָּפַל — **for an animal or bird that fell** to the ground is considered to be *tereifah* and is prohibited for consumption. אֵין לוֹ הֶיתֵּר — **It cannot be permitted** עַד שֶׁרוֹאִין אַחַר כָּךְ שֶׁהָלַךְ ד' אַמּוֹת הִילּוּךְ יָפֶה — **unless one later sees that it walks four** *amos* **with a regular gait.**[47] וְגַם בִּכְבָשִׂים וּבַעֲגָלִים צְרִיכִין לִיזָּהֵר בָּזֶה מְאוֹד — **With sheep and calves, too, one must be very careful about this.**

§24 בִּימֵי הַקַּיִץ שָׁכִיחַ מְאוֹד בְּבַר־אַוְזוֹת — **In the summer, it is very common with geese** שֶׁנִּמְצָאוּ בּוּעוֹת קְטַנּוֹת כְּמִין יַבֶּלֶת (ווארצלען) בִּבְנֵי מֵעַיִים — **that there**

---

44. That is, if a Jew's level of observance is unknown, one may not purchase food from him, but one may eat with him in his home. This is because many who are lax in regard to selling nonkosher food nevertheless refrain from eating it themselves. When in doubt, therefore, one may assume that the host's own food is kosher (see *Shach* 119:4). However, if there is reason to believe that the food in the Jew's home may not be kosher, one may not eat there.

45. Depending on the circumstances, it may need to be *kashered* (see *Yoreh Deah* 122:9). [See above, note 42, regarding pots left in one's home with a non-Jewish housekeeper.]

46. Animals or fowl that suffer from certain mortal defects are considered *tereifah* and are prohibited from being eaten. The specific defects that render an animal *tereifah* were transmitted to Moshe at Sinai and handed down by the Sages in the Oral Law. These defects and their laws are discussed at length in *Yoreh Deah* §29-60.

47. An *amah* is between 18.9 and 22.7 inches (48-57.7 cm.; see Appendix A). If the bird walked four *amos* in a normal fashion after falling, it is presumed not to be a *tereifah* (see *Yoreh Deah* 58:6).

48. The warts can sometimes block the

LAWS OF FORBIDDEN FOODS — SIMAN 46:25 146

(ווארצלען) בִּבְנֵי מֵעַיִים וְהַרְבֵּה נִטְרָפוֹת עַל יְדֵי כָּךְ[48], עַל כֵּן צְרִיכִין לִיזָּהֵר מְאוֹד לִבְדּוֹק הַבְּנֵי מֵעַיִים וּכְשֶׁנִּמְצָא בּוּעוֹת קְטַנּוֹת, יַעֲשֶׂה שְׁאֵלַת חָכָם.

כה. אֵין לָשִׁין עִיסָּה בְּחָלָב, שֶׁמָּא יֹאכַל הַפַּת עִם בָּשָׂר[49]. וְאִם לָשׁ, כָּל הַפַּת אָסוּר, אֲפִילוּ לְאָכְלוֹ לְבַדּוֹ, גְּזֵירָה שֶׁמָּא יֹאכְלוֹ עִם בָּשָׂר. וְאִם הָיָה דָבָר מוּעָט כְּדֵי אֲכִילָה פַּעַם אַחַת, אוֹ שֶׁשִּׁינָּה צוּרַת הַפַּת, שֶׁיְּהֵא נִיכָּר שֶׁלֹּא לְאָכְלוֹ עִם בָּשָׂר, מוּתָּר. וְכֵן הַדִּין אִם לָשׁ עִיסָּה עִם שׁוּמָּן שֶׁל בָּשָׂר. וְאֵין לֶאֱפוֹת שׁוּם פַּת עִם פלאדין, אוֹ פשטידא, בְּתַנּוּר, דְּחַיְישִׁינַן שֶׁמָּא יָזוּב מִן הַחֶמְאָה, אוֹ מִן הַשּׁוּמָּן, תַּחַת הַפַּת[50]. וְאִם זָב

are small blisters, resembling warts, found on the intestines, וְהַרְבֵּה נִטְרָפוֹת עַל יְדֵי כָּךְ — and many of them become *tereifah* on account of this.[48] עַל כֵּן צְרִיכִין לִיזָּהֵר מְאוֹד לִבְדּוֹק הַבְּנֵי מֵעַיִים — **Therefore, one must be very careful to examine the intestines,** וּכְשֶׁנִּמְצָא בּוּעוֹת קְטַנּוֹת — **and when small blisters are found,** יַעֲשֶׂה שְׁאֵלַת חָכָם — **one must inquire of a halachic authority** regarding the status of the goose.

§25 Kitzur now discusses certain restrictions that apply to baking bread:

אֵין לָשִׁין עִיסָּה בְּחָלָב — **One may not knead dough with milk** (in place of water, or in addition to it), שֶׁמָּא יֹאכַל הַפַּת עִם בָּשָׂר — for there is a concern that **perhaps one will** unknowingly **eat the bread with meat.**[49] וְאִם לָשׁ — **And if one did knead** and bake dairy bread, כָּל הַפַּת אָסוּר, אֲפִילוּ לְאָכְלוֹ לְבַדּוֹ — then **the entire** loaf of **bread is prohibited, even from being eaten by itself,** without any accompanying food. גְּזֵירָה שֶׁמָּא יֹאכְלוֹ עִם בָּשָׂר — This is **a decree** enacted out of concern that **perhaps it will be eaten with meat.** וְאִם הָיָה דָבָר מוּעָט — **However, if** the loaf **was of a small measure,** כְּדֵי אֲכִילָה פַּעַם אַחַת — **sufficient** only **to be eaten at one sitting,** אוֹ שֶׁשִּׁינָּה צוּרַת הַפַּת — **or if one made an unusually shaped bread,** שֶׁיְּהֵא נִיכָּר שֶׁלֹּא לְאָכְלוֹ עִם בָּשָׂר — **so that it should be recognizable** as intended **not to be eaten with meat,** מוּתָּר — then **it is permitted.** וְכֵן הַדִּין אִם לָשׁ עִיסָּה עִם שׁוּמָּן שֶׁל בָּשָׂר — **And the law is the same if one kneaded dough with meat gravy,** i.e., the bread is completely prohibited unless it is a single-serving size or a distinctive shape.

וְאֵין לֶאֱפוֹת שׁוּם פַּת עִם פלאדין, אוֹ פשטידא, בְּתַנּוּר — **And** similarly, **one should not bake any bread in an oven along with a dairy-filled loaf or a meat-filled loaf,** דְּחַיְישִׁינַן שֶׁמָּא יָזוּב מִן הַחֶמְאָה, אוֹ מִן הַשּׁוּמָּן, תַּחַת הַפַּת — **for we are concerned** that **perhaps some butter or gravy will** ooze out of the filled loaf, **flow beneath the bread** and become absorbed by the bread, and the bread might then be eaten with food of the opposite type.[50] וְאִם זָב תַּחְתָּיו — **If** one did bake bread together with a dairy-filled

intestines or cause them to be punctured, which would render the goose *tereifah* (*Rama, Yoreh Deah* 46:6).

49. Since bread is commonly eaten together with other foods, the Sages instructed that one not make bread containing dairy or meat ingredients. One must leave it *pareve*, so that it can be eaten at any meal. One may, however, bake a loaf that is visibly *filled* with a meat or dairy ingredient, for since its status is apparent to all, there is no concern that it will be eaten at the wrong meal (*Pri Megadim, Sifsei Daas* 97:1 and *Aruch HaShulchan* 97:5).

50. This concern applies when they are being baked upon the same surface, such that the butter or gravy might reach the bread (see *Aruch HaShulchan* 97:11). However, in the next *se'if* we will see that there is a further concern even when they are separated.

תַּחְתָּיו, דִּינוֹ כְּאִלּוּ נִילוֹשׁ עִמּוֹ, דְּאָסוּר לְאָכְלוֹ אֲפִילּוּ לְבַדּוֹ[51].

כו. **פַּת[52] שֶׁאֲפָאוֹ עִם הַצְּלִי בְּתַנּוּר אֶחָד — אִם הָיָה הַתַּנּוּר סָתוּם וְהַצְּלִי מְגוּלֶּה, אָסוּר הַפַּת לְאָכְלוֹ בְּחָלָב[53]. אֲבָל אִם הַצְּלִי הָיָה מְכוּסֶּה, אוֹ שֶׁהָיָה הַתַּנּוּר פָּתוּחַ וְהוּא תַנּוּר גָּדוֹל כְּתַנּוּרִים שֶׁלָּנוּ[54], מוּתָּר[55]. וּמִכָּל מָקוֹם, לְכַתְּחִלָּה יֵשׁ לִיזָּהֵר שֶׁלֹּא לִצְלוֹת בָּשָׂר בְּתַנּוּר שֶׁאוֹפִין בּוֹ פַּת, דְּחַיְישִׁינַן שֶׁמָּא יָזוּב מִן הַשּׁוּמָן תַּחַת הַפַּת, וַאֲפִילּוּ הַצְּלִי הוּא בְּמַחֲבַת יֵשׁ לָחוּשׁ[56].**

---

or meat-filled loaf, and butter or gravy **did flow beneath it,** **דִּינוֹ כְּאִלּוּ נִילוֹשׁ עִמּוֹ** — then **it has the same law as if it had been kneaded with it** (i.e., it is as though the bread were kneaded with butter or gravy), **דְּאָסוּר לְאָכְלוֹ אֲפִילּוּ לְבַדּוֹ** — meaning **that one is prohibited from eating it even by itself.**[51]

§26 Initially, one may not roast meat and dairy foods together in an oven, even if they do not touch each other, because the aroma of the meat may permeate the dairy food. Similarly, one may not bake bread in an oven while roasting meat, since meat aroma might permeate the bread.[52] Kitzur discusses the law pertaining after the fact:

פַּת שֶׁאֲפָאוֹ עִם הַצְּלִי בְּתַנּוּר אֶחָד — Regarding **bread that was baked** together **with roasting** meat, **in one oven,** the law is as follows: **אִם הָיָה הַתַּנּוּר סָתוּם וְהַצְּלִי מְגוּלֶּה** — **If the oven was sealed and the roasting** meat **was uncovered,** **אָסוּר הַפַּת לְאָכְלוֹ בְּחָלָב** — **the bread is prohibited to be consumed** together **with milk.**[53] **אֲבָל אִם הַצְּלִי הָיָה מְכוּסֶּה** — **However, if the roasting** meat **was covered,** **אוֹ שֶׁהָיָה הַתַּנּוּר פָּתוּחַ וְהוּא תַנּוּר גָּדוֹל כְּתַנּוּרִים שֶׁלָּנוּ** — **or the oven was open** (i.e., it was not fully sealed) **and it is large, like our ovens,**[54] **מוּתָּר** — then the bread is **permitted** to be eaten with milk.[55] **וּמִכָּל מָקוֹם, לְכַתְּחִלָּה יֵשׁ לִיזָּהֵר** — **Nevertheless,** even if the oven is vented and it is large, **one should initially be careful** **שֶׁלֹּא לִצְלוֹת בָּשָׂר בְּתַנּוּר שֶׁאוֹפִין בּוֹ פַּת** — **not to roast meat in an oven in which one is baking bread,** **דְּחַיְישִׁינַן שֶׁמָּא יָזוּב מִן הַשּׁוּמָן תַּחַת הַפַּת** — **for** an additional reason; i.e., that **we are concerned that perhaps gravy** from the meat **will flow beneath the bread.** **וַאֲפִילּוּ הַצְּלִי הוּא בְּמַחֲבַת** — **And even when** the meat is being **roasted in a pan,** **יֵשׁ לָחוּשׁ** — **it is** proper **to be concerned.**[56]

---

51. The bread might be forbidden even if butter or gravy oozed out of the filled dough and was not observed flowing directly underneath the bread (see *Shach, Taz* et al. to *Yoreh Deah* 97:1). Even if nothing was seen oozing out of the loaf, the bread may not necessarily be permitted, due to the considerations discussed in the next *se'if* (see *Shach* 97:2).

52. See *Yoreh Deah* 108:1.

53. It is permitted, however, to eat the bread by itself or with a meat meal (unlike the law of bread *containing* milk or gravy, discussed in the previous *se'if*). The concern for aroma is not sufficient to forbid the bread completely; it is merely cause for stringency initially (*lechatchilah*). Since it is initially possible to eat the bread with a non-dairy meal, one must do so (see *Rama, Yoreh Deah* 108:1 and *Shach* 97:4).

54. For the precise definition of a "large" oven, see *Yoreh Deah* ibid. and 97:3.

55. In a small or tightly sealed oven, the aroma of the meat (which bears some of the meat's essence) might permeate the bread, rendering it meaty. In a large oven that is vented, the aroma is less concentrated, and is very unlikely to permeate the bread. Therefore, after the fact, the bread is permitted even with milk (see *Rama* and *Shach* ibid.).

56. *Rama, Yoreh Deah* 97:1. Although when the meat is in a pan no gravy can flow over to the bread, initially it should not be placed in the oven with the bread due to the concern for its aroma (*Aruch HaShulchan* 97:11).

כז. תַּנּוּר שֶׁזָּב בְּקַרְקַע שֶׁלּוֹ שׁוּמָּן אוֹ חָלָב, צָרִיךְ הֶיסֵּק כְּדִין[57] עַד שֶׁיֵּלְכוּ הַגֶּחָלִים עַל פְּנֵי כוּלּוֹ וְיִתְלַבֵּן.

כח. תַּרְנְגוֹלִים מְסוֹרָסִים נוֹהֲגִים לְאָכְלָם, מִשּׁוּם דְּסוֹמְכִין דְּמִסְתָּמָא הָעַכּוּ״ם הַמְסָרֵס הוּא אוּמָּן וּבָקִי בְּדָבָר שֶׁלֹּא יַעֲשֶׂה בַּתְּפִירָה אֵיזֶה רֵיעוּתָא בִּבְנֵי מֵעַיִים (וְעַיֵּין לְקַמָּן סִימָן קצ״א סְעִיף ו׳)[58]. אֲבָל אִם נִמְצָא בָּהֶן אֵיזֶה רֵיעוּתָא, אֲפִילּוּ רַק שֶׁאֵינָן מוּנָּחִין כָּרָאוּי, הֲרֵי הֵן אֲסוּרִין[59].

כט. בִּקְצָת מְקוֹמוֹת נוֹהֲגִין הָעַכּוּ״ם הַמְפַטְּמִין אֲוָוזוֹת לְמָכְרָן לְיִשְׂרְאֵלִים שֶׁדּוֹקְרִין אוֹתָן תַּחַת כַּנְפֵיהֶם בְּמַחַט וְכַדּוֹמֶה כְּדֵי שֶׁיִּתְתַּפֵּחַ הַבָּשָׂר וְיִתְרָאוּ שְׁמֵנוֹת וְיֵשׁ בָּזֶה שְׁאֵלַת חָכָם אִם הֵן כְּשֵׁרוֹת אוֹ לֹא[60] (עַיֵּין שו״ת אִמְרֵי אֵשׁ יוֹרֶה דֵעָה סִימָן כ״ד).

---

§27 **תַּנּוּר שֶׁזָּב בְּקַרְקַע שֶׁלּוֹ שׁוּמָּן אוֹ חָלָב** — **An oven that had** meat **gravy or milk flow onto its floor** **צָרִיךְ הֶיסֵּק כְּדִין** — **must be heated up as per the laws** of *kashering*,[57] **עַד שֶׁיֵּלְכוּ הַגֶּחָלִים עַל פְּנֵי כוּלּוֹ וְיִתְלַבֵּן** — and accordingly, may not be used for baking bread (or any food of the opposite type from the substance that oozed onto the oven floor) **until coals pass over its entire** surface **and it becomes white hot.**

§28 Kitzur returns to *tereifah* issues:

תַּרְנְגוֹלִים מְסוֹרָסִים נוֹהֲגִים לְאָכְלָם — **It is common practice to eat chickens that have been castrated,** even though a chicken can become *tereifah* if the intestines are punctured when the incision is stitched. **מִשּׁוּם דְּסוֹמְכִין** — This is **because we rely** on the reasoning **דְּמִסְתָּמָא הָעַכּוּ״ם הַמְסָרֵס הוּא אוּמָּן וּבָקִי בְּדָבָר** — **that presumably the idolater who castrated** the chicken **was skilled and knowledgeable in the procedure,** **שֶׁלֹּא יַעֲשֶׂה בַּתְּפִירָה אֵיזֶה רֵיעוּתָא בִּבְנֵי מֵעַיִים** — such **that he would not cause any damage to the intestines while stitching** the incision. **(וְעַיֵּין לְקַמָּן סִימָן קצ״א סְעִיף ו׳** — **See below, 191:6.**[58]**)** **אֲבָל אִם נִמְצָא בָּהֶן אֵיזֶה רֵיעוּתָא** — **However, if there is any flaw found in them,** **אֲפִילּוּ רַק שֶׁאֵינָן מוּנָּחִין כָּרָאוּי** — **even** if no perforation is visible and the flaw is **merely** that the intestines **are not lying** in place **properly,** **הֲרֵי הֵן אֲסוּרִין** — the chickens **are prohibited.**[59]

§29 **בִּקְצָת מְקוֹמוֹת** — **In some places,** **נוֹהֲגִין הָעַכּוּ״ם הַמְפַטְּמִין אֲוָוזוֹת לְמָכְרָן לְיִשְׂרְאֵלִים** — **it is the practice of the idolaters who fatten geese to sell to Jews,** **שֶׁדּוֹקְרִין אוֹתָן תַּחַת כַּנְפֵיהֶם בְּמַחַט וְכַדּוֹמֶה** — **to puncture them beneath their wings with a needle or the like,** **כְּדֵי שֶׁיִּתְתַּפֵּחַ הַבָּשָׂר וְיִתְרָאוּ שְׁמֵנוֹת** — **so that the flesh will become swollen and they will appear fat.** **וְיֵשׁ בָּזֶה שְׁאֵלַת חָכָם אִם הֵן כְּשֵׁרוֹת אוֹ לֹא** — **The question must be put to a halachic authority as to whether or not they are kosher.**[60] **(עַיֵּין שו״ת אִמְרֵי אֵשׁ יוֹרֶה דֵעָה סִימָן כ״ד)** — **See** ***Responsa Imrei Eish,***

---

57. [The laws of *kashering* are detailed in *Siman* 116.] *Kashering* is necessary because the oven presumably absorbed some meaty or milky residue, which could become absorbed in whatever food is subsequently baked in it. See *Yoreh Deah* 97:2.

58. There, Kitzur discusses the prohibition against castrating animals. [It is on account of the prohibition that he assumes here that the one who performed the castration was not a Jew.]

59. See *Shach, Yoreh Deah* 46:10.

60. In this situation, as well as the following one, there is concern that perhaps an internal organ was punctured, which would render the creature *tereifah.*

וְכֵן בְּהֵמָה אֲשֶׁר לִפְעָמִים מֵחֲמַת רוֹב אֲכִילָה מִסְתַּכֶּנֶת וּרְפוּאָתָהּ שֶׁדּוֹקְרִין אוֹתָהּ בְּמַרְצֵעַ נֶגֶד הַכָּרֵס יֵשׁ בָּזֶה גַּם כֵּן שְׁאֵלַת חָכָם אִם הִיא כְּשֵׁרָה (עַיֵּין טוּב טַעַם וָדַעַת סִימָן ע״ה).

ל. נוֹהֲגִין לַעֲשׂוֹת פֵּירוֹת מְרוּקָחִין, שֶׁנּוֹתְנִים אֶת הַפֵּירוֹת תּוֹךְ צְלוֹחִית וּמְכַסִּין וְקוֹשְׁרִין אֶת פִּיו בְּשַׁלְפּוּחִית בְּהֵמָה וְכָךְ מַעֲמִידִין אוֹתוֹ לְתוֹךְ תַּנּוּר חַם שֶׁיִּרוּקְחוּ הַפֵּירוֹת[61], צְרִיכִין לִיזָּהֵר שֶׁיְּהֵא הַשַּׁלְפּוּחִית מִבְּהֵמָה כְּשֵׁרָה וְהוּכְשַׁר גַּם בִּמְלִיחָה וַהֲדָחָה כָּרָאוּי[62].

לא. בְּאֵרוֹת וּנְהָרוֹת שֶׁמּוּחְזָקִין שֶׁיֵּשׁ בְּמֵימֵיהֶם תּוֹלָעִים, אָסוּר לִשְׁתּוֹתָן עַד שֶׁיְּסַנְּנוּ אוֹתָן[63], וַאֲפִילוּ בְּדִיעֲבַד אִם בִּישֵּׁל בְּאוֹתָן מַיִם, יֵשׁ לֶאֱסוֹר

Yoreh Deah §24.) **וְכֵן בְּהֵמָה** — **Similarly,** in the case of **an animal** **אֲשֶׁר לִפְעָמִים מֵחֲמַת רוֹב אֲכִילָה מִסְתַּכֶּנֶת** — **that,** as **sometimes** occurs, **becomes endangered due to excessive eating,** **וּרְפוּאָתָהּ** — **and its remedy is** **שֶׁדּוֹקְרִין אוֹתָהּ בְּמַרְצֵעַ נֶגֶד הַכָּרֵס** — **that one pierces its** abdomen **with an awl** at the point **corresponding to** the location of **the stomach,** **יֵשׁ בָּזֶה גַּם כֵּן שְׁאֵלַת חָכָם אִם הִיא כְּשֵׁרָה** — **this, too, must be asked of a Rabbinic authority as to whether it is kosher.** (**עַיֵּין טוּב טַעַם וָדַעַת סִימָן ע״ה** — **See** *Responsa Tuv Taam VaDaas* §75.)

§30 **נוֹהֲגִין לַעֲשׂוֹת פֵּירוֹת מְרוּקָחִין** — **It is common practice to make fruit preserves** **שֶׁנּוֹתְנִים אֶת הַפֵּירוֹת תּוֹךְ צְלוֹחִית** — **by placing the fruit into a container,** **וּמְכַסִּין וְקוֹשְׁרִין אֶת פִּיו בְּשַׁלְפּוּחִית בְּהֵמָה** — **covering and tying the mouth** of the container **with the womb of an animal,** **וְכָךְ מַעֲמִידִין אוֹתוֹ לְתוֹךְ תַּנּוּר חַם** — **and placing it thus into a hot oven,** **שֶׁיִּרוּקְחוּ הַפֵּירוֹת** — **so that the fruit should become preserved.**[61] **צְרִיכִין לִיזָּהֵר שֶׁיְּהֵא הַשַּׁלְפּוּחִית מִבְּהֵמָה כְּשֵׁרָה** — **One must be careful,** however, **that the womb should be that of a kosher animal,** **וְהוּכְשַׁר גַּם בִּמְלִיחָה וַהֲדָחָה כָּרָאוּי** — **which had also been properly *kashered*** (prepared for kosher use), **by** having been **salted and rinsed** to remove its blood.[62]

§31 The remainder of the *Siman* deals mainly with the prohibition of consuming vermin:

בְּאֵרוֹת וּנְהָרוֹת שֶׁמּוּחְזָקִין שֶׁיֵּשׁ בְּמֵימֵיהֶם תּוֹלָעִים — Regarding **wellsprings and rivers about which it has been established that their waters contain worms,** **אָסוּר לִשְׁתּוֹתָן** — **it is prohibited to drink** from their waters **עַד שֶׁיְּסַנְּנוּ אוֹתָן** — **until they have been strained.**[63] **וַאֲפִילוּ בְּדִיעֲבַד** — **Even after the fact,** **אִם בִּישֵּׁל בְּאוֹתָן מַיִם** — **if one cooked** food **in those waters,** **יֵשׁ לֶאֱסוֹר** — **it should be** considered

---

61. Fruit preserved in this manner lasts a long time without becoming spoiled.

62. See *Siman* 36, where this process is outlined. As the fruit warms in the oven, steam rises, penetrates the womb and becomes suffused with its taste, and then descends and becomes mixed into the fruit. If the womb has not been *kashered,* the steam will render the fruit nonkosher (see *Pri Megadim, Sifsei Daas* 87:33). [We learn here that the cover of a pot becomes infused with the flavor of food cooked in the pot, and then releases the flavor when used further. Thus, one must avoid covering a meaty pot with a dairy pot-cover, and vice versa. In any situation where a pot was covered with a cover of the opposite type, even if the food cooked was *pareve,* one must seek halachic guidance.]

63. Only some of the vermin that develop in water are prohibited. The vermin that develop in *standing* bodies of water, such as cisterns of rainwater, are not forbidden until they emerge from the water. [Upon emerging, they become

(עַיֵּין חָכְמַת אָדָם)[64]. וְכֵן אָסוּר לִשְׁרוֹת בְּמַיִם זֶה בָּשָׂר, אוֹ לְהָדִיחַ בָּהֶם דְּבַר מַאֲכָל, כִּי הַתּוֹלָעִים נִדְבָּקִים בְּמַאֲכָל.

לב. כְּשֶׁמְּסַנְּנִין אֶת הַמַּיִם, צְרִיכִים לִיזָּהֵר לְסַנְּנוֹ דֶּרֶךְ מַפָּה, שֶׁלֹּא יִהְיֶה בְּאֶפְשָׁרִי לַעֲבוֹר אֲפִילוּ תוֹלָע דַּק שֶׁבְּדַקִּין[65].

לג. חוֹמֶץ שֶׁהִתְלִיעַ אָסוּר עַל יְדֵי סִינּוּן[66], כִּי אֲפִילוּ[67] תוֹלָע דַּק שֶׁבְּדַקִּין שֶׁנִּתְהַוָּה בְּחוֹמֶץ עוֹבֵר דֶּרֶךְ כָּל מַפָּה, וְהַסִּינּוּן גָּרוּעֵי גַּרְעֵיהּ וְיוֹתֵר טוֹב שֶׁלֹּא לְסַנְּנוֹ, כִּי הַתּוֹלָע הַמִּתְהַוָּה בְּמַשְׁקִים שֶׁבְּכֵלִים אֵינוֹ נֶאֱסָר כָּל זְמַן שֶׁלֹּא פֵּירַשׁ

---

prohibited, due to the assumption that the water contained worms. (עַיֵּין חָכְמַת אָדָם — See *Chochmas Adam* 38:5).[64] וְכֵן אָסוּר לִשְׁרוֹת בְּמַיִם זֶה בָּשָׂר — **Similarly, it is prohibited to soak meat in these waters,** אוֹ לְהָדִיחַ בָּהֶם דְּבַר מַאֲכָל — **or to rinse** any **food item in them,** כִּי הַתּוֹלָעִים נִדְבָּקִים בְּמַאֲכָל — **for the worms** in the water will **cling to the food.**

§32 כְּשֶׁמְּסַנְּנִין אֶת הַמַּיִם — **When straining water,** צְרִיכִים לִיזָּהֵר לְסַנְּנוֹ דֶּרֶךְ מַפָּה — **one must be careful to strain it through a** type of **cloth** שֶׁלֹּא יִהְיֶה בְּאֶפְשָׁרִי לַעֲבוֹר אֲפִילוּ תוֹלָע דַּק שֶׁבְּדַקִּין — through **which it would be impossible for even the tiniest of worms to pass.**[65]

§33 חוֹמֶץ שֶׁהִתְלִיעַ — **Vinegar that developed worms** אָסוּר עַל יְדֵי סִינּוּן — **is prohibited** even **upon being strained,**[66] כִּי אֲפִילוּ[67] תוֹלָע דַּק שֶׁבְּדַקִּין שֶׁנִּתְהַוָּה בְּחוֹמֶץ — **for the very tiny worms that develop in vinegar** עוֹבֵר דֶּרֶךְ כָּל מַפָּה — **can pass through any cloth.** וְהַסִּינּוּן גָּרוּעֵי גַּרְעֵיהּ — Indeed, **straining** the vinegar **is detrimental to it** וְיוֹתֵר טוֹב שֶׁלֹּא לְסַנְּנוֹ — **and it is preferable to not strain it,** כִּי הַתּוֹלָע הַמִּתְהַוָּה בְּמַשְׁקִים שֶׁבְּכֵלִים — **for a worm that develops in a liquid that is** contained **in a vessel** אֵינוֹ נֶאֱסָר כָּל זְמַן שֶׁלֹּא פֵּירַשׁ — **does not become prohibited until**

---

prohibited and remain so even if they return to the water.] By contrast, vermin that develop in the *flowing* water of rivers and springs are prohibited even if they never emerged from the water (see *Yoreh Deah* 84:1; these laws are derived from Scripture in *Chullin* 66b-67a). Therefore, if a river or spring contains worms, one may not drink its water without straining it.

64. One could reason that, when the water was cooked, any worms that were present came apart and then became nullified in the water. [Nullification is possible, once the worm is not a complete creature.] Accordingly, the water and any food cooked in it would be permitted. *Chochmas Adam* explains, however, that since the presence of worms is a *certainty* while their decomposition is merely a *possibility,* we cannot act leniently.

65. In this *se'if,* Kitzur refers not only to water that comes from rivers and wells, but also to standing water, such as rainwater that has been collected in cisterns. The worms that develop in this water are not prohibited until they emerge from the water, but they can become prohibited through the straining itself. If one uses a strainer with holes, perhaps a worm will initially be held back by the strainer, thus emerging from the water and becoming prohibited, but will then manage to work its way through the strainer and re-enter the water (*Chochmas Adam* 38:7; see *Yoreh Deah* 84:4). Kitzur therefore cautions that, when straining any water, one must be certain to use a cloth that will not allow any vermin to pass through.

66. That is, it becomes prohibited specifically after being strained, as Kitzur goes on to explain. [Vinegar, as well as any other liquid, is like standing water, in that vermin that develop in it become prohibited only upon emerging from the liquid (see *Yoreh Deah* ibid.).]

67. [The word אֲפִילוּ, which appears in the text of the Lemberg edition, seems to have been inserted erroneously, perhaps due to the similar wording found in the previous *se'if.*]

וְעַל יְדֵי הַסִּינּוּן אִיכָּא לְמֵיחַשׁ שֶׁמָּא יִפְרוֹשׁ עַל הַמְסַנֶּנֶת וְאַחַר כָּךְ יַחֲזוֹר[68]. וְהַמֻּבְחָר לְהַרְתִּיחַ תְּחִלָּה אֶת הַחוֹמֶץ וּלְסַנְּנוֹ אַחַר כָּךְ, דְּמֵאַחַר שֶׁהַתּוֹלָע מֵת עַל יְדֵי הָרְתִיחָה שׁוּב לֹא יַעֲבוֹר בְּסִינּוּן[69].

לד. תּוֹלָעִים הַגְּדֵלִים בְּפֵירוֹת בְּעוֹדָם בִּמְחוּבָּר אֲסוּרִין, אַף עַל פִּי שֶׁלֹּא פֵּירְשׁוּ מִמָּקוֹם לְמָקוֹם[70]. וְלִפְעָמִים נִמְצָא בִּפְרִי, וְכֵן בְּפוֹלִין וְקִטְנִיּוֹת, כְּמִין נְקוּדָּה שְׁחוֹרָה וְהוּא מָקוֹם שֶׁהִתְחִיל הַתּוֹלַעַה לְהִתְרַקֵּם, וְצָרִיךְ לִיטְּלוֹ מִשָּׁם בָּעוֹמֶק, דְּאָסוּר כְּמוֹ הַתּוֹלַעַת עַצְמָהּ[71].

---

it emerges from the liquid, וְעַל יְדֵי הַסִּינּוּן — **and as a result of straining** אִיכָּא לְמֵיחַשׁ — **there is a concern** שֶׁמָּא יִפְרוֹשׁ עַל הַמְסַנֶּנֶת — that **perhaps** a worm **will emerge** from the liquid **onto the strainer** וְאַחַר כָּךְ יַחֲזוֹר — **and then return** into the liquid.[68] וְהַמֻּבְחָר — If one desires to strain vinegar, **the best** option is לְהַרְתִּיחַ תְּחִלָּה אֶת הַחוֹמֶץ — **to first boil up the vinegar,** וּלְסַנְּנוֹ אַחַר כָּךְ — **and to strain it afterward,** דְּמֵאַחַר שֶׁהַתּוֹלָע מֵת עַל יְדֵי הָרְתִיחָה — **for after the worm has died through the boiling,** שׁוּב לֹא יַעֲבוֹר בְּסִינּוּן — **it will no longer pass through** the cloth **while being strained.**[69]

§34 תּוֹלָעִים הַגְּדֵלִים בְּפֵירוֹת בְּעוֹדָם בִּמְחוּבָּר — **Worms that develop in fruits while they are still connected** to the tree אֲסוּרִין — **are prohibited,** אַף עַל פִּי שֶׁלֹּא פֵּירְשׁוּ מִמָּקוֹם לְמָקוֹם — **even though they have not emerged from** their original **location** and crept **to** another **location.**[70] וְלִפְעָמִים נִמְצָא בִּפְרִי — Moreover, **sometimes there is found in fruit,** וְכֵן בְּפוֹלִין וְקִטְנִיּוֹת — **as well as in beans and legumes,** כְּמִין נְקוּדָּה שְׁחוֹרָה — **a type of black spot** וְהוּא מָקוֹם שֶׁהִתְחִיל הַתּוֹלַעַה לְהִתְרַקֵּם — **that is** actually **the location at which a worm has begun to take form.** וְצָרִיךְ לִיטְּלוֹ מִשָּׁם בָּעוֹמֶק — **One must remove it from there,** cutting **to the** full **depth** to which it penetrated the fruit, דְּאָסוּר כְּמוֹ הַתּוֹלַעַת עַצְמָהּ — **for it is prohibited just like an actual worm.**[71]

---

68. Thus, even if the vinegar contained worms, it was permitted before it was strained, and becomes prohibited after the straining because of the worms that may have emerged and then re-entered it (see *Chochmas Adam* 38:8). It is therefore better to leave vinegar unstrained than to strain it.

69. This option can be used for vinegar that was mistakenly strained as well. Although it might contain prohibited worms that emerged from the liquid and returned to it, the vinegar can be boiled and then strained again, in order to remove the worms.

70. The Torah prohibits consumption of creeping creatures (see *Vayikra* 11:41). This includes a worm that has crept on the ground or on any other surface. If a worm developed in a fruit after it became detached from the tree, and the worm has not yet emerged from the fruit, it is not prohibited, for this worm never crept upon the ground or upon any surface other than the fruit in which it originated (see *Yoreh Deah* 84:3). [Similarly, worms that develop in fish or cheese do not become prohibited until they emerge and creep upon a surface other than that in which they developed. See *se'ifim* 43-44.] However, if the worm developed in a fruit that is still attached to the tree, it is prohibited despite never having crept upon the ground, for the fruit itself is viewed as an extension of the ground to which it is connected (see *Chullin* 67a-b).

71. Although this worm is still at too early a stage in its development for it to actually creep, it is prohibited, since it is of a species that creeps, and it developed in an attached fruit, which is tantamount to the ground itself (Responsa of *Rashba* §275; see *Rama, Yoreh Deah* 84:6).

לה. כָּל[72] פְּרִי שֶׁדַּרְכּוֹ לְהַתְלִיעַ בְּעוֹדוֹ מְחוּבָּר, אִם עָבְרוּ עָלָיו י״ב חוֹדֶשׁ מִשֶּׁנִּתְלַשׁ, מוּתָּר, כִּי כָּל בְּרִיָּה שֶׁאֵין בּוֹ עֶצֶם אֵינוֹ מִתְקַיֵּים י״ב חוֹדֶשׁ, וּכְבָר נַעֲשָׂה כְּעַפְרָא בְּעָלְמָא. וּמִשּׁוּם חֲשָׁשׁ שֶׁמָּא הִתְלִיעוּ בְּתָלוּשׁ צְרִיכִין לְבָדְקָן וּלְהַשְׁלִיךְ הַתּוֹלָעִים וְהַיַּבְחוּשִׁין שֶׁנִּמְצְאוּ בַּחוּץ[73]. וְאַחַר[74] כָּךְ יִתְּנֵם לְמַיִם צוֹנְנִים וִיעָרְבֵן יָפֶה יָפֶה וְיַעֲלוּ הַתּוֹלָעִים וְהַמְנוּקָּבִים לְמַעְלָה וְיַשְׁלִיכֵם. וְאַחַר כָּךְ יִתְּנֵם בְּמַיִם רוֹתְחִין, שֶׁאִם נִשְׁאַר בּוֹ תּוֹלַעַת, יָמוּת מִיָּד וְלֹא יִפְרוֹשׁ[75]. וְאֵין לִסְמוֹךְ עַל זֶה רַק בְּקִטְנִיּוֹת

§35 Foods in which infestation is common must be examined for insects before they may be eaten. Fruits that commonly develop worms while attached to the tree must be opened and examined internally.[72] Kitzur discusses details of this law:

כָּל פְּרִי שֶׁדַּרְכּוֹ לְהַתְלִיעַ בְּעוֹדוֹ מְחוּבָּר — With respect to **any fruit that commonly develops worms while still attached** to the tree, **אִם עָבְרוּ עָלָיו י״ב חוֹדֶשׁ מִשֶּׁנִּתְלַשׁ** — **if twelve months have passed since it was picked, מוּתָּר** — **it is permitted** without internal inspection. **כִּי כָּל בְּרִיָּה שֶׁאֵין בּוֹ עֶצֶם אֵינוֹ מִתְקַיֵּים י״ב חוֹדֶשׁ** — This is **because any creature that has no bones,** such as a worm, **cannot survive for twelve months, וּכְבָר נַעֲשָׂה כְּעַפְרָא בְּעָלְמָא** — **and** thus, even if there was a worm in the fruit while it was attached, one may assume that **it has already** disintegrated and **become like mere dust. וּמִשּׁוּם חֲשָׁשׁ שֶׁמָּא הִתְלִיעוּ בְּתָלוּשׁ** — However, **due to the concern that** the fruits **became wormy after being picked, צְרִיכִין לְבָדְקָן** — **one must examine them** externally **וּלְהַשְׁלִיךְ הַתּוֹלָעִים וְהַיַּבְחוּשִׁין שֶׁנִּמְצְאוּ בַּחוּץ** — **and discard the worms and gnats that are found on the outside** of the fruits.[73]

The preceding suffices for one who intends to eat the fruits raw. For one who intends to cook them, an additional procedure is required:[74]

וְאַחַר כָּךְ יִתְּנֵם לְמַיִם צוֹנְנִים וִיעָרְבֵן יָפֶה יָפֶה — **One should then place** the fruits **into cool water and agitate them thoroughly, וְיַעֲלוּ הַתּוֹלָעִים וְהַמְנוּקָּבִים לְמַעְלָה וְיַשְׁלִיכֵם** — so that **the worms and the** worm-**punctured** fruits **will rise** to the surface, **and he will discard them. וְאַחַר כָּךְ יִתְּנֵם בְּמַיִם רוֹתְחִין** — **Then, one should place them** (the remaining fruits) **into boiling water, שֶׁאִם נִשְׁאַר בּוֹ תּוֹלַעַת** — **so that if a worm has remained in one** of them, **יָמוּת מִיָּד וְלֹא יִפְרוֹשׁ** — **it will die immediately, without emerging** from the fruit.[75] **וְאֵין לִסְמוֹךְ עַל זֶה רַק בְּקִטְנִיּוֹת**

---

72. See *Shulchan Aruch, Yoreh Deah* 84:8 with *Shach* §23.

73. Fruits that have a tendency to become infested while still upon the tree are more likely to develop worms after they are picked. Thus, even when there is no concern of internal infestation, they require external examination (*Aruch HaShulchan* 84:68). When there is no concern for infestation at all, no examination is required (*Shach* ibid.).

74. We have learned that worms that form inside fruits after they became detached are not forbidden until they emerge from the fruit and crawl. Thus, once the worms on the surface have been discarded, one may eat the fruits raw, since any internal worm is permitted. If the fruits are cooked, however, we must consider the possibility that before being cooked, a worm may emerge and crawl on the water, or on the surface of the fruit or pot, and then become mixed with the cooking fruit. One must therefore employ the following procedure, to eliminate any worm that may be inside a fruit before cooking (see *Shulchan Aruch, Yoreh Deah* 84:8 with *Beur HaGra* §24).

75. Placing the fruits into boiling water ensures that any remaining worms will be killed before they have a chance to emerge from the fruits and crawl. Nevertheless, we do not rely on boiling alone to eliminate the worms, because it is not guaranteed to kill them before they can emerge from the fruit and crawl. Only after the majority of the worms have been removed

וַעֲדָשִׁים וְכַדּוֹמֶה[76], וְדַוְקָא לְאַחַר י״ב חוֹדֶשׁ[77].

לו. כָּל הַפֵּירוֹת שֶׁצְּרִיכִין בְּדִיקָה צָרִיךְ לִפְתּוֹחַ כָּל אַחַת וְאַחַת וּלְהַשְׁלִיךְ אֶת הַגַּרְעִינִין לְמַעַן יוּכַל לְבָדְקָן יָפֶה יָפֶה. וּצְרִיכִין לִיזָּהֵר בָּזֶה מְאוֹד כְּשֶׁמְּרַקְּחִין פֵּירוֹת בִּדְבַשׁ וְצוּקֶר. וְכֵן כְּשֶׁעוֹשִׂין לעקפאר[78]. וְלָא מְהַנֵּי מַה שֶּׁבָּדַק מִקְצָתָן, וַאֲפִילוּ בָּדַק אֶת הָרוֹב, לָא מְהַנֵּי אֶלָּא צָרִיךְ לִבְדּוֹק כָּל פְּרִי וּפְרִי[79].

לז. לִפְעָמִים נִמְצָא בְּקֶמַח וְכַיּוֹצֵא בּוֹ תּוֹלָעִים גְּדוֹלִים וְסַגֵּי כְּשֶׁמְּנַפֶּה אוֹתוֹ בְּנָפָה שֶׁאֵין הַתּוֹלָעִים עוֹבְרִים. אֲבָל אִם נִמְצְאוּ בּוֹ מילבן לָא מְהַנֵּי הַנָּפָה.

וַעֲדָשִׁים וְכַדּוֹמֶה — However, **one should not rely on this** procedure, **except with legumes, lentils, and the like,** which have no pits,[76] **וְדַוְקָא לְאַחַר י״ב חוֹדֶשׁ** — **and only after twelve months** have passed from when the fruit was picked.[77]

§36 **כָּל הַפֵּירוֹת שֶׁצְּרִיכִין בְּדִיקָה** — With **all fruits that require** internal **examination, צָרִיךְ לִפְתּוֹחַ כָּל אַחַת וְאַחַת** — **one must open each and every one** of them **וּלְהַשְׁלִיךְ אֶת הַגַּרְעִינִין** — **and discard the pits, לְמַעַן יוּכַל לְבָדְקָן יָפֶה יָפֶה** — **in order that he be able to examine them very well. וּצְרִיכִין לִיזָּהֵר בָּזֶה מְאוֹד** — **One must be very careful about this** requirement **כְּשֶׁמְּרַקְּחִין פֵּירוֹת בִּדְבַשׁ וְצוּקֶר** — **when preserving fruit in honey and sugar, וְכֵן כְּשֶׁעוֹשִׂין לעקפאר** — **as well as when making** ***lekvar*** (prune jam).[78] **וְלָא מְהַנֵּי מַה שֶּׁבָּדַק מִקְצָתָן** — When there is a batch of fruit that requires examination, **it does not suffice to examine some of them, וַאֲפִילוּ בָּדַק אֶת הָרוֹב** — **and even** if **one examined the majority** of the batch and found it insect-free, **לָא מְהַנֵּי** — **this does not suffice** to permit the remainder; **אֶלָּא צָרִיךְ לִבְדּוֹק כָּל פְּרִי וּפְרִי** — **rather, one must examine each and every** individual **fruit.**[79]

§37 **לִפְעָמִים נִמְצָא בְּקֶמַח וְכַיּוֹצֵא בּוֹ תּוֹלָעִים גְּדוֹלִים** — **Sometimes, large worms are discovered in flour or the like, וְסַגֵּי כְּשֶׁמְּנַפֶּה אוֹתוֹ בְּנָפָה** — **and** in order to remove them, **it is sufficient to sift it through a sieve, שֶׁאֵין הַתּוֹלָעִים עוֹבְרִים** — **as the worms cannot pass through. אֲבָל אִם נִמְצְאוּ בּוֹ מילבן** — **However, if mites are discovered in it, לָא מְהַנֵּי הַנָּפָה** — **sifting does not suffice,** since mites can pass through the sieve.

---

through the soaking in cold water do we rely on the boiling to eliminate the few worms that may remain (*Shach* ibid. §24).

76. Although worms that develop inside fruit are not prohibited until they emerge, if a worm develops in the pit of a fruit and then comes out of the pit onto the pit's surface, it is considered as having emerged, and becomes prohibited. Thus, the described method of cleansing a fruit would not suffice for fruits that contain pits, since a worm may already have "emerged" inside the fruit before being placed in the boiling water. That worm is prohibited even though it never left the fruit. This method, therefore, is effective only for legumes or lentils, which have no pits (*Maharshal,* cited by *Shach* ibid. §27). *Shach,* however, disagrees and rules that this procedure may be relied upon for all fruits.

77. Even if a fruit has no pit, if it is less than twelve months old, it may contain a worm that developed while it was still attached to the tree. Such a worm is forbidden even though it never emerged from the fruit (see note 70). Therefore, the boiling procedure is ineffective (see *Shach* 84:25).

If one cooked infested fruit without following the procedure described here, the cooked product might be forbidden even after the fact. See *Shulchan Aruch* 84:8.

78. If there are worm-infested fruits in the jam, the entire batch might become prohibited.

79. Since infestation is common, we do not rely on examination of the majority of the batch (*Rama, Yoreh Deah* 84:8).

וּמִי שֶׁיֵּשׁ לוֹ חִיטִּין מְתוּלָּעִין, יַעֲשֶׂה שְׁאֵלַת חָכָם אֵיךְ יִטְחָנֵם[80].

לח. כָּל דָּבָר שֶׁהִתְלִיעַ, וְהוּא דָּבָר שֶׁאֵין הַדֶּרֶךְ לְבוֹדְקוֹ מִתּוֹלָעִים, אָסוּר לְמָכְרוֹ לְעַכּוּ"ם כְּשֶׁיֵּשׁ לָחוּשׁ שֶׁמָּא יַחֲזוֹר וְיִמְכְּרֶנּוּ לְיִשְׂרָאֵל[81]. וּמוּתָּר לַעֲשׂוֹת מִמֶּנּוּ יֵין שָׂרָף[82]. וְלֹא חַיְישִׁינַן שֶׁמָּא יָבוֹא בוֹ לִידֵי תַקָּלָה לְאוֹכְלוֹ כָּךְ[83], וּבִלְבַד שֶׁלֹּא יַשְׁהֶנּוּ זְמַן רַב[84].

לט. הַרְבֵּה מִינֵי יְרָקוֹת שֶׁמּוּחְזָקִין בְּתוֹלָעִים. וְיֵשׁ שֶׁמּוּחְזָקִין בְּמִילְבָן. וּמַה שֶׁהַנָּשִׁים אוֹמְרוֹת שֶׁמְּהַבְהֲבִין אֶת הַיָּרָק בָּאֵשׁ, אֵינוֹ מוֹעִיל[85]. וְיֵשׁ מִינֵי פֵּירוֹת, וְכֵן מִינֵי

וּמִי שֶׁיֵּשׁ לוֹ חִיטִּין מְתוּלָּעִין — One who has wheat kernels that are **infested with worms** **יַעֲשֶׂה שְׁאֵלַת חָכָם אֵיךְ יִטְחָנֵם — must inquire of a halachic authority** regarding **how** he may proceed **to grind them.**[80]

§38 **כָּל דָּבָר שֶׁהִתְלִיעַ, וְהוּא דָּבָר שֶׁאֵין הַדֶּרֶךְ לְבוֹדְקוֹ מִתּוֹלָעִים** — Any food **item that developed worms, but is a** type of **item that** does **not usually** need to be **inspected for worms,** i.e., it is generally insect-free, **אָסוּר לְמָכְרוֹ לְעַכּוּ"ם — may not be sold to an idolater** **כְּשֶׁיֵּשׁ לָחוּשׁ שֶׁמָּא יַחֲזוֹר וְיִמְכְּרֶנּוּ לְיִשְׂרָאֵל — when there is a** basis for **concern that perhaps he will sell it back to a Jew.**[81] **וּמוּתָּר לַעֲשׂוֹת מִמֶּנּוּ יֵין שָׂרָף — One is,** however, **permitted to** keep the food and **make whiskey from it,**[82] **וְלֹא חַיְישִׁינַן שֶׁמָּא יָבוֹא בוֹ לִידֵי תַקָּלָה — and we are not concerned** that **perhaps this will lead him to a pitfall,** **לְאוֹכְלוֹ כָּךְ** — in **which he** or a member of his household **will eat it as is** instead of making whiskey from it.[83] **וּבִלְבַד שֶׁלֹּא יַשְׁהֶנּוּ זְמַן רַב — But** this permit is **subject to the qualification that one may not retain it for a long** period of **time.**[84]

§39 **הַרְבֵּה מִינֵי יְרָקוֹת שֶׁמּוּחְזָקִין בְּתוֹלָעִים — Many types of vegetables are commonly** infested **with worms,** **וְיֵשׁ שֶׁמּוּחְזָקִין בְּמִילְבָן — and there are some that are commonly** infested **with mites.** **וּמַה שֶׁהַנָּשִׁים אוֹמְרוֹת שֶׁמְּהַבְהֲבִין אֶת הַיָּרָק בָּאֵשׁ — And that which the women say, that they singe the vegetables in fire** and this rids them of their infestation, **אֵינוֹ מוֹעִיל — is not effective.** Rather, these species must be examined before consumption.[85] **וְיֵשׁ מִינֵי פֵּירוֹת, וְכֵן מִינֵי**

---

80. If the wheat is heavily infested, it should not be used (*Shach* ibid. §39). If it is mildly infested, grinding is permitted under certain conditions (see *Shulchan Aruch* 84:14, with *Shach* §40).

81. Since the Jew would not expect the item to be infested, he might unsuspectingly eat it without inspection and consume the vermin. To protect the buyer from this unwitting transgression, one must avoid selling it to an idolater if he might sell it back to a Jew (see *Taz, Yoreh Deah* 84:9). Generally, this means that one may not sell the idolater a large amount of the product, which he might sell, but one may sell him a small amount that is suitable for personal use (*Shach* ibid. §17).

82. Since the whiskey will contain only the taste of the grain, and not the actual kernels, it can be made even from kernels that are infested with worms. For elaboration of the reason, see *Taz* ibid.

83. Although we prohibit the sale of this item to an idolater for fear that it might be consumed by an unwitting Jew who does not expect it to be infested, we need not prohibit the owner from retaining it for whiskey for the same reason. Since the current owner is aware of its infestation, he will certainly not allow it to be eaten by a Jew. [See, however, *Taz* (ibid.), who prohibits it on account of this concern.]

84. Rather, one must use it for whiskey soon, lest the infestation be forgotten and the food be eaten by a Jew.

85. *Chochmas Adam* 38:15. Nowadays, many

יְרָקוֹת, שֶׁמּוּחְזָקִין כָּל כָּךְ בְּתוֹלָעִים עַד שֶׁכִּמְעַט אִי אֶפְשַׁר לְבָדְקָן. וְרָאוּי לְכָל יְרֵא שָׁמַיִם שֶׁלֹּא לְאָכְלָן כְּלָל. וְיֵשׁ מִינֵי פֵּירוֹת שֶׁהַגַּרְעִינִין מוּחְזָקִים בְּתוֹלָעִים וְאָסוּר לְאָכְלוֹ[86]**.**

מ. בְּאֱגוֹזִים שְׁכִיחִים מְאוֹד מִילְבִן. וְהַמִּבְחָן לָזֶה: כְּשֶׁלּוֹקְחִין אֶת הָאוֹכֶל מִתּוֹךְ הַקְּלִיפָּה וּמַכִּין בַּקְּלִיפָּה עַל אֵיזֶה מָקוֹם חַם קְצָת, יוֹצְאִין מִילְבִן שֶׁנִּשְׁאֲרוּ בְּתוֹךְ הַקְּלִיפָּה. וּצְרִיכִין לִיזָּהֵר בָּזֶה מְאוֹד.

מא. לִפְעָמִים נִמְצָא בְּפֵירוֹת מְרוּקָּחִים בִּדְבַשׁ וְצוּקֶער שֶׁיֵּשׁ לְמַעְלָה סָבִיב הַכְּלִי מִילְבִן, יְנַקּוּ אוֹתוֹ הֵיטֵב, וְיִקְחוּ קְצָת גַּם מִן הַמַּאֲכָל עַד שֶׁיְּהֵא בָרוּר שֶׁלֹּא נִשְׁאַר בְּתוֹךְ הַמַּאֲכָל[87]**.**

יְרָקוֹת — Moreover, **there are some types of fruit, as well as some types of vegetables, שֶׁמּוּחְזָקִין כָּל כָּךְ בְּתוֹלָעִים — that are commonly so** infested **with** worms and mites **עַד שֶׁכִּמְעַט אִי אֶפְשַׁר לְבָדְקָן — that it is almost impossible to examine them** properly and fully rid them of their infestation. **וְרָאוּי לְכָל יְרֵא שָׁמַיִם שֶׁלֹּא לְאָכְלָן כְּלָל — It is appropriate for every God-fearing** person **to avoid eating them entirely. וְיֵשׁ מִינֵי פֵּירוֹת שֶׁהַגַּרְעִינִין מוּחְזָקִים בְּתוֹלָעִים — There also are** some **types of fruit whose pits are commonly** infested **with worms, וְאָסוּר לְאָכְלוֹ — and it is prohibited to eat them** (i.e., the pits).[86]

§40 **בְּאֱגוֹזִים שְׁכִיחִים מְאוֹד מִילְבִן — It is very common for nuts** to be infested with **mites, וְהַמִּבְחָן לָזֶה — and the** way to **determine** the presence **of this** infestation is as follows: **כְּשֶׁלּוֹקְחִין אֶת הָאוֹכֶל מִתּוֹךְ הַקְּלִיפָּה — When removing the edible** portion **from the shell, וּמַכִּין בַּקְּלִיפָּה עַל אֵיזֶה מָקוֹם חַם קְצָת — if one strikes the shell against something warm, יוֹצְאִין מִילְבִן שֶׁנִּשְׁאֲרוּ בְּתוֹךְ הַקְּלִיפָּה — mites that have remained in the shell will emerge. וּצְרִיכִין לִיזָּהֵר בָּזֶה מְאוֹד — One must be very careful about this** infestation.

§41 **לִפְעָמִים נִמְצָא בְּפֵירוֹת מְרוּקָּחִים בִּדְבַשׁ וְצוּקֶער — Sometimes, it is found with fruits** that have been **preserved in honey and sugar, שֶׁיֵּשׁ לְמַעְלָה סָבִיב הַכְּלִי מִילְבִן — that there are mites around** the walls of **the container, above** the fruit. **יְנַקּוּ אוֹתוֹ הֵיטֵב** — In this situation, **one must clean it** (i.e., the mouth of the container) **well, וְיִקְחוּ קְצָת גַּם מִן הַמַּאֲכָל — and also remove some of the food, עַד שֶׁיְּהֵא בָרוּר שֶׁלֹּא נִשְׁאַר בְּתוֹךְ הַמַּאֲכָל — until it is certain that no** mites **remain in the food.**[87]

---

species of fruits and vegetables that would usually be infested are bug-free as a result of insecticide use. Ideally, one should still check these species for infestation, since some farmers do not use insecticides. However, in the event that they were not checked and it is no longer possible to do so (such as when they were chopped or grated), one may assume that they were sprayed and are bug-free. Nevertheless, a scrupulous person should refrain from eating these species unless they were checked (*Igros Moshe, Yoreh Deah* I, §35; II, §25; and *Orach Chaim* IV, §91:3).

86. See *Chochmas Adam* 38:18 and *Aruch HaShulchan, Yoreh Deah* 84:63.

87. These mites generally remain on the container, rather than in the fruit. One must remove the upper portion of the fruit only as a precaution against the possibility that some of them descended into the fruit (*Chochmas Adam* 38:23).

מב. חָתַךְ פְּרִי, אוֹ צְנוֹן, בְּסַכִּין וְחָתַךְ גַּם הַתּוֹלַעַת שֶׁהָיָה בָּהֶם, יְקַנֵּחַ אֶת הַסַּכִּין הֵיטֵב, וְגַם מִן הַצְּנוֹן, אוֹ מִן הַפְּרִי, יִקְלוֹף קְצָת בִּמְקוֹם הַחֲתָךְ[88].

מג. בְּתוֹךְ הַדָּגִים נִמְצְאוּ לִפְעָמִים תּוֹלָעִים בַּמּוֹחַ, אוֹ בַּכָּבֵד, אוֹ בַּמֵּעַיִם, אוֹ בַּפֶּה, אוֹ בָּאָזְנַיִם[89], וּבִפְרָט בְּדָג הַנִּקְרָא העכט יֵשׁ בּוֹ תּוֹלָעִים דַּקִּים וַאֲרוּכִּים. וּבְמָקוֹם הַשְּׁכִיחַ, צְרִיכִין בְּדִיקָה. וְכֵן בְּהערינג שְׁכִיחַ בְּתוֹךְ הֶחָלָב תּוֹלָעִים דַּקִּים וּצְרִיכִין בְּדִיקָה. וְיֵשׁ מְקוֹמוֹת שֶׁיֵּשׁ עַל הַדָּגִים מִבַּחוּץ אֵצֶל הַסְּנַפִּירִין, וְגַם עַל הַסְּנַפִּירִין, וּבְתוֹךְ הַפֶּה וַאֲחוֹרֵי הָאָזְנַיִם שְׁרָצִים קְטַנִּים מְאוֹד וְהֵם עֲגוּלִים כַּעֲדָשָׁה. וּצְרִיכִין לִבְדוֹק שָׁם וּלְגָרְרָן הֵיטֵב.

---

§42 **חָתַךְ פְּרִי, אוֹ צְנוֹן, בְּסַכִּין — If one cut a fruit or a radish with a knife,** **וְחָתַךְ גַּם הַתּוֹלַעַת שֶׁהָיָה בָּהֶם — and** while doing so **also cut through a worm that was inside them,** **יְקַנֵּחַ אֶת הַסַּכִּין הֵיטֵב — one must wipe the knife off well,** **וְגַם מִן הַצְּנוֹן, אוֹ מִן הַפְּרִי, יִקְלוֹף קְצָת בִּמְקוֹם הַחֲתָךְ — and also peel off a bit of the radish or fruit at the place where it was cut.**[88]

§43 **בְּתוֹךְ הַדָּגִים נִמְצְאוּ לִפְעָמִים תּוֹלָעִים — Sometimes, worms are found in fish,** **בַּמּוֹחַ, אוֹ בַּכָּבֵד, אוֹ בַּמֵּעַיִם, אוֹ בַּפֶּה, אוֹ בָּאָזְנַיִם — in the brain, liver, intestines, mouth, or gills.**[89] **וּבִפְרָט בְּדָג הַנִּקְרָא העכט — Specifically, in the fish called** *hecht* (pike), **יֵשׁ בּוֹ תּוֹלָעִים דַּקִּים וַאֲרוּכִּים — there are** sometimes **long tiny worms.** **וּבְמָקוֹם הַשְּׁכִיחַ, צְרִיכִין בְּדִיקָה — Where this is common, they** (i.e., the fish) **must be examined.** **וְכֵן בְּהערינג שְׁכִיחַ בְּתוֹךְ הֶחָלָב תּוֹלָעִים דַּקִּים — Similarly, it is common with herring** that **in the milky liquid** there are **tiny worms,** **וּצְרִיכִין בְּדִיקָה — and they must** therefore **be examined.** **וְיֵשׁ מְקוֹמוֹת — There are also places** **שֶׁיֵּשׁ עַל הַדָּגִים מִבַּחוּץ אֵצֶל הַסְּנַפִּירִין — where the fish have, on their exterior, near the fins,** **וְגַם עַל הַסְּנַפִּירִין, וּבְתוֹךְ הַפֶּה וַאֲחוֹרֵי הָאָזְנַיִם — and also on the fins, in the mouth, and behind the gills,** **שְׁרָצִים קְטַנִּים מְאוֹד — very small insects** **וְהֵם עֲגוּלִים כַּעֲדָשָׁה — that are round like lentils.** **וּצְרִיכִין לִבְדוֹק שָׁם וּלְגָרְרָן הֵיטֵב —** In places where this infestation occurs, **one must examine there** (i.e., these parts of the fish), **and,** if any insects are found, **scrape them off thoroughly.**

---

88. When it cut through the worm, the knife became smeared with its residue, which in turn became smeared upon the fruit as it was cut further. Therefore, one must peel off the surface that was cut, and also clean the knife before it is used again. Ordinarily, if a non-kosher knife is used to cut a sharp food, such as a radish, we refrain from eating the entire food, because (nonkosher) flavor absorbed in a knife spreads through a sharp food (more readily than through a bland food). In the current situation, however, it suffices to peel away the surface that touched the knife (which contains actual residue), because the flavor imparted by the worm is repulsive, and it is not considered significant enough to render the entire food forbidden (*Taz* 96:13, *Chochmas Adam* 38:27).

89. Worms that develop in fish are permitted, as long as they have not emerged. Any worms found in the flesh of a fish are presumed to have developed within the fish and are permitted. However, the worms found in the organs listed here may have come from the water and found their way inside the fish; they are therefore prohibited. (*Shulchan Aruch, Yoreh Deah* 84:16; *Chochmas Adam* 38:28).

90. If something is repulsive to most people,

מד. תּוֹלָעִים הַנִּמְצָאִים בִּגְבִינָה — אִם אֵינָן נִמְאָסִין עָלָיו, מוּתָּרִין[90], כָּל זְמַן שֶׁלֹּא פֵּירְשׁוּ לְגַמְרֵי[91].

מה. הַרְבֵּה אַזְהָרוֹת הִזְהִירָה הַתּוֹרָה בִּשְׁרָצִים, וְעוֹבְרִין עֲלֵיהֶן בְּכַמָּה לָאוִין, וּמְטַמְּאִין אֶת הַנֶּפֶשׁ כִּדְכְתִיב (ויקרא יא, מג) "וְנִטְמֵתֶם בָּם". וְלָכֵן צָרִיךְ הָאָדָם לִיזָּהֵר בִּמְאוֹד מְאוֹד שֶׁלֹּא יִכָּשֵׁל בָּהֶם.

מו. הַשּׁוֹאֵל לְמוֹרֶה הוֹרָאָה אֵיזֶה שְׁאֵלָה וַאֲסָרוֹ, אָסוּר לוֹ לִשְׁאוֹל עוֹד לְמוֹרֶה הוֹרָאָה

---

§44 תּוֹלָעִים הַנִּמְצָאִים בִּגְבִינָה — **Worms that are discovered in cheese** אִם אֵינָן נִמְאָסִין עָלָיו, מוּתָּרִין — **are permitted, if one is not disgusted by them.**[90] כָּל זְמַן שֶׁלֹּא פֵּירְשׁוּ לְגַמְרֵי — However, they are permitted only **as long as they have not entirely left** the cheese.[91]

§45 הַרְבֵּה אַזְהָרוֹת הִזְהִירָה הַתּוֹרָה בִּשְׁרָצִים — **The Torah issued many prohibitions regarding** the consumption of **vermin,** וְעוֹבְרִין עֲלֵיהֶן בְּכַמָּה לָאוִין — **and one violates numerous transgressions on account of** eating any of **them.** וּמְטַמְּאִין אֶת הַנֶּפֶשׁ — **Moreover, they contaminate the soul,** כִּדְכְתִיב — **as is written** (*Vayikra* 11:43) regarding the consumption of vermin: "וְנִטְמֵתֶם בָּם" — *lest you become contaminated through them.* וְלָכֵן צָרִיךְ הָאָדָם לִיזָּהֵר בִּמְאוֹד מְאוֹד שֶׁלֹּא יִכָּשֵׁל בָּהֶם — **A person must therefore be extremely vigilant to avoid stumbling by** mistakenly eating any of **them.**

§46 Kitzur concludes the *Siman* with a guideline for one who makes a halachic inquiry:

הַשּׁוֹאֵל לְמוֹרֶה הוֹרָאָה אֵיזֶה שְׁאֵלָה — **One who,** due to an uncertainty regarding the status of a food, **poses the question before a halachic authority,** וַאֲסָרוֹ — **who pronounced** the food **prohibited,** אָסוּר לוֹ לִשְׁאוֹל עוֹד לְמוֹרֶה הוֹרָאָה אַחֵר — **may not pose that question before another halachic authority,** in the hope of a more lenient

---

it is prohibited even to one who is personally not repulsed by it (see above, 33:9, for the details of this prohibition). Apparently, the small worms found in cheese are not considered repulsive to the majority of people. Thus, if one is personally not repulsed by them, he is permitted to eat them (see *Rama* 84:16).

91. This law, that the worms become prohibited when they have entirely left the cheese, is from *Rama* (ibid.), and is the subject of debate among halachic authorities. Some maintain that the worms that develop in cheese are not included in the Biblical prohibition against vermin, and were prohibited by the Sages only to prevent the appearance of wrongdoing (lest one be perceived as consuming forbidden vermin). Thus, when it is obvious that the vermin developed in the cheese, they may be eaten.

According to this view, they do not become prohibited until they are removed from the *dish* containing the cheese. While still in the dish it is obvious that they developed in the cheese, so they are permitted even though they left the cheese itself (see *Shach, Yoreh Deah* 84:46).

Others, however, maintain that vermin that develop in cheese are prohibited Biblically, but only after they left the cheese. Now, while a worm that develops in fruit becomes prohibited even if it emerges onto the surface of the fruit (see note 76), the vermin that develop in cheese do not become prohibited until they leave the cheese entirely. Since the vermin develop on the *surface* of the cheese in the first place, they are not viewed as having "left" the cheese until they have departed it completely.

Thus, according to this view, if a worm is still creeping or even jumping upon the surface of the cheese, it is not prohibited. But once it has crept onto the dish that contains the cheese, it does become prohibited (*Pri Chadash* 84:53, cited by *Pri Megadim* 84:46 and *Chochmas*

אַחֵר, אֶלָּא אִם כֵּן הוֹדִיעוֹ שֶׁכְּבָר הוֹרָה הָרִאשׁוֹן לֶאֱסוֹר[92].

ruling, **אֶלָּא אִם כֵּן הוֹדִיעוֹ שֶׁכְּבָר הוֹרָה הָרִאשׁוֹן לֶאֱסוֹר** — **unless he notifies** the second halachic authority **that the first** halachic authority **already ruled** and **prohibited** the food.[92]

Adam 38:29).

92. When the first halachic authority issued his ruling, the item became prohibited. Even if a second halachic authority later rules leniently, the first ruling stands. However, if the second halachic authority can convince the first one that he erred, and he rescinds his ruling, then the item becomes permitted once again. [Thus, Kitzur permits asking a second authority after notifying him that a ruling was already issued, so that the second authority is aware that the item will remain prohibited unless the previous ruling is retracted.] For a fuller treatment of this subject, see *Rama, Yoreh Deah* 242:31 with *Shach* §54-58 and *Aruch HaShulchan* §60-61.

159 LAWS OF WINE OF IDOLATERS — SIMAN 47:1

סימן מז

הִלְכוֹת סְתָם יֵינָם וְהֶכְשֵׁר הַכֵּלִים מִמֶּנּוּ[1,2]

וּבוֹ כ״ב סְעִיפִים

א. סְתָם יֵינָם[3] בַּזְּמַן הַזֶּה, וְכֵן מַגַּע עוֹבֵד כּוֹכָבִים בְּיַיִן שֶׁלָּנוּ — יֵשׁ אוֹמְרִים דְּאֵינוֹ אָסוּר רַק בִּשְׁתִיָּה, וְלֹא בַהֲנָאָה[4]. וְלָכֵן מוּתָּר לְיִשְׂרָאֵל לִגְבּוֹת בְּחוֹבוֹ סְתָם יֵינָם,

SIMAN 47

THE LAWS OF WINE OF IDOLATERS, AND RENDERING UTENSILS USED WITH SUCH WINE FIT FOR KOSHER USE

CONTAINING 22 *SE'IFIM*

§1 The Prohibition Nowadays / **§2** Therapeutic Bath / **§3** Cooked Wine / **§4** Mixed Into a Cooked food / **§5** Diluted Wine and Raisin Wine / **§6** *Temed* / **§7** Vats of Pressed Grapes / **§8** Peels and Seeds / **§9** If an Idolater Added Water / **§10** Wine Vinegar / **§11** Whiskey / **§12** Tartar / **§13** Indirect Contact / **§14** Shipping Wine / **§15** Producing Kosher Wine / **§16** Utensils Used for Short-term / **§17** Storage Utensils / **§18** Glass Utensils / **§19** Residual Moisture / **§20** Hot Wine / **§21** Winemaking Equipment / **§22** After Twelve Months

Wine poured in idolatrous service becomes יֵין נֶסֶךְ, *nesech wine* (wine of libation), and a Jew is Biblically prohibited from drinking or having any benefit from it (*Avodah Zarah* 29b). As an extension of this prohibition and in order to prevent intermarriage,[1] the Rabbis prohibited drinking or benefiting from *any* wine of idolaters (סְתָם יֵינָם, literally, *their ordinary wine*), or even wine of a Jew that has been touched or poured[2] by an idolater, even if this was not done in service to his deity (see *Shulchan Aruch, Yoreh Deah* 123:1).

§1 **סְתָם יֵינָם** — With regard to the **wine of idolaters,**[3] **בַּזְּמַן הַזֶּה** — **nowadays,** when it is uncommon for them to offer a wine libation to their deities, **וְכֵן מַגַּע עוֹבֵד כּוֹכָבִים בְּיַיִן שֶׁלָּנוּ** — **and so too if an idolater touches our wine** nowadays, **יֵשׁ אוֹמְרִים** — **there are those** authorities **who say** **דְּאֵינוֹ אָסוּר רַק בִּשְׁתִיָּה** — **that it is prohibited only for drinking,** **וְלֹא בַהֲנָאָה** — **and not for benefit.**[4] **וְלָכֵן מוּתָּר לְיִשְׂרָאֵל לִגְבּוֹת בְּחוֹבוֹ סְתָם יֵינָם** — **Therefore, a Jew may accept wine of idolaters**

---

1. See *Avodah Zarah* 36b (see also *Shach* and *Taz,* beginning of *Yoreh Deah* §123).

2. There are many variables that must be taken into account regarding wine that has been touched or poured by an idolater; see *Yoreh Deah* §123-§125. A halachic authority must be consulted.

3. Literally, *their ordinary wine;* see introduction to this *Siman.*

4. Even though deriving benefit from an idolater's wine was included in the original prohibition, nevertheless, according to this opinion, wine of the idolater of our time who does not offer wine libations to his deity, is not subject to the full scope of the original prohibition, and is not prohibited for benefit; see *Yoreh Deah* 123:1. [However, the prohibition of *drinking* the wine of an idolater is in no way diminished, and the halachic authorities relate at length

מִפְּנֵי דְּהָוֵי כְּמַצִּיל מִידֵיהֶם[5]. וְהוּא הַדִּין בִּשְׁאָר הֶפְסֵד, כְּגוֹן, אִם עָבַר וְקָנָה. אֲבָל לְכַתְּחִלָּה אָסוּר לִקְנוֹת כְּדֵי לְהִשְׂתַּכֵּר בּוֹ. וְיֵשׁ מְקִילִין גַּם בָּזֶה, וְטוֹב לְהַחֲמִיר[6].

ב. מוּתָּר לַעֲשׂוֹת מֶרְחָץ מִסְּתָם יֵינָם לְחוֹלֶה שֶׁאֵין בּוֹ סַכָּנָה[7].

ג. יַיִן כָּשֵׁר שֶׁנִּתְבַּשֵּׁל, דְּהַיְינוּ שֶׁהִרְתִּיחַ וְנִתְמַעֵט מִמִּדָּתוֹ עַל יְדֵי הָרְתִיחָה[8], אִם נָגַע בּוֹ עַכּוּ״ם מוּתָּר אֲפִילוּ בִּשְׁתִיָּה[9]. אֲבָל יַיִן שֶׁנּוֹתְנִין לְתוֹכוֹ לַעֲנָה

---

as payment of a debt owed to him, מִפְּנֵי דְּהָוֵי כְּמַצִּיל מִידֵיהֶם — **because it is equivalent to rescuing** his debt **from them.**[5] וְהוּא הַדִּין בִּשְׁאָר הֶפְסֵד — **The same applies with regard to** any **other** potential financial **loss;** כְּגוֹן, אִם עָבַר וְקָנָה — **for example, if one transgressed** the prohibition (see below) **and purchased** wine from an idolater, he need not discard the wine, but may benefit from it and sell it to another idolater. אֲבָל לְכַתְּחִלָּה — **But, initially,** אָסוּר לִקְנוֹת כְּדֵי לְהִשְׂתַּכֵּר בּוֹ — **one may not purchase** wine from an idolater **in order to profit from it.** וְיֵשׁ מְקִילִין גַּם בָּזֶה — **There are,** however, **those** authorities **who are lenient in this** matter **as well,** and allow one to initially purchase wine from an idolater in order to profit from it. וְטוֹב לְהַחֲמִיר — **Nevertheless, it is preferable to conduct oneself stringently** and not do business with the wine of idolaters.[6]

§2 מוּתָּר לַעֲשׂוֹת מֶרְחָץ מִסְּתָם יֵינָם — **It is permitted to prepare a** therapeutic **bath using wine of idolaters** לְחוֹלֶה שֶׁאֵין בּוֹ סַכָּנָה — **for an ill person,** even if he **is not in** mortal **danger.**[7]

§3 Not all wine products are subject to the prohibition of wine of an idolater. The *se'ifim* that follow discuss the status of wine that was altered in some manner: יַיִן כָּשֵׁר שֶׁנִּתְבַּשֵּׁל — With regard to **kosher wine that has been cooked** דְּהַיְינוּ שֶׁהִרְתִּיחַ — **(that is, it has been heated** וְנִתְמַעֵט מִמִּדָּתוֹ עַל יְדֵי הָרְתִיחָה — to the extent that it began to evaporate **and has diminished in quantity due to the heating),**[8] אִם נָגַע בּוֹ עַכּוּ״ם — the halachah is that **if an idolater touched it** after it was cooked, מוּתָּר אֲפִילוּ בִּשְׁתִיָּה — **it is permitted even for drinking.**[9] אֲבָל יַיִן שֶׁנּוֹתְנִין לְתוֹכוֹ לַעֲנָה

---

the severe consequences for transgressing this prohibition (see *Chochmas Adam* 75:1).]

5. Since there is a real concern that if one does not accept the wine offered as payment he may never recover his money, one may rely on the opinion that it is permitted to have benefit from it nowadays, and accept the wine in order to sell it to another idolater.

6. See *Kitzur* below, 72:2, who rules that the wine of one who publicly desecrates the Shabbos has the same status as wine of an idolater. Rabbi Moshe Feinstein rules that although the custom is indeed not to drink wine touched by one who desecrates the Shabbos, one may give him wine to drink (*Igros Moshe, Orach Chaim* V, §37:8; see also *Igros Moshe, Orach Chaim* III, §22 and *Yoreh Deah* IV, §58:3).

7. This is permitted because of the more lenient status of today's idolaters (see *Rama, Yoreh Deah* 155:3 with *Shach* §16); see above, note 4. Nevertheless, this is permitted only for one who is ill (*Shach* 155:17). In fact, even one who is ill may not eat or drink such wine, unless his life is in danger (*Rama, Yoreh Deah* 145:3; see *Beur HaGra* there §19).

8. According to Rabbi Moshe Feinstein, once the temperature of the wine has reached 175° F [79.4° C] it is considered "cooked" regarding this law (*Igros Moshe, Yoreh Deah* II, §52 and *Even HaEzer* IV, §108; see also *Yoreh Deah* III, §31, where he states that one can be lenient and consider it cooked once it has reached a temperature of 165° F [73.9° C]).

9. Among the reasons offered for this are: (a) Idol worshipers do not use cooked wine in their

שֶׁקּוֹרִין ווערמוטה[10] — כָּל שֶׁשֵּׁם יַיִן עָלָיו, וְלֹא נִתְבַּשֵּׁל, נֶאֱסַר.

ד. תַּבְשִׁיל שֶׁיַּיִן מְעוֹרָב בּוֹ וְאֵינֶנּוּ נִיכָּר, אֲפִילוּ עֲדַיִין לֹא הִרְתִּיחַ, אֵינוֹ נֶאֱסָר בְּמַגַּע עַכּוּ"ם[11].

ה. יַיִן מָזוּג — אִם יֵשׁ בּוֹ שִׁשָּׁה חֲלָקִים מַיִם, בָּטֵל הַיַּיִן[12] וְאֵינוֹ נֶאֱסָר בְּמַגַּע עַכּוּ"ם. אֲבָל יַיִן צִמּוּקִין, דְּהַיְינוּ שֶׁנָּתַן מַיִם עַל הַצִּמּוּקִים, הֲרֵי זֶה כְּיַיִן גָּמוּר — עַיֵּין לְקַמָּן סוֹף סִימָן נ"ג[13].

ו. הַתֶּמֶד, דְּהַיְינוּ מַיִם שֶׁנּוֹתְנִים עַל הַחַרְצַנִּים אוֹ עַל הַשְּׁמָרִים[14] — כֹּל שֶׁהוּא מְשׁוּבָּח לִשְׁתִיָּה, אֵין לְהַתִּירוֹ אִם נָגַע בּוֹ עַכּוּ"ם[15].

שֶׁקּוֹרִין ווערמוטה — But wine to which the wormwood herb[10] was added, (which is called "vermouth") **כָּל שֶׁשֵּׁם יַיִן עָלָיו — as long as it is** still **called "wine," וְלֹא נִתְבַּשֵּׁל — and has not been cooked, נֶאֱסַר — is prohibited** if an idolater touches it, even though its taste has changed.

§4 **תַּבְשִׁיל** — Regarding **a food** that is being **cooked שֶׁיַּיִן מְעוֹרָב בּוֹ — that has wine mixed into it, וְאֵינֶנּוּ נִיכָּר — and** the wine **is not discernible, אֲפִילוּ עֲדַיִין לֹא הִרְתִּיחַ** — the halachah is that **even if it has not yet heated up, אֵינוֹ נֶאֱסָר בְּמַגַּע עַכּוּ"ם — it does not become prohibited as a result of an idolater touching it.**[11]

§5 **יַיִן מָזוּג** — The halachah regarding **diluted wine** is that **אִם יֵשׁ בּוֹ שִׁשָּׁה חֲלָקִים מַיִם— if it has** a ratio of **six parts water** to one part wine, **בָּטֵל הַיַּיִן — the wine is nullified,**[12] **וְאֵינוֹ נֶאֱסָר בְּמַגַּע עַכּוּ"ם — and is not prohibited through the contact of an idolater. אֲבָל יַיִן צִמּוּקִין — But raisin wine דְּהַיְינוּ שֶׁנָּתַן מַיִם עַל הַצִּמּוּקִים — that is** made by **pouring water onto raisins** and allowing them to soak in it **הֲרֵי זֶה כְּיַיִן גָּמוּר — is considered regular wine; עַיֵּין לְקַמָּן סוֹף סִימָן נ"ג — see below, end of *Siman* 53.**[13]

§6 **הַתֶּמֶד** — Regarding ***temed,*** **דְּהַיְינוּ מַיִם שֶׁנּוֹתְנִים עַל הַחַרְצַנִּים אוֹ עַל הַשְּׁמָרִים — that is, water that is poured onto grape seeds or lees**[14] and left to soak, **כֹּל שֶׁהוּא מְשׁוּבָּח לִשְׁתִיָּה** — the halachah is that **as long as it is of drinking quality, אֵין לְהַתִּירוֹ אִם נָגַע בּוֹ עַכּוּ"ם — it is not to be permitted if an idolater touched it.**[15]

---

religious rites (*Rambam, Hil. Maachalos Asuros* 11:9), and (b) it was uncommon for wine to be cooked, and, as a rule, Rabbinic decrees do not apply to uncommon cases (*Rosh, Avodah Zarah* 2:13).

10. The wormwood plant yields a bitter extract that is used to flavor certain wines, significantly altering their taste.

11. If , however, the actual wine is discernible (for example, it remained floating on the top of the mixture), it is prohibited if an idolater touches it (*Rama* 123:5).

12. I.e., its presence is not significant in this mixture, and is not halachically classified as "wine" with regard to this halachah. This is the case even if the taste of wine is discernible (see *Rama, Yoreh Deah* 123:8; *Mishnah Berurah* 204:33; and *Igros Moshe, Yoreh Deah* I, §63).

13. There, Kitzur discusses the particulars of this type of wine with regard to the laws of blessings.

14. Lees are the sediment that is found when an alcoholic beverage is fermented.

15. Although *temed* must fill certain specific criteria in order to be considered wine with regard to reciting the blessing of *borei pri hagafen* [*Who creates the fruit of the vine*] and other laws, nevertheless, as long as it is fit for drinking, it is not to be permitted if an idolater touched it, since it can be mistaken for actual wine (*Yoreh Deah* 123:9).

ז. עֲנָבִים דְּרוּכוֹת בְּגִיגִית — כֵּיוָן שֶׁנִּמְשַׁךְ מִמֶּנּוּ אֲפִילוּ מְעַט[16], אוֹ שֶׁשָּׁאַב מִמֶּנּוּ יַיִן בִּכְלִי, נִקְרָא הַכֹּל יַיִן וְנֶאֱסָר בְּמַגַּע עכו״ם, אֲפִילוּ לֹא נָגַע אֶלָּא בַּחַרְצַנִּים וּבַזָּגִים[17]. וְלָכֵן גִּיגִיּוֹת עֲנָבִים דְּרוּכוֹת עוֹמְדוֹת בְּבֵית עכו״ם יֵשׁ לֶאֱסוֹר שֶׁמָּא הִמְשִׁיךְ מִמֶּנָּה. וְאָסוּר לִדְרוֹךְ עַל יְדֵי עכו״ם, אֲפִילוּ בְּגִיגִית פְּקוּקָה[18].

ח. יֵשׁ לְהִזָּהֵר מִלְּהוֹצִיא אֶת הַחַרְצַנִּים וְהַזָּגִים מִן הַגִּתּוֹת עַל יְדֵי עכו״ם, אֲפִילוּ לְאַחַר שֶׁהוֹצִיאוּ מֵהֶם יַיִן רִאשׁוֹן וְשֵׁנִי, כִּי שֶׁמָּא יֵשׁ עֲלֵיהֶם עוֹד טוֹפַח יַיִן[19].

---

§7 In the winemaking process, the juice of the grape is extracted by pressing the grapes on the inclined floor of the treading basin of a winepress or in a vat, which has an opening that can be unplugged to allow the juice from the pressed grapes to flow out (see *Yoreh Deah* 123:17 and *Taz* §14). This *se'if* defines the point at which the juice in a vat is considered "wine," and therefore prohibited if touched by an idolater:

עֲנָבִים דְּרוּכוֹת בְּגִיגִית — With regard to **grapes that are pressed in a vat,** **כֵּיוָן שֶׁנִּמְשַׁךְ מִמֶּנּוּ אֲפִילוּ מְעַט** — the rule is that **once even a small amount** of wine **flowed forth from** the vat as a result of the pressing,[16] **אוֹ שֶׁשָּׁאַב מִמֶּנּוּ יַיִן בִּכְלִי** — **or,** even if it did not flow, but **one drew wine from it with a utensil,** **נִקְרָא הַכֹּל יַיִן** — **all** the liquid in the vat **is considered wine,** **וְנֶאֱסָר בְּמַגַּע עכו״ם** — **and becomes prohibited through the contact of an idolater,** **אֲפִילוּ לֹא נָגַע אֶלָּא בַּחַרְצַנִּים וּבַזָּגִים** — **even if he only touched the peels and seeds** of the grapes.[17] **וְלָכֵן** — **Therefore,** **גִּיגִיּוֹת עֲנָבִים דְּרוּכוֹת** — **vats of pressed grapes** **עוֹמְדוֹת בְּבֵית עכו״ם** — that are **standing in the house of an idolater** **יֵשׁ לֶאֱסוֹר** — **are to be** deemed **prohibited,** **שֶׁמָּא הִמְשִׁיךְ מִמֶּנָּה** — **out of concern that** the idolater **may have drawn** wine **from** the vat, thus conferring upon the liquid the status of wine, causing it to become prohibited.

וְאָסוּר לִדְרוֹךְ עַל יְדֵי עכו״ם — **It is prohibited to have** the grapes **pressed by an idolater,** **אֲפִילוּ בְּגִיגִית פְּקוּקָה** — **even in a plugged vat.**[18]

§8 **יֵשׁ לְהִזָּהֵר מִלְּהוֹצִיא אֶת הַחַרְצַנִּים וְהַזָּגִים מִן הַגִּתּוֹת עַל יְדֵי עכו״ם** — **One should be careful not to have an idolater remove the peels and seeds from the winepresses** **אֲפִילוּ לְאַחַר שֶׁהוֹצִיאוּ מֵהֶם יַיִן רִאשׁוֹן וְשֵׁנִי** — **even after the wine of the first and second** pressings **was extracted from them,** **כִּי שֶׁמָּא יֵשׁ עֲלֵיהֶם עוֹד טוֹפַח יַיִן** — **out of concern that there may still be moisture of wine on them.**[19]

---

16. That is, by way of the opening in the vat, through which the juice flows out. See introduction to this *se'if.* [With regard to a winepress, see *Yoreh Deah* 123:17 and *Chochmas Adam* 76:2.]

17. The moisture on the peels and seeds becomes prohibited (see below, *se'if* 19), and prohibits the wine (see *Yoreh Deah* 123:17 with *Shach* §32; *Chochmas Adam* 76:2).

18. When the vat is plugged the juice cannot flow from it, and it will therefore not attain the halachic status of "wine" throughout the process. Even so, one may not have an idolater press it, because if that were allowed, one may come to permit an idolater to press the grapes even after wine has been drawn from the vat, thus prohibiting the wine (*Rama, Yoreh Deah* 123:21).

19. Any moisture would become prohibited when the idolater touches it. See *Yoreh Deah* 123:10 with commentaries.

ט. עַכּוּ״ם שֶׁשָּׁפַךְ מַיִם לְתוֹךְ הַיַּיִן — אִם נִתְכַּוֵּין לְמוֹזְגוֹ[20], אָסוּר בִּשְׁתִיָּה[21]. וְאִם לֹא נִתְכַּוֵּין לְמוֹזְגוֹ, וַאֲפִילּוּ הוּא סָפֵק, מוּתָּר.

י. חוֹמֶץ יַיִן שֶׁנַּעֲשָׂה מִיַּיִן כָּשֵׁר — אִם הוּא חָזָק כָּל כָּךְ שֶׁמְּבַעְבֵּעַ כְּשֶׁשּׁוֹפְכִין אוֹתוֹ עַל הָאָרֶץ, שׁוּב אֵינוֹ נֶאֱסָר בְּמַגַּע עַכּוּ״ם. אֲבָל אִם נַעֲשָׂה מִסְּתָם יֵינָם[22], לְעוֹלָם הוּא בְּאִיסּוּרוֹ.

יא. וְכֵן יַיִן שָׂרָף שֶׁנַּעֲשָׂה מִסְּתָם יֵינָם, וְכֵן מֵהַחַרְצַנִּים וְהַזָּגִים וְהַשְּׁמָרִים, הֲרֵי הוּא כְּיַיִן עַצְמוֹ[23]. אֲבָל הַנַּעֲשֶׂה מִיַּיִן כָּשֵׁר, אוֹ לְאַחַר שֶׁנַּעֲשָׂה יַיִן שָׂרָף, אֵין מַגַּע עַכּוּ״ם אוֹסַרְתּוֹ.

יב. ווייִנשטיין[24] — נִתְפַּשֵּׁט הַמִּנְהָג לְהַתִּיר, כֵּיוָן שֶׁאֵין בּוֹ הֲנָאָה לְחֵיךְ[25].

---

§9 עַכּוּ״ם שֶׁשָּׁפַךְ מַיִם לְתוֹךְ הַיַּיִן — Regarding **an idolater who poured water into wine,** the halachah is as follows: אִם נִתְכַּוֵּין לְמוֹזְגוֹ — **If he intended to dilute it,**[20] אָסוּר בִּשְׁתִיָּה — **it is prohibited for drinking;**[21] וְאִם לֹא נִתְכַּוֵּין לְמוֹזְגוֹ — **but if he did not intend to dilute it,** וַאֲפִילּוּ הוּא סָפֵק — **or even if there is doubt** as to what his intention was, מוּתָּר — **it is permitted.**

§10 חוֹמֶץ יַיִן שֶׁנַּעֲשָׂה מִיַּיִן כָּשֵׁר — Regarding **wine vinegar that was produced from kosher wine,** אִם הוּא חָזָק כָּל כָּךְ — **if it is so strong** שֶׁמְּבַעְבֵּעַ כְּשֶׁשּׁוֹפְכִין אוֹתוֹ עַל הָאָרֶץ — **that it bubbles when it is poured on the ground,** שׁוּב אֵינוֹ נֶאֱסָר בְּמַגַּע עַכּוּ״ם — **it no longer becomes prohibited through** the **contact of an idolater,** for it is no longer considered wine. אֲבָל אִם נַעֲשָׂה מִסְּתָם יֵינָם — **But if** the vinegar **was produced from the wine of idolaters**[22] לְעוֹלָם הוּא בְּאִיסּוּרוֹ — **it remains prohibited forever** (i.e., no matter how strong it subsequently becomes).

§11 וְכֵן יַיִן שָׂרָף שֶׁנַּעֲשָׂה מִסְּתָם יֵינָם — **Similarly, brandy that was produced from wine of idolaters,** וְכֵן מֵהַחַרְצַנִּים וְהַזָּגִים וְהַשְּׁמָרִים — **or from peels, seeds, or lees** that remained after the idolaters pressed grapes into wine, הֲרֵי הוּא כְּיַיִן עַצְמוֹ — **is considered like actual wine** and is prohibited.[23] אֲבָל הַנַּעֲשֶׂה מִיַּיִן כָּשֵׁר — **However,** with regard to brandy **that was produced from kosher wine,** אוֹ לְאַחַר שֶׁנַּעֲשָׂה יַיִן שָׂרָף — the halachah is that **once it becomes brandy** אֵין מַגַּע עַכּוּ״ם אוֹסַרְתּוֹ — **contact of an idolater does not cause it to become prohibited,** i.e., it is no longer considered "wine."

§12 ווייִנשטיין — Regarding **tartar**[24] of an idolater, נִתְפַּשֵּׁט הַמִּנְהָג לְהַתִּיר — **it has become the widespread custom to permit it** כֵּיוָן שֶׁאֵין בּוֹ הֲנָאָה לְחֵיךְ — **since it does not** offer **pleasure to the palate.**[25]

---

20. In earlier times, wine was very strong and would be diluted before drinking.

21. When he intends to dilute it he can easily come to touch it (see *Shach, Yoreh Deah* 125:13).

22. That is, before it became vinegar it was already prohibited due to the prohibition of wine of idolaters.

23. Blended whiskey that contains a small amount of wine of an idolater is permitted if the prohibited wine amounts to one-seventh of the total or less. It is nevertheless fitting for a pious individual to avoid drinking it (*Igros Moshe, Yoreh Deah* I, §62-64).

24. Tartar (or cream of tartar) is a residue that accumulates on the walls of wine barrels. It is used in baking powder and medicine.

25. Some authorities prohibit tartar of an

יג. מַגַּע עַכּוּ"ם עַל יְדֵי דָּבָר אַחֵר, וְכֵן הַבָּא מִכֹּחוֹ, יַעֲשֶׂה שְׁאֵלַת חָכָם[26].

יד. הַשּׁוֹלֵחַ יַיִן עַל יְדֵי עַכּוּ"ם צָרִיךְ לְהַשְׁגִּיחַ הֵיטֵב בְּכָל מָקוֹם שֶׁיֵּשׁ בַּרְזָא אוֹ מְגוּפָא לַחְתּוֹם שָׁם בִּשְׁנֵי חוֹתָמוֹת[27].

טו. יִשְׂרָאֵל שֶׁעוֹשֶׂה יֵינוֹ שֶׁל עַכּוּ"ם בְּהֶכְשֵׁר כְּדֵי לְמָכְרוֹ אַחַר כָּךְ לְיִשְׂרְאֵלִים יֵשׁ בָּזֶה כַּמָּה חִילּוּקֵי דִּינִים, וְלִפְעָמִים אֲפִילוּ שְׁתֵּי חוֹתָמוֹת וְגַם מַפְתֵּחַ לֹא מְהַנֵּי, וְצָרִיךְ לִשְׁאוֹל לְמוֹרֶה הוֹרָאָה כְּדַת מַה לַּעֲשׂוֹת. וְשׁוֹמֵר נַפְשׁוֹ[28] יִרְחַק מִיַּיִן כָּזֶה.

---

§13 **מַגַּע עַכּוּ"ם עַל יְדֵי דָּבָר אַחֵר** — With regard to **contact of an idolater** with wine **by means of another object** (e.g., he touched the wine with a stick) **וְכֵן הַבָּא מִכֹּחוֹ** — **as well as** wine **that came** forth **from his force** (e.g., he lifted the barrel and wine spilled out), **יַעֲשֶׂה שְׁאֵלַת חָכָם** — **one must consult a halachic authority** as to whether the wine is permitted or not.[26]

§14 The following two *se'ifim* discuss how to ensure the integrity of wine in the possession of an idolater and of wine being produced from grapes belonging to an idolater.

הַשּׁוֹלֵחַ יַיִן עַל יְדֵי עַכּוּ"ם — **One who ships** kosher **wine with an idolater** **צָרִיךְ לְהַשְׁגִּיחַ הֵיטֵב** — **must take great care** **בְּכָל מָקוֹם שֶׁיֵּשׁ בַּרְזָא אוֹ מְגוּפָא** — that **every place** on the container **where there is a spigot or stopper** **לַחְתּוֹם שָׁם בִּשְׁנֵי חוֹתָמוֹת** — **should be sealed with two seals.**[27]

§15 **יִשְׂרָאֵל שֶׁעוֹשֶׂה יֵינוֹ שֶׁל עַכּוּ"ם בְּהֶכְשֵׁר** — The process by which **a Jew produces the wine of an idolater** (i.e., from an idolater's grapes) **so that it will be kosher,** **כְּדֵי לְמָכְרוֹ אַחַר כָּךְ לְיִשְׂרְאֵלִים** — **in order to subsequently sell it to Jews,** **יֵשׁ בָּזֶה כַּמָּה חִילּוּקֵי דִּינִים** — **is subject to a number of detailed laws.** **וְלִפְעָמִים אֲפִילוּ שְׁתֵּי חוֹתָמוֹת וְגַם מַפְתֵּחַ לֹא מְהַנֵּי** — **At times, even** securing the wine with **two seals as well as a** lock and **key is not effective** to permit the wine in this situation. **וְצָרִיךְ לִשְׁאוֹל לְמוֹרֶה הוֹרָאָה** — **One must consult a halachic authority** **כְּדַת מַה לַּעֲשׂוֹת** — **with regard to the proper procedure.** **וְשׁוֹמֵר נַפְשׁוֹ יִרְחַק מִיַּיִן כָּזֶה** — **Nevertheless, one who guards his soul**[28] **will avoid such wine.**

§16 A utensil that was used for the wine of an idolater is unfit for kosher use until all residue of the prohibited wine has been removed. The remainder of the *Siman* is devoted to discussing how this is accomplished:

---

idolater. However, even according to these authorities, if it was heated in a utensil, the utensil is permitted after twelve months have passed (*Shaar HaTziyun* 452:31); see below, *se'if* 22.

26. Wearing gloves when pouring wine does not constitute "contact by means of another object." Therefore, any wine [with the exception of kosher wine that has been heated to the temperature cited above in note 8] touched or poured by a waiter who is an idolater is certainly prohibited, even if he is wearing gloves (*Igros Moshe, Yoreh Deah* II, §51).

27. This ensures that the idolater will not pour out any wine in a manner that would cause the wine to become prohibited, as we will be aware if he tampers with the seals.

28. That is, he meticulously avoids any situation that can result in spiritual harm.

טז. כֵּלִים שֶׁל סְתָם יֵינָם, אִם הֵם כֵּלִים שֶׁאֵין הַדֶּרֶךְ לְהַחֲזִיק בָּהֶן יַיִן אֶלָּא זְמַן קָצָר, וְגַם לֹא הָיָה בָהֶן הַיַּיִן מֵעֵת לְעֵת[29], בֵּין שֶׁהֵם שֶׁל עוֹר, בֵּין שֶׁהֵם שֶׁל עֵץ וְשֶׁל זְכוּכִית וְשֶׁל אֶבֶן וְשֶׁל מַתָּכוֹת, אִם אֵינָן מְזוּפָּתִין[30], מְדִיחָן הֵיטֵב בְּמַיִם ג׳ פְּעָמִים וּמוּתָּרִים[31]. וְאִם הֵן מְזוּפָּתִין, יֵשׁ לָהֶם דִּין אַחֵר. וְכֵן כְּלֵי חֶרֶס יֵשׁ לָהֶן דִּין אַחֵר[32].

יז. כֵּלִים הָעֲשׂוּיִים לְהַכְנִיס בָּהֶם יַיִן לְקִיּוּם, דְּהַיְינוּ שֶׁמְּיַחֲדִין אוֹתָן לְהַחֲזִיק בָּהֶם יַיִן לְכָל הַפָּחוֹת ג׳ יָמִים, אַף עַל פִּי שֶׁהַכְּלִי הוּא שֶׁל יִשְׂרָאֵל וְהָעַכּוּ״ם הֶחֱזִיק בּוֹ אֶת הַיַּיִן רַק זְמַן מוּעָט, מִכָּל מָקוֹם צָרִיךְ הֶכְשֵׁר עַל יְדֵי עִירוּי. דְּהַיְינוּ, שֶׁמְּמַלְּאִין אֶת הַכְּלִי מַיִם עַל כָּל גְּדוֹתָיו[33] וְיַעֲמוֹד כָּךְ לְכָל הַפָּחוֹת כ״ד שָׁעוֹת מֵעֵת לְעֵת, וְאַחַר כָּךְ שׁוֹפֵךְ אֶת הַמַּיִם וְנוֹתֵן בּוֹ מַיִם שְׁנִיִּים וְיַעֲמוֹד כָּךְ לְכָל הַפָּחוֹת מֵעֵת לְעֵת,

---

כֵּלִים שֶׁל סְתָם יֵינָם — The method for rendering **utensils** used **for wine of idolaters** fit for kosher use is dependent on the type of utensil and its use: **אִם הֵם כֵּלִים שֶׁאֵין הַדֶּרֶךְ לְהַחֲזִיק בָּהֶן יַיִן אֶלָּא זְמַן קָצָר** — **If they are utensils that are used to hold wine for only a short time, וְגַם לֹא הָיָה בָהֶן הַיַּיִן מֵעֵת לְעֵת — and the** nonkosher **wine did not remain in them for a twenty-four-hour period,**[29] **בֵּין שֶׁהֵם שֶׁל עוֹר** — the halachah regarding such utensils is that **whether they are** made **of leather בֵּין שֶׁהֵם שֶׁל עֵץ וְשֶׁל זְכוּכִית וְשֶׁל אֶבֶן וְשֶׁל מַתָּכוֹת — or of wood, glass, stone, or metal, אִם אֵינָן מְזוּפָּתִין — if they are not coated with pitch,**[30] **מְדִיחָן הֵיטֵב בְּמַיִם ג׳ פְּעָמִים — one washes them well with water three times וּמוּתָּרִים — and they are permitted.**[31] **וְאִם הֵן מְזוּפָּתִין — But if they are coated with pitch יֵשׁ לָהֶם דִּין אַחֵר — they are subject to a different,** more stringent, **halachah. וְכֵן כְּלֵי חֶרֶס — Earthenware utensils as well יֵשׁ לָהֶן דִּין אַחֵר — are subject to a different,** more stringent, **halachah.**[32]

§17 כֵּלִים הָעֲשׂוּיִים לְהַכְנִיס בָּהֶם יַיִן לְקִיּוּם — Regarding **utensils that are made to hold wine for storage, דְּהַיְינוּ — that is, שֶׁמְּיַחֲדִין אוֹתָן לְהַחֲזִיק בָּהֶם יַיִן לְכָל הַפָּחוֹת ג׳ יָמִים — they are designated to hold wine for at least three days, אַף עַל פִּי שֶׁהַכְּלִי הוּא שֶׁל יִשְׂרָאֵל** — the halachah is that **even though the utensil belongs to a Jew וְהָעַכּוּ״ם הֶחֱזִיק בּוֹ אֶת הַיַּיִן רַק זְמַן מוּעָט — and the idolater stored** forbidden **wine in it for only a short time, מִכָּל מָקוֹם צָרִיךְ הֶכְשֵׁר עַל יְדֵי עִירוּי — nevertheless it must be rendered kosher through the** ***irui*** (pouring) **process. דְּהַיְינוּ — This** process **is accomplished** as follows: **שֶׁמְּמַלְּאִין אֶת הַכְּלִי מַיִם עַל כָּל גְּדוֹתָיו — The utensil is filled with water to overflowing,**[33] **וְיַעֲמוֹד כָּךְ לְכָל הַפָּחוֹת כ״ד שָׁעוֹת מֵעֵת לְעֵת — and it should remain standing this way for a period of at least twenty-four consecutive hours. וְאַחַר כָּךְ שׁוֹפֵךְ אֶת הַמַּיִם — Afterward, one pours out the water, וְנוֹתֵן בּוֹ מַיִם שְׁנִיִּים — and replaces it with a second** filling **of water, וְיַעֲמוֹד כָּךְ לְכָל הַפָּחוֹת מֵעֵת לְעֵת — and it is to remain standing this way for** another **period of at least**

---

29. Lit., *from time [of the day] to [the same] time [again].* See end of next *se'if.*

30. A coating of pitch would often be applied to utensils as a sealant. Pitch absorbs wine; thus, such utensils are subject to more stringent requirements in order to render them kosher.

31. See below, note 37.

32. An earthenware utensil is treated more stringently since its walls absorb the wine. With regard to this halachah, porcelain is considered earthenware (see *Mishnah Berurah* 451:163; see also *Igros Moshe, Yoreh Deah* I, end of §43).

33. Cold water may be used (see *Mishnah Berurah* 451:118).

LAWS OF WINE OF IDOLATERS — SIMAN 47:18-19 **166**

וְכֵן עוֹשֶׂה פַּעַם שְׁלִישִׁית. וְאֵין צְרִיכִין שֶׁיִּהְיוּ הַג' מֵעֵת לְעֵת דַּוְקָא רְצוּפִין. וְאִם עָמְדוּ
בּוֹ הַמַּיִם כַּמָּה יָמִים וְלֹא שְׁפָכָם לֹא עָלָה לוֹ אֶלָּא לְמֵעֵת לְעֵת אַחַת. יֵשׁ אוֹמְרִים
דְּאִם הַיַּיִן הָיָה בּוֹ מֵעֵת לְעֵת לֹא מִיתְכַּשֵּׁר בְּעֵירוּי, מִשּׁוּם דְּכָבוּשׁ כִּמְבוּשָׁל[34] וּבָעֵי
הַגְעָלָה[35]. וּבִמְקוֹם שֶׁאֵין צוֹרֶךְ גָּדוֹל יֵשׁ לְהַחֲמִיר כֵּן[36].

יח. כְּלֵי זְכוּכִית כֵּיוָן שֶׁהֵם חֲלָקִים וְקָשִׁים, אַף עַל פִּי שֶׁמַּכְנִיסִין בָּהֶן יַיִן לְקִיּוּם, סַגִּי
לְהוּ בַּהֲדָחַת ג' פְּעָמִים[37].

יט. כְּלִי שֶׁהָיָה בּוֹ יַיִן שֶׁלָּנוּ וְעֵירוּ אֶת הַיַּיִן וּבְעוֹד שֶׁהָיָה הַכְּלִי טוֹפֵחַ עַל מְנָת
לְהַטְפִּיחַ נָגַע שָׁם עַכּוּ"ם, סַגִּי לֵיהּ בַּהֲדָחָה ג' פְּעָמִים, אַף עַל פִּי שֶׁהוּא כְּלִי

---

twenty-four hours. וְכֵן עוֹשֶׂה פַּעַם שְׁלִישִׁית — Then he does the same a third time. וְאֵין צְרִיכִין שֶׁיִּהְיוּ הַג' מֵעֵת לְעֵת דַּוְקָא רְצוּפִין — The three twenty-four-hour periods need not be consecutive with one another; one may wait between them. וְאִם עָמְדוּ בּוֹ הַמַּיִם כַּמָּה יָמִים — However, even if the water remained standing in the utensil for a number of days consecutively, וְלֹא שְׁפָכָם — and he did not pour it out, לֹא עָלָה לוֹ אֶלָּא לְמֵעֵת לְעֵת אַחַת — it only counts for one twenty-four-hour period. יֵשׁ אוֹמְרִים — There are those authorities who say דְּאִם הַיַּיִן הָיָה בּוֹ מֵעֵת לְעֵת — that if the wine of idolaters was in the utensil for a twenty-four-hour period, לֹא מִיתְכַּשֵּׁר בְּעֵירוּי — the utensil can no longer be rendered kosher through irui, מִשּׁוּם דְּכָבוּשׁ כִּמְבוּשָׁל — due to the principle of "that which is soaked is like that which is cooked,"[34] וּבָעֵי הַגְעָלָה — and it therefore requires hagalah.[35] וּבִמְקוֹם שֶׁאֵין צוֹרֶךְ גָּדוֹל — In a situation where there is no great need to be lenient, יֵשׁ לְהַחֲמִיר כֵּן — one should be stringent in this regard (and conduct himself in accordance with this view).[36]

§18 כְּלֵי זְכוּכִית — With regard to glass utensils, כֵּיוָן שֶׁהֵם חֲלָקִים וְקָשִׁים — since they are smooth and hard, אַף עַל פִּי שֶׁמַּכְנִיסִין בָּהֶן יַיִן לְקִיּוּם — the halachah is that even if wine is put into them for storage, סַגִּי לְהוּ בַּהֲדָחַת ג' פְּעָמִים — it nevertheless suffices to render them kosher by rinsing them out well three times.[37]

§19 כְּלִי שֶׁהָיָה בּוֹ יַיִן שֶׁלָּנוּ — A utensil that had our (i.e., kosher) wine in it וְעֵירוּ אֶת הַיַּיִן — and the wine was poured out, וּבְעוֹד שֶׁהָיָה הַכְּלִי טוֹפֵחַ עַל מְנָת לְהַטְפִּיחַ — and while the residual moisture on the walls of the utensil could still moisten an object to the degree that that object could in turn moisten something else, נָגַע שָׁם עַכּוּ"ם — an idolater touched it there, i.e., where it was moist, סַגִּי לֵיהּ בַּהֲדָחָה ג' פְּעָמִים — it suffices to rinse it out three times, אַף עַל פִּי שֶׁהוּא כְּלִי

---

34. Generally, if a solid was left soaking in a liquid for twenty-four hours, they impart flavor into each other as if the two were cooked together. Therefore, these authorities hold that the method of purging required for a utensil that was used with prohibited hot wine is required here. See further.

35. Hagalah is the process of purging with hot water any flavor that was absorbed in the walls of a utensil. This method is employed to permit the usage of a utensil that was previously used for hot prohibited food; see below, se'if 20.

This process is described below, Siman 116.

36. Rabbi Moshe Feinstein (Igros Moshe, Yoreh Deah III, §32) asserts that irui suffices even in this situation, and it is not necessary to be stringent at all.

37. This method is effective only if the utensil is cleaned of all sediments. Therefore, a bottle with a narrow neck or any other utensil that cannot be fully cleaned of sediments that may have adhered to its inside walls cannot be rendered fit for kosher use (see Mishnah Berurah 451:156).

167 LAWS OF WINE OF IDOLATERS — SIMAN 47:20-22

שֶׁמַּכְנִיסִין בּוֹ לְקִיּוּם.

כ. הָא דִּמְהַנֵּי הֲדָחָה אוֹ עִירוּי זֶהוּ כְּשֶׁלֹּא נִשְׁתַּמֵּשׁ בּוֹ יַיִן רַק בְּצוֹנֵן, אֲבָל אִם נִשְׁתַּמֵּשׁ בּוֹ בְּחַמִּין, צָרִיךְ הַגְעָלָה כְּמוֹ מִשְּׁאָר אִיסּוּרִין.

כא. כְּלֵי הַגַּת, אַף עַל פִּי שֶׁאֵין מַכְנִיסִין בָּהֶם יַיִן לְקִיּוּם, כֵּיוָן שֶׁמִּשְׁתַּמְּשִׁין בָּהֶם יַיִן בְּשֶׁפַע חֲמִירֵי וּצְרִיכִין שְׁאֵלַת חָכָם אֵיךְ לְהַכְשִׁירָן.

כב. כָּל הַכֵּלִים שֶׁיָּשְׁנוּ י״ב חֳדָשִׁים מוּתָּרִים, כִּי בְּוַדַּאי כָּלָה כָל לַחְלוּחִית יַיִן שֶׁבָּהֶם. וַאֲפִילוּ נָתַן לְתוֹכָן מַיִם תּוֹךְ י״ב חוֹדֶשׁ, אֵין בְּכָךְ כְּלוּם.

שֶׁמַּכְנִיסִין בּוֹ לְקִיּוּם — even though it is a utensil into which wine **is put for storage.**

§20 **הָא דִּמְהַנֵּי הֲדָחָה אוֹ עִירוּי** — The ruling **that rinsing or *irui* is effective** in the previously mentioned cases **זֶהוּ כְּשֶׁלֹּא נִשְׁתַּמֵּשׁ בּוֹ יַיִן רַק בְּצוֹנֵן — applies only when** the utensil **was used exclusively with cold wine. אֲבָל אִם נִשְׁתַּמֵּשׁ בּוֹ בְּחַמִּין — However, if it was used with hot** wine, **צָרִיךְ הַגְעָלָה כְּמוֹ מִשְּׁאָר אִיסּוּרִין — it requires *hagalah*, as** is the halachah **with other prohibited** substances that were absorbed through heat into the walls of a utensil.

§21 **כְּלֵי הַגַּת** — With regard to **utensils of the winepress** (i.e., winemaking equipment), **אַף עַל פִּי שֶׁאֵין מַכְנִיסִין בָּהֶם יַיִן לְקִיּוּם** — the halachah is that **even though wine is not stored in them, כֵּיוָן שֶׁמִּשְׁתַּמְּשִׁין בָּהֶם יַיִן בְּשֶׁפַע — since wine is used in them in abundance חֲמִירֵי — they are** treated **stringently, וּצְרִיכִין שְׁאֵלַת חָכָם אֵיךְ לְהַכְשִׁירָן — and** the question of **how to render them kosher must be posed to a competent halachic authority.**

§22 **כָּל הַכֵּלִים שֶׁיָּשְׁנוּ י״ב חֳדָשִׁים — All utensils** used for wine of idolaters **that have** "**aged**" for **twelve months,** i.e., twelve months have passed since their last use with wine **מוּתָּרִים — are permitted, כִּי בְּוַדַּאי — for it is certain כָּלָה כָל לַחְלוּחִית יַיִן שֶׁבָּהֶם** — that **all moisture of the** prohibited **wine has dissipated. וַאֲפִילוּ נָתַן לְתוֹכָן מַיִם תּוֹךְ י״ב חוֹדֶשׁ — And even if he placed water into** the utensils **during** those **twelve months, אֵין בְּכָךְ כְּלוּם— it is of no consequence,** for that does not prevent the residual moisture from dissipating.

BERACHOS UPON FOOD MADE OF THE FIVE SPECIES OF GRAIN — SIMAN 48 168

סימן מח

דִּינֵי בְּרָכוֹת עַל מַאֲכָלִים מֵחֲמֵשֶׁת מִינֵי דָּגָן[1,2,3,4,5,6,7]

וּבוֹ י׳ סְעִיפִים

SIMAN 48

LAWS OF BERACHOS UPON FOODS MADE OF THE FIVE SPECIES OF GRAINS

CONTAINING 10 *SE'IFIM*

§1-4 Laws of *Pas Haba'ah B'kisnin* / **§5-6** Cooked or Fried Dough / **§7** Cooked or Fried Bread / **§8** Proper Blessing on Mixture of Dough Products and Liquid / **§9** Food Made From Bread Crumbs / **§10** Predominance of Grain Products in Mixtures

Foods made from the five types of grain (wheat, barley, spelt, oats or rye) [1] constitute a class of their own with regard to the halachos of blessings. Their special status derives from the fact that each of these five grains is a dietary staple that attains its highest form in bread, which, in turn, is the mainstay of any meal.[2] Our Sages established a separate blessing for these grains: *borei minei mezonos* (*Who creates species of nourishment*).[3]

When grain is made into bread, the basic staple of all meals, it has reached its highest possible level of importance as food, and requires *netilas yadayim*,[4] the *hamotzi* blessing prior to eating it,[5] and the recital of *Bircas HaMazon* [Grace After Meals] afterward.[6]

Baked items that are prepared in a way in which they are not used as a staple of a meal (e.g., pies, cakes) can, in certain cases, still be considered to be a "bread-type" food (*pas*). As such, they are subject to the halachos of standard bread in certain circumstances. *Se'ifim* 1-4 set out which preparations are included in this classification, and the halachos that apply to these foods.

Another aspect of the importance of grain products is evident in the laws of *ikar v'tafeil* (primary and subordinate foods).[7] When assessing a mixture

---

1. [Regarding the halachah of rice, see below, 52:17.]

2. See *Responsa* of *Chasam Sofer, Orach Chaim* §50.

3. On grains that are eaten raw or roasted (for example, if one eats raw or roasted kernels of wheat), one generally recites the same blessing upon them as upon any food that grows from the ground: *borei pri ha'adamah* (*Who creates the fruit of the ground*). The special status of foods made from grain is reached only when they are cooked or baked; see below, *se'if* 8, and *Orach Chaim* 208:2 with *Mishnah Berurah*.

4. I.e., *washing the hands*. For the halachos of *netilas yadayim*, see above, *Siman* 40.

5. בָּרוּךְ אַתָּה ה׳ אֱלֹהֵינוּ מֶלֶךְ הָעוֹלָם הַמּוֹצִיא לֶחֶם מִן הָאָרֶץ, *Blessed are You,* HASHEM, *our God, King of the universe, Who brings forth bread from the earth*. See above, 41:1.

6. For the halachos of *Bircas HaMazon*, see above, *Siman* 44.

7. These halachos are set out at length below, *Siman* 54.

169 BERACHOS UPON FOOD MADE OF THE FIVE SPECIES OF GRAIN — SIMAN 48:1-2

א. לֶחֶם שֶׁהוּא מֵחֲמֵשֶׁת מִינֵי דָגָן, אֶלָּא שֶׁהוּא פַּת הַבָּאָה בְּכִיסְנִין[8], אִם אוֹכֵל מִמֶּנּוּ פָּחוֹת מִשִּׁיעוּר קְבִיעוּת סְעוּדָה[9], אֵינוֹ צָרִיךְ נְטִילַת יָדַיִם, וְאֵין מְבָרְכִין עָלָיו "הַמּוֹצִיא", אֶלָּא "בּוֹרֵא מִינֵי מְזוֹנוֹת" וּלְאַחֲרָיו "עַל הַמִּחְיָה"[10]. אֲבָל אִם אוֹכֵל מִמֶּנּוּ שִׁיעוּר קְבִיעוּת סְעוּדָה, אֲזַי דִּינוֹ כְּלֶחֶם גָּמוּר — צָרִיךְ נְטִילַת יָדַיִם וּמְבָרְכִין עָלָיו "הַמּוֹצִיא" וּלְאַחֲרָיו בִּרְכַּת הַמָּזוֹן[11].

ב. מַהוּ פַּת הַבָּאָה בְּכִיסְנִין: יֵשׁ אוֹמְרִים שֶׁהוּא פַּת שֶׁנַּעֲשָׂה כְּמִין כִּיסִים[12] מְמוּלָּא בְּפֵירוֹת אוֹ בְּבָשָׂר אוֹ בִגְבִינָה (עַיֵּין אֶבֶן הָעוֹזֵר)[13] וְכַיּוֹצֵא בוֹ[14], וְכֵן כְּשֶׁנַּעֲשָׂה כְּמוֹ

---

of different foods to decide which is the appropriate blessing to recite, the fact that one of the foods is a grain product strongly influences the halachah. These halachos are set out in *se'if* 8 and *se'if* 10, below.

§1 לֶחֶם — A **bread**-type food שֶׁהוּא מֵחֲמֵשֶׁת מִינֵי דָגָן — **that is made of** one of **the five species of grains,** אֶלָּא שֶׁהוּא פַּת הַבָּאָה בְּכִיסְנִין — that was not prepared as bread, **but as *pas haba'ah b'kisnin,***[8] has the following halachah: אִם אוֹכֵל מִמֶּנּוּ פָּחוֹת מִשִּׁיעוּר קְבִיעוּת סְעוּדָה — **If one eats of such food less than the amount** that constitutes **a set meal,**[9] then its halachah is unlike that of bread; אֵינוֹ צָרִיךְ נְטִילַת יָדַיִם — that is, ***netilas yadayim* is not required** before **it** is eaten, וְאֵין מְבָרְכִין עָלָיו "הַמּוֹצִיא" — **and we do not recite** the ***hamotzi*** blessing **upon** eating **it.** אֶלָּא — **Rather,** "בּוֹרֵא מִינֵי מְזוֹנוֹת"— before eating it one recites the blessing of ***borei minei mezonos,*** וּלְאַחֲרָיו — **and after** eating **it** "עַל הַמִּחְיָה" — he recites the blessing of ***Al HaMichyah.***[10] אֲבָל — **However,** אִם אוֹכֵל מִמֶּנּוּ שִׁיעוּר קְבִיעוּת סְעוּדָה — **if one eats of such food an amount** that constitutes **a set meal,** אֲזַי דִּינוֹ כְּלֶחֶם גָּמוּר — **then its halachah is the same as standard bread:** צָרִיךְ נְטִילַת יָדַיִם — ***netilas yadayim* is required** before eating, וּמְבָרְכִין עָלָיו "הַמּוֹצִיא" — **and one recites the *hamotzi*** blessing **upon it,** וּלְאַחֲרָיו בִּרְכַּת הַמָּזוֹן — **and after** eating **it, *Bircas HaMazon.***[11]

§2 מַהוּ פַּת הַבָּאָה בְּכִיסְנִין — **What is *"pas haba'ah b'kisnin"*?** יֵשׁ אוֹמְרִים — **Some** authorities **say** שֶׁהוּא פַּת שֶׁנַּעֲשָׂה כְּמִין כִּיסִים — **that it is a bread**-type food **that is prepared as a kind of pocket**[12] מְמוּלָּא בְּפֵירוֹת — **filled with fruit,** אוֹ בְּבָשָׂר אוֹ בִגְבִינָה — **or** with **meat or cheese** (עַיֵּין אֶבֶן הָעוֹזֵר — **see *Even HaOzeir*** to 168:7-8),[13] וְכַיּוֹצֵא בוֹ — **or** a **similar** filling,[14] וְכֵן כְּשֶׁנַּעֲשָׂה כְּמוֹ

---

8. In general terms, this refers to baked goods that are usually not used as the main bread of a meal or to accompany a main course. See text and notes to *se'if* 2 for the characteristics, composition, and laws of such bread. Henceforth, we will refer to it simply as *kisnin*-bread.

9. Kitzur defines *kevias seudah,* "a set meal," in *se'if* 3, below.

10. Literally, *for the nourishment.* See below, 51:7-10, regarding the halachos of this *berachah acharonah* (final blessing).

11. *Kisnin*-bread is generally not classified as standard bread, since it is not usually eaten as or with a meal, but primarily as a snack. It is only when it is actually eaten as a meal, i.e., one eats the amount of *kisnin*-bread that constitutes a set meal, that it attains the status of standard bread (*Mishnah Berurah* 168:23).

12. Accordingly, the word כִּיסְנִין is derived from the word כִּיס, *pocket;* thus, פַּת הַבָּאָה בְּכִיסְנִין means *bread that comes in* [*the form of*] *pockets.*

13. *Even HaOzeir* writes that contrary to the opinion of some authorities, a meat or cheese filling is the same as a fruit filling, and gives the dough the halachah of *kisnin*-bread; see following note.

14. I.e., honey, sugar, nuts, almonds, or seasoning (*Shulchan Aruch* 168:7). The filling referred to here must be significant enough to be very clearly tasted, and to significantly

BERACHOS UPON FOOD MADE OF THE FIVE SPECIES OF GRAIN — SIMAN 48:2 170

פלאדין[15]. וְיֵשׁ אוֹמְרִים שֶׁהוּא פַּת שֶׁנִּילוֹשׁ בְּשֶׁמֶן אוֹ בְשׁוּמָּן אוֹ בִדְבַשׁ אוֹ בְחָלָב אוֹ בְבֵיצִים[16] אוֹ בִשְׁאָר מֵי פֵירוֹת[17], אֲפִילוּ עֵירַב בּוֹ גַּם מַיִם אֶלָּא שֶׁהוּא הַמּוּעָט[18]. וַאֲנַן נַקְטִינַן כְּדִבְרֵי שְׁנֵיהֶם לְהָקֵל[19] וּמַחֲזִיקִין אֵלּוּ וָאֵלּוּ לְפַת הַבָּאָה בְּכִיסְנִין[20].

פלאדין — and also those that are prepared like *flodin*.[15] **וְיֵשׁ אוֹמְרִים — However, there are those** authorities **who say שֶׁהוּא פַּת שֶׁנִּילוֹשׁ בְּשֶׁמֶן — that** *pas haba'ah b'kisnin* **refers to a bread**-dough **that was kneaded with oil אוֹ בְשׁוּמָּן — or with fat אוֹ בִדְבַשׁ — or with honey אוֹ בְחָלָב — or with milk אוֹ בְבֵיצִים — or with eggs**[16] **אוֹ בִשְׁאָר מֵי פֵירוֹת — or with other fruit juices.**[17] **אֲפִילוּ עֵירַב בּוֹ גַּם מַיִם — Even if water was mixed into** the dough **as well,** it is still classified as *kisnin*-bread, **אֶלָּא שֶׁהוּא הַמּוּעָט — as long as** the water **was the minority** of the liquid used.[18] **וַאֲנַן נַקְטִינַן כְּדִבְרֵי שְׁנֵיהֶם — We hold by both of these opinions, לְהָקֵל — following the lenient application** of each,[19] **וּמַחֲזִיקִין אֵלּוּ וָאֵלּוּ לְפַת הַבָּאָה בְּכִיסְנִין — and we therefore treat both these and those** foods **as a *"pas haba'ah b'kisnin."***[20]

---

affect its taste, such as in a fruit-filled pie (see *Mishnah Berurah* 168:28; *Beur Halachah* 168:7 s.v. שכמעט הדבש). Because of the filling, people do not usually eat this as the primary bread of a meal. Therefore, even in a case where one eats only the dough and none of the filling, it is not treated as standard bread (*Mishnah Berurah* ibid. §27).

In the case of meat and cheese fillings, many authorities hold that its classification depends on how the pastry is prepared. When it is clearly meant to be a snack, such as small pastries with bits of cheese or meat inside that are commonly served as a dessert (e.g., a cheese danish), then it is considered *kisnin*-bread according to this opinion. In certain preparations, however, a dough baked with a filling of meat or cheese is served as a meal in itself. In these cases, we do not treat the preparation as a snack of filled dough, but rather as a main dish (i.e., the filling of meat or cheese) that is served together with the bread (i.e., the dough in which it is encased). In such cases, the pastry is treated as standard bread and the *hamotzi* blessing should be recited. See *Mishnah Berurah* 168:94 and *Beur Halachah* 168:17 s.v. פשטיד״א. Kitzur, however, citing *Even HaOzeir*, makes no such distinction; see previous note.

15. I.e., a cake with layers of dough and fruit baked with honey, similar to contemporary apple strudel or baklava.

16. See *Mishnah Berurah* 168:94.

17. See *Mishnah Berurah* (168:85), who cites many authorities who hold that frying a dough in oil so that the taste of the oil is dominant also renders it *kisnin*-bread, even if it is subsequently baked.

18. The dominant taste must also be that of the flavoring and additives, and not the flour (*Mishnah Berurah* 168:33). [An example of this would be regular chocolate cake, coffee cake, or honey cake.]

[According to this explanation of "*kisnin*-bread," the word "*kisnin*" is derived from a toasted grain (כִּיסְנִין) that was customarily eaten after a meal for its healthful effect on the heart (see *Eruvin* 29b). This grain would be served with pastries such as those described here (i.e., kneaded with oil, fat, or honey, etc.). Thus, according to this opinion, פַּת הַבָּאָה בְּכִיסְנִין means "*bread that is served with toasted grain*" (*Rashi* to *Berachos* 41b s.v. פת הבאה).]

19. That is, eating either of these preparations does not require one to wash *netilas yadayim*, or recite *hamotzi* and *Bircas HaMazon*. See Appendix of Kitzur's editorial glosses regarding one who ate a *kezayis* (olive's volume; see Appendix A) of both of these types of *kisnin*-bread.

20. *Shulchan Aruch* (168:7) cites a third definition of *kisnin*-bread: A dough, even if kneaded with only flour and water, that was baked in a way that results in a hard, dry, brittle cracker (e.g., biscuits, hard pretzels). [According to this view, כִּיסְנִין is derived from the Aramaic word meaning hard, dry bread; see *Targum* to *Yehoshua* 9:5 (*Aruch*, s.v. כסן).] Since it is not usually eaten as a primary bread, it does not have the halachah of standard bread, and is considered *kisnin*-bread (see *Mishnah Berurah* 168:35). *Shulchan Aruch* concludes that we follow all three opinions, and all three types of baked goods are classified as *kisnin*-bread.

171 BERACHOS UPON FOOD MADE OF THE FIVE SPECIES OF GRAIN — SIMAN 48:3

ג. שִׁיעוּר קְבִיעַת סְעוּדָה לַאו בְּדִידֵיהּ מְשַׁעֲרִינַן, אֶלָּא בְּרוֹב בְּנֵי אָדָם[21] כַּמָּה שֶׁרְגִילִין לֶאֱכוֹל בִּסְעוּדַּת צָהֳרַיִם אוֹ בִסְעוּדַּת עֶרֶב[22] לִשְׂבּוֹעַ[23]. אִם הוּא אָכַל כְּשִׁיעוּר זֶה, אַף עַל פִּי שֶׁהוּא אֵינוֹ שָׂבֵעַ, מִכָּל מָקוֹם דִּינוֹ כְּמוֹ לֶחֶם[24]. וְאִם אָכַל פַּת זֶה עִם לִפְתָּן[25], מְשַׁעֲרִין גַּם כֵּן אִם אֲחֵרִים הָיוּ אוֹכְלִין אוֹתוֹ בְּלִפְתָּן הָיוּ שְׂבֵעִים[26].

§3 Kitzur now defines what constitutes a "set meal," and is thus subject to the requirements set forth at the end of *se'if* 1.

שִׁיעוּר קְבִיעַת סְעוּדָה — The amount that constitutes a "set meal" לַאו בְּדִידֵיהּ מְשַׁעֲרִינַן — is not measured for each individual **by his own** personal standard. **אֶלָּא בְּרוֹב בְּנֵי אָדָם** Rather, it is measured **by the** standards of the majority of people:[21] **כַּמָּה שֶׁרְגִילִין לֶאֱכוֹל — A "set meal" is the amount that** most people **would normally eat בִּסְעוּדַּת צָהֳרַיִם אוֹ בִסְעוּדַּת עֶרֶב — in a noon or evening meal,**[22] **לִשְׂבּוֹעַ —** when eating **to satisfy** their hunger.[23] **אִם הוּא אָכַל כְּשִׁיעוּר זֶה — If an individual eats this amount** of *kisnin*-bread, **אַף עַל פִּי שֶׁהוּא אֵינוֹ שָׂבֵעַ — even if he is not satiated, מִכָּל מָקוֹם דִּינוֹ כְּמוֹ לֶחֶם — it nevertheless has the halachic status of bread.**[24] **וְאִם אָכַל פַּת זֶה עִם לִפְתָּן — If he ate the** *kisnin*-**bread with an accompaniment,**[25] **מְשַׁעֲרִין גַּם כֵּן — then we also** must **determine אִם אֲחֵרִים הָיוּ אוֹכְלִין אוֹתוֹ בְּלִפְתָּן — whether others, eating this** amount of *kisnin*-bread **with accompaniment, הָיוּ שְׂבֵעִים — would be satiated.** If they would, it attains the status of bread.[26]

21. *Beur Halachah* (168:6 s.v. אע״פ שהוא קובע) writes that this refers to the majority of people in one's age group. Thus, a child or an elderly person follows the eating habits of the majority of his age group for whom a lesser amount may be considered a "set meal." See also *Igros Moshe, Orach Chaim* III, §32 (cited below, note 26), who writes that in this determination we follow the eating habits of each particular country as well.

22. That is, one of the regular full meals of the day.

23. *Mishnah Berurah* (168:24) cites an opinion that puts the amount of a "set meal" at the volume of four eggs, which is considerably less than this amount. [For the purposes of this halachah, this equals approximately the volume of 8 fl. oz. (see *Shi'urei HaMitzvos* §27).] *Mishnah Berurah* writes that while the halachah does not follow this opinion, it is better to avoid this situation either by eating less than the volume of four eggs (which all agree is not a "set meal"), and reciting the *mezonos* blessing beforehand and *Al HaMichyah* afterward (when required), or by eating at least an amount that most people would eat for a regular morning or evening meal (which all agree is a "set meal"), and washing *al netilas yadayim* and reciting the *hamotzi* blessing beforehand and *Bircas HaMazon* afterward.

24. I.e., even if this amount will not satiate that particular person, it is considered a set meal since it is an amount with which most people are satiated, and eat for a full meal. One person's individual level of satiety is not taken into account when it is at variance with the normal situation of the vast majority of people [בָּטְלָה דַעְתּוֹ אֵצֶל כָּל אָדָם] (*Rosh, Berachos* 6:30). See above, note 21.

25. For example, he ate the *kisnin*-bread with meat (see *Mishnah Berurah* 168:24).

26. That is, although most people would not have been satiated with the same amount of *kisnin*-bread eaten by itself, for the purposes of this halachah we look at the entire meal — the *kisnin*-bread together with the accompaniment, which combined is equal to an amount with which most people would be satiated. [See *Magen Avraham* 168:13.]

According to Rabbi Moshe Feinstein, this amount is determined by the amount of regular bread one would eat at such a meal. Thus, if one ate that amount of *kisnin*-bread together with a meal and was satiated from the entire meal, he is required to recite *Bircas HaMazon*.

Rabbi Feinstein further writes that in Western countries where bread is eaten only sparingly during the meal, the amount of *kisnin*-bread or cake that would constitute a "set meal" *when eaten with other foods* is considerably less than

BERACHOS UPON FOOD MADE OF THE FIVE SPECIES OF GRAIN — SIMAN 48:4 172

וְאִם אָכַל בְּלֹא לְפִתָּן שִׁיעוּר קָטָן וְהוּא שָׂבֵעַ וַאֲחֵרִים אִם הָיוּ אוֹכְלִין כָּךְ לֹא הָיוּ שְׂבֵעִים אֶלָּא שֶׁאִם הָיוּ אוֹכְלִין אוֹתוֹ עִם לְפִתָּן הָיוּ שְׂבֵעִים, הָוֵי לֵיהּ גַּם כֵּן דִּין לֶחֶם[27].

ד. אִם מִתְּחִלָּה הָיָה בְּדַעְתּוֹ לֶאֱכוֹל רַק מְעַט וּבֵירַךְ בּוֹרֵא מִינֵי מְזוֹנוֹת וְאַחַר כָּךְ נִמְלַךְ לֶאֱכוֹל שִׁיעוּר קְבִיעַת סְעוּדָה, אִם בָּזֶה שֶׁהוּא רוֹצֶה לֶאֱכוֹל עוֹד אֵין בּוֹ שִׁיעוּר קְבִיעַת סְעוּדָה אֶלָּא בְּצֵירוּף מַה שֶּׁאָכַל קוֹדֶם, אוֹכֵל כָּךְ[28] וּמְבָרֵךְ אַחַר כָּךְ בִּרְכַּת הַמָּזוֹן. אֲבָל אִם בָּזֶה שֶׁהוּא רוֹצֶה לֶאֱכוֹל עוֹד יֵשׁ בּוֹ שִׁיעוּר קְבִיעַת סְעוּדָה,

---

There is one situation in which we do not compare the effects of the meal that he ate to the effects of a similar meal on the majority of people: וְאִם אָכַל בְּלֹא לְפִתָּן שִׁיעוּר קָטָן — **If he ate a small amount** of *kisnin*-bread *without* accompaniment וְהוּא שָׂבֵעַ — **and he was satiated** with this amount, וַאֲחֵרִים אִם הָיוּ אוֹכְלִין כָּךְ — **but others,** i.e., the majority of people, **had they eaten this** amount לֹא הָיוּ שְׂבֵעִים — **would not be satiated,** אֶלָּא שֶׁאִם הָיוּ אוֹכְלִין אוֹתוֹ עִם לְפִתָּן הָיוּ שְׂבֵעִים — [although according to the rule set out above, we should follow the habits of the majority of people, and disregard the fact that he is satiated with less], **however,** in this case, since **if they would have eaten that** amount **with an accompaniment, they would have been satiated,** הָוֵי לֵיהּ גַּם כֵּן דִּין לֶחֶם — in this case **the** *kisnin*-bread that he ate **also attains the halachic status of bread.**[27]

§4 אִם מִתְּחִלָּה — **If at first,** when he began to eat, הָיָה בְּדַעְתּוֹ לֶאֱכוֹל רַק מְעַט — **he was planning to eat only a small amount** of *kisnin*-bread וּבֵירַךְ בּוֹרֵא מִינֵי מְזוֹנוֹת — **and he** therefore **recited the** ***borei minei mezonos*** **blessing** before eating (as per *se'if* 1), וְאַחַר כָּךְ נִמְלַךְ — **but afterward,** in middle of eating, **he changed his mind** לֶאֱכוֹל שִׁיעוּר קְבִיעַת סְעוּדָה — and decided **to eat the amount of a "set meal,"** the halachah in this case is as follows: אִם בָּזֶה שֶׁהוּא רוֹצֶה לֶאֱכוֹל עוֹד — **If that which he wishes to eat further** אֵין בּוֹ שִׁיעוּר קְבִיעַת סְעוּדָה — **does not contain the amount of a "set meal"** אֶלָּא בְּצֵירוּף מַה שֶּׁאָכַל קוֹדֶם — **unless it is combined with what he ate earlier,** אוֹכֵל כָּךְ — then **he should continue eating in this way,** i.e., without washing *netilas yadayim* and reciting *hamotzi.*[28] וּמְבָרֵךְ אַחַר כָּךְ בִּרְכַּת הַמָּזוֹן — **After** he finishes eating, **he should recite** ***Bircas HaMazon,*** since all the food he has eaten taken together constitutes an amount of a "set meal." אֲבָל — **However,** אִם בָּזֶה שֶׁהוּא רוֹצֶה לֶאֱכוֹל עוֹד — **if that which he still wishes to eat** יֵשׁ בּוֹ שִׁיעוּר קְבִיעַת סְעוּדָה — **contains** on its own **the amount of a "set meal,"**

---

the volume of four eggs. Thus, when one attends a wedding or banquet, and eats only a small amount of *kisnin*-bread, if he also eats other foods, which, together with the small amount of *kisnin*-bread would constitute a set meal, he would be obligated to wash his hands (*netilas yadayim*) and recite *Bircas HaMazon* upon the *kisnin*-bread. See *Igros Moshe, Orach Chaim* I, §56; III, §32, IV, §41.

27. Here, we do not disregard his particular level of satiety as being contrary to the normal level of satiety of the majority of people (as above, notes 21 and 24), since the common person would also be satiated with this amount if it were eaten together with an accompaniment (*Mishnah Berurah* 168:24).

28. See *Shaar HaTziyun* (168:21), who points out that in this case, since he had originally planned to eat only a small amount, and then changed his mind and decided to eat more, he must recite a new *berachah rishonah* (first blessing). Thus, although he is not required to recite *hamotzi* since he is not planning on eating a large amount, he must nevertheless recite *borei minei mezonos* before continuing to eat.

173 BERACHOS UPON FOOD MADE OF THE FIVE SPECIES OF GRAIN — SIMAN 48:5

צָרִיךְ לִיטוֹל יָדָיו וּלְבָרֵךְ בִּרְכַּת הַמּוֹצִיא עַל מַה שֶּׁהוּא רוֹצֶה לֶאֱכוֹל. אֲבָל בִּרְכַּת עַל הַמִּחְיָה אֵינוֹ צָרִיךְ לְבָרֵךְ עַל מַה שֶּׁאָכַל, לְפִי שֶׁיִּצְטָרֵף עִם מַה שֶּׁיֹּאכַל וְיִפְטוֹר בְּבִרְכַּת הַמָּזוֹן[29].

ה. עִיסָּה[30] שֶׁנִּילוֹשָׁה בְּמַיִם[31] וּבְלִילָתָהּ[32] רַכָּה — אִם אֲפָאוֹ בְּתַנּוּר, אוֹ אֲפִילוּ בְאִלְפָּס בְּלֹא מַשְׁקֶה, וַאֲפִילוּ מָשַׁח אֶת הָאִלְפָּס בְּשׁוּמָן שֶׁלֹּא יִשָּׂרֵף הָעִיסָּה, זֶה לֹא חָשׁוּב

צָרִיךְ לִיטוֹל יָדָיו — then before he continues, **he must wash his hands** for *netilas yadayim* **וּלְבָרֵךְ בִּרְכַּת הַמּוֹצִיא — and recite the *hamotzi* blessing** **עַל מַה שֶּׁהוּא רוֹצֶה לֶאֱכוֹל — upon that which he wishes to eat.** **אֲבָל בִּרְכַּת עַל הַמִּחְיָה אֵינוֹ צָרִיךְ לְבָרֵךְ — However, he need not recite the *Al HaMichyah* blessing** **עַל מַה שֶּׁאָכַל — upon** the food **that he has eaten** until that point, **לְפִי שֶׁיִּצְטָרֵף עִם מַה שֶּׁיֹּאכַל — because** with regard to the obligation of *berachah acharonah* (final blessing), **that** which he ate **is combined with that which he will** still **eat** **וְיִפְטוֹר בְּבִרְכַּת הַמָּזוֹן — and will** thus **be exempted** from its own *berachah acharonah* **with the *Bircas HaMazon*** that he will recite when he concludes his meal.[29]

§5 In the following *se'ifim,* Kitzur sets out the halachos for those grain preparations that do not attain the status of "*pas*":[30]

עִיסָּה שֶׁנִּילוֹשָׁה בְּמַיִם — With respect to **dough that was kneaded with water,**[31] **וּבְלִילָתָהּ רַכָּה** — even **if it has a loose consistency,**[32] the law is as follows: **אִם אֲפָאוֹ בְּתַנּוּר — If it was baked in an oven,** **אוֹ אֲפִילוּ בְאִלְפָּס בְּלֹא מַשְׁקֶה — or even** if it was baked **in a pan** but **without liquid,** it is considered as bread. **וַאֲפִילוּ מָשַׁח אֶת הָאִלְפָּס בְּשׁוּמָן — Even if the pan was smeared with fat** **שֶׁלֹּא יִשָּׂרֵף הָעִיסָּה — so that the dough should not burn,** **זֶה לֹא חָשׁוּב מַשְׁקֶה — that is not considered** to be cooked

29. If one recited the *hamotzi* blessing on *kisnin*-bread because he intended to eat to satiety, and then he changed his mind and decided to eat less, he is not required to recite the *mezonos* blessing, and he may continue eating *kisnin*-bread. This is because the blessing he recited was the correct one at the time he recited it, as *kisnin*-bread is considered regular bread if one plans on eating it to satiety (*Igros Moshe, Orach Chaim* II, §54; *Yoreh Deah* III, §120:2).

See below, 77:14, for discussion of the pertinent halachos regarding one who ate *kisnin*-bread after reciting *Kiddush* on Shabbos morning.

30. Until this point we have been dealing with baked goods that are classified as "*pas,*" that is, bread-type foods. As we have learned, depending on the method of preparation, *pas* can have either the halachah of standard bread (requiring *netilas yadayim, hamotzi,* and *Bircas HaMazon*), or *kisnin*-bread (upon which one recites *mezonos* when it is not eaten as a set meal). However, as long as they were baked in an oven, they are all classified as "*pas.*"

Generally speaking, an item made from the five grains, that was not baked at all as part of its preparation, does not attain the halachah of *pas,* and therefore cannot be classified as regular bread, nor as *kisnin*-bread. Therefore, one who eats such an item, even as a set meal, will always recite *mezonos* before eating and *Al HaMichyah* afterward. In the following *se'ifim,* Kitzur sets out the parameters of this halachah: exactly which methods of preparation produce *pas* and which do not, and which processes can make an item that was already *pas* lose this status even after it was baked.

31. I.e., it was not kneaded with oil or fruit juices, etc., in which case it may be classified as *kisnin*-bread; see above, *se'if* 2, second opinion.

32. I.e., it cannot stay in one place without spreading, i.e., a loose batter (see *Meiri, Pesachim* 37a). See below, *se'if* 8, regarding dough with a thick consistency that was not baked in an oven.

BERACHOS UPON FOOD MADE OF THE FIVE SPECIES OF GRAIN — SIMAN 48:5 174

מַשְׁקֶה וְדִינוֹ כְּמוֹ לֶחֶם גָּמוּר. וַאֲפִילוּ אוֹכֵל מִמֶּנּוּ רַק כְּזַיִת[33], צָרִיךְ נְטִילַת יָדַיִם[34] וְ"הַמּוֹצִיא" וּבִרְכַּת הַמָּזוֹן[35]. וְאִם טִגְּנוֹ בְּמַשְׁקֶה, לַאו לֶחֶם הוּא, אֲפִילוּ אוֹכֵל מִמֶּנּוּ כְּדֵי שְׂבִיעָה[36]. וְכֵן אוֹתָן רְקִיקִין שֶׁהֵן דַּקִּין מְאוֹד שֶׁאוֹפִין בִּדְפוּס בֵּין שְׁנֵי בַּרְזְלִין[37], אֵין לָהֶם דִּין לֶחֶם, וַאֲפִילוּ אוֹכֵל מֵהֶם כְּדֵי שְׂבִיעָה, מְבָרֵךְ רַק "בּוֹרֵא מִינֵי מְזוֹנוֹת" וּלְאַחֲרָיו "עַל הַמִּחְיָה"[38]. וְלִפְעָמִים עוֹשִׂין עִיסָּה רַכָּה מְאוֹד[39], דְּהַיְינוּ שֶׁנּוֹתְנִין קֶמַח וּמַיִם בִּקְדֵרָה וּמְעָרְבִין אוֹתָם בְּכַף וְשׁוֹפְכִין אוֹתָהּ עַל עֲלֵי יְרָקוֹת וְנֶאֱפֶה בְּתַנּוּר עַל הֶעָלִים, אָז יֵשׁ לוֹ דִּין פַּת הַבָּא בְּכִיסְנִין[40].

---

in a liquid, וְדִינוֹ כְּמוֹ לֶחֶם גָּמוּר — and it therefore has the halachic status of regular bread. וַאֲפִילוּ אוֹכֵל מִמֶּנּוּ רַק כְּזַיִת — Thus, even if one eats only a *kezayis*[33] of this bread, צָרִיךְ נְטִילַת יָדַיִם — he is required to wash *netilas yadayim*[34] וְ"הַמּוֹצִיא" וּבִרְכַּת הַמָּזוֹן — and to recite *hamotzi* before eating it, and *Bircas HaMazon* afterward.[35]

וְאִם טִגְּנוֹ בְּמַשְׁקֶה — However, if he fried the dough in a liquid לַאו לֶחֶם הוּא — then it is not considered bread at all, אֲפִילוּ אוֹכֵל מִמֶּנּוּ כְּדֵי שְׂבִיעָה — even if he eats an amount that would fully satiate.[36]

וְכֵן אוֹתָן רְקִיקִין — Likewise, those wafers שֶׁהֵן דַּקִּין מְאוֹד — that are very thin, שֶׁאוֹפִין בִּדְפוּס בֵּין שְׁנֵי בַּרְזְלִין — that are baked in a mold between two pieces of iron,[37] אֵין לָהֶם דִּין לֶחֶם — do not have the halachic status of bread; וַאֲפִילוּ אוֹכֵל מֵהֶם כְּדֵי שְׂבִיעָה — thus, even if he eats enough wafers to fully satiate, מְבָרֵךְ רַק "בּוֹרֵא מִינֵי מְזוֹנוֹת" — he recites only *borei minei mezonos* before eating it, וּלְאַחֲרָיו "עַל הַמִּחְיָה" — and after eating it, *Al HaMichyah.*[38]

וְלִפְעָמִים עוֹשִׂין עִיסָּה רַכָּה מְאוֹד — At times, people make a dough of very loose consistency;[39] דְּהַיְינוּ שֶׁנּוֹתְנִין קֶמַח וּמַיִם בִּקְדֵרָה — that is, they put flour and water in a pot וּמְעָרְבִין אוֹתָם בְּכַף — and mix them with a spoon. וְשׁוֹפְכִין אוֹתָהּ עַל עֲלֵי יְרָקוֹת — They then take this batter and pour it on vegetable leaves, וְנֶאֱפֶה בְּתַנּוּר עַל הֶעָלִים — and it is baked in an oven on the leaves; אָז יֵשׁ לוֹ דִּין פַּת הַבָּא בְּכִיסְנִין — this preparation has the halachic status of *pas haba'ah b'kisnin.*[40]

---

33. Approximately .6-1.1 fl. oz. (17.3-33.3 cc.); see Appendix A.

34. Regarding the obligation to recite the *al netilas yadayim* blessing when eating only a *kezayis,* see above, 40:1, with note 8.

35. It is not considered to be cooked, but baked, and therefore it is classified as regular bread, upon which one recites *hamotzi* before eating it, and *Bircas HaMazon* even upon eating only a *kezayis* (see above, 44:5). [The *hamotzi* blessing is required when eating any amount of standard bread, even less than a *kezayis.*] Similarly, if a batter of the same consistency was prepared with fruit juice instead of water, and then baked as described in this *se'if,* it would be considered *kisnin*-bread, since it was baked, not cooked.

36. That is, it does not even attain the halachic status of *kisnin*-bread that is considered to be bread when eaten to satiety, as explained above, *se'if* 1. Therefore, he recites *borei minei mezonos* before eating it and *Al HaMichyah* afterward.

37. *Shaar HaTziyun* 168:36 describes the process as follows: A loose batter is made of flour, and poured onto a hot iron mold. Then, another hot iron mold is brought down onto the first. When the two molds are pressed together, the heat of the molds bakes the batter into a thin wafer.

38. Since it is so thin and flimsy, it [does not resemble bread in any way and] has none of the halachos of "*pas*" (see *Mishnah Berurah* 168:38; *Shaar HaTziyun* 168:36).

39. See Appendix of Kitzur's editorial glosses for further discussion of this case.

40. If one eats an amount of a set meal of this preparation, he is required to recite *hamotzi* and

175 BERACHOS UPON FOOD MADE OF THE FIVE SPECIES OF GRAIN — SIMAN 48:6-7

ו. עִיסָּה שֶׁנִּתְבַּשֵּׁל וְאַחַר כָּךְ נֶאֱפָה, כְּגוֹן בייגיל, פרעצין, לֶחֶם גָּמוּר הוּא[41], וְדַוְקָא כְּשֶׁנֶּאֱפָה הֵיטֵב (עַיֵּין פְּרִי מְגָדִים סִימָן קס״ח, אֵשֶׁל אַבְרָהָם, סְעִיף קָטָן ל״ט)[42].

ז. לֶחֶם גָּמוּר שֶׁבִּשְּׁלוֹ, אוֹ טִגְּנוֹ בְּחֶמְאָה וְכַדּוֹמֶה, אֲפִילוּ הֶעֱבִיר מִמֶּנּוּ תּוֹאַר לֶחֶם, כְּגוֹן שֶׁטְּחוֹ בְּבֵיצִים, אִם יֵשׁ בַּפְּרוּסָה כְּזַיִת, כָּל דִּין לֶחֶם עָלָיו[43]. וְאִם אֵין בְּכָל פְּרוּסָה כְּזַיִת[44], אַף עַל פִּי שֶׁעַל יְדֵי הַבִּישׁוּל נָפְחוּ וְיֵשׁ בְּכָל פְּרוּסָה כְּזַיִת, אוֹ שֶׁנִּדְבַּק עַל יְדֵי הַבִּישׁוּל וְנַעֲשָׂה גּוּשׁ גָּדוֹל, וַאֲפִילוּ יֵשׁ עֲלֵיהֶם תּוֹאַר לֶחֶם, מִכָּל מָקוֹם אֵין לוֹ דִּין לֶחֶם וּמְבָרְכִין עָלָיו רַק "בּוֹרֵא מִינֵי מְזוֹנוֹת" וּלְאַחֲרָיו "עַל הַמִּחְיָה", וַאֲפִילוּ אָכַל כְּדֵי שְׂבִיעָה. וְאִם לֹא בִּישְּׁלָן, אֶלָּא שֶׁעֵירָה עֲלֵיהֶם רוֹטֶב רוֹתֵחַ, הָוֵי סָפֵק בְּרָכָה

---

§6 עִיסָּה שֶׁנִּתְבַּשֵּׁל — **Dough that was cooked** in water וְאַחַר כָּךְ נֶאֱפָה — **and afterward was baked,** כְּגוֹן בייגיל — **such as bagels** פרעצין — **and soft pretzels,** לֶחֶם גָּמוּר הוּא — **are** considered to be **standard bread;**[41] וְדַוְקָא כְּשֶׁנֶּאֱפָה הֵיטֵב — **but only if they were baked well** (עַיֵּין פְּרִי מְגָדִים סִימָן קס״ח אֵשֶׁל אַבְרָהָם סְעִיף קָטָן ל״ט — **see** *Pri Megadim, Siman* 168, *Eishel Avraham* §39).[42]

§7 לֶחֶם גָּמוּר — Regarding **regular** baked **bread** שֶׁבִּשְּׁלוֹ — **that was** then **cooked,** אוֹ טִגְּנוֹ בְּחֶמְאָה וְכַדּוֹמֶה — **or fried in butter or the like,** אֲפִילוּ הֶעֱבִיר מִמֶּנּוּ תּוֹאַר לֶחֶם — **even if** in this process **it lost its bread-like appearance,** כְּגוֹן שֶׁטְּחוֹ בְּבֵיצִים — **such as if it were smeared with eggs,** the halachah is אִם יֵשׁ בַּפְּרוּסָה כְּזַיִת — **as long as the piece** that he is eating **is** at least the size of **a** ***kezayis,*** כָּל דִּין לֶחֶם עָלָיו — **all of the halachos of** standard **bread apply to it.**[43] וְאִם אֵין בְּכָל פְּרוּסָה כְּזַיִת — **However, if none of the pieces** that he is eating **were** originally[44] as large as **a** *kezayis,* אַף עַל פִּי שֶׁעַל יְדֵי הַבִּישׁוּל נָפְחוּ — **even if they swelled as a result of the cooking,** וְיֵשׁ בְּכָל פְּרוּסָה כְּזַיִת — **so that** now **each piece is the size of a** *kezayis,* אוֹ שֶׁנִּדְבַּק עַל יְדֵי הַבִּישׁוּל — **and** even **if during the cooking process** the pieces **became attached** to each other, וְנַעֲשָׂה גּוּשׁ גָּדוֹל — **becoming one large mass,** וַאֲפִילוּ יֵשׁ עֲלֵיהֶם תּוֹאַר לֶחֶם — **and even if the pieces** still **retain their bread-like appearance,** מִכָּל מָקוֹם אֵין לוֹ דִּין לֶחֶם — **they nevertheless do not have the halachic status of bread.** וּמְבָרְכִין עָלָיו רַק "בּוֹרֵא מִינֵי מְזוֹנוֹת" — **One recites only the** ***borei minei mezonos*** **blessing** before eating **it,** וּלְאַחֲרָיו "עַל הַמִּחְיָה" — **and after** eating **it,** ***Al HaMichyah,*** וַאֲפִילוּ אָכַל כְּדֵי שְׂבִיעָה — **even if one ate an amount that would** fully **satiate.**

וְאִם לֹא בִּישְּׁלָן — **If one did not cook** the pieces of bread, אֶלָּא שֶׁעֵירָה עֲלֵיהֶם רוֹטֶב רוֹתֵחַ — **but poured a boiling broth over them,** הָוֵי סָפֵק בְּרָכָה — **then the** proper

---

Bircas HaMazon. [This applies only in a case where the resulting item is very soft and thin. If it is not soft and thin, it has the halachic status of regular bread (*Mishnah Berurah* 168:37).]

41. See below, *se'if* 8, which states that if it was only cooked in water and not baked, it would not have the halachah of *pas* at all.

42. *Pri Megadim* writes that if they were put into the oven only long enough to develop a crust, they are not considered bread.

43. Thus, if one of the pieces is at least a *kezayis,* he should recite *hamotzi* on that piece and exempt the rest of the pieces, even if they are smaller than a *kezayis* (*Mishnah Berurah* 168:53). Although dough that was only cooked is not considered to be bread (see *se'if* 5 and *se'if* 8), nevertheless, here, where the bread was already baked, it does not lose its status as bread upon being cooked (see *Mishnah Berurah* ibid. §69) unless the pieces are smaller than a *kezayis.*

44. *Mishnah Berurah* 168:54.

מִשּׁוּם דִּמְסַפְּקָא לָן אִי עֵירוּי חָשׁוּב בִּישׁוּל לְעִנְיָן זֶה אוֹ לֹא, וְאֵין לֶאֱכוֹל זֹאת אֶלָּא בְּתוֹךְ הַסְּעוּדָה[45]. וְאִם לֹא בִישְּׁלָן, אֶלָּא שְׁרָאָן בְּמַשְׁקִים, אוֹ בְּמָרָק וְכַדּוֹמֶה, וְאֵין בַּפְּרוּסוֹת כְּזַיִת, בָּזֶה תָּלוּי אִם יֵשׁ בָּהֶן תּוֹאַר לֶחֶם אוֹ לֹא. שֶׁאִם יֵשׁ לָהֶן תּוֹאַר לֶחֶם, הָוֵי לְהוּ דִּין לֶחֶם גָּמוּר, וְאִם אֵין לָהֶן תּוֹאַר לֶחֶם, אֵין לָהֶם דִּין לֶחֶם[46], וַאֲפִילּוּ אָכַל כְּדֵי שְׂבִיעָה, מְבָרֵךְ רַק "בּוֹרֵא מִינֵי מְזוֹנוֹת" וּלְאַחֲרָיו "עַל הַמִּחְיָה"[47]. אִם נִשְׁתַּנָּה מַרְאֶה הַמַּשְׁקִין מֵחֲמַת הַפְּרוּסוֹת, בְּיָדוּעַ שֶׁנֶּאֱבַד מֵהֶם תּוֹאַר לֶחֶם[48]. וְכֵן אִם נִשְׁרוּ בְּיַיִן אָדוֹם[49], אֵין לָהֶם עוֹד תּוֹאַר לֶחֶם.

אִי — blessing is a matter of doubt, מִשּׁוּם דִּמְסַפְּקָא לָן — because we are unsure עֵירוּי חָשׁוּב בִּישׁוּל לְעִנְיָן זֶה אוֹ לֹא — whether altering the pieces by pouring is equivalent to cooking with regard to this halachah or not. וְאֵין לֶאֱכוֹל זֹאת — Therefore, one should not eat this food אֶלָּא בְּתוֹךְ הַסְּעוּדָה — except during a bread meal when he has already washed *netilas yadayim* and recited the *hamotzi* blessing on regular bread.[45]

וְאִם לֹא בִישְּׁלָן — If one did not cook the pieces of bread, אֶלָּא שְׁרָאָן בְּמַשְׁקִים — but rather soaked them in a liquid אוֹ בְּמָרָק וְכַדּוֹמֶה — or in a broth, or the like, וְאֵין בַּפְּרוּסוֹת כְּזַיִת — and the pieces are not the size of a *kezayis*, בָּזֶה תָּלוּי — in this case the halachah depends אִם יֵשׁ בָּהֶן תּוֹאַר לֶחֶם אוֹ לֹא — on whether the pieces retained a bread-like appearance or not. שֶׁאִם יֵשׁ לָהֶן תּוֹאַר לֶחֶם — If they do retain a bread-like appearance הָוֵי לְהוּ דִּין לֶחֶם גָּמוּר — then they retain the halachah of standard bread; וְאִם אֵין לָהֶן תּוֹאַר לֶחֶם — but if they no longer have a bread-like appearance אֵין לָהֶם דִּין לֶחֶם — then they no longer have the halachic status of bread,[46] וַאֲפִילּוּ אָכַל כְּדֵי שְׂבִיעָה — and even if he ate an amount that would fully satiate, מְבָרֵךְ רַק "בּוֹרֵא מִינֵי מְזוֹנוֹת" — he recites only *borei minei mezonos* before eating it וּלְאַחֲרָיו "עַל הַמִּחְיָה" — and *Al HaMichyah* after eating it.[47]

אִם נִשְׁתַּנָּה מַרְאֶה הַמַּשְׁקִין — If, during the soaking, the color of the liquid changed מֵחֲמַת הַפְּרוּסוֹת — as a result of the pieces of bread, בְּיָדוּעַ שֶׁנֶּאֱבַד מֵהֶם תּוֹאַר לֶחֶם — then the pieces have certainly lost their bread-like appearance.[48] וְכֵן אִם נִשְׁרוּ בְּיַיִן אָדוֹם — Likewise, if the pieces were soaked in red wine,[49] אֵין לָהֶם עוֹד תּוֹאַר לֶחֶם — they no longer are considered to have a bread-like appearance.

---

45. Since there is a question whether to recite *hamotzi* or *mezonos* on such bread, one should eat this food only when it does not require any blessing at all, that is, during a bread meal. [Generally, any food eaten during a meal is exempted from its own blessing by the *hamotzi* blessing that was recited upon the bread at the beginning of the meal (see above, 43:1; see also *se'if* 6 there).]

46. However, if the pieces were a *kezayis* or larger, they retain the status of bread regardless of their appearance (*Shulchan Aruch* 168:10).

47. If the bread was merely crumbled but not soaked, even if the pieces are extremely small, they retain the halachic status of bread, since the fact that they no longer look like bread is only due to their small size; they were not essentially altered in any way (see *Shulchan Aruch* 168:10; *Mishnah Berurah* 168:60, 63). See below, *se'if* 9, regarding crumbs that were further altered and made into a different food.

48. When the halachah depends on the pieces retaining their bread-like appearance (such as when they are soaked), the whitish color of the soaking water is an indication that they have indeed lost that appearance (see *Mishnah Berurah* 168:63).

49. Regarding white wine, see *Beur Halachah* to 168:12 s.v. ביין אדום.

177 BERACHOS UPON FOOD MADE OF THE FIVE SPECIES OF GRAIN — SIMAN 48:8

ח. עִיסָּה שֶׁנִּילוֹשָׁה אֲפִילוּ בְּמַיִם לְבַד[50] וּבִישְּׁלָהּ – מְבָרֵךְ עָלָיו "בּוֹרֵא מִינֵי מְזוֹנוֹת" וּלְאַחֲרָיו "עַל הַמִּחְיָה", אֲפִילוּ אָכַל שִׁיעוּר שְׂבִיעָה[51]. וְכֵן גְּרִיסִין (גרויפען) שֶׁנַּעֲשִׂין מֵחֲמֵשֶׁת מִינֵי דָגָן וּבִישְּׁלָן – מְבָרְכִין עֲלֵיהֶן גַּם כֵּן "בּוֹרֵא מִינֵי מְזוֹנוֹת" וּלְאַחֲרֵיהֶן "עַל הַמִּחְיָה"[52], אֲפִילוּ אָכַל שִׁיעוּר שְׂבִיעָה. וְאִם[53] אוֹכְלָן עִם הַמָּרָק, וְכֵן מַאֲכָלֵי עִיסָּה שֶׁאוֹכְלִין עִם הַמָּרָק, אוֹ עִם הֶחָלָב, שֶׁנִּתְבַּשְּׁלוּ בָּהּ, אֵין

§8 **עִיסָּה שֶׁנִּילוֹשָׁה אֲפִילוּ בְּמַיִם לְבַד — Dough, even if it was kneaded with water only,**[50] **וּבִישְּׁלָהּ — but** rather than baking it in an oven, **one cooked it** in water, **מְבָרֵךְ עָלָיו "בּוֹרֵא מִינֵי מְזוֹנוֹת"— one recites *borei minei mezonos*** before eating it **וּלְאַחֲרָיו "עַל הַמִּחְיָה" — and *Al HaMichyah* after** eating **it, אֲפִילוּ אָכַל שִׁיעוּר שְׂבִיעָה — even when he ate an amount that** fully **satiates.**[51] **וְכֵן גְּרִיסִין (גרויפען) — Likewise,** a dish of cooked **grits שֶׁנַּעֲשִׂין מֵחֲמֵשֶׁת מִינֵי דָגָן — that was made** from one of **the five species of grain וּבִישְּׁלָן — and then cooked** in water, **מְבָרְכִין עֲלֵיהֶן גַּם כֵּן "בּוֹרֵא מִינֵי מְזוֹנוֹת" — one recites *borei minei mezonos* before eating it as well וּלְאַחֲרֵיהֶן "עַל הַמִּחְיָה" — and after** eating it, ***Al HaMichyah*,**[52] **אֲפִילוּ אָכַל שִׁיעוּר שְׂבִיעָה — even if he ate an amount that would** fully **satiate.**

Kitzur now sets out which *berachah* is appropriate for a mixture of grain foods and other foods.[53] This *se'if* discusses a mixture of grain food and liquids; *se'if* 10 discusses a mixture of grain food and solids.

וְאִם אוֹכְלָן עִם הַמָּרָק — If one eats these foods together **with broth, וְכֵן מַאֲכָלֵי עִיסָּה שֶׁאוֹכְלִין עִם הַמָּרָק — as well as foods made from dough that one eats** together **with broth, אוֹ עִם הֶחָלָב, שֶׁנִּתְבַּשְּׁלוּ בָּהּ — or with the milk in which they are cooked, אֵין**

50. This is in contrast to dough that was kneaded with other liquids, which even if baked in an oven does not attain the halachah of standard bread; see above, *se'if* 2.

51. Dough that was baked after it was cooked in water does attain the halachic status of bread (see above, *se'if* 6). Similarly, if, after it was baked, it was cooked, it does not lose its status of bread (depending on its size), as set out in the previous *se'if.* Here, the only process with which this dough was treated was cooking; it therefore never attains the halachah of *pas* at all (see *Mishnah Berurah* 168:69;72).

According to many authorities, however, when a regular dough was originally kneaded with the intention of baking it into bread, then it is considered bread even if it was ultimately cooked, as long as it has the appearance of bread. See *Mishnah Berurah* (ibid. §75), who writes that this opinion is followed in a case where one eats of this bread to satiety, and he must therefore recite *Bircas HaMazon* upon a meal of such bread. See *Beur Halachah* to 168:13 s.v. ונהגו להקל.

Furthermore, even when the dough is made with the intention that it will be cooked, not baked, a God-fearing individual should be concerned for the opinion that holds that such dough is to be considered regular bread as long as the pieces are at least a *kezayis* and they have the general appearance of bread. He should therefore eat such products only after reciting *hamotzi* on regular bread with the intention that the *hamotzi* blessing exempt this item from its *berachah rishonah* obligation (see *Shulchan Aruch* and *Rama* 168:13; *Mishnah Berurah* ibid. §76-78; *Beur Halachah* s.v. ויורא שמים).

52. See *Mishnah Berurah* (208:3), which states that, depending on the type of preparation, the proper blessing for cooked grits may be *ha'adamah;* see also below, 52:17.

53. When two foods are eaten together, a blessing is recited only on the primary food (עִקָּר); the subordinate food (טָפֵל) does not require its own blessing. [These halachos are discussed at length below, *Siman* 54.] When it comes to mixtures of foods, it must be determined which component of the mixture is the primary one and which is the subordinate (see below, 55:5-6). Here, Kitzur sets out the halachah as it pertains to the mixtures commonly eaten with grain foods. As we will see

BERACHOS UPON FOOD MADE OF THE FIVE SPECIES OF GRAIN — SIMAN 48:8 178

צָרִיךְ לְבָרֵךְ עַל הַמָּרָק וְהֶחָלָב, כִּי הֵמָּה טְפֵלִים וּבְטֵלִים לְגַבֵּיהֶן.[54] אֲבָל אִם בִּישֵּׁל רַק מְעַט לְבִיבוֹת אוֹ גְרִיסִין, וְעִיקַּר כַּוָּונָתוֹ רַק בִּשְׁבִיל הָרוֹטֶב אוֹ הֶחָלָב, בְּעִנְיָן זֶה אֵינָן בְּטֵלִין וּמְבָרֵךְ עֲלֵיהֶן "שֶׁהַכֹּל"[55], וְאַף עַל פִּי שֶׁאוֹכֵל גַּם הַלְּבִיבוֹת וְהַגְּרִיסִין, אֵין הָרוֹטֶב וְהֶחָלָב בְּטֵלוֹת, כֵּיוָן שֶׁהֵן הָעִיקָּר[56]. וּמִכָּל מָקוֹם[57], כְּדֵי לַעֲשׂוֹת עַל צַד הַיּוֹתֵר טוֹב רָאוּי לְבָרֵךְ תְּחִלָּה "שֶׁהַכֹּל" עַל הָרוֹטֶב אוֹ עַל הֶחָלָב לְבַד וְלִשְׁתּוֹת קְצָת, וְאַחַר כָּךְ יְבָרֵךְ עַל הַלְּבִיבוֹת אוֹ הַגְּרִיסִין "בּוֹרֵא מִינֵי מְזוֹנוֹת" (עַיֵּין מַחֲצִית הַשֶּׁקֶל סִימָן

צָרִיךְ לְבָרֵךְ עַל הַמָּרָק וְהֶחָלָב — there is no need to recite a blessing on the broth or the milk, but only on the grain product that he is eating with them, **כִּי הֵמָּה טְפֵלִים — for the liquids are** considered **subordinate וּבְטֵלִים לְגַבֵּיהֶן — and insignificant in relation to** the *mezonos* foods.[54]

אֲבָל — However, אִם בִּישֵּׁל רַק מְעַט לְבִיבוֹת אוֹ גְרִיסִין — if one cooked a liquid with **only a small amount of dumplings or grits, וְעִיקַּר כַּוָּונָתוֹ — and his primary interest** in this dish **רַק בִּשְׁבִיל הָרוֹטֶב אוֹ הֶחָלָב — is only the broth or the milk, בְּעִנְיָן זֶה אֵינָן בְּטֵלִין — in this case** the liquid **is not** considered to be **insignificant, וּמְבָרֵךְ עֲלֵיהֶן "שֶׁהַכֹּל" — and one must therefore recite upon them,** i.e., the liquids, their proper blessing of *shehakol.*[55] **וְאַף עַל פִּי שֶׁאוֹכֵל גַּם הַלְּבִיבוֹת וְהַגְּרִיסִין — And even though he is eating the dumplings and the grits as well, אֵין הָרוֹטֶב וְהֶחָלָב בְּטֵלוֹת —** still, **the liquid and the milk are not** considered **insignificant, כֵּיוָן שֶׁהֵן הָעִיקָּר — since they are** his **primary** interest in this dish.[56] **וּמִכָּל מָקוֹם — Nevertheless,** there remains some level of doubt regarding this;[57] **כְּדֵי לַעֲשׂוֹת עַל צַד הַיּוֹתֵר טוֹב —** therefore, **in order to act** regarding these *berachos* **in the ideal fashion רָאוּי לְבָרֵךְ תְּחִלָּה "שֶׁהַכֹּל" — it is appropriate to first recite the** *shehakol* **blessing עַל הָרוֹטֶב אוֹ עַל הֶחָלָב לְבַד — upon the broth or the milk by itself, וְלִשְׁתּוֹת קְצָת — and to drink a bit** of the liquid, **וְאַחַר כָּךְ יְבָרֵךְ עַל הַלְּבִיבוֹת אוֹ הַגְּרִיסִין "בּוֹרֵא מִינֵי מְזוֹנוֹת" — and afterward to recite the** *borei minei mezonos* **blessing upon the dumplings or the grits** (עַיֵּין מַחֲצִית הַשֶּׁקֶל סִימָן

---

in these halachos, grain foods are often an exception to some of the standard rules of blessings on primary and subordinate foods.

54. One who eats chicken soup with matzah balls (dumplings) needs to recite only a *mezonos* if every spoonful of soup eaten will contain some of the matzah ball.

With regard to the common case of eating cereal and milk, as long as there is a regular amount of milk added to the cereal, and the milk is added to contribute to the taste or to help swallow the cereal, one is to recite only the blessing upon the cereal. This is the halachah even if one is thirsty and enjoys the milk as well. However, if more milk than is common is added to the cereal, the milk is considered a separate drink that he is drinking together with the cereal. In this case (regardless of whether he was thirsty at the time), he must recite the *shehakol* blessing on the milk (see below, 52:2). Sugar is always considered subordinate to the cereal, and does not require a separate blessing when added. In contrast, fruit or banana sliced into the cereal is *not* subordinate to the cereal, and requires its own blessing (*Igros Moshe, Orach Chaim* IV, §43; I, §71).

55. See below, 52:2, for the halachos of this blessing.

56. However, they do not make the grain foods subordinate to them either, as will be explained at the end of the *se'if.* Therefore, a blessing is required on both the solid food and the liquid.

57. That is, there is an opinion that the grain food is considered so important that it renders even the majority of liquid in which it was cooked subordinate to it, and would therefore exempt the broth with its blessing of *mezonos.*

179 BERACHOS UPON FOOD MADE OF THE FIVE SPECIES OF GRAIN — SIMAN 48:9-10

ר״ה סְעִיף קָטָן ו׳)[58], שֶׁגַּם הֵמָּה אֵינָן טְפֵלוֹת, אַף עַל פִּי שֶׁאֵין הַכַּוָּנָה בִּשְׁבִילָן, לְפִי שֶׁמִּין דָּגָן הוּא חָשׁוּב וְאֵינוֹ נַעֲשֶׂה טָפֵל לְהַפְסִיד בִּרְכָתוֹ כֹּל שֶׁבָּא לִיתֵּן טַעַם בַּקְּדֵירָה[59].

ט. מַאֲכָלִים שֶׁעוֹשִׂים מִמַּצָּה כְּתוּשָׁה אוֹ מִלֶּחֶם מְפוֹרָר (קנעדיל, קרעמזיל) שֶׁמְּעָרְבִים אוֹתָן בְּשׁוּמָן וּבֵיצִים וְחָלָב וְגוֹבְלִין וּמְבַשְּׁלִין, אוֹ מְטַגְּנִין אוֹתָן, מְבָרְכִין עֲלֵיהֶן ״בּוֹרֵא מִינֵי מְזוֹנוֹת״ וּלְאַחֲרֵיהֶם ״עַל הַמִּחְיָה״[60].

י. דְּבָרִים מִמִּינֵי דָגָן שֶׁבִּישְּׁלָן עִם שְׁאָר מִינִים, כְּמוֹ שֶׁהוּא הַדֶּרֶךְ שֶׁמְּבַשְּׁלִין פֵּרוּרֵי עִיסָּה עִם פּוֹלִין אוֹ קִטְנִיּוֹת (פערפאל עם באנדליך או ערבסין),

---

שֶׁגַּם הֵמָּה אֵינָן טְפֵלוֹת — ר״ה סְעִיף קָטָן ו׳ — see *Machatzis HaShekel* 205:6).[58] Both blessings are necessary here **since** the grain foods **are also not subordinate** to the broth, אַף עַל פִּי שֶׁאֵין הַכַּוָּנָה בִּשְׁבִילָן — **despite the fact that they are not the primary interest** of the one eating the broth. לְפִי שֶׁמִּין דָּגָן הוּא חָשׁוּב — The reason for this is **that grain** by its nature is **inherently significant,** וְאֵינוֹ נַעֲשֶׂה טָפֵל — **and does not become subordinate** to another food לְהַפְסִיד בִּרְכָתוֹ — to the point that it **loses its** own obligation of its *mezonos* **blessing,** כֹּל שֶׁבָּא לִיתֵּן טַעַם בַּקְּדֵירָה — **as long as it serves to add flavor to the dish.**[59]

§9 מַאֲכָלִים שֶׁעוֹשִׂים מִמַּצָּה כְּתוּשָׁה — **Foods that are made from matzah meal** אוֹ מִלֶּחֶם מְפוֹרָר — **or from breadcrumbs** (קנעדיל, קרעמזיל — for example, a **dumpling** or matzah-meal **pancake**) שֶׁמְּעָרְבִים אוֹתָן — **that** are prepared **by mixing** the crumbs or small pieces בְּשׁוּמָן וּבֵיצִים וְחָלָב — **with fat, eggs, or milk,** וְגוֹבְלִין — **kneading them,** וּמְבַשְּׁלִין, אוֹ מְטַגְּנִין אוֹתָן — **and** then **cooking or frying them,** מְבָרְכִין עֲלֵיהֶן ״בּוֹרֵא מִינֵי מְזוֹנוֹת״ — **one is to recite *borei minei mezonos*** before eating them וּלְאַחֲרֵיהֶם ״עַל הַמִּחְיָה״ — **and *Al HaMichyah* after** eating **them.**[60]

§10 דְּבָרִים מִמִּינֵי דָגָן — Food **items** made **from the** five **species of grains** שֶׁבִּישְּׁלָן עִם שְׁאָר מִינִים — **that were cooked with other kinds** of food, כְּמוֹ שֶׁהוּא הַדֶּרֶךְ — **as is the common practice,** שֶׁמְּבַשְּׁלִין פֵּרוּרֵי עִיסָּה עִם פּוֹלִין אוֹ קִטְנִיּוֹת — **that bits of dough are cooked with beans or legumes** (פערפאל עם באנדליך או ערבסין — as

---

58. *Machatzis HaShekel* there explains that ordinarily, when eating two foods, neither of which is subordinate to the other, if the blessing for one is *mezonos* and the blessing for the other is *shehakol,* the *mezonos* should be recited first (see below, *Siman* 55). In this case, however, there is some doubt as to whether the broth is subordinate to the grain foods or not. Thus, if one would recite *mezonos* first, there is a possibility that he would exempt the broth from any requirement of its own blessing. Therefore, in this case, we reverse the order: The *shehakol* is recited first on the broth; this leaves the grain foods with a definite requirement of a blessing, since grain foods never lose their own requirement, as Kitzur explains.

Igros Moshe (*Orach Chaim* I, §69) rules that preferably one should first recite *mezonos* on the dumpling, and then recite a *shehakol* on another food with the intention of also exempting the broth from its *shehakol* obligation. If there is no *shehakol* food available, he should nevertheless recite a *mezonos* on the dumpling and then a *shehakol* on the soup, because the *mezonos* blessing should always precede the *shehakol* blessing. [This is based on a variant reading of *Magen Avraham* 205:6.]

59. Or to make the dish more satisfying (see *Mishnah Berurah* 208:8); see below, *se'if* 10.

60. This is so even if the resulting pieces are larger than a *kezayis* and even if he ate many of them. If, however, the matzah meal or bread crumbs were kneaded with water and baked, they would be considered regular bread, and would require a *hamotzi* (*Mishnah Berurah* 168:59). See Appendix of Kitzur's editorial glosses for further discussion.

BERACHOS UPON FOOD MADE OF THE FIVE SPECIES OF GRAIN — SIMAN 48:10 180

וַאֲפִילוּ מִין אֶחָד הוּא הָרוֹב, מִכָּל מָקוֹם כֵּיוָן שֶׁכָּל אֶחָד מוּבְדָּל בִּפְנֵי עַצְמוֹ[61] צָרִיךְ לְבָרֵךְ שְׁתֵּי בְרָכוֹת[62], דְּהַיְינוּ שֶׁמְּבָרֵךְ תְּחִלָּה עַל קְצָת פֵּירוּרֵי עִיסָּה "בּוֹרֵא מִינֵי מְזוֹנוֹת"[63] וְאוֹכְלָן, וְאַחַר כָּךְ מְבָרֵךְ עַל קְצָת פּוֹלִין "בּוֹרֵא פְּרִי הָאֲדָמָה" וְאוֹכְלָן, וְאַחַר כָּךְ אוֹכְלָן בְּיַחַד וְהָרוֹטֶב הוּא טָפֵל וְאֵינוֹ צָרִיךְ לְבָרֵךְ עָלֶיהָ (וְעוֹד שֶׁהֲרֵי נִפְטְרָה בְּבִרְכַּת "בּוֹרֵא פְּרִי הָאֲדָמָה", כִּדְלְקַמָּן סִימָן נ"ג סְעִיף ב')[64]. אֲבָל אִם נִתְמָעֲכוּ וְנִתְעָרְבוּ יַחַד, כְּגוֹן מַאֲכָל שֶׁעוֹשִׂין שֶׁמְּעָרְבִין קֶמַח וּבֵיצִים וּגְבִינָה וּמְטַגְּנִים אוֹ מְבַשְּׁלִים אוֹתוֹ, אַף עַל פִּי שֶׁהַקֶּמַח הוּא הַמּוּעָט, מִכָּל מָקוֹם כֵּיוָן שֶׁהוּא מֵחֲמֵשֶׁת מִינֵי דָּגָן הוּא חָשׁוּב[65] וּמְבָרְכִין עָלָיו "בּוֹרֵא מִינֵי מְזוֹנוֹת"

---

in the dish of **farfel together with beans or chickpeas),** **וַאֲפִילוּ מִין אֶחָד הוּא הָרוֹב** — **even if one of the components** in this mixture **constitutes the majority** of the dish, **מִכָּל מָקוֹם** — **nevertheless,** **כֵּיוָן שֶׁכָּל אֶחָד מוּבְדָּל בִּפְנֵי עַצְמוֹ** — **since each** of the ingredients **is separate** and **individually** recognizable,[61] **צָרִיךְ לְבָרֵךְ שְׁתֵּי בְרָכוֹת** — **one must recite two blessings;**[62] **דְּהַיְינוּ** — **that is,** **שֶׁמְּבָרֵךְ תְּחִלָּה עַל קְצָת פֵּירוּרֵי עִיסָּה "בּוֹרֵא מִינֵי מְזוֹנוֹת"** — **one should first recite the** ***borei minei mezonos*** **blessing** on **some** of the **bits of dough,**[63] **וְאוֹכְלָן** — **and eat** some of **them,** **וְאַחַר כָּךְ** — **and after that,** **מְבָרֵךְ עַל קְצָת פּוֹלִין "בּוֹרֵא פְּרִי הָאֲדָמָה"** — **he should recite the** ***borei pri ha'adamah*** **blessing on some of the beans,** **וְאוֹכְלָן** — **and eat** some of **them.** **וְאַחַר כָּךְ אוֹכְלָן בְּיַחַד** — **After this, he may eat them together.** **וְהָרוֹטֶב הוּא טָפֵל** — **The liquid** that is part of this dish **is** considered **subordinate** to the rest of the dish **וְאֵינוֹ צָרִיךְ לְבָרֵךְ עָלֶיהָ** — **and one is not required to recite a** separate **blessing upon it.** **(וְעוֹד שֶׁהֲרֵי נִפְטְרָה** — **Additionally,** the liquid **is exempt** from its own blessing **בְּבִרְכַּת "בּוֹרֵא פְּרִי הָאֲדָמָה"** — because it is included **in the** ***borei pri ha'adamah*** **blessing** that was recited over the beans, **כִּדְלְקַמָּן סִימָן נ"ג סְעִיף ב'** — **as explained below, 53:2).**[64]

אֲבָל — **However,** **אִם נִתְמָעֲכוּ וְנִתְעָרְבוּ יַחַד** — **if** the two ingredients were not separate, but **mashed and mixed together,** **כְּגוֹן מַאֲכָל שֶׁעוֹשִׂין** — **such as a food that is prepared** **שֶׁמְּעָרְבִין קֶמַח וּבֵיצִים וּגְבִינָה** — **by mixing** together **flour, eggs, and cheese,** **וּמְטַגְּנִים אוֹ מְבַשְּׁלִים אוֹתוֹ** — **and frying or cooking** this mixture; **אַף עַל פִּי שֶׁהַקֶּמַח הוּא הַמּוּעָט** — in this case, **although the flour is only the minority** of the dish, **מִכָּל מָקוֹם** — **nevertheless,** **כֵּיוָן שֶׁהוּא מֵחֲמֵשֶׁת מִינֵי דָּגָן** — **since it is** flour **of one of the five species of grains** **הוּא חָשׁוּב** — **it is** considered the most **significant** component of the mixture,[65] **וּמְבָרְכִין עָלָיו "בּוֹרֵא מִינֵי מְזוֹנוֹת"** — **and one recites**

---

61. See *Mishnah Berurah* 212:1.

62. According to Kitzur, when the foods are individually recognizable, we do not say that one should recite only the blessing on the primary food, but rather a separate blessing is required for each food. According to *Mishnah Berurah* (212:1), however, in this case, one should recite only the blessing on the food that is in the majority (see *Shaar HaTziyun* 212:2); see below, 54:5, with notes. See also Appendix of Kitzur's editorial glosses for further discussion.

63. See below, 55:5, which states that the *mezonos* is recited first in this case.

64. There, Kitzur explains that the appropriate blessing for a vegetable broth (the liquid that results from cooking vegetables in water) is *borei pri ha'adamah,* even if it is consumed by itself.

65. If none of the components were a grain product, the blessings would follow the ingredient that makes up the majority of the dish; see below, 54:5.

181 BERACHOS UPON FOOD MADE OF THE FIVE SPECIES OF GRAIN — SIMAN 48:10

וְאַחֲרָיו "עַל הַמִּחְיָה"[66]. וְאָמְנָם דַּוְקָא כְּשֶׁנּוֹתְנִים אֶת הַקֶּמַח בִּשְׁבִיל שֶׁיִּתֵּן טַעַם[67], אֲבָל אִם לוֹקְחִין רַק מְעַט קֶמַח לְדֶבֶק בְּעָלְמָא כְּמוֹ שֶׁהוּא הַדֶּרֶךְ שֶׁמְּתַקְּנִין מִינֵי לְפִתָּן בִּמְעַט קֶמַח, וְכֵן אוֹפִין מַעֲשֵׂה אוֹפֶה מִשְּׁקֵדִים וְצוּקֶער וּבֵיצִים וְנוֹתְנִים בּוֹ רַק מְעַט קֶמַח לְדֶבֶק בְּעָלְמָא, אָז בָּטֵל הַקֶּמַח וְאֵין מְבָרְכִין רַק עַל הָעִיקָּר[68]. וְכֵן רוֹטֶב

---

before eating this food the blessing of ***borei minei mezonos,*** **וְאַחֲרָיו "עַל הַמִּחְיָה"** — **and after** eating **it,** ***Al HaMichyah.***[66]

An exception to the above rule regarding a mixture that contains a grain product: **וְאָמְנָם דַּוְקָא** — **However,** a small amount of flour is considered the dominant ingredient **only** **כְּשֶׁנּוֹתְנִים אֶת הַקֶּמַח** — **when the flour is added** to the dish **בִּשְׁבִיל שֶׁיִּתֵּן טַעַם** — **in order to impart flavor** to the dish.[67] **אֲבָל אִם לוֹקְחִין רַק מְעַט קֶמַח** — **However, if one takes only a small amount of flour** **לְדֶבֶק בְּעָלְמָא** — and adds it to the dish **merely as a binding agent,** **כְּמוֹ שֶׁהוּא הַדֶּרֶךְ** — **as is common** **שֶׁמְּתַקְּנִין מִינֵי לְפִתָּן בִּמְעַט קֶמַח** — **in the case of different kinds of relishes that are prepared with a small amount of flour** added; **וְכֵן אוֹפִין מַעֲשֵׂה אוֹפֶה מִשְּׁקֵדִים וְצוּקֶער וּבֵיצִים** — **and also** in the case of **baked goods that are baked with almonds, sugar, and eggs,** **וְנוֹתְנִים בּוֹ רַק מְעַט קֶמַח** — **and just a small amount of flour is added to it** **לְדֶבֶק בְּעָלְמָא** — **merely to bind** these ingredients together, **אָז בָּטֵל הַקֶּמַח** — **in these cases, the flour is** considered **insignificant** **וְאֵין מְבָרְכִין רַק עַל הָעִיקָּר** — **and one is to recite the blessing only on the primary** ingredient in the mixture.[68] **וְכֵן רוֹטֶב** — **Likewise,**

---

66. See *Mishnah Berurah* (208:48), which states that although one recites *mezonos* before eating a food that has any amount of grain, one recites *Al HaMichyah* only if one ate a *kezayis* of the grain in the mixture within the time frame of *k'dei achilas pras* (see below, 51:5). See *Igros Moshe, Orach Chaim* IV, §41, which states that with regard to *berachah acharonah* this time frame is a bit less than three minutes. If one did eat a *kezayis* of the mixture but not a *kezayis* of grain within the time of *k'dei achilas pras,* one should recite the *berachah acharonah* of *Borei Nefashos* (for halachos of the *Borei Nefashos* blessing, see below, *Siman* 51).

A common application of this halachah occurs when eating exactly a *kezayis* of cake. One who eats only a *kezayis* of cake has in fact not eaten a complete *kezayis* of grain, since the cake is made up of other ingredients (e.g., sugar, flavorings) as well. According to the above rule that one does not recite *Al HaMichyah* if one did not eat a *kezayis* of grain within the time of *k'dei achilas pras,* one should not recite *Al HaMichayah* in this case, but rather *Borei Nefashos.* Nevertheless, common custom, as cited by *Mishnah Berurah* (208:48), is to recite *Al HaMichyah* in this case. Although *Mishnah Berurah* offers a justification for this custom, he nevertheless concludes that one should ideally avoid this situation (either by eating less than a *kezayis* of cake, or by eating enough cake so that he ate a *kezyis* of grain). *Igros Moshe* (*Orach Chaim* I, §71) does not accept the justification for the custom offered by *Mishnah Berurah,* and does not permit one to recite *Al HaMichyah* upon eating less than a *kezayis* of grain in the cake within the requisite time frame. Nevertheless, *Igros Moshe* also does not permit one to recite *Borei Nefashos* when eating exactly a *kezayis,* as this would be contrary to common custom. He therefore asserts that one must avoid the situation (in the manner mentioned above).

67. Or to make the dish more filling (*Mishnah Berurah* 208:8).

68. Likewise, if flour was added only to give the food a certain aroma or color, it is not considered the dominant ingredient (see *Shulchan Aruch* 204:12).

Regarding a pie with a *mezonos* pie crust, or an ice cream sandwich with *mezonos* wafers, the proper blessing depends on the intention of the eater. One who enjoys both the pie and the crust, or both the ice cream and the wafers, must recite a *mezonos* on the pie crust or wafer and the appropriate blessing for the

BERACHOS UPON FOOD MADE OF THE FIVE SPECIES OF GRAIN — SIMAN 48:10 182

שֶׁמְּבַשְּׁלִין וּמְתַקְּנִין אוֹתָהּ עִם קְצָת קֶמַח קָלוּי וּמְטוּגָּן בְּחֶמְאָה, אֵין מְבָרְכִין עַל הָרוֹטֶב כִּי אִם "שֶׁהַכֹּל". אֲבָל אִם הוּא בּוֹרֵר אֶת הַפֵּירוּרִים הַמְטוּגָּנִין וְאוֹכְלָן בִּפְנֵי עַצְמָן צָרִיךְ לְבָרֵךְ עֲלֵיהֶם "בּוֹרֵא מִינֵי מְזוֹנוֹת", וְאִם אוֹכֵל מֵהֶם כְּזַיִת צָרִיךְ לְבָרֵךְ אַחֲרֵיהֶן "עַל הַמִּחְיָה" וְכוּ'.

---

on a broth **שֶׁמְּבַשְּׁלִין וּמְתַקְּנִין אוֹתָהּ** — **that is cooked and prepared** **עִם קְצָת קֶמַח קָלוּי וּמְטוּגָּן בְּחֶמְאָה** — **with a bit of toasted flour, fried in butter,** **אֵין מְבָרְכִין עַל הָרוֹטֶב כִּי אִם "שֶׁהַכֹּל"** — **one recites only the** ***shehakol*** **blessing upon the broth.** **אֲבָל** — **However,** even in this case, **אִם הוּא בּוֹרֵר אֶת הַפֵּירוּרִים הַמְטוּגָּנִין** — **if he picks out the fried bits of flour** from the broth **וְאוֹכְלָן בִּפְנֵי עַצְמָן** — **and eats them by themselves,** **צָרִיךְ לְבָרֵךְ עֲלֵיהֶם "בּוֹרֵא מִינֵי מְזוֹנוֹת"** — **he must recite the** ***borei minei mezonos*** **blessing upon them,** **וְאִם אוֹכֵל מֵהֶם כְּזַיִת** — **and if he eats a** ***kezayis*** **of them,** **צָרִיךְ לְבָרֵךְ אַחֲרֵיהֶן "עַל הַמִּחְיָה" וְכוּ'** — **he must recite** ***Al Ha-Michyah*** **etc. after** eating **them.**

---

pie filling or the ice cream. However, if he does not care at all for the *mezonos* part, he should recite only the blessing upon the pie filling or ice cream (*Igros Moshe, Orach Chaim* IV, §43).

183 BLESSINGS FOR WINE AND HATOV VEHAMEITIV — SIMAN 49:1

סימן מט

דִּין בִּרְכַּת הַיַּיִן וּבִרְכַּת הַטּוֹב וְהַמֵּטִיב

וּבוֹ ט״ז סְעִיפִים

א. עַל הַיַּיִן מְבָרְכִין "בּוֹרֵא פְּרִי הַגָּפֶן"[1], וּלְאַחֲרָיו "עַל הַגֶּפֶן" וְכוּ'[2]. וְאֵין חִילּוּק בַּיַּיִן, אֲפִילּוּ הוּא עֲדַיִין תּוֹסֵס[3], וַאֲפִילּוּ זָב מֵעַצְמוֹ, וַאֲפִילּוּ יַיִן מְבוּשָּׁל[4], אוֹ קוּנְדִּיטִין, דְּהַיְינוּ שֶׁנָּתְנוּ לְתוֹכוֹ דְּבַשׁ וּבְשָׂמִים[5], אוֹ לַעֲנָה שֶׁהוּא מַר, אֲפִילּוּ הַיַּיִן מֵרִיחַ כְּחוֹמֶץ, כֵּיוָן שֶׁיֵּשׁ לוֹ טַעַם יַיִן הָוֵי יַיִן לְעִנְיַן בְּרָכָה. אֲבָל אִם נִתְחַמֵּץ בְּעִנְיָן שֶׁיֵּשׁ בְּנֵי אָדָם

SIMAN 49

THE HALACHOS OF THE BLESSING FOR WINE AND THE BLESSING OF HATOV VEHAMEITIV

CONTAINING 16 *SE'IFIM*

§1-3 Which Wines Require *Borei Pri HaGafen* / **§4-6** Blessing Upon Wine Exempts All Beverages / **§7** Reciting the Blessing During a Meal / **§8-12** Reciting *HaTov VeHaMeitiv* Upon a Second Wine / **§13-14** Drinking With Another / **§15** Reciting *HaTov VeHaMeitiv* for Others / **§16** The Cup of *Bircas HaMazon*

§1 **עַל הַיַּיִן מְבָרְכִין "בּוֹרֵא פְּרִי הַגָּפֶן"** — **Upon wine,** before partaking of it, **one recites the blessing:** *Baruch Atah Ado-noy Elokeinu Melech HaOlam, borei pri hagafen, Blessed are You,* H*ASHEM*, *our God, King of the Universe,* ***Who creates fruit of the vine,***[1] **וּלְאַחֲרָיו "עַל הַגֶּפֶן" וְכוּ'** — **and after** drinking **it,** one recites the blessing of *Al HaGefen,* ***For the vine,*** **etc.**[2] **וְאֵין חִילּוּק בַּיַּיִן** — With regard to this halachah **there is no difference in the** type of **wine,** **אֲפִילּוּ הוּא עֲדַיִין תּוֹסֵס** — **even if it is still bubbling,**[3] **וַאֲפִילּוּ זָב מֵעַצְמוֹ** — **and even if** the wine was not pressed from the grapes, but **flowed by itself.** **וַאֲפִילּוּ יַיִן מְבוּשָּׁל** — The same is true **even** for **wine that has been cooked,**[4] **אוֹ קוּנְדִּיטִין** — **or** for ***kunditin,*** **דְּהַיְינוּ שֶׁנָּתְנוּ לְתוֹכוֹ דְּבַשׁ וּבְשָׂמִים** — **that is,** wine **into which honey or spices were added,**[5] **אוֹ לַעֲנָה שֶׁהוּא מַר** — **or** if **wormwood** was added, **which is bitter.** **אֲפִילּוּ הַיַּיִן מֵרִיחַ כְּחוֹמֶץ** — **Even if the wine smells like vinegar,** **כֵּיוָן שֶׁיֵּשׁ לוֹ טַעַם יַיִן** — **as long as it tastes like wine,** **הָוֵי יַיִן לְעִנְיַן בְּרָכָה** — **it is** considered **wine with regard to** its **blessing.** **אֲבָל אִם נִתְחַמֵּץ** — **However, if it became sour** **בְּעִנְיָן שֶׁיֵּשׁ בְּנֵי אָדָם**

1. Wine is unique among beverages and therefore the Sages instituted a special blessing to be recited upon drinking it (see *Berachos* 35b).

2. See below, 51:7-8.

3. I.e., a very new wine that is still in the process of fermentation, resulting in bubbling.

4. This applies regardless of whether it was cooked when it was already wine, or whether the grapes or raisins from which the wine was produced were cooked (*Mishnah Berurah* 202:4).

5. Even if the honey and spices each constitute a third or more of this beverage, and its taste is greatly affected by these ingredients, the wine remains the most significant ingredient, and *borei pri hagafen* is recited (*Mishnah Berurah* 202:5,6).

שֶׁנִּמְנָעִין לִשְׁתּוֹתוֹ מִפְּנֵי חֲמִיצָתוֹ, יֵשׁ סָפֵק בְּבִרְכָתוֹ (וְאַף שֶׁיָּכוֹל לְבָרֵךְ בִּתְחִלָּתוֹ "שֶׁהַכֹּל"[6], עֲדַיִין יֵשׁ סָפֵק בִּבְרָכָה[7] אַחֲרוֹנָה). וְלָכֵן, אֵין לִשְׁתּוֹתוֹ אֶלָּא אִם כֵּן יְבָרֵךְ תְּחִלָּה[8] עַל יַיִן טוֹב (דִּין יֵין צִמּוּקִים — עַיֵּין לְקַמָּן סוֹף סִימָן נ"ג).

ב. הַחַרְצַנִּים שֶׁהוֹצִיאוּ מֵהֶם הַיַּיִן רַק עַל יְדֵי דְרִיכָה וְלֹא נֶעֶצְרוּ בְּבֵית הַבַּד[9], אִם נָתְנוּ עֲלֵיהֶם מַיִם, אֲפִילוּ לֹא מָצְאוּ יוֹתֵר מִמַּה שֶּׁנָּתְנוּ, אוֹ אֲפִילוּ מָצְאוּ פָּחוֹת,[10] מִכָּל מָקוֹם אִם טַעְמוֹ[11] יַיִן, מְבָרְכִין עָלָיו "בּוֹרֵא פְּרִי הַגָּפֶן"[12]. אֲבָל אִם

שֶׁנִּמְנָעִין לִשְׁתּוֹתוֹ מִפְּנֵי חֲמִיצָתוֹ — **to the point where some people would refrain from drinking it due to its sourness,** יֵשׁ סָפֵק בְּבִרְכָתוֹ — **there is a question as to its** proper **blessing.** (וְאַף שֶׁיָּכוֹל לְבָרֵךְ בִּתְחִלָּתוֹ "שֶׁהַכֹּל") — **Although one may recite the blessing of** ***shehakol*** **before** drinking it,[6] עֲדַיִין יֵשׁ סָפֵק בִּבְרָכָה אַחֲרוֹנָה — **there is still a question as to** its ***berachah acharonah*** [final blessing].)[7] וְלָכֵן, אֵין לִשְׁתּוֹתוֹ — **Therefore, one should not drink it** אֶלָּא אִם כֵּן יְבָרֵךְ תְּחִלָּה — **unless he first recites a blessing** עַל יַיִן טוֹב — **upon good wine.**[8] (דִּין יֵין צִמּוּקִים — עַיֵּין לְקַמָּן סוֹף סִימָן נ"ג — For the **laws of raisin wine, see below, end of** ***Siman*** **53.**)

§2 After the juice has been extracted from the grapes, the grape seeds may undergo an additional soaking process to produce a wine-like beverage. This *se'if* discusses the halachah of this beverage regarding the blessing of *borei pri hagafen.*

הַחַרְצַנִּים שֶׁהוֹצִיאוּ מֵהֶם הַיַּיִן — Regarding **grape seeds from which wine was extracted** רַק עַל יְדֵי דְרִיכָה — **only through treading,** וְלֹא נֶעֶצְרוּ בְּבֵית הַבַּד — **but they were never crushed** under the beam of **the winepress,**[9] אִם נָתְנוּ עֲלֵיהֶם מַיִם — **if water was** then **poured onto them** and allowed to steep, the resulting beverage is considered wine. אֲפִילוּ לֹא מָצְאוּ יוֹתֵר מִמַּה שֶּׁנָּתְנוּ — **Even if** at the conclusion of this process **they did not find more** liquid **than what they added,** אוֹ אֲפִילוּ מָצְאוּ פָּחוֹת — **or even if they found less** than they added,[10] מִכָּל מָקוֹם אִם טַעְמוֹ יַיִן — **nevertheless, if** this drink **tastes**[11] **like wine,** מְבָרְכִין עָלָיו "בּוֹרֵא פְּרִי הַגָּפֶן" — **one recites upon it the blessing of** ***borei pri hagafen.***[12] אֲבָל אִם

---

6. See below, 50:2, which states that the *shehakol* blessing may be recited in cases where the halachah regarding the proper *berachah rishonah* (first blessing) is in doubt.

7. If it is considered wine, one is obligated to recite the *Al HaGefen* blessing after drinking it; if it is not considered wine, he may not recite that blessing (see *Beur Halachah* 204:4 s.v. כל and *Machatzis HaShekel* 204:14).

8. And drinks an amount requiring a *berachah acharonah;* see below, 51:2. Thus, he may exempt the sour wine from both a *berachah rishonah* and a *berachah acharonah;* see below, *se'ifim* 4-6).

9. That is, the process through which the juice was first extracted was treading by foot, not pressing in a winepress. The treading process does not force out all the moisture from the seeds as does pressing.

10. In either scenario, since they found no additional liquid, it could be taken as an indication that no juice (or very little) was extracted from the grapes.

11. And smells (*Mishnah Berurah* 204:32,36).

12. Even if no additional liquid was found, we may assume that the juice that was in the grape seeds came out, and water was absorbed in its place (*Orach Chaim* 204:6).

However, if the drink contains six parts water to one part grape seeds, it cannot be considered wine, regardless of the taste (see following *se'if; Shaar HaTziyun* 204:29).

נֶעֶצְרוּ הַחַרְצַנִּים בְּבֵית הַבַּד[13] וְאַחַר כָּךְ נָתְנוּ עֲלֵיהֶם מַיִם, אוֹ שֶׁנָּתְנוּ מַיִם עַל שִׁמְרֵי יַיִן[14], אֵינוֹ אֶלָּא כְּמַיִם[15].

ג. יַיִן שֶׁנִּתְעָרֵב בְּמַיִם — אִם אֵין בַּיַּיִן אֶלָּא אֶחָד מִשִּׁשָּׁה חֲלָקִים שֶׁבַּמַּיִם, וַדַּאי בָּטֵל הַיַּיִן[16] וְאֵינוֹ רַק כְּמַיִם. וְאִם יֵשׁ בּוֹ יַיִן יוֹתֵר — אִם דֶּרֶךְ אַנְשֵׁי הַמָּקוֹם לִמְזוֹג אוֹתוֹ כָּל כָּךְ וְלִשְׁתּוֹתוֹ בִּמְקוֹם יַיִן, מְבָרֵךְ עָלָיו "בּוֹרֵא פְּרִי הַגָּפֶן"[17] וּלְאַחֲרָיו "עַל הַגֶּפֶן". וְאִם לֹא, בָּטְלָה דַעְתּוֹ.

ד. כְּשֵׁם שֶׁהַפַּת אִם קָבַע עָלָיו פּוֹטֵר כָּל מִינֵי מַאֲכָל[18], כָּךְ הַיַּיִן אִם קוֹבֵעַ אֶת עַצְמוֹ לִשְׁתּוֹת יַיִן[19] פּוֹטֵר שְׁאָר מַשְׁקִין מִבְּרָכָה רִאשׁוֹנָה וּמִבְּרָכָה אַחֲרוֹנָה[20],

---

נֶעֶצְרוּ הַחַרְצַנִּים בְּבֵית הַבַּד — **However, if** in the first extraction process, **the grape seeds were crushed** under the beam of **the winepress,**[13] **וְאַחַר כָּךְ נָתְנוּ עֲלֵיהֶם מַיִם** — **and then water was poured onto them, אוֹ שֶׁנָּתְנוּ מַיִם עַל שִׁמְרֵי יַיִן** — **or** in a case **where water was poured onto the wine lees,**[14] **אֵינוֹ אֶלָּא כְּמַיִם** — the resulting beverage **is only like water,** and *shehakol* is recited upon drinking it.[15]

§3 **יַיִן שֶׁנִּתְעָרֵב בְּמַיִם** — Regarding **wine that was mixed with water: אִם אֵין בַּיַּיִן אֶלָּא אֶחָד מִשִּׁשָּׁה חֲלָקִים שֶׁבַּמַּיִם** — **If the** ratio of **wine** to water in the mixture **is only one** part wine **to six parts** (or more) **water, וַדַּאי בָּטֵל הַיַּיִן** — **the wine is definitely nullified** in the mixture,[16] **וְאֵינוֹ רַק כְּמַיִם** — **and it is** considered **only like water. וְאִם יֵשׁ בּוֹ יַיִן יוֹתֵר** — **If there is more** than this percentage of **wine** in the mixture, **אִם דֶּרֶךְ אַנְשֵׁי הַמָּקוֹם לִמְזוֹג אוֹתוֹ כָּל כָּךְ** — then, **if it is common for the people of** that **place to dilute it that much, וְלִשְׁתּוֹתוֹ בִּמְקוֹם יַיִן** — **and to drink it in the place of wine, מְבָרֵךְ עָלָיו "בּוֹרֵא פְּרִי הַגָּפֶן"** — **he recites upon it the blessing of** ***borei pri hagafen,***[17] **וּלְאַחֲרָיו "עַל הַגֶּפֶן"** — **and after** drinking **it,** he recites ***Al HaGefen.*** **וְאִם לֹא** — However, **if** they do **not** drink this diluted mixture in place of wine, **בָּטְלָה דַעְתּוֹ** — **one's intention** to consider it as such **is insignificant,** and *shehakol* is recited.

§4 **כְּשֵׁם שֶׁהַפַּת** — **Just as** with **bread, אִם קָבַע עָלָיו** — **if one establishes** his meal around **it, פּוֹטֵר כָּל מִינֵי מַאֲכָל** — the blessing one recites on it **exempts all types of food** from the requirement to recite a separate *berachah rishonah* (first blessing) and *berachah acharonah,*[18] **כָּךְ הַיַּיִן** — **so too wine: אִם קוֹבֵעַ אֶת עַצְמוֹ לִשְׁתּוֹת יַיִן** — **If one drinks wine in a set manner,**[19] **פּוֹטֵר שְׁאָר מַשְׁקִין מִבְּרָכָה רִאשׁוֹנָה וּמִבְּרָכָה אַחֲרוֹנָה** — the blessings recited before and after drinking the wine **exempt** the obligation to recite **a *berachah rishonah*** **and *berachah acharonah*** **upon other beverages.**[20]

---

13. The weight of the beam forces out almost all the moisture in the grapes (*Mishnah Berurah* 204:35).

14. Lees are the sediment that is formed when an alcoholic beverage is fermented.

15. The *shehakol* blessing is recited for water and most beverages; see below, 52:2.

16. Even if the taste of wine is discernible in the mixture (*Mishnah Berurah* 204:33).

17. In order for *borei pri hagafen* to be recited it must also taste and smell like wine (*Mishnah Berurah* 204:32).

18. See above, 43:1.

19. Lit., "establishes himself to drink wine." See commentaries to *Orach Chaim* 174:2 for discussion of the precise meaning of this condition, and how much wine must be drunk.

20. I.e., if he drinks a beverage that would normally require a *shehakol* beforehand and *borei nefashos* (below, 51:1) afterward, neither is required.

וְדַוְקָא אִם הַמַּשְׁקִין הָיוּ עוֹמְדִין לְפָנָיו בְּשָׁעָה שֶׁבֵּירַךְ עַל הַיַּיִן, אוֹ שֶׁהָיָה עַל כָּל פָּנִים בְּדַעְתּוֹ לִשְׁתּוֹת אוֹתָן מַשְׁקִים. אֲבָל אִם לֹא הָיָה לְפָנָיו, וְלֹא הָיְתָה דַעְתּוֹ עֲלֵיהֶן, הָוֵי סָפֵק אִם צָרִיךְ לְבָרֵךְ עֲלֵיהֶן אוֹ לֹא[21]. עַל כֵּן יִמְנַע אֶת עַצְמוֹ מֵהֶם עַד לְאַחַר שֶׁיְּבָרֵךְ בְּרָכָה אַחֲרוֹנָה עַל הַיַּיִן[22], אוֹ (שבירך) [שֶׁיְּבָרֵךְ] עַל אֵיזֶה דְבַר מַאֲכָל "שֶׁהַכֹּל" וִיכַוֵּין לִפְטוֹר גַּם אֶת הַמַּשְׁקִין[23].

ה. אִם לֹא קָבַע אֶת עַצְמוֹ לִשְׁתּוֹת יַיִן, אֶלָּא שָׁתָה דֶּרֶךְ אַרְעַי, וְגַם לֹא הָיָה דַּעְתּוֹ לִשְׁתּוֹת מַשְׁקִים אֲחֵרִים, אָז וַדַּאי צָרִיךְ לְבָרֵךְ בְּרָכָה רִאשׁוֹנָה עַל מַשְׁקִים אֲחֵרִים. אֶלָּא, דְּאַכַּתִּי אִיכָּא סָפֵק בִּבְרָכָה אַחֲרוֹנָה אִם נִפְטְרָה בְּבִרְכַּת "עַל הַגֶּפֶן" שֶׁיְּבָרֵךְ עַל הַיַּיִן, אוֹ לֹא. עַל כֵּן, יֵשׁ לֶאֱכוֹל אֵיזֶה פְּרִי

וְדַוְקָא אִם הַמַּשְׁקִין הָיוּ עוֹמְדִין לְפָנָיו — This is true **only if these beverages were standing before him** **בְּשָׁעָה שֶׁבֵּירַךְ עַל הַיַּיִן** — **at the time that he recited the blessing upon the wine,** **אוֹ שֶׁהָיָה עַל כָּל פָּנִים בְּדַעְתּוֹ** — **or, at least he had the intention** while he was reciting the blessing for the wine **לִשְׁתּוֹת אוֹתָן מַשְׁקִים** — **to drink those beverages.** **אֲבָל אִם לֹא הָיָה לְפָנָיו** — **However, if** the drinks **were not before him** when he recited the blessing upon the wine, **וְלֹא הָיְתָה דַעְתּוֹ עֲלֵיהֶן** — **and he had no intention** of drinking **them,** **הָוֵי סָפֵק אִם צָרִיךְ לְבָרֵךְ עֲלֵיהֶן אוֹ לֹא** — **it is questionable whether he is required to recite a blessing upon them or not.**[21] **עַל כֵּן** — **Therefore,** **יִמְנַע אֶת עַצְמוֹ מֵהֶם** — **one should refrain from** drinking **them** **עַד לְאַחַר שֶׁיְּבָרֵךְ בְּרָכָה אַחֲרוֹנָה עַל הַיַּיִן** — **until after he has recited a *berachah acharonah* for the wine.**[22] **אוֹ (שבירך) [שֶׁיְּבָרֵךְ] עַל אֵיזֶה דְבַר מַאֲכָל "שֶׁהַכֹּל"** — **Alternatively, he should recite *shehakol* on some** other **food,** **וִיכַוֵּין לִפְטוֹר גַּם אֶת הַמַּשְׁקִין** — **while also intending to exempt the beverages.**[23]

§5 **אִם לֹא קָבַע אֶת עַצְמוֹ לִשְׁתּוֹת יַיִן** — **If one did not drink wine in a set manner,** **אֶלָּא שָׁתָה דֶּרֶךְ אַרְעַי** — **but drank** it **in a casual fashion,** **וְגַם לֹא הָיָה דַּעְתּוֹ לִשְׁתּוֹת מַשְׁקִים אֲחֵרִים** — **and he also had no intention of drinking other beverages,** **אָז וַדַּאי צָרִיךְ לְבָרֵךְ בְּרָכָה רִאשׁוֹנָה** — **then he certainly must recite a *berachah rishonah*** **עַל מַשְׁקִים אֲחֵרִים** — **for other beverages** that he subsequently drinks. **אֶלָּא, דְּאַכַּתִּי אִיכָּא סָפֵק** — **However, there is still a question** **בִּבְרָכָה אַחֲרוֹנָה** — **regarding the *berachah acharonah*** for those other beverages, **אִם נִפְטְרָה בְּבִרְכַּת "עַל הַגֶּפֶן"** — **whether they are exempted by the blessing of *Al HaGefen*** **שֶׁיְּבָרֵךְ עַל הַיַּיִן, אוֹ לֹא** — **that he will recite for the wine, or not.** **עַל כֵּן, יֵשׁ לֶאֱכוֹל אֵיזֶה פְּרִי** — **Therefore,**

---

21. *Mishnah Berurah* (174:3) cites a number of authorities who maintain that if one drinks wine in a set manner, other beverages would be exempted by the blessing for the wine even if they were not before him, unless they were served after the wine was finished. However, because many authorities are of the opinion that nowadays people do not drink wine in a set manner, he recommends that, ideally, all drinks that are to be exempted by the wine should be before the person when he recites the blessing of *borei pri hagafen* (see *Shaar HaTziyun* 174:8). Cf. Appendix of Kitzur's editorial glosses.

22. This avoids any question regarding the blessing, because after reciting the *berachah acharonah* the effectiveness of the original blessing has certainly ceased, and he must recite a *berachah rishonah* upon anything that he drinks.

23. In this case, the *berachah acharonah* for the wine will also exempt the other drinks from another *berachah acharonah;* see next *se'if* (see *Mishnah Berurah* 208:73).

שֶׁיְּבָרֵךְ אַחֲרֶיהָ "בּוֹרֵא נְפָשׁוֹת רַבּוֹת" לִפְטוֹר גַּם אֶת הַמַּשְׁקִין[25].

ו. הַמְקַדֵּשׁ עַל הַיַּיִן[26] וְדַעְתּוֹ לִשְׁתּוֹת יֵין שָׂרָף אוֹ קַאפֶע יֵשׁ סָפֵק אִם נִפְטְרוּ בִּבְרָכָה שֶׁעַל הַיַּיִן אוֹ לֹא[27]. עַל כֵּן, יֵשׁ לוֹ לְכַוֵּין שֶׁלֹּא לְפָטְרָם, וְאַף עַל פִּי כֵן יְבָרֵךְ עַל מְעַט צוּקֶר "שֶׁהַכֹּל" לִפְטוֹר גַּם אֶת הַמַּשְׁקִין.

---

one should eat a fruit שֶׁיְּבָרֵךְ אַחֲרֶיהָ "בּוֹרֵא נְפָשׁוֹת רַבּוֹת" — **in order to recite** the blessing of *Borei nefashos rabbos, **Who creates numerous living things,*** **afterward,**[24] לִפְטוֹר גַּם אֶת הַמַּשְׁקִין — **to exempt the beverages as well** from their obligation of *berachah acharonah.*[25]

§6 In the previous two *se'ifim*, Kitzur discussed three cases: (1) When he drank wine in a set manner *and* had in mind to drink other beverages, in which case the *berachah rishonah* on wine exempts the *berachah* on the other beverages (*se'if* 4). (2) When he drank wine in a set manner and did *not* have in mind to drink other beverages, where Kitzur rules that it is questionable (ibid.). (3) When he did *not* drink wine in a set manner, and did *not* have in mind to drink other beverages, in which case he must recite a *berachah rishonah* on the other beverages (*se'if* 5). Kitzur now addresses the law pertaining to a fourth case that has not been discussed: When one did *not* drink wine in a set manner, but *did* have in mind to drink other beverages.

הַמְקַדֵּשׁ עַל הַיַּיִן — On Shabbos, **one who recites *Kiddush* over wine**[26] וְדַעְתּוֹ לִשְׁתּוֹת יֵין שָׂרָף אוֹ קַאפֶע — **and intends to drink whiskey or coffee** afterward, יֵשׁ סָפֵק אִם נִפְטְרוּ בִּבְרָכָה שֶׁעַל הַיַּיִן אוֹ לֹא — **it is questionable if** these drinks **are exempted by the blessing upon the wine, or not.**[27] עַל כֵּן, יֵשׁ לוֹ לְכַוֵּין שֶׁלֹּא לְפָטְרָם — **Therefore, he should** specifically have **intention not to exempt those** drinks with his blessing of *borei pri hagafen.* וְאַף עַל פִּי כֵן — **But even so,** יְבָרֵךְ עַל מְעַט צוּקֶר "שֶׁהַכֹּל" — he should not recite the *shehakol* blessing upon the whiskey or coffee, but rather **he should recite the *shehakol* blessing on a bit of sugar** לִפְטוֹר גַּם אֶת הַמַּשְׁקִין — **to exempt the** obligation to recite that blessing upon the **drinks as well.**

---

24. *Borei nefashos* is the *berachah acharonah* recited after eating fruit (below, 51:1). Since this same blessing is recited after beverages (besides wine), one may recite a single *borei nefashos* for the fruit and beverage.

25. If the halachah is that the beverages require their own *berachah acharonah* of *borei nefashos*, he will thus be able to fulfill that requirement with the *borei nefashos* that he will recite for the fruit.

Mishnah Berurah (208:72) rules that in a case when he did not drink in a set manner, and he also did not have those beverages before him when he recited the blessing on the wine, he must certainly recite a separate *berachah acharonah* on the other beverages (*Borei Nefashos*), besides the *berachah acharonah* on the wine (*Al HaGefen*).

26. The laws of *Kiddush* are set out below, *Siman* 77.

27. In *se'if* 4, we have seen that one who drinks wine in a set manner and has in mind to drink other beverages certainly need not recite a *berachah rishonah* upon the other beverages. When one recites *Kiddush* over a cup of wine and is not drinking wine in a set manner, there is a halachic doubt whether he must recite a *berachah rishonah* upon the other beverages. *Mishnah Berurah* (174:3, and *Beur Halachah* 174:2 s.v. יין פוטר) rules that the *berachah rishonah* upon the wine exempts the *berachah* upon other beverages even if he did not drink wine in a set manner, as long as the other beverages were before him at the time. He asserts, however, that is proper in this case that one should drink at least a *melo lugmav*, a cheekful (see *Kelalim*), of wine if other drinks are to be exempted. This amount provides some sustenance, and therefore has the significance to exempt other drinks.

ז. כְּשֶׁמְּבָרֵךְ עַל הַיַּיִן בְּתוֹךְ הַסְּעוּדָה וְיֵשׁ שָׁם גַּם אֲנָשִׁים אֲחֵרִים[28] יֹאמַר ״סַבְרִי רַבּוֹתַי״[29], רוֹצֶה לוֹמַר, תְּנוּ דַעְתֵּיכֶם לִשְׁמוֹעַ, כְּדֵי שֶׁיַּפְסִקוּ מֵאֲכִילָתָן לִשְׁמוֹעַ הַבְּרָכָה[30].

ח. שָׁתוּ מִיַּיִן אֶחָד, בֵּין בְּתוֹךְ הַסְּעוּדָה, בֵּין שֶׁלֹּא בְּתוֹךְ הַסְּעוּדָה, וְהֵבִיאוּ לָהֶם יַיִן אַחֵר, אֵינוֹ מְבָרֵךְ עָלָיו ״בּוֹרֵא פְּרִי הַגָּפֶן״, כֵּיוָן שֶׁלֹּא נִמְלַךְ וְלֹא אַסַּח דַּעְתֵּיהּ מִיַּיִן, אֲבָל מְבָרֵךְ עָלָיו ״הַטּוֹב וְהַמֵּטִיב״[31]. וְכֵן אִם הֵבִיאוּ לָהֶם עוֹד יַיִן שְׁלִישִׁי

---

§7 **כְּשֶׁמְּבָרֵךְ עַל הַיַּיִן בְּתוֹךְ הַסְּעוּדָה — If one recites a blessing on wine during a meal,** **וְיֵשׁ שָׁם גַּם אֲנָשִׁים אֲחֵרִים — and other people are present,**[28] **יֹאמַר ״סַבְרִי רַבּוֹתַי״ — he should** first **say: "*Savri, rabbosai.*"**[29] **רוֹצֶה לוֹמַר** — With this, **his intention is to say,** **תְּנוּ דַעְתֵּיכֶם לִשְׁמוֹעַ — "Pay attention to hear** the blessing," **כְּדֵי שֶׁיַּפְסִקוּ מֵאֲכִילָתָן לִשְׁמוֹעַ הַבְּרָכָה — so that they will interrupt their eating to listen to the blessing.**[30]

§8 The remainder of the *Siman* is devoted to discussing the laws of the *HaTov VeHaMeitiv* blessing, which is recited when, after partaking of wine, a new wine is introduced.

שָׁתוּ מִיַּיִן אֶחָד — If they were drinking from one type of **wine,** **בֵּין בְּתוֹךְ הַסְּעוּדָה — whether during a meal** **בֵּין שֶׁלֹּא בְּתוֹךְ הַסְּעוּדָה — or not during a meal,** **וְהֵבִיאוּ לָהֶם יַיִן אַחֵר — and another** type of **wine was brought to them,** **אֵינוֹ מְבָרֵךְ עָלָיו ״בּוֹרֵא פְּרִי הַגָּפֶן״** — a second ***borei pri hagafen* is not recited upon** the second wine. **כֵּיוָן שֶׁלֹּא נִמְלַךְ** — The original blessing remains in effect **since this is not** a case where, after deciding to stop drinking, they **reconsidered** when the second wine was served. **וְלֹא אַסַּח דַּעְתֵּיהּ מִיַּיִן — Rather, they had not diverted their attention from** drinking any more **wine.** **אֲבָל מְבָרֵךְ עָלָיו ״הַטּוֹב וְהַמֵּטִיב״ — However, they recite upon** the second wine **the blessing,** *Baruch Atah Ado-noy Elokeinu Melech HaOlam, HaTov VeHaMeitiv, Blessed are You,* HASHEM, *our God, King of the Universe,* ***Who is good, and Who does good.***[31] **וְכֵן אִם הֵבִיאוּ לָהֶם עוֹד יַיִן שְׁלִישִׁי — Likewise, if a**

---

28. I.e., he wishes to recite the blessing upon the wine for all of the assembled. [That is, following the rule of שׁוֹמֵעַ כְּעוֹנֶה, *listening is like responding,* they will listen intently to his blessing and thus satisfy their own obligation to recite the blessing upon the wine that they will drink.]

29. Literally: *"Is it your intention, gentlemen?"* (see *Rama* 174:8). This serves as an invitation to those assembled to be exempted with the blessing now being recited. If they wish to be exempted, they must listen to the blessing, as Kitzur explains. See next note.

30. When he calls their attention to his blessing with the words *Savri, rabbosai,* they stop eating and listen intently to the blessing (*Mishnah Berurah* 174:43). See also *Beur Halachah* (174:8 s.v. וכן נוהגין), who notes that not all authorities agree with the practice of one person exempting others with the *berachah* over wine drunk during the meal.

31. The blessing of *HaTov VeHaMeitiv* is an expression of thankfulness for the bountiful blessings that Hashem showers upon us, as is evident in the abundance of wine that we have available. Furthermore, any physical indulgence, particularly drinking wine, can lead to frivolity. The Sages therefore instituted the blessing of *HaTov VeHaMeitiv*, which mirrors the blessing of *HaTov VeHaMeitiv* from *Bircas HaMazon,* which was instituted to thank Hashem for allowing the victims of the massacre at Beitar to be brought to burial (see below, *Siman* 51, note 22). The allusion to this tragic episode should have a sobering effect on one's mood (*Mishnah Berurah* (175:2) citing *Rabbeinu Bachya*; see also *Meshech Chochmah, Devarim* 8:10, for additional explanations of this blessing).

189 BLESSINGS FOR WINE AND HATOV VEHAMEITIV — SIMAN 49:9-10

מְבָרְכִים גַּם כֵּן עָלָיו "הַטּוֹב וְהַמֵּטִיב", וְכֵן עַל הַרְבֵּה (מֵעוּבְדָא דְּרַבִּי[32] עַל כָּל חָבִית וְחָבִית שֶׁהָיָה פּוֹתֵחַ הָיָה מְבָרֵךְ "הַטּוֹב וְהַמֵּטִיב").

ט. וְאִם הָיָה נִמְלָךְ מַמָּשׁ בְּאוֹפֶן שֶׁצָּרִיךְ לְבָרֵךְ שֵׁנִית "בּוֹרֵא פְּרִי הַגָּפֶן" (עַיֵּין לְקַמָּן סִימָן נ"ז), מְבָרֵךְ תְּחִלָּה "הַטּוֹב וְהַמֵּטִיב", וְאַחַר כָּךְ "בּוֹרֵא פְּרִי הַגָּפֶן"[33].

י. הָא דִּמְבָרְכִין "הַטּוֹב וְהַמֵּטִיב" דַּוְקָא בִּסְתָם, שֶׁאֵינוֹ יָדוּעַ שֶׁהַשֵּׁנִי גָּרוּעַ מִן הָרִאשׁוֹן[34], אַף עַל פִּי שֶׁאֵינוֹ יָדוּעַ אִם הוּא מְשׁוּבָּח מִן הָרִאשׁוֹן. אֲבָל אִם יָדוּעַ שֶׁהוּא גָּרוּעַ מִן הָרִאשׁוֹן, אֵין מְבָרְכִין עָלָיו. אַךְ כְּשֶׁהוּא בָּרִיא לְגוּף יוֹתֵר מִן הָרִאשׁוֹן,

---

third wine was brought to them, מְבָרְכִים גַּם כֵּן עָלָיו "הַטּוֹב וְהַמֵּטִיב" — **they recite upon it the blessing of *HaTov VeHaMeitiv* as well.** וְכֵן עַל הַרְבֵּה — **So too for** even **many** wines that are served one after the other. (מֵעוּבְדָא דְּרַבִּי — This is derived **from the practice of Rebbi,**[32] עַל כָּל חָבִית וְחָבִית שֶׁהָיָה פּוֹתֵחַ — who, **for every barrel** of wine **that he would open,** הָיָה מְבָרֵךְ "הַטּוֹב וְהַמֵּטִיב" — **would recite the blessing of *HaTov VeHaMeitiv*.)**

§9 וְאִם הָיָה נִמְלָךְ מַמָּשׁ — **If one** made a **definite** decision to stop drinking, and then **reconsidered** and decided to drink more, בְּאוֹפֶן שֶׁצָּרִיךְ לְבָרֵךְ שֵׁנִית "בּוֹרֵא פְּרִי הַגָּפֶן" — **in a manner that he is obligated to recite the blessing of *borei pri hagafen* again** if he is now served a second wine (עַיֵּין לְקַמָּן סִימָן נ"ז — for halachos of what constitutes "reconsidering," regarding this halachah, **see below, Siman 57**), מְבָרֵךְ תְּחִלָּה "הַטּוֹב וְהַמֵּטִיב"— **he should first recite the blessing of *HaTov VeHaMeitiv*** on the second wine, וְאַחַר כָּךְ "בּוֹרֵא פְּרִי הַגָּפֶן" — **and after that,** he should recite the blessing of ***borei pri hagafen*.**[33]

§10 הָא דִּמְבָרְכִין "הַטּוֹב וְהַמֵּטִיב" — **One recites the blessing of *HaTov VeHaMeitiv*** דַּוְקָא בִּסְתָם — **only** when the quality of the second wine is **undetermined,** שֶׁאֵינוֹ יָדוּעַ שֶׁהַשֵּׁנִי גָּרוּעַ מִן הָרִאשׁוֹן — that is, **when it is not known that the second** wine **is inferior to the first,**[34] אַף עַל פִּי שֶׁאֵינוֹ יָדוּעַ אִם הוּא מְשׁוּבָּח מִן הָרִאשׁוֹן — **even if it is** also **not known that it is superior to the first** wine. אֲבָל אִם יָדוּעַ שֶׁהוּא גָּרוּעַ מִן הָרִאשׁוֹן— **However, if it is known that** the second wine **is inferior to the first,** אֵין מְבָרְכִין עָלָיו — **one does not recite** the *HaTov VeHaMeitiv* **blessing upon it.** אַךְ כְּשֶׁהוּא בָּרִיא לְגוּף יוֹתֵר מִן הָרִאשׁוֹן — **However, if the** second wine **is more beneficial**

---

32. The great Tanna and redactor of the Mishnah, Rabbi Yehudah HaNasi, was known as "Rebbi." The practice cited here appears in *Yerushalmi Berachos* 6:8.

33. *HaTov VeHaMeitiv* is not a replacement for the required blessing on wine. It is an *additional* blessing that was established for the purpose of expressing gratitude on the abundance of wine. Therefore, whenever the original *borei pri hagafen* is no longer valid one must recite that blessing on the additional wine as well. See also *Shaar HaTziyun* 175:2.

34. If the first wine is old wine and the second wine is new wine, one should not recite the *HaTov VeHaMeitiv* blessing unless he is sure that the second one is at least as good (*Mishnah Berurah* 175:10).

If one is unsure which wine is superior, he may recite *borei pri hagafen* for one, and *HaTov VeHaMeitiv* for the other. However, it is preferable to remove one bottle from the table and recite *borei pri hagafen* for the remaining bottle; when the second wine is served, he recites *HaTov VeHaMeitiv* (*Mishnah Berurah* 175:14). [See, however *Mishnah Berurah* §4, who writes that *HaTov VeHaMeitiv* should not be recited if, when *borei pri hagafen* was recited, the second wine was in the house and he intended to drink from it.]

אַף עַל פִּי שֶׁהוּא גָרוּעַ בְּטַעַם, מְבָרְכִין עָלָיו "הַטּוֹב וְהַמֵּטִיב"[35].

יא. אֲפִילוּ הָיָה לָהֶם מִתְּחִלָּה שְׁתֵּי יֵינוֹת, אֶלָּא שֶׁלֹּא הָיוּ לְפָנָיו יַחַד כְּשֶׁבֵּירַךְ "בּוֹרֵא פְּרִי הַגָּפֶן", מְבָרֵךְ עַל הַשֵּׁנִי הַמְשׁוּבָּח "הַטּוֹב וְהַמֵּטִיב". אֲבָל אִם הָיוּ שְׁתֵּיהֶם לְפָנָיו עַל הַשֻּׁלְחָן, אֵינוֹ מְבָרֵךְ "הַטּוֹב וְהַמֵּטִיב", אֶלָּא "בּוֹרֵא פְּרִי הַגָּפֶן" מְבָרֵךְ עַל הַמְשׁוּבָּח לִפְטוֹר גַּם אֶת הַגָּרוּעַ[36].

יב. אֵין מְבָרְכִין "הַטּוֹב וְהַמֵּטִיב" אֶלָּא אִם יֵשׁ עוֹד מִן הַיַּיִן הָרִאשׁוֹן וְרוֹצִים לִשְׁתּוֹת אֶת הַשֵּׁנִי מִשּׁוּם שִׁינּוּי יַיִן. אֲבָל אִם מֵחֲמַת שֶׁהַיַּיִן הָרִאשׁוֹן כָּלָה מְבִיאִין אֶת הַשֵּׁנִי, אֵין מְבָרְכִין עָלָיו[37].

יג. אֵין מְבָרְכִין "הַטּוֹב וְהַמֵּטִיב" אֶלָּא כְּשֶׁיֵּשׁ אַחֵר עִמּוֹ[38] שֶׁהוּא שׁוֹתֶה גַּם כֵּן מִשְּׁתֵּי

---

to one's health than the first one, אַף עַל פִּי שֶׁהוּא גָרוּעַ בְּטַעַם **— even if the taste** of the second wine **is inferior** to that of the first one, מְבָרְכִין עָלָיו "הַטּוֹב וְהַמֵּטִיב" **— he recites the blessing of *HaTov VeHaMeitiv* upon it.**[35]

§11 אֲפִילוּ הָיָה לָהֶם מִתְּחִלָּה שְׁתֵּי יֵינוֹת **— Even if they originally had two wines** אֶלָּא שֶׁלֹּא הָיוּ לְפָנָיו יַחַד כְּשֶׁבֵּירַךְ "בּוֹרֵא פְּרִי הַגָּפֶן" **— but they were not both before him when he recited the blessing of *borei pri hagafen,*** מְבָרֵךְ עַל הַשֵּׁנִי הַמְשׁוּבָּח "הַטּוֹב וְהַמֵּטִיב" **— he should recite the blessing of *HaTov VeHaMeitiv* on the second, superior wine.** אֲבָל אִם הָיוּ שְׁתֵּיהֶם לְפָנָיו עַל הַשֻּׁלְחָן **— However, if they were both before him on the table,** אֵינוֹ מְבָרֵךְ "הַטּוֹב וְהַמֵּטִיב" **— he should not recite the blessing of *HaTov VeHaMeitiv,*** אֶלָּא "בּוֹרֵא פְּרִי הַגָּפֶן" מְבָרֵךְ עַל הַמְשׁוּבָּח **— rather, he should recite** the blessing of ***borei pri hagafen* on the superior** wine לִפְטוֹר גַּם אֶת הַגָּרוּעַ **— to exempt the inferior** wine **as well.**[36]

§12 אֵין מְבָרְכִין "הַטּוֹב וְהַמֵּטִיב" **— One does not recite the blessing of *HaTov VeHaMeitiv*** אֶלָּא אִם יֵשׁ עוֹד מִן הַיַּיִן הָרִאשׁוֹן **— unless there is still some of the first wine** remaining, וְרוֹצִים לִשְׁתּוֹת אֶת הַשֵּׁנִי **— and they wish to drink the second** wine מִשּׁוּם שִׁינּוּי יַיִן **— for a change of wines.** אֲבָל אִם מֵחֲמַת שֶׁהַיַּיִן הָרִאשׁוֹן כָּלָה מְבִיאִין אֶת הַשֵּׁנִי **— However, if they bring in the second** wine **because the first wine is finished,** אֵין מְבָרְכִין עָלָיו **— the blessing** of *HaTov VeHaMeitiv* **is not recited** on the second wine.[37]

§13 אֵין מְבָרְכִין "הַטּוֹב וְהַמֵּטִיב" **— One does not recite the blessing of *HaTov VeHaMeitiv*** אֶלָּא כְּשֶׁיֵּשׁ אַחֵר עִמּוֹ **— unless there is another person with him**[38] שֶׁהוּא שׁוֹתֶה גַּם כֵּן מִשְּׁתֵּי הַיֵּינוֹת **— who is also drinking from both**

---

35. If the taste is significantly worse, *HaTov VeHaMeitiv* should not be recited (*Mishnah Berurah* 175:12).

If one had white wine followed by red wine, the white wine is assumed to be healthier for him than the red wine. However, if he knows that the red wine is a better wine, he recites *HaTov VeHaMeitiv* upon the red wine (see *Mishnah Berurah* 175:13).

36. In the event that he erred and recited *borei pri hagafen* on the inferior wine, *HaTov VeHaMeitiv* should be recited on the second wine (*Mishnah Berurah* 175:5).

37. If more wine is served only after the completion of the first, the serving of the second wine is not considered a display of abundance that warrants a separate blessing (*Mishnah Berurah* 175:3).

38. They must be part of the same group, and not in different rooms (*Mishnah Berurah* 175:15).

191 BLESSINGS FOR WINE AND HATOV VEHAMEITIV — SIMAN 49:14-15

הַיֵּינוֹת[39], דְּהָכִי מַשְׁמַע: "הַטּוֹב" — לוֹ, "וְהַמֵּטִיב" — לַחֲבֵירוֹ[40]. וְהוּא הַדִּין אִם אִשְׁתּוֹ וּבָנָיו עִמּוֹ[41]. אֲבָל אִם הוּא יְחִידִי, אֵינוֹ מְבָרֵךְ.

יד. הָאוֹרֵחַ שֶׁמֵּיסֵב אֵצֶל בַּעַל הַבַּיִת — אִם הַבַּעַל הַבַּיִת נוֹתֵן אֶת הַקַּנְקַן עַל הַשֻּׁלְחָן שֶׁיִּשְׁתֶּה מִי שֶׁיִּרְצֶה, כְּמוֹ שֶׁעוֹשִׂין בִּסְעוּדוֹת גְּדוֹלוֹת, אִם כֵּן הַיַּיִן הוּא כְּמוֹ בְּשׁוּתָּפוּת, וּמְבָרְכִין "הַטּוֹב וְהַמֵּטִיב". אֲבָל אִם הַבַּעַל הַבַּיִת נוֹתֵן לְכָל אֶחָד כּוֹסוֹ, אֵין מְבָרְכִין "הַטּוֹב וְהַמֵּטִיב", כֵּיוָן שֶׁאֵין לָהֶם שׁוּתָּפוּת בַּיַּיִן, וַאֲפִילּוּ הַבַּעַל הַבַּיִת אֵינוֹ מְבָרֵךְ.

טו. אֶחָד יָכוֹל לְבָרֵךְ לְהוֹצִיא אֶת כּוּלָּם[42], וְיֹאמַר תְּחִלָּה "סַבְרִי" וְכוּ', שֶׁיִּתְּנוּ לֵב לִשְׁמוֹעַ וְיַעֲנוּ "אָמֵן", שֶׁיֵּצְאוּ בְּבִרְכָתוֹ[43]. וְדַוְקָא כְּשֶׁיֵּשׁ לְכָל אֶחָד כּוֹסוֹ לְפָנָיו

---

wines.[39] **דְּהָכִי מַשְׁמַע — For this is the connotation** of this blessing, **"הַטּוֹב" לוֹ — "*Who is good*"** referring **to him, "וְהַמֵּטִיב" לַחֲבֵירוֹ — "*and Who does good,*"** referring **to his fellow.**[40] **וְהוּא הַדִּין אִם אִשְׁתּוֹ וּבָנָיו עִמּוֹ — The same halachah** applies **if** it is **his wife and children** who **are with him** to partake of the wine.[41] **אֲבָל אִם הוּא יְחִידִי — However, if he is** drinking wine **alone, אֵינוֹ מְבָרֵךְ — he does not recite the blessing** of *HaTov VeHaMeitiv.*

§14 The law mentioned in the previous *se'if* — that one does not recite the blessing of *HaTov VeHaMeitiv* unless there is another person with him — is subject to an additional condition, which is that both people must share the wine. If one person is partaking of wine that is owned by the other person, *HaTov VeHaMeitiv* is not recited (see *Mishnah Berurah* 175:15). In this *se'if,* Kitzur explains how a guest may qualify. **הָאוֹרֵחַ שֶׁמֵּיסֵב אֵצֶל בַּעַל הַבַּיִת — A guest who is dining at his host's** meal may qualify for the recitation of *HaTov VeHaMeitiv* in the following case: **אִם הַבַּעַל הַבַּיִת נוֹתֵן אֶת הַקַּנְקַן עַל הַשֻּׁלְחָן — If the host places the bottle** of wine **on the table שֶׁיִּשְׁתֶּה מִי שֶׁיִּרְצֶה — so that whoever wishes, may drink, כְּמוֹ שֶׁעוֹשִׂין בִּסְעוּדוֹת גְּדוֹלוֹת — as is done at large feasts, אִם כֵּן הַיַּיִן הוּא כְּמוֹ בְּשׁוּתָּפוּת — if so, it is as if the wine is jointly owned, וּמְבָרְכִין "הַטּוֹב וְהַמֵּטִיב" — and they recite the blessing of *HaTov VeHaMeitiv.* אֲבָל אִם הַבַּעַל הַבַּיִת נוֹתֵן לְכָל אֶחָד כּוֹסוֹ — However, if the host serves each** guest **a cup** of wine **for himself, אֵין מְבָרְכִין "הַטּוֹב וְהַמֵּטִיב" — they do not recite the blessing of *HaTov VeHaMeitiv,* כֵּיוָן שֶׁאֵין לָהֶם שׁוּתָּפוּת בַּיַּיִן — since they are not partners in the wine, וַאֲפִילּוּ הַבַּעַל הַבַּיִת אֵינוֹ מְבָרֵךְ —** and in this case **even the host does not recite the blessing,** since he is not sharing his wine with others.

§15 אֶחָד יָכוֹל לְבָרֵךְ לְהוֹצִיא אֶת כּוּלָּם — One person may recite the blessing of *HaTov VeHaMeitiv* **and thereby exempt all** those present.[42] **וְיֹאמַר תְּחִלָּה "סַבְרִי" וְכוּ' — He should precede** his blessing **by saying: "*Savri,*"** etc. **שֶׁיִּתְּנוּ לֵב לִשְׁמוֹעַ וְיַעֲנוּ "אָמֵן"** — so that **they will pay attention to listen and respond with Amen, שֶׁיֵּצְאוּ בְּבִרְכָתוֹ — in order that they may be exempted with his blessing.**[43] **וְדַוְקָא כְּשֶׁיֵּשׁ לְכָל אֶחָד כּוֹסוֹ לְפָנָיו** — This may be done **only if everyone** present **has his own**

---

39. See following *se'if.*

40. For another application of this, see below, 59:1.

41. Although those present must have a share in the wine in order for this blessing to be recited (see following *se'if*), since one is obligated to support his family, it is as if they all have a joint ownership in the wine (*Mishnah Berurah* 175:15).

42. See above, note 30.

43. See above, *se'if* 7.

BLESSINGS FOR WINE AND HATOV VEHAMEITIV — SIMAN 49:16 192

שֶׁיִּטְעוּם מִיָּד שֶׁלֹּא יְהֵא הֶפְסֵק בֵּין הַבְּרָכָה לִשְׁתִיָּה.

טז. אִם מְבָרֵךְ בִּרְכַּת הַמָּזוֹן עַל כּוֹס יַיִן אַחֵר, אֵינוֹ צָרִיךְ לְבָרֵךְ עָלָיו "הַטּוֹב וְהַמֵּטִיב" שֶׁהוּא יוֹצֵא בְּמַה שֶּׁאָמַר בְּבִרְכַּת הַמָּזוֹן "הַטּוֹב וְהַמֵּטִיב"[44].

---

cup of wine **before him,** שֶׁיִּטְעוּם מִיָּד — **so that** each person **can immediately partake** of the wine, שֶׁלֹּא יְהֵא הֶפְסֵק בֵּין הַבְּרָכָה לִשְׁתִיָּה — **so that there should be no interruption between the blessing and the drinking.**

§16 אִם מְבָרֵךְ בִּרְכַּת הַמָּזוֹן — **If one recites** *Bircas HaMazon* עַל כּוֹס יַיִן אַחֵר — **upon a cup of wine that is** of a **different** type from the wine drunk during the meal, אֵינוֹ צָרִיךְ לְבָרֵךְ עָלָיו "הַטּוֹב וְהַמֵּטִיב" — **he need not recite the blessing of** *HaTov VeHaMeitiv* **upon it,** שֶׁהוּא יוֹצֵא — **for he has already fulfilled his obligation** בְּמַה שֶּׁאָמַר בְּבִרְכַּת הַמָּזוֹן "הַטּוֹב וְהַמֵּטִיב" — **by saying** *HaTov VeHaMeitiv* **in** *Bircas HaMazon.*[44]

---

44. The fourth blessing of *Bircas HaMazon* has the same theme as the *HaTov VeHaMeitiv* blessing recited over wine. In fact, it too is referred to as the blessing of *HaTov VeHaMeitiv*, as these are the essential words of the blessing.

193 BLESSINGS BEFORE FOOD, DRINK, AND FRAGRANCES — SIMAN 50:1

סימן נ

כְּלָלִים בִּבְרָכָה רִאשׁוֹנָה מִבִּרְכַּת הַנֶּהֱנִין

וּבוֹ ט״ז סְעִיפִים

א. כְּתִיב (תהלים כד, א) ״לַה׳ הָאָרֶץ וּמְלוֹאָהּ״, שֶׁהַכֹּל הוּא כְּמוֹ הֶקְדֵּשׁ, וּכְמוֹ שֶׁאָסוּר לֵיהָנוֹת מִן הַהֶקְדֵּשׁ עַד לְאַחַר הַפִּדְיוֹן, וְהַנֶּהֱנֶה מִן הַהֶקְדֵּשׁ בְּלֹא פִּדְיוֹן מָעַל, כְּמוֹ כֵּן אָסוּר לֵיהָנוֹת מִן הָעוֹלָם הַזֶּה בְּלֹא בְרָכָה, וְהַבְּרָכָה הוּא הַפִּדְיוֹן[1].

SIMAN 50

GENERAL RULES OF BLESSINGS BEFORE FOOD, DRINK, AND FRAGRANCES

CONTAINING 16 *SE'IFIM*

§1 Obligation To Bless Hashem Before Eating / **§2** When in Doubt as to the Proper Blessing / **§3** Reciting the Blessing While Holding the Item, or in Its Presence / **§4** Dropping the Item After Reciting the Blessing / **§5** Pause Between Blessing and Eating / **§6** Pouring out Harmful Water / **§7** Tasting / **§8** Eating for Medicinal Purposes / **§9** Eating or Drinking To Dislodge an Item From One's Throat / **§10** Reciting the Blessing After Putting the Item in One's Mouth / **§11-12** Reciting One Blessing for Two Items / **§13-16** Change of Location After Reciting the Blessing

Kitzur has previously detailed the general laws regarding blessings, as well as the proper intention and reverence for blessings, in *Siman* 6. In our *Siman,* Kitzur will discuss the laws relating specifically to blessings recited for various pleasures.

§1 **כְּתִיב ״לַה׳ הָאָרֶ וּמְלוֹאָהּ״ — It is written** (*Tehillim* 24:1): ***To Hashem* belongs the *earth and its fullness,*** **שֶׁהַכֹּל הוּא כְּמוֹ הֶקְדֵּשׁ** — which means that **everything** in this world **is like consecrated** Temple **property; וּכְמוֹ שֶׁאָסוּר לֵיהָנוֹת מִן הַהֶקְדֵּשׁ עַד לְאַחַר הַפִּדְיוֹן — just as it is forbidden to derive benefit from consecrated property until it has been redeemed, וְהַנֶּהֱנֶה מִן הַהֶקְדֵּשׁ בְּלֹא פִּדְיוֹן מָעַל — and one who does derive benefit from consecrated property before** it has been **redeemed has violated** its sanctity, **כְּמוֹ כֵּן אָסוּר לֵיהָנוֹת מִן הָעוֹלָם הַזֶּה בְּלֹא בְרָכָה — likewise, it is forbidden to derive benefit from this world without** reciting **a blessing** first. **וְהַבְּרָכָה הוּא הַפִּדְיוֹן — The blessing is the redemption,** which permits the food to be eaten.[1]

---

1. The verse, *To Hashem belongs the earth and its fullness,* implies that man's use of the earth's resources would constitute trespass on God's property. This apparently contradicts another verse (*Tehillim* 115:16), which reads: הַשָּׁמַיִם שָׁמַיִם לַה׳ וְהָאָרֶץ נָתַן לִבְנֵי־אָדָם, *As for the heavens — the heavens are Hashem's, but the earth He has given to mankind,* which implies that the earth is man's to use. The Gemara (*Berachos* 35a-b) resolves the difficulty by saying that the verse which states that the earth belongs to Hashem refers to *before* one recites a blessing, while the verse which states that Hashem has given the earth to man refers to *after* one recites a blessing.

וְהַנֶּהֱנֶה בְּלֹא בְרָכָה כְּאִלּוּ מָעַל בְּקָדְשֵׁי ה׳ יִתְבָּרֵךְ שְׁמוֹ. וְאֵין שִׁיעוּר לִבְרָכָה רִאשׁוֹנָה, שֶׁאֲפִילּוּ אוֹכֵל, אוֹ שׁוֹתֶה, כָּל שֶׁהוּא, חַיָּיב לְבָרֵךְ בְּרָכָה רִאשׁוֹנָה[2].

ב. אַף עַל פִּי שֶׁבְּדִיעֲבַד אִם טָעָה וּבֵירַךְ ״שֶׁהַכֹּל״ עַל כָּל דָּבָר[3], אֲפִילּוּ עַל פַּת וְעַל יַיִן, יָצָא (כִּדְלְקַמָּן סִימָן נ״ו), לְכַתְּחִלָּה אָסוּר לַעֲשׂוֹת כֵּן. אֶלָּא, צָרִיךְ לִלְמוֹד לְהָבִין אֵיזֶה בְּרָכָה יְבָרֵךְ עַל כָּל מִין וּמִין[4]. וְאַךְ בְּדָבָר שֶׁאִי אֶפְשַׁר לוֹ לְהִתְבָּרֵר מֵאֵיזֶה מִין הוּא, אוֹ שֶׁנִּסְתַּפְּקוּ הַפּוֹסְקִים וְאִי אֶפְשַׁר לְהַכְרִיעַ, אָז יוֹצְאִין בְּבִרְכַּת ״שֶׁהַכֹּל״. וְאִם הוּא דָבָר שֶׁיָּכוֹל לְפָטְרוֹ בְּתוֹךְ הַסְּעוּדָה עָדִיף טְפֵי[5].

ג. הַדָּבָר שֶׁמְּבָרְכִין עָלָיו לְאָכְלוֹ, אוֹ לִשְׁתּוֹתוֹ, אוֹ לְהָרִיחַ בּוֹ[6], אוֹ לַעֲשׂוֹת בּוֹ מִצְוָה[7],

---

וְהַנֶּהֱנֶה בְּלֹא בְרָכָה — Therefore, **one who derives benefit** from this world **without reciting a blessing** **כְּאִלּוּ מָעַל בְּקָדְשֵׁי ה׳ יִתְבָּרֵךְ שְׁמוֹ** — is viewed **as if he has violated** property that has been **sanctified to God, may His Name be blessed.** **וְאֵין שִׁיעוּר לִבְרָכָה רִאשׁוֹנָה** — **There is no** minimum **measure for** a food or drink to require the recitation of **a *berachah rishonah*** (first blessing), **שֶׁאֲפִילּוּ אוֹכֵל, אוֹ שׁוֹתֶה, כָּל שֶׁהוּא** — **for even if one eats or drinks a minute amount,** **חַיָּיב לְבָרֵךְ בְּרָכָה רִאשׁוֹנָה** — **he is obligated to recite a *berachah rishonah*.**[2]

§2 **אַף עַל פִּי שֶׁבְּדִיעֲבַד** — **Although** the halachah is that, **after the fact,** **אִם טָעָה וּבֵירַךְ ״שֶׁהַכֹּל״ עַל כָּל דָּבָר** — **if one had mistakenly recited the blessing of** *shehakol nihyah bidvaro, through Whose word **everything** came to be,*[3] **on any** food, **אֲפִילּוּ עַל פַּת וְעַל יַיִן** — **even on bread or wine,** **יָצָא** — **he has fulfilled** his obligation **(כִּדְלְקַמָּן סִימָן נ״ו)** — as explained **below, *Siman* 56**:4), **לְכַתְּחִלָּה אָסוּר לַעֲשׂוֹת כֵּן** — nevertheless, **it is forbidden to do so initially,** i.e., one may not recite the *shehakol* blessing on any food for which he does not know the correct blessing. **אֶלָּא, צָרִיךְ לִלְמוֹד לְהָבִין** — **Rather, one must learn to determine** **אֵיזֶה בְּרָכָה יְבָרֵךְ עַל כָּל מִין וּמִין** — **which blessing he should recite over every type** of food.[4] **וְאַךְ בְּדָבָר שֶׁאִי אֶפְשַׁר לוֹ לְהִתְבָּרֵר מֵאֵיזֶה מִין הוּא** — **Only, on an item that is impossible to identify of which type it is,** **אוֹ שֶׁנִּסְתַּפְּקוּ הַפּוֹסְקִים** — **or** an item about which **the halachic authorities are in doubt** regarding its classification, **וְאִי אֶפְשַׁר לְהַכְרִיעַ** — **and it is impossible to arrive at a decision** regarding its halachic status, **אָז יוֹצְאִין בְּבִרְכַּת ״שֶׁהַכֹּל״** — **then one may fulfill his obligation by** reciting **the *shehakol* blessing.** **וְאִם הוּא דָבָר שֶׁיָּכוֹל לְפָטְרוֹ בְּתוֹךְ הַסְּעוּדָה** — **If it is an item that can be included in a** bread **meal so that it will be exempted** from its own blessing,[5] **עָדִיף טְפֵי** — **it is preferable** to eat it during such a meal.

§3 **הַדָּבָר שֶׁמְּבָרְכִין עָלָיו** — Regarding **an item upon which one is reciting a blessing,** **לְאָכְלוֹ, אוֹ לִשְׁתּוֹתוֹ** — whether he wishes **to eat or drink it,** **אוֹ לְהָרִיחַ בּוֹ** — **or to smell it,**[6] **אוֹ לַעֲשׂוֹת בּוֹ מִצְוָה** — **or to perform a mitzvah with it,**[7]

---

2. This is in contrast to the *berachah acharonah* (final blessing), which is required only when one eats a minimum amount; see below, 51:2.

3. The halachos of the *shehakol* blessing are set out below, 52:2-3.

4. I.e., he should either ask a competent halachic authority, or study the laws of blessings himself (see *Mishnah Berurah* 202:84). [If he studied the laws and still could not determine the proper blessing, he may recite a *shehakol*.]

5. Generally, any food normally eaten during a meal is exempted from its own blessing with the *hamotzi* blessing that was recited upon the bread at the beginning of the meal (see above 43:1; see also *se'if* 6 there).

6. The laws of the blessings for fragrances are set out below, *Siman* 58.

7. For example, the cup of wine for *Bircas*

צָרִיךְ שֶׁיִּקַּח אוֹתוֹ קוֹדֶם הַבְּרָכָה בְּיַד יְמִינוֹ[8], וִיכַוֵּין אֵיזֶה בְּרָכָה הוּא צָרִיךְ לְבָרֵךְ עָלָיו כְּדֵי שֶׁכְּשֶׁיַּזְכִּיר אֶת הַשֵּׁם, שֶׁהוּא עִיקַּר הַבְּרָכָה, יֵדַע מַה שֶּׁיְּסַיֵּים וִיבָרֵךְ[9]. וְאִם לֹא אֲחָזוֹ כְּלָל, אֶלָּא שֶׁהָיָה לְפָנָיו כְּשֶׁבֵּירַךְ עָלָיו, יָצָא. אֲבָל אִם לֹא הָיָה לְפָנָיו כְּלָל כְּשֶׁבֵּירַךְ, אֶלָּא שֶׁהֵבִיאוּ לוֹ אַחַר כָּךְ, אַף עַל פִּי שֶׁבִּשְׁעַת הַבְּרָכָה הָיְתָה דַעְתּוֹ עָלָיו, לֹא יָצָא וְצָרִיךְ לְבָרֵךְ שֵׁנִית[10].

ד. נָטַל בְּיָדוֹ פְּרִי לְאָכְלוֹ וּבֵירַךְ עָלָיו וְנָפַל מִיָּדוֹ וְנֶאֱבַד, אוֹ נִמְאַס[11] עַד שֶׁאֵינוֹ רָאוּי לַאֲכִילָה[12], וְכֵן אִם בֵּירַךְ עַל כּוֹס מַשְׁקֶה וְנִשְׁפַּךְ הַכּוֹס, אִם יֵשׁ

צָרִיךְ שֶׁיִּקַּח אוֹתוֹ קוֹדֶם הַבְּרָכָה בְּיַד יְמִינוֹ — he must take it in his right hand before the blessing is recited,[8] **וִיכַוֵּין אֵיזֶה בְּרָכָה הוּא צָרִיךְ לְבָרֵךְ עָלָיו — and he should have in mind which blessing he must recite over it, כְּדֵי שֶׁכְּשֶׁיַּזְכִּיר אֶת הַשֵּׁם — so that when he utters the Name** of Hashem, **שֶׁהוּא עִיקַּר הַבְּרָכָה — which is the most significant** component **of the blessing, יֵדַע מַה שֶּׁיְּסַיֵּים וִיבָרֵךְ— he will** already **know how he will conclude the blessing.**[9] **וְאִם לֹא אֲחָזוֹ כְּלָל — If he did not hold** the item **at all, אֶלָּא שֶׁהָיָה לְפָנָיו כְּשֶׁבֵּירַךְ עָלָיו — but it was in front of him when he recited the blessing on it, יָצָא — he has fulfilled his obligation. אֲבָל אִם לֹא הָיָה לְפָנָיו כְּלָל כְּשֶׁבֵּירַךְ — However, if it was not in front of him at all when he recited the blessing, אֶלָּא שֶׁהֵבִיאוּ לוֹ אַחַר כָּךְ — rather, it was brought to him afterward, אַף עַל פִּי שֶׁבִּשְׁעַת הַבְּרָכָה הָיְתָה דַעְתּוֹ עָלָיו — even though he had that** item **in mind when he recited the blessing, לֹא יָצָא — he has not fulfilled his obligation וְצָרִיךְ לְבָרֵךְ שֵׁנִית — and he is required to recite the blessing a second time.**[10]

§4 נָטַל בְּיָדוֹ פְּרִי לְאָכְלוֹ — If one took a fruit in his hand in order **to eat it, וּבֵירַךְ עָלָיו — and he recited the blessing over it, וְנָפַל מִיָּדוֹ וְנֶאֱבַד — and** then **it fell from his hand and was lost, אוֹ נִמְאַס עַד שֶׁאֵינוֹ רָאוּי לַאֲכִילָה — or it became repulsive**[11] **to the point that it became inedible;**[12] **וְכֵן אִם בֵּירַךְ עַל כּוֹס מַשְׁקֶה — and likewise, if he recited a blessing on a cup of beverage, וְנִשְׁפַּךְ הַכּוֹס — and the cup spilled** (and he cannot retrieve even a single drop of the beverage), then the validity of the original blessing in both situations depends on the following: **אִם יֵשׁ**

HaMazon (above, 45:4), *Kiddush*, or *Havdalah* (below, 96:7).

8. A left-handed person should grasp it in his left hand (*Mishnah Berurah* 206:18). See Kitzur above, 45:4.

9. That is, one should not begin to recite the blessing, saying the Name of Hashem (בָּרוּךְ אַתָּה ה׳, *Blessed are You,* Hashem), and only then stop and think how he must conclude that particular blessing. See below, 56:5, regarding one who began reciting one blessing and then realized that he is actually supposed to be reciting a different blessing.

10. See below, end of note 13. *Mishnah Berurah* (206:19) writes that if the food was in a [closed] bin when he recited the blessing, and he need only remove the food from the bin to eat it, he need not repeat the blessing. *Mishnah Berurah* cites *Pri Megadim*, who writes that this may apply in any other case where it is certain that the food will be available for him to eat, even if it is in a different room that is adjacent to the one in which he recites the blessing. However, one should avoid such situations in order to minimize any interruption between the blessing and eating, and so that he may hold the food while reciting the blessing.

If one wishes to drink from a water fountain, he may recite the blessing although the water he will be drinking has not yet come forth from the spout (see *Orach Chaim* 206:6).

11. For example, if he opened the fruit and it was found to be rotten (see *Mishnah Berurah* 206:24).

12. If any part of the fruit [even a small amount] is still edible, that portion should be eaten, thus avoiding the need for another blessing (*Mishnah Berurah* 206:24).

לְפָנָיו עוֹד מִמִּין זֶה וְגַם דַּעְתּוֹ הָיְתָה לֶאֱכוֹל אוֹ לִשְׁתּוֹת יוֹתֵר מִמַּה שֶּׁלָּקַח בְּיָדוֹ, אִם כֵּן הָיְתָה הַבְּרָכָה גַּם עַל הַנִּשְׁאָר וְאֵינוֹ צָרִיךְ לְבָרֵךְ שֵׁנִית, אֲבָל בִּסְתָם לֹא חָלָה הַבְּרָכָה רַק עַל מַה שֶּׁהָיָה בְּיָדוֹ, וְצָרִיךְ לְבָרֵךְ שֵׁנִית[13]. וְכֵן אֲפִילוּ אִם הָיָה דַּעְתּוֹ לֶאֱכוֹל אוֹ לִשְׁתּוֹת יוֹתֵר, אֶלָּא שֶׁלֹּא הָיָה לְפָנָיו בִּשְׁעַת הַבְּרָכָה וְהוּבָא לוֹ עַתָּה, צָרִיךְ לְבָרֵךְ שֵׁנִית[14], אֲפִילוּ בְּעִנְיָן שֶׁאִם הָיָה אוֹכֵל אוֹ שׁוֹתֶה אֶת הָרִאשׁוֹן לֹא הָיָה צָרִיךְ לְבָרֵךְ עַל זֶה שֶׁהוּבָא לוֹ[15], הָכָא שָׁאנִי.

לְפָנָיו עוֹד מִמִּין זֶה — **If there is additional** fruit or drink **of that type before him** **וְגַם דַּעְתּוֹ הָיְתָה לֶאֱכוֹל אוֹ לִשְׁתּוֹת יוֹתֵר מִמַּה שֶּׁלָּקַח בְּיָדוֹ** — **and he also intended to eat or drink more than** just **what he was holding in his hand,** **אִם כֵּן הָיְתָה הַבְּרָכָה גַּם עַל הַנִּשְׁאָר** — **if so, the blessing applied to the remaining** fruit or drink **as well,** **וְאֵינוֹ צָרִיךְ לְבָרֵךְ שֵׁנִית** — **and he need not recite the blessing a second time**; rather, he should immediately partake of the fruit or drink that is before him. **אֲבָל בִּסְתָם** — **However, when** one had **no specific** intent, **לֹא חָלָה הַבְּרָכָה רַק עַל מַה שֶּׁהָיָה בְּיָדוֹ** — **the blessing takes effect only on what was in his hand,** **וְצָרִיךְ לְבָרֵךְ שֵׁנִית** — **and he must** therefore **recite the blessing a second time** before eating or drinking anything else.[13] **וְכֵן אֲפִילוּ אִם הָיָה דַּעְתּוֹ לֶאֱכוֹל אוֹ לִשְׁתּוֹת יוֹתֵר** — **Likewise, even if he intended to eat or drink more** than what was in his hand, **אֶלָּא שֶׁלֹּא הָיָה לְפָנָיו בִּשְׁעַת הַבְּרָכָה** — **but** that additional food or drink **was not before him when he recited the blessing,** **וְהוּבָא לוֹ עַתָּה** — **and now,** after the fruit dropped or the drink spilled, **it was brought before him,** **צָרִיךְ לְבָרֵךְ שֵׁנִית** — **he must recite the blessing a second time.**[14] **אֲפִילוּ בְּעִנְיָן** — This law applies **even if the situation is such** **שֶׁאִם הָיָה אוֹכֵל אוֹ שׁוֹתֶה אֶת הָרִאשׁוֹן** — **that had he eaten or drunk** some **of the first** food (that has fallen), **לֹא הָיָה צָרִיךְ לְבָרֵךְ עַל זֶה שֶׁהוּבָא לוֹ** — **he would not have been required to recite a blessing on what was brought to him,** since once he partook of the first food, it would be exempted with the original blessing.[15] **הָכָא שָׁאנִי** — For **here,** where the blessing that he recited never took effect on the food upon which he recited the blessing, **it is different.**

13. Since his original blessing served no purpose, he should first say *Baruch Shem kevod malchuso le'olam va'ed,* "Blessed is the Name of His glorious kingdom for all eternity," which is said when one recites a blessing in vain (*Orach Chaim* 206:6; above, 6:4; see there for the proper procedure if this happens before one finished reciting the blessing).

Mishnah Berurah (206:26) rules that if there was additional food of the same type in front of him, then even if he did not *specifically* have in mind to eat that food as well, he should partake of that food without repeating the blessing, for it is considered as if the blessing were intended for that food as well, since it was in front of him.

14. See previous note. *Mishnah Berurah* (ibid.) rules that in a case where one specifically intended to partake of additional food, even if it was not before him at the time of the blessing, he should partake of that food and not repeat the blessing.

15. In certain cases, if one recited a blessing and partook of a food, and then more food that is subject to that blessing was brought, he does not recite a new blessing on the food that was subsequently brought. One of the factors governing this law is whether he had intended to eat the second food at the time of the blessing (see below, 57:2). Kitzur distinguishes between that case, where he partook of the first food, and here, where he did not have a chance to partake of the food.

197   ~◦   BLESSINGS BEFORE FOOD, DRINK, AND FRAGRANCES — SIMAN 50:5

ה. צָרִיךְ שֶׁלֹּא יַפְסִיק יוֹתֵר מִכְּדֵי דִיבּוּר בֵּין הַבְּרָכָה לַאֲכִילָה. וַאֲפִילוּ בִּשְׁעַת
לְעִיסָה אָסוּר לְהַפְסִיק עַד שֶׁיִּבְלַע16 (דְּהָא עַל הַלְּעִיסָה אֵינוֹ צָרִיךְ בְּרָכָה
כְּדִלְקַמָּן סְעִיף ז')17. וְאִם הִפְסִיק בְּדִיבּוּר בֵּין הַבְּרָכָה לַאֲכִילָה18 שֶׁלֹּא מֵעִנְיַן
הָאֲכִילָה, צָרִיךְ לַחֲזוֹר וּלְבָרֵךְ19. אֲבָל אִם שָׁהָה בִּשְׁתִיקָה, אֵינוֹ צָרִיךְ לַחֲזוֹר
וּלְבָרֵךְ20. וּשְׁהִיָּה שֶׁהוּא לְצוֹרֶךְ הָאֲכִילָה לֹא חֲשִׁיב הֶפְסֵק כְּלָל. וְלָכֵן, כְּשֶׁרוֹצֶה
לֶאֱכוֹל פְּרִי גָדוֹל וְלַחְתּוֹךְ מִמֶּנּוּ חֲתִיכוֹת, יְבָרֵךְ כְּשֶׁהַפְּרִי שָׁלֵם, מִשּׁוּם דְּמִצְוָה
לְבָרֵךְ עַל הַשָּׁלֵם, וְהַשְּׁהִיָּה לֹא הֲוֵי הֶפְסֵק, מִשּׁוּם שֶׁהִיא לְצוֹרֶךְ הָאֲכִילָה. אַךְ
כְּשֶׁרוֹצֶה לֶאֱכוֹל אֵיזֶה פְּרִי וְאֵין לוֹ יוֹתֵר, וְיֵשׁ לָחוּשׁ שֶׁמָּא פְּרִי זוֹ מְתוּלַעַת

---

§5 צָרִיךְ שֶׁלֹּא יַפְסִיק יוֹתֵר מִכְּדֵי דִיבּוּר — One must not pause for a period of time greater than *k'dei dibbur* [lit., *the amount (of time) of an utterance*; approximately 1-2 seconds; see *Kelalim*] בֵּין הַבְּרָכָה לַאֲכִילָה — between reciting the blessing and beginning to eat (i.e., chew) the food. וַאֲפִילוּ בִּשְׁעַת לְעִיסָה — Moreover, even while one is chewing the first bite of food, אָסוּר לְהַפְסִיק עַד שֶׁיִּבְלַע — it is forbidden to interrupt until he has swallowed some of it,[16] (דְּהָא עַל הַלְּעִיסָה אֵינוֹ צָרִיךְ) בְּרָכָה — for the act of chewing itself does not require a blessing, כְּדִלְקַמָּן סְעִיף ז' — as explained below, *se'if* 7).[17]

וְאִם הִפְסִיק בְּדִיבּוּר בֵּין הַבְּרָכָה לַאֲכִילָה — If one interrupted by speaking[18] between reciting the blessing and eating the food, שֶׁלֹּא מֵעִנְיַן הָאֲכִילָה — about something unrelated to the eating of the food, צָרִיךְ לַחֲזוֹר וּלְבָרֵךְ — he must repeat the blessing.[19] אֲבָל אִם שָׁהָה בִּשְׁתִיקָה — However, if he only paused in silence, אֵינוֹ צָרִיךְ לַחֲזוֹר וּלְבָרֵךְ — he need not repeat the blessing.[20] וּשְׁהִיָּה שֶׁהוּא לְצוֹרֶךְ הָאֲכִילָה — Any pause that is for the purpose of that which he is eating לֹא חֲשִׁיב הֶפְסֵק כְּלָל — is not considered an interruption at all. וְלָכֵן — Therefore, כְּשֶׁרוֹצֶה לֶאֱכוֹל פְּרִי גָדוֹל — when one wishes to eat a large fruit וְלַחְתּוֹךְ מִמֶּנּוּ חֲתִיכוֹת — and to cut pieces from it, יְבָרֵךְ כְּשֶׁהַפְּרִי שָׁלֵם — he should recite the blessing while the fruit is whole, מִשּׁוּם דְּמִצְוָה לְבָרֵךְ עַל הַשָּׁלֵם — because it is a mitzvah to recite a blessing on a whole item, וְהַשְּׁהִיָּה לֹא הֲוֵי הֶפְסֵק — and the pause after the blessing while he cuts the fruit is not considered an interruption מִשּׁוּם שֶׁהִיא לְצוֹרֶךְ הָאֲכִילָה — because it is for the purpose of eating the fruit. אַךְ כְּשֶׁרוֹצֶה לֶאֱכוֹל אֵיזֶה פְּרִי — However, if one wishes to eat a fruit, וְאֵין לוֹ יוֹתֵר — and he has no more than one fruit, וְיֵשׁ לָחוּשׁ שֶׁמָּא פְּרִי זוֹ מְתוּלַעַת — and there is reason for concern

---

16. Even a small amount (*Mishnah Berurah* 167:35). See following note.

17. There should be no interruption between the recitation of the blessing and the act that requires the blessing. Since chewing does not require a blessing, the blessing does not take effect until he actually swallows some of the food.

If one did speak after chewing but before swallowing, *Mishnah Berurah* (167:35) is in doubt as to whether he must recite another blessing. He cites *Chayei Adam*, that if, before speaking, he swallowed even a taste of the food while chewing, he should definitely

not recite a blessing again (see also *Beur Halachah* 167:6 s.v. ולא).

18. Even one word (*Mishnah Berurah* 206:12).

19. One should not interrupt even to respond Amen to another blessing, or to respond to *Kaddish, Kedushah,* or *Borchu* (*Mishnah Berurah* 206:12; see *Shaar HaTziyun* 215:2).

20. Although one may not pause after reciting the blessing, if he does, regardless of the length of the pause, he need not recite the blessing again, as long as he did not divert his attention from the blessing (*Mishnah Berurah* 206:12).

שֶׁאֵינָהּ רְאוּיָה לַאֲכִילָה, יִפְתְּחֶנָּה וְיִבְדְּקֶנָּה קוֹדֶם הַבְּרָכָה[21].

ו. הַשּׁוֹתֶה מַיִם וְשׁוֹפֵךְ מְעַט קוֹדֶם שְׁתִיָּיתוֹ מִשּׁוּם חֲשַׁשׁ מַיִם הָרָעִים[22], יִשְׁפּוֹךְ קוֹדֶם שֶׁיַּתְחִיל לְבָרֵךְ, וְלֹא אַחַר הַבְּרָכָה, מִשּׁוּם בִּזָּיוֹן הַבְּרָכָה[23].

ז. הַטּוֹעֵם אֶת הַתַּבְשִׁיל אִם צָרִיךְ מֶלַח, וְכַיּוֹצֵא בּוֹ[24], וּפוֹלֵט, אֵינוֹ צָרִיךְ לְבָרֵךְ[25]. אֲבָל אִם בּוֹלֵעַ, יֵשׁ סָפֵק אִם צָרִיךְ לְבָרֵךְ כֵּיוָן שֶׁהוּא בּוֹלֵעַ, אוֹ אֵין צָרִיךְ לְבָרֵךְ כֵּיוָן שֶׁאֵין כַּוָּונָתוֹ לַאֲכִילָה[26]. וְלָכֵן, יִזָּהֵר שֶׁיְּכַוֵּין לֵיהָנוֹת מִמֶּנּוּ בְּתוֹרַת

---

that this fruit is infested with worms שֶׁאֵינָהּ רְאוּיָה לַאֲכִילָה — **which would render it inedible,** יִפְתְּחֶנָּה וְיִבְדְּקֶנָּה קוֹדֶם הַבְּרָכָה — **he should open it and examine it before** reciting **the blessing.**[21]

§6 הַשּׁוֹתֶה מַיִם וְשׁוֹפֵךְ מְעַט קוֹדֶם שְׁתִיָּיתוֹ — **One who drinks water and pours off a small amount before drinking,** מִשּׁוּם חֲשַׁשׁ מַיִם הָרָעִים — **due to the concern of harmful water,**[22] יִשְׁפּוֹךְ קוֹדֶם שֶׁיַּתְחִיל לְבָרֵךְ — **should pour it off before he begins to recite the blessing** וְלֹא אַחַר הַבְּרָכָה — **and not after the blessing,** מִשּׁוּם בִּזָּיוֹן הַבְּרָכָה — **so as** to avoid **disgracing the blessing.**[23]

§7 הַטּוֹעֵם אֶת הַתַּבְשִׁיל אִם צָרִיךְ מֶלַח, וְכַיּוֹצֵא בּוֹ — **One who tastes a dish** to determine **if it needs salt or the like,**[24] וּפוֹלֵט — **and then spits it out** without swallowing, אֵינוֹ צָרִיךְ לְבָרֵךְ — **does not need to recite a blessing** before tasting it.[25] אֲבָל אִם בּוֹלֵעַ — **However, if one swallows** the food he is tasting, יֵשׁ סָפֵק — **it is subject to** the following **doubt:** אִם צָרִיךְ לְבָרֵךְ — Do we say that **he is required to recite a blessing** כֵּיוָן שֶׁהוּא בּוֹלֵעַ — **since he did swallow** the food, אוֹ אֵין צָרִיךְ לְבָרֵךְ — **or does he not have to recite a blessing** כֵּיוָן שֶׁאֵין כַּוָּונָתוֹ לַאֲכִילָה — **since he had no intention of eating the food,** but only of tasting it.[26] וְלָכֵן יִזָּהֵר — **Therefore, one** who does this **should take care** before putting the food into his mouth שֶׁיְּכַוֵּין לֵיהָנוֹת מִמֶּנּוּ בְּתוֹרַת

---

21. In this case he cannot wait until after the blessing to cut it open, because if it were found to be inedible the blessing will have been recited in vain.

When eating nuts, one should remove the shell before reciting the blessing so that there should not be a long pause between the blessing and eating, and to ensure that the nut is indeed edible (*Mishnah Berurah* ibid.).

22. See *Chullin* 105b, where the Gemara discusses the reason for this practice (see also *Tosafos* to *Chullin* 106a s.v. חזונהו).

23. Once a blessing has been recited over a food, it appears disrespectful to throw some of it out. This action should also be avoided so as not to interrupt between the blessing and drinking (*Mishnah Berurah* 206:12).

24. Or if food has already been prepared, and one tastes it simply to find out if it is palatable (*Mishnah Berurah* 210:13).

25. The obligation to recite a blessing is only when one is "eating" a food. Tasting without swallowing is certainly not considered eating at all, even though his palate has pleasure from tasting the dish or chewing the food (*Mishnah Berurah* 210:15).

26. These two positions are recorded in *Shulchan Aruch* 210:2. According to the latter opinion, even though he actually swallows the food, since his intention was not for a regular act of eating, but only to taste it, it is not included in the obligation to recite a *berachah rishonah* or *berachah acharonah* (see *Mishnah Berurah* 210:13). However, even according to this opinion, one who tastes and swallows more than a *revi'is* (2.9 fl. oz.-5.1 fl. oz. [86.4 cc.-150 cc.]; see Appendix A) of liquid must recite the blessing upon it, since drinking that amount is considered "eating," not "tasting" (*Shulchan Aruch* 210:2). See *Mishnah Berurah* there (§14), who cites authorities who hold that with regard to solid food, the maximum amount that may be tasted without a

אֲכִילָה וִיבָרֵךְ עָלָיו וְיִבְלַע.

ח. הָאוֹכֵל אוֹ שׁוֹתֶה לִרְפוּאָה[27] — אִם הוּא דָּבָר מוּטְעָם[28] וְנֶהֱנֶה מִמֶּנּוּ[29], מְבָרֵךְ עָלָיו לְפָנָיו וּלְאַחֲרָיו בְּרָכָה הָרְאוּיָה לוֹ. וַאֲפִילוּ הוּא דְּבַר אִיסּוּר, כֵּיוָן שֶׁהַתּוֹרָה הִתִּירָה לוֹ עַתָּה[30], צָרִיךְ הוּא לְבָרֵךְ עָלָיו[31]. וְאִם הוּא דָּבָר מַר שֶׁאֵינוֹ נֶהֱנֶה מִמֶּנּוּ, אֵינוֹ מְבָרֵךְ עָלָיו. הַשּׁוֹתֶה בֵּיצָה חַיָּה לְצַחְצֵחַ קוֹלוֹ, אַף שֶׁאֵינוֹ נֶהֱנֶה מִטַּעְמוֹ, נֶהֱנֶה הוּא מִמְּזוֹנוֹ דְּמֵיזַן זָיִין, וּמְבָרֵךְ עָלָיו.

ט. נִכְנַס לוֹ דָּבָר בִּגְרוֹנוֹ וְשׁוֹתֶה מַשְׁקִין, אוֹ אוֹכֵל חֲתִיכַת פַּת, לְבָלְעוֹ, אוֹ שְׁאָר דָּבָר שֶׁנֶּהֱנֶה מִמֶּנּוּ, צָרִיךְ לְבָרֵךְ עָלָיו לְפָנָיו וּלְאַחֲרָיו. אֲבָל אִם שׁוֹתֶה מַיִם שֶׁלֹּא לִצְמָאוֹ,

---

אֲכִילָה — to intend to derive benefit from the food **by eating it**, as opposed to just tasting it; **וִיבָרֵךְ עָלָיו וְיִבְלַע — and he should recite the blessing and swallow** the food.

§8 הָאוֹכֵל אוֹ שׁוֹתֶה לִרְפוּאָה — If one eats or drinks a food or drink **for medical purposes,**[27] the requirement to recite a blessing depends on the following: **אִם הוּא דָּבָר מוּטְעָם — If it is something that has a pleasant taste**[28] **וְנֶהֱנֶה מִמֶּנּוּ — and he has pleasure** eating **it,**[29] **מְבָרֵךְ עָלָיו לְפָנָיו וּלְאַחֲרָיו בְּרָכָה הָרְאוּיָה לוֹ — he recites the** appropriate **blessings before and after** eating it. **וַאֲפִילוּ הוּא דְּבַר אִיסּוּר — Even if it is something that is** normally **forbidden** to eat, **כֵּיוָן שֶׁהַתּוֹרָה הִתִּירָה לוֹ עַתָּה** — nevertheless, **since the Torah permitted it for him now** that he is ill,[30] **צָרִיךְ הוּא לְבָרֵךְ עָלָיו — he must recite a blessing on it.**[31] **וְאִם הוּא דָּבָר מַר — If** that which he is eating for medicinal purposes **is bitter** **שֶׁאֵינוֹ נֶהֱנֶה מִמֶּנּוּ — and he thus does not derive pleasure from** eating **it,** **אֵינוֹ מְבָרֵךְ עָלָיו — he does not recite a blessing upon it.** **הַשּׁוֹתֶה בֵּיצָה חַיָּה — One who drinks a raw egg** **לְצַחְצֵחַ קוֹלוֹ — in order to refine his voice,** **אַף שֶׁאֵינוֹ נֶהֱנֶה מִטַּעְמוֹ — although he does not benefit from its taste,** **נֶהֱנֶה הוּא מִמְּזוֹנוֹ — he does benefit from the nourishment,** **דְּמֵיזַן זָיִין — because** an egg **provides nourishment.** **וּמְבָרֵךְ עָלָיו — Therefore he recites a blessing on it.**

§9 נִכְנַס לוֹ דָּבָר בִּגְרוֹנוֹ — If something lodged in one's throat **וְשׁוֹתֶה מַשְׁקִין, אוֹ אוֹכֵל חֲתִיכַת פַּת — and he takes a drink** (other than water; see below) **or eats a piece of bread** **לְבָלְעוֹ — to** help him **swallow** what is stuck, **אוֹ שְׁאָר דָּבָר שֶׁנֶּהֱנֶה מִמֶּנּוּ — or** if he eats **any other item from which he derives pleasure,** even though he is eating it only for the purpose of dislodging food in his throat, **צָרִיךְ לְבָרֵךְ עָלָיו לְפָנָיו וּלְאַחֲרָיו — he is required to recite a blessing before and after** eating **it.**
אֲבָל אִם שׁוֹתֶה מַיִם שֶׁלֹּא לִצְמָאוֹ — However, if he drinks water when he is not thirsty,

---

blessing is a *kezayis* (between .6 fl. oz. and 1.1 fl. oz. [17.3-33.3 cc.]; see Appendix A). Rabbi Moshe Feinstein (*Igros Moshe, Orach Chaim* I, §80) concurs with this view.

27. Even if the food is consumed only by sick people (*Mishnah Berurah* 204:55).

28. *Shaar HaTziyun* (204:37) adds that even if it does not have a pleasant taste, as long as it does not have a bad taste, a blessing is required if one's palate derives pleasure from it.

29. This applies even if he has no desire to eat the food, and is doing so solely for medical reasons; if one's palate derives pleasure from it, a blessing is recited (*Mishnah Berurah* 204:43).

30. Kitzur is speaking of a dangerously ill person, who is permitted to eat any food that is necessary for his health (see below, 192:7).

31. Otherwise, one may not recite a blessing upon a forbidden food (*Orach Chaim* 196:1; see *Mishnah Berurah* there §4).

If a sick person must eat on Yom Kippur, the same rule applies, and a blessing is recited (below, 133:18).

אֶלָּא כְּדֵי לְהַבְלִיעַ מַה שֶּׁנִּכְנַס לוֹ בִּגְרוֹנוֹ, אוֹ לְצוֹרֶךְ אַחֵר[32], לֹא יְבָרֵךְ[33], לְפִי שֶׁאֵין הֲנָאָה לְאָדָם בִּשְׁתִיַּית הַמַּיִם אֶלָּא כְּשֶׁהוּא שׁוֹתֶה לִצְמָאוֹ[34].

י. שָׁכַח וְהִכְנִיס אוֹכָלִין לְתוֹךְ פִּיו בְּלֹא בְרָכָה — אִם הוּא דָבָר שֶׁאַף אִם יַפְלִיטוֹ לֹא יְהֵא נִמְאָס, יַפְלִיטוֹ לְתוֹךְ יָדוֹ וִיבָרֵךְ עָלָיו. וְלֹא יְבָרֵךְ עָלָיו בְּעוֹדוֹ בְּפִיו, מִשּׁוּם דִּכְתִיב (תהלים עא, ח) "יִמָּלֵא פִי תְּהִלָּתֶךָ"[35]. וְאִם הוּא דָבָר שֶׁאִם יַפְלִיטוֹ יְהֵא נִמְאָס, כֵּיוָן דְּאָסוּר לְאַבֵּד אוֹכָלִין[36], מְסַלְּקוֹ בְּפִיו לְצַד אֶחָד וּמְבָרֵךְ עָלָיו. וְאִם אֵירַע לוֹ כֵּן בְּמַשְׁקִין, שֶׁאִי אֶפְשַׁר לוֹ לְסַלְּקָן לְצַד אַחֵר[37], אֲזַי אִם יֵשׁ לוֹ עוֹד מַשְׁקִין יִפְלוֹט אֵלּוּ לְאִיבּוּד. וְאִם אֵין לוֹ יוֹתֵר וְהוּא דָחוּק עַל זֶה הַמְּעַט שֶׁבְּתוֹךְ פִּיו, בּוֹלְעָן וִיבָרֵךְ אַחַר כָּךְ בְּרָכָה רִאשׁוֹנָה[38].

אֶלָּא כְּדֵי לְהַבְלִיעַ מַה שֶּׁנִּכְנַס לוֹ בִּגְרוֹנוֹ — but just for the sake of helping him swallow what is lodged in his throat, אוֹ לְצוֹרֶךְ אַחֵר — or for any purpose other than to quench his thirst,[32] **לֹא יְבָרֵךְ — he should not recite a blessing,**[33] **לְפִי שֶׁאֵין הֲנָאָה לְאָדָם בִּשְׁתִיַּית הַמַּיִם — for a person has no enjoyment from drinking water אֶלָּא כְּשֶׁהוּא שׁוֹתֶה לִצְמָאוֹ — unless it is to quench his thirst.**[34]

§10 שָׁכַח וְהִכְנִיס אוֹכָלִין לְתוֹךְ פִּיו בְּלֹא בְרָכָה — If one forgot and put food in his mouth without reciting **a blessing,** he should proceed as follows: **אִם הוּא דָבָר שֶׁאַף אִם יַפְלִיטוֹ לֹא יְהֵא נִמְאָס — If it is something that even if he would spit it out — it would not become repulsive, יַפְלִיטוֹ לְתוֹךְ יָדוֹ — he should spit it out into his hand, וִיבָרֵךְ עָלָיו — and** then **recite a blessing upon it** and eat it. **וְלֹא יְבָרֵךְ עָלָיו בְּעוֹדוֹ בְּפִיו — He should not recite a blessing upon it while it is still in his mouth, מִשּׁוּם דִּכְתִיב — because it is written** (*Tehillim* 71:8): **"יִמָּלֵא פִי תְּהִלָּתֶךָ" — *My mouth shall be filled with Your praise.***[35] **וְאִם הוּא דָבָר** — However, **if it is something שֶׁאִם יַפְלִיטוֹ יְהֵא נִמְאָס — that will become repulsive if he spits it out, כֵּיוָן דְּאָסוּר לְאַבֵּד אוֹכָלִין** — he should not spit it out, **since it is forbidden to ruin food;**[36] **מְסַלְּקוֹ בְּפִיו לְצַד אֶחָד** — rather, **he should move it to one side of his mouth וּמְבָרֵךְ עָלָיו — and recite the blessing over it. וְאִם אֵירַע לוֹ כֵּן בְּמַשְׁקִין — If this occurred with beverages, שֶׁאִי אֶפְשַׁר לוֹ לְסַלְּקָן לְצַד אַחֵר — which are impossible to move to another side** of the mouth,[37] **אֲזַי אִם יֵשׁ לוֹ עוֹד מַשְׁקִין — then, if he has more of the beverage, יִפְלוֹט אֵלּוּ לְאִיבּוּד — he should spit out what is in his mouth,** although it **will go to waste.** He should then recite the blessing and drink of the beverage. **וְאִם אֵין לוֹ יוֹתֵר — If he has no more** of the beverage, **וְהוּא דָחוּק עַל זֶה הַמְּעַט שֶׁבְּתוֹךְ פִּיו — and he is pressed** to keep **the small amount** remaining **in his mouth** because he needs the nourishment, **בּוֹלְעָן — he may swallow** the beverage, **וִיבָרֵךְ אַחַר כָּךְ בְּרָכָה רִאשׁוֹנָה — and after that he should recite a *berachah rishonah.***[38]

32. For example, to swallow a pill.

33. However, if he happens to be thirsty, he must recite a blessing (*Mishnah Berurah* 204:42).

34. *Mishnah Berurah* (204:40) adds that if one has any pleasure from drinking the water, it is to be taken as an indication that he is somewhat thirsty, and a blessing should be recited.

35. This indicates that when one praises Hashem, the blessing (or other form of praise) should be the only thing in his mouth.

36. See above, 42:9.

37. If there is a very small amount of liquid in his mouth, and he is able to recite a blessing, albeit with difficulty, he should do so (*Mishnah Berurah* 172:1).

38. *Mishnah Berurah* (172:5) rules that in such a case, a *berachah rishonah* is *not* recited.

(דְּכֵיוָן דְּנִזְכַּר בְּעוֹדוֹ בְּפִיו דּוֹמֶה קְצָת לְעוֹבֵר לַעֲשִׂיָּיתוֹ), אֲבָל בְּרָכָה אַחֲרוֹנָה לֹא יְבָרֵךְ[39]. אַךְ אִם הוּא יַיִן וְשָׁתָה רְבִיעִית, יְבָרֵךְ גַּם בְּרָכָה אַחֲרוֹנָה[40].

יא. הָיוּ לְפָנָיו שְׁנֵי מִינִים שֶׁבִּרְכוֹתֵיהֶם שָׁווֹת, כְּגוֹן אֱגוֹז וְתַפּוּחַ[41], שֶׁיָּכוֹל לְבָרֵךְ עַל אֶחָד וְלִפְטוֹר גַּם הַשֵּׁנִי, חַיָּיב לַעֲשׂוֹת כֵּן, וְאָסוּר לוֹ לְבָרֵךְ עַל אֶחָד בְּכַוָּונָה שֶׁלֹּא לִפְטוֹר אֶת הַשֵּׁנִי כְּדֵי לְבָרֵךְ גַּם עָלָיו בִּפְנֵי עַצְמוֹ, מִשּׁוּם דְּאָסוּר לִגְרוֹם בְּרָכָה שֶׁאֵינָהּ צְרִיכָה. וִיבָרֵךְ עַל הַיּוֹתֵר חָשׁוּב (כְּדִלְקַמָּן סִימָן נ״ה) וְנִפְטָר הַשֵּׁנִי, אַף עַל פִּי שֶׁלֹּא הָיְתָה כַּוָּונָתוֹ לְפָטְרוֹ[42]. אֲבָל אִם בֵּירַךְ עַל זֶה שֶׁאֵינוֹ חָשׁוּב, אֵינוֹ נִפְטָר

(דְּכֵיוָן דְּנִזְכַּר בְּעוֹדוֹ בְּפִיו — Although a *berachah rishonah* is generally recited only before eating or drinking, in this case, **since he remembered** to recite a blessing **while** the beverage **was still in his mouth,** דּוֹמֶה קְצָת לְעוֹבֵר לַעֲשִׂיָּיתוֹ — **it is somewhat similar to** reciting the blessing **before the act** of drinking it.) אֲבָל בְּרָכָה אַחֲרוֹנָה לֹא יְבָרֵךְ — **However, he should not recite a** ***berachah acharonah.***[39] אַךְ אִם הוּא יַיִן — **However, if** this occurred **with wine,** וְשָׁתָה רְבִיעִית — **and he drank a** ***revi'is,*** יְבָרֵךְ גַּם בְּרָכָה אַחֲרוֹנָה — **he should recite a** ***berachah acharonah*** **as well.**[40]

§11 הָיוּ לְפָנָיו שְׁנֵי מִינִים — **If one has two types** of food **before him** שֶׁבִּרְכוֹתֵיהֶם שָׁווֹת — **whose blessings are the same,** כְּגוֹן אֱגוֹז וְתַפּוּחַ — **such as a nut and an apple,**[41] שֶׁיָּכוֹל לְבָרֵךְ עַל אֶחָד — and **he can** thus **recite a blessing over one of them** וְלִפְטוֹר גַּם הַשֵּׁנִי — **and exempt** the requirement to recite a blessing upon **the second** food, חַיָּיב לַעֲשׂוֹת כֵּן — **he is obligated to do so;** וְאָסוּר לוֹ לְבָרֵךְ עַל אֶחָד — **it is forbidden to recite a blessing over one** of them בְּכַוָּונָה שֶׁלֹּא לִפְטוֹר אֶת הַשֵּׁנִי — **with the intention not to exempt the second,** כְּדֵי לְבָרֵךְ גַּם עָלָיו בִּפְנֵי עַצְמוֹ — **in order to recite a blessing for it as well on its own,** מִשּׁוּם דְּאָסוּר לִגְרוֹם בְּרָכָה שֶׁאֵינָהּ צְרִיכָה — **because it is forbidden to cause** the recitation of **an unnecessary blessing** (see above, 6:4). וִיבָרֵךְ עַל הַיּוֹתֵר חָשׁוּב — Thus, when one wishes to eat two foods that require the same blessing, **he is to recite the blessing over** the food **that is more significant** (כְּדִלְקַמָּן סִימָן נ״ה — in accordance with the rules detailed **below,** in ***Siman* 55,** *se'ifim* 1-3), וְנִפְטָר הַשֵּׁנִי, אַף עַל פִּי שֶׁלֹּא הָיְתָה כַּוָּונָתוֹ לְפָטְרוֹ — **and the second one is exempted even if he had no** specific **intention to exempt it** with his blessing.[42] אֲבָל אִם בֵּירַךְ עַל זֶה שֶׁאֵינוֹ חָשׁוּב — **However, if he recited a blessing over** the food **that is not as significant,** אֵינוֹ נִפְטָר

39. Since he is already required to recite the *berachah rishonah* after drinking it, he should not recite the *berachah acharonah* (even if he drank the minimum amount to require a *berachah acharonah*; see below, 51:2), as these two blessings (*berachah rishonah* and *berachah acharonah*) are never to be recited consecutively (see *Magen Avraham* 172:3). However, according to *Mishnah Berurah* (172:3,5), who maintains that the *berachah rishonah* is not recited after drinking (see previous note), one should recite the *berachah acharonah* after drinking.

40. In this case (see previous note), two blessings may be recited consecutively, since according to some authorities, the obligation to recite a *berachah acharonah* on wine is of Biblical origin (*Magen Avraham* 172:3; see below, 51:7).

41. The proper blessing upon both of these is *borei pri ha'eitz*, "Who creates the fruit of the tree" (below, 52:1).

42. It is exempted because it was before him when he recited the blessing (*Mishnah Berurah* 211:32). Regarding a case where the second food was brought in afterward, see below, 57:2-3, and *Mishnah Berurah* ibid.

הֶחָשׁוּב[43] אֶלָּא אִם כֵּן הָיָה דַעְתּוֹ לְפָטְרוֹ[44]. אֲבָל אִם בֵּירַךְ בִּסְתָם צָרִיךְ לַחֲזוֹר וּלְבָרֵךְ עַל הֶחָשׁוּב, דְּאֵינוֹ בְּדִין שֶׁיִּפְטוֹר שֶׁאֵינוֹ חָשׁוּב לְחָשׁוּב דֶּרֶךְ גְּרָרָא[45].

יב. אֲבָל אִם הֵם שְׁנֵי מִינִים, כְּגוֹן פְּרִי הָעֵץ וּפְרִי הָאֲדָמָה, אוֹ דָבָר שֶׁבִּרְכָתוֹ "שֶׁהַכֹּל", אַף עַל גַּב דִּבְדִיעֲבַד אִם בֵּירַךְ עַל כּוּלָּם "שֶׁהַכֹּל", אוֹ שֶׁבֵּירַךְ עַל פְּרִי הָעֵץ "בּוֹרֵא פְּרִי הָאֲדָמָה" יָצָא[46], מִכָּל מָקוֹם לְכַתְחִלָּה אָסוּר לַעֲשׂוֹת כֵּן, אֶלָּא יְבָרֵךְ עַל כָּל אֶחָד וְאֶחָד בְּרָכָה הַמְיוּחֶדֶת לוֹ, וּבִרְכַּת "בּוֹרֵא פְּרִי הָעֵץ" קוֹדֶמֶת[47] (עַיֵּין לְקַמָּן

הֶחָשׁוּב — the more **significant** food **is not exempted**[43] **אֶלָּא אִם כֵּן הָיָה דַעְתּוֹ לְפָטְרוֹ** — **unless he** specifically **intended to exempt it;**[44] **אֲבָל אִם בֵּירַךְ בִּסְתָם** — **but if he recited the blessing** over the less significant food **with no specific** intent, **צָרִיךְ לַחֲזוֹר וּלְבָרֵךְ עַל הֶחָשׁוּב** — **he must repeat the blessing over the** more **significant** food, **דְּאֵינוֹ בְּדִין** — **because it is not reasonable שֶׁיִּפְטוֹר שֶׁאֵינוֹ חָשׁוּב לְחָשׁוּב דֶּרֶךְ גְּרָרָא** — **that the** blessing of the **less significant** food **should exempt the** more **significant** food **in an incidental fashion.**[45]

§12 **אֲבָל אִם הֵם שְׁנֵי מִינִים** — **However, if these were two** different **types** of food, i.e., they are not subject to the same *berachah rishonah,* **כְּגוֹן פְּרִי הָעֵץ וּפְרִי הָאֲדָמָה** — **such as fruits and vegetables, אוֹ דָבָר שֶׁבִּרְכָתוֹ "שֶׁהַכֹּל"** — **or** if the second food is **something for which the** ***shehakol*** **blessing is recited, אַף עַל גַּב דִּבְדִיעֲבַד** — **although after the fact אִם בֵּירַךְ עַל כּוּלָּם "שֶׁהַכֹּל"** — **if he had recited** ***shehakol*** **on any** one **of them, אוֹ שֶׁבֵּירַךְ עַל פְּרִי הָעֵץ "בּוֹרֵא פְּרִי הָאֲדָמָה"** — **or he recited the blessing of** *borei pri ha'adamah,* ***Who creates the fruit of the ground*** (the proper blessing for a vegetable), **on a fruit, יָצָא** — **he has fulfilled** his **obligation,**[46] **מִכָּל מָקוֹם לְכַתְחִלָּה אָסוּר לַעֲשׂוֹת כֵּן** — **nevertheless, he may not do this initially; אֶלָּא יְבָרֵךְ עַל כָּל אֶחָד וְאֶחָד בְּרָכָה הַמְיוּחֶדֶת לוֹ** — **rather, he is to recite upon each** food **the blessing designated for that** food. **וּבִרְכַּת "בּוֹרֵא פְּרִי הָעֵץ" קוֹדֶמֶת** — **The blessing of** *borei pri ha'eitz,* ***Who creates the fruit of the tree,*** **is recited before** the other blessings of *borei pri ha'adamah* and *shehakol*[47] **(עַיֵּין לְקַמָּן**

---

43. Even if it was before him when he recited the blessing (*Mishnah Berurah* 211:32).

44. When one recites a blessing with specific intent to exempt another food with the same blessing, it is exempted, even if the second food is more significant, and even if it is not before him at the time (*Shaar HaTziyun* 212:22).

45. I.e., when there are two foods before him that share the same blessing, and one recites the blessing upon the less significant one, the blessing cannot apply to the more significant one without specific intent on the part of the one reciting the blessing to exempt it.

As mentioned by Kitzur, "significance" of a food follows certain definite parameters that are outlined in *Siman* 55. In some cases, there is a halachic dispute regarding which food is to be considered more significant in respect to reciting the blessing upon it. *Mishnah Berurah* (211:33) writes that in a case where one has two foods before him that are subject to the same blessing, and there is a halachic dispute regarding which food is to be considered more significant with respect to reciting the blessing upon it, one should specifically have in mind when reciting the blessing to exempt the second food as well.

46. See below, 56:2, 4.

47. That is, he should recite the blessing of *borei pri ha'eitz* and eat the fruit before reciting the blessing and eating the other foods. However, if he likes the other food better, or it is one of the Seven Species of the produce of Eretz Yisrael, he recites the blessing on that food first (see below, 55:1).

סִימָן נ״ה סְעִיף ד׳)[48]. וַאֲפִילוּ יֵשׁ לְפָנָיו יַיִן וַעֲנָבִים וְרוֹצֶה לִשְׁתּוֹת יַיִן קוֹדֵם וּמְבָרֵךְ ״בּוֹרֵא פְּרִי הַגָּפֶן״, אַף עַל פִּי שֶׁאִם הוּא מִתְכַּוֵּין לִפְטוֹר בִּבְרָכָה זוֹ גַּם הָעֲנָבִים יָכוֹל (לפטרו) [לְפָטְרָן][49], מִכָּל מָקוֹם לְכַתְּחִלָּה לֹא יַעֲשֶׂה כֵּן, אֶלָּא יְכַוֵּין שֶׁלֹּא לִפְטוֹר אֶת הָעֲנָבִים, כְּדֵי לְבָרֵךְ גַּם עֲלֵיהֶם בְּרָכָה הַמְתוּקֶּנֶת שֶׁהִיא ״בּוֹרֵא פְּרִי הָעֵץ״[50].

יג. בְּכָל הַדְּבָרִים, חוּץ מִן הַפַּת (שֶׁנִּתְבָּאֵר דִּינוֹ בְּסִימָן מ״ב סְעִיף י״ט כ׳ כ״א)[51], אִם שִׁינָּה מְקוֹמוֹ, אַף עַל פִּי שֶׁלֹּא הִסִּיחַ דַּעְתּוֹ, נֶחְשָׁב כְּמוֹ הֶיסֵּחַ הַדַּעַת. וְלָכֵן, מִי שֶׁאוֹכֵל אוֹ שָׁתָה בְּחֶדֶר אֶחָד וְאַחַר כָּךְ הוֹלֵךְ לְחֶדֶר אַחֵר לִגְמוֹר שָׁם אֲכִילָתוֹ וּשְׁתִיָּיתוֹ,

---

סִימָן נ״ה סְעִיף ד׳ — see below, 55:4).[48] **וַאֲפִילוּ יֵשׁ לְפָנָיו יַיִן וַעֲנָבִים — Even if one has wine and grapes before him,** **וְרוֹצֶה לִשְׁתּוֹת יַיִן קוֹדֵם — and he wishes to drink the wine before** eating the grapes, **וּמְבָרֵךְ ״בּוֹרֵא פְּרִי הַגָּפֶן״ — and he recites** *borei pri hagafen, **Who creates the fruit of the vine,*** over the wine, **אַף עַל פִּי שֶׁאִם הוּא מִתְכַּוֵּין — even though if he would intend** **לִפְטוֹר בִּבְרָכָה זוֹ גַּם הָעֲנָבִים — to exempt the grapes with this blessing** (*borei pri hagafen*) **as well,** **יָכוֹל (לפטרו) [לְפָטְרָן] — he can exempt them** with that blessing,[49] **מִכָּל מָקוֹם לְכַתְּחִלָּה לֹא יַעֲשֶׂה כֵּן — nevertheless, it is forbidden to do so** initially. **אֶלָּא יְכַוֵּין שֶׁלֹּא לִפְטוֹר אֶת הָעֲנָבִים — Rather,** when reciting *borei pri hagafen,* **he should intend not to exempt the grapes,** **כְּדֵי לְבָרֵךְ גַּם עֲלֵיהֶם בְּרָכָה הַמְתוּקֶּנֶת — so that he may recite the designated blessing upon them as well,** **שֶׁהִיא ״בּוֹרֵא פְּרִי הָעֵץ״ — which is *borei pri ha'eitz.***[50]

§13 בְּכָל הַדְּבָרִים — With regard to all foods, **חוּץ מִן הַפַּת — with the exception of bread,** (**שֶׁנִּתְבָּאֵר דִּינוֹ בְּסִימָן מ״ב סְעִיף י״ט כ׳ כ״א — whose laws are explained** above, **42:19-21**),[51] **אִם שִׁינָּה מְקוֹמוֹ — if one changed his location** while eating, **אַף עַל פִּי שֶׁלֹּא הִסִּיחַ דַּעְתּוֹ — even though he did not divert his attention** from eating, **נֶחְשָׁב כְּמוֹ הֶיסֵּחַ הַדַּעַת — the** change in location **is regarded as** if he had **diverted** his **attention.** **וְלָכֵן — Therefore,** **מִי שֶׁאוֹכֵל אוֹ שָׁתָה בְּחֶדֶר אֶחָד — one who is eating or drinking in one room,** **וְאַחַר כָּךְ הוֹלֵךְ לְחֶדֶר אַחֵר — and then goes to a different room** **לִגְמוֹר שָׁם אֲכִילָתוֹ וּשְׁתִיָּיתוֹ — to complete his eating or**

---

48. There, Kitzur details the laws regarding the precedence of these blessings.

49. See below, 56:1; *Mishnah Berurah* 208:69; and *Igros Moshe, Orach Chaim* I, §84.

50. As long as he did not *specifically intend* to exempt the grapes with the *borei pri hagafen* blessing, he should recite the *borei pri ha'eitz* blessing when he later eats the grapes (*Mishnah Berurah* 208:69).

51. According to Kitzur, the laws of this *se'if* apply to *all* foods except bread, which is generally not subject to the requirement that its *berachah rishonah* be repeated if one leaves the place where he recited the blessing. See above, 42:19, with notes 50 and 53 for the reason why bread is not included in this halachah and for further discussion of its halachos.

Others, however, maintain that other products of the five grains besides bread, and according to some opinions, even fruits of the Seven Species (the grains and species are enumerated below, 51:7) are subject to the same halachah as bread (*Shulchan Aruch* 178:5; see *Mishnah Berurah* §45). *Mishnah Berurah* (ibid.; see also §26 and 184:12) cites *Gra,* who rules like the opinion that maintains that grain products (but not fruit of the Seven Species) are considered like bread with regard to this halachah. In Kitzur's editorial glosses to this *se'if,* Kitzur concedes that one should endeavor to avoid such a situation when eating fruits of the Seven Species and certainly when eating grain products, since the matter is subject to dispute. See there for further discussion.

אֲפִילוּ מִמִּין הָרִאשׁוֹן, וַאֲפִילוּ אוֹחֵז בְּיָדוֹ אֶת הַמַּאֲכָל אוֹ הַמַּשְׁקֶה וְנוֹשְׂאוֹ אֶל הַחֶדֶר הָאַחֵר, מִכָּל מָקוֹם צָרִיךְ לְבָרֵךְ עָלָיו שָׁם מֵחָדָשׁ בְּרָכָה רִאשׁוֹנָה[52]. אֲבָל בְּרָכָה אַחֲרוֹנָה עַל מַה שֶּׁאָכַל תְּחִלָּה אֵינוֹ צָרִיךְ, כִּי הַבְּרָכָה שֶׁיְּבָרֵךְ בְּסוֹף תַּעֲלֶה לִשְׁתֵּיהֶן.

יד. וְכֵן אִם הָלַךְ לַחוּץ וְאַחַר כָּךְ חוֹזֵר לִמְקוֹמוֹ לִגְמוֹר אֲכִילָתוֹ, צָרִיךְ לְבָרֵךְ מֵחָדָשׁ בְּרָכָה רִאשׁוֹנָה. בַּמֶּה דְּבָרִים אֲמוּרִים כְּשֶׁהוּא אוֹכֵל לְבַדּוֹ, אוֹ כְּשֶׁהוּא אוֹכֵל עִם אֲחֵרִים וְכוּלָּם (שינוי) [שִׁינּוּ] אֶת מְקוֹמָם, אֲבָל אִם אֶחָד נִשְׁאַר עַל מְקוֹמוֹ, אֲזַי גַּם אֵלּוּ שֶׁהָלְכוּ כֵּיוָן שֶׁדַּעְתָּם לַחֲזוֹר לְכָאן אֶל זֶה שֶׁנִּשְׁאַר כָּאן וְלִגְמוֹר כָּאן אֲכִילָתָן, לָכֵן כְּשֶׁחוֹזְרִין וְאוֹכְלִין אוֹ שׁוֹתִין, אֵינָם צְרִיכִים לְבָרֵךְ מֵחָדָשׁ,

---

drinking there, אֲפִילוּ מִמִּין הָרִאשׁוֹן — **even** if he will eat **from the same type** of food that he had been eating, וַאֲפִילוּ אוֹחֵז בְּיָדוֹ אֶת הַמַּאֲכָל אוֹ הַמַּשְׁקֶה — **and even if he is holding the food or drink in his hand** וְנוֹשְׂאוֹ אֶל הַחֶדֶר הָאַחֵר — **and he carries it into the other room,** מִכָּל מָקוֹם — **nevertheless,** צָרִיךְ לְבָרֵךְ עָלָיו שָׁם מֵחָדָשׁ בְּרָכָה רִאשׁוֹנָה — **he must recite the *berachah rishonah* there anew.**[52] אֲבָל בְּרָכָה אַחֲרוֹנָה עַל מַה שֶּׁאָכַל תְּחִלָּה אֵינוֹ צָרִיךְ — **However, he is not required** to recite **a *berachah acharonah* on** the food **that he ate first** (i.e., in the first room), כִּי הַבְּרָכָה שֶׁיְּבָרֵךְ בְּסוֹף — **because the *berachah* acharonah that he will recite at the conclusion** of his eating in the second room תַּעֲלֶה לִשְׁתֵּיהֶן — **will cover** that which was eaten in **both** places.

§14 וְכֵן אִם הָלַךְ לַחוּץ — **Likewise, if one left** the room where he was eating any food (except bread), וְאַחַר כָּךְ חוֹזֵר לִמְקוֹמוֹ — **and then returned to his place** לִגְמוֹר אֲכִילָתוֹ — **in order to finish eating,** צָרִיךְ לְבָרֵךְ מֵחָדָשׁ בְּרָכָה רִאשׁוֹנָה — **he must recite the *berachah rishonah* anew** upon his return. בַּמֶּה דְּבָרִים אֲמוּרִים — **When do these** rules **apply?** כְּשֶׁהוּא אוֹכֵל לְבַדּוֹ — **When he is eating alone,** אוֹ כְּשֶׁהוּא אוֹכֵל עִם אֲחֵרִים וְכוּלָּם (שינוי) [שִׁינּוּ] אֶת מְקוֹמָם — **or, when he is eating with others and they all changed their location,** i.e., they moved to another place. אֲבָל אִם אֶחָד נִשְׁאַר עַל מְקוֹמוֹ — **However, if** he was eating with others, and at least **one** person **remained in his place,** אֲזַי גַּם אֵלּוּ שֶׁהָלְכוּ — **then even those who did leave** all have the same status as the one who stayed. כֵּיוָן שֶׁדַּעְתָּם לַחֲזוֹר לְכָאן — **For since they intend to return here** אֶל זֶה שֶׁנִּשְׁאַר כָּאן — **to** rejoin **the one who remained** וְלִגְמוֹר כָּאן אֲכִילָתָן — **and to finish eating here,** לָכֵן כְּשֶׁחוֹזְרִין וְאוֹכְלִין אוֹ שׁוֹתִין — **therefore when they return and eat or drink,** אֵינָם צְרִיכִים לְבָרֵךְ מֵחָדָשׁ — **they**

---

52. See *Mishnah Berurah* (178:11-12), which states that if, when beginning to eat he intended to go from room to room in the same house, or even from one floor to another in the same house, he may do so, and he certainly need not recite the blessing anew. In addition, *Beur Halachah* (178:1 s.v. בבית אחד) writes that if one did not have in mind when reciting the blessing to go from room to room in the same house, although he should not initially leave the room, if he did, he should *not* recite the *berachah rishonah* again.

Rabbi Moshe Feinstein writes (*Igros Moshe, Orach Chaim* II, §57) that one who goes outside while sucking a candy or chewing gum and had recited a blessing while preparing to leave his home, may continue eating even other candies (if he has them with him or if he could expect that he would obtain more) without reciting a new blessing (see *Shulchan Aruch* 178:4 and *Mishnah Berurah* 178:42). If he recited a blessing *before* preparing to leave home, he should stop eating before leaving and recite a new blessing after leaving the house (see there further).

205 BLESSINGS BEFORE FOOD, DRINK, AND FRAGRANCES — SIMAN 50:15-16

דְּכֵיוָן שֶׁנִּשְׁאַר כָּאן אֶחָד לֹא נִתְבַּטֵּל הַקְּבִיעוּת וְכוּלָּם חוֹזְרִין לִקְבִיעוּתָן וְנֶחְשָׁב הַכֹּל כִּסְעוּדָה אֶחָד[53].

טו. בְּחֶדֶר אֶחָד מִפִּינָּה לְפִינָּה, אַף עַל פִּי שֶׁהַחֶדֶר גָּדוֹל מְאוֹד, לֹא הָוֵי שִׁינּוּי מָקוֹם[54].

טז. אִם אוֹכֵל פֵּירוֹת בְּגַן שֶׁהוּא מוּקָּף מְחִיצוֹת וּבֵירַךְ עַל פֵּירוֹת מֵאִילָן אֶחָד עַל דַּעַת לֶאֱכוֹל גַּם מֵאִילָנוֹת אֲחֵרוֹת, יָכוֹל לֶאֱכוֹל גַּם מֵאִילָנוֹת אֲחֵרוֹת, אַף עַל פִּי שֶׁאֵינוֹ רוֹאֶה מְקוֹמוֹ, כֹּל שֶׁלֹּא הֵסִיחַ דַּעְתּוֹ, וְאֵין צָרִיךְ לְבָרֵךְ שֵׁנִית. אֲבָל אִם אֵין הַגַּן מוּקָּף מְחִיצוֹת, וּמִכָּל שֶׁכֵּן מִגַּן זֶה לְגַן אַחֵר, לֹא מְהַנֵּי דַּעְתּוֹ[55].

---

are not required to recite the blessing anew, **דְּכֵיוָן שֶׁנִּשְׁאַר כָּאן אֶחָד** — for since **one** person **remained here, לֹא נִתְבַּטֵּל הַקְּבִיעוּת** — **the permanence** of the original group **was not terminated, וְכוּלָּם חוֹזְרִין לִקְבִיעוּתָן** — **and all** those who left are considered to be **returning to their set place** when they come back. **וְנֶחְשָׁב הַכֹּל כִּסְעוּדָה אֶחָד** — **Thus, all** of the eating, both before they left and after they returned, **is considered one meal.** [53]

§15 בְּחֶדֶר אֶחָד מִפִּינָּה לְפִינָּה — If one goes **from one corner to another in the same room, אַף עַל פִּי שֶׁהַחֶדֶר גָּדוֹל מְאוֹד** — **even if it is a very large room, לֹא הָוֵי שִׁינּוּי מָקוֹם** — **it is not** considered **a change of location** that would require another blessing.[54]

§16 אִם אוֹכֵל פֵּירוֹת בְּגַן — **If one is eating fruit in a garden שֶׁהוּא מוּקָּף מְחִיצוֹת** — **that is surrounded by walls, וּבֵירַךְ עַל פֵּירוֹת מֵאִילָן אֶחָד** — **and he recited a blessing over the fruits of one tree עַל דַּעַת לֶאֱכוֹל גַּם מֵאִילָנוֹת אֲחֵרוֹת** — **with the intention of eating** fruit **from other trees as well, יָכוֹל לֶאֱכוֹל גַּם מֵאִילָנוֹת אֲחֵרוֹת** — **he may eat from** the **other trees as well, אַף עַל פִּי שֶׁאֵינוֹ רוֹאֶה מְקוֹמוֹ** — **even if he cannot see his** original **place** where he recited the blessing as he moves among the trees, **כֹּל שֶׁלֹּא הֵסִיחַ דַּעְתּוֹ** — **as long as he has not diverted his attention** from eating, **וְאֵין צָרִיךְ לְבָרֵךְ שֵׁנִית** — **and he is not required to recite the blessing a second time. אֲבָל אִם אֵין הַגַּן מוּקָּף מְחִיצוֹת** — **However, if the garden is not surrounded by walls, וּמִכָּל שֶׁכֵּן מִגַּן זֶה לְגַן אַחֵר** — **and certainly** if one moves **from this garden to another garden, לֹא מְהַנֵּי דַּעְתּוֹ** — **his** initial **intention** while he recited the blessing that he will change his location **is not effective** to allow the blessing to cover both places, and he is required to recite the blessing anew.[55]

---

53. However, if they wish to continue eating in another place, they must recite a new blessing (*Mishnah Berurah* 178:31).

54. This halachah applies even if he is not able to see his present location from where he began eating [such as where his view is blocked by a partition or furniture] (*Mishnah Berurah* 178:9; see above, note 52).

55. Kitzur rules that in order for the first blessing to be effective it is necessary for the entire area to be surrounded by walls, as well as for the person to have had in mind that he will eat from the other trees, as well. *Mishnah Berurah* (178:37-38) cites authorities who maintain that either an enclosure by walls, *or* having specific intent to eat from the other trees, is effective for the blessing to include the fruit of the other trees as well (see *Shaar HaTziyun* 178:31).

GENERAL RULES OF BERACHAH ACHARONAH — SIMAN 51:1-2 206

סימן נא

כְּלָלִים בִּבְרָכָה אַחֲרוֹנָה

וּבוֹ טו סְעִיפִים

א. עַל פֵּירוֹת הָאִילָן, חוּץ מִשִּׁבְעַת הַמִּינִים (כִּדְלְקַמָּן סְעִיף ז), וְעַל כָּל פֵּירוֹת הָאֲדָמָה וִירָקוֹת, וְכָל דָּבָר שֶׁאֵין גִּדּוּלוֹ מִן הָאָרֶץ[1], מְבָרֵךְ לְאַחֲרֵיהֶם "בּוֹרֵא נְפָשׁוֹת" וְכוּ'[2]. וַאֲפִילוּ אָכַל וְשָׁתָה, נִפְטָר בִּבְרָכָה אַחַת.

ב. בְּרָכָה אַחֲרוֹנָה, וְכֵן בִּרְכַּת הַמָּזוֹן, אֵין מְבָרְכִין אֶלָּא אִם כֵּן אָכַל כְּשִׁיעוּר, דְּהַיְינוּ כְּזַיִת[3]. אֲבָל עַל פָּחוֹת מִכְּשִׁיעוּר אֵין צָרִיךְ בְּרָכָה אַחֲרוֹנָה. וְעַל מַשְׁקִין — יֵשׁ אוֹמְרִים דְּאֵינוֹ חַיָּיב בִּבְרָכָה אַחֲרוֹנָה אֶלָּא אִם כֵּן שָׁתָה רְבִיעִית[4], וְיֵשׁ אוֹמְרִים דְּגַם

SIMAN 51

GENERAL RULES OF BERACHAH ACHARONAH

CONTAINING 15 *SE'IFIM*

§1 *Borei Nefashos* / §2 Minimum Amount for *Berachah Acharonah* / §3 A Complete Item / §4-6 Combinations and Time Frame for the Minimum Amount / §7 Blessing Upon the Seven Species / §8-9 Variations of the *Mei'ein Shalosh* Blessing / §10 Like *Bircas HaMazon* / §11 Version and Explanation of *Borei Nefashos* / §12 *Mei'ein Shalosh* and *Borei Nefashos* / §13 Reciting the Blessing in the Place Where One Ate / §14-15 Reciting the Blessing After Digestion

§1 עַל פֵּירוֹת הָאִילָן — **On the fruits of a tree,** חוּץ מִשִּׁבְעַת הַמִּינִים — **with the exception of the Seven Species** כִּדְלְקַמָּן סְעִיף ז) — **as** explained **below,** *se'if* 7), וְעַל כָּל פֵּירוֹת הָאֲדָמָה וִירָקוֹת — **and on any produce** that grows **from the ground, and** on any **vegetables,** וְכָל דָּבָר שֶׁאֵין גִּדּוּלוֹ מִן הָאָרֶץ — **and anything that does not grow from the ground,**[1] מְבָרֵךְ לְאַחֲרֵיהֶם "בּוֹרֵא נְפָשׁוֹת" וְכוּ' — **one recites** the blessing of *Borei Nefashos,* ***Who creates living things,*** **etc., after** eating **them.**[2] וַאֲפִילוּ אָכַל וְשָׁתָה — **Even if one** both **ate and drank,** נִפְטָר בִּבְרָכָה אַחַת — both food and drink **are exempted by** reciting **one blessing.**

§2 בְּרָכָה אַחֲרוֹנָה, וְכֵן בִּרְכַּת הַמָּזוֹן — A ***berachah acharonah*** (final blessing), **as well as** *Bircas HaMazon* (Grace after Meals), אֵין מְבָרְכִין אֶלָּא אִם כֵּן אָכַל כְּשִׁיעוּר — **is recited only if one ate the** minimum **amount,** דְּהַיְינוּ כְּזַיִת — **which is a** ***kezayis.***[3] אֲבָל עַל פָּחוֹת מִכְּשִׁיעוּר — **However,** upon **eating less than** this **amount** אֵין צָרִיךְ בְּרָכָה אַחֲרוֹנָה — **one is not required** to recite **a** ***berachah acharonah.*** וְעַל מַשְׁקִין — **Upon beverages,** יֵשׁ אוֹמְרִים דְּאֵינוֹ חַיָּיב בִּבְרָכָה אַחֲרוֹנָה — **some** authorities **say that one is not obligated** to recite **a** ***berachah acharonah*** אֶלָּא אִם כֵּן שָׁתָה רְבִיעִית — **unless he drank a** ***revi'is,***[4] וְיֵשׁ אוֹמְרִים — **and some** authorities **say** דְּגַם

---

1. Even water (*Mishnah Berurah* 207:2).

2. The text and explanation of the *Borei Nefashos* blessing are set out below, *se'if* 11.

3. The volume of an olive. Here, this is between 1 fl. oz. and 1.1 fl. oz. (29.6 cc.-33.3 cc.); see further, *Mishnah Berurah* 486:1.

4. This is between 2.9 fl. oz. and 5.1 fl. oz. (86.4 cc.-150 cc.); see Appendix A.

עַל מַשְׁקִין אִם שָׁתָה כְּזַיִת חַיָּיב בִּבְרָכָה אַחֲרוֹנָה. וְלָכֵן, לָצֵאת מִידֵי סְפֵיקָא יֵשׁ לִיזָּהֵר שֶׁלֹּא לִשְׁתּוֹת אֶלָּא פָּחוֹת מִכְּזַיִת אוֹ רְבִיעִית[5]. וְאֵין חִילּוּק בֵּין יֵין שָׂרָף לִשְׁאָר מַשְׁקִים[6].

ג. דָּבָר שֶׁהוּא כִּבְרִיָּיתוֹ, דְּהַיְינוּ אֱגוֹז אֶחָד אוֹ שְׁאָר פְּרִי, וַאֲפִילוּ קִטְנִיּוֹת אַחַת[7], יֵשׁ אוֹמְרִים, אַף עַל פִּי שֶׁאֵין בּוֹ כְּזַיִת, מִכָּל מָקוֹם כֵּיוָן שֶׁהוּא פְּרִי שָׁלֵם מְבָרְכִין אַחֲרָיו בְּרָכָה אַחֲרוֹנָה, וְיֵשׁ חוֹלְקִין. לָכֵן, לָצֵאת מִידֵי סָפֵק אֵין לֶאֱכוֹל פָּחוֹת מִכְּזַיִת[8]. וְאִם נִתְחַלֵּק הַדָּבָר קוֹדֶם הָאֲכִילָה[9], בָּטֵל מִמֶּנּוּ חֲשִׁיבוּתֵיהּ וּלְכוּלֵּי עָלְמָא אֵין מְבָרְכִין עָלָיו בְּרָכָה אַחֲרוֹנָה בְּפָחוֹת מִכְּזַיִת.

ד. כָּל הָאוֹכָלִין מִצְטָרְפִין לִכְזַיִת[10], וְאִם אָכַל כַּחֲצִי זַיִת מִדָּבָר שֶׁמְּבָרְכִין אַחֲרָיו "בּוֹרֵא

עַל מַשְׁקִין — that on beverages as well, אִם שָׁתָה כְּזַיִת חַיָּיב בִּבְרָכָה אַחֲרוֹנָה — if one drank only a *kezayis,* one must recite a *berachah acharonah.* וְלָכֵן, לָצֵאת מִידֵי סְפֵיקָא — Therefore, to avoid any doubt, יֵשׁ לִיזָּהֵר — one should take care שֶׁלֹּא לִשְׁתּוֹת אֶלָּא פָּחוֹת מִכְּזַיִת — to drink only either less than a *kezayis,* אוֹ רְבִיעִית — or to drink a *revi'is* or more.[5] וְאֵין חִילּוּק בֵּין יֵין שָׂרָף לִשְׁאָר מַשְׁקִים — There is no difference between liquor and any other drinks regarding this halachah.[6]

§3 דָּבָר שֶׁהוּא כִּבְרִיָּיתוֹ — Regarding **something that is a "whole creation,"** דְּהַיְינוּ אֱגוֹז אֶחָד — **such as a single nut** אוֹ שְׁאָר פְּרִי — **or any other** complete **fruit,** וַאֲפִילוּ קִטְנִיּוֹת אַחַת — **or even one** complete **bean,**[7] יֵשׁ אוֹמְרִים — **some** authorities say that אַף עַל פִּי שֶׁאֵין בּוֹ כְּזַיִת — **even if it is not** the size of **a *kezayis,*** מִכָּל מָקוֹם כֵּיוָן שֶׁהוּא פְּרִי שָׁלֵם — **nevertheless, since it is a complete fruit,** מְבָרְכִין אַחֲרָיו בְּרָכָה אַחֲרוֹנָה — **one recites a *berachah acharonah* after** eating it. וְיֵשׁ חוֹלְקִין — **However, some** authorities **disagree.** לָכֵן — **Therefore,** לָצֵאת מִידֵי סָפֵק — **in order to avoid** a situation of **doubt,** אֵין לֶאֱכוֹל פָּחוֹת מִכְּזַיִת — **one should not eat** such food in a quantity of **less than a *kezayis.***[8] וְאִם נִתְחַלֵּק הַדָּבָר קוֹדֶם הָאֲכִילָה — **If the item was divided before it was eaten,**[9] בָּטֵל מִמֶּנּוּ חֲשִׁיבוּתֵיהּ — **its significance is nullified,** וּלְכוּלֵּי עָלְמָא אֵין מְבָרְכִין עָלָיו בְּרָכָה אַחֲרוֹנָה — **and all** authorities **agree that a *berachah acharonah* is not recited over it** בְּפָחוֹת מִכְּזַיִת — **if** one ate **less than a *kezayis.***

§4 כָּל הָאוֹכָלִין מִצְטָרְפִין לִכְזַיִת — **All** types of **food combine to** complete **a *kezayis,*** requiring a *berachah acharonah* to be recited.[10] וְאִם אָכַל כַּחֲצִי זַיִת — **If one ate half a *kezayis*** מִדָּבָר שֶׁמְּבָרְכִין אַחֲרָיו "בּוֹרֵא נְפָשׁוֹת רַבּוֹת" — **of something after**

5. Less than a *kezayis* certainly does not require a *berachah acharonah*; more than a *revi'is* certainly does. Drinking between a *kezayis* and a *revi'is* would put one into a situation of doubt as to whether or not to make a *berachah acharonah.* See below, note 31; see also *Mishnah Berurah* 210:12.

6. See *Ba'er Heiteiv* 210:2.

7. Or a complete small fish (*Shaar HaTziyun* 210:20).

8. If one did eat a complete fruit, he does not recite a *berachah acharonah* unless he ate a *kezayis* (see *Orach Chaim* 110:1; *Igros Moshe, Orach Chaim* I, §78).

9. Even if a small piece was cut off, or a small portion disintegrated when the fruit was cooked (*Mishnah Berurah* 210:8). Similarly, if the pit was removed, the fruit is no longer considered to be in its original state (*Rama* 210:1; see *Mishnah Berurah* there §7 and §9).

10. I.e., if a person ate a small amount of a few kinds of foods, as long as all of the foods add up to a *kezayis,* he is obligated to recite the *berachah acharonah* upon those foods, as Kitzur proceeds to explain.

נְפָשׁוֹת רַבּוֹת״ וְכַחֲצִי זַיִת מִדָּבָר שֶׁמְּבָרְכִין עָלָיו בְּרָכָה מֵעֵין שָׁלֹשׁ[11], אוֹ אֲפִילוּ כַּחֲצִי זַיִת פַּת מְבָרֵךְ לְאַחֲרֵיהֶן ״בּוֹרֵא נְפָשׁוֹת רַבּוֹת״[12]. וְנִרְאֶה לִי דְּהוּא הַדִּין אִם אָכַל כַּחֲצִי זַיִת מִפֵּירוֹת שֶׁמְּבָרְכִין לְאַחֲרֵיהֶן ״עַל הָעֵץ״[13] וְכַחֲצִי זַיִת מִמִּין שֶׁמְּבָרְכִין לְאַחֲרָיו ״עַל הַמִּחְיָה״, אוֹ כַּחֲצִי זַיִת פַּת (דְּהַשְׁתָּא אֵין כָּאן שׁוּם מִין שֶׁבְּרָכָה אַחֲרוֹנָה שֶׁלּוֹ ״בּוֹרֵא נְפָשׁוֹת רַבּוֹת״, מִכָּל מָקוֹם) מְבָרֵךְ לְאַחֲרֵיהֶן ״בּוֹרֵא נְפָשׁוֹת רַבּוֹת״ (עַיֵּין מַחֲצִית הַשֶּׁקֶל סִימָן ר״י סְעִיף קָטָן א׳)[14]. וְאִם אָכַל כַּחֲצִי זַיִת מִמִּין שֶׁמְּבָרְכִין לְאַחֲרָיו ״עַל הַמִּחְיָה״ וְכַחֲצִי זַיִת פַּת, מְבָרֵךְ לְאַחֲרֵיהֶן ״עַל הַמִּחְיָה״. וּשְׁתִיָּה עִם אֲכִילָה אֵין מִצְטָרְפִין[15].

which one recites *Borei Nefashos Rabbos,* **וְכַחֲצִי זַיִת — and half a *kezayis* מִדָּבָר שֶׁמְּבָרְכִין עָלָיו בְּרָכָה מֵעֵין שָׁלֹשׁ — of something for which the *Mei'ein Shalosh*** (i.e., *abridgment of three*) **blessing**[11] **is recited, אוֹ אֲפִילוּ כַּחֲצִי זַיִת פַּת — or even if the** other **half a *kezayis*** was **bread, מְבָרֵךְ לְאַחֲרֵיהֶן ״בּוֹרֵא נְפָשׁוֹת רַבּוֹת״ — he recites the blessing of *Borei Nefashos Rabbos*** after eating **them.**[12] **וְנִרְאֶה לִי — It appears to me דְּהוּא הַדִּין אִם אָכַל כַּחֲצִי זַיִת מִפֵּירוֹת — that this is also the halachah if one ate half a *kezayis* of fruit שֶׁמְּבָרְכִין לְאַחֲרֵיהֶן ״עַל הָעֵץ״ — upon which** *Al HaEitz, for the tree,*[13] **is recited after** eating **them, וְכַחֲצִי זַיִת מִמִּין שֶׁמְּבָרְכִין לְאַחֲרָיו ״עַל הַמִּחְיָה״ — and half of a *kezayis* of a type** of food **after which** *Al HaMichyah, for the nourishment,* **is recited, אוֹ כַּחֲצִי זַיִת פַּת —** or even **if the second half of a *kezayis*** was **bread, (דְּהַשְׁתָּא אֵין כָּאן שׁוּם מִין שֶׁבְּרָכָה אַחֲרוֹנָה שֶׁלּוֹ ״בּוֹרֵא נְפָשׁוֹת רַבּוֹת״ — in which case no type** of food **was eaten whose *berachah acharonah* is *Borei Nefashos Rabbos,* מִכָּל מָקוֹם** — nevertheless), **מְבָרֵךְ לְאַחֲרֵיהֶן ״בּוֹרֵא נְפָשׁוֹת רַבּוֹת״ — he recites *Borei Nefashos Rabbos* after** eating **them (עַיֵּין מַחֲצִית הַשֶּׁקֶל סִימָן ר״י סְעִיף קָטָן א׳ — see *Machatzis HaShekel* 210:1).**[14] **וְאִם אָכַל כַּחֲצִי זַיִת — If one ate half of a *kezayis* מִמִּין שֶׁמְּבָרְכִין לְאַחֲרָיו ״עַל הַמִּחְיָה״ — of a type** of food **after which *Al HaMichyah* is recited, וְכַחֲצִי זַיִת פַּת — and also half a *kezayis* of bread, מְבָרֵךְ לְאַחֲרֵיהֶן ״עַל הַמִּחְיָה״ — he recites *Al HaMichyah* after** eating **them. וּשְׁתִיָּה עִם אֲכִילָה אֵין מִצְטָרְפִין — Drinking and eating do not combine** to complete the requisite amount for any *berachah acharonah.*[15]

11. This blessing has three basic forms (see below, *se'if* 7): *Al HaMichyah*, "for the nourishment," upon eating foods made from the five types of grain; *Al HaEitz*, "for the fruit," upon eating fruit of the Seven Species; and *Al HaGefen*, "for the vine," upon drinking wine. See below, *se'ifim* 7-8, where Kitzur elaborates upon the background and halachos of this blessing.

12. Although the Sages instituted a special blessing for the Seven Species, in certain cases *Borei Nefashos* can be considered an appropriate blessing for all foods. Thus, when one did not consume the requisite amount to require the *Mei'ein Shalosh* blessing or *Bircas HaMazon*, one can exempt that food with the recitation of *Borei Nefashos*.

13. As explained above (note 11), *Al HaEitz* and *Al HaMichyah* (which follows in Kitzur) are forms of the *Mei'ein Shalosh* blessing. See below, *se'if* 7.

14. *Machatzis HaShekel* cites halachic authorities who maintain that if one eats even less than a *kezayis* of a fruit of the Seven Species, *Borei Nefashos* is recited. Although the halachah does not follow this view when the fruit is eaten by itself, it can be used to support the opinion that if a *kezayis* of combined (Seven Species and non-Seven Species) foods was consumed, one should recite *Borei Nefashos*.

15. Just as all foods combine to the amount of *kezayis* with regard to *berachah acharonah*, so too do all beverages combine with each other to the amount of *revi'is* (*Mishnah Berurah* 210:1). However, foods and beverages, because they each have a different minimum amount for the *berachah acharonah* requirement (see *se'if* 2), do not combine. [Rabbi

ה. אָכַל כַּחֲצִי זַיִת וְשָׁהָה וְחָזַר וְאָכַל כַּחֲצִי זַיִת – אִם מִתְּחִלַּת הָאֲכִילָה הָרִאשׁוֹנָה עַד סוֹף הָאֲכִילָה לֹא הָיָה זְמַן יוֹתֵר כִּי אִם כְּדֵי אֲכִילַת פְּרָס16, מִצְטָרְפִין שְׁתֵּי הָאֲכִילוֹת וּמְבָרֵךְ בְּרָכָה אַחֲרוֹנָה17. אֲבָל אִם שָׁהָה יוֹתֵר, אֵין מִצְטָרְפִין18. וּבִשְׁתִיָּה אֲפִילוּ שָׁהָה פָּחוֹת מִזֶּה, אֵין מִצְטָרְפִין19.

§5 **אָכַל כַּחֲצִי זַיִת — If one ate half a *kezayis*** of food **וְשָׁהָה וְחָזַר וְאָכַל כַּחֲצִי זַיִת — and then paused, and again ate half a *kezayis*, אִם מִתְּחִלַּת הָאֲכִילָה הָרִאשׁוֹנָה — if, from the beginning of eating the first** half of the *kezayis* **עַד סוֹף הָאֲכִילָה — until the conclusion of eating** the second half of the *kezayis*, **לֹא הָיָה זְמַן יוֹתֵר — the time** that elapsed **was not longer כִּי אִם כְּדֵי אֲכִילַת פְּרָס — than *k'dei achilas pras*,**[16] **מִצְטָרְפִין שְׁתֵּי הָאֲכִילוֹת — the two acts of eating combine** to form one act of eating a full *kezayis*, **וּמְבָרֵךְ בְּרָכָה אַחֲרוֹנָה — and one recites the** appropriate ***berachah acharonah*.**[17] **אֲבָל אִם שָׁהָה יוֹתֵר — However, if he paused for longer** than that amount of time, **אֵין מִצְטָרְפִין — the** two acts of eating **do not combine** to form one act of eating a complete *kezayis*.[18] **וּבִשְׁתִיָּה — With regard to drinking, אֲפִילוּ שָׁהָה פָּחוֹת מִזֶּה — even if he paused less than this** amount of time between two acts of drinking, drinking less than a *revi'is* each time, **אֵין מִצְטָרְפִין** — the two acts of drinking **do not combine** to form one act of drinking a complete *revi'is*.[19]

Moshe Feinstein (*Igros Moshe, Orach Chaim* I, §74) rules that one who drank half a *revi'is* of wine and half a *revi'is* of another beverage should recite the *Borei Nefashos* blessing (see *Shaar HaTziyun* 210:4, who is unsure).]

One who eats a vegetable broth, and eats less than a *kezayis* of vegetables and less than a *revi'is* of the liquid, is not obligated to recite a *berachah acharonah*, even when they are eaten together (*Igros Moshe, Orach Chaim* I, §75 and *Even HaEzer* I, §114). If a food is eaten together with a liquid, and the liquid aids the eating of the food (e.g., such as food that is served in a sauce, or salad with dressing, or bread dipped in liquid), the solid and liquid combine for a *kezayis*, and the *berachah acharonah* of the solid is recited (*Mishnah Berurah* 210:1).

16. Literally, *the amount* [of time it takes] *to eat a half-loaf* [of bread], referring to the standard loaf in the times of the Mishnah (see *Rashi* to *Eruvin* 82b s.v. חציה לבית המנוגע). This time span ranges, depending on the context of the halachah, from 2 to 9 minutes according to the various authorities. See *Igros Moshe, Orach Chaim* IV, §41, who maintains that one is required to recite a *berachah acharonah* only if he consumes a *kezayis* in a time span of less than three minutes.

17. If one ate less than a *kezayis*, then left the house and returned, even immediately, and ate the rest of the *kezayis*, there is a question as to whether the two acts of eating can be considered one with regard to the obligation to recite a *berachah acharonah*. *Mishnah Berurah* (210:1) does not rule, but cites *Magen Avraham* (210:1), who is inclined to rule that one should recite the *berachah acharonah*. Rabbi Moshe Feinstein (*Igros Moshe, Orach Chaim* I, §77) concurs with *Magen Avraham's* view.

18. *Mishnah Berurah* (210:1) cites *Pri Megadim*, which states that when eating bread, as long as he ate to satiety, he must recite *Bircas HaMazon*, even if he did not eat a *kezayis* within the time of *k'dei achilas pras* (however, see *Shaar HaTziyun* ibid., §10, who questions this opinion). Rabbi Moshe Feinstein (*Igros Moshe, Orach Chaim* I, §76) rules that if one did not eat the *kezayis* of bread during this time frame, even if he did eat to satiety, he should not recite *Bircas HaMazon*. Nevertheless, one should avoid this situation and attempt, when eating to satiety, to eat a *kezayis* of bread within *k'dei achilas pras*.

19. According to this opinion, one can recite the *berachah acharonah* for drinking a *revi'is* only if he drinks it within the time frame that most people would drink a *revi'is* (*Mishnah Berurah* 210:1). [See *Shaar HaTziyun* ibid. §11 and *Haggadah Kol Dodi* §2 for how to determine this length of time.] *Mishnah Berurah* (ibid.) cites other authorities (including the *Gra*), who rule that the amount of time to consider drinking a *revi'is* of a beverage as one act of drinking is also *k'dei achilas pras*.

ו. שָׁתָה מַשְׁקֶה חַמָּה בִּמְעַט מְעַט (כְּמוֹ טהע קאפע), כֵּיוָן שֶׁאֵינוֹ שׁוֹתֶה בְּפַעַם אַחַת כְּשִׁיעוּר, אַף עַל פִּי שֶׁדֶּרֶךְ שְׁתִיָּיתָהּ בְּכָךְ, מִכָּל מָקוֹם אֵין מִצְטָרְפִין וְאֵינוֹ מְבָרֵךְ בְּרָכָה אַחֲרוֹנָה[20].

ז. בְּשִׁבְעָה מִינִים נִשְׁתַּבְּחָה אֶרֶץ יִשְׂרָאֵל דִּכְתִיב (דברים ח, ח) "אֶרֶץ חִטָּה וּשְׂעֹרָה וְגֶפֶן וּתְאֵנָה וְרִמּוֹן אֶרֶץ זֵית שֶׁמֶן וּדְבָשׁ" (שם פסוקים ט-י) וּבָתַר הָכִי כְּתִיב "אֶרֶץ אֲשֶׁר לֹא בְמִסְכֵּנֻת תֹּאכַל בָּהּ לֶחֶם ... וְאָכַלְתָּ וְשָׂבָעְתָּ וּבֵרַכְתָּ" וְגוֹ', וְכֵיוָן שֶׁבְּלֶחֶם מְבוֹאָר בַּתּוֹרָה "וְאָכַלְתָּ וְשָׂבָעְתָּ וּבֵרַכְתָּ", לָכֵן עַל הַלֶּחֶם מֵחֲמֵשֶׁת מִינֵי דָגָן, שֶׁהֵן "חִטָּה וּשְׂעֹרָה" הַמְפוֹרָשִׁין, וּמִכּוּסְמִין וְשִׁבּוֹלֶת שׁוּעָל וְשִׁיפוֹן, שֶׁהֵם גַּם כֵּן נִכְלָלִין בְּ"חִטָּה וּשְׂעֹרָה"[21], מְבָרְכִין אַחֲרָיו בִּרְכַּת הַמָּזוֹן, שֶׁהֵן שָׁלֹשׁ בְּרָכוֹת שְׁלֵמוֹת[22]

§6 שָׁתָה מַשְׁקֶה חַמָּה בִּמְעַט מְעַט — **If one drinks a hot beverage in small increments,** (כְּמוֹ טהע קאפע) — **such as tea** or **coffee),** כֵּיוָן שֶׁאֵינוֹ שׁוֹתֶה בְּפַעַם אַחַת כְּשִׁיעוּר — **since he does not drink the** requisite **amount at one time,** אַף עַל פִּי שֶׁדֶּרֶךְ שְׁתִיָּיתָהּ בְּכָךְ — **even though this is the way** people **drink it,** מִכָּל מָקוֹם אֵין מִצְטָרְפִין — **nevertheless,** the small amounts **do not combine** to be considered one act of drinking a *revi'is,* וְאֵינוֹ מְבָרֵךְ בְּרָכָה אַחֲרוֹנָה — **and one does not recite a *berachah acharonah.***[20]

§7 בְּשִׁבְעָה מִינִים נִשְׁתַּבְּחָה אֶרֶץ יִשְׂרָאֵל — **The Land of Israel is praised for seven species,** דִּכְתִיב — **as it is written** (*Devarim* 8:8): "אֶרֶץ חִטָּה וּשְׂעֹרָה וְגֶפֶן וּתְאֵנָה וְרִמּוֹן — ***a Land of wheat, barley, grape, fig, and pomegranate;*** אֶרֶץ זֵית שֶׁמֶן וּדְבָשׁ" — ***a Land of oil-olives and honey.*** וּבָתַר הָכִי כְּתִיב — **Following that, it is written** (ibid., verses 9-10): "אֶרֶץ אֲשֶׁר לֹא בְמִסְכֵּנֻת תֹּאכַל בָּהּ לֶחֶם ... — ***a Land where you will eat bread without poverty ...*** וְאָכַלְתָּ וְשָׂבָעְתָּ וּבֵרַכְתָּ" וְגוֹ' — ***You will eat and you will be satisfied, and bless*** Hashem, **etc.** וְכֵיוָן שֶׁבְּלֶחֶם מְבוֹאָר בַּתּוֹרָה — **Since, with regard to bread the Torah expressed** the directive of "וְאָכַלְתָּ וְשָׂבָעְתָּ וּבֵרַכְתָּ" — ***You will eat and you will be satisfied, and bless*** Hashem (referring to *Bircas HaMazon*), לָכֵן עַל הַלֶּחֶם מֵחֲמֵשֶׁת מִינֵי דָגָן — **therefore, upon** eating **bread** made **of one of the five grains,** שֶׁהֵן "חִטָּה וּשְׂעֹרָה" הַמְפוֹרָשִׁין — **which are wheat and barley, which are explicit** in the verse, וּמִכּוּסְמִין וְשִׁבּוֹלֶת שׁוּעָל וְשִׁיפוֹן — as well as **rye, oats, and spelt,** שֶׁהֵם גַּם כֵּן נִכְלָלִין בְּ"חִטָּה וּשְׂעֹרָה" — **which are also included in** the category **of wheat and barley,**[21] מְבָרְכִין אַחֲרָיו בִּרְכַּת הַמָּזוֹן — ***Bircas HaMazon* is recited afterward.** שֶׁהֵן שָׁלֹשׁ בְּרָכוֹת שְׁלֵמוֹת — *Bircas HaMazon* **consists of three complete blessings**[22]

20. *Mishnah Berurah* (ibid.) comments that this is a major point of dispute between halachic authorities, but that common practice is not to recite a *berachah acharonah* (see also opinion of *Gra* cited in previous note). He adds that people who are scrupulous in their actions allow the last *revi'is* of the hot drink to cool and then drink it without interruption, thus avoiding any question; he encourages following this practice.

21. Spelt is considered to be a sub-species of wheat; rye and oats are sub-species of barley (see *Rashi, Berachos* 44a s.v. חמשת המינים).

22. That is, as opposed to *Al HaMichyah,* which is an abridgement of these blessings. The three blessings are: (1) בִּרְכַּת הַזָּן, *the Blessing to the One Who Nourishes,* which was formulated by Moshe Rabbeinu in gratitude for the manna with which Hashem sustained the Jewish people in the Wilderness. (2) בִּרְכַּת הָאָרֶץ, *the Blessing for the Land* (beginning נוֹדֶה לְּךָ, *We thank You*), which was formulated by Yehoshua when the Jewish people entered Eretz Yisrael. (3) בּוֹנֵה

וְגַם בִּרְכַּת "הַטּוֹב וְהַמֵּטִיב" (שֶׁנִּתְקַן אַחַר כָּךְ בְּיַבְנֶה)[23]. אֲבָל כֹּל שֶׁאֵינוֹ לֶחֶם גָּמוּר, אֶלָּא מִינֵי מְזוֹנוֹת מֵאֵלּוּ חֲמֵשֶׁת מִינֵי דָגָן[24], וְכֵן עַל הַגֶּפֶן, דְּהַיְינוּ יַיִן וְגַם עֲנָבִים בֵּין לַחִים בֵּין יְבֵשִׁים בֵּין גְּדוֹלִים בֵּין קְטַנִּים[25], וּתְאֵנִים וְרִמּוֹנִים וְזֵיתִים וּתְמָרִים, שֶׁהֵם "דְּבַשׁ" הָאָמוּר בַּתּוֹרָה, לְפִי שֶׁמֵּהֶם זָב הַדְּבַשׁ, עַל כָּל אֵלּוּ מְבָרְכִין בְּרָכָה אַחֲרוֹנָה בְּרָכָה אַחַת מֵעֵין שָׁלֹשׁ, שֶׁהִיא כּוֹלֶלֶת בְּקִיצּוּר הַשָּׁלֹשׁ בְּרָכוֹת וְגַם "הַטּוֹב וְהַמֵּטִיב" שֶׁבְּבִרְכַּת הַמָּזוֹן[26].

ח. בִּבְרָכָה מֵעֵין שָׁלֹשׁ שֶׁלְּאַחַר מִינֵי מְזוֹנוֹת פּוֹתֵחַ "עַל הַמִּחְיָה וְעַל הַכַּלְכָּלָה" וְחוֹתֵם "וְנוֹדֶה לְּךָ עַל הָאָרֶץ וְעַל הַמִּחְיָה, בָּרוּךְ אַתָּה ה׳ עַל הָאָרֶץ וְעַל הַמִּחְיָה

וְגַם בִּרְכַּת "הַטּוֹב וְהַמֵּטִיב" — **as well as the blessing of** *HaTov VeHaMeitiv,* ***Who is good and Who does good*** **(שֶׁנִּתְקַן אַחַר כָּךְ בְּיַבְנֶה** — **that was instituted** at a **later** time, **in Yavneh).**[23] **אֲבָל כֹּל שֶׁאֵינוֹ לֶחֶם גָּמוּר** — **However, anything that is not** considered **actual bread, אֶלָּא מִינֵי מְזוֹנוֹת מֵאֵלּוּ חֲמֵשֶׁת מִינֵי דָגָן** — **but** are **kinds of** foods upon which the ***mezonos*** blessing is recited, **made from these five types of grain;**[24] **וְכֵן עַל הַגֶּפֶן, דְּהַיְינוּ יַיִן** — **as well as upon the "grape"** mentioned in the above verse, **which refers to wine; וְגַם עֲנָבִים בֵּין לַחִים בֵּין יְבֵשִׁים** — **as well as** actual **grapes, whether moist or dry, בֵּין גְּדוֹלִים בֵּין קְטַנִּים** — **large or small;**[25] **וּתְאֵנִים וְרִמּוֹנִים וְזֵיתִים** — **and** upon **figs, pomegranates, and olives; וּתְמָרִים, שֶׁהֵם "דְּבַשׁ" הָאָמוּר בַּתּוֹרָה** — **and** upon **dates, which are the honey referred to by the Torah** in the above verse **לְפִי שֶׁמֵּהֶם זָב הַדְּבַשׁ** — **because honey flows from them; עַל כָּל אֵלּוּ מְבָרְכִין בְּרָכָה אַחֲרוֹנָה** — **upon** eating **all these, we recite,** as **a** ***berachah acharonah,*** **בְּרָכָה אַחַת מֵעֵין שָׁלֹשׁ** — **the** ***Mei'ein Shalosh*** **blessing. שֶׁהִיא כּוֹלֶלֶת בְּקִיצּוּר הַשָּׁלֹשׁ בְּרָכוֹת** — **This** blessing **includes a concise** version **of the three blessings, וְגַם "הַטּוֹב וְהַמֵּטִיב" שֶׁבְּבִרְכַּת הַמָּזוֹן** — **as well as** the blessing of ***HaTov VeHaMeitiv,*** **of** ***Bircas HaMazon.***[26]

§8 In this *se'if,* Kitzur sets out the three variations of the *Mei'ein Shalosh* blessing, and the various combinations thereof.

בִּבְרָכָה מֵעֵין שָׁלֹשׁ שֶׁלְּאַחַר מִינֵי מְזוֹנוֹת — When reciting **the** ***Mei'ein Shalosh*** **blessing after** eating **grain products, פּוֹתֵחַ "עַל הַמִּחְיָה וְעַל הַכַּלְכָּלָה"** — **one opens** the blessing with *Blessed are You, HASHEM, our God, King of the universe,* ***for the nourishment and the sustenance,*** **וְחוֹתֵם "וְנוֹדֶה לְּךָ עַל הָאָרֶץ וְעַל הַמִּחְיָה** — **and concludes with** the phrase ***and we thank You for the Land and for the nourishment.*** **בָּרוּךְ אַתָּה ה׳ עַל הָאָרֶץ וְעַל הַמִּחְיָה וְעַל הַכַּלְכָּלָה"** — ***Blessed are You,*** ***HASHEM,*** ***for the Land,***

יְרוּשָׁלָיִם, *Builder of Yerushalayim* (beginning רַחֵם, *Have mercy*), which was formulated in stages by King David and King Shlomo, and refers to Yerushalayim and the Temple (see *Berachos* 48b).

23. This blessing was composed in gratitude to Hashem for preserving the bodies of the victims of the Roman massacre at Beitar, and for eventually allowing them to be brought to burial (*Berachos* 48b).

24. In *Siman* 48, Kitzur explains the halachic difference between "actual bread" and other grain preparations. See there also for cases in which certain grain preparations may be awarded the status of bread.

25. As long as they are fully ripe; see *Mishnah Berurah* 202:14-15.

26. See *Mishnah Berurah* (208:50), who explains how each of the blessings is represented in the *Mei'ein Shalosh* blessing.

וְעַל הַכַּלְכָּלָה״[27]. וְעַל הַיַּיִן פּוֹתֵחַ ״עַל הַגֶּפֶן וְעַל פְּרִי הַגֶּפֶן״ וְחוֹתֵם ״עַל הָאָרֶץ וְעַל פְּרִי הַגָּפֶן, בָּרוּךְ אַתָּה ה׳ עַל הָאָרֶץ וְעַל פְּרִי הַגָּפֶן״[28]. וְעַל הַפֵּירוֹת פּוֹתֵחַ ״עַל הָעֵץ וְעַל פְּרִי הָעֵץ״, וְחוֹתֵם ״עַל הָאָרֶץ וְעַל הַפֵּירוֹת, בָּרוּךְ אַתָּה ה׳ עַל הָאָרֶץ וְעַל הַפֵּירוֹת״ (וּבְאֶרֶץ יִשְׂרָאֵל[29], אוֹ אֲפִילוּ בְּחוּץ לָאָרֶץ אִם אָכַל מִפֵּירוֹת אֶרֶץ יִשְׂרָאֵל, אוֹמֵר ״עַל הָאָרֶץ וְעַל פֵּירוֹתֶיהָ״)[30]. אָכַל מִינֵי מְזוֹנוֹת וְגַם שָׁתָה יַיִן – כּוֹלֵל שְׁנֵיהֶם בִּבְרָכָה אַחַת[31], וְכֵן פֵּירוֹת וְיַיִן. וַאֲפִילוּ עֲנָבִים וְיַיִן, פֵּירוֹת וּמִינֵי מְזוֹנוֹת, אוֹ אֲפִילוּ מִינֵי מְזוֹנוֹת וְיַיִן וּפֵירוֹת, כּוֹלֵל שְׁלָשְׁתָּן. וְיַקְדִּים ״עַל הַמִּחְיָה״, וְאַחַר כָּךְ ״עַל הַגֶּפֶן״,

---

for the nourishment, and for the sustenance.[27] וְעַל הַיַּיִן — **Upon drinking wine,** פּוֹתֵחַ ״עַל הַגֶּפֶן וְעַל פְּרִי הַגֶּפֶן״ — **one begins** the blessing **with** the words *for the vine and for the fruit of the vine,* וְחוֹתֵם ״עַל הָאָרֶץ וְעַל פְּרִי הַגָּפֶן — **and concludes** *and we thank You* ***for the Land and for the fruit of the vine.*** בָּרוּךְ אַתָּה ה׳ עַל הָאָרֶ וְעַל פְּרִי הַגֶּפֶן״ — ***Blessed are You, Hashem, for the Land and for the fruit of the vine.***[28] וְעַל הַפֵּירוֹת — **Upon eating fruit** of the Seven Species (including grapes), פּוֹתֵחַ ״עַל הָעֵץ וְעַל פְּרִי הָעֵץ״ — **one begins** the blessing **with** ***for the tree and the fruit of the tree,*** וְחוֹתֵם ״עַל הָאָרֶץ וְעַל הַפֵּירוֹת — **and concludes with** *and we thank You* ***for the Land and for the fruit.*** בָּרוּךְ אַתָּה ה׳ עַל הָאָרֶץ וְעַל הַפֵּירוֹת״ — ***Blessed are You, Hashem, for the Land and for the fruit.*** (וּבְאֶרֶץ יִשְׂרָאֵל) — **In Eretz Yisrael,**[29] אוֹ אֲפִילוּ בְּחוּץ לָאָרֶץ אִם אָכַל מִפֵּירוֹת אֶרֶץ יִשְׂרָאֵל — **or even in the Diaspora if one ate of the fruit of Eretz Yisrael,** אוֹמֵר ״עַל הָאָרֶץ וְעַל פֵּירוֹתֶיהָ״ — **he should say,** ***for the Land and "its" fruit.***)[30] אָכַל מִינֵי מְזוֹנוֹת — **If one ate grain products** וְגַם שָׁתָה יַיִן — **and also drank wine,** כּוֹלֵל שְׁנֵיהֶם בִּבְרָכָה אַחַת — **he should include both of them in one blessing.**[31] וְכֵן פֵּירוֹת וְיַיִן — **Likewise,** if he ate **fruit and** drank **wine,** וַאֲפִילוּ עֲנָבִים וְיַיִן — **or even** ate **grapes and** drank **wine,** פֵּירוֹת וּמִינֵי מְזוֹנוֹת — or ate **fruit and grain products,** אוֹ אֲפִילוּ מִינֵי מְזוֹנוֹת וְיַיִן וּפֵירוֹת — **or even grain products, wine, and fruit,** כּוֹלֵל שְׁלָשְׁתָּן — **he should include** all **three** foods in the *Mei'ein Shalosh* blessing. וְיַקְדִּים ״עַל הַמִּחְיָה״ — In combining the various phrases within the blessing, **he should first say** the phrase ***for the nourishment,*** וְאַחַר כָּךְ ״עַל הַגֶּפֶן״ — **and then** say ***for the vine,***

---

27. According to the *Mishnah Berurah* (208:50), the words וְעַל הַכַּלְכָּלָה, *and for the sustenance*, are not recited at the conclusion of the blessing (see *Shaar HaTziyun* there §52).

28. If, after drinking wine, one concludes with the words וְעַל הַפֵּירוֹת, *and for the fruit*, he has fulfilled his obligation (*Mishnah Berurah* 208:56).

29. If one is eating fruit [of the Seven Species] that grew in Eretz Yisrael (see *Mishnah Berurah* 208:51).

30. This is in order to praise Hashem for having given us the Land that has produced these fruits (*Mishnah Berurah* 202:53). If one is unsure whether the fruit grew in Eretz Yisrael or not, he should conclude with the words וְעַל הַפֵּירוֹת, *and for the fruit* (ibid. §54).

31. As will be explained further. See Kitzur below (77:14), which states that when one drinks wine and eats *mezonos* upon which one will recite the *Al HaMichyah* blessing, he is required to drink at least a *revi'is* of wine so as to include the wine in the *Al HaMichyah* blessing. *Igros Moshe, Orach Chaim* II, §109, however, writes that it is *proper* (but one is not required) to add the words "*for the wine*" if he drank *less* than a *kezayis* of wine together with the *mezonos*. If one ate, in addition to the *mezonos, more* than a *kezayis* of wine but *less* than a *revi'is*, since there is halachic doubt as to the obligation of the *berachah acharonah* for the wine (see above, *se'if* 2), he is *required* to add the words "*for the wine*" into the *berachah acharonah* for the *mezonos*.

וְאַחַר כָּךְ "עַל הָעֵץ"[32]. וּכְשֶׁכּוֹלֵל "עַל הַמִּחְיָה" עִם שְׁאָר מִין לֹא יֹאמַר בַּחֲתִימָה "וְעַל הַכַּלְכָּלָה"[33], אֶלָּא יֹאמַר "בָּרוּךְ אַתָּה ה׳ עַל הָאָרֶץ וְעַל הַמִּחְיָה וְעַל פְּרִי הַגָּפֶן", אוֹ "עַל הַמִּחְיָה וְעַל הַפֵּירוֹת", אוֹ "עַל הַמִּחְיָה וְעַל פְּרִי הַגֶּפֶן וְעַל הַפֵּירוֹת"[34]. וּכְבָר נִדְפַּס הַנּוּסְחָא בְּסִידוּרִים. וְצָרִיךְ כָּל אִישׁ יִשְׂרָאֵל לִהְיוֹת בָּקִי בִּבְרָכָה זוֹ בְּעַל פֶּה.

ט. בְּשַׁבָּת וְיוֹם טוֹב וְרֹאשׁ חֹדֶשׁ מַזְכִּירִין בָּהּ מֵעֵנְיָנָא דְיוֹמָא[35]. וְאִם שָׁכַח וְלֹא הִזְכִּיר, אֵין מַחֲזִירִין אוֹתוֹ.

י. יֵשׁ לְהַחֲמִיר בִּבְרָכָה זוֹ כְּמוֹ בְּבִרְכַּת הַמָּזוֹן בִּדְבָרִים שֶׁנִּזְכְּרוּ בְּסִימָן מ״ד סְעִיף ו׳[36].

וְאַחַר כָּךְ "עַל הָעֵץ" — and then *for the tree.*[32] **וּכְשֶׁכּוֹלֵל "עַל הַמִּחְיָה" עִם שְׁאָר מִין** — **When one includes** the phrase *for the nourishment* together **with** one of the phrases for the **other types** of food, **לֹא יֹאמַר בַּחֲתִימָה "וְעַל הַכַּלְכָּלָה"** — **he should not say** ***and for the sustenance*** **at the conclusion** of the blessing as he does when reciting this blessing for grain products only.[33] **אֶלָּא יֹאמַר** — **Rather, he should say "בָּרוּךְ אַתָּה ה׳ עַל הָאָרֶץ וְעַל הַמִּחְיָה וְעַל פְּרִי הַגָּפֶן"** — ***Blessed are You,*** ***Hashem, for the Land, and for the nourishment, and for the fruit of the vine,*** **אוֹ "עַל הַמִּחְיָה וְעַל הַפֵּירוֹת"** — **or,** *for the Land, and* ***for the nourishment, and for the fruit,*** **אוֹ "עַל הַמִּחְיָה וְעַל פְּרִי הַגֶּפֶן וְעַל הַפֵּירוֹת"** — **or,** *for the Land, and* ***for the nourishment and for the fruit of the vine and for the fruit.***[34] **וּכְבָר נִדְפַּס הַנּוּסְחָא בְּסִידוּרִים** — **The text** of this blessing **is already printed in** ***siddurim*** (prayer books), **וְצָרִיךְ כָּל אִישׁ יִשְׂרָאֵל לִהְיוֹת בָּקִי בִּבְרָכָה זוֹ** — **and every Jewish person should be proficient in this blessing** **בְּעַל פֶּה** — and be able to recite it **by heart.**

§9 בְּשַׁבָּת וְיוֹם טוֹב וְרֹאשׁ חֹדֶשׁ — **On Shabbos, festivals, and Rosh Chodesh** (first day of the New Month), **מַזְכִּירִין בָּהּ מֵעֵנְיָנָא דְיוֹמָא** — **we mention in** the *Mei'ein Shalosh* blessing a phrase relating to **the theme of the day.**[35] **וְאִם שָׁכַח וְלֹא הִזְכִּיר** — **If one forgot and did not mention it,** **אֵין מַחֲזִירִין אוֹתוֹ** — **he does not repeat the blessing.**

§10 יֵשׁ לְהַחֲמִיר בִּבְרָכָה זוֹ — **One should be stringent with this blessing** (*Mei'ein Shalosh*) **כְּמוֹ בְּבִרְכַּת הַמָּזוֹן** — **just like** ***Bircas HaMazon,*** **בִּדְבָרִים שֶׁנִּזְכְּרוּ בְּסִימָן מ״ד סְעִיף ו׳** — **with** regard to **the things mentioned in** ***Siman*** **44,** ***se'if*** **6.**[36]

---

32. If he ate only two of the three categories, he should recite the applicable two in the order that they are set out here.

33. As noted above (note 27), according to the *Mishnah Berurah*, the words וְעַל הַכַּלְכָּלָה, *and for the sustenance*, are never recited at the conclusion of the blessing.

34. If one omits וְעַל פְּרִי הַגֶּפֶן, *and for the fruit of the vine,* he does not need to repeat the blessing (*Mishnah Berurah* 208:61).

35. On Shabbos, we add the words וּרְצֵה וְהַחֲלִיצֵנוּ בְּיוֹם הַשַּׁבָּת הַזֶּה, *And may it be pleasing to You to give us rest on this Shabbos day;* on Rosh Chodesh, וְזָכְרֵנוּ לְטוֹבָה בְּיוֹם רֹאשׁ הַחֹדֶשׁ הַזֶּה, *And remember us for goodness on this Rosh Chodesh;* on festivals, ... וְשַׂמְּחֵנוּ בְּיוֹם חַג, *And gladden us on this festival of ...* (the appropriate festival is inserted). These phrases are added before the concluding words of the blessing, ... כִּי אַתָּה ה׳ טוֹב וּמֵטִיב לַכֹּל וְנוֹדֶה לְּךָ עַל הָאָרֶץ וְעַל, *For You,* Hashem*, are good and do good to all and we thank You for the Land and for ...*

36. Such as reciting the blessing while seated, in an upright position, and wearing an outer garment and hat. [*Shulchan Aruch* (184:10) and *Mishnah Berurah* (ibid. §35) mention only the requirement to be seated.]

יא. בְּבִרְכַּת "בּוֹרֵא נְפָשׁוֹת" יֵשׁ אוֹמְרִים[37] "שֶׁבָּרָאתָ", וְיֵשׁ אוֹמְרִים "שֶׁבָּרָא", וְכֵן עִיקָּר[38]. וּפֵירוּשׁ שֶׁל הַבְּרָכָה הִיא: "בּוֹרֵא נְפָשׁוֹת רַבּוֹת וְחֶסְרוֹנָן"[39] — שֶׁבָּרָא הַנְּפָשׁוֹת וְגַם מַחְסוֹרָם, דְּהַיְינוּ כָּל צָרְכֵי סִיפּוּקָן שֶׁהֵם דְּבָרִים הֶכְרֵחִיִּים לְצוֹרֶךְ קִיּוּם חִיּוּתָן, כְּמוֹ הַלֶּחֶם וְהַמַּיִם, וְגַם "עַל כָּל" שְׁאָר הַדְּבָרִים "שֶׁבָּרָא" שֶׁאֵינָם הֶכְרֵחִיִּים כָּל כָּךְ אֶלָּא לְהִתְעַנֵּג בָּהֶם[40], כְּמוֹ פֵּירוֹת וְכַדּוֹמֶה. אָנוּ מְבָרְכִים אוֹתְךָ, "חַי הָעוֹלָמִים"[41]. צְרִיכִין לוֹמַר הַחֵית בְּפַתָּח[42] (הַגָּאוֹן מהר"א ווילְנָא זצ"ל הִסְכִּים עִם הַפּוֹסְקִים שֶׁכָּתְבוּ לַחְתּוֹם הַבְּרָכָה בְּשֵׁם וְלוֹמַר "בָּרוּךְ אַתָּה ה' חַי הָעוֹלָמִים")[43].

---

§11 **בְּבִרְכַּת "בּוֹרֵא נְפָשׁוֹת" יֵשׁ אוֹמְרִים** — **In the blessing of** *Borei Nefashos*,[37] **some** say the word **"שֶׁבָּרָאתָ"** — *that You have created*, **וְיֵשׁ אוֹמְרִים "שֶׁבָּרָא"** — **and some say,** *that He has created*, **וְכֵן עִיקָּר** — **and** the latter **is the principal** ruling to be followed.[38] **וּפֵירוּשׁ שֶׁל הַבְּרָכָה הִיא** — **The meaning of the blessing is:** **"בּוֹרֵא נְפָשׁוֹת רַבּוֹת וְחֶסְרוֹנָן"**— ***Who creates numerous living things and their needs,***[39] **שֶׁבָּרָא הַנְּפָשׁוֹת וְגַם מַחְסוֹרָם** — meaning, that **He created the living things along with that which they need,** **דְּהַיְינוּ כָּל צָרְכֵי סִיפּוּקָן** — **that is, everything that is required for their necessities,** **שֶׁהֵם דְּבָרִים הֶכְרֵחִיִּים לְצוֹרֶךְ קִיּוּם חִיּוּתָן** — **which are the essential things needed to keep them alive,** **כְּמוֹ הַלֶּחֶם וְהַמַּיִם** — **such as bread and water.** **וְגַם "עַל כָּל" שְׁאָר הַדְּבָרִים "שֶׁבָּרָא"** — **In addition** to that, the blessing continues, *for all* **the other things** *that He has created* **שֶׁאֵינָם הֶכְרֵחִיִּים כָּל כָּךְ** — **that are not as essential,** **אֶלָּא לְהִתְעַנֵּג בָּהֶם** — **but** were created **to be enjoyed,**[40] **כְּמוֹ פֵּירוֹת וְכַדּוֹמֶה** — **such as fruit and the like.** **אָנוּ מְבָרְכִים אוֹתְךָ, "חַי הָעוֹלָמִים".** — **We bless You,** Hashem, Who is ***the Life of the worlds.***[41] **צְרִיכִין לוֹמַר הַחֵית בְּפַתָּח** — **And one must pronounce the** *ches* (of the word חַי) vowelized **with a** *patach*.[42] **(הַגָּאוֹן מהר"א ווילְנָא זצ"ל** — **The Gaon, Rabbi Eliyahu** of **Vilna, of blessed memory,** **הִסְכִּים עִם הַפּוֹסְקִים שֶׁכָּתְבוּ** — **agreed with the halachic authorities who have written** **לַחְתּוֹם הַבְּרָכָה בְּשֵׁם** — **to conclude the** *Borei Nefashos* **blessing with** Hashem's **Name,** **וְלוֹמַר "בָּרוּךְ אַתָּה ה' חַי הָעוֹלָמִים"** — **by saying** ***Blessed are You, Hashem, the Life of the worlds.)***[43]

---

37. The full text of the blessing according to Kitzur is: בָּרוּךְ אַתָּה ה' אֱלֹהֵינוּ מֶלֶךְ הָעוֹלָם בּוֹרֵא נְפָשׁוֹת רַבּוֹת וְחֶסְרוֹנָן עַל כָּל מַה [שֶׁבָּרָא] [שֶׁבָּרָאתָ] לְהַחֲיוֹת בָּהֶם נֶפֶשׁ כָּל חָי. בָּרוּךְ חַי הָעוֹלָמִים, *Blessed are You, Hashem, our God, King of the universe, Who creates numerous living things and their needs; for all that [He has created] [You have created] with which to gratify every living being. Blessed is He, the Life of the worlds.* Kitzur now elaborates on the meaning of this blessing and addresses which one of the words in brackets should be said.

38. *Mishnah Berurah* (207:3) writes that each place should follow its own custom.

39. *Mishnah Berurah* writes (207:3, and *Shaar HaTziyun* ibid. §2) that the word is וְחֶסְרוֹנָם (*vechesronam*), with a *mem*, and not וְחֶסְרוֹנָן (*vechesronan*), with a *nun*.

40. This is the meaning of the words: עַל כָּל מַה שֶּׁבָּרָא לְהַחֲיוֹת בָּהֶם נֶפֶשׁ כָּל חָי, *for all that He has created with which to gratify every living being* (see *Mishnah Berurah* 207:5).

41. I.e., Hashem is the life-giver of both this world and the World to Come (*Abudraham*).

42. I.e., it should be pronounced *chai ha'olamim*, not *chei ha'olamim*. See, however, *Mishnah Berurah* (207:3), who rules that it is pronounced *chei ha'olamim*.

43. [The Vilna Gaon subscribes to the opinion that חֵי is pronounced with a *tzerei* — see *Beur HaGra* to *Orach Chaim* §207.] *Mishnah Berurah* (207:5) writes that the common practice does not follow this opinion, but rather concludes בָּרוּךְ חֵי הָעוֹלָמִים, *Blessed is He, the Life of the worlds.*

יב. אֲבָל פֵּירוֹת שֶׁבְּרָכָה אַחֲרוֹנָה שֶׁלָּהֶם בְּרָכָה מֵעֵין שָׁלֹשׁ וְגַם פֵּירוֹת הָעֵץ שֶׁבְּרָכָה אַחֲרוֹנָה שֶׁלָּהֶן הוּא "בּוֹרֵא נְפָשׁוֹת", מְבָרֵךְ בְּרָכָה מֵעֵין שָׁלֹשׁ, וְכֵיוָן שֶׁהוּא מַזְכִּיר בָּהֶם פְּרִי עֵץ נִפְטָרִים בָּזֶה כָּל פְּרִי הָעֵץ שֶׁאָכַל[44]. אֲבָל אִם נִתְחַיֵּיב בְּרִכַּת "בּוֹרֵא נְפָשׁוֹת" עַל מִין אַחֵר, אֵינוֹ נִפְטָר בִּבְרָכָה מֵעֵין שָׁלֹשׁ, וִיבָרֵךְ תְּחִלָּה בִּרְכַּת מֵעֵין שָׁלֹשׁ וְאַחַר כָּךְ בּוֹרֵא נְפָשׁוֹת.

יג. לְכַתְּחִלָּה אָסוּר לְאָדָם לָצֵאת מִמְּקוֹמוֹ[45] אוֹ לַעֲסוֹק בְּאֵיזֶה דָבָר[46] עַד שֶׁיְּבָרֵךְ בְּרָכָה אַחֲרוֹנָה שֶׁמָּא יִשְׁכַּח מִלְּבָרֵךְ. וּבְדִיעֲבַד כְּשֶׁיָּצָא מִמְּקוֹמוֹ, אִם הוּא צָרִיךְ לְבָרֵךְ "בּוֹרֵא נְפָשׁוֹת רַבּוֹת", יָכוֹל לְבָרֵךְ בְּמָקוֹם שֶׁהוּא שָׁם. אֲבָל אִם צָרִיךְ לְבָרֵךְ בְּרָכָה מֵעֵין שָׁלֹשׁ, צָרִיךְ שֶׁיַּחֲזוֹר לִמְקוֹמוֹ, כְּמוֹ בְּבִרְכַּת הַמָּזוֹן לְעֵיל סִימָן מ"ד סְעִיף ט'[47].

---

§12 **אֲבָל פֵּירוֹת שֶׁבְּרָכָה אַחֲרוֹנָה שֶׁלָּהֶם בְּרָכָה מֵעֵין שָׁלֹשׁ** — **If one ate fruit for which** the appropriate *berachah acharonah* is the *Mei'ein Shalosh* blessing (*Al HaEitz*), i.e., fruits of the Seven Species, **וְגַם פֵּירוֹת הָעֵץ שֶׁבְּרָכָה אַחֲרוֹנָה שֶׁלָּהֶן הוּא "בּוֹרֵא נְפָשׁוֹת"** — **and he also ate fruit of the tree for which the *berachah acharonah* is *Borei Nefashos,*** i.e., fruits that are not of the Seven Species, **מְבָרֵךְ בְּרָכָה מֵעֵין שָׁלֹשׁ** — **he recites the *Mei'ein Shalosh* blessing** after eating and that is sufficient, **וְכֵיוָן שֶׁהוּא מַזְכִּיר בָּהֶם פְּרִי עֵץ** — for **since he mentions in this** blessing the **fruit of the tree,** **נִפְטָרִים בָּזֶה כָּל פְּרִי הָעֵץ שֶׁאָכַל** — **all fruits that he has eaten are exempted with this** *berachah acharonah.*[44] **אֲבָל אִם נִתְחַיֵּיב בְּרִכַּת "בּוֹרֵא נְפָשׁוֹת" עַל מִין אַחֵר** — **However, if he is required** to recite **the blessing of *Borei Nefashos* for a different type** of food (i.e., not a fruit) that he ate, **אֵינוֹ נִפְטָר בִּבְרָכָה מֵעֵין שָׁלֹשׁ** — that food **is not exempted by the *Mei'ein Shalosh*** blessing. **וִיבָרֵךְ תְּחִלָּה בִּרְכַּת מֵעֵין שָׁלֹשׁ** — In this case, **he first recites the *Mei'ein Shalosh*** blessing, **וְאַחַר כָּךְ בּוֹרֵא נְפָשׁוֹת** — **and after that *Borei Nefashos.***

§13 **לְכַתְּחִלָּה אָסוּר לְאָדָם לָצֵאת מִמְּקוֹמוֹ** — **Initially,** after eating, **one is forbidden to leave his place**[45] **אוֹ לַעֲסוֹק בְּאֵיזֶה דָבָר** — **or to engage in anything** else[46] **עַד שֶׁיְּבָרֵךְ בְּרָכָה אַחֲרוֹנָה** — **until he has recited a *berachah acharonah,*** **שֶׁמָּא יִשְׁכַּח מִלְּבָרֵךְ** — **lest he forget to recite** this **blessing.** **וּבְדִיעֲבַד כְּשֶׁיָּצָא מִמְּקוֹמוֹ** — However, **if after the fact, he did leave his place,** **אִם הוּא צָרִיךְ לְבָרֵךְ "בּוֹרֵא נְפָשׁוֹת רַבּוֹת"** — **if he needs to recite** the blessing of ***Borei Nefashos Rabbos,*** **יָכוֹל לְבָרֵךְ בְּמָקוֹם שֶׁהוּא שָׁם** — **he may recite it at the place where he is** then. **אֲבָל אִם צָרִיךְ לְבָרֵךְ בְּרָכָה מֵעֵין שָׁלֹשׁ** — **But if he needs to recite the *Mei'ein Shalosh* blessing,** **צָרִיךְ שֶׁיַּחֲזוֹר לִמְקוֹמוֹ** — **he must return to** the original **place** where he ate, **כְּמוֹ בְּבִרְכַּת הַמָּזוֹן לְעֵיל סִימָן מ"ד סְעִיף ט'** — **just as** he must when reciting *Bircas HaMazon,* as set out **above, 44:9.**[47]

---

44. *Mishnah Berurah* (207:1) writes that if, after eating only fruit that was not from the Seven Species, one mistakenly recited *Al HaEitz,* he has also fulfilled his obligation.

45. If one intends to return immediately, he is permitted to leave (*Shaar HaTziyun* 178:26).

46. See above, 42:19.

47. *Mishnah Berurah* (184:12) cites *Gra,* who rules that only grain products are subject to the halachah that one must return to his original place to recite their *berachah acharonah* (*Al HaMichyah*), not fruit of the Seven Species or wine.

יד. אָכַל וְשָׁתָה וְלֹא בֵּירַךְ מִיָּד בְּרָכָה אַחֲרוֹנָה, יָכוֹל לְבָרֵךְ עַד שְׁעַת עִיכּוּל, דְּהַיְינוּ כָּל זְמַן שֶׁאֵינוֹ תָּאֵב לֶאֱכוֹל פֵּירוֹת[48], וּלְאַחַר שְׁתִיָּה כָּל זְמַן שֶׁאֵינוֹ צָמֵא. וּלְאַחַר זְמַנִּים אֵלּוּ אֵינוֹ יָכוֹל לְבָרֵךְ עוֹד. וּמִי שֶׁאֵינוֹ בָּקִי לְשַׁעֵר רָאוּי לוֹ כְּשֶׁנִּזְכַּר שֶׁלֹּא בֵּירַךְ בְּרָכָה אַחֲרוֹנָה, יְבָרֵךְ עַל מִין מִמִּין שֶׁאָכַל וִיבָרֵךְ בְּרָכָה אַחֲרוֹנָה לִפְטוֹר גַּם אֶת הָרִאשׁוֹן.

טו. אָכַל אוֹ שָׁתָה וְהֵקִיא לֹא יְבָרֵךְ בְּרָכָה אַחֲרוֹנָה דְּלֹא גָּרַע מִנִּתְעַכֵּל.

---

§14 אָכַל וְשָׁתָה וְלֹא בֵּירַךְ מִיָּד בְּרָכָה אַחֲרוֹנָה — **If one ate or drank and did not immediately recite a *berachah acharonah*,** יָכוֹל לְבָרֵךְ עַד שְׁעַת עִיכּוּל — **he may recite it until the time** the food has been **digested,** דְּהַיְינוּ כָּל זְמַן שֶׁאֵינוֹ תָּאֵב לֶאֱכוֹל פֵּירוֹת — **that is,** after eating fruit, **as long as he has no desire to eat fruit,**[48] וּלְאַחַר שְׁתִיָּה — **and after drinking,** כָּל זְמַן שֶׁאֵינוֹ צָמֵא — **as long as he is not thirsty.** וּלְאַחַר זְמַנִּים אֵלּוּ — **After these times** have passed, אֵינוֹ יָכוֹל לְבָרֵךְ עוֹד — **he may no longer recite a *berachah*** *acharonah.* וּמִי שֶׁאֵינוֹ בָּקִי לְשַׁעֵר — **One who cannot gauge** this time, רָאוּי לוֹ — **it is proper for him,** כְּשֶׁנִּזְכַּר שֶׁלֹּא בֵּירַךְ בְּרָכָה אַחֲרוֹנָה — **when he remembers that he has not recited a *berachah acharonah*,** יְבָרֵךְ עַל מִין מִמִּין שֶׁאָכַל — **to recite** another ***berachah*** *rishonah* **on the** same **type** of food **that he** previously **ate** (i.e., one that is subject to the same *berachah acharonah*), וִיבָרֵךְ בְּרָכָה אַחֲרוֹנָה — **and** then **eat it and recite a *berachah acharonah*** לִפְטוֹר גַּם אֶת הָרִאשׁוֹן — **to exempt the first** food **as well.**

§15 אָכַל אוֹ שָׁתָה וְהֵקִיא — **One who ate or drank and then vomited** לֹא יְבָרֵךְ בְּרָכָה אַחֲרוֹנָה — **should not recite a *berachah acharonah*,** דְּלֹא גָּרַע מִנִּתְעַכֵּל — **because this is no less** of a reason not to recite a *berachah acharonah* **than** if the food is already **digested.**

---

48. See above, 44:8.

217 HA'EITZ, HA'ADAMAH, AND SHEHAKOL BLESSINGS — SIMAN 52:1

סִימָן נב

דִּינֵי בִּרְכַּת "בּוֹרֵא פְּרִי הָעֵץ" וּ"בוֹרֵא פְּרִי הָאֲדָמָה" וְ"שֶׁהַכֹּל"

וּבוֹ ח"י סְעִיפִים

א. עַל פֵּירוֹת הַגְּדֵלִים בְּאִילָן מְבָרְכִין "בּוֹרֵא פְּרִי הָעֵץ". וְעַל פֵּירוֹת הַגְּדֵלִים בָּאֲדָמָה וְהֵם כָּל מִינֵי לִיפְתָּן[1] וִירָקוֹת וְקִטְנִיּוֹת וְטאטארקע וַעֲשָׂבִין מְבָרְכִין "בּוֹרֵא פְּרִי הָאֲדָמָה". וְלֹא נִקְרָא אִילָן אֶלָּא זֶה שֶׁהָעֲנָפִים שֶׁלּוֹ נִשְׁאָרִים גַּם בַּחוֹרֶף וּמוֹצִיא אַחַר כָּךְ עָלִים מִן הָעֲנָפִים, וַאֲפִילוּ הֵם דַּקִּין כִּגְבְעוֹלֵי פִשְׁתָּן. אֲבָל אִם הָעֲנָפִים כָּלִים לְגַמְרֵי

SIMAN 52

LAWS OF THE BOREI PRI HA'EITZ, BOREI PRI HA'ADAMAH, AND SHEHAKOL BLESSINGS

CONTAINING 18 *SE'IFIM*

§1 Fruits and Vegetables / **§2** Non-Plant Foods / **§3** Mushrooms and Truffles / **§4-6** Commonly Eaten Cooked or Raw / **§7** Inferior Fruit / **§8** Wild Plants / **§9** Ancillary Growths / **§10** Seeds / **§11** Almonds / **§12-14** Unripe Fruit / **§15** Sucking Juice From an Inedible Fruit / **§16** Recognizable Form / **§17** Rice, Millet / **§18** Sugar, Cinnamon, Licorice

§1 **עַל פֵּירוֹת הַגְּדֵלִים בְּאִילָן — Upon produce that grows on a tree,** **מְבָרְכִין "בּוֹרֵא פְּרִי הָעֵץ" — we recite the** following **blessing:** *Baruch Atah Ado-noy Elokeinu Melech HaOlam, borei pri ha'eitz — Blessed are You, Hashem, our God, King of the universe,* ***Who creates the fruit of the tree.*** **וְעַל פֵּירוֹת הַגְּדֵלִים בָּאֲדָמָה — Upon produce that grows from the ground,** **וְהֵם כָּל מִינֵי לִיפְתָּן — which** includes **all types of root vegetables,**[1] **וִירָקוֹת וְקִטְנִיּוֹת וְטאטארקע וַעֲשָׂבִין — vegetables, legumes** (such as beans or peas), **buckwheat, and herbage,** **מְבָרְכִין "בּוֹרֵא פְּרִי הָאֲדָמָה" — we recite the** following **blessing:** *Baruch Atah Ado-noy Elokeinu Melech HaOlam, borei pri ha'adamah — Blessed are You, Hashem, our God, King of the universe,* ***Who creates the fruit of the ground.***

Borei pri ha'eitz is recited only on the fruit of a tree, not other plants. Here, Kitzur explains the halachic distinction between plants and trees:

וְלֹא נִקְרָא אִילָן — A plant **is not classified** as **a tree** with regard to this halachah **אֶלָּא זֶה שֶׁהָעֲנָפִים שֶׁלּוֹ נִשְׁאָרִים גַּם בַּחוֹרֶף — unless it is** a plant **whose branches remain throughout the winter as well** as the summer, **וּמוֹצִיא אַחַר כָּךְ עָלִים מִן הָעֲנָפִים — and produces** new **leaves from the branches after** the winter, **וַאֲפִילוּ הֵם דַּקִּין כִּגְבְעוֹלֵי פִשְׁתָּן — even if** these branches **are as thin as stalks of flax.** **אֲבָל אִם הָעֲנָפִים כָּלִים לְגַמְרֵי בַּחוֹרֶף — However, if the branches disappear completely in the**

1. E.g., carrots and turnips (see *Mishnah Berurah* 205:18).

HA'EITZ, HA'ADAMAH, AND SHEHAKOL BLESSINGS — SIMAN 52:2-3 218

בַּחוֹרֶף וְאֵינוֹ נִשְׁאָר רַק הַשּׁוֹרֶשׁ, לֹא נִקְרָא אִילָן וּמְבָרְכִין עַל הַפֵּירוֹת "בּוֹרֵא פְּרִי הָאֲדָמָה"[2].

ב. עַל דָּבָר שֶׁאֵין גִּידוּלוֹ מִן הָאָרֶץ כְּמוֹ בָּשָׂר דָּגִים חָלָב גְּבִינָה, וְכֵן עַל כָּל מִינֵי מַשְׁקִים, חוּץ מִן הַיַּיִן[3] וְשֶׁמֶן זַיִת[4], מְבָרְכִין "שֶׁהַכֹּל". וְתֵיבַת "נִהְיָה" יֵשׁ לוֹמַר הַיּוּד בְּקָמַץ[5].

ג. כְּמֵיהִין וּפִטְרִיּוֹת (שוואמען), אַף עַל פִּי שֶׁהֵן גְּדֵלִין מִלַּחְלוּחִית הָאָרֶץ, יְנִיקָתָן אֵינָהּ מִן הָאָרֶץ אֶלָּא מִן הָאֲוִיר[6], וְלָכֵן אֵינָן נִקְרָאִין פְּרִי הָאֲדָמָה וּמְבָרְכִין עֲלֵיהֶן "שֶׁהַכֹּל".

---

winter, וְאֵינוֹ נִשְׁאָר רַק הַשּׁוֹרֶשׁ — **and only the root** of the plant **remains,** לֹא נִקְרָא אִילָן — **it is not classified as a tree,** וּמְבָרְכִין עַל הַפֵּירוֹת "בּוֹרֵא פְּרִי הָאֲדָמָה" — **and we recite the *borei pri ha'adamah* blessing on its fruit.**[2]

§2 עַל דָּבָר שֶׁאֵין גִּידוּלוֹ מִן הָאָרֶץ — **Upon** eating **something that does not grow from the ground,** כְּמוֹ בָּשָׂר דָּגִים חָלָב גְּבִינָה — **such as meat, fish, milk,** and **cheese,** וְכֵן עַל כָּל מִינֵי מַשְׁקִים — **as well as upon all types of beverages,** חוּץ מִן הַיַּיִן וְשֶׁמֶן זַיִת — **except for** grape **wine**[3] **and olive oil,**[4] מְבָרְכִין "שֶׁהַכֹּל" — **we recite the** following **blessing:** *Baruch Atah Ado-noy Elokeinu Melech HaOlam, shehakol nihyah bidvaro, Blessed are You, HASHEM, our God, King of the universe, through Whose word **everything** came to be.* וְתֵיבַת "נִהְיָה" — In the word "***nihyah***," יֵשׁ לוֹמַר הַיּוּד בְּקָמַץ — **the "*yud*" should be pronounced with a *kamatz*,** i.e., it should be pronounced *nihyah*, not *nihyeh*.[5]

§3 כְּמֵיהִין וּפִטְרִיּוֹת (שוואמען) — **Mushrooms and truffles,** אַף עַל פִּי שֶׁהֵן גְּדֵלִין מִלַּחְלוּחִית הָאָרֶץ — **although they grow from the moisture of the ground,** יְנִיקָתָן אֵינָהּ מִן הָאָרֶץ — **their nourishment is not** drawn **from the ground,** אֶלָּא מִן הָאֲוִיר — **but** rather **from the air.**[6] וְלָכֵן אֵינָן נִקְרָאִין פְּרִי הָאֲדָמָה — **Therefore they are not classified as *produce of the ground*,** and the blessing of *borei pri ha'adamah*, "Who creates the fruit of the ground," cannot be recited upon them; וּמְבָרְכִין עֲלֵיהֶן "שֶׁהַכֹּל" — instead, **we recite the *shehakol* blessing upon them.**

---

2. *Mishnah Berurah* (203:3) writes that upon berries that grow on bushes whose branches remain during the winter, although technically the proper blessing is *borei pri ha'eitz*, common custom is to recite *borei pri ha'adamah*. Rabbi Moshe Feinstein writes (*Igros Moshe, Orach Chaim* I, §85) that this applies only to those bushes that are three *tefachim* high (approximately 10-11 inches; see Appendix A) or less; upon bushes that are higher than that, one should recite *borei pri ha'eitz*. Furthermore, Rabbi Feinstein writes that the custom cited by *Mishnah Berurah* is not universal; there were places where common custom was to recite *borei pri ha'eitz* upon berries from lower bushes as well. Therefore, in a place where the custom is not known, or if one does not know the height of the bush from which the berries came, one should recite *borei pri ha'eitz*.

3. Upon which the proper blessing is *borei pri hagafen*, "Who creates the fruit of the vine." See above, 49:1-3, and *Shulchan Aruch* 272:2 for further discussion. For the laws of raisin wine, see below, 53:6. Upon any other type of wine (besides grape wine), the *shehakol* blessing is recited (*Mishnah Berurah* 202:47).

4. In principle, the proper blessing to be recited upon olive oil is *borei pri ha'eitz* (below, 53:1). However, see below, 54:8, which states that in practice this blessing is rarely recited.

5. Other authorities hold that the proper pronunciation is "*nihyeh*" (see *Shaarei Teshuvah* 204:8).

6. I.e., they are nourished by the moisture of the ground that they absorb through the air; see *Berachos* 40b.

219 HA'EITZ, HA'ADAMAH, AND SHEHAKOL BLESSINGS — SIMAN 52:4

ד. אֵין מְבָרְכִין "בּוֹרֵא פְּרִי הָעֵץ", אוֹ "בּוֹרֵא פְּרִי הָאֲדָמָה" אֶלָּא עַל דָּבָר שֶׁהוּא טוֹב לֶאֱכוֹל חַי וְגַם הַדֶּרֶךְ הוּא לְאָכְלוֹ חַי[7]. אֲבָל אִם אֵין הַדֶּרֶךְ לְאָכְלוֹ חַי אֶלָּא בִּמְבוּשָּׁל, אַף עַל פִּי שֶׁהוּא טוֹב לְמַאֲכָל גַּם כְּשֶׁהוּא חַי, מִכָּל מָקוֹם אֵינוֹ חָשׁוּב כָּל כָּךְ וְאֵין מְבָרְכִין עָלָיו בִּרְכָתוֹ אֶלָּא כְּשֶׁאוֹכְלוֹ מְבוּשָּׁל[8], אֲבָל אִם אֲכָלוֹ חַי אֵינוֹ מְבָרֵךְ עָלָיו אֶלָּא "שֶׁהַכֹּל"[9]. וְכָבוּשׁ הֲרֵי הוּא כִּמְבוּשָּׁל[10], וְלָכֵן עַל כְּרוּב (קרויט) כָּבוּשׁ מְבָרְכִין "בּוֹרֵא פְּרִי הָאֲדָמָה"[11]. וְכֵן מָלִיחַ[12] הוּא כִּמְבוּשָּׁל לְעִנְיָן זֶה.

---

§4 אֵין מְבָרְכִין "בּוֹרֵא פְּרִי הָעֵץ", אוֹ "בּוֹרֵא פְּרִי הָאֲדָמָה" — **We do not recite the** ***borei pri ha'eitz*** **or** ***borei pri ha'adamah*** **blessings** upon a raw fruit or a vegetable אֶלָּא עַל דָּבָר שֶׁהוּא טוֹב לֶאֱכוֹל חַי — **unless it is something that is suitable to be eaten raw,** וְגַם הַדֶּרֶךְ הוּא לְאָכְלוֹ חַי — **and common practice is to eat it raw.**[7] אֲבָל אִם אֵין הַדֶּרֶךְ לְאָכְלוֹ חַי — **However, if it is not common practice to eat it raw,** אֶלָּא בִּמְבוּשָּׁל — **but only cooked,** אַף עַל פִּי שֶׁהוּא טוֹב לְמַאֲכָל גַּם כְּשֶׁהוּא חַי — **even if it is also good to eat when it is raw,** מִכָּל מָקוֹם אֵינוֹ חָשׁוּב כָּל כָּךְ — **nevertheless it is not considered so significant** in its raw state, וְאֵין מְבָרְכִין עָלָיו בִּרְכָתוֹ — **and we do not recite its blessing** of *ha'eitz* or *ha'adamah* upon eating it אֶלָּא כְּשֶׁאוֹכְלוֹ מְבוּשָּׁל — **unless one eats it cooked;**[8] אֲבָל אִם אֲכָלוֹ חַי — **but if he eats it raw,** אֵינוֹ מְבָרֵךְ עָלָיו אֶלָּא "שֶׁהַכֹּל" — **he recites only the** ***shehakol*** **blessing upon it.**[9]

וְכָבוּשׁ הֲרֵי הוּא כִּמְבוּשָּׁל — A **pickled** food **is like a cooked** food.[10] וְלָכֵן עַל כְּרוּב (קרויט) כָּבוּשׁ — **Therefore,** on **pickled cabbage** מְבָרְכִין "בּוֹרֵא פְּרִי הָאֲדָמָה" — **we recite** ***borei pri ha'adamah.***[11] וְכֵן מָלִיחַ הוּא כִּמְבוּשָּׁל לְעִנְיָן זֶה — **Likewise, a salted** food[12] **is like a cooked** food **with regard to this** halachah.

---

7. The halachah in each locale is determined independently by the habits of its own residents (*Mishnah Berurah* 205:5; *Shaar HaTziyun* 205:3; *Beur Halachah* 205:1 s.v. שטובים חיים).

8. If a fruit or vegetable was planted with the intention that it will be prepared by cooking, it does not reach its optimal status as a fruit or vegetable until it is prepared in that way. Thus, in places where the common practice is to eat a certain fruit or vegetable only cooked, one cannot refer to it as *pri ha'eitz* (fruit of the tree), or *pri ha'adamah* (fruit of the ground) until it is cooked (see *Mishnah Berurah* 202:64; *Rashi, Berachos* 36a s.v. הכא אית ליה, and 38b s.v. שלקו).

9. *Mishnah Berurah* (205:3) writes that if most people also eat it uncooked and it tastes good that way, *borei pri ha'adamah* is recited (see *Shaar HaTziyun* §2). [Elsewhere, *Mishnah Berurah* indicates that even if a significant amount of people eat it that way (and not necessarily a majority), it still retains its blessing; see *Mishnah Berurah* 202:61, *Beur Halachah* 202:10 s.v. על אותן המים.]

If one mistakenly recited *borei pri ha'adamah* on a raw vegetable that tastes better when cooked, he has fulfilled the requirement, and should not recite another blessing (*Mishnah Berurah* 206:3).

A fruit or vegetable that is fit to be eaten both raw and cooked is subject to the *ha'eitz* or *ha'adamah* blessing when eaten either raw or cooked (*Orach Chaim* 205:1 with *Mishnah Berurah* §1). Thus, carrots, which are eaten raw as well as cooked, are subject to the blessing of *borei pri ha'adamah* whether eaten raw or cooked (*Igros Moshe, Orach Chaim* I, §66).

10. I.e., if a fruit or vegetable is commonly eaten only pickled, one should recite the *shehakol* blessing when eating it "raw."

11. Today, the appropriate blessing upon eating raw cabbage in a salad or coleslaw is *borei pri ha'adamah*, since it is the common practice to eat it that way (see *Mishnah Berurah* 205:4).

12. [In this context, a "salted" food refers to a food that has been sitting in salt for many days (see *Rashi, Berachos* 38b s.v. שאכל זית מליח).]

ה. עַל הַצְּנוֹן מְבָרְכִין "בּוֹרֵא פְּרִי הָאֲדָמָה". וְכֵן עַל שׁוּמִים וּבְצָלִים כְּשֶׁהֵן רַכִּין וְדַרְכּוֹ לְאָכְלָן חַיִּין, אַף עַל פִּי שֶׁעַל פִּי הָרוֹב אֵין אוֹכְלִין אוֹתָן רַק עִם פַּת, מִכָּל מָקוֹם גַּם אִם אוֹכְלָן בְּלֹא פַּת מְבָרְכִין עֲלֵיהֶן "בּוֹרֵא פְּרִי הָאֲדָמָה"[13]. אֲבָל אִם הִזְקִינוּ שֶׁהֵם חֲרִיפִים מְאוֹד וְאֵין דַּרְכָּן לְאָכְלָן חַיִּין, מִי שֶׁאֲכָלָן חַיִּין מְבָרֵךְ עֲלֵיהֶם "שֶׁהַכֹּל"[14].

ו. דְּבָרִים שֶׁהֵם טוֹבִים יוֹתֵר כְּשֶׁהֵם חַיִּין מִכְּשֶׁהֵם מְבוּשָּׁלִים, שֶׁהַבִּישּׁוּל מְגָרֵעַ אוֹתָן, אֵין מְבָרְכִין עֲלֵיהֶם כְּשֶׁהֵם מְבוּשָּׁלִים אֶלָּא "שֶׁהַכֹּל", וְאַף עַל פִּי שֶׁבִּישְּׁלָן עִם בָּשָׂר וְעַל יְדֵי הַבָּשָׂר נִשְׁתַּבְּחוּ, מִכָּל מָקוֹם אָז הַבָּשָׂר הוּא הָעִיקָּר וְאֵין מְבָרְכִין עֲלֵיהֶן אֶלָּא "שֶׁהַכֹּל"[15]. אֲבָל אִם בִּישְּׁלָן בְּאוֹפֶן שֶׁהֵן הָעִיקָּר וּמִכָּל מָקוֹם נִשְׁתַּבְּחוּ,

---

§5 עַל הַצְּנוֹן — On a radish מְבָרְכִין "בּוֹרֵא פְּרִי הָאֲדָמָה" — we recite the *borei pri ha'adamah* blessing. וְכֵן עַל שׁוּמִים וּבְצָלִים כְּשֶׁהֵן רַכִּין — Likewise, on garlic and onions when they are soft, וְדַרְכּוֹ לְאָכְלָן חַיִּין — and it is the common practice to eat them raw, אַף עַל פִּי שֶׁעַל פִּי הָרוֹב — even though most often אֵין אוֹכְלִין אוֹתָן רַק עִם פַּת — people eat them only together with bread, מִכָּל מָקוֹם גַּם אִם אוֹכְלָן בְּלֹא פַּת מְבָרְכִין עֲלֵיהֶן "בּוֹרֵא פְּרִי הָאֲדָמָה" — still, we recite *borei pri ha'adamah* on them when eating them without bread as well.[13] אֲבָל אִם הִזְקִינוּ — However, if they are aged שֶׁהֵם חֲרִיפִים מְאוֹד — and have developed a very sharp taste, וְאֵין דַּרְכָּן לְאָכְלָן חַיִּין — and it is therefore unusual to eat them raw מִי שֶׁאֲכָלָן חַיִּין — one who does eat them raw מְבָרֵךְ עֲלֵיהֶם "שֶׁהַכֹּל" — should recite the *shehakol* blessing upon them.[14]

§6 דְּבָרִים שֶׁהֵם טוֹבִים יוֹתֵר כְּשֶׁהֵם חַיִּין — Fruit or vegetables that are better when they are raw מִכְּשֶׁהֵם מְבוּשָּׁלִים — than when they are cooked, שֶׁהַבִּישּׁוּל מְגָרֵעַ אוֹתָן — because the cooking process diminishes their taste, אֵין מְבָרְכִין עֲלֵיהֶם כְּשֶׁהֵם מְבוּשָּׁלִים — upon eating them when they are cooked we do not recite the blessing of *ha'eitz* or *ha'adamah,* אֶלָּא "שֶׁהַכֹּל" — but only the *shehakol* blessing. וְאַף עַל פִּי שֶׁבִּישְּׁלָן עִם בָּשָׂר — Even if these foods were cooked with meat וְעַל יְדֵי הַבָּשָׂר נִשְׁתַּבְּחוּ — and they were improved by the flavor imparted by the meat, מִכָּל מָקוֹם אָז הַבָּשָׂר הוּא הָעִיקָּר — nevertheless, in that case, the meat is the primary food in the mixture, וְאֵין מְבָרְכִין עֲלֵיהֶן אֶלָּא "שֶׁהַכֹּל" — and we therefore recite only the *shehakol* blessing upon them.[15] אֲבָל אִם בִּישְּׁלָן בְּאוֹפֶן שֶׁהֵן הָעִיקָּר — However, if one cooked them in a way that they are the primary ingredient, וּמִכָּל מָקוֹם נִשְׁתַּבְּחוּ —

---

13. *Mishnah Berurah* (205:5) rules that in places where these vegetables are eaten only with bread, one should always recite *shehakol* on them when eating them alone. Rabbi Moshe Feinstein (*Igros Moshe, Orach Chaim* I, §64) concurs with this view, and writes that the blessing for onions and garlic, whether raw or cooked, is *shehakol*. However, on fried onions one recites the *ha'adamah* blessing because the frying process improves the taste of the onions and they are commonly eaten this way (*Mishnah Berurah* 205:7; see the following *se'if*). [If the onions are coated in a batter containing flour and then fried, the proper blessing is *borei minei mezonos*; see above, 48:10.]

14. See *Mishnah Berurah* (203:14), which cites a difference of opinion regarding the correct blessing for sharp radishes that are usually eaten only with bread. Rabbi Moshe Feinstein (*Igros Moshe, Orach Chaim* I, §62) writes that when eating these radishes without bread one should recite *shehakol*, but that in order to avoid any question one should preferably eat these radishes only with bread [in which case there is no obligation to recite a blessing upon the radish at all (above, 43:1)].

15. Below, 54:1. *Mishnah Berurah* (205:7) writes that this applies only if the vegetables

221 HA'EITZ, HA'ADAMAH, AND SHEHAKOL BLESSINGS — SIMAN 52:7-8

כְּגוֹן שֶׁטִּיגְּנָן בְּשׁוּמָּן אוֹ בִּדְבַשׁ וְכַיּוֹצֵא בוֹ, מְבָרְכִין עֲלֵיהֶן הַבְּרָכָה הָרְאוּיָה לָהֶן, דְּמַה לִי אִם נִתְבַּשְּׁלוּ בְּמַיִם אוֹ בְּשׁוּמָּן וּדְבַשׁ.

ז. מִינֵי פֵּירוֹת הַגְּרוּעִים הַגְּדֵלִים עַל אֲטָדִים וְקוֹצִים אוֹ בִּשְׁאָר אִילָנוֹת שֶׁיָּצְאוּ מֵאֲלֵיהֶן וְלָא נָטְעֵי לְהוּ אִינְשֵׁי, כְּמוֹ תַּפּוּחֵי יַעַר וְכַדּוֹמֶה, שֶׁכְּשֶׁהֵם חַיִּין אֵינָן רְאוּיִין לַאֲכִילָה, אַף עַל פִּי שֶׁבִּישְׁלָן אוֹ טִיגְּנָן בִּדְבַשׁ וְצוּקֶער וְהֵן רְאוּיִין לַאֲכִילָה, אֵין מְבָרְכִין עֲלֵיהֶן אֶלָּא "שֶׁהַכֹּל"[16]. אֲבָל לוּזִין (האזעלנוסל), אַף עַל פִּי שֶׁגְּדֵלִים בְּיַעַר, חֲשׁוּבִים הֵם וּמְבָרְכִים עֲלֵיהֶם "בּוֹרֵא פְּרִי הָעֵץ".

ח. עֲשָׂבִים הַגְּדֵלִים מֵאֲלֵיהֶם בְּלִי זְרִיעָה, אַף עַל פִּי שֶׁהֵן רְאוּיִין לֶאֱכוֹל חַיִּין, וַאֲפִילוּ בִּישְׁלָן מַאֲכָל חָשׁוּב, מִכָּל מָקוֹם כֵּיוָן שֶׁאֵין זוֹרְעִין אוֹתוֹ אֵינוֹ חָשׁוּב פְּרִי וּמְבָרְכִין עָלָיו "שֶׁהַכֹּל". אֲבָל סַעלאט[17] וְכַדּוֹמֶה שֶׁנִּזְרַע מְבָרְכִין עָלָיו "בּוֹרֵא פְּרִי הָאֲדָמָה".

---

and still they were improved through the cooking process, כְּגוֹן שֶׁטִּיגְּנָן בְּשׁוּמָּן אוֹ בִּדְבַשׁ וְכַיּוֹצֵא בוֹ — **for example, if he fried them in fat or honey or the like,** מְבָרְכִין עֲלֵיהֶן הַבְּרָכָה הָרְאוּיָה לָהֶן — **we recite upon them their appropriate blessing** of *ha'eitz* or *ha'adamah.* דְּמַה לִי אִם נִתְבַּשְּׁלוּ בְּמַיִם — **For what difference does it make if it was cooked in water** (in which case *ha'eitz* or *ha'adamah* is recited) אוֹ בְּשׁוּמָּן וּדְבַשׁ — or if it was cooked **in fat or honey?** In either case, the cooking process is not detrimental to the food, but improves it.

§7 מִינֵי פֵּירוֹת הַגְּרוּעִים — For **inferior types of fruit** הַגְּדֵלִים עַל אֲטָדִים וְקוֹצִים — **that grow on brambles and thornbushes,** אוֹ בִּשְׁאָר אִילָנוֹת שֶׁיָּצְאוּ מֵאֲלֵיהֶן — **or from other trees that have sprouted on their own** וְלָא נָטְעֵי לְהוּ אִינְשֵׁי — **and were not planted by man,** כְּמוֹ תַּפּוּחֵי יַעַר וְכַדּוֹמֶה — **such as wild apples and similar** fruit, שֶׁכְּשֶׁהֵם חַיִּין אֵינָן רְאוּיִין לַאֲכִילָה — **which, in their raw state are inedible,** אַף עַל פִּי שֶׁבִּישְׁלָן אוֹ טִיגְּנָן בִּדְבַשׁ וְצוּקֶער — **even if one cooked or fried them in honey or sugar,** וְהֵן רְאוּיִין לַאֲכִילָה — **and they are** now **edible,** אֵין מְבָרְכִין עֲלֵיהֶן אֶלָּא "שֶׁהַכֹּל" — **we recite only the *shehakol*** blessing upon them (not *borei pri ha'eitz*).[16] אֲבָל לוּזִין (האזעלנוסל) — **However, hazelnuts,** אַף עַל פִּי שֶׁגְּדֵלִים בְּיַעַר — **although they grow** wild **in the forest,** חֲשׁוּבִים הֵם — **are** considered a **significant** food, וּמְבָרְכִים עֲלֵיהֶם "בּוֹרֵא פְּרִי הָעֵץ" — **and we recite the *borei pri ha'eitz*** blessing **upon them.**

§8 עֲשָׂבִים הַגְּדֵלִים מֵאֲלֵיהֶם בְּלִי זְרִיעָה — **Herbage that sprouted on its own without being planted** by man, אַף עַל פִּי שֶׁהֵן רְאוּיִין לֶאֱכוֹל חַיִּין — **even if they are edible raw,** וַאֲפִילוּ בִּישְׁלָן מַאֲכָל חָשׁוּב — **even if one cooked them** and they have now become **a significant food,** מִכָּל מָקוֹם כֵּיוָן שֶׁאֵין זוֹרְעִין אוֹתוֹ — **nevertheless, since this** type of herbage **is not planted,** אֵינוֹ חָשׁוּב פְּרִי — **it is not considered a *pri*,** *fruit,* וּמְבָרְכִין עָלָיו "שֶׁהַכֹּל" — **and we recite the *shehakol* blessing** upon it. אֲבָל סַעלאט וְכַדּוֹמֶה — **However,** with regard to **lettuce,**[17] **or a similar** vegetable שֶׁנִּזְרַע — **that was planted,** מְבָרְכִין עָלָיו "בּוֹרֵא פְּרִי הָאֲדָמָה" — **we recite the**

---

were added solely to enhance the flavor of the meat, in which case they are not a significant part of the dish. However, if the vegetables were added for themselves as well, i.e., to be eaten as part of the dish, they retain their own significance and *borei pri ha'adamah* should be recited.

16. If the trees were cultivated by man, even if the fruits are not eaten raw, one recites *borei pri ha'eitz* upon them after they are cooked (*Beur Halachah* 203:4 s.v. אילני סרק).

17. See *Mishnah Berurah* 205, end of *se'if* 4.

HA'EITZ, HA'ADAMAH, AND SHEHAKOL BLESSINGS — SIMAN 52:9 222

וְגַם בַּעֲשָׂבִים הַגְּדֵלִים מֵאֲלֵיהֶם, אִם יֵשׁ בָּהֶם פֵּירוֹת חֲשׁוּבִים, כְּגוֹן יאגדיס ומאלניס[18], מְבָרְכִין עֲלֵיהֶן "בּוֹרֵא פְּרִי הָאֲדָמָה"[19].

ט. דָּבָר שֶׁאֵינוֹ עִיקַּר הַפְּרִי אֵינוֹ חָשׁוּב כְּמוֹ הַפְּרִי עַצְמוֹ אֶלָּא יוֹרֵד מַדְרֵגָה אַחַת[20], שֶׁאִם הוּא עֵץ מְבָרְכִין עַל הַטָּפֵל "בּוֹרֵא פְּרִי הָאֲדָמָה"[21], וְאִם הִיא פְּרִי הָאֲדָמָה מְבָרְכִין עַל הַטָּפֵל "שֶׁהַכֹּל". וְלָכֵן אִילָן צְלָף (קאפערנבוים)[22] שֶׁעָלִין שֶׁלּוֹ רְאוּיִין לַאֲכִילָה, וְיֵשׁ בֶּעָלִין כְּמִין תְּמָרִים בּוֹלְטִים, כְּמוֹ בְעָלִין שֶׁל עֲרָבָה, וַאֲבִיּוֹנוֹת — הֵן עִיקַּר הַפְּרִי, וְקַפְרִיסִין — הֵן הַקְּלִיפָּה שֶׁסָּבִיב הַפְּרִי, כְּמוֹ קְלִיפּוֹת הָאֱגוֹזִין, וּרְאוּי גַּם כֵּן לַאֲכִילָה: עַל הָאֲבִיּוֹנוֹת שֶׁהֵן עִיקַּר הַפְּרִי מְבָרֵךְ "בּוֹרֵא פְּרִי הָעֵץ", וְעַל הֶעָלִין וְעַל הַתְּמָרוֹת וְעַל הַקַּפְרִיסִין —

---

borei pri ha'adamah* blessing upon it.** וְגַם בַּעֲשָׂבִים הַגְּדֵלִים מֵאֲלֵיהֶם — **In addition,** types of **herbage that grow on their own,** i.e., they are not cultivated, אִם יֵשׁ בָּהֶם פֵּירוֹת חֲשׁוּבִים — **if they have** some type of **significant fruit** growing **on them,** כְּגוֹן יאגדיס ומאלניס — **such as** ***yagdes **and** ***malines,***[18] מְבָרְכִין עֲלֵיהֶן "בּוֹרֵא פְּרִי הָאֲדָמָה" — **we recite the** ***borei pri ha'adamah*** **blessing upon** eating **them.**[19]

§9 דָּבָר שֶׁאֵינוֹ עִיקַּר הַפְּרִי — **Something** that grows on a plant, **that is not the primary fruit,** אֵינוֹ חָשׁוּב כְּמוֹ הַפְּרִי עַצְמוֹ — **is not considered** as **significant as the fruit itself;** אֶלָּא יוֹרֵד מַדְרֵגָה אַחַת — **rather, it descends one level** with regard to the appropriate blessing.[20] שֶׁאִם הוּא עֵץ — That is, **if it** grows on **a tree,** מְבָרְכִין עַל הַטָּפֵל "בּוֹרֵא פְּרִי הָאֲדָמָה" — **we recite the** ***borei pri ha'adamah*** **blessing on the ancillary** growth;[21] וְאִם הִיא פְּרִי הָאֲדָמָה — **and if it** grows as part of **a vegetable,** מְבָרְכִין עַל הַטָּפֵל "שֶׁהַכֹּל" — **we recite the** ***shehakol*** **blessing on the ancillary** growth. וְלָכֵן אִילָן צְלָף (קאפערנבוים) — **Therefore,** regarding **the caper tree,**[22] שֶׁעָלִין שֶׁלּוֹ רְאוּיִין לַאֲכִילָה — **whose leaves are edible,** וְיֵשׁ בֶּעָלִין כְּמִין תְּמָרִים בּוֹלְטִים — **and the leaves** also **have date-like protuberances** that are also edible כְּמוֹ בְעָלִין שֶׁל עֲרָבָה — **similar to** the protuberances of **the leaves of a willow** tree; וַאֲבִיּוֹנוֹת — הֵן עִיקַּר הַפְּרִי — **and it also has berries, which are the main "fruit"** of this tree, וְקַפְרִיסִין — הֵן הַקְּלִיפָּה שֶׁסָּבִיב הַפְּרִי — as well as ***kafrisin*****, which are the husks encasing the fruit,** כְּמוֹ קְלִיפּוֹת הָאֱגוֹזִין — **resembling nut shells,** וּרְאוּי גַּם כֵּן לַאֲכִילָה — **and they are also edible;** the halachah regarding the appropriate blessing for each part, based on the rules set forth above, is as follows: עַל הָאֲבִיּוֹנוֹת שֶׁהֵן עִיקַּר הַפְּרִי — **Upon the berries, which are the primary fruit,** מְבָרֵךְ "בּוֹרֵא פְּרִי הָעֵץ" — **one recites the** ***borei pri ha'eitz*** **blessing.** וְעַל הֶעָלִין וְעַל הַתְּמָרוֹת וְעַל הַקַּפְרִיסִין — **On the leaves, the**

---

18. These refer to kinds of berries; see *Mishnah Berurah* 203:1,3. Some identify יאגדיס as *blueberries*, and מאלניס as *raspberries*.

19. See above, note 2. Upon wild strawberries one recites *borei pri ha'adamah*; see *Mishnah Berurah* 203:3, and *Igros Moshe*, *Orach Chaim* I, §86.

20. The more specific a blessing is, the more significant it is. Of the blessings *ha'eitz*, *ha'adamah*, and *shehakol*, *borei pri ha'eitz* is most significant, then *borei pri ha'adamah*, and then *shehakol*. In the case of this *se'if*, whichever blessing would ordinarily be appropriate for that plant (if it grew on a tree, *ha'eitz*; on the ground, *ha'adamah*), it descends one level to the blessing just under it in order of significance.

21. However, if one did recite *borei pri ha'eitz*, he has fulfilled his obligation, since it does grow on a tree (*Mishnah Berurah* 206:3).

22. I.e., the caper bush, a low, trailing shrub whose buds are used for pickling and spices.

223 HA'EITZ, HA'ADAMAH, AND SHEHAKOL BLESSINGS — SIMAN 52:9

"בּוֹרֵא פְּרִי הָאֲדָמָה"[23]. וְכֵן עֲלֵי וְורָדִי[ם] (רֹאזֶענבּלֶעטֶער) שֶׁנִּרְקְחוּ בִּדְבַשׁ וְצוּקֶער[24] מְבָרְכִין "בּוֹרֵא פְּרִי הָאֲדָמָה", אַף עַל פִּי שֶׁגְּדֵלִים בְּאִילָן[25], מִפְּנֵי שֶׁאֵינָן עִיקַּר הַפְּרִי. וְכֵן קְלִיפּוֹת מֶערַאנצִין שֶׁנִּרְקְחוּ בִּדְבַשׁ וְצוּקֶער מְבָרְכִין עֲלֵיהֶם "בּוֹרֵא פְּרִי הָאֲדָמָה"[26], וְעַל קְלִיפּוֹת קִישׁוּאִין שֶׁמְּטַגְּנִין בִּדְבַשׁ וְצוּקֶער מְבָרְכִין "שֶׁהַכֹּל". וְעַל הַשַּׁרְבִיטִין מֵהַקִּטְנִיּוֹת שֶׁזּוֹרְעִין בְּשָׂדוֹת, אַף עַל פִּי שֶׁהֵן מְתוּקִים, אִם אֲכָלָן בְּלֹא הַקִּטְנִיּוֹת, מְבָרְכִין עֲלֵיהֶם "שֶׁהַכֹּל"[27]. וְאֵלּוּ שֶׁזּוֹרְעִים בְּגַנּוֹת עַל דַּעַת לְאוֹכְלָן חַיִּין בְּשַׁרְבִיטֵיהֶן, אֲפִילּוּ כְּשֶׁאוֹכֵל הַשַּׁרְבִיטִין לְחוּד, יֵשׁ לְבָרֵךְ "בּוֹרֵא פְּרִי הָאֲדָמָה"[28].

---

date-like protuberances, and the husks, "בּוֹרֵא פְּרִי הָאֲדָמָה" — one recites *borei pri ha'adamah.*[23] וְכֵן עֲלֵי וְורָדִי[ם] (רֹאזֶענבּלֶעטֶער) שֶׁנִּרְקְחוּ בִּדְבַשׁ וְצוּקֶער — Likewise, on rose-petals that were preserved in honey and sugar,[24] מְבָרְכִין "בּוֹרֵא פְּרִי הָאֲדָמָה" — we recite the *borei pri ha'adamah* blessing, אַף עַל פִּי שֶׁגְּדֵלִים בְּאִילָן — even though these petals grow on a "tree,"[25] מִפְּנֵי שֶׁאֵינָן עִיקַּר הַפְּרִי — because they are not the primary product of this tree. וְכֵן קְלִיפּוֹת מֶערַאנצִין שֶׁנִּרְקְחוּ בִּדְבַשׁ וְצוּקֶער — Likewise, upon orange rinds that were preserved in honey and sugar, מְבָרְכִין עֲלֵיהֶם "בּוֹרֵא פְּרִי הָאֲדָמָה" — we recite the *borei pri ha'adamah* blessing upon them.[26] וְעַל קְלִיפּוֹת קִישׁוּאִין שֶׁמְּטַגְּנִין בִּדְבַשׁ וְצוּקֶער — On peels of cucumbers that are fried in honey and sugar, מְבָרְכִין "שֶׁהַכֹּל" — we recite the *shehakol* blessing. וְעַל הַשַּׁרְבִיטִין מֵהַקִּטְנִיּוֹת שֶׁזּוֹרְעִין בְּשָׂדוֹת — On the pods of the peas that are sown in the fields, אַף עַל פִּי שֶׁהֵן מְתוּקִים — even though they have a sweet taste, אִם אֲכָלָן בְּלֹא הַקִּטְנִיּוֹת — if one eats them without the peas, מְבָרְכִין עֲלֵיהֶם "שֶׁהַכֹּל" — the *shehakol* blessing should be recited upon them.[27] וְאֵלּוּ שֶׁזּוֹרְעִים בְּגַנּוֹת עַל דַּעַת לְאוֹכְלָן — However, those peas that are planted in gardens חַיִּין בְּשַׁרְבִיטֵיהֶן — with the intention of eating them raw, with their pods, אֲפִילּוּ כְּשֶׁאוֹכֵל הַשַּׁרְבִיטִין לְחוּד — then, even when one eats the pods by themselves יֵשׁ לְבָרֵךְ "בּוֹרֵא פְּרִי הָאֲדָמָה" — he should recite the *borei pri ha'adamah* blessing.[28]

---

23. See *Shaar HaTziyun* (202:41), who cites an opinion that since nowadays the caper tree is not planted at all for the sake of its leaves and husks, the appropriate blessing for any peripheral product is *shehakol.* However, *Igros Moshe* (*Orach Chaim* I, §59) rules that even today the appropriate blessing upon these parts of the caper is *borei pri ha'adamah.*

24. See above, 46:30, regarding the process of making preserves.

25. See above, *se'if* 1, regarding the classification of a "tree" with regard to this halachah.

26. *Mishnah Berurah* (202:39) rules that the appropriate blessing is *shehakol,* but if one recited *borei pri ha'eitz* or *borei pri ha'adamah,* he has fulfilled his obligation. See above, note 23, and *Chazon Ish, Orach Chaim* 33:2.

27. If they are eaten together with the peas, they do not require a separate blessing, as the *borei pri ha'adamah* blessing that one recites for the beans exempts the pods as well. See following note.

28. *Mishnah Berurah* (204:9) writes that both when they are planted to be eaten raw, and when they are planted for the peas, the blessing for the pods is a subject of dispute among the halachic authorities. *Mishnah Berurah* therefore suggests that they should be eaten only together with the peas, in which case the *borei pri ha'adamah* blessing that one recites for the peas exempts the pods as well. However, one who does eat the pods by themselves, even if they are planted to be eaten that way, should recite the *shehakol* blessing. See *Igros Moshe, Orach Chaim* I, §57, who rules like Kitzur that upon pods grown in the garden to be eaten raw one should recite the *borei pri ha'adamah* blessing.

HA'EITZ, HA'ADAMAH, AND SHEHAKOL BLESSINGS — SIMAN 52:10-11 224

י. גַּרְעִינִין שֶׁל פֵּירוֹת — אִם הֵם מְתוּקִים[29], מְבָרֵךְ עֲלֵיהֶן "בּוֹרֵא פְּרִי הָאֲדָמָה"[30], אֲבָל גַּרְעִינִים הַמָּרִים[31] אֵינָם נֶחְשָׁבִים כְּלָל, וְאִם אוֹכְלָן כָּךְ, (אינן) (אֵינוֹ) מְבָרֵךְ עֲלֵיהֶם כְּלָל. וְאִם מִתְקָן עַל יְדֵי הָאוּר וְכַדּוֹמֶה, מְבָרֵךְ עֲלֵיהֶם "שֶׁהַכֹּל".

יא. שְׁקֵדִים הַמָּרִים כְּשֶׁהֵם קְטַנִּים, שֶׁאָז עִיקַּר אֲכִילָתָן הִיא הַקְּלִיפָּה שֶׁאֵינָהּ מָרָה וְעַל דַּעַת כֵּן נוֹטְעִין אוֹתָן, מְבָרֵךְ עֲלֵיהֶן "בּוֹרֵא פְּרִי [הָ]עֵץ". וּכְשֶׁהֵם גְּדוֹלִים שֶׁאָז עִיקַּר הָאֲכִילָה הוּא מַה שֶּׁבִּפְנִים וְהוּא מַר, אִם אוֹכְלָן כָּךְ, אֵינוֹ מְבָרֵךְ כְּלָל. אֲבָל אִם מִתְקָן עַל יְדֵי הָאוּר, אוֹ דָּבָר אַחֵר, כֵּיוָן דִּפְרִי נִינְהוּ וְגַם עַל דַּעַת כֵּן נוֹטְעִין אוֹתָן, מְבָרֵךְ עֲלֵיהֶן "בּוֹרֵא פְּרִי הָעֵץ". שְׁקֵדִים הַמְחוּפִּין בְּצוּקֶר, אַף עַל פִּי שֶׁהַצּוּקֶר הוּא הָרוֹב, מִכָּל מָקוֹם מְבָרְכִין עֲלֵיהֶם "בּוֹרֵא פְּרִי הָעֵץ"[32].

---

§10 גַּרְעִינִין שֶׁל פֵּירוֹת — With regard to **fruit pits,** אִם הֵם מְתוּקִים — **if they are sweet,**[29] מְבָרֵךְ עֲלֵיהֶן "בּוֹרֵא פְּרִי הָאֲדָמָה" — **one recites the** ***borei pri ha'adamah*** **blessing upon them.**[30] אֲבָל גַּרְעִינִים הַמָּרִים — **However, pits that are bitter** to the point of being inedible[31] אֵינָם נֶחְשָׁבִים כְּלָל — **are not considered** to be a food **at all,** וְאִם אוֹכְלָן כָּךְ — **and if one eats them like that,** i.e., in their bitter state, (אינן) (אֵינוֹ) מְבָרֵךְ עֲלֵיהֶם כְּלָל — **he should not recite any blessing.** וְאִם מִתְקָן עַל יְדֵי הָאוּר וְכַדּוֹמֶה — However, **if he sweetens them by** roasting them over a **fire, or** using **a similar** technique, מְבָרֵךְ עֲלֵיהֶם "שֶׁהַכֹּל" — **he recites the** ***shehakol*** **blessing upon them.**

§11 שְׁקֵדִים הַמָּרִים — Regarding the proper blessing upon eating **bitter almonds:** כְּשֶׁהֵם קְטַנִּים — **When they are small,** שֶׁאָז עִיקַּר אֲכִילָתָן הִיא הַקְּלִיפָּה — **at which point they are eaten primarily for their husk,** שֶׁאֵינָהּ מָרָה — **which is not bitter,** וְעַל דַּעַת כֵּן נוֹטְעִין אוֹתָן — **and they are planted with this intention,** i.e., for their husks to be eaten at this stage, מְבָרֵךְ עֲלֵיהֶן "בּוֹרֵא פְּרִי [הָ]עֵץ" — **one recites** ***borei pri ha'eitz*** **upon** eating **them.** וּכְשֶׁהֵם גְּדוֹלִים — **When they** have grown **large,** שֶׁאָז עִיקַּר הָאֲכִילָה הוּא מַה שֶּׁבִּפְנִים — **at which point they are eaten primarily for** the nut that is **inside** the husk, וְהוּא מַר — **and** the nut **is bitter** when raw, אִם אוֹכְלָן כָּךְ — **if one eats them in this state,** אֵינוֹ מְבָרֵךְ כְּלָל — **he does not recite any blessing.** אֲבָל אִם מִתְקָן עַל יְדֵי הָאוּר — **However, if he sweetened them by** roasting them over the **fire,** אוֹ דָּבָר אַחֵר — **or** by using **another** technique that improves their flavor, כֵּיוָן דִּפְרִי נִינְהוּ — **then, since it is** considered **a** *pri*, **"fruit,"** וְגַם עַל דַּעַת כֵּן נוֹטְעִין אוֹתָן — **and also, they were planted with this intention,** i.e., that they will be eaten after being processed, מְבָרֵךְ עֲלֵיהֶן "בּוֹרֵא פְּרִי הָעֵץ" — **he recites upon them the** ***borei pri ha'eitz*** **blessing.**

שְׁקֵדִים הַמְחוּפִּין בְּצוּקֶר — Regarding **sugar-coated almonds,** אַף עַל פִּי שֶׁהַצּוּקֶר הוּא הָרוֹב — **even though the** amount of **sugar** in this preparation **is greater** than the amount of actual almond, מִכָּל מָקוֹם מְבָרְכִין עֲלֵיהֶם "בּוֹרֵא פְּרִי הָעֵץ" — **nevertheless, we recite the** ***borei pri ha'eitz*** **blessing upon them.**[32]

---

29. I.e., their taste is somewhat pleasant (*Mishnah Berurah* 202:23).

30. See Appendix of Kitzur's editorial glosses. If one mistakenly recited *borei pri ha'eitz,* he has fulfilled his obligation (*Mishnah Berurah* 202:23).

31. *Mishnah Berurah* 202:24.

32. The almond is considered the main component of this food. See below, 54:5, and note 15 there.

225 HA'EITZ, HA'ADAMAH, AND SHEHAKOL BLESSINGS — SIMAN 52:12-13

וְקאלמוס[33] מְחוּפֶּה בְּצוּקֶר מְבָרְכִין רַק "שֶׁהַכֹּל", כִּי הַקאלמוס אֵינוֹ פְּרִי.

יב. פֵּירוֹת שֶׁלֹּא נִגְמַר בִּישׁוּלָן עַל הָאִילָן, אֲפִילוּ בִּישְׁלָן אוֹ טִיגְּנָן בִּדְבַשׁ וְכַדּוֹמֶה, כְּמוֹ שֶׁהוּא הַדֶּרֶךְ לְטַגֵּן פֵּירוֹת שֶׁלֹּא נִגְמְרוּ בִּדְבַשׁ אוֹ צוּקֶער, מְבָרֵךְ עֲלֵיהֶם "שֶׁהַכֹּל"[34]. אַךְ עַל אֶתְרוֹג מְטוּגָּן בִּדְבַשׁ אוֹ בְּצוּקֶער יֵשׁ לְבָרֵךְ "בּוֹרֵא פְּרִי הָעֵץ"[35].

יג. נוֹבְלוֹת, וְהֵן פֵּירוֹת שֶׁנִּשְׁרְפוּ מִן הַחוֹם וְנָבְלוּ וְנָפְלוּ מִן הָאִילָן קוֹדֶם שֶׁנִּתְבַּשְּׁלוּ, כֵּיוָן שֶׁהוּא דָּבָר שֶׁנִּתְקַלְקֵל, אֵין מְבָרְכִין עָלָיו רַק "שֶׁהַכֹּל". וְכֵן פַּת שֶׁעִיפְּשָׁה[36], וְתַבְשִׁיל שֶׁנִּתְקַלְקֵל קְצָת, מְבָרְכִין עֲלֵיהֶן "שֶׁהַכֹּל"[37]. אֲבָל אִם נִתְקַלְקְלוּ לְגַמְרֵי עַד שֶׁאֵינָן רְאוּיִין לַאֲכִילָה, אֵין מְבָרְכִין עֲלֵיהֶן כְּלָל. וְכֵן חוֹמֶץ גָּמוּר

וְקאלמוס מְחוּפֶּה בְּצוּקֶר — For calamus[33] that is coated in sugar מְבָרְכִין רַק "שֶׁהַכֹּל" — we recite only the *shehakol* blessing, כִּי הַקאלמוס אֵינוֹ פְּרִי — because the calamus is not a *pri*, fruit.

§12 פֵּירוֹת שֶׁלֹּא נִגְמַר בִּישׁוּלָן עַל הָאִילָן — Fruits that did not complete their ripening process on the tree, אֲפִילוּ בִּישְׁלָן אוֹ טִיגְּנָן בִּדְבַשׁ וְכַדּוֹמֶה — even if they were subsequently cooked or fried in honey or the like, כְּמוֹ שֶׁהוּא הַדֶּרֶךְ — as is the manner of the common practice לְטַגֵּן פֵּירוֹת שֶׁלֹּא נִגְמְרוּ בִּדְבַשׁ אוֹ צוּקֶער — to fry unripe fruit in honey or sugar, מְבָרֵךְ עֲלֵיהֶם "שֶׁהַכֹּל" — one recites upon them the *shehakol* blessing.[34] אַךְ עַל אֶתְרוֹג — However, upon an *esrog* מְטוּגָּן בִּדְבַשׁ אוֹ בְּצוּקֶער — that has been fried in honey or sugar, יֵשׁ לְבָרֵךְ "בּוֹרֵא פְּרִי הָעֵץ" — one should recite the *borei pri ha'eitz* blessing.[35]

§13 נוֹבְלוֹת, וְהֵן פֵּירוֹת שֶׁנִּשְׁרְפוּ מִן הַחוֹם — Regarding *novlos*, which are fruit that were scorched while on the tree by the heat of the sun וְנָבְלוּ וְנָפְלוּ מִן הָאִילָן קוֹדֶם שֶׁנִּתְבַּשְּׁלוּ — and withered and fell from the tree before they were ripened, כֵּיוָן שֶׁהוּא דָּבָר שֶׁנִּתְקַלְקֵל — the halachah is that since a fruit such as this is something that is ruined, אֵין מְבָרְכִין עָלָיו — we do not recite the blessing of *borei pri ha'eitz* upon it; רַק "שֶׁהַכֹּל" — we recite only *shehakol*. וְכֵן פַּת שֶׁעִיפְּשָׁה — Likewise, with regard to bread that has spoiled[36] וְתַבְשִׁיל שֶׁנִּתְקַלְקֵל קְצָת — and a cooked dish that spoiled slightly, מְבָרְכִין עֲלֵיהֶן "שֶׁהַכֹּל" — we recite upon them the *shehakol* blessing.[37] אֲבָל אִם נִתְקַלְקְלוּ לְגַמְרֵי — However, if they are completely spoiled עַד שֶׁאֵינָן רְאוּיִין לַאֲכִילָה — to the point of inedibility, אֵין מְבָרְכִין עֲלֵיהֶן כְּלָל — we do not recite any blessing upon them at all. וְכֵן חוֹמֶץ גָּמוּר — Likewise,

---

33. A tall, perennial wetland plant that was evidently not commonly eaten.

34. This applies only if the fruits were completely inedible in their raw state. Regarding the proper blessing for fruits (whether eaten raw or sweetened by cooking) that ripened to the point that they were edible to some extent (that is, they would be eaten in pressing situations), see *Mishnah Berurah* 202:18-19, 21, and *Beur Halachah* 202:2 s.v. ושאר כל אילן.

35. See Appendix of Kitzur's editorial glosses, where he explains why an *esrog* is different.

36. And he is eating the spoiled part. Certainly when eating a different part of the bread that is not spoiled one must recite *hamotzi* before eating it and *Bircas HaMazon* afterward, as when eating any bread (*Shaar HaTziyun* 204:1).

37. Regarding the proper *berachah acharonah* (final blessing) to be recited upon spoiled bread, *Beur Halachah* (204:1 s.v. ופת שעיפשה) writes that if one did *not* eat to satiety, he should not recite *Bircas HaMazon* (Grace After Meals), but *Borei Nefashos*. However, he does not give a final ruling with regard to the proper *berachah acharonah* in a case where one ate such bread to satiety.

HA'EITZ, HA'ADAMAH, AND SHEHAKOL BLESSINGS — SIMAN 52:14-15 226

(שֶׁמְּבַעְבֵּעַ כְּשֶׁשּׁוֹפְכִין אוֹתוֹ עַל הָאָרֶץ) אֵין מְבָרְכִין עָלָיו כְּלָל. וְאִם עֵרְבוֹ בְּמַיִם עַד שֶׁרָאוּי לִשְׁתִיָּה, מְבָרְכִין עָלָיו "שֶׁהַכֹּל".

יד. וְיֵשׁ מִינֵי פֵּירוֹת שֶׁדַּרְכָּן בְּכָךְ שֶׁאֵינָן מִתְבַּשְּׁלוֹת לְעוֹלָם עַל הָאִילָן, אֶלָּא אַחַר שֶׁנּוֹטְלִין מִן הָאִילָן מְנִיחִין אוֹתָן בְּתוֹךְ קַשׁ וְתֶבֶן וְכַדּוֹמֶה וְעַל יְדֵי כָּךְ מִתְבַּשְּׁלִין, כְּגוֹן הָאֲגָסִים הַקְּטַנִּים (אשריצן), כֵּיוָן שֶׁדַּרְכָּן בְּכָךְ מְבָרְכִין עֲלֵיהֶן "בּוֹרֵא פְּרִי הָעֵץ"[38].

טו. יֵשׁ מִינֵי פֵּירוֹת שֶׁאֵין בָּהֶם אֶלָּא שְׂרָף בְּעָלְמָא כָּנוּס בְּתוֹךְ הַחַרְצַנִּים (וְנִקְרָאִים קאלינוס) וְאֵינָן רְאוּיִין לַאֲכִילָה, אֶלָּא מוֹצְצִין אוֹתָן וְזוֹרְקִין הַקְּלִיפּוֹת, מְבָרְכִין עַל מְצִיצָה זוֹ "שֶׁהַכֹּל" (דְּכֵיוָן שֶׁעִיקָּרוֹ אֵינוֹ אֶלָּא לְמַשְׁקֶה הַיּוֹצֵא מִמֶּנּוּ אֵין עָלָיו שֵׁם פְּרִי כְּלָל), וַאֲפִילוּ הוּא בּוֹלֵעַ גַּם הַקְּלִיפָּה וְהַגַּרְעִין אֵינוֹ מְבָרֵךְ רַק "שֶׁהַכֹּל"[39].

---

with regard to **totally** fermented **vinegar** (שֶׁמְּבַעְבֵּעַ כְּשֶׁשּׁוֹפְכִין אוֹתוֹ עַל הָאָרֶץ — if it is so fermented **that it bubbles when poured on the ground**) אֵין מְבָרְכִין עָלָיו כְּלָל — **we do not recite any blessing upon it at all.** וְאִם עֵרְבוֹ בְּמַיִם עַד שֶׁרָאוּי לִשְׁתִיָּה — **If he mixed it with water until it is potable,** מְבָרְכִין עָלָיו "שֶׁהַכֹּל" — then **we recite the *shehakol* blessing upon it.**

§14 וְיֵשׁ מִינֵי פֵּירוֹת שֶׁדַּרְכָּן בְּכָךְ — **However, there are certain types of fruit that their standard process** of growth and consumption **is in this way:** שֶׁאֵינָן מִתְבַּשְּׁלוֹת לְעוֹלָם עַל הָאִילָן — **They never ripen** while **on the tree;** אֶלָּא אַחַר שֶׁנּוֹטְלִין מִן הָאִילָן — **rather, after they are picked from the tree,** מְנִיחִין אוֹתָן בְּתוֹךְ קַשׁ וְתֶבֶן וְכַדּוֹמֶה — **they place them in hay or straw or the like,** וְעַל יְדֵי כָּךְ מִתְבַּשְּׁלִין — **and this causes them to ripen,** כְּגוֹן הָאֲגָסִים הַקְּטַנִּים (אשריצן) — as, **for example,** is the case with **small pears.** כֵּיוָן שֶׁדַּרְכָּן בְּכָךְ — The halachah in this case is that even though they are removed from the tree while still unripe, **since this is their standard process** of growth and consumption, מְבָרְכִין עֲלֵיהֶן "בּוֹרֵא פְּרִי הָעֵץ" — **we recite the *borei pri ha'eitz* blessing upon them.**[38]

§15 יֵשׁ מִינֵי פֵּירוֹת שֶׁאֵין בָּהֶם — **There are** certain **types of fruit that do not contain** any edible part אֶלָּא שְׂרָף בְּעָלְמָא כָּנוּס בְּתוֹךְ הַחַרְצַנִּים — **except for mere sap accumulated inside the seeds** (וְנִקְרָאִים קאלינוס — **and they are called "guilder rose"**). וְאֵינָן רְאוּיִין לַאֲכִילָה — **The** fruits themselves **are not edible;** אֶלָּא מוֹצְצִין אוֹתָן — **rather, people suck out their** contents וְזוֹרְקִין הַקְּלִיפּוֹת — **and discard the peels.** מְבָרְכִין עַל מְצִיצָה זוֹ "שֶׁהַכֹּל" — **We recite the *shehakol* blessing upon this sucking out of** the juice; (דְּכֵיוָן שֶׁעִיקָּרוֹ אֵינוֹ אֶלָּא לְמַשְׁקֶה הַיּוֹצֵא מִמֶּנּוּ — **since the primary** component of the fruit **is the liquid that comes out of it,** אֵין עָלָיו שֵׁם פְּרִי כְּלָל — **it cannot be classified as a *pri*, fruit, at all).** וַאֲפִילוּ הוּא בּוֹלֵעַ גַּם הַקְּלִיפָּה וְהַגַּרְעִין — **Even if one also swallows the peel and the pit,** אֵינוֹ מְבָרֵךְ רַק "שֶׁהַכֹּל" — **he should recite only the *shehakol* blessing.**[39]

---

38. Since these fruit are cultivated to be removed from the tree before being fully ripe, they are not considered "ruined" and cannot be classified with the *novlos* of the previous *se'if* (for further background of this halachah, see Appendix of Kitzur's editorial glosses).

39. Since the peel and pit are not fit for consumption, one does not recite a blessing upon them (*Mishnah Berurah* 203:3).

227 HA'EITZ, HA'ADAMAH, AND SHEHAKOL BLESSINGS — SIMAN 52:16

טז. אֵין מְבָרְכִין "בּוֹרֵא פְּרִי הָעֵץ" וּ"בוֹרֵא פְּרִי הָאֲדָמָה" אֶלָּא כְּשֶׁנִּיכָּר בְּמִקְצָת שֶׁהוּא פְּרִי[40], אֲבָל אִם נִתְרַסֵּק עַד שֶׁאֵינוֹ נִיכָּר כְּלָל מַה הוּא, כְּגוֹן לעקפאר (פאווידלא לאטווערג) שֶׁמְּבַשְּׁלִין מִשְּׁזוּפִין, וְקִטְנִיּוֹת שֶׁרִיסְּקָן לְגַמְרֵי[41], וְכַדּוֹמֶה, מְבָרְכִין עֲלֵיהֶם "שֶׁהַכֹּל"[42]. וּבְדִיעֲבַד אִם בֵּירַךְ עֲלֵיהֶם בְּרָכָה הָרְאוּיָה לָהֶן, יָצָא[43]. וְאִם רוֹב דֶּרֶךְ אֲכִילַת אוֹתָן פֵּירוֹת הוּא עַל יְדֵי רִיסּוּק שֶׁמְּרַסְּקִין אוֹתָן לְגַמְרֵי, מְבָרְכִין עֲלֵיהֶן אַף לְכַתְּחִלָּה בְּרָכָה הָרְאוּיָה לָהֶן.

§16 אֵין מְבָרְכִין "בּוֹרֵא פְּרִי הָעֵץ" — **We do not recite the** *borei pri ha'eitz* **blessing** upon a fruit וּ"בוֹרֵא פְּרִי הָאֲדָמָה" — **or the** *borei pri ha'adamah* **blessing** upon a vegetable אֶלָּא כְּשֶׁנִּיכָּר בְּמִקְצָת שֶׁהוּא פְּרִי — **unless it is somewhat evident that it is** indeed **a fruit** or vegetable.[40] אֲבָל אִם נִתְרַסֵּק — **However, if it was** finely **mashed** עַד שֶׁאֵינוֹ נִיכָּר כְּלָל מַה הוּא — **to the point that its identity is completely unrecognizable,** כְּגוֹן לעקפאר (פאווידלא לאטווערג) — **for example, jam** שֶׁמְּבַשְּׁלִין מִשְּׁזוּפִין, וְקִטְנִיּוֹת — **that** is made by **cooking plums, and legumes** (such as beans or peas) שֶׁרִיסְּקָן לְגַמְרֵי — **that are thoroughly mashed,**[41] וְכַדּוֹמֶה — **and similar** foods, מְבָרְכִין עֲלֵיהֶם "שֶׁהַכֹּל" — **we recite upon them the** *shehakol* **blessing.**[42] וּבְדִיעֲבַד — **After the fact,** אִם בֵּירַךְ עֲלֵיהֶם בְּרָכָה הָרְאוּיָה לָהֶן — **if one recited the blessing that was** originally **appropriate for them,** i.e., *borei pri ha'eitz* for mashed fruit and *borei pri ha'adamah* for mashed vegetables, יָצָא — **he has fulfilled his obligation.**[43] וְאִם רוֹב דֶּרֶךְ אֲכִילַת אוֹתָן פֵּירוֹת — **If the way these fruits are mostly eaten** הוּא עַל יְדֵי רִיסּוּק — **is** after they have gone **through a mashing process,** שֶׁמְּרַסְּקִין אוֹתָן לְגַמְרֵי — in which **they are completely mashed** to create a type of jam, מְבָרְכִין עֲלֵיהֶן אַף לְכַתְּחִלָּה בְּרָכָה הָרְאוּיָה לָהֶן — then **even initially we recite upon them the blessing that was** originally **appropriate for them.** Thus, the original blessing should be recited if one of the following two factors are present: the fruit or vegetable is still recognizable, *or* most people eat it this way.

---

40. *Mishnah Berurah* (202:40) comments that a fruit or vegetable will retain its original blessing even if it is mashed, as long as it keeps its solid form. Thus, upon mashed potatoes one recites *borei pri ha'adamah.*

41. *Mishnah Berurah* (202:41) describes the process of preparing this jam as cooking the fruits until they are entirely dissolved.

42. This case is actually the subject of dispute among the authorities (see *Shulchan Aruch* 202:7). *Rama* (ibid., as explained by *Mishnah Berurah* there, §42) writes that although it would seem that the proper blessing here is the original blessing (*ha'eitz* or *ha'adamah*), one should recite the *shehakol* blessing upon this food [so as to fulfill his obligation according to all opinions (see above, 50:2)].

43. See previous note. If one ate a fruit of the Seven Species prepared in this way, one is faced with a dilemma regarding the proper *berachah acharonah*: If the proper *berachah rishonah* (first blessing) is *ha'eitz* (see previous note), then the *berachah acharonah* is *Al HaEitz* (above, 51:7-8); if the proper *berachah rishonah* is *shehakol*, the *berachah acharonah* is *Borei Nefashos. Mishnah Berurah* (202:42) writes that due to the dispute among the authorities regarding the proper blessing, one should try to eat other foods that require *Al HaEitz* and *Borei Nefashos* in order to recite those blessings regardless of the status of the mashed fruit that he ate. If this is not possible, since the proper *berachah rishonah* here is actually *ha'eitz* (see previous note), he may recite *Al HaEitz* as the *berachah acharonah.* Since reciting *shehakol* as the *berachah rishonah* and *Al HaEitz* as the *berachah acharonah* is somewhat contradictory, *Igros Moshe* (*Yoreh Deah* II, §25) writes that one should try to avoid this situation.

HA'EITZ, HA'ADAMAH, AND SHEHAKOL BLESSINGS — SIMAN 52:17 228

יז. אוֹרֶז[44] וְדוֹחַן (הירז וְרייז) שֶׁנִּתְבַּשְּׁלוּ[45], אִם לֹא נִתְמָעֲכוּ, מְבָרֵךְ עֲלֵיהֶם "בּוֹרֵא פְּרִי הָאֲדָמָה". וְאִם נִתְמָעֲכוּ[46], אוֹ שֶׁטָּחַן וְעָשָׂה מֵהֶן פַּת, יֵשׁ חִילּוּק בֵּין אוֹרֶז לְדוֹחַן. כִּי מִצַּד הַדִּין עַל הָאוֹרֶז מְבָרֵךְ "בּוֹרֵא מִינֵי מְזוֹנוֹת"[47] וְעַל הַדּוֹחַן "שֶׁהַכֹּל", אֶלָּא שֶׁיֵּשׁ לָנוּ סָפֵק אִם אוֹרֶז הִיא הירז וְדוֹחַן רייז, אוֹ לְהֵיפּוּךְ. לָכֵן, יְרֵא שָׁמַיִם לֹא יֹאכַל בֵּין הירז בֵּין רייז שֶׁנִּתְמָעֲכוּ אֶלָּא בְּתוֹךְ הַסְּעוּדָה[48]. וּבִשְׁעַת הַדְּחָק שֶׁאֵין לוֹ פַּת, מְבָרֵךְ בֵּין עַל הירז בֵּין עַל רייז "שֶׁהַכֹּל"

§17 Complete kernels of grain (wheat, barley, spelt, oats, and rye) are considered "*pri ha'adamah,*" *fruit* (or *produce*) *of the ground*, and when eaten in that form their blessing is *borei pri ha'adamah.*[44] However, once they have begun to be processed and cooked into a nourishing food, the proper blessing is *borei minei mezonos* (*Who creates species of nourishment*); see above, 48:8.

In this *se'if,* Kitzur discusses whether the grains of millet and rice are also included in this halachah.

אוֹרֶז וְדוֹחַן (הירז וְרייז) שֶׁנִּתְבַּשְּׁלוּ — Millet and rice[45] that were cooked, אִם לֹא נִתְמָעֲכוּ — if they were not crushed, מְבָרֵךְ עֲלֵיהֶם "בּוֹרֵא פְּרִי הָאֲדָמָה" — one recites the *borei pri ha'adamah* blessing upon them. וְאִם נִתְמָעֲכוּ — If they were crushed[46] **אוֹ שֶׁטָּחַן וְעָשָׂה מֵהֶן פַּת — or if he ground them and made bread from their** flour, **יֵשׁ חִילּוּק בֵּין אוֹרֶז לְדוֹחַן** — then **there is a difference between millet and rice: כִּי מִצַּד הַדִּין — For insofar as the** actual **halachah, עַל הָאוֹרֶז מְבָרֵךְ "בּוֹרֵא מִינֵי מְזוֹנוֹת"** — when they are crushed or made into bread **one recites the blessing of *borei minei mezonos*** (*Who creates species of nourishment*) **upon** that which is called "***orez,***"[47] **וְעַל הַדּוֹחַן "שֶׁהַכֹּל" — and *shehakol* upon** that which is called "***dochan.***" **אֶלָּא שֶׁיֵּשׁ לָנוּ סָפֵק — However, we are unsure** as to the identity of these grains, **אִם אוֹרֶז הִיא הירז וְדוֹחַן רייז, אוֹ לְהֵיפּוּךְ** — i.e., **if "*orez*" is millet and "*dochan*" rice, or vice-versa. לָכֵן, יְרֵא שָׁמַיִם לֹא יֹאכַל בֵּין הירז בֵּין רייז שֶׁנִּתְמָעֲכוּ — Therefore, a God-fearing person should not eat crushed rice or millet אֶלָּא בְּתוֹךְ הַסְּעוּדָה — unless it is during a meal.**[48] **וּבִשְׁעַת הַדְּחָק — In a pressing situation, שֶׁאֵין לוֹ פַּת— when he has no bread** with which to exempt these foods, **מְבָרֵךְ בֵּין עַל הירז בֵּין עַל רייז "שֶׁהַכֹּל" — he should recite the *shehakol* blessing upon both millet and rice** [when

44. See *Shulchan Aruch* 208:4 and *Igros Moshe, Orach Chaim* I, §68 for further conditions regarding this halachah.

45. Although *Kitzur* refers to אוֹרֶז and דוֹחַן as millet and rice, respectively, it will soon become clear that these definitions are subject to dispute.

46. This includes even a slight crushing of the kernels, and possibly even the removal of the husks, as is done with our white rice (*Mishnah Berurah* 208:15, 26).

47. When this grain is eaten in its cooked form or after it has been made into bread, it satisfies and nourishes a person, as do the five species of grain. Therefore, the blessing of *borei minei mezonos,* "Who creates species of nourishment," is appropriate. However, the final blessing of *Al HaMichyah* or *Bircas HaMazon* is reserved only for the five grains, due to their significance (see above, 51:7). After eating *orez* (see next note), however, one recites only the *Borei Nefashos* blessing (*Mishnah Berurah* 208:28-29).

48. Generally, any food eaten within the context of a meal that has bread is exempt from a separate obligation to recite upon it a *berachah rishonah* (above, *Siman* 43).

Mishnah Berurah (208:25) rules, based on the consensus of many authorities, including the Gaon of Vilna, that אוֹרֶז is in fact rice, and therefore, the appropriate blessing is *borei minei mezonos* (see also *Beur Halachah* 208:8 s.v. על פת, *Shaar HaTziyun* loc. cit. §31).

229 HA'EITZ, HA'ADAMAH, AND SHEHAKOL BLESSINGS — SIMAN 52:18

וּלְאַחֲרֵיהֶם "בּוֹרֵא נְפָשׁוֹת". עַל פַּת הֶעָשׂוּי מִקִּטְנִיּוֹת (טענגרא קיקריטץ, מעלייי"ע, טירקישען ווייץ)[49], אֲפִילוּ בִּמְקוֹמוֹת שֶׁדַּרְכָּן בְּלֶחֶם זֶה, מְבָרְכִין עָלָיו "שֶׁהַכֹּל"[50] (עַיֵּין פְּרִי מְגָדִים סִימָן ר"ח מִשְׁבְּצוֹת סְעִיף קָטָן י"א[51] וְשִׁיּוּרֵי בְרָכָה סִימָן ר"ז). דִּין עֵירַב קְמָחִין[52] עַיֵּין בְּשֻׁלְחָן עָרוּךְ סִימָן ר"ח סְעִיף ט'[53].

יח. עַל הַצוּקער מְבָרֵךְ שֶׁהַכֹּל[54]. וְכֵן הַמּוֹצֵץ קָנִים מְתוּקוֹת שֶׁהַכֹּל. וְכֵן צימרינד וְלאקריטץ שֶׁכּוֹסְסִין וּבוֹלְעִין רַק טַעַם וּפוֹלְטִין הָעִיקָּר מְבָרְכִין שֶׁהַכֹּל.

---

they are crushed or made into bread], **וּלְאַחֲרֵיהֶם "בּוֹרֵא נְפָשׁוֹת"** — **and after** eating **them,** he should recite *Borei Nefashos.*

עַל פַּת הֶעָשׂוּי מִקִּטְנִיּוֹת — **For bread that is made from** legumes **(טענגרא קיקריטץ, מעלייי"ע, טירקישען ווייץ** — corn),[49] **אֲפִילוּ בִּמְקוֹמוֹת שֶׁדַּרְכָּן בְּלֶחֶם זֶה** — **even in places where they normally** eat **such bread, מְבָרְכִין עָלָיו "שֶׁהַכֹּל"** — **we recite the** ***shehakol*** **blessing upon** eating **it.**[50] **(עַיֵּין פְּרִי מְגָדִים סִימָן ר"ח מִשְׁבְּצוֹת סְעִיף קָטָן י"א וְשִׁיּוּרֵי בְרָכָה סִימָן ר"ז** — **See** ***Pri Megadim, Siman*** **208,** ***Mishbetzos*** *Zahav* **§11,**[51] **and** ***Shiyurei Berachah, Siman*** **207.) דִּין עֵירַב קְמָחִין** — For **the laws of** the blessing for **flour** from **mixed** sources,[52] **עַיֵּין בְּשֻׁלְחָן עָרוּךְ סִימָן ר"ח סְעִיף ט'** — **see** ***Shulchan Aruch,*** *Orach Chaim* **208:9.**[53]

§18 עַל הַצוּקער מְבָרֵךְ שֶׁהַכֹּל — **Upon sugar one recites the** ***shehakol*** **blessing.**[54] **וְכֵן הַמּוֹצֵץ קָנִים מְתוּקוֹת** — **Likewise, if one sucks sweet stalks** of sugar cane (or a similar plant), **שֶׁהַכֹּל** — he should recite ***shehakol.*** **וְכֵן צימרינד וְלאקריטץ** — **Likewise,** for the **cinnamon and licorice** plants **שֶׁכּוֹסְסִין וּבוֹלְעִין רַק טַעַם** — **that one chews and swallows only** the **taste וּפוֹלְטִין הָעִיקָּר** — **and spits out the main** portion of the plant, **מְבָרְכִין שֶׁהַכֹּל** — **we recite the** ***shehakol*** **blessing.**

---

49. These are all words of various dialects (Yiddish and Hungarian) for corn (maize).

50. *Borei pri ha'adamah* is not appropriate here because the kernel is not in its original state and these grains are not usually used for bread. This halachah also applies to bread made from millet, legumes, or grains other than wheat, barley, oats, rye, and spelt. The *berachah acharonah* for such bread is not *Bircas HaMazon* (which is recited only for bread of the five grains), but *Borei Nefashos* (see *Mishnah Berurah* 208:33).

51. *Pri Megadim* there argues that in regions where corn is used primarily for bread, *ha'adamah* should be recited. See, however, *Mishnah Berurah* (208:33), who writes that it is preferable to eat it only in the course of a bread meal so as to avoid the question of which blessing to recite. [The halachic authorities, when discussing corn, base their opinions upon the common use for corn in their times and countries. See, for example, *Responsa* of *Chasam Sofer* cited in *Mishnah Berurah* ibid., which states that the corn of his day was planted primarily as feed for fowl, and was rarely used for human consumption. With regard to this and all similar questions one must consult contemporary halachic authorities whose decision will be based on the conditions of farming and marketing of the day and the specific region.]

52. I.e., a mixture of flour from one of the five grains (wheat, barley, oats, rye, and spelt), together with other flour.

53. See also *Igros Moshe, Orach Chaim* I, §70.

54. Many authorities maintain that the correct blessing for sugar is *borei pri ha'eitz* because it is the primary product of the sugar cane, which remains standing from year to year. Although the halachah does not follow these opinions, if one did recite *borei pri ha'eitz* or even *borei pri ha'adamah* for sugar, he has fulfilled his obligation. Likewise, on sugar made from beets one should recite *shehakol.* If one recited *borei pri ha'adamah*, he should not then recite *shehakol,* for he has fulfilled his obligation (*Mishnah Berurah* 202:76; see *Beur Halachah* 202:15 s.v. על הסוקא"ר at length).

סימן נג

דִּין רוֹטֶב וּמַשְׁקֶה שֶׁל פֵּירוֹת וִירָקוֹת

וּבוֹ ו׳ סְעִיפִים

א. כָּל הַפֵּירוֹת וִירָקוֹת שֶׁסְּחָטָן וְהוֹצִיא מֵהֶן מַשְׁקִין מְבָרֵךְ עַל הַמַּשְׁקִין "שֶׁהַכֹּל", וְכֵן דְּבַשׁ הַזָּב מִן הַתְּמָרִים[1], כִּי אֵין מַשְׁקֶה נִקְרָאָה פְּרִי[2] רַק הַיַּיִן וְשֶׁמֶן זַיִת[3]. וְהַיַּיִן שֶׁהוּא חָשׁוּב מְאֹד[4] קָבְעוּ לוֹ בְּרָכָה מְיוּחֶדֶת "בּוֹרֵא פְּרִי הַגָּפֶן". וְשֶׁמֶן

SIMAN 53

THE LAW REGARDING BROTH AND JUICE OF FRUITS AND VEGETABLES

CONTAINING 6 *SE'IFIM*

§1 Fruit Juice, Wine, Olive Oil / **§2-3** Broth / **§4** Water Used for Pickling / **§5** Other Liquids / **§6** Raisin Wine

This *Siman* discusses the appropriate blessing on fruit and vegetable juices, and on liquids in which fruits or vegetables were cooked or soaked.

§1 כָּל הַפֵּירוֹת וִירָקוֹת — Concerning **all fruits and vegetables** שֶׁסְּחָטָן וְהוֹצִיא מֵהֶן מַשְׁקִין — **that one squeezed and extracted** their **juice,** מְבָרֵךְ עַל הַמַּשְׁקִין "שֶׁהַכֹּל" — **one recites the blessing of** *shehakol nihyah bidvaro, through Whose word **everything** came to be,* **upon the juice.** וְכֵן דְּבַשׁ הַזָּב מִן הַתְּמָרִים — **The same** blessing, *shehakol,* is recited on **honey that oozes from dates.**[1] כִּי אֵין מַשְׁקֶה נִקְרָאָה פְּרִי — **For no juice** of a fruit **is classified as** the actual **fruit**[2] רַק הַיַּיִן וְשֶׁמֶן זַיִת — **except wine and olive oil.**[3]

וְהַיַּיִן — Now, for **wine,** שֶׁהוּא חָשׁוּב מְאֹד — **which has great significance,**[4] קָבְעוּ לוֹ בְּרָכָה מְיוּחֶדֶת — the Sages **instituted a unique blessing** to be recited **for it:** "בּוֹרֵא פְּרִי הַגָּפֶן" — *Baruch Atah Ado-noy Elokeinu Melech HaOlam borei pri hagafen, Blessed are You Hashem, our God, King of the universe,* ***Who creates the fruit of the vine.*** וְשֶׁמֶן

---

1. This is also true of honey that was extracted by crushing or squeezing the dates (*Mishnah Berurah* 202:45). [The sweet, thick juice of the date or other fruit is known as "honey" (see *Rashi* to *Devarim* 26:2 s.v. ודבש).]

2. As explained by the Gemara (*Berachos* 38a), the juice of a fruit [whether it oozed out on its own or was extracted by crushing or squeezing] is not considered the essence of the fruit (in which case the appropriate blessing would be *borei pri ha'eitz*, "Who creates the fruit of the tree"), but is deemed to be merely the "sweat" [i.e., moisture] of the fruit. Therefore, the blessing on apple cider and other fruit juices is *shehakol* (*Mishnah Berurah* 202:47).

3. The principal use of grapes and olives is for the production of wine and olive oil (*Shulchan Aruch HaRav* 202:10; see *Beur Halachah* 202:15 s.v. על הסוקא״ר). Therefore, it is fitting that they should be subject to the blessing of the fruit itself, *borei pri ha'eitz*. Nevertheless, with regard to wine, the Sages instituted a unique blessing, as Kitzur proceeds to explain.

4. Since wine both satiates hunger and gladdens the heart, it is appropriate to offer special praise to the One Who created such exceptional fruit (see *Mishnah Berurah* 202:2, citing *Berachos* 35b; *Beur Halachah* 202:1 s.v. פה״ע). See above, *Siman* 49, for the particulars of when this blessing is recited.

231 BROTH AND JUICE OF FRUITS AND VEGETABLES — SIMAN 53:2

זַיִת שֶׁהוּא גַּם כֵּן חָשׁוּב, אִם נֶהֱנֶה מִמֶּנּוּ בְּעִנְיָן שֶׁהוּא צָרִיךְ לְבָרֵךְ עָלָיו, מְבָרְכִין עָלָיו "בּוֹרֵא פְּרִי הָעֵץ" (כְּדִלְקַמָּן סִימָן נ"ד סְעִיף ח')[5].

ב. פֵּירוֹת[6] שֶׁאֵין דַּרְכָּן לְבִישׁוּל אֶלָּא לְאָכְלָן חַיִּין, אִם בִּשְּׁלָן, מְבָרֵךְ עַל הָרוֹטֶב "שֶׁהַכֹּל"[7]. אֲבָל פֵּירוֹת שֶׁדַּרְכָּן לְיַבְּשָׁן וּלְבַשְּׁלָן[8] וְהֵן שְׁכִיחוֹת לָרוֹב וְנָטְעֵי לְהוּ אַדַּעְתָּא דְהָכִי[9], אִם בִּשְּׁלָן[10] כְּדֵי לֶאֱכוֹל הַפֵּירוֹת וְגַם לִשְׁתּוֹת אֶת הָרוֹטֶב,

זַיִת שֶׁהוּא גַּם כֵּן חָשׁוּב — Concerning **olive oil, which is also significant,** **אִם נֶהֱנֶה מִמֶּנּוּ** — **if one derives benefit from** consuming **it** **בְּעִנְיָן שֶׁהוּא צָרִיךְ לְבָרֵךְ עָלָיו** — **in a manner that he must recite a blessing upon it,** **מְבָרְכִין עָלָיו "בּוֹרֵא פְּרִי הָעֵץ"** — then **he recites upon it the blessing of** *borei pri ha'eitz, **Who creates the fruit of the tree*** **(כְּדִלְקַמָּן סִימָן נ"ד סְעִיף ח')** — **as** explained **below, 54:8).**[5]

§2 This *se'if* differentiates between the blessing on the broth of fruits that were grown for raw consumption and the broth of fruits that were planted for the purpose of being dried and cooked.[6]

פֵּירוֹת שֶׁאֵין דַּרְכָּן לְבִישׁוּל — With regard to those **fruits that are not normally cooked,** **אֶלָּא לְאָכְלָן חַיִּין** — **but are eaten raw,** **אִם בִּשְּׁלָן** — **if one cooked them,** **מְבָרֵךְ עַל הָרוֹטֶב "שֶׁהַכֹּל"** — **one recites the *shehakol* blessing upon the broth.**[7] **אֲבָל פֵּירוֹת שֶׁדַּרְכָּן לְיַבְּשָׁן וּלְבַשְּׁלָן** — **But fruits whose** usual **manner is to be dried and cooked,**[8] **וְהֵן שְׁכִיחוֹת לָרוֹב** — **and they are found in abundance** **וְנָטְעֵי לְהוּ אַדַּעְתָּא דְהָכִי** — **and are planted for that purpose,**[9] **אִם בִּשְּׁלָן כְּדֵי לֶאֱכוֹל הַפֵּירוֹת** — **if he cooked them**[10] **in order to eat the fruit** **וְגַם לִשְׁתּוֹת אֶת הָרוֹטֶב** — **and also to drink the**

---

5. Kitzur explains there that, generally, olive oil is not subject to its own blessing, because if one drinks it on its own, it has a detrimental effect and no blessing is recited on it at all; and if it is mixed with other ingredients, it is considered subordinate to the other ingredients and will be exempted with the blessing of the other ingredients (this is in accordance with the halachos governing the blessings upon primary and subordinate foods, detailed in that *Siman*). It is only when one drinks olive oil in a mixture for medicinal purposes that he recites the *borei pri ha'eitz* blessing, for then his primary intent is for the oil.

6. In earlier times, when no means of wide-scale distribution and practical storage of fresh fruits existed, fruits were often preserved by drying them, after which they were stored to be cooked and eaten at a later time. Since large amounts of produce could not be used immediately, fruits that were planted in abundance were almost certainly grown for drying and cooking.

7. A blessing on the broth is required only when one drinks the broth by itself. If, however, he drinks the broth while eating the fruit, we assume he was primarily interested in the fruit and he recites a *borei pri ha'eitz* on it (see above, 52:6); no blessing is recited on the broth, as it is deemed to be subordinate; see above, 48:10 (see *Mishnah Berurah* 202:54 with *Shaar HaTziyun* §66 for further discussion; see also *Mishnah Berurah* 205:9).

8. Kitzur is describing common practice in those times, which (as was explained above, note 6) was to plant crops in abundance for the purpose of drying the produce and then cooking them at a later time. However, the same ruling applies if they are planted for cooking without being dried first, for the ultimate issue here is whether they were planted for the purpose of cooking (see *Mishnah Berurah* 202:52).

9. This depends upon the original intention at the time of planting, not upon what is usual once they were dried. Thus, if the fruits are normally eaten raw, then although some people dry them, and once they are dried it is common to cook them, they are still considered fruits whose usual manner is not to be eaten cooked, and subject to the previous ruling of Kitzur, that one recites *shehakol* on their broth (*Mishnah Berurah* 202:52).

10. The same applies if he soaked them in

BROTH AND JUICE OF FRUITS AND VEGETABLES — SIMAN 53:2 232

מְבָרֵךְ עַל הָרוֹטֶב "בּוֹרֵא פְּרִי הָעֵץ", וַאֲפִילוּ אֵינוֹ אוֹכֵל מִן הַפֵּירוֹת. וְכֵן קִטְנִיּוֹת וִירָקוֹת בְּמָקוֹם שֶׁדַּרְכָּן לְבַשְּׁלָן לְאָכְלָן וְגַם לִשְׁתּוֹת הָרוֹטֶב, מְבָרֵךְ עַל הָרוֹטֶב "בּוֹרֵא פְּרִי הָאֲדָמָה", וַאֲפִילוּ אֵינוֹ אוֹכֵל מִן הַמַּאֲכָל. (וְהַחִילוּק שֶׁבֵּין זֶה לְמָה שֶׁנִּתְבָּאֵר בְּסָעִיף א' — יֵשׁ אוֹמְרִים מִשּׁוּם דְּהָתָם אֵין דַּרְכָּן בְּכָךְ לִסְחוֹט אֶת הַפֵּירוֹת אוֹ יְרָקוֹת לְהוֹצִיא מֵימֵיהֶן וְהָכָא דַּרְכָּן בְּכָךְ[11], וְיֵשׁ אוֹמְרִים מִשּׁוּם דְּיוֹתֵר נִכְנָס טַעַם הַפְּרִי וְהַיָּרָק בְּמַיִם שֶׁמְּבַשְּׁלִין אוֹתָן בָּהֶם מֵאֲשֶׁר הוּא בְּמַשְׁקֶה שֶׁזָּב מֵהֶן[12].)

---

broth, **מְבָרֵךְ עַל הָרוֹטֶב "בּוֹרֵא פְּרִי הָעֵץ"** — **he recites the** ***borei pri ha'eitz*** **blessing on the broth,** **וַאֲפִילוּ אֵינוֹ אוֹכֵל מִן הַפֵּירוֹת** — **even if he is not partaking of the fruit.** **וְכֵן קִטְנִיּוֹת וִירָקוֹת** — **So too with regard to legumes and vegetables:** **בְּמָקוֹם שֶׁדַּרְכָּן לְבַשְּׁלָן** — **In a place where the** usual **manner is to cook them** **לְאָכְלָן וְגַם לִשְׁתּוֹת הָרוֹטֶב** — **in order to eat them as well as to drink the broth,** **מְבָרֵךְ עַל הָרוֹטֶב "בּוֹרֵא פְּרִי הָאֲדָמָה"** — **one recites the blessing of** *borei pri ha'adamah,* ***Who creates the fruit of the ground,*** **on the broth,** **וַאֲפִילוּ אֵינוֹ אוֹכֵל מִן הַמַּאֲכָל** — **even if he is not eating the** solid **food.**

Kitzur contrasts this ruling, that the blessing on the broth of a fruit or vegetable is *ha'eitz* or *ha'adamah* even though he is not partaking of the actual fruit or vegetable, with the ruling of *se'if* 1, that the blessing on juice extracted from a fruit or vegetable is *shehakol*:

(וְהַחִילוּק שֶׁבֵּין זֶה לְמָה שֶׁנִּתְבָּאֵר בְּסָעִיף א') — **The** reason for the **difference between this and what was explained in** ***se'if*** **1** is a matter of dispute: **יֵשׁ אוֹמְרִים** — **Some** authorities **say** **מִשּׁוּם דְּהָתָם אֵין דַּרְכָּן בְּכָךְ** — that the blessing on juice extracted by squeezing the fruit or vegetable is *shehakol* **because there** it speaks of a case where **it is not the** usual **manner** **לִסְחוֹט אֶת הַפֵּירוֹת אוֹ יְרָקוֹת לְהוֹצִיא מֵימֵיהֶן** — **to squeeze the fruits or vegetables in order to extract their juice,** **וְהָכָא דַּרְכָּן בְּכָךְ** — **while here it is the** usual **manner** to cook these fruits or vegetables for their broth.[11] **וְיֵשׁ אוֹמְרִים** — **And there are** other authorities **who say** **מִשּׁוּם דְּיוֹתֵר נִכְנָס טַעַם הַפְּרִי וְהַיָּרָק** — that it is **because the flavor of the** actual **fruit and vegetable is absorbed to a greater extent** **בְּמַיִם שֶׁמְּבַשְּׁלִין אוֹתָן בָּהֶם** — **in the water in which they are cooked,** **מֵאֲשֶׁר הוּא בְּמַשְׁקֶה שֶׁזָּב מֵהֶן** — **than it is** present **in the juice that flows from them.)**[12]

---

water for a minimum of 24 hours and the water absorbed their flavor (*Shulchan Aruch* 202:10 and *Mishnah Berurah* §51-52 with *Shaar HaTziyun* §60; *Mishnah Berurah* 205:8). See below, *se'if* 4, with regard to pickling.

11. According to this opinion (*Rashba* to *Berachos* 38a s.v. דבש), the *borei pri ha'eitz* blessing is not appropriate on juice of fruits that are usually not squeezed for their juice, nor is it appropriate on the broth of fruits that are usually not cooked. [In addition, in order for *borei pri ha'eitz* to be the appropriate blessing according to this opinion, the fruit trees must be planted for that purpose, as mentioned by Kitzur earlier.]

12. This opinion (*Rosh, Berachos* 6:18) distinguishes between a *broth,* in which the liquid absorbs the actual flavor of the fruit or vegetable, and a squeezed *juice,* which does not contain the essence of the fruit. According to this opinion, even if the fruit *is* usually squeezed for its juice, one recites *shehakol* on the juice (see *Mishnah Berurah* 205:14).

Since no decision is rendered in this dispute, the *shehakol* blessing (which is an all-encompassing blessing; see above, 50:2) is recited as long as the conditions of both opinions have not been fulfilled. Thus, *ha'eitz* is recited only in the case presented by Kitzur in this *se'if,* that is, on the broth of a fruit that is usually cooked (and was planted for this purpose). [Nevertheless, one who mistakenly recited *borei pri ha'eitz* on the juice of a fruit

233 BROTH AND JUICE OF FRUITS AND VEGETABLES — SIMAN 53:3

אֲבָל אִם אֵין כַּוָּנַת הַבִּישׁוּל רַק בִּשְׁבִיל הַפֵּירוֹת אוֹ הַיְרָקוֹת, אֲזַי כְּשֶׁאֵינוֹ אוֹכֵל מִן הַפֵּירוֹת וְהַיְרָקוֹת אֶלָּא שׁוֹתֶה אֶת הָרוֹטֶב לְבַד, מְבָרֵךְ "שֶׁהַכֹּל". וְאִם בִּישְׁלָן עִם בָּשָׂר בְּיַחַד, אֲפִילוּ אִם כַּוָּנַת הַבִּישׁוּל גַּם בִּשְׁבִיל הָרוֹטֶב, לְעוֹלָם מְבָרֵךְ עַל הָרוֹטֶב "שֶׁהַכֹּל", כִּי הַבָּשָׂר הוּא הָעִיקָּר[13].

ג. פֵּירוֹת שֶׁשְּׁרָאָן אוֹ בִּישְׁלָן רַק בִּשְׁבִיל הָרוֹטֶב מְבָרֵךְ עָלָיו "שֶׁהַכֹּל", וְלָכֵן מְבָרְכִין עַל קאפע וְעַל טהע "שֶׁהַכֹּל"[14]. וְכֵן עַל הַשֵּׁכָר, בֵּין שֶׁהוּא מִתְּמָרִים בֵּין שֶׁהוּא מִשְּׂעוֹרִים.

Kitzur addresses the condition mentioned earlier, that the blessing on the broth is *ha'eitz* or *ha'adamah* only when it was cooked for the sake of both the fruit and the broth:

אֲבָל אִם אֵין כַּוָּנַת הַבִּישׁוּל רַק בִּשְׁבִיל הַפֵּירוֹת אוֹ הַיְרָקוֹת — But if the purpose of the cooking is only for the sake of the fruits or vegetables, i.e., the purpose is to prepare cooked fruit or vegetables, not fruit or vegetable broth, **אֲזַי כְּשֶׁאֵינוֹ אוֹכֵל מִן הַפֵּירוֹת וְהַיְרָקוֹת — then, if one does not eat the fruits or vegetables** **אֶלָּא שׁוֹתֶה אֶת הָרוֹטֶב לְבַד — but only drinks the broth,** **מְבָרֵךְ "שֶׁהַכֹּל" — he recites the *shehakol* blessing.** **וְאִם בִּישְׁלָן עִם בָּשָׂר בְּיַחַד — However, if he cooked** the fruits or vegetables **together with meat,** **אֲפִילוּ אִם כַּוָּנַת הַבִּישׁוּל גַּם בִּשְׁבִיל הָרוֹטֶב — even if the purpose of the cooking was for the sake of the broth as well,** **לְעוֹלָם מְבָרֵךְ עַל הָרוֹטֶב "שֶׁהַכֹּל" — he always recites the *shehakol* blessing on the broth,** **כִּי הַבָּשָׂר הוּא הָעִיקָּר — for the** flavor of the **meat** in the broth **is primary.**[13]

§3 פֵּירוֹת שֶׁשְּׁרָאָן אוֹ בִּישְׁלָן רַק בִּשְׁבִיל הָרוֹטֶב — With regard to **fruits that were soaked or cooked solely for the sake of the broth,** **מְבָרֵךְ עָלָיו "שֶׁהַכֹּל" — one recites the *shehakol* blessing on** the broth. **וְלָכֵן מְבָרְכִין עַל קאפע וְעַל טהע "שֶׁהַכֹּל" — Therefore, we recite the *shehakol* blessing on coffee and tea.**[14] **וְכֵן עַל הַשֵּׁכָר — The same** blessing, *shehakol,* is recited **on beer,** **בֵּין שֶׁהוּא מִתְּמָרִים בֵּין שֶׁהוּא מִשְּׂעוֹרִים — whether it is** produced **from dates or from barley.**

---

that is usually squeezed for its juice does not have to recite another blessing, since he has recited the proper blessing according to the first opinion (see *Shaar HaTziyun* 205:21; cf. ibid. 202:54). Conversely, one who recited *borei pri ha'eitz* on the broth of a fruit that is not normally cooked does not recite another blessing, since this is the appropriate blessing according to the second opinion (*Mishnah Berurah* 202:53).]

13. When eating a mixture of foods, one recites the blessing upon the primary ingredient, as explained below, *Siman* 54. Therefore, one who eats the broth of a meat and vegetable stew by itself recites only *shehakol,* which is the blessing on the meat, since the flavor of the meat in the broth is considered more important than the flavor of the vegetables.

However, the meat takes precedence only when the broth was originally cooked together with both meat and vegetables. If one first cooked the broth with the vegetables only, the broth assumes the *ha'adamah* blessing of the vegetables, which it retains even if he subsequently adds meat to the vegetables and broth and cooks them together (*Mishnah Berurah* 205:12-13, as explained by *Igros Moshe, Orach Chaim* I, §81).

If one eats the vegetables together with the broth, the *ha'adamah* blessing recited on the vegetables exempts the broth as well. Moreover, one must recite *ha'adamah* on the vegetables even if he is also eating the meat, for the vegetables are not considered secondary to the meat (*Mishnah Berurah* 205:13).

14. For coffee and tea are brewed only for the sake of the beverage, not for the coffee beans or tea leaves.

BROTH AND JUICE OF FRUITS AND VEGETABLES — SIMAN 53:4 234

ד. יְרָקוֹת אוֹ פֵּירוֹת שֶׁכּוֹבְשִׁין אוֹתָן בְּמַיִם שֶׁיִּתְחַמְּצוּ, אַף עַל פִּי שֶׁדַּרְכָּן בְּכָךְ (כְּגוֹן גורקען אוגרקיס ראטהע ריבען צוויקעל בארקעס קרויט), מִכָּל מָקוֹם אֵין מְבָרְכִין עַל הָרוֹטֶב כִּי אִם "שֶׁהַכֹּל". וְאַף עַל פִּי שֶׁטַּעַם הַיָּרָק וְהַפְּרִי בָּרוֹטֶב, מִכָּל מָקוֹם הוֹאִיל וְאֵין עִיקַּר הַכְּבִישָׁה בִּשְׁבִיל שֶׁיִּתְּנוּ טַעַם בַּמַּיִם אֶלָּא בִּשְׁבִיל שֶׁגַּם הֵמָּה בְּעַצְמָם יְתוּקְּנוּ עַל יְדֵי הַכְּבִישָׁה, לָכֵן מְבָרְכִין רַק "שֶׁהַכֹּל". וּמִכָּל מָקוֹם, אִם אָכַל תְּחִלָּה אֶת הַיָּרָק וּבֵירַךְ "בּוֹרֵא פְּרִי הָאֲדָמָה" וְאַחַר כָּךְ רוֹצֶה לִשְׁתּוֹת גַּם הָרוֹטֶב, יֵשׁ סָפֵק אִם צָרִיךְ לְבָרֵךְ עַל הָרוֹטֶב כִּי שֶׁמָּא יָצָא בְּבִרְכַּת "בּוֹרֵא פְּרִי הָאֲדָמָה" גַּם עַל הָרוֹטֶב[15]. לָכֵן לֹא יַעֲשֶׂה כֵּן[16].

---

§4 יְרָקוֹת אוֹ פֵּירוֹת — **Vegetables or fruits** שֶׁכּוֹבְשִׁין אוֹתָן בְּמַיִם שֶׁיִּתְחַמְּצוּ — **that are soaked in** salt**water so that they should become pickled,** אַף עַל פִּי שֶׁדַּרְכָּן בְּכָךְ — **even if these vegetables are commonly** pickled, (כְּגוֹן גורקען אוגרקיס ראטהע ריבען צוויקעל בארקעס קרויט — **such as gherkins, cucumbers, rhubarbs, gourds, beets, or cabbage)** מִכָּל מָקוֹם אֵין מְבָרְכִין עַל הָרוֹטֶב כִּי אִם "שֶׁהַכֹּל" — **nevertheless, we recite only the *shehakol* blessing on the liquid.** וְאַף עַל פִּי שֶׁטַּעַם הַיָּרָק וְהַפְּרִי בָּרוֹטֶב — **For even though the flavor of the vegetable or fruit is** present **in the liquid,** מִכָּל מָקוֹם — **nevertheless,** הוֹאִיל וְאֵין עִיקַּר הַכְּבִישָׁה בִּשְׁבִיל שֶׁיִּתְּנוּ טַעַם בַּמַּיִם — **since the main** purpose **of the soaking is not to impart the flavor** of the vegetables or fruits **into the water,** אֶלָּא בִּשְׁבִיל שֶׁגַּם הֵמָּה בְּעַצְמָם יְתוּקְּנוּ עַל יְדֵי הַכְּבִישָׁה — **but rather so that they themselves** (i.e., the fruits or vegetables) **should also become improved through the soaking** (i.e., so that they should become pickled), לָכֵן מְבָרְכִין רַק "שֶׁהַכֹּל" — **therefore, we recite only the *shehakol* blessing** on the liquid. וּמִכָּל מָקוֹם, אִם אָכַל תְּחִלָּה אֶת הַיָּרָק — **However, if one first ate the vegetable** וּבֵירַךְ "בּוֹרֵא פְּרִי הָאֲדָמָה" — **and recited the *borei pri ha'adamah* blessing** on it, וְאַחַר כָּךְ רוֹצֶה לִשְׁתּוֹת גַּם הָרוֹטֶב — **and afterward, he wishes to drink the liquid as well,** יֵשׁ סָפֵק אִם צָרִיךְ לְבָרֵךְ עַל הָרוֹטֶב — **there is a halachic doubt as to whether he is required to recite a blessing on the liquid,** כִּי שֶׁמָּא יָצָא בְּבִרְכַּת "בּוֹרֵא פְּרִי הָאֲדָמָה" גַּם עַל הָרוֹטֶב — **for perhaps he has also exempted** his obligation **on the liquid with the *borei pri ha'adamah* blessing.**[15] לָכֵן לֹא יַעֲשֶׂה כֵּן — **Therefore, one should not do this.**[16]

---

15. Although Kitzur has ruled that one is to recite *shehakol* on the liquid, this is actually based on a halachic doubt, for the proper blessing on the liquid may be *ha'adamah*. Therefore, once one has recited *ha'adamah* on the vegetables, he no longer recites *shehakol* on the liquid, since it may have been exempted with the blessing on the vegetables (see *Machatzis HaShekel* and *Pri Megadim, Mishbetzos Zahav* 202:24).

16. Rather, he should avoid drinking the liquid after eating the vegetable. [Alternatively, he may recite *shehakol* on something else and exempt the liquid with that blessing (see *Mishnah Berurah* 202:54).]

[If one eats the vegetables *together* with the liquid, no additional blessing is required, as the *ha'adamah* blessing recited on the vegetables exempts the liquid as well, since the liquid is subordinate to the vegetables; see above, note 13 (see *Mishnah Berurah* 202:54). In fact, according to *Mishnah Berurah* there, even when one wishes to eat the vegetables and drink the liquid afterward, the *ha'adamah* blessing recited on the vegetables will generally be effective for the broth as well (see *Shaar HaTziyun* there §26).]

235 BROTH AND JUICE OF FRUITS AND VEGETABLES — SIMAN 53:5-6

ה. וְכֵן פֵּירוֹת וִירָקוֹת וְקִטְנִיּוֹת וְכַדּוֹמֶה שֶׁבִּשְּׁלָן בְּמַשְׁקֶה שֶׁיֵּשׁ לָהּ טַעַם בְּעַצְמוּתָהּ, כְּגוֹן בְּחוֹמֶץ אוֹ בְּבארשט אוֹ בְּחָלָב, מְבָרְכִין עַל הָרוֹטֶב "שֶׁהַכֹּל"[17]. וְאִם אָכַל תְּחִלָּה אֶת הַמַּאֲכָל יֵשׁ סָפֵק אִם אֵין הָרוֹטֶב נִפְטָרָה בִּבְרָכָה זֹאת[18].

ו. צִמּוּקִין שֶׁיֵּשׁ בָּהֶן לַחְלוּחִית כָּל כָּךְ שֶׁאִם הָיוּ דוֹרְכִין אוֹתָן יֵצֵא מֵהֶן[19] דִּבְשָׁן, אִם כְּתָשָׁן וְשָׁרָה אוֹתָן בְּמַיִם לְצוֹרֶךְ שְׁתִיָּה, וְלֹא לְצוֹרֶךְ אֲכִילַת הַצִּמּוּקִין, אִם שָׁרוּ ג׳ יָמִים וְתוֹסֵס וּלְאַחַר ג׳ יָמִים עֵירָה מֵהֶם אֶת הַמַּשְׁקֶה לִכְלִי אַחֵר, הֲרֵי מַשְׁקֶה זוֹ יַיִן גָּמוּר מְבָרְכִין עָלָיו "בּוֹרֵא פְּרִי הַגָּפֶן" וּלְאַחֲרָיו בְּרָכָה מֵעֵין שָׁלֹשׁ, וּבְכָל מָקוֹם שֶׁצְּרִיכִין כּוֹס יַיִן יוֹצְאִין בּוֹ[20]. וּצְרִיכִין לִרְאוֹת שֶׁיִּהְיוּ הַצִּמּוּקִין יוֹתֵר מֵחֵלֶק שִׁשִּׁית שֶׁבַּמַּיִם

---

§5 וְכֵן פֵּירוֹת וִירָקוֹת וְקִטְנִיּוֹת וְכַדּוֹמֶה — **Similarly,** with regard to **fruits, vegetables, legumes, and the like** שֶׁבִּשְּׁלָן בְּמַשְׁקֶה — **that one cooked in a liquid** שֶׁיֵּשׁ לָהּ טַעַם בְּעַצְמוּתָהּ — **that has its own flavor,** כְּגוֹן בְּחוֹמֶץ אוֹ בְּבארשט אוֹ בְּחָלָב — **such as** if one cooked these items **in vinegar, in borscht, or in milk,** מְבָרְכִין עַל הָרוֹטֶב "שֶׁהַכֹּל" — the halachah is that **we recite the *shehakol* blessing on the liquid.**[17] וְאִם אָכַל תְּחִלָּה אֶת הַמַּאֲכָל — **But if he first ate the** solid **food** and recited its appropriate blessing, יֵשׁ סָפֵק אִם אֵין הָרוֹטֶב נִפְטָרָה בִּבְרָכָה זֹאת — **there is a halachic doubt as to whether or not the liquid is exempted with this blessing.**[18]

§6 Kitzur now details how raisins may be processed to produce a beverage that is halachically considered wine:

צִמּוּקִין שֶׁיֵּשׁ בָּהֶן לַחְלוּחִית כָּל כָּךְ — **Raisins that have enough moisture** שֶׁאִם הָיוּ דוֹרְכִין אוֹתָן יֵצֵא מֵהֶן דִּבְשָׁן — **that if one were to crush them,**[19] **their "honey,"** i.e., the thick extract of the raisin, **would emerge,** אִם כְּתָשָׁן וְשָׁרָה אוֹתָן בְּמַיִם — **if one** took such raisins and **crushed them and soaked them in water** לְצוֹרֶךְ שְׁתִיָּה, וְלֹא לְצוֹרֶךְ אֲכִילַת הַצִּמּוּקִין — **for the purpose of drinking** the liquid **and not for the sake of eating the raisins,** אִם שָׁרוּ ג׳ יָמִים וְתוֹסֵס — the halachah is that **if they were soaked for three days and they were bubbling** due to fermentation, וּלְאַחַר ג׳ יָמִים עֵירָה מֵהֶם אֶת הַמַּשְׁקֶה לִכְלִי אַחֵר — **and after three days he poured out the juice into a different utensil,** הֲרֵי מַשְׁקֶה זוֹ יַיִן גָּמוּר — **this juice is considered** halachically to be **actual wine;** מְבָרְכִין עָלָיו "בּוֹרֵא פְּרִי הַגָּפֶן" — before drinking it **we recite *borei pri hagafen* on it** וּלְאַחֲרָיו בְּרָכָה מֵעֵין שָׁלֹשׁ — **and after** drinking **it,** we recite **the *Mei'ein Shalosh* blessing** (i.e., *Al HaGefen;* above, 51:7-8). וּבְכָל מָקוֹם שֶׁצְּרִיכִין כּוֹס יַיִן יוֹצְאִין בּוֹ — **And wherever a cup of wine is required** (e.g., *Kiddush, Havdalah*),[20] **we can fulfill** our obligation **with it.** וּצְרִיכִין לִרְאוֹת — **But** when producing this wine, **we must see** to it שֶׁיִּהְיוּ הַצִּמּוּקִין יוֹתֵר מֵחֵלֶק שִׁשִּׁית שֶׁבַּמַּיִם — **that the raisins constitute more than one-sixth** of the volume **of the water** in which they are soaked.

---

17. Since the liquid has a taste of its own, it is to be considered on its own, and the blessing of the vegetables does not play a role in determining its blessing (*Mishnah Berurah* 208:12). Therefore, the blessing of *shehakol*, which is the appropriate blessing for milk (above, 52:2), vinegar (ibid. §13), and borscht (see *Mishnah Berurah* 205:8; cf. *Mishnah Berurah* there §12) is recited.

18. Since there are those who maintain that the proper blessing on the liquid is *ha'adamah* even when it has a taste of its own (see *Shaar HaTziyun* 218:19). See note 16.

19. Without first soaking them (*Mishnah Berurah* 202:59).

20. *Kiddush* and *Havdalah* are recited over a cup of wine at the onset and completion of Shabbos, respectively; below, 77:1.

BROTH AND JUICE OF FRUITS AND VEGETABLES — SIMAN 53:6 236

וּמְשַׁעֲרִין אֶת הַצִּמּוּקִין כְּמוֹ שֶׁהָיוּ בְּלַחוּתָן קוֹדֶם שֶׁנִּתְיַיבְּשׁוּ (עַיֵּין שַׁעֲרֵי תְּשׁוּבָה סִימָן ר״ד סְעִיף ה׳)[21]. וְדַוְקָא כְּשֶׁנַּעֲשָׂה עַל יְדֵי שְׁרִיָּיה כְּמוֹ שֶׁנִּתְבָּאֵר. אֲבָל אִם בִּישֵּׁל הַצִּמּוּקִין בְּמַיִם, אֵינוֹ נַעֲשֶׂה יַיִן עַל יְדֵי הַבִּישּׁוּל[22] (כֵּן כָּתַב בְּסֵפֶר הַחַיִּים וּדְלֹא כְּמוֹ שֶׁכָּתַב בְּסֵפֶר חַיֵּי אָדָם הִלְכוֹת שַׁבָּת כְּלָל ו׳ סְעִיף ז׳)[23]. (וְאִם שָׁרָה אוֹ בִּישֵּׁל אֶת הַצִּמּוּקִין עַל דַּעַת לֶאֱכוֹל גַּם אֶת הַצִּמּוּקִין יֵשׁ כַּמָּה סְפֵיקוֹת בִּבְרָכָה שֶׁעַל הַמַּשְׁקֶה[24].)

וּמְשַׁעֲרִין אֶת הַצִּמּוּקִין — When making this calculation, **the** volume of the **raisins is reckoned** **כְּמוֹ שֶׁהָיוּ בְּלַחוּתָן קוֹדֶם שֶׁנִּתְיַיבְּשׁוּ** — **according to** the size that **they were when they were moist, before they were dried** **(עַיֵּין שַׁעֲרֵי תְּשׁוּבָה סִימָן ר״ד סְעִיף ה׳ — see *Shaarei Teshuvah* to 204:5).**[21]

וְדַוְקָא — **However,** it is considered wine **only** **כְּשֶׁנַּעֲשָׂה עַל יְדֵי שְׁרִיָּיה** — **when it was processed by soaking** the raisins, **כְּמוֹ שֶׁנִּתְבָּאֵר** — **as I have written.** **אֲבָל אִם בִּישֵּׁל הַצִּמּוּקִין בְּמַיִם** — **But if one cooked the raisins in water,** **אֵינוֹ נַעֲשֶׂה יַיִן עַל יְדֵי הַבִּישּׁוּל** — **it does not become wine through this cooking.**[22] **(כֵּן כָּתַב בְּסֵפֶר הַחַיִּים** — **It is thus written in *Sefer HaChaim,*** **וּדְלֹא כְּמוֹ שֶׁכָּתַב בְּסֵפֶר חַיֵּי אָדָם הִלְכוֹת שַׁבָּת כְּלָל ו׳ סְעִיף ז׳** — **and** the halachah is **not as is written in *Sefer Chayei Adam,* Laws of Shabbos 6:7.)**[23]

(וְאִם שָׁרָה אוֹ בִּישֵּׁל אֶת הַצִּמּוּקִין — **If one soaked or cooked the raisins** **עַל דַּעַת לֶאֱכוֹל גַּם אֶת הַצִּמּוּקִין** — **with the intention of eating the raisins** (besides for drinking their juice) **יֵשׁ כַּמָּה סְפֵיקוֹת בִּבְרָכָה שֶׁעַל הַמַּשְׁקֶה** — **there are a number of halachic doubts with regard to the** proper **blessing on the** resulting **beverage.)**[24]

---

21. For further discussion, see *Shulchan Aruch* 272:6, with *Mishnah Berurah* and *Beur Halachah.*

22. Unless it has fermented for three days after being cooked (see *Mishnah Berurah* 272:22).

23. According to *Chayei Adam*, one may cook raisins, strain the wine, and use it [immediately] for *Kiddush*. [The view of *Chayei Adam* is the primary opinion cited by *Mishnah Berurah* (272:22), with the stringent view of *Sefer HaChaim* cited as a dissenting opinion.]

24. See *Shulchan Aruch* 202:11 with *Mishnah Berurah* for a discussion of this case.

237 LAW OF PRIMARY AND SUBORDINATE FOODS — SIMAN 54:1

סימן נד

דִּין עִיקָּר וְטָפֵל

וּבוֹ ט׳ סְעִיפִים

א. אִם אוֹכֵל שְׁנֵי דְבָרִים, אוֹ אוֹכֵל וְשׁוֹתֶה, וְהָאֶחָד עִיקָּר אֶצְלוֹ וְהַשֵּׁנִי הוּא טָפֵל לוֹ שֶׁאֵין כַּוָּונָתוֹ לְאָכְלוֹ אֶלָּא בִּשְׁבִיל הָעִיקָּר וְאִם לֹא הָיָה לוֹ אֶת הָעִיקָּר לֹא הָיָה אוֹכֵל כְּלָל אֶת הַטָּפֵל, כְּגוֹן שֶׁחָלַשׁ לִבּוֹ וּכְדֵי לְחַזֵּק לִבּוֹ אוֹכֵל דָּג מָלִיחַ אוֹ צְנוֹן, אֶלָּא מִפְּנֵי שֶׁהֵם דְּבָרִים חֲרִיפִים אוֹכֵל גַּם מְעַט פַּת אוֹ דָּבָר אַחֵר לְמַתֵּק הַחֲרִיפוּת[1], וְכֵן אִם מִתְאַוֶּה לִשְׁתּוֹת יֵין שָׂרָף וְשׁוֹתֶה וּבִכְדֵי לְמַתֵּק הַחֲרִיפוּת אוֹכֵל אַחֲרָיו מְעַט פַּת אוֹ אֵיזֶה פְּרִי, מְבָרֵךְ רַק עַל הָעִיקָּר וְעַל הַטָּפֵל אֵינוֹ צָרִיךְ לְבָרֵךְ,

---

SIMAN 54

THE LAW OF PRIMARY AND SUBORDINATE FOODS

CONTAINING 9 *SE'IFIM*

§1-4 One Food Eaten as a Result of Another / **§5** Foods Cooked Together / **§6** Solid and Liquid / **§7** Spices With Sugar / **§8** Olive Oil / **§9** Preserves

This *Siman* addresses the halachah with regard to the requirement of a blessing on a food that is being eaten in combination or in conjunction with another food.

§1 **אִם אוֹכֵל שְׁנֵי דְבָרִים — If one is eating two items** of food, **אוֹ אוֹכֵל וְשׁוֹתֶה — or if one is eating** a food **and drinking** a beverage, **וְהָאֶחָד עִיקָּר אֶצְלוֹ — and one of** the two foods **is primary to him** **וְהַשֵּׁנִי הוּא טָפֵל לוֹ — while the second is subordinate to it,** **שֶׁאֵין כַּוָּונָתוֹ לְאָכְלוֹ — such that his purpose in eating** the second food **is not** for its taste or nourishment **אֶלָּא בִּשְׁבִיל הָעִיקָּר — but only due to** his eating of **the primary** food, **וְאִם לֹא הָיָה לוֹ אֶת הָעִיקָּר — and if he would not be** eating **the primary** food **לֹא הָיָה אוֹכֵל כְּלָל אֶת הַטָּפֵל — he would not eat the subordinate one at all;** **כְּגוֹן שֶׁחָלַשׁ לִבּוֹ — for example,** if **he felt weak,** **וּכְדֵי לְחַזֵּק לִבּוֹ — and in order to regain his strength** **אוֹכֵל דָּג מָלִיחַ אוֹ צְנוֹן — he eats salted fish** [e.g., herring] **or radish,** **אֶלָּא מִפְּנֵי שֶׁהֵם דְּבָרִים חֲרִיפִים — but since they are sharp** **אוֹכֵל גַּם מְעַט פַּת אוֹ דָּבָר אַחֵר — he eats a bit of bread, as well, or something else** **לְמַתֵּק הַחֲרִיפוּת — to neutralize the sharpness;**[1] **וְכֵן אִם מִתְאַוֶּה לִשְׁתּוֹת יֵין שָׂרָף — or, similarly, if he desires to drink liquor,** **וְשׁוֹתֶה — and he drinks it,** **וּבִכְדֵי לְמַתֵּק הַחֲרִיפוּת — and in order to neutralize the sharpness,** **אוֹכֵל אַחֲרָיו מְעַט פַּת אוֹ אֵיזֶה פְּרִי — he eats a bit of bread or a fruit afterward,** **מְבָרֵךְ רַק עַל הָעִיקָּר —** the halachah is that **he recites the blessing only on the primary** food (i.e., the fish or the liquor). **וְעַל הַטָּפֵל אֵינוֹ צָרִיךְ לְבָרֵךְ — On**

---

1. According to the understanding of many authorities (cited by *Shaar HaTziyun* 212:9), herring is considered primary with respect to the bread only when one originally ate it in order to regain his strength. If, however, he ate it because he desired to eat herring, the bread would not be subordinate to the herring, and one would be required to wash his hands [and recite *al netilas yadayim;* above, *Siman* 40] and recite the *hamotzi* blessing on the bread, even though he is eating it only because he ate the herring.

לֹא לְפָנָיו וְלֹא לְאַחֲרָיו, כִּי נִפְטָר בִּבְרָכָה שֶׁעַל הָעִיקָר[2]. וְגַם נְטִילַת יָדַיִם אֵינוֹ צָרִיךְ[3].

ב. וְדַוְקָא אִם אוֹכֵל אֶת הָעִיקָר תְּחִלָּה וְאַחַר כָּךְ אֶת הַטָּפֵל[4,5], וּבְשָׁעָה שֶׁבֵּירַךְ עַל הָעִיקָר הָיָה דַעְתּוֹ לֶאֱכוֹל גַּם אֶת הַטָּפֵל, אוֹ שֶׁהוּא רָגִיל בְּכָךְ דְּהָוֵי כְּאִלּוּ הָיְתָה דַעְתּוֹ לְכָךְ[6], וְאוֹכֵל אֶת הַטָּפֵל בְּאוֹתוֹ מַעֲמָד לְאַפּוּקֵי אִם הָלַךְ בֵּינְתַיִם לְחֶדֶר אַחֵר[7], שֶׁאָז צָרִיךְ לְבָרֵךְ גַּם עַל הַטָּפֵל[8].

---

the subordinate food (the bread or fruit), **however, he need not recite a blessing,** **לֹא לְפָנָיו וְלֹא לְאַחֲרָיו** — i.e., **neither beforehand nor afterward,** **כִּי נִפְטָר בִּבְרָכָה שֶׁעַל הָעִיקָר** — **because it is exempted** from its own blessing **with the blessing on the primary** food.[2] **וְגַם נְטִילַת יָדַיִם אֵינוֹ צָרִיךְ** — **Nor is he required to wash *netilas yadayim*** in this case (if the subordinate food is bread).[3]

§2 Kitzur notes a number of conditions necessary for the above rule to apply:

וְדַוְקָא — **But** this applies **only** **אִם אוֹכֵל אֶת הָעִיקָר תְּחִלָּה** — **if he eats the primary** food **first** **וְאַחַר כָּךְ אֶת הַטָּפֵל** — **and then the subordinate** one,[4] and not the other way around.[5]

וּבְשָׁעָה שֶׁבֵּירַךְ עַל הָעִיקָר — Furthermore, it applies only if **at the time that he recited the blessing on the primary** food **הָיָה דַעְתּוֹ לֶאֱכוֹל גַּם אֶת הַטָּפֵל** — **he had in mind to eat the subordinate** food **as well,** **אוֹ שֶׁהוּא רָגִיל בְּכָךְ** — **or he was accustomed to** eat this subordinate food after the primary food, **דְּהָוֵי כְּאִלּוּ הָיְתָה דַעְתּוֹ לְכָךְ** — **which is the equivalent of having this** specifically **in mind.**[6]

וְאוֹכֵל אֶת הַטָּפֵל בְּאוֹתוֹ מַעֲמָד — Third, it applies only when **he eats the subordinate at the same time** that he eats the primary food, **לְאַפּוּקֵי אִם הָלַךְ בֵּינְתַיִם לְחֶדֶר אַחֵר** — **as opposed to** a case **where he went in the interim** (i.e., between eating the primary and subordinate foods) **to another room,**[7] **שֶׁאָז צָרִיךְ לְבָרֵךְ גַּם עַל הַטָּפֵל** — **in which case he must recite a blessing on the subordinate** food **as well.**[8]

---

2. See below, note 11.

If one ate less than a *kezayis* [the volume of an olive (between .6 fl. oz. and 1.1 fl. oz; 17.3 cc.- 33.3 cc.); see Appendix A] of a salty food followed by a *kezayis* of bread to neutralize its sharpness, he recites the *Borei Nefashos* blessing afterward (*Igros Moshe, Orach Chaim* IV, §42). [*Borei Nefashos* is normally recited after eating a *kezayis* of fish; above, 51:1.]

3. According to *Mishnah Berurah* (158:10), one who will be eating a minimum of a *kezayis* of bread should wash his hands to fulfill the obligation of *netilas yadayim*. However, he does not recite the *al netilas yadayim* blessing even if he will eat as much as an egg's volume of bread (which is larger than a *kezayis*). [The laws of *netilas yadayim*, "washing the hands," are set out above, *Siman* 40. Normally, one who will be eating bread must first wash his hands, and, if he will be eating an egg's volume of bread must also recite the blessing of *al netilas yadayim;* ibid, *se'if* 1 (see note 8 there).]

4. And [certainly] if he eats them at the same time (*Rama* 212:1).

5. The case of eating the subordinate food first followed by the primary food is discussed in the following *se'if.*

6. If he did not have in mind to eat the subordinate food, it is not exempted with the blessing on the primary food. *Mishnah Berurah* (212:4) rules that in such a case, one recites the *shehakol* blessing on the subordinate food, regardless of the food's usual blessing; see next *se'if.*

7. This condition is a reference to the halachos governing the requirement to recite a new blessing when one changes his place after reciting a blessing (see *Mishnah Berurah* 212:4). These halachos have been detailed above, 50:13-16. See note s 51-53 there for *Mishnah Berurah's* position on this matter.

8. See above, note 6.

ג. וְכֵן אִם אוֹכֵל מִתְּחִלָּה אֶת הַטָּפֵל וְאַחַר כָּךְ אֶת הָעִיקָּר, כְּגוֹן שֶׁרוֹצֶה לִשְׁתּוֹת יַיִן אוֹ יַיִן שָׂרָף וּכְדֵי שֶׁלֹּא לִשְׁתּוֹת אַלִּיבָּא רֵיקָנָא אוֹכֵל תְּחִלָּה אֵיזֶה דָּבָר קָטָן, צָרִיךְ לְבָרֵךְ גַּם עַל הַטָּפֵל. אָמְנָם כֵּיוָן שֶׁהוּא רַק טָפֵל עַתָּה, יֵשׁ אוֹמְרִים דְּיָרַד מִבִּרְכָתוֹ וְאֵין מְבָרְכִין עָלָיו (רַק) "שֶׁהַכֹּל"[9], וְיֵשׁ חוֹלְקִין[10]. וּלְהוֹצִיא אֶת עַצְמוֹ מִידֵי סְפֵיקָא יִשְׁתֶּה תְּחִלָּה קְצָת מִן הָעִיקָּר וִיבָרֵךְ עָלָיו לִפְטוֹר אֶת הַטָּפֵל.

ד. אִם כַּוָּנָתוֹ לִשְׁנֵיהֶם, כְּגוֹן שֶׁהוּא שׁוֹתֶה יַיִן שָׂרָף וְאוֹכֵל גַּם מִינֵי כִּיסְנִין וְדוּבְשָׁנִין (האניג קוכען), אוֹ מִרְקַחַת וְכַדּוֹמֶה, צָרִיךְ לְבָרֵךְ עַל שְׁנֵיהֶם[11]. וִיבָרֵךְ תְּחִלָּה עַל

---

§3 Kitzur addresses the first condition of the previous *se'if*:

וְכֵן אִם אוֹכֵל מִתְּחִלָּה אֶת הַטָּפֵל — Similarly, if the first condition was not satisfied, and **he first eats the subordinate** **וְאַחַר כָּךְ אֶת הָעִיקָּר — and afterward,** he eats **the primary;** **כְּגוֹן — for example,** **שֶׁרוֹצֶה לִשְׁתּוֹת יַיִן אוֹ יַיִן שָׂרָף — if he wishes to drink wine or liquor,** **וּכְדֵי שֶׁלֹּא לִשְׁתּוֹת אַלִּיבָּא רֵיקָנָא — and in order not to drink on an empty stomach** [literally, *empty heart*] **אוֹכֵל תְּחִלָּה אֵיזֶה דָּבָר קָטָן — he first eats a small amount** of food, **צָרִיךְ לְבָרֵךְ גַּם עַל הַטָּפֵל —** in this case **he must also recite a blessing on the subordinate** food. **אָמְנָם —** Now, even though the food that he is eating so that he should not be drinking on an empty stomach requires its own blessing, **nevertheless,** **כֵּיוָן שֶׁהוּא רַק טָפֵל עַתָּה — since now** that food **is merely subordinate** to the drink, **יֵשׁ אוֹמְרִים דְּיָרַד מִבִּרְכָתוֹ —** some authorities **say that it descends from** its regular status with regard to **its blessing,** **וְאֵין מְבָרְכִין עָלָיו (רַק) "שֶׁהַכֹּל" — and we recite only the *shehakol* blessing on it.**[9] **וְיֵשׁ חוֹלְקִין — There are, however, those** authorities **who dispute** this ruling, and maintain that the subordinate retains its standard blessing.[10] **וּלְהוֹצִיא אֶת עַצְמוֹ מִידֵי סְפֵיקָא — In order to remove oneself from** a situation of **doubt,** **יִשְׁתֶּה תְּחִלָּה קְצָת מִן הָעִיקָּר — one should first drink some of the primary** (i.e., the wine or liquor), **וִיבָרֵךְ עָלָיו — and recite a blessing on it** **לִפְטוֹר אֶת הַטָּפֵל — in order to exempt the subordinate,** for when the primary food is eaten first, no blessing is required on the subordinate food.

§4 **אִם כַּוָּנָתוֹ לִשְׁנֵיהֶם — If,** when eating two foods, **his intention is** not solely for one of them, with the other being purely subordinate, but rather he wants **to** eat **both of them,** **כְּגוֹן — for example,** **שֶׁהוּא שׁוֹתֶה יַיִן שָׂרָף — he is drinking liquor** **וְאוֹכֵל גַּם מִינֵי כִּיסְנִין — and also eating types of filled pastries,** **וְדוּבְשָׁנִין (האניג קוכען) — honey cakes,** **אוֹ מִרְקַחַת וְכַדּוֹמֶה — preserves, or the like,** **צָרִיךְ לְבָרֵךְ עַל שְׁנֵיהֶם — he must recite a blessing on both.**[11] **וִיבָרֵךְ תְּחִלָּה עַל**

---

9. Although the blessing on the primary food covers the subordinate food when one eats subordinate food afterward, nevertheless, when he eats the subordinate food first, the blessing recited afterward on the primary food cannot exempt what he ate previously. Thus, since one may not partake of a food without reciting a blessing (see above, 50:1), a blessing must be recited when partaking of the subordinate food (*Mishnah Berurah* 212:9). Nonetheless, since the food is not being eaten for its own sake, its standard blessing is not appropriate. Therefore, he recites the all-encompassing blessing, שֶׁהַכֹּל נִהְיָה בִּדְבָרוֹ, *through Whose word everything came to be*; above, 50:2 (see *Mishnah Berurah* 212:10 and *Beur Halachah* 212:1 s.v. ואינו מברך).

10. See *Mishnah Berurah* 212:10 with *Shaar HaTziyun* §24.

11. In this case, he must recite the blessing on the pastries because he is eating them for their own sake as well. Similarly, one who eats bread after liquor in order to neutralize its

LAW OF PRIMARY AND SUBORDINATE FOODS — SIMAN 54:5 — 240

הַכִּיסָנִין, אוֹ עַל הַמִּרְקַחַת, שֶׁהֵם חֲשׁוּבִים, וְאַחַר כָּךְ מְבָרֵךְ עַל הַיַּיִן שָׂרָף[12]. וּמִכָּל
שֶׁכֵּן אִם אוֹכֵל פַּת כִּיסָנִין וְשׁוֹתֶה גַם כֵּן קָאפֶע, שֶׁצָּרִיךְ לְבָרֵךְ עַל שְׁנֵיהֶם, דְּהַיְינוּ
תְּחִלָּה עַל הַפַּת כִּיסָנִין וְאַחַר כָּךְ עַל הַקָּאפֶע, שֶׁהֲרֵי כַּוָּנָתוֹ לִשְׁנֵיהֶם[13].

ה. שְׁנֵי מִינִים שֶׁנִּתְבַּשְּׁלוּ יַחַד, אִם כָּל מִין מוּבְדָּל לְעַצְמוֹ, מְבָרֵךְ עַל כָּל מִין בִּפְנֵי
עַצְמוֹ בְּרָכָה הָרְאוּיָה לוֹ[14]. אֲבָל אִם נִתְמַעֲכוּ וְנִתְדַּבְּקוּ, אֲזַי אַזְלִינַן בָּתַר רוּבָּא

הַכִּיסָנִין, אוֹ עַל הַמִּרְקַחַת — He should first recite the blessing on the pastries or preserves, שֶׁהֵם חֲשׁוּבִים — for they are more significant, וְאַחַר כָּךְ מְבָרֵךְ עַל הַיַּיִן שָׂרָף — and afterward recite the blessing on the liquor.[12] וּמִכָּל שֶׁכֵּן אִם אוֹכֵל פַּת כִּיסָנִין — And certainly if he is eating pastries וְשׁוֹתֶה גַם כֵּן קָאפֶע — and also drinking coffee, שֶׁצָּרִיךְ לְבָרֵךְ עַל שְׁנֵיהֶם — the halachah is that he must recite a blessing on both. דְּהַיְינוּ תְּחִלָּה עַל הַפַּת כִּיסָנִין — That is, first *mezonos* on the pastries, וְאַחַר כָּךְ עַל הַקָּאפֶע — and afterward *shehakol* on the coffee, שֶׁהֲרֵי כַּוָּנָתוֹ לִשְׁנֵיהֶם — for his intention is for both.[13]

§5 Thus far, Kitzur has discussed the halachos of the primary food exempting the subordinate food when one food is being eaten as a result of the other. Kitzur now goes on to discuss the halachos of primary and subordinate foods as they apply to a *mixture* of two foods.

שְׁנֵי מִינִים שֶׁנִּתְבַּשְּׁלוּ יַחַד — The rule regarding **two types** of food **that were cooked together** is: אִם כָּל מִין מוּבְדָּל לְעַצְמוֹ — **If each type** of food **is distinguishable** within the mixture, מְבָרֵךְ עַל כָּל מִין בִּפְנֵי עַצְמוֹ בְּרָכָה הָרְאוּיָה לוֹ — **one recites on each type** of food **its appropriate blessing.**[14] אֲבָל אִם נִתְמַעֲכוּ וְנִתְדַּבְּקוּ — **However, if they were mashed and became stuck together,** אֲזַי אַזְלִינַן בָּתַר רוּבָּא — **we then**

---

effect is exempt from reciting a blessing on the bread only if he is not hungry, and is eating the minimal amount necessary in order to neutralize the effect of the liquor. Otherwise, it cannot be considered subordinate, and a separate blessing is required. Since ascertaining one's ultimate intention is often not a simple matter, halachic authorities advise that, in order to avoid questions of a possible requirement of reciting the *al netilas yadayim* and *hamotzi* blessings, one should avoid eating bread for the purpose of neutralizing the effect of liquor (see *Mishnah Berurah* 212:5 with *Shaar Ha-Tziyun* §19).

12. This is based on the order of precedence of blessings set forth in the next *Siman*. [The blessing should be recited first on the pastries or preserves even if the liquor is more desirable to him (*Mishnah Berurah* 211:16; see *Beur Halachah* 211:3 s.v. וכן).]

13. See Appendix of Kitzur's editorial glosses.

Kitzur is discussing a case in which one drinks the coffee and eats the pastry separately. According to *Mishnah Berurah* (168:65),

even if one eats the pastry and coffee together by dipping the pastry into coffee, a separate blessing should be recited on each one. In order to avoid all halachic questions in such a case, *Mishnah Berurah* suggests that one first recite the *mezonos* blessing on the pastry (without dipping it), and then recite the *shehakol* blessing upon some sugar and taste a bit of sugar by itself. In this way, the coffee is exempted by the *shehakol* blessing recited upon the sugar.

14. This is the opinion of *Chayei Adam* (51:13). *Mishnah Berurah* (212:1), however, rules that when two distinct types of food are mixed together on the plate and both are significant (see next note), one recites only the blessing on the food that constitutes the majority. *Mishnah Berurah* (*Beur Halachah* 212:1 s.v. אם) advises that one who wishes to be stringent, and act in compliance with the opinion of *Chayei Adam* as well, should mash the minority food and mix it with the majority food; he may then recite the blessing of the majority food and eat them both together, as Kitzur rules below.

וּמַה שֶּׁהוּא הָרוֹב זֶהוּ עִיקָּר וּמְבָרְכִין עָלָיו וְהַשֵּׁנִי נִפְטָר[15]. אַךְ אִם אֶחָד הוּא מֵחֲמֵשֶׁת מִינֵי דָגָן, אַף עַל פִּי שֶׁהוּא הַמִּיעוּט, הוּא הָעִיקָּר, כְּמוֹ שֶׁנִּתְבָּאֵר בְּסִימָן מ״ח סְעִיף י׳, עַיֵּין שָׁם[16].

ו. מַאֲכָל שֶׁנָּתַן לְתוֹכוֹ חָלָב אוֹ מָרָק לְאָכְלָם בְּיַחַד, אִם עִיקַּר כַּוָּנָתוֹ הַמַּאֲכָל, אֲזַי מְבָרֵךְ רַק עָלָיו וְהֶחָלָב אוֹ הַמָּרָק טְפֵלִים. וְאִם כַּוָּנָתוֹ רַק עַל הַמָּרָק וְהֶחָלָב, מְבָרֵךְ עֲלֵיהֶם וְהַמַּאֲכָל הוּא טָפֵל. וְאִם כַּוָּנָתוֹ עַל שְׁנֵיהֶם (וְאֵין בִּרְכוֹתֵיהֶן שָׁווֹת), מְבָרֵךְ תְּחִלָּה עַל הַמַּאֲכָל וְאוֹכֵל מִמֶּנּוּ מְעַט, וְאַחַר כָּךְ מְבָרֵךְ ״שֶׁהַכֹּל״ עַל הַמָּרָק אוֹ עַל הֶחָלָב. וְאֵין הוֹלְכִין בָּזֶה אַחַר הָרוֹב[17]. וַאֲפִילוּ אִם הַמַּאֲכָל הוּא מִין דָּגָן[18],

---

follow the majority, **וּמַה שֶּׁהוּא הָרוֹב זֶהוּ עִיקָּר** — **and that which is the majority is** considered the **primary;** **וּמְבָרְכִין עָלָיו** — **thus, we recite the blessing upon it,** **וְהַשֵּׁנִי נִפְטָר** — **and the other,** minority food, **is exempted.**[15]

אַךְ אִם אֶחָד הוּא מֵחֲמֵשֶׁת מִינֵי דָגָן — **However, if one** of the foods **is one of the five species of grain,** **אַף עַל פִּי שֶׁהוּא הַמִּיעוּט, הוּא הָעִיקָּר** — **even if it is the minority** food in the mixture, **it is** nevertheless considered **the primary** food of the mixture, **כְּמוֹ שֶׁנִּתְבָּאֵר בְּסִימָן מ״ח סְעִיף י׳** — **as I have explained in** ***Siman*** **48,** ***se'if*** **10;** **עַיֵּין שָׁם** — **see there.**[16]

§6 **מַאֲכָל שֶׁנָּתַן לְתוֹכוֹ חָלָב אוֹ מָרָק לְאָכְלָם בְּיַחַד** — The halachah regarding **a solid food into which one mixed milk or broth in order to eat them together** is: **אִם עִיקַּר כַּוָּנָתוֹ הַמַּאֲכָל** — **If his primary intent is** to eat **the** solid **food,** **אֲזַי מְבָרֵךְ רַק עָלָיו** — **then he recites a blessing only on** the solid, **וְהֶחָלָב אוֹ הַמָּרָק טְפֵלִים** — **and the milk or broth is** considered **subordinate,** and thus exempt from a blessing. **וְאִם כַּוָּנָתוֹ רַק עַל הַמָּרָק וְהֶחָלָב** — **If, however, his intent was only for the broth or the milk,** **מְבָרֵךְ עֲלֵיהֶם** — **he recites the** appropriate **blessing on** the broth or the milk, **וְהַמַּאֲכָל הוּא טָפֵל** — **and the** solid **food is subordinate** and exempt from a blessing. **וְאִם כַּוָּנָתוֹ עַל שְׁנֵיהֶם** — **And if his intention was** to eat **both** **(וְאֵין בִּרְכוֹתֵיהֶן שָׁווֹת** — **and their blessings are not the same),** **מְבָרֵךְ תְּחִלָּה עַל הַמַּאֲכָל וְאוֹכֵל מִמֶּנּוּ מְעַט** — **he first recites the blessing on the** solid **food and eats a bit of it,** **וְאַחַר כָּךְ מְבָרֵךְ ״שֶׁהַכֹּל״ עַל הַמָּרָק אוֹ עַל הֶחָלָב** — **and afterward he recites the** ***shehakol*** **blessing on the broth or on the milk.** **וְאֵין הוֹלְכִין בָּזֶה אַחַר הָרוֹב** — **Our** determination of the proper procedure **in this case does not follow the** status of the **majority** of the food.[17] **וַאֲפִילוּ אִם הַמַּאֲכָל הוּא מִין דָּגָן** — **And even if the** solid **food is a type of grain,**[18]

---

15. *Mishnah Berurah* (212:1) rules that if one of them is significant and the other one is not [see there for particulars], only the blessing of the significant ingredient is recited, even if it constitutes a minority of the mixture (see also *Beur Halachah* 212:1 s.v. אם).

16. Kitzur explains there that due to its inherent importance, a product of the five species of grain (wheat, barley, oats, spelt, and rye) is considered primary in a mixture even if it constitutes only a minority of the mixture, provided that it was added for flavor. Therefore, according to Kitzur, if the two types are mashed together (and according to *Mishnah Berurah,* cited in note 14, even if they are separate), one recites only *borei minei mezonos,* regardless of the amount of grain. See Kitzur there and *Mishnah Berurah* 212:1 for further discussion; see also *Shulchan Aruch* 208:3 and 208:6 with *Mishnah Berurah.*

17. I.e., unlike two solid foods that were blended together, regarding which Kitzur ruled in the previous *se'if* that one recites the blessing on the one that is the majority, with regard to mixtures of liquids and solids the rule is different.

18. Which is normally considered primary in a

אֵינוֹ נֶחְשָׁב עִיקָּר לְעִנְיָן זֶה[19]. (וּמַאֲכָל שֶׁנִּתְבַּשֵּׁל בְּמַיִם אוֹ בְחָלָב — עַיֵּין לְעֵיל סִימָן מ"ח וְסִימָן נ"ג.)

ז. בְּשָׂמִים שְׁחוּקִים שֶׁעֵירְבָן עִם צוּקֶר[20] — הַבְּשָׂמִים הֵם הָעִיקָּר וּמְבָרְכִין עֲלֵיהֶם בְּרָכָה הָרְאוּיָה לָהֶן[21]. עַל אֱגוֹז מִישְׁקַאט — "בּוֹרֵא פְּרִי [הָ]עֵץ". עַל צִימְרִינְד — "בּוֹרֵא פְּרִי הָאֲדָמָה". וְכֵן עַל זַנְגְּבִיל (אוּנְגְבֶער) — "בּוֹרֵא פְּרִי הָאֲדָמָה".

אֵינוֹ נֶחְשָׁב עִיקָּר לְעִנְיָן זֶה — it is not considered primary in this case.[19] (**וּמַאֲכָל שֶׁנִּתְבַּשֵּׁל בְּמַיִם אוֹ בְחָלָב** — Regarding **a food that was cooked in water or milk,** **עַיֵּין לְעֵיל סִימָן מ"ח וְסִימָן נ"ג — see above, *Siman* 48** *se'if* 10 **and *Siman* 53** *se'ifim* 2,3, and 5.)

§7 Kitzur now discusses cases in which a secondary ingredient is added to enhance the flavor of, or negate a detrimental effect of, the primary food:

בְּשָׂמִים שְׁחוּקִים שֶׁעֵירְבָן עִם צוּקֶר — Regarding **ground spices**[20] **that were mixed with sugar, הַבְּשָׂמִים הֵם הָעִיקָּר — the spices are** considered the **primary** **וּמְבָרְכִין עֲלֵיהֶם בְּרָכָה הָרְאוּיָה לָהֶן — and we recite upon** the spices that have been mixed with sugar **their appropriate blessing,**[21] as follows: **עַל אֱגוֹז מִישְׁקַאט — On nutmeg, "בּוֹרֵא פְּרִי [הָ]עֵץ"** — the blessing is *borei pri ha'eitz,* ***Who creates the fruit of the tree;*** **עַל צִימְרִינְד — on cinnamon, "בּוֹרֵא פְּרִי הָאֲדָמָה"** — *borei pri ha'adamah,* ***Who creates the fruit of the ground;*** **וְכֵן עַל זַנְגְּבִיל (אוּנְגְבֶער) — on ginger, as well, "בּוֹרֵא פְּרִי הָאֲדָמָה"** — the blessing is ***borei pri ha'adamah.***

---

mixture, regardless of amount (see previous *se'if* and note 16).

19. Rabbi Moshe Feinstein rules that one who eats dry breakfast cereal together with milk recites a blessing only on the cereal (even if he is thirsty and derives pleasure from the milk as well). However, if he adds significantly more milk than the amount normally eaten with the cereal, he must also recite a blessing on the milk even if he is not thirsty, since he derives pleasure from the milk and it is clearly noticeable on its own. Pieces of fruit that were added to the cereal (such as sliced banana) are always considered independent and require a separate blessing. One does not recite a separate blessing on sugar that he adds to the cereal, as it is always considered subordinate to the rest (*Igros Moshe, Orach Chaim* IV, §43; see below, note 21).

If one eats chicken soup with matzah balls (that are made of one of the five species of grain), he recites the *mezonos* blessing on the matzah balls and does not need to recite a separate blessing on the soup. If, however, he eats the soup separately, a *shehakol* would be required. To avoid any question, it is best to eat a bit of matzah ball along with each spoonful of soup, and recite only a *mezonos* (*Igros Moshe* ibid.).

20. Even if they have been so finely ground that their original form is totally lost (*Mishnah Berurah* 203:12).

21. When one food is added to another in order to enhance its taste, the main food is considered primary and the added ingredient subordinate. Even if the mixture contains more sugar than spices, the spices are nevertheless primary, since the sugar serves only to sweeten the mixture (*Mishnah Berurah* 203:13).

If one eats a cracker with cheese or another spread, the cracker is considered primary and the spread is subordinate even if he desires the spread as well. Unlike one who eats a pastry after liquor both to neutralize its effect and for the sake of the pastry (in which case two blessings are required; see above, note 11), in this case, where the added food is being eaten together with the primary food as an accompaniment to the primary food, no blessing is required even if he also desires the added ingredient (*Mishnah Berurah* 212:6; see *Shaar HaTziyun* §20-21). See above, *Siman* 48, note 67.

ח. הַשּׁוֹתֶה שֶׁמֶן זַיִת כְּמוֹ שֶׁהוּא אֵינוֹ מְבָרֵךְ עָלָיו כְּלָל, מִפְּנֵי שֶׁהוּא מַזִּיק לוֹ. וְאִם עֵירְבוֹ עִם שְׁאָר דְּבָרִים, הוּא הַטָּפֵל וּמְבָרֵךְ רַק עַל הָעִיקָּר. אַךְ אִם יֵשׁ לוֹ אֵיזֶה מֵיחוּשׁ שֶׁהוּא צָרִיךְ אֶת הַשֶּׁמֶן לִרְפוּאָה וּבִכְדֵי שֶׁלֹּא יַזִּיק לוֹ הוּא מְעָרְבוֹ בִּשְׁאָר דָּבָר, מֵאַחַר שֶׁעִיקַּר כַּוָּונָתוֹ עַל הַשֶּׁמֶן, אַף עַל פִּי שֶׁהוּא הַמּוּעָט, מְבָרֵךְ עָלָיו בִּרְכָתוֹ, שֶׁהִיא "בּוֹרֵא פְּרִי הָעֵץ", וּפוֹטֵר אֶת הַדָּבָר אַחֵר[22]. וְאִם הוּא צָמֵא וְעִיקַּר כַּוָּונָתוֹ לִשְׁתּוֹת לִצְמָאוֹ, אֶלָּא שֶׁאַגַּב הוּא נוֹתֵן בּוֹ שֶׁמֶן לִרְפוּאָה, מְבָרֵךְ רַק עַל הַמַּשְׁקֶה. וְכֵן הַדִּין אִם נוֹתֵן לְתוֹךְ הַמַּשְׁקֶה אֱגוֹז מוּשְׁקַאט אוֹ צִימְרִינְד אוֹ אוּנְגְבֶר, דְּאַזְלִינַן אַחַר הַכַּוָּונָה[23].

ט. כָּל[24] מִינֵי מִרְקַחַת, הַדְּבַשׁ וְהַצּוּקֶער הֵן טְפֵלִים וּמְבָרְכִים עַל עִיקַּר הַפְּרִי

---

§8 **הַשּׁוֹתֶה שֶׁמֶן זַיִת כְּמוֹ שֶׁהוּא — One who drinks olive oil as is** (i.e., not mixed with other food) **אֵינוֹ מְבָרֵךְ עָלָיו כְּלָל — recites no blessing on it at all,** **מִפְּנֵי שֶׁהוּא מַזִּיק לוֹ — because it has a harmful effect on him** when consumed on its own; **וְאִם עֵירְבוֹ עִם שְׁאָר דְּבָרִים — but if he mixed it with other things** **הוּא הַטָּפֵל — it is** considered **subordinate,** **וּמְבָרֵךְ רַק עַל הָעִיקָּר — and one recites the blessing only on the primary** food with which it is mixed. **אַךְ אִם יֵשׁ לוֹ אֵיזֶה מֵיחוּשׁ — However, if one is suffering from an ailment** **שֶׁהוּא צָרִיךְ אֶת הַשֶּׁמֶן לִרְפוּאָה — for which he requires the olive oil for medicinal purposes,** **וּבִכְדֵי שֶׁלֹּא יַזִּיק לוֹ — and in order that** the olive oil **should not harm him,** **הוּא מְעָרְבוֹ בִּשְׁאָר דָּבָר — he mixes it with something else** (i.e., a beverage), **מֵאַחַר שֶׁעִיקַּר כַּוָּונָתוֹ עַל הַשֶּׁמֶן —** in this case, **since his primary intention is for the oil,** **אַף עַל פִּי שֶׁהוּא הַמּוּעָט — even though it constitutes the minority** of the mixture, **מְבָרֵךְ עָלָיו בִּרְכָתוֹ — he recites on it its** appropriate **blessing,** **שֶׁהִיא "בּוֹרֵא פְּרִי הָעֵץ" — which is** ***borei pri ha'eitz*** (see above, 53:1), **וּפוֹטֵר אֶת הַדָּבָר אַחֵר — and it exempts the other item with** which it was mixed.[22] **וְאִם הוּא צָמֵא — However, if one is thirsty,** **וְעִיקַּר כַּוָּונָתוֹ לִשְׁתּוֹת לִצְמָאוֹ — and his primary intention** in drinking the beverage **is to quench his thirst** **אֶלָּא שֶׁאַגַּב הוּא נוֹתֵן בּוֹ שֶׁמֶן לִרְפוּאָה — and only incidentally does he add oil into** the beverage **for medicinal purposes,** **מְבָרֵךְ רַק עַל הַמַּשְׁקֶה — he recites only the blessing on the beverage** into which it was mixed. **וְכֵן הַדִּין אִם נוֹתֵן לְתוֹךְ הַמַּשְׁקֶה — The same applies if he adds to a beverage** **אֱגוֹז מוּשְׁקַאט אוֹ צִימְרִינְד אוֹ אוּנְגְבֶר — nutmeg, cinnamon, or ginger,** **דְּאַזְלִינַן אַחַר הַכַּוָּונָה —** i.e., **that we follow the intention** of the one who is drinking it when determining the appropriate blessing.[23]

§9 Kitzur addresses the proper blessing to be recited upon foods that were preserved in sugar or honey:[24]

כָּל מִינֵי מִרְקַחַת — In all types of preserves, **הַדְּבַשׁ וְהַצּוּקֶער הֵן טְפֵלִים — the honey and sugar are** considered **subordinate,** **וּמְבָרְכִים עַל עִיקַּר הַפְּרִי — and we** therefore

---

22. Likewise, if one drinks olive oil for medicinal purposes and eats a bit of bread together with it to avoid the detrimental effect of the olive oil, the blessing on the oil exempts the bread (*Igros Moshe, Orach Chaim* I, §58).

23. E.g., if one mixes nutmeg into a beverage for use as an anti-diarrhea agent, its blessing depends upon whether he is drinking it because he is thirsty or for its therapeutic benefit (*Mishnah Berurah* 202:80; see there for further discussion).

24. See above, 46:30, for a description of the process.

בִּרְכָתוֹ הָרְאוּיָה לוֹ, וְעַיֵּין לְעֵיל סִימָן נ״ב.

recite on the actual fruit, and not on the other ingredients, **בִּרְכָתוֹ הָרְאוּיָה לוֹ** — **its appropriate blessing; וְעַיֵּין לְעֵיל סִימָן נ״ב — see above, *Siman* 52.**[25]

25. As explained in *se'if* 9 there, the blessing is dependent on whether the preserves were made with fruit or with other parts of the plant, such as leaves or peels.

245 LAW OF PRECEDENCE OF BLESSINGS — SIMAN 55:1

סימן נה

דִּין קְדִימָה בִּבְרָכוֹת

וּבוֹ ה׳ סְעִיפִים

א. מִי שֶׁיֵּשׁ לְפָנָיו מִינֵי פֵּירוֹת הַרְבֵּה וְהוּא רוֹצֶה לֶאֱכוֹל מִכּוּלָּם[1], אִם בִּרְכוֹתֵיהֶן שָׁווֹת[2], יְבָרֵךְ עַל זֶה שֶׁהוּא חָבִיב לוֹ וְחָפֵץ בּוֹ יוֹתֵר[3], וְאִם שְׁנֵיהֶם שָׁוִים לוֹ בַּחֲבִיבוּת, אֲזַי אִם יֵשׁ בֵּינֵיהֶם מִמִּין שִׁבְעָה שֶׁנִּשְׁתַּבְּחָה בָּהֶן אֶרֶץ יִשְׂרָאֵל (עַיֵּין לְעֵיל סִימָן נ״א

SIMAN 55

THE LAW OF PRECEDENCE OF BLESSINGS

CONTAINING 5 *SE'IFIM*

§1 Different Types of Fruits / §2-3 The Seven Species / §4 *Ha'eitz, Ha'adamah* and *Shehakol* / §5 *Mezonos, Hamotzi* and *Hagafen*

When one has various foods before him that are all subject to the same blessing, the blessing is recited on only one of the foods and the others are exempted with that blessing (see above, 50:11). In order to give the blessing its proper respect, one should recite the blessing on the most significant and best-liked food (see *Chayei Adam* 57:1). This *Siman* addresses how to determine upon which food the blessing is to be recited, as well as the proper order of blessings when one has various foods before him that are subject to different blessings.

§1 מִי שֶׁיֵּשׁ לְפָנָיו מִינֵי פֵּירוֹת הַרְבֵּה — The order of precedence with regard to the recital of the blessing for **one who has before him many** different **types of produce** (i.e., fruits and vegetables), וְהוּא רוֹצֶה לֶאֱכוֹל מִכּוּלָּם — **and wishes to partake of all of them,**[1] is as follows: אִם בִּרְכוֹתֵיהֶן שָׁווֹת — **If their blessings are the same** (i.e., they all require the blessing of *borei pri ha'eitz,* "Who creates the fruit of the tree," or all require the blessing of *borei pri ha'adamah,* "Who creates the fruit of the ground"),[2] in which case the blessing is recited upon one item to exempt the rest, יְבָרֵךְ עַל זֶה שֶׁהוּא חָבִיב לוֹ וְחָפֵץ בּוֹ יוֹתֵר — **he recites the blessing on the one that he likes and desires the most.**[3] וְאִם שְׁנֵיהֶם שָׁוִים לוֹ בַּחֲבִיבוּת — **If he likes two of them equally,** אֲזַי אִם יֵשׁ בֵּינֵיהֶם מִמִּין שִׁבְעָה שֶׁנִּשְׁתַּבְּחָה בָּהֶן אֶרֶץ יִשְׂרָאֵל — **then, if among them there is a fruit of the Seven Species for which Eretz Yisrael is praised** (עַיֵּין לְעֵיל סִימָן נ״א

1. If, however, he plans to eat only one type of fruit, or if there is currently only one type of fruit before him [even if another type will be brought in afterward], he simply recites the blessing on that fruit (*Rama* 211:5, *Mishnah Berurah* 211:1,31).

2. The halachos of these blessings are set out above, *Siman* 52.

3. [See Appendix of Kitzur's editorial glosses.] According to *Mishnah Berurah* (211:6,35), the fruit that he *usually* prefers is considered favored even if he presently desires a different one. Thus, one who wishes to eat an apple and an orange and usually prefers apples over oranges, but now desires the orange, should recite the blessing and eat a small amount of the apple. He may then eat the orange, and afterward finish the apple (*Mishnah Berurah* 211:10; see also ibid. §11 and *Beur Halachah* 211:1 s.v. וי״א).

סְעִיף ז׳)[4], יְבָרֵךְ עַל זֶה, אַף עַל פִּי שֶׁאֵינוֹ אֶלָּא חֲצִי פְּרִי וְהַשְּׁאָר הֵן שְׁלֵימוֹת. וְאִם אֵין בֵּינֵיהֶם מִמִּין שִׁבְעָה, אִם אֶחָד שָׁלֵם וְאֶחָד אֵינוֹ שָׁלֵם, שָׁלֵם עָדִיף[5]. וְכֵן אִם אֵין בִּרְכוֹתֵיהֶן שָׁווֹת, אֶלָּא שֶׁאֶחָד בִּרְכָתוֹ "בּוֹרֵא פְּרִי הָעֵץ" וְאֶחָד בִּרְכָתוֹ "בּוֹרֵא פְּרִי הָאֲדָמָה", שֶׁצָּרִיךְ לְבָרֵךְ עַל שְׁנֵיהֶם, אִם הָאֶחָד חָבִיב עָלָיו יְבָרֵךְ תְּחִלָּה עַל הֶחָבִיב[6], וְאִם שְׁנֵיהֶם שָׁוִים לוֹ, יְבָרֵךְ תְּחִלָּה עַל זֶה שֶׁהוּא מִמִּין שִׁבְעָה, אֲפִילוּ הוּא חֲצִי. וְאִם אֵין בֵּינֵיהֶם מִמִּין שִׁבְעָה, שָׁלֵם עָדִיף. וְאִם שְׁנֵיהֶם שְׁלֵמִים אוֹ שְׁנֵיהֶם חֲסֵרִים, יַקְדִּים "בּוֹרֵא פְּרִי הָעֵץ" לְ"בוֹרֵא פְּרִי הָאֲדָמָה"[7].

סְעִיף ז׳ — see above, *Siman* **51**, *se'if* **7** for a list of the Seven Species),[4] **יְבָרֵךְ עַל זֶה** — **he should recite the blessing on that one,** **אַף עַל פִּי שֶׁאֵינוֹ אֶלָּא חֲצִי פְּרִי** — **even** if that one **is only half of a fruit** **וְהַשְּׁאָר הֵן שְׁלֵימוֹת** — **and the others are whole.** **וְאִם אֵין בֵּינֵיהֶם מִמִּין שִׁבְעָה** — **And if there are none of the Seven Species among them,** **אִם אֶחָד שָׁלֵם** — **if one** fruit **is whole** **וְאֶחָד אֵינוֹ שָׁלֵם** — **and the** other **one is not whole,** **שָׁלֵם עָדִיף** — the **whole** fruit **is** given **priority,** and he should recite the blessing over that one.[5]

וְכֵן אִם אֵין בִּרְכוֹתֵיהֶן שָׁווֹת — **The same** applies **if their blessings are not the same,** **אֶלָּא שֶׁאֶחָד בִּרְכָתוֹ "בּוֹרֵא פְּרִי הָעֵץ"** — **but, rather, the blessing for one is** ***borei pri ha'eitz,*** **וְאֶחָד בִּרְכָתוֹ "בּוֹרֵא פְּרִי הָאֲדָמָה"** — **and the blessing for** the other **one is** ***borei pri ha'adamah,*** **שֶׁצָּרִיךְ לְבָרֵךְ עַל שְׁנֵיהֶם** — **in which case he is required to recite a blessing on both;** the same guidelines are followed in order to determine which blessing is to be recited first, as follows: **אִם הָאֶחָד חָבִיב עָלָיו** — **If he likes one** more, **יְבָרֵךְ תְּחִלָּה עַל הֶחָבִיב** — **he should first recite a blessing on the one that he likes.**[6] **וְאִם שְׁנֵיהֶם שָׁוִים לוֹ** — **If he** likes **both equally,** **יְבָרֵךְ תְּחִלָּה עַל זֶה שֶׁהוּא מִמִּין שִׁבְעָה** — **he should first recite a blessing on the** fruit **that is of the Seven Species** for which Eretz Yisrael is praised, **אֲפִילוּ הוּא חֲצִי** — **even if it is a half** of a fruit. **וְאִם אֵין בֵּינֵיהֶם מִמִּין שִׁבְעָה** — **And if there are none of the Seven Species among them,** **שָׁלֵם עָדִיף** — the one that is a **whole** fruit **has priority,** and its blessing takes precedence. **וְאִם שְׁנֵיהֶם שְׁלֵמִים אוֹ שְׁנֵיהֶם חֲסֵרִים** — **If they are both whole or both not whole,** **יַקְדִּים "בּוֹרֵא פְּרִי הָעֵץ"** — **he gives precedence to** the one that requires ***borei pri ha'eitz*** **לְ"בוֹרֵא פְּרִי הָאֲדָמָה"** — **over** the one that requires ***borei pri ha'adamah.***[7]

---

4. These fruits are also enumerated in the introduction to the following *se'if.*

5. Thus, according to Kitzur, the order of precedence is: (1) preferred fruit; (2) fruit of the Seven Species; (3) whole fruit.

However, *Mishnah Berurah* (see 211:13, with *Shaar HaTziyun* §8) rules that if the blessings of the fruit are the same, precedence is accorded first to one of the Seven Species, followed by the one that is whole, and finally, by the preferred food.

Thus, one who had grapes (which are one of the Seven Species) and an apple before him, and prefers apples over grapes, would, according to Kitzur, recite the *ha'eitz* blessing on the apples, since according to Kitzur the preferred fruit takes precedence over fruit of the Seven Species. According to *Mishnah Berurah,* the Seven Species take precedence over the preferred fruit; therefore, he would recite the blessing on the grapes. In a case where the Seven Species is not a consideration, for example, if neither fruit is of the Seven Species, such as apples and oranges, and the one that he prefers is cut up while the other is whole, according to Kitzur he recites the blessing on the preferred one, and according to *Mishnah Berurah* on the whole one.

6. [See note 3.] In this case, *Mishnah Berurah* (211:9) concurs with the order cited by Kitzur.

7. As a general rule, a more specific blessing has more significance than a less specific

247   LAW OF PRECEDENCE OF BLESSINGS — SIMAN 55:2

ב. אִם כּוּלָן הֵן מִמִּין שִׁבְעָה וְשָׁוִים לוֹ בַּחֲבִיבוּת צָרִיךְ לְהַקְדִּים אֶת זֶה שֶׁהִקְדִּימוֹ
הַפָּסוּק⁸. וְ"אֶרֶץ" בַּתְרָא שֶׁנֶּאֱמַר בַּפָּסוּק הִפְסִיק אֶת הַסֵּדֶר⁹. נִמְצָא לְפִי זֶה כִּי
תְּמָרִים קוֹדֶם לַעֲנָבִים, לְפִי שֶׁתְּמָרִים הֵם שֵׁנִי לְ"אֶרֶץ" בַּתְרָא וַעֲנָבִים הוּא שְׁלִישִׁי
לְ"אֶרֶץ" קַמָּא¹⁰. וְדַוְקָא עֲנָבִים, אֲבָל יַיִן כֵּיוָן שֶׁהוּא דָּבָר חָשׁוּב וְקָבְעוּ לוֹ בְּרָכָה
לְעַצְמוֹ, הוּא קוֹדֶם לְכָל הַפֵּירוֹת¹¹.

---

§2 The Seven Species for which Eretz Yisrael was praised are enumerated by the Torah in the verse (*Devarim* 8:8): אֶרֶץ חִטָּה וּשְׂעֹרָה וְגֶפֶן וּתְאֵנָה וְרִמּוֹן אֶרֶץ זֵית שֶׁמֶן וּדְבָשׁ, *A land of wheat, barley, grape, fig, and pomegranate; a land of oil-olives and date-honey.* The order of appearance in this verse reflects the importance of each of these fruits in relation to one another.

אִם כּוּלָן הֵן מִמִּין שִׁבְעָה — **If all of** the fruits that he wishes to eat **are of the Seven Species** וְשָׁוִים לוֹ בַּחֲבִיבוּת — **and he likes** them all **equally,** צָרִיךְ לְהַקְדִּים אֶת זֶה שֶׁהִקְדִּימוֹ הַפָּסוּק — **he must give precedence to the one that the verse placed earlier** and recite the blessing on that one.[8] וְ"אֶרֶץ" בַּתְרָא שֶׁנֶּאֱמַר בַּפָּסוּק — **Now, the latter "***eretz***"** (*land*) **stated in the verse** הִפְסִיק אֶת הַסֵּדֶר — **interrupts the order.** Therefore, the species appearing in the second section of the verse are accorded precedence based on their position in relation to the *second* "*eretz.*"[9] נִמְצָא לְפִי זֶה — **It thus emerges** כִּי תְּמָרִים קוֹדֶם לַעֲנָבִים — **that dates take precedence over grapes** (i.e., if one has dates and grapes before him, and wishes to eat both, he recites the blessing of *borei pri ha'eitz* on the dates), לְפִי שֶׁתְּמָרִים הֵם שֵׁנִי לְ"אֶרֶץ" בַּתְרָא — **for dates are second to the latter** *eretz* וַעֲנָבִים הוּא שְׁלִישִׁי לְ"אֶרֶץ" קַמָּא — **while grapes are third to the first** *eretz*.[10] וְדַוְקָא עֲנָבִים — **But** this applies only **to grapes;** אֲבָל יַיִן — **wine, however,** כֵּיוָן שֶׁהוּא דָּבָר חָשׁוּב — **since it is a significant item,** וְקָבְעוּ לוֹ בְּרָכָה לְעַצְמוֹ — **and it was accorded its own unique blessing** (*borei pri hagafen,* "Who creates the fruit of the vine"), הוּא קוֹדֶם לְכָל הַפֵּירוֹת — **precedes all fruit,** even dates.[11]

---

blessing. Although both *ha'eitz* and *ha'adamah* are specific blessings (see below, *se'if* 4), nevertheless, *ha'eitz* is considered somewhat more specific since it is limited to the fruit of the tree, while *ha'adamah* is applicable to all produce that grows from the ground, including fruit of the tree (for this reason the *ha'adamah* blessing is indeed valid, after the fact, for fruit of the tree as well; see below, 56:2). Therefore, when no other factors play a role, *ha'eitz* is to be recited first (see *Mishnah Berurah* 211:18).

8. Whatever appears earlier in the verse is considered more important and takes precedence with regard to determining upon which fruit to recite the blessing. For example, one who wishes to eat grapes, figs, and pomegranates would recite *borei pri ha'eitz* on the grapes, and exempt the figs and pomegranates that appear later in the verse. [Wheat and barley take precedence only when they are in the form of bread, cake, or a cooked dish; see

next *se'if* (see *Mishnah Berurah* 211:19; cf. ibid. §27 and §35).]

9. The word *land* appears twice in the verse, with the first five species appearing after the first "*land*" and the final two after the second: *A land* of (1) wheat, (2) barley, (3) grape, (4) fig, and (5) pomegranate; *a land* of (1) oil-olives and (2) date-honey. This serves as an indication that the species appearing following the second "*land*" take precedence over fruit that are further from the first "*land*" (*Mishnah Berurah* 211:21). Therefore, olives and dates (which immediately follow the second "*land*") take precedence over grapes and figs, which are third and fourth from the first "*land.*"

10. The order of precedence of the *fruit* of the Seven Species is thus: (1) olives; (2) dates; (3) grapes; (4) figs; and (5) pomegranates. The status of barley and other grains will be addressed below, note 14.

11. *Hagafen,* however, does not normally

ג. הָא דְיֵשׁ מַעֲלָה לְמִין שִׁבְעָה דַּוְקָא כְּשֶׁנִּגְמְרָה הַפְּרִי, אֲבָל פְּרִי שֶׁלֹּא נִגְמְרָה אֵין לָהּ מַעֲלָה, דְּלָא מִשְׁתַּבַּח קְרָא בְּמִידֵי דְּלָא חֲזֵי[12]. וְכֵן אִם אוֹכְלוֹ שֶׁלֹּא כְּדֶרֶךְ הֲנָאָתוֹ, כְּגוֹן הַכּוֹסֵס[13] חִטָּה, אֵין לָהּ קְדִימָה[14].

ד. אִם יֵשׁ לְפָנָיו דָּבָר שֶׁבִּרְכָתוֹ "בּוֹרֵא פְּרִי הָעֵץ" אוֹ "בּוֹרֵא פְּרִי הָאֲדָמָה" וְגַם דָּבָר שֶׁבִּרְכָתוֹ "שֶׁהַכֹּל"[15] וְרוֹצֶה לֶאֱכוֹל מִשְּׁנֵיהֶם, בִּרְכַּת "בּוֹרֵא פְּרִי הָעֵץ" וּבִרְכַּת "בּוֹרֵא פְּרִי הָאֲדָמָה" קוֹדְמוֹת, שֶׁהֵן חֲשׁוּבוֹת לְפִי שֶׁהֵן מְבוֹרָרוֹת יוֹתֵר

§3 Kitzur now cites a number of situations in which the Seven Species do not take precedence over other food:

הָא דְיֵשׁ מַעֲלָה לְמִין שִׁבְעָה — The superiority of the Seven Species is considered **דַּוְקָא כְּשֶׁנִּגְמְרָה הַפְּרִי — only once the fruit has fully developed. אֲבָל פְּרִי שֶׁלֹּא נִגְמְרָה אֵין לָהּ מַעֲלָה — But a fruit that is not fully developed has no superiority** based on its being one of the Seven Species, **דְּלָא מִשְׁתַּבַּח קְרָא בְּמִידֵי דְּלָא חֲזֵי — for the verse does not extol** the virtues of the land **with something unfit** for consumption.[12] **וְכֵן אִם אוֹכְלוֹ שֶׁלֹּא כְּדֶרֶךְ הֲנָאָתוֹ — Similarly, if he eats** the food **in** a way that is **not the usual manner of consumption, כְּגוֹן הַכּוֹסֵס חִטָּה — such as one who chews**[13] **wheat** kernels, **אֵין לָהּ קְדִימָה — it does not take precedence.**[14]

§4 The next *se'ifim* address cases in which a food is given precedence due to the greater significance of its blessing rather than due to its own significance:

אִם יֵשׁ לְפָנָיו — If one has before him דָּבָר שֶׁבִּרְכָתוֹ "בּוֹרֵא פְּרִי הָעֵץ" אוֹ "בּוֹרֵא פְּרִי הָאֲדָמָה" — a food **whose blessing is either *borei pri ha'eitz*** or ***borei pri ha'adamah,*** **וְגַם דָּבָר שֶׁבִּרְכָתוֹ "שֶׁהַכֹּל" — as well as something whose blessing is *shehakol,***[15] **וְרוֹצֶה לֶאֱכוֹל מִשְּׁנֵיהֶם — and he wishes to partake of both, בִּרְכַּת "בּוֹרֵא פְּרִי הָעֵץ" — the blessing of *borei pri ha'eitz* וּבִרְכַּת "בּוֹרֵא פְּרִי הָאֲדָמָה" — and the blessing of *borei pri ha'adamah* קוֹדְמוֹת — take precedence,** i.e., one should recite the blessing on that food and partake of it first. **שֶׁהֵן חֲשׁוּבוֹת — For those** blessings **are** more **significant** than the blessing of *shehakol,* **לְפִי שֶׁהֵן מְבוֹרָרוֹת יוֹתֵר — since they**

precede the *hamotzi* or *mezonos* blessings; see below, *se'if* 5. The halachos of the *borei pri hagafen* blessing are set out above, 49:1-7.

12. The superiority of the Seven Species is based on the verse that extols the Land of Israel as possessing these Seven Species. Therefore, if a fruit is not one for which the verse would extol the land, e.g., it is not fully developed, it does not possess the quality of the Seven Species with regard to this halachah.

13. Consuming something in an abnormal manner is referred to as *chewing.* [This term is used here, since eating kernels is not the optimal manner of consuming wheat; see next note.]

14. Wheat is usually ground into flour for bread and cake, or eaten as a cooked dish. In such cases, its blessing (which is generally *hamotzi* or *mezonos,* depending on what the wheat is made into; see above, *Siman* 48) precedes that of other species, even if he likes the others better; see below, *se'if* 5 (see *Shulchan Aruch* 211:6 with *Mishnah Berurah*).

When wheat kernels are eaten raw [or toasted], the appropriate blessing is *borei pri ha'adamah.* As Kitzur rules here, this blessing does not take precedence over the blessing of any fruit (see *Shulchan Aruch* 211:5). See *Mishnah Berurah* 211:27 and §35 for an opposing view; see also *Shaar HaTziyun* 211:11.

15. The halachos of the blessing of *shehakol niheyah bidvaro,* "through Whose word everything came to be," are set out above, *Siman* 52.

שֶׁאֵינָן פּוֹטְרוֹת אֶלָּא מִין אֶחָד, וְ״שֶׁהַכֹּל״ הִיא בְּרָכָה כּוֹלֶלֶת הַרְבֵּה. וַאֲפִילוּ אִם זֶה שֶׁבִּרְכָתוֹ ״שֶׁהַכֹּל״ הוּא חָבִיב לוֹ יוֹתֵר, מִכָּל מָקוֹם צָרִיךְ לְהַקְדִּים ״בּוֹרֵא פְּרִי הָעֵץ״ אוֹ ״בּוֹרֵא פְּרִי הָאֲדָמָה״[16].

ה. בִּרְכַּת ״בּוֹרֵא מִינֵי מְזוֹנוֹת״ קוֹדֶמֶת גַּם לְבִרְכַּת הַיַּיִן, וּמִכָּל שֶׁכֵּן ״הַמּוֹצִיא״[17], שֶׁהֲרֵי הִיא קוֹדֶמֶת גַּם לְבִרְכַּת ״בּוֹרֵא מִינֵי מְזוֹנוֹת״[18]. וְלָכֵן בְּשַׁבָּת וְיוֹם טוֹב כְּשֶׁמְּקַדֵּשׁ עַל הַיַּיִן, צָרִיךְ לְכַסּוֹת אֶת הַפַּת, שֶׁלֹּא יִרְאֶה בּוֹשְׁתּוֹ שֶׁמַּקְדִּימִין לוֹ בִּרְכַּת

are more specific, שֶׁאֵינָן פּוֹטְרוֹת אֶלָּא מִין אֶחָד — in that they are effective only for one type of food (i.e., *ha'eitz* on fruit and *ha'adamah* on vegetables), וְ״שֶׁהַכֹּל״ הִיא בְּרָכָה כּוֹלֶלֶת הַרְבֵּה — whereas *shehakol* is a blessing that encompasses many types of food. וַאֲפִילוּ אִם זֶה שֶׁבִּרְכָתוֹ ״שֶׁהַכֹּל״ הוּא חָבִיב לוֹ יוֹתֵר — Even if he likes this food whose blessing is *shehakol* better, מִכָּל מָקוֹם — nevertheless, צָרִיךְ לְהַקְדִּים ״בּוֹרֵא פְּרִי הָעֵץ״ אוֹ ״בּוֹרֵא פְּרִי הָאֲדָמָה״ — he must give precedence to *borei pri ha'eitz* or *borei pri ha'adamah,* and first recite the blessing upon the food that requires that blessing.[16]

§5 בִּרְכַּת ״בּוֹרֵא מִינֵי מְזוֹנוֹת״ קוֹדֶמֶת גַּם לְבִרְכַּת הַיַּיִן — **The blessing of *borei minei mezonos* also takes precedence over the blessing on wine** (*borei pri hagafen*). וּמִכָּל שֶׁכֵּן ״הַמּוֹצִיא״ — **And most certainly the blessing of *hamotzi*** takes precedence over the blessing on wine,[17] שֶׁהֲרֵי הִיא קוֹדֶמֶת גַּם לְבִרְכַּת ״בּוֹרֵא מִינֵי מְזוֹנוֹת״ — for *hamotzi* **also takes precedence over the blessing of *borei minei mezonos.***[18] וְלָכֵן בְּשַׁבָּת וְיוֹם טוֹב — **Therefore, on Shabbos and Yom Tov,** כְּשֶׁמְּקַדֵּשׁ עַל הַיַּיִן — **when one recites *Kiddush* on wine** צָרִיךְ לְכַסּוֹת אֶת הַפַּת — **he must cover the bread,** שֶׁלֹּא יִרְאֶה בּוֹשְׁתּוֹ — **so that it not witness its embarrassment** שֶׁמַּקְדִּימִין לוֹ בִּרְכַּת

16. Both the *ha'adamah* and the *ha'eitz* blessings are considered "specific" blessings in relation to the *shehakol* blessing; therefore, they take precedence despite other factors present, such as a desired food. *Borei pri ha'adamah* and *borei pri ha'eitz* also take precedence over *shehakol* even when *shehakol* is being recited upon one of the Seven Species, e.g., upon date honey; above, 53:1 (*Shaar HaTziyun* 211:9). With regard to each other, however, although *ha'eitz* is somewhat more specific than *ha'adamah*, this is not taken into account when other factors are present, as Kitzur explained at the end of *se'if* 1, above.

17. Like wine, which is significant and was accorded its own blessing (see above, *se'if* 2), wheat and barley are also subject to their own blessing (*hamotzi* or *mezonos*) when they are prepared as a cooked dish, cake, or bread. And since wheat and barley precede wine in the verse's list of the Seven Species, their blessing takes precedence over *hagafen* (see *Shulchan Aruch* 211:6, and *Mishnah Berurah* there §35). Even *hamotzi* or *mezonos* recited on food made from the other grains (rye, oats, and spelt) takes precedence over wine, since these grains are considered sub-species of wheat and barley with respect to this halachah (see *Mishnah Berurah* 211:24).

18. This is so even if the food whose blessing is *mezonos* is more significant and is liked better (see *Rama* 211:5 with *Mishnah Berurah* 211:30). [Kitzur is speaking of a case where the food that requires *mezonos* is not being eaten as part of a meal, and thus requires its own blessing even if eaten during the meal (see above, 43:6). If the *mezonos* food is eaten as part of the meal, there is no question of precedence, since its blessing is exempted with the blessing of *hamotzi* recited at the beginning of the meal; ibid., *se'if* 1 (*Mishnah Berurah* 211:28).]

Thus, *hamotzi* precedes all other blessings. *Mezonos,* even on a dish of rye, oats, and spelt, follows *hamotzi* in the order of precedence, and takes precedence over all other blessings, including the blessing on one of the Seven Species (see *Shulchan Aruch* 211:6 and *Mishnah Berurah* §35). See above, note 14.

הַיַּיִן[19]. וְכֵן בְּשַׁחֲרִית שֶׁמְּקַדֵּשׁ וְאוֹכֵל אַחַר כָּךְ מִינֵי מְזוֹנוֹת[20], צָרִיךְ לְכַסּוֹתָן בִּשְׁעַת הַקִּידּוּשׁ.

הַיַּיִן — that we give precedence to the blessing on wine (which is recited during *Kiddush*) **over its** blessing.[19] **וְכֵן בְּשַׁחֲרִית — Similarly, on** Shabbos **morning, שֶׁמְּקַדֵּשׁ — when one recites *Kiddush* וְאוֹכֵל אַחַר כָּךְ מִינֵי מְזוֹנוֹת — and afterward eats types of** food for which the blessing is *borei minei* ***mezonos,***[20] **צָרִיךְ לְכַסּוֹתָן בִּשְׁעַת הַקִּידּוּשׁ — he must cover** such food **at the time of *Kiddush.***

---

19. See below, 77:8, for another reason for this practice; see also *Mishnah Berurah* 271:41.

20. See below, 77:14, regarding this practice.

Summary of the Laws of Precedence of Blessings

The following is the order (based on Kitzur's rulings in our *Siman*) that is to be followed when reciting the blessing on various foods

[1] *Hamotzi*[a]
[2] *Mezonos*[b]
[3] *Hagafen*
[4] **Desired fruit or vegetable**[c]
[5] **Fruit of the Seven Species: (a) olive, (b) date, (c) grape, (d) fig, (e) pomegranate**
[6] **Whole fruit or vegetable**[d]
[7] *Ha'eitz*
[8] *Ha'adamah*
[9] *Shehakol*

a. The order of preference is: wheat bread, barley bread, spelt bread, rye bread, oat bread (see *Mishnah Berurah* 168:12-13). [Note: Rye bread sold commercially is produced with a majority of wheat flour, and should be treated as wheat bread.] See above, 41:8-12, for further rules regarding the precedence of various types of bread.

b. See previous footnote and *Mishnah Berurah* 211:35.

c. See note 3 in this *Siman*. According to *Mishnah Berurah*, the desired fruit or vegetable takes precedence only with regard to the *sequence* of blessings, i.e., when one is *ha'eitz* and the other *ha'adamah*. When both are *ha'eitz* or *ha'adamah*, a fruit of the Seven Species and a whole fruit or vegetable takes precedence over the desired fruit or vegetable (see *Shulchan Aruch* 211:1-2, with *Mishnah Berurah* and *Shaar HaTziyun*). See note 5.

d. See *Shaar HaTziyun* (211:5) with regard to the level of precedence awarded to a whole fruit or vegetable if one is *ha'eitz* and the other *ha'adamah*.

251 LAW REGARDING AN ERROR IN BLESSINGS — SIMAN 56:1

סימן נו

דִּינֵי טָעוּת בִּבְרָכוֹת

וּבוֹ ז׳ סְעִיפִים

א. טָעָה וּבֵירַךְ עַל לֶחֶם גָּמוּר "בּוֹרֵא מִינֵי מְזוֹנוֹת", אוֹ עַל פַּת כִּיסְנִין "הַמּוֹצִיא"[1], יָצָא[2]. אֲבָל אִם בֵּירַךְ עַל תַּבְשִׁיל, אֲפִילוּ מִמִּינֵי דָגָן, "הַמּוֹצִיא"[3], לֹא יָצָא. טָעָה וּבֵירַךְ עַל עֲנָבִים "בּוֹרֵא פְּרִי הַגָּפֶן"[4], יָצָא. וְכֵן אִם טָעָה בִּבְרָכָה אַחֲרוֹנָה

SIMAN 56

THE LAW REGARDING AN ERROR IN BLESSINGS

CONTAINING 7 *SE'IFIM*

§1 *Mezonos* and *Hamotzi; Hagafen* on Grapes / **§2** *Ha'adamah* and *Ha'eitz* / **§3** *Ha'eitz* on Wine / **§4** *Shehakol* / **§5** Error in Intent / **§6** Within the Time of *K'dei Dibbur* / **§7** After the Time of *K'dei Dibbur*

This *Siman* discusses the halachos pertaining to one who mistakenly uttered a blessing that was inappropriate for the food upon which it was recited.

§1 טָעָה וּבֵירַךְ עַל לֶחֶם גָּמוּר "בּוֹרֵא מִינֵי מְזוֹנוֹת" — **If one erred and recited the blessing of** *borei minei mezonos, **Who creates species of nourishment,*** **on actual bread** (rather than the required blessing of *hamotzi lechem min ha'aretz,* "Who brings forth bread from the earth"), אוֹ עַל פַּת כִּיסְנִין "הַמּוֹצִיא" — **or he recited *hamotzi* on *kisnin*-bread** (rather than *mezonos*),[1] יָצָא — **he has fulfilled** his obligation.[2] אֲבָל אִם בֵּירַךְ עַל תַּבְשִׁיל, אֲפִילוּ מִמִּינֵי דָגָן, "הַמּוֹצִיא" — **But if one** mistakenly **recited the *hamotzi* blessing on a cooked dish — even** one made from one **of the** five **species of grain,**[3] לֹא יָצָא — **he has not fulfilled** his obligation, since such dishes cannot in any way qualify as bread.

טָעָה — **If one erred** וּבֵירַךְ עַל עֲנָבִים "בּוֹרֵא פְּרִי הַגָּפֶן" — **and recited the blessing of** *borei pri hagafen, **Who creates the fruit of the vine,*** **on grapes**[4] יָצָא — **he has fulfilled** his obligation. וְכֵן אִם טָעָה בִּבְרָכָה אַחֲרוֹנָה — **So too, if one erred in** his

---

1. See above, *Siman* 48, for a definition of *kisnin*-bread (*se'if* 2), and how to ascertain the proper blessing for different preparations of grain products.

2. After the fact, *borei minei mezonos* is effective for bread, as it is the general blessing for all grain products (see *Beur Halachah* 167:10 s.v. במקום). See below, note 15, regarding one who recited *mezonos* on other foods.

See *Nishmas Adam* (glosses to *Chayei Adam*) 58:1 for the basis of the ruling that one who recited *hamotzi* on *kisnin*-bread has fulfilled his obligation. [Rabbi Moshe Feinstein (*Igros Moshe, Yoreh Deah* III, §120.2) advises that in such a case, a scrupulous individual should eat no more than the minimal amount that he consumed following the blessing.]

3. Wheat, barley, oats, spelt, and rye. For example, he recited *hamotzi* on a dish of oatmeal or pasta, for which the proper blessing is *mezonos* (see *Shulchan Aruch* 208:2). [*Hamotzi* is recited only on baked bread made from grain of the five species.]

4. The blessing of *borei pri hagafen*, "Who creates the fruit of the vine," was instituted to be recited for wine, not for grapes (above, 49:1). The proper blessing for grapes is *borei pri ha'eitz*, "Who creates the fruit of the tree."

וּבֵירַךְ "עַל הַגֶּפֶן"[5], יָצָא, שֶׁהֲרֵי גַּם הָעֲנָבִים פְּרִי הַגֶּפֶן הֵם.

ב. טָעָה וּבֵירַךְ עַל פְּרִי הָעֵץ "בּוֹרֵא פְּרִי הָאֲדָמָה"[6], אוֹ שֶׁהָיוּ שְׁתֵּיהֶן לְפָנָיו[7] וְטָעָה וְהִקְדִּים לְבָרֵךְ עַל פְּרִי הָאֲדָמָה וְנִתְכַּוֵּין לִפְטוֹר בָּזֶה גַּם אֶת פְּרִי הָעֵץ[8], יָצָא, שֶׁהֲרֵי גַּם הָעֵץ יוֹנֵק מִן הָאֲדָמָה[9]. אֲבָל אִם בֵּירַךְ עַל פְּרִי הָאֲדָמָה "בּוֹרֵא פְּרִי הָעֵץ", לֹא יָצָא[10]. וְלָכֵן, אִם הוּא מְסוּפָּק בְּאֵיזֶה פְּרִי אִם הוּא פְּרִי הָעֵץ אוֹ פְּרִי הָאֲדָמָה,

---

recitation of the ***berachah acharonah*** (final blessing) after eating grapes, **וּבֵירַךְ "עַל הַגֶּפֶן"** — **and recited the blessing of** *Al HaGefen, **for the vine,*** rather than *Al HaEitz, for the tree,*[5] **יָצָא** — **he has fulfilled** his obligation, **שֶׁהֲרֵי גַּם הָעֲנָבִים פְּרִי הַגֶּפֶן הֵם** — **for grapes too are the "fruit of the vine."**

§2 **טָעָה** — **If one erred** **וּבֵירַךְ עַל פְּרִי הָעֵץ "בּוֹרֵא פְּרִי הָאֲדָמָה"** — **and recited the blessing of** *borei pri ha'adamah, **Who creates the fruit of the ground,*** **on a fruit of the tree,**[6] **אוֹ שֶׁהָיוּ שְׁתֵּיהֶן לְפָנָיו** — **or, if both** a fruit and a vegetable **were before him,**[7] **וְטָעָה** — **and he erred** **וְהִקְדִּים לְבָרֵךְ עַל פְּרִי הָאֲדָמָה** — **and recited the** *borei pri ha'adamah* **blessing on the vegetable first,** **וְנִתְכַּוֵּין לִפְטוֹר בָּזֶה גַּם אֶת פְּרִי הָעֵץ** — **and he intended to exempt thereby the fruit of the tree,**[8] **יָצָא** — **he has fulfilled** his requirement for the blessing on the fruit of the tree, **שֶׁהֲרֵי גַּם הָעֵץ יוֹנֵק מִן הָאֲדָמָה** — **because the tree also draws nourishment from the ground.**[9]

אֲבָל אִם בֵּירַךְ עַל פְּרִי הָאֲדָמָה "בּוֹרֵא פְּרִי הָעֵץ" — **But if one recited** *borei pri ha'eitz, **Who creates the fruit of the tree,*** **on a vegetable,** **לֹא יָצָא** — **he has not fulfilled** his obligation.[10]

וְלָכֵן, אִם הוּא מְסוּפָּק בְּאֵיזֶה פְּרִי — **Therefore, if one is in doubt with regard to a "fruit"** **אִם הוּא פְּרִי הָעֵץ אוֹ פְּרִי הָאֲדָמָה** — **whether it is** halachically considered

---

5. The blessing of *Al HaGefen* is recited after drinking wine, and *Al HaEitz* after eating fruit of the Seven Species, including grapes (above, 51:8).

6. The halachos of the blessings of *borei pri ha'eitz,* "Who creates the fruit of the tree," and *borei pri ha'adamah,* "Who creates the fruit of the ground," are set out above, *Siman* 52.

7. Or even if the fruit was not before him (*Mishnah Berurah* 206:7). [We have used the term "vegetable" here when referring to anything upon which the proper blessing is *borei pri ha'adamah*, "Who creates the fruit of the ground." These halachos are outlined at length above, *Siman* 52.]

8. See above, 50:12 and 55:1, for the proper procedure with regard to reciting the blessing upon a fruit and a vegetable.

9. Although the proper blessing on the fruit of the tree is *borei pri ha'eitz,* nevertheless, since ultimately the nourishment of these fruits is drawn from the ground, the blessing of *borei pri ha'adamah*, "Who creates the fruit of the ground," is not inappropriate. Therefore, even if he intentionally recited *ha'adamah* on a fruit that requires *ha'eitz,* he has fulfilled the requirement (*Mishnah Berurah* 206:1).

10. The *borei pri ha'eitz* blessing is totally inappropriate for a vegetable or the like that grows from the ground. [Even if one recited *ha'eitz* on the fruit of a tree whose trunk does not survive the winter (whose blessing is *ha'adamah;* see above, 52:1), he has not fulfilled his obligation, since such fruit are considered fruit of the ground, not of the tree (*Mishnah Berurah* 206:2). However, one who recites *ha'eitz* on a fruit that does grow on the tree, but is not subject to *borei pri ha'eitz* because it is not sufficiently developed or is not the primary fruit of the tree (see above, 52:9-12), has fulfilled his obligation (*Mishnah Berurah* ibid. §3).]

וְאִי אֶפְשַׁר לוֹ לְבָרֵר בְּשׁוּם אוֹפֶן, יְבָרֵךְ עָלָיו "בּוֹרֵא פְּרִי הָאֲדָמָה"[11].

ג. טָעָה וּבֵירַךְ עַל הַיַּיִן "בּוֹרֵא פְּרִי הָעֵץ", אִם נִזְכַּר מִיָּד, יֹאמַר תּוֹךְ כְּדֵי דִיבּוּר[12] "בּוֹרֵא פְּרִי הַגָּפֶן". וְאִם לֹא נִזְכַּר מִיָּד, יָצָא בְּדִיעֲבַד[13].

ד. עַל כָּל דָּבָר, אֲפִילוּ עַל הַפַּת וְעַל הַיַּיִן, אִם טָעָה וּבֵירַךְ "שֶׁהַכֹּל", יָצָא[14] — וְעַיֵּין לְעֵיל סִימָן נ' סְעִיף ב'[15].

---

a fruit or a vegetable with regard to the proper blessing, וְאִי אֶפְשַׁר לוֹ לְבָרֵר בְּשׁוּם אוֹפֶן — **and it is impossible for him to clarify** the matter **in any way,** יְבָרֵךְ עָלָיו "בּוֹרֵא פְּרִי הָאֲדָמָה" — **he should recite the** ***borei pri ha'adamah*** **blessing upon it.**[11]

§3 טָעָה — Regarding **one who erred** וּבֵירַךְ עַל הַיַּיִן "בּוֹרֵא פְּרִי הָעֵץ" — **and recited** ***borei pri ha'eitz*** **on wine,** אִם נִזְכַּר מִיָּד — **if he remembered immediately,** יֹאמַר תּוֹךְ כְּדֵי דִיבּוּר — **he should say within** *k'dei dibbur,* ***the time of an utterance:***[12] "בּוֹרֵא פְּרִי הַגָּפֶן" — ***borei pri hagafen.*** וְאִם לֹא נִזְכַּר מִיָּד — **If, however, he did not remember immediately,** יָצָא בְּדִיעֲבַד — **he has fulfilled** his obligation **after the fact.**[13]

§4 עַל כָּל דָּבָר — **Regarding any** food **item,** אֲפִילוּ עַל הַפַּת וְעַל הַיַּיִן — **even bread or wine,** אִם טָעָה — **if one erred** וּבֵירַךְ "שֶׁהַכֹּל" — **and recited** upon it **the** ***shehakol*** **blessing,** יָצָא — **he has fulfilled** his obligation.[14] וְעַיֵּין לְעֵיל סִימָן נ' סְעִיף ב' — **See above,** ***Siman*** **50,** ***se'if*** **2.**[15]

---

11. This applies whether his doubt is based on his lack of knowledge regarding the botanic particulars of the fruit or due to an established halachic doubt as to the correct blessing. If, however, he is in doubt because he did not study the laws of blessings, he may not exempt himself with the *borei pri ha'adamah* blessing, and is required to seek clarification as to the correct blessing before he eats; see above, 50:2 (see *Mishnah Berurah* 202:84 and *Shulchan Aruch* 206:1, with *Mishnah Berurah* §4).

12. *K'dei dibbur* is the amount of time that it takes to greet one's teacher with the words *Shalom alecha rebbi* (Peace upon you, my master); see *Kelalim.* As a general rule, two statements that were made without pausing for "the time of an utterance" between them are considered as having been made together. See also *Mishnah Berurah* 206:12 with *Shaar HaTziyun* §10.

13. As a product of grapes, wine is also "fruit of the tree." Thus, after the fact, *borei pri ha'eitz,* "Who creates the fruit of the tree," can be considered appropriate. See Kitzur's editorial glosses, where Kitzur states that it would appear that the same law applies if he recited *borei pri ha'adamah,* "Who creates the fruit of the ground," over wine.

14. *Shehakol niheyah bidvaro,* "Through Whose word everything came to be," is the most encompassing blessing, and can therefore be considered an appropriate blessing for any food item. See next note. [The laws of the *shehakol* blessing are set out above, *Siman* 52.]

15. *Kitzur* explains there that this holds true only after the fact; initially, one may not do this. See 50:2 for further discussion, and above, note 11.

According to opinions cited by *Mishnah Berurah* (see *Beur Halachah* 167:10 s.v. במקום), one who recites *borei minei mezonos* on any food other than water and salt has fulfilled his obligation, and is not required to recite the proper blessing before eating it. Rabbi Moshe Feinstein advises that since this is valid only after the fact, one who did this should refrain from eating more than a single mouthful until he has an opportunity to leave his place in a manner that would require him to recite a new blessing; see above, 50:13-15 (see *Igros Moshe, Orach Chaim* IV, §40:1).

ה. אַף עַל פִּי שֶׁלְּכַתְחִלָּה צָרִיךְ לְדַקְדֵּק וּלְכַוֵּין עַל מַה שֶּׁהוּא מְבָרֵךְ (כְּמוֹ שֶׁנִּתְבָּאֵר בְּסִימָן נ׳ סְעִיף ג׳), מִכָּל מָקוֹם בְּדִיעֲבַד אִם טָעָה בְּכַוָּונָה, כְּגוֹן שֶׁלָּקַח בְּיָדוֹ כּוֹס קָסָבַר שֶׁהוּא יַיִן וּבֵירַךְ עַל דַּעַת שֶׁהוּא יַיִן וְקוֹדֶם שֶׁאָמַר "בּוֹרֵא פְּרִי הַגָּפֶן" נִזְכַּר שֶׁהוּא מַיִם אוֹ שֵׁכָר וְסִיֵּים "שֶׁהַכֹּל נִהְיָה בִּדְבָרוֹ", אֵין צָרִיךְ לַחֲזוֹר וּלְבָרֵךְ, דְּמִשּׁוּם טָעוּת בְּכַוָּונָה אֵין צָרִיךְ לַחֲזוֹר וּלְבָרֵךְ. וְכָל שֶׁכֵּן אִם טָעָה בְּהִיפּוּךְ, שֶׁהָיָה סָבוּר שֶׁהוּא שֵׁכָר אוֹ מַיִם וּבֵירַךְ עַל דַּעַת לוֹמַר "שֶׁהַכֹּל" וְקוֹדֶם שֶׁאָמַר "שֶׁהַכֹּל" נִזְכַּר שֶׁהוּא יַיִן וְסִיֵּים "בּוֹרֵא פְּרִי הַגָּפֶן", שֶׁיָּצָא, שֶׁהֲרֵי אֲפִילוּ אִם הָיָה מְסַיֵּים כְּפִי הַכַּוָּונָה הָיָה יוֹצֵא[16].

ו. אֲפִילוּ אִם סִיֵּים כָּל הַבְּרָכָה בְּטָעוּת, אֶלָּא שֶׁנִּזְכַּר תּוֹךְ כְּדֵי דִיבּוּר וְתִיקֵּן אֲמִירָתוֹ,

---

§5 The remainder of our *Siman* discusses the halachah regarding one whose error was based on a mistake with regard to the identity of the food upon which he recited the blessing:

אַף עַל פִּי שֶׁלְּכַתְחִלָּה צָרִיךְ לְדַקְדֵּק — Although ideally, when one begins reciting a blessing, **he must take care** **וּלְכַוֵּין עַל מַה שֶּׁהוּא מְבָרֵךְ — to have intent** for the appropriate blessing for the item **upon which he is reciting the blessing** (**כְּמוֹ שֶׁנִּתְבָּאֵר בְּסִימָן נ׳ סְעִיף ג׳ — as was explained in *Siman* 50, *se'if* 3**), **מִכָּל מָקוֹם בְּדִיעֲבַד — nevertheless, after the fact,** **אִם טָעָה בְּכַוָּונָה — if he erred in his intent,** his blessing is still valid. **כְּגוֹן — For example,** **שֶׁלָּקַח בְּיָדוֹ כּוֹס — if he took a cup in hand** **קָסָבַר שֶׁהוּא יַיִן — thinking that it** contains **wine,** **וּבֵירַךְ עַל דַּעַת שֶׁהוּא יַיִן — and he** began **reciting the blessing based on the assumption that it is wine,** **וְקוֹדֶם שֶׁאָמַר "בּוֹרֵא פְּרִי הַגָּפֶן" — but before he recited** the words ***"borei pri hagafen,"*** **נִזְכַּר שֶׁהוּא מַיִם אוֹ שֵׁכָר — he realized that it was water or beer,** **וְסִיֵּים "שֶׁהַכֹּל נִהְיָה בִּדְבָרוֹ" — and he concluded** his blessing with the words ***"shehakol nihyah bidvaro,"*** which is the appropriate blessing for water or beer, **אֵין צָרִיךְ לַחֲזוֹר וּלְבָרֵךְ — he is not required to recite the blessing again.** **דְּמִשּׁוּם טָעוּת בְּכַוָּונָה — For on account of an error in intent** **אֵין צָרִיךְ לַחֲזוֹר וּלְבָרֵךְ — one is not required to repeat the blessing.** **וְכָל שֶׁכֵּן אִם טָעָה בְּהִיפּוּךְ — And certainly if he erred in the opposite way —** **שֶׁהָיָה סָבוּר שֶׁהוּא שֵׁכָר אוֹ מַיִם — that is, he thought that it** contained **beer or water,** **וּבֵירַךְ עַל דַּעַת לוֹמַר "שֶׁהַכֹּל" — and he** began **reciting the blessing with the intent to say *"shehakol,"*** **וְקוֹדֶם שֶׁאָמַר "שֶׁהַכֹּל" נִזְכַּר שֶׁהוּא יַיִן — but before he said** the word ***"shehakol"* he realized that it is wine,** **וְסִיֵּים "בּוֹרֵא פְּרִי הַגָּפֶן" — and he concluded** with the words ***"borei pri hagafen"*** — **שֶׁיָּצָא** — the law is **that he has fulfilled** his obligation. **שֶׁהֲרֵי אֲפִילוּ אִם הָיָה מְסַיֵּים כְּפִי הַכַּוָּונָה** — In this case the blessing is certainly valid, **for even if he would have concluded according to his** original **intent** (i.e., *shehakol nihyah bidvaro*), **הָיָה יוֹצֵא — he would have fulfilled** his obligation.[16]

§6 **אֲפִילוּ אִם סִיֵּים כָּל הַבְּרָכָה בְּטָעוּת** — In fact, the same ruling applies **even if he concluded the entire blessing in error,** **אֶלָּא שֶׁנִּזְכַּר תּוֹךְ כְּדֵי דִיבּוּר — but he remembered within** the time of ***k'dei dibbur***[17] **וְתִיקֵּן אֲמִירָתוֹ — and he corrected**

---

16. Because after the fact, one who recites *shehakol* on any food has fulfilled his obligation; see above, *se'if* 4.

17. See above, note 12.

255 LAW REGARDING AN ERROR IN BLESSINGS — SIMAN 56:7

כְּגוֹן שֶׁלָּקַח כּוֹס מַיִם אוֹ שֵׁכָר קָסָבַר שֶׁהוּא יַיִן וּבֵירַךְ "בּוֹרֵא פְּרִי הַגָּפֶן" וְנִזְכַּר מִיָּד שֶׁהוּא מַיִם אוֹ שֵׁכָר וְסִיֵּים "שֶׁהַכֹּל נִהְיָה בִּדְבָרוֹ", וְכָךְ הָיְתָה אֲמִירָתוֹ "בּוֹרֵא פְּרִי הַגָּפֶן שֶׁהַכֹּל נִהְיָה בִּדְבָרוֹ", יָצָא.

ז. וְאִם לֹא נִזְכַּר תּוֹךְ כְּדֵי דִיבּוּר, צָרִיךְ לְבָרֵךְ מֵחָדָשׁ בִּרְכַּת "שֶׁהַכֹּל", אִם הוּא רוֹצֶה לִשְׁתּוֹת כּוֹס זֶה. וְאִם הָיָה בְּדַעְתּוֹ לִשְׁתּוֹת גַּם יַיִן אַחֵר, יִקַּח יַיִן וְיִשְׁתֶּה מִיָּד[18] וְאֵינוֹ צָרִיךְ בְּרָכָה שְׁנִיָּה כֹּל שֶׁלֹּא הִפְסִיק בְּדִיבּוּר[19] (עַיֵּין לְעֵיל סִימָן נ׳ סְעִיף ד׳ וּסְעִיף ה׳)[20]. וַאֲפִילּוּ טָעַם תְּחִלָּה מִן הַכּוֹס וְעַל יְדֵי טְעִימָתוֹ נוֹדַע לוֹ שֶׁהוּא מַיִם אוֹ שֵׁכָר, מִכָּל מָקוֹם

---

his words. **כְּגוֹן — For example, שֶׁלָּקַח כּוֹס מַיִם אוֹ שֵׁכָר — he took a cup of water or beer** in hand, **קָסָבַר שֶׁהוּא יַיִן — thinking that it was wine, וּבֵירַךְ "בּוֹרֵא פְּרִי הַגָּפֶן" — and recited the** entire **blessing of *borei pri hagafen*** on it **וְנִזְכַּר מִיָּד שֶׁהוּא מַיִם אוֹ שֵׁכָר — and immediately realized that it was water or beer, וְסִיֵּים "שֶׁהַכֹּל נִהְיָה בִּדְבָרוֹ" — and concluded** the blessing again with the words ***"shehakol niheyah bidvaro,"*** **וְכָךְ הָיְתָה אֲמִירָתוֹ — such that his words were as follows: "בּוֹרֵא פְּרִי הַגָּפֶן שֶׁהַכֹּל נִהְיָה בִּדְבָרוֹ" — *"borei pri hagafen, shehakol nihyah bidvaro,"*** **יָצָא — he has fulfilled** his obligation.

§7 וְאִם לֹא נִזְכַּר תּוֹךְ כְּדֵי דִיבּוּר — But if, in the above case, **he did not realize** that it was not wine in the cup **within** the time of ***k'dei dibbur*****,** **צָרִיךְ לְבָרֵךְ מֵחָדָשׁ בִּרְכַּת "שֶׁהַכֹּל" — he must recite the blessing of *shehakol* anew** **אִם הוּא רוֹצֶה לִשְׁתּוֹת כּוֹס זֶה — if he wishes to drink this cup** of water or beer. **וְאִם הָיָה בְּדַעְתּוֹ לִשְׁתּוֹת גַּם יַיִן אַחֵר — If,** at the time he erroneously recited the *borei pri hagafen* blessing, **he intended to drink other wine as well, יִקַּח יַיִן וְיִשְׁתֶּה מִיָּד — he should take wine and immediately drink it,** so that his blessing should not have been recited in vain.[18] **וְאֵינוֹ צָרִיךְ בְּרָכָה שְׁנִיָּה — And he need not** recite **a second blessing** of *borei pri hagafen* (even though there was a pause following the blessing longer than the time of *k'dei dibbur*) **כֹּל שֶׁלֹּא הִפְסִיק בְּדִיבּוּר — as long as he did not interrupt by speaking;**[19] **(עַיֵּין לְעֵיל סִימָן נ׳ סְעִיף ד׳ וּסְעִיף ה׳) — see above, *Siman* 50, *se'if* 4 and *se'if* 5).**[20] **וַאֲפִילּוּ טָעַם תְּחִלָּה מִן הַכּוֹס — And even if he first took a taste from the cup, וְעַל יְדֵי טְעִימָתוֹ נוֹדַע לוֹ שֶׁהוּא מַיִם אוֹ שֵׁכָר — and by tasting it he became aware that it was water or beer, מִכָּל מָקוֹם — nevertheless,**

---

18. According to *Mishnah Berurah* (209:8), if there was wine in front of him, even if he did not have specific intention to drink more, he should drink some of the wine without reciting a new blessing. See also above, 50:4, and note 13 there.

19. Uttering even a single word not related to the blessing or to the meal is considered an interruption (*Mishnah Berurah* 206:12 and 167:37). Even saying *Baruch Shem kevod malchuso le'olam va'ed* ("Blessed is the Name of His glorious kingdom for all eternity," normally said when one recites Hashem's Name in vain; see above, 6:4) constitutes an interruption here (*Shaar HaTziyun* 209:12).

20. In *se'if* 4 there, Kitzur discusses the laws pertaining to one who recited a blessing on a food but was unable to partake of it. In *se'if* 5, he rules that although initially one may not wait more than the time of *k'dei dibbur* between reciting the blessing and eating the food, nevertheless, one who did wait is not required to repeat the blessing as long as he did not interrupt with speech.

לֹא הָוֵי הֶפְסֵק בְּדִיעֲבַד[21] (וּלְעִנְיַן קִידּוּשׁ עַיֵּין לְקַמָּן סִימָן ע״ז סְעִיף י״ב).

לֹא הָוֵי הֶפְסֵק בְּדִיעֲבַד — it is not considered an interruption after the fact.[21] **(וּלְעִנְיַן קִידּוּשׁ עַיֵּין לְקַמָּן סִימָן ע״ז סְעִיף י״ב — With regard to *Kiddush*,** i.e., what to do if after reciting *Kiddush*, one realized that the cup of *Kiddush* contained a beverage other than wine, **see below, *Siman* 77, *se'if* 12.)**

---

21. Thus, he should drink wine immediately so that the *borei pri hagafen* blessing should not have been recited in vain.

257 ONE RECITED A BLESSING ON FOOD AND WAS BROUGHT MORE — SIMAN 57:1

סימן נז

דִּין בֵּירַךְ עַל מַאֲכָל אוֹ מַשְׁקֶה וְאַחַר כָּךְ הֵבִיאוּ לוֹ עוֹד

וּבוֹ ז׳ סְעִיפִים

א. בֵּירַךְ עַל הַלֶּחֶם וְלֹא הָיָה בְדַעְתּוֹ לֶאֱכוֹל יוֹתֵר מִמַּה שֶּׁהֵכִין לוֹ, כְּגוֹן שֶׁקָּנָה לוֹ לֶחֶם אוֹ גְלוּסְקָא וְסָבַר שֶׁיִּהְיֶה לוֹ דַּי, וְשׁוּב נִתְאַוָּה לֶאֱכוֹל יוֹתֵר וְשָׁלַח לִקְנוֹת לוֹ עוֹד, אֲפִילוּ יֵשׁ לְפָנָיו עוֹד מִמַּה שֶּׁהֵכִין לוֹ בַּתְּחִלָּה[1], מִכָּל מָקוֹם צָרִיךְ לְבָרֵךְ שֵׁנִית ״הַמּוֹצִיא״ עַל מַה שֶּׁהֵבִיאוּ לוֹ מִשּׁוּם דַּהֲוֵי נִמְלָךְ[2]. אֲבָל מִי שֶׁיֵּשׁ לוֹ לֶחֶם בְּבֵיתוֹ וְחָתַךְ לְעַצְמוֹ חֲתִיכָה, שֶׁהָיָה סָבַר שֶׁיִּהְיֶה לוֹ דַּי, וְאַחַר כָּךְ נִתְאַוָּה

SIMAN 57

THE LAW OF ONE WHO RECITED A BLESSING ON FOOD OR DRINK AND WAS SUBSEQUENTLY BROUGHT MORE

CONTAINING 7 *SE'IFIM*

§1 Purchasing or Slicing Additional Bread / §2 Specific Intent / §3 No Specific Intent / §4 More Important Fruit / §5 Different Types / §6 A Guest / §7 Multiple Cups of Wine

As we have seen (above, 50:11), the effectiveness of a blessing is not limited to the specific item upon which the blessing was recited. A single blessing is effective for additional food of the same type, and even for other foods that are subject to the same blessing, provided that they were included in the original intent of the one who is reciting the blessing. This *Siman* delineates the conditions and limitations of this provision.

§1 **בֵּירַךְ עַל הַלֶּחֶם — If one recited a blessing on bread** **וְלֹא הָיָה בְדַעְתּוֹ לֶאֱכוֹל יוֹתֵר מִמַּה שֶּׁהֵכִין לוֹ — and did not intend to eat more than what he prepared for himself,** **כְּגוֹן — for example,** **שֶׁקָּנָה לוֹ לֶחֶם אוֹ גְלוּסְקָא — he purchased bread or a roll for himself,** **וְסָבַר שֶׁיִּהְיֶה לוֹ דַּי — thinking that it would suffice for his** needs, **וְשׁוּב נִתְאַוָּה לֶאֱכוֹל יוֹתֵר — and afterward he desired to eat more,** **וְשָׁלַח לִקְנוֹת לוֹ עוֹד — and sent** someone **to purchase more** bread **for him,** **אֲפִילוּ יֵשׁ לְפָנָיו עוֹד מִמַּה שֶּׁהֵכִין לוֹ בַּתְּחִלָּה —** in such a case, **even if there is more of what he originally prepared for himself** still left **in front of him,**[1] **מִכָּל מָקוֹם — nevertheless,** **צָרִיךְ לְבָרֵךְ שֵׁנִית ״הַמּוֹצִיא״ עַל מַה שֶּׁהֵבִיאוּ לוֹ — he must recite *hamotzi* again on what they brought him,** **מִשּׁוּם דַּהֲוֵי נִמְלָךְ — for it is** deemed **a change of mind,** and the new bread is not included in the original blessing.[2]

אֲבָל מִי שֶׁיֵּשׁ לוֹ לֶחֶם בְּבֵיתוֹ — However, if one has bread in his home, **וְחָתַךְ לְעַצְמוֹ חֲתִיכָה — and,** in preparation for his meal, **he cut a piece for himself,** **שֶׁהָיָה סָבַר שֶׁיִּהְיֶה לוֹ דַּי — because he thought that it would suffice** for **his** meal, **וְאַחַר כָּךְ נִתְאַוָּה**

1. This is in contrast to the halachah below in *se'if* 3, in which having some of the original food left over is a criterion.

2. In this case, his actions attest to the fact that he originally planned to eat only one roll; otherwise he would have purchased more in the first place (see *Mishnah Berurah* 174:18).

ONE RECITED A BLESSING ON FOOD AND WAS BROUGHT MORE — SIMAN 57:2-3 258

לְיוֹתֵר וְחָתַךְ לוֹ עוֹד, אַף עַל פִּי שֶׁאֵין לוֹ עוֹד מִן הָרִאשׁוֹן, אֵין צָרִיךְ לְבָרֵךְ שֵׁנִית דְּזֶה לֹא מִקְרֵי נִמְלַךְ כִּי הַדֶּרֶךְ הוּא כָּךְ[3].

ב. בֵּירַךְ עַל הַפֵּירוֹת שֶׁהוּא אוֹכֵל וְהֵבִיאוּ לוֹ אַחַר כָּךְ עוֹד פֵּירוֹת, אִם בִּשְׁעַת הַבְּרָכָה הָיְתָה דַעְתּוֹ עַל כָּל מַה שֶּׁיָּבִיאוּ לוֹ, אֲזַי אֲפִילוּ אִם אֵין לוֹ עוֹד מֵהָרִאשׁוֹנוֹת, וַאֲפִילוּ אֵינָן מִמִּין הָרִאשׁוֹן אֶלָּא שֶׁבִּרְכוֹתֵיהֶן שָׁווֹת, אֵינוֹ צָרִיךְ לְבָרֵךְ שֵׁנִית עַל אֵלּוּ שֶׁהֵבִיאוּ לוֹ[4]. וְאִם הוּא נִמְלַךְ מַמָּשׁ, דְּהַיְינוּ שֶׁמִּתְּחִלָּה לֹא הָיָה דַעְתּוֹ לֶאֱכוֹל רַק אֵלּוּ שֶׁהֵם לְפָנָיו וְאַחַר כָּךְ נִמְלַךְ לֶאֱכוֹל יוֹתֵר, אֲזַי אֲפִילוּ הֵם מִמִּין הָרִאשׁוֹן וְגַם יֵשׁ לְפָנָיו עוֹד גַּם מֵהָרִאשׁוֹנוֹת, מִכָּל מָקוֹם צָרִיךְ לְבָרֵךְ שֵׁנִית עַל אֵלּוּ שֶׁהֵבִיאוּ לוֹ.

ג. וְאִם מִתְּחִלָּה הָיְתָה דַעְתּוֹ סְתָם לֹא כָּךְ וְלֹא כָּךְ, אֲזַי יֵשׁ חִילוּק: שֶׁאִם

לְיוֹתֵר — and afterward he desired more **וְחָתַךְ לוֹ עוֹד — and cut more** bread **for himself, אַף עַל פִּי שֶׁאֵין לוֹ עוֹד מִן הָרִאשׁוֹן — even though he has no more of the original** piece of bread left **אֵין צָרִיךְ לְבָרֵךְ שֵׁנִית — he need not recite another blessing, דְּזֶה לֹא מִקְרֵי נִמְלַךְ — for it is not considered a change of mind, כִּי הַדֶּרֶךְ הוּא כָּךְ — since it is the** normal **manner to do this.**[3]

§2 **בֵּירַךְ עַל הַפֵּירוֹת שֶׁהוּא אוֹכֵל** — If **one recited a blessing on the fruit that he is eating, וְהֵבִיאוּ לוֹ אַחַר כָּךְ עוֹד פֵּירוֹת — and they brought more fruit to him afterward,** the halachah is as follows: **אִם בִּשְׁעַת הַבְּרָכָה הָיְתָה דַעְתּוֹ עַל כָּל מַה שֶּׁיָּבִיאוּ לוֹ — If at the time of the blessing he had in mind** that the blessing should apply to **all that they will bring him, אֲזַי אֲפִילוּ אִם אֵין לוֹ עוֹד מֵהָרִאשׁוֹנוֹת — then even if he has no more of the first** fruit left, **וַאֲפִילוּ אֵינָן מִמִּין הָרִאשׁוֹן — and even if** the fruits that he was later brought **were not of the same type as the first one, אֶלָּא שֶׁבִּרְכוֹתֵיהֶן שָׁווֹת — as long as their blessings are the same, אֵינוֹ צָרִיךְ לְבָרֵךְ שֵׁנִית עַל אֵלּוּ שֶׁהֵבִיאוּ לוֹ — he need not recite a second blessing on those that they brought him.**[4] **וְאִם הוּא נִמְלַךְ מַמָּשׁ — If,** on the other hand, **he had a definite change of mind, דְּהַיְינוּ — that is, שֶׁמִּתְּחִלָּה לֹא הָיָה דַעְתּוֹ לֶאֱכוֹל רַק אֵלּוּ שֶׁהֵם לְפָנָיו — he originally only intended to eat those** items **that were before him, וְאַחַר כָּךְ נִמְלַךְ לֶאֱכוֹל יוֹתֵר — and afterward he changed his mind** and decided **to eat more, אֲזַי אֲפִילוּ הֵם מִמִּין הָרִאשׁוֹן — then, even if** the fruits that were brought **are of the** same **type as the first, וְגַם יֵשׁ לְפָנָיו עוֹד גַּם מֵהָרִאשׁוֹנוֹת — and he also** still **has before him more of the first ones, מִכָּל מָקוֹם צָרִיךְ לְבָרֵךְ שֵׁנִית עַל אֵלּוּ שֶׁהֵבִיאוּ לוֹ — he must nevertheless recite a second blessing on those that they brought him** now.

§3 **וְאִם מִתְּחִלָּה הָיְתָה דַעְתּוֹ סְתָם לֹא כָּךְ וְלֹא כָּךְ — But if** when he **originally** recited the blessing on the fruit that he was eating, **he did not have specific intent one way or the other,** and he was brought more fruit afterward, **אֲזַי יֵשׁ חִילוּק — then it**

---

3. Since it is normal for a person who thought that one piece would suffice to later decide to take additional pieces (and he did not clearly indicate that this was *not* his intent), all that he subsequently eats is also included in his original blessing (see *Mishnah Berurah* 174:18).

4. According to opinions cited by *Mishnah Berurah* (206:22), one who has sat down for a fixed session of eating fruit need not recite another blessing on fruits that are brought in afterward even if he had no specific intent, for the additional fruits are included in his original intention.

בְּשָׁעָה שֶׁהֵבִיאוּ לוֹ הַשְּׁנִיּוֹת לֹא הָיָה לוֹ עוֹד מֵהָרִאשׁוֹנוֹת צָרִיךְ לְבָרֵךְ שֵׁנִית[5], אֲבָל אִם הָיָה לוֹ אָז עוֹד מֵהָרִאשׁוֹנוֹת יֵשׁ סָפֵק אִם צָרִיךְ לְבָרֵךְ שֵׁנִית עַל הַשְּׁנִיּוֹת אוֹ אֵינוֹ צָרִיךְ[6]. לָכֵן טוֹב לִיזָּהֵר שֶׁכְּשֶׁהוּא מְבָרֵךְ תְּהֵא דַעְתּוֹ עַל כָּל מַה שֶּׁיָּבִיאוּ לוֹ. וְאִם לֹא הָיְתָה דַעְתּוֹ כָּךְ אֶלָּא בִסְתָמָא, כֵּיוָן דְּאִיכָּא סְפֵיקָא בִּבְרָכָה יֵשׁ לוֹ לִמְנוֹעַ אֶת עַצְמוֹ מִלְּאָכְלָם.

ד. הֵבִיאוּ לוֹ פְּרִי שֶׁהוּא חָשׁוּב וְחָבִיב עָלָיו יוֹתֵר מִן הָרִאשׁוֹנוֹת, אוֹ שֶׁהוּא מִמִּין שִׁבְעָה[7], אֲפִילוּ יֵשׁ לְפָנָיו עוֹד מֵהָרִאשׁוֹנוֹת, צָרִיךְ לְבָרֵךְ עַל זֶה שֶׁהֵבִיאוּ לוֹ[8]. כִּי מַה שֶּׁאֵינוֹ חָשׁוּב אֵינוֹ יָכוֹל לִפְטוֹר אֶת הֶחָשׁוּב דֶּרֶךְ גְּרָרָא אֶלָּא דַּוְקָא

---

depends upon the following: שֶׁאִם בְּשָׁעָה שֶׁהֵבִיאוּ לוֹ הַשְּׁנִיּוֹת — **If at the time when they brought him the second** batch of fruit לֹא הָיָה לוֹ עוֹד מֵהָרִאשׁוֹנוֹת — **he no longer had any of the first** fruits **left,** צָרִיךְ לְבָרֵךְ שֵׁנִית — **he must recite a second blessing;**[5] אֲבָל אִם הָיָה לוֹ אָז עוֹד מֵהָרִאשׁוֹנוֹת — **but if he had some of the first** fruits left, יֵשׁ סָפֵק — **there is a** halachic **doubt** אִם צָרִיךְ לְבָרֵךְ שֵׁנִית עַל הַשְּׁנִיּוֹת אוֹ אֵינוֹ צָרִיךְ — **whether or not he needs to recite a second blessing on the second** batch of fruit.[6] לָכֵן טוֹב לִיזָּהֵר — **Therefore, it is advisable to be careful** שֶׁכְּשֶׁהוּא מְבָרֵךְ — **when one recites a blessing,** תְּהֵא דַעְתּוֹ עַל כָּל מַה שֶּׁיָּבִיאוּ לוֹ — **to have in mind** that his blessing should encompass **whatever they may bring him.** וְאִם לֹא הָיְתָה דַעְתּוֹ כָּךְ — **And if he did not have this in mind,** אֶלָּא בִסְתָמָא — **but rather, he had no specific** intent, כֵּיוָן דְּאִיכָּא סְפֵיקָא בִּבְרָכָה — **since there is a doubt with regard to the blessing,** יֵשׁ לוֹ לִמְנוֹעַ אֶת עַצְמוֹ מִלְּאָכְלָם — **he should refrain from eating** the fruits that are subsequently brought to him.

§4 הֵבִיאוּ לוֹ — **If they brought to one** who previously recited a blessing on fruit and had no specific intent when reciting the blessing, פְּרִי שֶׁהוּא חָשׁוּב וְחָבִיב עָלָיו יוֹתֵר מִן הָרִאשׁוֹנוֹת — **a fruit that is more significant and desirable to him than the first ones,** אוֹ שֶׁהוּא מִמִּין שִׁבְעָה — **or that is** one **of the Seven Species** with which Eretz Yisrael was praised[7] (and the first food was not one of the Seven Species), אֲפִילוּ יֵשׁ לְפָנָיו עוֹד מֵהָרִאשׁוֹנוֹת — the halachah is that **even if he still has some of the first** fruit (upon which he recited the blessing) left **before him,** צָרִיךְ לְבָרֵךְ עַל זֶה שֶׁהֵבִיאוּ לוֹ — **he must recite a** new **blessing on this** fruit **that they brought him.**[8] כִּי מַה שֶּׁאֵינוֹ חָשׁוּב — **For** the blessing on **the one that is not** as **significant** אֵינוֹ יָכוֹל לִפְטוֹר אֶת הֶחָשׁוּב דֶּרֶךְ גְּרָרָא — **cannot exempt the significant one incidentally,** אֶלָּא דַּוְקָא

---

5. According to *Mishnah Berurah* (206:22), this applies only if it was not the exact same food; for example, he was eating apples and was brought oranges. However, if he was eating apples and was brought more apples, he need not recite a blessing even if none of the original apples were left when the new ones were brought.

6. *Mishnah Berurah* (206:22) rules that in this case one need not recite a blessing (unless it was an entirely different species; see below, *se'if* 5).

7. The Seven Species with which Eretz Yisrael was praised are enumerated by the Torah in *Devarim* 8:8: אֶרֶץ חִטָּה וּשְׂעֹרָה וְגֶפֶן וּתְאֵנָה וְרִמּוֹן אֶרֶץ זֵית שֶׁמֶן וּדְבָשׁ, *A land of wheat, barley, grape, fig, and pomegranates; a land of oil-olives and date-honey.* See above, 51:7.

8. According to *Mishnah Berurah* (211:32), even if the more important one was in front of him when he recited the blessing, he must have it specifically in mind in order to exempt it. Otherwise he must recite a new blessing (see ibid. §33 for an exception). See below, *se'if* 6, with note 11.

ONE RECITED A BLESSING ON FOOD AND WAS BROUGHT MORE — SIMAN 57:5 260

בְּשֶׁנִּתְכַּוֵּין לְפָטְרוֹ (כִּדְלְעֵיל סִימָן נ׳ סְעִיף י״א).

ה. בֵּירַךְ עַל הַשֵּׁכָר וְנִתְכַּוֵּין לִפְטוֹר כָּל מַה שֶּׁיָּבִיאוּ לוֹ מִבִּרְכַּת ״שֶׁהַכֹּל״ וְהֵבִיאוּ לוֹ דָּגִים, אֵינוֹ צָרִיךְ לְבָרֵךְ עַל הַדָּגִים. אֲבָל אִם הָיְתָה דַעְתּוֹ סְתָם, אֲפִילוּ אִם בְּשָׁעָה שֶׁהֵבִיאוּ אֶת הַדָּגִים עֲדַיִין הָיָה שֵׁכָר לְפָנָיו, מִכָּל מָקוֹם צָרִיךְ לְבָרֵךְ עַל הַדָּגִים[9], וְלֹא דָמֵי לְפֵירוֹת אֲפִילוּ שֶׁאֵלּוּ תַּפּוּחִים וְאֵלּוּ אֱגוֹזִים מִכָּל מָקוֹם הַכֹּל מִין אוֹכֶל הוּא, אֲבָל שֵׁכָר וְדָגִים הֵמָּה לְגַמְרֵי שְׁנֵי מִינִים מְחוּלָּקִים — זֶה אוֹכֶל וְזֶה מַשְׁקֶה. וְאֵינָן פּוֹטְרִין זֶה אֶת זֶה אֶלָּא אִם כֵּן הָיוּ לְפָנָיו בִּשְׁעַת בְּרָכָה אוֹ שֶׁהָיְתָה דַעְתּוֹ עֲלֵיהֶם[10].

בְּשֶׁנִּתְכַּוֵּין לְפָטְרוֹ — unless he had specific **intent to exempt it** **(כִּדְלְעֵיל סִימָן נ׳ סְעִיף י״א — as above,** ***Siman*** **50,** ***se'if*** **11).**

§5 בֵּירַךְ עַל הַשֵּׁכָר — If one recited a *shehakol* **blessing on beer, וְנִתְכַּוֵּין לִפְטוֹר כָּל מַה שֶּׁיָּבִיאוּ לוֹ — and he had in mind to exempt** with this blessing **whatever** food item **they will bring him מִבִּרְכַּת ״שֶׁהַכֹּל״ — whose blessing is** ***shehakol*** (above, 52:2-3), **וְהֵבִיאוּ לוֹ דָּגִים — and they brought him fish, אֵינוֹ צָרִיךְ לְבָרֵךְ עַל הַדָּגִים — he need not recite an** additional **blessing on the fish. אֲבָל אִם הָיְתָה דַעְתּוֹ סְתָם — However, if he had no specific intention, אֲפִילוּ אִם בְּשָׁעָה שֶׁהֵבִיאוּ אֶת הַדָּגִים — even if at the time when they brought** him **the fish עֲדַיִין הָיָה שֵׁכָר לְפָנָיו —** some of **the beer was still in front of him, מִכָּל מָקוֹם צָרִיךְ לְבָרֵךְ עַל הַדָּגִים — he must nevertheless recite a blessing on the fish.**

Kitzur contrasts this with a previous ruling:

וְלֹא דָמֵי לְפֵירוֹת — It is not similar to fruits,[9] **אֲפִילוּ שֶׁאֵלּוּ תַּפּוּחִים —** for with regard to fruits **even if these** first ones **are apples וְאֵלּוּ אֱגוֹזִים — and these** second ones **are nuts, מִכָּל מָקוֹם הַכֹּל מִין אוֹכֶל הוּא — they are nevertheless all a type** of solid **food. אֲבָל שֵׁכָר וְדָגִים — Beer and fish, however, הֵמָּה לְגַמְרֵי שְׁנֵי מִינִים מְחוּלָּקִים — are two totally distinct types; זֶה אוֹכֶל וְזֶה מַשְׁקֶה — one is a** solid **food and the other is a beverage. וְאֵינָן פּוֹטְרִין זֶה אֶת זֶה — Therefore, they do not exempt each other אֶלָּא אִם כֵּן הָיוּ לְפָנָיו בִּשְׁעַת בְּרָכָה — unless they were in front** of the person **at the time** he recited **the blessing, אוֹ שֶׁהָיְתָה דַעְתּוֹ עֲלֵיהֶם — or he had intention to** eat **them.**[10]

---

9. In *se'if* 3, Kitzur ruled that if one recited the blessing on the fruit without specific intent to eat more fruit, and was brought more fruit while he had some of the first fruit left, there is a doubt whether he must recite a blessing on the second fruit (see note 5 there).

10. **In summary:** If one recites a blessing upon one food and more food is subsequently brought to him, the halachah is as follows:

(1) If the food was bread:
- a. If it is evident from his actions that he did not intend to eat more, he must recite a new blessing.
- b. If his intention was not clear, but he simply did not plan originally to eat more, he need not recite a new blessing.

(2) Upon other food:
- a. If he had specific intent for all foods subject to this blessing, no further blessing is necessary.
- b. If he had intent only for the food that was before him, a new blessing is necessary in all cases.
- c. If he had no specific intent, then:
  - (i) If the second food is more significant and desirable or one of the Seven Species, *or*, if he first recited a blessing upon a beverage and then he was brought a solid food, *or*, if none of the original food was left before him, a blessing is

261 ONE RECITED A BLESSING ON FOOD AND WAS BROUGHT MORE — SIMAN 57:6-7

ו. כָּל זֹאת לֹא מַיְירֵי אֶלָּא בְּאָדָם הָאוֹכֵל מִשֶּׁלּוֹ, אֲבָל אִם הוּא אוֹכֵל אֵצֶל חֲבֵרוֹ כֵּיוָן שֶׁבֵּירַךְ עַל מִין אֶחָד פּוֹטֵר כָּל מַה שֶּׁיָּבִיאוּ לוֹ, אֲפִילוּ אֵין לוֹ עוֹד מֵהָרִאשׁוֹנִים[11], דְּהַכֹּל תָּלוּי בְּדַעַת הַבַּעַל הַבַּיִת[12]. אַךְ אִם נִמְלַךְ מַמָּשׁ, אָז צָרִיךְ לְבָרֵךְ שֵׁנִית. וְאִם לֹא הָיָה בְּדַעַת בַּעַל הַבַּיִת לְהָבִיא יוֹתֵר רַק לְבַקָּשַׁת הָאוֹרְחִים נָתַן לָהֶם, גַּם כֵּן אֵינָן צְרִיכִין לְבָרֵךְ, לְפִי שֶׁהָאוֹרְחִים סוֹמְכִין בְּדַעְתָּם שֶׁהַבַּעַל הַבַּיִת מִסְתָמָא יִתֵּן לָהֶם כָּל צָרְכָּם.

ז. מִי שֶׁבָּא לִסְעוּדָה[13] וְנָתְנוּ לוֹ כּוֹס וּבֵירַךְ עָלָיו וְאַחַר כָּךְ שׁוּב נָתְנוּ לוֹ כּוֹסוֹת,

---

§6 כָּל זֹאת לֹא מַיְירֵי אֶלָּא בְּאָדָם הָאוֹכֵל מִשֶּׁלּוֹ — This entire discussion **pertains only to a person who is eating his own** food. **אֲבָל אִם הוּא אוֹכֵל אֵצֶל חֲבֵרוֹ — However, if he is eating at his fellow's** home, the halachah is that **כֵּיוָן שֶׁבֵּירַךְ עַל מִין אֶחָד — once he has recited a blessing on one type, פּוֹטֵר כָּל מַה שֶּׁיָּבִיאוּ לוֹ — it exempts all** food **that they will serve him** that is subject to that blessing, **אֲפִילוּ אֵין לוֹ עוֹד מֵהָרִאשׁוֹנִים — even if** when he was served the second food **he has no more of the first** ones upon which he recited the blessing before him,[11] **דְּהַכֹּל תָּלוּי בְּדַעַת הַבַּעַל הַבַּיִת — for it is entirely dependent upon the intent of the host.**[12] **אַךְ אִם נִמְלַךְ מַמָּשׁ — Nevertheless, if** the guest **had a definite change of mind** (i.e., he first made a conscious decision not to eat more and then changed his mind), **אָז צָרִיךְ לְבָרֵךְ שֵׁנִית — he must then recite a second blessing. וְאִם לֹא הָיָה בְּדַעַת בַּעַל הַבַּיִת לְהָבִיא יוֹתֵר — Even if the host had no intention of serving more, רַק לְבַקָּשַׁת הָאוֹרְחִים נָתַן לָהֶם — and only** in response **to the request of the guests did he give them** more, **גַּם כֵּן אֵינָן צְרִיכִין לְבָרֵךְ — they still need not recite a blessing, לְפִי שֶׁהָאוֹרְחִים סוֹמְכִין בְּדַעְתָּם — for the guests expect שֶׁהַבַּעַל הַבַּיִת מִסְתָמָא יִתֵּן לָהֶם כָּל צָרְכָּם — that the host will presumably serve them whatever they need.**

§7 מִי שֶׁבָּא לִסְעוּדָה — Regarding **one who came to a meal,**[13] **וְנָתְנוּ לוֹ כּוֹס — and they gave him a cup** of wine **וּבֵירַךְ עָלָיו — and he recited a blessing on it, וְאַחַר כָּךְ שׁוּב נָתְנוּ לוֹ כּוֹסוֹת — and afterward, they gave him additional cups** of wine,

---

required (according to *Mishnah Berurah,* this last condition is considered only if he was brought a different type of food).

(ii) If some of the original food was left, the ruling in this case is subject to a halachic doubt, and one should refrain from eating further (according to *Mishnah Berurah* one may eat further without reciting another blessing).

11. In this case, the second food does not require a new blessing even if it is more significant than the first food upon which he recited the blessing (*Beur Halachah* 211:5 s.v. ובלבד).

12. Because the guests are aware that the host customarily brings out many types of food, one after the other (*Mishnah Berurah* 179:17).

Rabbi Moshe Feinstein writes (*Igros Moshe, Orach Chaim* I, §125) that this halachah applies only when one was invited for the purpose of eating. One who visits his fellow for any other reason, and was offered something to eat, has no basis upon which to assume that the host will bring different types of food, and must therefore recite another blessing upon any other food that he is served that was not present when he recited the first blessing.

13. This is referring to one who was a casual visitor rather than a guest who was invited for the meal (*Mishnah Berurah* 174:19, 179:14). See end of next note.

ONE RECITED A BLESSING ON FOOD AND WAS BROUGHT MORE — SIMAN 57:7 262

אִם הַמִּנְהָג הוּא כֵּן, מִסְתָמָא הָיְתָה דַעְתּוֹ עַל כּוּלָּם וְאֵינוֹ צָרִיךְ לְבָרֵךְ עוֹד.

the halachah is that **אִם הַמִּנְהָג הוּא כֵּן** — **if it is the custom** to do **this,** i.e., to give several cups of wine to a visitor, **מִסְתָמָא הָיְתָה דַעְתּוֹ עַל כּוּלָּם** — **presumably, his** original **intent was** to exempt **all of them, וְאֵינוֹ צָרִיךְ לְבָרֵךְ עוֹד** — **and he is not required to recite another blessing** upon subsequent cups.[14]

14. It is nevertheless preferable that the visitor specifically have in mind at the time of the original blessing that it should exempt whatever will be served (*Mishnah Berurah* 179:16). In a place where there is no custom to offer a number of cups of wine to a visitor, the visitor must recite a blessing on each cup that he is served (see *Orach Chaim* 179:4). [An invited guest, however, is not dependent on this custom (*Shaar HaTziyun* 179:18), and need not recite a blessing on each cup (see *Mishnah Berurah* 179:17); see previous *se'if.*]

263 LAWS OF BLESSINGS FOR FRAGRANCES — SIMAN 58:1

סימן נח

דִּין בִּרְכַּת הָרֵיחַ

וּבוֹ י״ד סְעִיפִים

א. כְּשֵׁם שֶׁאָסוּר לְאָדָם לֵיהָנוֹת מִמַּאֲכָל אוֹ מַשְׁקֶה קוֹדֶם שֶׁיְּבָרֵךְ, כָּךְ אָסוּר לוֹ לֵיהָנוֹת מֵרֵיחַ טוֹב קוֹדֶם שֶׁיְּבָרֵךְ עָלָיו שֶׁנֶּאֱמַר (תהלים קנ, ו) ״כֹּל הַנְּשָׁמָה תְּהַלֵּל יָהּ״. אֵיזֶהוּ דָבָר שֶׁהַנְּשָׁמָה נֶהֱנֵית מִמֶּנּוּ וְאֵין הַגּוּף נֶהֱנֶה מִמֶּנּוּ? הֱוֵי אוֹמֵר: זֶה הָרֵיחַ (ברכות מג, ב)[1]. אֲבָל לְאַחֲרָיו אֵינוֹ צָרִיךְ לְבָרֵךְ, מִשּׁוּם דִּכְשֶׁמַּפְסִיק הָרֵיחַ מֵחוֹטְמוֹ כְּבָר עָבְרָה הֲנָאָתוֹ וְהָוֵי כְּמוֹ אוֹכֶל שֶׁנִּתְעַכֵּל בְּמֵעָיו[2].

SIMAN 58

THE LAWS OF BLESSINGS FOR FRAGRANCES

CONTAINING 14 *SE'IFIM*

§1 The Blessing Upon Fragrance / **§2** Fragrant Fruit / **§3** Fragrant Trees / **§4** Fragrant Herbs / **§5** Non-plant Fragrances / **§6** Balsam Oil / **§7** Reciting the Wrong Blessing / **§8** Fragrant Water or Oil / **§9** Precedence of Blessings / **§10** Incense / **§11** Intended for Fragrance / **§12** Spice Shop / **§13** Fragrance Without a Source / **§14** Forbidden Sources of Fragrance

In this *Siman,* Kitzur discusses the appropriate blessing to be recited upon each kind of fragrance, and other halachos regarding the recitation of these blessings.

§1 **כְּשֵׁם שֶׁאָסוּר לְאָדָם לֵיהָנוֹת מִמַּאֲכָל אוֹ מַשְׁקֶה — Just as it is forbidden for a person to derive benefit from food or drink קוֹדֶם שֶׁיְּבָרֵךְ — without first reciting a blessing** upon it, **כָּךְ אָסוּר לוֹ לֵיהָנוֹת מֵרֵיחַ טוֹב — so too, it is forbidden for him to derive benefit from a pleasing fragrance קוֹדֶם שֶׁיְּבָרֵךְ עָלָיו — without first reciting a blessing upon it, שֶׁנֶּאֱמַר — as** the verse (*Tehillim* 150:6) **states: ״כֹּל הַנְּשָׁמָה תְּהַלֵּל יָהּ״ — *Let all souls praise God.*** The verse speaks of the *soul* (rather than the body) expressing the praise of Hashem. **אֵיזֶהוּ דָבָר שֶׁהַנְּשָׁמָה נֶהֱנֵית מִמֶּנּוּ** — The Sages ask: **What is something from which the soul derives pleasure, וְאֵין הַגּוּף נֶהֱנֶה מִמֶּנּוּ — but from which the body does not derive pleasure? הֱוֵי אוֹמֵר: זֶה הָרֵיחַ — You must say that this is the fragrant smell** (*Berachos* 43b).[1]

אֲבָל לְאַחֲרָיו אֵינוֹ צָרִיךְ לְבָרֵךְ — Nevertheless, after enjoying a pleasant fragrance **one is not obligated to recite a blessing** as one does after partaking of food (see above, *Simanim* 51 and 54), **מִשּׁוּם דִּכְשֶׁמַּפְסִיק הָרֵיחַ מֵחוֹטְמוֹ — for once the scent no longer reaches his nose, כְּבָר עָבְרָה הֲנָאָתוֹ — his enjoyment has ceased וְהָוֵי כְּמוֹ אוֹכֶל שֶׁנִּתְעַכֵּל בְּמֵעָיו — and it is** thus **similar to food that has already been digested in his intestines,** upon which a *berachah acharonah* (final blessing) is not recited.[2]

---

1. Since smells do not enter the body in the same tangible form as do food and drink, smell is considered, by comparison to eating, a "pleasure of the soul" (see *Aruch HaShulchan* 216:1).

2. See above, 51:14. See *Mishnah Berurah* 216:4 for another reason.

ב. כֵּיצַד מְבָרֵךְ עַל הָרֵיחַ הַטּוֹב? אִם זֶה שֶׁיּוֹצֵא מִמֶּנּוּ הָרֵיחַ הוּא פְּרִי שֶׁהוּא רָאוּי לַאֲכִילָה, בֵּין שֶׁהוּא פְּרִי הָעֵץ בֵּין שֶׁהוּא פְּרִי הָאֲדָמָה, אַף עַל פִּי שֶׁאֵינוֹ רָאוּי לַאֲכִילָה אֶלָּא עַל יְדֵי תַעֲרוֹבֶת, כְּגוֹן אֱגוֹז מִישקאט ציטראן וְאֶתְרוֹג (בִּשְׁאָר יְמוֹת הַשָּׁנָה חוּץ סוּכּוֹת שֶׁיִּתְבָּאֵר בְּסִימָן קל״ז סְעִיף ז׳), מִכָּל מָקוֹם כֵּיוָן שֶׁעִיקָּרוֹ לַאֲכִילָה מְבָרֵךְ ״אֲשֶׁר נָתַן (וְיֵשׁ אוֹמְרִים ״הַנּוֹתֵן) רֵיחַ טוֹב בַּפֵּירוֹת״[3]. וְדַוְקָא כְּשֶׁנִּתְכַּוֵּין לְהָרִיחַ בּוֹ, אֲבָל אִם לֹא נִתְכַּוֵּין לְהָרִיחַ אֶלָּא לַאֲכִילָה וְהָרֵיחַ בָּא לוֹ מִמֵּילָא, אֵינוֹ צָרִיךְ לְבָרֵךְ עַל הָרֵיחַ[4]. הַמֵּרִיחַ בְּקאפע קָלוּי שֶׁיֵּשׁ לוֹ רֵיחַ טוֹב[5] מְבָרֵךְ ״אֲשֶׁר נָתַן רֵיחַ טוֹב בַּפֵּירוֹת״.

ג. אִם זֶה שֶׁיּוֹצֵא מִמֶּנּוּ הָרֵיחַ הוּא עֵץ, אוֹ מִין עֵץ[6], מְבָרֵךְ ״בּוֹרֵא עֲצֵי בְשָׂמִים״

---

§2 There are five different blessings for fragrances. The proper blessing is determined by the source of the fragrance:

כֵּיצַד מְבָרֵךְ עַל הָרֵיחַ הַטּוֹב — What blessing does one recite on a pleasant fragrance? אִם זֶה שֶׁיּוֹצֵא מִמֶּנּוּ הָרֵיחַ — If the item from which the fragrance emanates הוּא **פְּרִי שֶׁהוּא רָאוּי לַאֲכִילָה — is edible produce,** בֵּין שֶׁהוּא פְּרִי הָעֵץ בֵּין שֶׁהוּא פְּרִי **הָאֲדָמָה — whether it is a fruit or a vegetable,** אַף עַל פִּי שֶׁאֵינוֹ רָאוּי לַאֲכִילָה אֶלָּא **עַל יְדֵי תַעֲרוֹבֶת — even if it is only fit to be eaten when mixed** with some other food, **כְּגוֹן אֱגוֹז מִישקאט ציטראן — such as nutmeg** or **a lemon,** **וְאֶתְרוֹג — as well as an** ***esrog*** **(בִּשְׁאָר יְמוֹת הַשָּׁנָה חוּץ סוּכּוֹת — all year round besides during the Succos holiday, שֶׁיִּתְבָּאֵר בְּסִימָן קל״ז סְעִיף ז׳ — as will be detailed** below, in ***Siman*** **137,** ***se'if*** 7), **מִכָּל מָקוֹם כֵּיוָן שֶׁעִיקָּרוֹ לַאֲכִילָה — nevertheless, since its main function is to be eaten, מְבָרֵךְ — he recites the** following **blessing: ״אֲשֶׁר נָתַן (וְיֵשׁ אוֹמְרִים ״הַנּוֹתֵן) רֵיחַ טוֹב בַּפֵּירוֹת״** — *Baruch Atah Ado-noy Elokeinu Melech HaOlam, asher nasan* (some say to substitute "*hanosein*" for "*asher nasan*"[3]) *rei'ach tov bapeiros, Blessed are You,* H*ASHEM*, *our God, King of the universe,* ***Who gave*** **(some say:** ***Who gives*), *a pleasant aroma to fruits.*** **וְדַוְקָא כְּשֶׁנִּתְכַּוֵּין לְהָרִיחַ בּוֹ** — The obligation to recite a blessing over fragrant fruits applies **only when one intends to smell** the fruit. **אֲבָל אִם לֹא נִתְכַּוֵּין לְהָרִיחַ אֶלָּא לַאֲכִילָה — However, if he did not intend to smell** the fruit, **but** merely **to eat it, וְהָרֵיחַ בָּא לוֹ מִמֵּילָא — and the fragrance reaches his** nose **on its own, אֵינוֹ צָרִיךְ לְבָרֵךְ עַל הָרֵיחַ — he need not recite a blessing over the fragrance.**[4] **הַמֵּרִיחַ בְּקאפע קָלוּי שֶׁיֵּשׁ לוֹ רֵיחַ טוֹב — One who smells roasted coffee that has a pleasant aroma**[5] **מְבָרֵךְ ״אֲשֶׁר נָתַן רֵיחַ טוֹב בַּפֵּירוֹת״ — should recite the blessing of** ***asher nasan rei'ach tov bapeiros.***

§3 **אִם זֶה שֶׁיּוֹצֵא מִמֶּנּוּ הָרֵיחַ הוּא עֵץ — If the source of the fragrance is a tree, אוֹ מִין עֵץ — or a tree-like** plant (i.e., a shrub),[6] **מְבָרֵךְ — one recites the** following **blessing: ״בּוֹרֵא עֲצֵי בְשָׂמִים״** — *Baruch Atah Ado-noy Elokeinu Melech*

---

3. *Mishnah Berurah* (216:9) rules that one should recite *asher nasan*, "Who gave."

4. If, when taking the fruit, he intended to both eat it and to smell it, he should first recite the blessing upon smelling and then the blessing upon eating. Alternatively, he may make the blessing upon eating, and eat a bit of the fruit while having the intention not to enjoy the smell; after this, he can make the second blessing and smell the fruit (*Mishnah Berurah* 216:10; see also *Beur Halachah* ibid. s.v. ולא נתכוין and או לאוכלו).

5. The case, as described by *Mishnah Berurah* (216:16), is one in which one smells the pleasurable scent emanating from hot ground coffee beans.

6. See following *se'if* regarding how to identify which species fall into the category of "shrub"

וְלָכֵן עַל הַהֲדַס וְעַל וֶרֶד שֶׁקּוֹרִין ראזען[7] וְעַל הַלְּבוֹנָה וְכַיּוֹצֵא מֵהֶם מְבָרְכִין "בּוֹרֵא עֲצֵי בְשָׂמִים", דְּכֵיוָן דְּעִיקָּרוֹ אֵינוֹ לַאֲכִילָה אֶלָּא לְהָרִיחַ לֹא הָוֵי פְּרִי[8]. עַל פִּלְפְּלִין וְעַל זַנְגְּבִיל (אונגבער) — יֵשׁ אוֹמְרִים דִּמְבָרְכִין, וְיֵשׁ אוֹמְרִים דְּאֵין מְבָרְכִין[9], עַל כֵּן אֵין לְהָרִיחַ בָּהֶם.

ד. עַל עֵשֶׂב וְיֶרֶק מְבָרְכִין "בּוֹרֵא עִשְׂבֵי בְשָׂמִים" (הָעַיִן בְּחִירִק[10] וְהַבֵּי"ת רְפוּיָה[11] כִּי הַחִירִק הוּא תְּנוּעָה קַלָּה[12] וְגַם הַבֵּי"ת שֶׁל "בְּשָׂמִים" רְפוּיָה[13,14] דְּסָמוּךְ

---

*HaOlam borei atzei vesamim, Blessed are You, Hashem, our God, King of the Universe, **Who creates fragrant trees.*** וְלָכֵן — **Therefore,** עַל הַהֲדַס וְעַל וֶרֶד שֶׁקּוֹרִין ראזען — **upon** smelling **a myrtle branch**[7] **or a rose,** וְעַל הַלְּבוֹנָה וְכַיּוֹצֵא מֵהֶם — **or upon frankincense or similar** fragrant plants, מְבָרְכִין "בּוֹרֵא עֲצֵי בְשָׂמִים" — **we recite the blessing of** *borei atzei vesamim.* דְּכֵיוָן דְּעִיקָּרוֹ אֵינוֹ לַאֲכִילָה אֶלָּא לְהָרִיחַ — **Since the primary** purpose of such items **is not for eating, but rather for** their **fragrance,** לֹא הָוֵי פְּרִי — **they are not considered "fruit,"** and the blessing of *hanosein rei'ach tov bapeiros,* "Who gave a pleasant aroma to fruits," is not appropriate.[8] עַל פִּלְפְּלִין וְעַל זַנְגְּבִיל (אונגבער) — **Upon** smelling **pepper or ginger,** יֵשׁ אוֹמְרִים דִּמְבָרְכִין — **some** authorities **rule that we recite a blessing,** וְיֵשׁ אוֹמְרִים דְּאֵין מְבָרְכִין — **and other** authorities **rule that we do not recite a blessing.**[9] עַל כֵּן אֵין לְהָרִיחַ בָּהֶם — **Therefore, one should** avoid this situation of uncertainty and **not smell them.**

§4 עַל עֵשֶׂב וְיֶרֶק — **Upon** fragrant **grasses and herbs,** מְבָרְכִין — **we recite the** following **blessing:** "בּוֹרֵא עִשְׂבֵי בְשָׂמִים" — *Baruch Atah Ado-noy Elokeinu Melech HaOlam borei isvei vesamim, Blessed are You, Hashem, our God, King of the Universe, **Who creates fragrant herbage.*** (הָעַיִן בְּחִירִק — **The** letter ***ayin*** (ע) of the word *isvei* (עשבי) is vowelized **with a *chirik,***[10] וְהַבֵּי"ת רְפוּיָה — **and the** letter ***beis*** (ב) of this word (עשבי), **is a soft** *veis,*[11] כִּי הַחִירִק הוּא תְּנוּעָה קַלָּה — **because the *chirik*** in the syllable that precedes it **is a "slight" vowel.**[12] וְגַם הַבֵּי"ת שֶׁל "בְּשָׂמִים" רְפוּיָה — **The letter *beis* in** the word ***vesamim*** (בְּשָׂמִים) **is also a soft** *veis,*[13] דְּסָמוּךְ לְאהו"י — following the rule of Hebrew grammar that the letter *beis*[14] is always

---

or "tree," and which under the category of "herb" with regard to this blessing.

7. On Succos, however, one may not smell the myrtle branch used with the *lulav* (see below, 137:7).

8. Although rose petals are edible (see above, 52:9), since their primary purpose is not to be used as food, one recites the *borei atzei vesamim* blessing. See *Shaar HaTziyun* 216:5 regarding rose oil and other products derived from parts of trees. Upon roses that grow from the ground and not on a shrub, one recites *borei isvei vesamim,* "Who creates fragrant herbage," as in the following *se'if* (*Mishnah Berurah* 216:17).

9. *Eliyahu Rabbah* (297:1) explains that the dispute hinges on whether spices such as pepper and ginger are considered "seasonings," which are meant to accompany food and are exempt from blessings for their fragrance, or if they are to be considered "smelling spices," whose *fragrance* is meant to be enjoyed, and, thus, require a blessing. See *Mishnah Berurah* 297:1.

10. Pronounced "*isvei,*" not "*esvei*" or "*eisvei.*"

11. It is not punctuated as a *beis* (בּ) [pronounced as a "b"], but as a *veis* (ב) [pronounced as a "v"]. The word עִשְׂבֵי is thus pronounced *isvei,* not *isbei.*

12. Not to be confused with the more common תְּנוּעָה קְטַנָּה, *"minor" vowel.* For explanation of this rule, see *Kesses HaSofer* (by the author of the Kitzur), introduction to second section, §24.

13. Thus, it is pronounced "*vesamim,*" not "*besamim.*"

14. This rule also applies to the letters ג, ד, כ, פ, ת (together referred to as בג"ד כפ"ת).

לְאֹהוּ"י)[15]. וְהַסִּימָן לֵידַע מַה הוּא עֵץ וּמַה הוּא יָרֶק — כָּל שֶׁהַגִּבְעוֹל הוּא קָשֶׁה
כְּגִבְעוֹל שֶׁל פִּשְׁתָּן וּמִתְקַיֵּים מִשָּׁנָה לְשָׁנָה וּמוֹצִיא עָלִין, זֶהוּ עֵץ. וְאוֹתָן שֶׁהַגִּבְעוֹל
לְעוֹלָם רַךְ, הֲוֵי "עִשְׂבֵי בְשָׂמִים"[16].

ה. אִם אֵינוֹ לֹא מִין עֵץ וְלֹא מִין עֵשֶׂב, כְּמוֹ הַמּוּסְק (פּיזאם)[17], מְבָרֵךְ עָלָיו "בּוֹרֵא
מִינֵי בְשָׂמִים". וְכֵן עַל שְׁווֹעַמְלִיךְ יְבֵשִׁים שֶׁיֵּשׁ לָהֶם רֵיחַ טוֹב, אִם מֵרִיחַ בָּהֶם
נִרְאֶה לִי דְּיֵשׁ לְבָרֵךְ "בּוֹרֵא מִינֵי בְשָׂמִים"[18].

ו. עַל שֶׁמֶן אֲפַרְסְמוֹן[19] הַגָּדֵל בְּאֶרֶץ יִשְׂרָאֵל[20], לַחֲשִׁיבוּתוֹ שֶׁגָּדֵל בְּאֶרֶץ יִשְׂרָאֵל
קָבְעוּ לוֹ בְּרָכָה בִּפְנֵי עַצְמָהּ, וּמְבָרְכִין עָלָיו "בּוֹרֵא שֶׁמֶן עָרֵב".

pronounced in its "hard" form when beginning a syllable except **when immediately preceded by** a syllable ending in the letter *aleph, hei, vav,* or *yud,* in which case it is pronounced as its "soft" form, as in our case, where it follows the word עִשְׂבֵי, *isvei.*)[15]

וְהַסִּימָן לֵידַע מַה הוּא עֵץ וּמַה הוּא יָרֶק — **The indication with which to determine what is a tree and what is an herb,** with regard to this halachah, is as follows: כָּל שֶׁהַגִּבְעוֹל הוּא קָשֶׁה כְּגִבְעוֹל שֶׁל פִּשְׁתָּן — **Any** plant whose stem is as firm as the stem of the flax plant, וּמִתְקַיֵּים מִשָּׁנָה לְשָׁנָה — **lasts from year to year,** וּמוֹצִיא עָלִין — **and produces leaves,** זֶהוּ עֵץ — **is considered a tree;** וְאוֹתָן שֶׁהַגִּבְעוֹל לְעוֹלָם רַךְ — those plants whose stems always remain soft הֲוֵי "עִשְׂבֵי בְשָׂמִים" — are **considered to be fragrant herbs.**[16]

§5 אִם אֵינוֹ לֹא מִין עֵץ וְלֹא מִין עֵשֶׂב — **If the source of the fragrance is neither a type of tree nor a type of herb,** כְּמוֹ הַמּוּסְק (פּיזאם) — **such as musk,**[17] מְבָרֵךְ עָלָיו — **one recites upon it** the following blessing: "בּוֹרֵא מִינֵי בְשָׂמִים" — **Baruch Atah Ado-noy Elokeinu Melech HaOlam borei minei vesamim, Blessed are You,** HASHEM, **our God, King of the Universe, Who creates species of fragrance.** וְכֵן עַל שְׁווֹעַמְלִיךְ יְבֵשִׁים — **Similarly, upon dried mushrooms** שֶׁיֵּשׁ לָהֶם רֵיחַ טוֹב — **that have a pleasant fragrance,** אִם מֵרִיחַ בָּהֶם — **if one smells them** נִרְאֶה לִי דְּיֵשׁ לְבָרֵךְ "בּוֹרֵא מִינֵי בְשָׂמִים" — it seems to me that **he is to recite the blessing of** *borei minei vesamim.*[18]

§6 עַל שֶׁמֶן אֲפַרְסְמוֹן — **Upon balsam oil**[19] הַגָּדֵל בְּאֶרֶץ יִשְׂרָאֵל — **that grows in the Land of Israel,** לַחֲשִׁיבוּתוֹ שֶׁגָּדֵל בְּאֶרֶץ יִשְׂרָאֵל — **because of its distinction due to the fact that it grows in the Land of Israel,**[20] קָבְעוּ לוֹ בְּרָכָה בִּפְנֵי עַצְמָהּ — **the** Sages **designated for it a unique blessing;** וּמְבָרְכִין עָלָיו — **thus, when smelling this oil we recite upon it** the following blessing: "בּוֹרֵא שֶׁמֶן עָרֵב" — **Baruch Atah Ado-noy Elokeinu Melech HaOlam borei shemen areiv — Blessed are You,** HASHEM, **our God, King of the Universe, Who creates pleasant oil.**

---

15. *Sefer Michlol* by *Radak,* 80a.

16. According to *Beur Halachah* (216:3 s.v. עצי בשמים), one recites the blessing of *borei atzei vesamim* ["Who creates fragrant trees"] only if the tree fulfills all the criteria of a tree with regard to the halachos of reciting *borei pri ha'eitz* upon its fruit (see above, 52:1). If it has a firm stem, but does not fulfill all of those criteria, one should recite the blessing of

borei minei vesamim ["Who creates species of fragrance"] (see below, *se'if 7*).

17. Musk is a scent derived from an animal source (*Mishnah Berurah* 216:7).

18. Mushrooms are not classified as "trees" nor as "herbs"; see above, 52:3.

19. This fragrance is derived from the sap of a balsam tree (*Mishnah Berurah* 216:22).

20. See *Shaar HaTziyun* 216:21, 25.

ז. בֵּירַךְ עַל שֶׁל עֵץ "עִשְׂבֵי בְשָׂמִים", (והן) (וְכֵן) לְהִיפּוּךְ, לֹא יָצָא[21]. אֲבָל אִם בֵּירַךְ "בּוֹרֵא מִינֵי בְשָׂמִים" עַל כָּל הַמִּינִים, יָצָא. וְלָכֵן, בְּכָל דָּבָר שֶׁהוּא מְסוּפָּק בְּבִרְכָתוֹ וְאִי אֶפְשַׁר לוֹ לְהִתְבָּרֵר[22], מְבָרֵךְ עָלָיו "בּוֹרֵא מִינֵי בְשָׂמִים"[23]. וְנִרְאֶה לִי דְּאִם בֵּירַךְ עַל פְּרִי הָעֵץ "בּוֹרֵא עֲצֵי בְשָׂמִים" יָצָא[24]. וְעַל כֵּן נִרְאֶה לִי כִּי עַל נעגליך וְכֵן עַל קְלִיפַּת מעראנצען וְצוטראנין יֵשׁ לְבָרֵךְ "בּוֹרֵא עֲצֵי בְשָׂמִים"[25].

ח. שֶׁמֶן, אוֹ מַיִם, שֶׁבִּשְּׂמוֹ בִּבְשָׂמִים[26], אִם בַּעֲצֵי בְשָׂמִים — מְבָרֵךְ "עֲצֵי בְשָׂמִים",

---

§7 בֵּירַךְ עַל שֶׁל עֵץ "עִשְׂבֵי בְשָׂמִים" — **If, upon** a fragrance derived **from a tree, one** mistakenly **recited the** *borei **isvei vesamim*** **blessing** (*Who creates fragrant herbs*), (והן) (וְכֵן) לְהִיפּוּךְ — **or the reverse,** i.e., one mistakenly recited the *borei atzei vesamim* blessing (*Who creates fragrant trees*) upon a fragrant herb, לֹא יָצָא — **he has not fulfilled his obligation.** אֲבָל אִם בֵּירַךְ "בּוֹרֵא מִינֵי בְשָׂמִים" — **However, if he recited** ***borei minei vesamim*** *(Who creates species of fragrance)* עַל כָּל הַמִּינִים — **upon any type of fragrance,** יָצָא — **he has fulfilled his obligation.**[21] וְלָכֵן, בְּכָל דָּבָר שֶׁהוּא מְסוּפָּק בְּבִרְכָתוֹ — **Therefore,** before smelling **any item about which he is unsure as to the** appropriate **blessing,** וְאִי אֶפְשַׁר לוֹ לְהִתְבָּרֵר — **and he is unable to have** the matter **clarified,**[22] מְבָרֵךְ עָלָיו "בּוֹרֵא מִינֵי בְשָׂמִים" — **he should recite upon it** ***borei minei vesamim.***[23]
וְנִרְאֶה לִי — **It appears to me** דְּאִם בֵּירַךְ עַל פְּרִי הָעֵץ "בּוֹרֵא עֲצֵי בְשָׂמִים" — **that if, upon** smelling a fragrant **fruit, one recited** ***borei atzei vesamim,*** יָצָא — **he has fulfilled his obligation.**[24] וְעַל כֵּן נִרְאֶה לִי — **Therefore, it appears to me** כִּי עַל נעגליך — **that upon** smelling **cloves** וְכֵן עַל קְלִיפַּת מעראנצען וְצוטראנין — **and upon** smelling **orange and lemon rinds,** יֵשׁ לְבָרֵךְ "בּוֹרֵא עֲצֵי בְשָׂמִים" — **one should recite the** ***borei atzei vesamim*** **blessing.**[25]

§8 שֶׁמֶן, אוֹ מַיִם, שֶׁבִּשְּׂמוֹ בִּבְשָׂמִים — Regarding **water or oil that was infused with fragrance from spices,**[26] the halachah is אִם בַּעֲצֵי בְשָׂמִים — **that if** it was infused **with** fragrance from **a** type of **fragrant tree,** מְבָרֵךְ "עֲצֵי בְשָׂמִים" — **then one**

---

21. The phrase *species of fragrance* refers to all types of fragrances, regardless of their origin. In contrast, the more specific blessings of *borei atzei vesamim* and *borei isvei vesamim* do not refer to any fragrances that are not derived from these respective sources.

22. See above, 50:2.

23. [In *se'if* 3 we have seen that when there is a doubt as to whether an item (in that case, pepper or ginger) requires a blessing before smelling it, one should avoid smelling it entirely. Here, however, it is certain that a blessing is required; the only doubt is as to the exact one. It is therefore appropriate to recite the general blessing of *borei minei vesamim* in this case.]

24. Although initially one must certainly recite the appropriate blessing, nevertheless, since a fruit is also a derivative of a tree, the blessing is effective.

25. It is questionable whether cloves and fruit rinds are to be viewed as fruit, and subject to the blessing of *asher nasan rei'ach tov bapeiros* ("Who gave a pleasant aroma to fruits"), or viewed as a product of the tree and subject to *borei atzei vesamim* ("Who creates fragrant trees"); see *Shaar HaTziyun* 216:12. Kitzur therefore concludes that one should recite *borei atzei vesamim,* which is effective regardless of which of these two blessings is the proper blessing. *Mishnah Berurah* (216:16), however, rules that due to the question with regard to the proper blessing upon cloves, one should recite *borei minei vesamim,* which is unquestionably effective (*Mishnah Berurah* does not discuss fruit rinds).

26. This refers to a case where at least some of the actual spices are still in the liquid; see further.

וְאִם בְּעִשְׂבֵי בְשָׂמִים — מְבָרֵךְ "בּוֹרֵא עִשְׂבֵי בְשָׂמִים", וְאִם הָיוּ בוֹ עֵצִים וַעֲשָׂבִים — מְבָרֵךְ "בּוֹרֵא מִינֵי בְשָׂמִים". וְכֵן בְּכָל מָקוֹם שֶׁיֵּשׁ רֵיחַ מְעוֹרָב מִמִּינִים שׁוֹנִים[27], מְבָרֵךְ "בּוֹרֵא מִינֵי בְשָׂמִים". אִם הוֹצִיאוּ הַבְּשָׂמִים[28] מִן הַשֶּׁמֶן וּמִן הַמַּיִם, יֵשׁ סָפֵק אִם מְבָרְכִים עֲלֵיהֶם כֵּיוָן שֶׁלֹּא נִשְׁאַר שָׁם הָעִיקָּר[29], עַל כֵּן אֵין לְהָרִיחַ בָּהֶם[30].

ט. הָיוּ לְפָנָיו פְּרִי הַמֵּרִיחַ וַעֲצֵי בְשָׂמִים וְעִשְׂבֵי בְשָׂמִים וּמִינֵי בְשָׂמִים, מְבָרֵךְ עַל כָּל אֶחָד בְּרָכָה הָרְאוּיָה לוֹ[31]. וּמַקְדִּים לְבָרֵךְ תְּחִלָּה עַל הַפְּרִי, וְאַחַר כָּךְ עַל הָעֵץ, וְאַחַר כָּךְ עַל עִשְׂבֵי בְשָׂמִים, וְאַחַר כָּךְ עַל מִינֵי בְשָׂמִים[32].

---

recites the blessing ***borei atzei vesamim*** (*Who creates fragrant trees*). **וְאִם בְּעִשְׂבֵי בְשָׂמִים** — **If** it was infused **with** fragrance from a type **of fragrant herb**, **מְבָרֵךְ "בּוֹרֵא עִשְׂבֵי בְשָׂמִים"** — **one recites the blessing *borei isvei vesamim*** (*Who creates fragrant herbs*). **וְאִם הָיוּ בוֹ עֵצִים וַעֲשָׂבִים** — **If** the water or oil **had** infused **in it** a combination of fragrances, from **trees and herbs**, **מְבָרֵךְ "בּוֹרֵא מִינֵי בְשָׂמִים"** — **one recites the blessing *borei minei vesamim*** (*Who creates species of fragrance*). **וְכֵן בְּכָל מָקוֹם** — **Similarly, in all circumstances** **שֶׁיֵּשׁ רֵיחַ מְעוֹרָב מִמִּינִים שׁוֹנִים** — **where a fragrance** emanates **from a combination of diverse species**, i.e., tree, herbs, and fruit sources,[27] **מְבָרֵךְ "בּוֹרֵא מִינֵי בְשָׂמִים"** — **one recites the blessing: *borei minei vesamim.*** **אִם הוֹצִיאוּ הַבְּשָׂמִים מִן הַשֶּׁמֶן וּמִן הַמַּיִם** — **If the spices were** completely[28] **removed from the oil or the water**, but the aroma remained, **יֵשׁ סָפֵק אִם מְבָרְכִים עֲלֵיהֶם** — **there is a** halachic **doubt whether** or not **a blessing is recited upon** the water or oil, **כֵּיוָן שֶׁלֹּא נִשְׁאַר שָׁם הָעִיקָּר** — **since the** original **source** of the fragrance **is no longer present.**[29] **עַל כֵּן אֵין לְהָרִיחַ בָּהֶם** — **Therefore, one should not smell** such fragrances.[30]

§9 **הָיוּ לְפָנָיו** — **If one had before him** the following items: **פְּרִי הַמֵּרִיחַ** — **a fragrant fruit,** **וַעֲצֵי בְשָׂמִים** — items from a **fragrant tree,** **וְעִשְׂבֵי בְשָׂמִים** — **fragrant herbs,** **וּמִינֵי בְשָׂמִים** — **and** other **kinds of fragrant items,** **מְבָרֵךְ עַל כָּל אֶחָד בְּרָכָה הָרְאוּיָה לוֹ** — **one should recite the appropriate blessing for each.**[31] **וּמַקְדִּים לְבָרֵךְ תְּחִלָּה עַל הַפְּרִי** — **First, he should recite the blessing upon the** fragrant **fruit;** **וְאַחַר כָּךְ עַל הָעֵץ** — **after that, upon the** fragrant item from the **tree;** **וְאַחַר כָּךְ עַל עִשְׂבֵי בְשָׂמִים** — **after that, upon the fragrant herbs;** **וְאַחַר כָּךְ עַל מִינֵי בְשָׂמִים** — **and after that, upon the other kinds of fragrances.**[32]

---

27. I.e., where different types of fragrant species are mixed or bundled together in such a manner that one cannot smell each type separately and recite its appropriate blessing. If possible, however, one should remove one [of each type] from the bundle and recite its appropriate blessing; see following *se'if* (see *Mishnah Berurah* 216:39 [a]).

28. *Mishnah Berurah* 216:29.

29. The remaining aroma may be considered too insignificant to be considered a fragrance upon which a blessing is required (*Mishnah Berurah* 216:31).

30. If other spices are available, one can recite the appropriate blessing over that spice and then enjoy the aroma emanating from the oil (*Mishnah Berurah* 216:32). If no other spice is available, *Mishnah Berurah* rules that one who does not wish to conduct himself stringently [and abstain from smelling it] may recite the blessing of *borei minei vesamim* and smell the oil or water.

31. That is, when each one can be taken separately. When each individual fragrance cannot be isolated, one recites *borei minei vesamim*; see previous *se'if*, and below, *se'if* 12.

32. The more specific blessings are to be recited before the less specific blessings; see above, 55:4. *Mishnah Berurah* (216:40) writes that if one normally prefers smelling herbs

י. מוּגְמָר[33], דְּהַיְינוּ שֶׁמְּשִׂימִין בְּשָׂמִים עַל גֶּחָלִים שֶׁיַּעֲלֶה רֵיחַ טוֹב, מְבָרְכִין עָלָיו מִשֶּׁיַּעֲלֶה הֶעָשָׁן קוֹדֶם שֶׁיַּגִּיעַ לוֹ הָרֵיחַ, כְּמוֹ בְּכָל בִּרְכַּת הַנֶּהֱנִין[34]. אֲבָל לֹא יְבָרֵךְ קוֹדֶם שֶׁעוֹלֶה הֶעָשָׁן, דִּבְעִינַן בְּרָכָה סָמוּךְ לַהֲנָאָה[35]. אִם הַמּוּגְמָר הוּא מִין עֵץ, מְבָרֵךְ "עֲצֵי בְשָׂמִים". וְאִם שֶׁל עֵשֶׂב — "עִשְׂבֵי בְשָׂמִים". וְאִם שֶׁל שְׁאָר מִינִים — (בו"מ) "(בּוֹרֵא מִינֵי בְשָׂמִים)". וְדַוְקָא כְּשֶׁמְּגַמֵּר בִּשְׁבִיל לְהָרִיחַ, אֲבָל מַה שֶּׁמְּעַשְּׁנִין בִּשְׁבִיל לְבַטֵּל הַסִּרְחוֹן, כְּדֶרֶךְ שֶׁנּוֹתְנִים בְּשָׂמִים אֵצֶל הַמֵּתִים, אֵין מְבָרְכִין עָלָיו כְּלָל.

---

§10 Generally, when reciting a blessing upon a fragrance, one should grasp the fragrant item in his right hand, recite the blessing, and then smell it (see above, 50:3). One should not recite the blessing before picking it up, since the blessing should be recited immediately prior to enjoying it. In this *se'if,* Kitzur details when the blessing should be recited upon a fragrance that one cannot hold in his hand while reciting the blessing.[33]

מוּגְמָר — When burning **incense,** **דְּהַיְינוּ שֶׁמְּשִׂימִין בְּשָׂמִים עַל גֶּחָלִים** — **that is,** the practice of **placing spices on burning coals** **שֶׁיַּעֲלֶה רֵיחַ טוֹב** — **in order to bring out a pleasant fragrance,** **מְבָרְכִין עָלָיו מִשֶּׁיַּעֲלֶה הֶעָשָׁן** — **one recites the blessing upon it after the smoke begins to rise** from the coals, **קוֹדֶם שֶׁיַּגִּיעַ לוֹ הָרֵיחַ** — but **before the aroma reaches him,** **כְּמוֹ בְּכָל בִּרְכַּת הַנֶּהֱנִין** — **as** one does **with any other blessing over physical pleasures.**[34] **אֲבָל לֹא יְבָרֵךְ קוֹדֶם שֶׁעוֹלֶה הֶעָשָׁן** — **However, one should not recite the blessing before the smoke rises,** **דִּבְעִינַן בְּרָכָה סָמוּךְ לַהֲנָאָה** — **for we require that the blessing** be recited **close to** the time when **the enjoyment** will take place.[35] **אִם הַמּוּגְמָר הוּא מִין עֵץ, מְבָרֵךְ "עֲצֵי בְשָׂמִים"** — **If the incense** was made from **a type of tree** or shrub, **he recites the blessing** *borei **atzei** vesamim* (*Who creates fragrant trees*); **וְאִם שֶׁל עֵשֶׂב** — **if** the incense was made **from a** fragrant **herb,** **"עִשְׂבֵי בְשָׂמִים"** — he recites *borei **isvei** vesamim* (*Who creates fragrant herbs*); **וְאִם שֶׁל שְׁאָר מִינִים** — **if** the incense comes **from some other** (non-plant) **species,** **(בו"מ) "(בּוֹרֵא מִינֵי בְשָׂמִים)"** — he recites ***borei minei vesamim*** (*Who creates species of fragrance*). **וְדַוְקָא כְּשֶׁמְּגַמֵּר בִּשְׁבִיל לְהָרִיחַ** — One recites the blessing **only when he is burning the incense in order to enjoy its fragrance.** **אֲבָל מַה שֶּׁמְּעַשְּׁנִין בִּשְׁבִיל לְבַטֵּל הַסִּרְחוֹן** — **However,** upon **the incense-smoke produced in order to neutralize a foul odor,** **כְּדֶרֶךְ שֶׁנּוֹתְנִים בְּשָׂמִים אֵצֶל הַמֵּתִים** — **such as when they place fragrances near** the bodies of **the dead,** **אֵין מְבָרְכִין עָלָיו כְּלָל** — **we do not recite any blessing at all.**

---

over the items from a fragrant tree or shrub, he should recite the blessing upon the herbs and smell them before reciting the blessing and smelling the item derived from fragrant trees (see above, 55:1).

When faced with two blessings, one upon eating food and another upon smelling the fragrance of another item, one should recite the blessing upon the food first (*Mishnah Berurah* 216:4).

33. See *Beur Halachah* 216:12 s.v. קודם שיגיע and *Tzlach* to *Berachos* 43a s.v. והא לא קארח.

34. As with all other blessings upon physical pleasure, one recites the blessing just before one begins to experience that pleasure, e.g., one recites the blessing upon food before beginning to eat or drink. In this case as well, one is to recite the blessing just before one begins to smell the pleasant fragrance.

35. To recite the blessing before the incense begins to burn is too far removed from the actual enjoyment. *Mishnah Berurah* (216:48) writes that in the event he did recite the blessing before the incense began to emit smoke, he has nevertheless fulfilled his obligation and should not repeat the blessing, as long as he did not interrupt between reciting the blessing and beginning to enjoy the fragrance (see above, 50:5).

יא. וְכֵן כָּל דָּבָר שֶׁאֵינוֹ עוֹמֵד לְהָרִיחַ, כְּגוֹן בְּשָׂמִים הַמּוּנָּחִים בְּחֶדֶר לִסְחוֹרָה[36], וְכֵן מוּגְמָר שֶׁמְּגַמְּרִין בּוֹ אֶת הַכֵּלִים שֶׁלֹּא נַעֲשָׂה לְהָרִיחַ בְּעַצְמוֹ רַק לִיתֵּן רֵיחַ בַּכֵּלִים, אֵין מְבָרְכִין עֲלֵיהֶם אַף עַל פִּי שֶׁהוּא מִתְכַּוֵּין לְהָרִיחַ[37].

יב. הַנִּכְנָס לְתוֹךְ חָנוּת שֶׁל בְּשָׂמִים אוֹ אפאטהעק[38] וְנִתְכַּוֵּין לְהָרִיחַ, מְבָרֵךְ "בּוֹרֵא מִינֵי בְשָׂמִים"[39], כִּי הַבְּשָׂמִים שֶׁבְּחָנוּת עוֹמְדִין לְהָרִיחַ דְּנִיחָא לֵיהּ לְבַעַל הֶחָנוּת שֶׁיָּרִיחוּ בְּנֵי אָדָם וְיִקְנוּ[40]. נִכְנָס וְיוֹצֵא, נִכְנָס וְיוֹצֵא, אִם הָיָה דַעְתּוֹ מִתְּחִלָּה לַחֲזוֹר, אֵינוֹ צָרִיךְ לְבָרֵךְ[41]. וְאִם הֵסִיחַ דַּעְתּוֹ, אוֹ שֶׁיָּצָא וְשָׁהָה זְמַן מְרוּבֶּה,

---

§11 וְכֵן כָּל דָּבָר שֶׁאֵינוֹ עוֹמֵד לְהָרִיחַ — **Similarly, any item that is not meant to be smelled** on its own, כְּגוֹן בְּשָׂמִים הַמּוּנָּחִים בְּחֶדֶר לִסְחוֹרָה — **such as spices in** a storage **room for commercial purposes,**[36] וְכֵן מוּגְמָר שֶׁמְּגַמְּרִין בּוֹ אֶת הַכֵּלִים — **or incense used to perfume garments,** שֶׁלֹּא נַעֲשָׂה לְהָרִיחַ בְּעַצְמוֹ — **that is not meant to be smelled by itself,** רַק לִיתֵּן רֵיחַ בַּכֵּלִים — **but only to impart a fragrance to garments,** אֵין מְבָרְכִין עֲלֵיהֶם — **we do not recite a blessing upon** smelling **them** אַף עַל פִּי שֶׁהוּא מִתְכַּוֵּין לְהָרִיחַ — **even if one intends to enjoy the fragrance.**[37]

§12 הַנִּכְנָס לְתוֹךְ חָנוּת שֶׁל בְּשָׂמִים — **One who enters a shop that sells spices,** אוֹ אפאטהעק — **or a pharmacy,**[38] וְנִתְכַּוֵּין לְהָרִיחַ — **and intends to smell** the fragrances there, מְבָרֵךְ "בּוֹרֵא מִינֵי בְשָׂמִים" — **recites the blessing** ***borei minei vesamim*** (*Who creates species of fragrance*),[39] כִּי הַבְּשָׂמִים שֶׁבְּחָנוּת עוֹמְדִין לְהָרִיחַ — **as the spices in the shop are meant to be smelled,** דְּנִיחָא לֵיהּ לְבַעַל הֶחָנוּת שֶׁיָּרִיחוּ בְּנֵי אָדָם — **for the owner of the shop wants people to smell** the fragrances וְיִקְנוּ — **so that they will** be motivated to **purchase** them.[40] נִכְנָס וְיוֹצֵא, נִכְנָס וְיוֹצֵא — **One who enters and leaves** a spice shop **several times,** אִם הָיָה דַעְתּוֹ מִתְּחִלָּה לַחֲזוֹר — **if** when he **originally** left, **he intended to return** shortly, אֵינוֹ צָרִיךְ לְבָרֵךְ — **he need not recite** another **blessing** upon his return.[41] וְאִם הֵסִיחַ דַּעְתּוֹ — **However, if he diverted his attention** from the spices, אוֹ שֶׁיָּצָא וְשָׁהָה זְמַן מְרוּבֶּה — **or if he left** the

---

36. This applies only when encountering the smell upon walking into the room. If one takes up these spices in his hand to smell them, he has granted them the status of items that are meant to be smelled, and he should recite the blessing (*Mishnah Berurah* 217:1).

37. If the incense was burned with the intention of enjoying the fragrance *and* imparting the fragrance into garments, a blessing is recited when smelling the incense (*Mishnah Berurah* 217:14).

38. In the past, medicines were commonly composed of ground herbs. A pharmacy (apothecary)was therefore a place likely to have a pleasant aroma emanating from many different species of herbs.

39. The fragrance that greets the customer upon entering the shop comes from multiple sources, and each individual source of fragrance cannot be isolated. Therefore, as Kitzur ruled in *se'if* 8, the general blessing *borei minei vesamim* is recited. Where each spice is distinct (as in *se'if* 9), a separate blessing is recited over each type (*Mishnah Berurah* 217:3).

40. This case is therefore distinct from that of the previous *se'if*, where the spices are put away in a storehouse and are not currently for sale; since those are not meant to be enjoyed, one does not recite a blessing upon smelling them. The aroma of spices in a shop, however, is meant to be enjoyed so as to motivate people to purchase them, and therefore requires a blessing (see *Mishnah Berurah* 217:1). [As noted by *Misgeres HaShulchan* (cited in *Beur Halachah* loc. cit.), this would not appear to apply in a pharmacy, where one's motivation is dependent upon his medical needs, not on the aroma of the medications. Although *Mishnah Berurah* offers a resolution to this issue, he nevertheless raises other issues with the application of this ruling to a pharmacy.]

41. Even if upon his return he smells a

אוֹ שֶׁנִּכְנַס לַחֲנוּת אַחֵר, צָרִיךְ לְבָרֵךְ בְּכָל פַּעַם[42].

יג. רֵיחַ שֶׁאֵין לוֹ עִיקָר, כְּגוֹן בְּגָדִים שֶׁהֵם מוּגְמָרִים, אוֹ שֶׁהָיוּ בְשָׂמִים מוּנָּחִים בִּכְלִי וְקָלַט רֵיחַ, וְכֵן הַמְמַשְׁמֵשׁ בְּאֶתְרוֹגִים, אוֹ בִשְׁאָר פֵּירוֹת הַמְרִיחִים, וְנִשְׁאַר בְּיָדוֹ אוֹ בְּבִגְדוֹ רֵיחַ, אֵין מְבָרְכִין עָלָיו.

יד. בְּסִימָן קנ״ב סְעִיף (י׳) [ח׳] יְבוֹאָר דְּאָסוּר לְהָרִיחַ בִּבְשָׂמִים[44] שֶׁל אִשָּׁה[43], וּבְסִימָן קס״ז סְעִיף ה׳ יְבוֹאָר דְּאָסוּר לְהָרִיחַ בְּרֵיחַ שֶׁנַּעֲשָׂה לַעֲבוֹדַת כּוֹכָבִים, וּמִכָּל שֶׁכֵּן דְּאָסוּר לְבָרֵךְ עֲלֵיהֶם.

---

shop **and delayed** his return **for a long time,** **אוֹ שֶׁנִּכְנַס לַחֲנוּת אַחֵר — or if he entered a different** spice **shop,** **צָרִיךְ לְבָרֵךְ בְּכָל פַּעַם — he must recite a blessing each time,** i.e., upon smelling the fragrance again, either upon returning to the first shop, or if he entered a second shop, upon smelling the fragrance there.[42]

§13 **רֵיחַ שֶׁאֵין לוֹ עִיקָר** — Regarding a **fragrance whose source is not present,** **כְּגוֹן בְּגָדִים שֶׁהֵם מוּגְמָרִים — for example, garments that were perfumed** with incense, **אוֹ שֶׁהָיוּ בְשָׂמִים מוּנָּחִים בִּכְלִי וְקָלַט רֵיחַ — or when spices were stored in a container and** the container **absorbed the scent;** **וְכֵן הַמְמַשְׁמֵשׁ בְּאֶתְרוֹגִים, אוֹ בִשְׁאָר פֵּירוֹת הַמְרִיחִים — similarly, one who handled *esrogim* or other fragrant fruit** **וְנִשְׁאַר בְּיָדוֹ אוֹ בְּבִגְדוֹ רֵיחַ — and the scent remained on his hands or clothing,** **אֵין מְבָרְכִין עָלָיו — we do not recite a blessing upon** smelling the garments, spice containers, or hands.

§14 **בְּסִימָן קנ״ב סְעִיף ח׳ יְבוֹאָר — In *Siman* 152, *se'if* 8, it will be set forth** **דְּאָסוּר לְהָרִיחַ בִּבְשָׂמִים שֶׁל אִשָּׁה — that it is prohibited** for a man **to smell a woman's**[43] **fragrances;**[44] **וּבְסִימָן קס״ז סְעִיף ה׳ יְבוֹאָר — in *Siman* 167, *se'if* 5, it will be set forth** **דְּאָסוּר לְהָרִיחַ בְּרֵיחַ שֶׁנַּעֲשָׂה לַעֲבוֹדַת כּוֹכָבִים — that it is forbidden to smell a fragrance produced for idol worship.** **וּמִכָּל שֶׁכֵּן דְּאָסוּר לְבָרֵךְ עֲלֵיהֶם — Certainly, then,** if one smells such fragrances, **it is forbidden to recite a blessing upon them.**

---

fragrance that he did not smell before, he need not recite another blessing, since the original blessing is still in effect (*Mishnah Berurah* 217:7). If one remained in the shop for an extended period of time, even if he diverted his attention from the fragrance, he need not recite a new blessing upon enjoying the fragrance again, since the fragrance was constantly present (*Shulchan Aruch* 217:1; *Mishnah Berurah* 217:4).

42. This halachah applies to anyone entering a spice shop. *Mishnah Berurah* (217:4) writes that the proprietor of the store should, upon entering the store for the first time in the day, intend to enjoy the fragrance and recite the blessing. Afterward he does not recite another blessing, even after leaving and then returning to the shop, since even when he leaves his shop, his intention [even if unexpressed] is always to return (*Mishnah Berurah* 217:4).

43. See also below 153:10, where Kitzur discusses a similar law pertaining to one's wife while she is a *niddah*.

44. I.e., fragrances worn by a woman (e.g., in a container around her neck) or carried in her hand or mouth (*Shulchan Aruch* 217:4), even if she is not wearing them at this time (*Mishnah Berurah* 217:17; see also Kitzur 152:10).

THE SHEHECHEYANU AND HATOV VEHAMEITIV BLESSINGS — SIMAN 59:1 272

סימן נט

דִּין בִּרְכַּת "שֶׁהֶחֱיָנוּ" וְ"הַטּוֹב וְהַמֵּטִיב"

וּבוֹ כ"א סְעִיפִים

א. עַל שְׁמוּעוֹת טוֹבוֹת[1] שֶׁשָּׁמַע מִפִּי אָדָם נֶאֱמָן שֶׁרָאָה אֶת הַדָּבָר, וּמִכָּל שֶׁכֵּן אִם הוּא בְּעַצְמוֹ רָאָה אֶת הַדָּבָר, אִם הִיא טוֹבָה רַק לוֹ לְבַדּוֹ[2], מְבָרֵךְ "שֶׁהֶחֱיָנוּ"[3]. וְאִם הִיא טוֹבָה לוֹ וְגַם לַאֲחֵרִים, מְבָרֵךְ "בָּרוּךְ אַתָּה ה' אֱלֹהֵינוּ מֶלֶךְ הָעוֹלָם הַטּוֹב וְהַמֵּטִיב", כְּלוֹמַר, טוֹב לוֹ וְגַם מֵטִיב לַחֲבֵרוֹ[4]. אִם בְּשָׁעָה שֶׁהוּא רוֹאֶה אוֹ שׁוֹמֵעַ אֶת הַשְּׁמוּעָה

SIMAN 59

THE LAWS OF THE SHEHECHEYANU AND THE HATOV VEHAMEITIV BLESSINGS

CONTAINING 21 *SE'IFIM*

§1 Blessings Over Good Tidings / **§2** Blessing Over Bad Tidings / **§3** Long-term Consequences / **§4** Everything for the Good / **§5** Upon the Birth of a Son / **§6** Upon the Death of a Relative / **§7-9** Upon Purchasing an Item / **§10** Upon Receiving a Gift / **§11** Upon Acquiring Torah Books / **§12** Insignificant Acquisitions / **§13** "Wear Out and Replace!" / **§14-17** Upon Enjoying New Fruits / **§18** *Shehecheyanu* on Fragrance / **§19** Enjoying God's Bounty / **§20-21** Seeing a Friend After an Absence

§1 עַל שְׁמוּעוֹת טוֹבוֹת — Upon good tidings[1] **שֶׁשָּׁמַע מִפִּי אָדָם נֶאֱמָן שֶׁרָאָה אֶת הַדָּבָר — that one heard from a trustworthy person who** personally **witnessed the occurrence, וּמִכָּל שֶׁכֵּן אִם הוּא בְּעַצְמוֹ רָאָה אֶת הַדָּבָר — and certainly if he himself saw the occurrence,** the halachah is **אִם הִיא טוֹבָה רַק לוֹ לְבַדּוֹ — that if** the occurrence **is beneficial to him alone,**[2] **מְבָרֵךְ "שֶׁהֶחֱיָנוּ" — he recites the *Shehecheyanu* blessing.**[3] **וְאִם הִיא טוֹבָה לוֹ וְגַם לַאֲחֵרִים — If** the occurrence **is beneficial to him as well as to others, מְבָרֵךְ — he should recite** the following **blessing: "בָּרוּךְ אַתָּה ה' אֱלֹהֵינוּ מֶלֶךְ הָעוֹלָם הַטּוֹב וְהַמֵּטִיב"** — *Baruch Atah Ado-noy Elokeinu Melech HaOlam, HaTov VeHaMeitiv,* ***Blessed are You,*** ***Hashem, our God, King of the universe, Who is good and does good.*** **כְּלוֹמַר** — The **meaning** of this blessing is, **טוֹב לוֹ** — God **"is good" to him,** i.e., to the one reciting the blessing, **וְגַם מֵטִיב לַחֲבֵרוֹ — and also "does good" to his fellow,** i.e., the other recipient of this beneficial occurrence.[4] **אִם בְּשָׁעָה שֶׁהוּא רוֹאֶה אוֹ שׁוֹמֵעַ אֶת הַשְּׁמוּעָה — If, at the time that he sees** the

---

1. That is, tidings that gladden the one who hears them (*Mishnah Berurah* 222:3).

2. For example, one who receives word that he is the sole recipient of an inheritance (see below, *se'if* 6).

3. The full text of the blessing is בָּרוּךְ אַתָּה ה' אֱלֹהֵינוּ מֶלֶךְ הָעוֹלָם שֶׁהֶחֱיָנוּ וְקִיְּמָנוּ וְהִגִּיעָנוּ לַזְּמַן הַזֶּה [*Baruch Atah Ado-noy Elokeinu Melech HaOlam, shehecheyanu vekiyemanu vehigi'anu la'zeman hazeh*], *Blessed are You,* Hashem, *our God, King of the universe, Who has kept us alive, and sustained us, and brought us to this season.* The halachos pertaining to this blessing are discussed in greater detail later in this *Siman.*

4. When the occurrence does not affect him at all, and only affects others, one does not recite a blessing.

אֵינוֹ יָכוֹל לְבָרֵךְ מֵחֲמַת גּוּפוֹ אוֹ מֵחֲמַת מְקוֹמוֹ[5]**, יָכוֹל לְבָרֵךְ אַחַר כָּךְ. וְכֵן בְּבִרְכַּת "דַּיַּין הָאֱמֶת".**

ב. חַיָּיב הָאָדָם לְבָרֵךְ אֶת ה׳ יִתְבָּרֵךְ שְׁמוֹ גַּם עַל הָרָעָה, שֶׁנֶּאֱמַר (דברים ו, ה) **"וְאָהַבְתָּ אֵת ה׳ אֱלֹהֶיךָ בְּכָל לְבָבְךָ וּבְכָל נַפְשְׁךָ וּבְכָל מְאֹדֶךָ"**[6] (ברכות נד, א). **"בְּכָל לְבָבְךָ" — בִּשְׁנֵי יְצָרֶיךָ, בְּיֵצֶר טוֹב וּבְיֵצֶר הָרַע**[7] **(פֵּירוּשׁ גַּם כְּשֶׁהוּא עוֹסֵק בְּעִנְיְנֵי עוֹלָם הַזֶּה יְקַיֵּים "בְּכָל דְּרָכֶיךָ דָעֵהוּ"** (משלי ג, ו) **עַיֵּין לְעֵיל סִימָן ל"א)**[8]**. "וּבְכָל נַפְשְׁךָ" — אֲפִילוּ הוּא נוֹטֵל אֶת נַפְשְׁךָ**[9]**. "וּבְכָל מְאֹדֶךָ" — בְּכָל מָמוֹנְךָ**[10]**. דָּבָר אַחֵר: "בְּכָל מְאֹדֶךָ" —**

---

occurrence or **hears the good tidings,** אֵינוֹ יָכוֹל לְבָרֵךְ — **he is unable to recite the blessing** מֵחֲמַת גּוּפוֹ אוֹ מֵחֲמַת מְקוֹמוֹ — **because** either **his body or his location** is unclean,[5] יָכוֹל לְבָרֵךְ אַחַר כָּךְ — **he may recite the blessing later** after washing his hands or leaving the unclean location. וְכֵן בְּבִרְכַּת "דַּיַּין הָאֱמֶת" — **The same applies to the blessing of** *Dayan HaEmes, **the true Judge,*** discussed in the following *se'if.*

§2 חַיָּיב הָאָדָם לְבָרֵךְ אֶת ה׳ יִתְבָּרֵךְ שְׁמוֹ — **Man is obligated to bless Hashem, may His Name be blessed,** גַּם עַל הָרָעָה — **even for bad** occurrences, שֶׁנֶּאֱמַר — as the verse **states** (*Devarim* 6:5): "וְאָהַבְתָּ אֵת ה׳ אֱלֹהֶיךָ — ***You shall love HASHEM, your God,*** בְּכָל לְבָבְךָ וּבְכָל נַפְשְׁךָ וּבְכָל מְאֹדֶךָ" — ***with all your heart, with all your soul, and with all your resources.*** The Sages (*Berachos* 54a) elaborate on each of these three requirements:[6] "בְּכָל לְבָבְךָ" — בִּשְׁנֵי יְצָרֶיךָ — "*With all your heart*" means **with your two inclinations,** בְּיֵצֶר טוֹב וּבְיֵצֶר הָרַע — **with the good inclination and with the evil inclination.**[7] (פֵּירוּשׁ — **This means,** גַּם כְּשֶׁהוּא עוֹסֵק בְּעִנְיְנֵי עוֹלָם הַזֶּה — that **even while one is engaged in worldly pursuits**, which is naturally the domain of the evil inclination, יְקַיֵּים "בְּכָל דְּרָכֶיךָ דָעֵהוּ" — **he should fulfill** the injunction of, ***In all of your ways you must know Him*** (*Mishlei* 3:6); עַיֵּין לְעֵיל סִימָן ל"א — **see above, *Siman* 31.**)[8] "וּבְכָל נַפְשְׁךָ" — "***With all your soul***" indicates that you should love Hashem אֲפִילוּ הוּא נוֹטֵל אֶת נַפְשְׁךָ — **even if He takes your life.**[9] "וּבְכָל מְאֹדֶךָ" — בְּכָל מָמוֹנְךָ — The words *bechol me'odecha, **"with all your resources,"*** indicate that you must love Hashem **with all of your money,** i.e., all of your possessions.[10] דָּבָר אַחֵר: "בְּכָל מְאֹדֶךָ" — **An alternative interpretation** of the words

---

5. See *Siman* 5, regarding the requisite state of cleanliness of body and location for one to recite a blessing.

6. The lesson regarding blessing Hashem for bad occurrences is taught at the end of this passage.

7. The Sages interpret the heart as a metaphor for the seat of craving and aspiration. The word לְבָבְךָ, *your heart,* could have been written לִבְּךָ. Homiletically, the extra ב indicates a second heart: Thus, one should love God with *both* his inclinations (*Re'ah, Berachos* 54a).

8. One should strive to harness all of his desires and make all of his activities acts of serving God. This can be achieved by refining even one's physically oriented actions by performing them with correct intentions, and not pursuing them merely as a means of fulfilling his needs and desires. Kitzur elaborates on this concept in *Siman* 31.

9. There are times when one must be prepared to sacrifice his life for the love of God. For example, one must give up his life rather than commit idolatry; see *Rambam, Hil. Yesodei HaTorah* 5:7.

10. There are times when one must give up all that he owns for the love of Hashem. See *Rama, Yoreh Deah* 157:1, and *Beur HaGra* 157:4-5, for the exact circumstances where this is applicable.

בְּכָל מִדָּה וּמִדָּה שֶׁהוּא מוֹדֵד לְךָ, בֵּין מִדָּה טוֹבָה בֵּין מִדָּה פּוּרְעָנִיּוֹת, הֱוֵי מוֹדֶה לוֹ[11]. מָה הוּא מְבָרֵךְ? עַל שְׁמוּעוֹת רָעוֹת מְבָרֵךְ "בָּרוּךְ אַתָּה ה' אֱלֹהֵינוּ מֶלֶךְ הָעוֹלָם דַּיַּן הָאֱמֶת"[12]. אִם בָּאוּ לוֹ כַּמָּה שְׁמוּעוֹת בְּבַת אַחַת, בֵּין טוֹבוֹת בֵּין רָעוֹת, דַּי לוֹ בִּבְרָכָה אַחַת[13]. וְחַיָּיב אָדָם לְבָרֵךְ גַּם עַל הָרָעָה בְּדֵעָה שְׁלֵמָה וּבְנֶפֶשׁ חֲפֵיצָה[14] כְּמוֹ שֶׁהוּא מְבָרֵךְ עַל הַטּוֹבָה, שֶׁנֶּאֱמַר (תהלים קא, א) "חֶסֶד וּמִשְׁפָּט אָשִׁירָה לְךָ ה' אֲזַמֵּרָה" — אִם חֶסֶד, "אָשִׁירָה", וְאִם מִשְׁפָּט "אָשִׁירָה". כִּי גַּם הָרָעָה לְעוֹבְדֵי ה' יִתְבָּרֵךְ שְׁמוֹ הִיא שִׂמְחָתָם וְטוֹבָתָם, כֵּיוָן שֶׁמְּקַבֵּל בְּאַהֲבָה מַה שֶּׁגָּזַר עָלָיו ה' יִתְבָּרֵךְ שְׁמוֹ, בֶּאֱמוּנָתוֹ כִּי הַכֹּל כַּפָּרַת עֲוֹנוֹתָיו. נִמְצָא כִּי בְּקַבָּלַת רָעָה זוֹ הוּא עוֹבֵד אֶת ה', וְהָעֲבוֹדָה הִיא שִׂמְחָה לוֹ[15].

---

bechol me'odecha: בְּכָל מִדָּה וּמִדָּה שֶׁהוּא מוֹדֵד לְךָ — **With every measure that He metes out to you,** בֵּין מִדָּה טוֹבָה בֵּין מִדָּה פּוּרְעָנִיּוֹת — **whether a good measure or a measure of punishment,** הֱוֵי מוֹדֶה לוֹ — **you are to** continue to **thank Him.**[11] מָה הוּא מְבָרֵךְ — **What blessing does he recite?** עַל שְׁמוּעוֹת רָעוֹת מְבָרֵךְ — **Upon** hearing **bad tidings he should recite the** following **blessing:** "בָּרוּךְ אַתָּה ה' אֱלֹהֵינוּ מֶלֶךְ הָעוֹלָם דַּיַּן הָאֱמֶת" — *Baruch Atah Ado-noy Elokeinu Melech HaOlam, Dayan HaEmes,* ***Blessed are You, Hashem, our God, King of the universe, the true Judge.***[12] אִם בָּאוּ לוֹ כַּמָּה שְׁמוּעוֹת בְּבַת אַחַת — **If several tidings reached him at one time,** בֵּין טוֹבוֹת בֵּין רָעוֹת — **whether** they were all **good** tidings **or bad** ones, דַּי לוֹ בִּבְרָכָה אַחַת — **it is sufficient for him** to recite **only one blessing** for all of the news.[13]

וְחַיָּיב אָדָם לְבָרֵךְ גַּם עַל הָרָעָה — **A person is obligated to recite the blessing over bad** tidings בְּדֵעָה שְׁלֵמָה וּבְנֶפֶשׁ חֲפֵיצָה — **with** the same **completeness of mind and willingness of spirit,**[14] כְּמוֹ שֶׁהוּא מְבָרֵךְ עַל הַטּוֹבָה — **as when he recites the blessing over good** tidings, שֶׁנֶּאֱמַר — **as** the verse **states** (*Tehillim* 101:1): "חֶסֶד וּמִשְׁפָּט אָשִׁירָה — ***Of kindness and judgment I shall sing;*** לְךָ ה' אֲזַמֵּרָה" — ***to You Hashem, I shall sing praise.*** אִם חֶסֶד, "אָשִׁירָה", וְאִם מִשְׁפָּט "אָשִׁירָה" — This means: **If** I am dealt **kindness, *I shall sing*; and if** I am dealt **justice,** i.e., punishment, then too, ***I shall sing.*** כִּי גַּם הָרָעָה — This is **because even the bad** occurrences, לְעוֹבְדֵי ה' יִתְבָּרֵךְ שְׁמוֹ — **to those who serve Hashem, may His Name be blessed,** הִיא שִׂמְחָתָם וְטוֹבָתָם — **are their joy, and** to **their benefit.** כֵּיוָן שֶׁמְּקַבֵּל בְּאַהֲבָה מַה שֶּׁגָּזַר עָלָיו ה' יִתְבָּרֵךְ שְׁמוֹ — **For when one accepts with love all that Hashem, may His Name be blessed, has decreed upon him,** בֶּאֱמוּנָתוֹ כִּי הַכֹּל כַּפָּרַת עֲוֹנוֹתָיו — **with his conviction that all** the troubles he endures **are** means of **atonement for his sins,** נִמְצָא — **the result is** כִּי בְּקַבָּלַת רָעָה זוֹ הוּא עוֹבֵד אֶת ה' — **that with the acceptance of this hardship he is** in fact **serving Hashem,** וְהָעֲבוֹדָה הִיא שִׂמְחָה לוֹ — **and** any act of **serving** Hashem **is** a source of **happiness to him.**[15]

---

11. The word מְאֹדֶךָ is understood here as cognate with the words מִדָּה, *measure*, and מוֹדֶה, *thank*. It is thus expounded to teach that one must thank Hashem for whichever measure He metes out, good or bad. In fulfillment of this injunction, the Sages instituted a blessing to be recited upon hearing bad tidings as well.

12. The intention of the blessing is to indicate our acceptance that all God does is just and righteous.

13. I.e., if he heard many good tidings, one blessing (*HaTov VeHaMeitiv*) is sufficient for all of the good tidings; and if he heard many bad tidings, one blessing (*Dayan HaEmes*) for all the bad tidings. This is true even if one did not hear of all the tidings at the same time, as long as he had not yet recited the blessing for the earlier tidings (*Shaar HaTziyun* 222:3).

14. I.e., he should recite the blessing without reservations, but willingly and with love.

15. Since the goal of every servant of Hashem is to do everything possible to serve Him, one

ג. הִגִּיעַ אֵלָיו טוֹבָה, אוֹ שֶׁשָּׁמַע שְׁמוּעָה טוֹבָה, אַף עַל פִּי שֶׁהַדְּבָרִים מַרְאִין שֶׁטּוֹבָה זוֹ תִּגְרוֹם לוֹ רָעָה, כְּגוֹן שֶׁמָּצָא מְצִיאָה וְאִם יִשְׁמַע הַדָּבָר לַמֶּלֶךְ יִקַּח כֹּל אֲשֶׁר לוֹ[16], מִכָּל מָקוֹם מְבָרֵךְ "הַטּוֹב וְהַמֵּטִיב"[17]. וְכֵן אִם נָגְעָה אֵלָיו רָעָה, אוֹ שָׁמַע שְׁמוּעָה רָעָה, אַף עַל פִּי שֶׁהַדְּבָרִים מַרְאִין שֶׁרָעָה זוֹ גּוֹרֶמֶת לוֹ טוֹבָה, כְּגוֹן שֶׁבָּא לוֹ שֶׁטֶף עַל שָׂדֵהוּ וּמַזִּיק תְּבוּאָתוֹ וּכְשֶׁיַּעֲבוֹר הַשֶּׁטֶף טוֹבָה הִיא לוֹ שֶׁהִשְׁקָה אֶת שָׂדֵהוּ, מִכָּל מָקוֹם מְבָרֵךְ "דַּיַּין הָאֱמֶת", שֶׁאֵין מְבָרְכִין עַל הֶעָתִיד לִהְיוֹת אֶלָּא עַל מַה שֶּׁאֵירַע עַתָּה[18].

ד. לְעוֹלָם יְהֵא אָדָם רָגִיל לוֹמַר: "כָּל מַה דְּעָבִיד רַחֲמָנָא, לְטַב עָבִיד" (ברכות ס, ב).

ה. יָלְדָה אִשְׁתּוֹ זָכָר, מְבָרֵךְ "הַטּוֹב וְהַמֵּטִיב"[19]. וְגַם הָאִשָּׁה תְּבָרֵךְ כֵּן. וְאִם

---

§3 הִגִּיעַ אֵלָיו טוֹבָה — **If he experienced a good** occurrence, אוֹ שֶׁשָּׁמַע שְׁמוּעָה טוֹבָה — **or if he heard a good tiding,** אַף עַל פִּי שֶׁהַדְּבָרִים מַרְאִין — **even though indications are** שֶׁטּוֹבָה זוֹ תִּגְרוֹם לוֹ רָעָה — **that this good** occurrence **will** eventually **cause him harm,** כְּגוֹן שֶׁמָּצָא מְצִיאָה — **for example,** if someone **found a lost object,** וְאִם יִשְׁמַע הַדָּבָר לַמֶּלֶךְ — **and if the king hears of this matter** יִקַּח כֹּל אֲשֶׁר לוֹ — **he will take away all of his possessions,**[16] מִכָּל מָקוֹם — **nevertheless,** מְבָרֵךְ "הַטּוֹב וְהַמֵּטִיב" — **one recites the blessing of *HaTov VeHaMeitiv*** upon finding the lost item.[17] וְכֵן אִם נָגְעָה אֵלָיו רָעָה — **Similarly, if a bad** occurrence **affected him** אוֹ שָׁמַע שְׁמוּעָה רָעָה — **or he heard bad tidings,** אַף עַל פִּי שֶׁהַדְּבָרִים מַרְאִין — **even though indications are** שֶׁרָעָה זוֹ גּוֹרֶמֶת לוֹ טוֹבָה — **that this bad** occurrence **will** eventually **cause him benefit,** כְּגוֹן שֶׁבָּא לוֹ שֶׁטֶף עַל שָׂדֵהוּ — **for example, if a flood inundated his field** וּמַזִּיק תְּבוּאָתוֹ — **and caused damage to his grain,** וּכְשֶׁיַּעֲבוֹר הַשֶּׁטֶף טוֹבָה הִיא לוֹ — **but when the flood** waters **recede it will be beneficial to him,** שֶׁהִשְׁקָה אֶת שָׂדֵהוּ — **as** the water **will have irrigated his field,** מִכָּל מָקוֹם מְבָרֵךְ "דַּיַּין הָאֱמֶת" — **he nevertheless recites the blessing of *Dayan HaEmes*,** שֶׁאֵין מְבָרְכִין עַל הֶעָתִיד לִהְיוֹת — **for we do not recite blessings** based **upon that which is yet to happen,** אֶלָּא עַל מַה שֶּׁאֵירַע עַתָּה — **but only for that which has taken place now.**[18]

§4 לְעוֹלָם יְהֵא אָדָם רָגִיל לוֹמַר — **A person should always be accustomed to say:** "כָּל מַה דְּעָבִיד רַחֲמָנָא — **Everything done by the Merciful One** (Hashem), לְטַב עָבִיד" — **He does for the good** (*Berachos* 60b).

§5 יָלְדָה אִשְׁתּוֹ זָכָר — **If one's wife gave birth to a** baby **boy** מְבָרֵךְ "הַטּוֹב וְהַמֵּטִיב" — **he recites the *HaTov VeHaMeitiv* blessing.**[19] וְגַם הָאִשָּׁה תְּבָרֵךְ כֵּן — **The**

---

will find joy even in accepting difficulties, as the act of accepting that which Hashem has decreed is itself a form of service to Hashem.

16. For example, he is concerned that the government would suspect him of stealing the object and punish him as a result (*Mishnah Berurah* 222:6).

17. [The blessing is nevertheless appropriate since we do not take the eventualities (which may, in fact, never occur) into consideration; see further in Kitzur, and next note.] If the benefit from the found item is shared by members of his household, he recites *HaTov VeHaMeitiv*; if only the finder benefits, the *Shehecheyanu* blessing is recited (*Mishnah Berurah* 222:6; see above, *se'if* 1).

18. We do not take into account the future possibility of reversed fortune, since we cannot be certain that the expected future result will actually happen (*Mishnah Berurah* 222:5). [If the anticipated eventuality does actually take place, then, if warranted, one would recite the appropriate blessing for that occurrence (*HaTov VeHaMeitiv* or *Dayan HaEmes*).]

19. The *HaTov VeHaMeitiv* blessing is appropriate since the birth of a son is good for both

מֵתָה הָאִשָּׁה בְּלִדְתָּהּ, מְבָרֵךְ "שֶׁהֶחֱיָנוּ"[20], דְּהָא לֵיכָּא הֲטָבָה לְאַחֲרִינֵי. וְכֵן אִם מֵת הָאָב קוֹדֶם שֶׁיְּלָדַתּוּ, הִיא מְבָרֶכֶת "שֶׁהֶחֱיָנוּ".

ו. מֵת אָבִיו אוֹ אֶחָד מִשְּׁאָר קְרוֹבָיו, אוֹ אֲפִילוּ אֵינוֹ קְרוֹבוֹ אֶלָּא שֶׁהוּא אָדָם כָּשֵׁר, וּמִכָּל שֶׁכֵּן תַּלְמִיד חָכָם שֶׁהוּא מִצְטַעֵר עָלָיו, מְבָרֵךְ "בָּרוּךְ אַתָּה ה' אֱלֹהֵינוּ מֶלֶךְ הָעוֹלָם דַּיַּין הָאֱמֶת". וְעַל שְׁאָר אָדָם שֶׁאֵינוֹ מִצְטַעֵר כָּל כָּךְ אוֹמֵר "בָּרוּךְ דַּיַּין אֱמֶת", בְּלֹא שֵׁם וּמַלְכוּת[21]. אִם נִשְׁאַר מֵאָבִיו מָמוֹן לִירַשׁ, מְבָרֵךְ גַּם כֵּן "שֶׁהֶחֱיָנוּ"[22]. וְאִם

woman (mother), too, recites this blessing. וְאִם מֵתָה הָאִשָּׁה בְּלִדְתָּהּ — If the woman died during childbirth מְבָרֵךְ "שֶׁהֶחֱיָנוּ" — then the father recites only the *Shehecheyanu* blessing,[20] דְּהָא לֵיכָּא הֲטָבָה לְאַחֲרִינֵי — for now there is no benefit of the birth of the son shared by anyone else (as explained above, *se'if* 1). וְכֵן אִם מֵת הָאָב קוֹדֶם שֶׁיְּלָדַתּוּ — Similarly, if the father died before the mother gave birth to the son, הִיא מְבָרֶכֶת "שֶׁהֶחֱיָנוּ" — she recites only the *Shehecheyanu* blessing upon the birth of her son.

§6 מֵת אָבִיו — **If one's father died** אוֹ אֶחָד מִשְּׁאָר קְרוֹבָיו — **or another of his relatives,** אוֹ אֲפִילוּ אֵינוֹ קְרוֹבוֹ — **or even** when **someone who is not his relative,** אֶלָּא שֶׁהוּא אָדָם כָּשֵׁר — **but was an upright individual,** passes away, וּמִכָּל שֶׁכֵּן תַּלְמִיד חָכָם — **and certainly if** the deceased **was a Torah scholar,** שֶׁהוּא מִצְטַעֵר עָלָיו — and is someone **for whom he is aggrieved** by his passing, מְבָרֵךְ — **he recites the** following **blessing:** "בָּרוּךְ אַתָּה ה' אֱלֹהֵינוּ מֶלֶךְ הָעוֹלָם דַּיַּין הָאֱמֶת" — *Baruch Atah Ado-noy Elokeinu Melech HaOlam, Dayan HaEmes,* ***Blessed are You,*** ***Hashem, our God, King of the universe, the true Judge.*** וְעַל שְׁאָר אָדָם — **Upon** the passing of **any other person,** שֶׁאֵינוֹ מִצְטַעֵר כָּל כָּךְ — **upon which he does not experience as much pain,** אוֹמֵר "בָּרוּךְ דַּיַּין אֱמֶת" — **he recites:** *Baruch Dayan HaEmes,* ***Blessed is the true Judge;*** בְּלֹא שֵׁם וּמַלְכוּת — that is, he recites the blessing **without mentioning the Name of Hashem or His sovereignty.**[21]

אִם נִשְׁאַר מֵאָבִיו מָמוֹן לִירַשׁ — **If an inheritance of money was left by one's father** who died, מְבָרֵךְ גַּם כֵּן "שֶׁהֶחֱיָנוּ" — **then,** in addition to the *Dayan HaEmes* blessing, **he also recites the blessing of *Shehecheyanu*.**[22] וְאִם יֵשׁ לוֹ עוֹד

him and his wife (see *se'if* 1). This blessing is to be recited even if he already has a number of sons (*Mishnah Berurah* 223:3). [See *Beur Halachah* (223:1 s.v. זכר) regarding whether a blessing is to be recited upon the birth of a boy when one already has many sons and no daughters and had desired a daughter.]

This blessing is recited immediately upon hearing the news of the birth of his son. When a daughter is born, the father recites the *Shehecheyanu* blessing upon seeing his daughter for the first time (*Mishnah Berurah* 223:1-2; *Igros Moshe, Orach Chaim* V, §43.5).

20. He should first recite *Dayan HaEmes* on his wife's passing (*Mishnah Berurah* 223:6).

21. Mention of "His sovereignty" refers to the words מֶלֶךְ הָעוֹלָם, *King of the universe,* which appear in the full version of a blessing.

The pain of the passing of one who is not kin is usually not strong enough to warrant the recitation of the full blessing with mention of Hashem's Name.

22. One first recites *Dayan HaEmes*, and afterward *Shehecheyanu*. Although one would prefer that his father remain alive and he would not inherit him, the blessing does not reflect one's happiness over a specific event, but rather the benefit received, even if it is mixed with pain and sorrow (*Mishnah Berurah* 223:9).

THE SHEHECHEYANU AND HATOV VEHAMEITIV BLESSINGS — SIMAN 59:7

יֵשׁ לוֹ עוֹד אַחִים לַחֲלוֹק בִּירוּשָׁה, אֲזַי בִּמְקוֹם בִּרְכַּת "שֶׁהֶחֱיָינוּ" מְבָרֵךְ "הַטּוֹב וְהַמֵּטִיב".[23]

ז. בָּנָה אוֹ קָנָה בַּיִת, אוֹ קָנָה כֵלִים אוֹ מַלְבּוּשִׁים חֲשׁוּבִים[24], אֲפִילוּ הָיוּ לוֹ כַּיּוֹצֵא בָּאֵלוּ תְּחִלָּה אֶלָּא שֶׁאֵלּוּ לֹא הָיוּ שֶׁלּוֹ מֵעוֹלָם[25] (לְאַפּוּקֵי מְכָרָן וְחָזַר וּקְנָאָן), וְהוּא שָׂמֵחַ בָּהֶם[26], מְבָרֵךְ "שֶׁהֶחֱיָינוּ"[27]. וְיֵשׁ לְבָרֵךְ בִּשְׁעַת הַקִּנְיָן, אוֹ גְּמַר הַבִּנְיָן, אַף עַל פִּי שֶׁעֲדַיִין לֹא נִשְׁתַּמֵּשׁ בָּהֶם, כִּי אֵין הַבְּרָכָה אֶלָּא עַל שִׂמְחַת הַלֵּב שֶׁהוּא שָׂמֵחַ בִּקְנִיָּיתָן[28].

אַחִים לַחֲלוֹק בִּירוּשָׁה — If he has other brothers with whom to divide the inheritance אֲזַי בִּמְקוֹם בִּרְכַּת "שֶׁהֶחֱיָינוּ" — then, rather than reciting the *Shehecheyanu* blessing, מְבָרֵךְ "הַטּוֹב וְהַמֵּטִיב" — he recites *HaTov VeHaMeitiv*.[23]

§7 בָּנָה אוֹ קָנָה בַּיִת — If one built or purchased a home, אוֹ קָנָה כֵלִים אוֹ מַלְבּוּשִׁים חֲשׁוּבִים — or purchased valuable utensils or clothing,[24] אֲפִילוּ הָיוּ לוֹ כַּיּוֹצֵא בָּאֵלוּ תְּחִלָּה — even if he already owned similar items previously, אֶלָּא שֶׁאֵלּוּ לֹא הָיוּ שֶׁלּוֹ מֵעוֹלָם — as long as he never owned these very items themselves[25] (לְאַפּוּקֵי מְכָרָן וְחָזַר וּקְנָאָן — this means to exclude items that he once owned, sold and then repurchased), וְהוּא שָׂמֵחַ בָּהֶם — and he is happy with their acquisition,[26] מְבָרֵךְ "שֶׁהֶחֱיָינוּ" — he recites the *Shehecheyanu* blessing.[27] וְיֵשׁ לְבָרֵךְ בִּשְׁעַת הַקִּנְיָן — One should recite the blessing at the time of the purchase אוֹ גְּמַר הַבִּנְיָן — or, in the case of building a new home, at the completion of the construction, אַף עַל פִּי שֶׁעֲדַיִין לֹא נִשְׁתַּמֵּשׁ בָּהֶם — although he has not yet used the items, כִּי אֵין הַבְּרָכָה אֶלָּא עַל שִׂמְחַת הַלֵּב שֶׁהוּא שָׂמֵחַ בִּקְנִיָּיתָן — for the blessing was instituted only as a means of expressing thanks for the joy in one's heart at the purchase, not for the enjoyment that results from using the item.[28]

---

23. Since others share the benefit with him, he recites *HaTov VeHaMeitiv*, as above, *se'if* 1 (*Mishnah Berurah* 223:10). If one has no brothers, but has a wife and children who will benefit from the inheritance together with him, *Beur Halachah* (223:2 s.v. אין לו אחים) rules that if the inheritance consists only of money, he recites *Shehecheyanu*, but if the inheritance includes other items as well from which his family will benefit, he should recite *HaTov VeHaMeitiv*.

24. One who purchases a new car should recite the *Shehecheyanu* blessing. If the car will be of benefit to other family members as well, he should recite *HaTov VeHaMeitiv* (*Igros Moshe, Orach Chaim* III, §80).

25. Even if they were owned by another, as long as they are new to him he is required to recite the blessing.

26. See below, *se'if* 12, that this will vary

according to the circumstances of each individual.

27. If the items purchased were for the use of his family as well, then *HaTov VeHaMeitiv* is recited (*Beur Halachah* 223:3 s.v. בנה בית חדש). If the purchase was made in partnership with others, each of the partners should recite *HaTov VeHaMeitiv*, as the benefit is shared among them. Similarly, if a community built a new synagogue, the entire community must recite the blessing. In this case, the blessing is recited aloud by the *chazzan* in the presence of the community, thus fulfilling their obligation (*Mishnah Berurah* 223:11).

28. The blessing is recited at the time of purchase only if it is ready to be used at that point. The blessing on items that are not yet complete, such as a suit that must be tailored before it can be worn, is recited before the first use, not at the time of purchase (*Mishnah Berurah* 223:17).

ח. וּכְשֶׁיִּלְבּוֹשׁ הַמַּלְבּוּשׁ יְבָרֵךְ "מַלְבִּישׁ עֲרוּמִּים"[29]. וְאַף שֶׁכְּבָר בֵּירַךְ שַׁחֲרִית "מַלְבִּישׁ עֲרוּמִּים" חוֹזֵר וּמְבָרֵךְ כְּשֶׁלּוֹבְשׁוֹ. אַךְ אִם לְבָשׁוֹ שַׁחֲרִית, נִפְטָר בִּבְרָכָה זֹאת. יֵשׁ אוֹמְרִים דְּהַקּוֹנֶה כּוֹבַע כְּשֶׁמְּשִׂימוֹ בְּרֹאשׁוֹ יְבָרֵךְ "עוֹטֵר יִשְׂרָאֵל בְּתִפְאָרָה"[30], וּבְאֵזוֹר יְבָרֵךְ "אוֹזֵר יִשְׂרָאֵל בִּגְבוּרָה"[31], וְיֵשׁ חוֹלְקִין. עַל כֵּן, טוֹב לְלָבְשָׁן פַּעַם הָרִאשׁוֹן שַׁחֲרִית וִיכַוֵּין לְפָטְרָן בִּבְרָכוֹת אֵלּוּ שֶׁאוֹמֵר אוֹתָן בְּסֵדֶר הַבְּרָכוֹת. קָנָה לוֹ טַלִּית שֶׁל מִצְוָה, אֲזַי לְאַחַר שֶׁעָשָׂה בּוֹ אֶת הַצִּיצִית יְבָרֵךְ "שֶׁהֶחֱיָינוּ"[32]. וְאִם לֹא בֵּירַךְ

§8 **וּכְשֶׁיִּלְבּוֹשׁ הַמַּלְבּוּשׁ — When one dons the** newly acquired **garment** for the first time, **יְבָרֵךְ "מַלְבִּישׁ עֲרוּמִּים" — he recites the following blessing:** *Baruch Atah Ado-noy Elokeinu Melech HaOlam, malbish arumim, Blessed are You, HASHEM, our God, King of the universe,* ***Who clothes the naked.***[29] **וְאַף שֶׁכְּבָר בֵּירַךְ שַׁחֲרִית "מַלְבִּישׁ עֲרוּמִּים" — Even if** it is later in the day, and **he already recited the blessing of *malbish arumim* in the morning,** as part of the Morning Blessings, **חוֹזֵר וּמְבָרֵךְ כְּשֶׁלּוֹבְשׁוֹ — he should recite the blessing again when putting on the garment** for the first time. **אַךְ אִם לְבָשׁוֹ שַׁחֲרִית — However, if he donned** the garment **in the morning,** and he will recite the blessing of *malbish arumim* as part of the Morning Blessings while wearing the garment for the first time, **נִפְטָר בִּבְרָכָה זֹאת — then he discharges** his obligation **with** that recitation of **this blessing.**

יֵשׁ אוֹמְרִים דְּהַקּוֹנֶה כּוֹבַע — Some authorities **say that when one purchases a hat, כְּשֶׁמְּשִׂימוֹ בְּרֹאשׁוֹ — when he places it on his head** for the first time **יְבָרֵךְ "עוֹטֵר יִשְׂרָאֵל בְּתִפְאָרָה" — he should recite the blessing of** *Oteir Yisrael besifarah,* ***Who crowns Israel with splendor.***[30] **וּבְאֵזוֹר יְבָרֵךְ "אוֹזֵר יִשְׂרָאֵל בִּגְבוּרָה"** — Similarly, **for a new belt, he should recite the blessing of** *Ozeir Yisrael bigvurah,* ***Who girds Israel with strength.***[31] **וְיֵשׁ חוֹלְקִין — Some disagree,** and maintain that these blessings are not to be recited when wearing a newly acquired hat or belt. **עַל כֵּן — Therefore,** to avoid the situation of a disputed obligation for a blessing, **טוֹב לְלָבְשָׁן פַּעַם הָרִאשׁוֹן שַׁחֲרִית — it is best to wear** these items **for the first time in the morning, וִיכַוֵּין לְפָטְרָן בִּבְרָכוֹת אֵלּוּ — and intend to discharge** his obligation of reciting a special blessing for the items **with his recitation of these blessings שֶׁאוֹמֵר אוֹתָן בְּסֵדֶר הַבְּרָכוֹת — that he recites in the** usual **arrangement of the** Morning **Blessings.**

קָנָה לוֹ טַלִּית שֶׁל מִצְוָה — If one purchased a new *tallis* for himself, אֲזַי לְאַחַר שֶׁעָשָׂה בּוֹ אֶת הַצִּיצִית — then, after he affixes the *tzitzis* tassels upon it, יְבָרֵךְ "שֶׁהֶחֱיָינוּ" — he should recite the *Shehecheyanu* blessing.[32] **וְאִם לֹא בֵּירַךְ אָז — If**

---

29. If the *Shehecheyanu* blessing is recited when the garment is worn for the first time (and not at the time of purchase; see previous note), it is recited after the blessing of *malbish arumim* (*Mishnah Berurah* 223:18).

30. The hat is referred to as a פְּאֵר, *splendor* (*Shemos* 39:28); see *Shulchan Aruch* 46:1.

31. Both of these blessings are also recited as part of the daily Morning Blessings.

32. When one buys a *tallis* before the *tzitzis* tassels are attached, he cannot recite the blessing at the time of purchase, for at that time it is incomplete and not ready for wear. Therefore, the blessing is deferred until after it is completed (see above, note 28, and *Mishnah Berurah* 22:1). One who buys a *tallis* complete with *tzitzis* should recite the blessing when he buys it. Regarding a *tallis katan* (above, 9:1), Rabbi Moshe Feinstein (*Igros Moshe, Orach Chaim* III, §80) rules that today, since most people do not consider a new *tallis katan* to be a noteworthy garment because the garment itself is not valuable, one does not recite *Shehecheyanu* when wearing it for the first time.

279 THE SHEHECHEYANU AND HATOV VEHAMEITIV BLESSINGS — SIMAN 59:9-10

אָז, יְבָרֵךְ בְּעִיטוּף הָרִאשׁוֹן לְאַחַר שֶׁבֵּירַךְ "לְהִתְעַטֵּף בַּצִּיצִית"[33].

ט. קָנָה כֵּלִים שֶׁמִּשְׁתַּמְּשִׁים בָּהֶם הוּא וּבְנֵי בֵיתוֹ – מְבָרֵךְ "הַטּוֹב וְהַמֵּטִיב"[34].

י. אִם נִתְּנוּ לוֹ בְּמַתָּנָה, מְבָרֵךְ "הַטּוֹב וְהַמֵּטִיב"[35], שֶׁהוּא טוֹבָה לוֹ וְגַם לְהַנּוֹתֵן טוֹבָה, כִּי אִם זֶה הַמְקַבֵּל הוּא עָנִי, הֲרֵי הִיא טוֹבָה לְהַנּוֹתֵן שֶׁזִּכָּהוּ הַשֵּׁם יִתְבָּרֵךְ לִיתֵּן צְדָקָה, וְאִם הַמְקַבֵּל הוּא עָשִׁיר, שָׂמֵחַ הַנּוֹתֵן שֶׁזֶּה מְקַבֵּל מִמֶּנּוּ מַתָּנָה[36].

---

he did not recite the blessing at that point, **יְבָרֵךְ בְּעִיטוּף הָרִאשׁוֹן** — he should recite the blessing of *Shehecheyanu* **the first** time that he **wraps** himself in the new *tallis*, **לְאַחַר שֶׁבֵּירַךְ "לְהִתְעַטֵּף בַּצִּיצִית"** — **after reciting the blessing of** *lehis'ateif batzitzis, **to wrap** ourselves **in tzitzis***.[33]

§9 **קָנָה כֵּלִים** — **One who purchased items** **שֶׁמִּשְׁתַּמְּשִׁים בָּהֶם הוּא וּבְנֵי בֵיתוֹ** — **that will be used by himself and by members of his household** **מְבָרֵךְ "הַטּוֹב וְהַמֵּטִיב"** — **recites the blessing of *HaTov VeHaMeitiv***, since others will share the benefit of the new items with him.[34]

§10 **אִם נִתְּנוּ לוֹ בְּמַתָּנָה** — **If** items **were given to him as a gift** **מְבָרֵךְ "הַטּוֹב וְהַמֵּטִיב"** — **he recites the blessing of *HaTov VeHaMeitiv***,[35] **שֶׁהוּא טוֹבָה לוֹ** — **since this** (the gift) **is a benefit for** the recipient **וְגַם לְהַנּוֹתֵן טוֹבָה** — **and** it is **also beneficial to the giver; כִּי אִם זֶה הַמְקַבֵּל הוּא עָנִי** — **because if the recipient is a poor person** **הֲרֵי הִיא טוֹבָה לְהַנּוֹתֵן** — **then** the gift **is beneficial to the giver, שֶׁזִּכָּהוּ הַשֵּׁם יִתְבָּרֵךְ לִיתֵּן צְדָקָה** — **for Hashem, may He be blessed, has granted him** the opportunity **to give charity; וְאִם הַמְקַבֵּל הוּא עָשִׁיר** — **and** even **if the recipient is wealthy, שָׂמֵחַ הַנּוֹתֵן** — **the giver is pleased** **שֶׁזֶּה מְקַבֵּל מִמֶּנּוּ מַתָּנָה** — **that this** wealthy person has honored him by having **accepted a gift from him.**[36]

---

33. Above, 9:8. Regarding one who purchased a new pair of *tefillin*, see *Beur Halachah* 22:1 s.v. קנה.

34. If he purchased garments for himself and other garments for members of his family, he recites *Shehecheyanu* for the clothing that he purchased for himself, and *HaTov VeHaMeitiv* for those purchased for his family members. The garments purchased for family members warrant the blessing of *HaTov VeHaMeitiv* even when only one individual will wear them, for the head of the household also derives pleasure from the fact that his family is well dressed (*Mishnah Berurah* 223:19).

One who purchases an engagement ring for his bride should recite *Shehecheyanu* at the time of purchase, for he enjoys the fact that he has a ring to give to her. When the bride receives it, she recites *Shehecheyanu* for the pleasure she derives from it, and she also recites *HaTov VeHaMeitiv,* because her groom, too, benefits from the fact that she now has an engagement ring (*Igros Moshe, Even HaEzer* IV, §84:2-3).

35. One does not recite a blessing upon receiving a gift of cash, since it is very embarrassing for the recipient to be dependent on another's gift of money; see *Mishnah Berurah* 223:20.

36. It is therefore considered a shared benefit when one receives a gift (see above, *se'if* 1). Nevertheless, the one who gave the gift does not recite any blessing (*Beur Halachah* 223:5 s.v. מברך הטוב והמטיב).

According to many other authorities, however, the *HaTov VeHaMeitiv* blessing is recited only where there is a shared *tangible* benefit. The satisfaction of giving charity or the honor of the wealthy person accepting his gift is not considered a tangible benefit, and in such a case the blessing of *Shehecheyanu,* not *HaTov VeHaMeitiv*, is appropriate (*Mishnah Berurah* 223:21).

THE SHEHECHEYANU AND HATOV VEHAMEITIV BLESSINGS — SIMAN 59:11-13 280

יא. עַל סְפָרִים חֲדָשִׁים שֶׁקָּנָה אֵינוֹ מְבָרֵךְ "שֶׁהֶחֱיָנוּ", מִשּׁוּם דְּמִצְוֹת לַאו לֵיהָנוֹת נִתְּנוּ[37].

יב. עַל דָּבָר שֶׁאֵינוֹ חָשׁוּב כָּל כָּךְ, כְּגוֹן חָלוּק אוֹ מִנְעָלִים וְאַנְפִּלָאוֹת, אֵין לְבָרֵךְ, וַאֲפִילוּ אִם הוּא עָנִי שֶׁשָּׂמֵחַ בָּהֶם. וְעָשִׁיר גָּדוֹל שֶׁקָּנָה כֵּלִים חֲדָשִׁים שֶׁרָאוּי לְבֵינוֹנִי לִשְׂמוֹחַ בָּהֶם, אֶלָּא שֶׁהוּא לְעָשְׁרוֹ אֵינָם חֲשׁוּבִים אֶצְלוֹ כָּל כָּךְ וְאֵינוֹ שָׂמֵחַ בָּהֶם, גַּם כֵּן לֹא יְבָרֵךְ[38].

יג. נוֹהֲגִין לוֹמַר לְמִי שֶׁלָּבַשׁ בֶּגֶד חָדָשׁ: "תְּבַלֶּה וּתְחַדֵּשׁ". וְעַל מִנְעָלִים אוֹ שְׁאָר בְּגָדִים שֶׁנַּעֲשׂוּ מֵעוֹרוֹת, אֲפִילוּ מִבְּהֵמוֹת וְחַיּוֹת טְמֵאוֹת, וַאֲפִילוּ אִם הָעוֹרוֹת הֵם תְּפוּרוֹת רַק תַּחַת הַבֶּגֶד, אֵין אוֹמְרִים "תְּבַלֶּה וּתְחַדֵּשׁ", כִּי אִם יְחַדֵּשׁ בֶּגֶד כָּזֶה,

---

§11 **עַל סְפָרִים חֲדָשִׁים שֶׁקָּנָה** — **Upon new** Torah **books that one purchased,** **אֵינוֹ מְבָרֵךְ "שֶׁהֶחֱיָנוּ"** — **one does not recite the** ***Shehecheyanu*** **blessing,** **מִשּׁוּם דְּמִצְוֹת לַאו לֵיהָנוֹת נִתְּנוּ** — **for the mitzvos were not given** to the Jewish people **for** the purpose of **deriving benefit** from them.[37]

§12 **עַל דָּבָר שֶׁאֵינוֹ חָשׁוּב כָּל כָּךְ** — **For an item that is not very significant,** **כְּגוֹן חָלוּק אוֹ מִנְעָלִים וְאַנְפִּלָאוֹת** — **such as a shirt, shoes, or socks,** **אֵין לְבָרֵךְ** — **one should not recite the** *Shehecheyanu* **blessing,** **וַאֲפִילוּ אִם הוּא עָנִי שֶׁשָּׂמֵחַ בָּהֶם** — **even** if the buyer **is a poor person who experiences joy** even **from** such an acquisition.[38] **וְעָשִׁיר גָּדוֹל שֶׁקָּנָה כֵּלִים חֲדָשִׁים** — **A very wealthy person who purchased new utensils** **שֶׁרָאוּי לְבֵינוֹנִי לִשְׂמוֹחַ בָּהֶם** — **that are such that an average person would be happy with** their acquisition, **אֶלָּא שֶׁהוּא לְעָשְׁרוֹ אֵינָם חֲשׁוּבִים אֶצְלוֹ כָּל כָּךְ** — **but he, due to his wealth, does not prize these items very much,** **וְאֵינוֹ שָׂמֵחַ בָּהֶם** — **and he is not made happy with** their acquisition, **גַּם כֵּן לֹא יְבָרֵךְ** — **should also not recite the** *Shehecheyanu* **blessing.**

§13 **נוֹהֲגִין לוֹמַר לְמִי שֶׁלָּבַשׁ בֶּגֶד חָדָשׁ** — **It is customary to tell someone wearing a new garment:** **"תְּבַלֶּה וּתְחַדֵּשׁ"** — ***"May you*** *merit to* ***wear out*** *this garment* ***and replace it with*** *a* ***new*** *one."* **וְעַל מִנְעָלִים אוֹ שְׁאָר בְּגָדִים שֶׁנַּעֲשׂוּ מֵעוֹרוֹת** — How-ever, **for shoes or other garments made of** animal **skins,** **אֲפִילוּ מִבְּהֵמוֹת וְחַיּוֹת טְמֵאוֹת** — **even** those made **from the hides of nonkosher animals and beasts,** **וַאֲפִילוּ אִם הָעוֹרוֹת הֵם תְּפוּרוֹת רַק תַּחַת הַבֶּגֶד** — **and even if the hides are only sewn** as a lining **underneath the garment,** **אֵין אוֹמְרִים "תְּבַלֶּה וּתְחַדֵּשׁ"** — **we do not say, "*May you*** *merit to* ***wear out*** *this garment* ***and replace it.*"** **כִּי אִם יְחַדֵּשׁ בֶּגֶד כָּזֶה** — **For in order**

---

37. *Shehecheyanu* is recited to thank Hashem for the enjoyment that comes from acquiring an item that provides tangible benefit. Now, the mitzvos were given to the Jewish people as a responsibility, not for the purpose of deriving benefit from them. Therefore, any benefit derived from performing a mitzvah, such as learning Torah, is not considered a benefit upon which this blessing should be recited. According to some authorities, however, one should recite *Shehecheyanu* when acquiring a new Torah book that he was striving to acquire, since the blessing is recited not upon the mitzvah use, but upon the acquisition (above, *se'if* 7), and he is happy to have acquired it. Therefore, one need not object to those who choose to recite such a blessing (*Mishnah Berurah* 223:13).

38. One recites the *Shehecheyanu* blessing only upon an item that the average person will not replace frequently (*Mishnah Berurah* 223:23-24).

צְרִיכִין מִתְּחִלָּה לְהָמִית בַּעַל חַי, וּכְתִיב (תהלים קנה, ט) "וְרַחֲמָיו עַל כָּל מַעֲשָׂיו"[39].

יד. פְּרִי[40] שֶׁהִיא מִתְחַדֶּשֶׁת מִשָּׁנָה לְשָׁנָה — בְּפַעַם הָרִאשׁוֹנָה שֶׁהוּא אוֹכְלָהּ בְּשָׁנָה יְבָרֵךְ "שֶׁהֶחֱיָנוּ"[41]. וִיבָרֵךְ תְּחִלָּה "שֶׁהֶחֱיָנוּ" וְאַחַר כָּךְ בִּרְכַּת הַפְּרִי[42]. וְאִם שָׁכַח וּבֵירַךְ תְּחִלָּה בִּרְכַּת הַפְּרִי, יָכוֹל לְבָרֵךְ גַּם אַחַר כָּךְ "שֶׁהֶחֱיָנוּ", וְלֹא הָוֵי הֶפְסֵק[43]. וְאִם לֹא בֵירַךְ בַּאֲכִילָה הָרִאשׁוֹנָה, שׁוּב אֵינוֹ מְבָרֵךְ. אִם יֵשׁ לְפָנָיו כַּמָּה מִינִים חֲדָשִׁים,

---

to replace such a garment, צְרִיכִין מִתְּחִלָּה לְהָמִית בַּעַל חַי — one must first kill a living creature to obtain its hide, וּכְתִיב "וְרַחֲמָיו עַל כָּל מַעֲשָׂיו" — and it is written (*Tehillim* 145:9): ***and His mercies are on all of His works.***[39]

§14 **פְּרִי שֶׁהִיא מִתְחַדֶּשֶׁת מִשָּׁנָה לְשָׁנָה — A fruit[40] that renews from year to year** (i.e., a seasonal fruit that is available only during certain times of the year), **בְּפַעַם הָרִאשׁוֹנָה שֶׁהוּא אוֹכְלָהּ בְּשָׁנָה — the first time that one eats it during the** new **year** (i.e., season) **יְבָרֵךְ "שֶׁהֶחֱיָנוּ" — he should recite the *Shehecheyanu* blessing.**[41] **וִיבָרֵךְ תְּחִלָּה "שֶׁהֶחֱיָנוּ" וְאַחַר כָּךְ בִּרְכַּת הַפְּרִי — One should first recite the *Shehecheyanu* blessing and** only **then the** appropriate **blessing on the fruit.**[42] **וְאִם שָׁכַח וּבֵירַךְ תְּחִלָּה בִּרְכַּת הַפְּרִי — If one forgot, and first recited the blessing on the fruit, יָכוֹל לְבָרֵךְ גַּם אַחַר כָּךְ "שֶׁהֶחֱיָנוּ" — he may still recite the *Shehecheyanu* blessing after** reciting the blessing on the fruit and before eating it, **וְלֹא הָוֵי הֶפְסֵק — and** the *Shehecheyanu* blessing **is not considered an interruption** between the blessing on the fruit and the eating.[43] **וְאִם לֹא בֵירַךְ בַּאֲכִילָה הָרִאשׁוֹנָה — If he did not recite the** *Shehecheyanu* **blessing the first time he ate** the fruit that season, **שׁוּב אֵינוֹ מְבָרֵךְ — he can no longer recite the blessing** on a subsequent occasion of eating that fruit.

אִם יֵשׁ לְפָנָיו כַּמָּה מִינִים חֲדָשִׁים — If one has before him several new species that he

---

39. Since God extends mercy to all of His creatures, we do not express a blessing in this manner, since it would amount to a blessing that an animal be killed.

40. This refers both to fruit from trees as well as [seasonal] "fruit" of the ground, such as pumpkins and melons (*Beur Halachah* 225:3 s.v. פרי חדש).

41. Fruits that never go out of season are not subject to the *Shehecheyanu* blessing, even if one has not eaten them for a very long time. By the same token, fruits that have two growing cycles each year are subject to *Shehecheyanu* twice annually (*Shulchan Aruch* and *Rama* 225:6).

Although fruits that grow seasonally, but are preserved by refrigeration throughout the year, should also be subject to the *Shehecheyanu* blessing if one knows that this particular fruit is from the new season, nevertheless, in practice, Rabbi Moshe Feinstein writes that (in deference to a dissenting opinion) since the recitation of the *Shehecheyanu* blessing over fruit is not an absolute requirement, there is basis to rule not to recite *Shehecheyanu* (*Igros Moshe, Orach Chaim* III, §34).

According to Rabbi Moshe Feinstein (*Igros Moshe, Orach Chaim* II, §58), it may be inappropriate to recite *Shehecheyanu* upon a fruit that was originally produced by grafting two species (a halachically prohibited act; see below, 174:1-2). Therefore, one should exempt it by reciting *Shehecheyanu* on another fruit eaten at the same time (see also *Beur Halachah* 225:1 s.v. פרי חדש).

42. *Borei pri ha'eitz* for a fruit or *borei pri ha'adamah* for a vegetable (the halachos of these blessings are found above, *Siman* 52).

43. Generally, one may not interrupt at all between the recitation of the blessing upon the food and eating the food; see above, 50:5. Alternatively, one may eat a bit of the fruit and then recite the *Shehecheyanu* blessing (*Mishnah Berurah* 225:11).

דַּי בְּבִרְכַּת ״שֶׁהֶחֱיָינוּ״ אַחַת לְכוּלָם. ב׳ מִינִים, אַף עַל פִּי שֶׁהֵם דּוֹמִים קְצָת, כְּמוֹ קִירשֶׁן וַויינְקסֶל, וַאֲפִילוּ אֵין חֲלוּקִין בְּשֵׁמוֹת אֶלָּא בְּטַעַם, כְּמוֹ תְּאֵנִים לְבָנִים וּתְאֵנִים שְׁחוֹרוֹת, אִם בֵּירַךְ ״שֶׁהֶחֱיָינוּ״ עַל מִין אֶחָד, כְּשֶׁנִּזְדַּמֵּן לוֹ אַחַר כָּךְ מִין הַשֵּׁנִי, מְבָרֵךְ גַּם עָלָיו ״שֶׁהֶחֱיָינוּ״, כִּי שְׁתֵּי שְׂמָחוֹת הֵן[44].

טו. אִם בֵּירַךְ ״שֶׁהֶחֱיָינוּ״ עַל עֲנָבִים, יֵשׁ אוֹמְרִים דְּאֵין צָרִיךְ לְבָרֵךְ עוֹד ״שֶׁהֶחֱיָינוּ״ עַל הַיַּיִן הֶחָדָשׁ[45], כִּי שִׂמְחָה אַחַת הוּא שֶׁהַיַּיִן יוֹצֵא מִן הָעֲנָבִים, וְיֵשׁ אוֹמְרִים דְּמִכָּל מָקוֹם צָרִיךְ לְבָרֵךְ ״שֶׁהֶחֱיָינוּ״ גַּם עַל הַיַּיִן הֶחָדָשׁ, מִשּׁוּם דְּיֵשׁ בּוֹ שִׂמְחָה יְתֵירָה מִבָּעֲנָבִים. וְעַל כֵּן, טוֹב שֶׁאִם בֵּירַךְ ״שֶׁהֶחֱיָינוּ״ עַל עֲנָבִים, אֲזַי כְּשֶׁשּׁוֹתֶה יַיִן חָדָשׁ יְבָרֵךְ תְּחִלָּה ״שֶׁהֶחֱיָינוּ״ עַל אֵיזֶה מִין חָדָשׁ לִפְטוֹר גַּם אֶת הַיַּיִן. אֲבָל אִם בֵּירַךְ תְּחִלָּה ״שֶׁהֶחֱיָינוּ״ עַל הַיַּיִן, לְכוּלֵּי עָלְמָא אֵינוֹ מְבָרֵךְ עוֹד עַל עֲנָבִים.

---

has not yet enjoyed this season, דַּי בְּבִרְכַּת ״שֶׁהֶחֱיָינוּ״ אַחַת לְכוּלָם — **one recitation of the *Shehecheyanu* blessing is sufficient for all of them.** ב׳ מִינִים — The halachah with regard to **two species,** אַף עַל פִּי שֶׁהֵם דּוֹמִים קְצָת — **even if they are slightly similar,** כְּמוֹ קִירשֶׁן וַויינְקסֶל — **such as sweet cherries and sour cherries,** וַאֲפִילוּ אֵין חֲלוּקִין בְּשֵׁמוֹת אֶלָּא בְּטַעַם — **and even if they do not differ in name but only in taste,** כְּמוֹ תְּאֵנִים לְבָנִים וּתְאֵנִים שְׁחוֹרוֹת — **such as white figs and black figs,** אִם בֵּירַךְ ״שֶׁהֶחֱיָינוּ״ עַל מִין אֶחָד — is that **if he recited the *Shehecheyanu* blessing on one type,** כְּשֶׁנִּזְדַּמֵּן לוֹ אַחַר כָּךְ מִין הַשֵּׁנִי — **when he later obtains the other type** מְבָרֵךְ גַּם עָלָיו ״שֶׁהֶחֱיָינוּ״ — **he should recite *Shehecheyanu*** on the second type **as well,** כִּי שְׁתֵּי שְׂמָחוֹת הֵן — **since** the two species **are two separate** sources of **joy.**[44]

§15 אִם בֵּירַךְ ״שֶׁהֶחֱיָינוּ״ עַל עֲנָבִים — **If one recited the *Shehecheyanu* blessing on grapes** from the new crop, יֵשׁ אוֹמְרִים — **some** authorities **say** דְּאֵין צָרִיךְ לְבָרֵךְ עוֹד ״שֶׁהֶחֱיָינוּ״ עַל הַיַּיִן הֶחָדָשׁ — **that he is no longer obligated to recite *Shehecheyanu* on the wine**[45] that comes from **the new** crop of grapes, כִּי שִׂמְחָה אַחַת הוּא — **because** both represent **one source of joy,** שֶׁהַיַּיִן יוֹצֵא מִן הָעֲנָבִים — **for wine is produced from grapes.** וְיֵשׁ אוֹמְרִים דְּמִכָּל מָקוֹם — **Other** authorities **say that, nevertheless,** צָרִיךְ לְבָרֵךְ ״שֶׁהֶחֱיָינוּ״ גַּם עַל הַיַּיִן הֶחָדָשׁ — **one must recite *Shehecheyanu* upon the wine** from **the new** season **as well,** מִשּׁוּם דְּיֵשׁ בּוֹ שִׂמְחָה יְתֵירָה מִבָּעֲנָבִים — **for** the wine **is a greater** source of **joy than grapes.** וְעַל כֵּן, טוֹב — **Therefore, it is proper** שֶׁאִם בֵּירַךְ ״שֶׁהֶחֱיָינוּ״ עַל עֲנָבִים — **that if he has** already **recited *Shehecheyanu* on the** new **grapes,** אֲזַי כְּשֶׁשּׁוֹתֶה יַיִן חָדָשׁ — **then when he drinks the new wine** for the first time יְבָרֵךְ תְּחִלָּה ״שֶׁהֶחֱיָינוּ״ עַל אֵיזֶה מִין חָדָשׁ — **he should first recite *Shehecheyanu* on some other new species** of fruit לִפְטוֹר גַּם אֶת הַיַּיִן — **to also discharge** his obligation of reciting *Shehecheyanu* **on the wine.** אֲבָל אִם בֵּירַךְ תְּחִלָּה ״שֶׁהֶחֱיָינוּ״ עַל הַיַּיִן — **However, if he first recited *Shehecheyanu* on the** new **wine,** לְכוּלֵּי עָלְמָא אֵינוֹ מְבָרֵךְ עוֹד עַל עֲנָבִים — **according to all** halachic authorities **he does not recite the** *Shehecheyanu* **blessing again on** the new **grapes.**

---

44. *Shaar HaTziyun* (225:18) notes that this halachah is in fact the subject of debate among the authorities. He concludes that it is best to avoid this halachic doubt by reciting *Shehecheyanu* over some other fruit of which he has not yet partaken this season.

45. See further in this *se'if* for a description of the wine being discussed.

283 THE SHEHECHEYANU AND HATOV VEHAMEITIV BLESSINGS — SIMAN 59:16-18

וְכָל זֶה דַּוְקָא כְּשֶׁהוּא שׁוֹתֶה אֶת הַיַּיִן כְּשֶׁהוּא תִּירוֹשׁ שֶׁהוּא נִיכָּר שֶׁהוּא יַיִן חָדָשׁ, אֲבָל אִם אֵינוֹ שׁוֹתֵהוּ עַד שֶׁהוּא יַיִן, אֲפִילוּ לֹא בֵּירַךְ "שֶׁהֶחֱיָנוּ" עַל עֲנָבִים, אֵינוֹ מְבָרֵךְ עָלָיו "שֶׁהֶחֱיָנוּ" מִשּׁוּם דְּאֵינוֹ נִיכָּר בֵּין חָדָשׁ לְיָשָׁן.

טז. אֵינוֹ מְבָרֵךְ "שֶׁהֶחֱיָנוּ" עַל הַבּוֹסֶר, אֶלָּא כְּשֶׁהִבְשִׁילוּ הָאֶשְׁכּוֹלוֹת עֲנָבִים. וְכֵן כָּל פְּרִי — אַחַר גְּמְרוֹ[46].

יז. נוֹהֲגִין שֶׁאֵין מְבָרְכִין "שֶׁהֶחֱיָנוּ" עַל יְרָקוֹת וּמִינֵי לְפָתוֹת מִפְּנֵי שֶׁהֵן מִתְקַיְּימוֹת זְמַן רַב עַל יְדֵי שֶׁמַּטְמִינִין אוֹתָן בְּקַרְקַע וּבְחוֹל, וְגַם הֵן מְצוּיִין[47], וְגַם אֵין בָּהֶם שִׂמְחָה כָּל כָּךְ[48].

יח. אֵין מְבָרְכִין "שֶׁהֶחֱיָנוּ" עַל הָרֵיחַ[49], מִשּׁוּם דְּמִן הָרֵיחַ נֶהֱנֶה הַנְּשָׁמָה[50] וְהַנְּשָׁמָה הִיא נִצְחִית[51].

וְכָל זֶה דַּוְקָא — **All of this** applies **only** **כְּשֶׁהוּא שׁוֹתֶה אֶת הַיַּיִן כְּשֶׁהוּא תִּירוֹשׁ** — **when he drinks the wine when it is still fresh wine** (i.e., it is not fully fermented), **שֶׁהוּא נִיכָּר שֶׁהוּא יַיִן חָדָשׁ** — **where it is evident that this** beverage **is** from the **new wine** crop. **אֲבָל אִם אֵינוֹ שׁוֹתֵהוּ עַד שֶׁהוּא יַיִן** — **However, if he does not drink it until it** has fully fermented into **wine**, **אֲפִילוּ לֹא בֵּירַךְ "שֶׁהֶחֱיָנוּ" עַל עֲנָבִים** — **even if he has not** yet **recited** ***Shehecheyanu*** **on the** new **grape** crop, **אֵינוֹ מְבָרֵךְ עָלָיו "שֶׁהֶחֱיָנוּ"** — **he does not recite** ***Shehecheyanu*** **on** the wine of the new crop, **מִשּׁוּם דְּאֵינוֹ נִיכָּר בֵּין חָדָשׁ לְיָשָׁן** — **since** the difference **between** wine of the **new** crop **and** wine of the **old** crop **is not** readily **apparent**.

§16 **אֵינוֹ מְבָרֵךְ "שֶׁהֶחֱיָנוּ" עַל הַבּוֹסֶר** — **One does not recite** ***Shehecheyanu*** **on unripe grapes**; **אֶלָּא כְּשֶׁהִבְשִׁילוּ הָאֶשְׁכּוֹלוֹת עֲנָבִים** — the blessing is recited **only when the clusters have ripened into** fully developed **grapes**. **וְכֵן כָּל פְּרִי** — **The same applies to all produce**: **אַחַר גְּמְרוֹ** — *Shehecheyanu* is recited only **once** the fruit **is fully developed**.[46]

§17 **נוֹהֲגִין שֶׁאֵין מְבָרְכִין "שֶׁהֶחֱיָנוּ"** — **The custom is that one does not recite the** ***Shehecheyanu*** **blessing** **עַל יְרָקוֹת וּמִינֵי לְפָתוֹת** — **upon vegetables and** vari**ous types of root vegetables** **מִפְּנֵי שֶׁהֵן מִתְקַיְּימוֹת זְמַן רַב** — **because they last for long periods of time** **עַל יְדֵי שֶׁמַּטְמִינִין אוֹתָן בְּקַרְקַע וּבְחוֹל** — **as a result of being buried in earth or sand**.[47] **וְגַם הֵן מְצוּיִין** — **Additionally, they are readily available** **וְגַם אֵין בָּהֶם שִׂמְחָה כָּל כָּךְ** — **and they also do not cause as much joy** as fruits.[48]

§18 **אֵין מְבָרְכִין "שֶׁהֶחֱיָנוּ" עַל הָרֵיחַ** — **We do not recite the** ***Shehecheyanu*** **blessing upon** smelling **fragrances**,[49] **מִשּׁוּם דְּמִן הָרֵיחַ נֶהֱנֶה הַנְּשָׁמָה** — **for it is the soul that enjoys fragrances**,[50] **וְהַנְּשָׁמָה הִיא נִצְחִית** — **and the soul is eternal**.[51]

---

46. However, one who did recite the *Shehecheyanu* blessing over an unripe fruit does not repeat the blessing when eating this fruit in its ripened state for the first time [provided that the first time it was eaten it was ripe enough to be subject to its appropriate blessing (e.g., *ha'eitz*); see above, 52:12] (*Mishnah Berurah* 225:12).

47. See above, note 40.

48. See above, note 41, and *Mishnah Berurah* 225:18 for further discussion of these halachos.

49. I.e., the scent of plants that are available only seasonally (*Mishnah Berurah* 225:16).

50. See above, 58:1, with note 1.

51. The blessing of *Shehecheyanu* (*Who has kept us alive, and sustained us ... to this season*) implies a transient existence. It would

THE SHEHECHEYANU AND HATOV VEHAMEITIV BLESSINGS — SIMAN 59:19-20 284

יט. עָתִיד אָדָם לִיתֵּן דִּין וְחֶשְׁבּוֹן עַל כָּל מַה שֶּׁרָאֲתָה עֵינוֹ וְלֹא אָכַל. רַבִּי אֶלְעָזָר הֲוֵי מְצַמְצֵם לֵיהּ פְּרִיטֵי וְקָנָה לוֹ מִכָּל דָּבָר פַּעַם אַחַת בַּשָּׁנָה וְאָכַל[52] (יְרוּשַׁלְמִי סוֹף קִידּוּשִׁין).

כ. הָרוֹאֶה אֶת חֲבֵירוֹ לְאַחַר שְׁלֹשִׁים יוֹם (עַיֵּין סִימָן שֶׁאַחַר זֶה סְעִיף י״ב) וְהוּא חָבִיב עָלָיו מְאֹד, וּמִכָּל שֶׁכֵּן אָדָם שֶׁהוּא גָּדוֹל מִמֶּנּוּ, כְּגוֹן אָבִיו אוֹ רַבּוֹ, וְשָׂמֵחַ בִּרְאִיָּיתוֹ, מְבָרֵךְ "שֶׁהֶחֱיָינוּ", אַף עַל פִּי שֶׁבְּתוֹךְ הַזְּמַן קִבֵּל מִמֶּנּוּ מִכְתָּב[53]. וְאִם רוֹאֵהוּ לְאַחַר י״ב חֹדֶשׁ מְבָרֵךְ "בָּרוּךְ אַתָּה ה׳ אֱלֹהֵינוּ מֶלֶךְ הָעוֹלָם[54] מְחַיֵּה הַמֵּתִים", (מִפְּנֵי שֶׁנִּשְׁכַּח מִן הַלֵּב כְּמוֹ שֶׁהַמֵּת נִשְׁכָּח לְאַחַר י״ב חֹדֶשׁ, דִּכְתִיב (תהלים לא, יג) "נִשְׁכַּחְתִּי כְּמֵת מִלֵּב

---

§19 עָתִיד אָדָם לִיתֵּן דִּין וְחֶשְׁבּוֹן — **In the future** judgment, **each person will be held accountable** (lit., [be required] to give judgment and accounting) עַל כָּל מַה שֶּׁרָאֲתָה עֵינוֹ וְלֹא אָכַל — **for everything that his eye has seen**, i.e., that he could have enjoyed, **that he did not eat.** רַבִּי אֶלְעָזָר הֲוֵי מְצַמְצֵם לֵיהּ פְּרִיטֵי — In fact, the Talmudic sage, **R' Elazar, would save pennies** וְקָנָה לוֹ מִכָּל דָּבָר פַּעַם אַחַת בַּשָּׁנָה וְאָכַל — **and purchase for himself** a bit **of every type of food once a year, and eat it**[52] (יְרוּשַׁלְמִי סוֹף קִידּוּשִׁין — *Talmud* ***Yerushalmi***, end of Tractate ***Kiddushin*** [4:12]).

§20 הָרוֹאֶה אֶת חֲבֵירוֹ לְאַחַר שְׁלֹשִׁים יוֹם — **One who sees his friend after** a separation of **thirty days** or longer (עַיֵּין סִימָן שֶׁאַחַר זֶה סְעִיף י״ב — **see following** *Siman, se'if* **12**, regarding the calculation of the thirty days), וְהוּא חָבִיב עָלָיו מְאֹד — **and** this friend **is very dear to him,** וּמִכָּל שֶׁכֵּן אָדָם שֶׁהוּא גָּדוֹל מִמֶּנּוּ — **and certainly** if he is **someone greater than himself**, i.e., someone whom he must honor, כְּגוֹן אָבִיו אוֹ רַבּוֹ — **such as his father or** Torah **teacher,** וְשָׂמֵחַ בִּרְאִיָּיתוֹ — **and he is happy to see** this person, מְבָרֵךְ "שֶׁהֶחֱיָינוּ" — **he should recite the** ***Shehecheyanu*** **blessing,** אַף עַל פִּי שֶׁבְּתוֹךְ הַזְּמַן — **even if during the time** of separation קִבֵּל מִמֶּנּוּ מִכְתָּב — **he had received letters from** him.[53]
וְאִם רוֹאֵהוּ לְאַחַר י״ב חֹדֶשׁ — **If he sees this person** for the first time **after twelve months** of separation, מְבָרֵךְ — **he should recite** the following **blessing:** "בָּרוּךְ אַתָּה ה׳ אֱלֹהֵינוּ מֶלֶךְ הָעוֹלָם מְחַיֵּה הַמֵּתִים" — *Baruch Atah Ado-noy Elokeinu Melech HaOlam,*[54] *mechayei hameisim,* ***Blessed are You, Hashem, our God, King of the universe, Who resuscitates the dead.*** (מִפְּנֵי שֶׁנִּשְׁכַּח מִן הַלֵּב — For this person **was forgotten from the heart** after such a long separation, כְּמוֹ שֶׁהַמֵּת נִשְׁכָּח לְאַחַר י״ב חֹדֶשׁ — **just as a deceased person is forgotten after twelve months,** דִּכְתִיב — **as it is written** [*Tehillim* 31:13]: "נִשְׁכַּחְתִּי כְּמֵת מִלֵּב — ***I have become forgotten as the***

---

therefore be incongruous to recite this blessing upon a pleasure that the soul, which is eternal, enjoys.

52. R' Elazar would seek the opportunity to show appreciation to God for every type of produce at least once a year (*Korban HaEidah* and *Pnei Moshe* ad loc.). On the basis of this statement of the *Talmud Yerushalmi*, the authorities rule that it is a mitzvah to eat some of each new crop every year to show appreciation for Hashem's creations (*Mishnah Berurah* 225:19).

53. *Mishnah Berurah* (225:2) rules that if one has received letters from the friend, or was informed of his welfare, he does not recite this blessing. If, however, one heard that his friend was ill, and when he met him, saw that he was healthy, one would certainly recite the *Shehecheyanu* blessing (*Shaar HaTziyun* 225:3).

54. See Appendix of editorial glosses of Kitzur.

הָיִיתִי כִּכְלִי אֹבֵד״ — מַה כְּלִי, מִי שֶׁאִבֵּד אוֹתוֹ וְלֹא מְצָאוֹ בְּתוֹךְ י״ב חֹדֶשׁ מִתְיָאֵשׁ מִמֶּנּוּ[55], אַף הַמֵּת נִשְׁכָּח מִן הַלֵּב לְאַחַר י״ב חֹדֶשׁ)[56], וְאֵינוֹ מְבָרֵךְ ״שֶׁהֶחֱיָנוּ״. אֲבָל אִם קִבֵּל מִמֶּנּוּ מִכְתָּב בְּתוֹךְ הַזְּמַן, אוֹ שֶׁשָּׁמַע בְּתוֹךְ הַזְּמַן מִשְּׁלוֹמוֹ, אֵינוֹ מְבָרֵךְ ״מְחַיֵּה הַמֵּתִים״, אֶלָּא ״שֶׁהֶחֱיָנוּ״. וְאֵין חִילּוּק בֵּין זְכָרִים לִנְקֵבוֹת, דַּאֲפִילּוּ הָאִישׁ שֶׁהוּא רוֹאֶה אֶת אִשְׁתּוֹ אוֹ אִמּוֹ אוֹ אֲחוֹתוֹ אוֹ בִּתּוֹ, וְכֵן הָאִשָּׁה שֶׁהִיא רוֹאָה אֶת בַּעְלָהּ אוֹ אָבִיהָ אוֹ אָחִיהָ אוֹ (בנו) (בְּנָהּ), מְבָרְכִין כֵּן.

כא. חֲבֵרוֹ שֶׁלֹּא רָאָה אוֹתוֹ מֵעוֹלָם, אֶלָּא שֶׁעַל יְדֵי מִכְתָּבִים שֶׁהֵרִיצוּ מִזֶּה לָזֶה נַעֲשׂוּ אוֹהֲבִים, אִם רוֹאֵהוּ אַחַר כָּךְ, אֵינוֹ מְבָרֵךְ עַל רְאִיָּתוֹ, דְּכֵיוָן שֶׁלֹּא הִתְרָאוּ מֵעוֹלָם פָּנִים אֶל פָּנִים אֵין הָאַהֲבָה גְּדוֹלָה כָּל כָּךְ שֶׁיְּהֵא שָׂמֵחַ בִּרְאִיָּתוֹ.

---

dead from the heart, הָיִיתִי כִּכְלִי אֹבֵד״ — ***I have become like a lost vessel.*** In what way are the dead analogous to a lost vessel? מַה כְּלִי — **Just as a utensil,** מִי שֶׁאִבֵּד אוֹתוֹ — **one who loses it** וְלֹא מְצָאוֹ בְּתוֹךְ י״ב חֹדֶשׁ — **and does not find it within twelve months** מִתְיָאֵשׁ מִמֶּנּוּ — **abandons hope of** retrieving **it,**[55] אַף הַמֵּת — **so** it is with **the dead** — נִשְׁכָּח מִן הַלֵּב לְאַחַר י״ב חֹדֶשׁ — they are **forgotten from the heart after twelve months.**)[56] וְאֵינוֹ מְבָרֵךְ ״שֶׁהֶחֱיָנוּ״ — When the *mechayei hameisim* blessing is recited, **one does not recite the *Shehecheyanu* blessing.** אֲבָל אִם קִבֵּל מִמֶּנּוּ מִכְתָּב בְּתוֹךְ הַזְּמַן — **However, if he received a letter from him during that time** אוֹ שֶׁשָּׁמַע בְּתוֹךְ הַזְּמַן מִשְּׁלוֹמוֹ — **or if he heard about his welfare during that time,** אֵינוֹ מְבָרֵךְ ״מְחַיֵּה הַמֵּתִים״, אֶלָּא ״שֶׁהֶחֱיָנוּ״ — **he does not recite the *mechayei hameisim* blessing, but rather** recites **the *Shehecheyanu* blessing.** וְאֵין חִילּוּק בֵּין זְכָרִים לִנְקֵבוֹת — **There is no distinction** with regard to this blessing **between males and females;** דַּאֲפִילּוּ הָאִישׁ — **even a man** שֶׁהוּא רוֹאֶה אֶת אִשְׁתּוֹ — **who sees his wife** after an extended separation, אוֹ אִמּוֹ אוֹ אֲחוֹתוֹ אוֹ בִּתּוֹ — **or his mother, sister, or daughter,** וְכֵן הָאִשָּׁה שֶׁהִיא רוֹאָה אֶת בַּעְלָהּ — **or a woman who sees her husband** after an extended separation, אוֹ אָבִיהָ אוֹ אָחִיהָ אוֹ (בנו) [בְּנָהּ] — **or her father, brother, or son,** מְבָרְכִין כֵּן — **recites the same blessing.**

§21 חֲבֵרוֹ שֶׁלֹּא רָאָה אוֹתוֹ מֵעוֹלָם — Regarding **one's friend whom he has never seen,** אֶלָּא שֶׁעַל יְדֵי מִכְתָּבִים שֶׁהֵרִיצוּ מִזֶּה לָזֶה — **but through** an exchange of **letters, sent from one to the other,** נַעֲשׂוּ אוֹהֲבִים — **they became close friends,** the halachah is אִם רוֹאֵהוּ אַחַר כָּךְ — that **if he meets** this friend **after** having developed this friendship, אֵינוֹ מְבָרֵךְ עַל רְאִיָּתוֹ — **he does not recite a blessing upon seeing him.** דְּכֵיוָן שֶׁלֹּא הִתְרָאוּ מֵעוֹלָם פָּנִים אֶל פָּנִים — For **since they have never before met face to face,** אֵין הָאַהֲבָה גְּדוֹלָה כָּל כָּךְ — **their love is not so strong** שֶׁיְּהֵא שָׂמֵחַ בִּרְאִיָּתוֹ — **to foster** so great **a happiness upon seeing him** as to warrant the reciting of a blessing.

---

55. One who finds a lost object must announce his find for up to twelve months from the time that it was found. After that, it is assumed that if the owner did not claim it, he has abandoned hope of ever retrieving it (see *Rashi* to *Berachos* 58b s.v. ככלי אובד).

56. Being reunited after an absence of twelve months is akin to seeing a friend after he has been brought back to life, hence the blessing of *mechayei hameisim*, "Who resuscitates the dead" (*Mishnah Berurah* 225:4; see there for another reason).

THE SHEHECHEYANU AND HATOV VEHAMEITIV BLESSINGS — SIMAN 59:21 · **286**

(דִּין "הַטּוֹב וְהַמֵּטִיב" עַל שִׁינּוּי יַיִן כָּתוּב בְּסִימָן מ"ט).

דִּין "הַטּוֹב וְהַמֵּטִיב" עַל שִׁינּוּי יַיִן כָּתוּב בְּסִימָן מ"ט) — The halachos regarding reciting the *HaTov VeHaMeitiv* blessing **upon a change of wine** during the meal **are written** above, **in** *Siman* **49,** *se'ifim* 8-16.)

287 BLESSINGS OVER SEEING VARIOUS PHENOMENA AND EVENTS — SIMAN 60:1

סימן ס

דִּין בִּרְכוֹת הָרְאִיָּה

וּבוֹ ט״ו סְעִיפִים

א. הָרוֹאֶה אִילָנֵי מַאֲכָל שֶׁמּוֹצִיאִין פֶּרַח[1] — מְבָרֵךְ ״בָּרוּךְ אַתָּה ה׳ אֱלֹהֵינוּ מֶלֶךְ הָעוֹלָם שֶׁלֹּא חִיסֵּר בְּעוֹלָמוֹ כְּלוּם וּבָרָא בוֹ בְּרִיּוֹת טוֹבוֹת וְאִילָנוֹת טוֹבוֹת לֵיהָנוֹת בָּהֶם בְּנֵי אָדָם״. וְאֵינוֹ מְבָרֵךְ אֶלָּא פַּעַם אַחַת בְּכָל שָׁנָה[2]. וְאִם אֵיחֵר מִלְּבָרֵךְ עַד שֶׁגָּדְלוּ הַפֵּירוֹת, לֹא יְבָרֵךְ עוֹד[3]. יֵשׁ אוֹמְרִים דְּאִם לֹא בֵּירַךְ בַּפַּעַם הָרִאשׁוֹן שֶׁרָאָה אֶת הַפְּרָחִים, שׁוּב לֹא יְבָרֵךְ (מַחֲצִית הַשֶּׁקֶל סִימָן רכ״ו)[4].

SIMAN 60

THE LAWS OF BLESSINGS OVER SEEING [VARIOUS PHENOMENA AND EVENTS]

CONTAINING 15 *SE'IFIM*

§1 Upon Seeing Fruit Trees Blossoming / **§2-3** Upon Witnessing Natural Phenomena / **§4** Upon Seeing a Rainbow / **§5** Upon Seeing Oceans and Tall Mountains / **§6-7** The Blessing of the Sun / **§8** At the Location of a Personal Miracle / **§9** Upon Seeing Great Scholars / **§10** Upon Seeing a King / **§11** Upon Seeing Graves / **§12** Interval Between Blessings / **§13-14** Upon Seeing Unusual Creations / **§15** Upon Seeing Beautiful Creations

§1 **הָרוֹאֶה אִילָנֵי מַאֲכָל שֶׁמּוֹצִיאִין פֶּרַח — One who sees fruit trees in bloom**[1] **מְבָרֵךְ — recites the** following **blessing:** **״בָּרוּךְ אַתָּה ה׳ אֱלֹהֵינוּ מֶלֶךְ הָעוֹלָם** — ***Blessed are You, Hashem, our God, King of the universe,*** **שֶׁלֹּא חִיסֵּר בְּעוֹלָמוֹ כְּלוּם** — ***Who did not leave anything lacking in His universe,*** **וּבָרָא בוֹ בְּרִיּוֹת טוֹבוֹת וְאִילָנוֹת טוֹבוֹת** — ***and created in it good creatures and good trees,*** **לֵיהָנוֹת בָּהֶם בְּנֵי אָדָם״** — ***through which to provide mankind pleasure.*** **וְאֵינוֹ מְבָרֵךְ אֶלָּא פַּעַם אַחַת בְּכָל שָׁנָה — One recites this blessing only once each year.**[2] **וְאִם אֵיחֵר מִלְּבָרֵךְ עַד שֶׁגָּדְלוּ הַפֵּירוֹת — If one delayed reciting the blessing until the fruit grew,** **לֹא יְבָרֵךְ עוֹד — he can no longer recite the blessing.**[3] **יֵשׁ אוֹמְרִים — Some** authorities **say** **דְּאִם לֹא בֵּירַךְ בַּפַּעַם הָרִאשׁוֹן שֶׁרָאָה אֶת הַפְּרָחִים — that if one did not recite the blessing the first time he saw the blossoms,** **שׁוּב לֹא יְבָרֵךְ — he does not recite the blessing** upon seeing the blossoms **again** (מַחֲצִית הַשֶּׁקֶל סִימָן רכ״ו — see *Machatzis HaShekel, Siman* 226).[4]

---

1. That is, when one sees the actual flower buds that will grow into fruit. One does not recite the blessing upon seeing the budding leaves (*Mishnah Berurah* 226:2).

2. Even if one sees several different types of fruit trees budding at different times, the blessing is recited only once annually (*Mishnah Berurah* 226:3).

3. *Mishnah Berurah* (226:4, *Shaar HaTziyun* §2) writes that if one did not see any fruit trees blossoming, but saw the fruit trees for the first time only after the fruit had already begun to grow, he may recite the blessing, as long as the fruit had not yet fully developed.

4. *Machatzis HaShekel* cites the differing opinions regarding this ruling. According to

BLESSINGS OVER SEEING VARIOUS PHENOMENA AND EVENTS — SIMAN 60:2 288

ב. עַל הַזִּיקִים, וְהוּא כּוֹכָב הַיּוֹרֶה כְּחֵץ בְּאוֹרֶךְ הַשָּׁמַיִם מִמָּקוֹם לְמָקוֹם וְנִמְשָׁךְ אוֹרוֹ כְּשֵׁבֶט, וְעַל הַכּוֹכָב שֶׁיֵּשׁ לוֹ זָנָב וְשֵׁבֶט שֶׁל אוֹרָה, וְעַל רַעֲדַת הָאָרֶץ, וְעַל רוּחוֹת שֶׁנָּשְׁבוּ בְּזַעַף[5], וְעַל הַבְּרָקִים[6], עַל כָּל אֶחָד מֵאֵלּוּ, מְבָרֵךְ "בָּרוּךְ אַתָּה ה' אֱלֹהֵינוּ מֶלֶךְ הָעוֹלָם עוֹשֶׂה מַעֲשֵׂה בְרֵאשִׁית". (וְאֵינוֹ מְבָרֵךְ עַל הַזִּיקִים כִּי אִם פַּעַם אַחַת בְּלַיְלָה, אַף עַל פִּי שֶׁרָאָה עוֹד כּוֹכָב אַחֵר רָץ. וְעַל הַכּוֹכָב שֶׁיֵּשׁ לוֹ זָנָב כֵּיוָן שֶׁבֵּירַךְ עָלָיו אֵינוֹ מְבָרֵךְ עוֹד, אֶלָּא כְּשֶׁלֹּא רָאָהוּ עַד לְאַחַר ל' יוֹם[7].) וְעַל הָרַעַם — אִם שְׁמָעוֹ לְאַחַר שֶׁעָבַר הַבָּרָק[8], מְבָרֵךְ "בָּרוּךְ אַתָּה ה' אֱלֹהֵינוּ מֶלֶךְ הָעוֹלָם שֶׁכֹּחוֹ וּגְבוּרָתוֹ מָלֵא עוֹלָם"[9]. וְאִם רָאָה אֶת הַבָּרָק וְשָׁמַע אֶת הָרַעַם בְּיַחַד, מְבָרֵךְ רַק בְּרָכָה אַחַת "עוֹשֶׂה מַעֲשֵׂה בְרֵאשִׁית"[10]. וְכֵן אִם בֵּירַךְ עַל הַבָּרָק "עוֹשֶׂה מַעֲשֵׂה בְרֵאשִׁית"

---

§2 עַל הַזִּיקִים — Upon seeing a meteor, וְהוּא כּוֹכָב הַיּוֹרֶה כְּחֵץ — which appears as a star that shoots like an arrow בְּאוֹרֶךְ הַשָּׁמַיִם מִמָּקוֹם לְמָקוֹם — and goes from place to place through the length of the sky, וְנִמְשָׁךְ אוֹרוֹ כְּשֵׁבֶט — and its light extends like a rod (i.e., a shooting star); וְעַל הַכּוֹכָב שֶׁיֵּשׁ לוֹ זָנָב וְשֵׁבֶט שֶׁל אוֹרָה — upon seeing a comet, which has a tail like a rod of light; וְעַל רַעֲדַת הָאָרֶץ — upon experiencing an earthquake; וְעַל רוּחוֹת שֶׁנָּשְׁבוּ בְּזַעַף — upon winds that blow with ferocity,[5] i.e., a hurricane or tornado; וְעַל הַבְּרָקִים — and upon seeing lightning;[6] עַל כָּל אֶחָד מֵאֵלּוּ, מְבָרֵךְ — upon witnessing any of these phenomena one recites the following blessing: "בָּרוּךְ אַתָּה ה' אֱלֹהֵינוּ מֶלֶךְ הָעוֹלָם עוֹשֶׂה מַעֲשֵׂה בְרֵאשִׁית" — *Baruch Atah Ado-noy Elokeinu Melech HaOlam, oseh maasei vereishis,* ***Blessed are You, Hashem, our God, King of the universe, Who makes the work of Creation.***
(וְאֵינוֹ מְבָרֵךְ עַל הַזִּיקִים כִּי אִם פַּעַם אַחַת בְּלַיְלָה — One recites the blessing upon seeing a meteor only once per night, אַף עַל פִּי שֶׁרָאָה עוֹד כּוֹכָב אַחֵר רָץ — even if he saw another meteor during the same night. וְעַל הַכּוֹכָב שֶׁיֵּשׁ לוֹ זָנָב — Upon seeing a comet, כֵּיוָן שֶׁבֵּירַךְ עָלָיו אֵינוֹ מְבָרֵךְ עוֹד — once he has recited the blessing upon it, he does not recite the blessing again, אֶלָּא כְּשֶׁלֹּא רָאָהוּ עַד לְאַחַר ל' יוֹם — unless he does not see it again for thirty days.)[7]
וְעַל הָרַעַם — Upon hearing thunder: אִם שְׁמָעוֹ לְאַחַר שֶׁעָבַר הַבָּרָק — if he heard it after the accompanying lightning has passed,[8] מְבָרֵךְ — he recites the following blessing: "בָּרוּךְ אַתָּה ה' אֱלֹהֵינוּ מֶלֶךְ הָעוֹלָם שֶׁכֹּחוֹ וּגְבוּרָתוֹ מָלֵא עוֹלָם" — *Baruch Atah Ado-noy Elokeinu Melech HaOlam shekocho u'gevuroso malei olam,* ***Blessed are You, Hashem, our God, King of the universe, Whose strength and power fill the universe.***[9] וְאִם רָאָה אֶת הַבָּרָק וְשָׁמַע אֶת הָרַעַם בְּיַחַד — If he saw the lightning and heard the thunder simultaneously, מְבָרֵךְ רַק בְּרָכָה אַחַת — he recites only one blessing, "עוֹשֶׂה מַעֲשֵׂה בְרֵאשִׁית" — that of *oseh maasei vereishis.*[10] וְכֵן — Similarly, אִם בֵּירַךְ עַל הַבָּרָק "עוֹשֶׂה מַעֲשֵׂה בְרֵאשִׁית" — if upon seeing lightning he

---

Mishnah Berurah (226:5), one may recite the blessing upon seeing the blossoms even if he had seen the blossoms before.

5. Or any unusually strong storm wind; see *Mishnah Berurah* 227:4.

6. See end of next *se'if.*

7. See below, *se'if* 12.

8. Or if he heard the thunder and did not see the lightning (*Mishnah Berurah* 227:5).

9. This blessing expresses praise to Hashem for implanting within natural phenomena the ability to demonstrate His power and inspire His creations to fear Him (*Mishnah Berurah* 227:7).

10. The custom is that when thunder is heard by itself, one recites only the blessing of

289 BLESSINGS OVER SEEING VARIOUS PHENOMENA AND EVENTS — SIMAN 60:3

וּבְתוֹךְ כְּדֵי דִיבּוּר לְהַבָּרָק נִשְׁמַע הָרַעַם, אֵינוֹ צָרִיךְ לְבָרֵךְ עָלָיו כִּי נִפְטַר בִּבְרָכָה שֶׁעַל הַבָּרָק[11]. אֵין מְבָרְכִין עַל הַבָּרָק אוֹ עַל הָרַעַם אֶלָּא תּוֹךְ כְּדֵי דִיבּוּר, אֲבָל אִם הִפְסִיק יוֹתֵר שׁוּב לֹא יְבָרֵךְ.

ג. כָּל זְמַן שֶׁלֹּא נִתְפַּזְּרוּ הֶעָבִים נִפְטָר בִּבְרָכָה אַחַת[12]. נִתְפַּזְּרוּ הֶעָבִים וְהַשָּׁמַיִם נִזְדַּכְּכוּ בֵּין בָּרָק לְבָרָק וּבֵין רַעַם לְרַעַם, צָרִיךְ לַחֲזוֹר וּלְבָרֵךְ[13]. וְהַבְּרָקִים שֶׁנִּרְאִים בְּלֹא רַעַם, אֶלָּא מֵחֲמַת הַחוֹם, אֵינָם כִּבְרָקִים מַמָּשׁ וְאֵין מְבָרְכִין עֲלֵיהֶם.

---

recited the *oseh maasei vereishis* blessing **וּבְתוֹךְ כְּדֵי דִיבּוּר לְהַבָּרָק נִשְׁמַע הָרַעַם** — **and within *k'dei dibbur*** (lit., *the amount [of time] of an utterance*; approximately 1-2 seconds; see *Kelalim*) of seeing **the lightning, the thunder was heard, אֵינוֹ צָרִיךְ לְבָרֵךְ עָלָיו — he need not recite a** separate **blessing upon** the thunder, **כִּי נִפְטַר בִּבְרָכָה שֶׁעַל הַבָּרָק — for** the obligation to recite a blessing upon the thunder **has been discharged with the blessing** recited **upon** seeing **the lightning.**[11] **אֵין מְבָרְכִין עַל הַבָּרָק אוֹ עַל הָרַעַם אֶלָּא תּוֹךְ כְּדֵי דִיבּוּר — One may recite the blessing over lightning or thunder only within *k'dei dibbur*** of the event. **אֲבָל אִם הִפְסִיק יוֹתֵר — However, if he paused longer** than this amount of time, **שׁוּב לֹא יְבָרֵךְ — he may no longer recite the blessing** until the next lightning bolt is seen or thunderclap is heard.

§3 כָּל זְמַן שֶׁלֹּא נִתְפַּזְּרוּ הֶעָבִים — As long as the clouds did not dissipate, נִפְטָר בִּבְרָכָה אַחַת — one is exempt from reciting any further blessings **with the one blessing** recited over the first lightning flash or thunderclap.[12] **נִתְפַּזְּרוּ הֶעָבִים וְהַשָּׁמַיִם נִזְדַּכְּכוּ** — However, **if the clouds dissipated and the sky cleared** completely **בֵּין בָּרָק לְבָרָק וּבֵין רַעַם לְרַעַם — between one flash of lightning and another, or between one thunderclap and the next, צָרִיךְ לַחֲזוֹר וּלְבָרֵךְ — he must recite the blessing again.**[13]

וְהַבְּרָקִים שֶׁנִּרְאִים בְּלֹא רַעַם — Lightning bolts that are seen without being followed with the sound of **thunder, אֶלָּא מֵחֲמַת הַחוֹם — but** are **caused by heat, אֵינָם כִּבְרָקִים מַמָּשׁ — are not** considered **actual lightning** flashes with regard to this halachah, **וְאֵין מְבָרְכִין עֲלֵיהֶם — and one does not recite a blessing upon** seeing **them.**

---

shekocho etc., and when lightning is seen one recites *oseh maasei vereishis.* (Technically, though, either blessing is appropriate for both thunder and lighting.) When both are experienced together, only the *oseh maasei vereishis* blessing is recited. If one recited instead *shekocho* etc. for both of them, he has also fulfilled his obligation (*Mishnah Berurah* 227:5).

11. This halachah does not appear in *Mishnah Berurah.* However, *Mishnah Berurah* (227:5) does write that one who saw lightning and recited *oseh maasei vereishis,* and had in mind to exempt the thunder that follows, should not recite a blessing on the thunder.

12. I.e., one should not recite any blessing over subsequent lightning flashes or thunderclaps during this storm.

13. Only when the sky is entirely cleared of clouds do we say that the storm has ended. If the wind blew the clouds apart but the sky remained cloudy, new blessings are not necessary on the subsequent lightning and thunder. On the following day, one should recite the blessings again even if the sky did not clear in between (*Mishnah Berurah* 227:8; see *Maamar Mordechai* 227:3, cited by *Kaf HaChaim* ad loc.).

BLESSINGS OVER SEEING VARIOUS PHENOMENA AND EVENTS — SIMAN 60:4-6 290

ד. הָרוֹאֶה[14] קֶשֶׁת[15] מְבָרֵךְ "בָּרוּךְ אַתָּה ה' אֱלֹהֵינוּ מֶלֶךְ הָעוֹלָם זוֹכֵר הַבְּרִית וְנֶאֱמָן בִּבְרִיתוֹ[16] וְקַיָּם בְּמַאֲמָרוֹ"[17]. אָסוּר לְהִסְתַּכֵּל הַרְבֵּה בַּקֶּשֶׁת[18].

ה. עַל הַיַּמִּים וְעַל הֶהָרִים הַגְּבוֹהִים הַמְפוּרְסָמִים בָּעוֹלָם מֵחֲמַת גָּבְהָם מְבָרֵךְ "עוֹשֶׂה מַעֲשֵׂה בְרֵאשִׁית"[19].

ו. הָרוֹאֶה חַמָּה בִּתְקוּפָתָהּ[20], וְהִיא מִכ"ח לְכ"ח שָׁנָה, שֶׁתְּקוּפַת נִיסָן[21] אָז בִּתְחִלַּת לֵיל

---

§4 In the days of Noach, Hashem made a covenant with the inhabitants of the world that He would not again destroy them with a flood. When Hashem is angered and the thought of destroying the world arises, He displays the rainbow as a sign of that covenant. When we see a rainbow we are to recognize this, and thank Hashem for preserving us.[14]

הָרוֹאֶה קֶשֶׁת — One who sees a rainbow[15] **מְבָרֵךְ — recites the** following **blessing: "בָּרוּךְ אַתָּה ה' אֱלֹהֵינוּ מֶלֶךְ הָעוֹלָם** — ***Blessed are You, Hashem, our God, King of the universe,*** **זוֹכֵר הַבְּרִית** — ***Who remembers the covenant,*** **וְנֶאֱמָן בִּבְרִיתוֹ** — ***is trustworthy in His covenant,***[16] **וְקַיָּם בְּמַאֲמָרוֹ"** — ***and fulfills His word.***[17] **אָסוּר לְהִסְתַּכֵּל הַרְבֵּה בַּקֶּשֶׁת — It is forbidden to gaze excessively at a rainbow.**[18]

§5 עַל הַיַּמִּים — Upon seeing **oceans, וְעַל הֶהָרִים הַגְּבוֹהִים — and upon** seeing **exceedingly tall mountains הַמְפוּרְסָמִים בָּעוֹלָם מֵחֲמַת גָּבְהָם — that are renowned in the world because of their** great **height, מְבָרֵךְ — one recites the blessing** of **"עוֹשֶׂה מַעֲשֵׂה בְרֵאשִׁית"** — *oseh maasei vereishis,* ***Who makes the work of Creation.***[19]

§6 הָרוֹאֶה חַמָּה בִּתְקוּפָתָהּ — One who sees the sun at the beginning of its cycle (lit., *at its turning point*),[20] **וְהִיא מִכ"ח לְכ"ח שָׁנָה** — an event **that** occurs **every twenty-eight years, שֶׁתְּקוּפַת נִיסָן אָז בִּתְחִלַּת לֵיל ד' — when the *tekufah* of Nissan**[21] **occurs at the beginning of the evening of the fourth day of the week,**

---

14. See *Bereishis* 9:8-17; *Rashi* ibid. v. 14. Since the rainbow appears as a result of mankind's wrongdoings, it is best not to inform others that there is a rainbow visible, as this amounts to talebearing (*Mishnah Berurah* 229:1).

15. It is unclear if this blessing is recited only when seeing the rainbow as a full arc, or if seeing even a partial arc is sufficient to require a blessing (*Beur Halachah* 229:1 s.v. הרואה).

16. Hashem keeps the covenant that He made and does not destroy the world even if there is an abundance of wickedness (*Mishnah Berurah* 229:4).

17. I.e., even if Hashem would not have made a covenant, He would still keep the words that He spoke (*Bereishis* 9:11), declaring that there would never again be a flood to destroy the earth (*Mishnah Berurah* 229:4).

18. Looking excessively at the rainbow weakens one's eyes. One should look at the rainbow [long enough to make note of it] and recite the blessing, and then not gaze at it any longer (*Mishnah Berurah* 229:5).

19. It is appropriate to praise Hashem when we recognize something that is in the same state as it was when created by Hashem during the six days of creation (*Mishnah Berurah* 228:1).

20. Once every twenty-eight years, the sun returns to the position in the heavens that it occupied at the time of its creation. The sun's arriving at *its original turning point* refers to the sun's returning to this position on the same day of the week and at the same hour of the day as the time that it was created (see *Mishnah Berurah* 229:6). See also *Bircas HaChammah,* ArtScroll Mesorah Publications, 2009.

21. The solar year is divided into four *tekufos* (seasons); see previous note. The beginning of these *tekufos* (also referred to as the "*tekufah*"), roughly corresponds to the equinoxes

291 BLESSINGS OVER SEEING VARIOUS PHENOMENA AND EVENTS — SIMAN 60:7

ד׳[22], מְבָרְכִין בְּיוֹם ד׳ בַּבּוֹקֶר[23] כְּשֶׁהִיא זוֹרַחַת ״בָּרוּךְ אַתָּה ה׳ אֱלֹהֵינוּ מֶלֶךְ הָעוֹלָם עוֹשֵׂה מַעֲשֵׂה בְרֵאשִׁית״. וְקוֹדֶם הַבְּרָכָה יֵשׁ לוֹמַר הַמִּזְמוֹר ״הַלְלוּיָהּ הַלְלוּ אֶת ה׳ מִן הַשָּׁמַיִם״ וְגוֹ׳ (תהלים קמח), וְאַחַר כָּךְ אוֹמְרִים הַבְּרָכָה, וְאַחַר כָּךְ ״אֵל אָדוֹן״ וְכוּ׳[24] עַד ״וְחַיּוֹת הַקּוֹדֶשׁ״, וְאַחַר כָּךְ מִזְמוֹר ״הַשָּׁמַיִם מְסַפְּרִים כְּבוֹד אֵל״ וְגוֹ׳ (תהלים יט), וְאַחַר כָּךְ ״עָלֵינוּ לְשַׁבֵּחַ״ וְקַדִּישׁ (כֶּרֶם שְׁלֹמֹה בְּשֵׁם הַגָּאוֹן בַּעַל חֲתַם סוֹפֵר זצ״ל)[25].

ז. לְכַתְּחִלָּה יֵשׁ לְבָרֵךְ בַּבּוֹקֶר מִיָּד בְּהָנֵץ הַחַמָּה, מִשּׁוּם דִּזְרִיזִין מַקְדִּימִין לְמִצְוָה. וְטוֹב אִם אֶפְשָׁר לְבָרֵךְ בַּאֲסִיפַת עָם, מִשּׁוּם דְּ״בְרָב עָם הַדְרַת מֶלֶךְ״ (משלי יד, כח)[26]

---

i.e., Tuesday evening,[22] **מְבָרְכִין בְּיוֹם ד׳ בַּבּוֹקֶר — recites the** following **blessing on Wednesday morning,**[23] **כְּשֶׁהִיא זוֹרַחַת — when** the sun **shines:** **״בָּרוּךְ אַתָּה ה׳ אֱלֹהֵינוּ מֶלֶךְ הָעוֹלָם עוֹשֵׂה מַעֲשֵׂה בְרֵאשִׁית״** — *Baruch Atah Ado-noy Elokeinu Melech HaOlam, oseh maasei vereishis, **Blessed are You, Hashem, our God, King of the universe, Who makes the work of Creation.***

וְקוֹדֶם הַבְּרָכָה — Before the blessing is recited, **יֵשׁ לוֹמַר הַמִּזְמוֹר ״הַלְלוּיָהּ הַלְלוּ אֶת ה׳ מִן הַשָּׁמַיִם״ וְגוֹ׳ — the Psalm** beginning with the words ***Halleluyah! Praise Hashem from the heavens*** (*Tehillim* Ch. 148) **should be recited. וְאַחַר כָּךְ אוֹמְרִים הַבְּרָכָה — After this, they recite the blessing** (*oseh maasei vereishis*), **וְאַחַר כָּךְ ״אֵל אָדוֹן״ וְכוּ׳ — followed by** the prayer, ***God the Master*, etc.**[24] **עַד ״וְחַיּוֹת הַקּוֹדֶשׁ״ — until** the end of that prayer with the words, ***and the holy Chayos.*** **וְאַחַר כָּךְ מִזְמוֹר ״הַשָּׁמַיִם מְסַפְּרִים כְּבוֹד אֵל״ וְגוֹ׳ — After this, the Psalm** beginning with the words ***The heavens declare the glory of God*** (*Tehillim* Ch. 19) is recited; **וְאַחַר כָּךְ ״עָלֵינוּ לְשַׁבֵּחַ״ וְקַדִּישׁ — and after this** the ***Aleinu leshabei'ach*** prayer, **and** then ***Kaddish.*** (**כֶּרֶם שְׁלֹמֹה בְּשֵׁם הַגָּאוֹן בַּעַל חֲתַם סוֹפֵר זצ״ל** — This arrangement of prayers is from ***Kerem Shlomo***, and is presented **in the name of the author of the** work ***Chasam Sofer*, of blessed memory.**)[25]

§7 **לְכַתְּחִלָּה יֵשׁ לְבָרֵךְ בַּבּוֹקֶר — Ideally, one should recite this blessing in the morning,** **מִיָּד בְּהָנֵץ הַחַמָּה — immediately at sunrise,** **מִשּׁוּם דִּזְרִיזִין מַקְדִּימִין לְמִצְוָה** — for **the zealous** perform a **mitzvah at the earliest opportunity.** **וְטוֹב אִם אֶפְשָׁר לְבָרֵךְ בַּאֲסִיפַת עָם — It is** also **good, if possible, to recite the blessing with a gathering of people,** **מִשּׁוּם דְּ״בְרָב עָם הַדְרַת מֶלֶךְ״ — since, *With the multitude of people is the glory of the King*** (*Mishlei* 14:28); i.e., the glory of Hashem is increased when many people join together to perform a mitzvah.[26]

---

and solstices. *Tekufas Nissan* marks the beginning of the spring season.

22. The sun was created and fixed in the heavens at the beginning of the fourth day of the week, i.e., at 6:00 p.m. on Tuesday evening. At that time it was positioned in the place where it is found at the beginning of *tekufas Nissan. Tekufas Nissan* takes place on Tuesday evening at 6:00 p.m. only once every twenty-eight years.

23. Since the sun is not visible in all places on the previous evening, the Sages ordained that the blessing be recited the next morning (*Ohr Pnei Moshe* §14).

24. A liturgical poem from the Shabbos morning prayers praising Hashem for the heavenly bodies.

25. See also *Responsa* of *Chasam Sofer, Orach Chaim* §56. Besides the required blessing, there is no single accepted text for this service, and other prayers have been added by various liturgists over the generations. For a full treatment of this subject, see *Bircas HaChammah*, ArtScroll Mesorah Publications, 2009, beginning p. 127.

26. Some authorities maintain that it is preferable to recite the blessing outside the synagogue after the morning services, so

BLESSINGS OVER SEEING VARIOUS PHENOMENA AND EVENTS — SIMAN 60:7 292

(וְיֵשׁ לְהַכְרִיז בְּיוֹם שֶׁלְּפָנָיו לְמַעַן יֵדְעוּ לְהִתְאַסֵּף). וְאִם אִי אֶפְשַׁר לְהִתְאַסֵּף תֵּיכֶף בַּבּוֹקֶר, אַל יִתְאַחֲרוּ בִּשְׁבִיל זֶה, אֶלָּא כָּל אֶחָד יְבָרֵךְ מִיָּד כְּשֶׁרוֹאֶה זְרִיחַת הַשֶּׁמֶשׁ, כִּי עִנְיַן זְרִיזִין מַקְדִּימִין דָּחֵי עִנְיַן "בְּרָב עָם"[27]. וּבְדִיעֲבַד אִם לֹא בֵּירַךְ בַּבּוֹקֶר, יָכוֹל לְבָרֵךְ עַד ג׳ שָׁעוֹת עַל הַיּוֹם, וּבִשְׁעַת הַדְּחָק עַד חֲצוֹת הַיּוֹם. וְלָכֵן, אִם בַּבּוֹקֶר יֵשׁ עֲנָנִים הַמְכַסִּים אוֹתָהּ, יַמְתִּין עַד קָרוֹב לַחֲצוֹת, אוּלַי תִּתְגַּלֶּה וִיבָרֵךְ בְּשֵׁם וּמַלְכוּת[28]. וְאִם לֹא נִתְגַּלָּה[29], יְבָרֵךְ בְּלֹא שֵׁם וּמַלְכוּת[30]. שְׁנַת קִידּוּשׁ הַחַמָּה הָיְתָה שְׁנַת תרכ״ט[31] וְתִהְיֶה אִם יִרְצֶה הַשֵּׁם בִּשְׁנַת תרנ״ז[32]. יְהִי רָצוֹן שֶׁנִּזְכֶּה לְאוֹר שִׁבְעַת יְמֵי בְרֵאשִׁית[33].

(וְיֵשׁ לְהַכְרִיז בְּיוֹם שֶׁלְּפָנָיו לְמַעַן יֵדְעוּ לְהִתְאַסֵּף) — **It is proper to announce** to the public **on the preceding day** that this blessing is to be recited the next day, **so that** the community members **know to gather.)** וְאִם אִי אֶפְשַׁר לְהִתְאַסֵּף תֵּיכֶף בַּבּוֹקֶר — **If it is not possible** for many people **to gather immediately in the morning,** אַל יִתְאַחֲרוּ בִּשְׁבִיל זֶה — **they should not delay** reciting the blessing **because of this.** אֶלָּא כָּל אֶחָד יְבָרֵךְ — **Rather, each individual should recite the blessing** מִיָּד כְּשֶׁרוֹאֶה זְרִיחַת הַשֶּׁמֶשׁ — **immediately upon seeing the sun shining,** כִּי עִנְיַן זְרִיזִין מַקְדִּימִין דָּחֵי עִנְיַן "בְּרָב עָם" — **for the precept of "*the zealous* perform mitzvos *at their earliest* opportunity" takes precedence over the precept of "*With the multitude of people* is the glory of the King."**[27]

וּבְדִיעֲבַד אִם לֹא בֵּירַךְ בַּבּוֹקֶר — **If it happened that one did not recite the blessing** first thing **in the morning,** יָכוֹל לְבָרֵךְ עַד ג׳ שָׁעוֹת עַל הַיּוֹם — **he can** still **recite the blessing until three hours into the day,** וּבִשְׁעַת הַדְּחָק עַד חֲצוֹת הַיּוֹם — **and in cases of** great **necessity,** he may recite the blessing **until noon.** וְלָכֵן — **Therefore,** אִם בַּבּוֹקֶר יֵשׁ עֲנָנִים הַמְכַסִּים אוֹתָהּ — **if in the morning there were clouds covering** the sun, יַמְתִּין עַד קָרוֹב לַחֲצוֹת — **one should wait until close to noon,** אוּלַי תִּתְגַּלֶּה — for **perhaps** the sun **will appear,** וִיבָרֵךְ בְּשֵׁם וּמַלְכוּת — **and** then **he should recite the** full **blessing with the Name** of Hashem **and His sovereignty.**[28] וְאִם לֹא נִתְגַּלָּה — **If** the sun **did not appear,**[29] יְבָרֵךְ בְּלֹא שֵׁם וּמַלְכוּת — **he should recite the blessing without** mentioning **the Name** of Hashem **and His sovereignty.**[30]

שְׁנַת קִידּוּשׁ הַחַמָּה הָיְתָה שְׁנַת תרכ״ט — **The year in which the "sanctification of the sun"**[31] last took place **was in the year 5629** (1869), וְתִהְיֶה אִם יִרְצֶה הַשֵּׁם בִּשְׁנַת תרנ״ז — **and it will** again **be, God willing, in the year 5657** (1897).[32] יְהִי רָצוֹן

---

as to enable the mitzvah to be performed in the company of a large assemblage (see *Responsa* of *Chasam Sofer, Orach Chaim* §56).

27. [See previous note.] Similarly, if clouds threaten to obscure the sun, one who sees the sun should recite the blessing immediately even alone (*Shaar HaTziyun* 229:1).

28. "His sovereignty" refers to the words מֶלֶךְ הָעוֹלָם, *King of the universe*, which appear in the full text of a blessing.

29. If the outline of the sun can be seen through the clouds one may still recite the full blessing. However, if even an outline cannot be seen, one may not recite the full blessing with Hashem's Name (*Mishnah Berurah* 229:8).

30. I.e., בָּרוּךְ עוֹשֶׂה מַעֲשֵׂה בְרֵאשִׁית, *Blessed [is He] Who makes the work of Creation.*

31. The appellation "sanctification of the sun," referring to the aforementioned blessing, is a colloquialism, borrowed from the term *kiddush levanah*, "sanctification of the moon" (below, 97:7-15), which is itself a borrowed term; see *Bircas HaChammah*, Mesorah Publications, 2009, p. 90.

32. As of this publication, the most recent occurrence of the blessing of the sun was 14 Nissan, Erev Pesach 5769 (April 8, 2009). The next two occurrences will be on 23 Nissan 5797 (April 8, 2037), and 2 Nissan 5825 (April 8, 2065).

293 BLESSINGS OVER SEEING VARIOUS PHENOMENA AND EVENTS — SIMAN 60:8

ח. מִי שֶׁעָשָׂה לוֹ הַקָּדוֹשׁ בָּרוּךְ הוּא נֵס שֶׁלֹּא כְּדֶרֶךְ הַטֶּבַע[34], כְּשֶׁרוֹאֶה אֶת הַמָּקוֹם שֶׁנַּעֲשָׂה לוֹ שָׁם הַנֵּס[35] מְבָרֵךְ "בָּרוּךְ אַתָּה ה' אֱלֹהֵינוּ מֶלֶךְ הָעוֹלָם שֶׁעָשָׂה לִי נֵס בַּמָּקוֹם הַזֶּה[36]" (וְעַיֵּין לְקַמָּן סִימָן ס"א סְעִיף ג')[37]. וְגַם בְּנוֹ וּבֶן בְּנוֹ, אֲפִילוּ אוֹתָם שֶׁנּוֹלְדוּ קוֹדֶם שֶׁנַּעֲשָׂה הַנֵּס, גַּם כֵּן מְבָרְכִין[38]. כֵּיצַד מְבָרְכִין? בְּנוֹ מְבָרֵךְ "שֶׁעָשָׂה נֵס לְאָבִי בַּמָּקוֹם הַזֶּה", וְאִם הֵם רַבִּים אוֹמְרִים "לְאָבִינוּ". בֶּן בְּנוֹ אוֹמֵר "לַאֲבוֹתַי",

---

שֶׁנִּזְכֶּה לְאוֹר שִׁבְעַת יְמֵי בְרֵאשִׁית — **May it be the will** of Hashem **that we merit the light of the Seven Days of Creation.**[33]

§8 מִי שֶׁעָשָׂה לוֹ הַקָּדוֹשׁ בָּרוּךְ הוּא נֵס — **Someone for whom the Holy One, blessed is He, performed a miracle,** שֶׁלֹּא כְּדֶרֶךְ הַטֶּבַע — **beyond the laws of nature,**[34] כְּשֶׁרוֹאֶה אֶת הַמָּקוֹם שֶׁנַּעֲשָׂה לוֹ שָׁם הַנֵּס — **upon seeing the place where the miracle was performed for him**[35] מְבָרֵךְ — **should recite the** following **blessing:** "בָּרוּךְ אַתָּה ה' אֱלֹהֵינוּ מֶלֶךְ הָעוֹלָם שֶׁעָשָׂה לִי נֵס בַּמָּקוֹם הַזֶּה" — *Baruch Atah Ado-noy Elokeinu Melech HaOlam, she'asah li nes bamakom hazeh,* ***Blessed are You,*** **Hashem, *our God, King of the universe, Who performed a miracle for me in this place***[36] (וְעַיֵּין לְקַמָּן סִימָן ס"א סְעִיף ג' — **see below, 61:3).**[37] וְגַם בְּנוֹ וּבֶן בְּנוֹ — **Also his son and grandson,** אֲפִילוּ אוֹתָם שֶׁנּוֹלְדוּ קוֹדֶם שֶׁנַּעֲשָׂה הַנֵּס — **even those** descendants **born before the miracle took place** (i.e., who did not personally benefit as a result of this miracle), גַּם כֵּן מְבָרְכִין — **also recite a blessing** when they visit this site.[38] כֵּיצַד מְבָרְכִין — **What blessing do they recite?** בְּנוֹ מְבָרֵךְ — **One's son recites:** "שֶׁעָשָׂה נֵס לְאָבִי בַּמָּקוֹם הַזֶּה" — *Baruch Atah Ado-noy Elokeinu Melech HaOlam, she'asah nes le'avi bamakom hazeh, Blessed are You,* Hashem, *King of the universe,* ***Who performed a miracle for my father in this place;*** וְאִם הֵם רַבִּים אוֹמְרִים "לְאָבִינוּ" — **if they are many** sons reciting the blessing in unison, **they say** *she'asah nes le'avinu bamakom hazeh, Who performed a miracle* ***for our father*** *in this place.* בֶּן בְּנוֹ אוֹמֵר "לַאֲבוֹתַי" — **A**

---

33. I.e., the future Redemption, when "*the light of the sun will be seven times as strong, like the light of [the] Seven Days*" (see *Yeshayah* 30:26 and *Rashi* there). During the Seven Days of Creation, there shone an extraordinary light that was seven times as strong as the light of the sun of this world; see *Toras Chaim* to *Sanhedrin* 91b.

34. For example, if a spring of water miraculously appears in the desert for a traveler who was in danger of dying of thirst or if one was run over by a vehicle and miraculously survived (see *Mishnah Berurah* 218:29, 32 and *Shaar HaTziyun* there §28).

35. That is, upon returning to the site of the miracle. At the time that the miracle took place he is obligated only to recite the *HaGomeil* blessing, as explained in the following *Siman* (*Mishnah Berurah* 218:15 and *Shaar HaTziyun* §6).

36. One does not recite the blessing within thirty days of his previous recitation of the blessing (*Mishnah Berurah* 218:15). When experiencing a miracle within the bounds of nature, one should recite the blessing without reciting the Name of Hashem and the words *Melech HaOlam*: בָּרוּךְ שֶׁעָשָׂה לִי נֵס בַּמָּקוֹם הַזֶּה, *Blessed [is He] Who performed a miracle for me in this place* (*Shulchan Aruch* 218:9).

37. There, Kitzur sets out other practices appropriate for one who was saved miraculously.

38. When visiting a place where a miracle was performed for a mother or grandmother, this blessing is also recited. However, it is not recited in a place where the miracle was performed for a spouse or for a child (*Beur Halachah* 218:4 s.v. וכל יוצאי ירכו). Great-grandchildren do not recite this blessing unless their grandparent (the son or daughter of the one for whom the miracle took place) was born after the miracle took place, in which case they too are considered to have personally benefited from the miracle (*Mishnah Berurah* 218:16, *Shaar HaTziyun* §7).

BLESSINGS OVER SEEING VARIOUS PHENOMENA AND EVENTS — SIMAN 60:9 294

וְאִם הֵם רַבִּים אוֹמְרִים "לַאֲבוֹתֵינוּ"[39]. וּמִי שֶׁנַּעֲשָׂה לוֹ נִסִּים הַרְבֵּה, בְּהַגִּיעַ לְאֶחָד מִכָּל הַמְּקוֹמוֹת[40] שֶׁנַּעֲשָׂה לוֹ נֵס צָרִיךְ לְהַזְכִּיר כָּל שְׁאָר הַמְּקוֹמוֹת, וְיִכְלוֹל כּוּלָּם בִּבְרָכָה אַחַת וְיֹאמַר "שֶׁעָשָׂה לִי נֵס בַּמָּקוֹם הַזֶּה וּבְמָקוֹם פְּלוֹנִי". וְכֵן בָּנָיו מַזְכִּירִין כָּל שְׁאָר הַמְּקוֹמוֹת.

ט. הָרוֹאֶה חָכָם גָּדוֹל בַּתּוֹרָה מִיִּשְׂרָאֵל מְבָרֵךְ "בָּרוּךְ אַתָּה ה' אֱלֹהֵינוּ מֶלֶךְ הָעוֹלָם שֶׁחָלַק מֵחָכְמָתוֹ לִירֵאָיו"[41] (לְפִי שֶׁיִּשְׂרָאֵל הֵם חֵלֶק אֱלֹהִי וּדְבֵקִים בּוֹ לָכֵן אוֹמֵר "שֶׁחָלַק")[42]. וְהָרוֹאֶה חָכָם גָּדוֹל בְּחָכְמַת הָעוֹלָם מֵאוּמּוֹת הָעוֹלָם[43], מְבָרֵךְ "בָּרוּךְ

---

grandson says *she'asah nes la'avosai, Who performed a miracle* ***for my fathers***; וְאִם הֵם רַבִּים אוֹמְרִים "לַאֲבוֹתֵינוּ" — **if they are many** grandsons, **they say** *she'asah nes la'avoseinu, Who performed a miracle* ***for our fathers.***[39]

וּמִי שֶׁנַּעֲשָׂה לוֹ נִסִּים הַרְבֵּה — **One who experienced many miracles,** בְּהַגִּיעַ לְאֶחָד מִכָּל הַמְּקוֹמוֹת שֶׁנַּעֲשָׂה לוֹ נֵס — **when he reaches one of any of the locations where a miracle was performed for him** and recites the blessing, צָרִיךְ לְהַזְכִּיר כָּל שְׁאָר הַמְּקוֹמוֹת — **must make mention of all the other places**[40] וְיִכְלוֹל כּוּלָּם בִּבְרָכָה אַחַת — **and include them all in one blessing.** וְיֹאמַר "שֶׁעָשָׂה לִי נֵס בַּמָּקוֹם הַזֶּה — **He should say,** *Blessed are You, Hashem, King of the universe,* ***Who performed a miracle for me in this place,*** וּבְמָקוֹם פְּלוֹנִי" — ***and in such and such place.*** וְכֵן בָּנָיו מַזְכִּירִין כָּל שְׁאָר הַמְּקוֹמוֹת — **His sons too,** when reciting the blessing for their father's miracle, **make mention of all the other places** when reciting the blessing in one location.

§9 הָרוֹאֶה חָכָם גָּדוֹל בַּתּוֹרָה מִיִּשְׂרָאֵל — **One who sees a great Jewish Torah scholar** מְבָרֵךְ — **recites** the following **blessing:** "בָּרוּךְ אַתָּה ה' אֱלֹהֵינוּ מֶלֶךְ הָעוֹלָם שֶׁחָלַק מֵחָכְמָתוֹ לִירֵאָיו" — *Baruch Atah Ado-noy Elokeinu Melech HaOlam, shechalak mei'chachmaso li'rei'av,* ***Blessed are You, Hashem, our God, King of the universe, Who has apportioned of His wisdom to those who fear Him.***[41] (לְפִי שֶׁיִּשְׂרָאֵל הֵם חֵלֶק אֱלֹהִי וּדְבֵקִים בּוֹ — **Because the Jewish people are the portion of God, and cling to Him,** לָכֵן אוֹמֵר "שֶׁחָלַק" — it is **therefore** appropriate here to **say** this blessing of ***Who apportioned.***)[42]

וְהָרוֹאֶה חָכָם גָּדוֹל בְּחָכְמַת הָעוֹלָם מֵאוּמּוֹת הָעוֹלָם — **One who sees a great non-Jewish scholar of the secular disciplines**[43] מְבָרֵךְ — **recites the** following **blessing:** "בָּרוּךְ

---

39. *Shulchan Aruch* (118:6) also cites the law of reciting a blessing upon seeing the place where a miracle was performed for one's Torah teacher. However, *Mishnah Berurah* rules that this applies only to a teacher who has taught him the majority of his Torah knowledge. This rarely applies to one's teacher in our days. Indeed, in his editorial glosses (see Appendix), Kitzur writes that he intentionally made no mention of this blessing

40. If, on the same day, one visited two or more locations where he experienced miracles, he must recite the blessing in each of the locations, even though he mentioned the other locations the first time he recited the blessing (*Mishnah Berurah* 218:19).

41. One should also recite *Shehecheyanu* upon seeing a great Torah scholar if thirty days have passed since he last saw the scholar (*Mishnah Berurah* 225:1).

42. With this, Kitzur explains the difference between the blessing recited over a Jewish Torah scholar and the blessing to be recited when seeing a non-Jewish scholar of secular disciplines (further in this *se'if*). Since Jews cling to God, we use the term שֶׁחָלַק, "*Who apportioned,*" denoting a grant that remains attached to its source, in contrast with שֶׁנָּתַן, "*Who gave,*" recited upon seeing non-Jewish scholars, which implies a gift removed from its source.

43. This does not apply to a scholar of other religions (*Mishnah Berurah* 224:10).

295 BLESSINGS OVER SEEING VARIOUS PHENOMENA AND EVENTS — SIMAN 60:10-11

אַתָּה ה׳ אֱלֹהֵינוּ מֶלֶךְ הָעוֹלָם שֶׁנָּתַן מֵחָכְמָתוֹ לְבָשָׂר וָדָם״.

י. הָרוֹאֶה מֶלֶךְ מִמַּלְכֵי אוּמּוֹת הָעוֹלָם[44], מְבָרֵךְ ״בָּרוּךְ אַתָּה ה׳ אֱלֹהֵינוּ מֶלֶךְ הָעוֹלָם שֶׁנָּתַן מִכְּבוֹדוֹ לְבָשָׂר וָדָם״, וַאֲפִילוּ אֵינוֹ רוֹאֶה אֶת הַמֶּלֶךְ מַמָּשׁ, אֶלָּא שֶׁהוּא רוֹאֶה בִּכְבוֹדוֹ וְיוֹדֵעַ בְּבֵירוּר שֶׁהַמֶּלֶךְ הוּא שָׁם יָכוֹל לְבָרֵךְ בְּרָכָה זוֹ. וְסוּמָא יְבָרֵךְ בְּלֹא שֵׁם וּמַלְכוּת[45]. וּמִצְוָה לְהִשְׁתַּדֵּל לִרְאוֹת בִּכְבוֹד מְלָכִים[46]. וְאִם רָאָה אוֹתוֹ פַּעַם אַחַת אַל יְבַטֵּל יוֹתֵר מִלִּימּוּדוֹ לִרְאוֹתוֹ, אֶלָּא אִם בָּא אַחַר כָּךְ בְּחַיִל יוֹתֵר וּבְכָבוֹד גָּדוֹל יוֹתֵר.

יא. הָרוֹאֶה קִבְרֵי יִשְׂרָאֵל, מְבָרֵךְ[47] ״בָּרוּךְ אַתָּה ה׳ אֱלֹהֵינוּ מֶלֶךְ הָעוֹלָם

״אַתָּה ה׳ אֱלֹהֵינוּ מֶלֶךְ הָעוֹלָם שֶׁנָּתַן מֵחָכְמָתוֹ לְבָשָׂר וָדָם״ — *Baruch Atah Ado-noy Elokeinu Melech HaOlam, shenasan mei'chachmaso levasar vadam,* ***Blessed are You, Hashem, our God, King of the universe, Who gave of His wisdom to flesh and blood.***

§10 הָרוֹאֶה מֶלֶךְ מִמַּלְכֵי אוּמּוֹת הָעוֹלָם — **If one sees a king of the non-Jewish nations of the world,**[44] מְבָרֵךְ — **he should recite the** following **blessing:** ״בָּרוּךְ אַתָּה ה׳ אֱלֹהֵינוּ מֶלֶךְ הָעוֹלָם — ***Blessed are You, Hashem, our God, King of the universe,*** שֶׁנָּתַן מִכְּבוֹדוֹ לְבָשָׂר וָדָם״ — ***Who has given of His glory to flesh and blood.*** וַאֲפִילוּ אֵינוֹ רוֹאֶה אֶת הַמֶּלֶךְ מַמָּשׁ — **Even if one cannot actually see the king** himself from his vantage point, אֶלָּא שֶׁהוּא רוֹאֶה בִּכְבוֹדוֹ — **but he does see the honor** accorded to the king וְיוֹדֵעַ בְּבֵירוּר שֶׁהַמֶּלֶךְ הוּא שָׁם — **and he knows with certainty that the king is there,** יָכוֹל לְבָרֵךְ בְּרָכָה זוֹ — **he may recite this blessing.** וְסוּמָא — **A blind person** who is incapable of seeing the king יְבָרֵךְ בְּלֹא שֵׁם וּמַלְכוּת — **should recite this blessing without** mentioning **the Name** of Hashem **or His sovereignty.**[45] וּמִצְוָה לְהִשְׁתַּדֵּל לִרְאוֹת בִּכְבוֹד מְלָכִים — **It is proper to attempt to see the honor accorded to kings.**[46] וְאִם רָאָה אוֹתוֹ פַּעַם אַחַת — **If one saw** this king **once before,** אַל יְבַטֵּל יוֹתֵר מִלִּימּוּדוֹ לִרְאוֹתוֹ — **he should not interrupt his Torah study further** in order **to see him** again, אֶלָּא אִם בָּא אַחַר כָּךְ — **unless he comes the next time** בְּחַיִל יוֹתֵר וּבְכָבוֹד גָּדוֹל יוֹתֵר — **with a larger entourage and a greater** display of **honor.**

§11 הָרוֹאֶה קִבְרֵי יִשְׂרָאֵל — **One who sees Jewish graves** מְבָרֵךְ — **should recite** the following **blessing:**[47] ״בָּרוּךְ אַתָּה ה׳ אֱלֹהֵינוּ מֶלֶךְ הָעוֹלָם — ***Blessed are***

---

44. This blessing is recited upon seeing any ruler who does not have any superior to whom he must answer, and who can pass final judgment involving life and death. Upon seeing any powerful government official, it is proper to recite the blessing without mention of the Name of Hashem and His Sovereignty. Thus, one would say: בָּרוּךְ שֶׁנָּתַן מִכְּבוֹדוֹ לְבָשָׂר וָדָם, *Blessed [is He] Who has given of His glory to flesh and blood* (*Mishnah Berurah* 224:12).

45. See *Mishnah Berurah* 224:11.

46. One who has witnessed honor accorded to non-Jewish kings will be able to contrast that honor with the glory that will attend the Messianic king when he arrives (see *Berachos* 58a).

47. According to some authorities, this applies only to seeing more than one grave, as the blessing is formulated in the plural (*Mishnah Berurah* 224:16). One is required to recite the blessing immediately upon seeing the graves, even if he did not yet enter the cemetery. However, he must see either graves or [horizontal] tombstones clearly. One who sees them only from a distance or knows that there are graves in the vicinity does not recite the blessing (*Igros Moshe, Orach Chaim* V, §37.10).

BLESSINGS OVER SEEING VARIOUS PHENOMENA AND EVENTS — SIMAN 60:12-13 296

אֲשֶׁר יָצַר אֶתְכֶם בַּדִּין" וְכוּ׳[48]. וְעַל קִבְרֵי עַכּוּ"ם אוֹמֵר "בּוֹשָׁה אִמְּכֶם מְאֹד חָפְרָה יוֹלַדְתְּכֶם הִנֵּה אַחֲרִית גּוֹיִם מִדְבָּר צִיָּה וַעֲרָבָה" (יִרְמְיָה נ׳ י"ב)[49].

יב. כָּל בִּרְכוֹת הָרְאִיָּה הַנִּזְכָּרוֹת[50], אִם חָזַר וְרָאָה אוֹתָן הַדְּבָרִים בְּעַצְמָם, אֵינוֹ חוֹזֵר וּמְבָרֵךְ אֶלָּא אִם כֵּן הָיָה בֵּין רְאִיָּה לִרְאִיָּה ל׳ יוֹם, דְּהַיְינוּ חוּץ מִיּוֹם הָרְאִיָּה הָרִאשׁוֹנָה וְחוּץ מִיּוֹם הָרְאִיָּה הַזֹּאת יִהְיוּ ל׳ יוֹם. אֲבָל אִם רוֹאֶה דָּבָר אַחֵר כָּזֶה שֶׁרָאָה אָז, כְּגוֹן מֶלֶךְ אַחֵר וּקְבָרִים אֲחֵרִים וְכַדּוֹמֶה, חוֹזֵר וּמְבָרֵךְ גַּם בְּתוֹךְ ל׳ יוֹם.

יג. הָרוֹאֶה כּוּשִׁי[51] וְגִיחוֹר, דְּהַיְינוּ שֶׁהוּא אָדוֹם הַרְבֵּה, וְהַלַּוְוקָן, דְּהַיְינוּ שֶׁהוּא לָבָן

You, Hashem, our God, King of the universe, אֲשֶׁר יָצַר אֶתְכֶם בַּדִּין" וְכוּ׳ — *Who fashioned you with justice,* etc.[48] וְעַל קִבְרֵי עַכּוּ"ם אוֹמֵר — Upon seeing graves of idolaters he should recite the verse: "בּוֹשָׁה אִמְּכֶם מְאֹד — *Your mother is very shamed,* חָפְרָה יוֹלַדְתְּכֶם — *the one who bore you is embarrassed,* הִנֵּה אַחֲרִית גּוֹיִם מִדְבָּר צִיָּה וַעֲרָבָה" — *behold, the final outcome of the nations is as a wilderness, a wasteland, and a desert* (יִרְמְיָה נ׳ י"ב — *Yirmiyah* 50:12).[49]

§12 כָּל בִּרְכוֹת הָרְאִיָּה הַנִּזְכָּרוֹת — Regarding **all the aforementioned blessings** recited **upon seeing** phenomena or events,[50] אִם חָזַר וְרָאָה אוֹתָן הַדְּבָרִים בְּעַצְמָם — **if one sees these very same phenomena again** אֵינוֹ חוֹזֵר וּמְבָרֵךְ — **he does not recite the blessing again,** אֶלָּא אִם כֵּן הָיָה בֵּין רְאִיָּה לִרְאִיָּה ל׳ יוֹם — **unless thirty days have passed between** the first time **he saw** them and the second time **he saw** them. דְּהַיְינוּ — **That is,** חוּץ מִיּוֹם הָרְאִיָּה הָרִאשׁוֹנָה — when **besides the first day** on which the phenomenon **was seen,** וְחוּץ מִיּוֹם הָרְאִיָּה הַזֹּאת — **and besides the day he saw it this time,** יִהְיוּ ל׳ יוֹם — **there are thirty days** intervening. אֲבָל אִם רוֹאֶה דָּבָר אַחֵר כָּזֶה שֶׁרָאָה אָז — **However, if he sees another phenomenon of the same type as the first,** כְּגוֹן מֶלֶךְ אַחֵר וּקְבָרִים אֲחֵרִים — **such as another king or other graves,** וְכַדּוֹמֶה — **and the like,** חוֹזֵר וּמְבָרֵךְ גַּם בְּתוֹךְ ל׳ יוֹם — **then he should recite the blessing again even within thirty days.**

§13 הָרוֹאֶה כּוּשִׁי — **If one sees a person with** unusually **black skin;**[51] וְגִיחוֹר — **or a** *gichor,* דְּהַיְינוּ שֶׁהוּא אָדוֹם הַרְבֵּה — **that is, a person with** unusually **red skin;** וְהַלַּוְוקָן — **or a** *lavkan,* דְּהַיְינוּ שֶׁהוּא לָבָן הַרְבֵּה — **that is, a person with**

---

48. The full text of the blessing: בָּרוּךְ אַתָּה ה׳ אֱלֹהֵינוּ מֶלֶךְ הָעוֹלָם אֲשֶׁר יָצַר אֶתְכֶם בַּדִּין וְזָן וְכִלְכֵּל אֶתְכֶם בַּדִּין וְהֵמִית אֶתְכֶם בַּדִּין וְיוֹדֵעַ מִסְפַּר כֻּלְּכֶם בַּדִּין וְהוּא עָתִיד לְהַחֲיוֹתְכֶם וּלְקַיֵּם אֶתְכֶם בַּדִּין. בָּרוּךְ אַתָּה ה׳ מְחַיֵּה הַמֵּתִים, *Blessed are You,* Hashem, *our God, King of the universe, Who fashioned you with justice, nourished and sustained you with justice, took your lives with justice, knows the sum total of you all with justice, and will restore and resuscitate you with judgment. Blessed are You,* Hashem, *Who resuscitates the dead.*

49. In this verse the prophet Yirmiyahu predicts the forthcoming destruction of the nations comprising the Babylonian empire in retaliation for having oppressed the Jewish people during their time of exile. It is appropriately recited when seeing the graves of idolaters, as the demise of the idolatrous nations is the fulfillment of the prophecy of doom for those who have oppressed us.

50. Except for thunder and lightning (see above, *se'if* 3), and the appearance of a rainbow (*Mishnah Berurah* 229:2).

51. See commentaries of *Rashi* (s.v. כושי) and *Rav Nissim Gaon* to *Berachos* 58b. [Note that the Kitzur was written in the 19th century in Hungary, where seeing black-skinned people was extremely rare. Nowadays, this blessing would obviously not be applicable.]

297 BLESSINGS OVER SEEING VARIOUS PHENOMENA AND EVENTS — SIMAN 60:14

הַרְבֵּה, וְהַקִּפֵּחַ, דְּהַיְינוּ שֶׁהוּא אָרוֹךְ וְדַק[52], וְהַנַּנָּס וְהַדְּרַקּוֹנָה, דְּהַיְינוּ מִי שֶׁהוּא מָלֵא יַבֶּלֶת, וּפְתוּיֵי הָרֹאשׁ שֶׁכָּל שַׂעֲרוֹתָיו דְּבוּקוֹת זוֹ בָּזוֹ[53], וְאֶת הַפִּיל, וְאֶת הַקּוֹף, מְבָרֵךְ "בָּרוּךְ אַתָּה ה' אֱלֹהֵינוּ מֶלֶךְ הָעוֹלָם מְשַׁנֶּה הַבְּרִיּוֹת". וְאֵינוֹ מְבָרֵךְ אֶלָּא בַּפַּעַם הָרִאשׁוֹן[54] שֶׁהַשִּׁנּוּי עָלָיו גָּדוֹל מְאוֹד[55].

יד. הָרוֹאֶה אֶת הַחִיגֵּר וְאֶת הַקִּטֵּעַ, דְּהַיְינוּ שֶׁנִּקְטְעוּ יָדָיו, וְאֶת הַסּוּמָא וּמוּכֵּה שְׁחִין וּבַהֲקָנִין, וְהוּא מִי שֶׁמְּנוּמָּר בִּנְקוּדוֹת לְבָנוֹת[56], אִם הֵם מִמְּעֵי אִמָּם, מְבָרֵךְ בַּפַּעַם הָרִאשׁוֹן שֶׁהוּא רוֹאֶה אוֹתָם "מְשַׁנֶּה הַבְּרִיּוֹת"[57]. וְאִם נִשְׁתַּנּוּ אַחַר כָּךְ וְהוּא מְצַעֵר עֲלֵיהֶם, מְבָרֵךְ "דַּיַּן הָאֱמֶת"[58].

---

unusually **white skin;** וְהַקִּפֵּחַ — **a** *kipe'ach,* דְּהַיְינוּ שֶׁהוּא אָרוֹךְ וְדַק — **that is, one who is excessively tall and thin** to the point that his slight frame seems to be unable to bear his height;[52] וְהַנַּנָּס — **a dwarf;** וְהַדְּרַקּוֹנָה — **a** *derakonah,* דְּהַיְינוּ מִי שֶׁהוּא מָלֵא יַבֶּלֶת — **that is, a person who is full of warts;** וּפְתוּיֵי הָרֹאשׁ — **a person whose hair is matted,** שֶׁכָּל שַׂעֲרוֹתָיו דְּבוּקוֹת זוֹ בָּזוֹ — that is, **all of his hair is attached** to the point that it looks like felt;[53] וְאֶת הַפִּיל, וְאֶת הַקּוֹף — **an elephant or a monkey;** מְבָרֵךְ — upon seeing any of these, **he recites the** following **blessing:** "בָּרוּךְ אַתָּה ה' אֱלֹהֵינוּ מֶלֶךְ הָעוֹלָם מְשַׁנֶּה הַבְּרִיּוֹת" — *Baruch Atah Ado-noy Elokeinu Melech HaOlam, meshaneh haberiyos,* ***Blessed are You,*** ***Hashem, our God, King of the universe, Who makes the creatures different.*** וְאֵינוֹ מְבָרֵךְ אֶלָּא בַּפַּעַם הָרִאשׁוֹן — **One recites this blessing only once** for each species[54] of people or animals mentioned above, שֶׁהַשִּׁנּוּי עָלָיו גָּדוֹל מְאוֹד — **when** their **unusual** appearance leaves a **great** impression **on him.**[55]

§14 הָרוֹאֶה אֶת הַחִיגֵּר — **One who sees a person who is lame;** וְאֶת הַקִּטֵּעַ — **or a person missing limbs,** דְּהַיְינוּ שֶׁנִּקְטְעוּ יָדָיו — **that is,** specifically **one whose hands are missing** (either from birth or they have been amputated, as explained below); וְאֶת הַסּוּמָא — **or a blind person;** וּמוּכֵּה שְׁחִין — **or a person smitten with boils;** וּבַהֲקָנִין — or a *bahakanin,* וְהוּא מִי שֶׁמְּנוּמָּר בִּנְקוּדוֹת לְבָנוֹת — **which is someone whose** skin **is spotted with white dots;**[56] אִם הֵם מִמְּעֵי אִמָּם — **if these conditions** have affected these individuals **from birth,** מְבָרֵךְ בַּפַּעַם הָרִאשׁוֹן שֶׁהוּא רוֹאֶה אוֹתָם — then **upon seeing them for the first time one recites the blessing of** "מְשַׁנֶּה הַבְּרִיּוֹת" — ***Who makes the creatures different.***[57] וְאִם נִשְׁתַּנּוּ אַחַר כָּךְ — **However, if they developed** these conditions **later** וְהוּא מְצַעֵר עֲלֵיהֶם — **and he is pained over their** fate, מְבָרֵךְ "דַּיַּן הָאֱמֶת" — **he should recite the** blessing of ***Dayan HaEmes*** (*The true Judge*), as he would after hearing of, or witnessing, distressing events.[58]

---

52. Consequently, he is bent over, giving the impression that his vertebrae are dislocated (see *Rashi* to *Bechoros* 45b). *Shulchan Aruch* (225:8) renders *kipe'ach* as obese; that is, he is unusually wide in proportion to his height.

53. *Rashi* to *Berachos* 58b s.v. פתויי ראש.

54. *Mishnah Berurah* 225:29.

55. *Mishnah Berurah* (225:29-30) rules that if one has not seen a person with this defect for thirty days, he should recite the blessing without reciting the Name of Hashem and the words *Melech HaOlam*. See note 57 below.

56. See *Mishnah Berurah* 225:24. In a place where such an individual is common, neither of the blessings cited here are recited upon seeing him (*Mishnah Berurah* ibid.).

57. *Shulchan Aruch* and *Rama* (225:9) debate whether this blessing is to be repeated upon seeing such an individual again after a thirty-day lapse. *Mishnah Berurah* (225:30) concludes that, in such a case, one should recite the blessing without reciting the Name of Hashem and the words *Melech HaOlam*.

58. See above, 59:2-3.

BLESSINGS OVER SEEING VARIOUS PHENOMENA AND EVENTS — SIMAN 60:15 298

טו. הָרוֹאֶה אִילָנוֹת טוֹבוֹת וּבְרִיּוֹת נָאוֹת, אֲפִילוּ עַכּוּ״ם (שֶׁרָאָה אוֹתוֹ בִּרְאִיָּה בְּעָלְמָא, כִּי אָסוּר לְהִסְתַּכֵּל בּוֹ), אוֹ בְּהֵמָה, מְבָרֵךְ ״בָּרוּךְ אַתָּה ה׳ אֱלֹהֵינוּ מֶלֶךְ הָעוֹלָם שֶׁכָּכָה לוֹ בְּעוֹלָמוֹ״. וְאֵינוֹ מְבָרֵךְ עֲלֵיהֶם אֶלָּא פַּעַם רִאשׁוֹנָה וְלֹא יוֹתֵר, לֹא עֲלֵיהֶם וְלֹא עַל אֲחֵרִים, אֶלָּא אִם כֵּן הָיוּ נָאִים מֵהֶם.

---

§15 **הָרוֹאֶה אִילָנוֹת טוֹבוֹת וּבְרִיּוֹת נָאוֹת** — **One who sees nice trees or beautiful creations,** **אֲפִילוּ עַכּוּ״ם** — **even an idolater** (**שֶׁרָאָה אוֹתוֹ בִּרְאִיָּה בְּעָלְמָא** — **upon whom he just glanced,** **כִּי אָסוּר לְהִסְתַּכֵּל בּוֹ** — **for it is forbidden to gaze upon him**),[59] **אוֹ בְּהֵמָה** — **or** even a pleasant looking **animal,** **מְבָרֵךְ** — **he recites the** following **blessing:** **״בָּרוּךְ אַתָּה ה׳ אֱלֹהֵינוּ מֶלֶךְ הָעוֹלָם שֶׁכָּכָה לוֹ בְּעוֹלָמוֹ״** — *Baruch Atah Ado-noy Elokeinu Melech HaOlam, shekachah lo be'olamo,* ***Blessed are You, Hashem, our God, King of the universe, Who has such in His universe.***[60] **וְאֵינוֹ מְבָרֵךְ עֲלֵיהֶם אֶלָּא פַּעַם רִאשׁוֹנָה וְלֹא יוֹתֵר** — **One recites this blessing only the first time** he sees this creation, **and no more,** **לֹא עֲלֵיהֶם וְלֹא עַל אֲחֵרִים** — **neither upon the** same creation **nor upon others** like it, **אֶלָּא אִם כֵּן הָיוּ נָאִים מֵהֶם** — **unless the** later ones **are more beautiful than** the first.

---

59. See *Magen Avraham* 225:20. One who worships idols is considered a wicked person upon whom one should not gaze (see *Megillah* 28a).

60. Today, the custom is not to recite this blessing, as it is difficult to define what exactly constitutes a beautiful creation. Instead, one should recite the blessing without Hashem's Name or Sovereignty: בָּרוּךְ שֶׁכָּכָה לוֹ בְּעוֹלָמוֹ, *Blessed [is He] Who has such in His universe* (see *Mishnah Berurah* 225:32 with *Shaar HaTziyun* §33).

299 BLESSINGS FOR SPECIFIC SITUATIONS — SIMAN 61:1

סימן סא

בִּרְכַּת הַגּוֹמֵל וְעוֹד קְצָת בְּרָכוֹת פְּרָטִיּוֹת

וּבוֹ י׳ סְעִיפִים

א. אַרְבָּעָה צְרִיכִים לְהוֹדוֹת[1]: יוֹרְדֵי הַיָּם כְּשֶׁיַּגִּיעוּ לִמְחוֹז חֶפְצָם, וְכֵן הוֹלְכֵי מִדְבָּרִיּוֹת אוֹ בִּשְׁאָר דֶּרֶךְ שֶׁמּוּחְזָק שֶׁיֵּשׁ בּוֹ סַכָּנָה[2] כְּשֶׁיַּגִּיעוּ לִמְחוֹז חֶפְצָם[3], וּבִכְלָל זֶה גַּם מִי שֶׁהָיָה בְּסַכָּנָה אַחֶרֶת וְנִיצַּל הֵימֶנָּה, כְּגוֹן שֶׁנָּפַל עָלָיו כּוֹתֶל אוֹ נְגָחוֹ שׁוֹר אוֹ

SIMAN 61

BIRCAS HAGOMEIL AND OTHER BLESSINGS FOR SPECIFIC SITUATIONS

CONTAINING 10 *SE'IFIM*

§1 Who Is Obligated To Recite the *HaGomeil* Blessing / **§2** When and Where To Recite the Blessing / **§3** Proper Procedures for One Who Experienced a Miracle / **§4** Prayer Before a Medical Procedure or Taking Medicine / **§5** Proper Response When Another Person Sneezes / **§6** Futile Prayers / **§7** Prayer When Measuring Grain / **§8** Bar Mitzvah Blessing and Feast / **§9-10** Blessings Upon Rain

When the Temple stood, a person who had been delivered from a life-threatening situation would bring a thanksgiving-offering (see *Rashi, Vayikra* 7:12). Nowadays, when the Temple is no longer standing, the Sages obligated one to thank God for saving him from a life-threatening peril by reciting *Bircas HaGomeil,* the thanksgiving blessing (see *Rosh, Berachos* 9:3). The following *Siman* discusses the details of this blessing, as well as several other blessings recited at significant events.

§1 **אַרְבָּעָה צְרִיכִים לְהוֹדוֹת** — People in **four** types of situations **must give thanks,** i.e., recite a special blessing of thanks:[1] **יוֹרְדֵי הַיָּם כְּשֶׁיַּגִּיעוּ לִמְחוֹז חֶפְצָם** — (1) **Seafarers when they reach their destination;** **וְכֵן הוֹלְכֵי מִדְבָּרִיּוֹת** — (2) **similarly, those who travel through the wilderness,** **אוֹ בִּשְׁאָר דֶּרֶךְ** — **or on any other route** **שֶׁמּוּחְזָק שֶׁיֵּשׁ בּוֹ סַכָּנָה** — **that is known to be dangerous,**[2] **כְּשֶׁיַּגִּיעוּ לִמְחוֹז חֶפְצָם** — must give thanks **when they reach their destination.**[3] **וּבִכְלָל זֶה גַּם** — Also **included in this category** **מִי שֶׁהָיָה בְּסַכָּנָה אַחֶרֶת** — **is one who was in any other dangerous situation** **וְנִיצַּל הֵימֶנָּה** — **and he was saved from it;** **כְּגוֹן שֶׁנָּפַל עָלָיו כּוֹתֶל** — **for example, a wall collapsed upon him,** **אוֹ נְגָחוֹ שׁוֹר** — **or an ox gored him,** **אוֹ**

---

1. See below, note 12. A minor is not required to recite this blessing (*Mishnah Berurah* 219:3). See below, note 11, regarding whether women are obligated.

2. According to Rabbi Moshe Feinstein, one recites the *HaGomeil* blessing after air travel of any distance (*Igros Moshe, Orach Chaim* II, §59).

3. Even if their journey was calm and uneventful (*Beur Halachah* 219:1 s.v. יורדי). When traveling on a trip of several days, one does not recite the blessing on any stopover along the way, but only at the conclusion of the trip (*Mishnah Berurah* 219:1 and *Shaar HaTziyun* loc. cit. §1).

שֶׁבָּאוּ עָלָיו לִסְטִים בַּדֶּרֶךְ וְשׁוֹדְדֵי לַיְלָה וְנִיצַל מֵהֶם וְכַדּוֹמֶה, וּמִי שֶׁהָיָה חוֹלֶה שֶׁיֵּשׁ בּוֹ סַכָּנָה, כְּגוֹן מַכָּה שֶׁל חָלָל אוֹ שֶׁהָיָה מוּטָל בְּמִטָּה ג׳ יָמִים מֵחֲמַת הַחוֹלִי[4] וְנִתְרַפֵּא וְהוֹלֵךְ עַל בּוּרְיוֹ, וּמִי שֶׁהָיָה חָבוּשׁ בְּבֵית הָאֲסוּרִים, אֲפִילּוּ רַק עַל עִסְקֵי מָמוֹן[5] וְיָצָא[6], וְסִימָנְךָ: ״וְכָל הַחַיִּי״ם יוֹדוּךָ סֶּלָה״[7] — חוֹלֶה, יִסּוּרִים, יָם, מִדְבָּר[8]. מַה מְּבָרֵךְ? ״בָּרוּךְ אַתָּה ה׳ אֱלֹהֵינוּ מֶלֶךְ הָעוֹלָם הַגּוֹמֵל לְחַיָּבִים טוֹבוֹת שֶׁגְּמָלַנִי כָּל טוֹב״[9]. וְהַשּׁוֹמְעִים אוֹמְרִים ״מִי שֶׁגְּמָלְךָ טוֹב הוּא יִגְמָלְךָ כָּל טוֹב סֶלָה״[10].

שֶׁבָּאוּ עָלָיו לִסְטִים בַּדֶּרֶךְ — or he was attacked by bandits while on the road, וְשׁוֹדְדֵי לַיְלָה — or set upon by **night marauders, וְנִיצַל מֵהֶם — and he was saved from them, וְכַדּוֹמֶה — or any similar** situation; **וּמִי שֶׁהָיָה חוֹלֶה שֶׁיֵּשׁ בּוֹ סַכָּנָה** — (3) **also, one who was gravely ill, כְּגוֹן מַכָּה שֶׁל חָלָל — such as** one who suffered **an internal injury, אוֹ שֶׁהָיָה מוּטָל בְּמִטָּה ג׳ יָמִים — or** one who **was bedridden for three days מֵחֲמַת הַחוֹלִי — due to an illness,**[4] **וְנִתְרַפֵּא וְהוֹלֵךְ עַל בּוּרְיוֹ — and he was healed and** now **walks around as a healthy person,** i.e., he has completely recovered; **וּמִי שֶׁהָיָה חָבוּשׁ בְּבֵית הָאֲסוּרִים** — (4) **also, one who was incarcerated in prison, אֲפִילּוּ רַק עַל עִסְקֵי מָמוֹן — even** if **only due to monetary matters,**[5] **וְיָצָא — and was released.**[6]

וְסִימָנְךָ — A mnemonic aid to remember these four situations: **״וְכָל הַחַיִּי״ם יוֹדוּךָ סֶּלָה״ — *Everything alive will gratefully acknowledge You forever!***[7] The four letters of the word חַיִּים, *alive,* form an acronym of these four situations: **חוֹלֶה — a person** who was **ill, יִסּוּרִים — one** who was **tormented** by being imprisoned, **יָם** — one who traveled the **sea, מִדְבָּר** — and one who journeyed through the **wilderness.**[8]

מַה מְּבָרֵךְ? — What blessing does he recite? ״בָּרוּךְ אַתָּה ה׳ אֱלֹהֵינוּ מֶלֶךְ הָעוֹלָם הַגּוֹמֵל לְחַיָּבִים טוֹבוֹת שֶׁגְּמָלַנִי כָּל טוֹב״ — *Baruch Atah Ado-noy Elokeinu Melech HaOlam, hagomeil l'chayavim tovos she'gemalani kol tov,* ***Blessed are You,*** ***Hashem, our God, King of the universe, Who bestows good things upon the guilty, Who has bestowed every goodness upon me.***[9] **וְהַשּׁוֹמְעִים אוֹמְרִים — Those who hear** the blessing **respond: ״מִי שֶׁגְּמָלְךָ טוֹב** — ***May He Who has bestowed goodness upon you*** **הוּא יִגְמָלְךָ כָּל טוֹב סֶלָה״ — *[continue to] bestow every goodness upon you forever.***[10]

4. Even if he was not gravely ill (see *Mishnah Berurah* 219:28; cf. *Beur Halachah* 219:8 s.v. כגון).

5. See *Beur Halachah* (219:1 s.v. חבוש), who rules that imprisonment for monetary violations does not warrant a blessing, unless one's life was in danger as a result of the incarceration.

6. One who experiences more than one of these situations at one time nonetheless recites the blessing only once (*Mishnah Berurah* 219:3).

7. This phrase is from the *Shemoneh Esrei* Prayer, in the *Modim* blessing.

8. In the context of this mnemonic, the phrase can be understood as saying: כָּל הַחַיִּים, *all who were subject to one of the four situations alluded to in the acronym* חיים — that is, חוֹלֶה, *ill;* יִסּוּרִים, *tormented in prison;* יָם, *traveled the sea;* or, מִדְבָּר, *traveled the wilderness* — יוֹדוּךָ סֶלָה, *shall gratefully acknowledge* the kindness of Hashem forever.

9. I.e., Hashem has bestowed His blessing upon me even though I am not deserving of it (*Mishnah Berurah* 219:4).

10. One fulfills his requirement even if those present do not respond (*Mishnah Berurah* 219:5).

ב. צָרִיךְ לְבָרֵךְ בְּרָכָה זֹאת בִּפְנֵי עֲשָׂרָה חוּץ מִמֶּנּוּ[11], וּשְׁנַיִם מֵהֶם יִהְיוּ תַּלְמִידֵי חֲכָמִים שֶׁעוֹסְקִים בַּהֲלָכוֹת, שֶׁנֶּאֱמַר (תהלים קז, לב) "וִירוֹמְמוּהוּ בִּקְהַל עָם וּבְמוֹשַׁב זְקֵנִים יְהַלְלוּהוּ"[12]. וְאִם אֵינָם נִמְצָאִים לוֹ תַּלְמִידֵי חֲכָמִים, אֵינוֹ מְעַכֵּב. וְנוֹהֲגִין לְבָרֵךְ כְּשֶׁעוֹלֶה לַתּוֹרָה לְאַחַר שֶׁבֵּירַךְ בְּרָכָה אַחֲרוֹנָה[13]. וּלְכַתְּחִלָּה אֵין לְאַחֲרָהּ יוֹתֵר מִג׳ יָמִים, וְלָכֵן אִם נִיצַל בְּיוֹם ב׳, יְבָרֵךְ מִיָּד בְּלֹא סֵפֶר תּוֹרָה, וְלֹא יַמְתִּין עַד יוֹם ה׳[14].

---

§2 צָרִיךְ לְבָרֵךְ בְּרָכָה זֹאת בִּפְנֵי עֲשָׂרָה — **One must recite this blessing in the presence of ten** men, חוּץ מִמֶּנּוּ — **not including** the one who is reciting the blessing **himself.**[11] וּשְׁנַיִם מֵהֶם יִהְיוּ תַּלְמִידֵי חֲכָמִים — **Two of these** ten **are to be Torah scholars** שֶׁעוֹסְקִים בַּהֲלָכוֹת — **who engage in** the study of **halachah,** שֶׁנֶּאֱמַר — **as** the verse **states** (*Tehillim* 107:32): "וִירוֹמְמוּהוּ בִּקְהַל עָם וּבְמוֹשַׁב זְקֵנִים יְהַלְלוּהוּ" — ***Let them exalt Him in the assembly of people, and in the session of the elders, praise Him.***[12] וְאִם אֵינָם נִמְצָאִים לוֹ תַּלְמִידֵי חֲכָמִים — **If Torah scholars are not available** to hear **his** blessing, אֵינוֹ מְעַכֵּב — **it does not prevent** him from reciting the blessing, i.e., he should recite it in the presence of any ten men.

וְנוֹהֲגִין לְבָרֵךְ כְּשֶׁעוֹלֶה לַתּוֹרָה — **The custom is to recite the blessing when he ascends to the Torah** reading לְאַחַר שֶׁבֵּירַךְ בְּרָכָה אַחֲרוֹנָה — **after he has recited the concluding blessing.**[13]

וּלְכַתְּחִלָּה אֵין לְאַחֲרָהּ יוֹתֵר מִג׳ יָמִים — **Initially, one should not delay** the recitation of this blessing for **more than three days** after his deliverance from danger. וְלָכֵן אִם נִיצַל בְּיוֹם ב׳ — **Therefore, if he was saved on Monday,** יְבָרֵךְ מִיָּד בְּלֹא סֵפֶר תּוֹרָה — **he should recite the blessing immediately, without** being called up to the Torah scroll, וְלֹא יַמְתִּין עַד יוֹם ה׳ — **and he should not wait until Thursday.**[14]

---

11. According to *Mishnah Berurah* (219:6), the one reciting the blessing may be counted as one of the ten. One who is not able to find ten men should wait up to thirty days with the hope that he will find ten. If he sees that he will not, he should recite the blessing without them (*Mishnah Berurah* 219:8).

Since the *HaGomeil* blessing should be recited in the presence of ten men, it is customary that women do not recite it, since it is improper for a woman to present herself in front of men for this purpose. However, some authorities rule that she should recite the blessing in the presence of ten women and one man (*Mishnah Berurah* 219:3). Rabbi Moshe Feinstein is quoted as ruling that a woman may recite the *HaGomeil* blessing in the presence of one man or one woman. If she is married she should preferably recite it in the presence of her husband (see *Igros Moshe, Orach Chaim* V, §14).

12. Psalm 107 exhorts people to praise Hashem for deliverance from the sea, wilderness, illness, or incarceration. It is from this Psalm that we derive the obligation to recite the *HaGomeil* blessing in these four situations. Verse 32 describes how this thanks should be rendered. It should be (1) בִּקְהַל עָם, *in an assembly of people*, referring to a gathering of no less than ten people (see *Rashi* to *Kesubos* 7b s.v. במקהלות), and (2) בְּמוֹשַׁב זְקֵנִים, *in a session of elders*. The word זָקֵן, *elder*, refers to a Torah scholar (see *Kiddushin* 32b); the plural "*elders*" indicates that there must be at least two.

13. The requirement to recite the blessing in the presence of ten men will be fulfilled at the Torah reading [discussed above, *Siman* 23], since the Torah is read only in the presence of ten [above, 15:1] (*Shulchan Aruch* 219:3).

14. The Torah is generally read only on Monday, Thursday, and Shabbos. One who experienced his deliverance after the Monday Torah reading should not wait the three days until the Thursday reading.

וְכֵן אִם הָיָה אָבֵל[15] שֶׁאֵינוֹ רַשַּׁאי לַעֲלוֹת לַתּוֹרָה[16], לֹא יַמְתִּין, אֶלָּא יְבָרֵךְ מִיָּד. אַךְ יְבָרֵךְ מְעוּמָּד[17] בִּפְנֵי עֲשָׂרָה, כְּמוֹ שֶׁנִּתְבָּאֵר. וּבְדִיעֲבַד אִם אֵיחֵר יוֹתֵר מִג׳ יָמִים, יָכוֹל לְבָרֵךְ גַּם אַחַר כָּךְ.

ג. מִי שֶׁנַּעֲשָׂה לוֹ נֵס, יֵשׁ לוֹ לְהַפְרִישׁ לִצְדָקָה מָמוֹן כְּפִי הַשָּׂגַת יָדוֹ וִיחַלֵּק לְלוֹמְדֵי תוֹרָה, וְיֹאמַר ״הֲרֵינִי נוֹתֵן מָעוֹת זֶה לִצְדָקָה וִיהִי רָצוֹן שֶׁיְּהֵא נֶחְשָׁב כְּאִלּוּ הִקְרַבְתִּי תוֹדָה״ (וְעַיֵּין סֵדֶר אֲמִירַת קָרְבַּן תּוֹדָה בְּסֵפֶר חַיֵּי אָדָם סוֹף חֵלֶק רִאשׁוֹן)[18]. וְטוֹב וְרָאוּי לוֹ לְתַקֵּן אֵיזֶה צָרְכֵי רַבִּים בָּעִיר. וּבְכָל שָׁנָה בַּיּוֹם הַזֶּה יִתְבּוֹדֵד לְהוֹדוֹת לַה׳ יִתְבָּרֵךְ שְׁמוֹ וּלְסַפֵּר אֶת הַנֵּס.

וְכֵן אִם הָיָה אָבֵל — Likewise, if he was a mourner,[15] **שֶׁאֵינוֹ רַשַּׁאי לַעֲלוֹת לַתּוֹרָה — who is not permitted to ascend to the Torah** reading,[16] **לֹא יַמְתִּין — he should not wait** until the mourning period is over, **אֶלָּא יְבָרֵךְ מִיָּד — but should recite the blessing immediately. אַךְ יְבָרֵךְ מְעוּמָּד** — Even though he is not reciting the blessing at the Torah reading, **he nevertheless is to recite the blessing standing,**[17] **בִּפְנֵי עֲשָׂרָה, כְּמוֹ שֶׁנִּתְבָּאֵר** — and **in the presence of ten** men, **as explained** above. **וּבְדִיעֲבַד — After the fact, אִם אֵיחֵר יוֹתֵר מִג׳ יָמִים — if one delayed more than three days, יָכוֹל לְבָרֵךְ גַּם אַחַר כָּךְ — he may recite the blessing even after** the preferred time has elapsed.

§3 This *se'if* discusses the proper procedure for someone who was miraculously saved from a dangerous situation.

מִי שֶׁנַּעֲשָׂה לוֹ נֵס — Someone for whom a miracle was performed that saved him from danger **יֵשׁ לוֹ לְהַפְרִישׁ לִצְדָקָה מָמוֹן כְּפִי הַשָּׂגַת יָדוֹ — should set aside money for charity commensurate with his means. וִיחַלֵּק לְלוֹמְדֵי תוֹרָה — He should distribute** this money **to those who study Torah, וְיֹאמַר — and declare: ״הֲרֵינִי נוֹתֵן מָעוֹת זֶה לִצְדָקָה** — ***I hereby give this money to charity,*** **וִיהִי רָצוֹן** — ***and may it be [Your] will*** **שֶׁיְּהֵא נֶחְשָׁב כְּאִלּוּ הִקְרַבְתִּי תוֹדָה״** — ***that*** *this donation* ***be considered as if I offered a thanksgiving-offering*** *in the Temple.* **(וְעַיֵּין סֵדֶר אֲמִירַת קָרְבַּן תּוֹדָה בְּסֵפֶר חַיֵּי אָדָם — See the order of the recitation of the thanksgiving-offering in *Chayei Adam,* סוֹף חֵלֶק רִאשׁוֹן — at the end of Volume 1.)**[18] **וְטוֹב וְרָאוּי לוֹ — It is** also **proper and appropriate for him לְתַקֵּן אֵיזֶה צָרְכֵי רַבִּים בָּעִיר —** to contribute to the **maintenance of some communal needs in the city.**

וּבְכָל שָׁנָה בַּיּוֹם הַזֶּה — Every year, on the anniversary of this occasion, **יִתְבּוֹדֵד לְהוֹדוֹת לַה׳ יִתְבָּרֵךְ שְׁמוֹ — he should seclude himself to give thanks to God, may His name be blessed, וּלְסַפֵּר אֶת הַנֵּס — and** also rejoice and **tell** others of **the miracle** that occurred to him.

---

15. I.e., he was within the seven days of mourning for a close relative.

16. See below, 210:3 and 219:2.

17. Although ideally one should stand, if he recited the blessing while seated, he has fulfilled his obligation (*Mishnah Berurah* 219:4).

18. Based on the principle that in the absence of the actual Temple service, the recitation of the verses and laws of a service is accepted by Hashem in place of that service, *Chayei Adam* sets out the verses and laws of the thanksgiving-offering, as well as an accompanying prayer, that should be recited by one who experienced a miracle. See also *Mishnah Berurah* 218:32.

ד. הַנִּכְנָס לְהַקִּיז דָּם[19], וְכֵן קוֹדֶם שֶׁיֹּאכַל אוֹ יִשְׁתֶּה אוֹ יַעֲשֶׂה אֵיזֶה דָּבָר לִרְפוּאָה, יִתְפַּלֵּל קוֹדֶם תְּפִלָּה קְצָרָה וְיֹאמַר "יְהִי רָצוֹן מִלְּפָנֶיךָ ה' אֱלֹהַי וֵאלֹהֵי אֲבוֹתַי שֶׁיִּהְיֶה לִי עֵסֶק זֶה לִרְפוּאָה כִּי רוֹפֵא חִנָּם אָתָּה"[20]. וְאִם דָּבָר זֶה שֶׁהוּא אוֹכֵל אוֹ שׁוֹתֶה לִרְפוּאָה צְרִיכִין לְבָרֵךְ עָלָיו (עַיֵּין לְעֵיל סִימָן נ' סְעִיף ח'), יֹאמַר תְּחִלָּה תְּפִלָּה זֹאת וְאַחַר כָּךְ יְבָרֵךְ (כֵּן נִרְאֶה לִי שֶׁלֹּא לְהַפְסִיק בֵּין הַבְּרָכָה לַאֲכִילָה)[21]. לְאַחַר שֶׁהִקִּיז דָּם, מְבָרֵךְ וְאוֹמֵר "בָּרוּךְ אַתָּה ה' אֱלֹהֵינוּ מֶלֶךְ הָעוֹלָם רוֹפֵא חוֹלִים".

ה. הַמִּתְעַטֵּשׁ — אוֹמֵר לוֹ חֲבֵרוֹ "אָסוּתָא"[22], וְהוּא יֹאמַר לוֹ "בָּרוּךְ תִּהְיֶה". וְאַחַר כָּךְ אוֹמֵר (בראשית מט, יח) "לִישׁוּעָתְךָ קִוִּיתִי ה' ", דְּהַמִּתְפַּלֵּל עַל חֲבֵרוֹ הוּא נַעֲנֶה תְּחִלָּה[23].

---

§4 **הַנִּכְנָס לְהַקִּיז דָּם — One who goes to let blood,**[19] **וְכֵן קוֹדֶם שֶׁיֹּאכַל אוֹ יִשְׁתֶּה — and, similarly, before one eats or drinks** for medicinal purposes **אוֹ יַעֲשֶׂה אֵיזֶה דָּבָר לִרְפוּאָה — or** before **performing any procedure for therapeutic purposes, יִתְפַּלֵּל קוֹדֶם תְּפִלָּה קְצָרָה — should first recite a short prayer וְיֹאמַר — by saying** the following: **"יְהִי רָצוֹן מִלְּפָנֶיךָ** — *May it be Your will,* **ה' אֱלֹהַי וֵאלֹהֵי אֲבוֹתַי** — *HASHEM, my God, and the God of my fathers,* **שֶׁיִּהְיֶה לִי עֵסֶק זֶה לִרְפוּאָה** — *that this endeavor should serve me as a remedy,* **כִּי רוֹפֵא חִנָּם אָתָּה"** — *for You are the Free Healer.*[20] **וְאִם דָּבָר זֶה — If this item שֶׁהוּא אוֹכֵל אוֹ שׁוֹתֶה לִרְפוּאָה — that he is eating or drinking for medicinal purposes צְרִיכִין לְבָרֵךְ עָלָיו — is** an item **over which one is required to recite a blessing, (עַיֵּין לְעֵיל סִימָן נ' סְעִיף ח' — see above, 50:8,** for the particulars of when a blessing is required on such items), **יֹאמַר תְּחִלָּה תְּפִלָּה זֹאת — he should first recite this prayer, וְאַחַר כָּךְ יְבָרֵךְ — and afterward he should recite the blessing** upon the food or drink **(כֵּן נִרְאֶה לִי — so it appears to me, שֶׁלֹּא לְהַפְסִיק בֵּין הַבְּרָכָה לַאֲכִילָה — so** as **not to interrupt between the blessing and the eating** by reciting the prayer after the blessing).[21]

לְאַחַר שֶׁהִקִּיז דָּם — After one let blood, מְבָרֵךְ וְאוֹמֵר — one should recite the following **blessing: "בָּרוּךְ אַתָּה ה' אֱלֹהֵינוּ מֶלֶךְ הָעוֹלָם** — *Blessed are You, HASHEM, our God, King of the universe,* **רוֹפֵא חוֹלִים"** — *Who heals the sick.*

§5 **הַמִּתְעַטֵּשׁ** — If **one sneezes, אוֹמֵר לוֹ חֲבֵרוֹ "אָסוּתָא" — his fellow should say** "*Asusa,*" "*Be healed!*"[22] **וְהוּא יֹאמַר לוֹ** — The one who sneezed **should** then **say to** his fellow: **"בָּרוּךְ תִּהְיֶה" — "You should be blessed," וְאַחַר כָּךְ אוֹמֵר — and afterward** the one who sneezed **should** also **say** (*Bereishis* 49:18): **"לִישׁוּעָתְךָ קִוִּיתִי ה' " — "*For Your salvation do I long, HASHEM,*" דְּהַמִּתְפַּלֵּל עַל חֲבֵרוֹ — because if one prays on behalf of his fellow, הוּא נַעֲנֶה תְּחִלָּה — he is answered first.**[23]

---

19. In earlier times, bloodletting was a common medical procedure.

20. He thus places his faith in Hashem as the true and only Healer rather than in the medical procedure (see *Mishnah Berurah* 230:6).

21. See above, 50:5.

22. Literally, *a remedy*. *Mishnah Berurah* (230:7) cites a Midrash that relates that until the times of the Patriarchs, illnesses did not exist. When it came time for a person to die, he would simply sneeze and suddenly die. So that people should be more aware of their impending demise, Yaakov Avinu prayed to Hashem that people should not die without first becoming ill. Thus, we say *Asusa* when a person sneezes, as if to wish that this sneeze should not be a harbinger of death.

23. The one who sneezed answers the wishes of *Asusa* with a prayer that his fellow be

ו. הַמִּתְפַּלֵּל עַל מַה שֶּׁעָבַר, כְּגוֹן שֶׁשָּׁמַע קוֹל צְוָחָה בָּעִיר וְאוֹמֵר "יְהִי רָצוֹן שֶׁלֹּא יְהֵא קוֹל זֶה בְּתוֹךְ בֵּיתִי", אוֹ שֶׁהָיְתָה אִשְׁתּוֹ מְעוּבֶּרֶת וּלְאַחַר מ׳ יוֹם מֵעִיבּוּרָהּ מִתְפַּלֵּל וְאוֹמֵר "יְהִי רָצוֹן שֶׁתֵּלֵד אִשְׁתִּי זָכָר", הֲרֵי זוֹ תְּפִלַּת שָׁוְא, כִּי מַה שֶּׁהָיָה הָיָה. אֲבָל בְּתוֹךְ מ׳ יוֹם מוֹעִיל תְּפִלָּה וְיָכוֹל לְהִתְפַּלֵּל[24]. וּלְאַחַר מ׳ יוֹם יָכוֹל לְהִתְפַּלֵּל שֶׁיְּהֵא הַוָּלָד זֶרַע קַיָּמָא טוֹב לַשָּׁמַיִם וְטוֹב לַבְּרִיּוֹת[25].

ז. הַנִּכְנָס לָמוֹד אֶת גָּרְנוֹ וְכַיּוֹצֵא בּוֹ, יִתְפַּלֵּל וְיֹאמַר "יְהִי רָצוֹן מִלְּפָנֶיךָ ה׳ אֱלֹהַי שֶׁתִּשְׁלַח בְּרָכָה בִּכְרִי הַזֶּה". הִתְחִיל לָמוֹד אוֹמֵר "בָּרוּךְ הַשּׁוֹלֵחַ בְּרָכָה בִּכְרִי הַזֶּה" (וְאוֹמֵר בְּלֹא שֵׁם וּמַלְכוּת)[26]. מָדַד וְאַחַר כָּךְ הִתְפַּלֵּל, הֲרֵי זוֹ תְּפִלַּת שָׁוְא,

---

§6 הַמִּתְפַּלֵּל עַל מַה שֶּׁעָבַר — **One who prays for that which is past,** כְּגוֹן שֶׁשָּׁמַע קוֹל צְוָחָה בָּעִיר — **for example: If he hears the sound of screaming in the city,** וְאוֹמֵר — **and he says:** "יְהִי רָצוֹן שֶׁלֹּא יְהֵא קוֹל זֶה בְּתוֹךְ בֵּיתִי" — ***May it be** Your **will that this cry should not be** taking place **within my house;*** אוֹ שֶׁהָיְתָה אִשְׁתּוֹ מְעוּבֶּרֶת — **or, if his wife is pregnant,** וּלְאַחַר מ׳ יוֹם מֵעִיבּוּרָהּ — **and after forty days into the pregnancy,** מִתְפַּלֵּל וְאוֹמֵר — **he prays and says:** "יְהִי רָצוֹן שֶׁתֵּלֵד אִשְׁתִּי זָכָר" — ***May it be** Your **will that my wife give birth to a boy,*** הֲרֵי זוֹ תְּפִלַּת שָׁוְא — **this** kind of prayer **is a prayer** recited **in vain** כִּי מַה שֶּׁהָיָה הָיָה — **because the event has already occurred** and cannot be changed. אֲבָל בְּתוֹךְ מ׳ יוֹם — **However, within the first forty days** of pregnancy, מוֹעִיל תְּפִלָּה — **prayer is effective** וְיָכוֹל לְהִתְפַּלֵּל — **and he may pray** regarding the child's gender.[24] וּלְאַחַר מ׳ יוֹם — **After forty days** into the pregnancy, יָכוֹל לְהִתְפַּלֵּל שֶׁיְּהֵא הַוָּלָד זֶרַע קַיָּמָא — **he may pray that the child be viable,** טוֹב לַשָּׁמַיִם וְטוֹב לַבְּרִיּוֹת — and that he develop to be **good toward Heaven and good toward** his fellow **creations**, i.e., that his actions find favor with Hashem and with people.[25]

§7 הַנִּכְנָס לָמוֹד אֶת גָּרְנוֹ — **One who enters to measure** the grain in **his silo,** וְכַיּוֹצֵא בּוֹ — **or a similar** activity, יִתְפַּלֵּל וְיֹאמַר — **should recite the** following **prayer:** "יְהִי רָצוֹן מִלְּפָנֶיךָ ה׳ אֱלֹהַי שֶׁתִּשְׁלַח בְּרָכָה בִּכְרִי הַזֶּה" — ***May it be Your will, Hashem, my God, that You bestow blessing on this pile** of grain.* הִתְחִיל לָמוֹד — **Once he began to measure** the grain אוֹמֵר — **he says:** "בָּרוּךְ הַשּׁוֹלֵחַ בְּרָכָה בִּכְרִי הַזֶּה" — ***Blessed is** the One **Who bestows blessing on this pile** of grain.* (וְאוֹמֵר בְּלֹא שֵׁם וּמַלְכוּת — **One recites** this blessing **without** reciting **the Name** of Hashem **or** mention of His **Sovereignty.**)[26] מָדַד וְאַחַר כָּךְ הִתְפַּלֵּל — **If he measured** his grain **and then prayed** for blessing to be bestowed upon it, הֲרֵי זוֹ תְּפִלַּת שָׁוְא — **his prayer is in**

---

blessed (בָּרוּךְ תִּהְיֶה). Since praying for another person itself is a reason for his own prayers to be answered, the one who said "You should be blessed" should take advantage of this opportunity, and immediately offer a short prayer for himself as well with the words לִישׁוּעָתְךָ קִוִּיתִי ה׳, *For Your salvation do I long, Hashem* (*Yam Shel Shlomo, Bava Kamma,* Chapter 8 §64).

24. During the first forty days of pregnancy, the unborn child is not yet formed, and prayer with regard to the gender can be effective (*Mishnah Berurah* 230:1).

25. Similarly, if he hears that there is a fire in the city, he may pray that even if the fire is in his house, his family be spared from harm (see *R' Yehonasan MiLunel, Berachos* 54a).

26. Most blessings begin with the words בָּרוּךְ אַתָּה ה׳ אֱלֹהֵינוּ מֶלֶךְ הָעוֹלָם, *Blessed are You, Hashem, our God, King of the universe.* This includes the two components that are generally necessary for a blessing to be valid: the Name of Hashem [ה׳ אֱלֹהֵינוּ, *Hashem, our God*] and His Sovereignty [מֶלֶךְ הָעוֹלָם, *King of the universe*] (see *Rambam, Hil. Berachos* 1:5). In this case,

שֶׁאֵין הַבְּרָכָה מְצוּיָה אֶלָּא בְּדָבָר הַנֶּעְלָם מִן הָעַיִן.

ח. מִי שֶׁנַּעֲשָׂה בְּנוֹ בַּר מִצְוָה[27], כְּשֶׁעוֹלֶה לַתּוֹרָה בַּפַּעַם הָרִאשׁוֹן[28] לְאַחַר שֶׁבֵּירַךְ בְּרָכָה אַחֲרוֹנָה עַל הַסֵּפֶר תּוֹרָה[29], מְבָרֵךְ הָאָב וְאוֹמֵר "בָּרוּךְ אַתָּה ה' אֱלֹהֵינוּ מֶלֶךְ הָעוֹלָם אֲשֶׁר פְּטָרַנִי מֵעוֹנְשׁוֹ שֶׁל זֶה"[30] (עַיֵּין בְּסֵפֶר חַיֵּי אָדָם)[31] וּמִצְוָה עַל הָאָדָם לַעֲשׂוֹת סְעוּדָה בְּיוֹם שֶׁנַּעֲשָׂה בְּנוֹ בַּר מִצְוָה, דְּהַיְינוּ בְּיוֹם שֶׁנִּכְנַס לִשְׁנַת י"ד[32]. וְאִם הַנַּעַר דּוֹרֵשׁ, הָוֵי סְעוּדַת מִצְוָה[33] אֲפִילוּ אֵינָהּ בְּאוֹתוֹ יוֹם.

---

vain, שֶׁאֵין הַבְּרָכָה מְצוּיָה אֶלָּא בְּדָבָר הַנֶּעְלָם מִן הָעַיִן — **for blessing is found only in something that is hidden from the eye,** i.e., its quantity is not known.

§8 מִי שֶׁנַּעֲשָׂה בְּנוֹ בַּר מִצְוָה — **One whose son becomes bar mitzvah,**[27] כְּשֶׁעוֹלֶה לַתּוֹרָה בַּפַּעַם הָרִאשׁוֹן — **when** the boy **ascends to** recite the blessings on **the Torah** reading **for the first time,**[28] לְאַחַר שֶׁבֵּירַךְ בְּרָכָה אַחֲרוֹנָה עַל הַסֵּפֶר תּוֹרָה — **after he has recited the concluding blessing** upon reading from **the** ***Sefer Torah*** (Torah scroll),[29] מְבָרֵךְ הָאָב וְאוֹמֵר — **the father recites the** following **blessing:** "בָּרוּךְ אַתָּה ה' אֱלֹהֵינוּ מֶלֶךְ הָעוֹלָם אֲשֶׁר פְּטָרַנִי מֵעוֹנְשׁוֹ שֶׁל זֶה" — *Baruch Atah Adonoy Elokeinu Melech HaOlam, asher petarani mei'onsho shel zeh,* ***Blessed are You, Hashem, our God, King of the universe, Who has freed me from the punishment of this boy***[30] (עַיֵּין בְּסֵפֶר חַיֵּי אָדָם — **see** ***Chayei Adam*** 65:3).[31] וּמִצְוָה עַל הָאָדָם לַעֲשׂוֹת סְעוּדָה — **It is a mitzvah for a person to arrange a feast** בְּיוֹם שֶׁנַּעֲשָׂה בְּנוֹ בַּר מִצְוָה — **on the day that his son becomes bar mitzvah;** דְּהַיְינוּ בְּיוֹם שֶׁנִּכְנַס לִשְׁנַת י"ד — **that is, on the day he begins his fourteenth year,** i.e., on his thirteenth birthday.[32] וְאִם הַנַּעַר דּוֹרֵשׁ — **If the boy delivers a** Torah **discourse,** הָוֵי סְעוּדַת מִצְוָה — **then** the meal **is** also **considered a "mitzvah feast,"**[33] אֲפִילוּ אֵינָהּ בְּאוֹתוֹ יוֹם — **even if it does not take place on that day,** i.e., on the day of his thirteenth birthday.

---

the blessing should be recited as written in the *se'if,* without mention of the Name of Hashem and His Sovereignty. See *Mishnah Berurah* 230:4 for the reason.

27. A boy becomes a bar mitzvah (i.e., *one who is obligated to observe the commandments of the Torah*), when he turns 13 years old, as Kitzur proceeds to explain. At this time, he is considered to have reached the age of legal majority; see above, 15:2.

28. Before this time he is generally not called to the Torah; see above, 23:24, and below, 79:9. When he reaches bar mitzvah he is called up to the Torah (see below, 78:11).

29. Or after the boy leads the prayers for the first time, thus demonstrating to all present that he is bar mitzvah (*Mishnah Berurah* 225:6).

30. Until a boy's bar mitzvah, it is the father's responsibility to train him to keep the mitzvos, and the father is held accountable if he fails this responsibility. After the bar mitzvah it becomes the responsibility of the boy to keep the mitzvos, and the father is thus free from this obligation and its potential for punishment (*Mishnah Berurah* 225:7). *Mishnah Berurah* points out, however, that the father is still obligated to reprove his son if he sees him acting incorrectly, just as with any other Jew.

31. *Chayei Adam* cites opinions that hold that this blessing should be recited without שֵׁם וּמַלְכוּת (mention of the Name of Hashem and His Sovereignty; see above, note 26), but rules that one may rely on the opinions that hold that the full blessing should be recited; see also *Mishnah Berurah* 225:8 for further discussion.

32. See above, 15:2, for further details regarding the exact day that a boy becomes bar mitzvah.

33. A סְעוּדַת מִצְוָה, *mitzvah feast,* is a meal that is itself a mitzvah (e.g., a Shabbos meal) or one that celebrates or facilitates a mitzvah (e.g., a feast at a wedding or *bris milah;* see below, 163:8).

ט. אִם הָיָה עֲצִירַת גְּשָׁמִים, אֲפִילּוּ בִּמְדִינוֹתֵינוּ שֶׁהַגְּשָׁמִים תְּדִירִים וְאֵינָן נֶעֱצָרִין כָּל כָּךְ, אִם אֵירַע שֶׁנֶּעֶצְרוּ כָּל כָּךְ עַד שֶׁהָיָה הָעוֹלָם בְּצַעַר, אֲזַי כְּשֶׁיָּרְדוּ הַגְּשָׁמִים, אִם יָרְדוּ כָּל כָּךְ וְרַבּוּ עַל הָאָרֶץ שֶׁמַּעֲלִים אֲבַעְבּוּעוֹת מִן הַמָּטָר וְהוֹלְכִין זֶה לִקְרַאת זֶה[34], צְרִיכִין לְבָרֵךְ עֲלֵיהֶם[35].

י. מַה מְּבָרֵךְ? אִם אֵין לוֹ שָׂדֶה, אוֹמֵר "מוֹדִים אֲנַחְנוּ לָךְ ה' אֱלֹהֵינוּ עַל כָּל טִפָּה וְטִפָּה שֶׁהוֹרַדְתָּ לָנוּ וְאִלּוּ פִינוּ מָלֵא שִׁירָה כַּיָּם" וְכוּ' (כְּמוֹ שֶׁהוּא בְּבִרְכַּת נִשְׁמַת)[36] עַד "וְיַקְדִּישׁוּ וְיַמְלִיכוּ אֶת שִׁמְךָ מַלְכֵּנוּ בָּרוּךְ אַתָּה ה' אֵל רוֹב הַהוֹדָאוֹת וְתִשְׁבָּחוֹת"[37]. וְאִם יֵשׁ לוֹ שָׂדֶה בְּשׁוּתָּפוּת עִם יִשְׂרָאֵל אַחֵר, מְבָרֵךְ "הַטּוֹב וְהַמֵּטִיב"[38].

---

§9 אִם הָיָה עֲצִירַת גְּשָׁמִים — **If there was a drought,** אֲפִילּוּ בִּמְדִינוֹתֵינוּ שֶׁהַגְּשָׁמִים תְּדִירִים — **even in our regions where it rains regularly** וְאֵינָן נֶעֱצָרִין כָּל כָּךְ — **and rain is not usually withheld,** i.e., there is usually no lack of rainfall, אִם אֵירַע שֶׁנֶּעֶצְרוּ כָּל כָּךְ — **in the event that** the rains **were withheld,** עַד שֶׁהָיָה הָעוֹלָם בְּצַעַר — **to the point where the population was in distress,** אֲזַי כְּשֶׁיָּרְדוּ הַגְּשָׁמִים — **then, when it does rain,** אִם יָרְדוּ כָּל כָּךְ וְרַבּוּ עַל הָאָרֶץ — **if** the rain **descended in such abundance on the earth** שֶׁמַּעֲלִים אֲבַעְבּוּעוֹת מִן הַמָּטָר — **that the rain creates bubbles** וְהוֹלְכִין זֶה לִקְרַאת זֶה — **and this** water on the ground **extends toward these** drops that continue to fall,[34] צְרִיכִין לְבָרֵךְ עֲלֵיהֶם — **a blessing should be recited upon** the rain.[35]

§10 מַה מְּבָרֵךְ — **What blessing does he recite?** אִם אֵין לוֹ שָׂדֶה — **If one does not own a field,** אוֹמֵר — **he recites** the following: "מוֹדִים אֲנַחְנוּ לָךְ ה' אֱלֹהֵינוּ — ***We give thanks to You,*** ***Hashem, our God,*** עַל כָּל טִפָּה וְטִפָּה שֶׁהוֹרַדְתָּ לָנוּ — ***for every single drop that You have brought down for us;*** וְאִלּוּ פִינוּ מָלֵא שִׁירָה כַּיָּם" וְכוּ' — ***were our mouths as full as song as the sea*** etc., (כְּמוֹ שֶׁהוּא בְּבִרְכַּת נִשְׁמַת — **following** the text of **the blessing of** the *Nishmas* Prayer),[36] עַד "וְיַקְדִּישׁוּ וְיַמְלִיכוּ אֶת שִׁמְךָ מַלְכֵּנוּ — **until** the phrase *all of them shall ... **sanctify and declare the sovereignty of Your Name, our King.*** בָּרוּךְ אַתָּה ה' — At that point, he should conclude with the words, ***Blessed are You, Hashem,*** אֵל רוֹב הַהוֹדָאוֹת וְתִשְׁבָּחוֹת" — ***God*** *Who is praised with* ***abundant thanksgivings and praises.***[37] וְאִם יֵשׁ לוֹ שָׂדֶה בְּשׁוּתָּפוּת עִם יִשְׂרָאֵל אַחֵר — **If one owns a field jointly with another Jew,** מְבָרֵךְ "הַטּוֹב וְהַמֵּטִיב" — **he recites the blessing of** *HaTov VeHaMeitiv,* ***Who is good and does good.***[38]

---

34. When a drop of rain falls into a puddle that has already formed on the ground, some droplets are displaced upward (*Rashi* to *Berachos* 59b).

35. See next *se'if.* In Eretz Yisrael, where there is no regular rainfall throughout the year, the first rainfall of the season is greatly anticipated and is cause for rejoicing. Therefore, *Beur Halachah* (221:1 s.v. אם היו) rules that even when there is no drought one should recite the blessing on the first rain of the season, but without שֵׁם וּמַלְכוּת (mention of Hashem's Name and His Sovereignty; see above, note 26).

36. This prayer, which begins with the words נִשְׁמַת כָּל חַי (*The soul of every living being*), is recited Shabbos and Yom Tov mornings before *Yishtabach*. Here, one begins from the words וְאִלּוּ פִינוּ, *were our mouths*, etc.

37. *Shulchan Aruch* (219:2) does not include the final word, וְתִשְׁבָּחוֹת, *and praises*. See *Beis Yosef* there.

38. See above, 59:1, which states that when one hears good tidings in which one shares the benefits with others as well, he recites the *HaTov VeHaMeitiv* blessing; if the tidings affect him alone, he recites the *Shehecheyanu* blessing.

וְאִם אֵין לוֹ שׁוּתָּף יִשְׂרָאֵל בַּשָּׂדֶה, אַף עַל פִּי שֶׁיֵּשׁ לוֹ אִשָּׁה וּבָנִים מְבָרֵךְ ״שֶׁהֶחֱיָינוּ״[39]. בִּרְכַּת ״הַטּוֹב וְהַמֵּטִיב״ וּבִרְכַּת ״שֶׁהֶחֱיָינוּ״, מְבָרֵךְ אַף עַל פִּי שֶׁאֵינוֹ רוֹאֶה אֶת הַגְּשָׁמִים אֶלָּא שֶׁהוּא שׁוֹמֵעַ שֶׁיּוֹרְדִים גְּשָׁמִים, אֲבָל בִּרְכַּת ״מוֹדִים אֲנַחְנוּ״ אֵינוֹ אוֹמֵר אֶלָּא מִי שֶׁהוּא רוֹאֶה אֶת הַגְּשָׁמִים.

וְאִם אֵין לוֹ שׁוּתָּף יִשְׂרָאֵל בַּשָּׂדֶה — If he has no Jewish partner in the ownership of the **field, אַף עַל פִּי שֶׁיֵּשׁ לוֹ אִשָּׁה וּבָנִים — even though he has a wife and children, מְבָרֵךְ ״שֶׁהֶחֱיָינוּ״** — he should not recite *HaTov VeHaMeitiv*, rather, **he should recite** the blessing of *Shehecheyanu, **Who kept us alive.***[39]

בִּרְכַּת ״הַטּוֹב וְהַמֵּטִיב״ וּבִרְכַּת ״שֶׁהֶחֱיָינוּ״ — The blessings of *HaTov VeHaMeitiv* and *Shehecheyanu,* מְבָרֵךְ אַף עַל פִּי שֶׁאֵינוֹ רוֹאֶה אֶת הַגְּשָׁמִים — one recites them **even if he does not** actually **see the rain, אֶלָּא שֶׁהוּא שׁוֹמֵעַ שֶׁיּוֹרְדִים גְּשָׁמִים — as long as he hears** from others **that it is raining. אֲבָל בִּרְכַּת ״מוֹדִים אֲנַחְנוּ״ — However, the blessing of** *Modim Anachnu, **We give thanks,*** **אֵינוֹ אוֹמֵר אֶלָּא מִי שֶׁהוּא רוֹאֶה אֶת הַגְּשָׁמִים — is to be recited only by one who sees the rain.** Thus, one who has no field and does not see the rain falling recites no blessing at all.

---

39. See previous note. According to *Mishnah Berurah* (221:4), if one has a wife and children, he should recite *HaTov VeHaMeitiv* since they can be considered "partners" with him, since they too share the benefit of the rain; see *Shaar HaTziyun* 221:2.

סימן סב

הִלְכוֹת מַשָּׂא וּמַתָּן

וּבוֹ י״ח סְעִיפִים

א. צָרִיךְ לִיזָּהֵר מְאוֹד שֶׁלֹּא לְהוֹנוֹת אֶת חֲבֵירוֹ. וְכָל הַמְאַנֶּה אֶת חֲבֵירוֹ, בֵּין שֶׁהַמּוֹכֵר מְאַנֶּה אֶת הַלּוֹקֵחַ[1] בֵּין שֶׁהַלּוֹקֵחַ מְאַנֶּה אֶת הַמּוֹכֵר[2], עוֹבֵר בְּלָאו, שֶׁנֶּאֱמַר (ויקרא כה, יד) ״וְכִי תִמְכְּרוּ מִמְכָּר לַעֲמִיתֶךָ אוֹ קָנֹה מִיַּד עֲמִיתֶךָ אַל תּוֹנוּ אִישׁ אֶת אָחִיו״[3]. וְהִיא הַשְּׁאֵלָה הָרִאשׁוֹנָה שֶׁשּׁוֹאֲלִין אֶת הָאָדָם בְּשָׁעָה שֶׁמַּכְנִיסִין אוֹתוֹ לְדִין: ״נָשָׂאתָ וְנָתַתָּ בֶּאֱמוּנָה?״

SIMAN 62

THE LAWS OF BUSINESS TRANSACTIONS

CONTAINING 18 *SE'IFIM*

§1-5 Overcharging and Underpaying / **§6** The Permissibility of Sales Promotions / **§7-8** Accuracy of Scales / **§9-10** Measuring Practices / **§11-12** The Prohibition Against Owning Inaccurate Instruments of Measure / **§13-14** Interfering With the Transactions of Another Jew / **§15** Withdrawing From a Transaction / **§16-17** Upholding Commitments Made to Others / **§18** The Order of Precedence When Selling to Others

§1 צָרִיךְ לִיזָּהֵר מְאוֹד שֶׁלֹּא לְהוֹנוֹת אֶת חֲבֵירוֹ — **One must be very careful not to defraud one's fellow** when setting the price for a transaction, וְכָל הַמְאַנֶּה אֶת חֲבֵירוֹ — for, **whoever does defraud his fellow,** בֵּין שֶׁהַמּוֹכֵר מְאַנֶּה אֶת הַלּוֹקֵחַ — regardless of **whether it is the seller who is defrauding the buyer** by overcharging him,[1] בֵּין שֶׁהַלּוֹקֵחַ מְאַנֶּה אֶת הַמּוֹכֵר — **or it is the buyer who is defrauding the seller** by underpaying,[2] עוֹבֵר בְּלָאו — **violates a prohibition,** שֶׁנֶּאֱמַר — **as** the verse **states** (*Vayikra* 25:14): ״וְכִי תִמְכְּרוּ מִמְכָּר לַעֲמִיתֶךָ אוֹ קָנֹה מִיַּד עֲמִיתֶךָ אַל תּוֹנוּ אִישׁ אֶת אָחִיו״ — ***When you make a sale to your fellow or make a purchase from the hand of your fellow, do not aggrieve one another.***[3] וְהִיא הַשְּׁאֵלָה הָרִאשׁוֹנָה שֶׁשּׁוֹאֲלִין אֶת הָאָדָם — Moreover, the Gemara (Shabbos 31a) tells us that **this is the first question asked of a person** בְּשָׁעָה שֶׁמַּכְנִיסִין אוֹתוֹ לְדִין — after he dies, **at the time he is brought to judgment** before the Heavenly tribunal: ״נָשָׂאתָ וְנָתַתָּ בֶּאֱמוּנָה?״ — **"Did you conduct business transactions with integrity?"**

---

1. The market determines the value of an item. In general, a seller is considered to be defrauding a buyer if he asks for a price that exceeds its current market value, and the unsuspecting buyer makes the purchase assuming that the requested price is a true reflection of the item's market value.

2. If an item in a store is underpriced, one is obligated to inform the storeowner (*Shulchan Aruch HaRav*, *Ona'ah* §3). Buying the item without notifying the owner of the item's true value is prohibited, even though the merchant made the mistake on his own.

3. Regarding the recourse available to the injured party when fraud has occurred, see *Shulchan Aruch, Choshen Mishpat* 227:2-4.

ב. כְּשֵׁם שֶׁיֵּשׁ אִיסּוּר אוֹנָאָה בְּמִקָּח וּמִמְכָּר, כָּךְ יֵשׁ אִיסּוּר אוֹנָאָה בִּשְׂכִירוּת וּבְקַבְּלָנוּת וּבְחִילּוּף מַטְבֵּעַ.

ג. הַנּוֹשֵׂא וְנוֹתֵן בֶּאֱמוּנָה אֵינוֹ חוֹשֵׁשׁ לְאוֹנָאָה. כֵּיצַד? "חֵפֶץ זֶה בְּכָךְ וְכָךְ לְקַחְתִּיו, כָּךְ אֲנִי רוֹצֶה לְהִשְׂתַּכֵּר בּוֹ", אַף עַל פִּי שֶׁהוּא נִתְאַנָּה בִלְקִיחָתוֹ וְכָל הַמִּתְאַנֶּה אֵינוֹ רַשַּׁאי לְהוֹנוֹת אֲחֵרִים בִּשְׁבִיל זֶה, מִכָּל מָקוֹם זֶה מוּתָּר, שֶׁהֲרֵי זֶה כִּמְפָרֵשׁ שֶׁלֹּא יִסְמוֹךְ עַל שִׁוּוּי הַמִּקָּח, אֶלָּא עַל הַדָּמִים שֶׁנָּתַן הוּא בַּעֲדוֹ[4].

ד. מִי שֶׁיֵּשׁ לוֹ אֵיזֶה דָבָר לְמִכּוֹר, אָסוּר לוֹ לְיַפּוֹתוֹ כְּדֵי לְרַמּוֹת בּוֹ, כְּגוֹן לְהַשְׁקוֹת בְּהֵמָה מֵי סוּבִּין שֶׁמְּנַפְּחִין וְזוֹקְפִין שַׂעֲרוֹתֶיהָ כְּדֵי שֶׁתֵּרָאֶה שְׁמֵנָה, אוֹ לִצְבּוֹעַ כֵּלִים יְשָׁנִים כְּדֵי שֶׁיִּתְרָאוּ כַּחֲדָשִׁים[5], וְכָל כַּיּוֹצֵא בָזֶה.

---

§2 כְּשֵׁם שֶׁיֵּשׁ אִיסּוּר אוֹנָאָה בְּמִקָּח וּמִמְכָּר — **Just as the prohibition against fraud applies** when engaging **in** transactions involving **buying and selling,** כָּךְ יֵשׁ אִיסּוּר אוֹנָאָה — **so does the prohibition against fraud apply** בִּשְׂכִירוּת — when setting the terms **for rentals,** וּבְקַבְּלָנוּת — **for contractual work,** וּבְחִילּוּף מַטְבֵּעַ — **and for money changing.**

§3 Even if a merchant was overcharged by his supplier, he may not pass on the higher costs to his customers. However, if he makes it clear that he is not setting the price for his customers based on the true value of the product, but on a "cost-plus" basis (his costs plus a specific profit margin), he is not considered to be defrauding his customers, as Kitzur explains in this *se'if.*

הַנּוֹשֵׂא וְנוֹתֵן בֶּאֱמוּנָה — **One who conducts business** [by disclosing his costs] **in good faith** אֵינוֹ חוֹשֵׁשׁ לְאוֹנָאָה — **need not be concerned regarding** the prohibition against **fraud.** כֵּיצַד — **How so?** "חֵפֶץ זֶה בְּכָךְ וְכָךְ לְקַחְתִּיו — If the seller tells the buyer, **"I purchased this item for such-and-such** amount, כָּךְ אֲנִי רוֹצֶה לְהִשְׂתַּכֵּר בּוֹ" — **and I want to realize such-and-such** amount of **profit from it,"** אַף עַל פִּי שֶׁהוּא נִתְאַנָּה בִלְקִיחָתוֹ — **then, even if he** (i.e., the merchant) **had been defrauded in its purchase** price when he bought the item, וְכָל הַמִּתְאַנֶּה אֵינוֹ רַשַּׁאי לְהוֹנוֹת אֲחֵרִים בִּשְׁבִיל זֶה — **and** although **one who was defrauded** (in this case, the merchant), **may not defraud another because of this,** מִכָּל מָקוֹם זֶה מוּתָּר — **nevertheless, it is permitted** to sell the item in this way, שֶׁהֲרֵי זֶה כִּמְפָרֵשׁ — **for it is as though he stipulated** to the buyer שֶׁלֹּא יִסְמוֹךְ עַל שִׁוּוּי הַמִּקָּח — **that he should not base** his perception of the worth of the transaction **upon the value of the** item **purchased,** אֶלָּא עַל הַדָּמִים שֶׁנָּתַן הוּא בַּעֲדוֹ — **but rather upon the** amount of **money that** the seller **paid in order to acquire it.**[4]

§4 מִי שֶׁיֵּשׁ לוֹ אֵיזֶה דָבָר לְמִכּוֹר — **One who has an item** that he wishes **to sell** אָסוּר לוֹ לְיַפּוֹתוֹ — **may not embellish its appearance** כְּדֵי לְרַמּוֹת בּוֹ — **in order to fool** a prospective buyer. כְּגוֹן לְהַשְׁקוֹת בְּהֵמָה מֵי סוּבִּין — **For example,** it is prohibited **to give an animal broth of bran to drink,** שֶׁמְּנַפְּחִין וְזוֹקְפִין שַׂעֲרוֹתֶיהָ — **which causes** the animal to become **bloated and its hair to stand erect,** כְּדֵי שֶׁתֵּרָאֶה שְׁמֵנָה — **in order that it appear fat,** אוֹ לִצְבּוֹעַ כֵּלִים יְשָׁנִים כְּדֵי שֶׁיִּתְרָאוּ כַּחֲדָשִׁים — **or to paint old utensils in order that they should appear to be new ones,**[5] וְכָל כַּיּוֹצֵא בָזֶה — **and any similar** deceptive **practice.**

---

4. This law is subject to a number of provisions (see *Choshen Mishpat* 227:27-28). A halachic authority should be consulted.

5. Certainly one may paint a utensil in order to improve its appearance, provided that the price that is set is appropriate for an old,

ה. וְכֵן אָסוּר לְעָרֵב מְעַט פֵּירוֹת רָעִים בְּהַרְבֵּה פֵּירוֹת יָפִים כְּדֵי לְמָכְרָם בְּחֶזְקַת יָפִים, אוֹ לְעָרֵב מַשְׁקֶה רָעָה בְּיָפֶה. וְאִם הָיָה טַעְמוֹ נִיכָּר, מוּתָּר לְעָרֵב, כִּי הַלּוֹקֵחַ יַרְגִּישׁ[6].

ו. מוּתָּר לְחֶנְוָנִי לַחֲלוֹק קְלָיוֹת וֶאֱגוֹזִים לְתִינוֹקוֹת כְּדֵי לְהַרְגִּילָם שֶׁיִּקְנוּ מִמֶּנּוּ. וְכֵן יָכוֹל לִמְכּוֹר בְּזוֹל יוֹתֵר מֵהַשַּׁעַר כְּדֵי שֶׁיִּקְנוּ מִמֶּנּוּ, וְאֵין בְּנֵי הַשּׁוּק יְכוֹלִין לְעַכֵּב עָלָיו[7].

ז. הַמּוֹדֵד אוֹ שׁוֹקֵל חָסֵר לַחֲבֵרוֹ, אוֹ אֲפִילוּ לְעַכּוּ״ם, עוֹבֵר בְּלָאו, שֶׁנֶּאֱמַר ״לֹא תַעֲשׂוּ עָוֶל ... בַּמִּדָּה בַּמִּשְׁקָל וּבַמְּשׂוּרָה״ (ויקרא יט, לה) (וְעַיֵּין לְקַמָּן סִימָן קפ״ב סְעִיף א׳ וּסְעִיף ד׳). וְעוֹנֶשׁ הַמִּדּוֹת וְהַמִּשְׁקָלוֹת קָשֶׁה מְאוֹד, שֶׁאִי אֶפְשַׁר לְמוֹדֵד אוֹ לְשׁוֹקֵל שֶׁקֶר

---

§5 **וְכֵן אָסוּר לְעָרֵב מְעַט פֵּירוֹת רָעִים בְּהַרְבֵּה פֵּירוֹת יָפִים** — **Similarly, it is prohibited to mix a few** pieces of **inferior produce with much superior produce** **כְּדֵי לְמָכְרָם בְּחֶזְקַת יָפִים** — **in order to sell them** all **as superior produce,** **אוֹ לְעָרֵב מַשְׁקֶה רָעָה בְּיָפֶה** — **or to mix an inferior beverage with a superior** one, thus obtaining the price of the better beverage even for the inferior one. **וְאִם הָיָה טַעְמוֹ נִיכָּר** — **However, if the taste** of the inferior beverage **would be discernable** even after being mixed, **מוּתָּר לְעָרֵב** — **then it is permissible to mix** the inferior beverage with the better one, **כִּי הַלּוֹקֵחַ יַרְגִּישׁ** — **for the buyer will detect** the presence of the inferior beverage when he tastes it before purchasing it.[6]

§6 **מוּתָּר לְחֶנְוָנִי לַחֲלוֹק קְלָיוֹת וֶאֱגוֹזִים לְתִינוֹקוֹת** — **It is permitted for a shopkeeper to distribute roasted kernels or nuts to children,** **כְּדֵי לְהַרְגִּילָם שֶׁיִּקְנוּ מִמֶּנּוּ** — **in order to accustom them to buy from him.** **וְכֵן יָכוֹל לִמְכּוֹר בְּזוֹל יוֹתֵר מֵהַשַּׁעַר** — **Similarly, it is permitted to sell** an item **for less than its market price** **כְּדֵי שֶׁיִּקְנוּ מִמֶּנּוּ** — **so that** people **will buy from him.** **וְאֵין בְּנֵי הַשּׁוּק יְכוֹלִין לְעַכֵּב עָלָיו** — **And fellow shopkeepers may not deter him** from doing this.[7]

§7 **הַמּוֹדֵד אוֹ שׁוֹקֵל חָסֵר** — **One who measures or weighs out less** than the amount being paid for, **לַחֲבֵרוֹ, אוֹ אֲפִילוּ לְעַכּוּ״ם** — when selling something **to his fellow** Jew, **or even to an idolater,** **עוֹבֵר בְּלָאו** — **violates a prohibition,** **שֶׁנֶּאֱמַר** — **as** the verse **states** (*Vayikra* 19:35): **״לֹא תַעֲשׂוּ עָוֶל ... בַּמִּדָּה בַּמִּשְׁקָל וּבַמְּשׂוּרָה״** — ***You shall not commit a perversion*** *in justice* ***in measures of length, weight, or volume*** **(וְעַיֵּין לְקַמָּן סִימָן קפ״ב סְעִיף א׳ וּסְעִיף ד׳)** — **see below, 182:1, 4,** regarding the prohibition against stealing from an idolater). **וְעוֹנֶשׁ הַמִּדּוֹת וְהַמִּשְׁקָלוֹת קָשֶׁה מְאוֹד** — Moreover, **the** Heavenly **punishment** for one who was dishonest with **measures and weights is very severe,** **שֶׁאִי אֶפְשַׁר לְמוֹדֵד אוֹ לְשׁוֹקֵל שֶׁקֶר** — **for it is** virtually **impossible for one who has measured or weighed deceitfully**

---

albeit refreshed, utensil. Kitzur is referring to one who beautifies the utensil externally so as to hide its flaws, and to charge for it as though it were new (*Tur, Choshen Mishpat* 228).

6. However, even in this case the seller may not rely on the fact that the buyer could taste it to misrepresent to the buyer the nature of the product; see *Pischei Teshuvah, Choshen Mishpat* 228:1.

7. A person may make it attractive for people to shop in his store. He may not, however, attempt to attract a customer who has already entered another store (see *Pischei Teshuvah, Choshen Mishpat* 156:8).

לָשׁוּב בִּתְשׁוּבָה הֲגוּנָה שֶׁאֵינוֹ יוֹדֵעַ מַה וּלְמִי יָשׁוּב[8], וְאַף שֶׁיַּעֲשֶׂה צָרְכֵי רַבִּים, אֵין זֹאת תְּשׁוּבָה הֲגוּנָה[9].

ח. כְּתִיב (דברים כה, יג-טו) "לֹא יִהְיֶה לְךָ בְּכִיסְךָ אֶבֶן וָאָבֶן גְּדוֹלָה וּקְטַנָּה. לֹא יִהְיֶה לְךָ בְּבֵיתְךָ אֵיפָה וְאֵיפָה גְּדוֹלָה וּקְטַנָּה[10]. אֶבֶן שְׁלֵמָה וָצֶדֶק יִהְיֶה לָּךְ, אֵיפָה שְׁלֵמָה וָצֶדֶק יִהְיֶה לָּךְ" וְגוֹ', וְתֵיבַת "בְּכִיסְךָ", וְכֵן תֵּיבַת "בְּבֵיתְךָ", נִרְאִין לִכְאוֹרָה כִּמְיוּתָּרִין[11]. וְדָרְשׁוּ רַבּוֹתֵינוּ ז"ל (בבא בתרא פט, א): "לֹא יִהְיֶה לְךָ בְּכִיסְךָ" מָמוֹן. מַה טַּעַם? מִשּׁוּם "אֶבֶן וָאָבֶן". "לֹא יִהְיֶה לְךָ בְּבֵיתְךָ" צְרָכֶיךָ. מַה טַּעַם? מִשּׁוּם "אֵיפָה וְאֵיפָה".

לָשׁוּב בִּתְשׁוּבָה הֲגוּנָה — **to properly repent,** שֶׁאֵינוֹ יוֹדֵעַ מַה וּלְמִי יָשׁוּב — **as he does not know what** amount, **or to whom, he must repay.**[8] וְאַף שֶׁיַּעֲשֶׂה צָרְכֵי רַבִּים — **And even if he** gives money to **fund public needs** to atone for this sin, אֵין זֹאת תְּשׁוּבָה הֲגוּנָה — **it is not a** fully **suitable** form of **repentance.**[9]

§8 In this *se'if,* Kitzur warns of the Heavenly punishment for dishonest measuring, and details the reward for one who is scrupulous when measuring:

כְּתִיב — **It is written** (*Devarim* 25:13-15): "לֹא יִהְיֶה לְךָ בְּכִיסְךָ אֶבֶן וָאָבֶן גְּדוֹלָה וּקְטַנָּה — ***You shall not have in your pouch a weight and a weight*** (i.e., two different weights), ***a large one and a small one.*** לֹא יִהְיֶה לְךָ בְּבֵיתְךָ אֵיפָה וְאֵיפָה גְּדוֹלָה וּקְטַנָּה — ***You shall not have in your house, a measure and a measure*** (i.e., two different measures), ***a large one and a small one.***[10] אֶבֶן שְׁלֵמָה וָצֶדֶק יִהְיֶה לָּךְ, אֵיפָה שְׁלֵמָה וָצֶדֶק יִהְיֶה לָּךְ" וְגוֹ' — ***A perfect and just*** (i.e., correct) ***weight shall you have, a perfect and just*** (i.e., correct) ***measure shall you have,*** **etc.** וְתֵיבַת "בְּכִיסְךָ" — In these verses, **the words "*in your pouch,*"** וְכֵן תֵּיבַת "בְּבֵיתְךָ" — **as well as the words "*in your house,*"** נִרְאִין לִכְאוֹרָה כִּמְיוּתָּרִין — **are seemingly unnecessary.**[11] וְדָרְשׁוּ רַבּוֹתֵינוּ ז"ל — **The Rabbis, of blessed memory** (*Bava Basra* 89a), therefore **expounded** these verses as a message regarding the punishment for violating these laws: "לֹא יִהְיֶה לְךָ בְּכִיסְךָ" מָמוֹן — In the context of this exposition, the words "*You shall not have in your pouch*" are understood as an independent statement, meaning: It can come about that ***you will not have in your pouch*** any **money.** מַה טַּעַם — **What would be the reason** for such a punishment? מִשּׁוּם "אֶבֶן וָאָבֶן" — It would be **as a result of** violating the prohibition of keeping ***a weight and a weight.*** "לֹא יִהְיֶה לְךָ בְּבֵיתְךָ" צְרָכֶיךָ — Similarly, it can come about that ***you will not have in your house*** **your necessities.** מַה טַּעַם — **What would be the reason** for such a punishment? מִשּׁוּם "אֵיפָה וְאֵיפָה" — It would be **as a result of** violating the prohibition of keeping

---

8. One cannot achieve full repentance for the sin of stealing without returning that which he stole; see below, 131:4.

9. See below, 182:7, which states that one who has stolen from many people and cannot now identify who they are, should provide funds for public needs so that those people from whom he has stolen will benefit from them. Here, Kitzur writes that although when there is no other option this is a partial remedy, it still does not offer full expiation.

10. I.e., a larger measure or weight to use when you buy, so that you will get a larger quantity, and a smaller measure or weight to use when you sell, so that you will give away less (*Rashi* ad loc.).

11. The verse could have simply stated, *You shall not have a weight and a weight ... You shall not have a measure and a measure,* as one is clearly prohibited from keeping false measures in any location.

אֲבָל "אֶבֶן שְׁלֵמָה וָצֶדֶק" אִם יִהְיוּ בְּבֵיתְךָ, "יִהְיֶה לָּךְ" מָמוֹן[12]. וְכֵן, "אֵיפָה שְׁלֵמָה וָצֶדֶק", אִם יִהְיוּ בְּבֵיתְךָ, יִהְיוּ לְךָ צְרָכֶיךָ. עוֹד אָמְרוּ רַבּוֹתֵינוּ ז"ל: מַה יַּעֲשֶׂה אָדָם וְיִתְעַשֵּׁר? יִשָּׂא וְיִתֵּן בֶּאֱמוּנָה, וִיבַקֵּשׁ רַחֲמִים מִמִּי שֶׁהָעוֹשֶׁר שֶׁלּוֹ, שֶׁנֶּאֱמַר (חגי ב, ח) **"לִי הַכֶּסֶף וְלִי הַזָּהָב"** (נִדָּה דַּף ע').

ט. צָרִיךְ לִמְדּוֹד וְלִשְׁקוֹל בְּעַיִן יָפָה, שֶׁיִּהְיֶה עוֹדֵף עַל הַמִּדָּה, שֶׁנֶּאֱמַר (דברים כה, טו) **"אֵיפָה שְׁלֵמָה וָצֶדֶק יִהְיֶה לָּךְ", מַה תַּלְמוּד לוֹמַר "וָצֶדֶק"? אָמְרָה תּוֹרָה: צַדֵּק מִשֶּׁלְּךָ וְתֵן לוֹ[13].**

י. צָרִיךְ לִמְדּוֹד כְּמִנְהַג הַמְּדִינָה, וְלֹא יְשַׁנֶּה כְּלָל. מָקוֹם שֶׁנָּהֲגוּ לִגְדּוֹשׁ, לֹא יִמְחוֹק, אֲפִילּוּ בִּרְצוֹן הַלּוֹקֵחַ שֶׁפִּיחֵת לוֹ מְדָמִים. וּמָקוֹם שֶׁנָּהֲגוּ לִמְחוֹק,

---

a measure and a measure. אֲבָל "אֶבֶן שְׁלֵמָה וָצֶדֶק" אִם יִהְיוּ בְּבֵיתְךָ — According to this interpretation, the next verse should be interpreted as follows: **However, if you will have in your house** *a perfect and just weight,* "יִהְיֶה לָּךְ" מָמוֹן — then *you will have* money.[12] וְכֵן — **Similarly,** "אֵיפָה שְׁלֵמָה וָצֶדֶק", אִם יִהְיוּ בְּבֵיתְךָ — **if you will have** *a perfect and just measure,* יִהְיוּ לְךָ צְרָכֶיךָ — then *you will have* **all your needs.** עוֹד אָמְרוּ רַבּוֹתֵינוּ ז"ל — **The Rabbis, of blessed memory, also said,** מַה יַּעֲשֶׂה אָדָם וְיִתְעַשֵּׁר — **What should a person do in order to become wealthy?** יִשָּׂא וְיִתֵּן בֶּאֱמוּנָה — **He should conduct business transactions with integrity,** וִיבַקֵּשׁ רַחֲמִים מִמִּי שֶׁהָעוֹשֶׁר שֶׁלּוֹ — **and he should plead for mercy from He to Whom wealth belongs,** שֶׁנֶּאֱמַר — **as** the verse **states** (*Chaggai* 2:8): "לִי הַכֶּסֶף וְלִי הַזָּהָב" — ***Mine is the silver, and Mine is the gold*** (נִדָּה דַּף ע' — *Niddah* **70b**).

§9 צָרִיךְ לִמְדּוֹד וְלִשְׁקוֹל בְּעַיִן יָפָה — **One must measure and weigh generously,** שֶׁיִּהְיֶה עוֹדֵף עַל הַמִּדָּה — **so that there will be more than** exactly **the** amount **measured,** שֶׁנֶּאֱמַר — **as** the verse **states** (*Devarim* 25:15): "אֵיפָה שְׁלֵמָה וָצֶדֶק יִהְיֶה לָּךְ" — ***A perfect and just weight shall you have.*** מַה תַּלְמוּד לוֹמַר "וָצֶדֶק" — After having stated that a person must have a perfect weight, **why must Scripture** also **say** ***just?*** אָמְרָה תּוֹרָה — The Sages explain (*Bava Basra* 88b) that **the Torah is saying:** צַדֵּק מִשֶּׁלְּךָ וְתֵן לוֹ — **Act justly with your own and give him** (i.e., the buyer) somewhat extra.[13]

§10 צָרִיךְ לִמְדּוֹד כְּמִנְהַג הַמְּדִינָה — **One must measure** in a manner **consistent with the practice of the country** in which the transaction is taking place, וְלֹא יְשַׁנֶּה כְּלָל — **and not deviate at all.** מָקוֹם שֶׁנָּהֲגוּ לִגְדּוֹשׁ — This means that **in a place where common practice is to heap** the contents above the top of the measure, לֹא יִמְחוֹק — **one should not level** its contents. אֲפִילּוּ בִּרְצוֹן הַלּוֹקֵחַ שֶׁפִּיחֵת לוֹ מְדָמִים — He may not do this **even** if it is **the wish of the buyer** that the measure will be level, **as** the buyer **will give** the seller **less money** than he would otherwise pay, since the measure is not heaped. וּמָקוֹם שֶׁנָּהֲגוּ לִמְחוֹק — **Similarly,**

---

12. This interpretation continues the exposition by splitting the phrases, to teach the Heavenly reward for keeping only fair weights and measures. Accordingly, the phrase יִהְיֶה לָּךְ, *you shall have*, is taken as a sentence on its own, meaning, *you shall have money*.

13. Since it is impossible for a weighing to be absolutely precise, the seller must act justly and give the buyer a little extra to ensure that he does not give him less than he deserves (see *Rashbam* ad loc.).

לֹא יִגְדּוֹשׁ, אֲפִילּוּ בִּרְצוֹן הַמּוֹכֵר שֶׁמּוֹסִיף לוֹ דָּמִים. כִּי הַתּוֹרָה הִקְפִּידָה עַל עִוּוּת הַמִּדּוֹת פֶּן תֵּצֵא תַּקָּלָה עַל יְדֵי זֶה שֶׁיִּרְאֶה הָרוֹאֶה שֶׁמּוֹדְדִין כָּךְ וְיִדְמֶה לוֹ שֶׁכָּךְ הִיא מִדַּת הָעִיר וְיִמְדּוֹד כֵּן לְאַחֵר שֶׁאֵינוֹ יוֹדֵעַ גַּם כֵּן אֶת הַמִּנְהָג וְיַטְעֵהוּ.

יא. חַיָּבִים רָאשֵׁי הַקָּהָל לְהַעֲמִיד מְמוּנִּים שֶׁיִּהְיוּ מְחַזְּרִים עַל הַחֲנֻיּוֹת, וְכָל מִי שֶׁנִּמְצָא אִתּוֹ מִדָּה חֲסֵרָה אוֹ מִשְׁקָל חָסֵר אוֹ מֹאזְנַיִם מְקוּלְקָלִים לְהַכּוֹתוֹ וּלְקָנְסוֹ כַּנִּרְאֶה בְּעֵינֵיהֶם.

יב. אָסוּר לְאָדָם לְהַשְׁהוֹת מִדָּה חֲסֵרָה בְּבֵיתוֹ אוֹ בַּחֲנוּתוֹ, אַף עַל פִּי שֶׁאֵינוֹ מוֹדֵד בָּהּ. וְאִם שׁוֹהֶה, עוֹבֵר בְּלָאו, שֶׁנֶּאֱמַר (דברים כה, יג-יד) "לֹא יִהְיֶה לְךָ בְּכִיסְךָ אֶבֶן וָאָבֶן גְּדוֹלָה וּקְטַנָּה. לֹא יִהְיֶה לְךָ בְּבֵיתְךָ אֵיפָה וְאֵיפָה גְּדוֹלָה וּקְטַנָּה"[14].

---

in a place where common practice is to level the contents with the top of the measure, **לֹא יִגְדּוֹשׁ — one may not heap** the contents above the measure. **אֲפִילּוּ בִּרְצוֹן הַמּוֹכֵר** — This too should not be done, **even** if it is **the wish of the seller, שֶׁמּוֹסִיף לוֹ דָּמִים — as** the buyer **is adding money to** the amount he would otherwise pay. **כִּי הַתּוֹרָה הִקְפִּידָה עַל עִוּוּת הַמִּדּוֹת** — Although simply not following the common practice does not constitute cheating, it is nevertheless prohibited, **for the Torah was stringent in regard to the distortion of measures** **פֶּן תֵּצֵא תַּקָּלָה** — and required that one follow the common practice, **lest it** otherwise **result in a pitfall, עַל יְדֵי זֶה שֶׁיִּרְאֶה הָרוֹאֶה שֶׁמּוֹדְדִין כָּךְ — for an observer might see that they measured as they did, וְיִדְמֶה לוֹ שֶׁכָּךְ הִיא מִדַּת הָעִיר — and would assume that this is the** accepted practice of **measuring in the city. וְיִמְדּוֹד כֵּן לְאַחֵר שֶׁאֵינוֹ יוֹדֵעַ גַּם כֵּן אֶת הַמִּנְהָג — And,** in the future, the observer **may measure this way** in his dealings **with another** person, **who is also unaware of the common practice, וְיַטְעֵהוּ — and** inadvertently **mislead him.**

§11 חַיָּבִים רָאשֵׁי הַקָּהָל לְהַעֲמִיד מְמוּנִּים — The community leaders are obligated to appoint officers שֶׁיִּהְיוּ מְחַזְּרִים עַל הַחֲנֻיּוֹת — who shall circulate among the stores, to ensure that all weights and measures are accurate. **וְכָל מִי שֶׁנִּמְצָא אִתּוֹ מִדָּה חֲסֵרָה — Anyone with whom there is found a measure lacking** its full size, **אוֹ מִשְׁקָל חָסֵר — or a weight lacking** from its designated weight, **אוֹ מֹאזְנַיִם מְקוּלְקָלִים — or a faulty scale, לְהַכּוֹתוֹ — they** (the community leaders) **are allowed to administer corporal punishment וּלְקָנְסוֹ — and to penalize him** monetarily, **כַּנִּרְאֶה בְּעֵינֵיהֶם — as they see fit.**

§12 אָסוּר לְאָדָם לְהַשְׁהוֹת מִדָּה חֲסֵרָה — It is prohibited for a person to retain a measure that lacks its full size **בְּבֵיתוֹ אוֹ בַּחֲנוּתוֹ — in his house or in his store, אַף עַל פִּי שֶׁאֵינוֹ מוֹדֵד בָּהּ — even if he does not measure with it. וְאִם שׁוֹהֶה, עוֹבֵר בְּלָאו — And if he does retain** a flawed measure, **he violates a prohibition, שֶׁנֶּאֱמַר — as** the verse **states** (*Devarim* 25:13-14): **"לֹא יִהְיֶה לְךָ בְּכִיסְךָ אֶבֶן וָאָבֶן גְּדוֹלָה וּקְטַנָּה — *You shall not have in your pouch a weight and a weight, a large one and a small one.* לֹא יִהְיֶה לְךָ בְּבֵיתְךָ אֵיפָה וְאֵיפָה גְּדוֹלָה וּקְטַנָּה" — *You shall not have in your house a measure and a measure, a large one and a small one.*[14]**

---

14. As stated, the prohibition is not only for using a flawed measure and cheating others, but even for retaining the flawed measure in one's possession.

וַאֲפִילוּ לַעֲשׂוֹת אֶת הַמִּדָּה עָבִיט לְמֵי רַגְלַיִם, אָסוּר[15], שֶׁמָּא יָבֹא מִי שֶׁאֵינוֹ יוֹדֵעַ וְיִמְדּוֹד בָּהּ. וְאִם יֵשׁ מִנְהָג בָּעִיר שֶׁאֵין מוֹדְדִין אֶלָּא בְּמִדָּה הָרְשׁוּמָה בְּרוֹשֶׁם הַיָּדוּעַ, וְזוֹ אֵינָהּ רְשׁוּמָה, מוּתָּר לְהַשְׁהוֹתָהּ.

יג. הַמְּחַזֵּיר אַחַר דָּבָר לִקְנוֹתוֹ אוֹ לְשָׂכְרוֹ, בֵּין קַרְקַע בֵּין מִטַּלְטְלִים, בֵּין מֵעַכּוּ״ם בֵּין מִיִּשְׂרָאֵל, וּכְבָר הוּשְׁווּ עַל הַדָּמִים, וְקוֹדֶם שֶׁגָּמְרוּ אֶת הַקִּנְיָן בָּא אַחֵר וּקְנָאוֹ אוֹ שְׂכָרוֹ, נִקְרָא רָשָׁע[16]. אֲבָל אִם עֲדַיִין לֹא הֻשְׁווּ עַל הַדָּמִים, אֶלָּא שֶׁהַמּוֹכֵר רוֹצֶה בְּכָךְ וְהַקּוֹנֶה רוֹצֶה בְּפָחוֹת, מוּתָּר לְאַחֵר לִקְנוֹתוֹ[17]. וְאָסוּר לְהַשִּׂיג גְּבוּל רֵעֵהוּ[18] בִּשְׂכִירוּת בָּתִּים וְכַדּוֹמֶה מֵעוֹבֵד כּוֹכָבִים[19].

וַאֲפִילוּ לַעֲשׂוֹת אֶת הַמִּדָּה עָבִיט לְמֵי רַגְלַיִם, אָסוּר — **It is even prohibited to make the** flawed **measure into a urine receptacle,**[15] **שֶׁמָּא יָבֹא מִי שֶׁאֵינוֹ יוֹדֵעַ וְיִמְדּוֹד בָּהּ** — **for perhaps one who is unaware** of its current use **would come to measure with it. וְאִם יֵשׁ מִנְהָג בָּעִיר** — However, **if there is a practice within the city שֶׁאֵין מוֹדְדִין אֶלָּא בְּמִדָּה הָרְשׁוּמָה בְּרוֹשֶׁם הַיָּדוּעַ** — **that one measures only with measures that are marked with a known mark** (such as a certification of accuracy), **וְזוֹ אֵינָהּ רְשׁוּמָה** — **and this** flawed measure **is not** so **marked, מוּתָּר לְהַשְׁהוֹתָהּ** — **it is permitted to retain it.**

§13 הַמְּחַזֵּיר אַחַר דָּבָר לִקְנוֹתוֹ אוֹ לְשָׂכְרוֹ — If **one** person **is endeavoring to purchase or rent an item, בֵּין קַרְקַע בֵּין מִטַּלְטְלִים** — regardless of **whether** it is **land or movable objects, בֵּין מֵעַכּוּ״ם בֵּין מִיִּשְׂרָאֵל** — and regardless of **whether** it is **from an idolater or a Jew, וּכְבָר הוּשְׁווּ עַל הַדָּמִים** — **and they have already agreed on a price, וְקוֹדֶם שֶׁגָּמְרוּ אֶת הַקִּנְיָן בָּא אַחֵר וּקְנָאוֹ אוֹ שְׂכָרוֹ** — **but before they completed the transaction, another** person **came and purchased it or rented it, נִקְרָא רָשָׁע** — then the second person **is called** a *rasha,* **a wicked person.**[16] **אֲבָל אִם עֲדַיִין לֹא הֻשְׁווּ עַל הַדָּמִים** — **However, if they have not yet agreed on a price; אֶלָּא שֶׁהַמּוֹכֵר רוֹצֶה בְּכָךְ וְהַקּוֹנֶה רוֹצֶה בְּפָחוֹת** — **rather** they are in the midst of their negotiations: **the seller wants such** a sum **and the buyer wants** to buy the item **for less, מוּתָּר לְאַחֵר לִקְנוֹתוֹ** — **then it is permitted for another** person **to buy it.**[17]

וְאָסוּר לְהַשִּׂיג גְּבוּל רֵעֵהוּ — **It is** also **prohibited to encroach upon the boundary of one's fellow** Jew[18] **בִּשְׂכִירוּת בָּתִּים וְכַדּוֹמֶה** — **in** regard to **renting houses or the like מֵעוֹבֵד כּוֹכָבִים** — **from idolaters.**[19]

---

15. Even though it is unlikely that it will ever be used again for measuring.

16. *Sma* (237:1) writes that a public announcement is made in the synagogue that he has committed an act of wickedness.

17. According to some authorities, even when they did not yet agree on a price, if the negotiations are in their final stage, and it is clear that, in the absence of any outside influence, the parties will shortly come to an agreement, another person may not interfere with a competing offer (see *Igros Moshe, Choshen Mishpat* I, §60).

18. In its literal sense, the prohibition of *hasagas gevul,* encroaching upon the boundary of one's fellow Jew, refers to one who actually moves the marker defining the boundary between his field and his neighbor's field (see *Devarim* 19:14). This term is also used when referring to the prohibition of unlawfully competing with one who has established a business or profession (see *Choshen Mishpat* 156:5-6), and is used here in a similar sense.

19. That is, if one Jew rented a house from an idolater, another Jew may not disregard the first Jew's position as prior tenant, and rent it from the idolater at the end of the term of the rental if the first Jew wishes to remain as the tenant; see *Chasam Sofer, Choshen Mishpat* 104, cited in *Pischei Teshuvah, Choshen Mishpat* 231:4; and *Nesivos HaMishpat* and other commentaries there for further discussion.

יד. הַנּוֹתֵן מָעוֹת לַחֲבֵרוֹ לִקְנוֹת לוֹ קַרְקַע אוֹ מִטַּלְטְלִין וְהָלַךְ הַשָּׁלִיחַ וְקָנָה אֶת הַחֵפֶץ בִּמְעוֹתָיו בִּשְׁבִיל עַצְמוֹ, הֲרֵי זֶה רַמַּאי[20]. וְאִם קְנָאוֹ מִמָּעוֹת שֶׁל הַמְשַׁלֵּחַ, מְחוּיָּב לִיתְּנוֹ לוֹ, אַף עַל פִּי שֶׁקְּנָאוֹ לְעַצְמוֹ.

טו. מִי[21] שֶׁנָּתַן אֲפִילוּ רַק מִקְצָת דָּמִים עַל הַמִּקָּח, אוֹ שֶׁרָשַׁם עַל הַמִּקָּח סִימָן בִּפְנֵי הַמּוֹכֵר, אוֹ שֶׁאָמַר לוֹ הַמּוֹכֵר רְשׁוֹם מִקָּחֲךָ, אַף עַל פִּי שֶׁהוּא בְּעִנְיָן שֶׁלֹּא קָנָה בָּזֶה[22], מִכָּל מָקוֹם כָּל הַחוֹזֵר בּוֹ, בֵּין הַלּוֹקֵחַ בֵּין הַמּוֹכֵר, לֹא עָשָׂה מַעֲשֵׂה יִשְׂרָאֵל, וְחַיָּיב לְקַבֵּל "מִי שֶׁפָּרַע", דְּהַיְינוּ שֶׁאוֹרְרִין אוֹתוֹ בְּבֵית דִּין וְאוֹמְרִים: "מִי שֶׁפָּרַע מֵאַנְשֵׁי

---

§14 הַנּוֹתֵן מָעוֹת לַחֲבֵרוֹ If **one gives money to his fellow** Jew לִקְנוֹת לוֹ קַרְקַע אוֹ מִטַּלְטְלִין — and appoints him to act as his agent **to purchase land or movable objects,** וְהָלַךְ הַשָּׁלִיחַ וְקָנָה אֶת הַחֵפֶץ בִּמְעוֹתָיו בִּשְׁבִיל עַצְמוֹ — and **the agent went and purchased the item for himself, with his own money,** הֲרֵי זֶה רַמַּאי — **this** agent **is** deemed **a deceitful person.**[20] וְאִם קְנָאוֹ מִמָּעוֹת שֶׁל הַמְשַׁלֵּחַ — However, **if he bought it with the money of the one who sent** him, מְחוּיָּב לִיתְּנוֹ לוֹ — **he must give it to him,** אַף עַל פִּי שֶׁקְּנָאוֹ לְעַצְמוֹ — **even if he had bought it for himself.**

§15 In order to transfer ownership of any property, whether through a sale or a gift, a formal act of acquisition (*kinyan*) must be made.[21] Even if a sale has been agreed upon and a price set, in the absence of a *kinyan*, the transaction can be reversed. Nevertheless, after the parties have reached a certain point in their understanding that the sale will be carried out, it is inappropriate to renege on that commitment. The level of obligation that each party has to carry through on the transaction depends on the stage at which one wishes to withdraw, as explained in the following *se'ifim*.

מִי שֶׁנָּתַן אֲפִילוּ רַק מִקְצָת דָּמִים עַל הַמִּקָּח — When **someone paid even only part of the price of the purchase,** אוֹ שֶׁרָשַׁם עַל הַמִּקָּח סִימָן — **or marked the purchase with an** identifying **mark** בִּפְנֵי הַמּוֹכֵר — **in the presence of the seller** (who did not object), אוֹ שֶׁאָמַר לוֹ הַמּוֹכֵר רְשׁוֹם מִקָּחֲךָ — **or if the seller told him "mark your purchase,"** אַף עַל פִּי שֶׁהוּא בְּעִנְיָן שֶׁלֹּא קָנָה בָּזֶה — then, **even if** the action that he took **was** performed **in a manner that it does not effect a *kinyan*** (transfer of the property),[22] מִכָּל מָקוֹם — **nevertheless,** כָּל הַחוֹזֵר בּוֹ — **anyone who reneges** on his commitment and withdraws from the transaction, בֵּין הַלּוֹקֵחַ בֵּין הַמּוֹכֵר — regardless of **whether** it is **the buyer or the seller** who withdraws, לֹא עָשָׂה מַעֲשֵׂה יִשְׂרָאֵל — **has not acted in a manner befitting a Jew,** וְחַיָּיב לְקַבֵּל "מִי שֶׁפָּרַע" — **and must receive** the curse of *mi shepara*, ***He Who demanded retribution*** דְּהַיְינוּ — **That is,** שֶׁאוֹרְרִין אוֹתוֹ בְּבֵית דִּין — **that they curse him in *beis din*** (Rabbinical court), וְאוֹמְרִים — **saying:** "מִי שֶׁפָּרַע מֵאַנְשֵׁי

---

20. Since the agent used his own money, the acquisition of the item for himself is effective. Nevertheless, he is deemed a deceitful person for reneging on his commitment to make the purchase on behalf of the one who sent him and purchasing it for himself instead.

21. Different types of *kinyanim* are used to effect the transfer of ownership of real estate and to effect the transfer of movable objects; see *Choshen Mishpat*: 190:1, 195:1, and 198:1.

22. That is, in a place where the custom is that marking the merchandise does not effect a *kinyan* (see *Choshen Mishpat* 201:1 and 204:6).

דּוֹר הַמַּבּוּל וּמֵאַנְשֵׁי דּוֹר הַפַּלָּגָה וּמֵאַנְשֵׁי סְדוֹם וַעֲמוֹרָה וּמִמִּצְרַיִם שֶׁטָּבְעוּ בַּיָּם[23], הוּא יִפָּרַע מִמִּי שֶׁאֵינוֹ עוֹמֵד בְּדִיבּוּרוֹ"[24].

טז. וְרָאוּי לוֹ לְאָדָם לַעֲמוֹד לוֹ בְּדִיבּוּרוֹ, שֶׁאֲפִילוּ לֹא נָתַן עֲדַיִין מָעוֹת וְלֹא רָשַׁם אֶת הַדָּבָר וְלֹא נִגְמַר הַקִּנְיָן, אִם הוּשְׁווּ עַל הַמְּחִיר, אֵין לְשׁוּם אֶחָד מֵהֶם לַחֲזוֹר. וּמִי שֶׁהוּא חוֹזֵר, בֵּין הַלּוֹקֵחַ וּבֵין הַמּוֹכֵר, הֲרֵי זֶה מִמְּחוּסְּרֵי אֲמָנָה, וְאֵין רוּחַ חֲכָמִים נוֹחָה הֵימֶנּוּ[25], כִּי רָאוּי לְאִישׁ יִשְׂרָאֵל לַעֲמוֹד בְּדִיבּוּרוֹ, כְּמוֹ שֶׁנֶּאֱמַר (צפניה ג, יג) "שְׁאֵרִית יִשְׂרָאֵל לֹא יַעֲשׂוּ עַוְלָה וְלֹא יְדַבְּרוּ כָזָב". וִירֵא שָׁמַיִם יֵשׁ לוֹ לְקַיֵּים אֲפִילוּ מַחֲשֶׁבֶת לִבּוֹ[26], שֶׁאִם חָשַׁב וְגָמַר בְּלִבּוֹ[27] לִמְכּוֹר לוֹ בְּסְכוּם זֶה וְהַלָּה לֹא יָדַע מִמַּחֲשַׁבְתּוֹ וְהוֹסִיף לוֹ עַל סְכוּם זֶה, לֹא יִקַּח מִמֶּנּוּ כִּי אִם סְכוּם זֶה

דּוֹר הַמַּבּוּל — **He Who exacted retribution from the people** who sinned **during the generation of the Flood,** **וּמֵאַנְשֵׁי דּוֹר הַפַּלָּגָה** — **and from the people** who sinned **during the generation of the Dispersion,** **וּמֵאַנְשֵׁי סְדוֹם וַעֲמוֹרָה** — **and from the people of Sodom and Gomorrah,** **וּמִמִּצְרַיִם שֶׁטָּבְעוּ בַּיָּם** — **and from the Egyptians who drowned in the sea,** due to their evil acts,[23] **הוּא יִפָּרַע** — **He will exact retribution** **מִמִּי שֶׁאֵינוֹ עוֹמֵד בְּדִיבּוּרוֹ"** — **from one who does not stand by his word.**[24]

§16 **וְרָאוּי לוֹ לְאָדָם לַעֲמוֹד לוֹ בְּדִיבּוּרוֹ** — **It is** indeed **appropriate for a person to stand by his words,** even if none of the above actions has been taken, **שֶׁאֲפִילוּ לֹא נָתַן עֲדַיִין מָעוֹת** — **i.e., even if he had not yet given any money,** **וְלֹא רָשַׁם אֶת הַדָּבָר וְלֹא נִגְמַר הַקִּנְיָן** — **and he had not marked the item, and the transaction had not been completed;** **אִם הוּשְׁווּ עַל הַמְּחִיר** — nevertheless, **if they have** already **agreed upon a price,** **אֵין לְשׁוּם אֶחָד מֵהֶם לַחֲזוֹר** — **neither of them should withdraw** from the transaction. **וּמִי שֶׁהוּא חוֹזֵר** — **And one who does withdraw,** **בֵּין הַלּוֹקֵחַ וּבֵין הַמּוֹכֵר** — **whether** it be **the buyer or the seller,** **הֲרֵי זֶה מִמְּחוּסְּרֵי אֲמָנָה** — **is** considered to be **among the untrustworthy,** **וְאֵין רוּחַ חֲכָמִים נוֹחָה הֵימֶנּוּ** — **and the Sages are not pleased with him.**[25] **כִּי רָאוּי לְאִישׁ יִשְׂרָאֵל לַעֲמוֹד בְּדִיבּוּרוֹ** — **For it is appropriate that a Jewish person stand by his words,** **כְּמוֹ שֶׁנֶּאֱמַר** — **as** the verse **states** (*Zephaniah* 3:13): **"שְׁאֵרִית יִשְׂרָאֵל לֹא יַעֲשׂוּ עַוְלָה וְלֹא יְדַבְּרוּ כָזָב"** — ***The remnant of Israel will not commit corruption, they will not speak falsehood.*** **וִירֵא שָׁמַיִם יֵשׁ לוֹ לְקַיֵּים אֲפִילוּ מַחֲשֶׁבֶת לִבּוֹ** — Moreover, **a God-fearing** Jew **should uphold even the thought** that had not been spoken but remained in **his heart.**[26] **שֶׁאִם חָשַׁב וְגָמַר בְּלִבּוֹ לִמְכּוֹר לוֹ בְּסְכוּם זֶה** — **That is, if** a **seller made an unspoken decision**[27] **to sell** an item **to** another **for a** specific **sum,** **וְהַלָּה לֹא יָדַע מִמַּחֲשַׁבְתּוֹ וְהוֹסִיף לוֹ עַל סְכוּם זֶה** — **and the other** (i.e., the one to whom he intended to sell) **did not know** of **his thoughts and offered him more than that sum,** **לֹא יִקַּח מִמֶּנּוּ כִּי אִם סְכוּם זֶה**

---

23. This is a listing of some of the more prominent examples in history when Hashem took vengeance on those who defied His will (see *Sma* 204:8). [The accounts of these punishments can be found in *Bereishis* Chs. 6-8; 11:1-9; Ch. 19, and *Shemos* Ch. 14.]

24. *Rama* (204:4) writes that *beis din* curses the person specifically, i.e., "He will exact retribution from *you* if you do not keep your word."

25. In this case, since no formal action has been taken, one is not liable to be cursed for withdrawing from the agreement.

26. Certainly a silent commitment is not binding, and one is not considered untrustworthy for failing to abide by it. However, a higher level of integrity requires that a person uphold even unspoken commitments.

27. Lit., *thought and concluded in his heart.*

שֶׁגָּמַר בְּלִבּוֹ, לְקַיֵּים מַה שֶּׁנֶּאֱמַר (תהלים טו, ב) "וְדֹבֵר אֱמֶת בִּלְבָבוֹ"[28]. וְכֵן הַלּוֹקֵחַ שֶׁגָּמַר בְּלִבּוֹ לִקְנוֹת בִּסְכוּם כָּךְ וְכָךְ, אֵין לוֹ לַחֲזוֹר בּוֹ. וְכֵן כָּל כַּיּוֹצֵא בָּזֶה בִּשְׁאָר דְּבָרִים שֶׁבֵּין אָדָם לַחֲבֵירוֹ יֵשׁ לוֹ לְקַיֵּים מַחְשְׁבוֹת לִבּוֹ אִם גָּמַר בְּלִבּוֹ לַעֲשׂוֹת אֵיזֶה טוֹבָה וְיֵשׁ בְּיָדוֹ לַעֲשׂוֹתָהּ. אֲבָל צָרְכֵי עַצְמוֹ, כֹּל שֶׁאֵין בָּהֶם סְרָךְ מִצְוָה[29] אֵין צָרִיךְ לְקַיֵּים, אֲפִילוּ מוֹצָא שְׂפָתָיו[30].

יז. וְכֵן מִי שֶׁאוֹמֵר לַחֲבֵרוֹ לִיתֵּן לוֹ אֵיזֶה מַתָּנָה קְטַנָּה, שֶׁזֶּה סָמַךְ דַּעְתּוֹ שֶׁבְּוַדַּאי יִתֵּן לוֹ, אִם חָזַר וְלֹא נָתַן לוֹ, הֲרֵי זֶה מִמְּחוּסְּרֵי אֲמָנָה. אֲבָל מַתָּנָה מְרוּבָּה אֵין בָּהּ חֶסְרוֹן אֲמָנָה, שֶׁהֲרֵי זֶה לֹא סָמַךְ דַּעְתּוֹ עַל זֶה. וּמִכָּל מָקוֹם בְּשָׁעָה שֶׁהוּא אוֹמֵר לִיתֵּן לוֹ צָרִיךְ לִהְיוֹת בְּדַעַת גְּמוּרָה, וְלֹא יְהֵא בְדַעְתּוֹ לְשַׁנּוֹת[31], כִּי לְדַבֵּר אֶחָד בְּפֶה

שֶׁגָּמַר בְּלִבּוֹ — he should not take the amount offered; **rather,** he should accept **only the amount that he had decided** to take. **לְקַיֵּים מַה שֶּׁנֶּאֱמַר** — He should feel bound to uphold his intentions, so as **to observe that which is written** (*Tehillim* 15:2) regarding the criteria for one to be assured a place in Heaven: **"וְדֹבֵר אֱמֶת בִּלְבָבוֹ"** — *and speaks truth within his heart.*[28] **וְכֵן הַלּוֹקֵחַ שֶׁגָּמַר בְּלִבּוֹ לִקְנוֹת בִּסְכוּם כָּךְ וְכָךְ** — **Likewise, a buyer who has made an unspoken decision to buy** an item **for a** specific **sum** **אֵין לוֹ לַחֲזוֹר בּוֹ** — **should not reverse himself.**

וְכֵן כָּל כַּיּוֹצֵא בָּזֶה בִּשְׁאָר דְּבָרִים שֶׁבֵּין אָדָם לַחֲבֵירוֹ — Likewise, in all similar situations of interactions **between man and his fellow,** **יֵשׁ לוֹ לְקַיֵּים מַחְשְׁבוֹת לִבּוֹ** — **one should uphold that which he concludes in his heart;** **אִם גָּמַר בְּלִבּוֹ לַעֲשׂוֹת אֵיזֶה טוֹבָה** — for example, **if he had made an unspoken decision to do some favor** for another person, **וְיֵשׁ בְּיָדוֹ לַעֲשׂוֹתָהּ — and he is able to do it,** he should. **אֲבָל צָרְכֵי עַצְמוֹ — However,** in regard to **his own needs,** **כֹּל שֶׁאֵין בָּהֶם סְרָךְ מִצְוָה — any** time **they do not involve mitzvah ramifications,**[29] **אֵין צָרִיךְ לְקַיֵּים אֲפִילוּ מוֹצָא שְׂפָתָיו — he is not required to uphold even that which was expressed by his lips.**[30]

§17 **וְכֵן מִי שֶׁאוֹמֵר לַחֲבֵרוֹ לִיתֵּן לוֹ אֵיזֶה מַתָּנָה קְטַנָּה — Similarly, one who tells his fellow that he will give him some small gift,** **שֶׁזֶּה סָמַךְ דַּעְתּוֹ שֶׁבְּוַדַּאי יִתֵּן לוֹ** — **since** (due to the small amount involved) the one who was told about the gift **would assume that** the one who indicated his intent to give the gift **would certainly give it to him,** **אִם חָזַר וְלֹא נָתַן לוֹ, הֲרֵי זֶה מִמְּחוּסְּרֵי אֲמָנָה — if** the giver **reneges and does not give it, he is** included **among the untrustworthy.** **אֲבָל מַתָּנָה מְרוּבָּה — However,** if he had said that he would give **a large gift** and neglected to do so, **אֵין בָּהּ חֶסְרוֹן אֲמָנָה — it is not** considered **untrustworthy** behavior, **שֶׁהֲרֵי זֶה לֹא סָמַךְ דַּעְתּוֹ עַל זֶה — for the one** who was promised the gift **does not rely on this** statement of intent, i.e., he is not totally confident that he will receive it. **וּמִכָּל מָקוֹם — Nevertheless,** although a person would not rely upon the promise of a large gift, **בְּשָׁעָה שֶׁהוּא אוֹמֵר לִיתֵּן לוֹ — at the time one says that he will give another** a gift, even a large one, **צָרִיךְ לִהְיוֹת בְּדַעַת גְּמוּרָה — it must be with a full intent** to give the gift, **וְלֹא יְהֵא בְדַעְתּוֹ לְשַׁנּוֹת — without any intention of changing** his mind.[31] **כִּי לְדַבֵּר אֶחָד בְּפֶה**

---

28. I.e., even what is in his heart must remain true.

29. See below, 67:4, which states that one who expresses a decision to do a mitzvah is obligated to keep his word.

30. As long as he did not take an oath to do that thing; see *Siman* 67.

31. Although one is not considered untrust-

וְאֶחָד בְּלֵב אָסוּר מִן הַתּוֹרָה, שֶׁנֶּאֱמַר (ויקרא יט, לו) "אֵיפַת צֶדֶק וְהִין צֶדֶק יִהְיֶה (לך) [לָכֶם]"[32]. מַה תַּלְמוּד לוֹמַר "הִין צֶדֶק", וַהֲלֹא הִין בִּכְלַל אֵיפָה הוּא[33]? אֶלָּא שֶׁיְּהֵא הֵן שֶׁלְּךָ וְלַאו שֶׁלְּךָ צֶדֶק[34]. וְכָל זֹאת לְעָשִׁיר, אֲבָל הָאוֹמֵר לִיתֵּן לְעָנִי, בֵּין מַתָּנָה מוּעֶטֶת בֵּין מַתָּנָה מְרוּבָּה, אֵינוֹ יָכוֹל לַחֲזוֹר בּוֹ מִן הַדִּין[35], מִפְּנֵי שֶׁנַּעֲשָׂה כְּמוֹ נֶדֶר, וַאֲפִילוּ גָּמַר בְּלִבּוֹ לִיתֵּן, צָרִיךְ לְקַיֵּים מַחֲשַׁבְתּוֹ[36].

יח. הָרוֹצֶה לִמְכּוֹר קַרְקַע אוֹ בַּיִת וּבָאוּ שְׁנַיִם — כָּל אֶחָד אוֹמֵר "אֲנִי אֶקַּח בְּדָמִים

וְאֶחָד בְּלֵב — **For expressing one** thing **verbally while meaning another** thing **in his heart** **אָסוּר מִן הַתּוֹרָה** — **is Biblically prohibited,** **שֶׁנֶּאֱמַר** — **as** the verse **states** (*Vayikra* 19:36): **"אֵיפַת צֶדֶק וְהִין צֶדֶק יִהְיֶה (לך) [לָכֶם]"** — ***You shall have** just scales, just weights,* ***a just*** (i.e., correct) ***eiphah and a just*** (i.e., correct) ***hin.***[32] **מַה תַּלְמוּד לוֹמַר "הִין צֶדֶק"** — **What is** the purpose of **the verse stating:** ***a just hin*****?** **וַהֲלֹא הִין בִּכְלַל אֵיפָה הוּא** — **Surely the** injunction to have a correct ***hin*** **is included in the** injunction to have a correct ***eiphah*** mentioned earlier in that verse![33] **אֶלָּא שֶׁיְּהֵא הֵן שֶׁלְּךָ וְלַאו שֶׁלְּךָ צֶדֶק** — The Sages therefore explained that the word *hin* is not simply referring to a measure, **rather,** it is teaches **that your "yes"** (*hein*) **and your "no,"** must **be correct** [i.e., truthful] (*Bava Metzia* 49a).[34]

וְכָל זֹאת לְעָשִׁיר — **All of the** above discussion (i.e., the difference between a large and small gift) **refers** only **to** a promise that has been made **to a wealthy person** (i.e., one who is not poor). **אֲבָל הָאוֹמֵר לִיתֵּן לְעָנִי** — **However, one who says** that he will **give** a gift **to a poor person,** **בֵּין מַתָּנָה מוּעֶטֶת בֵּין מַתָּנָה מְרוּבָּה** — then, **regardless of whether** the commitment was for **a small gift or** for **a large gift,** **אֵינוֹ יָכוֹל לַחֲזוֹר בּוֹ מִן הַדִּין** — **he may not renege** even **according to** the strict letter **of the law,**[35] **מִפְּנֵי שֶׁנַּעֲשָׂה כְּמוֹ נֶדֶר** — **for such a commitment** to give charity **is considered as a vow.** **וַאֲפִילוּ גָּמַר בְּלִבּוֹ לִיתֵּן** — **And even if one has** only **made an** unspoken **decision to give,** **צָרִיךְ לְקַיֵּים מַחֲשַׁבְתּוֹ** — **he must uphold his intention.**[36]

§18 **הָרוֹצֶה לִמְכּוֹר קַרְקַע אוֹ בַּיִת** — If **one wishes to sell land or a house,** **וּבָאוּ שְׁנַיִם** — **and two** prospective buyers **come** **כָּל אֶחָד אוֹמֵר "אֲנִי אֶקַּח בְּדָמִים**

---

worthy if he fails to abide by a statement that he will give a large gift, it is not permissible to make such statements without any intention of upholding them.

32. An *eiphah* and a *hin* are both units of volume. An *eiphah* is equivalent to 72 *lugin*, while a *hin* is equivalent to 12 *lugin* (*Rashi* to *Bava Metzia* 49a s.v. הין).

33. Considering that the Torah is concerned about the slightest deviation from a large measure such as an *eiphah*, surely it is concerned about a deviation from a smaller measure such as a *hin* (since the deviation will be proportionally larger). Why then does the Torah mention a *hin* in addition to an *eiphah*? (*Ritva* to *Bava Metzia* 49a).

34. The word הִין (*hin*), can be read like הֵין (*hein*), which means "yes" in Aramaic. Accordingly, the Torah's mention of "a correct *hin*" can be interpreted as teaching: When one says "yes" or "no," he should make sure that it is correct; i.e., when making a verbal commitment one must be sincere.

35. I.e., here it is not merely pious behavior to keep one's word, but it is an absolute requirement.

36. Although generally a vow is binding only if spoken (below, 67:6), an unspoken commitment to charity is also considered a vow, and must be fulfilled (*Rama, Yoreh Deah* 258:13). For laws of vows and oaths, see below, *Siman* 67.

אֵלּוּ״, וְאֵין אֶחָד מֵהֶם בַּעַל הַמֶּצֶר[37] — אִם הָיָה אֶחָד מֵהֶם מִיּוֹשְׁבֵי עִירוֹ וְהַשֵּׁנִי מֵעִיר אַחֶרֶת, בֶּן עִירוֹ קוֹדֵם. הָיוּ שְׁנֵיהֶם מִיּוֹשְׁבֵי עִירוֹ וְאֶחָד מֵהֶם שְׁכֵנוֹ, שְׁכֵנוֹ קוֹדֵם. וְאִם הַשֵּׁנִי הוּא חֲבֵרוֹ הָרָגִיל עִמּוֹ וּשְׁכֵנוֹ אֵינוֹ רָגִיל עִמּוֹ כְּלָל, חֲבֵרוֹ קוֹדֵם. הָיָה אֶחָד מֵהֶם חֲבֵרוֹ וְאֶחָד מֵהֶם קְרוֹבוֹ, חֲבֵרוֹ קוֹדֵם, שֶׁנֶּאֱמַר (משלי כז, י) ״טוֹב שָׁכֵן קָרוֹב מֵאָח רָחוֹק״[38]. אֲבָל לִשְׁאָר כָּל אָדָם קְרוֹבוֹ קוֹדֵם, חוּץ מִתַּלְמִיד חָכָם שֶׁקּוֹדֵם וַאֲפִילּוּ לִשְׁכֵנוֹ וַחֲבֵרוֹ הָרָגִיל אֶצְלוֹ[39]. אֲבָל אִם הָיָה אֶחָד מֵהֶם בַּעַל הַמֶּצֶר, הוּא קוֹדֵם לְכוּלָּם[40]. אֲפִילּוּ לְאַחַר שֶׁמְּכָרוֹ לְאַחֵר יָכוֹל בַּעַל הַמֶּצֶר לִיתֵּן אֶת הַדָּמִים לְהַלּוֹקֵחַ

״אֵלּוּ״ — and **each one says, "I will buy it for this** amount of **money,"** (i.e., they are both willing to pay the same price), **וְאֵין אֶחָד מֵהֶם בַּעַל הַמֶּצֶר — and neither of them is the owner of** the property that shares **the boundary** of the property being sold,[37] **אִם הָיָה אֶחָד מֵהֶם מִיּוֹשְׁבֵי עִירוֹ** — then, **if one of them was a resident of** the seller's **city** **וְהַשֵּׁנִי מֵעִיר אַחֶרֶת — and the second was from another city, בֶּן עִירוֹ קוֹדֵם — the resident of his city has precedence. הָיוּ שְׁנֵיהֶם מִיּוֹשְׁבֵי עִירוֹ — If they were both residents of** the seller's **city, וְאֶחָד מֵהֶם שְׁכֵנוֹ — and one of them is his neighbor, שְׁכֵנוֹ קוֹדֵם — then his neighbor has precedence. וְאִם הַשֵּׁנִי הוּא חֲבֵרוֹ הָרָגִיל עִמּוֹ** — However, **if the second** prospective buyer **is a friend with whom he is on familiar terms, וּשְׁכֵנוֹ אֵינוֹ רָגִיל עִמּוֹ כְּלָל — and he is not on familiar terms with his neighbor at all, חֲבֵרוֹ קוֹדֵם** — then **his friend has precedence. הָיָה אֶחָד מֵהֶם חֲבֵרוֹ** — If **one of them is his friend וְאֶחָד מֵהֶם קְרוֹבוֹ — and the other is his relative, חֲבֵרוֹ קוֹדֵם** — then **his friend has precedence, שֶׁנֶּאֱמַר — as** the verse **states** (*Mishlei* 27:10): **״טוֹב שָׁכֵן קָרוֹב מֵאָח רָחוֹק״ — *A close neighbor is better than a distant brother.***[38] **אֲבָל לִשְׁאָר כָּל אָדָם — However, in regard to all other people קְרוֹבוֹ קוֹדֵם — his relative has precedence, חוּץ מִתַּלְמִיד חָכָם — except for a Torah scholar, שֶׁקּוֹדֵם — for** a Torah scholar **has precedence, וַאֲפִילּוּ לִשְׁכֵנוֹ וַחֲבֵרוֹ הָרָגִיל אֶצְלוֹ — even over his neighbor or his friend with whom he is on familiar terms.**[39]

אֲבָל אִם הָיָה אֶחָד מֵהֶם בַּעַל הַמֶּצֶר — However, if one of the prospective buyers **is the owner of** the property situated on **a boundary** of the property being sold (i.e., he owns an adjacent property), **הוּא קוֹדֵם לְכוּלָּם — he has precedence over them all** (i.e., over the neighbor, the close friend, and even over the Torah scholar).[40] **אֲפִילּוּ לְאַחַר שֶׁמְּכָרוֹ לְאַחֵר — Moreover, even after** the seller **sold it to someone else, יָכוֹל בַּעַל הַמֶּצֶר לִיתֵּן אֶת הַדָּמִים לְהַלּוֹקֵחַ — the owner of the** property that is on the **boundary**

37. One who owns such a property has special rights, as explained later in this *se'if.*

38. A "close neighbor" refers to a friend. If the neighbor is not also a friend, the relative has precedence (*Rama, Choshen Mishpat* 175:50 and 253:29).

39. The preceding guidelines are recommendations and are not enforceable (*Rashi* to *Bava Metzia* 108b).

40. There is a great advantage for a person to own two adjacent properties rather than two non-adjacent ones. [In the case of a farm, being able to work both fields together makes it easier to plant and plow the fields. Similarly, owning two adjacent lots enables one to combine them and build a larger house.] Thus, for the neighbor, this particular property offers a tremendous benefit, while for an outside buyer, there is nothing special about this particular property; he can just as well purchase an equivalent property elsewhere. Halachah therefore gives the neighbor special rights to buy that property.

וּלְסַלֵּק אוֹתוֹ. וַאֲפִילוּ הַלּוֹקֵחַ הוּא תַלְמִיד חָכָם, וְשָׁכֵן, וְקָרוֹב לַמּוֹכֵר, וְהַמִּצְרָן הוּא עַם הָאָרֶץ, וְרָחוֹק מִן הַמּוֹכֵר[41], הַמִּצְרָן קוֹדֵם[42] וּמְסַלֵּק אֶת הַלּוֹקֵחַ[43]. וְכָל קְדִימוֹת אֵלּוּ מִצְוֹת חֲכָמִים הֵם, לְקַיֵּים מַה שֶּׁנֶּאֱמַר (דברים ו, יח) **״וְעָשִׂיתָ הַיָּשָׁר וְהַטּוֹב בְּעֵינֵי ה׳ (אלהיך)״.**

---

can give money to the buyer, וּלְסַלֵּק אוֹתוֹ — and remove him from the property. **וַאֲפִילוּ הַלּוֹקֵחַ הוּא תַלְמִיד חָכָם, וְשָׁכֵן, וְקָרוֹב לַמּוֹכֵר — Even if the buyer is a Torah scholar and a neighbor and a close** friend **of the seller, וְהַמִּצְרָן הוּא עַם הָאָרֶץ, וְרָחוֹק מִן הַמּוֹכֵר — and the owner of the adjacent property is an unlearned person and has no connection**[41] **to the seller, הַמִּצְרָן קוֹדֵם — the owner of the adjacent property has precedence,**[42] **וּמְסַלֵּק אֶת הַלּוֹקֵחַ — and can remove the buyer** from the property.[43]

וְכָל קְדִימוֹת אֵלּוּ — All of these levels **of precedence מִצְוֹת חֲכָמִים הֵם — were instructed by the Sages, לְקַיֵּים מַה שֶּׁנֶּאֱמַר** — in order **to fulfill that which is stated** (*Devarim* 6:18): **״וְעָשִׂיתָ הַיָּשָׁר וְהַטּוֹב בְּעֵינֵי ה׳ (אלהיך)״ — *You shall do what is fair and good in the eyes of HASHEM.***

---

41. Literally, *distant from*, i.e., he is neither a relative nor a close friend of the seller.

42. Unlike the order of precedence outlined in the beginning of this *se'if* (see note 39), the right of the owner of a bordering property is enforceable, and the purchaser can be forced to relinquish the property.

43. The laws regarding the right of the owner of the adjacent property are many and complex. They can be found in *Choshen Mishpat*, *Siman* 175.

321 PROHIBITION OF VERBAL ABUSE AND DECEIVING PEOPLE — SIMAN 63:1

סימן סג

אָסוּר לְהוֹנוֹת בִּדְבָרִים וְלִגְנוֹב דַּעַת הַבְּרִיּוֹת

וּבוֹ ה׳ סְעִיפִים

א. כְּשֵׁם שֶׁאוֹנָאָה אֲסוּרָה בְּמִקָּח וּמִמְכָּר, כָּךְ אֲסוּרָה אוֹנָאָה בִדְבָרִים[1], שֶׁנֶּאֱמַר (ויקרא כה, יז) "וְלֹא תוֹנוּ אִישׁ אֶת עֲמִיתוֹ וְיָרֵאתָ מֵאֱלֹהֶיךָ", זוֹ אוֹנָאַת דְּבָרִים[2]. וּגְדוֹלָה אוֹנָאַת דְּבָרִים מֵאוֹנָאַת מָמוֹן, שֶׁזֶּה נִיתָּן לְהִשָּׁבוֹן וְזֶה לֹא נִיתָּן לְהִשָּׁבוֹן[3], זֶה בְּמָמוֹנוֹ וְזֶה בְּגוּפוֹ[4]. וְהַצּוֹעֵק עַל אוֹנָאַת דְּבָרִים נַעֲנֶה מִיָּד. וְצָרִיךְ לִיזָּהֵר בְּיוֹתֵר מֵאוֹנָאַת אִשְׁתּוֹ שֶׁלֹּא לְצַעֲרָהּ בִּדְבָרִים, לְפִי שֶׁהָאִשָּׁה רַכָּה בְטֶבַע וְעַל צַעַר מְעַט הִיא בוֹכָה, וְהַשֵּׁם יִתְבָּרֵךְ מַקְפִּיד עַל הַדְּמָעוֹת, וְשַׁעֲרֵי דְמָעוֹת לֹא נִנְעֲלוּ[5].

SIMAN 63

THE PROHIBITION OF VERBAL ABUSE AND DECEIVING PEOPLE

CONTAINING 5 *SE'IFIM*

§1 The Severity of Hurting Verbally / **§2-3** Examples of Hurting Verbally / **§4-5** The Prohibition of Deception

§1 **כְּשֵׁם שֶׁאוֹנָאָה אֲסוּרָה בְּמִקָּח וּמִמְכָּר** — **Just as harming** another **is forbidden in business** (e.g., price fraud), as detailed in the previous *Siman*, **כָּךְ אֲסוּרָה אוֹנָאָה בִדְבָרִים** — **so too it is forbidden to hurt** another person **verbally,**[1] **שֶׁנֶּאֱמַר** — **as the** verse **states** (*Vayikra* 25:17): **"וְלֹא תוֹנוּ אִישׁ אֶת עֲמִיתוֹ וְיָרֵאתָ מֵאֱלֹהֶיךָ"** — ***Each of you shall not aggrieve his fellow, and you shall fear your God;*** **זוֹ אוֹנָאַת דְּבָרִים** — **this refers to hurting verbally.**[2] **וּגְדוֹלָה אוֹנָאַת דְּבָרִים מֵאוֹנָאַת מָמוֹן** — **Hurting verbally is a greater** sin **than monetary fraud,** **שֶׁזֶּה נִיתָּן לְהִשָּׁבוֹן** — **for** with regard to **this**, i.e., monetary fraud, **restitution is possible,** **וְזֶה לֹא נִיתָּן לְהִשָּׁבוֹן** — **and** with regard to **this**, i.e., hurting verbally, **restitution is not possible.**[3] **זֶה בְּמָמוֹנוֹ** — **This,** i.e., monetary fraud, affects only the victim's **money,** **וְזֶה בְּגוּפוֹ** — **whereas this,** i.e., hurting verbally, affects the victim's very **self.**[4]

וְהַצּוֹעֵק עַל אוֹנָאַת דְּבָרִים — **One who cries out** to Hashem **due to** the pain of **being hurt verbally** **נַעֲנֶה מִיָּד** — **is answered immediately.** **וְצָרִיךְ לִיזָּהֵר בְּיוֹתֵר מֵאוֹנָאַת אִשְׁתּוֹ** — **One must be exceedingly wary of** verbally **hurting his wife,** **שֶׁלֹּא לְצַעֲרָהּ בִּדְבָרִים** — and take care **not to cause her pain with words,** **לְפִי שֶׁהָאִשָּׁה רַכָּה בְטֶבַע** — **because a woman has a soft nature** **וְעַל צַעַר מְעַט הִיא בוֹכָה** — **and she** is liable **to cry** even **from a small** amount of **pain.** **וְהַשֵּׁם יִתְבָּרֵךְ מַקְפִּיד עַל הַדְּמָעוֹת** — This is of utmost severity, because **Hashem, may He be blessed, is strict** when one causes another to shed **tears,** **וְשַׁעֲרֵי דְמָעוֹת לֹא נִנְעֲלוּ** — **and the** heavenly **gates of tears have not been locked.**[5]

---

1. Examples of such prohibited behavior will appear in the *se'ifim* that follow.
2. See *Bava Metzia* 58b.
3. Money can be replaced, but the pain caused by a verbal wrong lingers on and often cannot be erased.
4. Many people feel more pain from hurtful words than from monetary loss (see *Sefer HaChinuch* §338).
5. The Gemara writes (*Bava Metzia* 59a) that

PROHIBITION OF VERBAL ABUSE AND DECEIVING PEOPLE — SIMAN 63:2 322

ב. כֵּיצַד הִיא אוֹנָאַת דְּבָרִים? לֹא יֹאמַר לַחֲבֵרוֹ "בְּכַמָּה אַתָּה רוֹצֶה לִיתֵּן חֵפֶץ זֶה", וְהוּא אֵינוֹ רוֹצֶה לִקְנוֹתוֹ[6]. הָיָה אֶחָד מְבַקֵּשׁ לִקְנוֹת תְּבוּאָה, לֹא יֹאמַר לוֹ "לֵךְ אֵצֶל פְּלוֹנִי", וְהוּא יוֹדֵעַ שֶׁאֵין לוֹ לִמְכּוֹר. אִם הָיָה חֲבֵרוֹ בַּעַל תְּשׁוּבָה, לֹא יֹאמַר לוֹ "זְכוֹר מַעֲשֶׂיךָ הָרִאשׁוֹנִים". אִם בָּאוּ יִסּוּרִים עַל חֲבֵרוֹ רַחֲמָנָא לִצְלַן, לֹא יֹאמַר לוֹ כְּדֶרֶךְ שֶׁאָמְרוּ חַבְרֵי אִיּוֹב לְאִיּוֹב[7] (איוב ד, ו-ז) "הֲלֹא יִרְאָתְךָ כִּסְלָתֶךָ ... זְכָר נָא מִי הוּא נָקִי אָבָד"[8] (וְהֵם שֶׁאָמְרוּ לוֹ כֵּן מִפְּנֵי שֶׁהָיָה מְעַוֵּת דְּבָרִים כְּלַפֵּי הַשְׁגָּחַת הַשֵּׁם יִתְבָּרֵךְ וּמִדּוֹתָיו). אִם שָׁאֲלוּ מֵאִתּוֹ אֵיזֶה דְּבַר חָכְמָה, לֹא יֹאמַר לְמִי שֶׁאֵינוֹ יוֹדֵעַ אוֹתָהּ חָכְמָה

---

§2 כֵּיצַד הִיא אוֹנָאַת דְּבָרִים — **What is considered hurting verbally?** לֹא יֹאמַר לַחֲבֵרוֹ — **One should not say to his fellow,** "בְּכַמָּה אַתָּה רוֹצֶה לִיתֵּן חֵפֶץ זֶה" — **"At what price do you wish to sell** me **this item?,"** וְהוּא אֵינוֹ רוֹצֶה לִקְנוֹתוֹ — **when,** in fact, **he does not wish to purchase it.**[6] הָיָה אֶחָד מְבַקֵּשׁ לִקְנוֹת תְּבוּאָה — Or if **a person is seeking to purchase grain,** לֹא יֹאמַר לוֹ — **one should not say to him,** "לֵךְ אֵצֶל פְּלוֹנִי" — **"Go to So-and-so,"** וְהוּא יוֹדֵעַ שֶׁאֵין לוֹ לִמְכּוֹר — **when he knows that** the person to whom he is sending him **has no** grain **to sell.** אִם הָיָה חֲבֵרוֹ בַּעַל תְּשׁוּבָה — Or, **if one's fellow was a penitent,** לֹא יֹאמַר לוֹ — **he should not say to him,** "זְכוֹר מַעֲשֶׂיךָ הָרִאשׁוֹנִים" — **"Remember your past deeds."** אִם בָּאוּ יִסּוּרִים עַל חֲבֵרוֹ רַחֲמָנָא לִצְלַן — Or, **if one's fellow is beset by suffering, God forbid,** לֹא יֹאמַר לוֹ — **he should not say to him,** כְּדֶרֶךְ שֶׁאָמְרוּ חַבְרֵי אִיּוֹב לְאִיּוֹב — **in the way that Iyov's colleagues said to Iyov** (*Iyov* 4:6-7):[7] "הֲלֹא יִרְאָתְךָ כִּסְלָתֶךָ — ***Could not your fear [of Hashem] have given you your confidence ...*** זְכָר נָא מִי הוּא נָקִי אָבָד" — ***Remember, please, which innocent person ever perished?***[8] (וְהֵם שֶׁאָמְרוּ לוֹ כֵּן — Iyov's friends, who did in fact say that to him, did not intend to cause pain; rather, **they said this to him** only מִפְּנֵי שֶׁהָיָה מְעַוֵּת דְּבָרִים — **because he was distorting issues** כְּלַפֵּי הַשְׁגָּחַת הַשֵּׁם יִתְבָּרֵךְ וּמִדּוֹתָיו — **regarding** fundamentals of faith such as **the Providence and Attributes of Hashem, may He be blessed.)** אִם שָׁאֲלוּ מֵאִתּוֹ אֵיזֶה דְּבַר חָכְמָה — Or, another example, **if one is asked a question that** requires **knowledge** of a certain subject, לֹא יֹאמַר לְמִי שֶׁאֵינוֹ יוֹדֵעַ אוֹתָהּ חָכְמָה — **he should not say to someone**

---

from the time the Holy Temple was destroyed the "gates of prayer" were locked, but the "gates of tears" were not. That is, although prayers alone are no longer answered as quickly or as readily as before (see *Meiri* ad loc.), when Hashem sees the tears of the injured, He swiftly punishes the perpetrator.

6. Such a comment constitutes hurting verbally since the merchant suffers unnecessary pain upon having been led to believe that he had a customer when, in fact, none ever existed (see also *Meiri*, *Bava Metzia* 58b).

7. After Iyov was beset by many tragedies, his friend Eliphaz set out (with two other friends) to comfort him, but after hearing Iyov's bitter reaction to his tragedies (*Iyov* Ch. 3), Eliphaz chastised him (see *Bava Basra* 16a-b).

8. Eliphaz's message to Iyov was: You should have used your fear of God to find confidence and hope. Remember, truly innocent people are never utterly destroyed; if you were truly innocent, these tragedies would never have befallen you (based on *Tosafos to Bava Metzia* 58b s.v. הלא; see also *Maharsha* ad loc.). [Such harsh criticism is categorized as hurting verbally because a person suffering tragic loss lacks the capacity to react constructively if he is told that his troubles are a result of his own misdeeds. Accordingly, this type of criticism hurts the person for no useful purpose. If someone really wants to help one who is suffering, he can gently remind him to examine his deeds (see *Berachos* 5b).]

323 PROHIBITION OF VERBAL ABUSE AND DECEIVING PEOPLE — SIMAN 63:3-5

"מָה אַתָּה (תשוב) [תָּשִׁיב] בַּדָּבָר הַזֶּה[9]?" וְכֵן כָּל כַּיּוֹצֵא בִּדְבָרִים אֵלּוּ שֶׁהֵם צַעַר הַלֵּב.

ג. מִי שֶׁיֵּשׁ לוֹ שֵׁם כִּינּוּי לִגְנַאי, אַף עַל פִּי שֶׁהוּא רָגִיל בְּאוֹתוֹ כִינּוּי וְאֵינוֹ מִתְבַּיֵּישׁ בּוֹ, אִם זֶה כַּוָּונָתוֹ לְבַיְּישׁוֹ, אָסוּר לִקְרוֹתוֹ בְּכִינּוּי זֶה, מִשּׁוּם אוֹנָאַת דְּבָרִים.

ד. אָסוּר לִגְנוֹב דַּעַת הַבְּרִיּוֹת (פֵּירוּשׁ לְרַמּוֹת בִּדְבָרִים, אַף עַל פִּי שֶׁאֵין בּוֹ חֶסְרוֹן מָמוֹן)[10], אֲפִילּוּ דַּעַת עַכּוּ"ם. לָכֵן אָסוּר לִמְכּוֹר לוֹ בְּשַׂר נְבֵלָה בְּחֶזְקַת שְׁחוּטָה[11]. אִם מוֹכֵר אֵיזֶה דָּבָר שֶׁיֵּשׁ בּוֹ מוּם, אַף עַל פִּי שֶׁהַדָּבָר שָׁוֶה כְּמוֹ שֶׁהוּא מוֹכְרוֹ לוֹ, מִכָּל מָקוֹם צָרִיךְ לְהוֹדִיעַ לְהַלּוֹקֵחַ אֶת הַמּוּם. (וּבְמַתָּנָה לֵיכָּא מִשּׁוּם גְּנֵיבַת דַּעַת.)

ה. לֹא יְבַקֵּשׁ מֵחֲבֵירוֹ שֶׁיֹּאכַל אֶצְלוֹ כְּשֶׁהוּא יוֹדֵעַ שֶׁלֹּא יֹאכַל[12]. לֹא יִתֵּן לוֹ מַתָּנָה

---

who is not knowledgeable in this subject, **"מָה אַתָּה (תשוב) [תָּשִׁיב] בַּדָּבָר הַזֶּה?"** — **"What would you respond regarding this matter?"**[9] **וְכֵן כָּל כַּיּוֹצֵא בִּדְבָרִים אֵלּוּ** — **Likewise, any** similar comments in cases that are **comparable to these** cases, **שֶׁהֵם צַעַר הַלֵּב** — in that **they are** the cause of **emotional pain**, are forbidden.

§3 **מִי שֶׁיֵּשׁ לוֹ שֵׁם כִּינּוּי לִגְנַאי** — So too, regarding **one who has a shameful nickname: אַף עַל פִּי שֶׁהוּא רָגִיל בְּאוֹתוֹ כִינּוּי** — **Even though he is used to** being called by **that name וְאֵינוֹ מִתְבַּיֵּישׁ בּוֹ** — **and is not embarrassed when it is used, אִם זֶה כַּוָּונָתוֹ לְבַיְּישׁוֹ** — nevertheless, **if one intends to embarrass him** by using it, **אָסוּר לִקְרוֹתוֹ בְּכִינּוּי זֶה** — **it is forbidden to call him that nickname, מִשּׁוּם אוֹנָאַת דְּבָרִים** — **as** that constitutes **hurting verbally.**

§4 **אָסוּר לִגְנוֹב דַּעַת הַבְּרִיּוֹת** — **It is forbidden to "steal the minds" of people** (**פֵּירוּשׁ לְרַמּוֹת בִּדְבָרִים** — the phrase "stealing the mind" **means, to deceive by** misleading **speech אַף עַל פִּי שֶׁאֵין בּוֹ חֶסְרוֹן מָמוֹן** — **even when there is no monetary** loss involved),[10] **אֲפִילּוּ דַּעַת עַכּוּ"ם** — **even the mind of an idolater. לָכֵן אָסוּר לִמְכּוֹר לוֹ** — **Therefore, it is forbidden to sell to** an idolater **בְּשַׂר נְבֵלָה בְּחֶזְקַת שְׁחוּטָה** — **the meat of a** ***neveilah***[11] **as if it were** properly **slaughtered. אִם מוֹכֵר אֵיזֶה דָּבָר שֶׁיֵּשׁ בּוֹ מוּם** — Likewise, **if one sells any item that has an imperfection, אַף עַל פִּי שֶׁהַדָּבָר שָׁוֶה** — **even though the item** is still **worth כְּמוֹ שֶׁהוּא מוֹכְרוֹ לוֹ** — the price for **which he is selling it to him, מִכָּל מָקוֹם צָרִיךְ לְהוֹדִיעַ לְהַלּוֹקֵחַ אֶת הַמּוּם** — **nevertheless, he must notify the buyer of the imperfection** (**וּבְמַתָּנָה לֵיכָּא מִשּׁוּם גְּנֵיבַת דַּעַת** — **Gifts are not subject to** the laws of **"stealing the mind,"** i.e., he does not have to notify the recipient of any imperfection.)

§5 **לֹא יְבַקֵּשׁ מֵחֲבֵירוֹ שֶׁיֹּאכַל אֶצְלוֹ** — **One should not invite his fellow to eat with him כְּשֶׁהוּא יוֹדֵעַ שֶׁלֹּא יֹאכַל** — **when he knows that he will** refuse the invitation and **not eat** with him.[12] **לֹא יִתֵּן לוֹ מַתָּנָה** — **One should not** offer to **give** his fellow **a gift**

---

9. The one who was questioned is embarrassed since he does not know how to respond.

10. Even one word of deception is forbidden; see *Rambam, Hilchos Dei'os* 2:6, at length.

11. *Neveilah* is meat of an animal or bird that was not slaughtered according to Torah law. It is forbidden for a Jew to eat, but permitted for a non-Jew. Although a non-Jew may eat such meat, he may prefer eating kosher meat for health reasons (see *Perishah, Choshen Mishpat* 228:6).

12. The indication of *Shulchan Aruch* (*Choshen Mishpat* 228:6) is that only persistent invitations are prohibited. As noted by

PROHIBITION OF VERBAL ABUSE AND DECEIVING PEOPLE — SIMAN 63:5 324

כְּשֶׁהוּא יוֹדֵעַ שֶׁלֹּא יְקַבֵּל. וְכֵן כָּל כַּיּוֹצֵא בָזֶה, שֶׁהוּא אֶחָד בַּפֶּה וְאֶחָד בַּלֵּב — יַרְאֶה לַחֲבֵרוֹ שֶׁהוּא מְכַבְּדוֹ וְאֵין כַּוָּנָתוֹ שְׁלֵמָה — אָסוּר. אֶלָּא יְהֵא תָמִיד פִּיו וְלִבּוֹ שָׁוִים[13] וְיִנְהוֹג בִּשְׂפַת אֱמֶת וְרוּחַ נָכוֹן וְלֵב טָהוֹר.

כְּשֶׁהוּא יוֹדֵעַ שֶׁלֹּא יְקַבֵּל — when he knows that he will not accept it. **וְכֵן כָּל כַּיּוֹצֵא בָזֶה — Likewise, any similar** behavior, **שֶׁהוּא אֶחָד בַּפֶּה וְאֶחָד בַּלֵּב — where** he expresses **one** thing **verbally** while meaning **another** thing is **in his heart, יַרְאֶה לַחֲבֵרוֹ שֶׁהוּא מְכַבְּדוֹ** — such as one who **displays respect for his friend וְאֵין כַּוָּנָתוֹ שְׁלֵמָה — but his intentions are not sincere, אָסוּר — is forbidden. אֶלָּא יְהֵא תָמִיד פִּיו וְלִבּוֹ שָׁוִים — Rather, one's words and intentions should always be identical,**[13] **וְיִנְהוֹג — and one should conduct** himself with the following attributes: **בִּשְׂפַת אֱמֶת וְרוּחַ נָכוֹן וְלֵב טָהוֹר — with truthful speech, a proper spirit, and a pure heart.**

Sma there (§8), to extend an invitation once or twice is viewed as standard protocol, and, in fact, if one does not extend an invitation it may be erroneously understood that the person was not invited due to his lowly stature.

13. I.e., he should mean what he says.

325 NOT TO CONDUCT BUSINESS WITH A FORBIDDEN ITEM — SIMAN 64:1

סימן סד

שֶׁלֹּא לַעֲשׂוֹת סְחוֹרָה בְּדָבָר הָאָסוּר

וּבוֹ ד׳ סְעִיפִים

א. כָּל דָּבָר שֶׁאָסוּר מִן הַתּוֹרָה בַּאֲכִילָה, אַף עַל פִּי שֶׁהוּא מוּתָּר בַּהֲנָאָה, אִם הוּא דָּבָר הַמְיוּחָד לְמַאֲכָל, אָסוּר לַעֲשׂוֹת בּוֹ סְחוֹרָה[1], אוֹ לְהַלְווֹת עָלָיו, וַאֲפִילוּ לִקְנוֹתוֹ לְהַאֲכִילוֹ לְפוֹעֲלוֹ עכּו״ם, אָסוּר[2]. אֲבָל דָּבָר שֶׁאֵינוֹ עוֹמֵד לַאֲכִילָה, כְּגוֹן סוּסִים וַחֲמוֹרִים, מוּתָּר לַעֲשׂוֹת בָּהֶם סְחוֹרָה[3]. וְחֵלֶב גַּם כֵּן מוּתָּר בִּסְחוֹרָה[4] שֶׁהֲרֵי נֶאֱמַר בּוֹ (ויקרא ז, כד) ״יֵעָשֶׂה לְכָל מְלָאכָה״[5].

SIMAN 64

NOT TO CONDUCT BUSINESS WITH A FORBIDDEN ITEM

CONTAINING 4 *SE'IFIM*

§1 Designated as Food / §2 A Forbidden Item Acquired Incidentally / §3 Collecting a Loan / §4 Forbidden by Rabbinic Law

§1 **כָּל דָּבָר שֶׁאָסוּר מִן הַתּוֹרָה בַּאֲכִילָה — Anything that is forbidden by Biblical law to be eaten, אַף עַל פִּי שֶׁהוּא מוּתָּר בַּהֲנָאָה — even though it is permitted to derive benefit from it, אִם הוּא דָּבָר הַמְיוּחָד לְמַאֲכָל — if it is something that is designated as food, אָסוּר לַעֲשׂוֹת בּוֹ סְחוֹרָה — it is forbidden to do business with it**[1] **אוֹ לְהַלְווֹת עָלָיו — or to lend money** to an idolater **against it**, i.e., to take forbidden food from the borrower as security for a loan. **וַאֲפִילוּ לִקְנוֹתוֹ לְהַאֲכִילוֹ לְפוֹעֲלוֹ עכּו״ם — Even to buy it for** the purpose of **feeding it to his worker** who is **an idolater אָסוּר — is forbidden.**[2] **אֲבָל דָּבָר שֶׁאֵינוֹ עוֹמֵד לַאֲכִילָה — However, things that are not designated for eating, כְּגוֹן סוּסִים וַחֲמוֹרִים — such as horses and donkeys, מוּתָּר לַעֲשׂוֹת בָּהֶם סְחוֹרָה — it is permitted to do business with them.**[3] **וְחֵלֶב גַּם כֵּן מוּתָּר בִּסְחוֹרָה — It is also permitted to do business with forbidden fat,**[4] **שֶׁהֲרֵי נֶאֱמַר בּוֹ — because it is stated regarding** forbidden fat (*Vayikra* 7:24): **״יֵעָשֶׂה לְכָל מְלָאכָה״ —** *The fat of an animal . . .* ***may be put to any use.***[5]

1. The authorities differ as to whether this prohibition is of Biblical or Rabbinic origin; see *Tosafos, Pesachim* 23a s.v. אמר קרא; *Tosafos Yom Tov, Shevi'is* 7:3; *Taz, Yoreh Deah* 117:1. See *Teshuvos HaRashba* (III §223), who explains that the prohibition in dealing in non-kosher foods is based on the concern that this might lead to some [accidental] consumption of one's merchandise.

Rabbi Moshe Feinstein writes (*Igros Moshe, Yoreh Deah* II, §37) that even if the food is in sealed cans or packages it may not be bought and sold. However, it is permitted to deal in prohibited food that is clearly marked for the consumption of animals, such as clearly labeled dog and cat food. This, however, does not apply to Biblically prohibited mixtures of milk and meat, for that is prohibited even for benefit (see above, 46:5). [Pet food may often contain such mixtures and may thus be subject to this prohibition as well. If one mistakenly purchased such food, a halachic authority must be consulted (see *Dagul Mervavah* 87:3; *Chasam Sofer, Responsa, Yoreh Deah* §92).]

2. See *Shach, Yoreh Deah* 117:3.

3. Since horses and donkeys are not raised for food, we are not concerned that as a result of dealing in them he may mistakenly come to eat them (*Teshuvos HaRashba* III, 223; see note 1).

4. The hard fats (suet) surrounding the stomach, loins, and liver are known as *cheilev,* "forbidden fat" (see *Yoreh Deah* 64 for a full listing), and may not be consumed.

5. *Shach* (*Yoreh Deah* 117:4) writes that this

NOT TO CONDUCT BUSINESS WITH A FORBIDDEN ITEM — SIMAN 64:2-3 326

ב. אִם נִזְדַּמֵּן לְאָדָם בְּאַקְרַאי דָּבָר אָסוּר, כְּגוֹן שֶׁצָּד דָּגִים וְעָלָה בִּמְצוּדָתוֹ דָּג טָמֵא, וְכֵן מִי שֶׁנִּזְדַּמְּנָה לוֹ נְבֵלָה וּטְרֵפָה[6] בְּבֵיתוֹ[7], מוּתָּר לְמָכְרָם כֵּיוָן שֶׁלֹּא נִתְכַּוֵּין לְכָךְ. וְצָרִיךְ לְמָכְרוֹ מִיָּד, וְלֹא יַמְתִּין עַד שֶׁתְּהֵא שְׁמֵנָה אֶצְלוֹ. וְיָכוֹל לְמָכְרָן גַּם עַל יְדֵי שָׁלִיחַ, אַף עַל פִּי שֶׁהַשָּׁלִיחַ יַרְוִיחַ בּוֹ[8], אֲבָל לֹא שֶׁיִּקְנֶה הַשָּׁלִיחַ לַחֲלוּטִין דְּאִם כֵּן הֲוָה אֶצְלוֹ סְחוֹרָה.

ג. וְכֵן מוּתָּר לִגְבּוֹת בְּחוֹבוֹ דְּבָרִים טְמֵאִים, וְיִמְכְּרֵם מִיָּד[9], דְּאָסוּר לְהַשְׁהוֹתָן כְּדֵי לְהִשְׂתַּכֵּר בָּהֶם. אֲבָל מוּתָּר לְהַשְׁהוֹתָן בִּכְדֵי שֶׁלֹּא יַפְסִיד מִן הַקֶּרֶן[10].

---

§2 **אִם נִזְדַּמֵּן לְאָדָם בְּאַקְרַאי דָּבָר אָסוּר — If a person happened** to acquire **a forbidden item, כְּגוֹן שֶׁצָּד דָּגִים — for example, he was fishing וְעָלָה בִּמְצוּדָתוֹ דָּג טָמֵא — and his net brought up a nonkosher fish; וְכֵן — likewise, מִי שֶׁנִּזְדַּמְּנָה לוֹ נְבֵלָה וּטְרֵפָה בְּבֵיתוֹ — one for whom a** ***neveilah*** **or** ***tereifah***[6] **came to be in his house;**[7] **מוּתָּר לְמָכְרָם —** in these cases, **it is permitted to sell them כֵּיוָן שֶׁלֹּא נִתְכַּוֵּין לְכָךְ — since he did not intend** to acquire them **for this** purpose. **וְצָרִיךְ לְמָכְרוֹ מִיָּד —** However, **he must sell it immediately, וְלֹא יַמְתִּין עַד שֶׁתְּהֵא שְׁמֵנָה אֶצְלוֹ — and not wait until it becomes fattened while in his possession. וְיָכוֹל לְמָכְרָן גַּם עַל יְדֵי שָׁלִיחַ — He may also sell it through a** Jewish **agent, אַף עַל פִּי שֶׁהַשָּׁלִיחַ יַרְוִיחַ בּוֹ — even if the agent will profit from this** deal.[8] **אֲבָל לֹא שֶׁיִּקְנֶה הַשָּׁלִיחַ לַחֲלוּטִין — However, the agent should not buy it from him completely, דְּאִם כֵּן —** for if he does so, **הֲוָה אֶצְלוֹ סְחוֹרָה — it is** considered **a** forbidden **business transaction on the part of** the agent.

§3 **וְכֵן — Similarly, מוּתָּר לִגְבּוֹת בְּחוֹבוֹ דְּבָרִים טְמֵאִים — it is permitted to collect nonkosher items in** payment **of a loan. וְיִמְכְּרֵם מִיָּד — However, he must sell them immediately,**[9] **דְּאָסוּר לְהַשְׁהוֹתָן כְּדֵי לְהִשְׂתַּכֵּר בָּהֶם —** because **it is forbidden to keep them** in his possession **in order to profit from them. אֲבָל מוּתָּר לְהַשְׁהוֹתָן — However, he may keep them בִּכְדֵי שֶׁלֹּא יַפְסִיד מִן הַקֶּרֶן — in order not to lose any of the principal.**[10]

---

permit applies only to the *cheilev* of kosher animals (even if its meat is forbidden, e.g., it was not slaughtered properly); however, one may not do business with the *cheilev* of non-kosher animals. [The verse cited by Kitzur here is speaking of kosher animals.]

6. A *neveilah* is an animal or bird that was not slaughtered according to Torah law. A *tereifah* is an animal or bird possessing one of a defined group of mortal physical defects (see *Rambam, Hilchos Maachalos Asuros* 4:6-9). The meat of such an animal or bird is forbidden even if it is slaughtered by *shechitah* (ritual slaughter).

7. E.g., he attempted to slaughter an animal according to the halachah, but the *shechitah* turned out to be invalid, rendering the animal a *neveilah*. Or, he discovers that the animal has a defect that renders it a *treifah*.

8. That is, it is permitted for the agent to sell it for the owner and profit from the sale.

Rabbi Moshe Feinstein (*Igros Moshe, Yoreh Deah* I, §51) permits one to be paid for transporting nonkosher food (or, for that matter, to provide services as a shipping company) provided that he has no share in the merchandise, since the prohibition applies only to doing business with nonkosher food that one owns.

9. He may not cook them in order to increase his profit, even if he sells them immediately thereafter (*Glosses of R' Akiva Eiger* to *Yoreh Deah* 117:1).

10. I.e., in a case where he would have to sell them at a loss if he does so immediately.

327 NOT TO CONDUCT BUSINESS WITH A FORBIDDEN ITEM — SIMAN 64:4

ד. דָּבָר שֶׁאֵין אִיסּוּרוֹ אֶלָּא מִדְּרַבָּנָן, כְּגוֹן גְּבִינוֹת שֶׁל נָכְרִי[11], מוּתָּר לַעֲשׂוֹת בּוֹ סְחוֹרָה.

---

§4 **דָּבָר שֶׁאֵין אִיסּוּרוֹ אֶלָּא מִדְּרַבָּנָן** — Regarding **items that are forbidden only by Rabbinic law,** **כְּגוֹן גְּבִינוֹת שֶׁל נָכְרִי** — **such as cheese** produced by **idolaters,**[11] **מוּתָּר לַעֲשׂוֹת בּוֹ סְחוֹרָה** — **it is permitted to do business with these** foods.

---

11. See above, 38:14.

סימן סה

הִלְכוֹת רִבִּית[1]

וּבוֹ ל׳ סְעִיפִים

א. לְפִי שֶׁנַּפְשׁוֹ שֶׁל אָדָם בְּטִבְעוֹ חוֹמֵד וּמִתְאַוֶּה אֶל הַמָּמוֹן, וְקָרוֹב יוֹתֵר שֶׁיְּהֵא הָאָדָם נִכְשָׁל בְּאִיסּוּר רִיבִּית מִבִּשְׁאָר אִיסּוּרִין שֶׁבְּמָמוֹן, כִּי בְּגָזֵל וְאוֹנָאָה וְכַדּוֹמֶה הֲרֵי זֶה מַשְׁגִּיחַ עַל עַצְמוֹ שֶׁלֹּא יְהֵא נִגְזָל וְשֶׁלֹּא יִתְאַנֶּה, וְגַם זֶה שֶׁהוּא רוֹצֶה לִגְזוֹל אוֹ לְהוֹנוֹת אֶת חֲבֵרוֹ לִפְעָמִים הוּא נִמְנָע מֵחֲמַת בּוּשָׁה אוֹ מֵחֲמַת יִרְאָה, מַה שֶּׁאֵינוֹ כֵן בְּרִיבִּית, כִּי הַלֹּוֶה נוֹתֵן לוֹ בִּרְצוֹנוֹ הַטּוֹב וְהוּא שָׂמֵחַ כִּי מָצָא מָקוֹם לִלְוֹת

SIMAN 65

THE LAWS OF INTEREST (RIBBIS)

CONTAINING 30 *SE'IFIM*

§1 The Stringency of the Prohibition of *Ribbis* / **§2** One Who Accepted *Ribbis* / **§3** Stipulated After the Loan / **§4** Borrower Adds on His Own / **§5** Gift of *Ribbis* / **§6** Advanced and Deferred *Ribbis* / **§7** Exchanging Loans / **§8** Benefiting the Lender / **§9** Words of *Ribbis* / **§10** Benefit of Gratitude / **§11** A *Se'ah* for a *Se'ah* / **§12** Collateral / **§13** Known Market Price / **§14-15** Selling Promissory Notes / **§16-17** Advancing Funds / **§18-20** Purchasing Merchandise for Resale in Another Place / **§21** Renting Real Estate / **§22** Laborer / **§23** Dowry / **§24-29** Transactions Involving an Idolater / **§30** An Apostate

This *Siman* deals with the prohibition against lending and borrowing money with interest (*ribbis*).[1] It opens with a discussion of the stringency of this prohibition.

§1 **לְפִי שֶׁנַּפְשׁוֹ שֶׁל אָדָם בְּטִבְעוֹ חוֹמֵד וּמִתְאַוֶּה אֶל הַמָּמוֹן — Since a person has a natural craving and desire for money,** the concern that a person will be drawn to transgress monetary prohibitions is greater than with other prohibitions. **וְקָרוֹב יוֹתֵר שֶׁיְּהֵא הָאָדָם נִכְשָׁל בְּאִיסּוּר רִיבִּית — Now, a person can more readily stumble with regard to the *ribbis* prohibition מִבִּשְׁאָר אִיסּוּרִין שֶׁבְּמָמוֹן — than with other monetary prohibitions, כִּי בְּגָזֵל וְאוֹנָאָה וְכַדּוֹמֶה — for with regard to theft and fraud and the like הֲרֵי זֶה מַשְׁגִּיחַ עַל עַצְמוֹ** — the potential victim **takes precautions שֶׁלֹּא יְהֵא נִגְזָל וְשֶׁלֹּא יִתְאַנֶּה — not to be a victim of theft or defrauded. וְגַם זֶה שֶׁהוּא רוֹצֶה לִגְזוֹל אוֹ לְהוֹנוֹת אֶת חֲבֵרוֹ — Additionally, one who is disposed to steal or defraud his fellow לִפְעָמִים הוּא נִמְנָע — will at times refrain מֵחֲמַת בּוּשָׁה אוֹ מֵחֲמַת יִרְאָה — out of shame or fear. מַה שֶּׁאֵינוֹ כֵן בְּרִיבִּית — This,** however, **is not so with regard to *ribbis*, כִּי הַלֹּוֶה נוֹתֵן לוֹ בִּרְצוֹנוֹ הַטּוֹב — for the borrower gives** it to the lender **of his own free will, וְהוּא שָׂמֵחַ** — and the borrower **is gratified כִּי מָצָא מָקוֹם לִלְוֹת — that**

---

1. [For a comprehensive treatement of the laws of *ribbis*, including their application vis-a-vis many modern-day situations (such as credit cards and foreign currency fluctuations), the reader is referred to *The Laws of Ribbis* by Rabbi Yisroel Reisman, Mesorah Publications, 1995.]

עַל כָּל פָּנִים בְּרִיבִּית, וְגַם הַמַּלְוֶה חוֹשֵׁב בְּדַעְתּוֹ כִּי הֲרֵי הוּא עוֹשֶׂה טוֹבָה גְדוֹלָה עִם הַלֹּוֶה שֶׁיּוּכַל לְהַרְוִיחַ בְּמָמוֹן זֶה כִּפְלֵי כִפְלַיִם יוֹתֵר מִן הָרִיבִּית, וְלָכֵן נָקֵל מְאוֹד שֶׁיְּהֵא הָאָדָם נִתְפַּתֶּה חַס וְשָׁלוֹם מִן הַיֵּצֶר הָרַע לִהְיוֹת נִכְשָׁל בְּאִיסּוּר זֶה. עַל כֵּן הֶחֱמִירָה תּוֹרָתֵנוּ הַקְּדוֹשָׁה מְאוֹד בְּאִיסּוּר זֶה וְהִרְבָּה לָאוִין נֶאֶמְרוּ בוֹ. הַמַּלְוֶה עוֹבֵר בְּשִׁשָּׁה לָאוִין[2], וְלֹא יָקוּם בִּתְחִיַּית הַמֵּתִים שֶׁנֶּאֱמַר (יחזקאל יח, יג) "בַּנֶּשֶׁךְ נָתַן וְתַרְבִּית לָקַח וָחָי לֹא יִחְיֶה". הַלֹּוֶה עוֹבֵר בִּשְׁלֹשָׁה לָאוִין[3]. הַסּוֹפֵר וְהָעֵדִים וְהֶעָרֵב עוֹבְרִים כָּל אֶחָד בְּלָאו אֶחָד[4]. וְכֵן הַסַּרְסוּר שֶׁהָיָה בֵינֵיהֶם אוֹ שֶׁסִּיֵּיעַ לְאֶחָד מֵהֶם, כְּגוֹן שֶׁהוֹרָה מָקוֹם

---

he found an opportunity to borrow, **עַל כָּל פָּנִים בְּרִיבִּית** — even if only on interest. **וְגַם הַמַּלְוֶה חוֹשֵׁב בְּדַעְתּוֹ** — Furthermore, the lender rationalizes, thinking to himself **כִּי הֲרֵי הוּא עוֹשֶׂה טוֹבָה גְדוֹלָה עִם הַלֹּוֶה** — that he is doing a great favor to the borrower, **שֶׁיּוּכַל לְהַרְוִיחַ בְּמָמוֹן זֶה כִּפְלֵי כִפְלַיִם יוֹתֵר מִן הָרִיבִּית** — for by investing this borrowed money, the borrower will be able to profit many times more than what he must pay in interest. **וְלָכֵן נָקֵל מְאוֹד** — It is therefore very easy **שֶׁיְּהֵא הָאָדָם נִתְפַּתֶּה חַס וְשָׁלוֹם מִן הַיֵּצֶר הָרַע** — for a person to be swayed, God forbid, by the evil inclination **לִהְיוֹת נִכְשָׁל בְּאִיסּוּר זֶה** — to stumble in this prohibition.

עַל כֵּן — Therefore, **הֶחֱמִירָה תּוֹרָתֵנוּ הַקְּדוֹשָׁה מְאוֹד** — our holy Torah dealt very stringently **בְּאִיסּוּר זֶה** — with regard to this prohibition, **וְהִרְבָּה לָאוִין נֶאֶמְרוּ בוֹ** — and many negative commandments were stated regarding it: **הַמַּלְוֶה עוֹבֵר בְּשִׁשָּׁה לָאוִין** — The lender transgresses six negative commandments[2] **וְלֹא יָקוּם בִּתְחִיַּית הַמֵּתִים** — and he will not rise with the future Resurrection of the Dead, **שֶׁנֶּאֱמַר** — as it is stated (*Yechezkel* 18:13): **"בַּנֶּשֶׁךְ נָתַן וְתַרְבִּית לָקַח וָחָי לֹא יִחְיֶה"** — *He gave on interest and took increase, shall he live? He shall not live!* **הַלֹּוֶה עוֹבֵר בִּשְׁלֹשָׁה לָאוִין** — The borrower transgresses three negative commandments.[3] **הַסּוֹפֵר וְהָעֵדִים וְהֶעָרֵב** — The scribe, the witnesses, and the guarantor **עוֹבְרִים כָּל אֶחָד בְּלָאו אֶחָד** — each transgress one negative commandment.[4] **וְכֵן הַסַּרְסוּר שֶׁהָיָה בֵינֵיהֶם** — So too the broker who was the intermediary between them **אוֹ שֶׁסִּיֵּיעַ לְאֶחָד מֵהֶם** — or who assisted one of them — **כְּגוֹן שֶׁהוֹרָה מָקוֹם**

---

2. They are: (1,2) By lending money at interest, the lender violates the two commandments of the verse (*Vayikra* 25:37): אֶת כַּסְפְּךָ לֹא תִתֵּן לוֹ בְּנֶשֶׁךְ, *Do not give him your money for interest,* וּבְמַרְבִּית לֹא תִתֵּן אָכְלֶךָ, *and do not give your food for increase.* [Both of these prohibitions apply whether one lends money, food, or anything else with interest.] (3) By collecting the interest payment, he violates the commandment: אַל תִּקַּח מֵאִתּוֹ נֶשֶׁךְ וְתַרְבִּית, *Do not take from him interest and increase* (ibid. v. 36). (4) By pressing the borrower for payment (this commonly occurs in the case of a loan made with interest), he violates the commandment: לֹא תִהְיֶה לוֹ כְּנֹשֶׁה, *Do not act toward him as a creditor* (*Shemos* 22:24). (5) By imposing the interest, he violates the commandment: לֹא תְשִׂימוּן עָלָיו נֶשֶׁךְ, *Do not lay interest upon him* (ibid.). (6) By causing the borrower to sin (by paying interest) the lender violates the commandment: וְלִפְנֵי עִוֵּר לֹא תִתֵּן מִכְשֹׁל, *and you shall not place a stumbling block before the blind* (*Vayikra* 19:14) (*Rashi* to *Bava Metzia* 75b s.v. מלוה).

3. The three negative commandments that the borrower violates are: (1) לֹא תַשִּׁיךְ לְאָחִיךָ, *You shall not cause your brother to take interest* (*Devarim* 23:20); (2) וּלְאָחִיךָ לֹא תַשִּׁיךְ, *But you may not cause your brother to take interest* (ibid. v. 21); (3) וְלִפְנֵי עִוֵּר לֹא תִתֵּן מִכְשֹׁל, *and you shall not place a stumbling block before the blind* (*Vayikra* 19:14).

4. I.e., לֹא תְשִׂימוּן עָלָיו נֶשֶׁךְ, *Do not lay interest upon him* (*Shemos* 22:24). [If the loan would not have been made without them, they also transgress the prohibition of וְלִפְנֵי עִוֵּר לֹא תִתֵּן מִכְשֹׁל, *and you shall not place a stumbling block before the blind* (*Vayikra* 19:14) (*Tosafos* to *Bava Metzia* 75b s.v. ערב).]

לְהַלְוֹּה לִלְוֹת, אוֹ שֶׁהוֹרָה מָקוֹם לְהַמַּלְוֶה לְהַלְווֹת, גַּם כֵּן עוֹבֵר בְּלָאו אֶחָד[5].

ב. מִי שֶׁנִּכְשַׁל וְלָקַח רִיבִּית מְחוּיָּב לְהַחֲזִירוֹ (מִלְּבַד רִיבִּית מוּקְדֶּמֶת וְרִבִּית מְאוּחֶרֶת דִּלְקַמָּן סְעִיף ו׳).

ג. אֲפִילוּ לֹא פָּסַק עִמּוֹ אֶת הָרִיבִּית בִּשְׁעַת הַלְוָאָה, אֶלָּא שֶׁהִלְוָה לוֹ בְּחִנָּם עַד זְמַן פְּלוֹנִי, אוֹ שֶׁמָּכַר לוֹ אֵיזֶה סְחוֹרָה בְּהַקָּפָה עַד זְמַן פְּלוֹנִי, אוֹ שֶׁחַיָּיב לוֹ בְּעִנְיָן אַחֵר לְשַׁלֵּם לוֹ יִהְיֶה מֵאֵיזֶה עִנְיָן שֶׁיִּהְיֶה, וּבְהַגִּיעַ זְמַן הַפֵּרָעוֹן פּוֹסֵק לוֹ אֵיזֶה דָּבָר בִּשְׁבִיל שֶׁיַּרְחִיב לוֹ אֶת הַזְּמַן, גַּם זֹאת הִיא רִיבִּית[6].

לְהַלְוֹּה לִלְוֹת — for example, he informed the borrower where he may obtain a loan, אוֹ שֶׁהוֹרָה מָקוֹם לְהַמַּלְוֶה לְהַלְווֹת — or he informed the lender where he may lend — גַּם כֵּן עוֹבֵר בְּלָאו אֶחָד — also transgresses one negative commandment.[5]

§2 מִי שֶׁנִּכְשַׁל וְלָקַח רִיבִּית — One who stumbled and took *ribbis* מְחוּיָּב לְהַחֲזִירוֹ — is required to return it (מִלְּבַד רִיבִּית מוּקְדֶּמֶת — excluding advance *ribbis* וְרִבִּית מְאוּחֶרֶת — and deferred *ribbis*; דִּלְקַמָּן סְעִיף ו׳ — see below, *se'if* 6, where these terms are defined).

§3 Not all interest is prohibited on the Biblical level. The Torah prohibits only *ribbis ketzutzah* (prearranged *ribbis*), i.e., when the obligation for its payment was agreed upon at the time of the loan. The following *se'if* discusses a case in which the obligation was not made at the time of the original loan, but may nevertheless be considered *ribbis ketzutzah.*

אֲפִילוּ לֹא פָּסַק עִמּוֹ אֶת הָרִיבִּית בִּשְׁעַת הַלְוָאָה — Even if the lender **did not stipulate at the time of the loan** that the borrower must pay him ***ribbis,* אֶלָּא שֶׁהִלְוָה לוֹ בְּחִנָּם עַד זְמַן פְּלוֹנִי — but he granted** the borrower **an interest-free loan until such-and-such time; אוֹ שֶׁמָּכַר לוֹ אֵיזֶה סְחוֹרָה בְּהַקָּפָה — or** in a case where **one sold some merchandise to another on credit עַד זְמַן פְּלוֹנִי — until such-and-such time; אוֹ שֶׁחַיָּיב לוֹ בְּעִנְיָן אַחֵר לְשַׁלֵּם לוֹ — or if one was liable to pay another due to some other matter, יִהְיֶה מֵאֵיזֶה עִנְיָן שֶׁיִּהְיֶה — be it for whatever matter it may be; וּבְהַגִּיעַ זְמַן הַפֵּרָעוֹן — and when the time for payment arrived** (i.e., when the loan or other obligation became due) **פּוֹסֵק לוֹ אֵיזֶה דָּבָר —** the debtor **commits** to pay the creditor **a certain** extra amount **בִּשְׁבִיל שֶׁיַּרְחִיב לוֹ אֶת הַזְּמַן — so that he extend the time** of the loan **for** the debtor, **גַּם זֹאת הִיא רִיבִּית — this is also considered *ribbis.***[6]

---

5. If they would not have made the loan without him, he transgresses the negative commandment of וְלִפְנֵי עִוֵּר לֹא תִתֵּן מִכְשֹׁל, *and you shall not place a stumbling block before the blind* (*Vayikra* 19:14). If the loan would have been made regardless, he transgresses a Rabbinic injunction (*Shulchan Aruch HaRav, Hil. Ribbis, se'if* 3).

It is prohibited to prepare documents for loans and other transactions that involve *ribbis* (*Igros Moshe, Choshen Mishpat* I, §93, citing *Rambam, Hilchos Malveh VeLoveh* 4:2 and *Shach, Yoreh Deah* 160:1). [People whose jobs entail preparing documents that may include clauses of *ribbis* (e.g., secretaries, salesmen, lawyers, paralegals, etc.) must be alert for this and present any questions to a competent halachic authority.]

6. This may in fact be Biblically prohibited (see introduction to this *se'if*), since a stipulation made at the time of an extension of a loan is legally equivalent to a stipulation made at the time of the initial lending (see *Yoreh Deah* 166:2).

ד. אֲפִילּוּ אִם הַלֹּוֶה נוֹתֵן לוֹ יוֹתֵר מִדַּעְתּוֹ בִּשְׁעַת הַפֵּרָעוֹן שֶׁלֹּא הִתְנָה עִמּוֹ, וְאֵינוֹ אוֹמֵר שֶׁנּוֹתְנוֹ לוֹ בִּשְׁבִיל רִיבִּית, גַּם כֵּן אָסוּר.

ה. אֲפִילּוּ אוֹמֵר לוֹ הַלֹּוֶה בִּשְׁעַת נְתִינַת הָרִיבִּית שֶׁהוּא נוֹתְנוֹ לוֹ בְּמַתָּנָה, גַּם כֵּן אָסוּר לְקַבְּלוֹ מִמֶּנּוּ[7]. אֲבָל אִם כְּבָר לָקַח מִמֶּנּוּ רִיבִּית וְהַמַּלְוֶה עוֹשֶׂה תְּשׁוּבָה וְרוֹצֶה לְהַחֲזִירוֹ לְהַלֹּוֶה וְהוּא מוֹחֵל לוֹ, מוּתָּר.

ו. אָסוּר לְהַקְדִּים אֶת הָרִיבִּית אוֹ לְאַחֵר אוֹתוֹ. כֵּיצַד? הָיָה רְאוּבֵן רוֹצֶה לִלְוֹת מִשִּׁמְעוֹן מָעוֹת וּמַקְדִּים וְשׁוֹלֵחַ לוֹ מַתָּנָה וּפֵירַשׁ לוֹ בִּשְׁבִיל שֶׁיַּלְוֵהוּ, אוֹ שֶׁהָיָה מַתָּנָה מְרוּבָּה דְּמִסְתָּמָא הָוֵי כְּאִלּוּ פֵּירַשׁ לוֹ שֶׁהִיא בִּשְׁבִיל שֶׁיַּלְוֵהוּ, זֶהוּ רִיבִּית מוּקְדֶּמֶת. לָוָה מִמֶּנּוּ וְהֶחֱזִיר לוֹ מְעוֹתָיו וְהָיָה שׁוֹלֵחַ לוֹ מַתָּנָה בִּשְׁבִיל מְעוֹתָיו

---

§4 The Sages extended the *ribbis* prohibition to include several additional situations. In the *se'ifim* that follow, a number of such situations are enumerated:

אֲפִילּוּ אִם הַלֹּוֶה נוֹתֵן לוֹ יוֹתֵר מִדַּעְתּוֹ בִּשְׁעַת הַפֵּרָעוֹן — Even if at the time of repayment the borrower, on his own, gives the lender **more** than he borrowed, **שֶׁלֹּא הִתְנָה עִמּוֹ** — an amount **that he did not** originally **stipulate to** give **him, וְאֵינוֹ אוֹמֵר שֶׁנּוֹתְנוֹ לוֹ בִּשְׁבִיל רִיבִּית — and he does not say that he is giving it as** ***ribbis,*** **גַּם כֵּן אָסוּר — it is also prohibited.**

§5 **אֲפִילּוּ אוֹמֵר לוֹ הַלֹּוֶה — Even** if **the borrower tells** the lender **בִּשְׁעַת נְתִינַת הָרִיבִּית — at the time when he is paying the** ***ribbis*** **שֶׁהוּא נוֹתְנוֹ לוֹ בְּמַתָּנָה** — **that he is giving it** to the lender **as a gift, גַּם כֵּן אָסוּר לְקַבְּלוֹ מִמֶּנּוּ — it is also forbidden to accept it from him.**[7]

אֲבָל אִם כְּבָר לָקַח מִמֶּנּוּ רִיבִּית — However, if the lender **already took** ***ribbis*** **from him, וְהַמַּלְוֶה עוֹשֶׂה תְּשׁוּבָה — and the lender repents** of this transgression **וְרוֹצֶה לְהַחֲזִירוֹ לְהַלֹּוֶה — and wishes to return it to the borrower, וְהוּא מוֹחֵל לוֹ — and** the borrower **forgives him** and waives its repayment, **מוּתָּר — it is permitted** for the lender to keep the money.

§6 **אָסוּר לְהַקְדִּים אֶת הָרִיבִּית — It is forbidden to advance the** ***ribbis*** **אוֹ לְאַחֵר אוֹתוֹ — or to defer it.**

These prohibitions are defined:

כֵּיצַד — What are these cases? **הָיָה רְאוּבֵן רוֹצֶה לִלְוֹת מִשִּׁמְעוֹן מָעוֹת — Reuven desired to borrow money from Shimon; וּמַקְדִּים וְשׁוֹלֵחַ לוֹ מַתָּנָה — therefore, he first sends** Shimon **a gift וּפֵירַשׁ לוֹ בִּשְׁבִיל שֶׁיַּלְוֵהוּ — and specifies that it is in order that he should lend him money, אוֹ שֶׁהָיָה מַתָּנָה מְרוּבָּה — or, it is a large gift, דְּמִסְתָּמָא — which,** due to its size, even **without specifying** its purpose, **הָוֵי כְּאִלּוּ פֵּירַשׁ לוֹ שֶׁהִיא בִּשְׁבִיל שֶׁיַּלְוֵהוּ — it is as if he specified that it is in order that** Shimon **should lend him** money, **זֶהוּ רִיבִּית מוּקְדֶּמֶת — this is advance** (pre-loan) ***ribbis.***

לָוָה מִמֶּנּוּ וְהֶחֱזִיר לוֹ מְעוֹתָיו — One who borrowed from someone **and repaid him, וְהָיָה שׁוֹלֵחַ לוֹ מַתָּנָה — and** he subsequently **sends** the lender **a gift בִּשְׁבִיל מְעוֹתָיו**

---

7. For *ribbis* is always awarded willingly, and it is nevertheless prohibited (*Shulchan Aruch HaRav, Hilchos Ribbis, se'if* 5, from *Tur, Yoreh Deah* §160). [This applies whether or not there was a stipulation at the time of the loan to pay *ribbis.*]

שֶׁהָיוּ בְּטֵלוֹת אֶצְלוֹ, וְזֶהוּ רִבִּית מְאוּחֶרֶת.

ז. אִם אֶחָד מַלְוֶה מְעוֹתָיו לַחֲבֵרוֹ עַל זְמַן מָה כְּדֵי שֶׁיַּחֲזוֹר זֶה וְיַלְוֵהוּ פַּעַם אַחֵר סַךְ יוֹתֵר לִזְמַן כָּזֶה, אוֹ סַךְ כָּזֶה לִזְמַן אָרוֹךְ יוֹתֵר, זֶה רִבִּית גָּמוּר[8]. וְאִם מַלְוֶה לוֹ עַל מְנָת שֶׁיַּלְוֶה לוֹ פַּעַם אַחֵר סַךְ כָּזֶה לִזְמַן כָּזֶה, יֵשׁ אוֹמְרִים שֶׁגַּם כֵּן אָסוּר, וְיֵשׁ אוֹמְרִים דְּמוּתָּר. וְיֵשׁ לְהַחֲמִיר. אַךְ אִם לֹא הִתְנוּ כֵן, אֶלָּא שֶׁהוּא מַלְוֶה לוֹ בִּרְצוֹנוֹ פַּעַם אַחֵר, אַף עַל פִּי שֶׁאֵינוֹ עוֹשֶׂה כֵּן אֶלָּא מֵחֲמַת שֶׁזֶּה גַם כֵּן כְּבָר הִלְוָהוּ, בָּזֶה יֵשׁ לְהָקֵל[9].

ח. צָרִיךְ הַמַּלְוֶה לִיזָּהֵר שֶׁלֹּא לֵיהָנוֹת מִן הַלֹּוֶה שֶׁלֹּא מִדַּעְתּוֹ כָּל זְמַן שֶׁמְּעוֹתָיו בְּיָדוֹ,

---

שֶׁהָיוּ בְּטֵלוֹת אֶצְלוֹ — as compensation **for** the lender's **money that remained idle in his** possession (i.e., the lender was unable to access the money) for the duration of the loan, **וְזֶהוּ רִבִּית מְאוּחֶרֶת** — **this is deferred** (post-payment) ***ribbis.***

§7 **אִם אֶחָד מַלְוֶה מְעוֹתָיו לַחֲבֵרוֹ עַל זְמַן מָה** — **If one lends his money to his fellow for a certain length of time** **כְּדֵי שֶׁיַּחֲזוֹר זֶה וְיַלְוֵהוּ פַּעַם אַחֵר** — **in order that his fellow should, in turn, lend him** money **at a different time** (i.e., it was stipulated at the time of the loan that the borrower must do so in return), **סַךְ יוֹתֵר לִזְמַן כָּזֶה** — whether it be **a larger amount** of money **for an equal** length of **time,** **אוֹ סַךְ כָּזֶה לִזְמַן אָרוֹךְ יוֹתֵר** — **or an equal amount for a longer period of time,** **זֶה רִבִּית גָּמוּר** — **this is actual *ribbis.***[8]

וְאִם מַלְוֶה לוֹ עַל מְנָת שֶׁיַּלְוֶה לוֹ פַּעַם אַחֵר — **If one lends** money **to another on the condition that** the borrower **should** in turn **lend** the lender **at another time** **סַךְ כָּזֶה לִזְמַן כָּזֶה** — **an equal amount for an equal** length of **time,** **יֵשׁ אוֹמְרִים שֶׁגַּם כֵּן אָסוּר** — **there are those who say that it is also prohibited,** **וְיֵשׁ אוֹמְרִים דְּמוּתָּר** — **and there are those who say that it is permitted.** **וְיֵשׁ לְהַחֲמִיר** — **One should conduct himself stringently,** and not make such a condition. **אַךְ אִם לֹא הִתְנוּ כֵן** — **However, if they did not make such a condition** at the time of the first loan, **אֶלָּא שֶׁהוּא מַלְוֶה לוֹ בִּרְצוֹנוֹ פַּעַם אַחֵר** — **but** the borrower **willingly lends** the original lender money **at a different time,** **אַף עַל פִּי שֶׁאֵינוֹ עוֹשֶׂה כֵּן אֶלָּא מֵחֲמַת שֶׁזֶּה גַם כֵּן כְּבָר הִלְוָהוּ** — **even if he is doing it only because this** fellow **also previously lent him,** **בָּזֶה יֵשׁ לְהָקֵל** — **in such** a case **one may** conduct himself **leniently.**[9]

§8 The Sages also prohibited the borrower from giving the lender various non-financial benefits. These are discussed in the *se'ifim* that follow.

צָרִיךְ הַמַּלְוֶה לִיזָּהֵר — **The lender must be careful** **שֶׁלֹּא לֵיהָנוֹת מִן הַלֹּוֶה שֶׁלֹּא מִדַּעְתּוֹ** — **not to derive benefit from the borrower** (for example, by using his tools) **without** the borrower's **knowledge,** **כָּל זְמַן שֶׁמְּעוֹתָיו בְּיָדוֹ** — **as long as** the lender's **money**

---

8. Even though the borrower is not paying him interest, but is merely agreeing to *lend* him money, nevertheless, since it is being stipulated that the loan must be greater, either in size or in duration, this constitutes *ribbis.*

9. Even in a case where there was no stipulation, it is permitted only in the manner that is being discussed here, that is, where the second loan is equal in amount and duration. It is not permitted if the second loan is for a larger amount or for a longer duration (see *Shulchan Aruch HaRav, Hilchos Ribbis, se'if* 6).

אֲפִילוּ בְּדָבָר שֶׁהָיָה עוֹשֶׂה לוֹ אַף אִם לֹא הִלְוָהוּ. שֶׁכֵּיוָן שֶׁנֶּהֱנֶה שֶׁלֹּא בִּרְשׁוּתוֹ נִרְאֶה שֶׁסּוֹמֵךְ עָלָיו שֶׁבִּשְׁבִיל מְעוֹתָיו שֶׁבְּיָדוֹ יִמְחוֹל לוֹ. אֲבָל אִם נֶהֱנֶה מִמֶּנּוּ מִדַּעְתּוֹ, מוּתָּר בְּדָבָר שֶׁהָיָה עוֹשֶׂה לוֹ אַף אִם לֹא הִלְוָהוּ, וּבִלְבַד שֶׁלֹּא יְהֵא דָּבָר שֶׁל פַּרְהֶסְיָא.[10]

ט. אִם לֹא הָיָה הַלֹּוֶה רָגִיל לְהַקְדִּים לְהַמַּלְוֶה שָׁלוֹם בְּפַעַם אַחֵר, אָסוּר לְהַקְדִּים לוֹ. וְאָסוּר לְכַבְּדוֹ בְּאֵיזֶה כִּיבּוּד בְּבֵית הַכְּנֶסֶת, אוֹ בְּמָקוֹם אַחֵר[11], אִם לֹא הָיָה רָגִיל כֵּן גַּם בְּפַעַם אַחֵר. וְכֵן שְׁאָר רִיבִּית דְּבָרִים בְּעָלְמָא אָסוּר שֶׁנֶּאֱמַר (דברים כג, כ) **״נֶשֶׁךְ כָּל דָּבָר אֲשֶׁר יִשָּׁךְ״[12], אֲפִילוּ דִּיבּוּר אָסוּר[13]. וְכֵן הַמַּלְוֶה מוּזְהָר עַל רִיבִּית דְּבָרִים**

---

is in the borrower's hands. **אֲפִילוּ בְּדָבָר שֶׁהָיָה עוֹשֶׂה לוֹ אַף אִם לֹא הִלְוָהוּ** — This restriction applies **even to something that** the borrower **would have done for** the lender **even if he had not lent him** the money. **שֶׁכֵּיוָן שֶׁנֶּהֱנֶה שֶׁלֹּא בִּרְשׁוּתוֹ** — **For since he is deriving benefit without** the borrower's **permission, נִרְאֶה שֶׁסּוֹמֵךְ עָלָיו** — **it appears that** the lender **relies upon him, שֶׁבִּשְׁבִיל מְעוֹתָיו שֶׁבְּיָדוֹ** — **that because of his money that is in the** borrower's **hands, יִמְחוֹל לוֹ** — **he will forgive him** and not protest, in which case it would constitute a *ribbis* violation. **אֲבָל אִם נֶהֱנֶה מִמֶּנּוּ מִדַּעְתּוֹ** — **But if he is benefiting from him with his knowledge, מוּתָּר** — **it is permitted, בְּדָבָר שֶׁהָיָה עוֹשֶׂה לוֹ אַף אִם לֹא הִלְוָהוּ** — **if it is something that he would have done for him even if he would not have lent him, וּבִלְבַד שֶׁלֹּא יְהֵא דָּבָר שֶׁל פַּרְהֶסְיָא** — **as long as it is not something** done **in public.**[10]

§9 **אִם לֹא הָיָה הַלֹּוֶה רָגִיל לְהַקְדִּים לְהַמַּלְוֶה** — **If the borrower was not accustomed** **שָׁלוֹם בְּפַעַם אַחֵר** — **to initiate a greeting to the lender at** any **other time, אָסוּר לְהַקְדִּים לוֹ** — the borrower **is prohibited from initiating** a greeting **to him** now that the lender has extended him a loan. **וְאָסוּר לְכַבְּדוֹ בְּאֵיזֶה כִּיבּוּד** — **And it is prohibited for** the borrower **to confer upon** the lender **an honor, בְּבֵית הַכְּנֶסֶת, אוֹ בְּמָקוֹם אַחֵר** — **in the synagogue or in some other place,**[11] **אִם לֹא הָיָה רָגִיל כֵּן גַּם בְּפַעַם אַחֵר** — **if he was not accustomed to do so at a different time.**

וְכֵן שְׁאָר רִיבִּית דְּבָרִים בְּעָלְמָא אָסוּר — **So too, other** types of **mere words of *ribbis* are prohibited, שֶׁנֶּאֱמַר** — **as it is written** (*Devarim* 23:20): **״נֶשֶׁךְ כָּל דָּבָר אֲשֶׁר יִשָּׁךְ״** — *You shall not cause your brother to take …* ***interest of anything that he may take as interest.*** The words **כָּל דָּבָר** (*anything*) can be translated to mean "any word."[12] **אֲפִילוּ דִּיבּוּר אָסוּר** — Thus, **even words are forbidden** where the words are uttered because of the loan.[13]

וְכֵן הַמַּלְוֶה מוּזְהָר עַל רִיבִּית דְּבָרִים — **The lender too is warned with regard to words**

---

10. Such as living in his courtyard or making use of his servants (*Yoreh Deah* 160:7).

11. E.g., to purchase an *aliyah* to the Torah for him (see *Shach, Yoreh Deah* 166:1, from *Maharshal*).

12. Although this verse is cited by the Gemara (*Bava Metzia* 75b) as the source for this prohibition, most authorities agree that this is not a Biblical derivation, and the prohibition is only Rabbinic in origin; see *Chochmas Adam* 131:11 (see also *Chelkas Binyamin* §160, *Tziyunim* §432).

13. Therefore, the borrower may not praise, express gratitude, or bless the lender in his presence (*Shulchan Aruch HaRav, se'if* 9; see also *Igros Moshe, Yoreh Deah* I, §80). One who borrowed money toward the costs of printing a *sefer* may not print a note containing an expression of thanks to the lender. He may, however, acknowledge the fact that Hashem rewards those who perform kindness with their money by writing "God's blessings are extended to So-and-so, who graciously lent funds for the publication of this volume" (*Igros Moshe* ibid.).

LAWS OF INTEREST (RIBBIS) — SIMAN 65:9-10 334

כְּגוֹן אִם אוֹמֵר לְהַלֹּוֶה הוֹדִיעֵנִי אִם יָבֹא פְּלוֹנִי מִמָּקוֹם פְּלוֹנִי. אַף עַל פִּי שֶׁאֵינוֹ מַטְרִיחוֹ אֶלָּא בַּאֲמִירָה בְּעָלְמָא[14], אִם לֹא הָיָה רָגִיל עִמּוֹ בְּזֶה קוֹדֶם לָכֵן וְעַתָּה סוֹמֵךְ עַל הַלְוָאָתוֹ לְצַוּוֹת עָלָיו מִפְּנֵי שֶׁהוּא נִכְנָע לוֹ, הֲרֵי זֶה רִיבִּית. וְאִם תֹּאמַר: וְהָא כְּתִיב (משלי כב, ז) "עֶבֶד לֹוֶה לְאִישׁ מַלְוֶה"[15]. זֶהוּ אֵינוֹ אֶלָּא לְעִנְיָן שֶׁאִם נָפַל בֵּינֵיהֶם דִּין וּדְבָרִים וְאוֹמֵר הַמַּלְוֶה נֵלֵךְ לְבֵית דִּין הַגָּדוֹל לָדוּן שָׁם וְהַלֹּוֶה אוֹמֵר לָדוּן כָּאן, מְחוּיָּב הַלֹּוֶה לֵילֵךְ כְּמוֹ שֶׁרוֹצֶה הַמַּלְוֶה, וְהַמַּלְוֶה אֵינוֹ מְחוּיָּב לָלֶכֶת לְבֵית דִּין הַגָּדוֹל שֶׁבְּמָקוֹם אַחֵר, מִשּׁוּם שֶׁנֶּאֱמַר "עֶבֶד לֹוֶה לְאִישׁ מַלְוֶה".

---

of *ribbis.* כְּגוֹן אִם אוֹמֵר לְהַלֹּוֶה — **For example, if he tells the borrower:** הוֹדִיעֵנִי אִם יָבֹא פְּלוֹנִי מִמָּקוֹם פְּלוֹנִי — **"Inform me if So-and-so arrives from such-and-such place."** אַף עַל פִּי שֶׁאֵינוֹ מַטְרִיחוֹ אֶלָּא בַּאֲמִירָה בְּעָלְמָא — **Although he is not troubling** the borrower to do **more than to merely say** something,[14] אִם לֹא הָיָה רָגִיל עִמּוֹ בְּזֶה קוֹדֶם לָכֵן — nevertheless, **if** the borrower **was not accustomed to do such a** favor **for** the lender **previously,** וְעַתָּה סוֹמֵךְ עַל הַלְוָאָתוֹ — **and** the lender **now relies on** the fact that **he** granted the borrower a **loan** לְצַוּוֹת עָלָיו — **to direct** the borrower to assist him, מִפְּנֵי שֶׁהוּא נִכְנָע לוֹ — **because** the borrower **is subservient to him,** הֲרֵי זֶה רִיבִּית — **this is** considered *ribbis.*

וְאִם תֹּאמַר — **Now, if you will ask:** וְהָא כְּתִיב — **But it is written** (*Mishlei* 22:7), "עֶבֶד לֹוֶה לְאִישׁ מַלְוֶה" — ***A debtor is a servant to the creditor?***[15] זֶהוּ אֵינוֹ אֶלָּא — The answer is that **this** rule applies **only** לְעִנְיָן שֶׁאִם נָפַל בֵּינֵיהֶם דִּין וּדְבָרִים — **in the event that a claim or argument arose between them,** וְאוֹמֵר הַמַּלְוֶה — **and the lender says,** נֵלֵךְ לְבֵית דִּין הַגָּדוֹל לָדוּן שָׁם — **"Let us travel to the Great *Beis Din*** (Rabbinical court) **to litigate there,"** וְהַלֹּוֶה אוֹמֵר לָדוּן כָּאן — **while the borrower says to litigate here,** in the local *Beis Din.* מְחוּיָּב הַלֹּוֶה לֵילֵךְ — In such a situation, **the borrower must go** כְּמוֹ שֶׁרוֹצֶה הַמַּלְוֶה — **as the lender wishes,** וְהַמַּלְוֶה אֵינוֹ מְחוּיָּב לָלֶכֶת לְבֵית דִּין הַגָּדוֹל שֶׁבְּמָקוֹם אַחֵר — **while the lender is not obligated to go to the Great *Beis Din* in another place** if the borrower wishes to go, מִשּׁוּם שֶׁנֶּאֱמַר — **because it is stated,** "עֶבֶד לֹוֶה לְאִישׁ מַלְוֶה" — ***A debtor is a servant to the creditor.*** This verse has no bearing, however, upon the *ribbis* prohibition.

§10 When one person hires another person to perform a service or when one patronizes another person's business, and does not pay him any more than what he would have paid a different worker or business owner, he has not actually given up anything tangible by patronizing this person over another. Nevertheless, he does receive the recipient's gratitude for having received the business. The Gemara (*Kiddushin* 58a-b, et al.) discusses whether the value of exercising one's option to patronize one person over another and thus receive that person's gratitude for having received the business (known as *tovas hanaah,* "benefit of gratitude") is considered financial value. This *se'if* will address the halachah of *tovas hanaah* as it pertains to the *ribbis* prohibition.

---

14. And the borrower can find out whether this person has arrived without expending any effort (*Shitah Mekubetzes* to *Bava Metzia* 75b).

15. This verse would appear to be teaching that it is incumbent upon the borrower to perform certain services on behalf of the lender.

י. אֲפִילּוּ טוֹבַת הֲנָאָה שֶׁאֵינוֹ מָמוֹן, אָסוּר לְהַמַּלְוֶה לֵיהָנוֹת מִן הַלֹּוֶה. כְּגוֹן שֶׁאִם הַמַּלְוֶה הוּא בַּעַל מְלָאכָה וְהַלֹּוֶה הַזֶּה אֵין דַּרְכּוֹ לִיתֵּן לוֹ מְלָאכָה בְּפַעַם אַחֵר רַק עַתָּה מֵחֲמַת שֶׁהִלְוָהוּ רוֹצֶה לָתֵת לוֹ מְלַאכְתּוֹ — אָסוּר[16].

יא. אָסוּר לְהַלְווֹת לְאֶחָד סְאָה[17] תְּבוּאָה שֶׁיַּחֲזִיר לוֹ אַחַר כָּךְ סְאָה תְּבוּאָה, אֲפִילּוּ מִין בְּמִינָהּ, כִּי שֶׁמָּא תִּתְיַיקֵּר בֵּינְתַּיִם הַתְּבוּאָה וְנִמְצָא זֶה מַחֲזִיר יוֹתֵר מִמַּה שֶּׁלָּוָה[18].

אֲפִילּוּ טוֹבַת הֲנָאָה — Even in a case of a "benefit of gratitude," **שֶׁאֵינוֹ מָמוֹן** — which **is not** considered to have true **financial value, אָסוּר לְהַמַּלְוֶה לֵיהָנוֹת מִן הַלֹּוֶה** — **the lender is forbidden to benefit from the borrower. כְּגוֹן** — **For example, שֶׁאִם הַמַּלְוֶה הוּא בַּעַל מְלָאכָה** — **if the lender is a workman, וְהַלֹּוֶה הַזֶּה אֵין דַּרְכּוֹ לִיתֵּן לוֹ מְלָאכָה בְּפַעַם אַחֵר** — **and on other occasions the borrower is not accustomed to provide him with work, רַק עַתָּה** — **only now, מֵחֲמַת שֶׁהִלְוָהוּ** — **since** this workman **has lent him** money, **רוֹצֶה לָתֵת לוֹ מְלַאכְתּוֹ** — the borrower **wishes to provide him with work, אָסוּר** — **it is prohibited.**[16]

§11 In this *se'if,* the prohibition known as lending "a *se'ah* for a *se'ah*" is detailed:

אָסוּר לְהַלְווֹת לְאֶחָד — **It is prohibited to lend someone סְאָה תְּבוּאָה** — **a *se'ah***[17] **of produce, שֶׁיַּחֲזִיר לוֹ אַחַר כָּךְ סְאָה תְּבוּאָה** — **in order that** the borrower **should later give him a *se'ah* of produce in return, אֲפִילּוּ מִין בְּמִינָהּ** — **even** if they are both of **the same kind** of produce. **כִּי שֶׁמָּא תִּתְיַיקֵּר בֵּינְתַּיִם הַתְּבוּאָה** — **For perhaps, in the meantime, the price of the produce will rise, וְנִמְצָא זֶה מַחֲזִיר יוֹתֵר מִמַּה שֶּׁלָּוָה** — **and it will turn out that this** borrower **is returning** goods that are **more** valuable **than those that he borrowed.**[18]

---

16. Unlike the typical case of *ribbis,* in this case, since (according to this opinion) the borrower's right to award this work to whomever he wishes is not considered a monetary benefit, and the borrower is paying him no more than what he would pay anyone else, he has not given anything extra to the lender, and no Biblical prohibition of *ribbis* has been transgressed. Nevertheless, since the lender is benefiting from having received, work that he would not have otherwise received, it is prohibited. [According to another opinion, *tovas hanaah* is considered to have intrinsic monetary value. According to that view, if one lends money with the stipulation that when he needs a worker he will award the job to the lender, that would be considered *ribbis ketzutzah* and be prohibited on a Biblical level (*Rama, Yoreh Deah* 160:23; see also *Beur HaGra* there §55; see also *Igros Moshe, Yoreh Deah* III, *Hil. Ribbis* 160:18).]

A lender may also not stipulate that the borrower refer customers to his business. According to *Igros Moshe* (ibid.), since there is a market value for the service of acting as a broker to attract customers, stipulating that the borrower perform this service constitutes *ribbis ketzutzah* and is, in fact, Biblically prohibited.

17. *Se'ah* is a measure of volume. This prohibition applies to any amount.

18. Although he is returning the exact same amount of produce that he borrowed, nevertheless, it is Rabbinically prohibited to return the more valuable produce, since what he is returning has greater value than what he borrowed. In order to avoid this situation, the Sages forbade the lending of goods unless one does it in the permitted manner cited by Kitzur in the line that follows, or in the permissible situations cited by Kitzur afterward.

This prohibition is not limited to produce. It applies to all goods and merchandise, except local currency (*Yoreh Deah* 162:1; see *Igros Moshe, Yoreh Deah* II, §114, who states that this exclusion applies even to our paper currency that is not tied to the value of gold or silver).

[Foreign currency is considered a commodity, and is treated as merchandise. For

אַךְ יַעֲשֶׂנּוּ דָמִים שֶׁאִם תִּתְיַיקֵּר הַתְּבוּאָה לֹא יִתֵּן לוֹ רַק הַדָּמִים[19]. וְאִם יֵשׁ לַלֹּוֶה אֲפִילּוּ רַק מְעַט מִמִּין זֶה, מוּתָּר לִלְוֹת אֲפִילּוּ כַּמָּה כּוֹרִין[20,21]. וְכֵן אִם יֵשׁ לוֹ לְאוֹתוֹ מִין שַׁעַר קָבוּעַ בְּשׁוּק, מוּתָּר לִלְוֹת, אַף עַל פִּי שֶׁאֵין לַלֹּוֶה כְּלוּם מִזֶּה הַמִּין[22]. וְכָל זֶה בְּמִין בְּמִינוֹ, אֲבָל מִין בְּשֶׁאֵינוֹ מִינוֹ, כְּגוֹן לְהַלְווֹת סְאָה חִיטִּין בִּסְאָה דוֹחַן, אָסוּר בְּכָל עִנְיָן, אַף עַל

אַךְ יַעֲשֶׂנּוּ דָמִים — Rather, to avoid this problem, when the loan of produce is made **he should convert it to** a loan of its **value,** by assessing its value and setting up the loan so that he is lending the *value* of the produce, not the produce itself. **שֶׁאִם תִּתְיַיקֵּר הַתְּבוּאָה לֹא יִתֵּן לוֹ רַק הַדָּמִים — Thus, if the price of the produce should rise, he will give only its** original **value** in return.[19]

Kitzur details two exceptions to the prohibition of lending goods for an equal amount of goods (a *se'ah* for a *se'ah*) without assessing its value. The first exception:
וְאִם יֵשׁ לַלֹּוֶה אֲפִילּוּ רַק מְעַט מִמִּין זֶה — If, at the time of the loan, **the borrower owns even a small amount of this kind** of produce that he wishes to borrow, **מוּתָּר לִלְוֹת אֲפִילּוּ כַּמָּה כּוֹרִין — it is permissible to borrow even several *kor***[20] of the same produce with the stipulation that he return that same amount of produce that he borrowed.[21]

The second exception:
וְכֵן אִם יֵשׁ לוֹ לְאוֹתוֹ מִין שַׁעַר קָבוּעַ בְּשׁוּק — So too, if that kind of produce **has a set market price, מוּתָּר לִלְוֹת — it is permissible to borrow** the produce, **אַף עַל פִּי שֶׁאֵין לַלֹּוֶה כְּלוּם מִזֶּה הַמִּין — even though the borrower does not have any of this kind** of produce.[22] In both of these cases payment may be made in the form of the produce borrowed even if the price rose in the interim.
וְכָל זֶה — This is all speaking **בְּמִין בְּמִינוֹ — of the same kind** of produce. **אֲבָל מִין בְּשֶׁאֵינוֹ מִינוֹ — However,** with regard to **unlike kinds** of produce, **כְּגוֹן לְהַלְווֹת סְאָה חִיטִּין בִּסְאָה דוֹחַן — for example to lend a *se'ah* of wheat in** order to receive **a *se'ah* of millet** in return, **אָסוּר בְּכָל עִנְיָן — it is prohibited under all circumstances, אַף עַל**

---

further discussion, see *The Laws of Ribbis* by Rabbi Yisroel Reisman, pp. 266, 273.]

[However, the prohibition of lending a *se'ah* for a *se'ah* does not apply to an article that is being lent for use and is afterward returned intact, such as a tool. Indeed, in such a case, even actual payment for the article's use is generally permitted, since it is not considered interest, but rent for the object, which is permissible; see *Yoreh Deah* §176 for further discussion.]

19. For example, if at the time of the loan, a *se'ah* of produce was worth $10, the loan must be set up as a loan with the value of $10. Thus, even if the price of the produce rises, and that amount of produce now sells for $12, he will not be obligated to pay more than $10 worth.

20. A larger measure [equal to thirty *se'ah*]. This is in fact true regardless of the amount.

21. In a case where the borrower owns the type of produce that he is borrowing, it is considered as if that produce is transferred to the lender at the time of borrowing. Thus, any fluctuation in price is viewed as having occurred in the lender's possession (*Rashi* to *Bava Metzia* 44b s.v. דינרי הוו ליה). This allowance extends even to a case in which the borrower owns a small amount of produce, and he may take out a loan of many times that amount on the basis of that produce [as to why this is so, see *Taz* 162:9 and *Shach* 162:16] (see *Rashi* ibid. 75a s.v. כמה כורין).

22. When the goods are readily available to all at a set price, it is viewed as if the borrower already has in his possession some of the type of goods that he is borrowing, in which case the prohibition of lending a *se'ah* for a *se'ah* does not apply [as to why this is so, see *Taz* 162:9 and *Shach* 162:16] (see *Beis Yosef* 162:3 from *Rashi* to *Bava Metzia* 72b s.v. אין לוין).

פִּי שֶׁהֵן בְּשַׁעַר אֶחָד וְיֵשׁ לוֹ דוֹחַן[23]. וּבְדָבָר קָטָן שֶׁאֵין הַדֶּרֶךְ לְהַקְפִּיד בְּיוֹקְרָא וְזוֹלָא, מוּתָּר בְּכָל עִנְיָן. וְלָכֵן מוּתֶּרֶת אִשָּׁה לְהַלְווֹת כִּכַּר לֶחֶם לַחֲבֶרְתָּהּ[24].

יב. הַמַּלְוֶה מָעוֹת עַל מַשְׁכּוֹן בַּיִת אוֹ שָׂדֶה אוֹ מָקוֹם בְּבֵית הַכְּנֶסֶת[25] וְהַמַּלְוֶה יִקַּח אֶת הַפֵּירוֹת מֵהַמַּשְׁכּוֹן, צָרִיךְ לִהְיוֹת בְּנַכְּיְיתָא, דְּהַיְינוּ שֶׁיְּנַכֶּה לוֹ מִן הַחוֹב דָּבָר קָצוּב לְכָל שָׁנָה, שֶׁזֶּהוּ יִהְיֶה הַשְּׂכִירוּת שֶׁנּוֹתֵן הַמַּלְוֶה. וַאֲפִילוּ הַשְּׂכִירוּת שָׁוָה יוֹתֵר מִמַּה

פִּי שֶׁהֵן בְּשַׁעַר אֶחָד — even if they have the same market price, וְיֵשׁ לוֹ דוֹחַן — and the borrower **has** a quantity of **millet** already in his possession.[23]

וּבְדָבָר קָטָן — Nevertheless, to lend a small item, שֶׁאֵין הַדֶּרֶךְ לְהַקְפִּיד בְּיוֹקְרָא וְזוֹלָא — regarding which one does not normally care about a rise or fall in price, מוּתָּר בְּכָל עִנְיָן — is permitted under all circumstances. וְלָכֵן מוּתֶּרֶת אִשָּׁה לְהַלְווֹת כִּכַּר לֶחֶם לַחֲבֶרְתָּהּ — Therefore, a woman may lend a loaf of bread to her friend.[24]

§12 One who lends money to another person may not benefit from the borrower's property. Thus, if a borrower pledges collateral for a loan, the lender may not benefit from that collateral (see below, 179:7) unless steps are taken to avoid the prohibition of *ribbis*, as detailed in this *se'if*:

הַמַּלְוֶה מָעוֹת עַל מַשְׁכּוֹן — One who lends money against collateral, בַּיִת אוֹ שָׂדֶה אוֹ מָקוֹם בְּבֵית הַכְּנֶסֶת — whether against **a house, a field, or a place in the synagogue,**[25] **וְהַמַּלְוֶה יִקַּח אֶת הַפֵּירוֹת מֵהַמַּשְׁכּוֹן — and** it is agreed that **the lender will receive the benefits of the collateral** as long as he holds it (i.e., by living in the house, reaping the fruit of the field, or occupying the place in the synagogue), **צָרִיךְ לִהְיוֹת בְּנַכְּיְיתָא — it must be done in a manner of deduction** so as to avoid the *ribbis* prohibition that would arise from receiving such benefits free of charge. **דְּהַיְינוּ שֶׁיְּנַכֶּה לוֹ מִן הַחוֹב — That is, he must deduct from the loan דָּבָר קָצוּב לְכָל שָׁנָה — a set amount for each year, שֶׁזֶּהוּ יִהְיֶה הַשְּׂכִירוּת שֶׁנּוֹתֵן הַמַּלְוֶה — and this will be the rent that the lender is paying** in return for his use of the property. Thus, he is not receiving free benefits in exchange for the loan. **וַאֲפִילוּ הַשְּׂכִירוּת שָׁוָה יוֹתֵר מִמַּה**

---

23. *Rama* 162:5. This applies to any type of goods or merchandise (*Shach* 162:15; for an explanation of this ruling, see *Igros Moshe, Yoreh Deah* III, *Hilchos Ribbis* 162:38).

24. The friend may later return another loaf of bread even if the price has risen in the meantime. This is because, for the most part, the price fluctuation is small, and is not considered meaningful to most people (*Mishnah Berurah* 450:2; see *Igros Moshe*, *Yoreh Deah* III, *Hil. Ribbis* 162:30, for further discussion). In fact, one may even borrow a small amount of bread on Erev Pesach [before the time of the prohibition of *chametz;* see below, 113:2] and return it after Pesach, even though at the time that he is returning the bread its price is considerably higher, since even such a difference in price is insignificant with regard to the small amount borrowed (*Mishnah Berurah* 450:2 with *Shaar HaTziyun* §4). See also below, 114:11.

One should not tell his fellow, "Join me for a meal in return for the meal that you once gave me," since it gives the appearance that he is repaying a loan, and, in the event that he provides him with a more elaborate meal, it would appear to be *ribbis.* If, however, one says, "Join me for a meal and I will join you another time," there are those who maintain that it is understood not as a loan, but as a graceful gesture so that the guest not feel embarrassed to accept the meal. In fact, since the offer to join the recipient for a meal at another time is not intended to serve as repayment, the latter may in return serve him a meal that is more elaborate than the one he received (*Rama, Orach Chaim* 170:13, as explained by *Mishnah Berurah* there §31-32; cf. *Taz* cited there).

25. In some congregations, one's place in the synagogue is purchased and belongs to the buyer.

שֶׁקָּצְבוּ בֵינֵיהֶם[26], מוּתָּר. אֲבָל לֹא יַחֲזִיר הַמַּלְוֶה וְיַשְׂכִּירוֹ לְהַלֹּוֶה עַצְמוֹ[27]. וְעוֹד יֵשׁ בְּעִנְיַן מַשְׁכַּנְתָּא הַרְבֵּה חִילּוּקֵי דִינִים, וְאֵין לַעֲשׂוֹת כִּי אִם עַל פִּי שְׁאֵלַת חָכָם.

יג. דָּבָר שֶׁיֵּשׁ לוֹ שַׁעַר יָדוּעַ אָסוּר לְמָכְרוֹ בְּיוֹתֵר מִן הַשַּׁעַר, מִפְּנֵי שֶׁמַּמְתִּין לוֹ אֶת הַמָּעוֹת[28]. אֲבָל דָּבָר שֶׁאֵין לוֹ שַׁעַר יָדוּעַ, אַף עַל פִּי שֶׁאִם הָיָה נוֹתֵן לוֹ עַתָּה אֶת הַמָּעוֹת הָיָה נוֹתְנוֹ לוֹ בְּפָחוֹת וּבִשְׁבִיל שֶׁהוּא מַמְתִּין אֶת הַמָּעוֹת מוֹכֵר לוֹ קְצָת בְּיוֹתֵר, מוּתָּר, וּבִלְבַד שֶׁלֹּא יַעֲלֵהוּ הַרְבֵּה (וְכָתַב בְּחַוּוֹת דַּעַת דְּהַיְינוּ שְׁתוּת אוֹ יוֹתֵר[29]) עַד שֶׁנִּיכָּר לַכֹּל שֶׁבִּשְׁבִיל הַמְתָּנַת הַמָּעוֹת הוּא מַעֲלֵהוּ. וְגַם אִם לֹא מַעֲלֵהוּ הַרְבֵּה, אֶלָּא שֶׁהוּא מְפָרֵשׁ וְאוֹמֵר "אִם תִּתֵּן לִי מִיָּד אֶת הַמָּעוֹת הֲרֵי לְךָ בְּי׳,

---

שֶׁקָּצְבוּ בֵינֵיהֶם — And even if the actual **value of the rental is more than** the amount of rent **that they agreed upon,**[26] **מוּתָּר — it is permitted. אֲבָל לֹא יַחֲזִיר הַמַּלְוֶה וְיַשְׂכִּירוֹ לְהַלֹּוֶה עַצְמוֹ — But the lender may not in turn rent it back to the borrower himself.**[27]

וְעוֹד יֵשׁ בְּעִנְיַן מַשְׁכַּנְתָּא הַרְבֵּה חִילּוּקֵי דִינִים — Additionally, there are many more particulars pertaining to the subject of a lender benefiting from **collateral. וְאֵין לַעֲשׂוֹת כִּי אִם עַל פִּי שְׁאֵלַת חָכָם — One should therefore not enter into** such a transaction **without consulting a Rabbinic authority.**

§13 When a person sells an item on credit, he is actually extending a loan to the purchaser for the purchase price. This *se'if* discusses whether a seller may charge more for his merchandise when he is extending credit.

דָּבָר שֶׁיֵּשׁ לוֹ שַׁעַר יָדוּעַ — An item that has a known market price אָסוּר לְמָכְרוֹ בְּיוֹתֵר מִן הַשַּׁעַר — may not be sold above the market price מִפְּנֵי שֶׁמַּמְתִּין לוֹ אֶת הַמָּעוֹת — due to the seller's **extending credit.**[28] **אֲבָל דָּבָר שֶׁאֵין לוֹ שַׁעַר יָדוּעַ — But an item that does not have a known market price — אַף עַל פִּי שֶׁאִם הָיָה נוֹתֵן לוֹ עַתָּה אֶת הַמָּעוֹת — even though if** the buyer **were to give** the seller **the money now הָיָה נוֹתְנוֹ לוֹ בְּפָחוֹת —** the seller **would give it to him for less, וּבִשְׁבִיל שֶׁהוּא מַמְתִּין אֶת הַמָּעוֹת — and since he is extending credit מוֹכֵר לוֹ קְצָת בְּיוֹתֵר — he sells it to him for somewhat more — מוּתָּר — it is permitted, וּבִלְבַד שֶׁלֹּא יַעֲלֵהוּ הַרְבֵּה — as long as he does not charge considerably more (וְכָתַב בְּחַוּוֹת דַּעַת — it is written in *Chavos Daas,*** *Yoreh Deah* 173:3, **דְּהַיְינוּ שְׁתוּת אוֹ יוֹתֵר — that** "considerably **more" is one-sixth or more),**[29] **עַד שֶׁנִּיכָּר לַכֹּל — to the extent that it is evident to all שֶׁבִּשְׁבִיל הַמְתָּנַת הַמָּעוֹת הוּא מַעֲלֵהוּ — that he is charging more because he is extending credit. וְגַם אִם לֹא מַעֲלֵהוּ הַרְבֵּה — And even if he does not charge considerably more, אֶלָּא שֶׁהוּא מְפָרֵשׁ וְאוֹמֵר — but explicitly tells him "אִם תִּתֵּן לִי מִיָּד אֶת הַמָּעוֹת — "If you give me the money now הֲרֵי לְךָ בְּי׳ — it is yours for ten**

---

26. I.e., he is deducting less than the normal market value of rent.

27. Renting the property back to the borrower may be considered actual *ribbis,* or, at the very least, have the appearance of *ribbis,* since he is now receiving payment directly from the borrower as a result of the loan (see *Beis Yosef* 164:1). See *Yoreh Deah* §164 with commentaries for further discussion.

28. Since the item has a set price, he is clearly charging more for extending credit, which constitutes *ribbis.* Therefore, in this case this is prohibited even if he did not explicitly state that he is charging more for this reason. See further in Kitzur.

29. For example, an item that he would have otherwise sold for $5 may not be sold on credit for $6.

וְאִם בְּהַקָּפָה תִּתֵּן לִי י״א״, אָסוּר[30]. וְכֵן אִם הַקּוֹנֶה קוֹנֶה אֶת הַסְּחוֹרָה בְּיוֹקֶר כְּדֵי לְמָכְרָהּ מִיָּד וּלְהַפְסִיד בִּשְׁבִיל שֶׁיִּהְיֶה הַמָּעוֹת בְּיָדוֹ אֵיזֶה זְמַן גַּם כֵּן אָסוּר[31] (מַהֲרַלְבַּ״ח וְסֵפֶר חֲתַם סוֹפֵר סִימָן קל״ז)[32].

---

coins, **וְאִם בְּהַקָּפָה** — **but if** you wish to purchase **on credit, תִּתֵּן לִי י״א״ — give me eleven," אָסוּר — it is** nevertheless **prohibited,** even though the difference is less than one-sixth.[30]

וְכֵן אִם הַקּוֹנֶה קוֹנֶה אֶת הַסְּחוֹרָה בְּיוֹקֶר — Similarly, even if none of the above prohibited circumstances were present, **for the purchaser to buy the merchandise at a high price** on credit **כְּדֵי לְמָכְרָהּ מִיָּד וּלְהַפְסִיד — for the purpose of reselling it immediately** (to someone who will pay without delay) **at a loss, בִּשְׁבִיל שֶׁיִּהְיֶה הַמָּעוֹת בְּיָדוֹ אֵיזֶה זְמַן — so that the money should be some time in his hand, גַּם כֵּן אָסוּר — is also prohibited**[31] **(מַהֲרַלְבַּ״ח וְסֵפֶר חֲתַם סוֹפֵר סִימָן קל״ז** — see ***Ralbach*** **§70 and *Responsa of Chasam Sofer, Yoreh Deah*** **§137).**[32]

§14 The *se'ifim* that follow introduce an innovative way of acquiring funds, which, although similar to *ribbis,* is nevertheless permitted (see *Rambam, Hilchos Malveh VeLoveh* 5:14).

---

30. A manufacturer or merchant may thus not set two prices, one if one pays cash and another higher price if one is postponing payment. This is prohibited even if the cash price is presented as a discount for cash sales, since the actual price is always assumed to be the price for cash, and one who is purchasing on credit is paying more for that option, which constitutes *ribbis* (see *Igros Moshe, Yoreh Deah* IV, 10:1; see also *Chochmas Adam* 139:5). A Rabbinic authority should be consulted to determine permissible pricing options.

31. For example, Reuven, who was in need of cash, offers to pay Shimon for some merchandise at the higher price of $100, and to pay him the next month. Shimon gives him the merchandise at the agreed-upon price, whereupon Reuven immediately resells the merchandise for the lower price of $90. Reuven thus obtains $90 for his use for a month, at which time he must pay Shimon $100 for the merchandise. In this case, since Reuven's intention in buying the merchandise was only to obtain money for his use for a period of time, after which point he will pay a higher amount, it is forbidden.

R' Shlomo Ganzfried (author of *Kitzur Shulchan Aruch*) was personally involved in a similar incident. R' Ganzfried sold merchandise on credit to a merchant, who in turn resold it at a loss (see *Chasam Sofer, Yoreh Deah* §137, cited by *Pischei Teshuvah* 173:1, for the particulars). R' Ganzfried posed to *Chasam Sofer* the question of whether any prohibition was involved in this transaction. In that case, *Chasam Sofer* ruled that it was a permitted transaction. His reasoning was based on the fact that the prohibition applies only when the original intention of the purchaser was to resell it immediately to obtain cash. In the case in which R' Ganzfried was involved, however, there was no reason to assume that the purchaser's original intention was to resell it immediately, since it involved a merchant, who dealt with this merchandise (and was, in fact, purchasing more of the same merchandise for cash). It is common for a merchant who purchases merchandise with the intention of selling it a later time to decide afterward to immediately resell the merchandise at a loss when a more lucrative investment opportunity comes his way.

32. In the case of *Ralbach*, Reuven (who did not have money available) approached Shimon, and requested of him to buy wool, which Reuven would then buy from him on credit at a higher price than Shimon had paid (see there for further particulars). *Ralbach* forbade such a transaction due to *ribbis* concerns. *Chasam Sofer* (ibid.) rules that this prohibition applies only when the one who is approached to purchase the merchandise (Shimon) does not deal with such merchandise. When he deals with such merchandise, it is permitted (see previous note).

יד. מִי שֶׁיֵּשׁ לוֹ שְׁטַר חוֹב עַל חֲבֵירוֹ, מוּתָּר לְמָכְרוֹ לְאַחֵר בְּפָחוֹת, וַאֲפִילוּ קוֹדֶם זְמַן הַפֵּרָעוֹן[33]. וְיִכְתּוֹב הַמּוֹכֵר לְהַלּוֹקֵחַ "אֲנִי מוֹכֵר לְךָ שְׁטָר זֶה, וּקְנֵי לְךָ אִיהוּ וְכָל שִׁעְבּוּדוֹ". וְצָרִיךְ שֶׁיְּהֵא הָאַחֲרָיוּת עַל הַלּוֹקֵחַ[34], רַק אַחֲרָיוּת שֶׁבָּא מֵחֲמַת הַמּוֹכֵר, כְּגוֹן שֶׁהַשְּׁטָר פָּרוּעַ וְכַדּוֹמֶה, יָכוֹל לִהְיוֹת עַל הַמּוֹכֵר. וּכְשֵׁם שֶׁיָּכוֹל לִמְכּוֹר אֶת הַשְּׁטָר לְאַחֵר בְּפָחוֹת, כְּמוֹ כֵן יָכוֹל לְמָכְרוֹ גַּם לְהַלֹּוֶה בְּעַצְמוֹ[35].

טו. וּבְאוֹפֶן זֶה יְכוֹלִין לְהוֹעִיל: כְּגוֹן רְאוּבֵן שֶׁצָּרִיךְ לְמָעוֹת בְּנִיסָן הוֹלֵךְ אֵצֶל שִׁמְעוֹן וְשִׁמְעוֹן נוֹתֵן לוֹ שְׁטַר חוֹב עַל עַצְמוֹ שֶׁהוּא חַיָּיב לִפְרוֹעַ לִרְאוּבֵן

מִי שֶׁיֵּשׁ לוֹ שְׁטַר חוֹב עַל חֲבֵירוֹ — **One who has a promissory note** drawn **against his fellow** מוּתָּר לְמָכְרוֹ לְאַחֵר בְּפָחוֹת — **may sell it to another** person **at a discount** from the amount of the original loan, וַאֲפִילוּ קוֹדֶם זְמַן הַפֵּרָעוֹן — **even before the time the payment** is due.[33] וְיִכְתּוֹב הַמּוֹכֵר לְהַלּוֹקֵחַ — **The seller is to write** the following **to the purchaser:** "אֲנִי מוֹכֵר לְךָ שְׁטָר זֶה — "I hereby **sell you this note;** וּקְנֵי לְךָ אִיהוּ וְכָל שִׁעְבּוּדוֹ" — **you shall** thus **acquire it and whatever lien it contains."** וְצָרִיךְ שֶׁיְּהֵא הָאַחֲרָיוּת עַל הַלּוֹקֵחַ — **The responsibility** (e.g., should the borrower default on the note) **must fall upon the purchaser;**[34] רַק אַחֲרָיוּת שֶׁבָּא מֵחֲמַת הַמּוֹכֵר — **only the responsibility that originates from the seller** — כְּגוֹן שֶׁהַשְּׁטָר פָּרוּעַ וְכַדּוֹמֶה — **such** as a claim **that the note has been paid, or the like** — יָכוֹל לִהְיוֹת עַל הַמּוֹכֵר — **may fall upon the seller.** וּכְשֵׁם שֶׁיָּכוֹל לִמְכּוֹר אֶת הַשְּׁטָר לְאַחֵר בְּפָחוֹת — **And just as** the lender **may sell the note to another person at a discount,** כְּמוֹ כֵן יָכוֹל לְמָכְרוֹ גַּם לְהַלֹּוֶה בְּעַצְמוֹ — **so too, he may also sell it to the borrower himself.**[35]

§15 Kitzur describes how funds may be acquired by means of a promissory note when someone does not currently own a promissory note:

וּבְאוֹפֶן זֶה יְכוֹלִין לְהוֹעִיל — **In this** following **manner** it **can be effective:** כְּגוֹן — **For example,** רְאוּבֵן שֶׁצָּרִיךְ לְמָעוֹת בְּנִיסָן — **Reuven, who is in need of money** now, **in** the month of **Nissan,** הוֹלֵךְ אֵצֶל שִׁמְעוֹן — **approaches Shimon,** וְשִׁמְעוֹן נוֹתֵן לוֹ שְׁטַר חוֹב עַל עַצְמוֹ — **and,** as a favor to Reuven, **Shimon gives him a promissory note** drawn **against himself** שֶׁהוּא חַיָּיב לִפְרוֹעַ לִרְאוּבֵן — **that he is obligated to**

33. A lender may sell a promissory note to a buyer, transferring to him the right to collect the debt. Invariably, the amount of the sale is less than the amount of the loan. In this way, the seller (lender) receives the money without the burden and risk involved in collecting the debt and (if the note is not yet due) without waiting for the loan to mature. The buyer takes upon himself the responsibility to collect the debt, but then profits by collecting more than what he paid for the note. Although in this case the buyer expends a certain amount of money and in due time collects more than he paid, it is not considered to be a form of *ribbis*, but rather a business transaction. This is because a promissory note is a financial instrument with a real market value. Thus, one who buys the note is not lending money; he is simply making a purchase.

34. For as long as the seller assumes responsibility for the debt (that is, to pay the amount of the loan to the buyer, in the event of default by the borrower), the note is still considered to belong to the seller, and has not truly been sold. What they have actually done is that the "buyer" has *lent* the "seller" the amount that he paid for the note (i.e., the amount of the original loan less the discount). When he collects the full amount of the loan from the original borrower or — in the event that the original borrower has no funds — from the "seller," it amounts to collecting interest (see *Taz, Yoreh Deah* 173:3).

35. For example, if the loan is for $1,000, and is not due for another six months, he may offer to sell it to the borrower for $900. The borrower will thus save $100 by repaying his debt six months earlier.

מֵאָה זְהוּבִים בְּחֹדֶשׁ תִּשְׁרֵי (וּכְנֶגֶד זֶה נוֹתֵן גַּם רְאוּבֵן שְׁטַר חוֹב כָּזֶה לְשִׁמְעוֹן שֶׁהוּא חַיָּיב לִפְרוֹעַ לוֹ מֵאָה זְהוּבִים בְּתִשְׁרֵי כְּדֵי שֶׁיְּהֵא שִׁמְעוֹן בָּטוּחַ), וְהוֹלֵךְ רְאוּבֵן וּמוֹכֵר אֶת הַשְּׁטָר חוֹב שֶׁיֵּשׁ לוֹ עַל שִׁמְעוֹן לְלֵוִי עַתָּה בְּנִיסָן בְּעַד תִּשְׁעִים זְהוּבִים[36]. (וּמִכָּל שֶׁכֵּן שֶׁאִם יֵשׁ לְשִׁמְעוֹן שְׁטַר חוֹב עַל יְהוּדָה אֲשֶׁר זְמַן הַפֵּרָעוֹן הוּא לְאַחַר זְמַן שֶׁהוּא יָכוֹל לְמָכְרוֹ לִרְאוּבֵן בְּהַקָּפָה עַד הַזְּמַן וּרְאוּבֵן יִתֵּן לוֹ שְׁטַר חוֹב עַל זֹאת, וְשׁוּב יִמְכּוֹר רְאוּבֵן אֶת הַשְּׁטָר חוֹב הַזֶּה בְּעַד כַּמָּה שֶׁיּוּכַל[37].) אֲבָל אִם רְאוּבֵן יִכְתּוֹב שְׁטַר חוֹב עַל עַצְמוֹ לְמָכְרוֹ לְשִׁמְעוֹן[38], אֲפִילּוּ עַל יְדֵי שָׁלִיחַ, אָסוּר[39].

---

pay Reuven **מֵאָה זְהוּבִים בְּחֹדֶשׁ תִּשְׁרֵי — one hundred gold pieces in the month of Tishrei** (six months from now) (**וּכְנֶגֶד זֶה — and, in exchange, נוֹתֵן גַּם רְאוּבֵן שְׁטַר חוֹב כָּזֶה לְשִׁמְעוֹן — Reuven also gives a similar promissory note to Shimon שֶׁהוּא חַיָּיב לִפְרוֹעַ לוֹ מֵאָה זְהוּבִים בְּתִשְׁרֵי — that he is obligated to pay him one hundred gold pieces in Tishrei, כְּדֵי שֶׁיְּהֵא שִׁמְעוֹן בָּטוּחַ — so that Shimon should be secure** that Reuven will pay him). **וְהוֹלֵךְ רְאוּבֵן — Reuven then goes וּמוֹכֵר אֶת הַשְּׁטָר חוֹב שֶׁיֵּשׁ לוֹ עַל שִׁמְעוֹן — and sells the promissory note that he has** drawn **against Shimon לְלֵוִי — to Levi, עַתָּה בְּנִיסָן בְּעַד תִּשְׁעִים זְהוּבִים — now, in Nissan, for ninety gold pieces.** Reuven has now received ninety gold pieces for use until Tishrei, at which time he will pay Shimon one hundred gold pieces, which Shimon pays to Levi.[36] (**וּמִכָּל שֶׁכֵּן שֶׁאִם יֵשׁ לְשִׁמְעוֹן שְׁטַר חוֹב עַל יְהוּדָה — And certainly if Shimon has a promissory note** drawn **against Yehudah, אֲשֶׁר זְמַן הַפֵּרָעוֹן הוּא לְאַחַר זְמַן — which is due after some time, שֶׁהוּא יָכוֹל לְמָכְרוֹ לִרְאוּבֵן בְּהַקָּפָה עַד הַזְּמַן — he may sell it to Reuven on credit until** that **time וּרְאוּבֵן יִתֵּן לוֹ שְׁטַר חוֹב עַל זֹאת — and Reuven will give him a promissory note** in return **for this. וְשׁוּב יִמְכּוֹר רְאוּבֵן אֶת הַשְּׁטָר חוֹב הַזֶּה — Reuven, in turn, will sell this note** that he bought from Shimon today **בְּעַד כַּמָּה שֶׁיּוּכַל — for as much as he could** receive for it.)[37] **אֲבָל אִם רְאוּבֵן יִכְתּוֹב שְׁטַר חוֹב עַל עַצְמוֹ** — Nevertheless, this is permissible only because he is selling it to a third party. **However, if Reuven were to write a promissory note** drawn **against himself, לְמָכְרוֹ לְשִׁמְעוֹן** — in order **to sell it to Shimon,**[38] **אֲפִילּוּ עַל יְדֵי שָׁלִיחַ — even** if he would do this **by means of an agent, אָסוּר — it is prohibited.**[39]

---

36. Although this is similar to *ribbis*, in that Reuven acquires 90 gold pieces today and it will cost him 100 gold pieces in six months, nevertheless, in fact, no actual loan occurred for which interest could have been assessed, since Reuven and Shimon have merely exchanged promissory notes. Later, when Reuven pays his obligation to Shimon, it is an independent transaction, unrelated to the money that he obtained from the promissory note that he received from him.

37. Here too, although Reuven will receive less for the promissory note today than he will eventually give Shimon when the loan matures, it is permitted, since when Shimon pays him, he is not paying back the money he received for the promissory note, but rather for an independent obligation that he took upon himself in exchange for the loan of another.

38. That is, Reuven seeks to obtain funds right now by writing a promissory note obligating himself to pay Shimon 100 gold pieces in six months, and "selling" that note to Shimon now for 90 gold pieces.

39. This does not constitute the sale of a loan, since no obligation exists until the promissory note changes hands. Thus, when he "sells" it to Shimon for 90 gold pieces, he has actually borrowed from Shimon those 90 gold pieces with the agreement that he will pay him back 100 gold pieces, and has thus transgressed the Biblical prohibition of *ribbis* (see *Chochmas Adam* 143:8).

טז. אָסוּר לִקְנוֹת תְּבוּאָה אוֹ שְׁאָר דָּבָר בְּהַקְדָּמַת מָעוֹת וְשֶׁיִּתֵּן לוֹ אֶת הַתְּבוּאָה לְאַחַר זְמַן דְּחַיְישִׁינַן שֶׁמָּא בֵינְתַיִם תִּתְיַקֵּר הַתְּבוּאָה אַחַר כָּךְ בִּזְמַן שֶׁיִּתֵּן לוֹ אֶת הַתְּבוּאָה נִמְצָא הַלּוֹקֵחַ נוֹטֵל יוֹתֵר מִשִּׁיעוּר מְעוֹתָיו בִּשְׁבִיל שֶׁהִקְדִּים אֶת הַמָּעוֹת[40]. אֲבָל אִם יֵשׁ לְהַמּוֹכֵר גַּם עַתָּה כָּל הַתְּבוּאָה שֶׁהוּא מוֹכֵר, אַף עַל פִּי שֶׁלֹּא יִתְּנָהּ לְהַלּוֹקֵחַ עַד לְאַחַר זְמַן, מוּתָּר. כִּי מַה שֶּׁיֵּשׁ לְהָאָדָם יָכוֹל לִמְכּוֹר אֲפִילוּ בְּזוֹל הַרְבֵּה כִּרְצוֹנוֹ[41]. וַאֲפִילוּ הַתְּבוּאָה לֹא נִגְמַר עֲדַיִין לִגְמְרֵי כָּרָאוּי, אֶלָּא שֶׁצְּרִיכָה עוֹד מְלָאכָה אַחַת אוֹ שְׁתֵּי מְלָאכוֹת, נֶחְשָׁב כְּאִלּוּ הִיא גְמוּרָה וּמוּתָּר. אֲבָל אִם מְחוּסֶּרֶת עוֹד שָׁלֹשׁ מְלָאכוֹת, אָסוּר (וְעַיֵּין בְּסִימָן שֶׁלְּאַחַר זֶה הֶיתֵּר לְהַקְדָּמַת מָעוֹת עַל סְחוֹרָה).

---

§16 This *se'if* discusses the halachah regarding advancing funds for produce or merchandise in order to take possession at a later date.

אָסוּר לִקְנוֹת תְּבוּאָה אוֹ שְׁאָר דָּבָר בְּהַקְדָּמַת מָעוֹת — It is prohibited to purchase produce or another item by advancing the funds **וְשֶׁיִּתֵּן לוֹ אֶת הַתְּבוּאָה לְאַחַר זְמַן** — in order **that** the seller **will give the produce** or merchandise **to** the buyer **at a later time,** **דְּחַיְישִׁינַן שֶׁמָּא בֵינְתַיִם תִּתְיַקֵּר הַתְּבוּאָה — for we are concerned that the price of the produce may rise in the meantime.** **אַחַר כָּךְ בִּזְמַן שֶׁיִּתֵּן לוֹ אֶת הַתְּבוּאָה** — Thus, **afterward, at the time when he will give him the produce,** **נִמְצָא הַלּוֹקֵחַ נוֹטֵל יוֹתֵר מִשִּׁיעוּר מְעוֹתָיו — it** will **turn out that the purchaser receives more** produce **than the value of the money** that he paid **בִּשְׁבִיל שֶׁהִקְדִּים אֶת הַמָּעוֹת — in return for advancing the money.**[40]

An exception to this prohibition:

אֲבָל אִם יֵשׁ לְהַמּוֹכֵר גַּם עַתָּה כָּל הַתְּבוּאָה שֶׁהוּא מוֹכֵר — But if now, too (i.e., at the time that he is receiving payment), **the seller has all of the produce that he is selling,** **אַף עַל פִּי שֶׁלֹּא יִתְּנָהּ לְהַלּוֹקֵחַ עַד לְאַחַר זְמַן, מוּתָּר — even though he will not give it to the purchaser until later, it is permitted.** **כִּי מַה שֶּׁיֵּשׁ לְהָאָדָם — For whatever a person** currently **owns** **יָכוֹל לִמְכּוֹר אֲפִילוּ בְּזוֹל הַרְבֵּה כִּרְצוֹנוֹ — he may sell as he wishes, even very inexpensively.**[41] **וַאֲפִילוּ הַתְּבוּאָה לֹא נִגְמַר עֲדַיִין לִגְמְרֵי כָּרָאוּי — And even if** the processing of **the produce has not yet been totally completed as required,** **אֶלָּא שֶׁצְּרִיכָה עוֹד מְלָאכָה אַחַת אוֹ שְׁתֵּי מְלָאכוֹת — but it still requires one or two processes** before it will be ready for the customer, **נֶחְשָׁב כְּאִלּוּ הִיא גְמוּרָה** — nevertheless, **it is considered complete,** **וּמוּתָּר — and it is permitted.** **אֲבָל אִם מְחוּסֶּרֶת עוֹד שָׁלֹשׁ מְלָאכוֹת — However, if it lacks three additional processes** in order to be ready for the customer, **אָסוּר — it is prohibited** to structure the deal in this manner. (**וְעַיֵּין בְּסִימָן שֶׁלְּאַחַר זֶה הֶיתֵּר לְהַקְדָּמַת מָעוֹת עַל סְחוֹרָה — See the *Siman* that follows** (66:8) for **a permissible manner to advance funds on merchandise** even when it is lacking three or more processes.)

---

40. One who advances funds for produce or merchandise is in effect extending a loan to the seller. Therefore, it would constitute *ribbis* if what he receives in return is worth more than what he has paid.

41. Therefore, even if the price does rise, the buyer is not seen as receiving more value than what he paid for due to the fact that he paid earlier, but rather, we view it as if he received at the time of the sale an expensive product for an inexpensive price. Nevertheless, even in this case the seller may not explicitly say that he is discounting the price due to his having paid early (*Rama* 173:7). [Note that here, unlike with regard to lending a *se'ah* for a *se'ah* in *se'if* 11, the seller must own the *entire* quantity of merchandise being sold at the time of the original payment.]

יז. וְאִם הוּקְבַּע הַשַּׁעַר לִתְבוּאָה[42], יָכוֹל לִקְנוֹת בְּהַקְדָּמַת מָעוֹת כְּפִי הַשַּׁעַר, אַף עַל פִּי שֶׁאֵין לְהַמּוֹכֵר כְּלוּם, שֶׁהֲרֵי אֲפִילוּ תִתְיַקֵּר אַחַר כָּךְ הַתְּבוּאָה אֵין הַלּוֹקֵחַ מַרְוִיחַ בְּמַה שֶׁהִקְדִּים אֶת הַמָּעוֹת כֵּיוָן שֶׁהָיָה יָכוֹל לִקְנוֹת אָז תְּבוּאָה בִּמְעוֹתָיו בְּשַׁעַר זֶה[43]. וּמֵאַחַר שֶׁפָּסַק בְּהֶיתֵּר, אַף עַל פִּי שֶׁנִּתְיַקְּרָה אַחַר כָּךְ הַתְּבוּאָה בִּשְׁעַת הַפֵּרָעוֹן וְאֵינוֹ רוֹצֶה לָתֵת לוֹ אֶת הַתְּבוּאָה שֶׁפָּסַק עָלֶיהָ, יָכוֹל לְשׁוּמָהּ עַל סְחוֹרָה אַחֶרֶת שֶׁיִּתֵּן לוֹ אוֹ שֶׁיִּתֵּן לוֹ מָעוֹת כְּשׁוֹוִי שֶׁל עַתָּה[44] (עַיֵּין בְּקוּנְטְרֵס שַׁעַר

---

§17 Another exception to the prohibition of advancing funds for produce or merchandise:

וְאִם הוּקְבַּע הַשַּׁעַר לִתְבוּאָה — If the market price for produce or merchandise **has been established,**[42] **יָכוֹל לִקְנוֹת בְּהַקְדָּמַת מָעוֹת כְּפִי הַשַּׁעַר — one may purchase** produce **at the market price by advancing funds, אַף עַל פִּי שֶׁאֵין לְהַמּוֹכֵר כְּלוּם — even if the seller has none** of the produce. **שֶׁהֲרֵי אֲפִילוּ תִתְיַקֵּר אַחַר כָּךְ הַתְּבוּאָה — For even if the price of the produce** or merchandise **were to subsequently rise, אֵין הַלּוֹקֵחַ מַרְוִיחַ בְּמַה שֶׁהִקְדִּים אֶת הַמָּעוֹת — the purchaser has not profited by advancing the funds, כֵּיוָן שֶׁהָיָה יָכוֹל לִקְנוֹת אָז תְּבוּאָה בִּמְעוֹתָיו בְּשַׁעַר זֶה — for he was able to purchase produce** or merchandise **at that time** on the open market **at this** same **price.**[43]

Thus, in the situations where it is permitted to advance payment (when the buyer has the merchandise or when the same merchandise is available on the open market for that price), it is permitted to accept the merchandise even if the price did indeed rise, since this transaction does not appear like *ribbis.* Kitzur now extends this ruling to cases where the seller wishes, at the time that the delivery is due, to give different merchandise in exchange for the merchandise that he owes the buyer:

וּמֵאַחַר שֶׁפָּסַק בְּהֶיתֵּר — Once the seller **has stipulated** to sell the produce for a certain price, **in a permissible manner** (i.e., either when he had the produce or if it was available on the open market for that price), **אַף עַל פִּי שֶׁנִּתְיַקְּרָה אַחַר כָּךְ הַתְּבוּאָה בִּשְׁעַת הַפֵּרָעוֹן** — then **even though the produce has risen in price afterward, at the time the payment** of the produce is due, **וְאֵינוֹ רוֹצֶה לָתֵת לוֹ אֶת הַתְּבוּאָה שֶׁפָּסַק עָלֶיהָ — if he does not wish to give him the produce that he has stipulated** to give, **יָכוֹל לְשׁוּמָהּ עַל סְחוֹרָה אַחֶרֶת שֶׁיִּתֵּן לוֹ — he may assess its** value **on other merchandise that he will give him, אוֹ שֶׁיִּתֵּן לוֹ מָעוֹת כְּשׁוֹוִי שֶׁל עַתָּה — or give him money according to its current value.**[44] (עַיֵּין בְּקוּנְטְרֵס שַׁעַר דֵּעָה בְּסוֹף הַסֵּפֶר שַׁעַר מִשְׁפָּט

---

42. That is, when an ample supply of a product is reaching the market and the price has stabilized.

43. When a person pays in advance for produce that was unavailable at that price, and then receives produce that rose in value from his time of purchase, it is seen as *ribbis*, since he is receiving more than he would otherwise have bought for that money only because he advanced the funds. However, when that amount of produce was available at that price in the open market at the time of his purchase, he is not seen as having gained anything by advancing the funds, because he could just as easily have bought it in the market at that time, in which case the produce would have risen in value in his possession.

Even in this case, however, one may not stipulate a lower price than the current market price at the time of payment.

44. For example, in a case where the buyer had advanced payment of $100 to the seller, and by the time the produce is due it has risen in price to $110, the seller, instead of giving him that produce, may exchange it for other merchandise that is worth $110, since that is the value of the produce that he owes him now. Not only may he give him

דֵּעָה בְּסוֹף הַסֵּפֶר שַׁעַר מִשְׁפָּט סִימָן קע"ה סְעִיף קָטָן ב׳ (הָרִאשׁוֹן), וּדְלֹא כְּמוֹ שֶׁכָּתַב בְּשֻׁלְחָן עָרוּךְ שֶׁל הַתַּנְיָא סְעִיף כ"ח)[45].

יח. מִי שֶׁיֵּשׁ לוֹ סְחוֹרָה שֶׁנִּמְכֶּרֶת כָּאן בְּזוֹל וּבְמָקוֹם אַחֵר בְּיוֹקֶר, וְאָמַר לוֹ חֲבֵירוֹ תְּנָה לִי סְחוֹרָה זֹאת וְאוֹלִיכֶנָּה לִמְקוֹם הַיּוֹקֶר וְאֶמְכְּרֶנָּה שָׁם וְאֶעֱשֶׂה צְרָכַי בְּמָעוֹת עַד זְמַן פְּלוֹנִי וְאֶפְרָעֶנָּה לְךָ כְּפִי מַה שֶּׁהָיָה שָׁוֶה שָׁם לְאַחַר נִכְּיוֹן הַהוֹצָאוֹת שֶׁעָלוּ עַל הַסְּחוֹרָה[46] — אִם הָאַחֲרָיוּת בַּהֲלִיכָה הָיָה עַל הַלּוֹקֵחַ, אָסוּר[47], וְאִם הָאַחֲרָיוּת עַל

(סִימָן קע"ה סְעִיף קָטָן ב׳ (הָרִאשׁוֹן — See *Kuntres Shaar Deah* at the end of *Sefer Shaar Mishpat, Siman* 175, *se'if katan* 2 [§1], **וּדְלֹא כְּמוֹ שֶׁכָּתַב בְּשֻׁלְחָן עָרוּךְ שֶׁל הַתַּנְיָא סְעִיף כ"ח — which is contrary to what is written in *Shulchan Aruch* of the *Tanya*,** *Hilchos Ribbis*, ***se'if* 28.)**[45]

§18 The discussion turns to various *ribbis* issues that may arise when one purchases merchandise in one town and resells it in a different town:

מִי שֶׁיֵּשׁ לוֹ סְחוֹרָה — If one who has merchandise שֶׁנִּמְכֶּרֶת כָּאן בְּזוֹל — that is sold locally at a low price וּבְמָקוֹם אַחֵר בְּיוֹקֶר — and in another place is sold **at a high price, וְאָמַר לוֹ חֲבֵירוֹ — was told by his fellow, תְּנָה לִי סְחוֹרָה זֹאת — "Give me this merchandise, וְאוֹלִיכֶנָּה לִמְקוֹם הַיּוֹקֶר — and I will bring it to the place** where it is sold at a **high price, וְאֶמְכְּרֶנָּה שָׁם — and I will sell it there, וְאֶעֱשֶׂה צְרָכַי בְּמָעוֹת עַד זְמַן פְּלוֹנִי — and I will make use of the money for my own needs until such-and-such time, וְאֶפְרָעֶנָּה לְךָ — when I will repay you כְּפִי מַה שֶּׁהָיָה שָׁוֶה שָׁם — according to what** the merchandise **was worth there, לְאַחַר נִכְּיוֹן הַהוֹצָאוֹת שֶׁעָלוּ עַל הַסְּחוֹרָה — after deducting the expenses that were expended on the merchandise,"**[46] whether the owner of the merchandise may accept this offer depends on its terms, as follows: **אִם הָאַחֲרָיוּת בַּהֲלִיכָה הָיָה עַל הַלּוֹקֵחַ — If the responsibility** for any mishap that occurs **while bringing** the merchandise to the other town **was borne by the purchaser** (i.e., the one who resells the merchandise in the other town), **אָסוּר — it is prohibited.**[47] **וְאִם הָאַחֲרָיוּת עַל הַמּוֹכֵר — But if the responsibility** was

---

other merchandise, but he may also give him $110 in cash in exchange for the produce. Although the buyer has given him $100 earlier and is now receiving $110, this is not seen as *ribbis*, since the seller is merely giving him the current value for the produce that he presently owes him.

45. According to *Shulchan Aruch HaRav*, if the price of the produce has risen, the seller may not exchange the produce with money, for since the buyer gave him a certain amount of money and is now receiving more money back in return, it appears too much like *ribbis*, and is prohibited.

46. For example, the merchandise can be sold for $800 locally (City A), and for $1,000 in City B. Shimon tells Reuven (the owner of the merchandise) that he will take the merchandise to City B, where he will sell it for $1,000. When he returns he will give the entire $1,000 that were the proceeds of the sale to Reuven, only deducting the actual expenses incurred in transporting and selling the merchandise. Although Shimon is not profiting from the sale, he does gain by having use of the money until the time that he must repay Reuven (see *Shulchan Aruch HaRav, Hil. Ribbis, se'if* 20).

47. Since the seller (Reuven) assumes no responsibility for any mishap, when Shimon receives the goods from Reuven it is viewed as an immediate sale of $800 worth of merchandise, in which Reuven, the seller, does not demand payment until a later time. By ultimately paying more than what the merchandise is worth *locally*, the buyer (Shimon) is paying *ribbis* in return for the use of the money.

הַמּוֹכֵר, מוּתָּר[48]**, וְהוּא שֶׁיִּתֵּן לְהַלּוֹקֵחַ אֵיזֶה דָבָר בִּשְׁבִיל טָרְחוֹ**[49]**.**

יט. מוּתָּר לְהַלְווֹת לַחֲבֵרוֹ ק׳ דִּינָרִין שֶׁיִּקְנֶה בָהֶם סְחוֹרָה עַל הַיָּרִיד, וּבְשׁוּבָם לְבֵיתָם יִתֵּן לוֹ הַלֹּוֶה ק״כ דִּינָרִין בַּעֲדָהּ, וּבִלְבַד שֶׁיְּקַבֵּל הַמַּלְוֶה אֶת הַסְּחוֹרָה וְיוֹלִיכֶנָּה לְבֵיתוֹ וְיִהְיֶה אַחֲרָיוּת הַדֶּרֶךְ עַל הַמַּלְוֶה, דְּהָוֵי כְּמוֹ שֶׁיֵּשׁ לוֹ חֵלֶק בְּרֶיוַח הַסְּחוֹרָה הוֹאִיל וּמְקַבֵּל עָלָיו אַחֲרָיוּת[50]**.**

כ. רְאוּבֵן שֶׁהוֹלֵךְ לְמָקוֹם שֶׁקּוֹנִים סְחוֹרָה בְּזוֹל יָכוֹל שִׁמְעוֹן לוֹמַר לוֹ הָבֵא לִי סְחוֹרָה

---

borne by the original **seller,** **מוּתָּר — it is permitted,**[48] **וְהוּא שֶׁיִּתֵּן לְהַלּוֹקֵחַ אֵיזֶה דָבָר בִּשְׁבִיל טָרְחוֹ — provided that** the original seller **pays the purchaser,** who resells the merchandise, **something for his effort.**[49]

§19 This *se'if* discusses a case involving someone who is at a fair in a different town, and wishes to borrow money from another person from his hometown in order to purchase merchandise at the fair.

מוּתָּר לְהַלְווֹת לַחֲבֵרוֹ ק׳ דִּינָרִין — One may lend his fellow 100 ***dinar*** **שֶׁיִּקְנֶה בָהֶם סְחוֹרָה עַל הַיָּרִיד — to purchase** 100 *dinar* worth of **merchandise at the fair,** **וּבְשׁוּבָם לְבֵיתָם** — with the stipulation that **when they return home,** **יִתֵּן לוֹ הַלֹּוֶה ק״כ דִּינָרִין בַּעֲדָהּ — the borrower will give him 120** ***dinar*** **for the merchandise,** **וּבִלְבַד שֶׁיְּקַבֵּל הַמַּלְוֶה אֶת הַסְּחוֹרָה — provided that the lender takes possession of the merchandise,** **וְיוֹלִיכֶנָּה לְבֵיתוֹ — and brings it home,** **וְיִהְיֶה אַחֲרָיוּת הַדֶּרֶךְ עַל הַמַּלְוֶה — and that the responsibility for** any mishap that occurs along **the way is borne by the lender.** **דְּהָוֵי כְּמוֹ שֶׁיֵּשׁ לוֹ חֵלֶק בְּרֶיוַח הַסְּחוֹרָה — For it is as if** the lender **has a portion in the profit of the merchandise,** **הוֹאִיל וּמְקַבֵּל עָלָיו אַחֲרָיוּת — since he accepts responsibility for** anything that may happen to **it.**[50]

§20 A similar case:

רְאוּבֵן שֶׁהוֹלֵךְ לְמָקוֹם שֶׁקּוֹנִים סְחוֹרָה בְּזוֹל — If Reuven is going to a place where merchandise is purchased inexpensively, **יָכוֹל שִׁמְעוֹן לוֹמַר לוֹ — Shimon may tell him,** **הָבֵא לִי סְחוֹרָה מִשָּׁם — "Bring me merchandise from there**

---

48. If the seller assumes responsibility, the merchandise is considered his until it is sold, and he is entitled to the full proceeds of the sale in the other town after deducting expenses. The buyer is considered to be no more than an agent to sell the seller's merchandise in the second town at a higher price (*Chochmas Adam* 139:18). When Shimon makes use of the proceeds of the sale, he is actually borrowing *that* amount from Reuven ($1,000 minus expenses), and he may repay that amount without a concern that he is paying *ribbis.*

49. As explained in the previous note, when the original owner assumes responsibility, the merchandise is considered his until it is sold, and the buyer is no more than an agent contracted to perform a service for him. If he does not reimburse him for this service, it emerges that the buyer has rendered a service to the original owner for the privilege of later borrowing the proceeds of the sale in the second town. This would constitute advance *ribbis* (see above, *se'if* 6). By compensating the buyer for his efforts, the *ribbis* issue is avoided (*Rosh, Bava Metzia* 5:22). See below, 66:1.

50. Since the lender is taking responsibility for any mishap along the way, it is considered as if no loan took place in the town where the agreement was made. Rather, the lender acquires ownership in the merchandise that gives him a right to its profits. Thus, when the borrower pays him 120 *dinar* for it, the lender is realizing profit on an investment, not interest on a loan (see *Taz* 173:31; see also *Chavos Daas, Beurim* 173:28).

מִשָּׁם וַאֲנִי אֶתֵּן לְךָ רֶיוַח כָּךְ וְכָךְ, וּבִלְבַד שֶׁתְּהֵא אַחֲרָיוּת הַסְּחוֹרָה עַל רְאוּבֵן עַד שֶׁהוּא מוֹסְרָהּ לְשִׁמְעוֹן[51].

כא. מוּתָּר לְהַרְבּוֹת שְׂכַר הַקַּרְקַע. כֵּיצַד? הִשְׂכִּיר לוֹ אֶת הֶחָצֵר[52] וְאָמַר לוֹ קוֹדֶם שֶׁהֶחֱזִיק בּוֹ "אִם תִּתֵּן לִי אֶת הַשְּׂכִירוּת מִיָּד, הֲרֵי הוּא לְךָ בִּי' זְהוּבִים לְשָׁנָה. וְאִם תְּשַׁלֵּם לִי בְּכָל חוֹדֶשׁ, תִּתֵּן לִי בְּעַד כָּל חוֹדֶשׁ אֶחָד זָהוּב"[53] — מוּתָּר. וְהַטַּעַם בָּזֶה מִשּׁוּם דְּמִצַּד הַדִּין שְׂכִירוּת אֵינָהּ מִשְׁתַּלֶּמֶת אֶלָּא לְבַסּוֹף, הִלְכָּךְ כַּאֲשֶׁר לוֹקֵחַ מִמֶּנּוּ זָהוּב בְּכָל חוֹדֶשׁ דַּהֲוָה לֵיהּ י"ב זְהוּבִים אֵין זֹאת שְׂכַר הַמְתָּנַת הַמָּעוֹת שֶׁהֲרֵי אֵינוֹ מְחוּיָּב לְשַׁלֵּם לוֹ בְּמוּקְדָּם. וּמַה שֶּׁאָמַר לוֹ "אִם תִּתֵּן לִי מִיָּד, הֲרֵי הִיא לְךָ בַּעֲשָׂרָה", אָז הָיָה מוֹחֵל לוֹ שְׁנֵי זְהוּבִים לְפִי שֶׁמַּקְדִּים לוֹ לְשַׁלֵּם

וַאֲנִי אֶתֵּן לְךָ רֶיוַח כָּךְ וְכָךְ — **and I will give you such-and-such** an amount **as profit,"** וּבִלְבַד שֶׁתְּהֵא אַחֲרָיוּת הַסְּחוֹרָה עַל רְאוּבֵן — **provided that the responsibility for the merchandise is borne by Reuven,** עַד שֶׁהוּא מוֹסְרָהּ לְשִׁמְעוֹן — **until he turns over the merchandise to Shimon.**[51]

§21 The following *se'ifim* discuss the laws of a discount for prepayment of rentals and wages.

מוּתָּר לְהַרְבּוֹת שְׂכַר הַקַּרְקַע — **It is permitted to add to the rental price of land** if the rent is not paid in advance. כֵּיצַד — **How** can this be done? הִשְׂכִּיר לוֹ אֶת הֶחָצֵר — **One** who **rented a courtyard**[52] to another person, וְאָמַר לוֹ קוֹדֶם שֶׁהֶחֱזִיק בּוֹ — **and** the owner **told** the renter **before he took possession of it,** "אִם תִּתֵּן לִי אֶת הַשְּׂכִירוּת מִיָּד — **"If you pay me the rent now,** הֲרֵי הוּא לְךָ בִּי' זְהוּבִים לְשָׁנָה — **it is** rented **to you for ten gold pieces per year,** וְאִם תְּשַׁלֵּם לִי בְּכָל חוֹדֶשׁ — **but if you pay me monthly** תִּתֵּן לִי בְּעַד כָּל חוֹדֶשׁ אֶחָד זָהוּב" — **give me one gold piece per month,"**[53] מוּתָּר — **it is permitted.** וְהַטַּעַם בָּזֶה — **And the reason for this is** מִשּׁוּם דְּמִצַּד הַדִּין — **since legally** שְׂכִירוּת אֵינָהּ מִשְׁתַּלֶּמֶת אֶלָּא לְבַסּוֹף — **rent is due only at the end** of its term, הִלְכָּךְ — **therefore,** כַּאֲשֶׁר לוֹקֵחַ מִמֶּנּוּ זָהוּב בְּכָל חוֹדֶשׁ — **when** the landlord **takes one gold piece from** the renter **per month,** דַּהֲוָה לֵיהּ י"ב זְהוּבִים — **which is twelve gold pieces** per year, אֵין זֹאת שְׂכַר הַמְתָּנַת הַמָּעוֹת — **it is not** considered **earnings for waiting for his money,** which is *ribbis.* On the contrary, the renter has merely fulfilled his obligation as required, שֶׁהֲרֵי אֵינוֹ מְחוּיָּב לְשַׁלֵּם לוֹ בְּמוּקְדָּם — **since he is not obligated to pay in advance.** וּמַה שֶּׁאָמַר לוֹ — **Thus, when** the landlord **tells him,** "אִם תִּתֵּן לִי מִיָּד, הֲרֵי הִיא לְךָ בַּעֲשָׂרָה" — **"If you pay** all of it **to me now, it is** rented **to you for ten** gold pieces," אָז הָיָה מוֹחֵל לוֹ שְׁנֵי זְהוּבִים — **he is forgoing two gold pieces** that he was due had he been paid monthly, לְפִי שֶׁמַּקְדִּים לוֹ לְשַׁלֵּם קוֹדֶם זְמַן הַפֵּרָעוֹן

---

51. Had the responsibility been borne by Shimon, it would be considered that Reuven, who advanced the funds for the purchase, actually lent the money to Shimon when he purchased the merchandise on his behalf. When Shimon pays more than the purchase price, it constitutes *ribbis.* This is avoided by having Reuven assume responsibility for the merchandise until Shimon receives it. Thus, as in the previous *se'if,* no loan has taken place; rather, it is considered Reuven's merchandise, which he subsequently resells to Shimon at a profit.

52. This applies to rentals of all types of real estate.

53. Thus, the price for paying in advance is 10 gold pieces, while the price for extending payment is 12 gold pieces.

קוֹדֶם זְמַן הַפֵּרָעוֹן, וְזֹאת מוּתָּר[54].

כב. וְדַוְקָא בִּשְׂכִירוּת קַרְקַע מוּתָּר לְהַרְבּוֹת בְּעִנְיָן הַזֶּה, מִפְּנֵי שֶׁהַקַּרְקַע נִקְנֵית לוֹ מִיָּד[55]. אֲבָל לְהַרְבּוֹת בִּשְׂכִירוּת פּוֹעֵל אָסוּר בְּעִנְיָן זֶה, דְּהַיְינוּ שֶׁאִם שׂוֹכֵר אֶת הָאָדָם שֶׁיַּעֲשֶׂה לוֹ מְלַאכְתּוֹ לְאַחַר זְמַן וּמַקְדִּים לוֹ שְׂכָרוֹ הַיּוֹם קוֹדֶם שֶׁנִּכְנַס לִמְלָאכָה וּבִשְׁבִיל זֶה יַעֲשֶׂה לוֹ אֶת הַמְּלָאכָה בְּפָחוֹת מִן הָרָאוּי, זֹאת אָסוּר, דְּכֵיוָן דְּהַפּוֹעֵל אֵינוֹ מִשְׁתַּעְבֵּד מֵהַשְׁתָּא הֲוָה לֵיהּ כְּמוֹ הַלְוָאָה[56]. אַךְ אִם הַפּוֹעֵל נִכְנָס לִמְלַאכְתּוֹ מִיָּד, אַף עַל פִּי שֶׁלֹּא יִגְמוֹר אֶת הַמְּלָאכָה עַד לְאַחַר יָמִים הַרְבֵּה, מוּתָּר לְהַקְדִּים לוֹ שְׂכָרוֹ

— **because** the renter **advanced payment before its due date,** וְזֹאת מוּתָּר — **and this is permitted.**[54]

§22 וְדַוְקָא בִּשְׂכִירוּת קַרְקַע מוּתָּר לְהַרְבּוֹת בְּעִנְיָן הַזֶּה — **But only with regard to rental of land is it permissible for him to add** to the rental amount **in this manner,** מִפְּנֵי שֶׁהַקַּרְקַע נִקְנֵית לוֹ מִיָּד — **because** the renter **acquires the land immediately,** and the payment is thus considered rent rather than a loan.[55] אֲבָל לְהַרְבּוֹת בִּשְׂכִירוּת פּוֹעֵל — **But to add to the wages of a laborer** אָסוּר בְּעִנְיָן זֶה — **is prohibited in this manner.** דְּהַיְינוּ — **That is,** שֶׁאִם שׂוֹכֵר אֶת הָאָדָם — **if one hires a person** שֶׁיַּעֲשֶׂה לוֹ מְלַאכְתּוֹ לְאַחַר זְמַן — **to do work for him at a later date,** וּמַקְדִּים לוֹ שְׂכָרוֹ הַיּוֹם — **and he advances his wages to him today** קוֹדֶם שֶׁנִּכְנַס לִמְלָאכָה — **before he commences work,** וּבִשְׁבִיל זֶה יַעֲשֶׂה לוֹ אֶת הַמְּלָאכָה בְּפָחוֹת מִן הָרָאוּי — **and in return, he will perform the labor at less than the appropriate** rate, זֹאת אָסוּר — **this is prohibited.** דְּכֵיוָן דְּהַפּוֹעֵל אֵינוֹ מִשְׁתַּעְבֵּד מֵהַשְׁתָּא — **For since the laborer is not committing** himself to engage in work **from now,** הֲוָה לֵיהּ כְּמוֹ הַלְוָאָה — the funds that the employer advances **are considered a loan.**[56] אַךְ אִם הַפּוֹעֵל נִכְנָס לִמְלַאכְתּוֹ מִיָּד — **However, if the worker commences work immediately** (i.e., the moment the funds are advanced, without any delay), אַף עַל פִּי שֶׁלֹּא יִגְמוֹר אֶת הַמְּלָאכָה עַד לְאַחַר יָמִים הַרְבֵּה — **even though he will not complete his work until after many days,** מוּתָּר לְהַקְדִּים לוֹ שְׂכָרוֹ — **it is permissible to advance his wages**

54. Only when one pays extra for *delaying* payment is it considered *ribbis*. Here, if he pays at the end of the month he is not delaying payment, since that is when the rent is due; when he pays less for paying at the beginning of the month he is actually receiving a discount for paying early, which is permitted. See *The Laws of Ribbis* by Rabbi Yisroel Reisman (1995, Mesorah Publications), Chapter 11, note 23, for a discussion regarding the difference between this and prepaying for merchandise. [A number of authorities maintain that if the local custom is to pay at the beginning of the rental term, this halachah does not apply, and it would be prohibited to stipulate a lower price for paying at the beginning of the month and a higher price for paying at the end of the month (see *Chochmas Adam* 136:10; cf. *Machaneh Ephraim, Hilchos Malveh, Dinei Ribbis, Siman* 31). In this case, a halachic authority must be consulted.]

55. I.e., even though he is only *obligated* to pay the rent at the end of each month, he acquires the rights to the property for the duration of the lease at the outset, when the agreement is made. Thus, even if he pays the entire amount at that time, he is not lending the owner money, but paying for the rental of the land that he has already acquired.

56. Since the worker is not committing himself to begin working now, the advance wages amount to nothing more than a loan that will be repaid later in the form of labor. Therefore, since he is accepting less than the appropriate rate in return for being paid in advance, when he later repays his debt with the more valuable labor, he has paid *ribbis*, which is prohibited.

בִּשְׁבִיל שֶׁיַּעֲשֶׂה בְּזוֹל, דְּכֵיוָן שֶׁיַּתְחִיל מִיָּד בַּמְּלָאכָה הֲוָה לֵיהּ שְׂכִירוּת וְלֹא הַלְוָאָה.[57]

כג. מוּתָּר לְהַרְבּוֹת בִּנְדוּנְיַת חֲתָנִים, כְּגוֹן שֶׁפָּסַק נְדוּנְיָא לְבִתּוֹ וְהִתְנָה עִם חֲתָנוֹ שֶׁכָּל שָׁנָה שֶׁיַּנִּיחַ אֶצְלוֹ אֶת הַנְּדוּנְיָא יִתֵּן לוֹ כָּךְ וְכָךְ שָׂכָר, מוּתָּר[58], שֶׁאֵין זֶה אֶלָּא כְּמוֹסִיף לוֹ נְדוּנְיָא, וּכְאִלּוּ אָמַר לוֹ "אֲנִי נוֹתֵן לְךָ מַתָּנָה כָּךְ וְכָךְ לִזְמַן פְּלוֹנִי, וְאִם לֹא אֶתֵּן לְךָ לִזְמַן פְּלוֹנִי, עוֹד אֲנִי מוֹסִיף לְךָ כָּךְ וְכָךְ", דְּמוּתָּר. וְדַוְקָא כְּשֶׁהִתְנוּ כֵּן מִיָּד בִּשְׁעַת כְּתִיבַת הַתְּנָאִים[59], דְּכֵיוָן דְּעַד עַתָּה לֹא הָיוּ עָלָיו שׁוּם חִיּוּב אִם כֵּן הַכֹּל הוּא חִיּוּב אֶחָד, אֲבָל אִם בִּשְׁעַת כְּתִיבַת הַתְּנָאִים נִתְחַיֵּיב בִּסְתָם סַךְ נְדוּנְיָא, וּבִשְׁעַת הַחֲתוּנָּה רוֹצִים לְהִתְפַּשֵּׁר לָתֵת לוֹ דְּבַר מָה בִּשְׁבִיל הַרְחָבַת הַזְּמַן —

בִּשְׁבִיל שֶׁיַּעֲשֶׂה בְּזוֹל — **in return for his performing** the labor **inexpensively.** **דְּכֵיוָן שֶׁיַּתְחִיל מִיָּד בַּמְּלָאכָה** — **For since he will begin the work immediately,** **הֲוָה לֵיהּ שְׂכִירוּת וְלֹא הַלְוָאָה** — the money **is deemed wages and not a loan.**[57]

§23 **מוּתָּר לְהַרְבּוֹת בִּנְדוּנְיַת חֲתָנִים** — **It is permitted to add to a wedding dowry.** **כְּגוֹן** — **For example:** **שֶׁפָּסַק נְדוּנְיָא לְבִתּוֹ** — **If one pledges a dowry for his daughter,** **וְהִתְנָה עִם חֲתָנוֹ** — **and** the father-in-law **stipulated with his son-in-law** **שֶׁכָּל שָׁנָה שֶׁיַּנִּיחַ אֶצְלוֹ אֶת הַנְּדוּנְיָא** — **that** for **each year that** the son-in-law **will allow the dowry to remain with** his father-in-law (i.e., that the son-in-law will delay collecting it), **יִתֵּן לוֹ כָּךְ וְכָךְ שָׂכָר** — his father-in-law **will give him such-and-such** an amount **as compensation,** **מוּתָּר** — **it is permitted,**[58] **שֶׁאֵין זֶה אֶלָּא כְּמוֹסִיף לוֹ נְדוּנְיָא** — **since this is merely as if he is providing additional dowry.** **וּכְאִלּוּ אָמַר לוֹ** — **And it is as if he told him,** **"אֲנִי נוֹתֵן לְךָ מַתָּנָה כָּךְ וְכָךְ לִזְמַן פְּלוֹנִי** — **"I am giving you a gift of such-and-such** an amount **by a certain time,** **וְאִם לֹא אֶתֵּן לְךָ לִזְמַן פְּלוֹנִי** — **and if I do not give** it to you **by** that **time,** **עוֹד אֲנִי מוֹסִיף לְךָ כָּךְ וְכָךְ"** — **I will increase** the gift by **such-and-such** an amount," **דְּמוּתָּר** — **which is permitted.** Since he does not yet owe him the money, he may incorporate such a condition as part of his dowry obligation. **וְדַוְקָא כְּשֶׁהִתְנוּ כֵּן מִיָּד בִּשְׁעַת כְּתִיבַת הַתְּנָאִים** — **But this is only if they made this stipulation immediately at the time of writing the** ***tenaim.***[59] **דְּכֵיוָן דְּעַד עַתָּה לֹא הָיוּ עָלָיו שׁוּם חִיּוּב** — **Since, until now, he had no obligation,** there is no debt; **אִם כֵּן הַכֹּל הוּא חִיּוּב אֶחָד** — **consequently, it is all** (i.e., the obligation and penalty) considered **a single obligation.** **אֲבָל אִם בִּשְׁעַת כְּתִיבַת הַתְּנָאִים נִתְחַיֵּיב בִּסְתָם סַךְ נְדוּנְיָא** — **However, if at the time of writing the** ***tenaim*** **he took on an unconditional obligation for the amount of the dowry,** **וּבִשְׁעַת הַחֲתוּנָּה רוֹצִים לְהִתְפַּשֵּׁר** — **and at the time of the wedding they wish to reach an agreement** **לָתֵת לוֹ דְּבַר מָה בִּשְׁבִיל הַרְחָבַת הַזְּמַן** — **to give** the son-in-law **something in return for extending the time,**

---

57. See *Bava Basra* 87a with *Rashbam, Rashba,* and *Shitah Mikubetzes,* for further discussion.

58. I.e., it is not considered as extending the duration of an obligation in exchange for additional payment (which is forbidden, as above, *se'if* 3), as Kitzur goes on to explain.

59. I.e., before the obligation is finalized.

The *tenaim* (literally, *conditions*) is a premarital contract containing the obligations agreed upon by both sides. [Nowadays, it is quite common to use a *tenaim* document that contains no monetary obligations at all, and is, for all practical purposes, merely ceremonial in nature. Therefore, one who wishes to add such a clause to an obligation of a dowry after the original marriage agreement has been agreed upon, must consult a halachic authority to determine at what point the obligation takes place.]

אָסוּר. וּצְרִיכִין לַעֲשׂוֹת בְּדֶרֶךְ הֶיתֵּר[60].

כד. יִשְׂרָאֵל שֶׁלָּוָה מֵעַכּוּ״ם בְּרִיבִּית וְיִשְׂרָאֵל אַחֵר יִהְיֶה עָרֵב — אִם הוּא בְּעִנְיָן שֶׁאֵין הָעַכּוּ״ם יָכוֹל לִתְבּוֹעַ תְּחִלָּה אֶלָּא אֶת הַלֹּוֶה, וְאַף כְּשֶׁלֹּא יִהְיֶה אֶפְשָׁר לִגְבּוֹת מִן הַלֹּוֶה אָז יָכוֹל לִתְבּוֹעַ מִן הֶעָרֵב — מוּתָּר. אֲבָל אִם הוּא בְּעִנְיָן שֶׁהָעַכּוּ״ם יָכוֹל לִתְבּוֹעַ תְּחִלָּה אֶת הֶעָרֵב, אִם כֵּן הָוֵי כְּאִלּוּ הֶעָרֵב לָוָה מִן הָעַכּוּ״ם וְהִלְוָה לְיִשְׂרָאֵל הַלֹּוֶה וְאָסוּר. וְכֵן עַכּוּ״ם שֶׁלָּוָה מִיִּשְׂרָאֵל בְּרִיבִּית וְיִשְׂרָאֵל אַחֵר הוּא עָרֵב — אִם הוּא בְּעִנְיָן שֶׁאֵין הַמַּלְוֶה יָכוֹל לִתְבּוֹעַ תְּחִלָּה אֶלָּא אֶת הָעַכּוּ״ם הַלֹּוֶה, וְאַף כַּאֲשֶׁר לֹא יִמְצָא אֵצֶל הָעַכּוּ״ם הַלֹּוֶה אָז יִגְבֶּה מִן הֶעָרֵב — מוּתָּר.

אָסוּר — it is prohibited, for this is a simple case of extending the time of an obligation in exchange for additional payment; see above, *se'if* 3. **וּצְרִיכִין לַעֲשׂוֹת בְּדֶרֶךְ הֶיתֵּר — And** in order to arrange this, **they must do it in a permissible manner.**[60]

§24 The *ribbis* prohibition does not apply to an idolater. One may thus both borrow money from, and lend money to, an idolater with interest. The final *se'ifim* of our *Siman* are primarily dedicated to a discussion of the laws of loans between a Jew and an idolater when another Jew has an involvement in the loan. The discussion begins with a presentation of the halachah regarding a loan made between a Jew and an idolater where another Jew is acting as a surety, guaranteeing payment of the loan.

יִשְׂרָאֵל שֶׁלָּוָה מֵעַכּוּ״ם בְּרִיבִּית — With regard to **a Jew who borrows from an idolater with interest, וְיִשְׂרָאֵל אַחֵר יִהְיֶה עָרֵב — and another Jew is to serve as guarantor, אִם הוּא בְּעִנְיָן — if the manner** of the obligation **is such שֶׁאֵין הָעַכּוּ״ם יָכוֹל לִתְבּוֹעַ תְּחִלָּה אֶלָּא אֶת הַלֹּוֶה — that the idolater may initially demand payment only from the borrower, וְאַף כְּשֶׁלֹּא יִהְיֶה אֶפְשָׁר לִגְבּוֹת מִן הַלֹּוֶה — and only when he is unable to collect from the borrower אָז יָכוֹל לִתְבּוֹעַ מִן הֶעָרֵב — may he then demand payment from the guarantor, מוּתָּר — it is permitted,** for the actual obligation is between the borrower and the lender, and one is permitted to pay *ribbis* to an idolater. Moreover, if the guarantor repays the idolater, the borrower must, when he has the funds, repay the entire amount (including the *ribbis*) to the guarantor. **אֲבָל אִם הוּא בְּעִנְיָן — But if the manner** of the obligation **is such שֶׁהָעַכּוּ״ם יָכוֹל לִתְבּוֹעַ תְּחִלָּה אֶת הֶעָרֵב — that the idolater may initially demand payment from the guarantor, אִם כֵּן — if so,** since the guarantor has assumed total responsibility for the loan, **הָוֵי כְּאִלּוּ הֶעָרֵב לָוָה מִן הָעַכּוּ״ם — it is as if the** Jewish **guarantor borrowed from the idolater, וְהִלְוָה לְיִשְׂרָאֵל הַלֹּוֶה — and,** in turn, **lent** the money **to the Jewish borrower** with interest, **וְאָסוּר — and this is prohibited,** as the Jewish borrower is prohibited from paying interest to the Jewish guarantor.

וְכֵן עַכּוּ״ם שֶׁלָּוָה מִיִּשְׂרָאֵל בְּרִיבִּית — So too, with regard to **an idolater who borrowed from a Jew with interest, וְיִשְׂרָאֵל אַחֵר הוּא עָרֵב — and another Jew serves as guarantor; אִם הוּא בְּעִנְיָן — if the manner** of the obligation **was** such **שֶׁאֵין הַמַּלְוֶה יָכוֹל לִתְבּוֹעַ תְּחִלָּה אֶלָּא אֶת הָעַכּוּ״ם הַלֹּוֶה — that the lender can initially demand payment only from the idolater who borrowed** the money, **וְאַף כַּאֲשֶׁר לֹא יִמְצָא אֵצֶל הָעַכּוּ״ם הַלֹּוֶה — and only when he cannot recover** the debt **from the idolater who borrowed אָז יִגְבֶּה מִן הֶעָרֵב — does he collect from the guarantor, מוּתָּר — it is**

60. See next *Siman*. A halachic authority familiar with the laws of *ribbis* should be consulted.

אֲבָל אִם הוּא בְּעִנְיָן שֶׁיָּכוֹל לִתְבּוֹעַ תְּחִלָּה גַּם אֶת הֶעָרֵב, אִם כֵּן הֶעָרֵב הוּא כְּמוֹ לֹוֶה וְאָסוּר. וְאִם הַיִּשְׂרָאֵל עָרֵב רַק בְּעַד הַקֶּרֶן וְלֹא בְעַד הָרִיבִּית — מוּתָּר. (בְּדִין יִשְׂרָאֵל שֶׁלָּוָה מִיִּשְׂרָאֵל וְיִשְׂרָאֵל אַחֵר יִהְיֶה עָרֵב, וְהַלֹּוֶה מְשַׁלֵּם לוֹ עֲבוּר זֶה שֶׁהַטַּ״ז וְהַשַּׁ״ךְ בִּנְקוּדוֹת הַכֶּסֶף מְקִילִין[61] — הִנֵּה דַּעַת הַחַוּוֹת דַּעַת לְהַחֲמִיר, עַיֵּין שָׁם.)

כה. עַכּוּ״ם שֶׁאָמַר לְיִשְׂרָאֵל ״לְוֵה בִּשְׁבִילִי מָעוֹת בְּרִבִּית מִיִּשְׂרָאֵל עַל מַשְׁכּוֹן זֶה״[62], אוֹ אֲפִילוּ אֵינוֹ נוֹתֵן לוֹ מַשְׁכּוֹן אֶלָּא שְׁטַר חוֹב, וְהַמַּלְוֶה סוֹמֵךְ אֶת עַצְמוֹ רַק עַל הַמַּשְׁכּוֹן אוֹ עַל הַשְּׁטָר שֶׁל הָעַכּוּ״ם, וְעַל הַשָּׁלִיחַ אֵין שׁוּם אַחֲרָיוּת — מוּתָּר. וַאֲפִילוּ אִם הַיִּשְׂרָאֵל הַשָּׁלִיחַ מֵבִיא אֶת הָרִבִּית לְהַמַּלְוֶה, מוּתָּר לְקַבְּלוֹ, וּבִלְבַד שֶׁהַלֹּוֶה יִגְמוֹר זֹאת בְּדַעְתּוֹ שֶׁכָּל אַחֲרָיוּת הַמַּשְׁכּוֹן וְהַמָּעוֹת בֵּין בַּהֲבָאָה בֵּין בַּחֲזָרָה[63]

---

permitted, since the obligation is between the lender and the idolater. **אֲבָל אִם הוּא בְּעִנְיָן שֶׁיָּכוֹל לִתְבּוֹעַ תְּחִלָּה גַּם אֶת הֶעָרֵב** — **But if the manner** of the obligation **was** such **that he may demand payment initially from the guarantor as well, אִם כֵּן הֶעָרֵב הוּא כְּמוֹ לֹוֶה** — **if so, the** Jewish **guarantor is like a borrower** (who borrowed money directly from another Jew) **וְאָסוּר** — **and it is prohibited. וְאִם הַיִּשְׂרָאֵל עָרֵב רַק בְּעַד הַקֶּרֶן** — **But if the Jew is a guarantor only for the principal וְלֹא בְעַד הָרִיבִּית** — **and not for the *ribbis*, מוּתָּר** — **it is permitted,** since the *ribbis* obligation is the sole responsibility of the idolater.

(**בְּדִין** — **With regard to the halachah** in the case of **יִשְׂרָאֵל שֶׁלָּוָה מִיִּשְׂרָאֵל** — one **Jew who borrows from a** second **Jew** without interest, **וְיִשְׂרָאֵל אַחֵר יִהְיֶה עָרֵב** — **and another Jew will serve as guarantor וְהַלֹּוֶה מְשַׁלֵּם לוֹ עֲבוּר זֶה** — **and the** Jewish **borrower pays** the guarantor **for this** service, **שֶׁהַטַּ״ז וְהַשַּׁ״ךְ בִּנְקוּדוֹת הַכֶּסֶף מְקִילִין** — both **the *Taz*** 170:3 **and *Shach* in *Nekudos HaKesef*** [ibid.] **rule leniently** and allow it;[61] **הִנֵּה דַּעַת הַחַוּוֹת דַּעַת לְהַחֲמִיר** — however, **note that the view of *Chavos Daas*** [ibid., *Beurim* §1] **is to rule stringently** and forbid it; **עַיֵּין שָׁם** — **see there.)**

§25 עַכּוּ״ם שֶׁאָמַר לְיִשְׂרָאֵל — If **an idolater tells a Jew, ״לְוֵה בִּשְׁבִילִי מָעוֹת בְּרִבִּית מִיִּשְׂרָאֵל עַל מַשְׁכּוֹן** — **"Borrow money on my behalf with interest from a Jew זֶה״** — **on this collateral,"**[62] **אוֹ אֲפִילוּ אֵינוֹ נוֹתֵן לוֹ מַשְׁכּוֹן** — **or even if he does not give him collateral, אֶלָּא שְׁטַר חוֹב** — **but rather,** he gives him **a promissory note, וְהַמַּלְוֶה סוֹמֵךְ אֶת עַצְמוֹ** — **and the** Jewish **lender** who receives it grants the loan because he **places his trust רַק עַל הַמַּשְׁכּוֹן אוֹ עַל הַשְּׁטָר שֶׁל הָעַכּוּ״ם** — **in the collateral or the note of the idolater alone, וְעַל הַשָּׁלִיחַ אֵין שׁוּם אַחֲרָיוּת** — **and the** Jewish **agent is not at all liable** for the loan, **מוּתָּר** — **it is permitted,** since the second Jew is lending to the idolater; the Jewish agent is merely a messenger to deliver the collateral or note. **וַאֲפִילוּ אִם הַיִּשְׂרָאֵל הַשָּׁלִיחַ מֵבִיא אֶת הָרִבִּית לְהַמַּלְוֶה** — **And even if the Jewish agent delivers the *ribbis* to the lender, מוּתָּר לְקַבְּלוֹ** — **it is permitted** for the Jewish lender **to accept it, וּבִלְבַד שֶׁהַלֹּוֶה יִגְמוֹר זֹאת בְּדַעְתּוֹ** — **provided that the lender makes a conscious commitment שֶׁכָּל אַחֲרָיוּת הַמַּשְׁכּוֹן וְהַמָּעוֹת** — **that the entire liability for** both **the collateral and money, בֵּין בַּהֲבָאָה בֵּין בַּחֲזָרָה** — **whether in bringing or returning,**[63]

---

61. Since the guarantor does not lend the money but merely guarantees payment, compensating him does not constitute *ribbis.*

62. That is, the Jew is merely acting as a messenger to bring the collateral from the idolater to the second Jew and to bring back the money he receives from him to the idolater.

63. That is, the Jewish lender accepts liability

הַכֹּל עַל אַחֲרָיוּתוֹ, וְעַל הַשָּׁלִיחַ לֹא יִהְיֶה שׁוּם אַחֲרָיוּת[64].

כו. וְכֵן יִשְׂרָאֵל שֶׁנָּתַן מַשְׁכּוֹן אוֹ שְׁטַר חוֹב לְיִשְׂרָאֵל חֲבֵרוֹ שֶׁיִּלְוֶה בִּשְׁבִילוֹ עַל זֶה מָעוֹת בְּרִיבִּית מֵעַכּוּ״ם — אִם הָעַכּוּ״ם אֵינוֹ סוֹמֵךְ רַק עַל הַמַּשְׁכּוֹן אוֹ עַל הַשְּׁטָר[65], וְעַל הַשָּׁלִיחַ אֵין שׁוּם אַחֲרָיוּת — מוּתָּר[66]. וְכֵן אִם הַיִּשְׂרָאֵל הַלְוָה תְּחִלָּה לְיִשְׂרָאֵל חֲבֵרוֹ עַל מַשְׁכּוֹן, וְאַחַר כָּךְ אָמַר לְהַמַּלְוֶה[67] "לְוֵה מָעוֹת מֵעַכּוּ״ם בְּרִיבִּית עַל מַשְׁכּוֹן זֶה וְעָלַי לְשַׁלֵּם הַקֶּרֶן וְהָרִיבִּית" — אִם הָעַכּוּ״ם סוֹמֵךְ אֶת עַצְמוֹ עַל הַמַּשְׁכּוֹן לְבַד — מוּתָּר[68].

הַכֹּל עַל אַחֲרָיוּתוֹ — is all his own responsibility, **וְעַל הַשָּׁלִיחַ לֹא יִהְיֶה שׁוּם אַחֲרָיוּת** — **and the agent will not be held liable at all.**[64]

§26 וְכֵן יִשְׂרָאֵל שֶׁנָּתַן מַשְׁכּוֹן אוֹ שְׁטַר חוֹב לְיִשְׂרָאֵל חֲבֵרוֹ — **Similarly,** with regard to **a Jew who gave collateral or a promissory note to his fellow Jew, שֶׁיִּלְוֶה בִּשְׁבִילוֹ עַל זֶה מָעוֹת בְּרִיבִּית מֵעַכּוּ״ם** — **so that, on its basis, he should** be his agent to **borrow on his behalf money with *ribbis* from an idolater,** the halachah is that **אִם הָעַכּוּ״ם אֵינוֹ סוֹמֵךְ רַק עַל הַמַּשְׁכּוֹן אוֹ עַל הַשְּׁטָר** — **if the idolater** grants the loan **relying only on the collateral or the** promissory **note,**[65] **וְעַל הַשָּׁלִיחַ אֵין שׁוּם אַחֲרָיוּת** — **and the agent has no obligation, מוּתָּר** — **it is permitted.**[66]

וְכֵן אִם הַיִּשְׂרָאֵל הַלְוָה תְּחִלָּה לְיִשְׂרָאֵל חֲבֵרוֹ עַל מַשְׁכּוֹן — **Similarly, if a Jew first lends another Jew** (interest-free) **on collateral, וְאַחַר כָּךְ אָמַר לְהַמַּלְוֶה** — **and afterward,** when the loan is due, the borrower **tells the lender:**[67] **"לְוֵה מָעוֹת מֵעַכּוּ״ם בְּרִיבִּית עַל מַשְׁכּוֹן זֶה** — **"Borrow money** (i.e., the amount that I owe you) **from an idolater, with interest, on the basis of this collateral** that I gave you, using that money to satisfy my loan from you, **וְעָלַי לְשַׁלֵּם הַקֶּרֶן וְהָרִיבִּית"** — **and** it will be incumbent **upon me to pay the principle and interest** to the idolater," **אִם הָעַכּוּ״ם סוֹמֵךְ אֶת עַצְמוֹ עַל הַמַּשְׁכּוֹן לְבַד** — the halachah is that **if the idolater** grants the loan **relying solely on the collateral,** and not on the one borrowing the money from him (the original lender), **מוּתָּר** — **it is permitted.**[68]

---

for any loss that may occur when bringing the collateral to the Jew and the money to the idolater, and then, at the end of the term, when returning the money to the Jew and the collateral to the idolater (*Yoreh Deah* 168:13). *Rama* (ibid. and *Darkei Moshe* §12) asserts that it is permitted even if the agent assumes responsibility when he is initially bringing the collateral to the Jew before the loan was made.

64. For if the agent is responsible for the loan, he is considered to have borrowed the money, which he lent afterward to the idolater. When the agent subsequently delivers the interest (given to him by the idolater) to the lender, he has paid interest on *his* own loan, which is prohibited.

65. That is, the idolater feels secure that the collateral will cover the loan and interest, and does not expect the Jewish agent to be responsible as a borrower or prohibited type of guarantor; see above, *se'if* 24 (see *Shach* 168:51; see also *Chelkas Binyamin* 168:167).

66. Since the agent is not responsible for the loan, the loan is a direct obligation between the borrower and the idolater.

If, however, the idolater is relying on the agent for payment, it is prohibited even if the owner of the collateral obligates himself to pay the idolater directly (see *Yoreh Deah* 168:1). Such issues commonly arise when someone who is unable to secure credit requests a friend or relative to take out a mortgage for him or to allow him to use his credit card. The one in whose name the loan was given is considered the borrower and paying interest on his behalf or reimbursing him for interest paid is prohibited (see *Igros Moshe, Yoreh Deah* III, §42).

67. *Chochmas Adam* 137:37.

68. Here too, since the original lender, who is now the agent of the borrower, is not responsible for the loan, and merely serves as a

כז. יִשְׂרָאֵל שֶׁהִלְוָה לְעַכּוּ״ם עַל מַשְׁכּוֹן בְּרִיבִּית כָּךְ וְכָךְ לְחֹדֶשׁ, וְאַחַר כָּךְ בָּא הַיִּשְׂרָאֵל לַחֲבֵרוֹ שֶׁהוּא יַלְוֶה לוֹ אֶת הַמָּעוֹת עַל מַשְׁכּוֹן זֶה, וְשֶׁהוּא יִטּוֹל אֶת הָרִיבִּית שֶׁיַּעֲלוּ מֵהַיּוֹם עַד הַפֵּרָעוֹן — מוּתָּר[69]. אֲבָל אִם הַיִּשְׂרָאֵל הָרִאשׁוֹן כְּבָר זָקַף אֶת הַקֶּרֶן עִם הָרִיבִּית לְכָל זְמַן הַהַלְוָאָה, הֲרֵי הַכֹּל הוּא כְּקֶרֶן שֶׁל יִשְׂרָאֵל וְאָסוּר לִלְווֹת עַל מַשְׁכּוֹן זֶה מִיִּשְׂרָאֵל חֲבֵרוֹ בְּרִיבִּית, דְּהָוֵי כְּאִלּוּ נָתַן אֶת הָרִיבִּית מִכִּיסוֹ[70].

כח. מְעוֹתָיו שֶׁל יִשְׂרָאֵל מוּפְקָדִים בְּיַד עַכּוּ״ם וְהִלְוָה אוֹתָם לְיִשְׂרָאֵל בְּרִבִּית — אִם הָיוּ בְּאַחֲרָיוּת הָעַכּוּ״ם שֶׁאִם יֹאבַד הַחוֹב יִתְחַיֵּיב הוּא לְשַׁלֵּם בִּמְעוֹתָיו —

---

§27 **יִשְׂרָאֵל שֶׁהִלְוָה לְעַכּוּ״ם עַל מַשְׁכּוֹן בְּרִיבִּית** — With regard to **a Jew** (Reuven) **who lent** money **to an idolater on collateral with interest,** **כָּךְ וְכָךְ לְחֹדֶשׁ** — at a rate of **such-and-such per month,** **וְאַחַר כָּךְ בָּא הַיִּשְׂרָאֵל לַחֲבֵרוֹ** — **and afterward,** this **Jew approaches his fellow** Jew (Shimon) **שֶׁהוּא יַלְוֶה לוֹ אֶת הַמָּעוֹת עַל מַשְׁכּוֹן זֶה** — and requests **that he** (Shimon) **lend him on this collateral** that Reuven received from the idolater **the** amount of **money** that Reuven lent to the idolater, **וְשֶׁהוּא יִטּוֹל אֶת הָרִיבִּית שֶׁיַּעֲלוּ מֵהַיּוֹם עַד הַפֵּרָעוֹן** — **and he** (Shimon) **will collect** from the idolater **the *ribbis* that is due from today until the time of repayment,** **מוּתָּר** — **it is permitted.**[69] **אֲבָל אִם הַיִּשְׂרָאֵל הָרִאשׁוֹן כְּבָר זָקַף אֶת הַקֶּרֶן עִם הָרִיבִּית לְכָל זְמַן הַהַלְוָאָה** — **But if the first Jew** (Reuven) **has already converted the principal together with the *ribbis* for the entire duration of the loan** to a single debt (i.e., the Jew and idolater calculated the principal and *ribbis,* and combined them into one debt), **הֲרֵי הַכֹּל הוּא כְּקֶרֶן שֶׁל יִשְׂרָאֵל** — **it is all** (i.e., both the original principal and the interest) **considered the principal of the Jew** (Reuven), **וְאָסוּר לִלְווֹת עַל מַשְׁכּוֹן זֶה מִיִּשְׂרָאֵל חֲבֵרוֹ בְּרִיבִּית** — **and it is prohibited** for Reuven **to borrow on interest from his fellow Jew on** the basis of this **collateral,** **דְּהָוֵי כְּאִלּוּ נָתַן אֶת הָרִיבִּית מִכִּיסוֹ** — **for** when the idolater pays the *ribbis,* **it is as if** Reuven **gave the *ribbis*** to Shimon **out of his own pocket.**[70]

§28 **מְעוֹתָיו שֶׁל יִשְׂרָאֵל מוּפְקָדִים בְּיַד עַכּוּ״ם** — Regarding **funds of a Jew that were deposited** as an investment **in the hands of an idolater,** **וְהִלְוָה אוֹתָם לְיִשְׂרָאֵל בְּרִבִּית** — **and** the idolater **lent them to a Jew with interest,** and the Jew who deposited the funds will receive that interest or a portion of it as a return on his investment, **אִם הָיוּ בְּאַחֲרָיוּת הָעַכּוּ״ם** — the halachah is that, **if the idolater bears responsibility for** the money, **שֶׁאִם יֹאבַד הַחוֹב יִתְחַיֵּיב הוּא לְשַׁלֵּם בִּמְעוֹתָיו** — **so that if the loan would be lost** (i.e., if the second Jew would default on the loan) the idolater **would be responsible to pay** the first Jew **from his own funds,** **מוּתָּר** — **it is permissible.**[71]

---

messenger between the borrower and idolater, it is permitted.

69. This is interpreted to be a sale of the collateral (see *Yoreh Deah* 168:18 with *Rama*), which, in turn, gives the purchaser rights to the loan. Therefore, the interest that accrues from the time of the sale until the end of the term of the loan is in fact directly due from the idolater to the second Jew who purchased the debt, and is thus permitted.

70. Once the interest has been added to the principal to form a single debt, the original owner of the debt (Reuven) is considered to already have rights to the unaccrued interest. When Reuven subsequently sells the debt, he must pay any interest that he receives from that point on to the current owner of the debt (Shimon). Thus, when the idolater pays the interest (that is actually due to Reuven, the original owner of the debt) to Shimon, who purchased the debt, it is as if the idolater is paying it on behalf of Reuven, which is prohibited.

מוּתָּר[71], וְאִם אֵינוֹ בְּאַחֲרָיוּת הָעַכּוּ״ם — אָסוּר[72]. וְלָכֵן בְּמָקוֹם שֶׁיֵּשׁ קְבוּצוֹת מָעוֹת [שפארקאסע] וְכַדּוֹמֶה שֶׁיֵּשׁ לְיִשְׂרְאֵלִים חֲלָקִים [אקציען] שָׁמָּה, וְיִשְׂרְאֵלִים לֹוִים מִשָּׁם בְּרִיבִּית, אַף עַל פִּי שֶׁהַמְּמוּנִּים הֵמָּה עַכּוּ״ם, מִכָּל מָקוֹם נִרְאֶה לִי דְּאִיסּוּר גָּמוּר הוּא. וְלָכֵן אָסוּר לִיתֵּן לְשָׁם מָעוֹת (כִּי שֶׁמָּא יִלְוֶה יִשְׂרָאֵל שֶׁאֵינוֹ הָגוּן), וְכֵן אָסוּר לִלְוֹת מִשָּׁם, כִּי שֶׁמָּא נָתַן לְשָׁם יִשְׂרָאֵל שֶׁאֵינוֹ הָגוּן[73].

וְאִם אֵינוֹ בְּאַחֲרָיוּת הָעַכּוּ״ם — But if the idolater does not bear responsibility for the money, **אָסוּר — it is prohibited.**[72]
וְלָכֵן — Therefore, **בְּמָקוֹם שֶׁיֵּשׁ קְבוּצוֹת מָעוֹת [שפארקאסע] וְכַדּוֹמֶה — in a place where there is a savings association or the like,** **שֶׁיֵּשׁ לְיִשְׂרְאֵלִים חֲלָקִים [אקציען] שָׁמָּה — and Jews have shares in it,** **וְיִשְׂרְאֵלִים לֹוִים מִשָּׁם בְּרִיבִּית — and** other **Jews borrow money from it with interest,** **אַף עַל פִּי שֶׁהַמְּמוּנִּים הֵמָּה עַכּוּ״ם — even though the managers** of the fund **are idolaters,** **מִכָּל מָקוֹם נִרְאֶה לִי דְּאִיסּוּר גָּמוּר הוּא — nevertheless,** since the liability in the case of a loss is incurred by the investors, **it appears to me that it is totally prohibited,** being considered a loan from a Jew to a Jew. **וְלָכֵן אָסוּר לִיתֵּן לְשָׁם מָעוֹת — Therefore, it is prohibited to deposit money there** **(כִּי שֶׁמָּא יִלְוֶה יִשְׂרָאֵל שֶׁאֵינוֹ הָגוּן — for a Jew who** conducts himself **improperly** [and is not concerned for the *ribbis* prohibition involved] **may borrow** from this savings association).
וְכֵן אָסוּר לִלְוֹת מִשָּׁם — Similarly, it is forbidden to borrow from there with interest, **כִּי שֶׁמָּא נָתַן לְשָׁם יִשְׂרָאֵל שֶׁאֵינוֹ הָגוּן — since a Jew** who conducts himself **improperly may have deposited** money **there.**[73]

---

71. Since the idolater is responsible for the loan, he is considered to have borrowed the money from the Jew, which he in turn lends to the other Jew. Since both transactions are performed with an idolater, it is permitted.

72. In this case, the loss incurred would be the responsibility of the first Jew who deposited his funds with the idolater, since the idolater did not assume responsibility for the loan to the second Jew. Therefore, the first Jew is considered to be lending the money to the second Jew, and it is therefore prohibited.

73. The question of the status of a company with both Jewish and non-Jewish shareholders has been the subject of considerable controversy, and is relevant not only to the laws of *ribbis,* but to a number of other laws as well, such as those of Shabbos and owning *chametz* on Pesach. The position taken by Kitzur, that even if a single Jew invests in a savings fund it is prohibited for a Jew to borrow from it with interest, was disputed by a number of other authorities of his time, including R' Y. S. Natanson, who, in a responsum to the author of *Kitzur Shulchan Aruch* (*Sho'el U'Meishiv, Mahadura Kamma* III:31) advised him to retract his ruling, and revise subsequent editions of Kitzur accordingly. Kitzur, however, remained steadfast in his ruling, and, in his editorial glosses, addresses R' Natanson's objection and raises the possibility that a number of similar situations may also be subject to the *ribbis* prohibition (see Appendix of Kitzur's editorial glosses).

In applying this ruling to today's banks, one must bear in mind that the setup of modern financial institutions is considerably more complex than in Kitzur's times. Indeed, with regard to owning shares in a company that does business on Shabbos, Rabbi Moshe Feinstein (*Igros Moshe, Even HaEzer* I, §7) rules that individual stock ownership is not significant, and is permitted as long as one does not own a controlling interest in the company. R' Y. S. Elyashiv, *shlita* (*Kovetz Teshuvos* III:124), applies *Igros Moshe*'s ruling regarding Shabbos to *ribbis.*

According to Rabbi Moshe Feinstein (*Yoreh Deah* II, §63; III, §41), this discussion pertains only to borrowing money from a bank, not with regard to a loan granted *to* a bank. Since banks are incorporated, its owners have no personal liability to repay the loan.

כט. שׁוּתָּפִין שֶׁצְּרִיכִין לִלְוֹת מָעוֹת בְּרִבִּית מֵעַכּוּ״ם יַעֲשׂוּ שְׁאֵלַת חָכָם אֵיךְ לַעֲשׂוֹת[74] (עַיֵּין ט״ז סִימָן ע׳ סְעִיף קָטָן ג׳ וְחַוּוֹת דַּעַת שָׁם סְעִיף קָטָן א׳ וּבְשֻׁלְחָן עָרוּךְ תַּנְיָא הִלְכוֹת רִבִּית סְעִיף ס״ד).

ל. מוּמָר אָסוּר לִלְוֹת מִמֶּנּוּ[75] בְּרִיבִּית[76], וְגַם לְהַלְווֹת לוֹ בְּרִיבִּית יֵשׁ לְהַחֲמִיר[77].

---

§29 **שׁוּתָּפִין שֶׁצְּרִיכִין לִלְוֹת מָעוֹת בְּרִבִּית מֵעַכּוּ״ם — Partners who need to borrow** money on interest **from an idolater** יַעֲשׂוּ שְׁאֵלַת חָכָם אֵיךְ לַעֲשׂוֹת — **must pose the question of how it is to be done to a Rabbinic authority**[74] (עַיֵּין ט״ז סִימָן ע׳ סְעִיף קָטָן ג׳ וְחַוּוֹת דַּעַת שָׁם סְעִיף קָטָן א׳ וּבְשֻׁלְחָן עָרוּךְ תַּנְיָא הִלְכוֹת רִבִּית סְעִיף ס״ד — see *Taz, Siman* 70, *se'if katan* 3; *Chavos Daas* there, *se'if katan* 1; *Shulchan Aruch HaTanya, Hil. Ribbis, se'if* 64).

§30 **מוּמָר אָסוּר לִלְוֹת מִמֶּנּוּ בְּרִיבִּית — It is forbidden to borrow from an apostate**[75] **with interest,**[76] **וְגַם לְהַלְווֹת לוֹ בְּרִיבִּית יֵשׁ לְהַחֲמִיר — and also with regard to lending him** money **with interest one should conduct himself stringently** and not lend him with interest.[77]

Therefore, Rabbi Moshe Feinstein rules that it is permissible to accept interest from a bank or other corporation even if it is *entirely* owned by Jews. However, it is prohibited to *pay* interest to a Jewish-owned corporation (i.e., where Jews own a controlling interest).

74. When two people take out a joint loan, each one is actually borrowing only half of the money. If the lender may demand payment in full from either one, each is a guarantor for the other, which is prohibited (see above, *se'if* 24).

75. This refers to a Jew who has totally forsaken the Jewish religion; for further discussion, see *Yoreh Deah* 159:2 with commentaries. One who transgresses a single mitzvah (even repeatedly) in order to satisfy his desires is certainly considered a Jew like any other, and one is required to lend him money interest-free (*Ahavas Chesed* 3:2); and it goes without saying that one may not borrow from him with interest.

76. See *Shach* 159:3.

77. See *Tur, Yoreh Deah* 159:2; *Ramban, Bava Metzia* 71b; and commentaries to *Shulchan Aruch, Yoreh Deah* 159:2.

355 LAWS OF ISKA — SIMAN 66:1

סימן סו

הִלְכוֹת עִיסְקָא[1]

וּבוֹ י״ב סְעִיפִים

א. הַנּוֹתֵן לַחֲבֵרוֹ מָעוֹת שֶׁיִּתְעַסֵּק בּוֹ וְהָרֶיוַח יִהְיֶה לַחֲצָאִין וְגַם הַהֶפְסֵד יִהְיֶה עַל שְׁנֵיהֶם בְּשָׁוֶה[2] — זֶהוּ נִקְרָא עִיסְקָא, וְאָסוּר מִפְּנֵי כִּי הַחֲצִי מִמָּעוֹת זֶה הוּא מִלְוֶה בְּיַד הַמְקַבֵּל שֶׁהֲרֵי הוּא בְּאַחֲרָיוּת שֶׁלּוֹ וְהוּא נוֹטֵל אֶת הָרֶיוַח וְגַם הַהֶפְסֵד עָלָיו,[3] וְהַחֲצִי

SIMAN 66

THE LAWS OF ISKA

CONTAINING 12 *SE'IFIM*

§1 The *Iska* / **§2-3** Permissible Stipulations and the *Heter Iska* / **§4** Acquiring a Portion of the Profit / **§5** After the Due Date / **§6** Text of the *Heter Iska* / **§7** Oral *Heter Iska* / **§8** *Heter Iska* for Advancing Payment for Merchandise / **§9** Writing an Ordinary Promissory Note / **§10** When There Is No Business Venture / **§11** Extending the Due Date / **§12** Raising Animals

This *Siman* details the laws of the *iska* (literally, *business*) agreement, in which one person provides the investment capital for a business venture and another person manages the business, with both sharing the profits and losses equally. This is the basis for what is known as the *heter iska,* which is a permissible alternative to lending money with *ribbis,*[1] by way of structuring the transaction as an *iska* rather than as a loan.

§1 **הַנּוֹתֵן לַחֲבֵרוֹ מָעוֹת שֶׁיִּתְעַסֵּק בּוֹ — One who gives his fellow funds to engage in a business venture** **וְהָרֶיוַח יִהְיֶה לַחֲצָאִין** — with the stipulation that **the profit will be divided equally** between them, **וְגַם הַהֶפְסֵד יִהְיֶה עַל שְׁנֵיהֶם בְּשָׁוֶה — and also** any **loss will be borne equally by both of them,**[2] **זֶהוּ נִקְרָא עִיסְקָא — this is referred to as an *iska,*** **וְאָסוּר — and it is prohibited.**

The basis for this prohibition:

מִפְּנֵי כִּי הַחֲצִי מִמָּעוֹת זֶה הוּא מִלְוֶה בְּיַד הַמְקַבֵּל — This is **because half of these funds are** considered **a loan in the hands of the recipient,** **שֶׁהֲרֵי הוּא בְּאַחֲרָיוּת שֶׁלּוֹ — for the responsibility** for this half **is upon him;** **וְהוּא נוֹטֵל אֶת הָרֶיוַח — he takes the profit** generated by this half if the venture succeeds, **וְגַם הַהֶפְסֵד עָלָיו — and also bears the loss** of this half if the venture suffers a loss.[3] **וְהַחֲצִי**

---

1. The prohibition of lending money with *ribbis* (interest) has been discussed in the previous *Siman.*

2. For example, the investor supplies capital of $1,000 and the venture realizes a profit of $200, making the total assets $1,200. The investor gets back his capital plus half the profits, viz. $1,100, while the recipient, who manages the investment, gets $100. If the enterprise suffers a loss and only $800 are left, the loss of $200 is also divided between them. The recipient must return $900 to the investor and thus each suffers a loss of $100.

3. When one person receives investment capital from another person and is expected to return the money regardless of whether the venture succeeds or fails, those funds are considered a loan. Therefore, since the investor

הוּא פִּקָּדוֹן אֶצְלוֹ שֶׁהֲרֵי הוּא בְּאַחֲרָיוּת הַנּוֹתֵן וְהוּא לוֹקֵחַ אֶת הָרֶיוַח מֵחֲצִי זֶה וְגַם הַהֶפְסֵד מֵחֲצִי זֶה עָלָיו[4], וְהַמְקַבֵּל שֶׁהוּא מִתְעַסֵּק וְטוֹרֵחַ בַּחֲצִי הַפִּקָּדוֹן שֶׁהוּא שַׁיָּיךְ לְהַנּוֹתֵן זֶהוּ רַק מִפְּנֵי שֶׁנּוֹתֵן לוֹ אֶת הַחֲצִי בְּהַלְוָאָה, וְהָוֵי רִיבִּית וְאָסוּר. וְיֵשׁ הֶיתֵּר לָזֶה אִם הַנּוֹתֵן נוֹתֵן לְהַמְקַבֵּל אֵיזֶה שָׂכָר בִּשְׁבִיל הֶעָמָל וְהַטּוֹרַח שֶׁהוּא מִתְעַסֵּק בְּחֶלְקוֹ[5]. וְיֵשׁ לִקְצוֹץ אוֹ שֶׁיִּתֵּן לוֹ מִיָּד בִּשְׁעַת נְתִינַת הַמָּעוֹת שְׂכָרוֹ. וְדֵי אֲפִילוּ בְּדָבָר[6] מוּעָט.

ב. יְכוֹלִין לְהַתְנוֹת שֶׁלֹּא יְהֵא הַמְקַבֵּל נֶאֱמָן לוֹמַר שֶׁהִפְסִיד מִן הַקֶּרֶן כִּי אִם עַל פִּי

הוּא פִּקָּדוֹן אֶצְלוֹ — The other **half** belongs to the investor and **is entrusted to** the recipient, **שֶׁהֲרֵי הוּא בְּאַחֲרָיוּת הַנּוֹתֵן — for the responsibility for** that half **is upon the investor; וְהוּא לוֹקֵחַ אֶת הָרֶיוַח מֵחֲצִי זֶה — he takes the profit from that half** if the venture succeeds, **וְגַם הַהֶפְסֵד מֵחֲצִי זֶה עָלָיו — and any loss to that half is borne by** the investor.[4] **וְהַמְקַבֵּל שֶׁהוּא מִתְעַסֵּק** — Now, **the recipient, who is engaging in business וְטוֹרֵחַ בַּחֲצִי הַפִּקָּדוֹן שֶׁהוּא שַׁיָּיךְ לְהַנּוֹתֵן — and expending effort on the half that has been entrusted to him, which belongs to the investor, זֶהוּ רַק מִפְּנֵי שֶׁנּוֹתֵן לוֹ אֶת הַחֲצִי בְּהַלְוָאָה — is doing so only because** the investor **is giving him the** other **half as a loan. וְהָוֵי רִיבִּית וְאָסוּר — This is *ribbis,* and is prohibited.**

וְיֵשׁ הֶיתֵּר לָזֶה — But there is a permissible manner **in which this** prohibition may be avoided, which is **אִם הַנּוֹתֵן נוֹתֵן לְהַמְקַבֵּל — if the investor gives the recipient אֵיזֶה שָׂכָר — some compensation בִּשְׁבִיל הֶעָמָל וְהַטּוֹרַח — for the toil and effort שֶׁהוּא מִתְעַסֵּק בְּחֶלְקוֹ — that he expends on** the investor's **portion.**[5] **וְיֵשׁ לִקְצוֹץ — And they should set** a specific amount at the outset of the agreement, **אוֹ שֶׁיִּתֵּן לוֹ מִיָּד בִּשְׁעַת נְתִינַת הַמָּעוֹת שְׂכָרוֹ — or he should give him his wages immediately at the time when the funds are given** for the investment. **וְדֵי אֲפִילוּ בְּדָבָר מוּעָט — And even a small amount**[6] **is sufficient** to avoid the *ribbis* prohibition.

§2 Kitzur now sets out further conditions that may permissibly be attached to the *iska* arrangement. The resulting agreement is one that can be used by one who seeks an assured specific return on his money without transgressing the *ribbis* prohibition, as will be explained in *se'if* 3.

יְכוֹלִין לְהַתְנוֹת — When setting up the *iska* arrangement, **they may stipulate שֶׁלֹּא יְהֵא הַמְקַבֵּל נֶאֱמָן — that the recipient should not be trusted לוֹמַר שֶׁהִפְסִיד מִן הַקֶּרֶן — to say that he incurred a loss of the principal כִּי אִם עַל פִּי עֵדִים**

---

and recipient are dividing the gains or losses, and the recipient of the *iska* is taking full responsibility for half of the investment, that half is considered a loan, which he is in turn investing in the venture at his own risk.

4. Since the investor is accepting full responsibility for half of the investment, he is considered to be investing his own funds in that half. The end result is that the investor and recipient are partners in the venture, with each one of them being responsible for half of the investment and each being entitled to the profits generated by his portion.

5. The recipient is thus not considered to be working for the investor because of the loan, but in exchange for the compensation that he gives him.

6. Such as a dollar, or even less (see *Igros Moshe, Yoreh Deah* II, §62; III, §41). If no amount was specified, a halachic authority should be consulted (see *Yoreh Deah* 177:2-4 with commentaries).

עֵדִים כְּשֵׁרִים, וְעַל הָרֶיוַח לֹא יְהֵא נֶאֱמָן כִּי אִם בִּשְׁבוּעָה[7].

ג. גַּם יְכוֹלִין לְהַתְנוֹת שֶׁהַבְּרֵירָה הוּא בְּיַד הַמְקַבֵּל, שֶׁאִם יִרְצֶה לָתֵת לְהַנּוֹתֵן כָּךְ וְכָךְ בְּעַד הַחֵלֶק הָרֶיוַח שֶׁלּוֹ, יְהֵא הָרְשׁוּת בְּיָדוֹ, וְכָל מוֹתַר הָרֶיוַח יִשָּׁאֵר לוֹ[8]. וְדֶרֶךְ זֶה הִיא נָכוֹן, כִּי מִסְתָמָא הַמְקַבֵּל לֹא יִרְצֶה לִישָּׁבַע[9] וְיִתֵּן לַנּוֹתֵן כְּפִי מַה שֶׁיִּקְצְבוּ בֵּינֵיהֶם. וְזֶהוּ הֶיתֵּר עִיסְקָא[10] הַנָּהוּג בֵּינֵינוּ[11]. וַאֲפִילוּ

כְּשֵׁרִים — **unless** it is substantiated **through the testimony of two valid witnesses.** **וְעַל הָרֶיוַח לֹא יְהֵא נֶאֱמָן כִּי אִם בִּשְׁבוּעָה** — **And on** any claim with regard to **the profit, he should not be trusted without** taking **an oath.**[7]

§3 **גַּם יְכוֹלִין לְהַתְנוֹת** — **They may also stipulate** **שֶׁהַבְּרֵירָה הוּא בְּיַד הַמְקַבֵּל** — **that the recipient has the option** **שֶׁאִם יִרְצֶה לָתֵת לְהַנּוֹתֵן כָּךְ וְכָךְ** — **that if he wishes to give the investor such-and-such** an amount **בְּעַד הַחֵלֶק הָרֶיוַח שֶׁלּוֹ** — **for the investor's portion of the profit,** **יְהֵא הָרְשׁוּת בְּיָדוֹ** — **he will be permitted to do so,** **וְכָל מוֹתַר הָרֶיוַח יִשָּׁאֵר לוֹ** — **while any additional profit will remain his.** If he does this, he will not be liable to an oath, since he has paid the maximum amount for which he may be liable to pay.[8] **וְדֶרֶךְ זֶה הִיא נָכוֹן** — **This way is** the **proper** one, **כִּי מִסְתָמָא הַמְקַבֵּל לֹא יִרְצֶה לִישָּׁבַע** — **for, presumably, the recipient will not wish to take an oath,**[9] **וְיִתֵּן לַנּוֹתֵן כְּפִי מַה שֶׁיִּקְצְבוּ בֵּינֵיהֶם** — **and he will give the investor** the amount **that they have stipulated between them,** regardless of the actual amount of the profit or loss. **וְזֶהוּ הֶיתֵּר עִיסְקָא הַנָּהוּג בֵּינֵינוּ** — **This is the *heter iska***[10]

---

7. That is, he will not be trusted to say that that there was no more profit than he declared, without taking an oath. The purpose of these conditions is to set up a situation in which the recipient will find it too difficult, or he will be unwilling to fulfill the required conditions, and he would instead choose to make payment as described below in the next *se'if.* [With regard to substantiating the loss through witnesses, see below, note 17.]

8. Using the example described above (note 2): They may stipulate that any profit realized above $200 will belong exclusively to the recipient. Thus, since the profit is shared equally, the investor will never have a claim to more than his $1000 principal and $100 profit. [Because of this stipulation, in the case that the recipient declares the full $200 profit from the venture, it is not necessary for him to take an oath that the profit was not greater, since the recipient will exercise his option to pay $100 in lieu of all profits.]

According to Rabbi Moshe Feinstein (*Igros Moshe, Yoreh Deah* II, §62; III, §40), the recipient must agree to invest in a venture where the expected return (according to the opinion of experts) is at least double the amount that the investor will be paid if the recipient does not take an oath. Thus, in our example, where it was stipulated that the recipient may pay $100 in lieu of taking an oath, the expected return on the $1000 invested must be a minimum of $200.

9. Due to its severity, people shun taking an oath even when their claim is true and legitimate. In order to further dissuade the recipient from taking an oath, the investor may stipulate that the oath be taken while holding a *Sefer Torah,* and even that it should be taken in the presence of the entire congregation at the time of the Torah reading in the synagogue, and that it include a curse upon his soul if he is not stating the truth (see *Igros Moshe, Yoreh Deah* II, §62; see also there III, §40-41).

10. *Heter iska,* "allowance through an *iska* venture," is a device through which one can be permissibly assured a specific return on his money without transgressing the *ribbis* prohibition. This is accomplished by means of an agreement, such as described above, that lays down terms and conditions for structuring the transaction such that it becomes an *iska* venture rather than a loan. Consequently, as with every *iska,* the investor's return has the legal status of a profit on an investment, which is permitted (provided that it is done in

אִם הַמְקַבֵּל יוֹדֵעַ אַחַר כָּךְ בְּעַצְמוֹ שֶׁלֹּא הִרְוִיחַ, אוֹ אֲפִילוּ אִם הִפְסִיד, יָכוֹל לִיתֵּן לְהַנּוֹתֵן אֶת הַקֶּרֶן עִם הָרֶיוַח שֶׁקָּצְבוּ בֵּינֵיהֶם, וְאֵין כָּאן שׁוּם אִיסּוּר, דְּכֵיוָן שֶׁיֵּשׁ עָלָיו חִיּוּב שְׁבוּעָה יָכוֹל לִפְטוֹר אֶת עַצְמוֹ בְּמָמוֹנוֹ מִן הַשְּׁבוּעָה[12].

ד. אֲבָל שֶׁיִּקְנֶה הַמְקַבֵּל אֶת חֵלֶק הָרֶיוַח שֶׁל הַנּוֹתֵן בְּכָךְ וְכָךְ, שֶׁיִּהְיֶה מְחוּיָּב לָתֵת לוֹ

---

that is customary among us.[11]

וַאֲפִילוּ אִם הַמְקַבֵּל יוֹדֵעַ אַחַר כָּךְ בְּעַצְמוֹ — And even if the recipient himself knows afterward שֶׁלֹּא הִרְוִיחַ — that he did not profit, אוֹ אֲפִילוּ אִם הִפְסִיד — or even if he incurred a loss, יָכוֹל לִיתֵּן לְהַנּוֹתֵן — he may still **give the investor אֶת הַקֶּרֶן עִם הָרֶיוַח שֶׁקָּצְבוּ בֵּינֵיהֶם — the** full **principal along with the profit that they agreed upon, וְאֵין כָּאן שׁוּם אִיסּוּר — and there is no** *ribbis* **prohibition involved. דְּכֵיוָן שֶׁיֵּשׁ עָלָיו חִיּוּב שְׁבוּעָה — For since he has an obligation to take an oath** (as set forth above in the previous *se'if*), **יָכוֹל לִפְטוֹר אֶת עַצְמוֹ בְּמָמוֹנוֹ מִן הַשְּׁבוּעָה — he may exempt himself from** taking **the oath with his money,** i.e., by paying the amount agreed upon.[12]

§4 In this *se'if,* Kitzur describes a method of ensuring a specific return on one's money without actually lending with interest. However, this method is nevertheless forbidden:

אֲבָל — However, שֶׁיִּקְנֶה הַמְקַבֵּל אֶת חֵלֶק הָרֶיוַח שֶׁל הַנּוֹתֵן בְּכָךְ וְכָךְ — an agreement **for the recipient to acquire the portion of the investor's profit** in return **for** payment of **such-and-such** an amount, **שֶׁיִּהְיֶה מְחוּיָּב לָתֵת לוֹ אַחַר כָּךְ — which would require**

---

a permissible manner, as set forth above, in *se'if* 1), rather than as interest on a loan. By stipulating the conditions delineated in the previous *se'if,* the investor is virtually certain that he will receive the agreed-upon return on his investment, since it is improbable that the recipient will fulfill the conditions that were stipulated in order to prove a loss or a lesser gain. On the other hand, the recipient will never have to pay more than the agreed-upon return if there was a larger profit, because he will exercise his right to pay a fixed amount. Nevertheless, since there is no *guarantee* of a profit, and, theoretically, the investor can, in fact, lose even half of his capital if it can be proven that the venture failed completely, therefore, as with every *iska,* he is an *investor* (on the investment portion), rather than a lender.

The authorities caution that the parties involved must be aware that the *heter iska* is not a magical device that permits lending with *ribbis,* but rather is a legal way of framing the transaction so that it constitutes an investment rather than a loan (see below, *se'if* 10; *Igros Moshe, Yoreh Deah* II, §62; see also *Igros Moshe, Yoreh Deah* I, §79 ד״ה ולכן and *Ahavas Chesed* Vol. 2, Ch. 15). [See, however, *Igros Moshe, Yoreh Deah* III, §41; see *The Laws of Ribbis,* by Rabbi Yisroel Reisman, Mesorah Publications, 1995, Chapter 23, note 3, for further discussion of these rulings.]

11. One should realize that although a properly drawn and executed *iska* document may be used without hesitation by someone who would otherwise be unable to lend money, one who is capable of lending money interest-free is required to do so. As Kitzur writes below (179:1), the mitzvah of granting an interest-free loan to a person in need is not merely meritorious, but is in fact obligatory. See also *Ahavas Chesed* Vol. 2, Ch. 15, where the Chofetz Chaim decries at length the practice of those who immediately upon earning a few rubles invest them for monetary gain, thus forgoing the immense spiritual profit awarded to one who fulfills the mitzvah of lending money to the needy for a relatively insignificant monetary profit.

12. That is, the extra money that he gives (that was not the result of a profit from the investment) is not given in return for the loan, but rather to exempt himself from his obligation to take an oath.

אַחַר כָּךְ כָּךְ וְכָךְ בְּכָל אוֹפֶן[13], זֶהוּ אָסוּר[14]. אֶלָּא, צָרִיךְ שֶׁיִּהְיֶה לְהַמְקַבֵּל הַבְּרֵירָה[15].

ה. נָתַן לוֹ עִיסְקָא עַל זְמַן וְנִתְעַכֵּב אֶצְלוֹ הַמָּעוֹת גַּם אַחַר זְמַן הַפֵּרָעוֹן צָרִיךְ הַמִּתְעַסֵּק לִיתֵּן לוֹ רֶיוַח גַּם בְּעַד הַזְּמַן שֶׁאַחַר כָּךְ, כִּי מִסְתָמָא נִשְׁאַר בְּיָדוֹ עַל תְּנַאי הָרִאשׁוֹן. וּמִכָּל מָקוֹם טוֹב יוֹתֵר לִכְתּוֹב תֵּיכֶף בְּתוֹךְ הַשְּׁטַר עִיסְקָא, שֶׁאִם יִשָּׁאֵר הַמָּעוֹת אֵצֶל הַמְקַבֵּל לְאַחַר הַזְּמַן, יִהְיֶה גַּם כֵּן בִּתְנַאי זֶה.

ו. נוּסַח שְׁטַר עִיסְקָא[16]: מוֹדֶה אֲנִי חָתוּם מַטָּה שֶׁקִּבַּלְתִּי לְיָדִי מֵאֵת ר׳ רְאוּבֵן הוֹרְוִויץ

---

him to give the investor **afterward** כָּךְ וְכָךְ בְּכָל אוֹפֶן — **such-and-such** an amount **regardless** of the amount of profit,[13] זֶהוּ אָסוּר — **is prohibited.**[14] אֶלָּא, צָרִיךְ שֶׁיִּהְיֶה לְהַמְקַבֵּל הַבְּרֵירָה — **Rather, it must be done** in a manner **that the recipient has the option** of exempting himself with an oath.[15]

§5 נָתַן לוֹ עִיסְקָא עַל זְמַן — **If** the investor **gave** the recipient funds as **an** ***iska*** **for a** certain length of **time,** וְנִתְעַכֵּב אֶצְלוֹ הַמָּעוֹת — **and the funds remained with** the recipient גַּם אַחַר זְמַן הַפֵּרָעוֹן — **beyond the time when payment** was due, צָרִיךְ הַמִּתְעַסֵּק לִיתֵּן לוֹ רֶיוַח — the recipient, **who is engaging in business, must give** the investor **profit** גַּם בְּעַד הַזְּמַן שֶׁאַחַר כָּךְ — **also for the time that** the money remained in his hands **after** the due date, כִּי מִסְתָמָא נִשְׁאַר בְּיָדוֹ עַל תְּנַאי הָרִאשׁוֹן — **for** the investment **presumably remained in his hand on the original terms.** וּמִכָּל מָקוֹם טוֹב יוֹתֵר לִכְתּוֹב תֵּיכֶף — **Nevertheless, it is preferable to specify immediately** from the onset בְּתוֹךְ הַשְּׁטַר עִיסְקָא — **in the** ***iska*** **document** שֶׁאִם יִשָּׁאֵר הַמָּעוֹת אֵצֶל הַמְקַבֵּל — **that if the funds remain with the recipient** לְאַחַר הַזְּמַן — **beyond the time** when payment is due, יִהְיֶה גַּם כֵּן בִּתְנַאי זֶה — **it will also be on the condition** of an *iska.*

§6 נוּסַח שְׁטַר עִיסְקָא: — Sample **text of an** ***iska*** **contract:**[16]

מוֹדֶה אֲנִי חָתוּם מַטָּה — ***I, the undersigned, hereby acknowledge*** שֶׁקִּבַּלְתִּי לְיָדִי מֵאֵת ר׳ רְאוּבֵן הוֹרְוִויץ מֵאוּנְגְוַואר — ***having received from***

---

13. That is, the recipient purchases the rights to the investor's share of the profit for a set amount, and thus pays that amount without need to take an oath.

14. Although it is standard business practice for an investor to sell his portion of the profit in a venture for a set amount, with the buyer receiving rights to all profits, whether large or small, nevertheless, in this case, when the investor makes such a deal with the recipient, it appears like interest on a loan, rather than profit on an investment, and is therefore prohibited (see *Shulchan Aruch HaRav, Hilchos Ribbis* §40; see also *Chochmas Adam* 142:12).

15. In such a case, it is not similar to interest on a loan since, if the profits were not realized or if there was a loss, the recipient has the option of taking an oath and not paying the stipulated amount.

16. One who writes a *heter iska* is strongly advised to confer with an authority who is experienced in these laws (see *Yaaros Devash* fol. 124a).

[*Chofetz Chaim,* in *Ahavas Chesed* Vol. 2, Ch. 15, cautions against being careless with regard to drawing up a proper *heter iska,* noting that if the *iska* document was not drawn up properly, the lender will be transgressing the prohibition of *ribbis,* which can affect whether one's soul will merit resurrection (see above, 65:1). Executing a document that contains provisions for *ribbis* is tantamount to writing and signing that the lender is denying the God of Israel; see *Bava Metzia* 71a.]

[See also Appendix D for the English text of a sample *heter iska* that R' Moshe Feinstein approved for use.]

מאונְגְוואר סך מֵאָה זְהוּבִים אעסטרייכישע וואהרונג בְּתוֹרַת עִיסְקָא לַחֲצִי שָׁנָה מִיּוֹם דִּלְמַטָּה, וְהִתְחַיַּיבְתִּי אֶת עַצְמִי שֶׁבְּכָל סְחוֹרָה טוֹבָה שֶׁתְּהֵא נִרְאֶה בְּעֵינַי שֶׁהִיא הַיּוֹתֵר קְרוֹבָה לְהַרְוִיחַ בָּהּ מְחוּיָּב אֲנִי לִקְנוֹת בְּעַד סַךְ הנ״ל, וְהֵם קוֹדְמִין לִמְעוֹתַי. וְכָל הָרֶיוַח שֶׁיִּתֵּן ה׳ לְיָדִי מֵאוֹתָהּ סְחוֹרָה יִהְיֶה הַמֶּחֱצָה לִי וְהַמֶּחֱצָה לר׳ רְאוּבֵן הנ״ל. וְכֵן חַס וְשָׁלוֹם לְהֶפְסֵד הוּא חֵלֶק כְּחֵלֶק. וּמִיָּד לְאַחַר כְּלוֹת חֲצִי שָׁנָה מִיּוֹם דִּלְמַטָּה אֲנִי מְחוּיָּב לְהַחֲזִיר לר׳ רְאוּבֵן הנ״ל אֶת הַקֶּרֶן וְגַם חֲצִי רֶיוַח שֶׁלּוֹ. וְלֹא יְהֵא לִי נֶאֱמָנוּת לוֹמַר הִפְסַדְתִּי אֶלָּא עַל פִּי שְׁנֵי עֵדִים כְּשֵׁרִים[17], וְעַל הָרֶיוַח לֹא אֱהֵא נֶאֱמָן רַק בִּשְׁבוּעָה. וְאוּלָם תְּנַאי הָיָה בֵּינֵינוּ שֶׁאִם אֶרְצֶה לִיתֵּן לוֹ בְּעַד חֵלֶק רֶיוַח שֶׁלּוֹ י׳ זְהוּבִים, אֲזַי אֵין לוֹ עָלַי שׁוּם תְּבִיעָה כִּי הַמּוֹתָר שַׁיָּיךְ לִי לְבַד, אֲפִילּוּ

סך מֵאָה זְהוּבִים אעסטרייכישע וואהרונג *R' Reuven Horowitz of Ungvar* בְּתוֹרַת עִיסְקָא — *the sum of one-hundred [Austrian] gold pieces as an iska venture* לַחֲצִי שָׁנָה מִיּוֹם דִּלְמַטָּה, — *for the duration of one-half of one year from the date entered below.* וְהִתְחַיַּיבְתִּי אֶת עַצְמִי שֶׁבְּכָל סְחוֹרָה טוֹבָה שֶׁתְּהֵא נִרְאֶה בְּעֵינַי שֶׁהִיא הַיּוֹתֵר קְרוֹבָה לְהַרְוִיחַ בָּהּ מְחוּיָּב אֲנִי לִקְנוֹת בְּעַד סַךְ הנ״ל, — *I have obligated myself to purchase with the aforementioned funds any suitable merchandise that, in my judgment, appears to be most likely to generate profits.* וְהֵם קוֹדְמִין לִמְעוֹתַי. — *These iska funds will be given priority for investment over my personal funds.*

וְכָל הָרֶיוַח שֶׁיִּתֵּן ה׳ לְיָדִי מֵאוֹתָהּ סְחוֹרָה יִהְיֶה הַמֶּחֱצָה לִי וְהַמֶּחֱצָה לר׳ רְאוּבֵן הנ״ל. — *Any profits that Hashem will grant me from the merchandise shall belong one-half to me and one-half to the aforementioned R' Reuven.* וְכֵן חַס וְשָׁלוֹם לְהֶפְסֵד הוּא חֵלֶק כְּחֵלֶק. — *Similarly, should any loss be incurred, God forbid, it shall be shared equally.* וּמִיָּד לְאַחַר כְּלוֹת חֲצִי שָׁנָה מִיּוֹם דִּלְמַטָּה — *Immediately upon the conclusion of the one-half-year term from the date entered below,* אֲנִי מְחוּיָּב לְהַחֲזִיר לר׳ רְאוּבֵן הנ״ל אֶת הַקֶּרֶן וְגַם חֲצִי רֶיוַח שֶׁלּוֹ. — *I shall be obligated to return to the aforementioned R' Reuven the principal as well as one-half of the profits.* וְלֹא יְהֵא לִי נֶאֱמָנוּת לוֹמַר הִפְסַדְתִּי אֶלָּא עַל פִּי שְׁנֵי עֵדִים כְּשֵׁרִים, — *I shall have no trustworthiness with regard to any claim that I have incurred a loss unless it has been substantiated through the testimony of two qualified witnesses.*[17]

וְעַל הָרֶיוַח לֹא אֱהֵא נֶאֱמָן רַק בִּשְׁבוּעָה. — *With regard to the profit, I shall not be trusted unless by means of taking an oath.* וְאוּלָם תְּנַאי הָיָה בֵּינֵינוּ — *However, it has been stipulated between us* שֶׁאִם אֶרְצֶה לִיתֵּן לוֹ בְּעַד חֵלֶק רֶיוַח שֶׁלּוֹ י׳ זְהוּבִים, — *that if I wish to give him, in lieu of his portion of the profit, the sum of ten gold pieces,* אֲזַי אֵין לוֹ עָלַי שׁוּם תְּבִיעָה — *that he shall then have no claim whatsoever against me.* כִּי הַמּוֹתָר שַׁיָּיךְ לִי לְבַד, — *Any additional profits are mine alone,* אֲפִילּוּ

17. Due to the concern that nowadays one may produce witnesses who will testify improperly, Rabbi Moshe Feinstein (*Igros Moshe, Yoreh Deah* II, §62) recommends that it be stipulated that the recipient must verify any claim of either a loss or lack of profit under solemn oath while holding a *Sefer Torah* (see above, note 9).

יְבוֹרַר שֶׁהָיָה הַרְבֵּה רֶיוַח. וְכָל דִּין תּוֹרַת נֶאֱמָנוּת לְבַעַל הַשְּׁטָר, אַף לְאַחַר זְמַן פֵּרָעוֹן. וְכָל זְמַן שֶׁלֹּא אַחֲזִיר אֶת הַמָּעוֹת הנ״ל הֵם בְּיָדִי בְּעִיסְקָא בְּאוֹפֶן הנ״ל. וְקִבַּלְתִּי שְׂכַר עֲמָלִי[18]. אוּנְגְּוַואר כ״ח שְׁבָט תרל״א לפ״ק. שִׁמְעוֹן אַייזֶענְשְׁטֵיין. בְּפָנֵינוּ עֵדִים[19]: לֵוִי בְּלוֹישְׁטֵיין, יְהוּדָה הוֹכְבֶּערְגֶער.

ז. אִם הַשָּׁעָה דְּחוּקָה וְאִי אֶפְשַׁר לָהֶם לִכְתּוֹב שְׁטַר עִיסְקָא, יְכוֹלִין לְהִתְנוֹת כָּל הַדְּבָרִים הנ״ל בְּעַל פֶּה.

ח. אִם מַקְדִּים מָעוֹת עַל סְחוֹרָה, יִכְתְּבוּ שְׁטַר הֶיתֵּר עִיסְקָא בְּעִנְיָן זֶה[20]:

יְבוֹרַר שֶׁהָיָה הַרְבֵּה רֶיוַח. — *even if it is determined that there was a large profit.* **וְכָל דִּין תּוֹרַת נֶאֱמָנוּת לְבַעַל הַשְּׁטָר,** — *Any credibility granted to the holder of the document* **אַף לְאַחַר זְמַן פֵּרָעוֹן.** — *shall continue to be in effect **after the payment is due.*** **וְכָל זְמַן שֶׁלֹּא אַחֲזִיר אֶת הַמָּעוֹת הנ״ל הֵם בְּיָדִי** — ***As long as I do not return the aforementioned funds*** **בְּעִיסְקָא בְּאוֹפֶן הנ״ל.** — ***they shall continue to be in my hands as an iska, in accordance with the above terms.***

וְקִבַּלְתִּי שְׂכַר עֲמָלִי. — ***I have received compensation for my efforts.***[18]

אוּנְגְּוַואר כ״ח שְׁבָט תרל״א לפ״ק. — ***Ungvar, 28 Shevat 5631***

שִׁמְעוֹן אַייזֶענְשְׁטֵיין. — ***Shimon Eisenstein***

בְּפָנֵינוּ עֵדִים: — ***Witnessed before us:***[19]

לֵוִי בְּלוֹישְׁטֵיין, — ***Levi Blaustein***

יְהוּדָה הוֹכְבֶּערְגֶער. — ***Yehudah Hochberger***

§7 אִם הַשָּׁעָה דְּחוּקָה — If they are pressed for time וְאִי אֶפְשַׁר לָהֶם לִכְתּוֹב שְׁטַר עִיסְקָא — and it is not possible for them to write an *iska* document, יְכוֹלִין לְהִתְנוֹת כָּל הַדְּבָרִים הנ״ל בְּעַל פֶּה — they may stipulate all of the previously mentioned particulars orally.

§8 In the previous *Siman* (*se'if* 16), we have seen that one may not advance payment for merchandise, due to issues of *ribbis.* This *se'if* details how one who wishes to advance payment for merchandise may accomplish this in a permissible manner.

אִם מַקְדִּים מָעוֹת עַל סְחוֹרָה — If one advances funds for merchandise, יִכְתְּבוּ שְׁטַר הֶיתֵּר עִיסְקָא בְּעִנְיָן זֶה — they should write a *heter iska* document in the following manner:[20]

---

18. This refers to the sum that the investor must give to the recipient in exchange for his managing the investment, as explained above, *se'if* 1.

19. Witnesses are not required for the *iska* document to be valid. They are included so that the terms of the document may be enforced if the recipient were to deny receiving the money.

20. The case: Reuven wishes to purchase five measures of spirits from Shimon for delivery in the month of Nissan, for which he is advancing 100 gold coins in Tishrei. Instead of giving the money now to Shimon in the form of payment for the future delivery of goods, the transaction is structured as an investment: Reuven advances an amount of 100 gold coins for investment in Shimon's distillery, and Shimon arranges that he can repay his principal as well as any profits in the form of five measures of spirits.

מוֹדֶה אֲנִי חָתוּם מַטָּה שֶׁקִּבַּלְתִּי מֵאֵת ר׳ רְאוּבֵן וַויינְשְׁטָאק מֵאוּנְגְוָואר (סאך) (סַךְ) מֵאָה זְהוּבִים אעסטרייכישע וואהרונג לְהִתְעַסֵּק בְּמָעוֹת זֶה בְּמַאשִׁין שֶׁאֲנִי מַחֲזִיק בִּכְפַר זָאהַאן[21] עַד רֹאשׁ חֹדֶשׁ נִיסָן הַבָּא עָלֵינוּ לְטוֹבָה. וְהָרֶיוַח שֶׁיַּעֲלֶה לְעֵרֶךְ מָעוֹת זֶה לְאַחַר נִכְּיוֹן כָּל הַהוֹצָאוֹת יִהְיֶה מֶחֱצָה שֶׁלִּי וּמֶחֱצָה לְר׳ רְאוּבֵן הנ״ל, וְכֵן חַס וְשָׁלוֹם הַהֶפְסֵד יִהְיֶה חֵלֶק כְּחֵלֶק. וּמִיָּד בְּרֹאשׁ חֹדֶשׁ נִיסָן הַבָּא עָלֵינוּ לְטוֹבָה אֲנִי מְחוּיָּב לְהַחֲזִיר לְר׳ רְאוּבֵן הנ״ל אֶת הַקֶּרֶן עִם חֵלֶק רֶיוַח שֶׁלּוֹ. וְלֹא אֶהֱא נֶאֱמָן לוֹמַר הִפְסַדְתִּי, אֶלָּא בְּבֵירוּר עַל פִּי שְׁנֵי עֵדִים כְּשֵׁרִים, וְעַל הָרֶיוַח לֹא אֶהֱא נֶאֱמָן כִּי אִם בִּשְׁבוּעָה. אַךְ זֹאת הוּתְנָה בֵּינֵינוּ, שֶׁאִם אֶרְצֶה בְּרֹאשׁ חֹדֶשׁ נִיסָן הַבָּא עָלֵינוּ לְטוֹבָה לִיתֵּן לְר׳ רְאוּבֵן הנ״ל בְּעַד הַקֶּרֶן וְגַם בְּעַד חֵלֶק רֶיוַח שֶׁלּוֹ

מוֹדֶה אֲנִי חָתוּם מַטָּה — *I, the undersigned, hereby acknowledge* שֶׁקִּבַּלְתִּי מֵאֵת ר׳ רְאוּבֵן וַויינְשְׁטָאק מֵאוּנְגְוָואר — *having received from R' Reuven Weinstock of Ungvar* (סאך) [סַךְ] מֵאָה זְהוּבִים אעסטרייכישע וואהרונג — *the sum of one-hundred [Austrian] gold pieces* לְהִתְעַסֵּק בְּמָעוֹת זֶה בְּמַאשִׁין שֶׁאֲנִי מַחֲזִיק בִּכְפַר זָאהַאן — *to engage in a business venture in the distillery*[21] *to which I hold the rights in the village of Zahan* עַד רֹאשׁ חֹדֶשׁ נִיסָן הַבָּא עָלֵינוּ לְטוֹבָה. — *until the upcoming Rosh Chodesh Nissan.* וְהָרֶיוַח שֶׁיַּעֲלֶה לְעֵרֶךְ מָעוֹת זֶה לְאַחַר נִכְּיוֹן כָּל הַהוֹצָאוֹת — *The portion of profits that results from this investment after deducting all expenses* יִהְיֶה מֶחֱצָה שֶׁלִּי וּמֶחֱצָה לְר׳ רְאוּבֵן הנ״ל, — *shall belong one-half to me and one-half to the aforementioned R' Reuven.* וְכֵן חַס וְשָׁלוֹם הַהֶפְסֵד יִהְיֶה חֵלֶק כְּחֵלֶק. — *Similarly, any loss incurred, God forbid, shall be shared equally.*

וּמִיָּד בְּרֹאשׁ חֹדֶשׁ נִיסָן הַבָּא עָלֵינוּ לְטוֹבָה — *Immediately upon the upcoming Rosh Chodesh Nissan,* אֲנִי מְחוּיָּב לְהַחֲזִיר לְר׳ רְאוּבֵן הנ״ל — *I shall be obligated to return to the aforementioned R' Reuven* אֶת הַקֶּרֶן עִם חֵלֶק רֶיוַח שֶׁלּוֹ. — *the principal as well as his portion of the profits.* וְלֹא אֶהֱא נֶאֱמָן לוֹמַר הִפְסַדְתִּי, — *I shall not be trusted to claim that I incurred a loss* אֶלָּא בְּבֵירוּר עַל פִּי שְׁנֵי עֵדִים כְּשֵׁרִים, — *unless it has been substantiated through the testimony of two qualified witnesses.*

וְעַל הָרֶיוַח לֹא אֶהֱא נֶאֱמָן — *With regard to the profit, I shall not be trusted* כִּי אִם בִּשְׁבוּעָה. — *unless by means of taking an oath.* אַךְ זֹאת הוּתְנָה בֵּינֵינוּ, — *However, it has been stipulated between us* שֶׁאִם אֶרְצֶה בְּרֹאשׁ חֹדֶשׁ נִיסָן הַבָּא עָלֵינוּ לְטוֹבָה — *that if I wish, upon the upcoming Rosh Chodesh Nissan,* לִיתֵּן לְר׳ רְאוּבֵן הנ״ל — *to give to the aforementioned R' Reuven* בְּעַד הַקֶּרֶן וְגַם בְּעַד חֵלֶק רֶיוַח שֶׁלּוֹ — *in*

---

21. According to Rabbi Moshe Feinstein (*Igros Moshe, Yoreh Deah* II, §62-63), the investor in an *iska* should *not* know the nature and details of the investment, since if the investor knows as a certainty that there was a loss (e.g., the business was destroyed by fire), he will be unable to require the recipient to take an oath. Rather, they should stipulate that the money is to be invested in any venture in which the expected return is at least double the agreed-upon amount that may be given in lieu of the profit, in order to exempt him from taking an oath (see above, note 8).

סַךְ חָמֵשׁ מִדּוֹת שפּירִיטוּס, אֲזַי אֵין לוֹ עָלַי עוֹד שׁוּם תְּבִיעָה יוֹתֵר. וְכָל דִּין תּוֹרַת נֶאֱמָנוּת לְבַעַל הַשְּׁטָר, אַף לְאַחַר זְמַן פֵּרָעוֹן. וְקִבַּלְתִּי שְׂכַר עֲמָלִי. אוּנְגְוַואר י״א תִּשְׁרֵי תרל״א לפ״ק. שִׁמְעוֹן בְּלוּמֶענְטָאהל. בְּפָנֵינוּ עֵדִים: לֵוִי בְּלוּישְׁטֵיין, יְהוּדָה הַלֵּוִי טויב.

ט. אִם הַנּוֹתֵן רוֹצֶה שֶׁהַמְקַבֵּל יִתֵּן לוֹ שְׁטַר חוֹב פָּשׁוּט וְאַמִּיץ כְּחֹק הַמְּדִינָה בִּכְדֵי שֶׁאִם הַמְקַבֵּל יְסָרֵב מִלִּפְרוֹעַ, אוֹ יָמוּת, יְהֵא לוֹ נָקֵל לִגְבּוֹת מְעוֹתָיו עַל יְדֵי עַרְכָּאוֹת[22], אֶלָּא שֶׁבְּעַל פֶּה הֵם מַתְנִים שֶׁהַמָּעוֹת הַזֶּה הִיא בְּתוֹרַת עִיסְקָא — לָא מְהַנֵּי, וַאֲפִילוּ הַשְּׁטָר אֵינוֹ אֶלָּא עַל הַקֶּרֶן לְבַד, דְּכֵיוָן שֶׁהַנּוֹתֵן יָכוֹל לִגְבּוֹת כָּל הַמָּעוֹת בִּשְׁטַר חוֹב שֶׁבְּיָדוֹ אֲפִילוּ אִם יִהְיֶה הֶפְסֵד בָּרוּר — אָסוּר. וַאֲפִילוּ אִם הַמְקַבֵּל מַאֲמִין לְהַנּוֹתֵן,

---

lieu of the principal as well as his portion of the profit סַךְ חָמֵשׁ מִדּוֹת שפּירִיטוּס, — *the amount of five measures of spirits,* אֲזַי אֵין לוֹ עָלַי עוֹד שׁוּם תְּבִיעָה יוֹתֵר. — *that he shall then have no further claim whatsoever against me.* וְכָל דִּין תּוֹרַת נֶאֱמָנוּת לְבַעַל הַשְּׁטָר, אַף לְאַחַר זְמַן פֵּרָעוֹן. — *Any credibility granted to the holder of the document shall continue to be in effect after the payment is due.* וְקִבַּלְתִּי שְׂכַר עֲמָלִי. — *I have received compensation for my efforts.*

אוּנְגְוַואר י״א תִּשְׁרֵי תרל״א לפ״ק. — *Ungvar, 11 Tishrei 5631*
שִׁמְעוֹן בְּלוּמֶענְטָאהל. — *Shimon Blumenthal*

בְּפָנֵינוּ עֵדִים: — *Witnessed before us:*
לֵוִי בְּלוּישְׁטֵיין, — *Levi Blaustein*
יְהוּדָה הַלֵּוִי טויב. — *Yehudah HaLevi Taub*

§9 One who is investing by means of a *heter iska* may wish to protect his investment by having a promissory note drawn up that is legally binding according to secular law, portraying the transaction as a loan. This *se'if* addresses whether this may be done.

אִם הַנּוֹתֵן רוֹצֶה שֶׁהַמְקַבֵּל יִתֵּן לוֹ — If the investor wants the recipient to give him שְׁטַר חוֹב פָּשׁוּט — an ordinary promissory note וְאַמִּיץ כְּחֹק הַמְּדִינָה — that is valid according to the law of the land, בִּכְדֵי שֶׁאִם הַמְקַבֵּל יְסָרֵב מִלִּפְרוֹעַ, אוֹ יָמוּת — so that in the event that the recipient refuses to make payment or dies, יְהֵא לוֹ נָקֵל לִגְבּוֹת מְעוֹתָיו עַל יְדֵי עַרְכָּאוֹת — the investor may collect his funds through the secular courts without difficulty,[22] אֶלָּא שֶׁבְּעַל פֶּה הֵם מַתְנִים — while they stipulate orally שֶׁהַמָּעוֹת הַזֶּה הִיא בְּתוֹרַת עִיסְקָא — that these funds are being given as an *iska,* לָא מְהַנֵּי — it is not effective in avoiding the issue of *ribbis,* **וַאֲפִילוּ הַשְּׁטָר אֵינוֹ אֶלָּא עַל הַקֶּרֶן לְבַד — even if the** promissory **note is only on the principal. דְּכֵיוָן שֶׁהַנּוֹתֵן יָכוֹל לִגְבּוֹת כָּל הַמָּעוֹת בִּשְׁטַר חוֹב שֶׁבְּיָדוֹ — Since, with the note that he is holding, the investor can collect all of the funds** invested, **אֲפִילוּ אִם יִהְיֶה הֶפְסֵד בָּרוּר — even in the event that there should be a definite loss, אָסוּר — it is** therefore **prohibited. וַאֲפִילוּ אִם הַמְקַבֵּל מַאֲמִין לְהַנּוֹתֵן — Moreover, even if the recipient trusts the**

---

22. That is, the investor is concerned that (despite the specific stipulations in the document requiring witnesses or an oath) if the secular courts are presented with a document that portrays the transaction as an investment he may find it difficult to collect the money that he is owed. [Note that it is normally prohibited to file a claim in a secular court. See below, 181:2-3, for the particulars of this prohibition. A halachic authority *must* be consulted.]

וְהוּא אָדָם חָסִיד, מִכָּל מָקוֹם לָא מְהַנֵּי. וַאֲפִילוּ אִם הַמְקַבֵּל נוֹתֵן לְהַנּוֹתֵן גַּם שְׁטַר עִיסְקָא שֶׁכָּתוּב בּוֹ כִּי הַמָּעוֹת שֶׁנִּכְתַּב בִּשְׁטַר חוֹב הוּא בְּתוֹרַת עִיסְקָא, גַּם כֵּן לָא מְהַנֵּי דְּאִיכָּא לְמֵיחַשׁ שֶׁמָּא הַנּוֹתֵן אוֹ יוֹרְשָׁיו יַעֲלִימוּ אַחַר כָּךְ אֶת הַשְּׁטַר עִיסְקָא וְיִגְבּוּ בִּשְׁטַר חוֹב[23]. וְאֵין הֶיתֵּר לָזֶה אֶלָּא שֶׁיַּשְׁלִישׁוּ אֶת הַשְּׁטַר עִיסְקָא בְּיַד שָׁלִישׁ, אוֹ שֶׁהַנּוֹתֵן יַחְתּוֹם אֶת עַצְמוֹ עַל הַשְּׁטַר עִיסְקָא וִיהֵא מוּנָּח בְּיַד הַמְקַבֵּל, אוֹ שֶׁיִּכְתְּבוּ עַל הַשְּׁטַר חוֹב שֶׁהוּא עַל פִּי אוֹפֶן הַמְבוֹאָר בִּשְׁטַר עִיסְקָא, אוֹ לְכָל הַפָּחוֹת יְיַחֲדוּ עֵדִים שֶׁהַשְּׁטַר חוֹב הוּא בְּתוֹרַת עִיסְקָא[24]. וּבְכָל אוֹפָנִים אֵלוּ, אֲפִילוּ אִם נִכְלַל בִּשְׁטַר חוֹב הַקֶּרֶן עִם הָרֶיוַח, שַׁפִּיר דָּמֵי.

---

investor, **וְהוּא אָדָם חָסִיד — and he is a pious man** who would not collect if it is not permitted (i.e., in the case of a proven loss), **מִכָּל מָקוֹם לָא מְהַנֵּי — nevertheless it is not effective. וַאֲפִילוּ אִם הַמְקַבֵּל נוֹתֵן לְהַנּוֹתֵן גַּם שְׁטַר עִיסְקָא — And even if the recipient gives the investor an *iska* document as well, שֶׁכָּתוּב בּוֹ כִּי הַמָּעוֹת שֶׁנִּכְתַּב בִּשְׁטַר חוֹב הוּא בְּתוֹרַת עִיסְקָא — in which it is written that the funds written in the promissory note are** actually being given **as an *iska*, גַּם כֵּן לָא מְהַנֵּי — it is also not effective, דְּאִיכָּא לְמֵיחַשׁ — for there is a concern שֶׁמָּא הַנּוֹתֵן אוֹ יוֹרְשָׁיו —** that **perhaps the investor or his heirs יַעֲלִימוּ אַחַר כָּךְ אֶת הַשְּׁטַר עִיסְקָא — will later conceal the *iska* document, וְיִגְבּוּ בִּשְׁטַר חוֹב — and collect with the promissory note.**[23] **וְאֵין הֶיתֵּר לָזֶה — There is no permissible manner to do this אֶלָּא שֶׁיַּשְׁלִישׁוּ אֶת הַשְּׁטַר עִיסְקָא בְּיַד שָׁלִישׁ — unless the *iska* document is deposited in the hands of a trustee, אוֹ שֶׁהַנּוֹתֵן יַחְתּוֹם אֶת עַצְמוֹ עַל הַשְּׁטַר עִיסְקָא — or the investor personally signs the *iska* document, וִיהֵא מוּנָּח בְּיַד הַמְקַבֵּל — and it is kept in the hands of the recipient, אוֹ שֶׁיִּכְתְּבוּ עַל הַשְּׁטַר חוֹב — or they write on the promissory note שֶׁהוּא עַל פִּי אוֹפֶן הַמְבוֹאָר בִּשְׁטַר עִיסְקָא — that its** actual obligation **is in the manner that is set forth in the *iska* document, אוֹ לְכָל הַפָּחוֹת יְיַחֲדוּ עֵדִים — or, at the very least, they designate witnesses** who can testify **שֶׁהַשְּׁטַר חוֹב הוּא בְּתוֹרַת עִיסְקָא — that the promissory note is** actually **according to the terms of an *iska*.**[24]

וּבְכָל אוֹפָנִים אֵלוּ — In any of these instances, אֲפִילוּ אִם נִכְלַל בִּשְׁטַר חוֹב הַקֶּרֶן עִם הָרֶיוַח — even if the promissory note contains both the principal and interest, שַׁפִּיר דָּמֵי — it is acceptable.

§10 In the following two *se'ifim,* Kitzur discusses the circumstances in which a *heter iska* is not effective, and what recourse the parties have in such cases.

---

23. This would thus jeopardize the enforceability of the *iska* document. Other authorities, however, are not concerned with this, and maintain that it does suffice to write a clause in the *iska* contract stating that it is the binding document and that the loan agreement was drawn up only as a source of recourse for the investor in the event that the recipient refuses to discharge his obligations as set forth in the *iska* contract. This position is taken by Rabbi Moshe Feinstein (*Igros Moshe, Yoreh Deah* II, §62; see also *Yoreh Deah* III, §38). Kitzur too, in his Appendix of editorial glosses, concedes that there is room for such a leniency; see there for a lengthy discussion. As with every *iska,* this should be done with the guidance of a halachic authority (see above, note 16).

24. Each of these measures ensures that the investor will not be able to deny the existence of an *iska* and collect with the promissory note.

י. שְׁטַר עִיסְקָא לָא מְהַנֵּי לְהַתִּיר אֶלָּא אִם הָאֱמֶת כֵּן הוּא שֶׁהוּא נוֹטֵל אֶת הַמָּעוֹת לַעֲשׂוֹת בּוֹ אֵיזֶה עֵסֶק. אֲבָל אִם אֵינוֹ נוֹטֵל אֶת הַמָּעוֹת לְצוֹרֶךְ עֵסֶק אֶלָּא לִפְרוֹעַ אֵיזֶה חוֹב וְכַדּוֹמֶה, אָז לָא מְהַנֵּי שְׁטַר עִיסְקָא, כֵּיוָן שֶׁהוּא שֶׁקֶר. אֲבָל יְכוֹלִין לַעֲשׂוֹת בְּאוֹפֶן זֶה, כְּגוֹן רְאוּבֵן שֶׁהוּא צָרִיךְ לְמָעוֹת וְיֵשׁ לוֹ אֵיזֶה סְחוֹרָה, אֲפִילוּ בְּמָקוֹם אַחֵר, יָכוֹל לְמָכְרָהּ לְשִׁמְעוֹן אֲפִילוּ בְּזוֹל גָּדוֹל וּבִתְנַאי שֶׁהַבְּרֵירָה בְּיַד רְאוּבֵן שֶׁאִם לֹא יִמְסְרֶנָּה לִידֵי שִׁמְעוֹן עַד יוֹם פְּלוֹנִי יִתֵּן לוֹ בַּעֲדָהּ כָּךְ וְכָךְ (שֶׁיִּהְיֶה לְשִׁמְעוֹן רֶיוַח כָּרָאוּי)[25], וְשִׁמְעוֹן יִתֵּן לִרְאוּבֵן אֶת הַמָּעוֹת וְיַעֲשׂוּ קִנְיַן סוּדָר[26] לְקִיּוּם הַמִּקָּח, דְּהַיְינוּ שֶׁשִּׁמְעוֹן הַלּוֹקֵחַ יִתֵּן קְצָת מִבִּגְדוֹ לִרְאוּבֵן שֶׁיִּתְפּוֹס בּוֹ וּבָזֶה הוּא קוֹנֶה אֶת הַסְּחוֹרָה שֶׁל רְאוּבֵן. וַאֲפִילוּ שֶׁלֹּא בִּפְנֵי עֵדִים וְהַסְּחוֹרָה הִיא בְּאַחֲרָיוּתוֹ שֶׁל שִׁמְעוֹן הַקּוֹנֶה[27].

שְׁטַר עִיסְקָא לָא מְהַנֵּי לְהַתִּיר — An ***iska*** **document is not effective to permit** an agreement **אֶלָּא אִם הָאֱמֶת כֵּן הוּא — unless in truth it is so, שֶׁהוּא נוֹטֵל אֶת הַמָּעוֹת לַעֲשׂוֹת בּוֹ אֵיזֶה עֵסֶק — that** the recipient **is taking the funds in order to invest them in a business venture. אֲבָל אִם אֵינוֹ נוֹטֵל אֶת הַמָּעוֹת לְצוֹרֶךְ עֵסֶק — But if he is not taking the funds for the purpose of a business venture, אֶלָּא לִפְרוֹעַ אֵיזֶה חוֹב וְכַדּוֹמֶה — but rather to repay some debt or the like, אָז לָא מְהַנֵּי שְׁטַר עִיסְקָא — the** ***iska*** **document would then not be effective, כֵּיוָן שֶׁהוּא שֶׁקֶר — since it is untrue. אֲבָל יְכוֹלִין לַעֲשׂוֹת בְּאוֹפֶן זֶה — But they may conduct** the transaction **in the following manner** and avoid the *ribbis* prohibition:

כְּגוֹן רְאוּבֵן שֶׁהוּא צָרִיךְ לְמָעוֹת — If, **for example, Reuven, who is in need of money, וְיֵשׁ לוֹ אֵיזֶה סְחוֹרָה, אֲפִילוּ בְּמָקוֹם אַחֵר — has some merchandise, even in a different place, יָכוֹל לְמָכְרָהּ לְשִׁמְעוֹן אֲפִילוּ בְּזוֹל גָּדוֹל — he may sell it to Shimon, even at a very low price, וּבִתְנַאי שֶׁהַבְּרֵירָה בְּיַד רְאוּבֵן — with the provision that the option is in Reuven's hands שֶׁאִם לֹא יִמְסְרֶנָּה לִידֵי שִׁמְעוֹן עַד יוֹם פְּלוֹנִי — that if he does not turn over** the merchandise **to Shimon before such-an-such date, יִתֵּן לוֹ בַּעֲדָהּ כָּךְ וְכָךְ — he will pay such-and-such** (i.e., a higher price) to Shimon **for it (שֶׁיִּהְיֶה לְשִׁמְעוֹן רֶיוַח כָּרָאוּי — so that Shimon may see a reasonable profit** from the transaction).[25] **וְשִׁמְעוֹן יִתֵּן לִרְאוּבֵן אֶת הַמָּעוֹת — Shimon is to** now **give Reuven the money, וְיַעֲשׂוּ קִנְיַן סוּדָר — and they must execute an "acquisition with the kerchief,"**[26] **לְקִיּוּם הַמִּקָּח — for the validation of the sale. דְּהַיְינוּ — This is** accomplished **שֶׁשִּׁמְעוֹן הַלּוֹקֵחַ יִתֵּן קְצָת מִבִּגְדוֹ לִרְאוּבֵן שֶׁיִּתְפּוֹס בּוֹ — by** having **Shimon, the purchaser, give Reuven,** the seller, **a bit of his clothing to take hold of, וּבָזֶה — and, in this manner, הוּא קוֹנֶה אֶת הַסְּחוֹרָה שֶׁל רְאוּבֵן — he acquires Reuven's merchandise. וַאֲפִילוּ שֶׁלֹּא בִּפְנֵי עֵדִים —** This is effective **even** if it was **not** performed **in the presence of witnesses. וְהַסְּחוֹרָה הִיא בְּאַחֲרָיוּתוֹ שֶׁל שִׁמְעוֹן הַקּוֹנֶה — The merchandise is** now **the responsibility of Shimon, the purchaser.**[27] Thus, the transaction is considered a sale, not a loan, and when the date of delivery

---

25. This is permitted since the one-time payment has the features of a penalty rather than interest (see *Shulchan Aruch HaRav, Hilchos Ribbis* §46).

26. This is a form of acquisition that transfers legal ownership of merchandise from the seller to the buyer even if the merchandise is not present at the place of the acquisition.

27. Once Shimon has made legal acquisition of the merchandise, any loss to the merchandise would be borne by Shimon. The transaction is thus effective immediately, and is not subject to the prohibition of advancing funds for a purchase where possession is taken only at a later date; see above, 65:16. See Appendix of Kitzur's editorial glosses.

יא. וְכֵן רְאוּבֵן שֶׁהָיָה חַיָּיב לְשִׁמְעוֹן מָעוֹת וּבְהַגִּיעַ זְמַן הַפֵּרָעוֹן אֵין לוֹ מָעוֹת לִרְאוּבֵן וְהִתְפַּשֵּׁר שֶׁשִּׁמְעוֹן יַמְתִּין לוֹ אֵיזֶה זְמַן, בָּזֶה גַּם כֵּן אֵין תַּקָּנָה בִּשְׁטַר עִיסְקָא, אֶלָּא שֶׁרְאוּבֵן יִמְכּוֹר לְשִׁמְעוֹן אֵיזֶה סְחוֹרָה שֶׁיֵּשׁ לוֹ בְּאוֹפֶן הנ״ל[28]. וְשִׁמְעוֹן יַחֲזִיר לוֹ אֶת הַשְּׁטָר חוֹב שֶׁהָיָה לוֹ עָלָיו מִכְּבָר וּרְאוּבֵן יִתֵּן לוֹ שְׁטָר עַל הַסְּחוֹרָה אֲשֶׁר קָנָה מֵאִתּוֹ בְּאוֹפֶן הנ״ל[29].

יב. יִשְׂרָאֵל שֶׁנּוֹתֵן לַחֲבֵירוֹ בְּהֵמָה לְגַדְּלָהּ וְשֶׁיַּחְלְקוּ אַחַר כָּךְ בָּרֶיוַח[30], דִּינוֹ כְּמוֹ שֶׁנָּתַן לוֹ מָעוֹת בְּעִיסְקָא[31] (וְעַיֵּין בְּיוֹרֶה דֵּעָה סִימָן קע״ז).

---

of the merchandise arrives and Reuven does not deliver the merchandise, it will be permissible for Reuven to pay Shimon the agreed-upon amount, even though he is paying more than he received from Shimon.

§11 **וְכֵן רְאוּבֵן שֶׁהָיָה חַיָּיב לְשִׁמְעוֹן מָעוֹת** — **So too,** with regard to **Reuven, who owed money to Shimon,** **וּבְהַגִּיעַ זְמַן הַפֵּרָעוֹן** — **and when the time of payment arrived,** **אֵין לוֹ מָעוֹת לִרְאוּבֵן** — **Reuven had no money,** **וְהִתְפַּשֵּׁר** — **and they reached an agreement** **שֶׁשִּׁמְעוֹן יַמְתִּין לוֹ אֵיזֶה זְמַן** — **that Shimon will defer** collection from **him for some time.** **בָּזֶה גַּם כֵּן אֵין תַּקָּנָה בִּשְׁטַר עִיסְקָא** — **Here too, there is no remedy** for Shimon to receive compensation **with an** ***iska*** **document,** since no money is being invested. **אֶלָּא שֶׁרְאוּבֵן יִמְכּוֹר לְשִׁמְעוֹן אֵיזֶה סְחוֹרָה שֶׁיֵּשׁ לוֹ בְּאוֹפֶן הנ״ל** — **Instead, Reuven should sell Shimon some of his merchandise in the manner mentioned above,**[28] **וְשִׁמְעוֹן יַחֲזִיר לוֹ אֶת הַשְּׁטָר חוֹב שֶׁהָיָה לוֹ עָלָיו מִכְּבָר** — **and Shimon will return the promissory note that was previously drawn against** Reuven. **וּרְאוּבֵן יִתֵּן לוֹ שְׁטָר עַל הַסְּחוֹרָה אֲשֶׁר קָנָה מֵאִתּוֹ** — **Reuven will then give him a note for the merchandise that he purchased from him,** **בְּאוֹפֶן הנ״ל** — **in the manner mentioned above.**[29]

§12 **יִשְׂרָאֵל שֶׁנּוֹתֵן לַחֲבֵירוֹ בְּהֵמָה לְגַדְּלָהּ** — Regarding **a Jew who gave his fellow an animal to raise,** **וְשֶׁיַּחְלְקוּ אַחַר כָּךְ בָּרֶיוַח** — **with** the agreement **that they should afterward divide the profit,**[30] **דִּינוֹ כְּמוֹ שֶׁנָּתַן לוֹ מָעוֹת בְּעִיסְקָא** — **the law** governing this case **is** the same **as if he gave him money for an** ***iska*** **venture**[31] (**וְעַיֵּין בְּיוֹרֶה דֵּעָה סִימָן קע״ז** — **see** ***Yoreh Deah, Siman*** **177,** *se'ifim* 1 and 23).

---

28. That is, by means of an "acquisition with the kerchief," as explained in the previous *se'if.*

29. That is, the note should state that Reuven is selling the merchandise to Shimon at a low price with the provision that if Reuven does not turn the merchandise over to Shimon before a certain date, Reuven will pay him a higher price for it. For example, if Reuven owes Shimon $1,000, Shimon may purchase the merchandise at that price, with Reuven agreeing to pay him $1,100 if he does not deliver the merchandise by a certain date. When that date arrives and the merchandise has not been delivered, Shimon will now receive $1,100 for the merchandise.

30. The owner of the animal is engaging the services of another person, such as a shepherd or farmer, to raise his animal, but rather than paying him an hourly or daily wage, they agree to divide the amount that the animal appreciates during the time that the animal was under his care.

31. As with every *iska* venture, half of the animal is considered to have been lent to the farmer while the remaining half belongs to the owner, and was entrusted to the farmer. As explained above, *se'if* 1, since the farmer is caring for the owner's portion only because he was lent the other half, it is prohibited as *ribbis* unless the owner compensates the farmer for his efforts (as well as paying for [half of] the animal's feed; see *Bris Yehudah,* Ch. 39, note 9).

367 LAWS OF VOWS AND OATHS — SIMAN 67:1

סימן סז

הִלְכוֹת נְדָרִים וּשְׁבוּעוֹת[1,2]

וּבוֹ י״א סְעִיפִים

א. אַל תְּהִי רָגִיל בִּנְדָרִים. כָּל הַנּוֹדֵר כְּאִלּוּ בּוֹנֶה בָּמָה[3] בִּשְׁעַת אִיסּוּר

SIMAN 67

THE LAWS OF VOWS AND OATHS

CONTAINING 11 *SEI'FIM*

§1-2 Avoiding Vows and Oaths / **§3** Vows for Charity / **§4** Oaths or Vows Relating to Mitzvos / **§5** Proper Vows / **§6** Expressed Correctly / **§7** Behavior That Constitutes a Vow / **§8** Annulling a Vow / **§9** Minimum Age / **§10-11** Revoking Vows

The Torah states (*Bamidbar* 30:3): אִישׁ כִּי יִדֹּר נֶדֶר לַה׳ אוֹ הִשָּׁבַע שְׁבֻעָה לֶאְסֹר אִסָּר עַל נַפְשׁוֹ לֹא יַחֵל דְּבָרוֹ וכו׳ — *If a man takes a vow to Hashem, or swears an oath to establish a prohibition upon himself, he shall not desecrate his word,* etc. This *Siman* discusses the laws of *nedarim* (vows) and *shevuos* (oaths),[1] two classes of oral declarations, and their legal consequences.[2]

§1 The *Siman* opens with the importance of avoiding taking oaths and vows (from *Nedarim* 22a, with explanation of *Ran* ad loc.):

אַל תְּהִי רָגִיל בִּנְדָרִים — One should not be accustomed to taking **vows. כָּל הַנּוֹדֵר — Whoever takes a vow, כְּאִלּוּ בּוֹנֶה בָּמָה —** it is **as if he builds a personal altar**[3] **בִּשְׁעַת אִיסּוּר הַבָּמוֹת — during the period when such altars are**

1. The English terms "*vow*" and "*oath*" include any type of solemn promise or pledge, and do not accurately reflect the halachic definitions of *nedarim* and *shevuos*. In this *Siman*, the term "vow" is to be taken as the halachic *neder* and the term "oath" is to be taken as the halachic *shevuah*. See next note.

2. Although a discussion all of the defining factors of the *neder* and *shevuah,* as well as an examination of all the possible variations of expressing oaths and vows, is beyond the scope of this work (see *Yoreh Deah* 204 *ff.* and 236 *ff.*), the chief distinction between the two is that a *neder* creates a prohibition upon an object, while a *shevuah* addresses the actions of a person, i.e., the one who takes the oath upon himself. As the Gemara states (*Nedarim* 2b): "A *neder* makes an object forbidden to the person, while a *shevuah* forbids the person to use the object."

Several halachic consequences result from this distinction. Most prominent is the rule that a *neder* takes effect only upon a physical matter that has substance, i.e., an object, whereas an oath takes effect even regarding a matter lacking substance. For example, the terminology of a vow cannot be used to forbid "a night's sleep" upon oneself, since sleep is not an object; however, one can prohibit sleep to his eyes with a vow (*Yoreh Deah* 213:1), or use the terminology of an oath to forbid himself to sleep for the night. [For more details, see *Yoreh Deah* §213.] Nevertheless, even such a vow would require annulment (described in *se'if* 8); see *Yoreh Deah* 206:5 and 213:1. Moreover, a vow can generally not be taken to require a person to do something, it can only create a prohibition upon him. There is, however, another type of vow, a vow of consecration (see note 7), which is an exception to this rule (*Rambam, Hil. Nedarim* 1:1-2). The vows addressed in *se'ifim* 3-5 are related to that type of vow.

3. This refers to any altar other than the one in the *Mishkan* (Tabernacle) or the *Beis HaMikdash* (Holy Temple).

LAWS OF VOWS AND OATHS — SIMAN 67:2 368

הַבָּמוֹת[4], וְהַמְקַיְּימוֹ[5] כְּאִלּוּ הִקְרִיב עָלָיו קָרְבָּן שֶׁחַיָּיב מִשּׁוּם שְׁחוּטֵי חוּץ[6], כִּי טוֹב יוֹתֵר שֶׁיִּשָּׁאַל עַל נִדְרוֹ וְיַתִּירוּ לוֹ. וְהָנֵי מִילֵּי בִּשְׁאָר נְדָרִים אֲבָל נִדְרֵי הֶקְדֵּשׁ[7] מִצְוָה לְקַיְּימָן שֶׁנֶּאֱמַר (תהלים קטז, יח) "נְדָרַי לַה' אֲשַׁלֵּם", וְלֹא יִשָּׁאַל עֲלֵיהֶם אֶלָּא בִּשְׁעַת הַדְּחָק.

ב. וְכֵן יִתְרַחֵק מִן הַשְּׁבוּעָה, אֲבָל אִם עָבַר וְנִשְׁבַּע עַל אֵיזֶה דָבָר, לֹא יִשָּׁאַל עָלֶיהָ, אֶלָּא יַעֲמוֹד בִּשְׁבוּעָתוֹ, אַף עַל פִּי שֶׁהוּא מִצְטַעֵר, שֶׁנֶּאֱמַר (תהלים טו, ד) "נִשְׁבַּע לְהָרַע וְלֹא יָמִר" וּכְתִיב אַחֲרָיו(שם פסוק ה) "עֹשֵׂה אֵלֶּה לֹא יִמּוֹט לְעוֹלָם"[8]. וְאֵין נִשְׁאָלִין עַל הַשְּׁבוּעָה אֶלָּא בִּשְׁעַת הַדְּחָק[9].

---

forbidden.[4] **וְהַמְקַיְּימוֹ — And one who fulfills** his vow, rather than seeking to have it annulled,[5] **כְּאִלּוּ הִקְרִיב עָלָיו קָרְבָּן — it is as if he offered a sacrifice upon it, שֶׁחַיָּיב מִשּׁוּם שְׁחוּטֵי חוּץ —** an act **for which one is liable for** the prohibition of **slaughtering** a consecrated animal **outside** the Temple.[6] **כִּי טוֹב יוֹתֵר — For it would have been better שֶׁיִּשָּׁאַל עַל נִדְרוֹ — if he had sought annulment for his vow, וְיַתִּירוּ לוֹ — so that they could permit for him** that which he forbade. **וְהָנֵי מִילֵּי בִּשְׁאָר נְדָרִים — However, this applies** only **to other vows,** that have only personal ramifications; **אֲבָל נִדְרֵי הֶקְדֵּשׁ — but vows of consecration**[7] **מִצְוָה לְקַיְּימָן —** are **a mitzvah to fulfill,** rather than to seek annulment for them, **שֶׁנֶּאֱמַר "נְדָרַי לַה' אֲשַׁלֵּם" —** as the verse **states** (*Tehillim* 116:18): ***My vows to Hashem I will fulfill.*** **וְלֹא יִשָּׁאַל עֲלֵיהֶם — One should not seek annulment for these** vows **אֶלָּא בִּשְׁעַת הַדְּחָק — unless in a pressing situation,** as determined by a halachic authority.

§2 וְכֵן יִתְרַחֵק מִן הַשְּׁבוּעָה — Likewise, one should distance himself from taking **oaths. אֲבָל אִם עָבַר וְנִשְׁבַּע עַל אֵיזֶה דָבָר — However, if he violated** this admonition **and swore regarding any matter, לֹא יִשָּׁאַל עָלֶיהָ — he should not seek annulment; אֶלָּא יַעֲמוֹד בִּשְׁבוּעָתוֹ — rather, he should keep his oath אַף עַל פִּי שֶׁהוּא מִצְטַעֵר — even if it causes him distress, שֶׁנֶּאֱמַר —** as the verse **states** (*Tehillim* 15:4): **"נִשְׁבַּע לְהָרַע וְלֹא יָמִר" — *One who can swear to*** *his* ***detriment without retracting.*** **וּכְתִיב אַחֲרָיו "עֹשֵׂה אֵלֶּה לֹא יִמּוֹט לְעוֹלָם" — And following that** verse, **it is written** (ibid. v. 5): ***He who does these shall not falter forever.***[8] **וְאֵין נִשְׁאָלִין עַל הַשְּׁבוּעָה — One may not seek annulment for an oath, אֶלָּא בִּשְׁעַת הַדְּחָק — unless in a pressing situation.**[9]

---

4. During most of Israel's history, with the exception of certain short periods, it was forbidden to offer sacrifices on such an altar (see *Zevachim* 112b).

5. Under certain circumstances a vow may be annulled. See below, *se'if* 8, for the process of annulling vows.

6. This severe prohibition is found in *Vayikra* 17:1-5. Just as it is forbidden for a person to expand upon the Torah's guidelines for divine service by building a personal altar, which is an additional, private place of worship, it is likewise inappropriate for one to add prohibitions to those of the Torah by making personal vows (see *Ran* to *Nedarim* 22a s.v. הנודר).

7. This law applies to consecration of animals to be brought as offerings (see *Rambam, Hil. Nedarim* 1:2 and 13:25), and, in the opinion of a number of authorities, applies to a vow of a gift to charity as well (see *Shach, Yoreh Deah* 203:2; see also *Chiddushei R' Akiva Eiger* to *Yoreh Deah* 203:3). This is apparently the opinion of Kitzur as well.

8. These verses list the attributes of one who is assured a place in Heaven. If one takes an oath, even to his own detriment, he should fulfill his oath and not retract it.

9. One may seek annulment if the oath is preventing him from performing a mitzvah (*Shach, Yoreh Deah* 230:2).

ג. צָרִיךְ לִיזָּהֵר שֶׁלֹּא יִדּוֹר שׁוּם דָּבָר, וַאֲפִילוּ לִצְדָקָה אֵין טוֹב לִידּוֹר. אֶלָּא, אִם יֵשׁ לוֹ בְּיָדוֹ מַה שֶּׁהוּא רוֹצֶה לִיתֵּן, יִתֵּן מִיָּד, וְאִם אֵין לוֹ, יַמְתִּין עַד שֶׁיִּהְיֶה לוֹ וְיִתֵּן בְּלֹא נֶדֶר. וְאִם פּוֹסְקִים צְדָקָה וְצָרִיךְ לִפְסוֹק עִמָּהֶם, יֹאמַר בְּפֵירוּשׁ שֶׁהוּא פּוֹסֵק בְּלִי נֶדֶר. וְכֵן כְּשֶׁמַּזְכִּירִין נְשָׁמוֹת[10] שֶׁנּוֹדְרִין לִצְדָקָה יֵשׁ לוֹמַר "בְּלִי נֶדֶר" (וְעַיֵּין לְעֵיל סִימָן ל"ד סְעִיף ט')[11]. אִם הוּא בְּעֵת צָרָה, מוּתָּר לוֹ לִנְדּוֹר.

ד. אִם דַּעְתּוֹ לִקְבּוֹעַ לוֹ אֵיזֶה לִימּוּד בַּתּוֹרָה, אוֹ לַעֲשׂוֹת אֵיזֶה מִצְוָה, וְהוּא יָרֵא פֶּן יִתְרַשֵּׁל אַחַר כָּךְ, אוֹ שֶׁהוּא מִתְיָרֵא פֶּן יְסִיתֵהוּ הַיֵּצֶר לַעֲשׂוֹת אֵיזֶה אִיסּוּר, אוֹ לְמָנְעוֹ מִלַּעֲשׂוֹת אֵיזֶהוּ מִצְוָה, מוּתָּר לוֹ לְזָרוּזֵי נַפְשֵׁיהּ בְּנֶדֶר אוֹ בִשְׁבוּעָה, דְּאָמַר רַב (נדרים ח, א): מִנַּיִן שֶׁנִּשְׁבָּעִין לְקַיֵּים אֶת הַמִּצְוָה לְזָרֵז אֶת עַצְמוֹ, אַף עַל

---

§3 צָרִיךְ לִיזָּהֵר שֶׁלֹּא יִדּוֹר שׁוּם דָּבָר — **One must be careful not to vow anything.** וַאֲפִילוּ לִצְדָקָה אֵין טוֹב לִידּוֹר — **Even** for the purpose of giving **to charity it is not proper to vow;** אֶלָּא, אִם יֵשׁ לוֹ בְּיָדוֹ — **rather, if he has in his possession** מַה שֶּׁהוּא רוֹצֶה לִיתֵּן — **that which he intends to give,** יִתֵּן מִיָּד — **he should give it immediately,** וְאִם אֵין לוֹ — **and if he does not have** the amount he wishes to give, יַמְתִּין עַד שֶׁיִּהְיֶה לוֹ — **he should wait until he has** that amount, וְיִתֵּן בְּלֹא נֶדֶר — **and** then **give it** to charity **without** first **taking a vow.** וְאִם פּוֹסְקִים צְדָקָה — **If** one is in a setting where people are **pledging to charity,** וְצָרִיךְ לִפְסוֹק עִמָּהֶם — **and he must pledge along with them,** יֹאמַר בְּפֵירוּשׁ — **he should say clearly** שֶׁהוּא פּוֹסֵק בְּלִי נֶדֶר — **that his pledge is without** the status of **a vow.** וְכֵן כְּשֶׁמַּזְכִּירִין נְשָׁמוֹת — **Likewise, during the memorial** service for departed **souls,**[10] שֶׁנּוֹדְרִין לִצְדָקָה — **in which** it is customary **to pledge** a donation **to charity,** יֵשׁ לוֹמַר "בְּלִי נֶדֶר" — **one should say, "I pledge without a vow"** (וְעַיֵּין לְעֵיל סִימָן ל"ד סְעִיף ט') — **see above, 34:9).**[11] אִם הוּא בְּעֵת צָרָה — **If one is going through a time of distress,** מוּתָּר לוֹ לִנְדּוֹר — **he is permitted to** make **a vow.**

§4 Although vows should generally be avoided, there are cases when it is permitted to take a vow:

אִם דַּעְתּוֹ לִקְבּוֹעַ לוֹ — **If one intends to designate for himself** אֵיזֶה לִימּוּד בַּתּוֹרָה — **a study** session **on any subject of Torah,** אוֹ לַעֲשׂוֹת אֵיזֶה מִצְוָה — **or** he intends **to perform any mitzvah,** וְהוּא יָרֵא פֶּן יִתְרַשֵּׁל אַחַר כָּךְ — **and he fears he may become lax** regarding one of these **at a later time,** אוֹ שֶׁהוּא מִתְיָרֵא פֶּן יְסִיתֵהוּ הַיֵּצֶר — **or if one fears that the** evil **inclination may entice him** לַעֲשׂוֹת אֵיזֶה אִיסּוּר — **to do something forbidden,** אוֹ לְמָנְעוֹ מִלַּעֲשׂוֹת אֵיזֶהוּ מִצְוָה — **or prevent him from doing some mitzvah,** מוּתָּר לוֹ לְזָרוּזֵי נַפְשֵׁיהּ בְּנֶדֶר אוֹ בִשְׁבוּעָה — **he may motivate himself by** taking **a vow or an oath.** דְּאָמַר רַב — This is in accordance with what **Rav said** (*Nedarim* 8a): מִנַּיִן שֶׁנִּשְׁבָּעִין לְקַיֵּים אֶת הַמִּצְוָה — **From where** is it derived **that one may take an oath to fulfill a mitzvah** לְזָרֵז אֶת עַצְמוֹ — **to motivate himself** אַף עַל

---

10. This refers to *Yizkor,* the prayer service in which the souls of the departed are remembered and charity is pledged in their memory. It is customarily recited on the three Festivals and Yom Kippur (see below, 133:21).

11. There, Kitzur discusses the halachos that apply to a pledge to charity, which, even without being worded as a vow, involve the potential of violating prohibitions.

פִּי שֶׁהוּא מוּשְׁבָּע וְעוֹמֵד מֵהַר סִינַי[12]? שֶׁנֶּאֱמַר (תהלים קיט, קו) "נִשְׁבַּעְתִּי וָאֲקַיֵּמָה לִשְׁמֹר מִשְׁפְּטֵי צִדְקֶךָ"[13]. וַאֲפִילוּ אִם לֹא אָמַר בִּלְשׁוֹן נֶדֶר אוֹ שְׁבוּעָה, אֶלָּא בְּדִיבּוּר בְּעָלְמָא, הָוֵי נֶדֶר וּמְחוּיָּיב לְקַיֵּים. וְלָכֵן צָרִיךְ הָאָדָם לִיזָּהֵר כְּשֶׁהוּא אוֹמֵר שֶׁיַּעֲשֶׂה אֵיזֶה דְּבַר מִצְוָה, שֶׁיֹּאמַר "בְּלִי נֶדֶר"[14]. וְטוֹב שֶׁיַּרְגִּיל הָאָדָם אֶת עַצְמוֹ כֵּן, אֲפִילוּ בְּאָמְרוֹ לַעֲשׂוֹת דְּבַר רְשׁוּת, כְּדֵי שֶׁלֹּא יִכָּשֵׁל חַס וְשָׁלוֹם בַּעֲוֹן נְדָרִים.

ה. מִי שֶׁנּוֹדֵר נְדָרִים כְּדֵי לְתַקֵּן מִדּוֹתָיו הֲרֵי זֶה זָרִיז וּמְשׁוּבָּח. כֵּיצַד? הֲרֵי שֶׁהָיָה זוֹלֵל וְנָדַר שֶׁלֹּא יֹאכַל בָּשָׂר אֵיזֶה זְמַן, אוֹ שֶׁהָיָה שׁוֹגֶה בַּיַּיִן וְאָסַר עָלָיו אֶת הַיַּיִן וּשְׁאָר מַשְׁקִין הַמְּשַׁכְּרִין, וְכֵן מִי שֶׁהָיָה מִתְגָּאֶה בְּיוֹפְיוֹ וְקִבֵּל עָלָיו נְזִירוּת[15] וְכַיּוֹצֵא

פִּי שֶׁהוּא מוּשְׁבָּע וְעוֹמֵד מֵהַר סִינַי — even though he stands under oath from the time of the Revelation at **Mount Sinai** to fulfill all the mitzvos?[12] **שֶׁנֶּאֱמַר** — For **as the** verse **states** (*Tehillim* 119:106): **"נִשְׁבַּעְתִּי וָאֲקַיֵּמָה לִשְׁמֹר מִשְׁפְּטֵי צִדְקֶךָ" — *I swore, and I will fulfill, to keep Your righteous ordinances.*[13] וַאֲפִילוּ אִם לֹא אָמַר בִּלְשׁוֹן נֶדֶר אוֹ שְׁבוּעָה — Even if one does not word** his intention **in the** formal **expression of a vow or oath, אֶלָּא בְּדִיבּוּר בְּעָלְמָא — but only as an ordinary expression** of intent, **הָוֵי נֶדֶר וּמְחוּיָּיב לְקַיֵּים — it** nonetheless **has the status of a vow, and he must keep it. וְלָכֵן צָרִיךְ הָאָדָם לִיזָּהֵר — Therefore, a person must be careful כְּשֶׁהוּא אוֹמֵר שֶׁיַּעֲשֶׂה אֵיזֶה דְּבַר מִצְוָה — when he says that he will do anything that is a mitzvah, שֶׁיֹּאמַר "בְּלִי נֶדֶר" — to** also **say "*b'li neder*"** (without a vow).[14] **וְטוֹב שֶׁיַּרְגִּיל הָאָדָם אֶת עַצְמוֹ כֵּן — It is proper for a person to accustom himself to this** practice of saying "*b'li neder,*" **אֲפִילוּ בְּאָמְרוֹ לַעֲשׂוֹת דְּבַר רְשׁוּת — even when saying that he will do a discretionary** (i.e., non-mitzvah) **act, כְּדֵי שֶׁלֹּא יִכָּשֵׁל חַס וְשָׁלוֹם בַּעֲוֹן נְדָרִים — so that he not** come to **stumble, God forbid,** into **the sin of** violating **vows.**

§5 מִי שֶׁנּוֹדֵר נְדָרִים — If one makes vows **כְּדֵי לְתַקֵּן מִדּוֹתָיו — in order to improve his character traits, הֲרֵי זֶה זָרִיז וּמְשׁוּבָּח — he is** acting with **alacrity and his** behavior **is praiseworthy. כֵּיצַד — What is a case** where this applies? **הֲרֵי שֶׁהָיָה זוֹלֵל — If one was gluttonous וְנָדַר שֶׁלֹּא יֹאכַל בָּשָׂר אֵיזֶה זְמַן — and he** therefore **vowed not to eat meat for a certain** amount of **time; אוֹ שֶׁהָיָה שׁוֹגֶה בַּיַּיִן — or, if one was overindulgent in wine וְאָסַר עָלָיו אֶת הַיַּיִן וּשְׁאָר מַשְׁקִין הַמְּשַׁכְּרִין — and forbade wine and other intoxicating beverages upon himself. וְכֵן מִי שֶׁהָיָה מִתְגָּאֶה בְּיוֹפְיוֹ — Likewise, one who was conceited about his beautiful appearance וְקִבֵּל עָלָיו נְזִירוּת — and he** therefore **accepted upon himself a *nezirus* vow,**[15] **וְכַיּוֹצֵא**

---

12. The entire Jewish nation — including generations yet unborn — entered into a covenant in the form of an oath at Mount Sinai to observe all of the Torah's commandments (see *Devarim* 28:69, *Shevuos* 39a, and *Bamidbar Rabbah* 9:54). In general, an oath cannot take effect upon something that is already the subject of a previous oath. Thus, without this teaching, it would have been assumed that an oath regarding any mitzvah would not take effect. The verse that Rav cites teaches that such an oath is effective (see *Nedarim* 8a with commentaries; see also *Ramban* to *Bamidbar* 30:3).

13. Nevertheless, contemporary authorities caution against taking vows or oaths under *any* circumstances (see further below, note 17).

14. That is, when accepting upon himself the mitzvah, he should say that he is doing so without the acceptance having the status of a vow.

15. A person who takes a vow of *nezirus* adopts the status of a *nazir,* who is forbidden to eat or drink grapes or grape products, to cut his hair, or to become contaminated by a human corpse. At the conclusion of his term

בָּזֶה, נְדָרִים כָּאֵלּוּ הֵמָּה עֲבוֹדַת הַשֵּׁם יִתְבָּרֵךְ שְׁמוֹ, וְעַל אֵלּוּ אָמְרוּ חֲכָמֵינוּ זִכְרוֹנָם לִבְרָכָה (אבות ג, יז): נְדָרִים סְיָג לִפְרִישׁוּת[16]. וּמִכָּל מָקוֹם גַּם בִּנְדָרִים כָּאֵלּוּ אֵין לוֹ לְאָדָם לְהַרְגִּיל אֶת עַצְמוֹ, אֶלָּא יֵשׁ לְהִתְגַּבֵּר עַל יִצְרוֹ גַּם בְּלֹא נְדָרִים[17].

ו. אֵין הַנֶּדֶר חָל אֶלָּא אִם הָיָה פִּיו וְלִבּוֹ שָׁוִים, אֲבָל אִם נָדַר בְּטָעוּת שֶׁלֹּא הָיָה דַעְתּוֹ כְּמוֹ שֶׁהוֹצִיא בִּשְׂפָתָיו[18], אוֹ שֶׁהִרְהֵר בְּלִבּוֹ נֶדֶר וְלֹא הוֹצִיא בִּשְׂפָתָיו, אֵין זֶה נֶדֶר.

ז. מִי שֶׁנָּהַג אֵיזֶה חוּמְרָא בִּדְבָרִים הַמּוּתָּרִים מִדִּינָא מֵחֲמַת סְיָג וְגָדֵר[19] וּפְרִישׁוּת, כְּגוֹן תַּעֲנִיּוֹת שֶׁבִּימֵי הַסְּלִיחוֹת[20], אוֹ שֶׁלֹּא לֶאֱכוֹל בָּשָׂר וְשֶׁלֹּא לִשְׁתּוֹת יַיִן

בָּזֶה — or some similar situation. **נְדָרִים כָּאֵלּוּ הֵמָּה עֲבוֹדַת הַשֵּׁם יִתְבָּרֵךְ שְׁמוֹ — Vows such as these are** part of **the service of Hashem, may His Name be blessed.** **וְעַל אֵלּוּ אָמְרוּ חֲכָמֵינוּ זִכְרוֹנָם לִבְרָכָה — Regarding these** vows, **our Sages of blessed memory, have stated** (*Avos* 3:17): **נְדָרִים סְיָג לִפְרִישׁוּת — Vows are a protective "fence" for abstinence.**[16] **וּמִכָּל מָקוֹם גַּם בִּנְדָרִים כָּאֵלּוּ — Nevertheless, even with regard to these types of vows,** **אֵין לוֹ לְאָדָם לְהַרְגִּיל אֶת עַצְמוֹ — a person should not accustom himself** to making them; **אֶלָּא יֵשׁ לְהִתְגַּבֵּר עַל יִצְרוֹ — rather, he should overcome his** evil **inclination** **גַּם בְּלֹא נְדָרִים — even without** the aid of **vows.**[17]

§6 **אֵין הַנֶּדֶר חָל — A** person's **vow does not take effect** **אֶלָּא אִם הָיָה פִּיו וְלִבּוֹ שָׁוִים — unless his words and his thoughts coincide;** **אֲבָל אִם נָדַר בְּטָעוּת — but if he expressed the vow incorrectly,** **שֶׁלֹּא הָיָה דַעְתּוֹ כְּמוֹ שֶׁהוֹצִיא בִּשְׂפָתָיו — that** is, what was in **his mind was not** the same **as** the words **that he verbalized,**[18] **אוֹ שֶׁהִרְהֵר בְּלִבּוֹ נֶדֶר — or if he thought** the words of **a vow in his heart** **וְלֹא הוֹצִיא בִּשְׂפָתָיו — but did not verbalize it,** **אֵין זֶה נֶדֶר — it does not have the status of a vow.**

§7 Although, in general, a vow must be verbalized to take effect (see previous *se'if*), nevertheless, some vows can take effect by virtue of a person having acted in a certain manner, as will be detailed in this *se'if*.

מִי שֶׁנָּהַג אֵיזֶה חוּמְרָא — One who conducts himself with **a stringency** **בִּדְבָרִים הַמּוּתָּרִים מִדִּינָא — with regard to matters that are permitted by halachah,** **מֵחֲמַת סְיָג וְגָדֵר וּפְרִישׁוּת — in order that** his stringency serve as **a** protective **"fence"** or **"enclosure,"**[19] or a form of **abstinence** — **כְּגוֹן תַּעֲנִיּוֹת שֶׁבִּימֵי הַסְּלִיחוֹת — such as fasting during the days of *Selichos*,**[20] **אוֹ שֶׁלֹּא לֶאֱכוֹל בָּשָׂר וְשֶׁלֹּא לִשְׁתּוֹת יַיִן — or**

---

as a *nazir*, he is required to bring sacrificial offerings in the *Beis HaMikdash* (Temple) and shave off the hair of his head; see *Bamidbar* 6:1-21. One who finds himself becoming conceited about his own beauty may take this vow and thus obligate himself to ultimately shave off his hair (see *Nedarim* 9b).

16. I.e., they are a protective measure that restrains one's tendency to indulge in physical pleasures.

17. In a letter to his son, Rabbi Moshe Feinstein (*Igros Moshe, Yoreh Deah* III, §96.9) strongly cautions him against taking vows even for the sake of Torah study or correcting character flaws.

18. For example, if he intended to take a vow not to eat wheat bread, but when he verbalized the vow he mistakenly said "barley bread," the vow does not take effect and both are permitted (*Yoreh Deah* 210:1).

19. That is, by prohibiting upon himself certain permitted conduct that could lead to transgressing a prohibition.

20. See below, 128:12.

מי״ז בְּתַמּוּז וְאֵילָךְ[21] וְכַיּוֹצֵא בּוֹ אֲפִילּוּ לֹא נָהַג כֵּן רַק פַּעַם הָרִאשׁוֹן אֶלָּא שֶׁהָיָה בְּדַעְתּוֹ לִנְהוֹג כֵּן לְעוֹלָם, אוֹ שֶׁנָּהַג כֵּן ג׳ פְּעָמִים אַף עַל פִּי שֶׁלֹּא הָיָה בְּדַעְתּוֹ לִנְהוֹג כֵּן לְעוֹלָם, וְלֹא הִתְנָה שֶׁיְּהֵא בְּלִי נֶדֶר וְרוֹצֶה לַחֲזוֹר מִפְּנֵי שֶׁאֵינוֹ בָּרִיא, צָרִיךְ הַתָּרָה[22], וְיִפְתַּח בַּחֲרָטָה[23] שֶׁהוּא מִתְחָרֵט עַל מַה שֶּׁנָּהַג כֵּן לְשֵׁם נֶדֶר. לָכֵן מִי שֶׁהוּא רוֹצֶה לִנְהוֹג בְּאֵיזֶה חוּמְרוֹת לְסְיָיג וּפְרִישׁוּת, יֹאמַר בַּתְּחִלָּה שֶׁאֵינוֹ מְקַבֵּל עָלָיו כֵּן בְּנֶדֶר[24], וְגַם יֹאמַר שֶׁאֵין בְּדַעְתּוֹ לִנְהוֹג כֵּן אֶלָּא בַּפַּעַם הַהִיא

---

refraining from eating meat and drinking wine מי״ז בְּתַמּוּז וְאֵילָךְ — from the seventeenth of *Tammuz* and onwards,[21] וְכַיּוֹצֵא בּוֹ — or any similar stringency — may by his actions effect a vow, in either of the following two ways: אֲפִילּוּ לֹא נָהַג כֵּן רַק פַּעַם הָרִאשׁוֹן — (1) **Even if he conducted himself in this way only one time,** אֶלָּא שֶׁהָיָה בְּדַעְתּוֹ לִנְהוֹג כֵּן לְעוֹלָם — **but he intended to continue this practice forever,** אוֹ שֶׁנָּהַג כֵּן ג׳ פְּעָמִים — **or** (2), **if he conducted himself this way three times,** אַף עַל פִּי שֶׁלֹּא הָיָה בְּדַעְתּוֹ לִנְהוֹג כֵּן לְעוֹלָם — **even if he did** ***not*** **intend to conduct himself in this way forever;** וְלֹא הִתְנָה שֶׁיְּהֵא בְּלִי נֶדֶר — in both of these cases, **if he did not stipulate that this** action **should not constitute a vow,** וְרוֹצֶה לַחֲזוֹר מִפְּנֵי שֶׁאֵינוֹ בָּרִיא — then, if **he wishes to discontinue** his practice **because he is not healthy** and is unable to continue that stringency, צָרִיךְ הַתָּרָה — his actions constitute a vow that **requires annulment.**[22]

וְיִפְתַּח בַּחֲרָטָה — The annulment can be made **by finding an "opening" based on regret;**[23] שֶׁהוּא מִתְחָרֵט עַל מַה שֶּׁנָּהַג כֵּן לְשֵׁם נֶדֶר — that is, **that** the one who had made the vow **regrets conducting himself in a manner that** his behavior **constituted a vow.** לָכֵן מִי שֶׁהוּא רוֹצֶה לִנְהוֹג בְּאֵיזֶה חוּמְרוֹת — **Therefore, one who wishes to conduct himself with any stringencies** לְסְיָיג וּפְרִישׁוּת — **as a** protective **"fence,"** or a form of **abstinence** יֹאמַר בַּתְּחִלָּה שֶׁאֵינוֹ מְקַבֵּל עָלָיו כֵּן בְּנֶדֶר — **should state at the outset**[24] **that** by following this conduct **he is not accepting it upon himself as a vow.** וְגַם יֹאמַר — **He should also say** שֶׁאֵין בְּדַעְתּוֹ לִנְהוֹג כֵּן אֶלָּא בַּפַּעַם הַהִיא — **that he**

---

21. Until after Tishah B'Av. See below, 122:1.

22. This halachah applies only to one who was aware that his conduct was within the letter of the law, and was conducting himself stringently. However, one who conducted himself in a certain way due to the mistaken understanding that it was halachically required that he do so (even if only to avoid a situation of halachic doubt), has not created a vow (*Igros Moshe, Yoreh Deah* I, §47).

23. There are two factors that can be a basis for the annulment of a vow: (a) חֲרָטָה, *regret* (that is, he regrets ever having taken the vow), and (b) פֶּתַח, *"opening"* (the determination that if certain circumstances would have been fully considered by the one making the vow at the time he declared it, he would not have made the vow in the first place). These serve as a basis for the vow to be declared as unintended, thereby allowing the person to be released from it (see following *se'if*). See *Yoreh Deah* 228:7 for further discussion of these factors. Now, unlike a פֶּתַח, (*"opening"*), חֲרָטָה (*regret*) is effective only if he has no interest in *ever* having been subject to the vow. If he feels that it was beneficial for him at some time, חֲרָטָה is not an effective basis for annulling the vow. Nevertheless, even in such a case, the annulment can be made by finding an "opening based on regret," which means that the regret of the one making the vow is itself used as an "opening" (that is, the annulment is based on the fact that had he realized that he would regret having taken the vow, he never would have made it); see *Shach* ad loc. §16. *Rama* (ibid.) writes that it is customary to annul a vow in that manner.

24. This statement must be made verbally (see *Yoreh Deah* 211:1 and *Shach* §2).

אוֹ בִּפְעָמִים שֶׁיִּרְצֶה וְלֹא לְעוֹלָם.

ח. כֵּיצַד מַתִּירִין אֶת הַנֶּדֶר אוֹ הַשְּׁבוּעָה? הוֹלֵךְ אֵצֶל שְׁלֹשָׁה אֲנָשִׁים בְּנֵי תוֹרָה וְאֶחָד מֵהֶם יִהְיֶה בָּקִי בְּהִלְכוֹת נְדָרִים שֶׁיֵּדַע אֵיזֶה נֶדֶר יְכוֹלִין לְהַתִּיר[25] וְאֵיזֶה מֵהֶן אֵינָן יְכוֹלִים לְהַתִּיר וְאֵיךְ מַתִּירִין[26], וְהֵם יַתִּירוּ לוֹ. וּמִי שֶׁנָּדַר בַּחֲלוֹם, טוֹב שֶׁיַּתִּירוּ לוֹ עֲשָׂרָה בְּנֵי תוֹרָה[27].

ט. אַף עַל פִּי שֶׁלְּעִנְיַן כָּל הַמִּצְוֹת שֶׁבַּתּוֹרָה אֵין הַבֵּן נַעֲשֶׂה גָּדוֹל עַד שֶׁיִּהְיוּ לוֹ שְׁלֹשׁ עֶשְׂרֵה שָׁנָה וְהֵבִיא שְׂעָרוֹת[28], וְהַבַּת אֵינָהּ גְּדוֹלָה עַד שֶׁיִּהְיוּ לָהּ שְׁתֵּים עֶשְׂרֵה שָׁנָה וְהֵבִיאָה סִימָנִים[29], אֲבָל לְעִנְיַן נֶדֶר וּשְׁבוּעָה יֵשׁ לָהֶם (קדומה) (קְדִימָה) שָׁנָה אַחַת, שֶׁהַקָּטָן בֶּן שְׁנֵים עֶשְׂרֵה שָׁנָה וְיוֹם אֶחָד[30], וְהַקְּטַנָּה בַּת אַחַד עָשָׂר שָׁנָה וְיוֹם אֶחָד,

---

intends to conduct himself in this way only this one time, אוֹ בִּפְעָמִים שֶׁיִּרְצֶה **— or those times that he wishes** to do so, וְלֹא לְעוֹלָם **— but not forever.** By doing so, he has avoided any possibility of establishing a vow, and he is not bound in the future by his present actions.

§8 כֵּיצַד מַתִּירִין אֶת הַנֶּדֶר אוֹ הַשְּׁבוּעָה **— How does one have vows and oaths annulled?** הוֹלֵךְ אֵצֶל שְׁלֹשָׁה אֲנָשִׁים בְּנֵי תוֹרָה **— He goes to three learned men,** וְאֶחָד מֵהֶם יִהְיֶה בָּקִי בְּהִלְכוֹת נְדָרִים **— and one of them should be proficient in the laws of vows** שֶׁיֵּדַע אֵיזֶה נֶדֶר יְכוֹלִין לְהַתִּיר **— so that he will know which vows can be annulled** וְאֵיזֶה מֵהֶן אֵינָן יְכוֹלִים לְהַתִּיר **— and which cannot be annulled,**[25] וְאֵיךְ מַתִּירִין **—** and he will also know **how vows are annulled,**[26] וְהֵם יַתִּירוּ לוֹ **— and they** may **annul it for him.** וּמִי שֶׁנָּדַר בַּחֲלוֹם, **— If** one **dreamt that he took a vow,** טוֹב שֶׁיַּתִּירוּ לוֹ עֲשָׂרָה בְּנֵי תוֹרָה **— it is proper for him to obtain annulment from ten learned** men.[27]

§9 אַף עַל פִּי שֶׁלְּעִנְיַן כָּל הַמִּצְוֹת שֶׁבַּתּוֹרָה **— Although with regard to all mitzvos in the Torah** אֵין הַבֵּן נַעֲשֶׂה גָּדוֹל **— a boy does not become an adult** עַד שֶׁיִּהְיוּ לוֹ שְׁלֹשׁ עֶשְׂרֵה שָׁנָה **— until he is thirteen years old** וְהֵבִיא שְׂעָרוֹת **— and has produced** two **hairs,**[28] וְהַבַּת אֵינָהּ גְּדוֹלָה **— and a girl does not become an adult** עַד שֶׁיִּהְיוּ לָהּ שְׁתֵּים עֶשְׂרֵה שָׁנָה **— until she is twelve years old** וְהֵבִיאָה סִימָנִים **— and exhibits** physical **signs** of adulthood,[29] אֲבָל לְעִנְיַן נֶדֶר וּשְׁבוּעָה **— but with regard to a vow or oath,** יֵשׁ לָהֶם (קדומה) [קְדִימָה] שָׁנָה אַחַת **— they** are subject to its laws **one year earlier:** שֶׁהַקָּטָן בֶּן שְׁנֵים עֶשְׂרֵה שָׁנָה וְיוֹם אֶחָד **— For a boy who is twelve years and one day old,**[30] וְהַקְּטַנָּה בַּת אַחַד עָשָׂר שָׁנָה וְיוֹם אֶחָד **— and a girl who is eleven years**

---

25. For example, *Rama* (*Yoreh Deah* 228:21) rules that a vow that is made "on public consensus" [עַל דַּעַת רַבִּים] cannot be annulled (see *Shach* 228:59 for further details of this law).

26. There are many details to be considered before annulling a vow, primarily, what constitutes an appropriate "*opening*" that will allow the annulment of the vow (see above, note 23). The entire process and its associated laws are explained in *Yoreh Deah* §228.

27. According to some opinions, a vow in a dream is treated with the same gravity as a *niduy,* excommunication, in a dream, which requires ten people to annul. Such a dream is seen as a possible message from Hashem, and ten people must be present to effect a change in a Divine edict (see *Shach* 334:53). See *Rama* (*Yoreh Deah* 210:2), who rules that if one has trouble gathering ten people of the proper stature, he may annul his vow before the standard panel of three.

28. See *Even HaEzer* 155:17-18.

29. See ibid.

30. That is, he has completed his 12th year

אֲפִילוּ לֹא הֵבִיאוּ סִימָנִים, אִם מְבִינִים לְשֵׁם מִי נָדְרוּ וְנִשְׁבְּעוּ — נִדְרֵיהֶן נֶדֶר וּשְׁבוּעָתָן שְׁבוּעָה. אֲבָל פְּחוּתִים מִזְּמַן זֶה, אֲפִילוּ מְבִינִים, אֵין דִּבְרֵיהֶם כְּלוּם. וּמִכָּל מָקוֹם גּוֹעֲרִין בָּהֶם וּמַכִּין אוֹתָן שֶׁלֹּא יַרְגִּילוּ לְשׁוֹנָם בִּנְדָרִים וּשְׁבוּעוֹת. וְאִם הוּא דָּבָר קָטָן וְקַל שֶׁאֵין בּוֹ עִינּוּי נֶפֶשׁ, גּוֹזְרִין עֲלֵיהֶן שֶׁיְּקַיְּימוּהוּ.

י. הָאָב[31] **מֵפִיר נִדְרֵי בִתּוֹ עַד שֶׁתִּתְבַּגֵּר, דְּהַיְינוּ שֶׁיִּהְיוּ לָהּ י״ב שָׁנָה וְשִׁשָּׁה חֳדָשִׁים, וְהוּא שֶׁלֹּא נִישֵּׂאת, וְהַבַּעַל מֵפִיר נִדְרֵי אִשְׁתּוֹ. כֵּיצַד מְפִירִין? אוֹמֵר ג׳ פְּעָמִים ״מוּפָר״, אוֹ ״בָּטֵל״, אוֹ שְׁאָר לְשׁוֹן הַמּוֹרֶה שֶׁהוּא עוֹקֵר אֶת הַנֶּדֶר מֵעִיקָּרוֹ**[32]**, בֵּין שֶׁאוֹמֵר כֵּן בְּפָנֶיהָ אוֹ שֶׁלֹּא בְּפָנֶיהָ, אֲבָל לְשׁוֹן הַתָּרָה לָא מְהַנֵּי בְּאָב וּבְבַעַל**[33]**. וְגַם אֵין יְכוֹלִין**

---

and one day old, **אֲפִילוּ לֹא הֵבִיאוּ סִימָנִים** — **even if they have not exhibited** physical **signs** of adulthood, **אִם מְבִינִים לְשֵׁם מִי נָדְרוּ וְנִשְׁבְּעוּ** — **if they understand in Whose Name they have taken the vow or oath,** **נִדְרֵיהֶן נֶדֶר וּשְׁבוּעָתָן שְׁבוּעָה** — **their vow is a** valid **vow and their oath is a** valid **oath.** **אֲבָל פְּחוּתִים מִזְּמַן זֶה** — **However,** children **younger than this age,** **אֲפִילוּ מְבִינִים** — **even if they** do **understand** to Whom such a declaration is made, **אֵין דִּבְרֵיהֶם כְּלוּם** — **their words have no effect,** and they do not assume the binding status of a vow or oath. **וּמִכָּל מָקוֹם** — **Nevertheless,** **גּוֹעֲרִין בָּהֶם וּמַכִּין אוֹתָן** — **one must reprimand them and corporally punish them,** **שֶׁלֹּא יַרְגִּילוּ לְשׁוֹנָם בִּנְדָרִים וּשְׁבוּעוֹת** — **so that they do not become accustomed to expressing vows and oaths.** **וְאִם הוּא דָּבָר קָטָן וְקַל** — **If** the vow expressed **is something that is small and easy** to fulfill, **שֶׁאֵין בּוֹ עִינּוּי נֶפֶשׁ** — **and there is no physical affliction** involved in fulfilling it, **גּוֹזְרִין עֲלֵיהֶן שֶׁיְּקַיְּימוּהוּ** — we **order them to fulfill it.**

§10 In addition to הַתָּרָה, *annulment*, a girl or woman may be released from her vow by her father or husband, through a process called הֲפָרָה, *revocation*. In the following *se'ifim*, Kitzur discusses how and in which circumstances revocation can be performed.[31]

הָאָב מֵפִיר נִדְרֵי בִתּוֹ עַד שֶׁתִּתְבַּגֵּר — **A father may revoke his daughter's vows until she attains full adulthood,** **דְּהַיְינוּ** — **that is,** **שֶׁיִּהְיוּ לָהּ י״ב שָׁנָה וְשִׁשָּׁה חֳדָשִׁים** — **when she becomes twelve years and six months old,** **וְהוּא שֶׁלֹּא נִישֵּׂאת** — **provided she was not married** by that age. **וְהַבַּעַל מֵפִיר נִדְרֵי אִשְׁתּוֹ** — **A husband may revoke his wife's vows** also. **כֵּיצַד מְפִירִין** — **How does one revoke** vows? **אוֹמֵר ג׳ פְּעָמִים** — **He says** the following **three times:** **״מוּפָר״, אוֹ ״בָּטֵל״** — **"It is revoked," or, "It is abolished,"** **אוֹ שְׁאָר לְשׁוֹן הַמּוֹרֶה** — **or any other expression that indicates** **שֶׁהוּא עוֹקֵר אֶת הַנֶּדֶר מֵעִיקָּרוֹ** — **that he is uprooting the vow completely.**[32] **בֵּין שֶׁאוֹמֵר כֵּן בְּפָנֶיהָ** — The revocation is effective **whether he says it in her presence,** **אוֹ שֶׁלֹּא בְּפָנֶיהָ** — **or not in her presence.** **אֲבָל לְשׁוֹן הַתָּרָה** — **However, the expression of annulment** (that is, the use of the word מוּתָּר, *it is annulled*) **לָא מְהַנֵּי** **בְּאָב וּבְבַעַל** — **is ineffective** when used **by a father or a husband.**[33] **וְגַם אֵין יְכוֹלִין**

---

and begun the first day of his 13th year. This is on the day that he turns 12 years old according to the Jewish calendar; see above, 15:2.

31. Revocation differs from annulment in that annulment annuls the vow retroactively, whereas revocation annuls the vow only from that point onward (*Yoreh Deah* 234:51). Other differences are discussed in the following *se'ifim*.

32. See *Taz, Yoreh Deah* 234:36.

33. This expression can be used only when the

לְהָפֵר רַק בְּיוֹם שָׁמְעָם, דְּהַיְינוּ אִם שָׁמְעוּ בִּתְחִלַּת הַלַּיְלָה, מְפִירִין כָּל הַלַּיְלָה וְכָל הַיּוֹם שֶׁלְּאַחֲרָיו[34], וְאִם שָׁמְעוּ בַּיּוֹם סָמוּךְ לְצֵאת הַכֹּכָבִים[35], אֵין מְפִירִין רַק עַד צֵאת הַכּוֹכָבִים, וְיוֹתֵר אֵינָן יְכוֹלִין לְהָפֵר[36]. בְּשַׁבָּת לֹא יֹאמַר לָהּ "מוּפָר לִיכִי" כְּמוֹ בְּחוֹל, אֶלָּא מְבַטֵּל בְּלִבּוֹ וְאוֹמֵר לָהּ "טְלִי אִכְלִי"[37] וְכַיּוֹצֵא בָּזֶה[38]. וְאִם הָאָב אוֹ הַבַּעַל אָמְרוּ תְּחִלָּה שֶׁהוּא מְרוּצֶּה עַל הַנֶּדֶר, אַף עַל פִּי שֶׁלֹּא אָמַר בְּפֵירוּשׁ, אֶלָּא שֶׁאָמַר לָשׁוֹן שֶׁהוּא מוֹרֶה שֶׁהוּא מְרוּצֶּה, וַאֲפִילוּ אִם רַק בְּלִבּוֹ חִישֵּׁב שֶׁהוּא מְרוּצֶּה בְּנִדְרָהּ, שׁוּב אֵינוֹ יָכוֹל לְהָפֵר.

לְהָפֵר רַק בְּיוֹם שָׁמְעָם — Additionally, they may revoke the vow **only on the day they heard** of it. **דְּהַיְינוּ אִם שָׁמְעוּ בִּתְחִלַּת הַלַּיְלָה — That is, if they heard** of it **at the beginning of the night, מְפִירִין כָּל הַלַּיְלָה וְכָל הַיּוֹם שֶׁלְּאַחֲרָיו — they may revoke** the vow during **the entire night and the entire following day;**[34] **וְאִם שָׁמְעוּ בַּיּוֹם — and if they heard** of the vow **during the day סָמוּךְ לְצֵאת הַכֹּכָבִים — close to nightfall,**[35] **אֵין מְפִירִין רַק עַד צֵאת הַכּוֹכָבִים — they may revoke it only until nightfall; וְיוֹתֵר אֵינָן יְכוֹלִין לְהָפֵר — beyond** that time **they cannot revoke it.**[36] **בְּשַׁבָּת לֹא יֹאמַר לָהּ "מוּפָר לִיכִי" — On Shabbos, he** (a father or husband) **should not say to her, "It is revoked for you," כְּמוֹ בְּחוֹל — as** he would say **on weekdays; אֶלָּא מְבַטֵּל בְּלִבּוֹ — rather, he should cancel** the vow **in his heart, וְאוֹמֵר לָהּ "טְלִי אִכְלִי" — and** then **say to her, "Take and eat,"**[37] **וְכַיּוֹצֵא בָּזֶה — or some similar** expression that indicates that he is revoking her vow.[38]

וְאִם הָאָב אוֹ הַבַּעַל אָמְרוּ תְּחִלָּה שֶׁהוּא — If the father or husband initially said מְרוּצֶּה עַל הַנֶּדֶר — that he is agreeable to the vow, אַף עַל פִּי שֶׁלֹּא אָמַר בְּפֵירוּשׁ — even though he did not say so **explicitly, אֶלָּא שֶׁאָמַר לָשׁוֹן שֶׁהוּא מוֹרֶה — but rather he said something that indicates שֶׁהוּא מְרוּצֶּה — that he is agreeable, וַאֲפִילוּ אִם רַק בְּלִבּוֹ חִישֵּׁב — and even if he** did not verbalize it, but **only thought in his heart שֶׁהוּא מְרוּצֶּה בְּנִדְרָהּ — that he is agreeable to her vow, שׁוּב אֵינוֹ יָכוֹל לְהָפֵר — he**

---

vow is annulled by a panel of three, through the method of הַתָּרָה, *annulment.* In addition, unlike הֲפָרָה, *revocation,* הַתָּרָה, *annulment,* can be performed only when the one who took the vow comes personally before the panel and asks for an annulment (*Yoreh Deah* 228:16).

34. A "day" in the Jewish calendar begins with the onset of night, and concludes with the end of the following day.

35. Literally, *the emergence of the stars;* see Appendix B. In any case where the husband or father heard of a vow or revoked a vow between sunset and nightfall, and, in fact, in *all* cases where a vow is made and a father or husband wishes to revoke it, a halachic authority must be consulted to determine if the vow can indeed be revoked. See *se'if* 11.

36. If the husband or father heard of the vow and remained silent because he was unaware that he was able to revoke the vow, that time does not count toward the one-day period; the one-day period begins from when he knows of the vow and realizes that he has the power to revoke it (*Yoreh Deah* 234:21).

37. That is, if she had prohibited a certain food upon herself, he should express his stand regarding the vow by telling her, "Take it and eat."

38. הַתָּרָה, *an annulment,* may not be performed on Shabbos unless it is for a Shabbos purpose (*Orach Chaim* 341; *Yoreh Deah* 228:3). *Mishnah Berurah* (341:1) explains that annulling a vow is an unnecessary bother, which must be avoided on Shabbos. *Revoking* a vow, however, is considered a necessary action, because if it is not done on Shabbos, the day will pass, along with the opportunity for revocation (*Shach* 234:40). Even so, in deference to the Shabbos, the usual expression of revocation should not be used.

(וְאִם תָּלְתָה הַנֶּדֶר בְּמַעֲשֶׂה[39] — עַיֵּין שַׁ"ךְ סִימָן רל"ד סְעִיף קָטָן מ"ה[40].)

יא. אֵיזֶה נְדָרִים יְכוֹלִין הָאָב אוֹ הַבַּעַל לְהָפֵר? דַּוְקָא דְּבָרִים שֶׁיֵּשׁ בָּהֶם עִינּוּי נֶפֶשׁ, כְּגוֹן רְחִיצָה[41] וְקִישּׁוּט כִּיחוּל וּפִרְכּוּס וְכַיּוֹצֵא בָּזֶה[42]. וְהַבַּעַל יָכוֹל לְהָפֵר גַּם דְּבָרִים שֶׁאֵין בָּהֶם עִינּוּי נֶפֶשׁ אִם הֵם מִן הַדְּבָרִים שֶׁבֵּין אִישׁ לְאִשְׁתּוֹ וְגוֹרְמִים אֵיבָה בֵּינֵיהֶם, אֲבָל אֵלּוּ אֵינָן מוּתָּרִים אֶלָּא כָּל זְמַן שֶׁהִיא יוֹשֶׁבֶת תַּחְתָּיו, וּלְאַחַר שֶׁנִּתְאַלְמְנָה אוֹ נִתְגָּרְשָׁה אֲסוּרָה בָּהֶן[43].

---

may no longer revoke it. **(וְאִם תָּלְתָה הַנֶּדֶר בְּמַעֲשֶׂה — Regarding** a case where a woman **took a vow contingent on a** specific **action,**[39] **עַיֵּין שַׁ"ךְ סִימָן רל"ד סְעִיף קָטָן מ"ה — see** ***Shach*****, 234:45.)**[40]

§11 אֵיזֶה נְדָרִים יְכוֹלִין הָאָב אוֹ הַבַּעַל לְהָפֵר — Which vows can the father or husband revoke? דַּוְקָא דְּבָרִים שֶׁיֵּשׁ בָּהֶם עִינּוּי נֶפֶשׁ — Only matters that involve self-affliction, כְּגוֹן רְחִיצָה וְקִישּׁוּט כִּיחוּל וּפִרְכּוּס — for example, if she prohibited upon herself **washing,**[41] **adornment, applying eye makeup, and rouge, וְכַיּוֹצֵא בָּזֶה — and the like.**[42] **וְהַבַּעַל יָכוֹל לְהָפֵר גַּם דְּבָרִים שֶׁאֵין בָּהֶם עִינּוּי נֶפֶשׁ —** In addition, **the husband may revoke even matters that do not involve self-affliction, אִם הֵם מִן הַדְּבָרִים שֶׁבֵּין אִישׁ לְאִשְׁתּוֹ — if they are matters that** affect the relationship **between man and wife וְגוֹרְמִים אֵיבָה בֵּינֵיהֶם — and cause hostility between them. אֲבָל אֵלּוּ — However,** when the husband revokes **these** vows, **אֵינָן מוּתָּרִים אֶלָּא כָּל זְמַן שֶׁהִיא יוֹשֶׁבֶת תַּחְתָּיו — they are permitted only during the time that she is living under his** auspices, i.e., he may revoke them only for the time that she is married to him, for it affects him only to that extent. **וּלְאַחַר שֶׁנִּתְאַלְמְנָה אוֹ נִתְגָּרְשָׁה — However, after she is widowed or divorced, אֲסוּרָה בָּהֶן — she is prohibited in the** matters that she prohibited upon herself.[43]

---

39. That is, she stipulated that the vow take effect only after a specific action has taken place. At issue is whether her father or husband may revoke the vow before the stipulation has been fulfilled.

40. *Shach* writes that if the stipulated action involves no self-affliction and would not cause hostility between the husband and wife (see following *se'if*), the husband may not revoke the vow until it has actually taken effect. If, however, the stipulated action would be considered a form of self-affliction or it can cause hostility between them, he may revoke it immediately.

41. Even for one day (*Yoreh Deah* 234:59).

42. If she took a vow prohibiting herself from eating any produce, even for one day, it is considered self-affliction, and her father or husband can revoke it (see *Yoreh Deah* 234:60, *Taz* 50).

43. *Yoreh Deah* (234:55) indicates that she is not bound by her vow even after she is divorced, because she might remarry her first husband. Only once she marries another man, at which point she can never remarry her first husband (*Devarim* 24:1-4), is she prohibited by her vow (which would then require annulment).

377 THE WAYFARER'S PRAYER AND OTHER MATTERS WHEN TRAVELING — SIMAN 68:1

סימן סח

דִּין תְּפִלַּת הַדֶּרֶךְ וּשְׁאָר דְּבָרִים שֶׁצְּרִיכִין לִיזָּהֵר בַּדֶּרֶךְ

וּבוֹ י״ב סְעִיפִים

א. הַיּוֹצֵא לְדֶרֶךְ, בֵּין מִבֵּיתוֹ בֵּין מִמָּקוֹם שֶׁהָיָה לָן בַּדֶּרֶךְ וְכֵן בַּחֲזָרָתוֹ לְבֵיתוֹ, לְאַחַר שֶׁיָּצָא מֵעִיבּוּרָהּ שֶׁל הָעִיר, דְּהַיְינוּ שִׁבְעִים אַמָּה וּשְׁנֵי שְׁלִישֵׁי אַמָּה[1] לְאַחַר שֶׁכָּלוּ כָּל הַבָּתִּים, מִתְפַּלֵּל תְּפִלַּת הַדֶּרֶךְ: יְהִי רָצוֹן מִלְּפָנֶיךָ ה׳ אֱלֹהֵינוּ וֵאלֹהֵי אֲבוֹתֵינוּ שֶׁתּוֹלִיכֵנוּ לְשָׁלוֹם וְכוּ׳. אוֹמְרָהּ בִּלְשׁוֹן רַבִּים[2], רַק ״וְתִתְּנֵנִי לְחֵן״ אוֹמֵר בִּלְשׁוֹן יָחִיד. וְיוֹתֵר טוֹב לְאָמְרָהּ לְאַחַר שֶׁיָּצָא מִיל מֵעִיבּוּרָהּ שֶׁל עִיר[3],

---

SIMAN 68

LAWS OF THE WAYFARER'S PRAYER AND OTHER MATTERS THAT ONE MUST OBSERVE WHEN TRAVELING

CONTAINING 12 *SE'IFIM*

§1-2 When To Recite *Tefillas HaDerech* / **§3** Adjacent to Another Blessing / **§4** Reciting While Riding / **§5** Once a Day / **§6** Practices When Embarking on a Journey / **§7** Ensuring Proper *Kashrus* / **§8** Praying While Traveling / **§9-10** Eating and *Bircas HaMazon* / **§11** Leaving on Friday / **§12** Protecting One's Money on Shabbos

§1 **הַיּוֹצֵא לְדֶרֶךְ — One who embarks on a journey, בֵּין מִבֵּיתוֹ — whether** he is leaving **from his house בֵּין מִמָּקוֹם שֶׁהָיָה לָן בַּדֶּרֶךְ — or from his place of lodging** when he is **on the road, וְכֵן בַּחֲזָרָתוֹ לְבֵיתוֹ — as well as when one is returning to his home, לְאַחַר שֶׁיָּצָא מֵעִיבּוּרָהּ שֶׁל הָעִיר —** at the beginning of his current trip, **after he leaves the outskirts of the city, דְּהַיְינוּ — that is, שִׁבְעִים אַמָּה וּשְׁנֵי שְׁלִישֵׁי אַמָּה — seventy *amos* and two-thirds of an *amah*[1] לְאַחַר שֶׁכָּלוּ כָּל הַבָּתִּים — beyond the furthest house of the city, מִתְפַּלֵּל תְּפִלַּת הַדֶּרֶךְ — recites** *Tefillas HaDerech*, ***the Wayfarer's Prayer,* יְהִי רָצוֹן מִלְּפָנֶיךָ —** which begins: ***May it be Your will,* ה׳ אֱלֹהֵינוּ וֵאלֹהֵי אֲבוֹתֵינוּ — *HASHEM, our God and the God of our forefathers,* שֶׁתּוֹלִיכֵנוּ לְשָׁלוֹם וְכוּ׳ — *that You lead us to peace,*** etc. **אוֹמְרָהּ בִּלְשׁוֹן רַבִּים — He recites it in plural form;[2] רַק ״וְתִתְּנֵנִי לְחֵן״ אוֹמֵר בִּלְשׁוֹן יָחִיד — only the phrase *and grant me grace* is recited in singular form. וְיוֹתֵר טוֹב לְאָמְרָהּ — And it is preferable to recite** this prayer **לְאַחַר שֶׁיָּצָא מִיל מֵעִיבּוּרָהּ שֶׁל עִיר —** only **after traveling one *mil*[3] beyond the outskirts of the city.**

---

1. Approximately 111-134 feet (34-41 meters); see Appendix A.

2. As is reflected by the words *"our God,"* and *"lead us."* When praying in plural form, one associates himself with the greater community, whose collective merit elevates his prayer (see *Mishnah Berurah* 110:19).

3. A *mil* is .6-.7 of a mile (.96-1.15 km.); see Appendix A.

THE WAYFARER'S PRAYER AND OTHER MATTERS WHEN TRAVELING — SIMAN 68:2-3 378

וּכְשֶׁהוּא כְּבָר בַּדֶּרֶךְ וְלָן בְּאֵיזֶה עִיר יָכוֹל לְאָמְרָהּ בַּבּוֹקֶר גַּם קוֹדֶם שֶׁיֵּצֵא[4].

ב. אֵין לְהִתְפַּלֵּל אוֹתָהּ אֶלָּא אִם כֵּן יֵשׁ לוֹ לָלֶכֶת לְכָל הַפָּחוֹת פַּרְסָה[5]. וּלְכַתְּחִלָּה יֵשׁ לוֹ לְהִתְפַּלֵּל בְּתוֹךְ פַּרְסָה הָרִאשׁוֹנָה. וְאִם שָׁכַח, יָכוֹל לְהִתְפַּלֵּל כָּל זְמַן שֶׁהוּא בַּדֶּרֶךְ, וּבִלְבַד שֶׁעֲדַיִין לֹא הִגִּיעַ לְתוֹךְ פַּרְסָה הַסְּמוּכָה לָעִיר שֶׁהוּא רוֹצֶה לָלוּן בָּהּ[6].

ג. תְּפִלַּת[7,8] הַדֶּרֶךְ צְרִיכִין לְאָמְרָהּ סָמוּךְ לִבְרָכָה אַחֶרֶת. וְלָכֵן, אִם יוֹצֵא בַּבּוֹקֶר וְאוֹמֵר בַּדֶּרֶךְ בִּרְכַּת הַשַּׁחַר, אוֹ שֶׁהָיָה לָן בַּדֶּרֶךְ בְּאֵיזוֹ עִיר (שֶׁאָז יָכוֹל לוֹמַר תְּפִלַּת הַדֶּרֶךְ

וּכְשֶׁהוּא כְּבָר בַּדֶּרֶךְ — If one is already on the road **וְלָן בְּאֵיזֶה עִיר — and has spent the night in a city** along the way, **יָכוֹל לְאָמְרָהּ בַּבּוֹקֶר — he may recite** *Tefillas HaDerech* **in the morning** **גַּם קוֹדֶם שֶׁיֵּצֵא — even before he embarks** on the next leg of his trip.[4]

§2 **אֵין לְהִתְפַּלֵּל אוֹתָהּ — One should not recite** this prayer **אֶלָּא אִם כֵּן יֵשׁ לוֹ לָלֶכֶת — unless he will be traveling** **לְכָל הַפָּחוֹת פַּרְסָה — at least** the distance of **one** ***parsah***.[5] **וּלְכַתְּחִלָּה יֵשׁ לוֹ לְהִתְפַּלֵּל — Ideally, he should recite the prayer** **בְּתוֹךְ פַּרְסָה הָרִאשׁוֹנָה — when he is still within** the **first** ***parsah*** of the city of his departure. **וְאִם שָׁכַח — If one forgot** to recite the prayer within this distance, **יָכוֹל לְהִתְפַּלֵּל כָּל זְמַן שֶׁהוּא בַּדֶּרֶךְ — he may recite it as long as he is on the road,** **וּבִלְבַד שֶׁעֲדַיִין לֹא הִגִּיעַ לְתוֹךְ פַּרְסָה הַסְּמוּכָה — provided that he has not yet arrived within one** ***parsah*** **לָעִיר שֶׁהוּא רוֹצֶה לָלוּן בָּהּ — of the city in which he intends to lodge.**[6]

§3 Typically, a blessing of significant length begins with the words בָּרוּךְ אַתָּה ה׳, *Blessed are You, Hashem*, and ends with a closing blessing.[7] In a series of blessings, only the first blessing opens with this phrase, while the rest of the blessings begin without it.[8] Since the text of *Tefillas HaDerech* does not begin with the words בָּרוּךְ אַתָּה ה׳, *Blessed are You, Hashem*, Kitzur advises that when reciting *Tefillas HaDerech*, one precede it with another, unrelated blessing, so as to put the *Tefillas HaDerech* within a "series" of blessings:

תְּפִלַּת הַדֶּרֶךְ צְרִיכִין לְאָמְרָהּ סָמוּךְ לִבְרָכָה אַחֶרֶת — *Tefillas HaDerech* should be recited following another blessing. **וְלָכֵן — Therefore,** **אִם יוֹצֵא בַּבּוֹקֶר — if one is departing in the morning** **וְאוֹמֵר בַּדֶּרֶךְ בִּרְכַּת הַשַּׁחַר — and is reciting the Morning Blessings en route,** **אוֹ שֶׁהָיָה לָן בַּדֶּרֶךְ בְּאֵיזוֹ עִיר — or if he has spent the night in a city** along the way **(שֶׁאָז יָכוֹל לוֹמַר תְּפִלַּת הַדֶּרֶךְ**

---

4. In this situation, one may recite *Tefillas HaDerech* at his place of lodging, when he makes preparations to continue his journey (*Mishnah Berurah* 110:29; see also below, *se'if* 3).

5. A *parsah* equals 8,000 *amos* (4 *mil*). This is equivalent to 2.4-2.87 miles (3.84-4.6 km.); see Appendix A.

Mishnah Berurah (110:30) explains that, generally speaking, a trip of less than a *parsah* is considered such a short distance that it does not pose any danger, and therefore, *Tefillas HaDerech* is not recited. However, one who is passing through a particularly dangerous area should recite *Tefillas HaDerech* even on a shorter trip.

6. If he reached within this distance, he should still recite *Tefillas HaDerech*, but should omit the concluding blessing of בָּרוּךְ אַתָּה ה׳ שׁוֹמֵעַ תְּפִלָּה, *Blessed are You, Hashem, Who hears prayer* (*Shulchan Aruch* 110:7).

7. For example, the *Asher Yatzar* blessing begins, בָּרוּךְ אַתָּה ה׳ ... אֲשֶׁר יָצַר, *Blessed are You, Hashem ... Who fashioned*, and concludes, בָּרוּךְ אַתָּה ה׳ רוֹפֵא כָל בָּשָׂר ..., *Blessed are You, Hashem, Who heals all flesh ...*

8. Such as the second and third blessings of *Bircas HaMazon*.

379 THE WAYFARER'S PRAYER AND OTHER MATTERS WHEN TRAVELING — SIMAN 68:4-5

גַּם קוֹדֶם שֶׁיֵּצֵא) וְאוֹמֵר, אֲפִילוּ קוֹדֶם שֶׁיֵּצֵא, בִּרְכַּת הַשַּׁחַר, יֹאמְרָהּ אַחַר בִּרְכַּת "הַגּוֹמֵל חֲסָדִים טוֹבִים לְעַמּוֹ יִשְׂרָאֵל". וְאִם הוֹלֵךְ לְאַחַר הַתְּפִלָּה מִבֵּיתוֹ, יֹאכַל אוֹ יִשְׁתֶּה אֵיזֶה דָּבָר עַל הַדֶּרֶךְ וִיבָרֵךְ בְּרָכָה אַחֲרוֹנָה וְסָמוּךְ לָהּ יֹאמַר תְּפִלַּת הַדֶּרֶךְ, אוֹ יָטִיל מַיִם וִיבָרֵךְ "אֲשֶׁר יָצַר" וְיִסְמְכָהּ לָהּ[9].

ד. יֵשׁ לְאוֹמְרָהּ בַּעֲמִידָה. וְאִם הוּא רוֹכֵב אוֹ הוֹלֵךְ בַּעֲגָלָה[10] — אִם אֶפְשָׁר לְהַעֲמִיד הַבְּהֵמָה[11], יַעֲמִידֶהָ מִשּׁוּם דְּרוֹכֵב כִּמְהַלֵּךְ דָּמֵי[12], וְאִם לָאו[13], אוֹמְרָהּ כָּךְ.

ה. אֵין אוֹמְרִים אוֹתָהּ אֶלָּא פַּעַם אַחַת בְּכָל יוֹם שֶׁהוּא הוֹלֵךְ[14], אֲבָל אִם חָנָה בְּאֵיזֶה עִיר עַל דַּעַת לָלוּן שָׁם וְאַחַר כָּךְ נִמְלַךְ וְיָצָא מִמֶּנָּה לַעֲבוֹר חוּצָה לָהּ אוֹ לָשׁוּב

גַּם קוֹדֶם שֶׁיֵּצֵא — in which case he may recite *Tefillas HaDerech* **even before leaving** the city, as above, *se'if* 1), **וְאוֹמֵר אֲפִילוּ קוֹדֶם שֶׁיֵּצֵא בִּרְכַּת הַשַּׁחַר — and he will be reciting the Morning Blessings even before departing, יֹאמְרָהּ אַחַר בִּרְכַּת "הַגּוֹמֵל חֲסָדִים טוֹבִים לְעַמּוֹ יִשְׂרָאֵל" — he should recite** *Tefillas HaDerech* **following** the last of the series of Morning Blessings, **the blessing of** *HaGomel chasadim tovim le'amo Yisrael,* ***Who bestows beneficent kindnesses upon His people Israel.*** **וְאִם הוֹלֵךְ לְאַחַר הַתְּפִלָּה מִבֵּיתוֹ — If one is leaving from his home** (i.e., he is not at a place of lodging along the way) **after** already having completed **the** morning **Prayers, יֹאכַל אוֹ יִשְׁתֶּה אֵיזֶה דָּבָר עַל הַדֶּרֶךְ — he should eat or drink something along the way, וִיבָרֵךְ בְּרָכָה אַחֲרוֹנָה — then recite the** appropriate ***berachah acharonah*** (final blessing), **וְסָמוּךְ לָהּ יֹאמַר תְּפִלַּת הַדֶּרֶךְ — and, following that** blessing, **he should recite** ***Tefillas HaDerech.*** **אוֹ יָטִיל מַיִם וִיבָרֵךְ "אֲשֶׁר יָצַר" — Alternatively, one may pass water and** then **recite the** ***Asher Yatzar*** **blessing, וְיִסְמְכָהּ לָהּ — and recite** *Tefillas HaDerech* **following that** *blessing.*[9]

§4 יֵשׁ לְאוֹמְרָהּ בַּעֲמִידָה — One should recite *Tefillas HaDerech* **while standing in one place. וְאִם הוּא רוֹכֵב אוֹ הוֹלֵךְ בַּעֲגָלָה — If one is riding** an animal **or traveling by wagon,**[10] **אִם אֶפְשָׁר לְהַעֲמִיד הַבְּהֵמָה — if it is possible to stop the animal,**[11] **יַעֲמִידֶהָ — one should stop it, מִשּׁוּם דְּרוֹכֵב כִּמְהַלֵּךְ דָּמֵי — since riding** an animal **is like walking.**[12] **וְאִם לָאו — If** it is **not** possible to stop the animal,[13] **אוֹמְרָהּ כָּךְ — he should recite** *Tefillas HaDerech* even **in that way,** i.e., while riding.

§5 אֵין אוֹמְרִים אוֹתָהּ אֶלָּא — *Tefillas HaDerech* **should be recited only פַּעַם אַחַת בְּכָל יוֹם שֶׁהוּא הוֹלֵךְ — once during each day that one is traveling.**[14] **אֲבָל אִם חָנָה בְּאֵיזֶה עִיר עַל דַּעַת לָלוּן שָׁם — However, if one stopped in a city with the intention of lodging there, וְאַחַר כָּךְ נִמְלַךְ וְיָצָא מִמֶּנָּה — but then reconsidered and left** that city **לַעֲבוֹר חוּצָה לָהּ אוֹ לָשׁוּב לְבֵיתוֹ — to continue onward or to return home,**

---

9. For the laws of *Asher Yatzar,* see above, *Siman* 4; for the laws of *berachah acharonah,* see *Siman* 51. In the event that none of these options are available to him, *Mishnah Berurah* (110:28) rules that he should simply recite *Tefillas HaDerech* by itself.

10. Or traveling by any other vehicle.

11. Or the car or other conveyance.

12. I.e., while walking it is difficult to concentrate properly on a prayer; while riding one is similarly challenged. However, he is not required to dismount or alight from the vehicle (*Shulchan Aruch* 110:4, *Mishnah Berurah* 110:23).

13. E.g., if stopping the vehicle will distract him from his journey (*Mishnah Berurah* 110:22).

14. I.e., if one is on a journey of many days, he must recite *Tefillas HaDerech* once every day of his journey (*Mishnah Berurah* 110:24).

THE WAYFARER'S PRAYER AND OTHER MATTERS WHEN TRAVELING — SIMAN 68:6 380

לְבֵיתוֹ, אוֹמְרָהּ פַּעַם שֵׁנִית[15]. אִם הוֹלֵךְ בַּיּוֹם וּבַלַּיְלָה, אוֹ שֶׁהָיָה לָן שֶׁלֹּא בִּמְקוֹם יִשּׁוּב[16], פַּעַם הָרִאשׁוֹן אוֹמְרָהּ בַּחֲתִימָה וּבִשְׁאָר הַיָּמִים אוֹמְרָהּ בְּלֹא חֲתִימָה, כִּי כָל זְמַן שֶׁלֹּא לָן בִּמְקוֹם יִשּׁוּב נֶחְשָׁב הַכֹּל לְדֶרֶךְ אֶחָד.

ו. טֶרֶם צֵאתוֹ לְדֶרֶךְ יֵשׁ לוֹ לִיתֵּן צְדָקָה, שֶׁנֶּאֱמַר (תהלים פה, יד) "צֶדֶק לְפָנָיו יְהַלֵּךְ וְיָשֵׂם לְדֶרֶךְ פְּעָמָיו"[17]. וְיֵשׁ לִיטּוֹל רְשׁוּת מֵהַגְּדוֹלִים שֶׁבָּעִיר שֶׁיְּבָרְכוּ אוֹתוֹ שֶׁיַּצְלִיחַ בְּדַרְכּוֹ, וְיֵשׁ לְהִשְׁתַּדֵּל שֶׁיְּלַוּוּ אוֹתוֹ אֵיזֶה אֲנָשִׁים[18]. וְהַמְלַוֶּה אֶת חֲבֵירוֹ כְּשֶׁהוּא פּוֹרֵשׁ מִמֶּנּוּ צָרִיךְ לַעֲמוֹד בִּמְקוֹמוֹ עַד שֶׁהַהוֹלֵךְ יִתְעַלֵּם מֵעֵינָיו (מהריעב"ץ)[19]. הַמְבָרְכִים לְהַהוֹלֵךְ בְּדֶרֶךְ לֹא יֹאמְרוּ לוֹ "לֵךְ בְּשָׁלוֹם", אֶלָּא "לֵךְ לְשָׁלוֹם", שֶׁהֲרֵי דָוִד אָמַר

אוֹמְרָהּ פַּעַם שֵׁנִית — he should recite *Tefillas HaDerech* **a second time.**[15] **אִם הוֹלֵךְ בַּיּוֹם וּבַלַּיְלָה — If one is traveling through the day and night, אוֹ שֶׁהָיָה לָן שֶׁלֹּא בִּמְקוֹם יִשּׁוּב — or if he lodges** overnight **in an unsettled area,**[16] he should not recite the complete *Tefillas HaDerech* every day; **פַּעַם הָרִאשׁוֹן אוֹמְרָהּ בַּחֲתִימָה** — rather, on the **first** day of travel **he should recite it with the concluding** blessing, **וּבִשְׁאָר הַיָּמִים אוֹמְרָהּ בְּלֹא חֲתִימָה — and on the subsequent days, he should recite it without the concluding** blessing. **כִּי כָל זְמַן שֶׁלֹּא לָן בִּמְקוֹם יִשּׁוּב** — Each day does not warrant its own complete *Tefillas HaDerech,* **for as long as he has not lodged in a settled area נֶחְשָׁב הַכֹּל לְדֶרֶךְ אֶחָד — the entire journey is considered to be one** continuous **trip** and the first *Tefillas HaDerech* remains in effect.

§6 טֶרֶם צֵאתוֹ לְדֶרֶךְ יֵשׁ לוֹ לִיתֵּן צְדָקָה — Before embarking on a trip one should give charity, **שֶׁנֶּאֱמַר — as** the verse **states** (*Tehillim* 85:14): **"צֶדֶק לְפָנָיו יְהַלֵּךְ וְיָשֵׂם לְדֶרֶךְ פְּעָמָיו"** — ***Righteousness will precede him, and he will set his footsteps on the way.***[17] **וְיֵשׁ לִיטּוֹל רְשׁוּת מֵהַגְּדוֹלִים שֶׁבָּעִיר — He should** also **take leave from the great men of the city, שֶׁיְּבָרְכוּ אוֹתוֹ שֶׁיַּצְלִיחַ בְּדַרְכּוֹ — so that they will bless him that his journey be successful. וְיֵשׁ לְהִשְׁתַּדֵּל — One should endeavor שֶׁיְּלַוּוּ אוֹתוֹ אֵיזֶה אֲנָשִׁים — that some people escort him** as he leaves.[18] **וְהַמְלַוֶּה אֶת חֲבֵירוֹ** — The procedure to be followed by **the one who escorts his fellow** at the beginning of his journey is **כְּשֶׁהוּא פּוֹרֵשׁ מִמֶּנּוּ — that when** the traveler **is departing from him, צָרִיךְ לַעֲמוֹד בִּמְקוֹמוֹ — he,** i.e., the one who is escorting him, **should remain in his place עַד שֶׁהַהוֹלֵךְ יִתְעַלֵּם מֵעֵינָיו** — and wait **until the traveler disappears from sight** (מהריעב"ץ — this halachah is **from R' Yaakov Emden ben Tzvi**).[19]
הַמְבָרְכִים לְהַהוֹלֵךְ בְּדֶרֶךְ — Those who wish to **bless one who is embarking on a journey לֹא יֹאמְרוּ לוֹ — should not say to him: "לֵךְ בְּשָׁלוֹם" — "Go in peace," אֶלָּא —** rather, they should say: **"לֵךְ לְשָׁלוֹם" — "Go to peace." שֶׁהֲרֵי דָוִד אָמַר**

---

15. The second leg of the journey is considered a new trip, since he had previously decided to stop for the day.

16. *Mishnah Berurah* (110:26) writes that if one spent only a short part of the night in an inn, but did not settle into the inn for the night, he does not recite *Tefillas HaDerech.*

17. In this context the word צֶדֶק refers to צְדָקָה, *charity*, which is to precede *his footsteps on the way.*

18. Having been escorted, even if only at the beginning of the trip, affords the traveler a measure of Divine protection; see *Sotah* 46b with *Maharsha.*

19. *Siddur* of R' Yaakov Emden, *Hil. Tefillas HaDerech U'Levayah.*

381 THE WAYFARER'S PRAYER AND OTHER MATTERS WHEN TRAVELING — SIMAN 68:6

לְאַבְשָׁלוֹם (שמואל־ב טו, ט) **״לֵךְ בְּשָׁלוֹם״ הָלַךְ וְנִתְלָה**[20]**, וְיִתְרוֹ שֶׁאָמַר לְמֹשֶׁה** (שמות ד, יח) **״לֵךְ לְשָׁלוֹם״ עָלָה וְהִצְלִיחַ**[21]**. כְּשֶׁהוּא בְדֶרֶךְ יַעֲסוֹק בַּתּוֹרָה, שֶׁנֶּאֱמַר** (דברים ו, ז) **״וּבְלֶכְתְּךָ בַדֶּרֶךְ״. וְיֹאמַר בְּכָל יוֹם אֵיזֶה מִזְמוֹרֵי תְהִלִּים בְּכַוָּנָה וְהַכְנָעָה. וְיִזָּהֵר שֶׁיְּהֵא לוֹ פַּת עִמּוֹ, אֲפִילוּ הוֹלֵךְ בְּמָקוֹם קָרוֹב. גַּם יֵשׁ לִיקַּח עִמּוֹ צִיצִית, שֶׁמָּא תִפְסוֹל לוֹ צִיצָה וְלֹא יַשִּׂיג אַחֶרֶת וְיִתְבַּטֵּל מִמִּצְוָה**[22]**. לְעוֹלָם יִכָּנֵס אָדָם בְּ״כִי טוֹב״ וְיֵצֵא בְּ״כִי טוֹב״. פֵּירוּשׁ: כְּשֶׁיִּכָּנֵס עַרְבִית לְבֵית הַמָּלוֹן יִכָּנֵס בְּעוֹד הַחַמָּה זוֹרַחַת, וּלְמָחָר יַמְתִּין עַד הָנֵץ הַחַמָּה וְיֵצֵא, וְאָז טוֹב לוֹ כְּמוֹ שֶׁנֶּאֱמַר** (בראשית א, ד) **״וַיַּרְא אֱלֹהִים אֶת הָאוֹר כִּי טוֹב״**[23]**. לֹא יֹאכַל הַרְבֵּה כְּשֶׁהוּא בְדֶרֶךְ**[24]**.**

לְאַבְשָׁלוֹם — For when King **David said to** his son **Avshalom** (*II Shmuel* 15:9): **״לֵךְ בְּשָׁלוֹם״** — **"Go in peace,"** **הָלַךְ וְנִתְלָה** — **he went and was hanged;**[20] **וְיִתְרוֹ שֶׁאָמַר לְמֹשֶׁה** — but when **Yisro said to Moshe** Rabbeinu (*Shemos* 4:18): **״לֵךְ לְשָׁלוֹם״** — **"Go to peace,"** **עָלָה וְהִצְלִיחַ** — **he arose and was successful.**[21]

כְּשֶׁהוּא בְדֶרֶךְ יַעֲסוֹק בַּתּוֹרָה — **When one is traveling he should engage in Torah** study, **שֶׁנֶּאֱמַר** — **as** the verse **states** (*Devarim* 6:7): **״וּבְלֶכְתְּךָ בַדֶּרֶךְ״** — *And you shall speak them* (words of Torah) ***while you go on the way.*** **וְיֹאמַר בְּכָל יוֹם אֵיזֶה מִזְמוֹרֵי תְהִלִּים** — **On every day** of travel, **he should recite a few chapters of *Tehillim*** (Psalms) **בְּכַוָּנָה וְהַכְנָעָה** — **with concentration and submission** to God.

וְיִזָּהֵר שֶׁיְּהֵא לוֹ פַּת עִמּוֹ — A traveler **should take care to have bread with him** **אֲפִילוּ הוֹלֵךְ בְּמָקוֹם קָרוֹב** — **even if he is traveling a short distance.** **גַּם יֵשׁ לִיקַּח עִמּוֹ צִיצִית** — **One should also take** *tzitzis*-strings **along with him,** **שֶׁמָּא תִפְסוֹל לוֹ צִיצָה** — **lest one of his** *tzitzis*-strings **become invalidated** **וְלֹא יַשִּׂיג אַחֶרֶת** — **and he will not be able to obtain another** string, **וְיִתְבַּטֵּל מִמִּצְוָה** — **and** thus remain **without the mitzvah.**[22]

לְעוֹלָם יִכָּנֵס אָדָם בְּ״כִי טוֹב״ — **A person should always enter** his lodging ***when "it is good"*** **וְיֵצֵא בְּ״כִי טוֹב״** — **and leave** his lodging ***when "it is good"*** **פֵּירוּשׁ** — **This means** that **כְּשֶׁיִּכָּנֵס עַרְבִית לְבֵית הַמָּלוֹן** — **when one arrives at the place of lodging at dusk,** **יִכָּנֵס בְּעוֹד הַחַמָּה זוֹרַחַת** — **he should enter while the sun is still shining.** **וּלְמָחָר יַמְתִּין עַד הָנֵץ הַחַמָּה** — **The next morning, he should wait until sunrise** **וְיֵצֵא** — **and** only **then** should **he leave.** **וְאָז טוֹב לוֹ** — If he follows this advice, **then it will be good for him,** **כְּמוֹ שֶׁנֶּאֱמַר** — **as it is stated** (*Bereishis* 1:4): **״וַיַּרְא אֱלֹהִים אֶת הָאוֹר כִּי טוֹב״** — ***and God saw that the light was good.***[23]

לֹא יֹאכַל הַרְבֵּה כְּשֶׁהוּא בְדֶרֶךְ — **One should not eat excessively while traveling.**[24]

---

20. See *II Shmuel* 18:9-15.

21. "*Go to peace*" indicates that the traveler should find peace and fulfillment at his destination, while "*go in peace*" is a blessing for the journey itself, but makes no mention of his welfare thereafter (*Maharsha* to *Berachos* 64a).

22. *Mishnah Berurah* (110:20) writes that it is proper for every God-fearing Jew to take his *tallis* and *tefillin* along on every trip, regardless of its length. Although one may intend to return home before the next morning, he might be forced to stay longer due to unforeseen circumstances.

23. Travel at night is dangerous; see *Pesachim* 2a and *Rashi* there s.v. בכי טוב. See *Mishnah Berurah* 110:28.

24. The strain of travel combined with the stress on his digestive system can be harmful.

THE WAYFARER'S PRAYER AND OTHER MATTERS WHEN TRAVELING — SIMAN 68:7-8 382

ז. בְּאַכְסַנְיָא שֶׁהוּא אוֹכֵל שָׁמָּה צָרִיךְ לְדַקְדֵּק אִם הַבַּעַל הַבַּיִת וְאַנְשֵׁי בֵיתוֹ הֵמָּה כְּשֵׁרִים וְנֶאֱמָנִים. וְאִם רוֹצֶה לֶאֱכוֹל בָּשָׂר בְּמָקוֹם שֶׁאֵינוֹ יָדוּעַ לוֹ, צָרִיךְ לַחְקוֹר וְלִדְרוֹשׁ הֵיטֵב מִי הוּא הַשּׁוֹחֵט וּמִי הוּא הָרַב הַמַּשְׁגִּיחַ עָלָיו, כִּי בַּעֲוֹנוֹתֵינוּ הָרַבִּים רַבָּה הַמִּכְשֵׁלָה, וְהַמַּשְׂכִּיל יָבִין[25], וּמִכָּל שֶׁכֵּן בְּיַיִן אֲשֶׁר בַּעֲוֹנוֹתֵינוּ הָרַבִּים רַבּוּ הַמִּתְפָּרְצִים, וּצְרִיכִין חֲקִירָה וּדְרִישָׁה[26].

ח. כְּשֶׁהוּא מִתְפַּלֵּל תְּפִלַּת שַׁחֲרִית בְּדֶרֶךְ יִזָּהֵר לְהִתְעַטֵּף בְּטַלִּית גָּדוֹל כְּמוֹ שֶׁהוּא מִתְפַּלֵּל בְּבֵית הַכְּנֶסֶת, כִּי הַטַּלִּית קָטָן[27] רָחוֹק שֶׁיִּהְיֶה כַּשִּׁיעוּר[28]. אִם הוֹלֵךְ בְּרַגְלָיו, אֲזַי כְּשֶׁאוֹמֵר הַפָּסוּק "שְׁמַע יִשְׂרָאֵל" וְגוֹ' וּ"בָרוּךְ שֵׁם כְּבוֹד מַלְכוּתוֹ לְעוֹלָם וָעֶד", צָרִיךְ לַעֲמוֹד[29] שֶׁיְּכַוֵּין לִבּוֹ הֵיטֵב. וְאִם רוֹכֵב אוֹ יוֹשֵׁב בַּעֲגָלָה[30] —

---

§7 בְּאַכְסַנְיָא שֶׁהוּא אוֹכֵל שָׁמָּה — **With** regard to **the place of lodging where one eats,** צָרִיךְ לְדַקְדֵּק — **he must carefully determine** אִם הַבַּעַל הַבַּיִת וְאַנְשֵׁי בֵיתוֹ — **if the host and his family** הֵמָּה כְּשֵׁרִים וְנֶאֱמָנִים — **are upstanding and trustworthy.** וְאִם רוֹצֶה לֶאֱכוֹל בָּשָׂר — **If one wishes to eat meat** בְּמָקוֹם שֶׁאֵינוֹ יָדוּעַ לוֹ — **in an unfamiliar place,** צָרִיךְ לַחְקוֹר וְלִדְרוֹשׁ הֵיטֵב — **he must investigate and inquire thoroughly** מִי הוּא הַשּׁוֹחֵט — **who the** ***shochet*** (ritual slaughterer) **is** וּמִי הוּא הָרַב הַמַּשְׁגִּיחַ עָלָיו — **and who the supervising rabbi is.** כִּי בַּעֲוֹנוֹתֵינוּ הָרַבִּים רַבָּה הַמִּכְשֵׁלָה — **For due to our numerous sins, there are many pitfalls** in the area of *kashrus,* וְהַמַּשְׂכִּיל יָבִין — **and an intelligent** person **will understand** on his own.[25] וּמִכָּל שֶׁכֵּן בְּיַיִן — **Certainly with regard to wine,** אֲשֶׁר בַּעֲוֹנוֹתֵינוּ הָרַבִּים רַבּוּ הַמִּתְפָּרְצִים — **with which, due to our numerous sins, there is a proliferation of those who breach** the standards of proper *kashrus,* וּצְרִיכִין חֲקִירָה וּדְרִישָׁה — **investigation and inquiry are necessary** to ascertain its *kashrus.*[26]

§8 כְּשֶׁהוּא מִתְפַּלֵּל תְּפִלַּת שַׁחֲרִית בְּדֶרֶךְ — **When one recites the Morning Prayers while on the road,** יִזָּהֵר לְהִתְעַטֵּף בְּטַלִּית גָּדוֹל — **he should take care to wrap himself in a** ***tallis,*** כְּמוֹ שֶׁהוּא מִתְפַּלֵּל בְּבֵית הַכְּנֶסֶת — **just as** he would do **when praying in the synagogue.** כִּי הַטַּלִּית קָטָן רָחוֹק שֶׁיִּהְיֶה כַּשִּׁיעוּר — He may not rely on the *tallis-katan*[27] **he is wearing, since it is unlikely that the** ***tallis-katan*** **reaches the** minimum **size** required.[28]

אִם הוֹלֵךְ בְּרַגְלָיו — **If he is** praying while **traveling by foot,** אֲזַי כְּשֶׁאוֹמֵר הַפָּסוּק "שְׁמַע יִשְׂרָאֵל" וְגוֹ' — **then when he recites the verse** of *Shema Yisrael,* ***Hear O Israel*** **etc.,** וּ"בָרוּךְ שֵׁם כְּבוֹד מַלְכוּתוֹ לְעוֹלָם וָעֶד" — **and** the phrase that follows, ***Blessed is the Name of His glorious kingdom for all eternity,*** צָרִיךְ לַעֲמוֹד — **he should stop** walking,[29] שֶׁיְּכַוֵּין לִבּוֹ הֵיטֵב — **so that he can concentrate properly** on what he is saying. וְאִם רוֹכֵב — **If he is riding** an animal אוֹ יוֹשֵׁב בַּעֲגָלָה — **or sitting in a wagon,**[30]

---

25. See Appendix of Kitzur's editorial glosses.

26. The kosher production of wine is governed by a unique and complex set of laws; see above, *Siman* 47.

27. Literally, *small cloak* or *garment.* This refers to the smaller *tzitzis* garment that is customarily worn throughout the day, in contrast to the larger *tzitzis* garment, the *tallis-gadol* (literally, *large cloak*), worn only during Morning Prayers.

28. See above, 9:1.

29. According to some authorities, one should remain in one place until he reaches the words עַל לְבָבֶךָ, *upon your heart* (*Mishnah Berurah* 63:11).

30. Or any vehicle.

383 THE WAYFARER'S PRAYER AND OTHER MATTERS WHEN TRAVELING — SIMAN 68:8

מוּתָּר[31]. וּבִתְפִלַּת שְׁמוֹנֶה עֶשְׂרֵה יַעֲמוֹד. וְאִם הוּא נָחוּץ לְדַרְכּוֹ — אִם יָכוֹל לַעֲמוֹד לְכָל הַפָּחוֹת בְּשָׁלֹשׁ בְּרָכוֹת רִאשׁוֹנוֹת וּבְשָׁלֹשׁ בְּרָכוֹת אַחֲרוֹנוֹת — מוּטָב[32], וְאִם לָאו — יִתְפַּלֵּל מְיוּשָּׁב בָּעֲגָלָה[33] וְיַעֲשֶׂה הַכְּרִיעוֹת מְיוּשָּׁב[34]. וְאָמְנָם טוֹב יוֹתֵר שֶׁיִּתְפַּלֵּל אֲפִילּוּ מִיָּד בַּעֲלוֹת הַשַּׁחַר[35], וְגַם מִנְחָה אֲפִילּוּ מִיָּד חֲצִי שָׁעָה אַחַר חֲצוֹת הַיּוֹם[36],

מוּתָּר — **it is permitted to** recite these verses without stopping.[31] **וּבִתְפִלַּת שְׁמוֹנֶה עֶשְׂרֵה** — However, **when** reciting **the** ***Shemoneh Esrei*** **Prayer,** **יַעֲמוֹד** — **he should stop** to pray. **וְאִם הוּא נָחוּץ לְדַרְכּוֹ** — **If he is pressed** for time **to continue his journey** and cannot remain in one place for the entire *Shemoneh Esrei,* **אִם יָכוֹל לַעֲמוֹד** — then, **if he is able to stop** **לְכָל הַפָּחוֹת בְּשָׁלֹשׁ בְּרָכוֹת רִאשׁוֹנוֹת** — **at least while** reciting **the first three blessings** of *Shemoneh Esrei* **וּבְשָׁלֹשׁ בְּרָכוֹת אַחֲרוֹנוֹת** — **and the last three blessings,** **מוּטָב** — **that is preferable.**[32] **וְאִם לָאו** — **If** he is **not** able to do so, **יִתְפַּלֵּל מְיוּשָּׁב בָּעֲגָלָה** — **he should pray while seated in the wagon,**[33] **וְיַעֲשֶׂה הַכְּרִיעוֹת מְיוּשָּׁב** — **and bow** his body at the appropriate places in the prayer **while seated.**[34] **וְאָמְנָם טוֹב יוֹתֵר** — **However, it is preferable** **שֶׁיִּתְפַּלֵּל אֲפִילּוּ מִיָּד בַּעֲלוֹת הַשַּׁחַר** — **to pray even as early as daybreak** before leaving, rather than praying en route while seated.[35]

וְגַם מִנְחָה — With regard to ***Minchah*** **as well,** it is preferable to pray before leaving, **אֲפִילּוּ מִיָּד חֲצִי שָׁעָה אַחַר חֲצוֹת הַיּוֹם** — **even as soon as half an hour after midday,**[36]

---

31. *Mishnah Berurah* (63:10) writes that if one is riding an animal, it is preferable to come to a halt while reciting this portion of *Shema.*

32. One should also stop to take three steps backward after ending the *Shemoneh Esrei* (*Shulchan Aruch* 94:5). *Mishnah Berurah* (94:18) adds that this applies as well to one who is walking.

33. If possible, he should turn his face toward Eretz Yisrael (*Mishnah Berurah* 94:15). See above, 18:10.

34. When traveling on an airplane, if it is difficult to stand and one will be disturbed if he does so, it is better to pray *Shemoneh Esrei* while seated; however, one should stand to bow in the required places (*Igros Moshe, Orach Chaim* IV, §20).

35. See above, 18:1, which states that the ideal time to recite the Morning *Shemoneh Esrei* begins at sunrise. In this circumstance, however, Kitzur rules that one should rather recite the *Shemoneh Esrei* Prayer as early as daybreak (cf. *Beur Halachah* 89:1 s.v. ואם התפלל, who maintains that one should wait until the light spreads across the eastern horizon). For the halachic definitions of these times, see Appendix B.

Shulchan Aruch and *Rama* (89:8) write that this halachah pertains only to *Shemoneh Esrei;* the proper time for *Shema,* however, as well as for donning *tallis* and *tefillin* with their blessings, is not until *"misheyakir"* (literally, *when one can recognize;* see Appendix B for explanation), which is not until later (see above, 9:9, 10:2, and 17:1). Thus, even if one must recite the *Shemoneh Esrei* earlier than *misheyakir,* nevertheless, if at all possible, he should not recite *Shema* and its blessings at that time (see also *Shulchan Aruch* 58:3). *Mishnah Berurah* (89:42), however, writes that common practice is not to recite *Shemoneh Esrei* earlier and *Shema* afterward, but rather to recite *Shemoneh Esrei* (even while seated) together with the rest of the *Shacharis* service at its proper time while traveling. See there for further discussion.

If one is traveling, and the only *minyan* available is beginning before *misheyakir,* he may join them if he calculates that by the time they reach *Borchu* it will be *misheyakir.* He should wait until after *Yishtabach* to put on *tallis* and *tefillin,* or put them on earlier without reciting the blessing, and move them slightly at that time (after *misheyakir*) and recite the blessing (see *Mishnah Berurah* 89:40 and *Igros Moshe, Orach Chaim* IV, §6).

36. See below, 69:2.

THE WAYFARER'S PRAYER AND OTHER MATTERS WHEN TRAVELING — SIMAN 68:9-10 384

כְּדֵי שֶׁיּוּכַל לְהִתְפַּלֵּל מְעוּמָּד וְכָרָאוּי. (הַשִּׁיעוּר שֶׁהוּא מְחוּיָּב לַחֲזוֹר אַחַר מַיִם וּכְדֵי לְהִתְפַּלֵּל בַּעֲשָׂרָה כָּתוּב בְּסִימָן י״ב סְעִיף ה׳ וּסְעִיף ח׳, עַיֵּין שָׁם.)

ט. הַמְהַלֵּךְ בַּדֶּרֶךְ וְהִגִּיעַ עֵת הָאוֹכֶל וְלֹא מָצָא מַיִם נִתְבָּאֵר בְּסִימָן מ׳ סְעִיף י״ד. וּבְסִימָן מ״ב סְעִיף י״ט נִתְבָּאֵר שֶׁהָאוֹכֵל פַּת אָסוּר לָצֵאת מִמְּקוֹמוֹ עַד שֶׁיְּבָרֵךְ בִּרְכַּת הַמָּזוֹן, וּבְסִימָן מ״ד סְעִיף ו׳ נִתְבָּאֵר שֶׁצָּרִיךְ לְבָרֵךְ מְיוּשָּׁב דַּוְקָא. וְאָמְנָם אִם אָכַל בַּדֶּרֶךְ כְּשֶׁהוּא מְהַלֵּךְ, מוּתָּר לְבָרֵךְ בִּרְכַּת הַמָּזוֹן גַּם כֵּן כְּשֶׁהוּא מְהַלֵּךְ, מִפְּנֵי שֶׁאֵין דַּעְתּוֹ מְיוּשֶּׁבֶת עָלָיו אִם יִצְטָרֵךְ לְהִתְעַכֵּב. אֲבָל אִם אָכַל מְיוּשָּׁב, גַּם בִּרְכַּת הַמָּזוֹן צָרִיךְ לְבָרֵךְ מְיוּשָּׁב.

י. קְצָת נוֹהֲגִין שֶׁבִּהְיוֹתָם בַּדֶּרֶךְ וְאוֹכְלִים בְּבֵית עַכּוּ״ם אֵין מְבָרְכִין בְּזִימּוּן[37] מִשּׁוּם דְּלָא הָוֵי קְבִיעוּת[38]. וּמִכָּל מָקוֹם אִם קָבְעוּ עַצְמָן שָׁם לֶאֱכוֹל בְּיַחַד,

---

כְּדֵי שֶׁיּוּכַל לְהִתְפַּלֵּל מְעוּמָּד וְכָרָאוּי — in order to be able to pray while standing and in the proper manner, and not have to pray while sitting.

(**הַשִּׁיעוּר שֶׁהוּא מְחוּיָּב לַחֲזוֹר אַחַר מַיִם** — The laws regarding **the measure** of distance **that one must travel to obtain water** for washing one's hands before praying, **וּכְדֵי לְהִתְפַּלֵּל בַּעֲשָׂרָה — and** the distance one must travel **to pray with** a *minyan,* a quorum of ten, **כָּתוּב בְּסִימָן י״ב סְעִיף ה׳ וּסְעִיף ח׳, עַיֵּין שָׁם — are written above, 12:5,8; see there** for details of those halachos.)

§9 **הַמְהַלֵּךְ בַּדֶּרֶךְ** — The halachah for **one who is traveling** **וְהִגִּיעַ עֵת הָאוֹכֶל — and mealtime has arrived,** **וְלֹא מָצָא מַיִם — but he has no water available** with which to wash his hands, **נִתְבָּאֵר בְּסִימָן מ׳ סְעִיף י״ד — is detailed above, in 40:14.** **וּבְסִימָן מ״ב סְעִיף י״ט נִתְבָּאֵר — In 42:19 it is explained** **שֶׁהָאוֹכֵל פַּת אָסוּר לָצֵאת מִמְּקוֹמוֹ — that one who eats bread may not leave his place** **עַד שֶׁיְּבָרֵךְ בִּרְכַּת הַמָּזוֹן — until he has recited** *Bircas HaMazon,* ***Grace After Meals;*** **וּבְסִימָן מ״ד סְעִיף ו׳ נִתְבָּאֵר — in 44:6 it is explained** **שֶׁצָּרִיךְ לְבָרֵךְ מְיוּשָּׁב דַּוְקָא — that one must recite** ***Bircas HaMazon*** **only while sitting.** **וְאָמְנָם — However,** **אִם אָכַל בַּדֶּרֶךְ כְּשֶׁהוּא מְהַלֵּךְ — if one ate on the road while he was walking,** **מוּתָּר לְבָרֵךְ בִּרְכַּת הַמָּזוֹן — he is permitted to recite** ***Bircas HaMazon*** **גַּם כֵּן כְּשֶׁהוּא מְהַלֵּךְ — while he is walking as well,** **מִפְּנֵי שֶׁאֵין דַּעְתּוֹ מְיוּשֶּׁבֶת עָלָיו — because his mind would be unsettled** **אִם יִצְטָרֵךְ לְהִתְעַכֵּב — if he would be required to wait,** and he would be unable to focus properly on the blessing. **אֲבָל אִם אָכַל מְיוּשָּׁב — However, if he was seated during his meal,** **גַּם בִּרְכַּת הַמָּזוֹן צָרִיךְ לְבָרֵךְ מְיוּשָּׁב — then he must recite** ***Bircas HaMazon*** **while sitting, as well.**

§10 **קְצָת נוֹהֲגִין** — **Some** people **follow the practice** **שֶׁבִּהְיוֹתָם בַּדֶּרֶךְ וְאוֹכְלִים בְּבֵית עַכּוּ״ם — that when traveling and eating in the house of an idolater,** **אֵין מְבָרְכִין בְּזִימּוּן — they do not recite** *Bircas Hamazon* **with** the ***zimun*** blessing,[37] **מִשּׁוּם דְּלָא הָוֵי קְבִיעוּת — because it is not** considered **a formal gathering,** and thus the *zimun* is not recited.[38] **וּמִכָּל מָקוֹם — Nevertheless,** **אִם קָבְעוּ עַצְמָן שָׁם לֶאֱכוֹל בְּיַחַד — if**

---

37. The halachos of the *zimun* blessing are set out above, *Siman* 45.

38. See above, 45:15. *Mishnah Berurah* (193:27) writes that it is customary to recite the *zimun.* If, however, the meal takes place during the daytime in a casual, informal setting, it is questionable whether there is a requirement of *zimun.* In this situation, he

385   THE WAYFARER'S PRAYER AND OTHER MATTERS WHEN TRAVELING — SIMAN 68:11

אֵינוּ נָכוֹן לְבַטֵּל הַזִּימוּן. וְיֹאמְרוּ³⁹ "הָרַחֲמָן הוּא יִשְׁלַח לָנוּ בְּרָכָה מְרוּבָּה בִּמְקוֹם
הֲלִיכָתֵנוּ וּבִמְקוֹם יְשִׁיבָתֵנוּ עַד עוֹלָם". וְאִם אוֹכְלִים מִשֶּׁל אֶחָד, יְכוֹלִין לוֹמַר "הָרַחֲמָן
הוּא יְבָרֵךְ אֶת בַּעַל הַבַּיִת הַזֶּה", וְקָאֵי עַל בַּעַל הַסְּעוּדָה, וְאִם לָאו, יֹאמַר "הָרַחֲמָן
הוּא יְבָרֵךְ אוֹתָנוּ", וְעַיֵּן לְעֵיל סוֹף סִימָן מ"ד.

יא. מִדִּינָא אָסוּר לֵילֵךְ בְּעֶרֶב שַׁבָּת יוֹתֵר מִן שָׁלֹשׁ פַּרְסָאוֹת,⁴⁰ בֵּין לְבֵיתוֹ בֵּין
לְמָקוֹם אַחֵר, כְּדֵי שֶׁיּוּכְלוּ לְהָכִין צָרְכֵי סְעוּדוֹת שַׁבָּת כָּרָאוּי, וּבִמְדִינוֹת
אֵלּוּ⁴¹ אֵין נִזְהָרִין בָּזֶה מִפְּנֵי שֶׁרוֹב בְּנֵי אָדָם מְכִינִים בִּרְוִיחַ. וּמִכָּל מָקוֹם צָרִיךְ

they did formally gather to eat a meal as a group,   אֵינוּ נָכוֹן לְבַטֵּל הַזִּימוּן — it is not proper to abstain from the mitzvah of *zimun*.

As described in the introduction to *Siman* 44, the *Bircas HaMazon* blessings are followed by a series of supplications, most of which begin with the word *HaRachaman*. One of these is a prayer that Hashem bless the house in which one ate, and the master of the house. When reciting the *Bircas HaMazon* in the house of an idolater,[39] this is replaced with the following: וְיֹאמְרוּ — They should recite: הָרַחֲמָן הוּא יִשְׁלַח לָנוּ בְּרָכָה מְרוּבָּה" — *The compassionate One! May He send us abundant blessing*   בִּמְקוֹם הֲלִיכָתֵנוּ וּבִמְקוֹם — *in the place of our travels and the place of our dwelling,*   יְשִׁיבָתֵנוּ עַד עוֹלָם" — *forever.* וְאִם אוֹכְלִים מִשֶּׁל אֶחָד — If they have eaten the food of one of those present,   יְכוֹלִין לוֹמַר — they may say: הָרַחֲמָן הוּא יְבָרֵךְ אֶת בַּעַל הַבַּיִת הַזֶּה" — *The compassionate One! May He bless the master of this house,*   וְקָאֵי עַל בַּעַל הַסְּעוּדָה — referring to the one who provided the meal.   וְאִם לָאו יֹאמַר — If they are not partaking of the food belonging to one of them, but each is partaking of his own food, each one should say: "הָרַחֲמָן הוּא יְבָרֵךְ אוֹתָנוּ — *The compassionate One! May He bless us.*   וְעַיֵּן לְעֵיל סוֹף סִימָן מ"ד — See above, end of *Siman* 44, regarding the text of the blessing when there is an idolater in the house.

§11 מִדִּינָא — According to the strict halachah,   אָסוּר לֵילֵךְ בְּעֶרֶב שַׁבָּת — it is forbidden to travel on Friday   יוֹתֵר מִן שָׁלֹשׁ פַּרְסָאוֹת — a distance greater than three *parsaos*,[40]   בֵּין לְבֵיתוֹ בֵּין לְמָקוֹם אַחֵר — whether one is traveling to one's home, or to any other place.   כְּדֵי שֶׁיּוּכְלוּ לְהָכִין צָרְכֵי סְעוּדוֹת שַׁבָּת כָּרָאוּי — The reason for this prohibition is to ensure that one has ample time to prepare for the Shabbos meals.   וּבִמְדִינוֹת אֵלּוּ — However, in these countries,[41]   אֵין נִזְהָרִין בָּזֶה — people are not commonly careful regarding this practice,   מִפְּנֵי שֶׁרוֹב בְּנֵי אָדָם מְכִינִים בִּרְוִיחַ — because most people prepare an abundant amount of food, and food is generally available even on short notice.   וּמִכָּל מָקוֹם — In any event,   צָרִיךְ כָּל

---

advises that the travelers eat separately, thus avoiding the question entirely.

39. See above, *Siman* 44, note 67.

40. 7.2-8.6 miles (11.5-13.8 kilometers); see Appendix A. According to *Pri Megadim*, if one is traveling on horseback or in a vehicle, he may cover any distance until a third of the

day has elapsed. According to *Bach*, if one is travelling in a vehicle, he may travel even after midday, as long as he stops in time to be ready for Shabbos (*Mishnah Berurah* 249:1; see there for further discussion).

41. *Kitzur* was written in Hungary, in Central Europe.

THE WAYFARER'S PRAYER AND OTHER MATTERS WHEN TRAVELING — SIMAN 68:12 386

כָּל אָדָם לִיזָּהֵר מְאוֹד שֶׁיִּכָּנֵס לְאוּשְׁפִּיזָא בְּעוֹד הַיּוֹם גָּדוֹל כִּי הַרְבֵּה חִילּוּל שַׁבָּת בָּא עַל יְדֵי מַה שֶּׁמִּתְאַחֲרִים. לָכֵן יְהֵא נִזְהָר מְאוֹד וְלֹא יְסִיתֶנּוּ הַיֵּצֶר לוֹמַר עוֹד הַיּוֹם גָּדוֹל וְדֶרֶךְ טוֹב.

יב. מִי שֶׁהוּא בְּיוֹם שַׁבַּת קוֹדֶשׁ בַּדֶּרֶךְ בְּמָלוֹן וְיֵשׁ לוֹ מָעוֹת, אִם יָכוֹל לְהַפְקִידָן אוֹ לְהַצְנִיעָן, אָסוּר לְהַחֲזִיקָן בְּכִיסוֹ שֶׁהֲרֵי הֵם מוּקְצֶה[42]. וְאִם מִתְיָרֵא שֶׁמָּא יִגְנְבוּם מִמֶּנּוּ יִתְפְּרֵם עֶרֶב שַׁבָּת בְּבִגְדוֹ, וְיֵשֵׁב בַּבַּיִת, וְלֹא יֵצֵא בָּהֶם בְּמָקוֹם שֶׁאֵין עֵירוּב[43]. אַךְ אִם יֵשׁ לָחוּשׁ שֶׁמָּא מֵחֲמַת זֶה שֶׁאֵינוֹ יוֹצֵא כָּל הַיּוֹם מִבֵּיתוֹ יַרְגִּישׁוּ שֶׁיֵּשׁ לוֹ מָעוֹת וְיִגְזְלֵם מִמֶּנּוּ, מוּתָּר לָצֵאת בָּהֶם כְּשֶׁהֵם תְּפוּרִים בְּבִגְדוֹ[44]. אֲבָל אִם הֵם בְּכִיסוֹ,

---

אָדָם לִיזָּהֵר מְאוֹד — **every person should take great care** **שֶׁיִּכָּנֵס לְאוּשְׁפִּיזָא** — **to enter the lodging** where he will spend Shabbos **בְּעוֹד הַיּוֹם גָּדוֹל** — **while there is still a significant** amount of time **left in the day,** **כִּי הַרְבֵּה חִילּוּל שַׁבָּת בָּא עַל יְדֵי מַה שֶּׁמִּתְאַחֲרִים** — **because numerous violations of** the laws of **Shabbos come about as a result of arriving late.** **לָכֵן יְהֵא נִזְהָר מְאוֹד** — **Therefore,** if one is traveling on Friday, **he should take great care** **וְלֹא יְסִיתֶנּוּ הַיֵּצֶר לוֹמַר** — **and not** allow the evil **inclination to entice him,** by **saying:** **עוֹד הַיּוֹם גָּדוֹל וְדֶרֶךְ טוֹב** — ***There is still much** time left **in the day, and the road is fine** for travel!*

§12 **מִי שֶׁהוּא בְּיוֹם שַׁבַּת קוֹדֶשׁ בַּדֶּרֶךְ בְּמָלוֹן** — **One who is traveling, and is** lodged **at an inn for the** duration of **the holy Shabbos** **וְיֵשׁ לוֹ מָעוֹת** — **and he has money** in his possession, **אִם יָכוֹל לְהַפְקִידָן אוֹ לְהַצְנִיעָן** — **if he is able to deposit** the money **for safekeeping, or hide it,** **אָסוּר לְהַחֲזִיקָן בְּכִיסוֹ** — **he may not keep** the money **in his pocket,** **שֶׁהֲרֵי הֵם מוּקְצֶה**— **because** the money **is** *muktzeh.*[42] **וְאִם מִתְיָרֵא שֶׁמָּא יִגְנְבוּם מִמֶּנּוּ** — **If** he is unable to effectively deposit or hide the money, and **he fears it will be stolen from him,** **יִתְפְּרֵם עֶרֶב שַׁבָּת בְּבִגְדוֹ** — **he should sew** the money **into his clothing before the onset of Shabbos,** **וְיֵשֵׁב בַּבַּיִת** — **and remain in the house;** **וְלֹא יֵצֵא בָּהֶם בְּמָקוֹם שֶׁאֵין עֵירוּב** — **he may not go outside to any place that has no** *eruv.*[43] **אַךְ אִם יֵשׁ לָחוּשׁ** — **However, if he is concerned** **שֶׁמָּא מֵחֲמַת זֶה שֶׁאֵינוֹ יוֹצֵא כָּל הַיּוֹם מִבֵּיתוֹ** — **that due to his not leaving his house the entire day** **יַרְגִּישׁוּ שֶׁיֵּשׁ לוֹ מָעוֹת** — people **will realize that he has** a significant amount of **money** with him, **וְיִגְזְלֵם מִמֶּנּוּ** — **and** they may **steal it from him,** **מוּתָּר לָצֵאת בָּהֶם** — **he may leave** the house **with the money** **כְּשֶׁהֵם תְּפוּרִים בְּבִגְדוֹ** — **if** the money **is sewn into his clothing.**[44] **אֲבָל אִם הֵם בְּכִיסוֹ** — **However, if money is** merely sitting **in his**

---

42. I.e., it may not be moved on Shabbos. The laws of *muktzeh* are set out below, *Siman* 88.

43. One may not carry items from one domain to another on Shabbos; an *eruv* permits this in certain circumstances. The laws of "carrying" on Shabbos are set out below, *Siman* 84; the laws of *eruv*, *Siman* 94.

44. Carrying money sewn into one's garment is an unusual method of carrying, and therefore does not present a Biblical transgression. While this is ordinarily forbidden by Rabbinic law, in this specific case the Sages did not prohibit it, as they were concerned, lest one panic when faced with a potential financial loss and dig a hole to hide his money, or perform some other Biblical Shabbos transgression. If one did not sew the money into his clothing before Shabbos and he must leave the house, he may carry it outside in another unusual manner, such as by placing it in his shoe. However, it is preferable for the money to be sewn in before Shabbos than to rely on other methods (see *Mishnah Berurah* 301:123).

387   THE WAYFARER'S PRAYER AND OTHER MATTERS WHEN TRAVELING — SIMAN 68:12

בְּכָל עִנְיָן אָסוּר. (עַיֵּין עוֹד בְּסִימָן קפ"ט דְּבָרִים שֶׁצְּרִיכִין לִיזָּהֵר בַּדֶּרֶךְ‎[45].)

pocket, and not sewn in,   בְּכָל עִנְיָן אָסוּר — it is forbidden in any case.

עַיֵּין עוֹד בְּסִימָן קפ"ט דְּבָרִים שֶׁצְּרִיכִין לִיזָּהֵר בַּדֶּרֶךְ — See also below, in *Siman* 189, regarding other **things about which one must take care when traveling.**)[45]

---

45. I.e., the halachos pertaining to helping another traveler when his animal can no longer manage its load.

LAWS OF THE MINCHAH PRAYER — SIMAN 69:1 388

סימן סט

דִּינֵי תְּפִלַּת מִנְחָה

וּבוֹ ט׳ סְעִיפִים

א. אָמַר רַבִּי חֶלְבּוֹ: אָמַר רַב הוּנָא: לְעוֹלָם יִזָּהֵר אָדָם בִּתְפִלַּת הַמִּנְחָה שֶׁהֲרֵי לֹא נַעֲנָה אֵלִיָּהוּ אֶלָּא בִּתְפִלַּת הַמִּנְחָה, שֶׁנֶּאֱמַר (מלכים-א יח, לו) ״וַיְהִי בַּעֲלוֹת הַמִּנְחָה[1] וַיִּגַּשׁ אֵלִיָּהוּ״[2]. וְהַטַּעַם שֶׁתְּפִלַּת הַמִּנְחָה הִיא חֲשׁוּבָה כָּל כָּךְ מִפְּנֵי כִּי תְּפִלַּת הַשַּׁחַר זְמַנָּהּ יְדוּעָה בַּבֹּקֶר בְּקוּמוֹ מִמִּטָּתוֹ יִתְפַּלֵּל מִיָּד קוֹדֶם שֶׁיְּהֵא טָרוּד בַּעֲסָקָיו, וְכֵן תְּפִלַּת עַרְבִית בַּלַּיְלָה זְמַנָּהּ יָדוּעַ בְּבוֹאוֹ לְבֵיתוֹ וְהוּא פָּנוּי מֵעֲסָקָיו,

---

SIMAN 69

THE LAWS OF THE MINCHAH PRAYER

CONTAINING 9 *SE'IFIM*

§1 Special Diligence With Regard to the *Minchah* Prayer / **§2** Time of *Minchah* / **§3** Engaging in Other Activities Before *Minchah* / **§4** Washing the Hands for *Minchah* / **§5** *Ashrei* and *Kaddish* / **§6** When the Congregation Begins Late / **§7** One Who Arrives Late for *Minchah* / **§8** *Tachanun* and *Kaddish* at Night / **§9** Reciting *Minchah* After the Congregation Ushered in Shabbos or the Festival

§1 Kitzur opens the *Siman* with a citation of a Talmudic teaching (*Berachos* 6b) that conveys the importance of being diligent with regard to the *Minchah* prayer:

אָמַר רַבִּי חֶלְבּוֹ: אָמַר רַב הוּנָא — R' Chelbo said in the name of Rav Huna: לְעוֹלָם יִזָּהֵר אָדָם בִּתְפִלַּת הַמִּנְחָה — A person should always be diligent with regard to the *Minchah* Prayer, שֶׁהֲרֵי לֹא נַעֲנָה אֵלִיָּהוּ אֶלָּא בִּתְפִלַּת הַמִּנְחָה — for the prophet Eliyahu was answered only through the *Minchah* Prayer, שֶׁנֶּאֱמַר — as it is stated (*I Melachim* 18:36): **״וַיְהִי בַּעֲלוֹת הַמִּנְחָה וַיִּגַּשׁ אֵלִיָּהוּ״ — *And it was at the time of the offering of the minchah*[1] *and Eliyahu approached* ...**[2] **וְהַטַּעַם שֶׁתְּפִלַּת הַמִּנְחָה הִיא חֲשׁוּבָה כָּל כָּךְ — The reason that the *Minchah* Prayer is so important מִפְּנֵי — is because** it has a quality not shared by the other two daily prayers: **כִּי תְּפִלַּת הַשַּׁחַר זְמַנָּהּ יְדוּעָה בַּבֹּקֶר — for the morning Prayer is** recited **at a specific time in the morning** (see above, 18:1), **בְּקוּמוֹ מִמִּטָּתוֹ יִתְפַּלֵּל מִיָּד — for when one arises from his bed** in the morning, **he prays immediately, קוֹדֶם שֶׁיְּהֵא טָרוּד בַּעֲסָקָיו — before he becomes preoccupied with his affairs; וְכֵן תְּפִלַּת עַרְבִית בַּלַּיְלָה — likewise, the evening Prayer at night זְמַנָּהּ יָדוּעַ** — is recited at a **specific time** (see below, 70:1-2), **בְּבוֹאוֹ לְבֵיתוֹ — when one comes home** at the end of the day **וְהוּא פָּנוּי מֵעֲסָקָיו — and he is free from his**

---

1. I.e., the *minchah* offering that accompanied the afternoon *tamid*-offering in the Temple (see *se'if* 2). The name of the afternoon prayer (*Minchah*) is based on this verse (see *Tosafos* to *Pesachim* 107a s.v. סמוך).

2. This refers to the time Eliyahu stood on Mount Carmel and confronted the prophets of Baal in order to demonstrate that Hashem is the true God. He placed a sacrifice upon an altar, without providing a fire to burn it. He then prayed that a fire would come down from heaven to consume the offering, and God answered his prayer (see *I Melachim* 18:19-40). Eliyahu deliberately waited until the time for praying *Minchah*, because this prayer is particularly effective (*Beurei HaGra* ad loc.).

אֲבָל תְּפִלַּת הַמִּנְחָה הוּא בְּעוֹד שֶׁהַיּוֹם גָּדוֹל וְהָאָדָם טָרוּד בַּעֲסָקָיו וְהוּא צָרִיךְ לָשִׂים אֶל לִבּוֹ וְלִפָּנוֹת מִכָּל עֲסָקָיו וּלְהִתְפַּלֵּל, עַל כֵּן שְׂכָרָהּ הַרְבֵּה מְאוֹד.

ב. **עִיקָּר**[3,4] **זְמַנָּהּ הוּא בְּט׳ שָׁעוֹת וּמֶחֱצָה וּלְמַעְלָה**[5]**, וְהִיא נִקְרֵאת מִנְחָה קְטַנָּה**[6]**. וּבִשְׁעַת הַדְּחָק, כְּגוֹן שֶׁהוּא צָרִיךְ לָצֵאת לַדֶּרֶךְ, אוֹ שֶׁהוּא צָרִיךְ לֶאֱכוֹל, יָכוֹל לְהִתְפַּלֵּל מִיָּד לְאַחַר שֵׁשׁ שָׁעוֹת וּמֶחֱצָה**[7]**, וְהִיא נִקְרֵאת מִנְחָה גְּדוֹלָה**[8]**. וְהֶמְשֵׁךְ זְמַנָּהּ הוּא לְכַתְּחִלָּה עַד שָׁעָה וּרְבִיעִית שָׁעָה קוֹדֶם הַלַּיְלָה וְלֹא יוֹתֵר, וְזֶה נִקְרָא פְּלַג**

---

affairs. **אֲבָל תְּפִלַּת הַמִּנְחָה** — However, the *Minchah* Prayer **הוּא בְּעוֹד שֶׁהַיּוֹם גָּדוֹל** — is recited **while there is much** time left **in the day** **וְהָאָדָם טָרוּד בַּעֲסָקָיו** — and **a person is** therefore **preoccupied with his affairs,** **וְהוּא צָרִיךְ לָשִׂים אֶל לִבּוֹ** — and he therefore **must be mindful** of his obligation **וְלִפָּנוֹת מִכָּל עֲסָקָיו וּלְהִתְפַּלֵּל** — **and free himself from all his affairs to pray** *Minchah.* **עַל כֵּן** — **Therefore,** **שְׂכָרָהּ הַרְבֵּה מְאוֹד** — **the reward** for the recitation of the *Minchah* Prayer **is very great.**

§2 The *Minchah* Prayer corresponds to the afternoon *tamid,* the daily afternoon-offering in the Temple.[3] Generally speaking, the time that the *Minchah* Prayer can be recited corresponds to the time that the *tamid*-offering could have been brought in the Temple, from six-and-a-half hours after sunrise[4] until evening. However, it is preferable to recite the *Minchah* prayer at certain specific times in the afternoon, as Kitzur explains in this *se'if.*

עִיקָּר זְמַנָּהּ הוּא בְּט׳ שָׁעוֹת וּמֶחֱצָה וּלְמַעְלָה — **The principal time** for reciting *Minchah* begins **from nine-and-one-half hours** after sunrise[5] **and onward;** **וְהִיא נִקְרֵאת מִנְחָה קְטַנָּה** — **this** time period **is called** *minchah ketanah,* ***lesser minchah.***[6] **וּבִשְׁעַת הַדְּחָק** — However, **in times of pressing need,** **כְּגוֹן שֶׁהוּא צָרִיךְ לָצֵאת לַדֶּרֶךְ** — **for example, if one needs to set out on a journey,** **אוֹ שֶׁהוּא צָרִיךְ לֶאֱכוֹל** — **or he needs to eat,** **יָכוֹל לְהִתְפַּלֵּל מִיָּד לְאַחַר שֵׁשׁ שָׁעוֹת וּמֶחֱצָה** — **he may recite the** *Minchah* **Prayer immediately after six-and-a-half hours have passed** from daybreak.[7] **וְהִיא נִקְרֵאת מִנְחָה גְּדוֹלָה** — **This** time period **is called** *minchah gedolah,* ***greater minchah.***[8]

וְהֶמְשֵׁךְ זְמַנָּהּ הוּא לְכַתְּחִלָּה — **Ideally, the** proper **time** for *Minchah* **extends** **עַד שָׁעָה וּרְבִיעִית שָׁעָה קוֹדֶם הַלַּיְלָה** — **until one-and-one-quarter hours before nightfall** **וְלֹא יוֹתֵר** — **and not later.** **וְזֶה נִקְרָא פְּלַג הַמִּנְחָה** — **This is called** *plag haminchah,* ***half***

---

3. *Berachos* 26b.

4. This is a half-hour (see *Shaar HaTziyun* 233:8) after halachic midday; see Appendix B.

5. Or, 3 ½ hours after *chaztos hayom,* halachic midday. Although the afternoon *tamid*-offering in the Temple could be brought earlier than this, in actual practice the offering of the *tamid* was generally deferred until 9 ½ hours into the day to allow the public more time for bringing their voluntary offerings (which are not permitted to be offered after the afternoon *tamid*). For this reason, it is ideal not to recite the *Minchah* Prayer until this time (*Mishnah Berurah* 233:1).

6. See note 9.

7. This was the earliest time that the afternoon *tamid*-offering could have been offered in the Temple; see above, note 5. Likewise, if it will not be possible for one to pray with a *minyan* (quorum) if he waits until later, he may recite *Minchah* at this time (*Mishnah Berurah* 233:1).

8. This time is called the "greater *Minchah,*" because the greater portion of the day remains; the "lesser *Minchah*" begins later in the day, when only a small portion of the day remains (see *Perishah* 232:5).

LAWS OF THE MINCHAH PRAYER — SIMAN 69:3 390

הַמִּנְחָה[9], כִּי מִשְּׁעַת מִנְחָה קְטַנָּה עַד הַלַּיְלָה הוּא שְׁתֵּי שָׁעוֹת וּמֶחֱצָה, וְהַחֵצִי מִזֶּה הִיא שָׁעָה וּרְבִיעִית. וּבְדִיעֲבַד אוֹ בִּשְׁעַת הַדְּחָק יָכוֹל לְהִתְפַּלֵּל עַד צֵאת הַכּוֹכָבִים[10]. וְכֵן נוֹהֲגִין עַתָּה בְּרוֹב הַקְּהִלּוֹת שֶׁמִּתְפַּלְּלִין מִנְחָה סָמוּךְ לַלַּיְלָה[11]. וְשָׁעוֹת אֵלּוּ הֵמָּה שָׁעוֹת זְמַנִּיּוֹת, דְּהַיְינוּ לְפִי עֵרֶךְ הַיּוֹם מִזְּרִיחַת הַחַמָּה עַד שְׁקִיעָתָהּ[12] מִתְחַלֵּק הַיּוֹם לְי״ב חֲלָקִים. וְאִם הַיּוֹם גָּדוֹל י״ח שָׁעוֹת, אֲזַי שָׁעָה וּמֶחֱצָה נֶחְשֶׁבֶת לְשָׁעָה.

ג. אָסוּר לְהַתְחִיל לֶאֱכוֹל, אֲפִילוּ סְעוּדָּה קְטַנָּה[13], סָמוּךְ לְמִנְחָה קְטַנָּה, וְ״סָמוּךְ״ הַיְינוּ חֲצִי שָׁעָה קוֹדֶם. וְאִם אֵינוֹ קוֹבֵעַ עַצְמוֹ לִסְעוּדָּה, אֶלָּא שֶׁאוֹכֵל אוֹ שׁוֹתֶה דֶּרֶךְ

minchah,[9] כִּי מִשְּׁעַת מִנְחָה קְטַנָּה עַד הַלַּיְלָה הוּא שְׁתֵּי שָׁעוֹת וּמֶחֱצָה — **because from the onset of *minchah ketanah* until nightfall is two-and-one-half hours,** וְהַחֵצִי מִזֶּה הִיא שָׁעָה וּרְבִיעִית — **and half of that is one-and-one-quarter hours.** וּבְדִיעֲבַד — **However, after the fact,** i.e., if it is already past this time, אוֹ בִּשְׁעַת הַדְּחָק — **or in a time of pressing need,** יָכוֹל לְהִתְפַּלֵּל עַד צֵאת הַכּוֹכָבִים — **one may recite the *Minchah* Prayer until the appearance of** three **stars.**[10] וְכֵן נוֹהֲגִין עַתָּה בְּרוֹב הַקְּהִלּוֹת — **The current custom of most congregations follows this,** שֶׁמִּתְפַּלְּלִין מִנְחָה סָמוּךְ לַלַּיְלָה — **as they recite** the ***Minchah*** Prayer **close to nightfall.**[11]

וְשָׁעוֹת אֵלּוּ הֵמָּה שָׁעוֹת זְמַנִּיּוֹת — **The hours** mentioned here **are "seasonal hours,"** דְּהַיְינוּ — **that is,** לְפִי עֵרֶךְ הַיּוֹם — their length is **determined by the length of the day.** מִזְּרִיחַת הַחַמָּה עַד שְׁקִיעָתָהּ — This is calculated as follows: **From sunrise until sunset**[12] מִתְחַלֵּק הַיּוֹם לְי״ב חֲלָקִים — **the day is divided into twelve** equal **segments;** וְאִם הַיּוֹם גָּדוֹל י״ח שָׁעוֹת — **thus, if the day lasts for eighteen** standard **hours,** אֲזַי שָׁעָה וּמֶחֱצָה נֶחְשֶׁבֶת לְשָׁעָה — **then** each **seasonal hour would be one-and-a-half** standard **hours.**

§3 Once the time for *Minchah* has arrived, it is prohibited, before reciting the Prayer, to begin any activity that may extend until the time of the *Minchah* Prayer passes:

אָסוּר לְהַתְחִיל לֶאֱכוֹל, אֲפִילוּ סְעוּדָּה קְטַנָּה — **It is forbidden** for one **to begin eating even a small meal**[13] סָמוּךְ לְמִנְחָה קְטַנָּה — from **close to the time of *minchah ketanah*** until he has recited the *Minchah* prayer. וְ״סָמוּךְ״ הַיְינוּ חֲצִי שָׁעָה קוֹדֶם — The term **"close to" means half an hour before.** וְאִם אֵינוֹ קוֹבֵעַ עַצְמוֹ לִסְעוּדָּה — **If he does not** eat **a proper meal,** אֶלָּא שֶׁאוֹכֵל אוֹ שׁוֹתֶה דֶּרֶךְ אַרְעַי — **but**

9. There is no indication in *Shulchan Aruch* or *Mishnah Berurah* that one should recite *Minchah* before *plag haminchah*. However, one who recites *Maariv* between *plag haminchah* and nightfall (see below, 70:1) should not recite *Minchah* after *plag haminchah* (see *Shulchan Aruch* and *Rama* 233:1 and *Mishnah Berurah* there). For further discussion, see below, 76:1.

10. *Tzeis hakochavim;* this refers to three medium-sized stars. See below, 70:1, with note 5; see also Appendix B.

11. *Mishnah Berurah* (233:14) cites many authorities who rule that once the sun disappears below the horizon, *Minchah* may no longer be recited. *Mishnah Berurah* rules that in cases of pressing need, one may recite *Minchah* up to 15 minutes before nightfall (*tzeis hakochavim*). However, one should rather pray before sundown alone than after sundown with the congregation (ibid.).

12. This is the opinion of *Gra* in calculating the beginning and end of the day. See, however, above, 17:1, and below, 139:10, where Kitzur follows the opinion of the *Magen Avraham*, in which the day begins at daybreak and ends at nightfall (see further in Appendix B regarding the calculation of these hours and the halachic definitions for these times). See also *Misgeres HaShulchan* to this *se'if.*

13. Even a Shabbos or Yom Tov meal is considered only a "small meal" (*Mishnah Berurah* 232:24); a "large meal" is described below.

אַרְעַי פֵּירוֹת אוֹ תַבְשִׁיל, אֲפִילוּ מֵחֲמֵשֶׁת מִינֵי דָגָן, יֵשׁ מַתִּירִין, אֲבָל יֵשׁ לְהַחֲמִיר גַּם בָּזֶה[14]**. וְכֵן אָסוּר לִיכָּנֵס לְמֶרְחָץ, אוֹ לְהִסְתַּפֵּר, סָמוּךְ לְמִנְחָה קְטַנָּה. וּסְעוּדָה גְדוֹלָה, כְּגוֹן סְעוּדַת נִישּׂוּאִין אוֹ בְּרִית מִילָה וְכַדּוֹמֶה, אָסוּר לְהַתְחִיל, אֲפִילוּ סָמוּךְ לְמִנְחָה גְדוֹלָה, דְּהַיְינוּ מֵחֲצוֹת הַיּוֹם אָסוּר, אֶלָּא יַמְתִּינוּ עַד זְמַן מִנְחָה גְדוֹלָה וְיִתְפַּלְּלוּ קוֹדֶם הַסְּעוּדָה. וּבְמָקוֹם שֶׁקּוֹרִין לְבֵית הַכְּנֶסֶת, וְהוּא רָגִיל לֵילֵךְ לְבֵית הַכְּנֶסֶת לְהִתְפַּלֵּל בְּצִיבּוּר, מוּתָּר לְהַתְחִיל סְעוּדָה קְטַנָּה סָמוּךְ לְמִנְחָה קְטַנָּה, וְגַם אַחַר כָּךְ, וּבִלְבַד שֶׁמִּיָּד שֶׁקּוֹרִין לְבֵית הַכְּנֶסֶת יַפְסִיק מִמַּה שֶׁהוּא עוֹסֵק לְהִתְפַּלֵּל. וּסְעוּדָה גְדוֹלָה סָמוּךְ לְמִנְחָה קְטַנָּה אָסוּר לְהַתְחִיל, אֲפִילוּ בְּמָקוֹם שֶׁקּוֹרִין לְבֵית הַכְּנֶסֶת, וַאֲפִילוּ סָמוּךְ לְמִנְחָה גְדוֹלָה יֵשׁ לְהַחֲמִיר.**

---

rather eats or drinks in an informal manner (as a snack) **פֵּירוֹת אוֹ תַבְשִׁיל, אֲפִילוּ מֵחֲמֵשֶׁת מִינֵי דָגָן** — **fruit or a cooked dish, even if it contains** one **of the five grains,** **יֵשׁ מַתִּירִין** — **some** authorities **permit** this to be eaten during that time. **אֲבָל יֵשׁ לְהַחֲמִיר גַּם בָּזֶה** — **However, one should be stringent in this** regard **as well.**[14]

וְכֵן אָסוּר לִיכָּנֵס לְמֶרְחָץ — **Likewise, it is forbidden to enter the bathhouse** to bathe **אוֹ לְהִסְתַּפֵּר** — **or to take a haircut** **סָמוּךְ לְמִנְחָה קְטַנָּה** — **close to the** time of ***minchah ketanah.***

וּסְעוּדָה גְדוֹלָה — With regard to **a "large meal,"** **כְּגוֹן סְעוּדַת נִישּׂוּאִין אוֹ בְּרִית מִילָה וְכַדּוֹמֶה** — **such as a wedding or circumcision feast or similar** occasion, **אָסוּר לְהַתְחִיל, אֲפִילוּ סָמוּךְ לְמִנְחָה גְדוֹלָה** — **it is forbidden to begin** it **even close to *minchah gedolah;*** **דְּהַיְינוּ מֵחֲצוֹת הַיּוֹם אָסוּר** — **i.e., it is forbidden from midday.** **אֶלָּא יַמְתִּינוּ עַד זְמַן מִנְחָה גְדוֹלָה** — **Rather, they should wait until the time of *minchah gedolah,*** **וְיִתְפַּלְּלוּ קוֹדֶם הַסְּעוּדָה** — **and** then **pray before the meal.** **וּבְמָקוֹם שֶׁקּוֹרִין לְבֵית הַכְּנֶסֶת** — **In a place where they call** the congregants **to the synagogue** for prayers, **וְהוּא רָגִיל לֵילֵךְ לְבֵית הַכְּנֶסֶת לְהִתְפַּלֵּל בְּצִיבּוּר** — **and one is accustomed to go to the synagogue to pray with the congregation,** **מוּתָּר לְהַתְחִיל סְעוּדָה קְטַנָּה** — that person **may begin a "small meal"** **סָמוּךְ לְמִנְחָה קְטַנָּה** — **close to the** time of ***minchah ketanah,*** **וְגַם אַחַר כָּךְ** — **and even after this** time has arrived, **וּבִלְבַד שֶׁמִּיָּד שֶׁקּוֹרִין לְבֵית הַכְּנֶסֶת** — **provided that immediately upon being called to the synagogue** **יַפְסִיק מִמַּה שֶׁהוּא עוֹסֵק לְהִתְפַּלֵּל** — **he interrupts his activities to** go to **pray.** **וּסְעוּדָה גְדוֹלָה סָמוּךְ לְמִנְחָה קְטַנָּה אָסוּר לְהַתְחִיל** — **However, it is forbidden to begin a large meal close to** the time of ***minchah ketanah*** **אֲפִילוּ בְּמָקוֹם שֶׁקּוֹרִין לְבֵית הַכְּנֶסֶת** — **even in a place where they call** the congregants **to the synagogue** to pray. **וַאֲפִילוּ סָמוּךְ לְמִנְחָה גְדוֹלָה יֵשׁ לְהַחֲמִיר** — Additionally, **one should be stringent** and avoid beginning a "large meal" **even close to** the time of ***minchah gedolah.***

---

14. According to *Mishnah Berurah* (232:34, 35), one may eat as much fruit as he desires, but food containing one of the five grains may be eaten only casually (as a snack), not as a meal. One should not drink more than the volume of an egg (two-thirds of a *revi'is*; see Appendix A) of intoxicating beverages, since that could prevent him from praying. However, other drinks may be consumed even in large amounts. One may eat as much as an egg-sized portion of bread in a casual manner (*Shulchan Aruch* 232:3).

ד. לִתְפִלַּת מִנְחָה צְרִיכִין גַּם כֵּן נְטִילַת יָדַיִם עַד הַפֶּרֶק, כְּמוֹ לִתְפִלַּת שַׁחֲרִית[15], וְכִמְבוֹאָר לְעֵיל בְּסִימָן י״ב (ו)סְעִיף ה׳ וּסְעִיף ו׳ (וְעַיֵּין חַיֵּי אָדָם כְּלָל ל״ג סְעִיף ו׳ וּבְשֻׁלְחָן עָרוּךְ שֶׁל הַתַּנְיָא סִימָן צ״ב בְּמַרְאֵה מָקוֹם אוֹת כ״ג)[16]. וְכֵן לִתְפִלַּת מַעֲרִיב, אִם הִפְסִיק בֵּין מִנְחָה[17]. וְכֵן לְמוּסָף, אִם הִפְסִיק בֵּין שַׁחֲרִית, צָרִיךְ לִיטּוֹל יָדָיו[18].

ה. אֵין[19] לוֹמַר "אַשְׁרֵי" שֶׁקּוֹדֶם מִנְחָה עַד שֶׁיְּהֵא מִנְיָן בְּבֵית הַכְּנֶסֶת, כְּדֵי שֶׁהַשְּׁלִיחַ צִבּוּר יֹאמַר הַקַּדִּישׁ עַל מַה שֶּׁאָמְרוּ בַּעֲשָׂרָה[20]. וְאִם אָמְרוּ "אַשְׁרֵי" בְּלֹא מִנְיָן, וְאַחַר כָּךְ נִשְׁלַם הַמִּנְיָן, יֹאמְרוּ אֵיזֶה מִזְמוֹר וְאַחַר כָּךְ יֹאמַר הַשְּׁלִיחַ צִבּוּר קַדִּישׁ. וְיֵשׁ לְהַשְּׁלִיחַ צִבּוּר לְהִתְעַטֵּף בְּטַלִּית קוֹדֶם "אַשְׁרֵי", שֶׁלֹּא לְהַפְסִיק בֵּין

---

§4 לִתְפִלַּת מִנְחָה צְרִיכִין גַּם כֵּן נְטִילַת יָדַיִם עַד הַפֶּרֶק — **For the** ***Minchah*** **Prayer, one is also required to wash his hands until the wrist,** כְּמוֹ לִתְפִלַּת שַׁחֲרִית — **just as it is** required **for the** ***Shacharis*** (Morning) **Prayer,**[15] וְכִמְבוֹאָר לְעֵיל בְּסִימָן י״ב (ו)סְעִיף ה׳ וּסְעִיף ו׳ — **as set out above, 12:5-6.** (וְעַיֵּין חַיֵּי אָדָם כְּלָל ל״ג סְעִיף ו׳ — **See** ***Chayei Adam*** **33:6** וּבְשֻׁלְחָן עָרוּךְ שֶׁל הַתַּנְיָא סִימָן צ״ב בְּמַרְאֵה מָקוֹם אוֹת כ״ג — **and the** ***Shulchan Aruch*** **of the** ***Tanya, Siman*** **92, note 23.)**[16] וְכֵן לִתְפִלַּת מַעֲרִיב — **Likewise,** one should wash his hands **for the** ***Maariv*** (Evening) **Prayer** אִם הִפְסִיק בֵּין מִנְחָה — **if there was an interruption between** ***Minchah*** **and** *Maariv.*[17] וְכֵן לְמוּסָף — **The same** halachah applies **to the** ***Mussaf*** Prayer: אִם הִפְסִיק בֵּין שַׁחֲרִית — **If there was an interruption between** ***Shacharis*** **and** *Mussaf,* צָרִיךְ לִיטּוֹל יָדָיו — **one must wash his hands.**[18]

§5 The *Minchah* Prayer begins with the recitation of *Ashrei*[19] by the congregation, followed by the *chazzan's* recitation of *Kaddish*, and then the congregational recitation of *Shemoneh Esrei*. Afterward, the *chazzan* repeats the *Shemoneh Esrei* aloud.

אֵין לוֹמַר "אַשְׁרֵי" שֶׁקּוֹדֶם מִנְחָה — **The** congregation **should not recite** ***Ashrei*** **that precedes the** ***Minchah*** *Shemoneh Esrei* עַד שֶׁיְּהֵא מִנְיָן בְּבֵית הַכְּנֶסֶת — **until there is a** ***minyan*** (quorum) of ten men **in the synagogue,** כְּדֵי שֶׁהַשְּׁלִיחַ צִבּוּר יֹאמַר הַקַּדִּישׁ עַל מַה שֶּׁאָמְרוּ בַּעֲשָׂרָה — **so that the** ***chazzan*** **can recite** the ***Kaddish*** before *Shemoneh Esrei* **on** the verses **that were said by ten** men.[20] וְאִם אָמְרוּ "אַשְׁרֵי" בְּלֹא מִנְיָן — **If they did recite** ***Ashrei*** **without a** ***minyan,*** וְאַחַר כָּךְ נִשְׁלַם הַמִּנְיָן — **and the** ***minyan*** **was subsequently completed,** יֹאמְרוּ אֵיזֶה מִזְמוֹר — **they should** then **recite a psalm,** וְאַחַר כָּךְ יֹאמַר הַשְּׁלִיחַ צִבּוּר קַדִּישׁ — **and then the** ***chazzan*** **should recite** ***Kaddish.***

וְיֵשׁ לְהַשְּׁלִיחַ צִבּוּר לְהִתְעַטֵּף בְּטַלִּית קוֹדֶם "אַשְׁרֵי" — **The** ***chazzan*** **should wrap himself in a** ***tallis*** **before** the recitation of ***Ashrei*** (rather than afterward) שֶׁלֹּא לְהַפְסִיק בֵּין

---

15. No blessing is recited when washing the hands for *Minchah* (*Mishnah Berurah* 233:17).

16. These two sources discuss the difference between the obligation of washing the hands when they are known to be unclean, and when they are not know to be unclean.

17. When he recites *Maariv* immediately following *Minchah*, he need not wash his hands again.

18. Even when *Mussaf* does not immediately follow *Shacharis*, as long as one did not leave the synagogue, it is assumed that he did not divert his attention from the cleanliness of his hands, and he need not wash his hands before reciting *Mussaf* (*Mishnah Berurah* 233:18).

19. *Tehillim,* Ch. 145, preceded by verses 84:5 and 144:15 of *Tehillim.*

20. See above, 15:1.

״אַשְׁרֵי״ לְקַדִּישׁ. וְאִם לֹא הָיָה טַלִּית עַד לְאַחַר שֶׁאָמַר ״אַשְׁרֵי״, יִתְעַטֵּף וְיֹאמַר אֵיזֶה פְּסוּקִים שֶׁעֲלֵיהֶם יֹאמַר קַדִּישׁ.

ו. אִם הַשָּׁעָה דְחוּקָה וְקָרוֹב לְלַיְלָה, מַתְחִיל הַשְּׁלִיחַ צִבּוּר מִיָּד אַחַר קַדִּישׁ הַשְּׁמוֹנֶה עֶשְׂרֵה בְּקוֹל רָם[21], וְהַצִּבּוּר לֹא יִתְפַּלְּלוּ, אֶלָּא שׁוֹמְעִים וְעוֹנִים[22] עַד שֶׁאָמַר ״הָאֵל הַקָּדוֹשׁ״, אָז עוֹנִים ״אָמֵן״ וּמִתְפַּלְּלִים בְּלַחַשׁ[23]. וְאִם הַשָּׁעָה דְחוּקָה בְּיוֹתֵר וְיֵשׁ לָחוּשׁ שֶׁאִם יַמְתִּינוּ עַל הַשְּׁלִיחַ צִבּוּר עַד לְאַחַר שֶׁיֹּאמַר ״הָאֵל הַקָּדוֹשׁ״ לֹא יְסַיְּמוּ תְּפִלָּתָם בְּעוֹד יוֹם[24], יְכוֹלִין לְהִתְפַּלֵּל מִיָּד עִם הַשְּׁלִיחַ צִבּוּר בְּלַחַשׁ מִלָּה בְּמִלָּה עַד ״הָאֵל הַקָּדוֹשׁ״[25]. וְטוֹב אִם אֶפְשָׁר שֶׁיְּהֵא לְכָל הַפָּחוֹת אֶחָד שֶׁיַּעֲנֶה עַל בִּרְכוֹת הַשְּׁלִיחַ צִבּוּר ״אָמֵן״.

״אַשְׁרֵי״ לְקַדִּישׁ — so that he does not have to interrupt between *Ashrei* and *Kaddish* by donning the *tallis* then. **וְאִם לֹא הָיָה טַלִּית עַד לְאַחַר שֶׁאָמַר ״אַשְׁרֵי״** — If **there was no *tallis*** available **until after he had recited *Ashrei,*** **יִתְעַטֵּף וְיֹאמַר אֵיזֶה פְּסוּקִים** — then, upon obtaining the *tallis,* **he should wrap himself** in it **and recite a** few Torah **verses** **שֶׁעֲלֵיהֶם יֹאמַר קַדִּישׁ** — **upon which he can** then **recite *Kaddish.***

§6 **אִם הַשָּׁעָה דְחוּקָה וְקָרוֹב לְלַיְלָה** — **If time is pressing and it is close to nightfall,** **מַתְחִיל הַשְּׁלִיחַ צִבּוּר מִיָּד אַחַר קַדִּישׁ** — **the *chazzan* should begin, immediately** after the ***Kaddish*** following *Ashrei,* **הַשְּׁמוֹנֶה עֶשְׂרֵה בְּקוֹל רָם** — to recite **the *Shemoneh Esrei* aloud.**[21] **וְהַצִּבּוּר לֹא יִתְפַּלְּלוּ** — **The congregation should not recite** the *Shemoneh Esrei* **Prayer** at that point, **אֶלָּא שׁוֹמְעִים וְעוֹנִים עַד שֶׁאָמַר ״הָאֵל הַקָּדוֹשׁ״** — **rather, they should listen and respond** appropriately[22] **until after the recitation of** the third blessing, *HaKeil HaKadosh, **the Holy God;*** **אָז עוֹנִים ״אָמֵן״ וּמִתְפַּלְּלִים בְּלַחַשׁ** — **they then respond** to that blessing **with Amen and pray** the *Shemoneh Esrei* **silently.**[23] **וְאִם הַשָּׁעָה דְחוּקָה בְּיוֹתֵר** — **If time is extremely pressing** **וְיֵשׁ לָחוּשׁ** — **and there is** reason to be **concerned** **שֶׁאִם יַמְתִּינוּ עַל הַשְּׁלִיחַ צִבּוּר** — **that if** the congregation **waits for the *chazzan*** **עַד לְאַחַר שֶׁיֹּאמַר ״הָאֵל הַקָּדוֹשׁ״** — **until after he recites** the blessing of ***HaKeil HaKadosh*** aloud, as above, **לֹא יְסַיְּמוּ תְּפִלָּתָם בְּעוֹד יוֹם** — **they will not** be able to **complete their prayers while it is still day,**[24] **יְכוֹלִין לְהִתְפַּלֵּל מִיָּד עִם הַשְּׁלִיחַ צִבּוּר בְּלַחַשׁ** — **they may immediately begin praying quietly, together with the *chazzan,*** **מִלָּה בְּמִלָּה עַד ״הָאֵל הַקָּדוֹשׁ״** — reciting with him **word by word, until** the blessing of ***HaKeil HaKadosh.***[25] **וְטוֹב אִם אֶפְשָׁר שֶׁיְּהֵא לְכָל הַפָּחוֹת אֶחָד** — **It is proper, if possible, that there be at least one** person who is not praying at that time, **שֶׁיַּעֲנֶה עַל בִּרְכוֹת הַשְּׁלִיחַ צִבּוּר ״אָמֵן״** — so that **he can respond to the blessings** recited **by the *chazzan*** with **Amen.**

---

21. I.e., instead of the congregation reciting *Shemoneh Esrei* first, followed by the *chazzan's* repetition, the *chazzan* begins by reciting the first part of *Shemoneh Esrei* aloud.

22. I.e., responding with Amen to each blessing and responding appropriately to the *Kedushah.*

23. I.e., from the beginning of *Shemoneh Esrei.* The *chazzan,* however, continues his recitation silently, continuing from the fourth blessing.

24. Kitzur indicates that the entire *Shemoneh Esrei* should be completed before nightfall; see also *Mishnah Berurah* 124:7 and 233:14.

25. This includes the recitation of *Kedushah,* and *Ledor Vador*; see following *se'if* (*Mishnah Berurah* 124:9). Afterward they should all continue reciting the *Shemoneh Esrei* silently. In all cases, the *Shemoneh Esrei* is followed by *Tachanun* (unless night has already fallen; see *se'if* 8) and *Kaddish Tiskabeil.*

ז. מִי שֶׁבָּא לְבֵית הַכְּנֶסֶת וּמָצָא צִבּוּר מִתְפַּלְלִין שְׁמוֹנֶה עֶשְׂרֵה, מִתְפַּלֵּל עִמָּהֶם שְׁמוֹנֶה עֶשְׂרֵה, וְיֹאמַר "אַשְׁרֵי" לְאַחַר הַשְּׁמוֹנֶה עֶשְׂרֵה[26]. וְאִם לֹא יוּכַל לִגְמוֹר שְׁמוֹנֶה עֶשְׂרֵה קוֹדֶם שֶׁיָּבֹא הַשְּׁלִיחַ צִבּוּר לִקְדוּשָּׁה, וְאִם יַמְתִּין עַד לְאַחַר שֶׁיִּגְמוֹר הַשְּׁלִיחַ צִבּוּר כָּל הַשְּׁמוֹנֶה עֶשְׂרֵה עִם הַקַּדִּישׁ יַעֲבוֹר זְמַן תְּפִלָּה[27], יַמְתִּין וְיִתְפַּלֵּל בְּלַחַשׁ עִם הַשְּׁלִיחַ צִבּוּר בַּחֲזָרַת הַתְּפִלָּה, מִלָּה בְּמִלָּה. וְיֹאמַר עִמּוֹ כָּל נוּסַח הַקְּדוּשָּׁה[28], וְגַם "לְדוֹר וָדוֹר" וְכוּ' כְּמוֹ שֶׁהוּא אוֹמֵר[29], וִיסַיֵּים עִמּוֹ בְּשָׁוֶה בִּרְכַּת "הָאֵל הַקָּדוֹשׁ" וּבִרְכַּת "שׁוֹמֵעַ תְּפִלָּה"[30], וְגַם "מוֹדִים" יֹאמַר בְּשָׁוֶה כְּדֵי שֶׁיִּשְׁחֶה עִם הַצִּבּוּר[31].

§7 **מִי שֶׁבָּא לְבֵית הַכְּנֶסֶת** — **If one who** has not yet recited *Minchah* **arrives at the synagogue** **וּמָצָא צִבּוּר מִתְפַּלְלִין שְׁמוֹנֶה עֶשְׂרֵה** — **and finds the congregation reciting the *Shemoneh Esrei*** of *Minchah,* **מִתְפַּלֵּל עִמָּהֶם שְׁמוֹנֶה עֶשְׂרֵה** — **he should recite the *Shemoneh Esrei* Prayer together with them** **וְיֹאמַר "אַשְׁרֵי" לְאַחַר הַשְּׁמוֹנֶה עֶשְׂרֵה** — **and** then **recite *Ashrei* after *Shemoneh Esrei*.**[26] **וְאִם לֹא יוּכַל לִגְמוֹר שְׁמוֹנֶה עֶשְׂרֵה** — However, **if** he sees that **he will not be able to complete the** silent ***Shemoneh Esrei*** **קוֹדֶם שֶׁיָּבֹא הַשְּׁלִיחַ צִבּוּר לִקְדוּשָּׁה** — **before the *chazzan* reaches *Kedushah,*** **וְאִם יַמְתִּין עַד לְאַחַר שֶׁיִּגְמוֹר הַשְּׁלִיחַ צִבּוּר** — **and if he would wait** to begin his silent *Shemoneh Esrei* **until the *chazzan* completes** **כָּל הַשְּׁמוֹנֶה עֶשְׂרֵה עִם הַקַּדִּישׁ** — **the entire** repetition of the ***Shemoneh Esrei* and the *Kaddish*** that follows it **יַעֲבוֹר זְמַן תְּפִלָּה** — **the time for the** *Minchah* **Prayer would pass,** [27] **יַמְתִּין** — **he should wait** until the congregation completes their silent prayers **וְיִתְפַּלֵּל בְּלַחַשׁ עִם הַשְּׁלִיחַ צִבּוּר בַּחֲזָרַת הַתְּפִלָּה** — **and** then **pray quietly together with the *chazzan* with his repetition of the *Shemoneh Esrei*** **Prayer,** **מִלָּה בְּמִלָּה** — reciting with him **word by word.** **וְיֹאמַר עִמּוֹ כָּל נוּסַח הַקְּדוּשָּׁה** — When reciting the *Shemoneh Esrei* with the *chazzan,* **he should recite the entire text of *Kedushah* together with him,**[28] **וְגַם "לְדוֹר וָדוֹר" וְכוּ'** — **as well as** the passage of *Ledor Vador,* ***From generation to generation,*** **etc.** **כְּמוֹ שֶׁהוּא אוֹמֵר** — **just as** the *chazzan* **says it.**[29] **וִיסַיֵּים עִמּוֹ בְּשָׁוֶה בִּרְכַּת "הָאֵל הַקָּדוֹשׁ" וּבִרְכַּת "שׁוֹמֵעַ תְּפִלָּה"** — **He should** take care **to complete the blessing of *HaKeil HaKadosh* and the blessing of** *Shomei'a Tefillah,* ***Who hears prayer*****, with** the *chazzan,* **in unison.**[30] **וְגַם "מוֹדִים" יֹאמַר בְּשָׁוֶה** — **He should also recite** *Modim,* ***We gratefully thank You*****, together with** the *chazzan,* **כְּדֵי שֶׁיִּשְׁחֶה עִם הַצִּבּוּר** — **so that he will bow together with the congregation.**[31]

---

26. *Magen Avraham* (108:5) cites *Zohar,* which states that one should not recite *Ashrei* after *Minchah* with the intention of fulfilling his obligation, but as one who reads any portion of the Torah (see *Mishnah Berurah* 108:14).

27. See *Mishnah Berurah* (109:14), which states that the following halachah applies not only when he would otherwise miss the time of *Minchah,* but also for any other valid need.

28. Including the introductory portions, *nekadeish* (or *nakdishach*), *le'umasam,* and *u'vedivrei*; see *Beur Halachah* 109:2 s.v. אבל.

29. In *Nusach Ashkenaz,* the *chazzan* recites this passage in his repetition instead of the standard opening of *Atah Kadosh.* When an individual is praying together with the *chazzan* in the manner described above, he should recite the *chazzan's* version.

30. See above, 20:11, which states that the Amen responses to these two blessings are obligatory. By completing the blessing at the same time as the *chazzan,* he does not need to respond, just as the *chazzan* himself recites the blessing and does not respond (*Mishnah Berurah* 109:12).

31. When the *chazzan* bows and recites *Modim,* each member of the congregation also bows and recites *Modim D'Rabbanan, "the Rabbis' Modim"* (see above, 20:5). It is inappropriate for one to be present and not bow

רַק בְּיוֹם תַּעֲנִית צִבּוּר לֹא יֹאמַר עִם הַשְּׁלִיחַ צִבּוּר "עֲנֵנוּ", אֶלָּא אוֹמְרוֹ בְּ"שׁוֹמֵעַ תְּפִלָּה", כְּמוֹ שְׁאָר יָחִיד[32]. וְכֵן[33] אִם רוֹצֶה לְהִתְפַּלֵּל מַעֲרִיב עִם הַצִּבּוּר, וְאִם יַמְתִּין עַד אַחַר חֲזָרַת הַשְּׁלִיחַ צִבּוּר אֶת הַתְּפִלָּה יִצְטָרֵךְ לְהִתְפַּלֵּל עַרְבִית בִּיחִידוּת, יִתְפַּלֵּל מִנְחָה עִם חֲזָרַת הַשְּׁלִיחַ צִבּוּר. וְאִם בָּא סָמוּךְ לִקְדוּשָּׁה, יַמְתִּין עַד לְאַחַר שֶׁיֹּאמַר הַשְּׁלִיחַ צִבּוּר "הָאֵל הַקָּדוֹשׁ", וְיַעֲנֶה "אָמֵן", וְאָז יִתְפַּלֵּל. וְאַף שֶׁיַּפְסִיד עֲנִיַּית אָמֵן שֶׁלְּאַחַר "שׁוֹמֵעַ תְּפִלָּה", וְגַם "מוֹדִים" (שֶׁהֵם חִיּוּבִים), מִכָּל מָקוֹם הָכִי עָדִיף טְפֵי מִלְּהַפְסִיד תְּפִלַּת עַרְבִית עִם הַצִּבּוּר[34], וּמִכָּל שֶׁכֵּן אִם הַשָּׁעָה עוֹבֶרֶת מִזְּמַן מִנְחָה

רַק בְּיוֹם תַּעֲנִית צִבּוּר — However, on a public fast day, לֹא יֹאמַר עִם הַשְּׁלִיחַ צִבּוּר "עֲנֵנוּ" — he should not recite *Aneinu, **Answer us,*** **with the** ***chazzan;*** **אֶלָּא אוֹמְרוֹ בְּ"שׁוֹמֵעַ תְּפִלָּה" — rather, he should recite it in** the blessing of ***Shomei'a Tefillah,*** **כְּמוֹ שְׁאָר יָחִיד — as** in the *Shemoneh Esrei* of **any other individual.**[32]

In many congregations, *Minchah* is followed immediately by *Maariv.*[33] Here, *Kitzur* guides a latecomer when he is faced with the choice of missing the opportunity to respond to an important part of either prayer:

וְכֵן אִם רוֹצֶה לְהִתְפַּלֵּל מַעֲרִיב עִם הַצִּבּוּר — Likewise, if one arrives at the synagogue after the congregation has started *Minchah,* and **he wishes to pray** ***Maariv*** **with the congregation, וְאִם יַמְתִּין עַד אַחַר חֲזָרַת הַשְּׁלִיחַ צִבּוּר אֶת הַתְּפִלָּה — and if he waits** to begin *Minchah* **until the** ***chazzan*** **completes the repetition** of the ***Shemoneh Esrei*** **Prayer** **יִצְטָרֵךְ לְהִתְפַּלֵּל עַרְבִית בִּיחִידוּת — he will have to pray** ***Maariv*** **alone,** i.e., without a *minyan,* **יִתְפַּלֵּל מִנְחָה עִם חֲזָרַת הַשְּׁלִיחַ צִבּוּר — he should pray** the ***Minchah*** *Shemoneh Esrei* **together with the** ***chazzan's*** **repetition,** as above.

וְאִם בָּא סָמוּךְ לִקְדוּשָּׁה — If one arrives close to ***Kedushah,*** **יַמְתִּין עַד לְאַחַר שֶׁיֹּאמַר הַשְּׁלִיחַ צִבּוּר "הָאֵל הַקָּדוֹשׁ" — he should wait until the** ***chazzan*** **completes** the blessing of ***HaKeil HaKadosh*** following *Kedushah.* **וְיַעֲנֶה "אָמֵן" —** At that point, **he should respond** with **Amen** to the blessing, **וְאָז יִתְפַּלֵּל — and recite the** *Minchah* **Prayer. וְאַף שֶׁיַּפְסִיד עֲנִיַּית אָמֵן — Even though he will lose** the opportunity to **respond** with **Amen שֶׁלְּאַחַר "שׁוֹמֵעַ תְּפִלָּה" — after** the blessing of ***Shomei'a Tefillah,*** **וְגַם "מוֹדִים" — as well as** the opportunity to recite ***Modim*** with the congregation **(שֶׁהֵם חִיּוּבִים — which are obligatory), מִכָּל מָקוֹם הָכִי עָדִיף טְפֵי — this is nevertheless better מִלְּהַפְסִיד תְּפִלַּת עַרְבִית עִם הַצִּבּוּר — than losing** the opportunity of reciting the ***Maariv*** **Prayer with the congregation.**[34] **וּמִכָּל שֶׁכֵּן אִם הַשָּׁעָה עוֹבֶרֶת מִזְּמַן מִנְחָה — Certainly, if the time for** ***Minchah*** **is about to pass,** one should recite

---

at this juncture, even if he is in the middle of his prayers. (See above, 20:5, regarding one who is holding at another point in his recitation of *Shemoneh Esrei* when the *chazzan* reaches *Modim.*)

32. On a fast day, the *chazzan* recites *Aneinu* as a separate blessing between the seventh and eight blessings of *Shemoneh Esrei* (i.e., between גּוֹאֵל יִשְׂרָאֵל, *Redeemer of Israel,* and רְפָאֵנוּ, *Heal us*). An individual recites it as part of the blessing of *Shomei'a Tefillah*; see above, 19:14 and 20:8.

33. See below, 70:1.

34. However, the response of *Yehei Shemei Rabba* takes precedence over praying with the congregation. Therefore, if by reciting *Shemoneh Esrei* at that time, he will miss the response of *Yehei Shemei Rabba* to the *Kaddish* following *Shemoneh Esrei*, he should rather wait until after *Kaddish*, and then recite *Shemoneh Esrei*, even though he will then lose the chance to recite *Maariv* with the congregation (*Mishnah Berurah* 109:4).

(וְעַיֵּין לְעֵיל סִימָן כ׳ סְעִיף י״א)[35].

ח. אִם[36] נִמְשְׁכָה תְּפִלַּת הַמִּנְחָה עַד הַלַּיְלָה, לֹא יֹאמְרוּ תַּחֲנוּן, כִּי אֵין אוֹמְרִים תַּחֲנוּן בְּלַיְלָה. וּצְרִיכִין לִיזָּהֵר וּלְהַשְׁגִּיחַ שֶׁלֹּא תִּמָּשֵׁךְ עַד הַלַּיְלָה מַמָּשׁ, כִּי אָז אֵין אוֹמְרִים קַדִּישׁ תִּתְקַבֵּל עַל הַתְּפִלָּה שֶׁהִתְפַּלְּלוּ בַּיּוֹם, כֵּיוָן שֶׁהַלַּיְלָה שַׁיָּיכָה לְיוֹם מָחֳרָת[37].

ט. מִי שֶׁבָּא בְּעֶרֶב שַׁבָּת לְמִנְחָה בְּבֵית הַכְּנֶסֶת וְהַקָּהָל כְּבָר קִבְּלוּ שַׁבָּת, אוֹ יוֹם טוֹב, דְּהַיְינוּ בְּשַׁבָּת אָמְרוּ "מִזְמוֹר שִׁיר לְיוֹם הַשַּׁבָּת" (תהלים צב), וּבְיוֹם טוֹב אָמְרוּ

Shemoneh Esrei together with the *chazzan's* repetition (וְעַיֵּין לְעֵיל סִימָן כ׳ סְעִיף **י״א — see above, 20:11).**[35]

§8 After the *chazzan's* repetition of *Shemoneh Esrei, Tachanun* is recited,[36] followed by the *chazzan's* recitation of *Kaddish Tiskabeil.* This *Kaddish* contains a plea that our *Shemoneh Esrei* prayer be accepted, beginning with the words תִּתְקַבֵּל צְלוֹתְהוֹן, *May our prayers be accepted.* After this *Kaddish,* the congregation recites *Aleinu.* The *Minchah* service is completed by the recitation of the mourner's *Kaddish.*

אִם נִמְשְׁכָה תְּפִלַּת הַמִּנְחָה עַד הַלַּיְלָה — If the *Minchah* Prayer extended until nightfall, לֹא יֹאמְרוּ תַּחֲנוּן — *Tachanun* should not be recited, כִּי אֵין אוֹמְרִים תַּחֲנוּן בְּלַיְלָה — because *Tachanun* is not recited at night. וּצְרִיכִין לִיזָּהֵר וּלְהַשְׁגִּיחַ — It is necessary to be vigilant and take care שֶׁלֹּא תִּמָּשֵׁךְ עַד הַלַּיְלָה מַמָּשׁ — that the service **not extend into the night itself, כִּי אָז אֵין אוֹמְרִים קַדִּישׁ תִּתְקַבֵּל — because then,** after nightfall, **the *Kaddish Tiskabeil* cannot be recited עַל הַתְּפִלָּה שֶׁהִתְפַּלְּלוּ בַּיּוֹם — for** the *Minchah Shemoneh Esrei* **Prayer that was recited during the day, כֵּיוָן שֶׁהַלַּיְלָה שַׁיָּיכָה לְיוֹם מָחֳרָת — because** in Jewish law **the night is** considered to be **part of the following day.**[37]

§9 Although Shabbos begins with sundown on Friday,[38] it may be ushered in earlier in the day by the congregation or by an individual (see below, 76:1, for the particulars). After the congregation ushers in the holy day, a latecomer who has not yet recited *Minchah* must take the following precautions:

מִי שֶׁבָּא בְּעֶרֶב שַׁבָּת לְמִנְחָה בְּבֵית הַכְּנֶסֶת — One who arrives at the synagogue on Friday afternoon **for the *Minchah*** Prayer **וְהַקָּהָל כְּבָר קִבְּלוּ שַׁבָּת, אוֹ יוֹם טוֹב — and the congregation has already ushered in the Shabbos or the festival, דְּהַיְינוּ — that is, בְּשַׁבָּת אָמְרוּ "מִזְמוֹר שִׁיר לְיוֹם הַשַּׁבָּת" — in the case of** ushering in **Shabbos they recited** (*Tehillim* Ch. 92) *Mizmor shir l'yom haShabbos,* ***A psalm, a song for the Shabbos day,*** **וּבְיוֹם טוֹב אָמְרוּ "בָּרְכוּ" — and in the case of**

---

35. There, Kitzur sets out the obligation to respond to *Kedushah, Modim,* and the blessings of *HaKeil HaKadosh* and *Shomei'a Tefillah,* and discusses how one should proceed if he comes late to the *Shacharis* Prayer.

36. For a complete discussion of the laws of *Tachanun,* see *Siman* 22.

37. That is, if the *Shemoneh Esrei* was recited by day, the *Kaddish Tiskabeil* cannot be recited for that *Shemoneh Esrei,* since with nightfall it is already considered the next day, and the supplication cannot be recited for a prayer recited on the previous day.

38. See below, 75:1.

"בָּרְכוּ", לֹא יִתְפַּלֵּל מִנְחָה בְּבֵית הַכְּנֶסֶת הַזֹּאת, אֶלָּא יֵלֵךְ חוּץ לְבֵית הַכְּנֶסֶת וְיִתְפַּלֵּל. וְאִם שׁוֹמֵעַ שֶׁהַשְּׁלִיחַ צִבּוּר אוֹמֵר "בָּרְכוּ", לֹא יַעֲנֶה עִם הַצִּבּוּר, שֶׁאִם יַעֲנֶה "בָּרְכוּ" שׁוּב אֵינוֹ רַשַּׁאי לְהִתְפַּלֵּל אַחַר כָּךְ תְּפִלָּה שֶׁל חוֹל[40]. (וְאִם טָעָה וְעָנָה, יִתְפַּלֵּל עַרְבִית שְׁתַּיִם כִּדְלְעֵיל סִימָן כ"א[41].) וְאִם בָּא סָמוּךְ לְקַבָּלַת שַׁבָּת וְיוֹם טוֹב, אַף עַל פִּי שֶׁלֹּא יוּכַל לִגְמוֹר הַשְּׁמוֹנֶה עֶשְׂרֵה קוֹדֶם שֶׁיְּקַבְּלוּ שַׁבָּת אוֹ יוֹם טוֹב, יָכוֹל לְהִתְפַּלֵּל כֵּיוָן שֶׁמַּתְחִיל בְּהֶיתֵּר[42].

---

ushering in **the festival they recited** *Borchu,*[39] **לֹא יִתְפַּלֵּל מִנְחָה בְּבֵית הַכְּנֶסֶת הַזֹּאת** — **should not recite** *Minchah* **in that synagogue. אֶלָּא יֵלֵךְ חוּץ לְבֵית הַכְּנֶסֶת וְיִתְפַּלֵּל** — **He should rather leave the synagogue and** then **pray. וְאִם שׁוֹמֵעַ שֶׁהַשְּׁלִיחַ צִבּוּר אוֹמֵר "בָּרְכוּ"** — **If he hears the** *chazzan* **saying** *Borchu,* **לֹא יַעֲנֶה עִם הַצִּבּוּר** — **he should not respond** *"Baruch Hashem HaMevorach ..."* **with the congregation, שֶׁאִם יַעֲנֶה "בָּרְכוּ"** — **for if he does respond** to *Borchu* **with** *"Baruch Hashem HaMevorach ...,"* and has joined them in ushering in Shabbos, **שׁוּב אֵינוֹ רַשַּׁאי לְהִתְפַּלֵּל אַחַר כָּךְ תְּפִלָּה שֶׁל חוֹל** — **he can no longer recite a weekday prayer.**[40] (**וְאִם טָעָה וְעָנָה** — **If he erred and responded, יִתְפַּלֵּל עַרְבִית שְׁתַּיִם** — **he** can no longer recite *Minchah* that day, and **must recite the** ***Maariv*** **Prayer twice, כִּדְלְעֵיל סִימָן כ"א** — **as** set out **above,** ***Siman*** **21.)**[41]

וְאִם בָּא סָמוּךְ לְקַבָּלַת שַׁבָּת וְיוֹם טוֹב — **If one** who did not yet recite *Minchah* **arrived close to the** congregation's **ushering in of Shabbos or the festival, אַף עַל פִּי שֶׁלֹּא יוּכַל לִגְמוֹר הַשְּׁמוֹנֶה עֶשְׂרֵה קוֹדֶם שֶׁיְּקַבְּלוּ שַׁבָּת אוֹ יוֹם טוֹב** — **even if,** were he to start praying *Minchah* at that point, **he would not be able to complete the** ***Shemoneh Esrei*** **before** the congregation **ushers in Shabbos or the festival, יָכוֹל לְהִתְפַּלֵּל** — **he may** still **recite the** *Minchah* **Prayer** in the synagogue, **כֵּיוָן שֶׁמַּתְחִיל בְּהֶיתֵּר** — **since he began** reciting the Prayer **while** he was **permitted** to do so.[42]

---

39. The *Maariv* service opens with the *chazzan* proclaiming: *"Borchu es Hashem HaMevorach"* — *Bless Hashem, the Blessed One*, to which the congregation (followed by the *chazzan*) responds: *"Baruch Hashem HaMevorach le'olam va'ed"* — *Blessed is Hashem, the Blessed One, for all eternity*. Normally, upon hearing the *chazzan* say *"Borchu ..."* even one who is not presently praying with the congregation should respond *"Baruch Hashem ..."* with the congregation.

40. According to Rabbi Moshe Feinstein, if, when responding with *Baruch Hashem* etc., he specifically had in mind not to usher in the Shabbos, he is not considered to have ushered in Shabbos for himself and he may pray *Minchah* afterward (*Igros Moshe, Orach Chaim* III, §37).

41. See there, *se'if* 6.

42. Nevertheless, even in this case it is better to pray outside the synagogue (*Mishnah Berurah* 263:63).

סִימָן ע

דִּינֵי תְּפִלַּת מַעֲרִיב[1,2,3]

וּבוֹ ה׳ סְעִיפִים

א. זְמַן קְרִיאַת שְׁמַע שֶׁל תְּפִלָּה שֶׁל עַרְבִית הוּא מִשֶּׁנִּרְאִין ג׳ כּוֹכָבִים קְטַנִּים[4], וּבְיוֹם הַמְעוּנָּן יַמְתִּין עַד שֶׁיֵּצֵא הַסָּפֵק מִלִּבּוֹ[5]. וְעַכְשָׁיו נוֹהֲגִין לְהִתְפַּלֵּל בְּצִבּוּר מַעֲרִיב תֵּיכֶף אַחַר מִנְחָה, אַף עַל פִּי שֶׁעֲדַיִין אֵינוֹ לַיְלָה, מִפְּנֵי טוֹרַח הַצִּבּוּר,

---

SIMAN 70

THE LAWS OF THE MAARIV PRAYER

CONTAINING 5 *SE'IFIM*

§1 Proper Time for *Maariv* and *Shema* / **§2** Eating Before *Maariv*; Latest Time for *Maariv* / **§3** Arriving Late to *Maariv* / **§4** *Baruch Hashem Le'Olam* and Announcements Before *Shemoneh Esrei* / **§5** Waiting for the Last Person

The *Maariv* service consists of two main sections. The first is the recitation of the *Shema* and its accompanying blessings. The recitation of *Shema* every evening is in fulfillment of the Biblical obligation (*Devarim* 6:7): וְדִבַּרְתָּ בָּם ... וּבְשָׁכְבְּךָ, *And you shall speak of them ... when you lie down*.[1] The recitation of *Shema* is preceded by two blessings and followed by two blessings.[2] The second section of the *Maariv* service is the *Shemoneh Esrei,* instituted by the Sages to parallel the nightly service in the Temple of burning any remaining sacrificial parts on the Altar.[3]

§1 **זְמַן קְרִיאַת שְׁמַע שֶׁל תְּפִלָּה שֶׁל עַרְבִית — The time for reciting the *Shema* of the *Maariv* prayer** **הוּא מִשֶּׁנִּרְאִין ג׳ כּוֹכָבִים קְטַנִּים — is when three small stars are visible** in the sky.[4] **וּבְיוֹם הַמְעוּנָּן — On a cloudy day,** when stars are not easily visible, **יַמְתִּין עַד שֶׁיֵּצֵא הַסָּפֵק מִלִּבּוֹ — one should wait until he no longer has any doubt**[5] that nightfall has arrived. **וְעַכְשָׁיו נוֹהֲגִין — Nowadays, the** prevalent **custom is** **לְהִתְפַּלֵּל בְּצִבּוּר מַעֲרִיב — that the congregation recites *Maariv*** **תֵּיכֶף אַחַר מִנְחָה — immediately after *Minchah*** **אַף עַל פִּי שֶׁעֲדַיִין אֵינוֹ לַיְלָה — even though it is not yet night,** **מִפְּנֵי טוֹרַח הַצִּבּוּר — due to the burden** it would cause

---

1. See introduction to *Siman* 17.

2. Mishnah, *Berachos* 11a. An additional blessing, בָּרוּךְ ה׳ לְעוֹלָם, *Blessed is Hashem forever,* was added later; see below, note 18.

3. See *Berachos* 26b.

4. Night actually begins when three stars of medium size are visible in the sky, but due to the concern that most people are unfamiliar with the different sizes of stars, we wait until three small stars are visible, to ensure that one does not recite *Shema* too early (*Mishnah Berurah* 235:1). From this point onward, Kitzur refers to this time as צֵאת הַכּוֹכָבִים, literally, *the emergence of stars,* henceforth rendered simply, *nightfall.* For further discussion regarding this time, see Appendix B. If one did recite the *Shema* before this point, he must repeat it after nightfall (*Shulchan Aruch* 235:1).

5. See Appendix B. [According to Rabbi Moshe Feinstein, in the New York area, this time is approximately 50 minutes after sunset; see note 23 to Appendix B.]

שֶׁהִיא טוֹרַח לֶאֱסוֹף הַצִּבּוּר שֵׁנִית[6], וּבִלְבַד שֶׁלֹּא יְהֵא קוֹדֶם פְּלַג הַמִּנְחָה[7], כִּי אָז אֲפִילּוּ בְּדִיעֲבַד אֵינָם יוֹצְאִין. וְאַשְׁרֵי לְמִי שֶׁמִּתְפַּלֵּל עַרְבִית בְּצִבּוּר בַּלַּיְלָה, וּבֵין מִנְחָה לְמַעֲרִיב עוֹסֵק בַּתּוֹרָה לְחַבֵּר הַלַּיְלָה עִם הַיּוֹם בַּתּוֹרָה שֶׁהוּא עִנְיָן גָּדוֹל[8]. וְעַל כָּל פָּנִים רָאוּי לְכָל יְרֵא שָׁמַיִם שֶׁאִם הִתְפַּלֵּל בְּצִבּוּר קוֹדֶם הַלַּיְלָה[9], לֹא יֹאכַל קוֹדֶם הַלַּיְלָה אֶלָּא יַמְתִּין, וּמִיָּד לְאַחַר צֵאת הַכּוֹכָבִים יִקְרָא ג׳ פָּרָשִׁיּוֹת שֶׁל קְרִיאַת שְׁמַע[10]. וּמִי שֶׁאֵינוֹ מִתְפַּלֵּל בְּצִבּוּר — אָסוּר לוֹ לְהִתְפַּלֵּל תְּפִלַּת עַרְבִית קוֹדֶם צֵאת הַכּוֹכָבִים.

ב. לְכַתְּחִלָּה צָרִיךְ לְהִתְפַּלֵּל עַרְבִית מִיָּד בְּצֵאת הַכּוֹכָבִים[11]. וְאָסוּר לְהַתְחִיל לֶאֱכוֹל

---

to the congregation if they would pray later, **שֶׁהִיא טוֹרַח לֶאֱסוֹף הַצִּבּוּר שֵׁנִית — for** if they would not pray *Maariv* immediately after *Minchah*, **the congregation would be bothered to gather a second time** for *Maariv*.[6] **וּבִלְבַד שֶׁלֹּא יְהֵא קוֹדֶם פְּלַג הַמִּנְחָה** — *Maariv* may be recited early **as long as it is not** recited **before** ***plag ha-minchah***,[7] **כִּי אָז אֲפִילּוּ בְּדִיעֲבַד אֵינָם יוֹצְאִין — for then, they do not fulfill their obligation even after the fact**, and they must pray again after *plag haminchah*. **וְאַשְׁרֵי לְמִי שֶׁמִּתְפַּלֵּל עַרְבִית בְּצִבּוּר בַּלַּיְלָה** — Although the above practice is permitted, **praised is one who prays *Maariv* with the congregation at night, וּבֵין מִנְחָה לְמַעֲרִיב עוֹסֵק בַּתּוֹרָה — and studies Torah between *Minchah* and *Maariv*, לְחַבֵּר הַלַּיְלָה עִם הַיּוֹם בַּתּוֹרָה — thus connecting night and day with Torah** study, **שֶׁהוּא עִנְיָן גָּדוֹל — which is a very worthy practice.**[8]

וְעַל כָּל פָּנִים — At the very least, רָאוּי לְכָל יְרֵא שָׁמַיִם — the **proper** way **for every God-fearing person** to conduct himself is **שֶׁאִם הִתְפַּלֵּל בְּצִבּוּר קוֹדֶם הַלַּיְלָה — that if he prayed** *Maariv* **with the congregation before nightfall, לֹא יֹאכַל קוֹדֶם הַלַּיְלָה — he should refrain from eating until evening;**[9] **אֶלָּא יַמְתִּין — rather, he should wait** until dark, **וּמִיָּד לְאַחַר צֵאת הַכּוֹכָבִים — and immediately after nightfall יִקְרָא ג׳ פָּרָשִׁיּוֹת שֶׁל קְרִיאַת שְׁמַע — recite the three passages of *Shema*,**[10] after which he may eat. **וּמִי שֶׁאֵינוֹ מִתְפַּלֵּל בְּצִבּוּר — One who is not praying** *Maariv* **with the congregation** **אָסוּר לוֹ לְהִתְפַּלֵּל תְּפִלַּת עַרְבִית קוֹדֶם צֵאת הַכּוֹכָבִים — may not recite the *Maariv* prayer before nightfall.**

§2 לְכַתְּחִלָּה צָרִיךְ לְהִתְפַּלֵּל עַרְבִית מִיָּד בְּצֵאת הַכּוֹכָבִים — Ideally, one should recite the *Maariv* prayer immediately at nightfall.[11] **וְאָסוּר לְהַתְחִיל לֶאֱכוֹל — It is**

---

6. In addition, *Mishnah Berurah* (235:8) points out that if *Maariv* would not be recited immediately after *Minchah*, many people would not return to the synagogue after dark, and perhaps some would miss praying *Maariv* entirely. Due to these concerns, the congregation is permitted to pray *Maariv* early.

Mishnah Berurah (235:9) writes that when reciting the *Shema* during an "early" *Maariv*, one should intend *not* to fulfill his Biblical obligation of reciting the evening *Shema*. After nightfall he should repeat the *Shema*, this time intending to fulfill the mitzvah.

7. One-and-a-quarter seasonal hours before the end of the day; see Appendix B.

8. It is likewise a worthy practice to engage in Torah study or prayer during the early morning, thus connecting the night with the day in holiness (see *Mishnah Berurah* 1:2 and above, 1:5).

9. See *Mishnah Berurah* 235:19 and 267:6 for further discussion.

10. Even if one intends to repeat the entire *Shema* as part of the recitation of the Bedtime *Shema* (see below, 71:4), it is preferable not to rely on this recitation for the fulfillment of his obligation, as that is not the function of the bedtime recital (*Mishnah Berurah* 235:12).

11. I.e., he should recite it at the first opportunity, as all mitzvos should be performed with alacrity (*Mishnah Berurah* 235:26).

אוֹ לַעֲשׂוֹת שׁוּם דָּבָר[12] חֲצִי שָׁעָה קוֹדֶם צֵאת הַכּוֹכָבִים[13], כְּמוֹ סָמוּךְ לְמִנְחָה קְטַנָּה[14] (עַיֵּין לְעֵיל סִימָן ס"ט סְעִיף ג'). וְאִם אֵין לוֹ פְּנַאי, כְּגוֹן שֶׁהוּא לוֹמֵד בָּרַבִּים, עַל כָּל פָּנִים לֹא יְאַחֵר יוֹתֵר מֵחֲצוֹת הַלַּיְלָה[15]. וּבְדִיעֲבַד אֲפִילוּ אַחַר חֲצוֹת עַד שֶׁלֹּא עָלָה עַמּוּד הַשַּׁחַר יָצָא[16].

ג. מִי שֶׁבָּא לְבֵית הַכְּנֶסֶת לִתְפִלַּת עַרְבִית וּמָצָא שֶׁהַצִּבּוּר עוֹמְדִין לְהִתְפַּלֵּל שְׁמוֹנֶה עֶשְׂרֵה, אֲפִילוּ עֲדַיִין אֵינוֹ לַיְלָה אֶלָּא מִפְּלַג הַמִּנְחָה וּלְמַעְלָה, מִתְפַּלֵּל עִמָּהֶם שְׁמוֹנֶה עֶשְׂרֵה[17], וְאַחַר כָּךְ כְּשֶׁיִּהְיֶה לַיְלָה אוֹמֵר הַקְּרִיאַת שְׁמַע עִם הַבְּרָכוֹת. וְאִם

---

forbidden to begin eating **אוֹ לַעֲשׂוֹת שׁוּם דָּבָר — or to do any activity,**[12] **חֲצִי שָׁעָה קוֹדֶם צֵאת הַכּוֹכָבִים** — within **a half hour before nightfall,**[13] **כְּמוֹ סָמוּךְ לְמִנְחָה קְטַנָּה** — **just as** these actions are forbidden **close to *minchah ketanah***[14] for someone who did not yet pray *Minchah* **(עַיֵּין לְעֵיל סִימָן ס"ט סְעִיף ג')** — **see above, 69:3).**

וְאִם אֵין לוֹ פְּנַאי — If one does not have time to recite *Maariv* immediately at nightfall, **כְּגוֹן שֶׁהוּא לוֹמֵד בָּרַבִּים — for instance, if he is teaching Torah to a group** of people, **עַל כָּל פָּנִים לֹא יְאַחֵר יוֹתֵר מֵחֲצוֹת הַלַּיְלָה** — he may delay his prayer, but **in any case not delay** reciting *Maariv* **past halachic midnight.**[15] **וּבְדִיעֲבַד אֲפִילוּ אַחַר חֲצוֹת** — However, **after the fact, even if it is past halachic midnight,** **עַד שֶׁלֹּא עָלָה עַמּוּד הַשַּׁחַר יָצָא** — if he recites *Maariv* **up until daybreak, he has fulfilled his obligation.**[16]

§3 **מִי שֶׁבָּא לְבֵית הַכְּנֶסֶת לִתְפִלַּת עַרְבִית — One who arrives at the synagogue for the** *Maariv* prayers **וּמָצָא שֶׁהַצִּבּוּר עוֹמְדִין לְהִתְפַּלֵּל שְׁמוֹנֶה עֶשְׂרֵה — and finds the congregation about to begin** *Shemoneh Esrei,* **אֲפִילוּ עֲדַיִין אֵינוֹ לַיְלָה — even if it is not yet night,** **אֶלָּא מִפְּלַג הַמִּנְחָה וּלְמַעְלָה — as long as it is after *plag haminchah,*** **מִתְפַּלֵּל עִמָּהֶם שְׁמוֹנֶה עֶשְׂרֵה — he should recite *Shemoneh Esrei* with them.**[17] **וְאַחַר כָּךְ כְּשֶׁיִּהְיֶה לַיְלָה — Later, after nightfall,** **אוֹמֵר הַקְּרִיאַת שְׁמַע עִם הַבְּרָכוֹת — he should recite *Shema* with** its accompanying **blessings.** **וְאִם**

---

12. This includes even taking a short nap (*Mishnah Berurah* 235:17).

13. *Mishnah Berurah* (ibid.) rules that one may study Torah until nightfall itself. Furthermore, if he appoints someone (who is not studying) to remind him to pray *Maariv* later, he may continue learning past nightfall as well.

14. *Minchah ketanah* begins two-and-a-half seasonal hours before nightfall (see above, 69:2; see also Appendix B).

15. According to Biblical law, the evening *Shema* may be recited until daybreak. The Sages instituted that the *Shema* be recited before *chatzos* (halachic midnight; see Appendix B), so that one not wait until the last moment, as this may result in his inadvertently missing the allotted time. See *Beur Halachah* (235:3 s.v. וזמנה).

One who is traveling in the evening and expects to reach his destination well before *chatzos* should not pray while en route, but should rather wait to pray at his destination. In such a case, a passenger may even sleep while traveling since he will surely awaken when he arrives at his destination (*Igros Moshe, Orach Chaim* V, §37.11; see *Mishnah Berurah* 89:42).

16. See Appendix B.

In case of an unavoidable circumstance, one may recite the *Shema* even after daybreak, as long as the sun has not yet appeared over the horizon. In such a situation, the blessings of *Hashkiveinu* and *Baruch Hashem le'olam* are omitted and *Shemoneh Esrei* is not recited (*Rama* 235:4, *Mishnah Berurah* 235:34).

17. If one can find another congregation that prays *Maariv* later, he should wait to pray with the second one, since it is preferable to recite the entire *Maariv* in the proper sequence (*Mishnah Berurah* 236:12).

הַצִּבּוּר עוֹמְדִין בְּאֶמְצַע קְרִיאַת שְׁמַע וּבִרְכוֹתֶיהָ וְיֵשׁ לוֹ שְׁהוּת לוֹמַר קוֹדֶם שֶׁיַּגִּיעוּ לִתְפִלַּת שְׁמוֹנֶה עֶשְׂרֵה קְרִיאַת שְׁמַע עִם הַבְּרָכוֹת עַד "שׁוֹמֵר עַמּוֹ יִשְׂרָאֵל לָעַד", יַעֲשֶׂה כֵּן, וִידַלֵּג "בָּרוּךְ ה' לְעוֹלָם" וכו'[18], וְאֵינוֹ צָרִיךְ לְאוֹמְרוֹ אַחַר כָּךְ לְאַחַר הַתְּפִלָּה[19] (מהריעב"ץ). וְאִם הוּא לֹא הִתְפַּלֵּל עֲדַיִין מִנְחָה, יִתְפַּלֵּל תְּפִלַּת שְׁמוֹנֶה עֶשְׂרֵה מִנְחָה בְּשָׁעָה שֶׁהַצִּבּוּר אוֹמְרִים קְרִיאַת שְׁמַע עִם הַבְּרָכוֹת[20] וְיִשְׁהֶה מְעַט, לְכָל הַפָּחוֹת כְּדֵי הִילּוּךְ ד' אַמּוֹת[21], וְיִתְפַּלֵּל אַחַר כָּךְ שְׁמוֹנֶה עֶשְׂרֵה עִם הַצִּבּוּר לְמַעֲרִיב,

---

הַצִּבּוּר עוֹמְדִין בְּאֶמְצַע קְרִיאַת שְׁמַע וּבִרְכוֹתֶיהָ — If, when he arrives, **the congregation is in the middle of** reciting ***Shema*** **and its** accompanying **blessings, וְיֵשׁ לוֹ שְׁהוּת לוֹמַר — and he has time to recite, קוֹדֶם שֶׁיַּגִּיעוּ לִתְפִלַּת שְׁמוֹנֶה עֶשְׂרֵה — before** the congregation **reaches the *Shemoneh Esrei*** **prayer, קְרִיאַת שְׁמַע עִם הַבְּרָכוֹת — *Shema* with the blessings עַד "שׁוֹמֵר עַמּוֹ יִשְׂרָאֵל לָעַד" — until** the conclusion of the *Hashkiveinu* blessing that ends with *shomer amo Yisrael la'ad,* ***Who protects His people Israel forever,*** **יַעֲשֶׂה כֵּן — he should do so. וִידַלֵּג "בָּרוּךְ ה' לְעוֹלָם" וכו' —** In this case **he should skip** the final blessing, *Baruch* HASHEM *le'olam,* ***Blessed is*** **HASHEM *forever,*** **etc.**[18] **וְאֵינוֹ צָרִיךְ לְאוֹמְרוֹ אַחַר כָּךְ לְאַחַר הַתְּפִלָּה — and he does not have to recite it later, after the** *Shemoneh Esrei* **Prayer**[19] **(מהריעב"ץ** — the source of this halachah is the *siddur* **of R' Yaakov Emden).**

וְאִם הוּא לֹא הִתְפַּלֵּל עֲדַיִין מִנְחָה — If one arrives to find the congregation reciting *Maariv,* and **he has not yet prayed *Minchah,*** **יִתְפַּלֵּל תְּפִלַּת שְׁמוֹנֶה עֶשְׂרֵה מִנְחָה — he should recite the *Shemoneh Esrei* of *Minchah*** **בְּשָׁעָה שֶׁהַצִּבּוּר אוֹמְרִים קְרִיאַת שְׁמַע עִם הַבְּרָכוֹת — while the congregation recites *Shema* with** its **blessings.**[20] **וְיִשְׁהֶה מְעַט —** Upon concluding *Minchah,* **he should pause briefly, לְכָל הַפָּחוֹת כְּדֵי הִילּוּךְ ד' אַמּוֹת — for at least the time it takes to walk four *amos,***[21] **וְיִתְפַּלֵּל אַחַר כָּךְ שְׁמוֹנֶה עֶשְׂרֵה עִם הַצִּבּוּר לְמַעֲרִיב — and afterward pray the *Shemoneh Esrei* of *Maariv* with**

---

18. This passage, consisting of a collection of Biblical verses and a concluding blessing, was introduced during the Geonic era. At that time, most people gathered in the fields for prayers. According to many authorities, this collection of verses was substituted for *Shemoneh Esrei* in order to shorten the service so that it could be completed before dark. The recitation of this passage was retained even after the practice of praying in the fields was discontinued (*Tur* 236, *Perishah* loc. cit. §9; see also *Bais Yosef* ibid. s.v. ומה שנוהגים).

However, the custom to recite *Baruch* HASHEM *le'olam* is not universal (see *Tur* ibid.). For example, common custom in Eretz Yisrael is not to recite it. It is preferable that one who lives in Eretz Yisrael and is accustomed not to say *Baruch* HASHEM *le'olam* not say it even when he is outside of Eretz Yisrael and is praying in a congregation that does say it. In such a case, he should extend his recitation of *Shema* so that he should finish the blessing of *Shomer amo Yisrael la'ad* when the congregation is finishing *Baruch* HASHEM *le'olam* (*Igros Moshe, Orach Chaim* II, §102). If, however, it is not possible for him to do this, and it will be evident to others that he is deviating from the custom in that place (for example, if he is the *chazzan*), he should recite *Baruch* HASHEM *le'olam* with the congregation (*Igros Moshe, Yoreh Deah* III, §96.8).

19. According to *Mishnah Berurah* (236:11), one should recite *Baruch* HASHEM *le'olam* even after *Shemoneh Esrei*, with the omission of the concluding blessing (בָּרוּךְ אַתָּה ה' הַמֶּלֶךְ בִּכְבוֹדוֹ וכו', *Blessed are You,* HASHEM, *the King in His glory,* etc.).

20. If one is able to pray *Maariv* with another congregation after nightfall, he should rather recite the *Shemoneh Esrei* of *Minchah* while the congregation is reciting the *Shemoneh Esrei* of *Maariv,* and then pray *Maariv* with the congregation that prays later (*Mishnah Berurah* 236:11).

21. Approximately 2-3 seconds.

וְאַחַר כָּךְ כְּשֶׁיִּהְיֶה לַיְלָה יֹאמַר קְרִיאַת שְׁמַע עִם הַבְּרָכוֹת.

ד. מִן "בָּרוּךְ ה' לְעוֹלָם" עַד "יִרְאוּ עֵינֵינוּ" יֵשׁ לוֹמַר בִּישִׁיבָה. וְאָסוּר לְהַפְסִיק מִן תְּחִלַּת "וְהוּא רַחוּם"[23] עַד לְאַחַר הַשְּׁמוֹנֶה עֶשְׂרֵה[24]. וּמַה שֶּׁהַשַּׁמָּשׁ מַכְרִיז "יַעֲלֶה וְיָבֹא", "טַל וּמָטָר"[25], לֹא הָוֵי הֶפְסֵק, מִשּׁוּם דְּהָוֵי צוֹרֶךְ הַתְּפִלָּה[26].

ה. אִם נִשְׁאַר אָדָם יְחִידִי מִתְפַּלֵּל מַעֲרִיב בְּבֵית הַכְּנֶסֶת בְּלַיְלָה, חַיָּיב חֲבֵרוֹ לְהַמְתִּין עַד שֶׁיְּסַיֵּים תְּפִלָּתוֹ כְּדֵי שֶׁלֹּא תִתְבַּלְבֵּל מַחֲשַׁבְתּוֹ. וְאִם הִתְחִיל לְהִתְפַּלֵּל בְּשָׁעָה שֶׁלֹּא יוּכַל לְסַיֵּים תְּפִלָּתוֹ עִם הַצִּבּוּר, אֵינוֹ חַיָּיב לְהַמְתִּין עָלָיו,

---

the congregation. וְאַחַר כָּךְ כְּשֶׁיִּהְיֶה לַיְלָה — Afterward, when it is night, יֹאמַר קְרִיאַת שְׁמַע עִם הַבְּרָכוֹת — he should recite *Shema* with its blessings.

§4 מִן "בָּרוּךְ ה' לְעוֹלָם" עַד "יִרְאוּ עֵינֵינוּ" — The verses **from** the beginning of ***Baruch* *HASHEM le'olam*** **until** *Yir'u eineinu, **May our eyes see,*** יֵשׁ לוֹמַר בִּישִׁיבָה — **should be recited while seated.**[22]

וְאָסוּר לְהַפְסִיק מִן תְּחִלַּת "וְהוּא רַחוּם" — **It is forbidden to interrupt** one's prayers **from the beginning of the recitation of** *V'Hu rachum, **He, the Merciful One,***[23] עַד לְאַחַר הַשְּׁמוֹנֶה עֶשְׂרֵה — **until the completion of the *Shemoneh Esrei*** Prayer.[24] וּמַה שֶּׁהַשַּׁמָּשׁ מַכְרִיז "יַעֲלֶה וְיָבֹא" — **The announcement of the *shamash*** (sexton) reminding the congregation to recite ***Yaaleh VeYavo*** "טַל וּמָטָר" — or to recite *v'sein* ***tal u'matar,***[25] לֹא הָוֵי הֶפְסֵק — **does not constitute an interruption** in his prayers מִשּׁוּם דְּהָוֵי צוֹרֶךְ הַתְּפִלָּה — **because it is required to** ensure the proper recital of **the prayers** by the congregation, and is therefore considered part of the service.[26]

§5 אִם נִשְׁאַר אָדָם יְחִידִי — **If there is a lone person left** מִתְפַּלֵּל מַעֲרִיב בְּבֵית הַכְּנֶסֶת בְּלַיְלָה — **reciting *Maariv* at night in the synagogue,** חַיָּיב חֲבֵרוֹ לְהַמְתִּין — **his fellow must wait** for him there עַד שֶׁיְּסַיֵּים תְּפִלָּתוֹ — **until he completes his prayers,** כְּדֵי שֶׁלֹּא תִתְבַּלְבֵּל מַחֲשַׁבְתּוֹ — **so that the concentration** of the one who is praying **is not disturbed** out of fear of remaining alone in the synagogue at night. וְאִם הִתְחִיל לְהִתְפַּלֵּל — **However, if he began his prayers** בְּשָׁעָה שֶׁלֹּא יוּכַל לְסַיֵּים תְּפִלָּתוֹ עִם הַצִּבּוּר — **at a time when it was no longer possible for him to complete his prayers together with the congregation,** אֵינוֹ חַיָּיב לְהַמְתִּין עָלָיו — his fellow **is not**

---

22. See *Mishnah Berurah* 236:10. [*Yir'u eineinu* begins the concluding blessing of this passage.]

23. It is customary to recite this verse (from *Tehillim* 78:38) before *Borchu* (*Mishnah Berurah* 236:1).

24. The prohibition of not interrupting from the recital of *V'Hu rachum* is not mentioned in *Mishnah Berurah*. He does, however, note that one may not interrupt during *Shema* and its blessings, as Kitzur writes above, *Siman* 16:1 (besides the exceptions mentioned in *Siman* 16). [One may also not interrupt between the blessings of *Shema* and *Shemoneh Esrei* (*Shulchan Aruch* 236:2).] *Mishnah Berurah* (236:1) states that those who speak between their response to *Borchu* and the beginning of their recitation of the first blessing of *Maariv* do so in violation of this halachah.

25. Or *Al HaNissim* (*Mishnah Berurah* 236:7). These additions to the *Shemoneh Esrei* are recited only at certain times during the year, as explained above, *Siman* 19. The *shamash* customarily announces these changes immediately before the congregation begins *Shemoneh Esrei*.

26. However, such an annoucement may not be made before the *Shacharis Shemoneh Esrei;* see *Shaar HaTziyun* 236:4.

שֶׁהֲרֵי מוֹכְחָא מִילְּתָא דַּאֲדַעְתָּא דְהָכִי נִכְנַס שֶׁאֵינוֹ מְפַחֵד[27].

obligated to wait for him, **שֶׁהֲרֵי מוֹכְחָא מִילְּתָא** — **for it is clear** **דַּאֲדַעְתָּא דְהָכִי נִכְנַס** — **that he entered** into this situation **with this in mind,** **שֶׁאֵינוֹ מְפַחֵד** — and **that he does not fear** being alone.[27]

27. It is, however, considered an act of piety to wait for him even in this situation (*Mishnah Berurah* 90:48).

THE NIGHTTIME ROUTINE — SIMAN 71:1 404

סימן עא
סֵדֶר הַלַּיְלָה
וּבוֹ ה׳ סְעִיפִים

א. אַחַר תְּפִלַּת עַרְבִית צָרִיךְ לִקְבּוֹעַ עֵת לַתּוֹרָה לְקַיֵּם "וְהָגִיתָ בּוֹ יוֹמָם וָלַיְלָה"[1] (יהושע א, ח). וְיֵשׁ לָחוּשׁ בַּלַּיְלָה אִם יֹאכַל תְּחִלָּה, תַּחְטְפֶנּוּ שֵׁינָה מִתּוֹךְ שֶׁהוּא יָגֵעַ וְהַטֶּבַע מְבַקֶּשֶׁת מְנוּחָה וְנִמְצָא מִתְבַּטֵּל מִתּוֹרָה, עַל כֵּן יֵשׁ לִיזָּהֵר שֶׁיִּקְבַּע לוֹ עֵת לִלְמוֹד קוֹדֶם הָאֲכִילָה. אַךְ, אִם הוּא רָעֵב וְלִבּוֹ חָלָשׁ שֶׁלֹּא אָכַל בַּיּוֹם לָשׂוֹבַע, יִטְעוֹם מִיָּד כְּדֵי לְיַשֵּׁב דַּעְתּוֹ, וְאַחַר כָּךְ יִלְמוֹד קְצָת, וְאַחַר כָּךְ יֹאכַל סְעוּדָתוֹ דֵּי צָרְכּוֹ, וְיַחֲזוֹר לִלְמוֹד תּוֹרָה אִישׁ אִישׁ כְּפִי הַשָּׂגָתוֹ. אָמְרוּ רַבּוֹתֵינוּ זִכְרוֹנָם לִבְרָכָה (ערובין סה, א): "לֹא אִיבְּרָא לַיְלָה אֶלָּא לְגִירְסָא", וְהַיְינוּ בְּלֵילֵי חוֹרֶף, וּמִכָּל מָקוֹם גַּם בַּלֵּילוֹת הַקְּצָרוֹת צָרִיךְ לִלְמוֹד מְעַט בְּכָל לַיְלָה לְקַיֵּם "וְהָגִיתָ בּוֹ

SIMAN 71
THE NIGHTTIME ROUTINE
CONTAINING 5 *SE'IFIM*

§1 Learning Torah at Night / §2 The Evening Meal / §3 Introspection and Repentance / §4 The Bedtime *Shema* / §5 Proper Sleeping Position

§1 אַחַר תְּפִלַּת עַרְבִית — After the *Maariv* service (see previous *Siman*) **צָרִיךְ לִקְבּוֹעַ עֵת לַתּוֹרָה** — one should keep a designated time for Torah study, **לְקַיֵּם "וְהָגִיתָ בּוֹ יוֹמָם וָלַיְלָה"** — to fulfill the directive of the verse (*Yehoshua* 1:8): *You shall contemplate it* [the Torah] *day and night.*[1] **וְיֵשׁ לָחוּשׁ בַּלַּיְלָה** — At night there is reason to be concerned **אִם יֹאכַל תְּחִלָּה** — that if one were to eat before studying **תַּחְטְפֶנּוּ שֵׁינָה** — he would be overcome by sleep, **מִתּוֹךְ שֶׁהוּא יָגֵעַ וְהַטֶּבַע מְבַקֶּשֶׁת מְנוּחָה** — since he is fatigued and the physical nature of a person seeks repose, **וְנִמְצָא מִתְבַּטֵּל מִתּוֹרָה** — and he will thus have neglected Torah study. **עַל כֵּן יֵשׁ לִיזָּהֵר** — Therefore, one should take care **שֶׁיִּקְבַּע לוֹ עֵת לִלְמוֹד קוֹדֶם הָאֲכִילָה** — to keep a designated time for study before eating. **אַךְ, אִם הוּא רָעֵב וְלִבּוֹ חָלָשׁ** — However, if he is hungry and he feels weak **שֶׁלֹּא אָכַל בַּיּוֹם לָשׂוֹבַע** — because he had not eaten a satisfying meal all day, **יִטְעוֹם מִיָּד כְּדֵי לְיַשֵּׁב דַּעְתּוֹ** — he should eat a small amount in order to settle his mind, **וְאַחַר כָּךְ יִלְמוֹד קְצָת** — and then he should study a bit. **וְאַחַר כָּךְ יֹאכַל סְעוּדָתוֹ דֵּי צָרְכּוֹ** — After that, he should eat a sufficient meal **וְיַחֲזוֹר לִלְמוֹד תּוֹרָה** — and then return to study Torah, **אִישׁ אִישׁ כְּפִי הַשָּׂגָתוֹ** — each person commensurate with his abilities.

אָמְרוּ רַבּוֹתֵינוּ זִכְרוֹנָם לִבְרָכָה — Our Rabbis, of blessed memory, stated (*Eruvin* 65a): **"לֹא אִיבְּרָא לַיְלָה אֶלָּא לְגִירְסָא"** — *Night was created specifically for the sake of Torah study.* **וְהַיְינוּ בְּלֵילֵי חוֹרֶף** — This refers to the long winter nights. **וּמִכָּל מָקוֹם גַּם בַּלֵּילוֹת הַקְּצָרוֹת** — However, even during the shorter nights **צָרִיךְ לִלְמוֹד מְעַט בְּכָל לַיְלָה** — one should study at least a little every night, **לְקַיֵּם "וְהָגִיתָ בּוֹ**

---

1. See above, *Siman* 27:1-2, for further discussion of the obligation to study Torah.

יוֹמָם וָלַיְלָה", וּמִן ט"ו בְּאָב וְאֵילָךְ יוֹסִיף מְעַט מְעַט. וְאָמַר רֵישׁ לָקִישׁ (עבודה זרה ג, ב): **כָּל הָעוֹסֵק בַּתּוֹרָה בַּלַּיְלָה חוּט שֶׁל חֶסֶד נִמְשָׁךְ עָלָיו בַּיּוֹם**[2]**, שֶׁנֶּאֱמַר** (תהלים מב, ט) **"יוֹמָם יְצַוֶּה ה' חַסְדּוֹ**[3] **וּבַלַּיְלָה שִׁירֹה עִמִּי" — מַה טַּעַם "יוֹמָם יְצַוֶּה ה' חַסְדּוֹ"? מִשּׁוּם "וּבַלַּיְלָה שִׁירֹה עִמִּי"**[4]**. וְאִיכָּא דְאָמְרֵי: אָמַר רֵישׁ לָקִישׁ: כָּל הָעוֹסֵק בַּתּוֹרָה בָּעוֹלָם הַזֶּה שֶׁהִיא דּוֹמָה לְלַיְלָה הַקָּדוֹשׁ בָּרוּךְ הוּא מוֹשֵׁךְ עָלָיו חוּט שֶׁל חֶסֶד בָּעוֹלָם הַבָּא שֶׁהוּא יוֹם שֶׁנֶּאֱמַר "יוֹמָם יְצַוֶּה ה' חַסְדּוֹ וּבַלַּיְלָה שִׁירֹה עִמִּי"**[5]**. וּמִכָּל שֶׁכֵּן, מִי שֶׁיֵּשׁ לוֹ חֹק קָבוּעַ לִלְמוֹד בְּכָל יוֹם**[6] **וְנִתְבַּטֵּל בַּיּוֹם, שֶׁהוּא צָרִיךְ לְהַשְׁלִים חָקוֹ בַּלַּיְלָה.**

"יוֹמָם וָלַיְלָה" — to fulfill the directive of the verse, ***You shall contemplate it day and night.*** **וּמִן ט"ו בְּאָב וְאֵילָךְ — From the fifteenth of** the month of ***Av*** **and onward,** as the nights grow longer, **יוֹסִיף מְעַט מְעַט — he should gradually increase** the time he spends learning at night.

Kitzur cites a Gemara (*Avodah Zarah* 3b) that highlights the significance of Torah study at night:

וְאָמַר רֵישׁ לָקִישׁ — Reish Lakish said: כָּל הָעוֹסֵק בַּתּוֹרָה בַּלַּיְלָה — Whoever engages in Torah study **at night חוּט שֶׁל חֶסֶד נִמְשָׁךְ עָלָיו בַּיּוֹם — is endowed with charm during the day,**[2] **שֶׁנֶּאֱמַר — as it states** (*Tehillim* 42:9): **"יוֹמָם יְצַוֶּה ה' חַסְדּוֹ וּבַלַּיְלָה שִׁירֹה עִמִּי" —** ***In the day Hashem will command His charm,***[3] ***and in the night His song was with me.*** **מַה טַּעַם "יוֹמָם יְצַוֶּה ה' חַסְדּוֹ"** — The Psalmist states: **What is the reason that** ***In the day Hashem will command His charm*** to descend upon me? **מִשּׁוּם "וּבַלַּיְלָה שִׁירֹה עִמִּי" — Because** ***in the night His song*** [of Torah] ***was with me.***[4]

A variant version of this teaching is now presented:

וְאִיכָּא דְאָמְרֵי — Others say this teaching is as follows: **אָמַר רֵישׁ לָקִישׁ — Reish Lakish said: כָּל הָעוֹסֵק בַּתּוֹרָה בָּעוֹלָם הַזֶּה — Whoever engages in Torah** study **in this world, שֶׁהִיא דּוֹמָה לְלַיְלָה — which is likened to night,** **הַקָּדוֹשׁ בָּרוּךְ הוּא מוֹשֵׁךְ עָלָיו חוּט שֶׁל חֶסֶד בָּעוֹלָם הַבָּא — the Holy One, Blessed is He, will endow him with charm in the World to Come, שֶׁהוּא יוֹם — which is** likened to **day, שֶׁנֶּאֱמַר — as it states: "יוֹמָם יְצַוֶּה ה' חַסְדּוֹ וּבַלַּיְלָה שִׁירֹה עִמִּי" —** ***In the day Hashem will command His kindness, and in the night His song was with me.***[5]

Kitzur continues:

וּמִכָּל שֶׁכֵּן — Certainly, מִי שֶׁיֵּשׁ לוֹ חֹק קָבוּעַ לִלְמוֹד בְּכָל יוֹם — one who has a set amount to study Torah **every day,**[6] **וְנִתְבַּטֵּל בַּיּוֹם — and** one day **he neglected to** complete that amount **during the day, שֶׁהוּא צָרִיךְ לְהַשְׁלִים חָקוֹ בַּלַּיְלָה — must fill his quota at night.**

---

2. Literally: *a thread of grace extends over him.* God makes him appear pleasant in the eyes of other people (*Rashi* ad loc.). *Maharsha* (ad loc.) explains that it is normal for one who remains awake all night to appear exhausted and short-tempered. This Gemara states that one who deprives himself of sleep at night in order to study Torah will be granted a thread of grace and will still have an appealing appearance.

3. In Reish Lakish's current exposition, חֶסֶד (in the word חַסְדּוֹ), normally rendered as *kindness,* is interpreted as a synonym for חֵן, *charm.* This usage appears in *Bereishis* 39:21 and *Esther* 2:17.

4. The term שִׁירָה, *song,* is used to describe the Torah in the verse (*Devarim* 31:19): וְעַתָּה כִּתְבוּ לָכֶם אֶת הַשִּׁירָה הַזֹּאת, *And now, write for yourselves this song* (*Maharsha* ad loc.).

5. I.e., because His song of Torah was with me in this world, which is likened to the night, therefore, in the World to Come, which is likened to the day, Hashem will command His kindness to descend upon me.

6. See above, 27:1.

ב. רָאוּי לְאָדָם בֵּינוֹנִי הַבָּרִיא לְמַעֵט בִּסְעוּדַת הַלַּיְלָה וּתְהֵא קַלָּה מִסְּעוּדַת הַיּוֹם, וְיַרְוִיחַ בָּזֶה אַרְבָּעָה דְבָרִים: א) יִשְׁמוֹר בְּרִיאוּתוֹ. ב) יְהֵא נִשְׁמָר בְּדָבָר רָע[7] שֶׁלֹּא יָבֹא לִידֵי מִקְרֵה לַיְלָה שֶׁבָּא מֵחֲמַת אֲכִילָה גַסָּה וּדְבָרִים הַמְחַמְּמִים. ג) שֶׁיִּהְיוּ חֲלוֹמוֹתָיו נוֹחִים וּמְיוּשָּׁבִים, כִּי מֵרוֹב אֲכִילָה וּשְׁתִיָּה הַרְבֵּה פְּעָמִים בָּאִים חֲלוֹמוֹת קָשִׁים וְזָרִים. ד) שֶׁלֹּא תִכְבַּד שֵׁינָתוֹ עָלָיו, וְיָקִיץ בַּזְּמַן הָרָאוּי. וְדַי לְאָדָם הַבָּרִיא לִישַׁן שִׁשָּׁה שָׁעוֹת[8]. וְיִזָּהֵר שֶׁלֹּא לִישַׁן בְּחֶדֶר יְחִידִי[9]. וְלֹא יִישַׁן בְּמָקוֹם חַם בְּיוֹתֵר וְלֹא בְמָקוֹם קַר בְּיוֹתֵר.

ג. רָאוּי לְכָל יְרֵא שָׁמַיִם שֶׁקּוֹדֶם הֲלִיכָתוֹ לִישַׁן יְפַשְׁפֵּשׁ בְּמַעֲשָׂיו שֶׁעָשָׂה כָּל הַיּוֹם, וְאִם יִמְצָא שֶׁעָשָׂה עֲבֵירָה, יִתְחָרֵט וְיִתְוַדֶּה עָלֶיהָ[10] וִיקַבֵּל עַל עַצְמוֹ בְּלֵב שָׁלֵם שֶׁלֹּא לַעֲשׂוֹתָהּ עוֹד, וּבִפְרָט בַּעֲבֵירוֹת הַמְּצוּיוֹת, כְּגוֹן חֲנִיפוּת שְׁקָרִים לֵיצָנוּת

---

§2 רָאוּי לְאָדָם בֵּינוֹנִי הַבָּרִיא — It is proper for the average healthy person לְמַעֵט בִּסְעוּדַת הַלַּיְלָה — to minimize the amount he eats during the evening meal, וּתְהֵא קַלָּה מִסְּעוּדַת הַיּוֹם — and it should consist of lighter food than the day meal. וְיַרְוִיחַ בָּזֶה אַרְבָּעָה דְבָרִים — He will achieve four things with this: (1) יִשְׁמוֹר בְּרִיאוּתוֹ — He will protect his health; (2) יְהֵא נִשְׁמָר בְּדָבָר רָע — he will be protected from an "evil thing,"[7] שֶׁלֹּא יָבֹא לִידֵי מִקְרֵה לַיְלָה — that is, he will thus avoid having a nocturnal emission, שֶׁבָּא מֵחֲמַת אֲכִילָה גַסָּה — which is often the result of overeating וּדְבָרִים הַמְחַמְּמִים — and eating foods that heat the body; (3) שֶׁיִּהְיוּ חֲלוֹמוֹתָיו נוֹחִים וּמְיוּשָּׁבִים — his dreams will be pleasant and calm, כִּי מֵרוֹב אֲכִילָה וּשְׁתִיָּה הַרְבֵּה פְּעָמִים — because often, as a result of excessive eating and drinking בָּאִים חֲלוֹמוֹת קָשִׁים וְזָרִים — one is visited by harsh and strange dreams; (4) שֶׁלֹּא תִכְבַּד שֵׁינָתוֹ עָלָיו — he will not fall into a deep slumber, וְיָקִיץ בַּזְּמַן הָרָאוּי — and he will awaken at the proper time. וְדַי לְאָדָם הַבָּרִיא — It is sufficient for a healthy person לִישַׁן שִׁשָּׁה שָׁעוֹת — to sleep for six hours a night.[8]

וְיִזָּהֵר — One should be careful שֶׁלֹּא לִישַׁן בְּחֶדֶר יְחִידִי — not to sleep alone in a room.[9] וְלֹא יִישַׁן בְּמָקוֹם חַם בְּיוֹתֵר — Additionally, one should not sleep in a very hot place וְלֹא בְמָקוֹם קַר בְּיוֹתֵר — or in a very cold place.

§3 רָאוּי לְכָל יְרֵא שָׁמַיִם — It is proper behavior for every God-fearing person שֶׁקּוֹדֶם הֲלִיכָתוֹ לִישַׁן — that before going to sleep יְפַשְׁפֵּשׁ בְּמַעֲשָׂיו שֶׁעָשָׂה כָּל הַיּוֹם — he should examine his actions of the entire day. וְאִם יִמְצָא שֶׁעָשָׂה עֲבֵירָה — If he finds that he has sinned, יִתְחָרֵט וְיִתְוַדֶּה עָלֶיהָ — he should regret his actions and confess his sin,[10] וִיקַבֵּל עַל עַצְמוֹ בְּלֵב שָׁלֵם — and accept upon himself with a sincere heart שֶׁלֹּא לַעֲשׂוֹתָהּ עוֹד — never to commit the sin again. וּבִפְרָט בַּעֲבֵירוֹת הַמְּצוּיוֹת — In particular, the commonly occurring sins, כְּגוֹן חֲנִיפוּת שְׁקָרִים לֵיצָנוּת לְשׁוֹן הָרַע

---

7. This usage is taken from *Devarim* 23:10.

8. *Mishnah Berurah* (238:2) writes that there is no fixed amount one should sleep each night; it depends on each individual's strength and stamina. However, one should not sleep more than necessary, so as not to minimize his Torah study.

9. Even if there are people in other rooms of the house, it is preferable to keep the door to the room open (see *Mishnah Berurah* 239:9 with *Shaar HaTziyun* §17). See above, 33:7, and note 12 there.

10. To obtain atonement for one's sins, it is essential to confess them before Hashem (see *Rambam, Hilchos Teshuvah* 1:1).

לְשׁוֹן הָרַע[11], צְרִיכִין בְּדִיקָה בְּיוֹתֵר[12]. גַּם יִתֵּן הָאָדָם אֶל לִבּוֹ לִמְחוֹל לְכָל אָדָם שֶׁחָטָא כְּנֶגְדּוֹ, שֶׁלֹּא יֵעָנֵשׁ שׁוּם אָדָם מֵחֲמָתוֹ[13], דְּאִיתָא בַּגְּמָרָא (שבת קמט, ב): כָּל מִי שֶׁחֲבֵרוֹ נֶעֱנַשׁ עַל יָדוֹ אֵין מַכְנִיסִין אוֹתוֹ בִּמְחִיצָתוֹ שֶׁל הַקָּדוֹשׁ בָּרוּךְ הוּא, וְיֹאמַר ג׳ פְּעָמִים "שָׁרֵי לְכָל מַאן דִּי צַעֲרַן", וְאַחַר כָּךְ יֹאמַר "רִבּוֹנוֹ שֶׁל עוֹלָם הֲרֵינִי מוֹחֵל" וְכוּ׳[14].

ד. אִם[15] לֹא קָרָא שָׁלֹשׁ פָּרָשִׁיּוֹת שֶׁל קְרִיאַת שְׁמַע[16] כְּשֶׁהָיָה לַיְלָה[17], אֲזַי יֹאמַר כָּל הַג׳ פָּרָשִׁיּוֹת בִּקְרִיאַת שְׁמַע שֶׁעַל הַמִּטָּה[18]. אֲבָל אִם אֲמָרָם בַּלַּיְלָה, אֵינוֹ צָרִיךְ לוֹמַר בִּקְרִיאַת שְׁמַע שֶׁעַל הַמִּטָּה כִּי אִם פָּרָשָׁה הָרִאשׁוֹנָה בִּלְבַד, וּמִכָּל מָקוֹם לְמִצְוָה מִן הַמּוּבְחָר יֹאמַר כָּל הַשָּׁלֹשׁ פָּרָשִׁיּוֹת. וְאַחַר כָּךְ אוֹמְרִים מִזְמוֹרֵי וּפְסוּקֵי דְרַחֲמֵי

— such as speaking words of **flattery, falsehoods, mockery,** and ***lashon hara***,[11] צְרִיכִין בְּדִיקָה בְּיוֹתֵר — **require meticulous examination** of one's deeds to root them out.[12] גַּם יִתֵּן הָאָדָם אֶל לִבּוֹ — At this time, **one should also be conscientious** לִמְחוֹל לְכָל אָדָם שֶׁחָטָא כְּנֶגְדּוֹ — **to forgive anyone who has sinned against him,** שֶׁלֹּא יֵעָנֵשׁ שׁוּם אָדָם מֵחֲמָתוֹ — **so that no person be punished on his account.**[13] דְּאִיתָא בַּגְּמָרָא — **For the Gemara states** (*Shabbos* 149b): כָּל מִי שֶׁחֲבֵרוֹ נֶעֱנַשׁ עַל יָדוֹ — **Anyone whose fellow is punished on his account** אֵין מַכְנִיסִין אוֹתוֹ בִּמְחִיצָתוֹ שֶׁל הַקָּדוֹשׁ בָּרוּךְ הוּא — **is not admitted to the enclosure of the Holy One, Blessed is He.** וְיֹאמַר ג׳ פְּעָמִים — **He should say** the following **three times:** "שָׁרֵי לְכָל מַאן דִּי צַעֲרַן" — **"I forgive anyone who has aggrieved me."** וְאַחַר כָּךְ יֹאמַר — **He should then say** the following prayer: "רִבּוֹנוֹ שֶׁל עוֹלָם הֲרֵינִי מוֹחֵל" וְכוּ׳ — ***Master of the universe, I hereby forgive*** etc.[14]

§4 The routine of *Krias Shema al HaMitah*, the Bedtime *Shema*, consists primarily of the recitation of *Shema* and the *HaMapil* blessing, and also includes various other prayers and verses. The recitation of this *Shema* immediately before retiring offers protection against the dangers of the night.[15]

אִם לֹא קָרָא שָׁלֹשׁ פָּרָשִׁיּוֹת שֶׁל קְרִיאַת שְׁמַע — **If,** when reciting *Maariv,* **one did not recite** all **three passages of** ***Shema***[16] כְּשֶׁהָיָה לַיְלָה — **when it was night,**[17] אֲזַי יֹאמַר כָּל הַג׳ פָּרָשִׁיּוֹת בִּקְרִיאַת שְׁמַע שֶׁעַל הַמִּטָּה — **then he should recite all three passages during the Bedtime** ***Shema.***[18] אֲבָל אִם אֲמָרָם בַּלַּיְלָה — **However, if he recited** all three passages **when it was** already **night,** אֵינוֹ צָרִיךְ לוֹמַר בִּקְרִיאַת שְׁמַע שֶׁעַל הַמִּטָּה — **he need not recite** all of **them during the Bedtime** ***Shema,*** כִּי אִם פָּרָשָׁה הָרִאשׁוֹנָה בִּלְבַד — **but only the first passage.** וּמִכָּל מָקוֹם — **Nevertheless,** לְמִצְוָה מִן הַמּוּבְחָר — in order **to** perform the **mitzvah** of reciting the Bedtime *Shema* **in the choicest way** יֹאמַר כָּל הַשָּׁלֹשׁ פָּרָשִׁיּוֹת — **he should recite all three passages** in any case. וְאַחַר כָּךְ אוֹמְרִים מִזְמוֹרֵי וּפְסוּקֵי דְרַחֲמֵי — **He should then**

11. Literally, *evil speech*, i.e., speaking negatively about another; see above, 30:1-6.

12. *Mishnah Berurah* (239:9) adds the sin of neglecting Torah study to the list of sins that require an added measure of examination.

13. In the merit of forgiving those who have wronged him, one attains a long life (*Mishnah Berurah* ibid.).

14. The complete prayer can be found in most *siddurim* (prayer books) in the section of the Bedtime *Shema*.

15. See *Berachos* 5a.

16. Cited above, introduction to *Siman* 17.

17. See above, 70:1.

18. He should do so with the intention of fulfilling the mitzvah of reciting the *Shema* and the mitzvah of remembering the Exodus from Egypt (*Mishnah Berurah* 239:1).

כְּמוֹ שֶׁנִּדְפַּס בְּסִידּוּרִים[19]. וְאוּלָם בְּרוֹב הַסִּידּוּרִים נִדְפַּס בִּרְכַּת הַמַּפִּיל קוֹדֶם קְרִיאַת שְׁמַע, וְיוֹתֵר טוֹב לוֹמַר בִּרְכַּת הַמַּפִּיל בַּסּוֹף, שֶׁתְּהֵא הַבְּרָכָה סְמוּכָה לְשֵׁינָה[20], וְיֹאמַר קְרִיאַת שְׁמַע עִם הַמִּזְמוֹרִים קוֹדֶם שֶׁהוֹלֵךְ לְמִטָּתוֹ, וּבִרְכַּת הַמַּפִּיל יֹאמַר כְּשֶׁהוּא עַל מִטָּתוֹ (עַיֵּין לְעֵיל סוֹף סִימָן ה')[21]. וְקוֹדֶם שֶׁיֵּלֵךְ לְמִטָּתוֹ, יֵלֵךְ אֶל הַמְּזוּזָה וְיָנִיחַ אֶצְבְּעוֹתָיו עָלֶיהָ וְיֹאמַר "ה' שׁוֹמְרִי" וְגוֹ'[22], וְאַחַר כָּךְ יֹאמַר ז' פְּעָמִים "בְּכָל דְּרָכֶיךָ" וְגוֹ' (משלי ג, ו)[23]. וּלְאַחַר שֶׁאָמַר בִּרְכַּת הַמַּפִּיל לֹא יֹאכַל וְלֹא יִשְׁתֶּה וְלֹא יְדַבֵּר עַד שֶׁיִּישַׁן[24]. אִם אֵינוֹ יָכוֹל לִישַׁן, יֹאמַר עוֹד הַפַּעַם קְרִיאַת שְׁמַע[25] וְהַמִּזְמוֹרִים וּפְסוּקֵי דְרַחֲמֵי, וְחוֹזֵר וְקוֹרֵא עַד שֶׁתַּחְטְפֶנּוּ שֵׁינָה[26]. אוֹ יֹאמַר כַּמָּה פְּעָמִים פְּסוּקִים אֵלוּ:

---

recite psalms and verses that make mention **of** God's **mercy,** **כְּמוֹ שֶׁנִּדְפַּס בְּסִידּוּרִים — as printed in the *siddurim*** (prayer books).[19] **וְאוּלָם בְּרוֹב הַסִּידּוּרִים — However, in most *siddurim*** **נִדְפַּס בִּרְכַּת הַמַּפִּיל קוֹדֶם קְרִיאַת שְׁמַע — the blessing of** *HaMapil, **Who casts** the bonds of sleep,* **is printed before** the *Shema,* **וְיוֹתֵר טוֹב לוֹמַר בִּרְכַּת הַמַּפִּיל בַּסּוֹף — but it is** actually **preferable to recite the *HaMapil* blessing at the conclusion** of the Bedtime prayers, **שֶׁתְּהֵא הַבְּרָכָה סְמוּכָה לְשֵׁינָה — so that the blessing** be recited **close to** the time of **sleep.**[20]

וְיֹאמַר קְרִיאַת שְׁמַע עִם הַמִּזְמוֹרִים — One should recite *Shema* and the aforementioned **psalms** **קוֹדֶם שֶׁהוֹלֵךְ לְמִטָּתוֹ — before going to his bed** for the night, **וּבִרְכַּת הַמַּפִּיל יֹאמַר כְּשֶׁהוּא עַל מִטָּתוֹ — and the *HaMapil* blessing** should be recited **when he** is already **in bed** (**עַיֵּין לְעֵיל סוֹף סִימָן ה'** — see above, end of *Siman* 5).[21] **וְקוֹדֶם שֶׁיֵּלֵךְ לְמִטָּתוֹ — Before going to bed,** **יֵלֵךְ אֶל הַמְּזוּזָה — he should approach the *mezuzah,*** **וְיָנִיחַ אֶצְבְּעוֹתָיו עָלֶיהָ — place his fingers upon it,** **וְיֹאמַר — and recite** the following: **"ה' שׁוֹמְרִי" וְגוֹ' — *HASHEM is my guardian,* etc.**[22] **וְאַחַר כָּךְ יֹאמַר ז' פְּעָמִים — He should then say** the following **seven times:** **"בְּכָל דְּרָכֶיךָ" וְגוֹ' — *In all your ways,*** *know Him* etc. (*Mishlei* 3:6).[23] **וּלְאַחַר שֶׁאָמַר בִּרְכַּת הַמַּפִּיל — After one has recited the *HaMapil* blessing,** **לֹא יֹאכַל וְלֹא יִשְׁתֶּה וְלֹא יְדַבֵּר — he should not eat, drink, or speak,** **עַד שֶׁיִּישַׁן — until he falls asleep.**[24] **אִם אֵינוֹ יָכוֹל לִישַׁן — If he cannot fall asleep,** **יֹאמַר עוֹד הַפַּעַם קְרִיאַת שְׁמַע — he should recite *Shema* again,**[25] **וְהַמִּזְמוֹרִים וּפְסוּקֵי דְרַחֲמֵי — as well as the psalms and verses** that make mention **of** God's **mercy.** **וְחוֹזֵר וְקוֹרֵא — He should continuously repeat** these passages **עַד שֶׁתַּחְטְפֶנּוּ שֵׁינָה — until he is overcome by sleep.**[26]

אוֹ יֹאמַר כַּמָּה פְּעָמִים פְּסוּקִים אֵלוּ — Alternatively, he should say the following verses

---

19. If one cannot recite the entire Bedtime *Shema* (e.g., he is ill), he may recite just the first passage of *Shema* and the *HaMapil* blessing (*Mishnah Berurah* 239:9).

20. *Mishnah Berurah* (239:2) suggests that one who is prone to falling asleep while reciting the Bedtime *Shema* should say *HaMapil* first.

21. There, Kitzur writes how one should recite a blessing when not fully dressed.

22. ה' שׁוֹמְרִי, ה' צִלְּךָ עַל יַד יְמִינֶךָ, *HASHEM is my Guardian; HASHEM is my protective Shade at my right hand* (cf. *Tehillim* 121:5); see above, 11:24.

23. The full verse reads: בְּכָל דְּרָכֶיךָ דָעֵהוּ וְהוּא יְיַשֵּׁר אֹרְחֹתֶיךָ, *In all your ways know Him, and He will smooth your paths.*

24. One who recited *Shema* and then becomes thirsty may drink and then repeat the first passage of *Shema*. However, if he has already recited the *HaMapil* blessing, he should be careful not to drink before going to sleep (*Mishnah Berurah* 239:4).

25. *Mishnah Berurah* (239:7) writes that only the first passage should be repeated, with the opening verse (*Shema Yisrael* etc.) omitted.

26. One may also think Torah thoughts until he falls asleep (*Mishnah Berurah* 239:6).

״תּוֹרָה צִוָּה לָנוּ״ וְגוֹ׳ (דברים לג, ד)[27], **״אֵשׁ תָּמִיד״ וְגוֹ׳** (ויקרא ו, ו)[28], **״סֵעֲפִים שָׂנֵאתִי״ וְגוֹ׳** (תהלים קיט, קיג)[29], **״אוֹר זָרֻעַ״ וְגוֹ׳** (שם צז, יא) [30], **עַד שֶׁתַּחְטְפֶנּוּ שֵׁינָה, וְהִיא סְגוּלָּה לְהִנָּצֵל מִמִּקְרֵה לַיְלָה, רַחֲמָנָא לִיצְלַן. וּתְהֵא כַּוָּנָתוֹ בְּשֵׁינָה לְחַזֵּק כֹּחוֹ לַעֲבוֹדַת קוֹנוֹ וַאֲזַי נֶחְשֶׁבֶת לוֹ לַעֲבוֹדַת שָׁמַיִם**[31]**. אִם צָרִיךְ לְשַׁמֵּשׁ מִטָּתוֹ, לֹא יֹאמַר תְּחִלָּה בִּרְכַּת הַמַּפִּיל, אֶלָּא אַחַר כָּךְ קוֹרֵא לְכָל הַפָּחוֹת פָּרָשָׁה הָרִאשׁוֹנָה שֶׁל קְרִיאַת שְׁמַע וְאוֹמֵר בִּרְכַּת הַמַּפִּיל**[32]**.**

ה. יַפְשִׁיט מַלְבּוּשָׁיו מֵעָלָיו וְלֹא יִישַׁן בְּמַלְבּוּשָׁיו. כְּשֶׁחוֹלֵץ מִנְעָלָיו וּפוֹשֵׁט בְּגָדָיו, חוֹלֵץ וּפוֹשֵׁט שֶׁל שְׂמֹאל תְּחִלָּה[33]**. וְלֹא יָנִיחַ מַלְבּוּשָׁיו תַּחַת מְרַאֲשׁוֹתָיו, כִּי מְשַׁכֵּחַ לִימּוּדוֹ**[34]**. וְצָרִיךְ לִיזָּהֵר מְאֹד לְהַרְגִּיל אֶת עַצְמוֹ לִשְׁכַּב עַל צִדּוֹ, וְאִיסּוּר גָּדוֹל לִשְׁכַּב פְּרַקְדָּן, דְּהַיְינוּ גַּבּוֹ לְמַטָּה וּפָנָיו לְמַעְלָה, אוֹ**

---

several times: **״תּוֹרָה צִוָּה לָנוּ״ וְגוֹ׳** — ***The Torah that** Moshe **commanded us,* etc.**[27] (*Devarim* 33:4); **״אֵשׁ תָּמִיד״ וְגוֹ׳** — ***A constant fire,* etc.**[28] (*Vayikra* 6:6); **״סֵעֲפִים שָׂנֵאתִי״ וְגוֹ׳** — ***The plotters of evil I hate,* etc.**[29] (*Tehillim* 119:113); **״אוֹר זָרֻעַ״ וְגוֹ׳** — ***Light is sown,* etc.**[30] (*Tehillim* 97:11). **עַד שֶׁתַּחְטְפֶנּוּ שֵׁינָה** — He should repeat these verses **until he is overcome by sleep.** **וְהִיא סְגוּלָּה לְהִנָּצֵל מִמִּקְרֵה לַיְלָה, רַחֲמָנָא לִיצְלַן** — **This is a mystical aid for attaining** Divine **protection against** experiencing **a nocturnal emission, God forbid.**

וּתְהֵא כַּוָּנָתוֹ בְּשֵׁינָה לְחַזֵּק כֹּחוֹ לַעֲבוֹדַת קוֹנוֹ — **One's purpose in sleeping should be to strengthen himself for the service of his Creator,** **וַאֲזַי נֶחְשֶׁבֶת לוֹ לַעֲבוֹדַת שָׁמַיִם** — **and then** this ordinarily mundane activity **is considered a service of God.**[31] **אִם צָרִיךְ לְשַׁמֵּשׁ מִטָּתוֹ** — **If one needs to engage in marital relations,** **לֹא יֹאמַר תְּחִלָּה בִּרְכַּת הַמַּפִּיל** — **he should not recite the *HaMapil* blessing first.** **אֶלָּא אַחַר כָּךְ קוֹרֵא** — **Rather, afterward he should recite** **לְכָל הַפָּחוֹת פָּרָשָׁה הָרִאשׁוֹנָה שֶׁל קְרִיאַת שְׁמַע** — **at least the first passage of *Shema,*** **וְאוֹמֵר בִּרְכַּת הַמַּפִּיל** — **and** then **say the *HaMapil* blessing.**[32]

§5 יַפְשִׁיט מַלְבּוּשָׁיו מֵעָלָיו — Before going to sleep, **one should undress** **וְלֹא יִישַׁן בְּמַלְבּוּשָׁיו** — **and not sleep in his clothing.** **כְּשֶׁחוֹלֵץ מִנְעָלָיו וּפוֹשֵׁט בְּגָדָיו** — **When one takes off his shoes and disrobes,** **חוֹלֵץ וּפוֹשֵׁט שֶׁל שְׂמֹאל תְּחִלָּה** — **he should take off** his **left** shoe **and remove the left** side of his garment **first, before** the right side.[33] **וְלֹא יָנִיחַ מַלְבּוּשָׁיו תַּחַת מְרַאֲשׁוֹתָיו** — **He should not place his clothing under his head,** **כִּי מְשַׁכֵּחַ לִימּוּדוֹ** — **for** this practice **causes one to forget his learning.**[34] **וְצָרִיךְ לִיזָּהֵר מְאֹד לְהַרְגִּיל אֶת עַצְמוֹ לִשְׁכַּב עַל צִדּוֹ** — **One should take extreme care to accustom himself to lie on his side.** **וְאִיסּוּר גָּדוֹל לִשְׁכַּב פְּרַקְדָּן** — **It is a grave sin to lie down *prakdan,***[35] **דְּהַיְינוּ גַּבּוֹ לְמַטָּה וּפָנָיו לְמַעְלָה** — **that is, his back**

---

27. The full verse reads: תּוֹרָה צִוָּה לָנוּ מֹשֶׁה מוֹרָשָׁה קְהִלַּת יַעֲקֹב, *The Torah that Moshe commanded us is the heritage of the congregation of Yaakov.*

28. The full verse reads: אֵשׁ תָּמִיד תּוּקַד עַל הַמִּזְבֵּחַ לֹא תִכְבֶּה, *A constant fire shall remain aflame on the Altar; it shall not be extinguished.*

29. The full verse reads: סֵעֲפִים שָׂנֵאתִי וְתוֹרָתְךָ אָהָבְתִּי, *The plotters of evil I hate, but I love Your Torah.*

30. The full verse reads: אוֹר זָרֻעַ לַצַּדִּיק וּלְיִשְׁרֵי לֵב שִׂמְחָה, *Light is sown for the righteous; and for the upright of heart, gladness.*

31. See above, 31:4.

32. Before reciting *Shema* he should wash his hands and make sure that his body is clean (*Mishnah Berurah* 239:5).

33. See above, 3:4.

34. See *Mishnah Berurah* 2:2.

35. See *Berachos* 13b. This is explained below, 151:2.

בְּהִיפּוּךְ פָּנָיו לְמַטָּה וְגַבּוֹ לְמַעְלָה, אֶלָּא דַוְקָא עַל צִדּוֹ. וְטוֹב שֶׁיִּשְׁכַּב בִּתְחִלַּת שֵׁינָתוֹ עַל צַד שְׂמֹאל וּבְסוֹף עַל צַד יָמִין, וְהוּא טוֹב לִבְרִיאַת הַגּוּף, כִּי הַכָּבֵד מוּנָּח בְּצַד יָמִין וְהָאִיצְטוֹמְכָא בְּצַד שְׂמֹאל וְכַאֲשֶׁר יַטֶּה עַל צַד שְׂמֹאל אֲזַי יְהֵא הַכָּבֵד עַל הָאִצְטוֹמְכָא וִיחַמְּמָהּ בְּחוּמּוֹ וּבָזֶה יִתְעַכֵּל הַמָּזוֹן מְהֵרָה, וְאַחֲרֵי שֶׁנִּתְעַכֵּל הַמָּזוֹן רָאוּי לוֹ שֶׁיַּטֶּה עַל צַד יָמִין כְּדֵי שֶׁתָּנוּחַ הָאִצְטוֹמְכָא וְיֵרֵד פְּסוֹלֶת הַמַּאֲכָל. וְלֹא יִתְהַפֵּךְ מִצַּד עַל צַד פְּעָמִים הַרְבֵּה. (הִלְכוֹת צְנִיעוּת יְבוֹאַר אִם יִרְצֶה ה׳ בְּסִימָן ק״נ.)

---

below and his face turned **upward,** **אוֹ בְּהִיפּוּךְ** — **or** to lie in **the reverse** position, **פָּנָיו לְמַטָּה וְגַבּוֹ לְמַעְלָה** — that is, with **his face** turned **downward and his back above. אֶלָּא דַוְקָא עַל צִדּוֹ** — **Rather,** one should lie **only on his side. וְטוֹב שֶׁיִּשְׁכַּב בִּתְחִלַּת שֵׁינָתוֹ עַל צַד שְׂמֹאל — It is best to lie on the left side for the beginning of his sleep, וּבְסוֹף עַל צַד יָמִין — and at the end, on his right side. וְהוּא טוֹב לִבְרִיאַת הַגּוּף** — This practice **has a positive effect on one's health, כִּי הַכָּבֵד מוּנָּח בְּצַד יָמִין — for the liver is located on the right side** of the body, **וְהָאִיצְטוֹמְכָא בְּצַד שְׂמֹאל — and the stomach on the left side. וְכַאֲשֶׁר יַטֶּה עַל צַד שְׂמֹאל — When one lies on his left** side, **אֲזַי יְהֵא הַכָּבֵד עַל הָאִצְטוֹמְכָא — then the liver** lies **on the stomach וִיחַמְּמָהּ בְּחוּמּוֹ — and** the liver **warms** the stomach **with** the liver's **heat, וּבָזֶה יִתְעַכֵּל הַמָּזוֹן מְהֵרָה — thus expediting the digestion of the food. וְאַחֲרֵי שֶׁנִּתְעַכֵּל הַמָּזוֹן — After the food has been digested,** later in the night, **רָאוּי לוֹ שֶׁיַּטֶּה עַל צַד יָמִין — it is proper for him to turn onto his right side, כְּדֵי שֶׁתָּנוּחַ הָאִצְטוֹמְכָא — so that his stomach can rest** from the digestive process, **וְיֵרֵד פְּסוֹלֶת הַמַּאֲכָל — and the waste** portion **of the food can descend** to the small intestine. **וְלֹא יִתְהַפֵּךְ מִצַּד עַל צַד פְּעָמִים הַרְבֵּה — One should not turn from side to side many times** during the night. **(הִלְכוֹת צְנִיעוּת יְבוֹאַר אִם יִרְצֶה ה׳ בְּסִימָן ק״נ) — The laws of modesty** with respect to marital relations **will be explained, God willing, in *Siman* 150.)**

411 ⌒ APPENDIX A – SHIURIM

⊷§ Appendix A

SHIURIM: HALACHIC MEASUREMENT EQUIVALENTS

The following chart describes the halachic measurements that are mentioned in the course of the Kitzur, in terms of their current equivalents. Three of the commonly held determinations regarding these equivalents are presented, those of *R' Chaim No'eh*, *R' Moshe Feinstein* and *Chazon Ish* (*R' Avraham Yeshayahu Karelitz*). Each of these measurements is presented in both English and metric units.[1]

[Regarding the measurements that were used by the Kitzur himself, see his *Kelalim* (Definition of Terms, printed in the beginning of this volume), where the *amah* is measured as approximately 1 Bohemian cubit, or three-quarters of a Viennese cubit. In modern terms this is approximately 23 in., or 58 cm. Note that this measure is approximately as large as the largest measure set forth in the chart below, that of the *Chazon Ish*. In contrast, regarding measures of volume, Kitzur's measurements are closer to the smaller measurements recorded here.][2]

© 2010, MPL	R' Chaim No'eh		R' Moshe Feinstein		Chazon Ish[3]	
	English	*Metric*	*English*	*Metric*	*English*	*Metric*
Length of Barleycorn[4] (אורך שעורה)	.4 in.[5]	10 mm.[5]	–	–	.44 in.	11 mm.
Thumb-breadth (אגודל)	.8 in.	2 cm.	.9 in.	2.3 cm.	.95 in.	2.4 cm.
Thumb-joint[6] (קשר אגודל)	1.6 in.	4 cm.	–	–	1.6 in.	4 cm.
3 Thumb-breadths	2.3 in.	6 cm.	2.6 in.	6.7 cm.	2.75 in.[7]	7 cm.[7]
1 Tefach = 4 Thumb-breadths	3.2 in.	8 cm.	3.6 in.	9 cm.	3.8 in.	9.6 cm.
2 Tefachim = 8 Thumb-breadths	6.3 in.	16 cm.	7.1 in.	18 cm.	7.6 in.	19.2 cm.
3 Tefachim = 12 thumb-breadths	9.5 in.	24 cm.	10.6 in.	27 cm.	11.4 in.	28.9 cm.
4 Tefachim	12.6 in.	32 cm.	14.2 in.	36 cm.	15.2 in.	38.5 cm.
³/₄ Amah	14.2 in.	36 cm.	15.9 in.	40.5 cm.	17.1 in.	43.3 cm.
Amah	18.9 in.	48 cm.	21.3 in.	54 cm.	22.7 in.	57.7 cm.

---

1. In many instances, the measurements have been rounded to one decimal place.

2. See *Kelalim*; see also *Mishnah Berurah* (486:1), who cites *Shaarei Teshuvah,* which states that one should follow the stringent view when fulfilling Biblical obligations. See below, note 11.

3. The measurements of the *Chazon Ish* set out in this chart are based on the measurement of 10 *tefachim* being the equivalent of 96.2 centimeters [37.9 inches] (see *Shiurei HaMitzvos* [§1] by *R' Yaakov Yisrael Kanievski,* printed as an

addendum to his *sefer Shiurin Shel Torah,* 1979 edition). From this measurement, the rest of the measurements are extrapolated (1 *tefach* = 9.62 cm. [3.8 in.], etc.). It should be noted, however, that when dealing with Biblical obligations, *Chazon Ish* advised using a more stringent measure. Thus, when stringency demands a larger measurement (such as with regard to the minimum length of the *tzitzis* strings when the strings were severed — see Kitzur 9:13), then all measurements should be based on a larger 2.5 centimeter (.98 in.) thumb-breadth (the thumb-breadth

APPENDIX A — SHIURIM ⟿ 412

© 2010, MPL	R' Chaim No'eh		R' Moshe Feinstein		Chazon Ish	
	English	Metric	English	Metric	English	Metric
10 Tefachim	31.5 in. (2.6 ft.)	80 cm.	35.4 in. (3 ft.)	90 cm.	37.9 in. (3.2 ft.)	96.2 cm.
4 Amos	75.6 in. (6.3 ft.)	1.92 m.	85 in. (7 ft. 1 in.)	2.2 m.	90.9 in. (7.6 ft.)	2.3 m.
4 x 4 Amos	39.7 sq. ft.	3.7 sq. m.	50.2 sq. ft.	4.66 sq. m.	57.4 sq. ft.	5.32 sq. m.
Mil (2,000 Amos)	.6 mile	.96 km.	.67 mile	1.1 km.	.7 mile	1.15 km.
4 Mil = 1 Parsah	2.4 mile	3.84 km.	2.68 mile	4.3 km.	2.87 mile	4.6 km.
Volume of a Quarter-Log (רביעית)	2.9 fl. oz.	86.4 cc	2.9-4.4 fl. oz.[8]	86-130.7 cc.[8]	5.1 fl. oz.	150 cc.
Volume of an Olive (כזית)	.6-1 fl. oz.[9]	17.3-28.8 cc.[9]	.7-1 fl. oz.[10]	20-29.6 cc.[10]	1.1 fl. oz.[11]	33.3 cc.[11]

being the basic unit of measurement; see above, *Kelalim*). Accordingly, one tefach will equal 10 cm. (3.9 in.), and one *amah* will equal 60 cm. (23.6 in.), etc.

Conversely, when a stringent approach would demand a smaller measurement (again, with regard to Biblical requirements), such as when measuring the maximum distance from the hole for the *tzitzis* to the corner of the garment (Kitzur 9:3), it has been recommended that one should take even the smaller system of measurement (that of *R' Chaim No'eh* in the chart) into account (see *Chazon Ish, Orach Chaim* 39:15; *Shiurei HaMitzvos* §3) See below, note 7.

For further discussion of the measures of the *Chazon Ish* as they apply to the various measurements and in relation to different mitzvos, see *Shiurin Shel Torah* by *R' Yaakov Yisrael Kanievski.*

4. This is the required width of *tefillin* straps; see Kitzur 10:13.

5. *R' Chaim No'eh* estimates this at .4 in. (10 mm.); however, he writes that .36 in. (9 mm.) may also suffice.

6. [The measurements that appear here from *R' Chaim No'eh* and *Chazon Ish* are their estimated measurements. Both recommend using 1.6 in. (4 cm.), but agree that 1.4 in. (3.5 cm.) may actually be sufficient.

7. See *Shiurei HaMitzvos* (§3), who recommends a maximum of 2.3 in. (6 cm.) for the distance between the edge of a garment and the hole for its *tzitzis* [he adds that it should certainly not exceed 2.7 in. (7 cm.)].

8. *R' Dovid Feinstein, shlita.* The larger measurement is to be used for Biblical obligations, while the smaller measure can be relied on for Rabbinic obligations.

9. The smaller measurements may be used for Rabbinic obligations, and the larger measurement should be followed when fulfilling a Biblical obligation. [The 1 fl. oz. (28.8 cc.) measure recorded here for the Biblical *kezayis* is slightly larger than the actual calculation of *R' Chaim No'eh* for this measure; however, he advises that when fulfilling a mitzvah that calls for eating a *kezayis*, one should eat this larger amount, to account for any food that remains lodged in the mouth and not swallowed.] See note 11.

10. The larger measurement is to be used for Biblical obligations, while the smaller measure can be relied upon for Rabbinic obligations.

11. This measure of 1.1 fl. oz. (33.3 cc.) is based on the determination of the *Chazon Ish* of an average size of our current eggs as 1.7 fl. oz. (50 cc.), and measuring a *kezayis* as $^2/_3$ of the volume of an egg. According to *Mishnah Berurah* (486:1), however, when fulfilling Biblical obligations, one should measure a *kezayis* as equivalent to the current size of one egg. This would yield a measurement of 1.7 fl. oz. (50 cc.) for a *kezayis*. See also *Kelalim.*

Note that even the 1.1 fl. oz. measurement is only to be used when the larger amount results in a stringency. When using a larger measure would result in leniency *Shiurei Mitzvos* (§24) writes that one must consider the possibility that an amount as small as the size of today's olives would be considered a *kezayis*. [For example, one who has eaten less than 1.1 fl. oz. of bread, but an amount as large as one of today's olives, would have a doubtful obligation to recite *Bircas HaMazon* and should see to it that his obligation is fulfilled (e.g. by eating the full 1.1 oz. measure; see *Kitzur* 44:5).]

413 APPENDIX B — ZEMANIM

Appendix B

זְמַנִּים, ZEMANIM: DIVISION OF HALACHIC TIMES THROUGHOUT THE DAY

The purpose of this Appendix is to provide an outline of the various halachic times commonly applicable over the course of a standard day. The halachos involved in determining these time periods are extremely complex, both from a halachic and a technical standpoint; a serious treatment of these halachos would require an in-depth study. This Appendix provides a list of the *zemanim* accompanied by a general definition of the terms and some of the halachos that apply during these times. Various opinions regarding some of the *zemanim* are noted, but by no means are all the opinions on any individual topic addressed.[1]

(1) שָׁעוֹת זְמַנִּיּוֹת, SHA'OS ZEMANIYOS — SEASONAL HOURS

Many of the *zemanim* are listed here as a certain number of hours into the day. For example, the latest time to recite *Shema* is three hours into the day; to pray *Shacharis,* four hours. Unless otherwise noted, these do not refer to our set hours of 60 minutes, but to hours in the Talmudic system of שָׁעוֹת זְמַנִּיּוֹת, *seasonal hours.* In this system, the night and day are divided into twelve equal segments regardless of the length of that particular day. Each of these segments is referred to as an "hour."

Thus, in the winter, when there are less than twelve standard daytime hours, each seasonal hour will be shorter than 60 minutes. Conversely, in the summer when there are more than twelve standard daylight hours, each seasonal hour will be longer than 60 minutes. Thus the "three hours" for the latest time for *Shema* actually represents a fourth of any given day; the "four hours" for *Shacharis* represents a third (*Rambam, Commentary* to *Berachos* 1:2; see *Orach Chaim* 58:1, 89:1, 233:1, and Kitzur 69:2).

There is a controversy as to how to measure the length of the "day" that is used as the basis of this calculation. *Magen Avraham* (58:1, 233:3, 443:3) maintains that the day is measured from daybreak (עֲלוֹת הַשַּׁחַר), until nightfall (צֵאת הַכּוֹכָבִים). *Gra,* however, maintains that the day begins at sunrise and ends at sunset.[2]

[Each seasonal hour will be shorter according to the calculation of the *Gra* than according to that of the *Magen Avraham,* since for the purposes of this calculation, *Gra* considers "day" to start with sunrise (which is after daybreak), and end with

1. This Appendix should therefore not be used to compute the start or end time of any of the daily *zemanim.* One can consult any of the reliable calendars that are available, which provide detailed halachic times for each day and location.

2. *Shenos Eliyahu* to *Berachos* 1:1; *Beur HaGra* to *Orach Chaim* 459:2. See Kitzur 17:1, 113:2 and 139:10, where he follows the opinion of *Magen Avraham;* see, however, Kitzur 69:2, where he appears to follow the opinion of *Gra.*

APPENDIX B — ZEMANIM ⟶ **414**

sunset (which is earlier than nightfall). Despite this, the three "hours" for *Shema* will always end earlier according to the *Magen Avraham,* since according to his calculation, we do not begin to count these hours from sunrise, but from the much earlier time of daybreak.]

(2) עֲלוֹת הַשַּׁחַר / עַמּוּד הַשַּׁחַר, ALOS HASHACHAR / AMUD HASHACHAR — DAYBREAK

❑ **Halachic Application:** One may not eat or involve himself in personal endeavors from daybreak until one prays *Shacharis* (Kitzur, *Siman* 8). One who prays *Shacharis* as early as *alos hashachar,* although it is not the optimal time, has fulfilled his obligation (ibid. 18:1).

❑ **Time:** *Alos hashachar* occurs some time before sunrise when light begins to appear on the horizon. *Mishnah Berurah* cites two opinions regarding exactly when this takes place. According to some authorities, *alos hashachar* occurs when the *first* light of dawn appear on the eastern horizon. Others hold that *alos hashachar* occurs a bit later, when the light spreads across the *entire* eastern horizon.[3]

The Gemara in *Pesachim* (94a) writes that an average person can walk four *mil*[4] from *alos hashachar* until the later occurrence of sunrise. According to some authorities, the time it takes to walk a *mil* is 18 minutes.[5] Thus, in their view, *alos* occurs 72 minutes before sunrise.[6] Others calculate the time it takes to walk a *mil* as 22.5 minutes. Accordingly, *alos* occurs 90 minutes before sunrise.[7]

However, there is another variable to be considered when calculating the time of *alos hashachar.* According to some authorities, the above numbers of minutes before sunrise (72 or 90) apply at all latitudes and at all times of the year.[8] Others, however, maintain that these numbers apply only in Eretz Yisrael on the equinox day. Thus, the time of *alos hashachar* will vary at other latitudes and seasons.[9]

---

3. *Mishnah Berurah* 58:18, with *Beur Halachah* to 85:4 ד"ה משעלה עה"ש; and *Mishnah Berurah* 89:2,3, with *Beur Halachah* to 89:1 ד"ה ואם התפלל.

4. See Appendix A.

5. *Yoreh Deah* 69:6; *Orach Chaim* 459:2; *Rama, Orach Chaim* 261:1.

6. *Rambam, Peirush HaMishnayos, Berachos* 1:1; see *Magen Avraham* 89:2.

7. *Beur HaGra, Orach Chaim* 459:2 ד"ה ושיעור; *Minhag Eretz Yisrael,* following *R' Y.M. Tukechinsky.*

8. Glosses of *Rav Henkin* to *Ezras Torah* calendar, *Tzom Gedaliah.*

9. According to these authorities, to calculate *alos hashachar* for other latitudes and seasons, we must first determine the angle of the sun (measured in degrees) at the time of *alos hashachar* in Eretz Yisrael on the spring or fall equinox (or any other location that has the latitudinal coordinates of Eretz Yisrael). This

number of degrees will become the true measure for *alos hashachar,* and can be applied to other latitudes and seasons of the year (*Beur HaGra, Orach Chaim* 261:2; *Yoreh Deah* 262:9; *Minhag Eretz Yisrael,* following *R' Y.M. Tukechinsky*). When the calculations are made, it emerges that at 72 minutes before sunrise the sun's position is 16.1 degrees beneath the horizon; 90 minutes before sunrise, the sun's position is 19.8 degrees beneath the horizon. These numbers are used by these authorities to calculate when *alos* will occur in any location on any given day.

There is yet another opinion, which fixes the halachic time of *alos* as when the sun's position is 18 degrees below the horizon (see *Melamed LeHo'il* 30; see also *Klei Nechoshes* from *R' Avraham Ibn Ezra, Shaar* 19). This opinion is based upon scientific observation of when the first light of dawn appears (following the first opinion cited from *Mishnah Berurah* in the text above).

(3) מִשֶׁיַּכִּיר, MISHEYAKIR — WHEN ONE CAN RECOGNIZE

❑ **Halachic Application**: The earliest time for donning *tallis* (Kitzur 9:9), *tefillin* (ibid. 10:2), and reciting the *Shema* (ibid. 17:1).

❑ **Time:** In *hilchos tzitzis* this time is described as when it is light enough to differentiate between the white and *techeiles* strings in *tzitzis* (Kitzur 9:9). In *hilchos tefillin* it is described as when it is light enough for one to recognize an acquaintance at a distance of four *amos* (ibid. 10:2). Both of these descriptions refer to the same time of day (*Mishnah Berurah* 58:2).

The time of *misheyakir* will vary according to location and time of year. Various estimates have been given for different locales, some as much as 60 minutes before sunrise in Eretz Yisrael, some as little as 35-40 minutes for the New York area. Many *zemanim* calendars note this time by degrees of the sun beneath the horizon.[10]

(4) הָנֵץ הַחַמָּה, HANETZ HACHAMAH ("NETZ") — SUNRISE

❑ **Halachic Application:** Mitzvos whose time of fulfillment is during the day should be performed only after sunrise (*Megillah* 20a). The optimal time for the recitation of *Shemoneh Esrei* is with sunrise (Kitzur 18:1).

❑ **Time:** *Hanetz hachamah* (commonly known simply as "*netz*") is generally understood to refer to the beginning of the appearance of the orb of the sun above the horizon. Some say, however, that it refers to some time before the entire orb of the sun rises above the horizon (see *Rama* 58:1; *Mishnah Berurah* 58:7).

(5) סוֹף זְמַן קְרִיאַת שְׁמַע, SOF ZEMAN KRIAS SHEMA — LATEST TIME TO RECITE SHEMA

❑ **Halachic Application:** The morning *Shema* must be recited by this time (see Kitzur 17:1).

❑ **Time:** Three seasonal hours from the beginning of the day, or, at the point that a quarter of the day has passed (see above, *Seasonal Hours,* for the two views regarding how seasonal hours are calculated).

(6) סוֹף זְמַן תְּפִלָּה, SOF ZEMAN TEFILLAH — LATEST TIME FOR SHACHARIS

❑ **Halachic Application:** One must pray *Shacharis* by this time (see Kitzur 18:1).

❑ **Time:** Four seasonal hours from the beginning of the day, or, at the point that a third of the day has passed (see above, *Seasonal Hours,* for the two views regarding how seasonal hours are calculated).

(7) חֲצוֹת הַיּוֹם, CHATZOS HAYOM — MIDDAY

❑ **Halachic Application:** Final time for praying *Shacharis* for one who did not pray earlier (see Kitzur 18:1).

❑ **Time:** Six hours from the beginning of the day. This is commonly calculated as half the time between sunrise and sunset.[11]

---

10 See *Igros Moshe*, *Orach Chaim* IV, §6; *Eidus LeYisrael* (*Rav Henkin*); *Kaf HaChaim* 18:18.

11. *Igros Moshe,* however, writes in several responsa (*Orach Chaim* I, §24; II, §20; IV, §62;

APPENDIX B — ZEMANIM ᴄ͛ᴼᴼ **416**

(8) מִנְחָה גְדוֹלָה, MINCHAH GEDOLAH — THE GREATER MINCHAH

❏ **Halachic Application:** Although this is before the ideal time for *Minchah,* one may pray *Minchah* beginning from this time in cases of need (see *Kitzur* 69:2; *Mishnah Berurah* 233:1).

❏ **Time:** One half-hour after Midday (six-and-a-half hours after the beginning of the day).[12]

(9) מִנְחָה קְטַנָּה, MINCHAH KETANAH — THE SMALLER MINCHAH

❏ **Halachic Application:** Ideally one should not pray *Minchah* prior to this time (ibid.).

❏ **Time:** Three-and-a-half seasonal hours after midday (nine-and-a-half hours from the beginning of the day).

(10) פְּלַג הַמִּנְחָה, PLAG HAMINCHAH — THE HALF MINCHAH

❏ **Halachic Application:** The Gemara (*Berachos* 27a), cites a disagreement whether one may pray *Minchah* from the time of *Minchah Ketanah* until nightfall, or whether the time for *Maariv* begins at *Plag HaMinchah.* The Gemara rules that each person may follow either opinion.[13]

❏ **Time:** Ten and three-quarter seasonal hours after the beginning of the day (or, one-and-a-quarter seasonal hours before the end of the day).

(11) שְׁקִיעָה, SHEKIAH — SUNSET

❏ **Halachic Application:** According to some authorities, *Minchah* may no longer be recited after sunset (see *Beur HaGra, Orach Chaim* 261:2). Other authorities hold that *Minchah* may be recited some time after sunset; see below. See *Mishnah Berurah* 233:14.

❏ **Time:** When the sun is no longer visible above the horizon.

(12) בֵּין הַשְּׁמָשׁוֹת, BEIN HASHEMASHOS — THE TRANSITION PERIOD BETWEEN DAYS[14]

At some point during *bein hashemashos,* a transition between day and night takes place, but it is unknown when this occurs. Thus, a given moment of *bein hashemashos* could be day [if the transition to night will occur later during *bein hashemashos*]; it could be night [if the transition occurred earlier], or it could be partly day and partly night [if the transition occurs during that very moment].[15] Since the moment of transition could conceivably occur either at the very beginning or at the very end of *bein hashemashos,* it is likewise possible that the *entire* period of *bein hashemashos* consists of night or day respectively.

---

and *Even HaEzer* I, §58), that the time of *chatzos* varies with the longitude; see there for further discussion.

12. See *Shaar HaTziyun* 233:8 as to whether this half-hour refers to 30 minutes or half of the seasonal hour of that day.

13. See *Orach Chaim* 233:1 and *Mishnah Berurah* ibid. 5-6 for further discussion. See

also *Kitzur* 69:2.

14. Literally, *between the suns;* "sun" is a synonym for "day" (see *Gur Aryeh* to Exodus 12:6; see also *Rashi, Shabbos* 134a ד"ה ולוקמיה).

15. See *Maharsha, Shabbos* 34b, in explanation of *Tosafos* ד"ה ספק לטומאה ולקרבן; cf. *Ritva* to *Yoma* 47b ד"ה אמר ר' יוחנן).

❑ **Halachic Application:** Due to this uncertainty, *bein hashemashos* must be treated with the stringency of both the previous and the following days. For example, one may not perform *melachah* (forbidden labor) during *bein hashemashos* on Friday, for the next day (Shabbos) may have already begun. By the same token, one may not perform melachah during *bein hashemashos* on Saturday, for it may still be the same day (Shabbos).

❑ **Time:** The Gemara (*Shabbos* 34b) states that *bein hashemashos* begins with "sunset," and lasts the amount of time it takes for an average person to walk 3/4 of a *mil* (or 1500 *amos*), after which it is considered night. There is some disagreement as to what that "sunset" refers to in relation to this definition. According to some authorities,[16] the Gemara here is referring to the standard meaning of sunset, when the orb of the sun disappears below the horizon. Therefore, if it takes 18 minutes to walk one *mil* (see above, *Alos HaShachar*), then *bein hashemashos* lasts 13.5 minutes. If it takes 22.5 minutes, then *bein hashemashos* lasts about 17 minutes after sunset. After this time, it is considered night.

Rabbeinu Tam, [17] however, asserts that the sunset referred to by the Gemara here is a "second sunset" — the "setting" of the sun's rays — which occurs well after the orb of the sun is no longer visible on the horizon.[18] According to *Rabbeinu Tam, bein hashemashos* begins at the time of the second sunset, and nightfall occurs somewhat later than this.[19]

(13) צֵאת הַכּוֹכָבִים, TZEIS HAKOCHAVIM — NIGHTFALL[20]

❑ **Halachic Application:** The previous day is considered to have definitely ended with nightfall. Thus, for example, at the end of Shabbos and Yom Tov it is permitted to perform *melachah* from this time.

❑ **Time:** *Mishnah Berurah* (235:1) writes simply that nightfall occurs when three medium-sized stars are visible in the night sky. For Biblical obligations we wait until three small stars are visible, so as to ensure beyond a doubt that three

16. *Rav Hai Gaon* and *Rav Sherira Gaon* (as cited in *Teshuvos Maharam Alashkar* §96; *Gra* to *Orach Chaim* 261:2 and *Yoreh Deah* 262:9).

17. *Rabbeinu Tam* is cited in *Tosafos* to *Shabbos* 35a ד״ה תרי and *Pesachim* 94a ד״ה ר״י; see *Shulchan Aruch, Orach Chaim* 261:2, and *Mishnah Berurah* ibid. 23-24.

18. *Rabbeinu Tam* bases this on the Gemara in *Pesachim* (94a) that states that a person can walk four *mil* (72 or 90 minutes) between sunset and nightfall (while the Gemara in *Shabbos* cited above states that *bein hashemashos* lasts only the time it takes to walk 3/4 of a *mil*). He reconciles these two sources by explaining that the Gemara in *Shabbos* refers to the "second sunset," while the Gemara in *Pesachim* refers to the first sunset.

19. The beginning of the second sunset can be calculated as 3 1/4 mil after the actual [first] sunset (either 58.5 or 73 1/8 minutes after sunset). See, however, *Tzeis HaKochavim* below, and end of note 21 there, which states that *bein hashemashos* may begin earlier than this even according to *Rabbeinu Tam.*

Igros Moshe (*Yoreh Deah* II, §79 and *Orach Chaim* IV, §62) writes that when possible, one should adhere to the stringent ramifications of both views cited above. Therefore, for example, on Friday evening one must abstain from performing *melachah* from sunset, because that is the beginning of *bein hashemashos* according to the first view cited above; and on Shabbos evening, one must continue to abstain from performing *melachah* until night has fallen even according to *Rabbeinu Tam.* See also *Mishnah Berurah* 261:23.

20. Literally, *the emergence of the stars.*

APPENDIX B — ZEMANIM 〜 **418**

medium-sized stars are visible (*Shulchan Aruch* 235:1 with *Taz* and *Magen Avraham* §1).[21]

Although, according to the first opinion mentioned in the previous section (*Bein HaShemashos*), nightfall should occur either 13.5 or about 17 minutes after actual sunset, while according to *Rabbeinu Tam* nightfall should not occur until four *mil* (either 72 or 90 minutes) after sunset, most authorities explain that even according to these opinions, it will always halachically be considered nightfall when three medium-sized stars are visible in the sky.[22] This time will vary from location to location.[23]

(14) חֲצוֹת הַלַּיְלָה, CHATZOS HALAILAH — MIDNIGHT

❏ **Halachic Application:** One must recite the *Maariv* prayer by *Chatzos HaLailah* (see Kitzur 70:2).

❏ **Time:** Twelve standard hours after *Chatzos HaYom*.

---

21. It is difficult to reconcile the absolute measures mentioned in the Gemara ($^3/_4$ *mil*, 4 *mil*), with the opinions of the halachic authorities who write that *tzeis hakochavim* varies from location to location; see *Mishnah Berurah* 261:22. *Gra* (*Beur HaGra, Orach Chaim* 261:2, *Yoreh Deah* 262:9) states that the $^3/_4$ *mil* measure is correct in Bavel (Babylonia) at the time of the equinox, and that *tzeis hakochavim* in other locations occurs when the sun is the same number of degrees beneath the horizon that it is in Bavel on the day of the equinox when the stars first become visible.

[Above (see *Bein HaShemashos* and note 15) it was stated that according to *Rabbeinu Tam*, *bein hashemashos* begins at the second sunset, either 58.5 or 73 $^1/_8$ minutes after actual sunset. Clearly, if *Rabbeinu Tam* agrees that nightfall occurs as soon as three stars are visible (which, as we have seen, occurs earlier than these times), *bein hashemashos* must also begin earlier. Some authorities therefore calculate the beginning of *bein hashemashos* according to *Rabbeinu Tam* as beginning $^3/_4$ of a *mil* (either 13.5 or 17 minutes) before the time that stars are actually visible. This is the opinion of Kitzur in his *Kelalim* (see there, *Bein HaShemashos*); this is also the opinion of *Chasam Sofer* (*Responsa, Orach Chaim* §80). See, however, *Igros Moshe, Orach Chaim* II, §79, who writes that the period of *bein hashemashos* will be even shorter in places where stars are visible less than 72 minutes after actual sunset.]

22. See, for example, *Responsa of Chasam Sofer, Orach Chaim* §80; *Minchas Kohen, Maamar* 2, Chapter 5; *Mishnah Berurah* 261:24 and *Beur Halachah* ibid. ד״ה קודם הלילה.

23. See *Igros Moshe, Orach Chaim* IV, §62 and *Yoreh Deah* II, §79), who writes that in the New York area stars are certainly visible by 50 minutes after sunset, and this time can certainly be regarded as "*tzeis hakochavim,*" nightfall, even according to *Rabbeinu Tam*.

APPENDIX OF KITZUR'S EDITORIAL GLOSSES

The author of the Kitzur wrote editorial glosses to his work, in which he expanded upon many of the subjects discussed in the Kitzur. These glosses appeared as footnotes in the 1884 edition upon which this edition is based. While these notes have appeared in other editions of the Kitzur, they have generally been intermingled with glosses of other commentators. In this Appendix, we present all of the Kitzur's original footnotes, as they appeared in the 1884 edition.

סי׳ ל״ה סעיף א

א. בספר שו״ת בנין ציון חלק א׳ סימן ק״ט שאלה: נוהגים העולם כשמשימין פרי האדמה שקורין קארטאפלע (ערדעפל) בעיסה שמפרישין בתחלה מעט כשיעור חלה טרם שמערבין קארטאפלען. ונראה לי טעם המנהג על פי המבואר ביורה דעה סימן שכ״ד סעיף י״א בשאור של אינו יהודי שמשימין אחר הפסח בעיסה שצריך להפריש יותר ממה שיש בהשאור שמא יפריש מן הפטור על החיוב. ואם כן הוא הדין כשיפריש חלה אחר שערבו פרי האדמה שמא יפריש חלה מהם. אבל נראה לי דלא דמי, שהרי דין זה שהוא מהתרומת הדשן (סי׳ ק״ץ) אינו אלא בשאור, אבל בשאר דברים, ואפלו בעיסה, אמרינן יש בילה וכו׳, ואפלו וכו׳, מכל מקום נראה לי דהכא כיון דנתפרדו הקארטאפעל לפרורין קטנים הוי כמו קמח בקמח דחשיב לח בלח, ואם כן פשיטא דיש בחלה מעט קמח, וחלה אין לה שיעור, ושפיר יכול לערב הקארטאפעל בשעת לישת הקמח קדם הפרשת עיסה לחלה. ועוד נראה לי ראיה ברורה לזה ממה שכתוב ביורה דעה סימן שכ״ד סעיף ט׳: העושה עיסה מחטים ואורז, אם יש בה טעם דגן וכו׳, עין שם, ופרשו התוספות (זבחים ע״ח ע״א ד״ה מתיב רבא) והרא״ש (הלכות קטנות, חלה סי׳ ח׳) הטעם משום דטעם כעקר דאוריתא, וכיון דפרי האדמה הם אינם מינו עם העיסה ויש בהם טעם דגן הם כמו קמח, ולא שייך מן הפטור על חיוב וכו׳, עד כאן לשונו. ולפי עניות דעתי נראין גם כן דבריו נכונים דהא עין רואה בהפרשת החלה שהוא בצק מגובל ולא הקארטאפלען. דהא הקארטאפלען לאו בר גיבול הן. ואף אם יש לחוש קצת שמא בתוך הכזית הזה יש איזה פרור מהאקארטאפעל שלא נתגבל בתוך העיסה, מנא לן לחוש לזה מאחר דמצד הדין חלה אין לה שיעור. והנה המחבר הנ״ל בתשובתו האריך קצת ונטה קו להחמיר. ולפי עניות דעתי אין דבריו מוכיחין ואין כאן מקומו להאריך. וביותר תמוה לי מה שכתב שם בסוף דבריו, וזה לשונו: ועוד נראה לי שיש לחוש, כיון שאם מערב הקארטאפעל מקודם, אף שיש טעם דגן בהם, מכל מקום גם טעמם נטעם בהעיסה, והרי לפי מה שכתב הט״ז סימן שכ״ד סעיף קטן ט״ו לא יפריש מהפשטידא, כיון שיש בו טעם בשר, אף שטעם הלחם לא בטל ממנה לגמרי, מכל מקום כיון שנטעם בו גם טעם אחר הוי כאינו מינו. ואם כן הוא הדין גם כן בבכי האי גונא וכו׳, עד כאן לשונו. תמיהני איך למד מדברי ט״ז אלו אשר כמו שהם לפנינו אין להם שחר, וכמו שכתוב בדגול מרבבה שלא ידע לזה טעם וריח. ובספר שערי דעה כתב להניח דבריו שיש בהם חסרון הניכר, עין שם. שוב (הראתי) [הראוני] מה שכתוב בליקוטי שו״ת חתם סופר חלק ששי סימן ח״י, והנראה לפי עניות דעתי כתבתי.

סי׳ ל״ח סעיף ה׳

ב. עין לקמן סימן ע״ב בהערה, דהמומר לחלל שבתות בפרהסיא דינו כעכו״ם גם לענין פת עכו״ם ובישולי עכו״ם כמו לכל דבר.

סי׳ ל״ט סעיף א׳

ג. דברים שכתבתי בסימן זה בארתי בעזרת השם בהערותי לספר חיי אדם.

סי׳ מ׳ סעיף ד

ד. בבית יוסף (אורח חיים ס׳ קס״א ד״ה שיעור; כסף משנה הל׳ ברכות ו:ד) כתב דדברי הרמב״ם סתומים. אבל בכסף משנה כתב כי יש לנו לומר דבשיטת הרי״ף רביה אמרה. ובהערותי לספר חיי אדם כתבתי בעזרת ה׳ הוכחה לזה, דהרמב״ם כהרי״ף סבירא ליה.

סי׳ מ׳ סעיף י״ב

ה. לפי מה שכתב המגן אברהם בסימן קס״א סעיף קטן ג׳, דאם רוב היד מכסה אפלו בדבר שאינו מקפיד, חוצץ, צריך לומר כי מה שכתב בשלחן ערוך שם סעיף ב׳: ״אף על פי שיש על ידיו ממשות״ וכו׳, הינו דוקא במיעוט היד, וסמך עצמו על מה שכתב בסעיף א׳, ודלא כמו שכתב בספר חיי אדם:״אפלו דבר שמכסה כל היד, אם דרכו בכך, אינו חוצץ״ וכו׳. ובהערותי שמה בארתי בעזרת ה׳ את הדבר, וגם כתבתי לתרץ קושית השבות יעקב (ח״א ס׳ ס״ט) שהביא המחצית השקל (סי׳ קס״א ס״ק ז), וכאן אין מקום להאריך.

סי׳ מ״ב סעיף י״ב

ו. לפי מה שכתב התוספות (בכורות מ״ד ע״ב ד״ה ואין) לחלק בין מים לשאר משקין, נראה דאין צריכין לחלק בין תוך הסעודה לשלא בתוך הסעודה. וגם פשטות הענין בעובדה דרב הונא משמע שהוא שלא בשעת סעודה.

סי׳ מ״ב סעיף י״ט

ז. כיון דלדעת הרי״ף (פסחים כ ע״א) והרמב״ם (הל׳ ברכות ד: ג-ה) והר״ח (רבינו חננאל פסחים קא ע״ב) בסימן קע״ח (ע׳ בית יוסף או״ח שם) גם בפת כל ששנה מקומו צריך לברך.

סי׳ מ״ב סעיף כ״א

ח. כי לדעת הפוסקים הנ״ל, אף אם היתה דעתו לכך, לא מהני לבית אחר.

סי׳ מ״ג סעיף א׳

ט. כמו כן כתב גם בספר חיי אדם (מג: א). ובאמת כי (בש״פ כתבו) [בש״ע כתב (או״ח קעז סע׳ א)]: ״דברים שדרך לקבע סעודה עליהם ללפת בהם את הפת״ וכו׳, וכן הוא לשון התוספות (ברכות מא ע״ב ד״ה הלכתא) והרא״ש (ברכות פרק ו סי׳ כו). ומלשון זה משמע דדברים שאין הדרך ללפת בהם את הפת, כגון, תפוחי אדמה, דוחן וכדומה, אפלו כוונת אכילתן לשבוע, צריך לברך עליהם. אבל מלשון תלמידי רבנו יונה (ברכות פ״ו, כט ע״א בדפי הרי״ף ד״ה אמר רב פפא) ורשב״א (ברכות מא ע״א ד״ה שלא מחמת), ועוד כמה פוסקים, מוכח דכל דבר שדרכו לאכלו בתוך הסעודה לשבוע אין מברכין עליו. וכן עמא דבר.

סי׳ מ״ג סעיף ו׳

י. כן כתב בספר חיי אדם (מג: ט-י). והנה בפירות כתבתי בסעיף ג׳ דאפלו היו מונחין על השלחן בשעת ברכת ״המוציא״ לא נפטרו, וכמו שכתב המגן אברהם סימן קע״ז סעיף קטן ב׳. וכן נראה ממה שכתב התוספות בברכות דף מ״ב הטעם דאין מברכין על המרור משום דרחמנא קבעיה חובה. אבל בכאן נראה, לפי עניות דעתי, הנכון כמו שכתב בספר חיי אדם (מג:ג) וכן כתב גם בשלטי גבורים (ברכות כט ע״א בדפי הרי״ף, ד״ה רש״י פי׳, אות ב׳), משום דכאן איכא ספיקי טובא: הרשב״א בחדושיו ברכות, דף מ״א ע״ב, כתב להדיא דאין מברכין על פת כיסנין שבתוך הסעודה (ודין לאחר הסעודה אינו נהוג בזמנינו), וכן נראה, לפי עניות דעתי, דעת תלמידי רבנו יונה בשם רבני צרפת (ברכות כט ע״א ד״ה ואומרים רבני צרפת) שם (ומה שכתב המגן אברהם בסימן קס״ח סעיף קטן כ״ב יש לישב). ולרש״י לא נזכר זאת כלל בגמרא. ועוד, הא אנן לא ידעינן מהו פת כיסנין, וכמו שכתב הדגול מרבבה ואבן העוזר (ס׳ קסח ד״ה

ובסעיף י״ג, קטע המתחיל ולפי זה) להשיג על המגן אברהם. על כן גם לפי עניות דעתי נראה שיש לסמך בזה על השלטי הגבורים.

סי׳ מ״ד סעיף א׳

יא. בגמרא (ברכות דף מ״ו ע״ב): ״מים אחרונים - בזמן שהם ה׳, מתחילין מן הגדול. ובזמן שהם מאה, מתחילין מן הקטן״ וכו׳, ופסקו כן בטור ושלחן ערוך (או״ח קפא: ו), ונמשכו אחריהם כל האחרונים ז״ל. ואנכי לא ראיתי מעולם שידקדקו בזה. ונראה לי משום דקים להו כהרי״ף (ברכות לד ע״ב) והרמב״ם (הל׳ ברכות ז:יב), וכמו שכתב בכסף משנה ובמגדול עז. גם בסמ״ג (עשה כז) וברבנו ירוחם (נתיב טז חלק ז) לא מצאתיו. והיותר תמוה, לפי עניות דעתי, על רבנו הטור, שהרי גם אביו הרא״ש, ז״ל, לא הביא דבר זה בדרך הילכתא, רק לקושיא ופרוקא בפרק ז׳ סוף סימן י״ד, עין שם. וגם על רבנו הבית יוסף ז״ל צריך עיון גדול שלא העיר בזה דבר.

סי׳ מ״ד סעיף י״ג

יב. בספר חיי אדם (מז:יח) לא כתב כן, וכבר השגתי שם עליו והבאתי שמה מה שכתב בברכי יוסף (או״ח קפח:ז).

סי׳ מ״ד סעיף י״ד

יג. כן הוכחתי בהערותי לספר חיי אדם שהעיקר לאמרו בפתיחה בשם ומלכות, והבאתי שמה שכן מבואר ברבינו ירוחם (נתיב יא חלק א) ובספר ארחות חיים (הל׳ ברכות אות נ), ושכן מוכח גם בקיצור פסקי הרא״ש (ז:כג), עין שם.

סי׳ מ״ד סעיף י״ז

יד. אבל בברכה אחרונה שעל הכוס שהוא שותה לאחר ברכת המזון (עין לקמן סימן צ״ו סעיף ד׳) נראה, לפי עניות דעתי, כיון שהוא שותה אותו כשהוא לילה, לא יזכיר של שבת (לאפוקי ממה ששמעתי מקצת בעלי תורה שאמרו להזכיר), עין מגן אברהם סימן קפ״ח סעיף קטן י״ח. שוב שמעתי שכן הורה גם אדוני מורי ורבי הגאון מהר״ם א״ש, זצ״ל, שלא להזכיר. ונראה פשוט דאם למחר ראש חדש, יזכיר של ראש חדש.

סימן מ״ה סעיף ו

טו. ומורי הגאון, הנ״ל, נהג שהמתין עד שאמר המזמן ״ברוך אתה ה׳״ ואז אמר ״ברוך הוא וברוך שמו״, ואחר כך התחיל הוא את הברכה.

סימן מ״ה סעיף ט

טז. בשולחן ערוך סימן ק״צ (סעי׳ ד): אם המברך אינו רוצה לטעום, יטעום אחד מהמסובין כשיעור וכו׳ וכתב בחידושי רבי עקיבא איגר דהמברך ברכת המזון (כיון שהוא לא ישתה) לא יברך ״בורא פרי הגפן״, אלא הטועם יברך, דדילמא ברכת המזון אינה טעונה כוס ולא הוי ברכת המצות ואינו יכול לברך בשביל אחר אם אינו מברך גם לעצמו. אבל בשו״ת חכם צבי סימן קס״ח כתב דדוקא המברך ברכת המזון צריך לברך גם על הכוס, וממילא דצריך הוא לשתות גם כן.

סימן מ״ה סעיף י

יז. עיין מחצית השקל (קצז: ו) ודבריו דחוקין. וכדברי הספר חמד משה (קצז:א) נראה לפי עניות דעתי העיקר.

סימן מ״ו סעיף ד

יח. עיין פתחי תשובה סימן פ״א סעיף קטן י׳. תשובות גור אריה יהודה סימן ק׳. טור יורה דעה סימן קי״ח קי״ט וספר כרם שלמה יורה דעה.

סימן מ״ח סעיף ב

יט. ממילא מובן שאם אוכל כזית ממין הראשון וגם כזית ממין השני, שהוא צריך נטילת ידים ו״המוציא״ וברכת המזון, דהא חד מינייהו ממה נפשך פת גמור הוא. ובעל חיי אדם בכלל נ״ד סימן ג׳ במחילת כבוד תורתו נתן בזה מקום לטעות בלשונו.

סימן מ״ח סעיף ה

כ. במגן אברהם סימן קס״ה סעיף קטן כ׳ היה נראה לומר לכאורה שהוא טעות סופר וצריך לומר ״אבל אם אינם דקים כל כך״ וכו׳. ומכל מקום לדינא נראה כמו שכתבנו דהא הט״ז בסוף סעיף קטן ט׳ כתב דהמין נאלסונקי אינם דקים כלל.

סימן מ״ח סעיף ט

כא. עיין מגן אברהם סימן קס״ח סעיף קטן כ״ח, והאחרונים ז״ל חלקו עליו. ותמיהני שלא העירו כי גדולי הפוסקים, הרי״ף והרמב״ם (הל׳ ברכות פרק ג הל׳ ח) והרא״ש ז״ל (ברכות פרק ו׳ סי׳ י), לא הביאו כלל הך אוקימתא (ברכות לז ע״ב) ״בשערסן״. ומוכח דסבירא להו דכיון דלמסקנא לא צריכין לה, גם לדינא לא קיימא לן הכי. וכמו אוקימתא ״בבא מלחם גדול״, ועיין נשמת אדם (כלל נד ס״ק ד׳). וגם נראה דהך ״בשערסן״ פירושו שגבלן במים, אבל בגבלן במי פירות, לא גרע מאם גבל קמח ממש במי פירות, דהוי ליה פת כסנין.

סימן מ״ח סעיף י

כב. כמו כן בספר חיי אדם כלל נ״ד סימן ט׳, ובפני אדם כתבתי שם שכן נראה לפי עניות דעתי, ושאין סתירה לזה מדברי הפרי מגדים בפתיחה אות י״א, כי שם מיירי שנתערבו ונתדבקו יחד ונעשו גוש אחד. וגם לישנא דרב ושמואל (ברכות לו ע״ב) דאמרי ״כל שיש בו מחמשת מיני דגן״ וכו׳, משמע שיש בו מעורב ומדובק. ועין טבול יום פרק ב׳ משנה ה׳: מעשה קדרה בקטניות. ויש גורסים וקטניות.

סימן מ״ט סעיף ד

כג. בט״ז סימן קע״ד, סעיף קטן ב׳, הביא דברי המרדכי, ובדגול מרבבה השיג עליו כי דעת המרדכי (ברכות רמז קנ) כדעת הסמ״ק דבזמן הזה אין קביעות ליין, ואנן קיימא לן בסימן רי״ג דמהני קביעות. ולפי עניות דעתי כיון דדעת התוספות (ברכות מא ע״ב ד״ה ויין) דלא קיימא לן כלל כרבי חייא, וגם הרמב״ם לא הביאו, די לנו לתפוס כדעת המרדכי.

סימן נ׳ סעיף יג

כד. המגן אברהם בסימן קע״ח (ס״ק יב) כתב דעל כל ז׳ מינים אינו צריך לברך בשינוי מקום משום דספק ברכות להקל, וכן כתב בספר חיי אדם (נט:טו). אבל בהערותי כתבתי כי מדקדוק לשון הרמ״א (או״ח קעח סע׳ ב) שכתב, וזה לשונו: ולכן מי שפסק סעודתו וכו׳ דהא פת צריך ברכה במקומו לכולי עלמא וכו׳, עד כאן לשונו, נראה, לפי עניות דעתי, כי דעתו רק בפת, כיון דלכולי עלמא צריך ברכה במקומו וליכא רק ספק אחד שמא הלכה כרב חסדא, ולכן הוי לקולא. אבל באינך ז׳ מינים, יש לברך, משום דאיכא תרי צדדים לברך - שמא הלכה כרב ששת (פסחים קא ע״ב), ואם תמצא לומר הלכה כרב חסדא, דלמא אינו צריך ברכה במקומו אלא פת בלבד. ומכל מקום, ודאי דלכתחלה יש ליזהר בכל ז׳ מינים שלא לשנות מקומו, ומכל שכן מיני דגן, דרוב הפוסקים סבירא להו דצריכין ברכה במקומו ולהפוסקים כרב חסדא אינן צריכין ברכה בשינוי מקום.

סימן נ״ב סעיף י

כה. כן כתב בספר גן המלך (אות ל׳) ובאבן העוזר (רב:ג). והפרי חדש (רב:ג) כתב לברך ״שהכל״ והסכים עמו בברכי יוסף (רב:ג). ולא ידעתי למה. וגם מלשון הרשב״א (ברכות לו

ע״ב ד״ה קליפי) משמע דדוקא גרעינין המרים לא נטעי להו אינשי אדעתא דהכי, אבל גרעינין המתוקים נראה דגם אדעתא דהכי נטעי להו.

סימן נ״ב סעיף יב

כו. כן נהג אדוני מורי ורבי הגאון מהר״ם א״ש זצ״ל. ואף כי האתרוגים המובאים למדינתינו עדיין לא נגמרו לגמרי, מכל מקום כיון שאנו יוצאין בהם ידי מצוה בעל כרחך דחשבינן להו לגמר פרי. וגם אדעתא דהכי נטעי להו לאכלו מרוקחין. ועיין שו״ת פנים מאירות חלק א׳ סוף סימן ס״ה כתב גם כן לברך עליהן ״בורא פרי העץ״.

סימן נ״ב סעיף יד

כז. אמת כי מלשון הטור בסימן ר״ד מוכח דאין מברכין עליהן רק ״שהכל״, והאחרונים ז״ל נחלקו בזה. ולפי עניות דעתי נראה העיקר לברך עליהן ״בורא פרי העץ״, כי לא שייך לומר שיהיו אלו בכלל נובלות שהן מין קללה. ובירושלמי (ברכות פרק ו הל׳ ג׳) איתא: ראה נובלות שנשרו אומר ״ברוך דיין האמת״ וכו׳, ואיך שייך לברך ״דיין האמת״ על דבר שהוא מצפה לו, והרי מין פירות שאינן מתבשלות לעולם על האילן מעיקרא אדעתא דהכי נטע את האילן והוא יושב ומצפה מתי ינשרו מן האילן להטמינם במקום שיתבשלו.

סימן נ״ד סעיף ד

כח. לא הוצרכתי לכתוב דין זה אלא מפני שראיתי למחבר אחד שכתב שהוא נוהג לברך על הפת כיסנין ולא על הקאפע מפני שהוא טפל. אבל מנהג כל גדולי ישראל אינו כן.

סימן נ״ה סעיף א

כט. בהערותי לספר חיי אדם כתבתי דבהגהות מימוניות (הל׳ ברכות פ״ו הל׳ יג) כתב דרבים העומדים בשיטת הרמב״ם ז״ל ושלפי עניות דעתי גם דעת הרי״ף ז״ל נראה כן. וכעת זכני ה׳ יתברך שמו לספר האשכול וראיתי שם בסימן כ״ט שגם בעל הנחל (נחל אשכול אות ג) הוכיח כן במשור דהרי״ף כהרמב״ם סבירא ליה.

סימן נ״ו סעיף ג

ל. האחרונים ז״ל נחלקו בזה. והנה בירושלמי (ברכות פ״ו הל׳ ב) איתא: תני: רבי יוסי אומר: כל המשנה על המטבע שטבעו חכמים, לא יצא ידי חובתו. רבי יהודה אומר: כל שנשתנה מברייתו ולא שינה ברכתו, לא יצא. רבי מאיר אומר וכו׳. ופירש מהרא״פ: ״כל שנשתנה מברייתו״ - כגון פת ויין, ולא שינה ברכתו, לא יצא, שאם אמר עליהם ״בורא פרי האדמה״ ו״בורא פרי העץ״, לא יצא. משמע דרבי יוסי סבירא ליה יצא. וקימא לן רבי יוסי ורבי יהודה, הלכה כרבי יוסי, ובפרט כי בש״ס דילן לא הובאו כלל דברי רבי יהודה, ואם כן מוכח לכאורה ההלכה דיצא ואולם בתוספתא איתא: רבי יהודה אומר: כל שנשתנה מברייתו ושינה ברכתו, יצא. וצריך עיון, ויש לישב. ודע כי לפי דעת הסוברים דאם בירך על היין ״בורא פרי העץ״ יצא נראה דהוא הדין אם בירך ״בורא פרי האדמה״.

סימן נ״ב סעיף ו

לא. המגן אברהם בסימן ר״ט סעיף קטן ג׳ כתב דבלא ידע שהוא מים, לא יצא לכמה פוסקים: התוספות (ברכות יב ע״א ד״ה לא) והמרדכי (ברכות רמז לב) ורש״י (ברכות שם) והרמב״ם (הל׳ ברכות פ״ח הל׳ יא). ומשמע דדעתו לפסוק הכי, וכן פסק בבאר היטב (ס״ק ג). וכן משמע מהמגן אברהם סוף הסימן, שכתב דאם כוונתו על האש מברך אחר כך על הבשמים (עין שם בדגול מרבבה, ודברי הפרי מגדים שם דחוקין). אך בסימן תפ״ז (ס״ק ב) כתב המגן אברהם דרוב הפוסקים סבירא ליה אף על פי שלא ידע, יצא. אבל לא הודיענו מי המה רוב הפוסקים, ואנחנו לא נדע זולת הרי״ף לפרוש הרא״ש ז״ל (ברכות פרק א ס׳ יד). והחק יעקב פסק שם (תפז ס״ק ב) דבלא ידע, לא יצא. ואולם באמת מה שהמגן אברהם מונה גם את רש״י בתוך הנך פוסקים

דלא יצא, אמת שגם הרשב״א בחידושיו (ברכות יב ע״א ד״ה הכי גריס) כתב כן, אבל רבינו יונה (ברכות ו ע״א ד״ה פתח) כתב דגם לדעת רש״י יצא. ונראה דלא פלטן מספיקא, ולקולא.

סימן נ״ט סעיף כ

לב. בשו״ת פנים מאירות, חלק א׳ סימן ס״ו, כתוב לברך ברכה זאת בלא הזכרת מלכות, כמו שהיא בתפלת שמונה עשרה. ובהערותי לספר חיי אדם כתבתי מה שלפי עניות דעתי יש לפקפק על ראיותיו. ועוד כתבתי כי לכאורה לשון הרמב״ם (הל׳ ברכות פרק י׳ הל׳ ב׳) מוכח כותיה, ושגם זאת יש לדחות - עין בית יוסף סוף סימן ר״ל שעל מה שכתב הרמב״ם ״ברוך אתה ה׳ רופא חולים״ כתב דמשמע דהוא הדין דמזכיר מלכות (וסמך על מה שכתב בפרק א׳ הלכה ה׳). וגם כתבתי מה שצריך עיון לפי עניות דעתי מתפלת ״צרכי עמך ישראל מרובין״, וכאן אין מקומו להאריך. וראיתי בסידורים שנדפסה ברכה זאת ד״מחיה המתים״ במלכות, ונראה דאין לשנות.

סימן ס׳ סעיף ח

לג. ברכת התלמיד על נס רבו השמטתי בכוונה.

סימן ס״ה סעיף כח

לד. עיין ביורה דעה סימן קס״ט סעיף כ״א וסעיף כ״ד. ואף דכאן גם מלוים ולוים עכו״ם מעורבים, הרי הט״ז (ס״ק לב) והש״ך (ס״ק עג) כתבו בשם הריב״ש דהוי ריבית דאורייתא, ובדאורייתא לא אמרינן ברירה. והא דהרמ״א בסימן ק״ס סעיף ט״ז בשם רש״י, בעל כרחך צריכין לחלק באיזה חילוק, עיין שם בחוות דעת (סע׳ קס, ביאורים ס״ק ח), ברמ״א שם, כתב בשם המוהרי״ק דאם השליח עושה שטר על שם המלוה הוה כאלו הלוה לו המלוה בעצמו ואסור משום דהשטר עביד ליה עיקר הלואה, וגם כאן עושים שטר על שם השותפין המלוים. ולכן, לפי עניות דעתי, אין כאן שום היתר, ועל המיקל להביא ראיה. ודע כי גם בענין הגורלות (לאזען) וכן הבטחת הילדים (קינדער אסעקיראציאון) אשר הריוח בא מרבית, וישראלים מעורבים בהם, אני נבוך מאוד אם יש בזה היתר.

סימן ס״ו סעיף ט

לה. נמשכתי בזה אחר הספר חכמת אדם [שכ״כ] שכך כתב בכלל קמ״ב סימן י״ג. ושוב נתעוררתי מחכם אחד כי בספר לקט הקמח (שנדפס בגליון היורה דעה) [נדפס בשו״ע יורה דעה אחרי סימן קעז] כתב נוסח (שער) [שטר] עיסקא ממהר״ם חאגי״ז ז״ל ומבואר שם שהיו עושין ב׳ שטרות. שטר עסקא בתנאים המבוארים ועוד שטר חוב פשוט ושניהם בידי הנותן. ולאחר העיון נראה כי דבר זה במחלוקת איתמר. כי הנה בתשובות שב יעקב סימן ל״ה היה המנהג שעשו שטר חוב גמור ולמטה כתבו בתורת עיסקא וכו׳. והוא בענין שיכולין לחתוך הכתב עיסקא מן החוב כתב ויהיה נשאר החוב כתב ביד המלוה בלי שום תנאי. וערער הרב השואל ז״ל ממה שכתב בשולחן ערוך סימן קע״ז סעיף כ״ד, וממה שכתב שם הרא״ש והטור דבתר שטרא אזלינן, והרי המלוה יכול לחתוך תנאי העיסקא. והגאון בעל שב יעקב ז״ל החזיק את המנהג הזה, דהא מלשון הרמב״ם והשולחן ערוך שכתבו טעם האיסור שמא ימות הנותן משמע דאם הנותן קיים והמקבל מודה שהיה ריוח חייב הוא לצאת ידי חובתו לשלם להנותן מה שמגיע לו לחלקו. ואך להרא״ש והטור דסבירא להו טעמא משום דבתר שטרא אזלינן, אסור. ומאחר דהוי פלוגתא דרבוותא אם כן על כל פנים בענין זה שכותבין החוב כתב רק על הקרן לחוד, דהאיסור רק משום דהוי קרוב לשכר ורחוק מהפסד, דהוא איסור דרבנן, הולכין אחר המיקל, בפרט דהחולקין הן רבים נגד הרא״ש והטור. עוד כתב שם דבנדון זה גם להרא״ש והטור ניחא, דהוי כמו שטר ושוברו עמו, ואף שבידו לחתכו, מהיכי תיתי יעשה זאת, אטו ברשיעי עסקינן, ועיין שם עוד בשב יעקב גם בתשובה שנית ושלישית (ועיין גם בספר גידולי תרומה). ולפי זה נראה דגם הדרך שהנהיג המהר״ם חאגי״ז בשני שטרות נכון הוא, דכיון ששני השטרות אגודים ביחד

הוי ליה שטר ושוברו עמו, ולרשיעי לא חיישינן. והנה בדגול מרבבה הקשה סתירת הרא״ש אהדדי, עיין שם מה שכתב. והן אמת כי לאחר המחילה מעצמותיו הקדושים דבריו נפלאו, דהא בדברי הרא״ש בכלל פ״ח סימן ז׳ ובכלל פ״ט סימן י׳ מבואר דגם בכתיב בשטר הקרן לחוד אסור ליקח את הריוח מטעם דבתר שטרא אזלינן, עיין שם. ולישב קצת דבריו שבכלל ס״ו יש לומר לפי עניות דעתי דמילתא פסיקתא קאמר, דאפלו למאן דאית ליה כשטרי מחוזנאי, אינו חייב כלום מאחר דלא היה התנאי בשעה שנתחייב במעות. ומכל מקום לדינא נראה לפי עניות דעתי נכונים דברי השב יעקב, דאם המקבל מודה שהיה ריוח, מחוייב ליתן כפי מה שהתנה. וגם במה שמתיר לכתוב העיסקא למטה מן החוב כתב. והוא הדין נמי במנהג המהר״ם חאגי״ז לכתוב שני שטרות. ואנכי מעיקרא נמשכתי אחרי דברי בעל חכמת אדם (ועיין מה שכתב שם גם בקונטרס בינת אדם) ואין כאן מקומו להאריך, והבוחר יבחר.

סימן ס״ו סעיף י

לו. בטורי זהב סימן קס״ז סעיף קטן א׳, וזה לשונו: וכתב בלבוש (סי׳ קסז) למצוא תקנה למלוין וכו׳, עד כאן לשונו, ועיין שם בנקודות הכסף. ובחוות דעת שם (ביאורים ס״ק א) כתב דהיתר זה תמוה דהא מבואר בסימן קע״ד דאם אומר כשיהיה לי מעות אחזיר לך דהוי ריבית קצוצה וכו׳, ונדחק שם לחלק בין הך דהריב״ש (שו״ת, תשובה שלה) להך דהלבוש, עיין שם, ודבריו מפוקפקים לפי עניות דעתי. והנה הריב״ש הוכיח דבריו ממתניתין דהלוהו על שדהו וכו׳ וכך היה ביתוס בן זונין עושה על פי חכמים, דכל שהוא משום קנס אין בו משום ריבית, דלא הוי אגר נטיר, מפני שאינו מרויח בהמתנה כלום, שהרי אפלו ממתין לו כל הג׳ שנים, אם הוא פרעו בסוף הזמן אינו מרויח כלל, ואם כן כשלא פרעו והוחלט לו אין כאן ריבית אלא קנס, עיין שם בריב״ש. ומיושב מה שכתב החוות דעת מהך דסימן קע״ד, דאם אומר ״לכשיהיה לי מעות אחזיר לך״, דהוי רבית קצוצה, דהתם ודאי הוי אגר נטיר שהוא מרויח בהמתנה. וגם הך דמהרי״ט (סימן כ״ג) שהביא החוות דעת מיירי במרויח בהמתנה כמבואר שם כדבריו, מה שאין כן בריב״ש ובלבוש. ועיין מה שכתב בספר פתחי תשובה סימן קע״ד סעיף קטן א׳ וסעיף קטן ב׳. ועיין שם בהגהות יד שאול שהראה לנו דברי התבואות שור בבכור שור מסכת בבא מציעא (דף סה ע״ב), עיין שם. ובשולחן ערוך של התניא (הל׳ רבית) סימן מ״ו הביא גם כן תקנה זאת להלכה. ועיין שם שכתב, וזה לשונו: ולהאומרים שכל קנס יש בו משום אסמכתא וכו׳, גם כאן צריך לקנות ממנו בבית דין חשוב, או שכתוב בשטר שקנו ממנו בבית דין חשוב, שזה מועיל אף שלא היה שם בית דין כלל רק שקנו ממנו בקנין סודר בפועל ממש. וצריכין להזהיר זאת לרבים שטועים בזה ואין קונין בקנין סודר כלל וגובין בשטרות אלו שלא כדין, עד כאן לשונו.

הערה לסימן ס״ח סעיף ז

לז. כתב הגאון בעל בית אפרים זצ״ל במאמר יפה לבדיקה (שבסוף היורה דעה החדש) כי לפעמים הרב אשר הוא מנסה ומסמיך את השוחט, הרב בעצמו אין לו הרגשה טובה בבדיקת הסכין. אזי, אם יש בעיר אנשים אחרים שיש להם הרגשה טובה ויודע בהם שהם יראים ושלמים, ומכל שכן אם המה גם כן שוחטים מומחים, יכול לסמוך עליהם אם הם אומרים לו שיש לזה הרגשה טובה. והא ודאי שכיח טובא שאפלו מי שהוא גדול בתורה אין לו הרגשה טובה ואינו יכול לנסות את השוחט. וההרגשה אינה תלויה במעלות התורה כלל. ולכן, הרב אשר הוא ירא שמים, אם אינו ברור לו שיש לו הרגשה טובה, אזי כשבא לפניו שוחט על הנסיון, אינו בוש לעמוד על בירור הדבר על ידי אחרים אשר יודע בהם שיש להם הרגשה טובה ושהם יראי שמים. אבל אם אינו כן, מי יודע? וכבר הרעיש על זה הגאון בעל כרתי ופלתי זצ״ל סימן א׳, כרתי סעיף קטן י״ב, כי לפעמים המורה בעצמו אשר נותן קבלה אין לו הרגשה והוא בוש לבדוק על ידי אחרים, ועל ידי זה רבה המכשלה, עיין שם. ואנו מה נאמר בדורות אלו אשר בעונותינו הרבים רבו המורים שאינם הגונים ה׳ ירחם עלינו.

⋴§ *Appendix D*

The following is the English text of a *heter iska* that was prepared under the direction of Rabbi Moshe Feinstein.[1]

HETER ISKA

I, _____, hereby certify that on _____,
    NAME OF BORROWER   DATE

I received the sum of _____ from _____,
                       AMOUNT   LENDER

half as a loan and half as an *iska* investment for a period of one year. I

pledge to use these monies for business and produce a profit of

_____, with half belonging to me and half belonging to
DOUBLE AMOUNT LENDER WANTS

_____. My payment for my work shall be _____.
               LENDER   SMALL SUM

I agree to not be believed about any loss or lack of profit, unless I produce

witnesses and swear to back my claim in shul before the Rav and congrega-

tion, at the time of the public reading of the Torah. And in any such

matters, the holder of this document shall be believed. If the money is not

returned at the end of one year, the business agreement shall continue,

with the same yearly terms, until it is returned.

Signed on _____, at _____
               DATE   PLACE

_____

_____ Witnesses (optional)

---

1. Rabbi Moshe Feinstein preferred this version to that used by Kitzur, as the payment made by the borrower is an actual share of profit. [By contrast, in Kitzur's version, the payment is made *in lieu* of the share of the profit.]
[This text was obtained from Rabbi Yosaif Asher Weiss, who prepared it in the early 1980's.]

427 INDEX

Index

NOTES FOR INDEX USAGE

This volume of Kitzur contains many hundreds of Halachos. The following index is intended to make it easier to find the pertinent Halachah quickly and intuitively. To help with that, we have preceded the general index with a list of topic headings; using this list, one can easily determine which entries in the index he or she should scan. Please note that this index covers only the areas addressed in this volume; please see the index to the Kleinman Edition Kitzur Shulchan Aruch – Volume 1, for the subjects discussed in that volume.

This index is intended only to help the reader find the relevant section in the Kitzur. One should not attempt to infer the proper Halachah from the wording of index entries.

This volume of the Kitzur contains the laws of berachos. To make it easier for the reader to find the appropriate berachah rishonah for particular foods discussed by the Kitzur, we have included an index entry titled "berachos: guide." This entry lists the specific foods (and fragrances) discussed in the volume (usually the Kitzur includes both berachah rishonah and acharonah in the same location); for more general topics, one can turn to the headings discussing specific berachos, such as berachos: mezonos.

The topic heading "dietary laws" lists all the other headings that would come under that rubric but are given their own topic entries.

To ensure consistency in each entry, when appropriate, the citations first list the Se'if(im) in a particular Siman in the Kitzur that discuss the Halachah; afterward, the applicable footnotes from that Siman are listed (denoted by the letter "n"; e.g., 48:n62 refers to Siman 48, footnote 62) in order. Se'ifim in other Simanim follow, and then the footnotes to that Siman. Therefore, it is possible that an entry will first list a Se'if at the end of a Siman, and then list a footnote from that Siman's start, a few pages earlier.

Many of the Halachos in this volume are related or interconnected. To help steer the reader to germane topic headings, many entries in the index have, at the end of that particular entry, a line that says "see" followed by relevant entries under other topic headings.

INDEX 428

TOPIC HEADINGS

Ahavas Hashem
animals
Al HaGefen
Al HaMichyah
Amen
Avel
avodas Hashem
bar mitzvah
basar b'chalav
bedtime Shema
berachos
berachos: Al HaEitz
berachos: Al HaGefen
berachos: Al HaMichyah
berachos: berachah acharonah,
    general rules
berachos: berachah rishonah, error in
berachos: berachah rishonah, general rules
berachos: berachah rishonah, limitations of
berachos: berachah rishonah, precedence in
berachos: Borei Nefashos
berachos: Dayan HaEmes
berachos: fragrances, blessings on
berachos: guide
berachos: ha'adamah
berachos: ha'eitz
berachos: hagafen
berachos: HaGomeil
berachos: har'iyah/over seeing
berachos: HaTov VeHaMeitiv, good tidings
berachos: HaTov VeHaMeitiv, wine
berachos: mechayei meisim
berachos: mezonos
berachos: miscellaneous
berachos: shehakol
berachos: Shehecheyanu
berachos: Tefillas HaDerech
Bircas HaGomeil
Bircas HaMazon
birds
bishul akum
blessing
blood
Borei Nefashos
bread
bread baked by an idolater
butter
business transactions
business transactions: forbidden items
business transactions: iska
business transactions: ribbis
challah, mitzvah of
challah, Shabbos

chalav akum
Chanukah
charity
chatzitzah
cheilev
cheese
children
Chol HaMoed
clothing
concentration
convert
Dayan HaEmes
dietary laws
drinking
eating
eggs
Erev Pesach
fats, forbidden
fearing God
fish
food cooked by an idolater
food, respect for
foods, forbidden
forgetfulness
fragrances, blessings on
ger
guests
ha'adamah
hadachah
ha'eitz
hamotzi
hand-washing, before meals
HaTov VeHaMeitiv, good tidings
HaTov VeHaMeitiv, wine
health
heart
heter iska
immersing utensils
ikar/tafel
insects
interest
kashering, meat or poultry
kashrus
kavanah
ketanim
Kiddush
king
liver
loans
loving God
lung
maid
mayim acharonim

429 INDEX

meal, blessings during
meal, conduct of
meal, eating/drinking before
meat
meat and milk
mechallel Shabbos
mechayei meisim
medical issues
melichah
mezonos
milk and meat
milk of a non-Jew
Minchah
miracle
mitzvah
mourner
neder
neis
netilas yadayim
nesech wine
night
oath
ona'as devarim
pas akum
pas haba'ah b'kisnin
Pesach, Erev
poultry
poverty
prayer
prayer: Maariv
prayer: Minchah
prayer: Mussaf
pressing circumstances
primary food/secondary food
Purim
rainbow

ribbis
right
rinsing
roasting
Rosh Chodesh
Rosh Hashanah
salting
sefer
service of Hashem
Shabbos
Shabbos, desecration of
Shabbos: Kiddush
she'as hadchak
shehakol
Shehecheyanu
Shema, bedtime
shevuah
sleep
soaking
speech
stam yeinam
Tefillas HaDerech
tevilas keilim
Torah
traveling
tzedakah
vow
wealth
wine
wine of a non-Jew
women
yayin nesech
Yiras Shamayim
Yom Kippur
Yom Tov
zimun

INDEX

Ahavas Hashem
    parameters of   59:2
animals
    abdomen pierced   46:29
    birds, feeding crumbs to   42:11
    elephant, blessing upon seeing   60:13
    feeding before meals   42:1
    feeding hamotzi piece to   41:4
    feeding human food to   42:9
    food for, business with   64:n1
    Hashem's mercy on   59:13, 59:n39
    monkey, blessing upon seeing   60:13
    raising investor's animal   66:12
    see meat; poultry
Al HaGefen
    see berachos: Al HaGefen
Al HaMichyah

    see berachos: Al HaMichyah
Amen
    after prayer or blessing   44:7
    to Bircas HaMazon   45:7
    to zimun   45:6, 45:20
Avel
    honored with zimun   45:5
    reciting Bircas HaGomeil   61:2
avodas Hashem
    being accountable for not eating what
        one sees   59:19
    by accepting hardship   59:2
    improving through vows   67:5
    in all one's ways   59:2
    showing appreciation for new produce
        each year   59:n52
    what Hashem does, is for good   59:4

INDEX 430

bar mitzvah
    father's blessing at   61:8
    feast for   61:8
basar b'chalav
    bread, cutting with dairy knife for meat
        and vice versa   46:12
    bread, using for meat and dairy meals
        46:7, 46:n14
    cheese, eating meat after   46:11, 46:12
    chewing meat without swallowing   46:9
    cooked in meat pot without meat
        46:10, 46:n21
    cut sharp food with dairy knife and put
        into meat dish and vice versa   46:13
    dentures, using with meat and milk
        46:n23
    eating milk and meat at same table
        46:6
    eggs found inside poultry   36:26
    koshering vessel from meat to
        dairy and vice versa   46:15, 46:n33
    meat found in teeth   46:9
    milk, almond/rice/soy, with meat
        46:14, 46:n32
    prohibition of   46:5
    salt-receptacles, different   46:7, 46:n15
    utensils interchanged   46:n17, 46:n62
    utensils, marked for dairy   46:8
    waiting to eat dairy after meat   46:9
    see foods, forbidden
bedtime Shema
    see night
berachos
    see berachos: miscellaneous
berachos: Al HaEitz
    mashed fruit   52:n43
    mistakenly recited for non-Seven
        Species fruit   51:n44
    structure of   51:8
    when also obligated in Borei Nefashos
        51:12
berachos: Al HaGefen
    combined with Al HaMichyah   51:8,
        51:n31
    forgot hagafen   50:10, 50:n40
    exempts other beverages from
        berachah   49:4, 49:5, 49:n25
    mistakenly recited for grapes   55:1
    obligation of   49:1
    structure of   51:8
berachos: Al HaMichyah
    amount necessary for   48:n66
    combined with Al HaGefen   51:8, 51:n31
    exactly a kezayis of cake   48:n66
    mezonos ingredients, mixed together
        48:10
    structure of   51:8

"v'al hakalkalah"   51:8, 51:n27
berachos: berachah acharonah, general rules
    bread, combining eating two different
        times   51:n18
    changing location before reciting
        51:13, 51:n47
    changed location while eating   51:n17
    combining different foods/drinks to
        require berachah acharonah
        51:4, 51:n15
    combining eating and drinking for
        berachah acharonah   51:4, 51:n15
    combining drinking two different times
        51:5, 51:n19
    combining eating two different times
        51:5
    delay in reciting   51:14
    drinking a hot beverage   51:6, 51:n20
    eating and drinking exempted with one
        blessing   51:1
    forgot "v'al pri hagafen"   51:n34
    how long after eating recited   51:14
    Mei'ein Shalosh, conduct during
        51:10, 51:n36
    Mei'ein Shalosh, knowing by heart   51:8
    Mei'ein Shalosh, mentioning Shabbos,
        festivals, Rosh Chodesh, and if
        forgotten   51:9
    minimum amount drank   51:2
    minimum amount eaten   51:2
    obligated in Al HaEitz and Borei
        Nefashos   51:12
    obligated in more than one Mei'ein
        Shalosh   51:8, 51:n31
    Seven Species, on   51:7
    vomited before reciting   51:15
    whole item (smaller than kezayis)   51:3
    see berachos: Al HaEitz; berachos: Al
        HaGefen; berachos: Al HaMichyah;
        berachos: Borei Nefashos
berachos: berachah rishonah, error in
    concluded incorrectly   56:7
    concluded incorrectly and corrected
        himself   56:6
    erred in intent but concluded correctly
        56:5
    ha'adamah instead of ha'eitz   56:2
    ha'eitz instead of ha'adamah   56:2
    ha'eitz instead of hagafen   56:3
    hagafen on grapes   56:1
    hamotzi instead of mezonos   56:1
    mezonos instead of any berachah   56:n15
    mezonos instead of hamotzi   56:1
    shehakol instead of any berachah   50:2,
        56:4
berachos:
    berachah rishonah, general rules

431 INDEX

changing location 50:13, 50:14, 50:15, 50:16, 50:n51, 50:n52
concentrating on 50:3
discarding item berachah recited on 50:6
forbidden item 50:8, 50:n31
forgot to recite 50:10, 50:n38, 50:n39
interrupting between berachah and swallowing 50:5, 50:n17
item in front of person 50:3, 50:n10
medical purposes 50:8
minimum amount eaten to require 50:1
no enjoyment – berachah? 50:8, 50.9
obligation to know proper berachah 50:2
pausing between berachah and eating 50:5
permits food to be eaten 50:1
pouring from cup before drinking 50:6
procedure for reciting 50:3
recited on less significant food 50:11
reciting designated berachah for each food 50:12
reciting on whole object 50:5
reciting with empty mouth 50:10
removing shell before 50:n21
ruined/spoiled food 52:13
secondary to primary plant item 52:9
shehakol works for all foods – parameters of 50:2
tasting with/without swallowing 50:7
to clear throat 50:9
unable to partake from object berachah was recited on 50:4, 50:n13
unknown 50:2, 56:4
unknown if ha'eitz or ha'adamah 56:2, 56:n11
unnecessary berachah 50:11
water 50:9
without, as if violated sanctified property 49:1
see berachos: berachah rishonah, error in; berachos: berachah rishonah, limitations of; berachos: berachah rishonah, precedence in; berachos: guide; berachos: ha'adamah; berachos: ha'eitz; berachos:hagafen; berachos: hamotzi; berachos:mezonos; berachos: shehakol
berachos: berachah rishonah, limitations of
guest – berachah includes everything 57:6, 57:n12
more fruit brought to him 57:2, 57:3, 57:n4, 57:n5, 57:n6

more significant fruit brought to him 57:4
original piece cut too small 57:1
purchased more after he recited 57:1
visitor – given cup of wine 57:7, 57:n14
was drinking and solid food brought 57:5
See summary of these laws at 57:n10.
berachos: berachah rishonah, precedence in
blessings on fragrances 58:9, 58:n32
food or fragrance first? 58:n32
hamotzi and mezonos precede hagafen 55:5
if berachos are the same 55:1, 55:n5
if berachos are not the same 55:1, 55:n7
Seven Species 55:2, 55:3, 55:n17
significant first 50:11
specific berachah precedes 55:1, 55:4, 55:n7
See summary of these laws at the conclusion of Siman 55.
berachos: Borei Nefashos
fruit (non-Seven Species) 51:1
meaning of 51:11
on less than a kezayis of grain in k'dei achilas pras 48:n66
text of 51:11, 51:n39, 51:n42. 51:n43
vegetables 51:1
water 51:1
when also obligated in Al HaEitz 51:12
berachos: Dayan HaEmes
bad that may lead to good 59:3
delaying recitation 59:1
intent while reciting 59:2
many tidings 59:2, 59:n13
obligation of 59:2
on a death 59:6, 59:n20
reason for 59:2
seeing someone disabled 60:14
without Hashem's Name 59:6
berachos: fragrances, blessings on
berachah proximate to smelling 58:10
borei atzei vesamim 58:3
borei isvei vesamim 58:4
borei minei vesamim 58:5
borei shemen areiv 58:6
combined smells 58:8, 58:n27
did not intend to smell 58:2
food or fragrance first? 58:n32
fruits 58:2
herbs 58:4
incense, burning 58:10
intended to eat and smell 58:n4
intended to smell 58:2
interrupted before smelling 58:n35

INDEX 432

items not meant to be smelled
58:11, 58:n37
neutralizing foul odor 58:10
not tree or herb 58:5
obligation of 58:1
pharmacy/apothecary,
entering/reentering 58:12, 58:n41,
58:n42
precedence in 58:9, 58:n32
reason for 58:1
recited wrong berachah 58:7
rei'ach tov bapeiros 58:2, 58:n3
shrubs/trees 58:3
source not present 58:13
spice shop, entering/re-entering 58:12,
58:n41, 58:n42
trees/shrubs 58:3
tree, definition of 58:4, 58:n16
unsure of correct berachah 58:7
vegetables 58:2
women's fragrances 58:14
see berachos: guide
berachos: guide
almonds, bitter 52:11
almonds, sugar-coated 52:11
bagels 48:6
balsam oil 58:6
beer 53:3
berries 52:n2
blueberries 52:n18
bread cooked/fried after baking 48:7
bread, not from five grains 52:n50
bread, spoiled 52:13, 52:n37
broth from cooked fruit/vegetables/
legumes 53:2, 53:n7
calamus 52:11
candy 50:n52
caper bush products 52:9, 52:n23
cereal and milk 48:n54, 54:n19
chewing gum 50:n52
chicken soup with matzah balls 48:n54,
48:n58, 54:n19
cinnamon plant 52:18, 54:7
cloves 58:7, 58:n25
coffee 53:3, 58:2, 58:n5
cornbread 52:17, 52:n51
cracker and cheese/spread 54:n21
cucumber peel 52:9
date honey 53:1
dough, cooked 48:8, 48:n51
dumpling 48:9
egg, raw 50:8
esrog 52:12, 58:2
frankincense 58:3
fruit in cereal 48:n54, 54:n19
fruit juice 53:1
fruit pits 52:10

fruits, inedible – juices sucked out 52:15
fruits, mashed 52:16, 52:n43
fruits, raw/cooked 52:4, 52:6
fruits, unripe 52:12, 52:14
fruits, wild 52:7
garlic 52:5, 52:n13
ginger 54:7, 58:3
grits, cooked 48:8, 48:n52
hazelnuts 52:7
honey from dates 53:1
ice cream sandwich 48:n68
jam 52:16
kernels of grain 48:n3
kneidel 48:9
lemon 58:2
lemon rind 58:7
licorice plant 52:18
liquid that item was cooked/soaked in
53:4, 53:5
mead 49:1
medical purposes 50:8
millet 52:17
mushrooms 52:3, 58:5
musk 58:5
myrtle 58:3, 58:n7
nutmeg 54:7, 58:2
oil, infused 58:8
olive oil 53:1, 53:8
onions 52:5, 52:n13
orange rind 58:7
orange rind, candied 52:9, 52:n26
pancakes 48:9
pas haba'ah b'kisnin 48:1
pastry and coffee 54:4, 54:n13
pea pods 52:9, 52:n28
pepper 58:3
pickled vegetables 52:4
pickle juice 53:4
pie with crust 48:n68
pits, fruit 52:10
potatoes, mashed 52:n40
preserves 54:9
pretzels, soft 48:6
radish 52:5, 52:n14
raisin wine 53:6
raspberries 52:n18
rice 52:17
rose 58:3, 58:n8
rose petals, candied 52:9
sugar/sugar cane 52:18
tea 53:3
truffles 52:3
vegetable juice 53:1
vegetables, cultivated 52:8
vegetables, mashed 52:16
vegetables, raw/cooked 52:4, 52:6
vegetables, wild 52:8, 52:n18

433 ~ INDEX

vinegar	52:13	recited in front of	61:2, 61:n11
wafers	48:5	recited standing	61:2, 61:n17
water	50:9	traveling, recited at conclusion	61:n3
water from water fountain	50:n10	who obligated in	61:1
water, infused	58:8	berachos: hamotzi	
wine	53:1	bagels	48:6
wine, spiced	49:1	bread cooked/fried after baking	48:7
see fragrances, blessings on; ikar/tafel;		bread soaked after baking	48:7
pas haba'ah b'kisnin		on "set meal" of pas haba'ah b'kisnin	
berachos: ha'adamah			48:3
berries	52:n2	pas haba'ah b'kisnin	48:1
garlic	52:5, 52:n13	pretzels, soft	48:6
grits, cooked	48:8, 48:n52	see berachah rishonah: mezonos;	
kernels of grain	40.n3	herachos; ikar/tafel; pas haba'ah	
onions	52:5, 52:n13	b'kisnin	
produce, definition of	52:1	berachos: har'iyah/over seeing	
radish	52:5, 52:n14	beautiful creations	60:15, 60:n60
recited on	52:1	Bircas haChammah	60:6, 60:7
ruined/spoiled food	52:13	comet	60:2
secondary item, on	52:9	disabilities	60:14
vegetables, cultivated	52:8	earthquake	60:2
vegetables, pickled	52:4	elephant	60:13
vegetables, raw/cooked	52:4	fruit tree in bloom	60:1
vegetables, wild	52:8	graves, Jewish/non-Jewish	60:11
see berachos		hurricane	60:2
berachos: ha'eitz		king, blind person's blessing	60:10
berries	52:n2	king, knows he is there	60:10
fruits, raw/cooked	52:4	king, sees	60:10
fruits, unripe	52:12, 52:14	lightning	60:2, 60:3, 60:n10
fruits, wild	52:7	meshaneh haberiyos	60:13, 60:14
hazelnuts	52:7	meteor	60:2
recited on	52:1	monkey	60:13
tree, definition of	52:1	mountains	60:5
berachos: hagafen		oceans	60:5
exempts other beverages from		official, blessing recited?	60:n44
berachah	49:4, 49:5, 49:6	oseh maasei vereishis	60:2, 60:5, 60:6
forgot to recite	50:10, 50:n40	place where miracle occurred	60:8
mead	49:1	rainbow	60:4
raisin wine	53:6	scholar, Jewish	60:9, 60:n41
"Savri" before	49:7	scholar, non-Jewish	60:9
sour wine	49:1	she'asah neis	60:8
spiced wine	49:1	shechalak mei'chachmaso li'rei'av	60:9
vinegar, smells like	49:1	shekachah lo be'olamo	60:15, 60:n60
water with steeped grape seeds	9:2	shekocho u'gevuroso	60:2
wines obligated in	49:1	shelo chiseir b'olamo	60:1
wine/water mixed	49:3	shenasan mei'chachmaso	
see HaTov VeHaMeitiv; wine; yayin		levasar vadam	60:9
nesech		shenasan m'kvodo levasar vadam	60:10
berachos: HaGomeil		skin, unusually colored	60:13
air travel	61:n2	storm clouds dissipated	60:3, 60:n13
avel, recites immediately	61:2	sun, beginning of cycle	60:6, 60:7
dangerous situation	61:1	thirty days between birchos har'iyah	
delaying recitation of	61:2, 61:n11		60:12
incarcerated but not in danger	61:1,	thunder	60:2, 60:3, 60:n10
	61:n5	tornado	60:2
multiple reasons to recite	61:n6	unusual physical conditions	60:13, 60:14
obligation to recite	61:1	winds	60:2

INDEX   **434**

zocheir habris   60:4
    see king; rainbow
berachos: HaTov VeHaMeitiv, good tidings
    at time of purchase   59:7, 59:n28
    birth of boy   59:5
    car, new   59:n24
    delaying recitation   59:1
    engagement ring, bride recites   59:n34
    good that may lead to harm   59:3
    home, new   59:7, 59:n27
    item as gift   59:10, 59:n36
    items for family members   59:9, 59:n34
    items, valuable   59:7, 59:9, 59:n27
    meaning of   59:1
    many tidings   59:2, 59:n13
    money, gift of   59:n35
    news of benefit to him and others   59:1
    obligation of   59:1
    on inheritance   59:6, 59:n23
    rain, after drought   61:10, 61:n39
    synagogue, new   59:n27
    when recited   59:1, 59:7
    see berachos: HaTov VeHaMeitiv, wine
berachos: HaTov VeHaMeitiv, wine
    after deciding not to drink   49:9
    both bottles already there   49:11
    exempting others with communal
      blessing   49:15
    first bottle finished   49:12
    guests   49:14
    intended to serve second wine   49:n34
    obligation of   49:8
    "Savri" before   49:15
    unsure of quality of second wine   49:10
    when drinking alone   49:13
    when second wine inferior   49:10
    wine of Bircas HaMazon   49:16
    wine not shared   49:14
    see berachos: HaTov VeHaMeitiv,
      good tidings
berachos: mechayei meisim
    on seeing someone after
      twelve months   59:20
    on seeing someone never seen before
      59:21
berachos: mezonos
    bread cooked/fried after baking   48:7
    breadcrumbs, made from   48:9
    bread soaked after baking   48:7
    dough, cooked   48:8, 48:n51
    dumpling   48:9
    grits, cooked   48:8
    kneidel   48:9
    matzah meal, made from   48:9
    pas haba'ah b'kisnin   48:1
    pancake   48:9
    wafers   48:5

    works for most foods – parameters of
      56:n15
    see berachos: hamotzi; berachos; ikar/
      tafel; pas haba'ah b'kisnin
berachos: miscellaneous
    after bloodletting   61:4
    before the mitzvah   40:5
    challah, mitzvah of   35:1
    compensatory, in Bircas HaMazon   44:12
    for bar mitzvah   61:8
    HaMapil blessing   71:4
    netilas yadayim   40:1, 40:5
    on rain after drought   61:9, 61:10
    on rain in Eretz Yisrael   61:n35
    tevilas keilim   37:1
    see meal, eating before
berachos: shehakol
    fruits, raw/cooked   52:4, 52:6
    fruits, wild   52:7
    garlic   52:5, 52:n13
    mushrooms   52:3
    onions   52:5, 52:n13
    pronunciation of   52:2, 52:n5
    radish   52:n14
    recited on   52:2
    ruined/spoiled food   52:13
    secondary item, on   52:9
    truffles   52:3
    vegetables, raw/cooked   52:4
    vegetables, wild   52:8
    wine, sour   49:1
    works for all foods – parameters of
      50:2, 56:4, 56:n11
    see ikar/tafel
berachos: Shehecheyanu
    at time of purchase   59:7, 59:n28
    birth of girl   59:n19
    car, new   59:n24
    clothing, new   59:7
    delaying recitation   59:1
    died in childbirth   59:5, 59:n20
    engagement ring, bride and groom
      recite   59:n34
    fragrances   59:18, 59:n51
    fruits, forgot to recite   59:14
    fruits, fully ripened   59:16, 59:n46
    fruits, grafted species   59:n41
    fruits, new   59:14, 59:n40
    fruits, once per season   59:n41
    fruits, on multiple   59:14
    fruits, preserved by refrigeration   59:n41
    fruits, similar   59:14, 59:n44
    good that may lead to harm   59:3
    grapes and wine of same season   59:15
    home, new   59:7
    husband died before son born   59:5
    insignificant item   59:12

435 ∿ INDEX

item as gift 59:10, 59:n36
items, valuable 59:7, 59:n38
many tidings 59:2, 59:n13
money, gift of 59:n35
news of personal benefit 59:1
obligation of 59:1
on inheritance 59:6, 59:n23
on seeing someone after thirty days
59:20, 59:n53
on seeing someone never seen before
59:21
rain, after drought 61:10
sefer, new 59:11, 59:n37
wealthy person 59:12
when recited 59:1, 59:7, 59:14, 59:n43
wine, fully fermented 59:15
tallis, on new 59:8, 59:n32
vegetables 59:17, 59:n40
see berachos: mechayei meisim;
clothing
berachos: Tefillas HaDerech
forgot to recite 68:2
once per day/trip 68:5
reciting after another blessing 68:3,
68:n9
reciting standing 68:4
text of 68:1
when recited 68:1, 68:2, 68:n5
without closing blessing 68:5
see traveling
Bircas HaGomeil
see berachos: HaGomeil
Bircas HaMazon
Al HaNissim, forgot 44:16
Amen after HaRachaman 44:7
additions to 44:10, 44:16, 44:17
amount that obligates in 44:5, 51:2
bread, on 51:7
concentration during 44:6
delay in reciting 44:8, 44:n32
dress during 44:6
forgot if recited 44:11, 44:n42
HaTov VeHaMeitiv on wine 49:16
idolater in house 44:18, 68:10
immediately after mayim acharonim
44:2
leader washes first 44:1
leaving before 42:19, 44:9,
44:n36, 44:n37
leaving tablecloth and bread during 44:3
meal spanned Shabbos/festival and
weekday 44:17
meal spanned two occasions 44:17
pas haba'ah b'kisnin 48:1
reasons for 44:1, 51:7
reciting along with the leader 45:7
removing/covering knives during 44:4

removing empty dishes before 45:4
Retzei 44:10
Retzei, forgot 44:12, 44:13, 44:15,
44:n45, 44:n47
sitting during 44:6
structure of 51:n22, 51:n23
traveling 44:n27, 68:10
unsure if recited 44:11, 44:n42
Yaaleh VeYavo 44:10
Yaaleh VeYavo, forgot 44:12, 44:13, 44:14,
44:15, 44:n45, 44:n59
Yom Kippur, on 44:n59
see mayim acharonim; meal, conduct
of; wine; zimun
birds
see animals
bishul akum
baking 38:n19
beer 38:12
bread made from legumes 38:3
candied fruit 38:11
coffee 38:12
cooked for ill Jew on Shabbos 38:9
dough belonging to Jew 38:5
egg 38:10
egg coating bread 38:4
food eaten raw 38:6
food generally eaten cooked 38:10
food requiring mixing 38:n21
foods included in prohibition 38:6
frying 38:n19
hot chocolate 38:12
insignificant food 38:6
Jew stoking fire 38:8, 38:n27
maidservant cooking for herself 38:8
maidservant cooking for Jews 38:7,
38:n26, 38:n27
pickling food 38:n19
reasons for prohibition 38:n20
roasting 38:6
smoking food 38:n19
tea 38:12
utensils used for 38:6, 38:8, 38:9, 38:n31
blessing
see berachos
blood
care not to consume 36:12
draining after salting 36:10
eggs, blood in 46:1, 46:n1, 46:n2
fish, blood of 46:2
gums, came out of 46:3
milk, blood found in 46:4
permissible circumstances 40:n76
prohibition of consuming 36:1
see rinsing; salting; soaking
Borei Nefashos
see berachos: Borei Nefashos

INDEX 436

bread
  baked with meat or dairy   46:26, 46:n53
  baked with meat or dairy loaf
         46:25, 46:n51
  Bircas HaMazon on   51:7
  blessing before/after   41:1, 51:7
  blessing on better loaf   41:8
  blessing on complete/larger loaf   41:3,
         41:8
  cooked/fried after baking, berachah on
         48:7
  cutting, on Shabbos   41:3, 41:4, 41:n18
  cutting, place to   41:3
  cutting, size of pieces   41:4
  cutting, small roll   41:3
  cutting with dairy knife for meat
    and vice versa   46:12
  dipping in salt   41:6, 41:n44
  distributing   41:7
  eating immediately after hamotzi 41:4
  interruptions before hamotzi   41:2
  kneaded with milk or meat   46:25,
         46:n49
  leaving on table after meal   44:3
  not from five grains, berachah   52:n50
  precedence for making hamotzi on
        41:8, 41:9, 41:10
  pre-cutting   41:3
  procedure for hamotzi   41:5
  soaked after baking, berachah on   48:7
  spoiled, berachah on   52:13, 52:n37
  using for meat and dairy meals
        46:7, 46:n14
  who to give hamotzi piece to   41:4
  see berachos: hamotzi; food, respect
    for; pas haba'ah b'kisnin
bread baked by an idolater
  see pas akum
butter
  local custom determines   38:15
  made from chalav akum   38:n48
  permissibility of eating from
    idolater   38:15
business transactions
  agent for buyer bought item himself
        62:14
  agreement, reneging on   62:15, 62:16
  attracting competitor's customer 62:n7
  buyers, precedence in selling to
        62:18, 62:n39
  charity, commitment to give   62:17
  commitment, carrying through on
       62:15, 62:16, 62:17
  community enforces weights and
    measure standards   62:11
  deceptive sales tactics   62:4, 62:5,
       62:n5, 63:4

  defrauded person cannot pass
    along his loss   62:3
  gift, reneging on promise of   62:17
  giveaways to attract customers   62:6
  honesty in speech   62:17
  informing seller if item is
    underpriced   62:n2
  importance of honesty in business
       62:1, 62:2
  interfering with pending transaction
       62:13, 62:n17
  mi shepara   62:15
  neighbor, precedence in selling to 62:18
  interfering with renter from idolater
       62:13, 62:n19
  selling for inflated price   62:n1
  setting selling price based on seller's
    expense   62:3, 62:n4
  tortious interference   62:13, 62:n17
  undercutting competitor's price   62:6
  weights and measures, dishonest
       62:7, 62:8
  weights and measures, inaccurate –
    possessing   62:12
  weighing and measuring according to
    local custom   62:10
  weighing and measuring generously
       62:9
  see business transactions: forbidden
    items; speech
business transactions: forbidden items
  agent, via an   64:2
  collecting as loan payment   64:3
  fats, forbidden   64:1, 64:n5
  food, animal   64:n1
  food, biblically forbidden   64:1
  food, forbidden but not used for 64:1
  food, rabbinically forbidden   64:3
  happened to acquire   64:2
  transporting   64:n8
business transactions: iska
  advancing money for later purchase
       66:8, 66:n27
  heter iska, definition   66:3, 66:n10
  heter iska, oral agreement   66:7
  heter iska, sample text   66:6, 66:8
  heter iska, witnesses to 66:n17, 66:n19
  investor's involvement in investment
       66:n21
  investor requiring promissory note
       66:9, 66:n23
  only for actual investment   66:10
  paying back loan via   66:11
  paying investor to avoid oath   66:3
  paying recipient for his effort
       66:1, 66:n6
  permissible method   66:1

437 INDEX

profit and loss split between investor
and recipient 66:1
purchase with penalty for non-delivery
66:10
raising another's animal 66:12
recipient buying investor's profit 66:4
recipient holding funds past term of
iska 66:5
stipulations permitted 66:2, 66:3, 66:n8
see business transactions: ribbis
business transactions: ribbis
advance ribbis 65:6
advancing money for later purchase
65:16, 65:17, 66:8, 66:n27
agent using money he earned for seller
65:18
apostate and ribbis 65:30
borrower buying merchandise and
buying it from lender 65:19
borrower chooses to lend back 65:7
borrower chooses to pay back more
65:4
borrower greeting lender 65:9
borrower honoring lender 65:9
borrower paying guarantor for his
services 65:24
borrower providing work to lender 65:10
borrower thanking lender 65:n13
borrower transgresses 65:1
borrowing from idolater on Jew's behalf
65:26
borrowing on behalf of an idolater 65:25
broker transgresses 65:1
buying for someone and charging
him more 65:20
buying on credit at higher than value
65:n32
buying on credit to sell at a loss
65:13, 65:n31
buying/selling promissory notes
65:14, 65:15
corporations 65:n73
credit card, using someone else's
65:n66
deferred ribbis 65:6
dowry, supplementing for delayed
payment 65:23
ease of transgression 65:1
extending time of loan 65:3
given as gift 65:5
guarantor for idolater's loan 65:24,
65:29, 65:n74
guarantor transgresses 65:1
idolater and ribbis 65:24
idolater lending Jew's investment
money to other Jew and paying
interest on investment 65:28

invitation to meal 65:n24
lender accepting interest from
idolater's loan from borrower 65:27
lender benefiting from borrower 65:8,
65:9
lender benefiting from collateral 65:12
lender stipulating that borrower lend
back more 65:7
lender stipulating to receive different
item than lent 65:11
lender stipulating to receive same
amount of item he lent 65:11
lender transgresses 65:1
lending item for use 65:n18
lending small item 65.11
mortgage, taking out for someone else
65:n66
partners borrowing from idolater 65:29
preparing documents for 65:n3
renting, charging more for delayed
payment 65:21, 65:n54
returning, if took 65:2, 65:5
savings association with Jewish
shareholders 65:28, 65:n73
scribe transgresses 65:1
seller charging more when extending
credit 65:13
severity of prohibition 65:1
store having cash price and credit price
65:n30
wages, discounting for prepayment 65:22
witnesses transgress 65:1
words of ribbis 65:9, 65:n13
see business transactions: iska
challah, mitzvah of
after baking 35:n11
after Pesach 35:5
amount separated 35:1, 35:n5
amount separated from 35:2, 35:5,
35:6, 35:n7
baked goods 35:n11
blessing on 35:1, 35:6, 35:n4, 35:n8
burning/disposing of separated piece
35:1, 35:n6
cake batter 35:n17
child, given to 35:n21
cooking dough 35:6
dough with eggs/fruit juice 35:7, 35:n21
dough obligated in 35:1, 35:2, 35:6,
35:7, 35:n8, 35:n11,
35:n16, 35:n17
dough of non-Jew 35:n16
doughs joined together 35:3, 35:n11
dough with potato 35:n3
Eretz Yisrael 35:1, 35:9, 35:n21, 35:n24
fermentation agent 35:4
from separate units 35:3, 35:n11, 35:n12

INDEX   **438**

frying dough 35:6
  if forgotten 35:9
  joining units with cover 35:3, 35:n11
  leavening agent, procedure for 35:4
  matzah, challah from 35:3, 35:n10,
    35:n12
  mezonos, challah for 35:n19
  non-Jew's dough 35:n16
  obligation of 35:1, 35:8
  Pesach, after 35:5
  Pesach, forgotten before 35:9
  procedure of 35:1, 35:n5, 35:n6
  protruding from vessel 35:3, 35:n11,
    35:n12
  Shabbos, if not separated before 35:9
  sourdough 35:4, 35:5, 35:n14, 35:n15
  vessel, combined in 35:3
  weight of dough 35:n8
  when already separated 35:n14
  when obligated 35:1
  who may eat 35:1
  without a blessing 35:6, 35:n8, 35:n21
  without owner's permission 35:8
  women's obligation 35:8
challah, Shabbos
  cutting into 41:3, 41:4, 41:n18
  making homemade 38:n5
  procedure for hamotzi 41:5
chalav akum
  cheese from 38:13
  children supervising 38:13
  commercial milk in the United States
    38:n40
  maidservants milking 38:13
  reason for prohibition 38:n40
  procedure for permitting 38:13
  prohibition of 38:13
  see butter; cheese
Chanukah
  Al HaNissim in Bircas HaMazon 44:16
charity
  before traveling 68:6
  commitment to give 62:17
chatzitzah
  netilas yadayim 40:11, 40:12, 40:n55
  tevilas keilim 37:10, 37:n26
cheilev
  spleen 36:23
cheese
  made from chalav akum 38:13
  made by a non-Jew 38:14
  procedure for permitting 38:14
  see butter; chalav akum
children
  distributing treats to attract patronage
    62:6
  feeding before animals 42:n1

  guests feeding them 42:17
  keeping kosher 46:1
  oaths 67:9
  prayer for unborn 61:6
  supervising milking 38:13
  tevilas keilim by 37:12
  vows 67:9, 67:10
  zimun 45:22
Chol HaMoed
  forgot Yaaleh VeYavo in
    Bircas Hamazon 44:14, 44:15
clothing
  belt, new 59:8
  buying new 59:7
  good wishes to someone who
    has new 59:13
  hat, new 59:8
  reciting malbish arumim on new 59:8
  tallis, new 59:8
concentration
  see kavanah
convert
  joining zimun 45:23
Dayan HaEmes
  see berachos: Dayan HaEmes
dietary laws
  see basar b'chalav; bishul akum; blood;
    bread; butter; challah, chalav akum;
    cheilev; cheese; eggs; mitzvah of;
    foods, forbidden; heart; liver; lung;
    maid; meat; mechallel Shabbos;
    pas akum; poultry; rinsing; roasting;
    salting; soaking; yayin nesech
drinking
  publicly 42:12
  watching 42:13
eating
  watching 42:13
eggs
  found inside poultry, meaty 36:26
Erev Pesach
  see Pesach, Erev
fats, forbidden
  see cheilev
fearing God
  see Yiras Shamayim
fish
  see foods, forbidden
food cooked by an idolater
  see bishul akum
food, respect for
  bread for other uses 42:8, 42:10
  bread, throwing 41:7, 42:9
  crumbs, care with 42:11
  feeding animals 42:9
  for common use 42:n32
  medicinal use 42:10

439 INDEX

picking up 42:9
sitting on 42:9
spitting out 50:10
throwing 42:9
wine, washing with 42:9
foods, forbidden
animal, abdomen pierced 46:29
beans/legumes, examining for worms
46:35, 46:73
beans/legumes, wormy 46:34
bird, thrown to ground before
slaughter 46:23
buying food from someone not
known to be observant of
kashrus laws 46:21
cheese, wormy 46:44
chickens, castrated 46:28
children keeping kosher 46:1
cooking kosher and nonkosher
proximately 46:20
cooking when only maidservant
home 46:20
cut food and worm with knife 46:42
eggs, blood in 46:1, 46:n1
eggs, checking 46:1, 46:n2
fish, blood of 46:2
fish, worms in 46:43, 46:n89
flour, wormy 46:37, 46:n80
food, sealer unknown 46:19
food, sending with idolater
or suspect Jew 46:16, 46:17, 46:18
food sent unsealed 46:18
food, wormy – retaining in home 46:38
food, wormy – selling to idolater
46:38, 46:n81
food, wormy – whiskey from 46:38
fruits, candied – mite-infested 46:41
fruits, examining for worms 46:35, 46:36,
46:n73, 46:n76, 46:n77
fruits, wormy 46:34, 46:n70
guest by someone not known to be
observant of kashrus laws
46:21, 46:n44
gums bled on food 46:3
geese, checking intestines 46:24
insects/worms, importance of vigilance
in avoiding 42:5, 46:45
item which one rabbi forbade, asking
another about 46:46
kashrus certification symbols 46:40
milk, blood found in 46:4
nuts, often mite-infested 46:40
oven, meat or milk spilled into 46:27
produce, infested and un-examinable
46:39
sealing sack for transport 46:17
sheep and calves, thrown to ground

before slaughter 46:23
utensil left in idolater's/craftsman's
house 46:22
vegetables, singeing to remove worms
46:38
vegetables, wormy 46:38, 46:n85
vinegar, wormy 46:33
water, straining 46:32
water, wormy 46:31, 46:n63
womb, used to make fruit preserves
46:30
see *basar b'chalav; bread*
forgetfulness
drying hands on clothes 40:5
fragrances, blessings on
see *berachos: fragrances*
ger
see *convert*
guests
berachah rishonah includes all foods
57:6
by someone not known to be
observant of kashrus laws
46:21, 46:n44
feeding host's children 42:17
HaTov VeHaMeitiv 49:14
having, atones for sins 44:4
pas akum brought to table for 41:9
precedence for zimun 45:n25
proper manners 42:18
woman guest drinking wine 42:16
ha'adamah
see *berachos: ha'adamah*
hadachah
see *rinsing*
ha'eitz
see *berachos: ha'eitz*
hamotzi
see *berachos: hamotzi*
hand-washing, before meals
after relieving oneself 40:15, 40:16,
40:n69
amount of water used for 40:4
and prosperity 40:4, 40:n15
bandage on hand 40:12, 40:n55
before Asher Yatzar 40:15, 40:16, 40:n69
before food dipped in liquid 40:17,
40:20, 40:n74
before food eaten with utensil 40:20
before preserves/preserved fruit 40:19
before reciting hamotzi 40:1
blessing before drying 40:5, 40:n23
both hands 40:n5
chatzitzah and 40:11, 40:12
covering hands instead of 40:14
discolored water 40:8
disqualified water 40:8, 40:10

INDEX 440

during meal 40:16
dressing on hand 40:12, 40:n55
drying the hands 40:5
each hand twice 40:5, 40:n24
fingernails, dirt under 40:11, 40:n50
food dipped in liquid 40:17, 40:20,
40:n74
food eaten with utensil 40:20
from a pump 40:7
from a whole vessel 40:2
from narrow spigot 40:13, 40:n59
hands clean before 40:11
hands colored/stained 40:12
immersing the hands 40:7, 40:n31
in a mikveh 40:7
in a river 40:7
in a spring 40:7
in snow 40:7
interruptions before hamotzi 41:2
"liquids" that make food require
washing 40:18, 40:19,
40:n21, 40:n81
narrow-mouthed vessel 40:4, 40:n17
no vessel available 40:n59
no water available 40:14
obligation to 40:1
one hand washing the other 40:9
pas haba'ah b'kisnin 48:1
pouring generously 40:4
procedure for 40:4, 40:5
reasons for obligation 40:1
rings, removing 40:11
scab on hand 40:n55
size of bread one washes for 40:1, 40:n8
touched impure spot during meal
40:16, 40:n69
touched impure spot while hands wet
40:6
traveler 40:14
twice on each hand 40:4
vessel that cannot stand upright 40:3
vessel used for 40:2
vessel with narrow mouth 40:4, 40:n17
vessel with uneven rim 40:2
water – becoming impure? 40:9,
40:n26, 40:n46
water, disqualified 40:8, 40:10
water – from human force 40:13
water – from unplugged barrel 40:13
water – used prior 40:8, 40:9
water that became repulsive 40:8, 40:n45
when meal interrupted 42:23
without a blessing 40:1, 40:16,
40:17, 40:n8, 42:23
without a vessel 40:7
HaTov VeHaMeitiv, good tidings
see berachos: HaTov VeHaMeitiv,

good tidings
HaTov VeHaMeitiv, wine
see berachos: HaTov VeHaMeitiv, wine
health
bloodletting 61:4
prayer before therapeutic action 61:4
sneezing 61:5
heart
eating 36:n29
preparation for soaking 36:18
heter iska
see business transactions: iska
immersing utensils
see tevilas keilim
ikar/tafel
broth with fried flour bits 48:10
cereal and milk 48:n54, 54:n19
chicken soup with matzah balls 48:n54,
48:n58, 54:n19
distinct components 48:10, 48:n62,
54:5, 54:n14
flour as binding agent 48:10
fruit in cereal 48:n54, 54:n19
ice cream sandwich 48:n68
liquid/sauce 48:10
majority non-mezonos, mixed together
48:n65
mezonos in liquid 48:8
minority mezonos, mixed together
48:10, 54:5
mixed beverage 54:8
mixed liquid with solid 54:6
mixed together 54:5
mixed with olive oil 54:8
pie with crust 48:n68
preserves 54:9
primary food, if both are 54:4
spices mixed with sugar 54:7
subordinate food, berachah on, if eaten
first 54:3, 54:n9
subordinate food, bread – netilas
yadayim? 54:1, 54:n3
subordinate food does not require
berachah 54:1, 54:2
taste enhancer 54:7
insects
see foods, forbidden
interest
see ribbis
kashering, meat or poultry
see salting
kashrus
see dietary laws
kavanah
during Bircas HaMazon 44:6
on berachah rishonah 50:2
ketanim

441 ◦ INDEX

see children
Kiddush
  see Shabbos: Kiddush
king
  blessing upon seeing   60:10
  blessing when present   60:10
  blind person's blessing   60:10
  official, blessing recited?   60:n44
  mitzvah to see honor accorded to   60:10
  when to interrupt Torah study to see
     60:10
liver
  soaked for 24 hours   36:2
  roasting to kasher   36:20, 36:21,
     36:n35, 36:n37
loans
  mitzvah to grant   66:n11
  see business transactions: iska; business
    transactions: ribbis
loving God
  see Ahavas Hashem
lung
  preparation for soaking   36:19
maid
  cooking for Jews   38:7
  cooking when home alone   46:20, 46:n42
  milking   38:13
  supervising her cooking   38:n26
  supervising rinsing meat   36:12
mayim acharonim
  amount of water for   44:n7
  care with water of   44:2
  drying hands after   44:2
  first to wash   44:1
  importance of   44:1, 44:n6
  interruptions after   44:2
  procedure of   44:1
  reasons for   44:1
  zimun cup poured before   45:2
meal, blessings during
  appetizers   43:3
  bread exempts from   43:1, 43:n4
  eating with bread   43:2, 43:3
  on baked goods   43:6
  on coffee   43:7
  on drinks   43:2
  on foods eaten as part of meal   43:1
  on foods sent by neighbors   43:1
  on fruit   43:3, 43:4, 43:5,
    43:n23, 43:n29
  on liquor   43:2
  on wine   43:2, 49:7
  see HaTov VeHaMeitiv
meal, conduct of
  beginning in one place and concluding
    in a second   42:19; 42:n52, 44:9
  conversing during   42:5

dinner   71:2
eating after completion, before Bircas
  HaMazon   42:23
eating bread during   41:n43, 43:n4
evening meal   71:2
feeding animals first   42:1
giving from, to cook   42:n38
giving from, to server   42:14, 42:n39
giving to one who will not wash or
  recite blessings   42:15, 42:n41
gluttonously   41:4, 42:2, 42:6
group eating together   42:20
leaving before Bircas HaMazon   42:19,
    44:9, 44:n36, 44:n37
leaving in middle of   42:19, 42:20,
    42:21, 42:n56, 44:9
manners during   42:2, 42:3, 42:4
planning to leave in middle of   42:21,
    42:n56
praying in middle of   42:22
precedence in eating   42:6
reciting Shir HaMaalos/Al Naharos Bavel
    42:5
removing empty dishes before
  Bircas HaMazon   45:4
salt on table   41:6
sleeping in middle of   42:22
standing during   42:2
supper   72:2
table, leaving until after Bircas
  HaMazon   44:3
table, respect for   41:6
table set   42:2
waiting for companion during   42:7
  see bread; drinking; eating; guests;
    mayim acharonim; meal, blessings
    during; wine
meal, eating/drinking before
  berachah acharonah on   39:1
  cakes/mezonos   39:3
  delay before meal   39:n11
  foods/drinks which will be eaten during
    meal   39:1, 39:n16
  liquor   39:2
  wine   39:2
meat
  cut after soaking   36:4
  discolored area found   36:n2
  drying after soaking   36:7
  frozen, salting   36:5
  placing in salt before salting   36:14
  removing head before soaking   36:13
  roasting to kasher   36:n32
  sending with idolater or suspect
    Jew   46:16, 46:17, 46:18
  see basar b'chalav; poultry; rinsing;
    salting; soaking

INDEX ⌇ **442**

meat and milk
   see *basar b'chalav*
mechallel Shabbos
   bread baked by   38:n17
   wine of   47:n6
mechayei meisim
   see berachos: mechayei meisim
medical issues
   see *health*
melichah
   see *salting*
mezonos
   see berachos: mezonos
milk and meat
   see *basar b'chalav*
milk of a non-Jew
   see *chalav akum*
Minchah
   see *prayer: Minchah*
miracle
   procedure for one who experienced
      41:3
mitzvah
   intent to do equivalent to vow   67:4
   showing love for   41:4
   vows and oaths as motivation to
      perform   67:4
mourner
   see *Avel*
neder
   see *vow*
neis
   see *miracle*
netilas yadayim
   see *hand-washing, before meals*
nesech wine
   see *yayin nesech*
night
   bedtime Shema   71:4
   eating before Torah study   71:1
   examining day's activity   71:3
   forgiving others   71:3
   HaMapil blessing   71:4
   marital relations and Shema   71:4, 71:n32
   minimizing evening meal   71:2
   repenting day's sins   71:3
   sleep, amount of   71:2, 72:n8
   sleep, conduct during   71:5
   sleeping alone   71:2
   sleep, purpose of   71:4
   Torah study at   71:1
   undressing, procedure for   71:5
   see *prayer: Maariv*
oath
   annulment discouraged   67:2
   avoiding   67:2
   children's   67:9

definition of   67:n2
motivation to perform mitzvah   67:4
   see *vow*
ona'as devarim
   see *speech*
pas akum
   bagels   38:n14
   baked by mechallel Shabbos   38:n17
   baked from Jew's dough   38:5
   baked on fat-smeared surface   38:4
   baked under Jewish supervision   38:n10
   baked with a Jew's participation   38:2
   bread made from legumes   38:3
   commercial bakery   38:n5
   egg coating   38:4
   forbidden breads made from   38:3
   from a baker   38:1, 38:n5
   homemade bread   38:1
   inferior for making hamotzi on   41:9
   no local baker   38:1
   pancakes   38:4
   pressing situation   38:1, 38:n8
   reason for prohibition   38:1
   regional variations   38:1
   Shabbos meals   38:n5
   while journeying   38:1
pas haba'ah b'kisnin
   ate a little and decided to eat more   48:4
   bagels   48:6
   batter, covered with   48:5
   berachah rishonah on   48:1
   cheese filling   48:2, 48:n14
   definition of   48:2, 48:n20
   definition of "set meal" for   48:3,
      48:n23, 48:n26
   dough, fried   48:5, 48:n17
   dough/batter, loose   48:5
   meat filling   48:2, 48:n14
   pan-baked/fried   48:5, 48:n17
   pretzels, soft   48:6
   wafers   48:5
   see *berachos: hamotzi; berachos:*
      mezonos
Pesach, Erev
   forgot to separate challah   35:9
poultry
   chickens, castrated   46:28
   cut after soaking   36:4
   discolored area found   36:n2
   draining blood from   36:10
   drying after soaking   36:7
   eggs found inside   36:26
   frozen, salting   36:5
   geese, checking intestines   46:24
   geese, punctured beneath wings   46:29
   opening for salting   36:9
   placing in salt before salting   36:14

443 ✑ INDEX

removing head before soaking 36:13
singeing before salting 36:28
thrown to ground before slaughter 46:23
zimun on 45:21
see meat; rinsing; salting; soaking
poverty
and respect for food 42:11
result of dishonest weights and
measures 62:8
prayer
before calculating assets 61:7
before therapeutic action 61:4
due to being hurt verbally 63:1
for another causes own prayer to be
answered 61:5
for unborn child 61:6
for the past 61:6
for wealth 62:8
while traveling 68:8, 68:n35
see prayer: Minchah
prayer: Maariv
activity before 70:2
Baruch Hashem le'olam 70:3, 70:4,
70:n18
did not yet recite Minchah 70:3
eating before 70:1, 70:2
hand-washing before 69:4
interrupting during 70:4, 70:n24
latecomer for 70:3, 70:n17
Shema, reciting 70:1, 70:n6, 70:n10
time for reciting 70:1, 70:n4, 70:2
Torah study after 71:1
Torah study before 70:1, 70:2, 70:n13
traveler 70:n15
waiting for last person in synagogue 70:5
prayer: Minchah
activity before 69:3
Ashrei, reciting with minyan 69:5
chazzan, wrapping in tallis 69:5
diligence required for 69:1
eating a meal before 69:3
hand-washing before 69:4
Kaddish Tiskabeil, reciting after nightfall
69:8
latecomer for 69:7, 70:3
latecomer for, before Shabbos 69:9
minchah gedolah 69:2
place where people are summoned to
69:3
plag haminchah, reward for 69:1
Tachanun, reciting at night 69:8
time for reciting 69:2, 69:n11, 69:n12
time for, running out 69:6
Torah study after 70:1
while traveling 68:8
prayer: Mussaf
hand-washing before 69:4

pressing circumstances
see she'as hadchak
primary food/secondary food
see ikar/tafel
Purim
Al HaNissim in Bircas HaMazon 44:16
rainbow
blessing upon seeing 60:4
gazing excessively at 60:4
informing people of 60:n14
ribbis
see business transactions: ribbis
right
first for netilas yadayim 40:4
rinsing
after salting 36:12
liver 36:20, 36:n35
supervising 36:12
see salting; soaking
roasting
liver 36:20, 36:21, 36:22, 36:n35, 36:n37
meat 36:n32
when too late for salting 36:n49
Rosh Chodesh
Bircas HaMazon, forgot Yaaleh VeYavo
in 44:14, 44:15
Mei'ein Shalosh, mentioning in 51:9
see Bircas HaMazon
Rosh Hashanah
forgot Yaaleh VeYavo in Bircas
HaMazon 44:14, 44:15
see Bircas HaMazon
salting
after 72 hours 36:27
before, placing meat in salt 36:14
bones, with/without marrow 36:16
draining blood after 36:10, 36:12, 36:17
eggs found in poultry 36:26
frozen meat 36:5
head not removed 36:13
head, procedure for 36:15
intestines/rectum 36:24
legs, procedure for 36:17
liver 36:20, 36:22
on a basket/board 36:10
over hair 36:15, 36:17
partially 36:n10
preparation for 36:1
procedure for 36:9, 36:12,
36:15, 36:16, 36:17
rinsing off afterward 36:12
salt, coarseness 36:8
singeing feather stubble before 36:28
spleen, procedure for 36:23
time required for 36:11
together with liver 36:22
too dry/too wet 36:7, 36:8

INDEX   **444**

udder 36:24
vessel for before 36:14
when water clear 36:3
see rinsing; soaking
sefer
Shehecheyanu on 59:11, 59:n37
service of Hashem
see avodas Hashem
Shabbos
Bircas HaMazon, Retzei in 44:10, 44:12,
44:13, 44:15
food cooked by non-Jew for ill person
on 38:9
gums bleeding 46:3
homemade challah 38:n5
knives, not removing on 44:4
lodging over Shabbos, money 68:12
Mei'ein Shalosh, mentioning in 51:9
Minchah before, after congregation
accepted Shabbos 69:9
reciting Shir HaMaalos at the end of
meal of 42:5
tevilas keilim on 37:13
traveling before 68:11
see Bircas HaMazon; challah, Shabbos;
mechallel Shabbos
Shabbos, desecration of
see mechallel Shabbos
Shabbos: Kiddush
covering bread/cake during 55:5
exempting other beverages from
berachah 49:6
she'as hadchak
annulling oath 67:2
bread, cutting with dairy knife for meat
and vice versa 46:12
bread, baked by idolater 38:1, 38:n8
not enough time for Minchah 69:6
not enough time for salting 36:11
not enough time for soaking 36:3
no vessel for netilas yadayim 40:14
repulsive water for netilas yadayim 40:n45
soaking in warm water 36:5
washing hands in snow 40:7
shehakol
see berachos: shehakol
Shehecheyanu
see berachos: Shehecheyanu
Shema, bedtime
see night
shevuah
see oath
sleep
see night
soaking
cut afterward 36:4
drying afterward 36:7

enables later salting 36:27
erev Shabbos, on 36:3
head, preparing for 36:15
heart, tearing before 36:18
longer than 24 hours 36:2
lung, cutting before 36:19
meat before salting 36:1
not enough time for 36:3
poultry, removing head before 36:13
reasons for 36:n1
spleen, preparing for 36:23
stomach of calf, preparing 36:25
vessel for, other uses 36:6, 36:n9
with cold water 36:1
with warm water 36:5
see rinsing; salting
speech
deceiving through 63:4
gift that will be declined 63:5
hurting one's wife with 63:1
hurting verbally, examples of 63:2
invitation that will be declined 63:5
nickname, degrading 63:3
prohibition of harming another
verbally 63:1
severity of sin of verbally hurting
another 63:1
truthful 63:5
words of ribbis 65:9, 65:n13
see oath; vow
stam yeinam
see yayin nesech
Tefillas HaDerech
see berachos: Tefillas HaDerech
tevilas keilim
aluminum utensils 37:n2
appliances, electric 37:n27
blessing on 37:1
blessing when manufacturer unknown
37:6, 37:n4
borrowed utensil 37:5, 37:13
chatzitzah 37:10, 37:n26
children, immersion by 37:12
china utensils 37:n7
cleanliness of immersed utensils 37:10
coffee-grinder 37:9
earthenware utensils 37:3
electric appliances 37:n27
establishment that did not immerse,
eating in 37:n14
factory owned by Jew but workers non-
Jews 37:6, 37:n16
glass utensils 37:1
how to immerse 37:10, 37:11
jugs 37:8
knife, slaughtering or skinning 37:8
matzah-forming tools 37:8

445 ✦ INDEX

metal utensils 37:1
obligation of 37:1
peppermill 37:9
pitchers 37:8
place of immersion 37:1, 37:2, 37:n3
porcelain utensils 37:3
poultry needle 37:8
rented utensil 37:5
Shabbos, on 37:13
shopkeeper's obligation 37:5
spit 37:8
toaster 37:n22
trays 37:8
trivet/tripod 37:8
using before immersion 37:1, 37:n14
utensil crafted or repaired 37:7
utensils bought containing food
    items 37:n23
utensils, narrow mouthed 37:11
utensils not used for ready food 37:8
utensils obligated in 37:1, 37:8
utensil that requires kashering 37:4
when immersion impossible 37:n33
wooden utensils 37:3
Yom Tov, on 37:13
Torah
completing day's quota of at night 71:1
designated study time in evening 71:1
importance of study at night 71:1
interrupting study of to see king 60:10
study between Minchah and Maariv 70:1
study while traveling 68:6
words of, during meal 42:5
traveling
air travel, HaGomeil 61:n2
before Shabbos 68:11
Bircas HaMazon while 44:n27, 68:10
blessing traveler 68:6
care to eat and drink kosher food 68:7
charity before 68:6
conduct while 68:6
escorting traveler 68:6
hand-washing while 40:14
lodging over Shabbos, money 68:12
praying while 68:8, 68:n35, 70:n15
preparations for 68:6, 68:n22
Torah study while 68:6
zimun while 68:10
see berachos: Tefillas HaDerech
tzedakah
see charity
vow
actions can create 67:7
annulment 67:7, 67:8, 67:n23
annulment encouraged 67:1
avoiding 67:1, 67:3
care to say "b'li neder" 67:4

children's 67:9
daughter's 67:10, 67:11
definition of 67:n2
dreamt that vow taken 67:8
expressed incorrectly 67:6
improving character traits through 67:5
intent to do mitzvah equivalent to vow
    67:4
motivation to perform mitzvah 67:4
of consecration, annulment
    discouraged 67:1
revoking daughter's or wife's 67:10, 67:11
thought but not verbalized 67:6
wife's 67:10, 67:11
see oath
wealth
and respect for food 42:11
prayer for 62:8
result of honest business practices 62:8
wine
blessing on, during meal 43:2
disqualified for zimun 45:3
mannered drinking of 42:2, 42:n8
preferable for zimun 45:1
washing hands with 42:9
woman drinking 42:16
see berachah rishonah: hagafen; HaTov
    VeHaMeitiv; yayin nesech
wine of a non-Jew
see yayin nesech
women
baking challah for Shabbos 38:n5
childbirth, blessings on 59:5, 59:n19
drinking wine at meal 42:16
easily hurt by words 63:1
fragrances, blessing on 58:14
lending food to friend 65:11
obligated in zimun 45:22
reciting HaGomeil 61:n11
revoking daughter's or wife's vows
    67:10, 67:11
supervising servants 36:12
taking challah 35:8
unsure if recited Bircas HaMazon 44:11
yayin nesech
cooked wine 47:3
diluted wine 47:5; 47:9
dish cooked with wine 47:6
doing business with 47:1
for ill person's use 47:2
idolater cleaning winepress 47:8
idolater diluted 47:9
idolater indirectly touched/moved 47:13
idolater pressing grapes 47:7
juice from vat/winepress 47:7
mechallel Shabbos 47:n6
parameters of prohibition 47:1

INDEX   **446**

producing kosher wine from idolater's
    grapes   47:15
raisin wine   47:5
sealing for transport   46:16, 47:14
sending with idolater or suspect
    Jew   46:16, 46:17, 46:18, 47:14
spiced wine   47:3
tartar   47:12
temed   47:6
touched by idolater   47:1, 47:13
touched/moved indirectly   47:13
uncooked wine   47:3
used to ferment beer   38:12
utensil, kosher, touched while moist
                            47:19
utensil, not used for twelve months
                            47:22
utensils used for, making kosher   47:16,
          47:17, 47:18, 47:19, 47:20
utensil, used with hot wine   47:20
vinegar   48:10
water with steeped grape seeds   47:6
where people are lax regarding   38:12
whiskey   47:11
winepress, juice in   47:7
winepress, making kosher   47:21
Yiras Shamayim
    and mayim acharonim   44:1
    and rinsing salted meat   36:12
    avoiding infested produce   46:39
    during Bircas HaMazon   44:6
    when unsure if recited Bircas
        HaMazon   44:n42
Yom Kippur
    berachos on food on   50:n31
    Bircas HaMazon on   44:n59
    fogot Yaaleh VeYavo in Bircas HaMazon
                          44:n59
Yom Tov
    Mei'ein Shalosh, mentioning in   51:9
    reciting Shir HaMaalos at the end of
        meal of   42:5
    tevilas keilim on   37:13
    Yaaleh VeYavo in Bircas HaMazon
          44:10, 44:12, 44:13, 44:14
    see Bircas HaMazon
zimun

already recited Bircas HaMazon   45:16
answering Amen to   45:6, 45:20
beverages performed with   45:1
chamar medinah   45:1, 45:n5
children and zimun   45:22
continuing meal after zimun   45:17
convert joining   45:23
cup filled before mayim acharonim
                           45:2
cup for, qualities of   45:4
did not eat with group   45:20
diners drinking   45:8
disqualified from joining   45:23
disqualified wine   45:3, 45:n11
drinking with others eating   45:10
forced to leave before   45:15
forgot Hashem's Name in   45:13
forgot to do   45:16
group separating   45:11, 45:12,
                    45:15, 45:n62
groups joining   45:19
how many need to eat bread   45:14
in idolater's home   68:10
interrupting meal for   45:17
joined a different zimun   45:16
joining two people eating   45:10
large gathering, how to do   45:18
leaving before   45:n62
leader drinking   45:9
obligation of   45:1
one ate pas akum   45:21
over a cup   45:1, 45:8, 45:n3
pagum wine   45:3, 45:8, 45:n11
precedence in being honored with
                    45:5, 45:n25
procedure of   45:4, 45:6, 45:7,
          45:8, 45:12, 45:n24
removing empty dishes before   45:4
seeking people for   45:10, 45:14
some ate meat/some dairy   45:21
ten eating together separating   45:12
three eating together separating 45:11
while traveling   68:10
with ten   45:12
with three   45:1
women obligated in   45:22
see Bircas HaMazon

The Twenty-four Books of Tanach

TORAH

Bereishis	בְּרֵאשִׁית	Genesis
Shemos	שְׁמוֹת	Exodus
Vayikra	וַיִּקְרָא	Leviticus
Bamidbar	בַּמִּדְבָּר	Numbers
Devarim	דְּבָרִים	Deuteronomy

NEVIIM / PROPHETS

Yehoshua	יְהוֹשֻׁעַ	Joshua
Shoftim	שׁוֹפְטִים	Judges
Shmuel	שְׁמוּאֵל	Samuel
Melachim	מְלָכִים	Kings
Yeshayah	יְשַׁעְיָה	Isaiah
Yirmiyah	יִרְמְיָה	Jeremiah
Yechezkel	יְחֶזְקֵאל	Ezekiel
Hoshea	הוֹשֵׁעַ	Hosea
Yoel	יוֹאֵל	Joel
Amos	עָמוֹס	Amos
Ovadiah	עוֹבַדְיָה	Obadiah
Yonah	יוֹנָה	Jonah
Michah	מִיכָה	Micah
Nachum	נָחוּם	Nahum
Chavakkuk	חֲבַקּוּק	Habakkuk
Tzefaniah	צְפַנְיָה	Zephaniah
Chaggai	חַגַּי	Haggai
Zechariah	זְכַרְיָה	Zechariah
Malachi	מַלְאָכִי	Malachi

KESUVIM / WRITINGS

Tehillim	תְּהִלִּים	Psalms
Mishlei	מִשְׁלֵי	Proverbs
Iyov	אִיּוֹב	Job
Shir HaShirim	שִׁיר הַשִּׁירִים	Song of Songs
Rus	רוּת	Ruth
Eichah	אֵיכָה	Lamentations
Koheles	קֹהֶלֶת	Ecclesiastes
Esther	אֶסְתֵּר	Esther
Daniel	דָּנִיֵּאל	Daniel
Ezra	עֶזְרָא	Ezra
Nechemiah	נְחֶמְיָה	Nehemiah
Divrei HaYamim	דִּבְרֵי הַיָּמִים	Chronicles

KITZUR SHULCHAN ARUCH YOMI CALENDAR

תשרי

☐	כד תשרי	24 Tishrei	1:1-4
☐	כה תשרי	25 Tishrei	1:5-2:4
☐	כו תשרי	26 Tishrei	2:5-3:1
☐	כז תשרי	27 Tishrei	3:2-End
☐	כח תשרי	28 Tishrei	4:1-5:1
☐	כט תשרי	29 Tishrei	5:2-8
☐	ל תשרי	30 Tishrei	5:9-6:16

חשון

☐	א חשון	1 Cheshvan	6: 17-3
☐	ב חשון	2 Cheshvan	6: 4-9
☐	ג חשון	3 Cheshvan	6:10-7:End
☐	ד חשון	4 Cheshvan	8: 1-5
☐	ה חשון	5 Cheshvan	8:6-9:3
☐	ו חשון	6 Cheshvan	9:4-9
☐	ז חשון	7 Cheshvan	9: 10-13
☐	ח חשון	8 Cheshvan	9: 14-End
☐	ט חשון	9 Cheshvan	10: 1-3
☐	י חשון	10 Cheshvan	10: 4-12
☐	יא חשון	11 Cheshvan	10: 13-19
☐	יב חשון	12 Cheshvan	10: 20-End
☐	יג חשון	13 Cheshvan	11: 1-11
☐	יד חשון	14 Cheshvan	11: 12-20
☐	טו חשון	15 Cheshvan	11:21-12:4
☐	טז חשון	16 Cheshvan	12: 5-10
☐	יז חשון	17 Cheshvan	12:11-13:1
☐	יח חשון	18 Cheshvan	13:2-14:3
☐	יט חשון	19 Cheshvan	14: 4-End
☐	כ חשון	20 Cheshvan	15: 1-6
☐	כא חשון	21 Cheshvan	15:7-End
☐	כב חשון	22 Cheshvan	16: 1-End
☐	כג חשון	23 Cheshvan	17: 1-7
☐	כד חשון	24 Cheshvan	17:8-18:2
☐	כה חשון	25 Cheshvan	18: 3-9
☐	כו חשון	26 Cheshvan	18: 10-14
☐	כז חשון	27 Cheshvan	18: 15-End
☐	כח חשון	28 Cheshvan	19: 1-7
☐	כט חשון	29 Cheshvan	19:8-10
☐	*ל חשון	*30 Cheshvan	19:11-13

כסלו

☐	א כסלו	1 Kislev	19:14-20:7
☐	ב כסלו	2 Kislev	20:8-21:2
☐	ג כסלו	3 Kislev	21:3-8
☐	ד כסלו	4 Kislev	21:9-22:End
☐	ה כסלו	5 Kislev	23:1-9
☐	ו כסלו	6 Kislev	23:10-15

☐	ז כסלו	7 Kislev	23:16-22
☐	ח כסלו	8 Kislev	23:23-End
☐	ט כסלו	9 Kislev	24:1-6
☐	י כסלו	10 Kislev	24:7-End
☐	יא כסלו	11 Kislev	25:1-26:2
☐	יב כסלו	12 Kislev	26:3-12
☐	יג כסלו	13 Kislev	26:13-21
☐	יד כסלו	14 Kislev	26:22-27:End
☐	טו כסלו	15 Kislev	28:1-10
☐	טז כסלו	16 Kislev	28:10-29:3
☐	יז כסלו	17 Kislev	29:4-10
☐	יח כסלו	18 Kislev	29:11-17
☐	יט כסלו	19 Kislev	29:18-30:3
☐	כ כסלו	20 Kislev	30:4-31:1
☐	כא כסלו	21 Kislev	31:2-32:1
☐	כב כסלו	22 Kislev	32:2-7
☐	כג כסלו	23 Kislev	32:8-18
☐	כד כסלו	24 Kislev	32:16-22
☐	כה כסלו	25 Kislev	139:1-4
☐	כו כסלו	26 Kislev	139:5-11
☐	כז כסלו	27 Kislev	139:12-19
☐	כח כסלו	28 Kislev	139:20-End
☐	כט כסלו	29 Kislev	32:23-End
☐	*ל כסלו	*30 Kislev	33:1-6

טבת

☐	א טבת	Teves 1	33:7-End
☐	ב טבת	Teves 2	34:1-4
☐	ג טבת	Teves 3	34:5-13
☐	ד טבת	Teves 4	34:14-35:7
☐	ה טבת	Teves 5	35:8-36:10
☐	ו טבת	Teves 6	36:11-26
☐	ז טבת	Teves 7	36:27-37:9
☐	ח טבת	Teves 8	37:10-38:8
☐	ט טבת	Teves 9	38:9-39:1
☐	י טבת	Teves 10	121:1-5
☐	יא טבת	Teves 11	39:2-40:4
☐	יב טבת	Teves 12	40:5-13
☐	יג טבת	Teves 13	40:14-End
☐	יד טבת	Teves 14	41:1-7
☐	טו טבת	Teves 15	41:8-42:5
☐	טז טבת	Teves 16	42:6-19
☐	יז טבת	Teves 17	42:20-43:3
☐	יח טבת	Teves 18	43:4-44:4
☐	יט טבת	Teves 19	44:5-13
☐	כ טבת	Teves 20	44:14-45:2
☐	כא טבת	Teves 21	45:3-8

KITZUR SHULCHAN ARUCH YOMI CALENDAR

☐	כב טבת	22 Teves	45:9-16
☐	כג טבת	23 Teves	45:17-46:3
☐	כד טבת	24 Teves	46:4-16
☐	כה טבת	25 Teves	46:17-29
☐	כו טבת	26 Teves	46:30-40
☐	כז טבת	27 Teves	46:41-47:7
☐	כח טבת	28 Teves	47:8-21
☐	כט טבת	29 Teves	47:22-48:5

שבט

☐	א שבט	1 Shevat	48:6-End
☐	ב שבט	2 Shevat	49:1-6
☐	ג שבט	3 Shevat	49:7-50:2
☐	ד שבט	4 Shevat	50:3-10
☐	ה שבט	5 Shevat	50:11-51:1
☐	ו שבט	6 Shevat	51:2-7
☐	ז שבט	7 Shevat	51:8-End
☐	ח שבט	8 Shevat	52:1-7
☐	ט שבט	9 Shevat	52:8-15
☐	י שבט	10 Shevat	52:16-53:2
☐	יא שבט	11 Shevat	53:3-54:3
☐	יב שבט	12 Shevat	54:4-55:1
☐	יג שבט	13 Shevat	55:2-56:5
☐	יד שבט	14 Shevat	56:6-57:5
☐	טו שבט	15 Shevat	57:6-58:7
☐	טז שבט	16 Shevat	58:8-59:1
☐	יז שבט	17 Shevat	59:2-8
☐	יח שבט	18 Shevat	59:9-19
☐	יט שבט	19 Shevat	59:20-60:5
☐	כ שבט	20 Shevat	60:6-13
☐	כא שבט	21 Shevat	60:14-61:5
☐	כב שבט	22 Shevat	61:6-62:3
☐	כג שבט	23 Shevat	62:4-14
☐	כד שבט	24 Shevat	62:15-63:1
☐	כה שבט	25 Shevat	63:2-64:End
☐	כו שבט	26 Shevat	65:1-8
☐	כז שבט	27 Shevat	65:9-15
☐	כח שבט	28 Shevat	65:16-22
☐	כט שבט	29 Shevat	65:23-End
☐	ל שבט	30 Shevat	66:1-6

אדר

☐	א אדר**	**1 Adar	66:7-10
☐	ב אדר	2 Adar	66:11-67:5
☐	ג אדר	3 Adar	67:6-End
☐	ד אדר	4 Adar	68:1-7
☐	ה אדר	5 Adar	68:8-69:1
☐	ו אדר	6 Adar	69:2-7
☐	ז אדר	7 Adar	69:8-70:End
☐	ח אדר	8 Adar	71:1-4
☐	ט אדר	9 Adar	71:5-72:4
☐	י אדר	10 Adar	72:5-10
☐	יא אדר	11 Adar	140:1-141:3
☐	יב אדר	12 Adar	141:4-13
☐	יג אדר	13 Adar	141:14-21
☐	יד אדר	14 Adar	141:22-142:5
☐	טו אדר	15 Adar	142:6-End
☐	טז אדר	16 Adar	72:11-19
☐	יז אדר	17 Adar	72:20-73:4
☐	יח אדר	18 Adar	73:5-End
☐	יט אדר	19 Adar	74:1-75:3
☐	כ אדר	20 Adar	75:4-9
☐	כא אדר	21 Adar	75:10-76:4
☐	כב אדר	22 Adar	76:5-13
☐	כג אדר	23 Adar	107:1-108:3
☐	כד אדר	24 Adar	108:4-109:6
☐	כה אדר	25 Adar	109:7-110:5
☐	כו אדר	26 Adar	110:6-12
☐	כז אדר	27 Adar	110:13-111:6
☐	כח אדר	28 Adar	111:7-13
☐	כט אדר	29 Adar	111:14-112:4

ניסן

☐	א ניסן	1 Nisan	112:5-113:7
☐	ב ניסן	2 Nisan	113:8-114:4
☐	ג ניסן	3 Nisan	114:5-12
☐	ד ניסן	4 Nisan	114:13-115:3
☐	ה ניסן	5 Nisan	115:4-116:4
☐	ו ניסן	6 Nisan	116:5-14
☐	ז ניסן	7 Nisan	116:15-117:4
☐	ח ניסן	8 Nisan	117:5-11
☐	ט ניסן	9 Nisan	117:12-118:4
☐	י ניסן	10 Nisan	118:5-8
☐	יא ניסן	11 Nisan	118:9-119:2
☐	יב ניסן	12 Nisan	119:3-5
☐	יג ניסן	13 Nisan	119:6-8
☐	יד ניסן	14 Nisan	119:9-End
☐	טו ניסן	15 Nisan	120:1-End
☐	טז ניסן	16 Nisan	101:1-102:1
☐	יז ניסן	17 Nisan	102:2-103-2
☐	יח ניסן	18 Nisan	103:3-11
☐	יט ניסן	19 Nisan	103:12-104:6
☐	כ ניסן	20 Nisan	104:7-End
☐	כא ניסן	21 Nisan	104:1-105:End
☐	כב ניסן	22 Nisan	76:14-22
☐	כג ניסן	23 Nisan	76:23-77:8
☐	כד ניסן	24 Nisan	77:9-15

KITZUR SHULCHAN ARUCH YOMI CALENDAR

☐	כה ניסן	25 Nisan	77:16-End
☐	כו ניסן	26 Nisan	78:1-7
☐	כז ניסן	27 Nisan	78:8-79:1
☐	כח ניסן	28 Nisan	79:2-End
☐	כט ניסן	29 Nisan	80:1-8
☐	ל ניסן	30 Nisan	80:9-17

אייר

☐	א אייר	1 Iyar	80:17-26
☐	ב אייר	2 Iyar	80:267-35
☐	ג אייר	3 Iyar	80:36-45
☐	ד אייר	4 Iyar	80:46-60
☐	ה אייר	5 Iyar	80:61-67
☐	ו אייר	6 Iyar	80:68-76
☐	ז אייר	7 Iyar	80:77-86
☐	ח אייר	8 Iyar	80:87-81:2
☐	ט אייר	9 Iyar	81:3-82:2
☐	י אייר	10 Iyar	82:3-8
☐	יא אייר	11 Iyar	82:9-83:2
☐	יב אייר	12 Iyar	83:3-84:4
☐	יג אייר	13 Iyar	84:5-15
☐	יד אייר	14 Iyar	84:16-85-3
☐	טו אייר	15 Iyar	85:4-86:5
☐	טז אייר	16 Iyar	86:6-87:6
☐	יז אייר	17 Iyar	87:7-17
☐	יח אייר	18 Iyar	87:18-88:1
☐	יט אייר	19 Iyar	88:2-6
☐	כ אייר	20 Iyar	88:7-14
☐	כא אייר	21 Iyar	88:15-89:3
☐	כב אייר	22 Iyar	89:4-90:4
☐	כג אייר	23 Iyar	90:5-14
☐	כד אייר	24 Iyar	90:15-91:1
☐	כה אייר	25 Iyar	91:2-13
☐	כו אייר	26 Iyar	91:14-92:2
☐	כז אייר	27 Iyar	92:3-End
☐	כח אייר	28 Iyar	93:1-94:2
☐	כט אייר	29 Iyar	94:3-8

סיון

☐	א סיון	1 Sivan	94:9-19
☐	ב סיון	2 Sivan	94:20-95:1
☐	ג סיון	3 Sivan	95:2-11
☐	ד סיון	4 Sivan	95:12-End
☐	ה סיון	5 Sivan	96:1-5
☐	ו סיון	6 Sivan	96:6-14
☐	ז סיון	7 Sivan	96:15-97:9
☐	ח סיון	8 Sivan	97:10-End
☐	ט סיון	9 Sivan	143:1-9
☐	י סיון	10 Sivan	143:10-18
☐	יא סיון	11 Sivan	143:19-144:6
☐	יב סיון	12 Sivan	144:7-145:6
☐	יג סיון	13 Sivan	145:7-20
☐	יד סיון	14 Sivan	145:21-146:End
☐	טו סיון	15 Sivan	147:1-148:End
☐	טז סיון	16 Sivan	149:1-11
☐	יז סיון	17 Sivan	149:12-150:5
☐	יח סיון	18 Sivan	150:6-13
☐	יט סיון	19 Sivan	150:14-151:5
☐	כ סיון	20 Sivan	151:6-152:7
☐	כא סיון	21 Sivan	152:8-End
☐	כב סיון	22 Sivan	153:1-9
☐	כג סיון	23 Sivan	153:10-154:1
☐	כד סיון	24 Sivan	154:2-End
☐	כה סיון	25 Sivan	155:1-6
☐	כו סיון	26 Sivan	155:7-End
☐	כז סיון	27 Sivan	156:1-157:3
☐	כח סיון	28 Sivan	157:4-158:End
☐	כט סיון	29 Sivan	159:1-6
☐	ל סיון	30 Sivan	159:7-160:5

תמוז

☐	א תמוז	1 Tamuz	160:6-161:8
☐	ב תמוז	2 Tamuz	161:9-17
☐	ג תמוז	3 Tamuz	161:18-162:5
☐	ד תמוז	4 Tamuz	162:6-11
☐	ה תמוז	5 Tamuz	162:12-163:4
☐	ו תמוז	6 Tamuz	163:5-164:4
☐	ז תמוז	7 Tamuz	164:5-165:3
☐	ח תמוז	8 Tamuz	165:4-11
☐	ט תמוז	9 Tamuz	165:12-166:3
☐	י תמוז	10 Tamuz	166:4-167:9
☐	יא תמוז	11 Tamuz	167:10-168:5
☐	יב תמוז	12 Tamuz	168:6-171:1
☐	יג תמוז	13 Tamuz	171:2-173:1
☐	יד תמוז	14 Tamuz	173:2-175:3
☐	טו תמוז	15 Tamuz	175:4-176:7
☐	טז תמוז	16 Tamuz	176:8-177:8
☐	יז תמוז	17 Tamuz	121:6-End
☐	יח תמוז	18 Tamuz	177:9-178:3
☐	יט תמוז	19 Tamuz	178:4-179:8
☐	כ תמוז	20 Tamuz	179:9-180:8
☐	כא תמוז	21 Tamuz	180:9-181:4
☐	כב תמוז	22 Tamuz	181:5-13
☐	כג תמוז	23 Tamuz	181:14-182:1
☐	כד תמוז	24 Tamuz	182:2-11
☐	כה תמוז	25 Tamuz	182:12-183:3
☐	כו תמוז	26 Tamuz	183:4-184:5

KITZUR SHULCHAN ARUCH YOMI CALENDAR

☐	כז תמוז	27 Tamuz	184:6-185:4
☐	כח תמוז	28 Tamuz	185:5-187:End
☐	כט תמוז	29 Tamuz	188:1-189:5

אב

☐	א אב	1 Av	189:6-191:End
☐	ב אב	2 Av	122:1-6
☐	ג אב	3 Av	122:7-11
☐	ד אב	4 Av	122:12-123:2
☐	ה אב	5 Av	123:3-124:3
☐	ו אב	6 Av	124:4-11
☐	ז אב	7 Av	124:12-20
☐	ח אב	8 Av	124:21-125:End
☐	ט אב	9 Av	126:1-End
☐	י אב	10 Av	127:1-10
☐	יא אב	11 Av	127:11-End
☐	יב אב	12 Av	192:1-7
☐	יג אב	13 Av	192:8-193:5
☐	יד אב	14 Av	193:6-End
☐	טו אב	15 Av	194:1-11
☐	טז אב	16 Av	194:12-195:7
☐	יז אב	17 Av	195:8-196:1
☐	יח אב	18 Av	196:2-8
☐	יט אב	19 Av	196:9-19
☐	כ אב	20 Av	196:20-197:5
☐	כא אב	21 Av	197:6-198:3
☐	כב אב	22 Av	198:4-14
☐	כג אב	23 Av	198:15-199:9
☐	כד אב	24 Av	199:10-200:2
☐	כה אב	25 Av	200:3-9
☐	כו אב	26 Av	200:10-202:1
☐	כז אב	27 Av	202:2-8
☐	כח אב	28 Av	202:9-203:2
☐	כט אב	29 Av	203:3-204:5
☐	ל אב	30 Av	204:6-205:3

אלול

☐	א אלול	1 Elul	205:4-206:6
☐	ב אלול	2 Elul	206:7-207:5
☐	ג אלול	3 Elul	207:6-208:9
☐	ד אלול	4 Elul	208:10-209:6
☐	ה אלול	5 Elul	209:7-210:End
☐	ו אלול	6 Elul	211:1-11
☐	ז אלול	7 Elul	211:12-212:End
☐	ח אלול	8 Elul	213:1-214:End
☐	ט אלול	9 Elul	215:1-216:End
☐	י אלול	10 Elul	217:1-219:1
☐	יא אלול	11 Elul	219:2-7
☐	יב אלול	12 Elul	219:8-220:4
☐	יג אלול	13 Elul	220:5-221:2
☐	יד אלול	14 Elul	221:3-End
☐	טו אלול	15 Elul	Klalim:
☐	טז אלול	16 Elul	128:1-4
☐	יז אלול	17 Elul	128:5-11
☐	יח אלול	18 Elul	128:12-End
☐	יט אלול	19 Elul	129:1-7
☐	כ אלול	20 Elul	129:8-13
☐	כא אלול	21 Elul	129:14-19
☐	כב אלול	22 Elul	129:20-End
☐	כג אלול	23 Elul	130:1-End
☐	כד אלול	24 Elul	131:1-4
☐	כה אלול	25 Elul	131:5-9
☐	כו אלול	26 Elul	131:10-16
☐	כז אלול	27 Elul	131:17-132:End
☐	כח אלול	28 Elul	133:1-8
☐	כט אלול	29 Elul	133:9-15

תשרי

☐	א תשרי	1 Tishrei	133:17-21
☐	ב תשרי	2 Tishrei	133:22-26
☐	ג תשרי	3 Tishrei	133:27-4:1
☐	ד תשרי	4 Tishrei	134:2-6
☐	ה תשרי	5 Tishrei	134:7-12
☐	ו תשרי	6 Tishrei	134:13-135:2
☐	ז תשרי	7 Tishrei	135:3-6
☐	ח תשרי	8 Tishrei	135:7-12
☐	ט תשרי	9 Tishrei	135:13-End
☐	י תשרי	10 Tishrei	136:1-2
☐	יא תשרי	11 Tishrei	136:3-End
☐	יב תשרי	12 Tishrei	137:1-7
☐	יג תשרי	13 Tishrei	137:8-138:1
☐	יד תשרי	14 Tishrei	138:2-End
☐	טו תשרי	15 Tishrei	98:1-7
☐	טז תשרי	16 Tishrei	98: 8-13
☐	יז תשרי	17 Tishrei	98:14-22
☐	יח תשרי	18 Tishrei	98: 33-32
☐	יט תשרי	19 Tishrei	98:33-99:2
☐	כ תשרי	20 Tishrei	99:3-100:4
☐	כא תשרי	21 Tishrei	100:5-10
☐	כב תשרי	22 Tishrei	100:11-16
☐	כג תשרי	23 Tishrei	100:17-End

* When Cheshvan has only 29 days, 19:8-20:2 are studied on 29 Cheshvan, and 20:3-7 are studied on 1 Kislev. When Kislev has only 29 days, 32:23-33:2 are studied on 29 Kislev, and 33:3-14 studied on 1 Teves.

** During a leap year, Adar I is used either to catch up on missed days or to review difficult halachos for a better understanding.

This volume is part of
THE ARTSCROLL® SERIES
an ongoing project of
translations, commentaries and expositions on
Scripture, Mishnah, Talmud, Midrash, Halachah,
liturgy, history, the classic Rabbinic writings,
biographies and thought.

For a brochure of current publications visit your local
Hebrew bookseller or contact the publisher:

Mesorah Publications, ltd

313 Regina Avenue / Rahway, New Jersey 07065
(718) 921-9000 / www.artscroll.com

Many of these works are possible
only thanks to the support of the
MESORAH HERITAGE FOUNDATION,
which has earned the generous support of concerned people,
who want such works to be produced
and made available to generations world-wide.
Such books represent faith in the eternity of Judaism.
If you share that vision as well,
and you wish to participate in this historic effort
and learn more about support and dedication opportunities –
please contact us.

Mesorah Heritage Foundation

313 Regina Avenue / Rahway, New Jersey 07065
(718) 921-9000 ext. 5 / www.mesorahheritage.org

Mesorah Heritage Foundation is a 501(c)3 not-for-profit organization.